THE SIXTIES

DATE DUE					

BY THE SAME AUTHOR

Uptown: Poor Whites in Chicago (coauthor)
Busy Being Born
The Whole World Is Watching: Mass Media in
  the Making and Unmaking of the New Left
Inside Prime Time
The Murder of Albert Einstein
The Twilight of Common Dreams: Why America
  Is Wracked by Culture Wars
The War Within: America's Battle Over Vietnam
Sacrifice

EDITED

Campfires of the Resistance: Poetry from the
  Movement
Watching Television

"The perfect blend of history, faith, and love in all its forms, this tale of second chances and brave choices swept me away. Laura Frantz brings colonial coastal Virginia to life so well, I could almost taste the salty sea breeze. Expertly crafted and elegantly penned, *A Heart Adrift* proves once again why this author ranks among my all-time favorites. Highly recommended for fans of historical fiction."

Jocelyn Green, Christy Award–winning
author of *Shadows of the White City*

"Laura Frantz has a way with story, lacing her books with hope and starlight. *A Heart Adrift* contains a considerable amount of both. It's a sweetly satisfying novel that is as addictive as the chocolates Esmée Shaw creates and Henri Lennox craves. A slow-burn romance aches with longing and the possibility of second chances, but it's the relationship between vastly different sisters that stole my heart: gentle Esmée, who finds all she's ever wanted against the backdrop of crashing waves and an isolated island, and vivacious Eliza, a woman who discovers everything she was always meant to be in the loss of all she thought she was.

"*A Heart Adrift* firmly anchors readers during the stirrings of the hardly remembered French and Indian War. And in the middle of that storm, it shines a light on providential grace and the beauty of redemptive love."

Kimberly Duffy, author of *A Tapestry
of Light* and *Every Word Unsaid*

"*A Heart Adrift* is a lush treatise on love lost and found at the intersection of ambition and desire. While Esmée was endearing to me as a woman with agency and intellect, persevering against the rigid constructs of her time period, Henri's passion to forge a life with the woman he loves while danger looms awakened every last one of my romantic sensibilities. Laura Frantz's rich tapestry of history and heroism is destined to dazzle readers of Susanna Kearsley and Diana Gabaldon—all while luring new fans with its intricate plot, delicious pacing, and welcome intrigue. This long-established queen of epic historical fiction is at the height of her game. And I know I speak for many when I happily say I cannot wait to see where she sweeps us away to next!"

Rachel McMillan, author of *The London
Restoration* and *The Mozart Code*

A HEART
Adrift

Books by Laura Frantz

The Frontiersman's Daughter
Courting Morrow Little
The Colonel's Lady
The Mistress of Tall Acre
A Moonbow Night
The Lacemaker
A Bound Heart
An Uncommon Woman
Tidewater Bride
A Heart Adrift

THE BALLANTYNE LEGACY

Love's Reckoning
Love's Awakening
Love's Fortune

A HEART

Adrift

a novel

LAURA FRANTZ

Revell

a division of Baker Publishing Group
Grand Rapids, Michigan

© 2022 by Laura Frantz

Published by Revell
a division of Baker Publishing Group
PO Box 6287, Grand Rapids, MI 49516-6287
www.revellbooks.com

Printed in the United States of America

Library of Congress Cataloging-in-Publication Data
Names: Frantz, Laura, author.
Title: A heart adrift : a novel / Laura Frantz.
Description: Grand Rapids, MI : Revell, a division of Baker Publishing Group, [2022]
Identifiers: LCCN 2021018771 | ISBN 9780800734978 (paperback) | ISBN 9780800741020 (casebound) | ISBN 9781493434121 (ebook)
Subjects: GSAFD: Love stories.
Classification: LCC PS3606.R4226 H43 2022 | DDC 813/.6—dc23
LC record available at https://lccn.loc.gov/2021018771

Scripture used in this book, whether quoted or paraphrased by the characters, is from the King James Version of the Bible.

Published in association with Books & Such Literary Management, 52 Mission Circle, Suite 122, PMB 170, Santa Rosa, CA 95409-5370, www.booksandsuch.com.

Baker Publishing Group publications use paper produced from sustainable forestry practices and post-consumer waste whenever possible.

22   23   24   25   26   27   28   7   6   5   4   3   2   1

To my heart sister,
Ginger Graham,
who reached home ahead of me.
I hope heaven has a beautiful library.

PROLOGUE

Sigh no more, ladies, sigh no more, men were deceivers ever;
One foot in sea, and one on shore, to one thing constant never.

Shakespeare

VIRGINIA COAST
APRIL 1745

With his back to the coastal wind, Henri Lennox settled his arms around Esmée Shaw, guiding her soft, pale hands with his tanned, callused fingers as they let the long silken line out. The pear-shaped kite caught on a gust, tugging at the string till it threatened to snap.

"Let it fly away from you bit by bit," he told her.

She did so, her laugh a surprised trill as the kite climbed higher. "Shall I let out more line?"

"Slowly, aye. With the right technique, you can even make it dance."

"What?"

"Just give a tug to the string now and again. Like this." He showed her as they gazed upward, the kite zigzagging against the azure sky, its tail a scarlet streak as it soared and dipped.

9

Wonder laced her tone. "Where did you get such a winsome creation?"

"The East Indies. They've been kite-flying for centuries. We colonials are just coming awake. Our kite lacks but one thing."

"Oh?" She tugged on the line and sent the kite dancing again.

He relaxed his hold on her hands, resting his jaw against her hatless head. She fit neatly beneath his chin, her back warm against his linen-clad chest, the wind riffling her carefully pinned hair like he longed to do with his fingers. He breathed in the telltale rose scent that seemed to imbue every ebony strand. "The kite lacks decoration. Our entwined initials should suit."

"Henri . . . how romantic." Her voice held a touch of teasing. "'Tis something I might fancy, not you."

"You've no idea what keeps me awake long nights at sea."

The afternoon sun sank behind them when it had been in their eyes minutes before. Had it not just been noon? At their feet was an empty basket, the remains of a *piquenique*. The cold meats, cheeses, and fruit had been devoured, even the little comfits molded in the shape of anchors from Shaw's Chocolate shop. Esmée's hat was atop the sand near her discarded shoes. Henri saw Admiral and Mrs. Shaw at a distance, slowly walking the beach with Esmée's younger sister.

He kissed his beloved's soft brow, his hands falling to her tightly cinched waist. "With you, time seems to melt away when I want it to stand still."

"If I could stop the clock, I would." She let out more line, head tipped back as the kite soared higher. "I want to run with it."

"In those petticoats?" Even as he asked it, she darted away from him. Lithe and laughing, she ran full tilt along the shore, a ruffled white wave breaking over her bare feet.

He started after her, stepping over her hat and slippers. The sand slowed him, his boots heavy, but he finally caught up with her. He untangled the kite string from her fingers and led her behind a dune that hid them from any onlookers.

"Henri, will you spoil my merriment?"

"My mind is more on kissing than kites, Esmée."

She caught her breath as he brought the kite string behind his back, out of her reach, while his free arm encircled her. She laid her head upon his chest, her long-lashed eyes closing. Emotion knotted his throat. Did she realize she held his heart? Not just a piece of it. The entire whole of it.

She raised her head, her green eyes soft yet wary. "*Don't*, Henri."

He brushed back a dark tendril of her hair. "Don't kiss you?"

"Don't tell me you're leaving again."

"All right, *ma belle*. I'll just kiss you then." The tender moment was theirs, the future be hanged. He kissed her soundly. Rather, she kissed him, her arms tightening around his neck as if anchoring him to the spot and preventing their parting. Sensations she alone was capable of rousing swam through him, widening eddies of desire shadowed by regret.

"Captain Lennox? Esmée?"

At the sound of the admiral's voice they drew apart, and inexplicably Henri let go of the line. The colorful kite kept soaring, borne on a west wind over the water, seeming to touch the clouds before vanishing from sight.

CHAPTER

one

Chocolate had been Captain Henri Lennox's one weakness. Was it still?

Pondering it, Esmée wiped cocoa-dusted hands on her apron and stood in the open doorway of the chocolate shop facing York's sail-studded harbor. The noon sun still held a touch of summer, drenching her in buttery yellow light.

A pint of honey-sweetened milk. Two dried Mexican chilies. One cinnamon stick. A crushed vanilla pod. All whisked into a steamy froth with a wooden molinillo.

That was how the captain preferred his chocolate. Though it had been ten years since she'd last seen him, Henri Lennox's memory still chafed like a saltwater rash. Would it always?

Overhead the shop's wooden sign swung noisily on its iron bracket in a contrary coastal wind. *Shaw's Chocolate.* Newly painted and adorned with a silver chocolate pot, it beckoned countless cocoa-craving customers.

At six o'clock, Esmée moved to close the door, trading the briny tang of the sea for the warm, rich scent of cocoa instead.

"Daughter, have you finished Lady Lightfoot's almonds?"

Esmée rounded the worktable as her father emerged from the adjoining coffeehouse that served as his office, his pleasure plain. Upon the long wooden countertop before them was tray after tray of confections. Esmée's favorites were the chocolate almonds, but she'd made several batches of sugared almonds too.

"Fit for the most fastidious matron in all the Tidewater," her father announced after close perusal. "And her annual ball."

Esmée smiled. "I've used cochineal and saffron to color them red and yellow—and spinach and berries for green and blue."

"Vibrant." He tossed a red confection into his mouth. "Delicious."

"I've more to do tomorrow if the weather continues cool, though I'm running short of orange flower water."

He crossed to the large bow-fronted window, taking in the moored vessels like the admiral of old. "We're overdue for a merchant fleet. We've too much illicit Dutch tea and silk handkerchiefs of late."

Was there a beat of regret in his voice? Did he miss his seafaring days? Alarm unfurled like a pirate's black flag inside her. Barnabas Shaw held himself erect, defying the stoop of age, his silver hair hidden beneath a white periwig, his garments tailored to his distinguished frame. He seemed preoccupied of late. A bit on edge. He claimed it was on account of all the bloodshed, but that seemed naught but a bad dream, the conflict on the distant frontier betwixt faraway England, France, and the Indians.

Or was he pondering her mother? Though Eleanor Shaw had been gone three years, it seemed far longer.

Turning, he faced Esmée. "Where is our summons to the ball? I've not had a look at it."

She unearthed a stack of papers beneath the counter, the gilt-edged invitation at the very bottom.

"Read it to me, if you would, as I've misplaced my spectacles."

She held the card aloft in the fading light. "'Pleasure Ball. While we live, let us live. Admiral Barnabas Shaw and Miss Esmée Shaw are

14

requested to attend the ball at Lightfoot Hall on Tuesday, seventh of October current, at seven o'clock p.m.'"

"Your sister is coming from Williamsburg, and we shall go together as a foursome."

"Eliza never misses a frolic." Esmée placed the invitation on a shelf. "She and Quinn are a popular pair. They dance divinely."

"As do you." At last he moved away from the window. "I shall be your proud escort. No doubt you'll not lack dance partners, even at eight and twenty. 'Tis not too late, you know . . ."

Not too late for love, for marriage.

The ongoing lament was now a familiar song. "I've no wish to wed and leave you, Father. An occasional frolic is enough for me. Besides, who would manage the shop? Your other business ventures take all your time. You don't even like chocolate."

He chuckled. "'Twas your mother's preoccupation. But she came by it honestly, being a chocolatier's daughter."

"A preoccupation I am happy to continue." Esmée eyed the almonds for any imperfections. "At least for now. I've none of Eliza's ambitions. I want to live simply. Be of benefit to somebody somewhere."

She reached for the commonplace book stuffed with recipes penned in Mama's faded, scrolling hand. The secrets of the chocolatier's trade. She'd not exchange the old book for a chest of buried treasure . . . or a husband.

Smoothing her soiled apron, Esmée set the chatelaine at her waist clanking. Crafted of sterling silver, it had been her mother's, a practical yet whimsical piece of jewelry she was rarely without.

"Be that as it may"—her father cleared his throat—"you were in love once."

His low words rolled across the empty shop like a rogue wave, swamping and nearly upending her. Schooling her astonishment, she stared at him. "A foolish infatuation I've since recovered from."

"Have you?" He kept his gaze on Water Street. "Or is it more you met a man who's made every would-be suitor of yours unworthy ever since?"

How pithy he could be. How wise. But how wrong he was about this antiquated matter.

"A man who set me aside for the sea." Esmée untied her apron and hung it from a wall peg. "A man who is deemed a respectable privateer in some circles but a pirate prince in others."

He looked at her then, no apology in his weather-beaten features. "I don't mean to nettle you, Daughter. I only mention it because there's been talk that Captain Lennox has returned to the colonies."

Her hands fisted in the folds of her skirt. Though she'd been about to retreat into the kitchen, all such practicalities flew out of her benumbed head.

"The scuttlebutt is he intends to finish the lighthouse on Indigo Island. And I must say I heartily approve. Virginia—Chesapeake Bay—has ne'er needed it so much as now. Guard ships are not enough. We must have a light."

The light that was my idea and he abandoned upon our heated parting.

Her father talked on, unaware of the maelstrom in her head and heart. "No doubt that and his usual business bring him back, owner and part owner of several vessels as he is."

Captain Lennox—Henri—hadn't been home for years, at least not on the streets of York. Last she knew he'd been sailing the trade routes of the Spanish Main, his many exploits printed in the *Virginia Gazette*. Of late he held the record for the fastest sailing time, some 240 miles in less than a day. Exploits she'd dismissed as more fancy than fact. Betimes he seemed more ghost, haunting the coast.

Haunting her.

She'd grown used to thinking him afar off, not hazarding a meeting on some side street in York or even Williamsburg. The very possibility of stumbling across him had her all aflutter, her claimed recovery in question.

"Time for supper." With a jangling of keys, her father locked the front door. "I'll walk up the hill and home with you after I dismiss the indentures."

She hardly heard him, lost as she was in the tattered memories of the past. His footsteps retreated, but his hard words outlasted him.

"You were in love once."

Absently she fiddled with her chatelaine, toying with the ornamental chain with its many pins and clasps. It bore several significant trinkets. A key. Scissors. A watch. A pincushion ball. A needle case. A heart-shaped vinaigrette and another for sweetmeats.

Even a tiny silver lighthouse.

CHAPTER
two

Henri's homecoming had been as silent and stealthy as he could make it. He'd struck his vessel's colors, emptied her of all crew, and moored the *Relentless* at the island's opposite end, facing the mainland and not the Atlantic. Now, climbing rickety, weathered steps to the stone cottage he once called home, Henri stowed his captaincy as he'd soon stow his tarred garments.

Behind him trod Cyprian, his steward and a native of the Mosquito Coast. Clad in trews and a Monmouth cap, he was still barefoot, as he was when on the deck.

"You needn't shadow me," Henri said over his shoulder. "You're as deserving of a pint and freedom as all the rest."

"Aye, sir. But first I must see this pile of sand ye call home—and the light tower ye oft speak of." Cyprian's dark eyes reflected new appreciation. "Are ye lord and master of all the island?"

"Such as it is, aye. But not the ordinary on Indigo's opposite end. That is Mistress Saltonstall's business."

"And who is this woman, sir?"

"The widow of one of my ablest sailors, God rest him," Henri replied, anticipating his next question. "When he died he left her enough prize money to build the ordinary."

"She will not care ye seek yer cottage instead?"

"Nay." Henri reached into the bosom of his shirt and withdrew a coral necklace. "Give her my regards. I'll pay her a visit in time. For now, she'll be hard-pressed to keep up with you henhearted numbskulls."

Cyprian laughed. "We shall drink and eat our fill and tie our hammocks to the trees tonight, then row to the mainland tomorrow?"

"I row to the mainland. You stay and careen the vessel."

"So my role as steward ends? Ye'll be alone tonight? Is that not lonesome?"

"Nay."

Even as he uttered the half-truth, Henri wished it back. How could he explain the pure pleasure of profound solitude after crowded months at sea? The disorienting process of regaining one's equilibrium as well as one's land legs, which were better acquired alone?

They came to the cottage, tarrying outside its locked door. His gaze swept the shore, the sunburnt grasses and sand, till it came to rest on the half-finished light tower rising like a smokeless candle over the beach.

Cyprian's mouth sagged when he saw it. Recovering himself, he gave an admiring whistle. "Ye'll finish the light?"

"It requires a stonemason and a glass top." Henri discarded the longing he felt when he looked at it. In memory it stood taller, needed less work. The keeper's cottage was finished, at least, though it would remain empty till the tower was done.

Would it always remind him of Esmée?

The boxy lines of his cottage—deceptively plain outwardly—were softened in the September gloaming. He unlocked the door, and it creaked open at the push of his hand. As Henri entered, Cyprian all but gaped on the threshold. Fine furnishings. Colorful Turkish carpets. Framed maps. Dutch paintings in gilt frames.

And dust.

A mouse skittered by his booted feet. He'd need a cat. The tiger-striped feline on board the *Relentless* would do.

"Fetch Clementine for me the next time you come round, aye?"

"Shall I bring the wee hammock she sleeps in?"

"Aye."

With a nod, Cyprian continued surveying this treasure chest of stone as Henri passed into the kitchen. His cupboards were bare of all but tinned tea and a few unopened bottles of Madeira, which was mostly for guests, as he drank little but bumboo and brackish water.

What he craved was chocolate.

As Henri poked and prodded his way about the cottage's four rooms, Cyprian grabbed a rag and wiped a Windsor chair clean in the parlor. The hearth bore a blackened log and soured ashes from Henri's homecoming five years before. He'd avoided York and done his business in Norfolk then. But this time he'd lay over longer. Attend to his investments and business ventures. At the very least deliver the letters from fellow seamen to kin on shore.

With a low whistle, Cyprian eyed the shelves that framed the fireplace like bookends. "So many books, sir, and I cannot make out a single word."

"Find someone to school you."

A ready grin. "Someone in petticoats."

With a wry smile, Henri sat down on the dusted chair. When he said no more, Cyprian saluted him and sailed out the open door in the direction of the Flask and Sword with urgency in his rolling gait.

In the utter stillness came the familiar lapping of water against the shore and the odd chorus of cicadas in the surrounding trees. The richly appointed room tilted and spun and finally settled. Henri fought to stay awake.

He was too weary to shed his sea-tainted garments. Too weary to quench his thirst. Too weary to even shut the door on the encroaching night. His head tilted forward, his bristled jaw nearly resting on his chest. His clasped hands, never far from the pistol at his middle, relaxed. He drifted . . . dreamed. In time his own snoring jarred him awake.

Or was it something else?

He blinked the sleep from his eyes. Tried to focus on a cobwebbed corner. Someone seemed a part of the velvety shadows now filling every crevice and cubbyhole, a rebuke in her unforgettable forest-green eyes.

Esmée Shaw.

That sent him to his feet. He slammed the door, locked it, and passed into his bedchamber with a prayer on his lips rather than a barely squelched epithet.

Let the words of my mouth and the meditation of my heart be acceptable in Thy sight, O Lord, my strength and my redeemer.

Within the confines of the Williamsburg milliner and mantua-maker, Esmée watched her sister turn slowly about in her new gown. A great quantity of silk and silver thread had been expended, every extravagance granted. Eliza Shaw Cheverton—Lady Drysdale—was everything Esmée was not. The wife of a leading Virginia official. Social. Beautiful. Daring. Queenly in height. And as round as five months of pregnancy could make her.

Eliza pirouetted despite the baby's bulk. "What say you about the color, Sister?"

Esmée caught her bottom lip between her teeth. "'Tis . . . eye-catching."

"Blindingly orange, you mean." Eliza's blue eyes glittered. "Like a pumpkin."

"'Tis an appropriate color for autumn. You'll make a striking entrance."

"I do believe the length needs altering." Mouth puckered with pins, Mistress Bell knelt and began fussing with the hem.

Eliza put a hand to her tawny hair, a mass of unpowdered curls. "You should see my towering wig, powdered to perfection and boasting a ship or two."

Eyes rounding, Esmée tried to envision such an elaborate coiffure. Eliza had a knack for influencing fashion with her shocking style. "You jest."

"Father will be amused." Taking out her new lace-tipped fan, Eliza stirred the heated air. "I do hope Lady Lightfoot's ball is on a cool night. Rainy, even. I can't imagine dancing in such heat, especially with two to consider."

"As your elder sister"—Esmée's gaze traveled to her sister's expanding middle—"I caution you against dancing at all." Even as she said it, she knew her hopes defied conventions. Gentry or no, women were rarely slowed by pregnancy, continuing to go and do till they became too uncomfortable. Eliza showed no signs of slowing her pace.

"Nonsense. Tell me again which of Mama's gowns you'll be wearing?"

"The saffron silk."

"Surely *you* jest." Eliza's distaste led to a theatrical shudder.

"The fabric is still lush, though the lace is yellowed with age."

"Old as it is, I'm surprised it's not moth-eaten." Eliza took command as she always did in such matters. "As for the lace, a misfortune easily remedied. I spied an exquisite length of blond Mechlin in the back room."

"Indeed." Mistress Bell finished her pinning. "I've also an exceptional Brussels lace."

Lips pursed, Eliza studied Esmée. "I suppose you'll go wigless and natural again. But 'tis just as well. 'Twould take a whole hogshead of powder to coat that black head of yours." Her fan fluttered harder. "What about jewels?"

Esmée brought a hand to her bare throat. "Mama's pearls."

"Pearls are passé. Father's emeralds pair well with so yellow a gown."

The largest emerald was big as a hen's egg. "Pearls are always my preference," Esmée said. Elegant. Unassuming. "As for Father's jewels, you know what will be said . . ."

"Ill-gotten gain," Eliza whispered dramatically, then gave a wicked laugh. "Let them whisper what they will. Father is beyond reproach—"

Esmée put a finger to her lips as Mistress Bell reentered the room, hands full of blue cards wrapped with lace. For a few minutes, her worries were pushed aside as she perused the offerings, finally deciding on the Mechlin bobbin lace, which Eliza insisted on paying for.

The fitting finished, Eliza hurried her down Nassau Street to their townhouse. If Esmée ever rued anything about her younger sister, it was Eliza's infernal rush.

"Look at the maples turning the very hue of my ball gown—and yours." Esmée slowed her pace, brittle leaves rustling underfoot. "Williamsburg is glorious in the fall."

Eliza turned her face skyward as a maple leaf drifted down. "Glorious indeed, and a wee bit more refined than York. All those jacks and rogues along the waterfront! I do wonder why you dally there when Quinn and I have opened our home to you. You could have a splendid season here . . . go husband hunting."

"But the chocolate shop—"

"Turn the shopkeeping over to the servants," Eliza told her. "Promise me you'll come and stay once the baby arrives, at least briefly."

"I know precious little about infants, but I'll be glad to help you if I can. Father may well come too. He's counting down till his first grandchild."

"I wonder if he will come. He was always at sea when we were small. I don't know how Mama managed it. Writing letters perpetually to some port that were rarely answered."

"Not a port. Ascension Island. I found an entire box of letters sealed with red wax from Father after Mama died, remember. All lovingly perused."

Sadness shaded Eliza's finely molded features. "Would that we had Mama instead."

They turned down a brick walkway that led past a grand magnolia tree to the Cheverton townhouse. A butler in livery opened the door before they'd set foot on the first step, greeting them and then sending to the kitchen for tea at Eliza's request.

Esmée left her lace purchase and straw hat in the foyer and followed Eliza into a newly refurbished parlor of Egyptian blue overlooking the rear garden. They sat, and a tea table between them was soon laid with the latest creamware tea service.

Eliza was unusually subdued. "Father's last exploits were the death of Mama."

Esmée didn't care to dwell on it. Many years had passed since they fled the pirate's den of Rhode Island, exchanging Block Island for York's sandy shores. Something nefarious had sent them south, with Father's northern enemies determined to lay him low. Escaping their net, he'd begun anew in Virginia, a respected admiral turned shipbuilder, merchant, tax assessor, and founding member of Grace Church.

Not the scourge of merchant vessels sailing the trade routes of the Spanish Main.

"Do you ever wonder why Father turned to privateering after so illustrious a naval career?" Eliza whispered.

Tea was brought, delaying Esmée's answer.

"Hyson or imperial?" her sister asked.

"Hyson with cream, please." Esmée looked out the window, where the last summer irises bent beneath the rising wind. The tea's delicate fragrance, usually soothing, failed to relieve. "Father's very lifeblood is salt water."

Eliza leaned in conspiratorially. "Speaking of maritime matters, there's tittle-tattle floating about that a certain sea captain has returned to Virginia."

Esmée felt a slight tremor as she lifted her cup. "Father said the same."

"Does that upset you? Your hand is shaking." Eliza's concern only elevated Esmée's unease. "I thought perhaps after so many years, you'd all but yawn at the mention of his name."

Yawn? Rather, yowl. "Henri Lennox remains a conundrum, then and now."

"Who is the captain anyway?" Eliza mused. "Respected privateer . . . or pirate?"

Esmée lifted her shoulders in a slight shrug. "'Tis ever been a puzzle separating pirates from privateers. People have a terrible thirst for gossip and believe the worst."

"I'll not align with his enemies and call him a pirate but rather a respected privateer and former commissioned officer of the Royal Navy." Eliza's hand slipped to her middle as if her maternity stays were laced too tightly. "Tell me again why you two parted. The details escape me after so long. All I can remember is the both of you being absolutely besotted."

Besotted. The word, once sweet, now seemed laughable.

"He chose the sea—his captaincy and ship—over me." Esmée took a silver spoon and stirred sugar into her cup. "And I could not conscience being left behind on shore."

"No doubt our family history has some bearing on your very messy parting. With Father away at sea so much, we hardly knew him. Mama was more widow. We seemed rather fatherless except we never lacked a thing. Even now, deeply involved in colonial maritime affairs, he is a riddle, always on the go and remarkably closemouthed."

Esmée knew firsthand her father's long silences—rife with unspoken regrets, she'd often thought—and the surprising recent words he did utter.

"You were in love once."

Even now, a sennight later, the words clung to her like pitch.

Desperate for a distraction, Esmée looked about the lovely parlor still smelling of fresh milk paint. Eliza's redecorating had no end. "I fear Father is missing Mama more rather than less as time goes by. Lately he seems especially restless. Preoccupied."

Eliza's alarmed eyes pinned her over the rim of her Sevres cup. "'Tis almost October, the month Mama passed. Surely that is the reason."

Was it?

Esmée forced a smile, more undone by Eliza's rare discomfiture than Father's moods. "Perhaps the Lightfoot pleasure ball is just the antidote for us all."

CHAPTER
three

⟨decorative flourish⟩

*H*enri rowed the five miles from Indigo Island to the mainland in under an hour, spurred on by seas so flat and smooth they resembled an opal. Such becalmed waters were usually a hindrance, stranding ships and starving crews nearer the equator. The doldrums were the bane of Atlantic sailors. But here off Virginia's coast, all was in his favor, though he wished for a light wind, if only to allay the late September sun beating at his back and dampening his linen shirt.

A sack of letters lay in the jolly boat's bottom, brought over eight thousand miles from Ascension Island to loved ones throughout Virginia. Since his own familial ties were so meagre, he'd had no letters to post. The lonesome lack sharpened his resolve to keep the tenuous ties of his fellow mariners intact.

Looking over his shoulder, he squinted beneath the brim of his cocked hat as York's sprawling façade took shape. His mental map of the thriving town was largely intact. Little had changed other than an array of new warehouses as befitted a port town. Water Street still boasted a staggering assortment of taverns and rum shops and bawdy houses, as plenteous as the ships glutting the harbor. On the cliff above, handsome, genteel homes looked down like disgruntled parishioners on the sinning street.

His gaze hung on one. The Shaw residence. He'd last ducked beneath the door's lintel at the age of five and twenty. Esmée was younger, a vision of midnight hair, eyes green as a Montserrat forest, and a smile that had once stood him still. What had ten years wrought? Likely she'd wed. Given her parents grandchildren.

His mind reached back to a memory long blocked, the day he and Esmée had first met. The *Relentless* had moored at Block Island, a stronghold of privateers, pirates, and assorted mariners in Rhode Island. He rarely sailed so far north, but unexpected business had taken him there.

Three young women had been walking the beach, a fragile April sun breaking through after a fearsome winter. They were shelling, bare of foot, skirts lifted above their ankles. Their lilting voices carried over the water as the *Relentless* docked, drawing the attention of his affection-starved crew. He'd rebuked them for gawking but was hard-pressed to rein himself in and follow his own admonishment.

And then, that very eve, he'd found himself at a supper party hosted by the prominent Williams family. In Esmée walked, her smile wide, her pale green gown beguiling. Henri was taken aback by her warmth, her genuineness. She was flushed by the sun, as curvaceous and inviting as tropical fruit.

"Captain Lennox," their hostess queried, "have you met Miss Esmée Shaw?"

Henri gave the requisite bow while Esmée curtsied prettily, hands clasped at her slim waist.

"The privateer?" she asked, her long-lashed gaze holding his. "Henri Lennox?"

Ahn-ree. Her French was perfect. Few pronounced his forename well. That alone left him half-smitten. "Should I bow out now?"

"Never fear." Her face dimpled into a laugh. "I don't believe half what the papers print."

"The truth is never so colorful, nay." He clasped his hands behind his back and struck a non-piratical pose. "You are the daughter of the renowned Admiral Shaw of Rhode Island."

"Soon to be situated in fair Virginia."

He regarded her closely. *What?*

"Father won't stray far from the sea. He's purchased a townhouse in the port town of York. We'll be opening a chocolate shop and coffeehouse on Water Street."

"Not far from my home off the Virginia capes."

Her expression was unsurprised. "You own an island, 'tis said."

"Indigo Island, aye."

"How did you come by it?"

"As payment of a debt owed me."

"Do you know its history?"

He smiled, enjoying their banter. "Perhaps the better question is, do you?"

"Father told me a ship heavily laden with indigo from Porto Bello foundered there in a storm a hundred years ago." Her eyes sparkled. "I should like to see your island."

Such bold words bordered on coquetry. But her eyes held such guileless interest he was charmed. "Indigo Island's shells are the finest I've seen beyond Hispaniola, the pearl of the Caribbean."

"You saw me shelling today as you docked." She extended her fan, its leaves painted with a ship, the edges lace tipped. "A handsome vessel you command, Captain Lennox."

The rest of their conversation was a pleasurable blur. If not for his unusual foray north, would they have ever met?

Shoving his musings aside and returning to the present, Henri pulled harder at the oars, then beached the jolly on a little-used stretch of white sand north of town. His senior-most crew had come ashore the day before, the rest careening the vessel and biding their time at Mistress Saltonstall's ordinary. His own day was a blank slate once he'd taken care of the post, the hours to fill as he willed.

By noon he'd walked the length and breadth of town, dined on York River oysters, and purchased supplies for Indigo Island. Word was spreading he'd returned, and by three o'clock, he'd been invited to a function that necessitated a visit to a tailor and some serious second thoughts.

Steeling his resolve, he entered the spacious shop of Brambly and Boone to find half a dozen tailors at a worktable before the large front window. September's waning light streamed over breeches and coats and waistcoats in various stages of construction. No shoddy cloth here.

"Good afternoon, sir." A small, bespectacled man emerged from a back room and gave a little bow. "Richard Boone, sir."

"Henri Lennox." He removed his hat, aware of his dishabille after a morning's row and a day about town. "I've come for a suit of clothes fit for a pleasure ball."

Respect smote the man's close-set eyes. "Ah, Lady Lightfoot's, no doubt, though there's a great deal of entertainment to be had in Williamsburg as well." He went to a glass case and retrieved paper ribbons with which to measure Henri. "Lennox, did you say? Captain Lennox of the *Relentless*?"

"The same," Henri replied, aware of every eye at the worktable now upon him.

"Honored, Captain. I promise you a suit of clothes that befits your rank and station. A quality wool broadcloth woven to a rich finish, perhaps. Our seamstress shall sew your shirt." Boone took a wheezing breath. "Have you any preferences, sir?"

"No pleated ruffles or other frippery," Henri said as the measuring ribbon stretched from his shoulder to his wrist.

"Mother-of-pearl buttons and a stock of the best linen, adorned at the end with fringe or knots, is my recommendation." Boone stood back and surveyed him. "Should I summon a wigmaker, sir?"

"No need." Wigs and powder were as unwelcome as ruffles and lace. The sea had stripped him to the barest essentials, including dress. While many good men on shore suffered want, others smothered themselves in velvet and silver thread. He'd not be among them. "But a shoemaker is in order."

"Consider it done." Boone's scrutiny shifted to Henri's booted feet. "Silver buckles and black leather seem in order as well."

"Agreed."

"We'll have your garments ready in two days' time. Will you be lodging at the Swan like so many watermen?"

"Nay. The Royal Oake on Church Street."

"Of course. A gentleman's establishment. Would you like your purchases delivered there, sir?"

"Obliged, aye."

"And will this be on credit, Captain? Or otherwise?"

"Spanish silver dollars."

"Ah." The sudden smile on the tailor's face promised a handsome suit indeed. Coin was always hard to come by in the colonies. "Very well, sir."

The Royal Oake's dining room boasted a table for twenty, and a dizzying array of dishes promised no one would emerge hungry. While the other lodgers lingered at table, Henri sought the silence of the parlor, where a case clock's ticking reminded him that time was all too fleeting. On a side table was a stack of Virginia newspapers from as far back as summer to the present day. He reached for the latest, the ink smudged from repeated perusals. Best familiarize himself with local matters, at least, before braving the ball and being asked his opinion on colonial politics or the ferocious fighting on the frontier.

"A gentleman cannot possibly ponder current events without a pipe." His hostess, Charlotte Oake, a comely widow who operated the inn with her aging father-in-law, held out not only a handsome filled pipe but a light. The pipe's clay bowl bore a Scottish unicorn on one side and an English lion on the other.

Pleasure warmed his words. "Your hospitality is unsurpassed."

"Bull's-eye tobacco." She smiled as she lit the pipe, and fragrant smoke purled between them. "Only the best for our guests."

At the sound of her father-in-law's voice, she moved away with a beguiling swish of her skirts while Henri returned to the most recent *Virginia Gazette*. International news, most of it disturbing. A plethora of notices for runaway slaves and indentures. And ads—a great many.

Yellow candlelight spread across the page, and his gaze landed on the last thing he wanted to see.

Sold here. Shaw's Superior Chocolate. Water Street, York. Soconusco, Caracas, and Maracaibo cocoa, the purest in the world. Greatly recommended by several eminent physicians for its lightness on the stomach and its great use in all consumptive cases. Two shillings sixpence per pound.

He set his jaw. His sweet tooth roared.

Pulling the pipe from between his teeth, Henri eyed the door through which his hostess had disappeared. Was there any chocolate to be had in the house?

He'd passed by Shaw's on his afternoon walk through town, the sweet, velvety aroma slowing his pace. He needed a pressed cake or two wrapped in paper and stamped with the Shaw insignia before returning to Indigo Island. 'Twas his one indulgence. Two shillings sixpence per pound exceeded a sailor's daily wage, if not a captain's.

On second thought, mayhap he'd avoid Shaw's altogether and see if there was any chocolate to be had in Williamsburg instead.

CHAPTER

four

Of all the things in the aromatic, tidy kitchen at Shaw's Chocolate, Esmée's favorite was the chocolate stone. Made of white Italian marble and placed at one end of the long worktable, it was the heart of a chocolatier's trade. Heated, the stone began melting the cocoa nibs even before she pressed her rolling pin to the brittle mass. She applied sure, even strokes born of years' experience by her mother's side, and the gritty nibs began to liquefy beneath her hands, releasing the most exquisite fragrance to be had indoors.

Around her the kitchen hummed, the indentured servants at different tasks. Simon was out back, grinding the cocoa at the hopper. Molly was but a few feet away from Esmée, molding a batch of soft, sugared chocolate in tiny tins, while Anna wrapped and stamped bricks of chocolate before carrying them to the storefront for display.

Father preferred Esmée out front. She drew customers as much as the merchandise, he oft said, remembering names and preferences and prior orders. But when her spirit grew troubled, she retreated to the kitchen, losing or at least solacing herself with the work. Within these walls were memories of her beloved mother, warm, rich, and sweet.

Shaw's Chocolate was Mama's doing. Mama's vision. But it was

Esmée's dowry and the place where she invested herself. One of two places where she felt a tie to her mother.

Even now her thoughts of a certain captain and a certain ship and a ball gown that lacked lace trim faded to the far reaches as she poured a waterfall of Maracaibo sugar onto the chocolate stone, then rolled and mixed the mass till all was smooth. Next, she reached for a small tin, extracted orange peel, added it to the mixture, then threw in a dash of vanilla and more sugar. Bittersweet became a more delicately flavored chocolate. With a swipe of her finger she sampled it, waiting a discerning second before her eyes went wide with delight.

Chocolate perfection.

Molly chuckled. "'Tis a wonder, mistress, yer not broad as a bulkhead with all the cocoa butter ye partake."

Smiling, Esmée took another lick. She *had* gained a stone since . . . She forced herself to finish the untimely thought. *Since the captain last saw me.* She took a wooden tool and scraped the melted chocolate into a waiting bowl to cool.

Anna stopped her stamping. "Is it true yer father has ordered a hand mill from Boston, Miss Shaw?"

Nodding, Esmée poured another pound of cocoa nibs onto the stone. "Not only a hand mill but a large grinder that produces one hundred weight of chocolate in six hours."

"I second that!" Simon shouted through the back door.

"Chocolate's becoming the beverage of choice for colonists," Esmée said, "if for no other reason than the crown's infernal tax on tea."

"Glad I am that cocoa sails straight from the Caribbean and England has no say." Molly began picking out the chocolates that didn't pass muster. "I'm drinking so much coffee lately I nearly forget what tea tastes like!"

Esmée ceased her rolling as Josiah poked his head into the kitchen from the shop entrance. "Widow Oake to see you, Miss Shaw."

"Let's trade places then." Esmée handed him the roller, washed her hands, and exchanged her soiled apron for a clean one with a readiness she was far from feeling.

"Good morning, Miss Shaw." The widow's chilly smile seemed no more genuine than paste gems. Beneath her beribboned hat, Charlotte Oake's eyes held no warmth. "I would rather deal with you than the help."

"What do you buy?" Esmée replied, hoping to conclude their business as quickly as possible. Charlotte's maid stood in back of her, wearing a timid smile.

Esmée's gaze flew from the calendar proclaiming it the first of October to the clock Father had taken down. Time seemed to stop when the Oakes appeared. The widow was fond of reminding Esmée she was not among York's founding families but an outsider, an easterner.

Still, Esmée tried to be cordial and fill the lengthy silence. "How goes it at the Royal Oake?"

"All our rooms are full at present." Charlotte moved about the charmingly arranged shop, her gloved hand touching this or that. "I'm in need of chocolate for our table. Certain gentlemen lodgers seem especially fond of such."

As Charlotte passed by a front window, her gown caught the light, the celestial blue silk cascading like a ruffled wave to her elegantly shod feet. From London, likely. Her father-in-law insisted on London-made goods.

Esmée gestured to the recently stocked shelves. "We've a new array of flavors—anise, Ceylon cinnamon, nutmeg, and Madagascar vanilla if you'd like a taste."

"Vanilla, then." When Esmée passed her a sample, Charlotte pursed her lips as if she'd been handed a lemon instead. "I find Shaw's no match for the chocolatiers in New York and Philadelphia."

Esmée bit her lip. She'd never visited the foremost city chocolatiers. Could those goods be that much superior? Though theirs was a humble shop, they did their best to turn out a quality product.

"How do you recommend preparing your hot beverages?" Charlotte asked.

"Hot cocoa? I simply add powdered chocolate and sugar to steamed milk, stirring all the while. Once it's off the fire, whir the milk mixture with a hand mill till frothy."

"Milk, not water?"

"Milk makes for a richer drink."

"I'll take this pewter chocolate pot with the lidded hand mill, then, though I cower at the price." Charlotte passed it to Esmée with a frown. "And five of your best bricks of chocolate." Drifting to the display of other confections, she pointed to a chocolate tart Molly had baked that morning. "And this."

As Esmée wrapped her purchases, she was nearly undone by the widow's scrutiny.

"How is your sister, Lady Drysdale? I rarely see her in York these days."

Though Eliza had been married two years, Esmée oft forgot her sister's formal title. "She is busy with Williamsburg pursuits now that she resides there."

"I'd heard you might open a second chocolate shop in the capital." Charlotte gestured for her maid to take the purchases. "'Tis said your sister has been talking of such. Rather a step down for a titled woman to still be meddling in matters of commerce, is it not?"

The jibe barely skimmed Esmée's conscience. *A second shop?* More indentures. More machinery. More labor. And more cross, inquiring customers like the Oakes. Esmée returned the matter to Eliza's lap.

"My sister shall be happy to enlighten you on the matter if you ask her." Esmée knotted the string binding the purchases and passed them over the counter to the maid.

"Come along, Verity," Charlotte said at last. "We've the chandler to see next."

The petty tension dissolved at the closing of the shop door, which soon jingled open again as other customers entered. Half an hour later Esmée returned to the kitchen to gather chocolate for a delivery while Simon readied the pony cart outside. 'Twas her day to visit the almshouse, following Mama's habit.

Leaving the indentures to mind the shop, Esmée took the reins in hand and sought the end of Water Street heading north, blessedly free of her sister's lofty trappings and title, no lady's maid in pursuit. After the heat of the shop, the afternoon seemed cool, clouds piled as high as meringue and snuffing the sun. The road to the almshouse followed the coast with a sweeping view of the water, thus making it more pleasure than chore. Already the coastal landscape wore the robust mantle of autumn.

She hadn't delivered cocoa since last May, as their season for chocolate making was short in the Southern colonies. Fall to spring was when they plied their trade, their sultry summers devoted to other business.

Out here amid the wind and salt tang of the sea, she felt far more at peace than in some fussy ballroom, yet Lady Lightfoot's assembly loomed, a sennight away. Esmée nearly groaned aloud.

"Not all balls are bad, mind you," Eliza oft said.

Once, Father had escorted them to the governor's palace in Williamsburg, past the imposing forecourt and into the immense rear ballroom that bore double doors with steps leading to an elaborate formal garden. There, like something out of a fairy tale, Eliza captured the attention of Quinn, Lord Drysdale. A felicitous match, Father said, when all the stars aligned and turned a simple Eliza Shaw into a titled lady.

Esmée was content to be the older sister and watch the romantic drama unfold. The congenial, handsome Quinn. The ebullient, beautiful Eliza. His prominent kin scandalized that their rising star of a relative might be tainted by the privateering past of his affianced's admiral father. In the end, rumors were quelled, the wedding commenced, and now Esmée herself was to become an aunt in a few months' time. What would life hand them next?

The pony cart bumped along, hitting a stone or two and churning up dust. The brown ribbon of road unwound ahead of her, little traveled. Father didn't like her traveling alone, but the pistol secured beneath the seat hadn't been used once. Never had she encountered a threat. 'Twas simply a lonesome path to a place most avoided.

Tugging on the reins, she paused on a grassy knoll overlooking tidelands and islands. Indigo Island was the farthest, its rocky shore like a raised shoulder shrugging her away. Somewhere on the island stood the unfinished lighthouse, tall but dark. The plan had been to complete it prior to her and the captain's nuptials. They'd agreed to dismiss custom and wed on the beach, then honeymoon in his cottage. Sunrises and sunsets were said to be spectacular from that speck of land, the quiet and privacy unsurpassed.

Lately she'd heard no more from Father about Captain Lennox's return. A pity he was so seldom home, all that beauty unappreciated. For all she knew he'd already set sail again and she could drop her guard like a hot iron, letting go of her dread at encountering him on every corner.

Snapping the reins, she guided the pony onto the road again. She had little need of the dashing, intriguing Henri Lennox in her life. Her days were full, even if her heart was still adrift. She would not allow herself the tiniest spark of intrigue at his rumored appearance. The captain had not found her worthy then, nor would he now. They were both older and wiser, long past any youthful infatuation.

Another half mile and she rolled into the courtyard before the cluster of brick buildings that made up the almshouse. Two women gathering nuts in their aprons beneath a hickory tree looked up as she passed. In a far yard men chopped firewood and broke stones for road building, while unseen women spun cloth and gardened or worked in the kitchen.

To live here was to punish the poor for being poor, Father said. Elderly outcasts, widows, destitute women, disabled men, and orphaned children led a cheerless existence. Upon the arms of their humble garments was a bit of red cloth marked with a *P*, as they were wards of the parish. This humbling distinction hurt Esmée too. Was it not enough they were here? A hundred untold stories lived in their somber, shrunken faces. Even the children seemed half-alive, deprived of affection and family and life's basic comforts.

Her heart gave a little leap as half a dozen youngsters broke free of their chores and rushed toward her, as taken by her pony as the cocoa she brought. A sharp rebuke by the female trustee stole their joy. Mistress Boles approached, chronically ill-tempered and grasping, followed by the cheerier and slightly younger Miss Grove.

"I've need of helping hands to unload." Esmée oft wondered if the children ever saw any of what she brought. "I've real sweetmeats this time, not dry bricks of cocoa. Come near and I'll give you each a treat as a reward for your labors."

Before the matron could protest, Esmée doled out the best of the bounty—raisins and extra chocolate almonds from Lady Lightfoot's order. Something like daylight spilled into their eager, childish faces, their open hands wrenching Esmée's heart.

"A waste of confections, I daresay," Mistress Boles muttered.

Steeling herself against the rising tide of heartache—and the stench of unwashed bodies and mended garments—Esmée watched Mistress Boles chase the children away. She called after them, "I wish I could bring you a hundredfold more."

"If only every soul in Virginia was as generous as you, we'd be called the poorhouse no longer," Miss Grove told her as the cart was emptied, the goods carried to the kitchen.

Esmée focused on Miss Grove's wavy hair, swept back severely beneath her mobcap. Her yellow dress, though faded, brought a burst of color. "What need have you of blankets and linens?"

"There is never enough, I confess. Your gift of stockings and caps last winter helped a great deal."

"Never enough of those either, once winter sets in. I've been knitting steadily all summer, as has my late mother's sewing society in York."

"I'm heartened to hear it." Miss Grove smiled, her complexion's spiderweb of wrinkles easing. "You'll be pleased to know the children are being schooled twice a week by an itinerant master . . ."

"Because there aren't sufficient funds to maintain one permanently," Esmée finished for her. "Is the schoolmaster fair? Kind?"

"Fair, perhaps. I've yet to meet many who are kind. Most seem overfond of the lash."

Mistress Boles reappeared, ending their honest conversation. She raised dull eyes heavenward. "Surely you'll be wanting to return to York, Miss Shaw. The clouds bode ill."

As does your countenance.

Schooling her dismay, Esmée made ready to leave. "Perhaps you and Miss Grove can make a list of all your needs and give it to me next visit. With prayer and industry, we shall remedy what we can."

A child snuck forward when Mistress Boles turned her back. "Thank'ee, Miss Shaw." Her freckled face softened in a smile. "Come back soon, if ye please. We've so few visitors and need a bit o' cheer."

The matron turned round again. Had she heard? "Shoo!" she shouted, then looked at Esmée again. "Jenny will as soon pick your pocket as give you a sly word."

Esmée knelt down till she was eye level with the scolded girl. "Of course I shall, sweet Jenny. Count on it."

Turning away, Esmée swiped at her eyes with a gloved hand as the wind tugged at the surrounding trees and sent the leaves adance in colorful disarray, adding a touch of whimsy to the disheartening scene. She'd always sensed God's Spirit in the wind. Surely He was near now, comforting society's castoffs, even brushing her damp cheek with an unseen hand.

Wasn't He?

Esmée climbed into the cart and took up the reins again. She waved goodbye, the pony lighter in step as the cart was now empty, though her heart was still burdened. Perhaps Lady Lightfoot's ball would be a good place to begin her almshouse entreaties.

CHAPTER

five

After a sennight, Henri began to feel as though he resided in York. His tailoring took longer than expected, requiring him to stay on at the Royal Oake, which left no time to return to Indigo Island before Lady Lightfoot's ball. He wasn't overly concerned, as his crew was a well-disciplined lot for the most part. They were deserving of a rest when they weren't at work on the vessel, anticipating the next as-yet-unknown sailing. He'd crossed paths with his quartermaster and ship's carpenter in town. A few of his crew were already selling wares at York's market— Monmouth caps and stockings they knitted. They gave him a hearty greeting, clearly glad to be ashore. Others were taking notice of their return from all quarters.

"Can it be Captain Lennox?" A burly, ham-fisted merchant stopped him midstride, walking stick in hand. "I'd heard you were again in York. Might I have a word with you about a shipping venture I have in mind?"

"Monday, mayhap," Henri put forth. "Where would you like to meet?"

"At Shaw's coffeehouse, none other. Say, two o'clock?"

With a nod, Henri continued his walk. Best get used to Shaw's, the preferred meeting place. Did the admiral hold a grudge over what had happened between him and his daughter?

He lifted his cocked hat to a passing carriage of colorful straw-hatted ladies, their lingering looks reminding him of Esmée again. How odd it felt to be a landsman. Yet the last few sailings had left him feeling that the ship had shrunk or he'd expanded, a grown man regarding everything in miniature.

York seemed more interesting than ever before. His stay had been sweetened with Shaw's cocoa at breakfast, and he'd not even had to darken the door of their shop. Nor had he seen any sign of Esmée anywhere, though he'd caught sight of her father at a distance, coming out of the customhouse on Main Street.

He'd always been fond of the admiral. Ten years had knocked him down a stone or two, but he still bore the erect carriage of a former commander, making him stand out on a bustling, hazardous street. Mistress Shaw he remembered as a force in her own right. Hospitable. A generous benefactress. A shrewd woman of trade.

He wouldn't dwell on their two daughters.

Shutting the door of the inn as quietly as he could still resulted in Widow Oake appearing. She sailed into the narrow hall, sleek as a shallop, as he set one foot on the stair to his rooms.

"Captain Lennox . . ." Her silver eyes held an unspoken invitation. "Father wanted me to tell you all is in hand for your transport to the ball tonight. Our coachman will come round at half past six."

"I'll be ready." He took the second step as a case clock thundered four o'clock. Plenty of time to prepare.

"Are you fond of dancing, Captain?"

Fond was generous. "Nay." He softened his reply with a half-smile. "I'd rather ply shark-infested waters."

She chuckled at his half jest. "Something tells me your attendance at the ball isn't due to your skill at allemandes and minuets."

"If it were, I'd not be invited."

"Might I wheedle *one* country dance out of you in our very own parlor at our next entertainment? A reel or jig?"

41

He gained another step. He'd seen less persistent pirates. "Mayhap."

Her smile was coy as he departed. Finally upstairs, he paused to admire the elaborate bell system his host had threaded on copper wire from lodgers' rooms down to the servants' quarters. A pull on an embroidered silk cord quickly gained him the hot water he needed. A water closet with a little door opening into the hall allowed a servant to attend to any needs without entering guests' rooms.

Once bathed, shaved, and dressed, he studied himself in the looking glass, something he rarely did aboard ship. All in all, his new suit left him looking like anyone else of genteel status in Virginia.

No doubt at the ball he would see many Virginians he knew and some he didn't.

And others he didn't want to.

"Are you skittish, Sister?"

Skittish? *In spades.*

Esmée locked eyes with Eliza as they finished dressing in their adjoining bedchambers of the York townhouse. Quinn was below with Father, waiting impatiently, probably.

"You seem unnaturally disquieted." Reaching out, Eliza tugged on a tightly coiled curl till it relaxed and draped over Esmée's shoulder.

"You know how I feel about these genteel gatherings." Esmée stared at her sister's elaborate coiffure, a powdered pouf over a foot high crowned with a ship, which had taken over two hours to achieve and left Eliza's lady's maid in tears. Even now the nautical headdress seemed to be listing despite its intricate scaffolding.

Eliza studied her with a canny eye. "So, the pearls win?"

Atop the dressing table an assortment of gems winked up at them in the candlelight, myriad velvet-lined jewelry cases open. Eliza dangled a glittering garnet on a gold chain, then exchanged it for another.

"I rarely wear anything but pearls." Esmée touched her throat where the necklace rested. "As for you, how about this star ruby Father brought Mama from the city of Karur in India?"

"How do you remember all the details?" Eliza fastened the ruby about her neck. "Your fondness for geography, I suppose. Celestial navigation has always been your strong suit."

"As society is yours."

"If you'd been a son, you might well have been a sailor," Eliza teased. "A jack."

With a last look at each other and the looking glass, they put on light silk capes a maid brought and went below. In the coach, the seven-mile distance would be easily managed despite the rutted road. Lady Lightfoot lived halfway between York and Williamsburg in a grand brick mansion named Lightfoot Hall, its ballroom a twin to the governor's palace in the capital, but as she and Dinwiddie were kin, no one made much of the likeness.

Esmée settled back on the upholstered seat, wishing the seven miles were seventy instead. But even that distance would not give her time to compose herself. "Pleasure" balls they were not. Already she was counting the hours till she could peel off her many layers while ruminating about all the things she'd said and done but shouldn't have. Yet she liked Lady Lightfoot. And she did not wish to offend by declining her gracious invitation. As she was not prone to lying, pleading illness didn't suit either. Let the ball be a ruse for raising funds for the almshouse.

Beside her, Eliza sat fussing with the pins in her hair. Her sister's shipwreck of a coiffure only added to Esmée's angst as she watched it barely clear the coach's narrow doorway. The men got in after them warily. Father looked resplendent in admiral attire, and no one could fault Quinn for his wardrobe, respected barrister and member of the governor's council that he was.

"How goes your marine atlas?" Quinn asked Father as he settled beside Eliza.

"A piece of work," Father replied, clearly pleased by the subject. "Charting the Atlantic coast is a tedious process, but if it improves navigation safety, 'tis well worth it."

"I heard the admiralty is hurrying you to finish on account of the French threat."

"Understandably with the enemy coming by sea . . ."

The men continued their talk as Eliza gave a final poke with a pin, and the ship seemed anchored at last. "You are my foil tonight, Sister. Unpowdered and unwigged. Plain pearls and remade gown."

Did Eliza suspect she tried to blend in with the paneling? "All the better."

"Did I mention Quinn's parents gifted me an heirloom tiara upon news of the baby? A shocking assortment of diamonds, Quinn says, that's been in the Cheverton family a century or better. Sadly, my in-laws remain in England but plan to sail unless a declaration of war is decided."

"When shall you wear the tiara?"

"As soon as it—and the heir—arrives."

Esmée took a deep breath, her stays overtight. "What makes you so sure the heir isn't a she?"

"We've only chosen names for a boy, so a boy it must be."

Esmée quelled her eye rolling. "Best ponder daughter's names, as the Almighty might have other designs."

"Quinn has his heart set on a son." Eliza lowered her voice as the men droned on. "I daren't suggest otherwise."

They rounded a curve that marked the last leg of their journey, sending Esmée sliding toward the window. She unclenched her fists from the folds of her gown to find her palms damp beneath her gloves. Her ordeal was at hand. How she wished for some of Eliza's joie de vivre, her ability to glide through whatever life dealt her, smiling and undaunted.

The coach rolled into the forecourt of the Lightfoot mansion behind a line of conveyances as liveried servants sprang into service. Esmée alighted from the coach on her father's arm, then followed Quinn and Eliza into the marbled hall, where a butler waited at the ballroom's entrance to announce them. Biting her lip, she fixed an eye on her sister's coiffure lest she need to right it, rather than the press of people on every side. There seemed an audible gasp at Eliza's entry, which soon subsided as other guests appeared.

Lady Lightfoot was known for her democratic guest list. Among

Virginia's bejeweled gentry were wealthy Scots merchants and other notables of questionable pedigree who'd risen to prominence in the colonies because of their wits and business acumen and advantageous marriages. They had few of the airs and graces of the titled and genteel but were far more interesting, at least to Esmée.

Her father steered her safely to a corner, where old friends greeted them. Eliza and Quinn, ever popular, were moving about, speaking to those they knew and some they didn't. From all appearances, her sister's headdress was staying the course.

"My dear Miss Shaw . . ." Lady Lightfoot's distinct tone cut through the hubbub as she passed in front of Esmée after greeting her father. For a widow of many years, she had retained her agile mind and slim figure. "I believe I spy a long-lost acquaintance of yours." With that, their hostess moved on in a glittering display of silk and feathers, leaving a trail of dread and trepidation in her wake.

Father watched her departure with a lift of his graying brows. "I suppose this means Captain Lennox is at hand."

Esmée scanned the ballroom, dismay leaving her breathless. "In truth, I never expected to see him here. He wasn't one for dancing. Nor did I expect Lady Lightfoot to mention him outright."

"She didn't name him, my dear, though I did detect a certain glint in her eye. Lady Lightfoot has ever been one for a trick or a little matchmaking." He gave Esmée a pained, apologetic half-smile. "Speaking of which . . ." His gaze strayed to the rear doorway, open and leading to the garden. Esmée's did the same.

There stood Henri Lennox, hands clasped behind his back, shoulders squared and expression resolute, looking for all the world like a commander at the helm of a ship in a storm. As if a ball was more a navigational hazard than the high seas.

Esmée took out a hand fan and cooled her face, wishing the painted silk device were the size of a sail and she could hide behind it. Her smothering anxiety was overshadowed by a rush of heartsore remembrance. All the captain's youthful lines had been chipped away into the sculpting of the hardened man he'd become. The jut of his jaw told her so, as did his sun-cast features more sharply chiseled. A face shaped by countless foreign ports and untold destinations. A gloss of black hair caught back with silk ribbon. Eyes of so cold an ocean blue they hurt her.

Ten long years.

She hardly knew him.

CHAPTER

Six

Amid so much finery and so many faces, Henri felt at sea. And when he'd barely rediscovered his land legs, he was expected to dance.

"Captain Lennox! Just the man I was hoping to encounter." Virginia's acting governor gave a formal bow, his wig powder flaking onto the shoulders of his velvet suit. "Lady Lightfoot assured me of your presence tonight but cautioned me against cornering you and denying you an evening's entertainment."

"On the contrary," Henri replied, warming to the official's forthright manner. "Corner away."

"After supper, certainly." Dinwiddie's broad Scots brogue warmed Henri's ears, as did his convivial wink. "I dare not earn the ire of every unmarried miss in the room straightaway."

The dancing commenced, a minuet stepped by the most prestigious and well placed among them, including a stunning young woman in a fanciful wig with a ship perched atop it. Henri's wry amusement faded as recognition kicked in. *Upon my soul . . .*

Eliza Shaw?

The certainty took hold as guests framed him on both sides. His hostess, Lady Lightfoot, was making straight for him.

"Captain Lennox, how utterly dashing you look."

Henri gave a little bow as she tapped his sleeve with her fan.

"I half expected to see you in naval uniform, but of course you are a free agent now and no longer one of His Majesty's officers." She smiled widely, eyes roaming the glittering assembly. "There are a number of young ladies here who are noticeably agog at your presence . . . including Admiral Shaw's daughter, a prior acquaintance of yours, is she not?"

Was Lady Lightfoot jesting? He'd not spied Esmée in the throng, though it was likely she'd be present. Given their acrimonious parting, *agog* was the last word he'd choose. *Aghast*, rather.

Lady Lightfoot moved on, and the young woman to his right smiled up at him. He'd rather partner with a roomful of complete strangers than the estranged Miss Shaw.

"A dance, Miss . . . ?"

"Miss Traverse." The young lady brightened at his forced words.

The minuet ended and a reel that all the Scots present excelled at was struck. Henri found himself caught up in the gaiety, the steps and turns easily recalled, his partner's pleasure tempering his impatience to get on with the evening.

When the dance ended, he excused himself, distracted by a naval officer in uniform who drew him into conversation with two York shipbuilders.

"Tell us about the *Relentless*, Captain Lennox," one gentleman said. "A three-masted ship of the line with seventy-four guns, aye? A gift from the governor of Nevis in the Caribbean for warring with buccaneers and securing shipping lanes in his province?"

His back to the ballroom, Henri spoke with ease about what he knew best, sharing details of his last cruise and the current careening on Indigo Island.

Another gentleman joined in. "You're the talk of all the coffee-houses on the coast, not to mention broadsides and newspapers, with your black jacks and lucrative prizes."

"Is it true you've captured more than thirty enemy ships in a twelve-month?" an officer asked. "Spanish, mostly, as well as notorious buccaneers?"

"Much of it hearsay," Henri countered. He shied from any praise or applause, though it was preferable to being vilified as a pirate. "As privateer, I simply align with colonial authorities in wanting the lawlessness by sea stopped."

"Well, I for one welcome your return to port amongst us proud Virginians. 'Tis hurricane season, after all."

Henri grimaced as a line began forming. He might be headed straight for a tempest with supper at hand.

The double doors of the dining room swung open. Like with dancing, those of highest rank went first, titled Virginia officials and whatnot, which left the Shaws somewhere in the middle. Quinn and Eliza were far ahead, at the front of the line behind Lady Lightfoot, thus removing one of Esmée's familiar underpinnings. Thankfully, Father was at hand, speaking with a Williamsburg merchant. Behind them was her dear friend Kitty Hart, followed by . . .

Captain Lennox.

Esmée fixed her gaze straight ahead, feeling as wooden as a ship's figurehead. Were his intense eyes boring into her stays-straightened back? Censuring her for sitting out the dancing more than she danced? Finding fault with her for being unpowdered and plain? Her plan to remain in the shadows backfired badly. Instead she'd gained unwanted attention because of her simplicity.

Breathe, lass.

Mightn't the captain have forgotten all about her? Perhaps she'd left so little a dent in his conscience that she was all but invisible now. Certainly he'd had other flirtations since. She certainly couldn't hold a candle to many of the young belles tonight in their whispering silks and winking gemstones.

The line crawled toward the dining room's entrance, supper smells mingling with fragrant beeswax candles. She put a hand to her waist to finger her chatelaine, something she oft did when distressed. But it was a habit of no use to her now, for she wasn't wearing it.

Places were sought, a great shuffling and fuss occurred, and Esmée found herself staring at the one remaining seat.

To the right of Henri Lennox.

All the other places around the immense table were taken, leaving her standing conspicuously. She dared not look at the captain, yet she felt his unease like a stone wall between them. Or was it her own discomfiture? She sat down and looked to her lap, a hammer tapping at her temples and threatening to flip her stomach.

How had they left it at the last? When they'd faced each other that final time in the Shaws' townhouse parlor, their voices rising notch by notch?

"Marry me, Esmée."

"I would, Henri, if not for the sea."

"So the sea is the only obstacle between us?"

"It robbed my mother of my father. I would not have it rob me of you."

"You would have me forsake my calling, then."

"Better your calling than your wife."

"Your stated reasons are your refusal, I take it."

She had made no reply. And then, a decade's absence.

Supper's seating arrangement left Henri feeling keelhauled—roped and thrown overboard only to be dragged under the ship's backbone to his doom. So far Esmée hadn't said a word. The long table was wide enough that conversations across it were impossible. He tried to say a few words to the elderly lady to his left who was stone-cold deaf. Esmée seemed in a similar predicament with the gentleman to her right, who was more absorbed by laughter and talk farther down. Awkwardness did not begin to describe the arrangement.

Henri swallowed. Removed all regret and blame from his tone. He stole a look at her. "How does one account for ten lost years, Miss Shaw?"

Esmée's pale hand stilled on her wine glass. The pearl ring she wore unearthed a long-buried memory. "One does not, Captain Lennox. Or, if left no choice, very carefully."

Silence.

He stared at the candelabra in front of him. "By some trick of fate, we have ended up side by side."

"*Fate*, sir?" Mockery curdled her tone. "I don't believe in it."

"Mayhap the Almighty is having a fine jest at our expense." He drummed his fingers lightly atop the damask tablecloth. "To your credit you were never one for theatrics or hysterics. You'll simply soldier on through supper and make the best of it."

"And you, stalwart seaman that you are, shall do the same." She shifted as if uncomfortable in her chair. "Despite the fact we are drawing noticeable attention."

He raised his gaze. No less than half a dozen pairs of eyes were on them. "People have long memories of thwarted love affairs."

"Indeed."

"Well, I for one have a few overdue inquiries," he said, then paused to swallow a sip of wine. "How is your dear mother?"

"Buried."

Nay. Dismayed, he let the news settle. Her terse answer begged details he could not ask about. "My deepest sympathies." He meant it. Eleanor Shaw had been an uncommon woman. A woman ahead of her time, or rather a woman who made good use of the time she'd been given.

"A question for a question," Esmée said as soup was served. "Why have you come ashore?"

He eyed the monogrammed bowl surmounted by the Lightfoot family crest that was set before him. Crab bisque? "I spent the last three years in the Summer Isles. I was beginning to forget Virginia."

To this she made no reply. The lukewarm soup was more enjoyable than their stilted conversation. Only a dozen more courses to go.

"How is your father?" he asked, having spied the admiral earlier in the evening. It was a far safer question.

"Adrift without my mother."

"And your sister?"

"'Tis my turn, Captain."

He wished for a little levity, but she was unsmiling. Intense. Gone was the warmth and approachability that had once marked her. Had she somehow assumed some of her sister's mercurial hauteur? If so, it was a cold, shrewd beauty that left him missing the Esmée of old.

"What of your own Virginia kin?" she asked, turning intelligent eyes on him.

"Deceased. The rest are in Scotland, if you recall. And France. I've none left in the colonies."

Her lengthy pause rattled him. "I'm . . . terribly sorry." She ran a spoon through her soup but made no move to eat it. "To answer your earlier question, my sister is as irrepressible as ever."

Down the long table came Eliza's unmistakable laugh. She was heavier than he remembered. *Enceinte?* And all aglitter from head to toe. In the press of guests he'd not gotten a good look at the bewigged gentleman who'd danced with her. Her husband?

"Your sister was always one to land on her feet," he murmured.

Esmée herself was dressed far more sedately. Her yellow gown seemed rather faded, but the lace draping her bodice and sleeves was exquisite, a foil to her bountiful black hair. And her pearls . . . She'd always preferred them. When in the South Seas he'd oft been reminded of that.

Fish was served along with dishes he later couldn't recall, so intent was he on their forced talk. Esmée pushed her food around her plate while he managed a few forkfuls. Had his presence stolen her appetite? Pale as she was, she resembled the wilting white roses at table's center. Hardly the enchanting creature he'd stored away in memory's darkest corner.

The silence chafed. Whose turn was it now? Though he wanted to convince himself he could navigate this encounter with aplomb, that her hold on him was irretrievably broken, he could not.

CHAPTER

seven

They seemed an island unto themselves. Little eddies of lively conversation on all sides of them made their forced, close proximity all the more painful. The silver fork grew heavy in Esmée's hand. Every bite seemed more difficult to swallow. All at once she felt far from a self-possessed woman of nearly thirty but rather childlike and fragile, throat tight and near tears.

Dear Hermione.

Sorrow made her sag and went unrelieved as supper wore on. Esmée felt blindsided by the news, further thrown off by the captain's stoicism reporting it, as if family were of no more merit than his crew and deserved little mention.

Once she and Hermione looked forward to being sisters-in-law. Eliza had been especially fond of her, though she'd lost touch with her after her rift with the captain. The Lennoxes had lived in a handsome house facing the waterfront in Norfolk back then. His father had been a respected shipbuilder there.

At least her own sister had been spared. Tonight Eliza was shining, her coiffure miraculously intact. She'd not stopped smiling all evening. Didn't her cheeks feel the strain? Father seemed to be enjoying himself too. At home, devoid of Mama, their suppers were quiet affairs. Here he seemed to forget himself, mingling with his fellows, making merry, and toasting this or that.

She took another tasteless bite. Captain Lennox was finally conversing with the woman on his left, the heavily rouged and powdered wife of a port official. Stealing another look at him, she fixed upon the scar above his brow, a thin, pale line she didn't recall. Concern softened her for an unguarded moment. She'd likely never know how it came to be there.

But it was the tattoo inked on his right wrist that most intrigued her. The Jerusalem cross? Five black crosses were etched beneath his silver-buttoned cuff, ever popular with mariners. Some shipboard artist's doing, no doubt. Was the accompanying Latin phrase, *Coram Deo*, also there? *In the presence of God.* Was that how he felt upon the sea in all its magnificence? In the Almighty's very presence?

Fingering her pearls, Esmée tried to strike up a conversation on her right as dessert was served, to no avail. So far, all her efforts on behalf of the almshouse had come to nil, making the evening a complete loss.

A small crystal dish was set before her—blackberry flummery. What she craved was chocolate. Cocoa bolstered, soothed, and satisfied while the flummery was sticky and cloyingly sweet. She darted a discreet look left. Captain Lennox sat back in his chair like lord and master, making no inroads on his dessert. He seemed sunk in thought, and she'd wager it wasn't flummery he was pondering.

Supper was nearly at an end, God be thanked. A two-hour ordeal that would require a fortnight's recovery. She nearly sighed aloud in relief.

As the dancing resumed, Esmée hovered near a partially open window, drawn by a cool breeze. She'd not danced in ages, though she was partial to the English country dances stepped by a number of couples. Once she'd been lauded as graceful, on par with Eliza. A wistful longing tugged at her, dusty memories of their former French dancing master sweet.

Watching couples assemble for a longways dance, she found herself drawn forward at the press of Kitty's gloved hand. Though she'd steered clear of the captain since supper, she could do so no longer. Someone had coerced him onto the ballroom floor. A young woman in shagreen silk waved her fan at him, looking as cunning as a fox in a henhouse.

Esmée's middle twisted, souring what little supper she'd partaken of. As lines formed, the captain stood across from her, not the fan-waving coquette. By accident or design? Accident, she would wager. She tried to smile and be at her dancing best lest anyone apprehend her fluttering nerves, a dozen unwelcome memories assailing her.

Once her dancing best had been with him.

Though he'd claimed to favor supporting the wall, he'd managed dancing admirably back then. And now?

As she thought it, more dancers assembled, and the green-gowned woman nudged her aside as if determined to partner with the captain. Esmée yielded as a flash of irritation gave way to a feeling far more startling. Disappointment? But there was no time to dwell on it. The music prompted them forward, and in time he did indeed become her partner. She placed her fingertips lightly in his upraised palm, more a whisper than a touch, her heart in her throat. Up and down the rows they went as one, dancing figures with all the other couples.

Increasingly breathless, she met his eyes again and again as they matched steps. The dance required it. To look away from one's partner was rude and sure to be noted. Each time their eyes and hands touched she felt a slight shift, an inexplicable thawing. His eyes . . . had they really been so silvery a blue? His face so handsomely weathered?

A tiny flicker of something long dead threatened to rekindle.

The next morning found Esmée at work, Lady Lightfoot's ball a hazy dream. Tying on an apron and toying with her chatelaine, she stood in the still-dark kitchen, breathing in vanilla and orange essence and cinnamon, letting her spirits settle. Everything still felt a bit off. The help weren't due for an hour or so, but evidence of the previous day's labor adorned every available counter and workplace. She'd barely been hungry for her hyson tea and dry toast at breakfast, so now she reached for a shell-shaped sweetmeat, letting its richness melt on her tongue.

But it in no way assuaged the previous night's encounter.

Sighing, she passed through the door into the shop, where the first ribbons of light streamed through the bow-fronted window. The majestic view of the harbor never failed to swell her heart—all those tall-masted brigs, schooners, and ships of the line commanded by stalwart, unflinching men the likes of Henri Lennox.

The stirring spectacle sent her back into the kitchen again, where she grabbed a broom and began sweeping an already pristine floor. She hummed a hymn. Eyed the clock. Perused account books and receipts. She would not wallow in sore memories or the sorry one they'd made last night. Like as not, the captain was still at Lady Light-foot's. She'd seen the way he'd been sequestered by Virginia's foremost officials at a break in the dancing, then once a cotillion resumed, he had disappeared into an antechamber.

She'd slipped outside into the garden, the moonlit darkness sweetly scented and consoling. Couples strolled about as she hid herself away in a folly at a far corner. Knowing Eliza, Esmée felt her hopes for an early exit fade. Pregnancy had not curbed her sister's high spirits or her nocturnal habits.

They'd finally returned home at three o'clock in the morning, Eliza still chattering like a magpie, Quinn snoring on the seat beside her, and Father as mute and contemplative as a monk. He'd gone into that antechamber with the captain and gentlemen. She'd witnessed it before fleeing to the garden. And the door had not reopened till long after midnight, at which point the men emerged without a hint of whatever had detained them. Nor had Father said a word since. This morning he'd slept well past his usual rising time of five o'clock. Eliza would be abed till noon, though Quinn usually sought out one of the coffeehouses to visit with his York friends.

Opening a sack of cocoa nibs, Esmée inhaled their familiar scent much as she did coffee. The roast was exactly right. Too long over the fire turned the cocoa bitter. Too little heat robbed it of flavor. Those Philadelphia roasters knew what they were about. The nibs had been winnowed free of chaff and were ready for refining.

She poured the entire sack into a large marble mortar while the chocolate stone heated at the hearth. Raising a pestle, she let loose all her angst and began pounding the nibs to dust. An airy brown powder rose and tickled her nose, sending her sneezing into her sleeve.

By the time the shop opened, a sheen of velvety chocolate covered the stone. A lick of her finger left grit on Esmée's tongue. Switching to a different roller, she continued crushing and adding sugar, even a bit of orange essence, Eliza's favorite. She stopped only when Anna came into the kitchen with a package in her arms.

"Miss Shaw, look at what was left on the front step." She held it out to Esmée, who stopped her rolling. "Your name is on the outside."

Esmée wiped her hands on her apron, took the package, and untied the string binding the wrapping paper. *The Complete Confectioner.*

Wonder bloomed. Bound in leather, the long-coveted book held a whiff of new ink. Or was it her imagination? Tentative, she opened it and marveled at the pristine pages unmarred by grease or chocolate. "You saw no one?"

"None, Miss Shaw. 'Twas just sitting by the door alongside a stray cat." Anna sniffed. "I'm surprised it wasn't thieved with all the riffraff on Water Street."

Clutching the book to her bodice, Esmée returned to the shop and perused the chocolate pots and accessories, excited to try a new recipe.

Who might the gift giver be?

eight

*H*enri hadn't reckoned on old houses having so many ghosts.

The keys from his father's solicitor hung heavy in his pocket as he unlocked the front door of the Norfolk townhouse on Prince Street. Dust overlaid the once busy entrance hall, running up the elaborately carved balustrade and coating every nick and scratch in a sandy powder, even dimming the crystal brilliance of the chandelier and windows. He shut the door and it echoed. A dismal sound.

Shrugging off the melancholy that had dogged him since coming into the city by coach, he strode across the foyer to the parlor, opening doors and traversing rooms with an eye for change. Paint—the rooms were overdue for it. The carpet was threadbare and nearly colorless with age. Dustcloths hid the furnishings except for an occasional chair leg or table end. But the paintings on the walls, seascapes and oils depicting his ancestors, seemed unchanged. 'Twas a well-built house. A handsome house. A place of many memories, most of them happy.

He climbed the stairs and entered the bedchambers, including his own before he'd gone away to sea. The narrow cot with its plain indigo counterpane . . . had he really lain there? Beneath a window was his writing table, old and scarred in the harsh light piercing the grime of the windowpane. There by the fireplace were knifed notches that marked his growth. He'd gone from a sickly baby to a man full grown at a towering six feet two inches and fourteen stone.

After breathing past the musty smell of unused rooms, he opened a door to the three-tiered portico. Here on the shaded second floor, a scattering of lightweight Windsor chairs and a small game table sat forlorn. He peered over the portico's railing into the walled garden below.

Roses were still abloom, a clash of pinks and oranges and yellows amid the drooping perennials and weeds. Nothing too amiss here that a sennight's work wouldn't mend. The sundial and dry fountain at the garden's heart eased him. Intact. He'd played many an hour around them as a lad. Some things, at least those cast in stone, didn't change.

The servants' quarters in the attic had him bending low not to scrape his head. Even with cocked hat beneath one arm, he still touched the low ceiling. Back down the winding stair he went to the foyer, then exited out a back door to sit on a bench and catch the sun's last rays as they brightened a battered arbor.

He stared at a twisted quince, once a favorite climbing tree. Age made one reflect, he guessed. At five and thirty, what would be said about him that truly mattered if he were to die tomorrow? That he sailed the high seas and was rarely at home.

Better ponder the pasts of those he loved. Memory took him down a hazy path, heart-tuggingly indistinct but painful as a cat-o'-nine-tails nonetheless. His mother had been most at home in the garden. She'd sewn dried lavender into the hems of her petticoats and linens, even concocted lavender lemon water. And Hermione . . . His sister had arranged for a pianoforte on small wheels to be pushed onto the portico in good weather. There were garden parties. Guests. Towering trays of marzipan and endless bowls of punch. His father had presided over all with characteristic good humor. Until that dark day at the docks.

What bitter irony that he'd once teased his father he'd someday go to sea in the very vessels his father constructed. He'd been jesting.

Though he'd long been enamored of shipbuilding, not once had he entertained the notion of sailing.

"By Jove, Son! Will you torment me in my old age with such far-flung notions?" His father had stared at him, his Scots temper roaring. "Am I to see you gone from here for months—years on end? The sea is a fickle mistress. She'll abuse you like Jonah and coerce some behemoth to swallow you and spit you out, only you might never return to us."

His mother bore his playfulness with a smile, her usual French effusiveness undimmed. "You'll be the handsomest jack to ever sail the high seas. 'Captain Lennox' sounds *magnifique*!"

"A privateer you'll be? 'Tis but a rude disguise," his sister teased. "Henri Lennox, buccaneer à la corsair! Will you share your prizes with us poor relations who'll be pining for you at home?"

Then, just shy of his sixteenth birthday, he'd been working late in his father's dockyard when a press-gang overtook him, the certificate of exemption he carried in his pocket of no consequence. Though the lad with him had gotten away, the gang pummeled him into a corner, tore up his paper, then took him aboard the HMS *Victory*.

Fueled by fury as well as ambition, he'd worked his way up from cabin boy to midshipman to officer till he'd used the Royal Navy to gain his own vessel and his own captaincy. And then, much like a courtship, as wooing as a siren's song, the sea had finally won him over. As commander, he'd been freed of rebellious shipmates and overbearing admirals. Freed to chart his course, choose his crew, and sail where he willed. This was what he'd been designed to do, though the Almighty had used an unjust impressment and the Royal Navy to accomplish it.

But now that he was back in Norfolk where it all began, his impressment seemed especially bittersweet. He'd missed much being at sea, not only the sorrows but the joys. If he'd been closer to home, might his parents' and sister's lives have been better? Easier? Might they still live? Their voices echoed in his head and heart, so bruising his eyes stung. It caused a man to reconsider. Who did he have? And who would come after him?

A bird trilled. A few colorful leaves drifted down, reddening his black coat and boots. Near at hand was an unkempt climbing rose. It bespoke . . . Esmée. He hadn't wanted her to intrude. Not even the thought of her. But she'd once been in this garden, making a mighty fuss over this very rose and especially the trellis-in-the-round at the garden's heart. In midsummer it resembled an overflowing flower basket.

His gaze slid to the west corner of the overgrown yew hedge where he'd kissed her. And she'd kissed him back.

"Captain Lennox, might that be you?"

A high, reedy voice trailed over the garden wall. He stood and walked toward the sound, envisioning the ancient lady on the other side. "It is I, Mistress Ludwick."

"Can it be? I've not seen you in an age! Mightn't you humor an old crone and show yourself?"

In moments he was at the iron gate that divided her garden from his. With a sweep of his hat, he bowed and then took in her parchment-paper face, white and lined but much as he remembered.

"How mournful it must be to return to an empty house once so full of life!"

He frowned. "I am wondering whether to sell or occupy."

"Sell? Your dear mother would resurrect herself if she knew!"

"But a man like myself, living here alone . . ." He looked back at the house, allowing himself a rare glib moment. "It begs a family. Life. Laughter."

"Indeed." She pursed her wrinkled lips. "A shame there's no Mistress Lennox or offspring to settle down here. But should you decide to reside in our fair city, that would follow in the blink of an eye, most assuredly, though I thought York had its hold on you. Indigo Island, rather."

"'Tis always wise to explore one's options, aye?" After the debacle at Lady Lightfoot's, Norfolk held unmistakable appeal.

"Don't tell me you're tiring of the sea." She studied him unblinkingly. "Ah, I do believe you are. I see it in your sun-weathered face, those honest eyes of yours."

He smiled at her sharp appraisal. "I'm no longer the wee lad you fed kissing comfits to, but you still know me."

"Of course I do. A man is merely an overgrown boy. You are wanting change. This place suits you. You could raise a family and be a man about town. Here there are no shadows to dodge."

Shadows. Did she suspect him of being a pirate? Or sense his personal safety was in question on the mainland?

"Fare thee well, Captain Lennox." She moved away, her gait slow yet graceful. "I do hope to see you again soon."

nine

The shop door jangled shut at noon, and finding herself alone, Esmée drifted toward the Dutch door separating the chocolate shop from the coffeehouse. Shipowners and merchants, politicians and literary men gathered in the spacious, beamed room that hummed with hearsay, headlines, and other matters whatever the season. Newspapers and broadsides were scattered about, the *Virginia Gazette* foremost.

This was how Esmée kept track of the captain after a fashion. Discreetly. Privately. Without involving anyone else. Once the ire of their parting had cooled, she was beset with an insatiable curiosity time could not dim.

How did such a man handle a failed love affair? By wintering in the Caribbean. Intercepting pirate ships preying upon merchant vessels. Testifying at the admiralty court in Boston. Recovering an abandoned Spanish wreck near Madagascar. Trading the aptly named *Bachelor's Delight* for the more enigmatic *Relentless*. If she had a shilling every time she read "Taken by the *Relentless*, Captain Lennox," she'd be a wealthy woman.

And now she knew how he handled a loathsome reunion. Stoically.

Handsomely. With nary a trace of trepidation. As if he'd forgotten all about her and recovered unscathed from their liaison of old.

While she herself was a tangle of tarred rope.

"Sister! Why on earth are you loitering at the coffeehouse door? Father forbids it!"

Eliza stood behind her, winking in merriment. The truth was, Father did forbid it, but Eliza cared not a whit. It was how she'd kept the attention of Quinn, a regular at Shaw's coffeehouse back then. Even now he was at his preferred corner table, one of their male indentures replenishing coffee and chocolate as he and his highborn friends talked taxes and tariffs.

"What is it you're clutching to your chest?" Eliza peered at *The Complete Confectioner* with a sharp eye.

"Anna found it on the shop steps this morn." Esmée had hardly set the book down. "The giver is a mystery."

Eliza's smile curled expectantly. "A secret admirer, perhaps?"

"Secret, aye. Admirer, nay."

"A gift from Captain Lennox is my guess. I saw the two of you at supper. Quite cozy after so long a separation."

"Cozy?" Esmée rolled her eyes. "You're in need of a pair of spectacles. We were simply thrown together quite unexpectedly and spent an excruciating supper, followed by dancing, trying to be polite while wondering what on earth we ever found attractive about each other in the first place."

"Ha! He's still a remarkably gallant devil, you must admit."

"A tattooed devil."

"Most mariners are." Eliza laughed and took the book from her. "I recall you and Mama trying to find this very volume with no success. Till now."

"'Tis so hard to come by, printed in England. The York and Williamsburg booksellers have not been able to obtain a single copy of it."

Eliza paged to the flyleaf with gloved hands. "I do wish he'd signed it. But of course, you might have burnt the book if he had."

"Shush. 'Tis too valuable a tome. I would simply have torn out his signature."

"Hmm. How long has it been since you two were enamored with each other?"

"It matters not. You've already asked me. 'Twas a foolish infatuation."

"I wonder." Eliza seemed to reconsider. "In and out of every foreign port as he is, and for so long, I suppose he has a paramour somewhere. Several, perhaps."

The notion nearly made Esmée squirm. "He made no mention of such."

"Of course he wouldn't confess such intimacies to you, his prior sweetheart. Nor would he ask such of you, being a gentleman of rank. Which begs the question . . . what *did* you two talk about?"

"Really, Eliza. Your interrogation knows no bounds." Esmée took the book back. "Though he did ask about you."

"Did he?" Eliza looked flattered. "How are his Norfolk kin?"

A pang shot through Esmée, arrow-sharp. "All have passed."

Eliza's face crumpled. "Poor Captain Lennox. I only knew of his father's death. 'Twas in the papers a few years ago, but Mama hid it from you."

"What?"

"She knew it might upset you. Unearth the past." Eliza sighed. "But I had no idea about Mrs. Lennox and Hermione. I do recall Hermione wedding a landowner of some merit."

The tightness in Esmée's chest expanded. Might Hermione have died in childbirth? Eliza, for all her fearlessness, had a mortal dread of such. So many failed to survive the ordeal and enjoy motherhood. Esmée's fervent prayer was that her sister be spared.

"I suppose the captain has returned to Indigo Island and I can breathe again," Esmée said. The thought was nettling. Sore. A bittersweet mix of things regretted romantically that would never be righted.

"More's the pity." Eliza went to the shop window and stared out at the teeming harbor. "Farewell, our masterful, commanding Captain Lennox."

Did her sister know something of his whereabouts? An imminent cruise? Quinn had gone into the anteroom with the other officials during the ball. Had the captain already set sail again? Esmée opened her mouth to ask, then closed it. She'd rather bite her tongue in two. What would knowing profit her?

Let the past pass.

"We must make the most of the time we've been given." Eliza spun away from the glass. "I asked Father if he could spare you in the near future. Quinn will be in meetings, as the assembly will soon be in session. Some nonsense over outlawing the importation of slaves."

"Nonsense? I beg to differ."

"*Nonsense* in that such a measure will never pass muster in slave-heavy Virginia." The mettle in Eliza's tone suggested it was a frequent topic of discussion in the Chevertons' townhouse. She softened, her eyes as imploring as a spaniel's. "Come, Esmée. I get frightfully lonesome."

Esmée set the book on the counter. "What of your many friends?"

"None suit like the company of my elder sister."

Before Esmée could reply, a customer entered and ended the matter, inquiring after a new chocolate pot.

"See you soon, Sister." Eliza smiled in farewell. "We shall have a splendid time in Williamsburg."

Beset by a headache, Esmée left the shop and walked uphill toward Main Street, knowing Quinn and Eliza had departed and the townhouse would be quiet. Since Mama had died, Father rarely arrived home till supper at eight o'clock. As usual, Esmée was greeted by their housekeeper, Mrs. Mabrey.

"A headache, you say?" Her lined face grew pinched with concern beneath her beribboned mobcap. "Some thyme tea should do. Shall I bring it to your bedchamber?"

"Father's study, thank you." Esmée removed her straw hat, set it on a foyer table, and moved past the stairwell into her father's bower. Instinctively she reached for his mahogany spyglass, standing at one window and training her sights on Indigo Island. On such a clear day every speck of sand glittered, trees swaying like the grass-skirted women her father told stories about. Somewhere she couldn't see sat the Flask and Sword, the boon of sailors. Captain Lennox was on the back side of the island in the cottage Father had told her about. He'd visited more than once, though not for years.

"Here you go, Miss Shaw."

"Thank you, Mrs. Mabrey."

The tea tray was placed on a small table near at hand, infusing the paneled room with an earthiness that mingled well with Father's pungent tobacco and heady brandy.

The housekeeper shut the door behind her, and Esmée returned to her musings. Sleeplessness pinched her eyes, and the ache gripping her temples throbbed unrelentingly. Returning the spyglass to its lined case, she sat down to her tea, then remembered the scrap of paper in her pocket. She laid it in her lap as she sipped from her cup. Her name, oft misspelled, was written flawlessly in a bold, masculine hand. The bookseller's? Or the giver's?

Despite her headache, a wee thrill couldn't be denied. A little intrigue in her chocolate-laden world was not amiss. Might Eliza be right? Could the giver be the captain?

She took out her old memories of him, sorting through each one like antique buttons in a box before settling on one that shone like glass. 'Twas when he'd whisked her south to meet his Norfolk family. What a fuss had come beforehand as trunks lay open and garments were examined and cast off in favor of something suitable.

"You ken what this means, dear daughter." Mama looked at her, a knowing glint in her eye.

Esmée, caught up in the novelty of a serious suitor, thought little beyond the present moment. "I know not except Captain Lennox wishes to acquaint me with Norfolk."

"'Tis a thoughtful move toward matrimony, if that is what you both want."

Torn between two hats—a straw bonnet with a cluster of silk violets and a beribboned bergère—Esmée turned this way and that before the looking glass. "Has Henri asked Father for my hand?"

"Perhaps he's waiting for his family's reception of you first. No doubt 'twill be as warm as ours of him. His mother is French, remember. I hope you'll say a few words with her in her native tongue."

Esmée had finally decided on the bergère. "How I wish I was as fluent as Eliza."

Now she hardly recalled their coach ride south to the old port town steeped in the tobacco trade. But all the rest seemed near as yesterday. There in the entry hall of a large brick townhouse, Henri had introduced her to his family as if she'd been royalty. Their kind regard of her had been equally memorable.

His mother, expressive and garrulous, took to her at once. She had Henri's ocean-blue eyes, calm as the sea on a summer's day. His father, a giant of a man, was a bit stern, his dark hair unpowdered, his dress Quaker-plain. And his sister, Hermione, as lovely as her name, was blessed with the same blue eyes and coal-black hair, a dimple in her chin.

And now they were all . . . gone. While he'd been away at sea, she guessed. How did the captain come to terms with that? Esmée wrestled with the emotion the dusty memory wrought. It seemed out of place here in this still room years after the fact.

If only the tea would assuage her head *and* her heart. All her carefully stowed feelings, any remaining tenderness toward him, had been hardened by long, barren years. Or so she thought. Seeing him again—his once beloved features, the silky hair she'd run her fingers through, the broad shoulders that seemed a bulwark against the world—made her realize the great void she'd experienced in his absence. Though Eliza and others had tried their hand at matchmaking and a few would-be suitors had come forward, Esmée had spurned them all, politely but firmly. Much to Eliza's dismay.

"My dream is to have children close in age," Eliza had confided. "Cousins are truly one of life's best gifts."

"I may well never marry. Not everyone is called to it. You'd best have as many children as the Lord allows to make up for my lack."

"Well, I shan't stop conspiring." Eliza winked at her brazenly. "'Tis what I do best!"

"Scheming is more like it," Esmée shot back, close to tears and trying to hide it. "Praying gets better results."

But somewhere along the way even she'd stopped praying. Whereas once Captain Lennox's safety and well-being on the seas were first in her heart, she'd jettisoned those petitions. Her fervent prayers went the way of her hopes and became floating wreckage. As the years passed, it hardly seemed to matter.

Hers was a heart adrift.

And the captain's sudden, unexpected return reminded her of all that.

"Daughter, are you unwell? I smell medicinal tea." Her father entered his study, a concerned eye on her as he stowed his walking stick and cocked hat. "'Tis rare I see you home so early in the day."

She forced a smile. "I might ask you the same, Father."

Yawning, he took a seat behind his desk. "One gets little done the day after a ball, I'm afraid."

Esmée poured a second cup of tea. Father disdained the stuff. "Shall I have Mrs. Mabrey bring you some coffee?"

"Nay, I drank my weight in it this morn. A bit of brandy will do." He uncapped the decanter on his desk and poured the amber liquid into a waiting glass. "Though what I crave is your mother's milk punch."

She studied him sympathetically as he drank deeply. "Perhaps we shall make some at Christmastide."

"I saw you standing at the Dutch door earlier, gazing into the coffeehouse." Rebuke was in his tone. The previous eve's late hour had turned him not only tired but testy.

"You know I like to peruse newspapers left by your customers. Since Eliza has invited me to the capital for an extended stay, I must keep current lest I be branded a bumpkin."

"I'll be happy to tell you any pressing news." He leaned back in his chair, gaze drawn to the windows at the screech of gulls. "For instance, Captain Lennox has returned to Indigo—"

"Father! I *need* no telling." Her rare outburst rattled the teacup in her hand, sloshing liquid onto her skirt.

He stared at her, fanning the flame in her face. "Pretend all you like. I'm not your doting father for naught. You've been completely addled since you first heard of his return. I only thought to take the worry from your countenance with news he's left the mainland."

She dabbed at the damp on her skirt with a handkerchief, her headache thundering again. "If my countenance is clouded, 'tis because I'm missing Mama, like you. And truth be told, I'm dreading Williamsburg society, where I am referred to as Lady Drysdale's spinster sister or Captain Lennox's jilted sweetheart."

"Not the respected businesswoman of York and patron of the parish almshouse."

"The former is far more savory." She gave a brittle smile. "Perhaps I shall try my hand at raising support among Eliza's genteel friends. That was my intent at the ball before I was . . . um . . ."

"Unmoored by Captain Lennox's arrival."

Rather, shipwrecked. "What other news should I be aware of?"

"I'm loath to heap more unwelcome reports on you, but there's said to be a large influx of French expelled from Acadia who'll soon be at Virginia's door. Not only that, there's been a dozen more arrivals at the almshouse, yet scarcely room to house them."

Her heart squeezed. "Who is among their number?"

"A drunkard. Two lewd women." Father was nothing if not forthright. "Four abandoned children. A lunatic. One destitute expectant mother. An invalid with no memory. I forget the rest."

"'Tis exactly what troubles me. Out of sight at the almshouse, they are all easily forgotten."

"You've had some success at providing care for the elderly in private homes here in York."

"Only four, sadly. Private benefactors are few."

"Then seek support from the wealthy in Williamsburg with my blessing."

"I'd rather spend time at the almshouse."

He poured a second brandy. "How like your mother you are. 'Twas all her visits to the poor that influenced you, accompanying her as you did. And in the end 'twas the death of her."

His mournful tone hurt her, but he spoke truth. Mama had contracted an illness at the almshouse that had indeed been her demise. As for Father, he was ever generous to the poor, but lodge or visit them he would not do. Yet pounds and pence only went so far. These unfortunates—shunned outcasts—needed to be seen, spoken to, touched.

He returned to the window and took up the spyglass she'd set down. At once she was cast back to the quarterdeck, windward side, where he'd stood as commander of his beloved man-of-war. Even at almost seventy he looked stalwart. Commanding.

"I nearly forgot." The spyglass came down. "Your sister told me to relay you're to see the milliner-mantuamaker ahead of our going to Williamsburg. Something about stripping you of your old gowns and infernal chatelaine and outfitting you in something splendid."

Esmée made a face. "Betimes I feel like the younger sister, not the elder."

He smiled indulgently, the deep, sun-weathered creases in his face softening. "Eliza will have her way."

Esmée smoothed a worn fold of her skirt, its once vibrant pattern faded. While she appreciated her sister's generosity—*extravagance*—it seemed at odds with her almshouse sympathies. She would not look like royalty and go there. Or anywhere.

"You might better benefit your cause if you didn't appear as if you were one step away from the almshouse yourself, my dear."

"I'm hopelessly disinterested in dress, Father." Her sister's ongoing fascination with fashion skimmed past her like a butterfly across a millpond. She felt a mere moth. "I'm guessing Eliza is planning an entire wardrobe for me."

"Your sister is generous to a fault." Her father's levity vanished. "Quinn humors her so, importing all manner of this or that and giving in to her every whim. I fear my grandchild shall be spoilt."

Esmée feared it too. Finishing her tea, she pushed up from the chair and excused herself. "Till supper, Father. I believe I'll go rest in my room."

CHAPTER
ten

aving had his fill of the mainland, Henri rowed back to the island, standing in the jolly and facing forward, a habit of old watermen who claimed it was less taxing and more navigable. Squinting in the sun's glare, he set his sights on the Flask and Sword, its beleaguered façade begging paint and repairs. A small sloop and dory were docked, both unknown to him. The ordinary never lacked for customers, whatever the season.

Some of his crew sat upon the beach. Others hung in hammocks stretched between wind-whipped trees. Still others toiled on the *Relentless* now beached on the island's bay side. A few waved a hand as Henri drew nearer.

Home.

Only Indigo Island didn't seem much like home, he'd been gone so long. Now it felt unfamiliar. Foreign. Like any seldom seen port or landing place.

He beached the jolly and made for the ordinary, boots sinking into white sand. His men knew his swift stride too well to slow him, other than a hand flung to a forehead as he passed. Into the ordinary he went, seeking his preferred corner by a wide window open to the salt air.

Without asking, Mistress Saltonstall fetched him a dram and set it down with a wide, gap-toothed smile. "Welcome, Captain Lennox, on this bonny October day."

"Obliged." Henri leaned back in his Windsor chair, his tattooed hand encircling the pewter cup. "How is Hermes?"

She seemed pleased he'd remembered the varmint's name. The monkey—a small marmoset from Peru—perched on her shoulder. Baring its teeth, Hermes gave a cackle before traveling to her other shoulder.

She winked. "Ornery as ever and a constant reminder of ye."

He'd gifted her Hermes after sailing to South America five years before. Eccentric as she was, she'd taken to the creature immediately, even teaching it tricks, to the amusement of the watermen who frequented her establishment.

"How goes it at York?" she asked, petting Hermes's long tail. "Norfolk, rather."

"Busy. Crowded." He took a drink. "Full of itself."

She laughed, her wrinkles collapsing in mirth. "Everything Indigo Island isn't."

He took another drink and willed the memory of Esmée away as he'd done a decade or better. Leaving him to his ponderings, Mistress Saltonstall moved on as Cyprian and the ship's drummer appeared, intent on his table.

"Hats off, lads," he said with a slight smile. Their land manners had yet to catch up with them.

They grabbed their caps and sat opposite him, eager as schoolboys.

"Where to next, sir?" they asked in unison.

"I know not." Port Royal was their hope. Or the lucrative Windward Passage between Cuba and Haiti. "How goes the careening?"

Cyprian grimaced. "Full of ship's worms as she is, we'll have to winter over right here." He looked at his tarred breeches. "The masts—or parts of 'em—had to be removed. We've not finished scraping 'er down."

"When that's done, I'll set you to work on the light," Henri said. "A stonemason has been hired and will be here shortly."

Their expressions brightened. This was far preferable to scraping down a worm-ridden vessel, truly. They began to chatter as Henri's gaze stretched beyond them to the ordinary's entrance. His four most trusted men ducked beneath the door's lintel—the Africans Tarbonde and Udo, his sailing master and quartermaster, followed by the Englishmen, sea chaplain Ned Autrey and ship surgeon Alistair Southack.

Hermes screeched at their entrance and fled behind the bar. Henri's two youngest crew followed suit and scurried out a side door, their seats left vacant for their superiors.

"Welcome back, sir," Tarbonde said with a grin, the country marks or tribal scars across his cheeks a perpetual reminder of just how far he was from his Ghanaian home.

More ale was served, but Henri waited till they'd quenched their thirst before satisfying their curiosity about his time on the mainland.

"You were missed," Southack said after a long sip. "Some of the crew respect no man's authority but yours."

"Other than a small tussle or two, all has been the doldrums." Udo took a long drink. "I trust your time in York was eventful since you tarried awhile."

Henri nodded, sharing the high points. "I got my bearings. Attended a ball. Was thrown from a horse."

They chuckled. Horsemanship was not one of his strengths. He'd been too long at sea.

"There's a great deal of war talk," he told them. "I spoke at length with Virginia officials."

"Ah, at last we get to the meat of the matter." Southack leaned in, eyes alive with anticipation.

Henri nodded. But how to condense hours of conversation? "The British are commissioning seamen to prey upon and plunder French ships, thereby cutting supply lines to enemy allies on the frontier."

Udo toyed with his pewter tankard. "Commit acts of freebooting?"

"Aye, all in the name of establishing English dominance on the high seas as well as North America and the Caribbean."

"'Tis a war, aye, or soon will be," Tarbonde said. "A contest over who wins America and other foreign interests."

"And the plunder?" Southack's gaze never left Henri. "If we risk our lives as privateers under an official letter of marque? Are all prizes taken given over to the British government?"

"A great many questions remain unanswered. And I've made no promises as to our involvement." Henri ran a hand over his unshaven face. "Closer to home, Virginia's government is desperate for reinforcements to protect Chesapeake Bay from pirates. This from the lord commissioner for trade and plantations and the secretary of state."

Udo frowned. "When will you learn more, sir?"

Henri looked out the window toward York. "In a sennight I'm to attend a meeting in Williamsburg. A gathering of officials and certain mariners of note, including Admiral Barnabas Shaw."

"Famed commander of the Royal Navy?" Tarbonde queried.

Southack's brow lifted. "Famed commander and former privateer turned pirate."

"Careful." Henri leveled his gaze at the surgeon. "The same has been said of us."

Ned regarded Henri warily. "In that same vein, be watchful of your enemies in the capital and elsewhere who would rejoice to see you brought low." His gaze slid to the Africans. "And slave catchers ashore who would like nothing better than to ensnare bona fide freemen."

The warning led to a sullen silence. Henri had nearly forgotten the high feeling against him among Virginia's planters and politicians. So much falsehood was printed about him by those who opposed him, it turned previously unbiased citizens against him as well. But he was most concerned about the Africans. Many of them were inked with the Jerusalem cross as he was, identifying themselves as his crew in a show of unity and pride.

"Let us talk of more pleasant matters. Like the ball. What I'd give to see a comely petticoat or two." Southack let out a long breath. "I'd gladly suffer a minuet."

Ned nodded. "As would I."

Henri understood. He knew they longed to escape their wooden world and form feminine ties. "'Tis your turn to go ashore. We've no imminent sailing to pursue to keep you from staying as long as you like. Not yet. But once on the mainland, be on your guard."

"Are you sure it's only a meeting you're going to in the capital?" Southack's wink was sly. "I seem to recall Admiral Shaw having several beautiful daughters."

"Only two," Henri corrected. "One is wed."

"Which leaves the second." Southack drummed impatient fingers atop the scarred table.

When Henri said nothing, his sea chaplain filled the silence. "Miss Esmée Shaw? A chocolatier who has a shop along the waterfront, or once did. Last we were in port, Shaw's supplied us with chocolate before we sailed."

"Shaw's will need to resupply us ahead of our next voyage," Udo said. "Six pounds of chocolate per man, much like the officers marching with Braddock's army."

"God rest Braddock's sorry soul," Ned breathed.

They observed a moment of silence for the fallen general. But in truth, the frontier was so far, the war threat felt even further removed.

Southack brightened. "So what is your recommendation for lodgings in York?"

"The Royal Oake should suffice," Henri said. "The bell system is rather extraordinary. And the owner has a very accommodating daughter who may not be able to withstand your charms."

Udo winked. "Though she withstood yours, no doubt, immune to matrimony as you are."

They all laughed soundly, and Tarbonde called for more ale.

Henri regarded them fondly. "If I wed, then I'd have to relax my cardinal rule of prohibiting married men as crew."

"With all due respect, your crew might be better for marrying," Ned replied.

"I'll not separate husbands and wives and families." The rule was ironclad. And it was Esmée who had been behind it.

Talk turned to other matters. But Esmée's memory, repeatedly tossed overboard, stubbornly resurfaced. And now he was no longer here by the open window with a salt breeze caressing his unshaven face. He was at the ball's supper again, seated beside her, a decade of ill feeling between them.

Though time and weather had simply lined him, she was remarkably changed. She'd grown rounder and even more beguiling, as if she'd snuck one too many chocolates in his absence. She was . . . voluptuous. And guarded. No longer the guileless girl he'd left behind.

And now the possessor of a hard-won copy of *The Complete Confectioner.*

CHAPTER
eleven

ethinks yer more buccaneer than privateer." Mistress Saltonstall gaped in outright astonishment as Henri shoveled sandy soil back into a deep hole. "Buried treasure, indeed, even if not ill-gotten!"

Dusk was layering Indigo Island in silvery shadows. It was his favorite time of day, be it by land or sea. "Remember this exact location. You're the only soul who knows besides me." His wink was likely lost on her in the gloaming. "And if it goes missing, I'll know who to blame."

"Hoot! I'm no long-gone fool or babbler. Yer stash is safe with me." She dug in her pocket, withdrew a silver ingot, and admired it. "Especially since ye see to the needs of so many and don't hoard yer prizes."

Tossing the shovel aside, Henri began covering the spot with brush, glad to have it done before dark. She lent a hand, dragging fallen pine branches and grapevines to help finish the task. He'd left caches she didn't know about in half a dozen places on the island, carefully marked on a map he had stashed beneath a floorboard in his cottage bedchamber.

Winded, she eyed him. "Tell me again how ye came by such a haul."

Henri straightened to his full height and took the flask she handed him. "A flotilla of Spanish ships wrecked off the coast of Florida in a late summer's gale. A great many pesos were lost and a great many regained, including the silver."

She whistled through gapped teeth. "Is it true what yer quartermaster said—that all them jacks drowned?"

"To the last man, God rest them."

"The Spaniards claiming those alligator-ridden waters are no doubt hotter than Hades over yer haul."

He swiped at his sweaty brow with his sleeve. "None witnessed our recovery of the cargo."

For all their blether claiming Florida, the Spanish had done little to settle it other than found St. Augustine and build an impenetrable stone fort. It was made of seashells, his men had scoffed, yet it had withstood twenty-seven days of cannon fire during the last British attack.

He took a drink. "I'm to return to the mainland and have need of riding instruction as there are so few carriages to be had. Any recommendations?"

"So, yer in need of a fine-blooded horse fit for a gentleman captain." Mistress Saltonstall's gaze held more mirth than he liked. "None better than Jago Wherry. He can be found at the quarter-mile races of a Saturday outside Williamsburg. Or the almshouse when his pockets are empty."

"He's a homeless gambler, then."

"Aye, but he kens horses, and everybody knows it. Tell him Polly sent ye. We were once acquainted in our youth." Born and bred in York, she knew any name Henri put to her. "So ye can't ride, Captain, being boat bound for so long?"

"Riding the waves is the sum of my experience, I'm afraid."

She chuckled and took back the flask.

"That and the horse latitudes," he added.

Her mirth vanished. "All those poor creatures thrown overboard in the windless passages. 'Tis a wonder America has any horses at all."

"Now Virginia abounds with them." He looked toward the fading sunset beyond York's distant lights. "And a great many excellent riders."

"Take care to buy yer mount from the Tayloes, who import the best breeds," she told him. "Then stable yer steed at Grant's on Ballard Street."

"Obliged. What can I bring you when I return from the mainland next?"

"Nary a thing, Captain." She looked sly again, a light in her pale eyes. "Since the rheumatism plagues me so on the island come foul weather, I may winter in York with my widowed sister. She keeps a snug little house on the outskirts. But ye can keep an eye on the Flask and Sword if ye stay on. And Hermes."

Henri opened his mouth to protest, but she'd already turned her back with a cackle and was soon well beyond hearing as she hurried to return to the ordinary before dark. He looked after her with welling dread.

Hermes. And a horse.

He didn't have a good feeling about this.

Esmée might have been royalty for all the attention the milliner-mantuamaker paid her . . . when she had paid her scant attention before.

Eliza must have spent a pretty penny. Madame Suchet was French by birth and styled herself a *marchande de modes*, her mellifluous accent and shop nothing short of sumptuous. Esmée rarely came here save for a length of lace or a pretty fan.

"Your Chinese silk gown is finished, but your cream brocade lacks lace," Madame Suchet said. "Lady Drysdale insists on Dutch linen petticoats and shifts, matching slippers for every gown, clocked silk stockings . . ." She paused as if all the details eluded her. "And a cape of purple broadcloth lined with white silk shag."

Esmée's senses swam as her gaze roamed the rich interior. Fans, gloves, stays, hats, and furbelows she had no name for adorned every available inch of space. Bedazzling. Overwhelming. Suffocating. She took a deep, discreet breath.

"Nothing but the first fashion here in York, with imported cloth arriving daily." Madame Suchet's smile was elusive, the shadows beneath her eyes telling. "I am in a battle royale with the Williamsburg milliner, an Englishwoman. Do you know her?"

Esmée fingered a peacock feather. "Barely."

"Miss Bell may claim the capital, but I am *la dame* of the harbor, all these handsome ships at my beck and call."

"You no doubt created many of the gowns for Lady Lightfoot's ball," Esmée said.

"*Oui*, including Lady Lightfoot's lavender ensemble." With a proud smile she draped the aforementioned cape about Esmée's shoulders. "Winter is coming, and Lady Drysdale wishes you to be warm."

In truth, Eliza wanted her dressed for Williamsburg society more than the weather, and for a sum that pricked Esmée's conscience. Was Quinn agreeable to such an expenditure? Did he even know? Granted, the Chevertons rivaled Virginia's ever-prosperous Byrds, but . . .

"Pish-posh! One would think you were a Philadelphia Quaker with your plain ways," Eliza had scolded recently. "Or indisposed to milliner-mantuamakers."

"Touché!" Esmée teased. "In a word, these ladies of trade furnish everything that sets off our beauty, increases our vanity, and renders us ridiculous, as has been said."

"Sister, you simply *must* stop perusing the coffeehouse papers!"

Esmée returned to the laborious if lovely present. The cape was removed, and a rustling chintz in various hues was draped over her for a final day gown. A fawning assistant helped with pins and suggestions. Esmée stifled a yawn, wishing for a cup of cocoa, as the forenoon was crisp.

"I shall have everything delivered to your residence the day before you leave for Williamsburg," Madame Suchet promised.

Thanking her, Esmée lingered by a display of ribbon near the door.

"You are admiring the silk taffety ribbon, no? How about a yard or two of this Parisian blue or pear green? Scarlet is also gaining ground, though sable is the preferred color." Madame Suchet took up the black and strung it round her own throat. "A ribbon choker necklace is all the rage."

Esmée took out her embroidered pocketbook. She'd not add to Eliza's account. "I'll take three yards of each, including the rose and purple."

Smiling, Madame Suchet bid her adieu and let the shopgirl handle the matter.

At last, purse lighter, Esmée walked uphill toward home. Once there she donned a riding habit, hiding the ribbons in a saddlebag when the groom brought her saddled horse round. Atop Minta and shivering beneath the muted midday sun, she moved past wagons and carts and hawkers going about their noisy business in town.

In minutes she'd gained the coastal road, cantering along its rutted path, pausing once to let her mare water at a creek and sample a patch of seagrass. She savored the seascape, a palette of blues and grays as the sun broke free of scattered clouds.

She'd timed her almshouse visit carefully, hoping the trustees would be elsewhere. Once she arrived, she had her wish. Mistress Boles was absent and Miss Grove was busy with the children. Glad for the lack of supervision, Esmée sat down at a long trestle table in the dining hall with sixteen almshouse women, including the new arrivals Father had mentioned. Quickly she learned their names. Lucy, Hannah, Jane, Arminda. They regarded her with wide-eyed surprise. Gentlewomen didn't oft dine with the destitute. Or were they staring at her riding habit? Eliza called it shabby, outmoded, but even if the green velvet was worn and the feathers limp with age, it was an extravagance they'd rarely beheld.

"Ye picked a good day to sup with us, Miss Shaw," one woman told her. "'Tis meat Monday."

Meat? Esmée glanced at her own plate. Could this paltry bit of bone and gristle be called that? Smiling nevertheless, she wondered how she'd eat a bite. Almshouse men were served before the women, while the children partook in their schoolroom.

"Will ye say grace, Miss Shaw?" came another timid query.

Joining hands, they bowed their heads. Esmée paused, sensing all the unspoken, unmet needs at hand. "Dear Lord, let it be our earnest prayer to serve Thee better day by day as we grow in grace and trust

Thee for our wants in soul and body. For these and all Thy blessings, God's holy name be praised for Christ's sake. Amen."

The shallow bowl of soup ladled out next bore a tiny potato and a sliver of parsnip. Esmée took up her spoon without complaint, aware of half a dozen eyes on her as if awaiting a wince of distaste.

Stale bread reminding her of ship's biscuits—with no butter—rounded out the meagre meal. She thought of the citrus delivered to their very door two days past from a ship newly returned from the Caribbean. These women were alarmingly thin, even the pregnant Alice. Such humble fare was barely enough to keep a bird alive.

"Thank ye for the chocolate ye brought last time," another woman murmured.

A few capped heads bobbed. The most talkative sat across from her. "We've had a bit in hot milk and it's divine. But seems like the trustees take the lion's share. Guess it's their due for puttin' up with the lot o' us."

Esmée managed another disagreeable spoonful. "Is Mistress Boles away often?"

"Her mother's ailin', so she hies to Tobacco Road now and again to tend to her."

They ate in companionable silence, a comment made now and then. Esmée soldiered on, trying to determine what was most needed near at hand. The mother-to-be required far more than the ribbon she'd brought. She'd seen better dressed indentures and slaves. The eldest among them bore sores on her wrinkled cheeks. What bathing facilities did these residents have? Nary a bath in a twelvemonth, it seemed for some. Surely there was no excuse for uncleanliness with the York River at hand.

"Before you return to work," Esmée said, "I beg you, tell me your most pressing want. Shoes? A comb? Pockets? A pinch of tea or a remedy from the York apothecary? A petticoat? Today I've only brought a bit of comely ribbon."

They rushed her at the mention, and when Esmée passed around the taffety ribbons, the women laughed and compared colors, proving poverty and age failed to dent an appreciation for pretty things.

Each woman then confided her most pressing need. Miss Grove returned to help, jotting down each whispered request with stylus and paper. The women left merrier than when she'd arrived, clutching their bit of finery as they returned to their assigned chores, be it garden or washhouse or kitchen.

Miss Grove handed the lengthy list over. "How can you possibly provide all these items, Miss Shaw?"

"I shan't provide them," Esmée said with a confident smile, pocketing the paper. "The Almighty shall."

Miss Grove gave a sigh. "My faith is small, I'm afraid. I've seen a great many broken promises and hearts here."

Esmée squeezed her hand before turning away. "I can assure you every need on the list shall be met, though it may take time."

She left the main building, the wind rising and threatening to unseat her hat. Minta was hobbled beneath a widespread oak wearing a leafy coat as colorful as the biblical Joseph's. Esmée started toward her, the sun in her eyes, before coming to a sudden stop. There, across a wide stretch of meadow, were two men and a handsome bay horse. A nicer mount she'd never seen save from the stables of the Tayloes or Lees.

Yet it wasn't the horse but the rider she lingered upon. Could it be? Only an uncanny resemblance, surely. Wasn't the captain back on his island? If so, his twin swung himself up in the saddle.

And promptly fell off the other side.

Oh, Henri.

Nay. *Captain Lennox.* She wouldn't allow herself the more intimate *Henri.*

Or would she?

If ever she'd wished him a humiliating moment, such played out before her very eyes. To see him so undone when he was usually all mastery and finesse was a shocking sight.

He stood, failed to dust himself off, and tried again. He succeeded on a second try, though he swayed a bit. She held her breath as the portly man on the ground gave some instruction. Jago Wherry? Reins in hand, the captain prodded the bay forward and began a slow, uncertain walk . . . in her direction.

The wind gusted and a shower of crisp leaves ended her gawking, adorning her beaver hat. Brushing them aside, she mounted her mare with great speed and a new appreciation for the riding lessons of her youth. Prodding Minta into motion, she rode toward York's smoke and spires far faster than she'd left them.

CHAPTER

twelve

enri's tumble from the saddle was far less jarring than the realization he had an audience. If it had been anyone other than Esmée, he wouldn't have minded. There she stood in a fetching tailored jacket and skirt of the palest green. A jaunty hat with several white feathers crowned her head. He regarded her just long enough for Jago Wherry to take note.

The canny Cornishman gave a chuckle. "'Twas Miss Shaw who caused ye to take a tumble, no doubt."

Henri smiled past his humiliation and turned his back on the comely vision as Esmée fled with far more grace than he was capable of. Reins firmly in hand, he gave up the thought of chasing after her. A far-fetched notion, as she was born to the saddle like any well-bred woman. He'd never catch up with her.

Wherry cleared his throat. "Riding is not so far afield from commanding a ship, aye, sir? Ye must control the direction and speed with great discernment and a minimum of meddling. Ye must let the horse—like the ship—do the work."

"A worthy comparison."

"Yer posture is without fault, but yer a bit stiff." Wherry took a step back. "'Tis all about balance. Ye must learn to think like the creature upon whose back ye sit."

"A tall order."

By hour's end Henri had grown comfortable with this, his third lesson, enough to manage a brisk walk if not a trot. "I believe I can make my way back to Grant's stables."

"Without breaking yer blessed neck, I hope."

"If I do, Trident is yours."

Wherry gave a wheezing laugh and scratched Trident's withers. "Ye learn quick, Captain. And a better horse cannot be had. Spritely but not too spirited. Even tempered. Surefooted."

"And long-suffering with a sea rover like myself."

"Ye have a way with Trident, calm and assured as ye are. That bodes well for ye both."

Henri reached into his waistcoat and withdrew coin enough to pay for Wherry's trouble. "We have a gentleman's agreement, aye? I'll not see my hard-earned cash wagered."

Wherry chuckled. "Come to the races, Captain, and ye might well change yer mind."

"Once I can ride there without cause for shame, I may take you up on it."

They parted, Henri taking the same road that had returned Esmée to town. She'd seemed to appear out of nowhere, as if he'd dreamed her standing there. What was she doing miles from York, and alone at that?

Thirsty and winded, Esmée slowed to a trot as she neared York. With the almshouse women fresh in mind, she spent the next hour visiting various shops to purchase what she could. Intent on the apothecary last, she abruptly changed course, avoiding Charlotte Oake as she came out of the bookbindery next door. Remounting Minta, saddlebags bulging, Esmée quickly considered her options and reined left.

Down an alley she went, intent on Matthews Street. At its end, the

Harts' residence beckoned with acres of fragrant flowers and ripening orchards. For many years, the Harts had imported upwards of hundreds of flowering species from a London nursery to adorn their corner of Virginia. 'Twas a beloved spot since the Shaws had only a small kitchen garden and a few straggling roses now that Mama was gone.

Kitty, her dearest friend, was an able businesswoman in her own right. Her antidote to the popular, male-dominated coffeehouses in the colony was to open a female-dominated tea garden. As usual, Kitty was outside, tending to the last of the season's trumpet flowers and tuberoses.

"Esmée!" Kitty tossed aside a spade, peeled off her soiled gloves, and hurried down a brick walkway to greet her. "Nary a penny is needed!" she joked about the usual entrance fee paid by visitors.

They embraced and passed beneath an arbor's rose-scented shade. Though it was October, the blooms continued lush. Empty wicker chairs called for an extended visit. In summer, musicians were hired to play as visitors strolled the attractive paths over several acres.

"You've been to the almshouse is my guess." Kitty's amber eyes sharpened. "But you seem rather . . . bestirred. Might that have something to do with the passing of a magnificent bay horse just moments ago carrying your captain?"

"*My* captain?" Esmée darted a glance at the road, safely distant. "Most decidedly *not*."

"'Twas what I always called him once upon a time," Kitty said unapologetically as they took their seats.

"We didn't cross paths, not this time. I simply saw him from afar as I left the almshouse."

"You're still recovering from being thrust together at Lady Lightfoot's ball, I suppose." Kitty picked a rose from overhead and brought it to her nose. "What a hullaballoo when the captain strode in! All the women regarding him as if he were Poseidon himself. He has as many admirers as naysayers, you know."

Naysayers was kind. *Enemies* was more accurate. There was no denying Henri had a colorful past. Impressed as a lad by the British navy—a form of white slavery, he'd once said—he'd since caused an uproar among slave-owning Virginians once he became commander of his own vessel.

"You're remembering the brig *Swallow*, as am I," Esmée said, focusing on a cardinal as it winged by with a swoosh of red.

"Captain Lennox was right to intercept it. To burn it." Kitty's voice was low, as they were not alone in the garden. "Would that all of those slavers suffer the same fate."

Only two days out off the coast of Cabinda in Africa, the *Swallow* had been intercepted by the *Relentless* and returned to port. Its cargo of several hundred slaves who were crammed between the hold and deck had been liberated, the ship's crew left on land as their vessel was torched.

Esmée flinched recalling it. "'Twas the utmost irony the ship was bound for Virginia. Thankfully, none could prove it was the captain, with it happening so far from our shores. And he wisely stayed away."

An absence of years Esmée knew all too well. For a time the *Swallow*'s burning had incensed slave owners and ignited a fierce debate on the ills of the trade, but the Middle Passage continued robust. Of all the American colonies, Virginia enslaved the most Africans, and they landed almost daily in dizzying numbers.

"Quakers and free Africans have long been crying out against slavery," Esmée said. "'Tis rumored a large portion of the captain's profiteering prizes help fund those who oppose it."

"And now the renowned Captain Lennox has returned to our shores. Quite courageously too, making so public an appearance at the ball and now about town."

Esmée bit her lip, pondering it all. "Father led me to believe he'd left York. I assumed he'd set sail again. Glad I am I'll soon be at Eliza's in Williamsburg. Perhaps I shall stay longer than planned."

"On account of the dashing captain?" Kitty laughed. "Though you hope to ignore him, why does it appear you are as enamored with him as at first?"

"Enamored?" Esmée shook her head so vehemently it set her hat's feathers dancing. "Do you have any inkling how mortifying it is to keep being reminded of a thwarted love affair at every turn?"

"Ah." Kitty studied her pensively. "What you need is cherry syllabub."

"Cherry?" Esmée brightened. She *was* thirsty. "Grog is more like it. 'Tis stronger."

"Grog? Bah!" Waving a hand, Kitty summoned a servant to bring refreshments. "Foul stuff fit for common sailors."

"Are you calling Captain Lennox common?"

"Hardly! But what is that to you?" Kitty's eyes narrowed with mirth. "Yet you seem all too ready to leap to his defense."

Esmée lapsed into stymied silence.

"I do believe he's even handsomer than I remember. And those eyes of his, serene one minute, then intense as a tropical storm the next—"

"You are no help at all."

Kitty leaned in with a sympathetic purr. "So, he still holds your heart, at least a bit of it."

Did he?

Esmée shook her head in denial. When he'd left long ago, she'd vowed to never let another man affect her so, her heart torn asunder at their impasse.

"Which reminds me . . ." Kitty brought her round with whiplash haste. "I read in yesterday's *Virginia Gazette* an advertisement that might interest you. 'Twas remarkable in its brevity. Simply, 'Wanted: Lighthouse keeper, Indigo Island.'"

Esmée listened, ripples of dismay widening inside her. She'd avoided the papers of late, not wanting to read more about the captain than she must. But now . . . "Have you a copy?"

"I shall ask Father what he did with it before you go. 'Tis all the talk about town. That and the captain's return. Reading it brought back all that you once told me. About your shared plan for the light."

"Once, yes." Surprise gave way to an immediate wounding. A second betrayal. Esmée vowed to return home and remove the little silver lighthouse from her chatelaine once and for all. "Long ago we'd planned to marry on the island and keep the light."

"But it goes back further, does it not? To childhood?"

Dear Kitty. Remembering all the poignant details. "You mean when I was small and Father took me to Massachusetts to see the Boston harbor light. The first of its kind in the colonies. I recall him carrying me up steep steps all the way to the top. Heaven's view, he said. I've never forgotten it."

Ever since, she'd carried that remarkable moment like an ember inside her, stoking it and breathing life into it as the years went by. Father had helped fan that dream. The Chesapeake with its treacherous capes and shifting sandbars needed a similar light, he'd often said.

With a little nod, Kitty placed the wilting rose on the table. "I heard Boston Light recently burned."

Esmée nodded, her dream now ashes too. "Father told me. He keeps in contact with the lightkeeper there."

The syllabub came, a cold, sweet distraction.

"I know the chocolate shop was your mother's dream, not yours," Kitty said. "Yet you've faithfully maintained it, and 'tis quite successful. Successful enough for you to leave it should you want to and simply keep it as your dowry."

"I adore chocolate, but 'tis not what sets my soul on fire," Esmée admitted.

"And the island and lighthouse do?"

How could she answer, having never experienced either? She took another sip, feeling oddly unburdened at their honest talk, knowing Kitty was a safe harbor. "What do you know of the captain's present whereabouts?"

"I have it on good authority that he's lodging at the Royal Oake when in town and that the widow Charlotte is rather smitten. You've not seen him at the shop?"

"He's not so much as darkened the door, though something curious happened the morn after the ball. A cookbook I've long coveted was found on the shop's doorstone. The booksellers here and in Williamsburg haven't been able to import any from London. So I wondered . . ."

"Might Captain Lennox be behind it?" Kitty looked hopeful. Far more hopeful than Esmée felt.

"I don't know what to think. 'Tis a riddle I'll likely never solve. Imagine my brazenly asking him if he'd gifted it to me, only to have him say nay." Esmée chuckled despite herself. "Though I would like to thank whoever it was that was so thoughtful. So generous."

"Why don't you give him a secret gift in return?"

"Nonsense."

"A riding crop, perhaps, now that he's become a horseman. I spied a handsome silver one with a tortoiseshell handle at Christie's store just yesterday."

Dare she?

Kitty pressed forward, clearly smitten with her plan. "Arrange for it to be delivered to the Royal Oake discreetly, as happened at your chocolate shop. Let Charlotte wonder as well. Hoodwink her into believing the captain is taken."

"How . . . bold." Esmée warmed to the plan nevertheless. "Amusing, even."

Kitty laughed, looking like a cat with cream. "'Tis romantic . . . intriguing."

"I pass by Christie's on the way home," Esmée said, still torn. "If the crop is still there, 'twill be his. If not . . ." Might that be her answer? "I'll let you know what transpires. But not a word to anyone, promise me. Not even your dear father."

"'Tis our secret. I'll keep you in my thoughts and prayers." Kitty's expression clouded briefly before her smile resurfaced. "You were never quite the same after Captain Lennox went away years ago. I'd be delighted if the former Esmée Shaw came around again."

CHAPTER
thirteen

Williamsburg in autumn nearly blinded him with color. Accustomed to the muted blues and grays of sea and sky save a brilliant sunset or sunrise aboard ship, Henri rode down Duke of Gloucestershire Street with a raptness that made him half forget his poor horsemanship. Countless oaks and maples rustled like a silk skirt in a brisk wind, sending a torrent of painted leaves swirling down onto dusty cobblestones.

He'd nearly forgotten Publick Times every April and October when the courts were in session, people overflowing every inch of Williamsburg. If he hadn't been invited to stay at the governor's palace, he doubted he'd find a room at one of the inns.

To his right was the Raleigh Tavern with its deep porch fronting the street, the din of crockery and men's voices from the taproom making him almost risk the spectacle of dismounting and tethering Trident to the hitch rail. He swallowed, his throat bone-dry, and gave the Raleigh a last, lingering glance. In one hand he held the reins, in another the mysterious riding crop used to cue his horse at intervals.

Wrapped in brown paper and string, it had been delivered to his lodging house just yesterday ahead of his leaving for Williamsburg.

Charlotte Oake had looked more perplexed than pleased as she presented it to him when he entered the foyer.

"For you, Captain," she'd told him, unsmiling. "A courier from Christie's store said this was to be given to you posthaste."

He took the package, wanting to open it privately, but curiosity got the best of him, so he tore open the paper. "No mention of the giver?"

"None." She gave no sign of leaving till he'd unwrapped it. "Do you have a secret admirer, sir?"

He stared at the crop, a costly piece of work. "One with decidedly good taste, if so."

Was Esmée trying to pay him back for his gifting her a book? Granted, *The Complete Confectioner* had long been in his possession. He'd thought, upon his return to Virginia five years before, to ask her forgiveness and give her the gift. But second thoughts had the tome going around the world with him instead, tucked beneath a stack of sailing manuals in a bookcase, a continual if barbed reminder of their broken tie.

Charlotte's features tightened. "How long will you be in Williamsburg, sir?"

He gave her no firm answer, as he hadn't one. He considered it now as he turned up Palace Green. The governor's brick residence with its ornamental iron gates at the far end was the undisputed crown jewel of the capital, away from the crowds and confusion of Virginia's largest town. He sought the palace's cobbled forecourt, where a groom waited to take his mount to the near stables.

Stiff and slightly saddle sore, Henri climbed stone steps to the palace's front door, gaze rising to the towering lanthorn impaling the October sky. The door opened, and a butler ushered him into a weapon-lined hall that seemed more military fort than palace.

"The governor is upstairs in the middle room with his officials, sir, but will see you in due time. I'll show you to your chamber."

Henri followed the liveried servant down a carpeted hall and up a stair to an enormous bedchamber. Compared to his cramped sea cabin aboard the *Relentless*, it was sumptuous—fit for a prince—and painted as yellow as a finch's wing. The bed linens bore a floral pattern all the rage on land these days. He was most drawn to the comfortable chair near a crackling hearth. Though the day wasn't cold, the room was airy, and night would soon set in with autumn's chill.

Restless, he crossed the thick carpet to one of two windows and pushed aside the ornate drapes. Palace Green stretched before him, his second-floor vantage point giving him a bird's-eye view.

His gaze drifted from the mustering militia to a man playing a fiddle to a bevy of laughing, chatting belles strolling in colorful procession past the palace gates. The ribbons on their wide straw hats fluttered behind them, their elegant skirts teased by the wind, all of them paired in twos but for the lone graceful straggler at the back . . .

Esmée?

He took a second look, gaze darting to the front of the column before returning to the rear again. Esmée followed at a distance, obviously content to keep her own pace. She paused to buy paper flowers from a barefoot young girl selling them on a corner.

Crossing his arms, he allowed himself an unhindered look at her. She was talking to the flower peddler, twirling the paper blossoms in one gloved hand. She'd always been kind. No airs about her. Her sister and entourage were now halfway down the other side of Palace Green as if they'd forgotten all about her. As usual, Eliza was leading the charge, undeterred by her pregnancy or anything else, for that matter. He watched them through the trees till they'd turned a distant corner by Bruton Parish Church.

Was Virginia so infernally small?

He was used to an ocean, and town had him tripping over people. Was it not uncanny that he and Esmée kept crossing paths? First the ball, then near the almshouse, and now this. What next? As she likely didn't associate with Virginia's officials, he doubted they'd move beyond this chance encounter from afar. No mention had been made of a rout or any other form of entertainment, not at the governor's palace, anyway. He could rest easy, mayhap. Finish his business with colonial officials and be gone.

He turned away from the window and sought the hearth, sinking down into the velvet-upholstered chair. A tug on the bell cord gained him something to allay his thirst. In minutes, a footman brought a silver tray and poured him a cup of strong, hot tea. Bohea, from the scent of it. A dram of French brandy rested beside it. Here it was a relief to escape the near constant shadow of Charlotte Oake, even if she did serve Shaw's chocolate.

The book he'd brought—Thomas à Kempis's *The Imitation of Christ*—awaited reading, one quote worth remembering.

Everywhere I have sought peace and not found it, except in a corner with a book.

He stretched out his legs, his boots near the elaborately cast brass andirons, and pondered. Why had the governor called him here? Something to do with the current conflict, no doubt. His gaze traveled to the window again, the sky so blue and the town so peaceful it was hard to believe there was a war nearing official declaration.

Surely Dinwiddie didn't want to make a soldier of him.

CHAPTER
fourteen

smée pressed her paper flowers to her nose in a fit of whimsy. Just ahead were Eliza and her friends, returning to tea at the Cheverton townhouse. They'd had a delightful stroll about town, mindful winter would soon set in with an icy vengeance. The autumn wind was rising, pressing against them as they passed Bruton Parish Church and continued toward Nassau Street. Eliza was laughing, spirits high on so lovely an afternoon.

Esmée warmed to the sound after a fretful two days. Upon her arrival, her sister was complaining of pains and the physic was sent for. With the baby not due till January, any trouble was unwelcome. Still, Eliza had insisted on entertaining friends and walking about and now presiding over tea. She waited on the steps for Esmée to catch up as her guests went over the threshold into the townhouse.

"Sister, how you dally!" Appearing amused and exasperated, Eliza gestured her inside, clearly ready to sit down. "What fuss over paper flowers!"

All six ladies swarmed into the parlor like colorful butterflies, removing hats and gloves before settling around a tea table. Esmée felt like the odd woman out. The present company did not make her feel unwelcome, but neither had they common ground, with their talk of parties and French fashion and the latest gossip to be had.

"What have you in hand there?" Lady Griffin asked her, leaning in and enveloping Esmée in a cloud of toilet water.

"Paper carnations and roses." Esmée held them out so she could see the painstaking care with which they were crafted.

"Clever." On Esmée's other side, Miss Cartwright wrinkled her pale nose. "But I prefer silk flowers from the milliner. Nothing so common as paper."

"Common? 'Tis artistry to me," Esmée replied. "Look at the parts of the flower from stamen to petals, all dyed such lovely hues. The child—Lottie is her name—would make a botanist proud. I asked her for a whole nosegay of them to last me through the winter."

"Well, they shan't wilt, truly," Lady Griffin said with a chuckle, eyes on the refreshments being brought into the room. "Though I fancy they won't retain their color either."

Across the table, the governor's eldest daughter, Rebecca Dinwiddie, took out her fan. "The flowers are lovely, though I'd rather talk chocolate, Miss Shaw. Your sister says you may well open a shop right here in Williamsburg."

Esmée opened her mouth to naysay it once again, then bit her tongue lest it only stir up Eliza's zeal for the plan. Would her sister never let go of the notion?

Eliza simply smiled, pouring tea into prewarmed cups for those who wanted it, making a great show of it with her Wedgwood tea service. The maid stood by with a porcelain chocolate pot new to Esmée, twisting the molinet between her hands to blend the beverage.

"Enough about chocolate," Miss Cartwright said, her color high. "You know what's said."

"Indeed, I do," Lady Griffin replied. "The fair sex is to be particularly careful how they meddle with romances, chocolate, novels, and the like."

"The *Virginia Almanac*, for one." Miss Cartwright's capped head bobbed. "Especially in the spring, as those inflamers are very dangerous."

"My dear sister, which is your preference?" Eliza asked, clearly amused by the conversation. "The very tepid-in-reputation tea? Or the more passionate and provoking hot chocolate?"

Esmée replied unashamedly, "Chocolate, please."

Smiling, Miss Dinwiddie raised her own chocolate cup. "I'm especially partial to Shaw's dark cocoa with orange essence, as is my father."

"Speaking of your father, our respected governor"—Lady Griffin fingered the opal choker about her neck—"do tell us about the next function he and your mother are rumored to be planning."

"Indeed, the new ballroom and supper room will host a splendid assembly this January."

"A holiday ball?" Miss Marriot exclaimed. "Enchanting!"

"Miss Shaw, will you join us, or have you other reasons to stay in York?" Miss Dinwiddie asked.

Another assembly. The frivolous cost of which could feed and clothe the almshouse till next Christmastide. What could Esmée say to this?

Judge not that ye be not judged.

Eliza pouted when Esmée failed to answer. "I shan't attend, for obvious reasons."

A tittering of sympathy went round the circle. Esmée sipped from her cup in silence, glad the conversation had gone another, less inflammatory direction. In the foyer she could hear her father and Quinn about to go out. They'd been summoned to the palace. Some sort of meeting that involved maritime matters. They wouldn't return till after supper, they'd said that morn, which left her and Eliza to their own devices.

"And you, Miss Shaw?" Lady Griffin seemed determined that Esmée answer. "Are you not fond of dancing? I believe I saw you at Lady Lightfoot's ball. And in the company of Captain Lennox, I daresay."

The room stilled. The ladies were looking at her over the rims of their cups. Heat climbed from Esmée's tightly laced stays to her powderless cheekbones. What could she say?

Eliza set her cup down. "My sister and Captain Lennox do not belong in the same sentence. They simply happened to be thrust together at Lady Lightfoot's table and later when dancing."

"Quite a shame, as he is so *very* eligible," Lady Griffin whispered, brows arched as if privy to inside information. "Though his detractors are many."

Esmée's pulse quickened. Feigning disinterest, she took another sip of chocolate. Had she been a fool to send the captain that riding crop? She could not blame Kitty. She'd wanted to do it, had been rather charmed by the suggestion . . . and therein revealed the state of her heart. She was not at all over Henri Lennox. Not one whit. She'd have to be confined to a casket first. How had she convinced herself over the long years that he had no hold on her?

Eliza flashed her dimpled smile and passed the tray of ginger cakes. "Let us talk less of dashing ship captains and more of the coming assembly."

"Have you heard?" Miss Cartwright brightened. "I was at the mantuamaker's just yesterday. She told me of a new fashion influenced by the secret language of flowers. By embroidering one's clothes, one conveys a message." She looked at one of the paper flowers Esmée had placed on the table. "A carnation means 'my heart aches for you.' A rose in bloom signifies love. I say we all embroider our gowns with meaningful flowers for the coming ball."

"You refer to my very colorful friend, Mary Wortley Montagu," Lady Griffin told them with a touch of pride. "She started the craze for a floral love language in England and the continent. It *is* rather amusing to consider which flowers we might choose."

Eliza was clearly smitten with the idea, her expression rapt. "If I could attend, I would buy up all the scarlet thread and smother my gown in bright red roses, which must symbolize passion."

"I would pick a white lily, which symbolizes purity." Miss Dinwiddie reached for another tea cake with a blush. "Father says that at seventeen I'm too young to consider a suitor."

"Bosh! Never too young—or too old!" Lady Griffin retorted, having outlived three husbands. "Love visits us at any age and often quite unexpectedly."

"What would you choose, Miss Marriot?" Esmée asked her. Of all the women present, she was the undisputed beauty, second to

Eliza, with her flawless skin and flaxen hair, and was reputed to have a great many admirers.

"Purple violet, I believe, though I have no inkling what it signifies."

"Daydreaming," Lady Griffin told her. "'Near them the Vi'let glows with odours blest and blooms in more than Tyrian purple drest.' Next time we gather I shall read from some of Lady Montagu's letters. They are quite eloquent."

"Tyrian purple, indeed." Eliza poured another round of tea and chocolate. "I spied silk of that very color at the mantuamaker's the other day. Needs be you ladies begin embroidering straightaway. January is not far off."

"Shall we meet here, then?" Miss Cartwright suggested. "Company always makes needlework more enjoyable. Unless it would tire you too terribly, that is, Lady Drysdale."

Esmée returned her attention to her sister, who'd reached down to pet her enormous Angora cat, Dulcet, that had crept into the parlor on furry white feet. Eliza looked tired. Half-moons rimmed her eyes, and she'd stifled more yawns than Esmée could count.

Straightening, Eliza flashed another smile. "I beg you, come. Embroidery is not my strong suit, but company keeps my mind off my coming confinement."

Did anyone else detect the note of dread in Eliza's voice?

"I'm nearly done with the babe's welcome gift," Esmée said. "I hope you like it." Declining another cup of tea, she reached for her sewing bag and took out her latest handwork. Tea drinking and talk didn't satisfy for long. She must be doing something.

Lady Griffin raised an eyebrow. "What have you there?"

Esmée threaded a needle with practiced ease. "Clouts and pilchers for the almshouse infants."

A quiet nearly as lengthy as that of Captain Lennox's mention ensued. The ladies looked on as she plied her needle.

"Ah, the almshouse." Lady Griffin's tone implied both distaste and indifference. "Overfull of a great many feebleminded as well as fallen women, not to mention beggarly, idle men."

"You might be surprised if you visited. I welcome you to accompany me." Careful to hide the ire she felt lest she hurt her cause, Esmée continued, "There are a great many orphaned children. And infirm elderly with no means or family to support them."

"I've heard conditions are dismal." Miss Cartwright turned troubled eyes on her. "How often are you there, Miss Shaw?"

"Every sennight, usually. More often if there's cause." Esmée raised her gaze and smiled at them in invitation. "If you cannot accompany me, I encourage you to give what you are willing—goods, foodstuffs, coin. Anything at all helps."

"Hearing about orphaned infants makes me melancholy." Eliza put a hand on her burgeoning middle. "Imagine being brought up homeless and even motherless. And then there are the children indentured almost before they are out of pudding caps and leading strings!"

Enlivened by too many cups of sugared tea, Eliza was in full theatrical mode, embarrassing Esmée but perhaps aiding her mission. Rebecca Dinwiddie looked shocked. Was the governor's daughter shielded from such harsh realities? Beside her, the sensitive Miss Cartwright sighed while Miss Marriot took out a handkerchief and dabbed her eyes.

Lady Griffin appeared unmoved. "Is that not how your saintly mother died, Miss Shaw? A malignant fever? Contracting her very death by patronizing the almshouse . . ." She shuddered and closed her eyes. "*Pesthouse* is more like it."

Chafed, Esmée continued stitching, though she had another idea of how best to use her needle. Lady Griffin was in dire need of deflating, her arrogance unchecked. "How hard your heart is, madam. My mother did indeed die from a malignant fever, but she could have gotten the same from the very streets of York or Williamsburg. The Almighty has the final say over life and death. 'Twas simply Mama's time or she would never have contracted it to begin with, pesthouse or no."

The ensuing silence grew strained. Miss Marriot coughed into her handkerchief. Had Esmée stirred a hornet's nest?

"How blithely you say such, Miss Shaw." Lady Griffin's haughty tone was Esmée's final undoing. "The Almighty I worship is a different being altogether, a Creator, certainly, but one who remains apart from His creation, giving us leave to act as we will. Personal responsibility and accountability are foremost."

"You speak of a clockwork universe, not divine Providence." Esmée finished one clout and moved to the next, eyes on her stitches. "If you read less of misguided deists and more of the Bible, we might be spared this futile conversation."

"Ladies, please." Eliza's wide eyes flashed a warning.

Esmée smiled at her, dispelling the tension, or so she hoped.

But Lady Griffin was not finished. "What of the danger to your sister and her unborn child with your frequent forays to the poor?"

Esmée replied, "I am seldom in Williamsburg and am vigilant about my own welfare in York. If I find myself ill, I shut myself off from everyone, especially my sister. No one has cause to worry."

"Glad I am to hear it," Lady Griffin concluded with a chill smile. "As for the almshouse, I suppose a shopkeeping, bluestocking spinster must be passionate about something."

Though the slight stung, it held a pithy truth.

Eliza opened her mouth to leap to her sister's defense, it seemed, then caught Esmée's warning glance and quieted. Only the Almighty could change Lady Griffin's heart. Or her own, for that matter. Biting her lip lest their banter develop into a full-blown row, Esmée drew a relieved breath as talk returned to the ball. But her mind remained on the almshouse and how to better it.

CHAPTER
fifteen

aptain Lennox, might I have the pleasure of your accompanying me home for supper tonight?" Quinn said.

Henri pushed up from his chair after two days of meetings in the middle room at the governor's palace, stomach rumbling in answer. "Obliged, Lord Drysdale."

"You've yet to meet my lovely wife. She's quite fond of company and conversation." Quinn, known far and wide for his hospitality, clapped a hand on Henri's shoulder. "And I hope you'll find our new French chef second to none here in Williamsburg, even the governor's own."

After a few more minutes exchanging farewells with a dozen or so officials, they left the governor's residence and began their walk down Palace Green. A late afternoon drizzle had done little in the way of dampening the revelry. Market Square was glistening, numerous stalls and hawkers offering all manner of Virginia goods.

"Fresh air is never more welcome than after being sequestered in the palace or the House of Burgesses," Quinn said with a relieved smile.

"Mind if we stop by the fruit seller?" Henri eyed the booth across the wide street. "Lady Drysdale might enjoy a pineapple or some bounty from the Summer Isles."

"No purchase quite like a gift." Quinn swung his walking stick with élan. "Do I detect a note of wistfulness in your tone? A longing for the Caribbean, Captain?"

"Mayhap. It nearly became home, as I was away from Virginia for so long."

"My family has a sugar plantation in Barbados. Dreadfully hot. Mosquitos as big as dinner plates," Quinn lamented. "I'm due to return soon on necessary business after the birth of my firstborn."

"I prefer Saint Barthélemy with the hidden coves of Anse du Gouverneur and the sandy beaches of Saline." Henri's pleasant tone turned wry. "French buccaneers, iguanas, and *le chocolat.*"

Quinn smiled his amusement. "You speak fluent French, no doubt."

"*Oui.*" Henri shrugged. "*Je peux communiquer de façon simple.*"

"There is nothing simple about you, Captain," Quinn replied as Henri selected two lush pineapples and paid in pieces of eight. "And I can't help but wonder whether you will risk the governor's dangerous proposition or decline and simply sail away to fairer destinations."

"I have some time to consider it, though the sea, sun, and sand are a powerful elixir," Henri confessed, his head still full of the arguments for and against the proposal in the governor's chambers. "At least we all agree something must be done to stop the French by sea lest we be ruled by the French on land."

"Agreed. But at what cost? Your very life, mayhap. And those of your men."

"War is the trade of kings, after all."

"Indeed." Quinn tipped his hat to someone in passing. "I'd much rather speak of our shared opposition of the slave trade."

"'Tis rare to find one with such convictions, especially in slave-heavy Virginia."

"A tragedy I strive to rectify, though I may see little done to abolish it in my lifetime." Quinn turned to him, his ever genial eyes grave. "But at least I can begin making changes on the sugar plantation I mentioned, replacing Africans with indentures."

"You have an air of Granville Sharp and other staunch abolitionists about you."

"I was trained at London's Temple Court with the best of them. And I've been inspired by your past burning of the *Swallow*, an audacious act that gained considerable attention and made a great many men and women consider their stance on the matter. Far more effective than printing a broadside or waxing eloquent about it in the newspapers."

"Nothing remotely eloquent about smelling a vessel before it's sighted. Or men, women, and children chained and lying in filth after only two days at sea." Though it had been eight years since the tragedy, the misery was burned into his memory like an African brand. "I have no words for those who captain such ships or claim human cargo, many of them our fellow Virginians."

"Woefully so." Quinn's eyes flashed. "'Tis a trade of the greatest inhumanity and an affront to God Almighty."

"Yet slavery remains the cornerstone of the British empire clear to the Caribbean."

"You had a taste of slavery yourself, being impressed in the Royal Navy, taken from your home and family and all you held dear."

"It hardly compares to the evil done the Africans, but aye, a small taste. The experience opened my eyes to those held against their will, their God-given rights violated."

They walked in silence for several moments, beyond the busy marketplace. Henri breathed deeply of the autumn air. Fall, despite its melancholy bent, had always been his favorite season.

"I'm a poor host bringing up such dark matters." Quinn quickened his pace, his voice lifting. "Let us dwell on the present instead. You are our honored guest, and I'm certain Cook has prepared something that will tempt your French sensibilities. My wife will entertain us after supper with the harpsichord, and if you choose to stay on, there will even be illuminations on Palace Green after dark."

They turned up Nassau Street with its deep shade and elegant townhouses, the gardens surrounding them still abloom and untouched by frost. A few welcoming lights shone in windows, lifting

Henri's pensive mood. If he refused the governor's offer, he could settle down. Have a wife who might even play the harpsichord. Hire a cook to turn out endless tantalizing dishes. Beget children to chase after. Cultivate landlocked friends like Quinn. It sounded . . . idyllic.

Impossible.

They mounted brick steps to a door opened by a stone-faced butler in livery.

"Good evening, sirs."

The foyer, fragrant with cooking herbs, was dominated by a curving staircase. Hats and coats discarded, they passed into a spacious, blue-paneled parlor. Feminine voices could be heard upstairs, and then came a light tread on the steps. Henri faced the doorway, ready to greet Lady Drysdale, whoever she might be. His acquaintance with Quinn was just a few days old, but they'd found common ground in the governor's oft heated meetings. Henri was impressed with the younger man's sound judgment and thorough knowledge of colonial affairs.

"Quinn, is that you?" The lovely voice heralded the appearance of a young woman in rustling crimson silk, her throat wrapped in rubies.

Henri's mind whirled.

Lady Drysdale née Eliza Shaw?

The wrench in his gut was offset by Eliza's trilling laugh. "Dear husband, have you played a prank on our unsuspecting captain?"

Though she seemed every bit as taken aback as he was, Eliza recovered well. Henri looked down at the pineapples he held, wishing himself back at the governor's palace. Had he judged Quinn wrong? Was this some sort of tawdry prank?

But it was Quinn who appeared the most confused. He shot a glance at Henri, then returned to his wife. "I was unaware Captain Lennox was known to you."

"Well . . ." Eliza flushed the hue of her gown. "Long ago, yes. We retain a great respect for him, of course, though we did not think to cross paths again."

"*We?*" her husband prodded.

A sigh. "My sister and myself. And Father, of course." Eliza swallowed and darted a glance at the foyer. "But mostly Esmée."

Understanding seemed to dawn on his host's face. "Blast!" Quinn blanched. "Forgive me, Captain. At least take back your pineapples—"

"A peace offering," Henri jested, still trying to grasp Eliza's very advantageous marriage to one of Virginia's foremost officials.

Thanking him, she came forward and took the fruit from his outstretched hands. "How did you know pineapples are my preference?"

A sudden movement in the foyer caused all eyes to shift to the doorway. Esmée, of course. Admiral Shaw was just behind her, obviously as delighted as his oldest daughter was not.

"Captain Lennox!" he all but thundered in the distressed silence. "What brings you to our door?"

"Lord Drysdale invited me to"—Henri's gaze hung on Esmée—"to cause a commotion."

They laughed, all but Esmée, whose tentative half-smile didn't reach her eyes. She came toward them, as comely as ever in a shimmering blue gown. He preferred it to her yellow ensemble at the ball. Blue was always eye-catching, mayhap because it reminded him of the sea. The silken fabric seemed like water poured over her, so flattering was the fit, every inch of cloth and lace accentuating her buxom figure.

"Best have it out in the open." Esmée came to stand between her father and Eliza. "Once upon a time Captain Lennox and I had a . . . an understanding."

"Of the romantic sort," Eliza finished with a genuine smile. "But 'tis ancient history, and today dawns anew. This evening, rather."

"Well, I for one don't believe in coincidences or chance meetings," Admiral Shaw said, showing no befuddlement. "When I left the governor's meetings early today, I never expected you'd be our guest. I couldn't be happier."

"Please, come into the dining room as supper is at hand." Eliza gestured toward a candlelit chamber, where a long table already bore steaming dishes. "'Tis much more informal than Lady Lightfoot's ball." She gave a charming wink in Henri's direction. "Though the seating arrangement is exactly the same."

CHAPTER

sixteen

smée sat down, Henri to her left. Across from them was Eliza, while Quinn and Father occupied the ends of the table. For a few seconds, the lovely flowers at table's center caught her eye and softened her dismay. Gotten from Eliza's formal garden in back of the townhouse, the last of summer's roses showed off their cream and scarlet hues, their scent heady.

Also heady was the man beside her. His hair was tousled by the windy walk here, and the faint facial lines, etched by wind and weather, were kinder by candlelight. His tailor, whoever that might be, needed applause. Henri was dressed for town, his dark broadcloth suit as striking as any she'd seen among Virginia gentlemen. She'd always found a well-dressed man appealing right down to his polished, buckled shoes. But more than that, she was impressed with Henri's graciousness and humor moments earlier as they'd navigated another hazardous meeting.

All too aware of him, she placed her serviette in her lap, taking a bit from this or that dish without thinking. Oh, if she could only say amusing things like Eliza, not sit here tongue-tied and awkward and wishing they didn't have so bittersweet a history to overcome.

But if they couldn't be lovers, might they be friends? She daren't hope for more. Her heart wasn't ready for more. Nor, she surmised in the stilted silence between them, was his.

"How fortunate we have French cuisine, Captain Lennox." Eliza's smile hadn't dimmed yet. "Our cook has made a delicious beef ragout that I hope you'll find delectable."

Henri smiled. "I'm sure I shall."

"And what is for dessert?" Quinn asked as a footman began to pour the wine.

"Your favorite apple tart, made with those pippins from the orchard," Eliza told him. "The rest will be pressed for cider."

"Take care to have some fruit set aside for winter. They oft improve with age. Much like fine wine"—Quinn looked up from sampling his beef ragout—"or romance."

Esmée stared at him. Was she being too sensitive, or was his comment meant for her and the captain? Quinn was, in his own way, as shrewd and forthright as Eliza. That he had a recent high regard of Henri there could be no doubt. Something was afoot beyond the usual supper invitation, surely. But what?

"So please inform me, gentlemen, of the happenings behind closed doors at the palace." Eliza posed the question foremost in Esmée's mind. "Or is it hushed?"

"Alas, too private and too dense for polite supper conversation, I'm afraid," Quinn replied, sending a small smile his wife's way and sparing his father-in-law and Henri an answer. "I'd much rather hear about your day."

Eliza set down her fork. "I shan't bore you with all the feminine details so will just say Esmée entertained us by debating deism and a clockwork universe with Lady Griffin." She smiled, a flash of triumph in her eyes. "Esmée won."

"Lady Griffin?" Her father's brow rose. "A rather dangerous sparring partner, is she not?"

Eliza continued, gleeful. "Esmée even invited her to the almshouse."

Quinn broke out in laughter. "Now *that* I would have liked to witness. My own parlor sounds far more riveting than palace chambers, I must say."

Esmée caught Henri's wry smile. Would he think her a shrew? Eccentric in her spinsterhood?

"Open and honest conversation is never amiss when handled civilly," she said quietly, losing what remained of her appetite. "I rather enjoyed meeting the governor's lovely daughter and Eliza's other friends."

"It does you much good to be amongst society, Lady Griffin aside. You are too often at the chocolate shop and almshouse," her father told her. He looked toward Henri. "Speaking of York, I hope you feel free to darken our door on Main Street when you're ashore. Or at least come by the coffeehouse."

"I may come to you injured and in need of a physic, as I've recently taken up riding."

Laughter rippled round the table. His newfound interest in horses intrigued Esmée. A daring endeavor after so long at sea. He fancied the freedom to be had on horseback, no doubt.

"How goes it offshore?" Eliza asked him, ever fascinated by those who lived in the barrier islands. "I hope your crew is well."

"Glad for a lull, most of them, after two years at sea. Having the Flask and Sword at their beck and call makes it even more agreeable." Henri took a sip of wine as a footman whisked his empty plate away. "Repairs are being made to the *Relentless* as we speak."

"If you're not anxious to return," Quinn offered, "why not accompany us to church in the morning?"

Esmée stared at Quinn. Though a dutiful churchgoer, he often napped during lengthy sermons, as did her sister.

Eliza offered her most charming smile. "If we could sweeten the offer with chocolate, Captain, would you agree?"

Would he?

Henri darted a glance at Esmée. Was he seeking her approval? His gaze traveled from her to her sister, leaving her a bit bereft. Once she'd grown lost in those sea-blue eyes, a silvery light in them when he was amused.

"Church?" A softness crept into his tone. "Most welcome after salt-spray services with a sea chaplain."

Would he attend with them, then? The wonder of it washed over her, and she sighed a little too audibly. Henri's intent gaze ricocheted back to her. She forced a smile and looked to her lap.

As soon as supper ended, thinking Henri might excuse himself and leave, Esmée was surprised to find herself seated beside him on the parlor sofa while Eliza played the harpsichord across the room. Her father and Quinn were deep in conversation by the hearth.

Henri leaned back, one arm along the sofa's curving arm. "So, tell me, when did your sister meet Lord Drysdale?"

Esmée was distracted, not by the question but by his nearness. Her full petticoats brushed against his leg and completely covered one of his buckled shoes. The room was cool, but she felt flushed. She needed to do something with her hands, only she didn't have a fan. Nor could she fiddle with her chatelaine, which was upstairs on the dressing table.

"They met a few years ago." Esmée was cast back to their courtship, far smoother than her own had been. "Quinn first spied her when at the York coffeehouse. Eliza was helping Mama in the chocolate shop. But it wasn't till Eliza was riding around Williamsburg in an open carriage that he decided to further their acquaintance. He happened to leave the Raleigh Tavern the precise moment she went by. And so she tossed him the love token she kept in her pocket as the carriage passed. 'Twas engraved with her initials and a heart."

A romantic story, making falling in love seem ridiculously easy. To her credit, Eliza hadn't known who Quinn was, other than a well-dressed gentleman, and couldn't be blamed for the fortune hunting some accused her of later at the governor's ball.

Henri ran a hand over his clean-shaven jaw. "Do you remember how we met?"

His quiet question was nearly lost as Eliza finished a robust Italian concerto, the notes soaring. They clapped, delaying Esmée's answer. Hoping for a quieter piece, she asked Eliza, "Won't you play Bach? *The Well-Tempered Clavier*, perhaps?"

"Why don't you?" Eliza replied good-naturedly. "'Tis your favorite, and you perform it better than I do."

Esmée gave a decided shake of her head. Nothing would tear her away from answering Henri's surprising question. "Please . . . play on."

With a slight lift of her shoulders, Eliza returned to her music.

As she struck the first note, Esmée toyed absently with the lace trim on her sleeve. "I do remember how we met." *Though I've tried to forget.*

Was he recalling finding her shelling on the beach? And later at the supper party? Her lowered gaze caught the slow fisting of his hand where it rested on the sofa, the Jerusalem cross plain.

"Mayhap the end of a matter is more important than the beginning." The gravity in his voice held her, much like the inked tattoo.

"Perhaps," she replied rather vacuously.

What more could she say? And what exactly did he mean? She looked at him in question, the drone of Quinn and her father's conversation and Eliza's quieter playing a thousand miles distant. He was not looking at her but straight ahead as if weighing his words. Charting his course.

"Are you . . . spoken for?" His was a bold query, made bolder by their broken past.

"My heart, you mean?" Her calm reply belied the roiling inside her.

"Aye." His eyes roamed her face as if trying to reconcile a decade's difference and all the events and people that might have come between them.

"I . . . nay." She paused, her need to know overpowering any shyness and turning around the question. "And you?"

"Aye." A curt nod of his tousled head sent her spirits to her shoes. "Betrothed to my ship. My crew. The sea."

Heat stained her face. "I regret saying such."

"You simply stated the truth, Esmée. Though at the time I was unwilling to hear it."

Esmée. Not *Miss Shaw.*

Her stomach flipped. His use of her given name muted the harsh memory somehow. A long-suppressed desire flickered deep inside her. How she wanted to say his name in return and not merely think it.

Captain seemed so formal, keeping him out of reach. *Henri* seemed a leap forward yet held the rusty disuse of years.

She swallowed. Fought to steady her nerves. "I—I am not the woman I was, Henri." Entreaty framed her words. "I regret a great many things."

His gaze cut to her again, held her eyes for a beat longer than propriety deemed necessary. The music had stopped, as had the room's conversation. All eyes were on them, bringing their heartfelt conversation to a sudden, maddening halt. Flushing again, Esmée looked away from him. How much had her family overheard?

From beyond the damask window drapery came a pop and a soaring white light. Through the glass, small rockets left starry streaks against the night sky.

"Glory! The illuminations have begun! We must join the festivities on Palace Green." Eliza led the way into the foyer, pausing to let Quinn fetch her cape against the chill before they exited out the door the butler had opened, Father after them.

Henri took Esmée's own cape in hand. "Is this yours?"

Nodding, she turned her back, letting him drape the purple garment over her shoulders before they followed the others outside. Skittery as he made her, she almost stumbled on the steps. His hand shot out to steady her, cupping her elbow in an endearing—and searing—gesture. Her heart, once aflutter, now began to knock about her chest like a fist on a door.

Woe to her if he didn't feel the same.

Together they walked toward the display, joining countless gaping, guffawing onlookers. The night assumed a kind of magic she'd not felt for so long that it seemed she'd been living in a trance since he left. With him beside her, the heavens glittering above, the mood one of festive jubilation all around, she came awake.

And it shook her to her new calamanco slippers that he might well walk away again.

CHAPTER

seventeen

Esmée was back in the chocolate shop three days hence, her chance encounter with Henri in Williamsburg seeming naught but a woozy dream. Until she saw him go past on his handsome horse, right down teeming Water Street, looking like he was born to the saddle. Was he still having lessons with Jago Wherry?

With no one else in the front of the shop to witness her befuddlement, she rushed to the bow-fronted window to see him tying up his mount at a hitch rail in front of the coffeehouse. Instantly her hands flew to her hair and cap, a bit untidy after a busy morning. Her apron bore a chocolate stain, so she whisked it off, only to look up again as he spoke with a woman in a wide, beribboned hat. Esmée's heart lurched.

Kitty?

Her friend was her exuberant self, her lithe form clad in lilac silk taffeta, her gloved hands gesticulating as she spoke. And she was . . . gesturing to the chocolate shop. A sudden clatter in the coffeehouse made Esmée jump. Broken cups? One glance at the Dutch door earned her nothing but the sight of a great many men reading papers or conversing amid a great many beverages.

When the shop door pushed open with a jingle of the bell, Esmée made a pretense of arranging chocolate pots and cups before the wide window.

"There you are!" Kitty closed the door, her lady's maid nowhere in evidence. "Be forewarned. You might well have a visitor."

"Captain Lennox?"

"The one and only. Apparently he has business in the coffeehouse." She looked toward the open Dutch door. "One never knows what he might do next. He's carrying that riding crop you gave him—"

"Shhhh," Esmée said, gesturing to the counter. "Would you like a sweet? We've a new batch of anise-flavored chocolates topped with sugared orange rind."

"I'd rather talk gentlemen," Kitty whispered.

"I'd rather *not*," Esmée whispered back with another glance at the door.

"There is no one near enough to eavesdrop. Your indentures must all be in the kitchen, and the coffeehouse is full of commotion." Kitty removed her gloves, still smiling. "Oh, this shop smells divine! No wonder you spend your days making confections."

Esmée held out a tray filled with hardening sweets, a wisp of orange rind atop each. Pippin knots, millefruit biscuits, preserved cherries, and apricot tartlets were Kitty's for the taking.

She chose an apricot tartlet, her eyes closing as she sampled a bite. "I've come to buy a pound or two of cocoa for drinking. With winter coming on, we must have hot chocolate."

"I've a quantity of especially good Caribbean cocoa." Esmée moved to a cupboard where the best was stored. "What with the French trouble by land and sea, our supplies are low."

"Ah, the French. How weary I am of war talk." Kitty watched as Esmée wrapped the whitish cocoa bricks in paper. "Why not visit us this afternoon? Our winter tearoom awaits, freshly painted and warmed by the Franklin stove Father ordered from Philadelphia."

"Sounds cozy." Esmée tied the bundle with string. "But I'm overdue at the almshouse, being away in Williamsburg as I was."

"Of course. I would offer to go with you, but . . ." Kitty wrinkled her nose. "I don't know how you abide the wretched conditions. The sadness."

The sadness. That was the worst of it. Betimes she couldn't bear it. Yet still she must go. "One young woman is nearing her confinement." Esmée checked the watch pinned to her chatelaine. A clock wasn't on the shop wall. Father wanted his customers to forget the time and dwell on confections. "I hope to take her some things that might help with the baby. Clouts and blankets and such." She'd finally gathered all the needs the almshouse women had confided last visit, and she felt a little like a child at Christmas in her desire to deliver them.

With a sigh, Kitty paid for her purchase. "Imagine a babe being born in that place. A ward of the parish, I suppose." She took the wrapped chocolate and started for the door. "Do come by when you can. We've much to talk about, like your churchgoing the past Sabbath with Captain Lennox. That has set both Williamsburg and York astir!"

Esmée smiled sheepishly. "How on earth did you come to learn of it?"

"I have a dear aunt who attends Bruton Parish, remember."

"Captain Lennox was Eliza and Quinn's guest, is all."

"I do wonder if that's all there is to the tattle." Kitty cast a final, probing look her way. The shop door jingled anew as she went out. "Farewell, dear friend!"

By the time Esmée left Shaw's Chocolate shortly after two o'clock, Captain Lennox's horse was no longer tethered before the coffeehouse. Something inside her dimmed at the apparent rebuff. Where had he gone?

Her answer came when she rode her mare down the coastal road toward the almshouse.

A figure on horseback in the distance drew nearer in a storm of dust. Jago Wherry? He sat atop Captain Lennox's handsome bay horse, headed back toward York.

"Good afternoon, Miss Shaw." He tipped his battered hat, looking pleased with the world.

"Good afternoon, Mr. Wherry. A fine mount you have there."

"Aye, 'tis not mine, Miss Shaw, but Captain Lennox's. I'm playing the groom and returning Trident to the stable."

Trident. The weapon of Poseidon, god of the sea. Why was she not surprised? She bit her lip before the next burning query escaped her.

Where is the captain?

But Jago, unless inebriated, was known to be close-lipped, and at this moment he was most decidedly sober. She cantered on, aswirl with her most recent encounter with Henri at Eliza's. Used to confining his memory to a small corner of her mind, she could do so no longer. He was back, larger than life, and she could not shake his intriguing questions.

"Do you remember how we met?"

"Are you . . . spoken for?"

Mostly she recalled his enigmatic answers.

"Mayhap the end of a matter is more important than the beginning."

"You simply stated the truth, Esmée. Though at the time I was unwilling to hear it."

He had called her by name, a name he once said he found beautiful and musical. Once he'd even teased her, calling her Esmée Shaw Lennox. She'd penned those very words over and over on scraps of paper when no one was looking, scrolling the *E* and *S* and *L* endlessly before throwing her daydreams into the hearth's fire.

The road before her took a winding turn along the sun-soaked coast. For all her woolgathering, she saw the beach and boat plain. A small jolly was leaving shore, filled to the brim with all sorts of boxes and kegs.

The small hopes she'd begun to cherish fled. He was leaving. Rowing away from her just as he'd sailed away years ago. Bound for Indigo Island and looking for all the world as if he wouldn't be back for some time, perhaps spending the winter there and taking a long-deserved rest after years at sea.

She took refuge behind a bunch of stately sea oats bronzed by autumn and tried to reconcile herself to his going. His coat and cocked hat were off, his sleeves rolled up, the thick muscles of his forearms like knotted cordwood. He plied the oars with an expertise born of experience, his linen shirt rippling like a white flag in the breeze. Gannets and gulls careened overhead as if inspecting his cargo.

Did he carry chocolate?

If he'd come into the shop, she would have given him a supply for his men, as they'd done one cruise. But he'd chosen the coffeehouse instead. That, in some way, seemed a rejection, a slight, even if exceedingly small. And yet the hurt loomed large. Overcome, feeling much like the little girl who'd fallen from an apple tree and had the wind knocked out of her, she bent her head.

Lord, help mend my still-broken heart.

Not feeling fit for company, she finally reined Minta in the direction of York. Till she'd collected herself, the almshouse must wait.

CHAPTER

eighteen

Henri felt a release as he pulled away from shore and slid into the current. With the governor's meetings behind him and an uncertain future ahead of him, he needed the sanctuary of Indigo Island to weigh his decision. A decision best made away from distractions like a belle in a blue silk gown bearing chocolate. Or anything resembling the bustle and fuss of Tidewater Virginia.

He plied the oars with all his might, the breeze buffeting him, the sun's sliding behind a cloud allowing him to study his launching point. He'd thought it secluded. Private. Just sand and scrub. He blinked and narrowed his eyes. A beat of amusement pulsed inside him and led to an outright grin.

Amid the tall beach grass and sea oats mingled with thick stands of bayberry and wax myrtle was a froth of white ostrich feathers. Just like the ones he'd spied atop Esmée's riding hat. Eliza's doing, likely. Esmée wasn't one for fripperies and seemed to have forgotten the telling feathers that now gave her away. Had she unwittingly followed him here? Passed Jago Wherry on her way to the almshouse? Whatever had transpired, there she was in her befeathered hat, spying on him.

He resisted the urge to wave or raise the spyglass for a closer look. Let her believe she remained out of sight. He turned his head sideways, his rowing rhythmic, his gaze on the infinite blue of the sea instead of the memory of her jade eyes. A man could as easily drown in those depths as the ocean.

Though something deep within urged him to take a second look, he was now safely beyond sight of her. The shoreline receded, Indigo Island at his back. His senses were soon assaulted by the smell of roasting oysters and beach bonfires and crying gulls.

Several of his crew threw up their hands or tossed their hats in the air at his return. He waved and rowed on, past the Flask and Sword where Cyprian was hanging linens out to dry, on toward the back of the island where his cottage rested on its rocky perch. He wanted peace. Solitude. The kind he'd not had in York or Williamsburg.

But he couldn't outrow Esmée.

Thoughts of her trailed him like a leaping dolphin riding the wake of a ship. Twice they'd been thrust together without warning. He'd even accepted Eliza's gracious invitation to attend church. Every head had turned as they'd entered, assuring him the past had not been forgotten as he'd hoped but was being resurrected. Esmée was left to traipse through the eddies of gossip ashore while he sought his island refuge.

He'd gone to Shaw's coffeehouse briefly on a matter of business. The adjoining Dutch door leading to the chocolate shop was a nearly irresistible invitation. But considering his openness with her as they'd sat in the townhouse parlor, distance seemed the wisest path. His own conflicted feelings about her needed unraveling first. She was not the young woman he remembered. Time had turned her into someone else entirely.

Once docked, he secured the mooring lines and began unloading cargo—foodstuffs and necessaries to last till his next trip to the mainland. By the time he'd heaved the last crate to a shed, he heard footsteps. Henri put a padlock on the door and turned to greet whoever it was that intruded on his desire to be alone.

'Twas Cyprian, a steaming kettle in one hand, a linen-wrapped loaf in the other, and a large smile on his deeply tanned face. "Good day to ye, sir."

"Aye, so it is." Henri stomped wet sand from his boots before he went inside the cottage. "What do you bring?"

"Some victuals from Mistress Saltonstall. She said ye'd be power-fully hungry and in no mood to make yer own supper."

Gratitude chased away any inconvenience. "She would be right." Henri took the kettle and set it on the table. Oyster stew, from the smell of it. The chill of late October seemed to call for such.

Cyprian unwrapped a loaf of wheaten bread and gazed upon it as if it were the Mughal emperor's jewels. Was he famished?

"Why don't you take supper with me and tell me what has trans-pired since I've been away?" Gesturing to a chair, Henri went to a near basin and washed his hands, trying to recall where he last saw utensils.

"Aye, sir. With pleasure." Cyprian set the bread down and took a seat, still smiling. "No butter or cheese, I'm sorry to say."

"Ah, but there is," Henri said over his shoulder as he went to fetch both from the stores he'd brought.

Cyprian lit a candle as the shadows deepened, casting fragile light over what proved to be a delicious supper. The lad talked between bites, allowing Henri to slow down and savor his meal. Mistress Saltonstall was an admirable cook.

"All yer officers are still on the mainland, sir . . . just us small jacks stayin' to keep to task on the ship . . . She's looking spry . . . but there's been some worries what with the weather . . . Old Jacques feels a hur-ricane in his bones . . . That creature, Hermes, got into some rum and turned lunatic, he did."

Nodding and chuckling, Henri waited till Cyprian fed him the last piece of news with a sound belch.

"Beg pardon, sir." He pushed back his empty bowl with a sated sigh. "Ye've taught me better."

"Belching isn't mutiny, Cyprian." With a wink, Henri brought out a small bag of candied lemon peel gotten from York. "Care for a sweet?"

Cyprian grinned back at him. "Have any chocolate, sir?"

Blast. "Nay. I have none." To his everlasting regret. Hot chocolate sounded good on a chilly eve. "Needs be I send you to the mainland for some before winter sets in."

"Would ye, sir?" Cyprian chewed on the lemon peel, eyes alive with anticipation. "Shaw's chocolate, aye?"

"None other."

"I do wonder, sir, why ye didn't go there yerself."

I nearly did. Henri shrugged. "No milk cow on the island, at least since I was here last. No cause for hot chocolate."

"Needs be we get a cow, then."

"Consult Mistress Saltonstall. She may have one hiding in the woods," Henri replied, thinking of the times they'd weathered a crossing with distressed animals for some menagerie in England. He'd put his foot down after transporting a duke's orangutan and an earl's zebra. All he wanted was a rat-catching cat aboard ship. Or a dog. A sudden meowing assured him the ship's cat, Clementine, was about her business.

Spent, Henri sat down in the Windsor chair facing the cold hearth while Cyprian jumped up, still chewing, and began laying a fire. Soon the cavernous, blackened hole glowed as red-gold as a tropical Maldives sunset, a few sparks flying past the andirons into the room.

"If ye don't mind my asking, sir . . . what's that curiosity on yer windowsill?"

Henri looked to where he'd left the mystery gift. "A riding crop. Something that requires a horse."

"Mayhap we need a horse and a cow, then."

"Nay!" Henri's vehemence sent his steward back a step. "I've no time for farming. Another cruise may be imminent."

"Well, sir, needs be I get back to the Flask and Sword lest ye say otherwise."

Henri looked about, noticing the shine of floorboards and essence of beeswax. "I suppose I have you to thank for making this cobwebbed cottage fit for habitation."

"Aye, Captain. I take my duties seriously whether aboard ship or off it."

"Good night, then. Sleep well."

The lad departed with a grin and the empty kettle.

After the hum of York and Williamsburg, the island seemed especially tranquil. Henri added another log to the fire and stepped outside, looking west toward the mainland. Tonight the sunset was quiet, no splash of spectacular color, no jaw-dropping hues. Lights twinkled from York, a beguiling vision in the gathering darkness.

How did Esmée spend her autumn eves?

She liked books . . . or once did. Endless cups of tea with cream and sugar. Talking by the fire in a favorite chair. Trouncing him at table games. That was the Esmée of old. The woman at the ball and in Eliza's parlor seemed different somehow. Understandably guarded. More than a bit discomfited in his company. Face-to-face with him again, she was even comelier than he remembered, if that was possible.

No doubt she couldn't say the same about him.

He felt a bit old. Achy. He rubbed his perpetually sunburned neck at the back, where his hair tailed from a black silk ribbon over his collar. His muscles were a bit stiff from riding horseback, something he'd begun to enjoy but might never master. He needed to return to the mainland, if only to ride again.

And give the governor and Virginia's officials his answer.

The water lapping against the rocks failed to solace him like usual. Night was filling in all the nooks and crannies of the island, whippoorwills calling among the darkening pines. The hearth's fire crackled at his back through the open door, calling him in from a chill eve that might lead to a black frost. Glad as he was to be back, the island suddenly felt a tad hollow, as did his cottage.

To say nothing of his heart.

CHAPTER

nineteen

The next day, Esmée arrived at the almshouse at a most inopportune time. Father had advised her against going. There'd been a frost, the ground hard as cast iron, and a bitter wind blew her nearly sideways as she traveled the coastal road. When she neared the spot where she'd watched Henri leave in the jolly, she prodded the gentle Minta into a near gallop as if to bypass the hurt of his leaving.

When she arrived, her gaze hung on the far field where Henri had had his riding lesson. Now crude shelters covered the ground, smoke from fires casting a haze about the camp. The French émigrés Father had told her about? Men, women, and children roamed about, heads bent, dejection about them. An occasional burst of mellifluous French wafted toward her.

No sooner had she hobbled Minta outside the women's quarters than an anguished cry rent the chilly air. Alice?

Last visit she was having ghost pains, the midwife called them. Was her travail now upon her? Within the bricked walls the cries echoed, making Esmée rue she'd not heeded Father.

Summoning help to carry in the items she'd brought for all the women, Esmée pondered leaving. Sheer duty propelled her forward till she stood on the second floor outside the birthing room.

Another cry raised the gooseflesh on her arms. This was what was in store for Eliza. *Heaven help us.* Eliza was not fond of pain or exerting herself. Or untimely interruptions.

Feeling slightly squeamish herself, Esmée uttered a silent prayer for both her sister and Alice. Next came a fragile but piercing howl, which had Mistress Boles calling for broth and bread and fresh linens.

Esmée began unpacking the needful things for Alice. Clouts. Blankets. Feeding cloths. Even a play-pretty or two as the babe grew.

"Miss Shaw." Looking relieved, Miss Grove approached with a bundle. "Mind the babe, please, just till Alice is set to rights. He's a robust little fellow."

The warm, squirming infant was placed in Esmée's outstretched arms. Rosebud pink and oddly wrinkled, the tiny boy blinked up at her in wonder. Did all babies have such blue eyes? She bounced him gently when his mouth puckered, determined to keep him quiet for his exhausted mother's sake. When he threatened to howl again, she caressed his velvety cheek, her voice more a whisper as she sang an old lullaby Mama had sung to Eliza.

"'Hush! The waves are rolling in, white with foam, white with foam. Father toils amid the din, but baby sleeps at home.'"

The babe's father was a soldier, she'd been told, gone to join up with Washington's army in the back country. The young mother hadn't heard from him since and, with no kin of her own, had sought refuge at the almshouse. Their future seemed bleak. Someone once said every child was a promise that God wanted the world to go on. But what a world it was, full of conflict and strife, regret and heartache.

Esmée overheard Miss Grove's kindly question. "What will you name the child, Alice?"

"I'll call him after my father, God rest him. A humble tinsmith but a God-fearing one." The answer came so quiet Esmée nearly missed it. "Alden Reed."

Mistress Boles sailed past Esmée with a terse greeting and a mention she was needed elsewhere.

Esmée entered and approached the bed. Surely Alice wanted to hold her child, at least till a meal was brought. "Little Alden is beautiful, Alice. And in need of his mother."

Alice smiled back at her wanly, perspiration calling out her pockmarked skin, her fair braid tousled like straw. "I'm sorry about all the fuss, Miss Shaw. A lady such as you shouldn't have to put up with such as me."

"Nonsense." Smiling, Esmée laid the baby in the crook of her arm. "He's beautiful. Your father would be proud."

"Aye, that he would be." She looked down at her infant as wondrously as Esmée hoped Eliza would look at hers in time. "And my husband too, when he returns from service."

As the linens were changed and a meal was brought, Esmée took her leave, following Miss Grove out. "I'd best hasten home as the weather is sharp. I just wanted to bring the women's things as promised. They're below in the trustees' office."

Miss Grove clasped her hand in thanks. "I don't know how we'd fare without you."

"'Tis but little. I see now the French refugees have come, and with them more needs."

They passed downstairs into the courtyard, where a lone oak had been spared the men's woodcutting. A few benches were scattered about with a view of the large common garden.

"The French encampment is growing." Arms folded against the chill, Miss Grove looked out on the field, which bore shriveling vines and a few plump pumpkins. "We're in charge of feeding them. The government has promised provisions, but I wonder if any will be forthcoming. Winter always means a lack as it is. The garden's long spent."

"I've heard they're to take the oath of allegiance to King George," Esmée said. "But I thought they might be moved further south to Georgia and the Carolinas." Unable to stomach the sight of so much poverty and all its accompanying ills, she looked toward the York River turned to pewter by thick, hovering clouds, the water adorned with vessels of all descriptions.

"I wish they would move on, though I know 'twill not be any easier elsewhere. A few fights have broken out between the almshouse men and the French. These newcomers are hungry and exhausted. Their spirits are low. Some are in forced isolation because of illness."

Lord, help. These French papists, considered enemies of the crown, weren't even of the same religion. Yet the king expected Virginia to host such a number? And deepen the almshouse woes besides?

"How long must you help them?"

"I cannot say. 'Tis another of the king's edicts that brook no argument." Miss Grove's tone turned entreating. "Might you acquire some meat for us in the meantime? Even bones will do. Something with which to make broth and feed many."

"Of course. I'll speak with the butchers in York."

"And pray, please, that we aren't beset with sickness like last season. With the cold came fevers and every imaginable malady, more than the physic could remedy, if we can even get a physic to come."

"Perhaps a visit to the apothecary would help, to have a supply of medicines beforehand."

Miss Grove's lined face eased only slightly. "'Twould be most welcome, as always."

"You're in no danger of running low on firewood, thankfully." Esmée had seen growing woodpiles deftly stacked all about the property. "Though a coal stove would be warmer, at least in the dining hall."

"We've plenty to warm us, thanks to the men's woodcutting. Coal is a luxury few can afford."

"'Tis never amiss to hope . . . dream." Esmée spoke softly, wanting to lift the discouragement in Miss Grove's beleaguered face. "I've no doubt you're in need of something yourself, carrying the weight of the women and children as you do."

"Mercy, Miss Shaw." The woman's surprise revealed she thought little of herself. A hand went to her hair. "A new cap wouldn't be amiss. This one is so worn it's now threadbare."

Two caps, then. Esmée bid her a warm goodbye, wishing she'd thought of it sooner.

"Take care, Miss Shaw, and God be with you till we meet again."

A barefoot lad fetched Minta. Esmée stepped atop the mounting block and sat sidesaddle. The biting autumn air did her good. She rode out with a last look at the forlorn French encampment before her thoughts ran ahead to Henri.

Nay. The captain is a conundrum I can do without.

'Twas only her aloneness, her loneliness, that sharpened her interest in him. Was it not? Just when she'd adjusted to life without him, made a resigned peace with his absence, he'd reappeared, renewing her girlish hopes and dreams. Alas, she'd soon turn thirty. Henri was older still. Yet when he was near, all the years seemed to slip away and she felt young again. And he was, if possible, even more intriguing than he used to be.

Or had her own spinsterish ways simply deepened her appreciation of him?

Restlessness churned like a current inside her. She felt on the cusp of something new, though she knew not what. Surely it wasn't in the form of a privateer with a questionable reputation.

Lord, what is it You have for me beyond the almshouse and chocolate shop?

CHAPTER

twenty

enri's most trusted men, recently returned from shore leave, sat before him in a semicircle at the ordinary's corner table. Despite Hermes's screeching and Mistress Saltonstall's robust chatter with a patron in the open doorway, he wasted no time telling them the latest turn of events.

"I have a recent communication from the frontier, sent by Colonel Washington to Governor Dinwiddie." Henri took out the letter given him, a sad testament to how the frontier fight with the French and Indians was faring, at least at the time the letter was penned. He held the letter aloft as he read, "'Regular troops exposed all those who were inclined to do their duty to almost certain death; and at length, in despite of every effort to the contrary, broke and ran as sheep before hounds, leaving the artillery, ammunition, provision, baggage, and in short everything a prey to the enemy, and when we endeavored to rally them in hopes of regaining the ground and what we had left upon it, it was with as little success as if we had attempted to have stopped the wild beasts of the mountains.'"

"Colonel Washington is referring to British regulars," Southack said with thinly veiled disgust. "Not Virginians."

"Aye, the king's army," Henri said. He read on in confirmation. "'The Virginia companies behaved like men and died like soldiers.'"

"And Braddock, the white-wigged general, was buried overmountain in an unmarked grave, so I heard." Udo shook his dark head. "Is this not Washington's third attempt to rout the French and take Fort Duquesne?"

"Aye." Henri nodded and folded the letter, noting the broken black seal. "And now the French general Montcalm is said to be on his way here."

"Which led to much ado in Williamsburg with the governor's council," Tarbonde surmised, his astute gaze holding Henri's own. "Have you made your decision, sir?"

"Nay."

Henri's reticence had them all studying him keenly. He was not one to dally. He could read their thoughts. And with a new French commander on the way . . .

He leaned back in his chair till it groaned. "If you were in my place, what would your decision be?"

A weighty pause. Rarely did he turn the question round. It seemed to stymie them.

"With Britain hurtling toward war with France and not just fighting Indians on the frontier, our involvement by sea seems critical," Southack finally said. "But just what is our stake in this?"

"We'd be issued a letter of marque and reprisal from the colonial government authorizing us to target French ships, capture them, and plunder them. We'd set sail in a newly commissioned vessel." He paused, noting their surprise. "We'd fly foreign flags, including French flags as decoys, if needs be."

"And the prizes?" they asked in unison.

"Delivered in part to the admiralty court in Philadelphia. Our share would be fifty percent of all prizes." Henri tapped the letter, thinking again of Braddock. "And one hundred percent of the danger."

"A risky endeavor." Ned expelled a breath, always the last to speak. His perspective as sea chaplain usually differed from the others'. "Though no doubt of great benefit to the colonial cause."

Henri nodded, no nearer his decision than he'd been when he'd first heard of the secret foray against the French at the governor's palace. Was that not in itself his answer? Yet when had he shied away from danger or aiding the British colonies?

"And if you say nay?" Ned questioned, folding his hands atop the edge of the table as if he were about to pray.

"If I—*we*—decline, other ships and crews will bear the commission," Henri stated matter-of-factly.

Southack grimaced. "And take both prizes and credit."

"Virginia's governor desires us at the helm," Henri said. Not only Virginia's governor but other colonial authorities as well. He stopped short of revealing anything vainglorious, further tempting them toward a very hazardous cruise.

"You cannot possibly be content to stay on Indigo Island with so dire a threat. Nor sail away on other business." Tarbonde studied him as if seeing him in a new light. "'Twould be a dereliction of duty."

"You could also further establish your reputation as one of privateer and not pirate as the naysayers have painted you," Southack said.

"What would be done with captives?" Udo queried when Henri made no reply. "You are known far and wide for fair treatment, but with the French declared our enemies . . ."

"They'd likely be used in prisoner exchanges or as leverage in treaties. Transported to prison ships." That alone gave Henri pause. There was no worse fate.

And it could be his and his crew's lot as well.

CHAPTER

twenty-one

Esmée took the tray of chocolate meringues from the kitchen into the shop, each looking like small storm clouds that matched the heavens over the harbor. Airy and sweet, the egg-white-and-sugar confections were among her favorites, pairing nicely with the chocolate tarts on display. With no one to witness her pilfering, she snuck one and let its ethereal goodness melt on her tongue, her stays expanding with every bite.

Sweet indeed. After a morning spent begging bones from the town's butchers, including a promised delivery, she had her reward. Now in the afternoon, business had ebbed, though the coffeehouse never seemed to quiet. Father was there today, distributing newspapers and handbills, conversing about the latest news in Virginia and beyond with any who cared to join him. His unmistakable voice comforted her as she went about her tasks, taking inventory, perusing the long-coveted *Complete Confectioner*, and overseeing orders for social gatherings and whatnot.

When the shop's bell jingled, she looked up from her work to find a stranger shutting the door behind him, his coattails whipped about

133

by a harbor wind. Knowing nearly everyone in York and even Williamsburg, Esmée discreetly took his measure but couldn't place him.

She gave the familiar shopkeeper's greeting, brushing tart crumbs from her apron. "Good afternoon, sir. What do you buy?"

Tucking his cocked hat beneath one arm, he came to a stop at the counter, gaze landing on the meringues and tarts before sliding to the mound of sugared almonds atop a large porcelain dish. Pleasure suffused his tanned features.

"I'm rather overcome," he said, eyes roving the shelves next.

She understood his dilemma, common to first timers. What *wouldn't* he choose?

"I've not had Shaw's chocolate since the last sailing," he told her with a smile. "Now I'm en route to visit kin in the country and I'd rather not arrive empty-handed."

Last sailing? He was no common jack, truly. "Chocolate almonds travel especially well, though chocolate tarts do not," she told him, charmed by his gracious manner. "Care to try an almond?" She held out the dish.

"I'll take them all," he replied after a bite. "Though I can't guarantee they'll last beyond Tobacco Road."

"If some go missing, none will be the wiser." Smiling, she began wrapping them for travel. "You speak of your kin. Might I know them?"

"Ah, no doubt. Forgive me for the frightful lack of introductions. Nathaniel Autrey, lately at sea."

"The Autreys of Mount Autrey?" She did not doubt it. He bore their wide forehead and cleft chin in addition to their telltale fiery locks. "An old Virginia family you have, sir."

"A very feminine one." He was referring to his maiden aunts, no doubt. "You know them, Miss . . . ?"

"Just who's forgetting introductions?" Flushing, Esmée handed him his wrapped chocolates. "I am Miss Shaw, the proprietress of Shaw's Chocolate. My father is—"

"Barnabas Shaw. The famed admiral." His admiration was not lost on her. "No doubt you and your father are acquainted with Captain Henri Lennox."

Nodding, she lowered her gaze. "My father especially."

"I'm sea chaplain of the *Relentless*, or have been these past many years."

A sea chaplain? All frigates and line-of-battle ships allowed them, though not all but the most devout commanders wanted them aboard. And they did far more than keep journals and hold divine service. She busied herself with his purchase. What more could she say? Would mention of Henri always affect her so? Turn a routine, chocolate-laden encounter bittersweet?

"Good day, Miss Shaw." He gave a slight, elegant bow before he went out. "I hope we meet again."

She crossed to the display window, watching him climb into a waiting coach, then drew back as his gaze returned to the shop. Might Henri be with him? As the coach pulled away with a lurch, she rested her eyes on the cloudy harbor, wishing she'd been a bit more forthright.

Are you on shore long, sir? Does Captain Lennox have any plans to set sail again? And are you always so charming at first meeting?

Henri walked the beach, frothy waves murmuring a monotonous lament against the shore with the incoming tide. His crew continued work on the *Relentless* on the island's south side. Cyprian, ill with a mild fever, lay in a hammock beneath oaks fast losing the last of their leaves. Southack hovered, ready to dispense whatever remedy was called for.

Henri stared down at the wave-washed sand, wishing his mind would come clean, but his thoughts were knotted as rigging. He felt akin to a dismasted ship. It had been nearly a fortnight since those gravely serious meetings in the palace. Governor Dinwiddie awaited his reply. All of British America teetered on the brink of war as matters on the frontier grew more explosive.

While he dallied.

For the first time in his entire naval career, he had no wish to return to sea. The *Relentless* could stay beached forever. Somewhere between the last few cruises and setting foot in York, he'd lost something. His moorings. His true north. His mind.

A few months before, a broken spar had knocked him down. Had that something to do with it? He still had headaches but thought himself mostly healed. Lifting a hand, he traced the scar above his left brow. Nay, he could not blame his indecision on an accident. He knew the real reason. But what would he say to Dinwiddie and his officials?

I've decided to forsake all duty to my country and let France gain the upper hand on the high seas, not only on the colonial frontier, while I attend dances and learn to ride and sip chocolate and try to woo the woman I lost a decade ago.

Headache or no, his prayers seemed to reach no farther than the cottage ceiling. The dilemma was even stealing his sleep.

Lord, make Your will plain to me.

"Captain." A familiar masculine voice turned him round.

"You're back," Henri said. Ned had been on the mainland for a sennight. Henri hadn't expected his return so soon.

"I am." Ned wore his town clothes, his buckled shoes digging deep into the sand as he walked toward Henri. A smile lit up his clean-shaven face. "I can wait no longer to share the glad news."

Henri fell into step beside him. "Glad news? Is there to be no war?"

A low laugh. "War is the farthest thing from my mind. I believe I've met the woman I'm going to marry—or begin courting, at least."

Henri's hand shot out instinctively. "Congratulations, then."

Ned shook with vigor, never missing a step. "I suppose you'll not relax your rule about banning married men as crew."

"Never. Especially newly married ones." Curiosity overcame him. "So, tell me about her."

A slow smile transformed Ned's ruddy features. "She rather bowled me over. I forgot my manners. I nearly forgot to remove my hat at first meeting."

Henri chuckled, stunned by his words. But Ned of all people deserved a helpmeet. A pastor, albeit a sea chaplain, shouldn't be alone.

"She's . . . perfect. Small in stature. Comes to about here." He thumped his hand just below his shoulder. "Hair as black as a Brazilian diamond. Eyes a peculiar shade of jade."

"Careful, you're downright poetic."

Ned laughed, a merry sound that further nettled Henri's tempestuous mood. "Isn't that what lovers do?"

"Does this beauty have a name?"

"Her name is as lovely as all the rest of her."

"A Williamsburg belle?"

"Nay. York."

"Where did you meet?"

"Shaw's Chocolate shop."

Henri snapped to attention. "Admiral Shaw's daughter?"

"The same. Miss Esmée Shaw."

Nay. A thousand times nay.

Henri stopped in his tracks. A sound kick in the gut would have made him gladder. For a few seconds he stood speechless. Then at last he asked, "Are you sure you weren't just entranced by a surfeit of chocolate?"

"Not at all. I visited her twice there. Once when I first got to York and then today before my leaving."

"Twice hardly equates to marriage." Henri shot him a chary look and resumed walking in the direction of the Flask and Sword. "Women are far more complex than they first appear."

"Where is your sense of romance, Captain?" Ned expelled a breath, eyes on distant York. "Once or twice is often all that's necessary."

"I would caution you of the lovesick sailor phenomenon. Lovesick chaplain, in your case." Henri assumed his commander's voice. "When one is away months or years at sea, anything remotely feminine appears utterly remarkable."

"In this case there is no such delusion." Ned studied him, a sympathetic light in his eye. "Have you never experienced it?"

Henri kicked at a pebble in his way. *Aye.* Had he not once felt the same? When Esmée had first entered a stuffy Rhode Island parlor, it was as if no other woman existed. Only Ned did not know of his and Esmée's former tie, having been aboard a schooner till joining the *Relentless* crew.

"Lest you think I've completely lost my reason, I questioned my kinfolk at Mount Autrey about the Shaws, especially Esmée," Ned said. "My aunts are a formidable hurdle—two of them, anyway."

"Well . . . go on," Henri muttered over his misery.

"I've made other discreet inquiries." Ned was as earnest as Henri had ever seen him, removing all hope that this was one big lark. "Her character is sterling. Not vain but virtuous. Kind. God-fearing. She stretches out her hand to the poor and visits the almshouse regularly. She is a woman of spirit and industry, managing the chocolate shop like her mother before her. For the life of me I cannot understand why she has never wed."

"A failed love affair, mayhap."

Ned's clenched brow eased. "Perhaps she was simply waiting for me."

Henri would hear no more. "In short, the perfect chaplain's wife."

"Exactly. And since my father and mother are long buried, I ask your blessing."

My blessing. "I suppose you've yet to tell her you're hardly a humble chaplain but kin to the Autreys."

"She did ask, hearing my surname. An insignificant detail."

Henri nodded. This was what he most admired about Ned. His humility. His utter disregard for earthly mammon. In truth, Esmée had all the makings of a genteel chaplain's wife. Together they could launch all sorts of charitable endeavors from Mount Autrey, one of the largest estates in Virginia, a veritable fount of funds.

"Now seems the time to leave the sea and settle down." The note of finality in Ned's voice seemed to seal the matter. "Though we've had many an adventure together of which I'm extremely grateful, Captain, my wanderlust has begun to tire, as we've oft discussed. I'm now intent on resigning my post, and I seek your blessing."

In a few choice words, Ned had stated Henri's own predicament. *My wanderlust has begun to tire. I'm intent on resigning my post.* So succinctly stated yet how infernally complicated. To leave the sea and settle down was Henri's burning desire and had been for some time.

For Ned it was entirely possible, while he himself felt shackled. By his reputation. His resources. His connections.

"I understand." Henri forced a smile, tried to summon some gladness for Ned beyond a half-hearted clap on the back. "But my blessing is hardly needed. I wish you the best in whatever you undertake." He took a breath and added, "There's never been a more worthy man for such a woman."

Ned's brow tightened anew. "You've oft talked of settling down yourself."

"And now a new endeavor has presented itself." Time ticked on. Virginia needed an answer. "I'm beginning to think I will always be at sea. Die at sea."

"No wife. No children." Ned shook his head mournfully. "Granted, able mariners are always needed, but in the end, is it worth it?"

Henri did not answer. Ned had raised the very question that would not let him be.

CHAPTER
twenty-two

terse letter came from Eliza.

Dear Sister,
  I have been visited by the three aunts from Mount Autrey.
Please hasten to Williamsburg where I await you impatiently.
Come see the leaves turn color if nothing else.

Your loving Eliza

A visit? Esmée hardly had time, what with begging bones and holding newborns and experimenting with the latest chocolate confections. But what Eliza wanted, Eliza eventually got. And Williamsburg *was* a magnificent panorama of color in autumn.

But what of the spinster aunts from Mount Autrey? Might this have something to do with Nathaniel Autrey?

Esmée pondered it all the way to Eliza's, wishing Father were awake and could distract her. Despite the rumbling coach hitting a bone-rattling bump or two, he dozed, a victim of too many late nights spent working on his marine atlas.

At last he came awake when they rode past Jane Vobe's tavern. "What is that divine smell?"

Esmée leaned nearer the coach's window. "Beef pasty, perhaps."

"I suppose 'tis too late to request the same for our supper from Eliza's kitchen."

"Pasties are a thoroughly English dish, remember."

"I dare not offend the French chef, you mean." He cleared his throat. "What was that marvelous concoction he served us last time when Captain Lennox came to dine?"

Esmée's mind was blank as new paper. Beef ragout? She hardly recalled it, given the company.

With a stifled yawn, her father returned his hat to his head. "I doubt I'll be back in time for supper anyway, as Dinwiddie is fond of conversing so late."

"I hope he serves you something amidst all that secrecy."

"Something Scottish, no doubt, as befits his humble roots." He looked out the window, occasionally raising a hand at passersby who recognized their coach.

She fisted her gloved hands in the folds of her skirts, knowing Henri was somehow at the very heart of these meetings. "Father, if I may be so bold, what have you to do with all this intrigue and conniving?"

To her relief he chuckled. "You make it sound downright villainous. Far more interesting than it is."

"Well? 'Tis how it appears to those of us on the outside."

"On the outside? You have a touch of Eliza's dramatic flair, 'twould seem." He waved again as they passed Bruton Parish Church. "The governor and his officials are merely consulting me about maritime matters in case there's to be a war."

War, war. Would they talk of nothing else? "You don't believe we're in danger of becoming French colonials rather than English ones?"

"Bah! You've been reading one too many broadsides and papers. Coffeehouses aren't called penny universities for naught."

Would he have her believe it was merely gossip? "Perhaps I need to revisit my French lessons of old."

"Which is why Captain Lennox is being considered for the task."

Her gaze narrowed on his shuttered face. "So there's a *task* to consider?" She tried to piece this confounding puzzle together. "Because the captain is part French and speaks French?"

And such mesmerizing French that it sounded like a song. A symphony. *Euphony*, Mama once called it. Years ago, Henri had not simply said goodbye. He'd leaned in, his breath warm against her ear, and whispered *ma belle* and other endearments. Even the memory, long relegated to the trash heap, sent her stomach plummeting to her shoes.

Her father smiled enigmatically, looking like the freebooter he had once been accused of being. "All in good time, my dear."

"No doubt it involves danger," she said grimly. "A prolonged cruise."

The coach lurched to a stop in the courtyard behind Quinn and Eliza's townhouse, sparing him further elaboration. Feeling like a kettle left too long at the fire, Esmée gathered her hat and gloves off the upholstered seat and stepped down once the door opened.

Would she ever have answers?

Dusk gathered about Henri like a gray cloak. Thieves were prevalent along the byways and backroads of rural Virginia. Few traveled at night because of it. He kept a loaded pistol close, careful of shifting shadows. He'd hoped to see Williamsburg by dark, but night was rushing in fast and another stop was required. The lights of the almshouse shone just ahead, and beyond it countless hovels of the French refugees, the smoke from their chimneys trailing crooked gray fingers into the darkening sky. Fragments of French conversation drifted to him as men and women sat outside smoking clay pipes.

Tonight was not the time to ponder their plight, these displaced souls now the bane of cash-strapped Virginia. But the sound of his mother's language never failed to move him, ushering in a dozen different recollections of her, each bittersweet.

He relaxed the reins, slowing Trident to a walk. He'd timed his arrival at the almshouse carefully so as not to attract attention, when most of the residents would be done with their labors and supper and in their rooms, if Jago Wherry had told him right.

The night watch was on patrol, halting him as he approached, lanthorn held high.

"I've business with the trustee, Mr. Boles," Henri told him, dismounting.

"Is he expecting ye, sir?"

"Nay, but he'll be glad of it."

With a nod, the watchman left him, and Henri opened his saddlebags. Soon he was escorted toward a small building that served as both living quarters and office for the supervisor of the entire almshouse. Wherry had spoken well of Boles but less so of the trustee matron. Henri regretted finding them both in one place, having tea by the fire, clearly taken aback by his sudden appearing—or rather irritated by the intrusion, judging from the matron's sour expression.

"And you are, sir?" Boles inquired politely, coming forward.

"Simply a benefactor and champion of the poor," Henri replied, heaving the sacks of specie atop Boles's desk. They jingled as they settled, rousing the matron, who abandoned her tea and came nearer.

"The bequest comes with conditions." Henri fixed a stern eye upon them both. "'Tis to be wisely stewarded for the benefit of all those beneath the almshouse roof—every man, woman, and child as well as the French émigrés in your midst. Not ferreted or spent selfishly by those in positions of authority such as yourselves." Here he held the eye of Mistress Boles. "I have contacts—informants, if you will—who will report to me any suspected double-dealing. Depending on how you conduct yourselves and manage the monies given you, more might be forthcoming in future."

Clearly skittish, Boles began untying the sacks. The knots finally gave way and he stood slack-jawed. Spanish pistoles and pieces of eight were common enough in the colonies, but rarely in such quantities.

"Sir—" Astonishment washed his weary face. "Gold doubloons and silver dollars? 'Tis a fortune."

"Aye. All in need of careful consideration and wise handling."

"May we not ask your name, kind sir?" the matron queried meekly. "Your occupation?"

"Nay." Not even Wherry knew about tonight. Henri wished he could have simply left the specie at the door. "Treat it as you would any endowment or bequest. But say nothing from whence it came."

"You have my word, sir," Boles replied without hesitation.

Their effusive thanks followed him as he went out the door, as glad to get away as he was to lighten Trident's load. Night riding was new to him—dangerously so. In the dark he couldn't see hazards in his path, but Trident seemed to have a sixth sense about him, hastening him to Williamsburg in good time beneath a full moon.

Generosity always left him with a warmth deep inside, an inextinguishable light in a world gone awry. What good were the prizes he'd gotten if not shared? Perhaps such would delight Esmée when she learned of it, even if she'd never know its source.

Truly, the smallest good deed was better than the grandest good intention.

The next afternoon found Esmée hurtling toward Mount Autrey with Eliza to pay a call to the aunts of Captain Lennox's sea chaplain. Though Esmée had never seen the vast estate, she'd heard of it. Her perplexity about their visit was second to her confusion about Nathaniel Autrey's relation to it. She'd thought him a distant relation. A poor sea chaplain and sailor. Eliza was having none of it.

"Really, Esmée." Eliza leaned back on the seat with a sigh. "You look as though you were on your way to a wake!"

"I'm simply pondering what all this means." Esmée smoothed her petticoats, which collided in silky profusion with her sister's. "So the aging aunts paid a visit to you and inquired about me. I don't suppose it was about the abundance of chocolate almonds their nephew brought them."

"Well, they did mention them rather glowingly."

"I don't know why such fuss over a man I conducted business with over the counter a time or two, charming though he was."

"If you would but pull your head out of your receipt books and mind the workings of the outside world . . ." Eliza gave that disarming smile she used when sly. "Your humble chaplain is more a ruse. Rumor has it he might well be the future heir to Mount Autrey and all it entails."

"So?"

Eliza's eyes narrowed in irritation. The baby was making her cross, keeping her up nights with indigestion. "*So*, he has expressed a fondness for you that set these dear ladies all aflutter. And it has nothing to do with Shaw's chocolate."

"Promise me this visit will be brief." But wasn't the reverend's message last Sunday at Grace Church about honoring others with the gift of time? Conscience pricked, Esmée quickly amended, "Though elderly ladies who are oft alone deserve more."

"Indeed." Eliza looked less ruffled. "Most unwed women would leap at the invitation. This bodes well for you and your future."

The coach bumped along the rutted road in dire need of the almshouse men's rocks. Esmée's stomach felt just as gravelly. This was not how she had envisioned her future playing out. Though it might sound unkind, Nathaniel Autrey was little more to her than one of Captain Lennox's crew. That alone made him interesting and of merit. She had no matrimonial aspirations whatsoever.

Still, she could not stem her awe at the beauty of Mount Autrey as they turned off Tobacco Road and moved past elaborate iron gates. The mansion sat on a knoll, lending to its arresting appearance. Of Flemish bond brick, it was a feat of architecture from its multiple porticos to its parterre gardens. Yet she couldn't ignore what kept the Autrey fortune afloat. That alone nullified any romantic prospects.

Eliza's steady gaze was unnerving. "I know what you're thinking, Sister. But you must say nothing of the enslaved here. 'Tis a fact of Virginia life and has ever been."

Even as Eliza spoke, scores of Africans labored in distant fields or scurried to and from the mansion and dependencies. For once the almshouse seemed less wretched. At least the poorest of the poor there were free.

Once the coach deposited them at the entrance amid a storm of dust, Esmée and Eliza climbed wide stone steps and were soon ushered into a wide, deep foyer where a staircase curved upward to three floors. The house was old. Immense. Esmée wasn't surprised when the butler's voice echoed. Into the nearest parlor they went, where three elderly women awaited them. All eyes speared Esmée. There was no other word to describe it. Summoning some of Eliza's charm, she greeted them warmly, again wondering what had led to this unexpected meeting.

"How good of you to visit us," said the aunt who looked to be the eldest, a snowy-haired matron with a diamond-encrusted chatelaine worn at her waist. It glittered as she moved toward several chairs and gestured for them to sit.

Esmée looked from her to the other two aunts. How on earth was it possible to distinguish them if all were the Mistresses Autrey? There was no doubt, however, as to which aunt held the key to the coveted tea chest. The smallest and plumpest wore spectacles and said nary a word while the other began to talk in low tones to the exotic bird kept in a cage by a draped window.

"Allow me to introduce Charis and Dorothy, my younger sisters." The eldest aunt gestured to them with a wrinkled, heavily ringed hand. "I am Margaret."

"Pleased to meet you all," Esmée said. She was at sea with names. Rarely did they make an impression. Eliza, on the other hand, had an astonishing ability to remember names *and* titles.

The five of them sat in low armchairs about the inlaid table. Esmée took in the elegant room redolent of beeswax and something she couldn't name. It smelled ancient . . . unaired. She longed to open a window or two. She craved the salty tang of the sea.

"As soon as I saw you on the drive, I rang for tea," Margaret told them.

Refreshments came, the equipage flawless, and were served in the biggest silver pot Esmée had ever seen. She placed her serviette in her lap, never more mindful of tea etiquette. These antique women looked as if they'd written the rules. Sugar first. Milk at the last, *after* the tea was poured. Eliza performed flawlessly, as usual. But not Esmée. A bit flustered, she added milk first.

146

"To put milk in your tea before sugar is to cross the path of love, perhaps never to marry," Dorothy said with a slight, reproving smile.

"Such an amusing superstition," Eliza countered between sips. "And may I say how I admire your spiral molded porcelain? Chelsea, I believe? And with handles, all the rage but still so rare."

"Chelsea, yes," Margaret said, holding her cup aloft. "No sense burning one's hands."

"I miss sipping from a dish," Dorothy told them, pouring the steaming tea into her saucer with nary a misplaced drop. "The old ways die hard."

"Have you a chocolate pot?" Esmée asked them.

Margaret made a face. "We are rather chary of cocoa, given what's printed about it in Europe—chocolate being one of many disorders that shorten lives."

"Oh? Our York physic espouses its health benefits—" Esmée startled as the bird squawked, her cup rattling in her saucer. "Of which there are many."

"Chocolate is but a lure for any who happen down Water Street," Dorothy said in whispered tones. "Heavens! A woman such as yourself doesn't plan to keep tending shop forever, do you? And at so disagreeable a place under the hill as Water Street!"

Did they disapprove of her trade or mainly her location? Though there were many women who kept shop, it was mostly left to the middling sort, of which these women were most decidedly not.

"I'm continuing in my mother's stead," Esmée told them quietly. "Proudly so. As for Water Street, little else could be had as far as buildings go when my father bought it. We're making the waterfront more respectable, I hope."

Charis held up her empty cup, eyes plaintive.

Dorothy clucked sympathetically. "Sister is in danger of rivaling Dr. Johnson's tea consumption at five and twenty cups in one sitting."

Truly, Charis's cups exceeded them all and she'd yet to speak a word. Was she mute?

A lengthy silence followed, with no explanation given about Charis's silent state.

"Tea amuses the evening, solaces the midnight, and welcomes the morning, I believe Dr. Johnson said." Unable to endure the tense silence, Esmée finished her own cup and placed an upturned spoon atop it. Would Eliza take the hint?

Her sister merely smiled serenely and stirred more milk into her cup. No doubt she was missing her pot of cream. Despite their means, these sisters appeared quite frugal.

"I've always thought hyson smells of roasted chestnuts," Dorothy told them.

Margaret focused on her sister. "Oh? I prefer souchong's delicate, floral flavor."

"And you, Miss Shaw? Which is your favorite?" Dorothy inquired.

"Gunpowder tea. Such a honeyed taste," Esmée replied as the mantel clock struck three. "'Tis the freshest on long trade routes, my father said."

"Ah, your father." Margaret's eyes narrowed. "The esteemed admiral from Rhode Island."

The sisters exchanged a furtive look.

"Which puts me in mind of Captain Lennox, cut of the same cloth," Charis told them. "Our nephew's daring sea captain."

Esmée nearly sighed aloud. Clearly Charis wasn't mute. And what a topic she'd chosen to expound upon! Would everything always circle back to Henri?

CHAPTER

twenty-three

*H*enri was on the verge of saying nay to the proposed mission, and he sensed that the governor's council, a body of astute, shrewd men, knew it. The temperature in the paneled room was cool, but tempers were a-simmer. And it had little to do with the French threat.

"Provisions for several months at sea are needed and as follows . . ."

Henri listened as quartermaster Udo detailed the provisions required for such a mission before the chamber of officials, who sat rapt if stony-faced and silent. That they were listening to an African, an able commander in his own right, was an extraordinary occurrence. That Udo was free was an affront to these slave-owning Virginians. But Henri would not pander to their preference to exclude his black crew. Nor would he set sail without them.

Udo's smooth, robust voice filled the chamber's farthest corners. "Thirteen tierces and forty-five barrels salt beef and pork. A cask of oats. Five hundred gallons rum. Three tons beer. Five hundred pounds cheeses and butter. Fruit to stave off scurvy. Vinegar. Four hundred pounds brown sugar . . ."

Minutes before, Henri himself had finished telling the council of the weapons and artillery required to take on any enemy ships encountered, a presentation that smacked of an unwanted war, dug deep into Virginia's depleted coffers, and raised many a testy question. On either side of him sat Tarbonde and Southack, as well as his first mate and master gunner, all experienced men who knew the sea and its many moods and dangers as well as himself.

His foremost ally among Virginia's officials was missing. Lord Drysdale—Quinn—had been called away on other business. Henri hoped he'd return by next meeting. Across from Quinn's empty seat sat Admiral Shaw, ever attentive, occasionally asking a well-placed question and keeping the conversation on course. For all his years—and Henri guessed him to be nearing seventy—his mind was rapier sharp, and he'd not lost his passion for maritime affairs. Which led to a question that had nothing to do with the present company . . .

Was Esmée also in Williamsburg?

He looked toward a window that bespoke an easterly breeze. The airtight chamber left one pining for the outdoors and a walk about town. The Raleigh flashed to mind, Carter's brick store beside it. He needed a shaving razor. A woolen frock coat against the chill. Some minor items to tide him over while he lodged at the Raleigh and the governor's business was being done.

"Captain Lennox, we are prepared to reward your crew with payment of three months' wages in advance of their service, in addition to all of the provisions outlined by your quartermaster."

Henri returned his attention to the governor as Udo sat down.

Dinwiddie said with some pride, "A new seventy-four-gun manof-war is at your behest, en route from the Wharton shipyard in Philadelphia to York."

Henri sensed his crew's surprise. They were not easily impressed, but this was a major coup for all. Only the newest and most capable ships were thus equipped. Wharton was the premier shipbuilder in all thirteen colonies.

Did they ken their captain wanted nothing to do with it?

All attention was on Henri again. He simply listened as Dinwiddie called for yet another meeting the next morning, at which time they would discuss the French navy and its ships of the line en route to British North America, as well as the latest intelligence coming from the harbor of Brest.

"I regret we must adjourn early today, gentlemen. I've death warrants to sign for deserters, a decision to be made on the issuance of paper money, appointments to be confirmed, and visiting Indian dignitaries to entertain." Dinwiddie put a hand to his high forehead, his normally florid face the hue of his powdered wig. "Till tomorrow, then. Ours is a most pressing matter that begs resolution by sennight's end."

Henri stood, his attention on the beleaguered official's back as he exited the chamber. The responsibilities of office dogged the governor, a true servant of the crown. Fatigue of body and vexation of mind were what plagued him, he'd told Henri earlier. As he was charged with taking back Fort Duquesne from the French on the frontier and trying to raise Virginia's fighting forces, a war by sea seemed another extraordinary complication.

"Won't you join us, Captain?" Southack asked him, moving toward the door. "A pint or two at the Raleigh seems in order, for some of us, at least."

"Later, mayhap," Henri said, putting on his hat. His black jacks would return to York and their lodgings at the Colored Seamen's Home on the outskirts. "For now I've other business to attend to."

He left the crowded room, slipping out the front door and the palace's forecourt onto the street, and noticed the Indian delegation recently come to town. The gathered Cherokee were beaded and befeathered, a tall chief having his portrait painted beneath a brilliant red maple. With Publick Times in October over, the town had a quieter feel, a thoughtful and more peaceful cadence.

He took a backstreet toward the Raleigh, trying to recall what it was he needed from Carter's store. He tipped his hat to a trio of straw-hatted young ladies who tittered and gawked at him as he passed. Comely as they were, they didn't hold a candle to Esmée.

Why was his every thought ensnared by her?

He pressed on, his coattails whipped about by the strengthening wind. Nigh on three o'clock. His stomach rumbled, making him consider supper options. After a day crowded with people and war talk, he wanted nothing more than the sanctuary of his lodgings and a fire to ward off the evening's chill. Quinn lent him a book from his growing personal library. Fielding's *The Journal of a Voyage to Lisbon.*

But first, Carter's store.

How good it felt to be out in the open air. Even without a harbor view, Williamsburg had a charm all its own. Eliza had wanted to send a maid in her stead, but Esmée felt the need to walk about alone while her sister napped. She hastened from Nassau Street toward the town's wide-set thoroughfare with a decisive step, as if anxious to outpace any memories of yesterday's tea. Mount Autrey cast quite a shadow in her thoughts. But for the moment she didn't care to contemplate being courted by the sea chaplain, despite Eliza's glee as they returned to the townhouse in the coach.

"Just think, Sister, we could be nearer neighbors. Mount Autrey lies just beyond Williamsburg. Not only that, you'd be ensconced at one of the oldest plantations in all Virginia, though the old aunties might take some getting used to."

"You can put all that out of your head once and for all." Esmée fingered her chatelaine, lingering on the tiny silver lighthouse. "I'm in no more danger of becoming an Autrey than you are being crowned queen of England."

For once Eliza had made no reply.

Pulling her cape closer about her, Esmée slowed by Williamsburg's jeweler. A woman jostled her as she went past, causing her to hold tighter to her pocketbook. Pickpockets were commonplace, be it here or York. She looked through the store's large front window, assessing pinchbeck broaches and necklaces displayed next to sobering mourning jewelry and the pointe naive diamond rings capable of writing on glass. She'd always been most drawn to simple posy rings with their poignant inscriptions exchanged by lovers.

Far off yet not forgot.

God above increase our love.
In Christ and thee my comfort be.
Meet me at midnight.
Yours in heart till death depart.

Charmed, she nearly pressed her nose to the glass but for her wide hat. The longing building inside her became a full-fledged ache.

Early in their courtship, Henri had hinted at giving her a posy ring. Why had he not? Rather, why did it matter? She turned on her heel with renewed purpose and walked on to Carter's store. Up the bricked steps and through the jingling door she went, always at home among her fellow merchants.

"What d'ye buy, Miss Shaw?" the shopkeeper asked, despite being busy with other customers.

"Pounce and wax." Esmée took in the many shelves and displays crowded with all manner of tempting goods in a dizzying array. She missed the familiar York shops, but truly Williamsburg dazzled.

The shopkeeper's voice carried pleasantly. "What you seek is at the back, in the south corner opposite the men's coats."

Thanking him, she slowly made her way in that direction, perusing cheesecake pans and ambergris wash balls, buttons and hand fans and handkerchiefs, China toy tea ware and imported garden seed. An embroidered bergère hat with velvet ribbons begged closer perusal, yellow silk roses adorning it. As she took the hat from its stand, she glanced past the display to the man in the near corner before a gilt-edged looking glass. And froze.

Henri?

What an arresting picture he made, even with his back to her. The coat he tried on was of fulled wool, suitable for winter, with a collar and deep cuffs. It fit his wide-set shoulders snugly before falling to the tops of his black boots. This one was a smoky gray, while the shop clerk held another in Prussian blue.

"Do you have a preference, sir?" the clerk asked.

A pause. Henri had a knack for weighing his words before speaking.

"The blue one," Esmée whispered behind their backs.

Brow arched, the clerk turned toward her, as did the captain. Surprise crossed both their faces, and then Henri shrugged off the gray coat and exchanged it for the blue one. With a bob of his head, the clerk bowed and excused himself, leaving them alone.

"Blue it is," Henri said with aplomb, turning back to the mirror.

Taking a deep breath, Esmée stepped clear of the hat display, forgetting she still clutched the bergère. Her head swam traitorously. She'd not eaten since breakfast, and then only sweet cake.

He looked at her reflection in the mirror, meeting her eyes. "So you are not only a chocolatier but a purveyor of men's garments."

"We are old friends, are we not?" She came to stand beside him, her wide petticoats brushing the leg of his breeches. "And as your friend I can make recommendations about your coat. Though the gray is handsome enough, you are altogether elevated in blue."

"Your turn." He faced her, gaze falling from her face to the hat she held. "Try it on."

He reached out a hand to hold the bergère as she pulled the hatpins from her hair and removed the plain bonnet she wore. As she set the hat in place, the admiration in his eyes warmed her all over. She scarcely consulted the looking glass. Yet she must have the hat.

"I know nothing of women's fashion, Miss Shaw, but it does become you . . . more than a little."

So they were back to formal names, were they? The sting of it poked a hole in her swelling pleasure. Still, she smiled at him, caught up in this cozy corner while the world spun around them.

"Thank you, Captain. I believe I shall buy it."

He took off the greatcoat and folded it over one arm while she removed her new hat. Stepping to the mirror, she pinned her old hat back into place.

"What brings you to Williamsburg?" The intensity of his gaze nearly made her forget his question.

"My father had meetings of which I'm sure you were a part. And I'm always happy to see my sister."

"Lord Drysdale was absent today. Please give him and Lady Drysdale my regards."

"I shall. We expect him home late this evening." She paused, awkwardness building. But she was unwilling to end their chance encounter. "Are you lodging in town?"

"At the Raleigh, as palace quarters are full. But alas, Williamsburg has no harbor. And no Shaw's Chocolate."

That cheered her, though he'd yet to darken their door. "You miss the sea."

"Aye, among other things."

Other things?

She would not let herself think she was one of them. Her eyes met his again, and she found his gaze warm and lively, as if holding some invitation.

He gestured for her to go ahead of him. She did so reluctantly, having forgotten the time. The clock on a far wall told five o'clock. Esmée wanted to still the mechanical hands stealing the moment away from her. She could easily have stood there all night. But the store was closing soon, and a queue of people waited to purchase their goods. Somehow a gentleman got between them, ending any further conversation.

And Esmée realized she had completely forgotten Eliza's pounce and wax.

CHAPTER

twenty-four

The November morning glowered, threatening rain, but nothing prevented Esmée from heading toward Matthews Street to see Kitty Hart. She'd begun to walk about York more often of late since returning from Williamsburg. Doing so helped clear her head. With those tall-masted ships in the harbor at her back, she wasn't reminded at every turn of Henri Lennox like she was when at the chocolate shop. On the other hand, she didn't need reminding, as he'd taken up permanent residence in her head *and* her heart.

"Good morning, Miss Shaw." A mob-capped servant bobbed a curtsy as Esmée drew near.

"Is Miss Hart at home?" Esmée asked, and the servant pointed the way.

The tea garden had been readied for winter, a somber sight after the recent black frost. Each flower bed seemed asleep, some covered with thatch, others with earth. At the heart of it all was the brick tearoom with its many windows, a wisp of smoke floating above it like a white flag. Esmée missed the music of the fountain and vendors strolling about selling refreshments. Many a romantic assignation had occurred here and still did.

Through the glass of the tearoom, Esmée saw Kitty bustling about in an apple-green gown. She approached, a gift of chocolate in hand. Nothing sounded so good as a steaming cup of tea or cocoa with her closest friend and confidante. If not for Kitty, who would she spill her secrets to?

"Esmée! Your timing is perfect. We just bid goodbye to our last guests." Smiling, Kitty embraced her and welcomed her in. "As soon as I saw you at the gate, I sent for tea. I've a fresh loaf of bread with newly churned butter and a jar of cherry preserves for just such an occasion."

That was Kitty's appeal, making much of an ordinary occurrence. Esmée took a seat nearest the coal stove, an ornate contraption that warmed every corner of the tearoom.

"'Tis delightful—warmer than wood!" Esmée stretched out cold fingers, her gloves in her lap. "Does it smoke?"

"More than I like. And coal dust is quite unattractive. I miss wood ash for fertilizing the garden to boot." Taking a seat opposite her, Kitty eyed a near coal bucket with fire tongs. "But Father is rather pleased with it. Soon all the lumber in the colonies will be gone and coal must suffice, he says."

Esmée passed her the chocolate. "A little something for when winter truly sets in."

"Winter, indeed. Have you heard? The almanac predicts early snows." With a shiver, Kitty opened the sack of shaved chocolate. "I shall weather the season in the tearoom, sipping hot chocolate and reading books."

"Shall you traipse through the snow?"

"Father is contemplating building a covered passage so we shan't get our feet wet. But enough of that." Kitty's expression turned imploring. "I'd much rather hear about you. I've not seen you riding by of late, not even in your coach."

"I've been in Williamsburg. Eliza is wanting company as she nears her confinement, and Father has meetings at the palace."

"I trust your sister is well. She's frequently mentioned in the *Gazette*. The baby has hardly slowed her in society."

"Irrepressible Eliza." Overwarm, Esmée worked the clasp of her cape free and let it slip from her shoulders. "She's already searching for a wet nurse and nursemaid."

"I didn't expect otherwise. As Lady Drysdale she would have help."

"I do wonder though . . ." Esmée paused, voicing her ongoing prayer. "I hope Eliza doesn't exchange family life for society."

"Many genteel women do." Kitty quieted as the maid came in with a tray. "A little gunpowder tea today, shall we?"

"Oh?" Esmée breathed in the welcome aroma. "I was just telling the ladies at Mount Autrey that gunpowder is my favorite."

"Mount Autrey?" Kitty studied her, then took up the sugar nippers to indulge her habit. "We have much to discuss, then."

With a slight lift of her shoulders, Esmé replied, "Their nephew, Nathaniel Autrey, is Captain Lennox's sea chaplain."

"The captain?" Kitty looked up from the sugar, wide-eyed. "My, how the plot does thicken . . ."

"A minor detail." Esmée busied herself with reaching for the cream pot. "You see, Chaplain Autrey visited me in the chocolate shop on two occasions and seems to have told his aunts he found me . . . agreeable."

"He's smitten, you mean." Kitty laughed. "Well, I wonder what Captain Lennox thinks of that!"

"Very little, I'm sure. 'Twould seem Chaplain Autrey will no longer be sailing but, according to his aunts, returning home to assume his rightful place, whatever that might be."

"With you by his side, no doubt. Is that where this fairy tale is leading? His aunts are rather ancient, and the sea chaplain could well be the heir, making you mistress of Mount Autrey."

Esmée looked askance at her. "How easy you make it sound when it is in fact quite complicated."

"How so?"

"Nathaniel Autrey seems gentlemanly enough, but . . ."

Kitty began pouring tea. "I suppose the question remains—do you want to see him?"

"Nay."

"Because your heart is already taken."

There was no fooling Kitty. Taking a steadying breath, Esmée confronted the matter head-on. "I regret that I still have . . . feelings for the captain." There, she had confessed it. Now perhaps she could amend the matter.

"Ten-year-*old* feelings. And have you seen the captain recently?"

"I have." Their recent encounter was all too fresh. She pondered it and took a sip of tea. "Quite by accident at Carter's store in Williamsburg Thursday last."

"I don't believe in accidents, nor coincidences, but rather divine instances," Kitty said, passing both butter and bread. "Especially in matters of the heart."

Esmée took cherry jam next, hardly knowing what she did, so sunk was she in the memory. "I helped him choose a greatcoat." Had his pleasure in the moment only been imagined? "He seemed to welcome my advice. We parted as friends."

"Friends." The disappointment in Kitty's tone rivaled Esmée's own.

If she could take the word back, she would. She'd only meant to smooth an awkward moment. *Friends* had seemed the perfect word to gloss over her imperfect feelings.

"How long has the captain been in Virginia since his return?" Kitty asked.

"Two months is my guess."

"And you've been thrust together how many times since?"

"Once at Lady Lightfoot's ball, then when Quinn invited him for supper and to see the illuminations on Palace Green, at church, and lastly at Carter's store. Though I did spy him going into Father's coffeehouse on one occasion."

"Has he not come by the chocolate shop?" At Esmée's nay, Kitty said, "Then that is your answer."

"Meaning he would have stopped by had he any feelings for me."

"Perhaps he's lost his fondness for cocoa," Kitty said gently, adding more sugar to her tea. "Or he's still somewhat burnt from your prior association and doesn't know how to proceed."

Esmée swallowed a bite, the dismay welling inside her rendering the refreshments tasteless. "Then what would you suggest? Your plan of . . . attack?"

Kitty laughed again. "How like your father you sound! Plan of attack, indeed." Her eyes glittered. Kitty liked nothing better than a little intrigue. "Well, I do have one daring idea . . ."

CHAPTER
twenty-five

Esmée clutched her cape tighter about her as she left the tearoom and walked home, noticing York's streets emptying fast in the face of a rising wind. Ships in the harbor pulled restively at their anchors, and Water Street seemed oddly quiet, as it always did in the face of great gusts. Such brought to mind the autumn squall of 1749, when a great many dismasted ships left their moorings and tobacco houses were overturned, all followed by a violent snowstorm. Kitty's prediction of an early winter might not be far off.

She began to hurry, head down, as great drops of rain spattered her cape, turning it from purple to black. Passing through the iron gate of their residence on fleet feet, she thought again of Kitty's bold proposition. *Daring idea* did not do it justice.

Up the steps she went. Their housekeeper, always having a sixth sense about such things, was at the door to greet her. "Come in, dear, and let me take your cape to dry by the fire. I can ready hot tea if you'd like."

"No need, thank you, as I've just been to the tearoom." Esmée removed her cape and smoothed her hair, looking toward Father's study at the end of the hall, where the door was shut. Father often had visitors.

"The admiral has asked not to be disturbed." Mrs. Mabrey whisked the cape away to the front parlor, where a fire roared in the grate. "Supper may be late. Cook has prepared your favorite, chicken fricassee."

"Ah, I must thank her. And I'll wait to eat with Father."

"Very well." She left for the kitchen belowstairs while Esmée started up the steps to the second floor.

At the sound of masculine laughter, she stopped. Company never much concerned her. Any number of merchants and townspeople came and went from Father's study on any given day. The fragrance of tobacco smoke, pungent and heady, snuck beneath the door. Many women abhorred it, but Esmée found it indescribably masculine and far better than snuff. The captain once smoked a handsome pipe with premium Tidewater tobacco. Did he still?

Her father's voice crested as if he were enjoying himself immensely. More laughter rumbled, followed by a voice she knew all too well, deep and heart-tuggingly distinct. Henri, without a doubt. A third man was present, his voice begging recognition, that failed to take root.

She hastened her steps. But before she was halfway up, the study door opened and a blue-coated figure stepped into the hall, closing the door behind him. Though she tried to tiptoe and avoid every creak in the stair, the whisper of her petticoats gave a warning.

The captain looked up and slowed his step. Was he on his way out? He stopped at the banister, resting one hand on the elaborately carved newel post at the stair's bottom. Their eyes locked. A moment of indecision racked her. Should she simply acknowledge him and continue her climb? Or return downstairs for conversation? Her feet, having a mind of their own, began their descent.

"Miss Shaw."

"Captain Lennox." She looked to the closed study door in question.

"I was on my way to my lodgings. Chaplain Autrey has asked to speak with your father alone."

Her stomach turned to jelly. She nodded, trying not to frown, remembering too late how disheveled she looked. Some of her upswept hair had escaped its pins and dangled about her shoulder. And Henri . . . he looked for all the world like he wanted to right it. She hovered on the bottom step, eye level with him now. Above his creamy neckcloth a faint line of color began to show.

"I don't mean to prevent you going upstairs," he told her.

"You didn't." She mulled her next words as the hall turned deathly quiet. "Another chance encounter, 'twould seem."

"We have a knack for those." He glanced toward the closed study door. "I came by to speak with the admiral about the light on Indigo Island."

"Of course," she replied, fingering her chatelaine. "How did that go?"

"He's in full agreement a keeper be found as soon as possible. Virginia's coastline, including the Chesapeake, has never been so vulnerable, despite guard ships."

Even now the names of foundering ships played in her head like a song. *La Galga. Invincible. Severn. Royal Fortune. Rebecca. Pembroke. Blackwall.* So many lives lost, not to mention treasure, including the herd of Spanish mustangs that swam to safety on one barrier island and were there still.

"So 'tis finished?" she asked quietly, almost sadly, as if she were outside the glass looking in.

"Finally, aye."

"Will you be its keeper?"

His face clouded, adding years. Was that a drift of silver through his dark hair or only a trick of the light? "'Twas the original plan . . . our plan, remember? But it seems I'm most needed at sea."

Nay, you are not.

His words weighted her, underscoring the chasm betwixt them. Separate paths. Separate ambitions. Separate lives.

"I'm considering several men who've applied for the position." With that he seemed to nail shut the coffin on their once shared dream.

Despite it, she gave way to a wistful longing. "I've always wanted to set foot on Indigo Island."

His eyes flashed surprise. "I nearly forgot you've not been there."

"'Tis beautiful, I hear. Serene. Is it true your cottage was built from Montserrat stone?" The question bordered on the intimate, but she forged ahead, uncaring. "And the lightkeeper's cottage is the same?"

"The both of them. Hurricane proof if not earthquake proof."

Hearing about him and his island life secondhand always chafed, but 'twas better than no news at all. "Mistress Saltonstall is a customer of ours," she said. "I suppose she's left the island for the winter."

"She has. Hermes remains behind."

Mistress Saltonstall's marmoset? She'd nearly forgotten Hermes. His antics were said to entertain tavern patrons far and wide. "I hope you've not been put in charge of him."

"Nay. The contrary creature is in the keeping of my steward."

"Poor thing. Might I send him some chocolate?"

"Oh, aye. Hermes is fond of your chocolate almonds especially."

"I meant your steward—"

"I ken what you meant, Esmée." He winked, the light remaining in his eyes. "Is there no laughter left in your soul?"

The gentle question was still more a dousing of cold water, though his return to her first name assuaged her somewhat. Tears hovered that had nothing to do with sweets but with his belonging to the sea. Of their shared lighthouse dream gone awry. She set her jaw lest she dig for a handkerchief.

Once they had laughed. His winking at her was commonplace. Once she'd felt she hadn't a care in the world with him near. Somehow time had turned her somber. Older, if not wiser. "I am not the woman—the girl—you remember. Ten years has wrought many changes."

He nodded, never taking his eyes off her. "Changes . . . not all of them welcome."

She looked to her slippers. She had no clue what raced through his thoughts, but half a dozen thorns were uppermost in hers. So many changes. Did he notice what a shell their townhouse had become without her mother and then Eliza? How she'd become unmoored, trying to salve her sorrow in her mother's endeavors, from chocolate shop to almshouse? How she was half-angry with him for forging ahead with the lighthouse and leaving her behind in his wake?

The study door opened. Esmée gave the captain a last, fleeting look before turning and hurrying upstairs lest Father and the sea chaplain see her.

CHAPTER

twenty-six

Supper that night was a quiet affair. Father seemed preoccupied, at least until dessert was served—his favorite flummery with brandied cherries.

"Cook has outdone herself," he said as a servant removed his supper plate and served dessert in small crystal dishes.

Fighting a headache, Esmée drank a cup of coffee, adding so much cream and sugar it reminded her of Kitty. Her mind was not on the meal, and it seemed her father knew it, for he regarded her thoughtfully.

"Cat got your tongue, Daughter?"

She moistened her lips, which had suddenly gone dry. "We have no cat, Father."

He chuckled as coffee was poured on his side of the too large table. Mama's and Eliza's places remained empty, gaping holes where laughter and talk had once been effortless. Esmée sipped from her cup without savoring the coffee.

"You're not going to ask me about our gentleman callers?" her father asked.

Surprised, she held her cup aloft and peered at him over the rim. "Since they met with you and not me, do you care to divulge it?"

His smile seemed rueful. "Chaplain Autrey—Ned, I believe the captain calls him—came specifically to ask about you."

"I'm flattered, but . . ." The thought of him romantically was no more palatable than before. "He has since left for Indigo Island, has he not?"

"Aye, but his plan is to quit the captain's crew and settle at Mount Autrey within a fortnight."

"With his maiden aunts."

"Whom you've met, thanks to Eliza's roistering."

"So far I've been catechized by his aunts, not courted by Chaplain Autrey."

Her father chuckled as he plied his spoon. "The man, however latent, may well be heir to a prosperous plantation in need of a mistress."

So Father approved, did he? Their terse talk felt more like verbal sparring. She sipped her coffee, waiting for the next volley.

"I was rather taken aback." He brought a serviette to his lips. "I thought the captain had come not to talk about the island's light but something else entirely."

His resumed courtship of her, perhaps?

"I find the light altogether fascinating," she replied, certain of where he was headed and desperate to turn the tide of conversation. "Such a beacon is overdue."

"Long overdue. The captain even made mention of it being your idea to begin with."

Had he? The words rang hollow.

"But I digress." Her father's face beneath his unpowdered wig looked grave. "With Chaplain Autrey's pursuit, you have an opportunity for change."

Her spoon hovered over her untouched flummery. "You would have me be the mistress of a plantation of over a hundred Africans, in direct opposition to our faith and even the Freedom Society you are a part of?"

"Nay. That is not my decision but yours. Yet it begs considering. As mistress, you might implement change."

But not the one she wanted. Not the change that would come from loving a man so much she'd face those challenges gladly.

Her headache thundered between her temples. She set down her spoon, half sick.

"I thought perhaps that after visiting the Autrey aunts, you had some regard for him," her father said.

"'Twas Eliza's doing. Repaying a social call."

"Will you receive him, then, once he is settled at Mount Autrey?"

Would she? The prospect was as appealing as yesterday's porridge. "I shan't play him false and encourage him. So, nay."

"Keep an open mind, Daughter." He motioned for more coffee as a servant reappeared. "When your mother and I were courting, she herself was unsure at first. Her family had higher hopes for her than a mere sailor. But I finally won them—and more importantly, her—over. I practiced patience until she came to know me better. With her by my side, I soon rose in the ranks of the Royal Navy. I'm a better man because of your mother, and there's not a day goes by that I don't wish she were still by my side. I simply want to see you settled, a family about you, like your sister."

Rarely did he speak of the past. Eliza's fortuitous match had been a joy to him. He was very fond of Quinn and anticipated his first grandchild. Esmée, on the other hand, had been at home with him all her life, nursed Mama till the end, and fully expected to do the same with him when his time came.

A niggling suspicion bloomed. Might he have another reason for seeing her settled? If she wed, would he return to sea as she suspected?

His gaze grew shrewd. "I sense you are still torn over Captain Lennox."

Could he see straight to her heart? *Torn* was an understatement. "Captain Lennox and I are now . . . friends." The word pained her no matter how much she used it. To be just friends made her especially heartsore.

"Friends? Glad I am to hear it." He nodded as if it confirmed something that had passed between him and the captain about the matter. "There are men made more for their professions than marriage.

Captain Lennox is one of them. He is too great an asset to the colonial cause—to England's cause—to remain ashore at such a critical juncture. The sooner you reconcile yourself to that fact, the better."

His firm words snuffed the last of her hopes. Why had she let hope take hold? Hope that Henri had had a change of heart. That he'd had enough of the sea. That they'd have a future together after long years apart.

"Sir . . ." The messenger at the door brought her father to his feet. "There's been a disturbance at the coffeehouse. Thievery, one of your indentures is saying."

With a last word to Esmée, her father excused himself to return to Water Street and the trouble there.

Esmée watched the candelabra cast shadows on the portraits of prior Shaws hanging upon the paneled walls, the beeswax candles melting lower and lower, her spirits with them. What did the Lord have in store for her? Was it in the form of Nathaniel Autrey and not Henri Lennox? Was she blinded by the one and not able to clearly see the other? She knew little of Nathaniel, but in truth, her would-be suitor was not of the same caliber. He was shorter, slender, and more softly spoken, with eyes so nondescript they almost held no color at all. But for his blaze of hair . . .

For the Lord seeth not as man seeth; for man looketh on the outward appearance, but the Lord looketh on the heart.

Duly chastised, Esmée closed her eyes and confessed all dissatisfaction. Who was she to discount the man if he was the Lord's choice for her? Many married for reasons other than love. Was it not better than life alone? Yet was that reasoning not flawed? Didn't Nathaniel Autrey deserve more than a half-hearted bride?

As for remaining a spinster, she'd grown used to her solitary state. But she did not sit idly by and lament she had no mate. Her hours were filled with family. The almshouse. Business. Friends. And she was about to become an aunt, if not a wife and mother.

Life was all about how you looked at it, was it not?

CHAPTER
twenty-seven

The next morn, Henri and his crew sailed from York with the tide. Theirs was a quiet passage, the blustery weather of the previous day and night a memory. The shallop soon had them across the Chesapeake, the island before them a shimmering mirage. High above the pines and dunes and beach heather rose the finished stone tower, soon to shine a piercing light to mariners. No more kindling sporadic bonfires on cliff tops to aid navigation, nor witnessing ships dashed to pieces on reefs or other perils of the deep.

"If there's to be a war, the light shall go dark lest the French be guided by it," the admiral had told Henri. "But in times of peace 'twill be a sure boon for ships coming and going, whether in stormy seas or no. Virginia should have risen to the occasion long ago."

"The Norfolk architect who designed it will soon make a final inspection," Henri replied, though the satisfaction he expected to feel was denied him. Why, he didn't know.

"You've seen it through to fruition and have shouldered considerable expense."

"'Tis a beauty at such a great height and crafted of local granite." Henri carefully enumerated the details that had occupied him since he'd first taken to the sea and seen countless lights around the globe. "Hanging oil lamps, at least twelve of them, though candles will suffice if oil is scarce. A platform around the light's lantern room will keep the glass free of snow and ice in bad weather. And a small cannon has been cast to answer ships in the fog."

"Much like the Boston harbor light." The admiral had looked pleased, even proud. "Lord willing, it shan't be so cursed."

Henri contemplated it now. Lord willing, it would only be a blessing, not just to the coming lightkeeper but to all those who encountered it. His vision was but one step from being realized. Nay, his and Esmée's vision. Though he'd seen the project to a finish, he'd not forgotten it was her idea from the first.

"There's but one matter that confounds me about Admiral Shaw."

Henri had nearly forgotten Ned was close. The chaplain moved nearer him in the bow.

"He seems somewhat reserved about my pursuit of his daughter," Ned confided, his tone perplexed. "And more than a little surprised."

"As I wasn't privy to what passed between you, I can offer little insight," Henri replied, trying to dismiss his meeting with Esmée on the stair. But every detail badgered him like sand fleas. Her fragile expression. Her wind-tossed hair tumbling to her shoulder. The beguiling way she held his gaze.

"I presumed my ties to Mount Autrey would be of more merit than being a simple sea chaplain."

"Admiral Shaw is an opponent of slavery. He may well wonder why a chaplain would espouse such by living there, even if you don't inherit the plantation."

"A predicament I've no peace with myself." Ned shook his head.

"You should know he and Mrs. Shaw were among the founders of a Rhode Island society for freeing those in bondage. His daughter is assuredly of the same mind."

"Then I am in a maddening quandary, am I not? A mere nephew, yet tainted by my relation. It does not help that the overseers are said to be cruel to Mount Autrey's slaves."

"Consider manumitting the enslaved Africans if it's in your power to do so. Employ tenant farmers instead."

"Like the mother country."

"Cease growing tobacco and turn to more profitable endeavors like grain and white wheat."

"You are ahead of your time, Captain. And you sound a farmer at heart, not a sailor."

"Truth be told, I've grown weary of the sea."

"Yet the governor and his minions are so desperate to foil the French they've agreed to all your terms, even your African crew."

Henri said no more as two jacks reached for the mooring lines with which to dock. With a lightness he didn't feel, Henri leapt to the pier.

Ned followed, expression still grim. "You've not yet said what you think of her."

Henri walked on, caught off guard by the question. Had the admiral told Ned of his and Esmée's former tie?

Finally he faced Ned, well out of earshot of the rest of the crew. "What do I think of her . . ." Heat sidled up his face, much as it had done when he was in the stairwell alone with her. Dare he say it? *Speak truthfully.* "I was in love with her once."

Ned's soberness turned to astonishment, and he parroted the words back to Henri. "In love with her?"

"*Once,*" Henri stated firmly. "I hardly know her now."

Ned stared at him. "You've never spoken of it."

"'Twas long ago. Before you came aboard. It seemed of little consequence."

"May I ask what happened to end your misalliance?"

"I scarce ken how to frame it." Henri shrugged. "She wanted me to stay on land. I craved the sea."

Ned looked aggrieved. "You spurned her."

"Nay." The mere thought raked Henri's composure. "'Twas mutual. And I do not care to remember."

"If 'tis still sore, then some feeling must remain."

Henri turned away, done with the conversation. "Tell the men I want a meeting at six bells in the forenoon."

LAURA FRANTZ

They parted, Henri going to look at the light tower but mostly at the finished keeper's cottage a stone's throw from it. A short, covered passage connected the two for protection in times of inclement weather. Pushing open the cottage door, he paused before entering, trying to see it with new eyes. He'd taken care to furnish it comfortably, culling items from his travels and carefully storing them in the ship's hold with the future lightkeeper in mind.

Twin Venetian wingback chairs upholstered in blue tapestry with a nautical theme rested by the fireplace. On a game table was a Russian scrimshaw cribbage set. Tole lanterns hung from the beamed ceiling, each unique. A teak shipwright's trunk adorned one plaster wall beneath a shelf that held a spyglass and tide tables. He was partial to the humble ship's barrel for storage in a kitchen corner and the handsome chest of drawers in the bedchamber, its painted surface of a ship at full sail. The generous bed was hung with soft if plain linens. Sparse, well intentioned, and well crafted, the cottage simply lacked a keeper.

His next order of business was to supply just that, one he could oversee till he sailed under a letter of marque for Virginia. Decision made, he still craved a different sort of future.

CHAPTER

twenty-eight

Surely babies were made to inspire hope, especially in the dreary days of November. As soon as Esmée sat down by the hearth's fire in Miss Grove's cramped almshouse quarters, Alice's baby boy in her arms, a sweet peace settled over her. Asleep, bundled in one of the blankets she'd made, a wee fist tucked under his dimpled chin, Alden was the picture of contentment.

"Such foul weather of late, though you seem to have brought the sunshine with you today, at least," Miss Grove told her as she cleared away the tea tray they'd partaken of. "'Tis good to have you back. We seldom have company, especially when the roads turn to mud and ice."

"I had to see how you all were faring, including this wee cherub." Esmée smoothed a wisp of the baby's russet hair showing beneath his bonnet. "And replenish your cocoa stores before winter sets in."

Miss Grove settled opposite her in the wing chair, a worn affair of scuffed walnut. "Of all the things you bring us, Shaw's hot chocolate is the unrivaled favorite of all the residents."

"I confess to an overfondness for it." Esmée looked out a near window, where the sun had the shine of May, not November. "When the snow flies and York comes to a standstill, there's little better."

"We've no one to bring us such fancies but you." Leaning forward, Miss Grove darted a glance at the door before saying conspiratorially, "Though I must tell you in secret, we are of late well supplied. Even with the French refugees on our doorstep."

"Well supplied? You don't mean all those bones I begged?"

Miss Grove chuckled, revealing a missing tooth. "Those bones are much appreciated. But nay, I'm referring to another benefactor. A furtive one. Not long ago a gentleman stopped by here under cover of darkness and met with Mr. Boles and his wife."

"Is this gentleman known to you?"

"Nay, and he insisted on remaining anonymous. The night watch did say he wasn't a great age but younger. Hatted and somewhat disguised." Her eyes shone. "He left an enormous sum with the express wish of seeing it well used. He spoke of having contacts who would apprise him of anything misspent."

Esmée warmed to the mystery. "Meaning the bulk of the money is to go to the poor for their well-being and comfort, not the trustees' pockets."

"Precisely. It seems to have struck some fear into the heart of the Boleses and even the lesser staff. Depending on how the behest is managed, more might be forthcoming. Or not."

Esmée felt stark relief. "'Tis hard to persuade people to be open-handed, yet this man did it unbidden."

"Perhaps the gentleman is known to you?"

"I know of no such gentleman. But I like that he did his giving in secret, as Scripture praises. No naming the almshouse after him."

"Indeed." Miss Grove's wide smile made her appear less careworn. "'That thine alms may be in secret: and thy Father which seeth in secret himself shall reward thee openly.'"

"Still, I am curious . . . and intrigued." Esmée looked down at the sleeping baby, her thoughts far afield. "'Tis good only God knows."

Miss Grove reached up a hand to touch the new mobcap Esmée had brought her. "Mr. Boles has even promised a chapel and a walled garden in spring now that we're not so dependent on parish levies."

"A chapel *and* garden? How delightful! Then I shall be doubly relieved all winter, knowing none here are in need." Esmée felt one burden lighter. How quickly life could take a turn. Only recently she'd been sitting at her father's table feeling as spent as the guttering candles, and now this.

Might the captain have done the benevolent deed? Or . . . had the sea chaplain decided to somehow curry her favor by giving to a cause dear to her heart?

"I've need of guidance." Ned paced before the hearth as rain drummed a steady rhythm on the cottage's shingled roof. Since their return to the island, the weather had been fitful. "You're the best one suited to offer advice, given you were once fond of the woman I now favor."

Henri leaned back in his wing chair, feet extended to the roaring fire. He could feel the heat through the worn soles of his boots. "Since I failed in that respect, mayhap you'd best consult Southack or Robbins."

"Southack, who cavorts with every native woman he sees? Or Robbins, so prudish a first mate he can't speak of a woman without a feverish blush?"

"What are you in need of knowing?" Henri asked grudgingly.

"How to proceed." Ned raked a hand through lank hair and came to a sudden stop. Leaning into the mantel, he seemed so perplexed that Henri bit his tongue lest he laugh. "I've gained her father's approval. Now hers is needed. But how do I call upon her? What should I bring?"

"Bring yourself." Henri moved to add another stick of wood to the fire. "State your intentions and see what she says."

"But—"

"Take care to not overthink it lest you appear a straw man. Speak from the heart."

"How easy you make it sound."

"You'll know soon enough if she favors you."

Ned looked to the Bible open on the table as if contemplating his most biblical option. "Perhaps I should ponder the Song of Songs first."

Henri uttered a warning. "Careful lest it inflame you before your time."

"What?"

"'Tis a biblical celebration of marriage, not courtship. An unabashedly sensuous book."

Ned assumed an injured look. "I am a chaplain, remember. I well know what it says, though in all truthfulness, I've not visited its passages in some time."

"Here's another caution." Henri cleared his throat, bracing himself against the onrush of carefully stowed memories. "Speak no French."

"French? Miss Shaw does not care for it?"

"It may remind her of my doing so and slow your pursuit."

"Touché, Captain." Understanding lit Ned's features. Then a shadow darkened his brow. "I confess she bears a striking resemblance to Verity."

Verity. Ned's betrothed who'd died of fever. As he'd never met her, Henri was in the dark.

"Same hair and eye color," Ned murmured mournfully. "Same penchant for confections."

"If your attraction is based on a dead woman," Henri told him curtly if kindly, "'tis rocky ground upon which to proceed."

"Well taken." Ned began pacing again, no small feat given the close quarters, and looked so troubled Henri sensed something more was on his mind than courtship.

"What weighs on you, Ned? Surely not the lovely Miss Shaw."

Ned shook his head. "The thought of living with my maiden aunts on a sprawling plantation is . . . daunting."

"'Tis nothing like the sea." Henri stared at the dog irons, pondering Ned's predicament. "Though if you can handle shipboard conditions as well as you did, several women and a great deal of acreage seem less burdensome."

"I'm considering a pastorate. A parish. There are many in need of shepherding in various places in Virginia and elsewhere."

"Why not preach and minister to the Africans within your sphere at Mount Autrey?"

"And be cast out of Virginia? Labeled a heretic?"

"Pray about it foremost."

"Aye, pray." Ned looked at Henri, his bloodshot eyes indicating a sleepless night or two. "I will miss your company and our wooden world."

Henri took hold of a black glass bottle, removed the seal, and poured them both a drink.

Ned took a bracing sip. "Vinho da roda."

"Aye. Madeira Terrantez. Aged by our last trip around the world."

"You brought that pipe of Madeira aboard when we were in the West Indies, if memory serves. Some five hundred bottles. This must be one of them."

They lapsed into silence, the drone of rain and snap of the fire a drowsy melody. Soon Ned departed in better spirits, leaving Henri alone. But his own thoughts were poor company, his feelings in chaos. Ned had stirred them up like storm petrels, those ominous birds that flew alongside ships, foretelling a gale. Here he sat, attempting to support his longtime sea chaplain, needing to pray for him at so critical a juncture . . .

When what he wanted was to throw him overboard.

He shut his eyes and took a deep, measured breath. *God, forgive me.*

CHAPTER

twenty-nine

*E*smée smoothed the lace sleeve of her gown, a lush rose brocade never before worn. She hovered on the stair landing of the Williamsburg townhouse, trying to warm to the idea of the party below. Voices floated up to her, scraps of spirit-sated conversation and laughter, inviting her to join in when what she craved was a quiet corner. A book. A window seat from which to watch the stormy weather.

'Twas Eliza's last soiree before her confinement. And what a soiree it was, with an ice sculpture adorning an enormous punch bowl and no end of savory items from the kitchen, even a table reserved for Shaw's chocolate in all its forms. A liveried servant was at hand to concoct hot cocoa, rich with cream and beaten to a froth and topped with West Indies spices.

Since Eliza had only hinted at the guest list, Esmée tried to prepare herself for elation or deep disappointment. The one voice she hoped to hear was lost to her, either missing or muffled by upwards of two dozen people.

She began her descent, glad the foyer was empty. A fan dangled from her wrist by a golden cord. With so many people in the parlor, she'd certainly need it. As she was missing her chatelaine, it gave her something to do with her hands.

"Esmée, there you are!" Eliza's voice rang out and turned every eye to her, if only momentarily.

Smiling rather stiffly, Esmée entered the melee, candlelight glittering off a great many gowns and jewels and faces. The governor was there with his wife and daughters. Rebecca Dinwiddie smiled at her, no doubt recalling their rather controversial tea of weeks before. Her own father held court by the marble fireplace, surrounded by old friends. Several officials, burgesses among them, gathered round the punch bowl, their conversation rousing and reminding her of the coffeehouse. No merchants here or any middling folk, just Williamsburg's leading lights as befitting Lord and Lady Drysdale.

"Miss Shaw, just the lady I was hoping to encounter."

She turned. Nathaniel Autrey gave a gallant bow to one side of the parlor door, as if awaiting her entrance. She tried not to stare, but she'd not seen him so well dressed nor smelling like a perfumery—eau de cologne? He wore a powderless wig tailed down his back with black silk ribbon. She nearly didn't recognize him.

Tongue-tied, she inclined her head, wishing for a little music. As there was to be no dancing, she braced herself for a long night of conversation.

"Are your aunts here?" she asked, gaze sweeping the crowded room.

"They rarely venture out in foul weather, given their advanced age."

"Of course." Relief flooded her. "You're brave to come. The wind is wilder by the hour."

"I can only imagine Indigo Island about now." Ignorant of her thoughts mired there, he looked briefly toward a window. "Hurricane season is still upon us." His eyes sought hers long enough to fill her face with fire. "Would you care for punch, Miss Shaw?"

At her smile and nod, he threaded his way through the parlor to the punch bowl being refilled while she seated herself on a vacant chair. Eliza's laughter rang out, reminding Esmée anew her sister had gotten a double portion of hostessing while she herself had not.

Though Eliza's entertaining was faultless, Esmée worked to stifle a yawn. It didn't help she'd visited the Williamsburg bookseller and had a novel waiting upstairs. The bestselling *Love in Excess* raised her father's brows and left Eliza laughing, but Esmée was drawn to the daring premise, challenging the custom that forbade women from declaring their romantic thoughts. Since when were men the only arbiters of affection?

Chaplain Autrey returned, two glasses in hand. She took the cold punch with gratitude, as the room was overwarm.

"So have you come to the mainland permanently? Left Indigo Island and the service of Captain Lennox?" she asked.

"I'm now at Mount Autrey, aye, trying to come to terms with my land legs." He looked down at her, studying her more closely than she wished. Or was she being too sensitive?

"What made you seek the sea to begin with?" She was sincerely curious, but the pained look on his face told her she'd misspoken. "I'm sorry, I—"

"Nay, Miss Shaw. 'Tis an honest question that deserves an honest answer." He stared down into his glass. "My betrothed died on the eve of our wedding. Verity was everything to me. Perhaps too much so. Idolatry, if you will. When she died I took to the sea, thinking to outrun her memory."

"And did you?"

"Nay. But I found instead the only One worthy of worship. And Verity's loss, while still painful, assumed its rightful place."

Esmée stared at him, forgetting herself. Could idols be of flesh and blood like Verity, not just carved stone or wood? She pondered this, unprepared for his next words.

"You undoubtedly know where my future interests lie where you're concerned, Miss Shaw."

"My father told me." Though she was well versed in resisting suitors, she still found it awkward, her palms damp. She gave an apologetic smile. "And being a forthright woman, some say a spinster, I thank you but must say I am not the wife you are desiring."

"I appreciate your honesty." Was it her imagination, or did his eyes twinkle? For so plain a rebuff, he weathered it well. "My fondness for chocolate may well have blinded me to the Lord's leading. And your agreement."

As if they'd orchestrated it, her sister drew near, a belle on each side of her. "Allow me to introduce Miss Carter and Miss Marriot." Eliza was all smiles, the Drysdale tiara she wore flashing in the candlelight. "They've yet to meet the new resident of Mount Autrey."

Turning her back on them, Eliza gave Esmée a piercing look. Knowing that look, Esmée followed her around the parlor's perimeter and into an alcove half-hidden by exotic potted plants.

"The governor's tongue has been loosed by too much punch," Eliza whispered with vehemence, her back against the wall. "He's been spilling details about all those closed-door meetings at the palace."

Esmée sensed it all had to do with Henri. Would Dinwiddie's revelations endanger his mission? She took another bracing sip of punch.

With a flutter of her fan, Eliza continued. "A declaration of war is imminent, and the battle will soon be fought by sea, not only by land. Stalwart captain that he is, Lennox will carry a letter of marque from the colonial government, acting as an ancillary of the Royal Navy."

The sweet punch soured on Esmée's tongue. She wanted to raise a hand to stay the words, understanding why Father had spared her the details. A grim mission indeed. "So Captain Lennox will command a vessel of war."

Dinwiddie was rabid for war, the newspapers printed, eager to defeat France with whatever manpower was available to him. Hadn't the irascible Scot ignited the frontier conflict by sending Colonel Washington west to begin with? She looked across the room at the governor speaking with Quinn and fellow burgesses so intently.

"But that is not all of it." Eliza's color was high, her voice a bit breathless. "Quinn is behaving quite strangely."

"What means you?"

Eliza darted a look in his direction. "At the last minute he cut half the guests from the guest list. Something about vain persons and dissemblers and evildoers, all of whom are the foremost critics of Captain Lennox."

Esmée felt a flicker of triumph. "Oh?"

"Brace yourself further." Eliza's fan fluttered harder. "He insists our party conclude before midnight."

With a look at the mantel clock, Esmée said, "Your parties oft last till dawn. Perhaps he is merely concerned for you and the baby—"

"Ha! He doesn't want to be late to Sabbath service. We haven't missed church for weeks now. He listens raptly to every word Reverend Dawson utters. He even wants to discuss his sermons once we are home."

"Fancy that," Esmée said dryly.

"Of late he's become an ardent admirer of Mr. Whitefield, the evangelist, and his writings and stance on slavery. I tell you, I have great cause for alarm."

"Sister, if you'd told me Quinn is in his cups, had insulted Reverend Dawson, and committed adultery, that would concern me. As it stands, I can only offer you my congratulations."

With a huff, Eliza moved on, her gown cleverly disguising the baby's bulk, leaving Esmée alone in the alcove. She finished her punch, and a servant came to replenish it. The hour was early, only nine o'clock. Esmée looked toward the window again as a gust of wind shook the pane.

What was the captain doing on such a night?

Hunkering down by the fire, likely. Once he'd been fond of books. They'd talked of poems and plays and novels. They played cribbage. She made them both flip, which frothed into foamy waves atop blue Meissen mugs. Feet to the hearth in her father's study, they heard the clock chime midnight many a time, but her parents said nary a word. It had been, in hindsight, the richest, most exhilarating time of her life.

If not his.

CHAPTER

thirty

Good day to you, Widow Radcliffe." Esmée smiled and helped the bent-backed woman to the chocolate shop door with her purchases, glad for so busy a morning, as it kept her mind off the heart-pounding present. But now, with no more customers at hand, a dreadful lull ensued, though one of the indentures was singing a slightly off-key tune in the kitchen.

Esmée moved to the front window, her vista mostly gray as winter approached. The days were growing shorter, the weather crisp as a Hewes crab apple. Next door, the coffeehouse hummed, patrons enjoying fresh-pressed cider. She could smell its spiced tang through the open Dutch door. Occasionally a gentleman would cross the threshold and buy a sweet to partake of with his beverage or carry home to a wife or sweetheart.

But not Henri Lennox.

She'd not seen him since their week-old encounter in the townhouse foyer when he'd been wearing the handsome coat she'd helped pick out at Carter's store. Though she looked for him—and his horse—about town or on the road between York and Williamsburg, he stayed hidden. The papers had ceased printing his whereabouts and business, giving rise to her belief he remained on Indigo Island.

Esmée rearranged the display window, moving chocolate pots and porcelain cups nearer the glass. Taking up a cluster of turkey feathers, she dusted, an unnecessary task, as Simon had done it just that morning. What once brought her a sense of satisfaction now turned to ashes no matter what she set her hand to. Blame it on the news heard at Eliza's soiree. She'd hardly slept since. It wasn't only Henri's future she was concerned with but her own. And enacting her plan required all the courage she could muster. It might all come to naught and haunt her the rest of her life, but still she must try.

Crossing the shop to the kitchen door, she bade Molly take her place. "I must go out and shan't return to the shop today. But Father is near should you need him."

Molly simply smiled, used to her midday jaunts, and exchanged her soiled apron for a clean one. "I'll gladly swap, Miss Shaw. I'm weary o' Josiah's singing."

Esmée removed her own apron and reached for her cloak. Hurriedly she passed by the chocolate stones heating at the hearth and was reminded of the cocoa grinder Father spoke of getting from Boston, capable of producing one hundred pounds of chocolate in six hours. No doubt the indentures would prefer that, freeing them from kitchen labor better spent elsewhere.

Down Water Street she went on foot, then took a sharp right up the rutted road that climbed to Main Street and their residence. She stopped at the stable, telling a hand to ready her mare. Minta nickered at her voice, anticipating a ride. It gave Esmée time to go to her bedchamber and change into her riding habit.

And reconsider her foolhardy plan.

She pressed on nonetheless, boots on and plumed hat pinned tightly, glad Mrs. Mabrey hadn't questioned her and Father was busy at the coffeehouse. He'd put a stop to her rashness at once if he found out. Yet as she turned down the lonely road that led to the almshouse, she felt an odd peace settle over her. From the top of her head to her leather soles, it seemed a cool draft of water passed through her, settling her, encouraging her, leading her. So stark was the absence of her recent turmoil that tears stung her eyes.

Was this what the Lord had for her then? This rash mission she'd undertaken in her own secret thoughts, only to be confirmed by Kitty? How was it possible to feel any peace? Yet peace was what she had. At least for the fleeting moment.

Lord, I am a foolish, lovestruck woman. Please guide me and keep me from harm.

She prodded Minta into a gallop, wanting her mission over with as soon as possible. 'Twas fortuitous Jago Wherry was getting wood in the saw lot away from the almshouse. The few men with him tipped their hats and moved away as she neared. He dropped his armload of wood as if sensing her business was with him as she reined in a few feet away. She rarely spoke with him, not since her mother was alive and they'd visited weekly. Wherry came and went as his fortunes rose and fell at the track and elsewhere.

"Good afternoon to you," Esmée said, staying atop her horse.

"G'day, Miss Shaw." He removed his hat, clutching its battered edges in workworn hands. "We don't oft see you unless you're pulling a cart full of relief."

"No need for that of late, thankfully." Did he know who had given the fortune to the almshouse? She took a breath, a bit winded from her ride. "I've come to ask something of you. A private matter."

He took a step nearer, his features sharpening. "At your service, ma'am."

"I want you to row me to Indigo Island." Her gaze held his. "Stone-cold sober."

A smile curled his thin lips. "But I've no boat, Miss Shaw."

"Well, you're clever enough to get one. And I'll reward you handsomely for it."

He pondered this, amusement and concern playing across his craggy face. "Ye've not set foot on the island before?"

"Never. 'Tis time." Even as she spoke the confident words, she had second thoughts. She felt a bit like Eliza with such scheming.

"Does the captain know of yer coming?"

186

"I'd rather he not."

"Um . . ." He seemed to reconsider.

"For all you know, I might be visiting Mistress Saltonstall," she said.

"I doubt it, given she's now on the mainland." He returned his hat to his head and peered at the glowering sky. "A bit chancy with November well upon us. When are ye thinking of going?"

"The next fair day."

He studied the sky. "Could be tomorrow . . . could be sennight's end." A nod. "I'll be ready."

"We'll meet at eight bells in that little cove where you saw the captain off."

"Yer the admiral's daughter, for sure." His chest shook with suppressed laughter. "I must warn ye yer taking a frightful risk. A northeaster could blow in, keeping ye on the island for days and days if ye do get there."

Esmée nearly sighed aloud. The sweet relief she'd felt—the elusive peace that flew in the face of this mad plan—began to crack beneath his caution.

Lord, help.

CHAPTER
thirty-one

The weather continued to defy Esmée and beg her to reconsider. There was plenty of time for Wherry to change his mind . . . or borrow a boat. Plenty of time for her to revisit her trust in this man, a stranger nearly, with a questionable reputation. But who else would she involve in her plan? Henri had entrusted Wherry to give him riding lessons. Was she wrong to rely on him as well?

Midweek, she stood at her rain-smeared bedchamber window, gazing past York to the Atlantic that beckoned. She fingered her chatelaine, intent on the little lighthouse. If all this went awry, she would hurl the tiny token into the sea. But . . .

Her Bible lay open on the table near her empty teacup. She'd been too preoccupied to partake of much breakfast. Only Kitty knew of her plan. Kitty was praying for her and watching the weather.

Father was absent while she waited, busy with matters in town. He even went to Williamsburg all of a sudden, as secretive as ever as to why, but Esmée was certain it had to do with Henri. Instead of it weakening her purpose, sensing Henri might set sail at any moment only hardened her resolve. She would act with grace and dignity despite her boldness, lest she spend the rest of her life ruing her cowardice and failure to move forward.

Lord, let me not make myself a fool by either rashness or overthinking the matter.

One verse in particular kept her grounded.

For God hath not given us the spirit of fear; but of power, and of love, and of a sound mind.

Even the timing was the Almighty's own. And the weather.

At last, sennight's end found Esmée in the agreed-upon cove. She stood on the sand, clutching her purse of coin, wondering if she'd dreamed the plan up. She was alone on the launching site. No vessel. No Wherry at hand. Had he succumbed to spirits and forgotten their agreement? Suddenly weary, she sat down upon a log and faced the wind.

The water was calm. Dead calm. And it might not be again for some time.

But the wily Cornishman did not disappoint. A sudden shout carried over the water. She turned in its direction. A handsome jolly raised her brows in admiration. Jago Wherry and a lad from the almshouse plied the oars. She wouldn't ask where Wherry had gotten the vessel. She prayed he'd not stolen it. Such boats usually hung from davits at a ship's stern when not in use.

He docked and helped her in, and she took a discerning if discreet breath. He didn't waft of spirits, though she spied a bottle half-hidden in rain gear stashed in the boat's bottom. With a practiced air he took up the oars again, reminding her of his history. Word was he'd once served under an Admiral of the Fleet in the Royal Navy. Surely she was in good hands.

From her stern seat she was rendered speechless, aware of a great many things at once. The still blue of the water on a nearly windless day, its fathomless depths a mirror of the heavens above. Was this what enticed the captain time and again?

While the men rowed, she took in York in a way denied her before. How small it looked. How insignificant. It faded from her line of sight as if melting like a confection on the horizon, all the ships at anchor like a child's toys. Down the relative safety of the York River and into the treacherous bay they went, all manner of vessels around them.

Breathless she was. Not from any exertion but from the risk she took. What if the jolly capsized? Whales did much mischief, upending boats without warning. What if—nay, she could not bear it—the island was less than she'd hoped and dreamed? She kept her eye on it beneath the shade of her cloak's hood as the flutter inside her intensified.

What if the captain was not there? Or—the latent realization turned her leaden—he'd already set sail or hired a lighthouse keeper?

She took in the mound of land resembling a sea turtle's back. There were more trees than she'd imagined. Wind-stunted pines. An abundance of seagrass. Gulls careening overhead. By the time they neared the island, the wind had strengthened, stirring her cloak and nearly pushing her hood back.

The light could not be seen yet, situated as it was on the backside of the island, facing the Atlantic. The captain's cottage was not far from it, or so Father once told her. The keeper's cottage too.

Where would she find Henri? And would Indigo Island become a beloved memory or another sore reminder?

CHAPTER
thirty-two

*T*was late November. Painfully aware of the time, Henri stood with arms folded, legs apart, and boots firmly planted on shifting sand as he watched his men coat the bottom of the *Relentless* with tar, tallow, and sulfur. Its potency carried in the rising wind, but it was a pleasant smell, at least to him, evidence of enormous effort. Behind him were the ship's guns and top masts that needed to be returned to the careened vessel before severe weather set in. His crew had finished with little time to spare. Even old Jacques's bones ached, a sworn precursor to a gale.

"Well done!" His voice rang out, meeting with huzzahs from all sides. "An extra half gill of rum at day's end for every man."

The beach where they'd chosen to work was ideal, shallow and secluded. Of all the coves and inlets on this seven-mile island, this was his favorite. It held the lush richness of the Caribbean, with warm azure waters and glittering sand but none of its venomous snakes.

"Blasted teredo worms!" he overheard Cyprian say from down the beach as he spat into the sand.

Tarbonde smiled patiently. "'Tis only the third careening we've endured this year."

191

"Next time we'll not stay so long in the Caribbean," Henri replied, thinking shipworms one of the few hazards of the tropics.

Southack scratched his chin. "Still no word from the governor about our departure?"

"Any day now," Henri replied quietly.

"The men are enjoying their freedom meanwhile," Southack said. "They've struck their tents and moved to the Flask and Sword since it's been shuttered for the winter. Generous of Mistress Saltonstall to offer up quarters while we wait. But I suppose you paid her handsomely to do it."

With a nod, Henri privately recounted her glee as they'd dickered about a price. She'd come away with a sack of silver ingots and a Burmese ruby she fancied besides.

"Captain." Udo approached, a list in hand. "I've sent to the mainland for another fortnight's victuals and drink. Jacques is quite at home in the tavern's kitchen . . ." His voice died away as he looked toward the water.

Henri, intent on the careening, widened his focus. Half a league out was a trim little jolly, three figures within. Two were at the oars, one of which was Jago Wherry. Another was in the stern, her purple cape fluttering against her full figure like a flag. He'd seen that comely garment before . . .

Esmée?

The bottom dropped out of his belly. Some of his crew were now gaping, forgetting their work. As the vessel floated by, Esmée turned her head toward him as if captured by the activity on shore and the hulking vessel that lay on its side like a beached behemoth. Were they on their way toward the end of the island? His cottage? Or the light?

Run, man.

Without a word to anyone, he bolted, kicking up sand as he sprinted toward the trees and trail that led to his end of the island. His boots clattered on the boardwalk. Winded, even dazed, he thrust open the door to his dwelling and made for the washstand in his bedchamber. He poured water into a basin and all but dunked his head in, ruing the bristles scrabbling his jaw, his uncombed hair. If ever he'd had the look of a pirate . . .

Rearing back, he toweled himself dry. Too late for a razor. Missing a comb, he ran both hands through his black mane, then tied the mass back with black ribbon. His garments would suffice. One unsatisfactory look in the mirror sent him from the bedchamber outside again.

To he knew not what.

While he awaited the next sighting of the vessel, he battled for composure. Why had Esmée come? Had Admiral Shaw fallen ill? Was she somehow bringing word from Lord Drysdale and Williamsburg?

His impatience was soon rewarded when the jolly sidled up to the pier. Despite the sea jaunt, Esmée looked as comely as he'd ever seen her. A queenly posture. Cape hood pushed back to reveal upswept hair with nary a pin awry. And a triumphant smile—was it slightly tremulous?—on her upturned face as he put out a hand to lift her to land. At least some of his fears were allayed.

"Good morning, Captain."

His heart beat hard against his rib cage. "To what do I owe the pleasure, Miss Shaw?"

"I've always wanted to see your island," she answered as lightly as if they were exchanging pleasantries about the weather. "And have a private word with you, if I may."

He darted a glance at Jago, who was busy with the mooring lines. "I'll escort you to my study, then."

"Thank you."

Hand cupping her elbow, he led her up the steps to his cottage, second-guessing himself all the way. Should he have taken her to the light instead? His study—did it look hurricane struck? Of late the chaos in his spirit was reflected in his normally tidy surroundings. Too late to right them. He opened the door for her reluctantly, and she entered in ahead of him, her face alive with interest.

"Your first visit to the island," he said, overcome by a guilty negligence.

She simply smiled again as he led her to his study. It wasn't as disheveled as he remembered, just dusty, and they both sat, the desk between them. Her attention drifted from him to the cowrie shell atop his desk. Removing her gloves, she reached out a hand to touch it.

"I've never seen the like," she said, looking a bit awed. "It has the shine of porcelain."

"They're most abundant in the Indian Ocean. A gift to me from the African chief liberated from the *Swallow*."

Her expression brightened. "Ah, the heroic deed that will not die."

He nearly flushed at her open admiration. Fisting his hands atop his desk, he wondered if his pleasure in her company showed on his face. "I'll be honest and say I'm rather thunderstruck by your coming. 'Tis not every day a lady of quality hazards a crossing to a barrier island in the chill of November."

"Expect the unexpected, 'tis said." Her quiet words rolled over him as her green gaze held his. "I've mainly come because I'm seeking the position of lightkeeper."

He swallowed, not entirely astounded, but still . . . "The position."

"After much thought . . ." Her lovely face turned pensive. "If you've not already decided on a keeper, that is."

He looked down at the papers before him, half a dozen men's names scrawled as possible appointees. None but two seemed fit for the task. Both were capable. Middle-aged and able-bodied. Proven Virginians who had seen military service.

"Why do you wish to turn lightkeeper instead of being the successful chocolatier and almshouse benefactress you are?" He felt beyond his ken questioning her, this woman who had his heart so entangled, but there must be some semblance of an interview even if he refused her the position.

"Shaw's Chocolate was my mother's business and the almshouse her heart's cause, though I've been glad to stand in her stead." She folded her hands atop her lap, her lush cape settling in lavender folds about her. "But in truth, I'm unnecessary to its continuance now that it's well established and worked by indentures. As for the almshouse, the poor will always be with us, sadly."

No refuting that. Scripture said the same. But another matter still tore at him. Ned's presence seemed to come between them, a question that begged settling once and for all. Did this mean she'd refused him? Even after he'd sought her father's permission to court her? The silence needed filling, but how to frame such a delicate question?

"Have you no other . . . opportunities, Es—Miss Shaw? Choices?"

She lowered her gaze, a pink cast to her features. "If you imply any suitors, nay. I am not meant to reside at Mount Autrey. And I have said as much to your sea chaplain."

Relief nearly made him light-headed. Still, there were other hurdles to overcome. "You realize island life is very different than living on the mainland."

"Understandably. But I would do my part for Virginia and the Chesapeake."

"You'd be the first lady lightkeeper in the colonies. Other than the woman in Rhode Island who took up the task when her keeper husband died."

"First of many, is my guess."

"What does your father say?"

A pause. "He knows nothing of my coming here." She looked past him to the map pinned to the wall behind him. "I am, I remind you, of an age to do what I will."

He'd not forgotten her age, nor his. Even now the pinch in his knees reminded him of the rheumatism that plagued aging seamen. "'Tis often lonesome and dangerous. As keeper you'd do far more than clean and polish glass."

"Do you doubt my abilities, Captain?"

"Nay, I admire you for rising to the challenge." He leaned forward, resting his forearms on the desk. "You make me think twice about the men who seek the appointment. None of them rowed out in a jolly to win the position."

She smiled, then grew serious again. "I can swim, surely a requirement. I keep a cool head under trying conditions. I prefer solitude to society." She took a breath. "I'm stronger than I look."

The sun slanted through a window, casting her in angelic light. It made her look . . . vulnerable. Too fragile for the rigors of lighthouse keeper.

"You must be thirsty." He gestured toward the bottle on a tray at the edge of his desk. "Madeira?"

With a nod, she reached into her pocket and produced a small brown package tied with twine. "Madeira pairs nicely with chocolate."

Her smile warmed him all over. He reached for the wine and poured it into two glasses engraved with fruiting vines while she unwrapped her offering.

"Chocolate meringues," she told him, passing him a confection. "Though I've also brought some almonds, as I recall your fondness for those long ago."

He'd had no Shaw's chocolate since his return to the island, and these were like a siren's song. Only there was no ship's mast to tie himself to so he could stay on course. He was now in dire straits, his good intentions sinking as he came under her spell again.

He passed her a glass, the wine a rich brown not unlike the chocolate. "Are you attempting to bribe me, Miss Shaw?"

Laughter lit her eyes. So she did have some merriment left in her soul. "Guilty, Captain Lennox—unashamedly so."

He raised his glass in a toast. "To the newly appointed lightkeeper of Indigo Island."

Lips parted, she stared back at him, her glass suspended in midair. "Surely you do not jest."

"On my honor."

Their rims clinked, and then they each took a celebratory sip. Next he sampled the meringue, the sugary goodness melting on his tongue.

"With conditions," he amended, hating the harsh sound of it.

"Conditions?"

"The first is that you'll not be here alone. A maidservant must accompany you."

"I know just the one from the almshouse."

"You'll be relieved every six weeks by an assistant, giving you leave to return to the mainland for a few days."

"Fair enough." Her posture seemed to relax, and she sat back in her chair, wine glass in hand, meringue in her lap.

"You'll keep a detailed log to be given to me or to colonial authorities upon request."

She listened, looking thoughtful.

"Your wages will be a hundred fifty pounds a year, payable in silver ingots or pieces of eight. Your preference."

She merely nodded pleasantly.

"And you'll prepare yourself for the onslaught of gossip that will ensue once the mainland gets word you're ensconced as lightkeeper here by the man who was once your would-be husband."

Her eyes flared, not at the mention of gossip, he guessed, but his calling out their former intimacy.

"Not only that, but a man who is even now awaiting orders of a letter of marque and who will be your nearest neighbor till that happens."

She took a bite of meringue, which slowed her reply. "Let them say what they will. I care not."

"Spoken like an admiral's daughter." He savored his Madeira and this rare moment. The look on her face bespoke a sudden hesitation. Had he alarmed her with such plain speaking?

"You're not appointing me to the position because my father is admiral or—" She wavered, groping for the words he already knew hovered on her tongue.

"Because I feel guilt or some sort of indebtedness to you because of our former impasse?" At her pained nod, he removed all doubt. "Nay. Your father as admiral doesn't hurt your cause, but you are entirely capable of keeping the light, come what may. I have no qualms on that account."

"Nor do I," she replied, a new gleam in her eye, lifting her glass in another toast.

CHAPTER
thirty-three

Henri's firm nay removed any doubt Esmée had about why he was appointing her lightkeeper. Still, her suddenly shifting world made her a little light-headed, which had nothing to do with the wine and everything to do with his proximity and her new position.

She, the lady lightkeeper of Indigo Island.

She'd expected some naysaying. An outright refusal. As if to ground herself, she touched the tiny silver lighthouse on her chatelaine beneath the folds of her cloak.

"May I see my future quarters?" she asked when they'd finished their refreshments.

"Of course. Right this way."

Out they went, her spirit and step more buoyant than when she'd arrived. The path connecting his cottage to the light and her quarters had recently been scattered with shells. Their footsteps crunched as they walked it, a distance mercifully short.

Or brow-raisingly brief.

If the wags got wind of it ... She shuttered the thought and followed him, eyes on his broad back until she laid eyes on her new home. *Home.* 'Twas not as she imagined it. 'Twas even better. Made of rubblestone and brick, the lighthouse shot into the sky some one hundred sixty feet high, its foundation staked into the ground with iron spikes. But 'twas the cottage that called to her. Quaint. Well-built. Its door and windows seemed almost in miniature, especially when the captain ducked beneath the lintel, his shoulders nearly touching the doorframe.

Once they were in the main room—the parlor—her gaze was everywhere at once. The cold hearth that begged for a warm fire vied for her attention, along with the simple furnishings that bespoke exotic ports. All was masculine and spare, something she would enjoy making her own. She'd put curtains at the windows and bring over a few of her treasured belongings to start.

"So, how does it strike you?" Henri stood back as she began to roam.

Withholding her answer, she passed into a bedchamber, its windows facing the sea. Would she hear its music night and day?

The kitchen was trim but adequate, with room enough for a small table and two chairs. Cooking vessels rested on the hearthstones. The room simply lacked a teapot and pretty porcelain cups. The larder was large, as befitting a home so far from a market. Supplies would need to be gotten, especially for the coming winter.

"At the risk of sounding too forward, I'm rather smitten," she finally said, garnering his smile.

They went outside, where the back of the cottage was level enough for a small garden. Next he took her into the light, up the twisting stair to the very top. The dizzying height and view stole her breath.

All around them rested lanterns waiting to be lit and a great many candles. Unkindled, the tower seemed a hollow place, a body without a soul. Echoing and awaiting its purpose. Henri was standing near her, one protective hand on her back as if the glass was not there at all and she was in danger of falling. She felt his hand through the thick folds of her cape. Warmth flooded her.

"Look, there's a sloop approaching." Her words were awed. She felt she looked down upon the open sea with the view of a gull.

The Atlantic seemed merry today, a brilliant blue, the wind making a lacy ruffle around the island's shores. She'd pray for days more fair than ill.

"Will the light withstand a hurricane?"

His reply was slow in coming. He placed a hand upon a beam. "Only the Almighty knows. But I had a Norfolk architect construct it like a ship for that very reason. The internal structure is of stalwart oak like a mast, the wood coated in oakum and pitch, much like a hull. The iron spikes you saw anchor the whole to the foundation."

"Since you've overseen it, I'll trust it in a storm."

The accolade hung in the tower's windless air. He looked down at her, making her feel small and awed and wonder if she was up to the task. If she'd ever wished she were a taller, stronger woman, 'twas now. His hand fell away, and he turned toward her, filling her view, his back against the glass.

"Esmée, tell me. Is this what you genuinely want?"

She looked up at him, missing the touch of his hand, wishing it at the small of her back again. Something burned in his eyes. A banked fire from of old? A familiar heat radiated between them. She felt it to her bones. He looked at her like he had before he'd kissed her that first time. Her own need sparked, making her place a hand on the front of his coat, not to push him away but to enfold the fine fabric in her fingers and draw him closer.

He leaned in, so intoxicatingly near she sighed. Her eyes closed as she awaited the brush of his lips.

"Captain Lennox, sir?" an unfamiliar voice said respectfully. "Surgeon Southack has need of ye at yer convenience."

Her hand fell away as Henri answered in a voice that echoed down the stairwell. "A half hour, then."

Intimacy gone, she started toward the steps, which seemed impossibly narrow and steep, more a hazard going down than up.

"Take my hand and let me go ahead of you," Henri told her.

She reached for him again, a rush of memories filling her. Once they'd held hands so often, it felt odd when they didn't. If his gloves had been off, she could have felt the strength of his fingers again, skin to skin, and the jagged scar along the thumb where a sword had once slashed him. She'd not asked him about the scar on his brow. Would she ever know its cause?

They took their time coming down lest she misstep and returned to the sunlit air. Jago and his oarsman were nowhere to be seen. Had they sought out the Flask and Sword to slake their thirst? The sun bespoke the afternoon, just ahead of her usual two o'clock dinner hour. The bit of wine and chocolate they'd shared still lingered on her tongue.

Henri gestured to a plot of leveled ground. "A fog cannon will be installed within a fortnight. But you won't have to fire it. One of my crew has been assigned that task."

They stood near the pier, the jolly bobbing in the water, the lighthouse at their backs. A comfortable silence ensued, rife with emotion.

She stifled the thornlike worry that reared its ugly head. *I know you are soon to sail under a letter of marque for the colonial government.* She wanted nothing to intrude on this day, this moment. This *peace.* Did he feel it too?

Curiosity got the better of her. "How do you come by your meals? I see no cook or housekeeper."

"Most of the time I take a long walk west to the Flask and Sword, where the *Relentless*'s cook has command of Mistress Saltonstall's kitchen."

"So you eat with your crew."

"Aye. And then I walk the beach home again. The sunsets are spectacular."

She looked west toward York, a thin line of green on the horizon. "I shall look forward to the sunrises too."

He studied her with an openness that told her they'd overcome some barrier, moved past the unease that had held them captive since his return. "I'll collect you by pinnace Saturday next in York's harbor. Bring anything you wish to make yourself at home here. And if you should change your mind—"

"I shan't."

Jago and the oarsman appeared as if materializing in thin air. "Ready to depart, Miss Shaw?"

She wasn't at all ready, but what choice did she have? If she had her druthers, the wind and the waves would keep her here. But the water was only slightly more ruffled now than when they'd left, a reminder of the hurdles to come. Telling friends and family. Fending off gossips.

She took a last look at the light and cottage with a keen yearning as Henri handed her into the boat. Raising the hood of her cape, she cast a look at him.

He stood unsmiling, looking thoughtful, making her wonder what he was pondering.

Lord willing, he'd still be here by Saturday next. She couldn't imagine the island without him.

CHAPTER
thirty-four

"You're *what*?" Eliza stared at Esmée as if she'd sprouted horns in their very parlor.

"I'm to be the new lightkeeper for Indigo Island," Esmée repeated, marveling at the calm that accompanied the decision, only slightly bestirred by her sister's disquiet.

"A female lightkeeper? All your novel reading is giving you fancies! I can't imagine it!"

"'Tis no different than any female tradeswoman," Esmée replied, taking a seat on the sofa. "We've female printers, bookbinders, blacksmiths. Even an apothecary."

"But my confinement—I—you won't be here for the baby's birth!"

"I'm hardly a midwife or nursemaid," Esmée said in soothing tones. "And every six weeks or so I'm to have shore leave."

"You know your sister is not one for society." Quinn took a seat beside his wife, stroking her hand as it rested on the sofa. "Nor is she at your beck and call."

A tear slid down Eliza's plump cheek. "But . . ."

"I'm rather proud." Father stood by the crackling hearth, arms crossed. "The admiral's daughter has achieved something I never thought or expected."

"'Tis partly Captain Lennox's doing," Esmée told them, passing Eliza a handkerchief. "He has had several interested parties, all men. I wasn't sure he'd take me seriously."

"He considers you because he's still in love with you," Eliza said with conviction. "I witnessed it in my own parlor but a month ago."

The men chuckled as Esmée shook her head. "'Tis not what it seems—"

"Oh? 'Tis what all Virginia will think!"

"Let the naysayers spew what they will," their father put in. "My daughter and Captain Lennox are above reproach."

Eliza managed a short, tearstained laugh. "You do have a bold bone after all, Sister, if a tad belated, running off with the captain this way."

Esmée sighed. "We are not—"

"What of the almshouse and your charitable endeavors?" Quinn interrupted gently, still smiling. "You will be missed."

"The almshouse has had a windfall of late." Esmée still longed to unravel that mystery. "An anonymous benefactor has given so generously, 'twill carry them through the winter and far beyond."

"And the chocolate shop?" Quinn queried.

Father cleared his throat. "I've just purchased a hand-operated machine from Boston. 'Tis time Esmée was relieved of her duties there."

Esmée warmed at her father's words, for she'd been unsure of his reaction. Eliza still looked sullen, her usual high spirits dampened by sleepless nights and indigestion. Even now she winced, moving a hand as if to counter an uncomfortable kick.

She continued to pout. "When does your island sojourn begin?"

Four more days. Each stroke of the clock brought Henri nearer. "Captain Lennox is coming this Saturday to collect me and my things."

Eliza persisted. "Why don't you two just elope? 'Tis what it amounts to, does it not?"

"Employment is not the same as elopement." Father sent a stern look Eliza's way. "Some felicitations are due your sister, are they not?

She has served all of us well, even caring for your mother till she passed, and is late to living a life of her own."

"I gather this is a resounding nay to Nathaniel Autrey's pursuit." Quinn's voice was absent of any censure. "I've just learned that lately he has been in the company of my cousin Elinor from Norfolk."

"Elinor?" Eliza's vexation vanished as surprise rushed in. "Why, she's homely enough to stop a clock. What on earth does he see in her?"

"Pretty is as pretty does, as Mama oft said," Esmée reminded her. "I've met Elinor, and she's lovely."

"Pish! Nor does she have any dowry I know of."

"Chaplain Autrey has little need of it, given he might inherit Mount Autrey one day." Quinn gave a small, knowing smile, which left Eliza eyeing him curiously.

"I wish Chaplain Autrey all my best." Esmée felt relief just saying it. "And his bride-to-be, whomever she is."

Quinn took a cup of punch the maid brought round while Eliza turned up her nose at a cup of chamomile tea before accepting it. "Will Captain Lennox replace him, do you think?" she asked.

"Likely, if he can find a man willing to serve on a ship of the line in dangerous waters." Father downed the last of his punch. "Not many would."

Weary of any ominous talk, Esmée steered the conversation in a safer direction. "You should see the cottage I'm to occupy. 'Tis like something from a fairy tale. There's even room for a small garden come spring."

Father held out his cup as the punch was replenished. "I'll visit you as often as I can. I've seen the lighthouse plans but not the finished structure."

"What of a maidservant?" Eliza asked between sips of tea.

"'Tis one of the captain's conditions." Esmée pondered the miss she had in mind. "I've already sought permission from the almshouse and the girl in question. Lucy Barlow is willing to accompany me. She's skilled in needlework and housework, including cookery. There's even a cozy room for her off the kitchen."

"I'm relieved," Eliza exclaimed. "'Twould not do to be the only woman on an island of men, even if they are under Captain Lennox's command."

"The island will soon be absent of all but a trusted guard." Father moved closer to the fire since the room's corners were cold, chilling Esmée with his words as well. "And Mistress Saltonstall shall return in spring."

"I do wonder," Quinn remarked, looking to Esmée, "if you won't tire of the isolation in time, having become used to town, with an ability to roam at will. The island is not unlike being shipbound, one would think."

"I hadn't thought of that," Esmée told him. "But time will tell."

"Promise you'll visit me once you return to shore." Eliza set her unfinished tea aside. "I simply must be the first to hear all about it."

"Of course I shall," Esmée reassured her. Eliza was not usually so cross. "Perhaps you'll even set foot on the island one day."

Eliza rolled her eyes, though a wry smile played at the corners of her mouth. "Another one of your fancies, Sister. I give you a fortnight before you're missing us and wanting to forsake your island duties."

thirty-five

smée turned the spyglass on York's harbor from the anonymity of her father's study, where she'd been waiting for the last quarter of an hour. A small crowd gathered at the landing just below Shaw's Chocolate. The *Relentless*'s pinnace had just docked amid the many frigates and merchantmen and sloops already at anchor—a cardinal among crows, from the attention it garnered. With its ornately decorated sterncastle and three masts, not to mention half a dozen crew, it looked dashing and fit for anything, if only to carry a chocolatier turned lightkeeper to a near island.

Her heart skipped as she watched Henri step onto the pier, his cape furling and unfurling like a sail in the November wind. A few jacks remained on the boat save two lads who accompanied him onto Water Street and up the hill to the Shaw residence. Breathless, she rushed to her bedchamber—her soon-to-be-former bedchamber—and readied to leave as Mrs. Mabrey greeted the captain in the hall below.

Soon three trunks, a chair and tea table, and several other items were loaded onto a waiting wagon. Esmée walked behind as the conveyance rumbled back down to the waterfront, glad to stretch her legs after two days of packing. Kitty was on hand, the two of them giddy as schoolgirls, for the day was clement and spirits were high. As the captain bowed from the waist when he greeted her again, Kitty blushed to the roots of her fair hair.

"So gallant," Kitty whispered to Esmée when his back was turned. "For a widow of one and thirty, even I feel a bit smitten."

Smiling, Esmée linked arms with her. "I shall miss you and your tea garden. But when I come ashore, we shall celebrate."

"And I shall come to the island in turn, spend the night at your cozy cottage, climb to the top of the light, and take in the princely view."

They chattered so exuberantly Henri turned around and smiled at them as they neared the water. Father was on hand, coming out of the coffeehouse to bid them farewell. His appearance caught the attention of one too many wags about town. Soon the papers would buzz with the news of Esmée Shaw leaving York.

Lucy arrived, brought from the almshouse by Jago Wherry in a pony cart. Her few belongings were in a small bag, a kitten included. For every new home needed a cat, did it not?

Esmée greeted Lucy, praying the both of them wouldn't be seasick, as the wind was brisk. Dressed in a plain striped cotton gown with a darker petticoat, a clean apron about her waist, and a bonnet framing her face, Lucy looked expectant and a tad fearful. Scuffed shoes and white-thread stockings were on her small feet. The humiliating mark of the almshouse was missing from her garments. But had she no cloak? Before Esmée could reach for the clasp of her own cape to give her, the captain removed his and draped it about the maid's shivering shoulders. Esmée smiled her thanks, touched by the small courtesy.

"'Tis colder on the open water than here in the harbor," he said, returning her gaze as he helped her into the pinnace.

Warmed by his touch, Esmée watched as Lucy smiled up at him, a bit wide-eyed at the gathering crowd. Seated in the vessel, Esmée steeled herself against the late autumn wind, her excitement building with every second.

"How long will it take, Miss Shaw?" Lucy asked beside her, her kitten in her lap.

"With those sails unfurled and the captain at the helm, no time at all."

Esmée let out a breath as the mooring lines were loosed. Jacks she'd never seen worked around her, the captain standing tall. The boat took to the open water, leaving her a bit winded as they gained speed. Every ripple seemed to roll through her in turn, not sickening but exhilarating. A far different ride than the slow-as-molasses row in the jolly. She looked out on the York River as they sailed into Chesapeake Bay, which winked sapphire blue in the sun. Beyond it lay a mound of land bitten by autumn's first frosts.

His island and now hers.

CHAPTER

thirty-six

The cottage was better than she'd left it. Pushing open the door, Lucy on her heels, Esmée could hardly contain her delight. A second Windsor chair had been placed near the hearth in the front parlor, the fire crackling merrily in welcome. Striped curtains were at the windows, making the cloth she'd brought unnecessary.

"My sailmakers have had a heyday outfitting your windows and your maid's bedding," Henri told her.

"You have a very able crew." Esmée went to a window, marveling at how well-stitched the curtains were. "Please thank them for me."

He supervised the men moving their belongings while she and Lucy wended their way through the cottage, exclaiming over this or that. A vase of dried flowers adorned the kitchen table. And not only flowers but a crusty loaf of bread and a small pot of salted butter. Thyme and roast chicken teased their senses, enticing Lucy to lift the lid off a pot in the embers.

"Jacques—the *Relentless*'s cook—prepared your supper." Henri stood in the kitchen doorway, answering the question Esmée wanted to ask.

Smiling, she turned toward him. "A warm welcome indeed. Won't you join us?"

He hesitated, his lips parting as if he was considering, then curving in an apologetic half-smile. "Another eve, mayhap. Tonight I'll leave you to get your bearings."

She nodded, pulled in a dozen different directions at once. Lucy was already in her room off the kitchen while the crew brought in the last of Esmée's trunks and furnishings, inquiring as to where she'd like them. When she looked up again, Henri had disappeared. But how far could he go with his quarters a stone's throw from her own?

By nightfall, they'd settled in and stripped Jacques's delicious chicken to the bone. Saving half a loaf of the bread for their morning tea, Esmée invited Lucy to sit by the fire in the small parlor. Taking out her sewing, Lucy stitched a handkerchief while Esmée read aloud from *Robinson Crusoe*, the kitten, Tibby, curled up at their feet.

"By this time it blew a terrible storm; indeed, and now I began to see terror and amazement in the faces of the seamen themselves. The master, though vigilant in the business of preserving the ship, yet as he went in and out of his cabin by me, I could hear him softly to himself say, several times, 'Lord be merciful to us! We shall all be lost! We shall all be undone!'"

Lucy's hands stilled, her needle midair. A moody wind began to blow about the cottage, adding to the moment's intensity. "D'ye think, mistress, that Captain Lennox would be so afraid of a storm?" she asked.

"Afraid of the storm, perhaps, but hopefully confident in the storm's Maker who can still the waves and even walk on them."

Lucy's capped head bobbed in vigor. "When ye asked me if I wanted to come to the island, I was a bit afraid, though it be a good deal better than the almshouse. But what if a rogue wave comes over us and sweeps us out to sea?"

"You must take care not to go out in foul weather. You and Tibby shall stay secure right here by the fire, at least for this winter, while I tend to the light and pray for safety."

"Yer as brave as the captain, mistress. To think ye must climb all those tower stairs no matter the weather!"

Esmée smiled, setting the book aside. "'Tis for the good of many, all those brave sailors who seek a safe harbor."

"Including the captain, aye." Tibby pressed against Lucy's skirts, and Lucy reached down a hand to stroke its caramel-streaked back. "Ye'll light his way back when he goes to sea again?"

The bittersweet thought intruded on Esmée's quiet joy. "I should hope so. And pray for his return."

"I'd best hie to bed and say my prayers so I can wake early and make our tea and toast." Yawning, Lucy scooped Tibby up and excused herself. "I shan't forget Mrs. Mabrey's peach preserves."

"A delightful breakfast awaits us."

At the close of her door, Esmée went to the window. With the tower unlit till tomorrow, the darkness was profound save the square of yellow gleaming from the captain's own cottage. Though she couldn't see it, she could hear the surf beating against the beach and the moan of the wind that drove it there. Yet she'd never felt so secure. So . . . serene.

Was God's leading not the way of peace? She sought the hearth again, already at home in her chair, thankful for all the little things Henri had superintended for her comfort. Or was she making it more significant than it actually was? He would, in truth, have done the same for any keeper, would he not? She settled back in her chair and tried not to think of his leaving. She mustn't let her present happiness and the blessing God had given her depend on the captain and his future.

CHAPTER

thirty-seven

he following day Henri pulled on his boots, the gray day beyond his cottage like a woolen blanket, in direct contrast to his sunny mood. The island smelled clean, as it always did after a windy lashing—of wet rocks and sodden sand and foamy treasures pushed ashore from the deep.

His first thought on awakening had been Esmée. Mayhap her last thought had been of him. He'd seen her at her parlor window around nine o'clock when he'd returned from his usual rounds before retiring. He nearly couldn't sleep. Thank heaven she wasn't on the other end of the island, miles distant. He chuckled. Thank heaven Hermes and crew were.

He stood and exchanged last night's rain gear for a woolen coat, his red Monmouth cap for a tan cocked hat. Used to being alone on his own stretch of beach, especially in the morning, he left the cottage to a pleasant surprise. Esmée was walking away from him as the tide went out, her purple cape aflutter. Every now and then she bent over to pick something up and examine it. Just like her shelling that day they'd first met.

He headed toward her, coming up from behind slowly so as not to startle her. "Good morning, Miss Shaw."

"A fine day to you, Captain."

He wanted to say *Esmée*, but a new formality had crept in with her position. It weighed on him, but he let it pass. "What have you there?"

She held out something blue and jagged. She'd said on her arrival she was hoping for a pearl.

"Sea glass." He took the piece and held it up to the light, its green tint visible. "Likely from a bottle of spirits. Pearls suit you better."

She smiled at him, her upswept hair pillowing a bit loosely about her face, two long curls over her shoulder. "I'll keep looking."

Farther down the beach he heard laughter. Cyprian was on hand, entertaining the maidservant, who had an egg basket on one arm. No doubt he'd visited the hens roosting at the Flask and Sword as a way of introduction. Clever, that.

"Tell me your maidservant's story," he said, falling into step beside her.

Esmée kept her eyes on the sand. "Lucy is but eighteen, orphaned after her parents died of fever. She was at the almshouse long enough to take a dislike to it. Being skilled with a needle, she was on her way to being bound out to a mantuamaker. When I gave her the choice to come with me, she readily assented. But I do wonder about keeping her isolated here long."

"At the moment she seems happy enough."

Laughter erupted again, Lucy's mingled with Cyprian's.

"Is that a monkey I spy on the shoulder of your cabin boy?" Esmée asked. "The renowned Hermes, I take it."

He chuckled. "You've yet to be formally introduced. Cyprian is my steward and has charge of Hermes for the time being."

"I've never seen a better dressed youth."

"Once he laid eyes on fair Lucy, he must have decided to bedeck himself in the finest garments to be had from the common chest."

"Ah, the slops chest, Father called it. Plunder."

"Aye, from seized enemy vessels."

The lad did look a tad ludicrous, having traded his humble working trousers and shirt of yesterday for ruffles and silk. But Lucy seemed to be enjoying the attention, and Henri would rather they be here than in the alleys and gin shops ashore.

"Tell me his story." Esmée looked at him, another wisp of hair tumbling down. With a gloved hand she looped it behind her ear, jarring the bonnet that matched her gown.

He was having a devil of a time trying to stay his hand and not right it for her, staunching his urge to throw her hat to the wind, take out all the pins, and tumble her hair further. "Cyprian is Portuguese. I found him begging at the port of Lisbon. He's served aboard the *Relentless* for several years and is well into manhood, though he looks younger."

"They've known such hardship already." Esmée's expression turned pensive. "Their laughter does me good. Let them have their amusement while they may."

They walked on in silence for a time, pausing now and again to examine something interesting on the beach. When he gave a little bow and held out another piece of sea glass, she curtsied prettily in return, making them both laugh.

"'Tis the blue of your gown," he remarked. "The one you wore when we first met."

She looked at him, near disbelief in her eyes. "I still have it but haven't worn it since—"

Since you left.

He'd tried to pin that blue down a thousand times in the last decade. Caribbean blue. Delft blue. Egyptian blue. Marine blue, the official color of British naval uniforms. Cobalt blue.

Lapis lazuli. Aye, that was it.

She squinted into the sunlight, and he looked to the sea and then the lighthouse when she said, "So shall we kindle the light tonight, you and I?"

How romantic she made it sound. A joint effort. The first of many, he hoped. "Aye, I want you to shadow me for a sennight or so, till we know the ins and outs of the tower and its workings and you're comfortable enough to handle it on your own."

"Will you be here a sennight more?" The shadow he'd found in her face when he'd seen her at Lady Lightfoot's ball returned, eclipsing her loveliness.

"I know not." How he wanted to throw any future cruise to the wind and remain right here. Even now he sensed there was more to her arrival than keeping the light. His appointing her as lightkeeper had been far from objective.

Would it all play out like it had years before when they'd first parted?

He sent his concerns heavenward, the sunlit moment weighed down by dark thoughts.

"Then we shall make the most of the time given us." Her smile was soft, a bit sad. It tore at him in a way little else did.

Gone was the spirited girl who had objected so strenuously to his going to sea. He hardly knew what to do with the composed woman in her place.

She took his extended hand, and he helped her over a rocky outcropping. "Is it true you forbid married men from joining your crew?"

He gave a nod. "Mostly out of respect to you."

Her green gaze came back to him. Tears stood in her eyes. His own throat closed and threatened to choke him.

At last he said, "I took to heart all you said back then—the toll on your family with your father away, your mother especially."

She leaned down and picked up a cracked shell. "I wish I'd known. It might have softened my regard of you."

He took a breath and revealed the rest. "I had a small chest of letters I wrote you but never sent."

The shell was discarded. "Do you have them still?"

His aye earned such a bittersweet look it sank his stomach to his boots.

"Might you give them to me after all?"

Would he? "The heartsick ponderings of a sailor?" He'd nearly thrown the chest overboard on more than one melancholy occasion. "Mayhap when I sail again."

"Please." The entreaty in her voice decided the matter.

"Do you forgive me for leaving?" He looked toward the line of smoke that marked the Flask and Sword's chimney. "For forsaking what we had?"

A gull swooped in, shattering the air with its cry.

"Only if you'll forgive me for making it an all-or-nothing arrangement." The mist in her eyes returned. "That was unconscionable."

"We were young. Foolish."

"And now?" Pensiveness limned her words. "We are . . ."

"Older. Wiser." He said the last word with a shake of his head. "Friends."

"Friends." Her echo came soft, a bit disappointed, he thought.

Hope took hold. "Unless you want to be otherwise."

She halted then and looked up at him, her sandy fingers full of beach treasures. "I scarcely know how to start over, if that's what you mean."

His heart began to pound. A deluge of emotion akin to a tropical monsoon swirled inside him. Never did he imagine this turn of events—having her here beside him, removing the distance between them in one stunning move. And now looking as if they might reconcile, fall in love again.

If they'd ever stopped loving each other to begin with.

"I want what you want, Henri." She began walking again, her full skirts dragging on the wet sand. "Maybe 'tis a bit like dancing," she said, a beguiling light in her eye. "I shall simply follow your lead."

He caught up to her, wanting to take her hand again yet wanting to be careful with her. Not wreck the both of them like before. How did one let go of the past and risk love again?

CHAPTER

thirty-eight

*T*he next day Henri sat with his officers at a tavern table, the rest of the crew spread out across the taproom. The Flask and Sword had never looked better, the floors mopped, every stick of furniture shiny as a newly minted shilling. Even Hermes looked content perched on a window ledge, eating pecans and occasionally emitting a shrill screech. Henri smiled his amusement, wishing Mistress Saltonstall back, if only to have another woman on the island. In the meantime, if there was a cruise, half a dozen of his men who were injured and ailing would remain behind, the penalty being caretakers of a cantankerous marmoset.

He finished his ale and set down his tankard, careful to avoid the letter of marque and reprisal lying atop the table. It had been delivered that afternoon by a courier of Virginia's governor in the name of the king, and Henri had just read it aloud. Their future mission sounded simple but was infinitely complex.

George the Second, by the grace of God, King of England, Scotland, and Ireland, defender of the faith, &c. To Captain Henri Lennox, commander of eighty men and mounting thirty carriage

*guns. You may, by force of arms, attack, subdue, and take all ships
and other vessels belonging to the inhabitants of France, on the
high seas, or between high-water and low-water marks . . .*

His crew's conversation had risen around him like a headwind
ever since.

"We're fully outfitted and ready to sail at a moment's notice."

"Lest fortune frown upon us, I shall place a silver coin beneath the
main mast when we weigh anchor."

"Superstitions don't become you. Coin be hanged. I saw you on
your knees petitioning Providence at the last violent squall."

"A misfortune the French often fly false flags, hoping to avoid
capture."

Hermes screeched at Cyprian's late entry, then ran to the lad, who
hoisted him on his shoulder. Laughter rumbled through the watching
men while Henri looked out a near window at the sunset.

"How many other privateers are operating under letters of marque,
Captain?" Tarbonde asked from across the table.

Henri came to attention. "New York leads the colonies in sending twenty-six privateers bearing three hundred fifty guns and nearly
three thousand men. Virginia is second in force."

A pronounced hush ensued as the gravity of their mission took hold.

Henri stood, bringing the din across the room to a slow halt. "I
need to tend the light."

Chuckling and elbowing greeted his announcement. "Don't you
have a lady lightkeeper for that, Captain?" Southack dared to ask.

With a wink, Henri settled his cocked hat on his head. "A lady
lightkeeper in training."

"No matter who tends it, 'tis most welcome," Cyprian said as Hermes
scrambled to his opposite shoulder. "Far better than the hilltop fires
of old."

Henri went out, glad for fresh air and quiet. His walk was an enviable one, energizing him after the tobacco smoke and chatter of
the tavern. The beach lay in winsome white curves all the way to his
end of the island, easily navigated by moonlight. He was beginning

to look forward to the hour when darkness descended. Once a trial to him, lonesome and full of memories, it now marked the time he could see Esmée.

By now she'd have finished her supper and was likely seated by the fire with Lucy. Esmée had mentioned knitting him stockings, even a hat and gloves—simple, practical things that a man had need of. He considered getting sheep so she'd have a supply of wool at hand, but that was in the distant future.

He rapped at the door, and it opened. Lucy gave him an unnecessary curtsy and excused herself, retreating to the kitchen. Esmée's eyes shone with quiet delight, another step away from the guarded woman she'd become.

"Good evening." He removed his hat as she rose from her seat.

"A good evening indeed." She gestured to the chair Lucy had vacated. "Won't you sit for a moment and warm up? 'Tis not quite dusk."

He did so, noticing all the little things she'd done to make the cottage hers. Over the hearth hung a landscape painting of a garden in bloom, while a smaller painting of her father's last ship rested on the mantel.

He leaned in to get a closer look. "A remarkable likeness of the *Indefatigable*."

"Mama painted it for him shortly before she died. 'Twas the great love of his life after her."

He added another log to the fire, thinking how cozy the cottage was compared to his own quarters. "Your mother was very gifted. And I'm sure very missed."

"Always." She returned to her knitting, her movements smooth and sure. "The oil landscape was in my York bedchamber. I've a fondness for gardens. Cook has a kitchen garden at our townhouse, but I've always dreamed of flowers. This painting gave me a little of what I lacked."

"In summer you'll find rose mallow, goldenrod, and wildflowers on the island."

"I've in mind roses, lavender, and larkspur. Even my favorite, sweet peas—the new variety of painted lady in particular. They symbolize goodbye, adieu, bon voyage."

"Don't remind me," he replied.

She eyed him in surprise, needles stilling.

"I'd rather remain and build you a wall to enclose your garden. Protect it from the wind."

"I can't imagine you doing something so small. Not when you've seen the gardens of Versailles and the Alhambra."

"Mayhap it's because I've seen them that my true north is now home."

"And is Indigo Island your home? Can you be content to live on an island so small?"

"My life has already been enlarged by your coming here, Esmée."

"You flatter me." Her needles picked up again, faster than before. "'Tis been but two days."

"The best days I've spent." Reaching out, he took her nearest hand, the yarn falling to her aproned lap. "I have no desire to sail."

"But has it not been decided?" She clutched his hand, her eyes sharp with intensity.

"I've a letter of marque and reprisal, aye." He continued to hold her hand and her gaze. "We could sail at any time now. We merely await word from Williamsburg."

And what a cruise it would be. An all-out battle. The potential loss of his ship, his crew, his life. He couldn't recount the close calls he'd had previously, both aboard ship and in foreign ports. Then, he hadn't half reckoned with the danger, but now . . .

"Imminent, then." She looked to the fire as it sputtered and hissed. "When once I had you not at all, even a little of you now is heaven-sent. Every second."

"Now you flatter me." His smile summoned her own. "But in truth, I feel the same."

They sat in sweet silence save for her knitting till a clock with a musical chime struck six. She was the first out of her chair, gathering her cloak and gloves. He held the door open, and they went out into moonlight and silence.

What he wanted was to gather her in his arms.

CHAPTER

thirty-nine

Esmée was far more aware of Henri than the task at hand. Up the steep stairs they went, his lantern throwing low light in the tower. The first time she'd climbed she'd been slightly winded, but now she hardly noticed. At the top she watched as he hung the lantern from a hook near the giant compass lamp, which held twenty-four lights.

"I've received confirmation our light can be seen by telescope from three leagues away."

Our light. How sweet the sound. They began to kindle each candle, and the tower was soon ablaze. When Henri was away, she'd have charge of them all. Red leather fire buckets filled with sand and water were at floor level. A tinderbox and brass candlesnuffer lay in a tray near at hand, a second lantern alongside it. Plenty of light to read by if the tower wasn't so cold. In summer she might bring a book.

Once the candles were illuminated, they stood by the glass facing the Atlantic. This was their ambition realized, a lighthouse for treacherous shoals and shifting sandbars, a warning of the infamous middle ground that marked Chesapeake Bay. No telling how many ships and lives had been lost there, casting crew and cargo into the deep.

And now she had a small part in it all.

Down the steps they went. She fully expected him to open the door at the tower's bottom as he usually did, lantern held high in the other hand. But instead he set the light on the floor, illuminating her yellow quilted petticoat and his dark breeches and boots, casting the rest of them in shadows.

"Esmée."

Her name, so tenderly spoken, sent a tremor through her, as did his sudden nearness a handbreadth away. She leaned into him, her knees a bit weak, her breath short.

He placed his hand on hers, holding it against his cheek. "I never stopped loving you, Esmée. No matter how far I sailed nor how many years passed, there's been none but you."

His words came slow and earnest, further mending the hurt the past had wrought. Her throat tightened, tears close. What could she say to this? She had no words. Only a tempest of fine feeling, joy foremost. Standing on tiptoe, she shut her eyes and pressed her lips to his. Their kiss was known yet different. Richer and sweeter than ever before. His arms went around her immediately, stronger than she remembered yet just as tender.

"*Ma belle.*" The old endearment hadn't lost its luster. His lips brushed her cheek and then her hair, his breath a tickle against her ear. "Was it you who gave me the riding crop?"

"I confess." Another kiss, long and lingering. Breathless, she rested her head against his chest. "And was it you who gave me the confectionary book?"

"Guilty."

"And 'twas you who blessed the almshouse so abundantly."

"I knew there was a need." He stroked her hair. "I knew it was important to you. And so it became important to me."

She looked up at him again. "Your doing so made it easier for me to come here, not worrying about their lack in another lean winter season."

"If you are as good a lightkeeper as an almshouse patron, of which I have no doubt, then Virginia is blessed indeed."

"Alas, you, Captain Lennox, are a terrible distraction."

His low laugh held a hint of mischief. "Who knew lighthouses were made for liaisons like this, Miss Shaw?"

He kissed her again, stealing her breath once more, his arms about her so warm and enveloping she forgot the cold stone and plummeting temperatures around them.

"I want this night to never end." His bristled cheek rested against her smooth one. His heartfelt words echoed her own unspoken thoughts. "Marry me, Esmée."

The words she'd heard years before now seemed doubly knee-bending as she grasped the enormity of the question. "When, Henri?"

"Upon my return. A few months, Lord willing."

"Then I shall, without question."

"All that matters to me is you will soon be mine at last. Esmée Shaw Lennox."

The wonderment of it stilled her tongue. Could it be? She'd come to the island with small hopes of being the lightkeeper or residing on the island at all. And now this . . .

"We'll redeem those lost years, you and I." His voice held a promise and the solemnity of a spoken vow. "Our future is finally at hand."

CHAPTER

forty

Esmée slowly awoke, her new bed not quite familiar with the sun slanting down through an equally unfamiliar window. She'd slept late, Henri having kept the last watch of the light. Tonight she would spell him in turn, but for now she lay beneath the counterpane and closed her eyes again, reliving those minutes in the tower when their shared passion spurred such sudden, unexpected declarations. It seemed naught but a vivid dream.

His lips against hers, trailing the curve of her neck . . . Burying his face in her hair. *Marry me, Esmée.* They'd stayed in the tower a long time, neither of them wanting to part. And even after that she'd lain awake, the feel and scent of him lingering.

Nay, she'd not dreamed it.

Pushing the covers back, she swung bare feet to the floor. Beneath the closed door came the beckoning scents of coffee and breakfast as Lucy clattered about the kitchen. From the parlor chimed the mantel clock. The fire in her bedchamber hearth gleamed red with a few sooty ashes that needed replenishing. All in good time.

Positioning her stays over her shift, she tied the front laces and dressed in layers as befitted the cold, then donned a woolen petticoat.

225

She unraveled the braid from her hair and began to pin it up, the small mirror over the dresser capturing her joyous expression instead of her usual pensive one.

Lucy's voice pushed past the door after a timid knock. "Mistress, will ye breakfast soon?"

"Coming," Esmée replied, pulling a shawl about her shoulders and pinning it in place with a crystal brooch.

The warmth of the kitchen was like an embrace, the hearth's robust fire making the teakettle sing. At the table were bowls of steaming porridge and a small pot of cream, bread and butter, and peach preserves.

"Good morning, Lucy." Esmée sat down, glad she'd brought over some of Mama's beloved porcelain china.

"And a beautiful morn it is." The maid sat down across from Esmée and poured them tea.

Stifling a yawn, Esmée took in the red-checkered gingham tablecloth spread with care and the shell centerpiece, her stomach rumbling. "I overslept without meaning to."

"Ye look refreshed. Sweet dreams, mayhap?"

"Aye, very sweet." She took a breath. "You shall be the first to know . . . Captain Lennox and I are to wed."

Lucy's mouth popped open, her eyes round as saucers. "When, mistress?"

"As soon as he returns from his next cruise."

"Oh, glad news indeed! Shall ye marry here on the island? The beach perhaps, or the deck of his ship?"

Esmée reached for the preserves, delighted by all the possibilities. "I haven't given it much thought."

Joy seemed to sit at the table with them, the sunshine a benevolent guest as it streamed across the table, illuminating gilt-edged cups and saucers. Unhindered by clouds, the sky beyond the kitchen window was as blue as the ocean below it.

"And yer gown, Miss Shaw?"

Esmée pondered it. She'd brought mostly serviceable garments, leaving all but two of her most costly gowns behind. "Perhaps the Spitalfields silk with the matching shoes I brought. And pearls."

"And yer bouquet?" Lucy, obviously schooled to weddings despite her humble station, looked perplexed.

"Seagrass and shells, perhaps?"

They laughed, trying to take the unexpected in.

"Ye'll need a bride's cake and a groom's cake. I'm guessing that French chef of the captain's could concoct something special."

"I should hope." Esmée sipped her tea, sure it was more likely Cyprian who drew Lucy than cake. "For now we'll keep the news between us two. Anticipate a special occasion."

Lucy's eyes shone with delight in a way they'd never done at the almshouse. "A frolic is most welcome, especially on the heels of a wedding."

An island wedding as opposed to one at Grace Church or the Shaws' formal parlor. Eliza might never forgive her, but Father would understand. A memorable wedding it would be with a crew of sailors as guests, perhaps even Hermes.

"We've much to look forward to. Glad I am to have such a capable young woman by my side to help me," Esmée said with gratitude, and Lucy flushed.

Breakfast done, Lucy set off to get milk from the Flask and Sword's lone cow while Esmée betook herself to the captain's cottage, comfortably close to her own. The shutters weren't closed, nor was the door locked.

Was Henri asleep?

She pushed open the cottage door, and there she found her beloved in a chair by the hearth. Even at rest he emanated an immense vitality she found irresistible. His hair was unkempt as if he'd run his hands through it, his still form draped by a woolen blanket.

She shut the door soundlessly and tiptoed to him, her heart on tiptoe as well.

CHAPTER
forty-one

A trace of perfumed soap brought Henri to his senses. Lavender? Nay, rose. *Esmée.* Her very essence. His limbs were heavy, his eyes closed. Fragments of their time in the tower washed over him like storm-tossed flotsam.

Was he dreaming again?

When warm lips met his own, he came fully awake. His bride-to-be knelt in front of him, blue skirts swirling around her in a frothy mass not unlike a wave.

Her voice held a teasing lilt he'd not heard in . . . years. "I wanted to ask if you'd repented of your bold question last night in the tower."

He chuckled. This was the Esmée of old shining through, the one he'd missed so desperately. "I have not nor will I ever, especially with a greeting such as that."

He leaned forward, holding her face between his hands. She looked as lovely as he was disheveled. But her gaze told him she liked his roguish, rumpled appearance. Drawing back, he reached into his pocket. Taking her left hand in his, he slowly slipped the jewelry on her finger. "I meant to give you this last night. But now seems a better time."

His mind flashed to Williamsburg as she said, "Did you see me gazing at posy rings on the street that day we met in Carter's store?"

"Nay." He brought her hand to his lips and kissed it.

Noticeably moved, she removed the ring, peering at the inscription within. "'In Christ and thee my comfort be.'" She stared down at it, a glitter of gold flowers and vines encircling her finger once she put it on again. "I've never seen one so beautiful, the words so fitting."

"Not too small nor too large?"

"'Tis perfect."

"Even after ten years," he murmured, relieved.

Her lashes lifted, her gaze beseeching. "You've had it all this time?"

He nodded. "It seems Providence was intent on being my comfort before I could have you as my bride."

"Oh, Henri . . ." Emotion made her voice tremble. "Had you brought it with you that terrible day? When we quarreled in the townhouse parlor and then parted?"

The memory had finally lost its barb if not its regret. "I returned to the ship and put it away in the trunk that would hold the letters I wrote you."

A single tear wet her cheek. She dashed it away with the back of her hand before he could reach for a handkerchief. "Which you'll give me on your leaving."

"If you still want them."

"Want them?" She took his hands in hers and squeezed. "They'll be my stay till you return. That and this." She looked to the ring again, more touched than he'd anticipated.

Despite her brave words, he saw sadness in her eyes—the dread of their future parting. He took her in his arms where she knelt, her head resting in the hollow of his shoulder. "If God has brought us this far, we've no fear of the future, Esmée."

They grew quiet, the companionable silence dear if emotionally laden. How would their lives have been different had they wed long ago?

"I cannot wait." She pulled away from him and stood, smoothing her skirts and the comely apron that cinched her waist. "For now I'll practice being your wife."

He looked on, amused, as she added wood to the fire and stoked it into a snapping, popping crimson. Next she took the blanket that he'd set aside, folding it neatly before going into the kitchen. He heard—rather guessed at—her movements as the crane creaked and water splashed in a teakettle.

So this was what wedded life would be like. Not going it alone. Not being surrounded by unending sea and crew. Not hearing the cottage echo. Her presence already infused it with her rose scent and warmth and liveliness. She was nearly his. Forever.

Yawning, he pushed up from his chair and sought his bedchamber, on the opposite end of the cottage where Esmée commandeered the kitchen. There he peered into the looking glass of his washstand, his bristled jaw begging a razor. He'd bathe and change clothes once she left. But for now he'd just ready for breakfast.

She began humming a low tune, and it buoyed him as he made his way back to the kitchen. She looked at home there, her expression serene, the table set for him. Despite his not having told her where anything was in the larder, she'd set bacon to frying and eggs awaited their turn. Toast too. But for now, tea.

"Mightn't you like coffee better?" She looked at him as he sat down and fisted his hands atop the table. "I see you have no chocolate."

"I'll like whatever it is you serve me."

She smiled, a pink tint to her cheeks. His own were ruddy from more than the razor. Despite their longstanding tie, there were a great many things to be discovered between them, both mundane and otherwise. As she poured his tea, Henri bowed his head in a silent prayer, thankful for far more than breakfast.

He'd barely finished setting down his fork when a voice boomed. "Captain Lennox, sir!"

The bellow came from beyond the cottage but brought him to his feet. Esmée looked at him, then passed to the nearest window. Together they looked out on not just the rise and fall of low waves hurrying to shore but a ship's bow cutting through the water like scissors through blue silk, its masts as tall as the oaks felled to make them, heavy guns on two decks. The *Intrepid*'s topsides were painted black, the figurehead of a woman striking.

Their intimacy of the hour before abruptly ended. A full crew of men scurried over the deck in all directions as the ship rounded the island and prepared to drop anchor. The hour had come.

CHAPTER
forty-two

Though Esmée had long grown used to vessels of every size and description, nothing could have prepared her for the sight of the ship that would take Henri away from her. Her heart quailed at the coming separation. The *Intrepid* was one of the handsomest ships of the line she'd ever seen, built to inspire awe among its allies and fear among its enemies. 'Twas a two-masted brigantine, outfitted superbly, guns and cannons on full display.

Henri turned back to her. "I fancy the figurehead resembles you."

"Should I be flattered?" Esmée thought it an odd likeness, dark hair and all. "I even have a yellow dress of that same color."

"Though expertly carved, she's very wooden. You're far lovelier." He winked at her. "You well know female figureheads are said to calm angry seas with their beauty."

"Not only that, when I was small Father told me fairies lived in the figurehead and watched over the crew." Her attention returned to the window. "He was telling me about the ship as it was being built. A maritime feat, he called it. And now yours to command."

"Pray I keep my wits about me."

"Why? You've never been otherwise."

"I've never been betrothed."

"Does this mean you must alter your rule about unmarried crew, Captain?"

"What is your recommendation, Miss Shaw?"

She smiled. She always seemed to be smiling of late. "Why not query your men?"

"Fair enough. This shall, God willing, be my final cruise."

Lucy's words echoed in her mind. Mightn't they marry on the ship's smoothly planed deck? A sort of declaration of her love for him, a way to redeem the past. A rebuke to the foolish girl she'd once been. But for now Henri had hold of her hand, leading her out the door.

Even anchored at a distance, the *Intrepid* loomed as large as the island itself, dwarfing everything except the light. In time, the jolly was lowered and several crew disembarked, intent on the landing.

When ashore, one man gave a little bow, cocked hat beneath one arm. "Richard Farr, sea chaplain, at your service." He lowered his bald head once again. "Miss Shaw, daughter of the renowned Admiral Shaw, I presume. I am an admirer of your father and his coffeehouse."

Charmed, Esmée greeted him just as warmly, thinking how different he was from Nathaniel Autrey. Behind him came several other new crew, lured more by the captain's reputation than the colonial government's lucrative sign-on bonus, Father had said. They regarded her with deference and downcast eyes, obeying Henri's command to repair to the Flask and Sword.

"This is Dr. Gerard, ship's surgeon." Henri made introductions to a tall, bespectacled man of middle age.

He bowed. "Good morning, Captain. At your service."

Two ship's surgeons? She'd thought only Southack would sail. The significance was not lost on her. Henri exchanged a few pleasantries with the newest medical officer before he walked on, joining those en route to the tavern.

"A full complement of hand-selected men," she mused, "including your Africans who form the foundation of your crew. Fiercely loyal, all of them, or so I've heard."

"'Tis what keeps ships afloat and mutiny at bay," he replied, attention still on the ship.

Esmée shaded her eyes, having forgotten her hat, as another figure in the full uniform of a naval officer walked toward them. "Father? What are you doing here?"

Her father embraced her, holding her tight as if she'd been gone months instead of days. His gray eyes sparkled, his navy felted cape expertly tailored. "And do you think I'd be absent from this launch? And the frolic beforehand?"

"Frolic?" She drew back as Henri explained there would be a bit of revelry before sailing. "Of course you must be in attendance, Father. 'Tis your lifeblood, this."

"Eliza nearly accompanied me. She misses her older sister dearly." He smiled enigmatically. "Of course she sent a little something to you. Her gift is in the captain's cabin."

"Does it require tending or feeding?" Esmée asked, knowing Eliza's preference for the outlandish.

"Neither, thankfully." Her father faced into the wind, pulling his cocked hat lower. "Now if you lightkeepers will excuse me, I'll be on my way."

"When you return, we'll show you the tower," Esmée told him with a squeeze of his arm.

"All in good time, my dear. For now I must quench my thirst and be among my maritime fellows." With a smile, he bid them farewell, following the well-trod path that wended through sheltering pines, the new chaplain accompanying him.

Alone with Henri, Esmée watched them go, then returned her attention to the ship.

"You look befuddled, *mon amour*," Henri said.

The endearment brought heat to her cheeks. "After years of sameness, I'm reeling from the unpredictable, however welcome."

He smiled and adjusted his own hat, the cockade a flourish of red and blue, the king's colors.

"Never mind me." She looked to the water. "Your ship awaits."

"How about a tour?"

Her plans for the morning were set aside. "Of course."

Into the waiting jolly they went, his gaze attentive lest she misstep. She'd not been on one of her father's ships for years. He'd had but one that rivaled the *Intrepid*. He still spoke of it fondly.

As they bridged the short distance, they were welcomed by the remaining crew on deck. Esmée stood to one side while Henri greeted the men, who then went about their duties.

She ran a hand along the taffrail. "Father said they launched from a secret location. Why not York's harbor?"

"Our mission is unknown to most. No need to garner undue attention or alert French spies."

He led her over the gleaming deck, walking forward and aft, his expression so schooled she couldn't guess what he was thinking. He opened the door to his quarters, the paneled chamber appointed in blue and gold and spanning the width of the stern. Its large windows faced away from the lighthouse and cottages and took in the sea instead.

He surveyed the bower before them with an amused appreciation, while she was nearly speechless. "The great cabin is fitted up rather like Eliza's parlor."

He showed her several interesting features, including his mahogany desk with brass loops that lashed it down during heavy weather and a china cupboard adorned with pewter and silver. A pleasing arrangement of sofa and chairs were atop a large turkey-red rug.

"Forward of the great cabin is my night cabin for sleeping. Small but adequate."

Her gaze landed on the richly appointed bed through the open doorway. "Hardly a hammock or cot."

Everything smelled of wood shavings within these timbered walls. Sunlight streamed through the stern's span of windows and gilded the dark paneling like gold dust. Despite her cape, she shivered. She'd always found it harsh that ships had no heat other than the galley's cookstove. Not even the captain's quarters.

Henri picked up a box wrapped in decorated paper and silk ribbon from atop his desk. Eliza's gift? She read the attached card.

Dearest Esmée,

A silhouettist came to town recently and amused us. He captured my profile perfectly, so I am giving it to you lest you forget your younger sister while stranded on that desolate island of yours.

Your loving Eliza

Delighted, Esmée held the paper up to the light, astonished a simple paper silhouette could capture so much of her comely sister.

"Shadow portraits." Henri smiled. "Or *à la Pompadour*, as the French call them."

How like Eliza to send something unusual. Esmée returned the gift to its velvet-lined box, wishing she missed Eliza—and the mainland—more than she did.

Henri came to stand behind her at the windows, enclosing her in his arms. "When I sail, I want to remember this." He rested his cheek against her upswept hair. "Your being here with me in this place, if only for a brief time."

Already she felt the emptiness of his going. The slight creaking of the ship and cradle-like motion of its gentle rocking gave her only an inkling of what shipboard life was like.

"How is it on the open sea?" Though Father had told her, she wanted to hear it from Henri himself.

"Noisy. Crowded. A great many sights and smells and sounds on board."

Was solitude as dear to him as it was to her? "Can you retire to your cabin and just be alone?"

"Rarely." His voice held a hint of pathos. "But mark my word, when I do I'll be thinking of you."

CHAPTER

forty-three

Back in the lightkeeper's cottage, Esmée and Lucy began preparing refreshments. Father and Henri were in the front parlor talking by the hearth. Scraps of conversation drifted to her as she placed cups in saucers and fetched spoons and sugar. Her father preferred gunpowder tea. Henri's choice was chocolate.

Her father had brought them several high-quality bricks. His silver pocket grater rested on the table, and she used it to shave some of the cocoa into warm milk, added sugar, and whisked it into a froth with a molinillo. Tasting it, she made a face. Had they vanilla? A few steps to the larder made all the difference. Not only vanilla but cinnamon, nutmeg, and star anise too.

Father's voice held the authority of his admiralty of old. "Here are more details concerning your mission from the governor . . ."

A rustle of papers. Henri made some remark she couldn't decipher. She carried in the tray, set it down, and served them. Henri's appreciation was not lost on her as he set the papers aside and took his cup. Her father poured tea into his saucer as was his custom, while she took a third chair nearest the fire and sipped her own.

Henri winked. "You do realize I'm marrying you for your cocoa making."

"I did wonder," she replied with a smile. "Shaw's Chocolate makes a delicious dowry."

Her father's pleasure was palpable. "Now that I'm aware your courtship has commenced, I shall be unstinting with our cocoa. As it stands, I made sure the galley holds a hefty supply since there'll be no visiting the premier cocoa growers in the Caribbean on this voyage."

"Nay." Henri stared into the fire, dark brows knit together like thread stitched too tight. "We'll bear away to the north, off the Virginia capes."

The pause that ensued was onerous, and Esmée felt a sudden, swift terror. She looked to a sleet-streaked windowpane that reminded her of their slippery walk to the light but an hour before, wishing someone—something—would intervene and prevent Henri's going.

Henri's gaze shifted to Esmée. Firelight played across her serene features, but he detected a shadow beneath. The looming cruise made a dismal backdrop to the evening.

"When shall you put to sea?" she asked, pulling her gaze from the window to meet his.

He gestured to the papers. "'Tis likely in Dinwiddie's correspondence . . . which I am in no hurry to read."

Her slight smile assured him not a whit. They'd not discussed the future in depth except in the vaguest terms. The sea had driven a wedge between them years before. Would it again?

The admiral finished his tea, and Esmée poured him more, trailing that telltale rose scent that had been his delight and undoing in the night. Though the *Intrepid* sat at anchor just offshore, its wintry decks fit for skating, this was not the time to broach the onerous task before him. He'd rather talk Christmas and weddings. But for the admiral—

"You do understand, Daughter, the critical nature of your betrothed's mission."

Esmée surprised Henri with her swift answer. "Intercept French supply ships en route to Scotia and their militias fighting on the western frontier."

Henri nodded, unwillingly drawn into the conversation. "Specifically, intercept and capture the fleet that bears three thousand French regulars en route to North American posts, along with a number of officers."

The admiral took another sip from his saucer. "Beware the newly launched *Raisonable*, a sixty-four-gun ship of the line and the pride of the French navy. Rather, be wary of Admiral Comte du Bois de la Motte and Pierre de Salvert." He rattled off the French names with admirable flair.

Esmée looked from her father to Henri again, her chin raised in a bid to be resolute. But he knew better. The admiral, however, enjoyed nothing more than discussing ships, strategy, and the coming conflict.

Henri shrugged. "One maneuvers. One encounters. One fires cannon. Then each of the two fleets retires and the ocean is as salt as ever, so the French navy says."

Though a low rumbling laugh built in the admiral's chest, Esmée's eyes glittered. "I shall fetch you more chocolate."

The sudden clutch in his belly was more ache. Admiral Shaw continued his tea drinking. The mantel clock struck seven, and at last Esmée returned to the parlor, looking more composed than when she'd left and bearing an entire chocolate pot.

To Henri's surprise—and relief—the admiral set down his empty cup with a yawn. "I shall leave you two lovebirds alone and retire to bed and dream of my seafaring days."

"Good night, Father." Esmée kissed him on the cheek. "'Tis a bit slippery tonight. Mind your step."

He went out, carrying a lantern, while she resumed her place by the fire.

"To our future," Henri said, lifting his cup and wanting to take the worry from her face. "'And if one prevail against him, two shall withstand him; and a threefold cord is not quickly broken.'"

"A beloved Scripture." She raised her cup to his. "Still, I would be aware of the realities of this cruise and pray accordingly."

"I'd rather tell you about the Patagonia coast, where countless but-terflies swarm the decks and rigging." He took a long, sweet drink. "Or the colorful coral beds off of the Turks and Caicos Islands."

"Nay, Henri."

"All right. The realities . . ." He lingered on the pale oval of her face and her remarkable eyes, arguably her best feature. "We could founder in heavy weather."

"You haven't yet."

"French buccaneers could trouble us. Or the Spanish."

"Not to mention their navies."

He took a deep breath. "We could be ambushed. Torched. Stranded. Imprisoned."

"Confined to a prison ship." She shuddered when she said it.

"The crew might mutiny."

"Nary a chance."

He studied the cocoa grounds at the bottom of his cup. "There ends all the hazards I can think of."

"'Tis enough." She poured herself a second cup. "I'd worry except for this. Surely the Lord didn't bring us together to tear us apart."

"Agreed. And your prayers go with me."

Her eyes held that glitter again. "There was a time I nearly gave up on prayer. I prayed and we parted. I prayed and my mother died. But I also prayed and good came to the almshouse, Eliza made a wonderful match, and you came back to me."

"It helps to remove yourself from the equation." All the times he'd wrestled in prayer returned to him like a rogue wave. "I've learned to pray 'Thy kingdom come, Thy will be done on earth as it is in heaven.'"

"'Tis a brave prayer."

"'Tis the best, most honest prayer."

They fell into a companionable silence, solaced by the snap of the fire and cups warm against their palms.

She looked at him pensively. "Tell me about the home you have in mind here."

Setting his cup aside, he added two chunks of pine to the leaping flames. "Before I sail I'll show you the place. If you agree, we can break ground in spring for a three-storied house with southern porches, a great many windows, and a walled garden."

Her eyes lit like the candle between them. Did talk of the future lessen the anxiety of the present? He felt it too, a subtle but tangible anticipation, the future no longer hazy. No longer consumed with missing the other.

"Might you draw me a sketch?" she asked.

At his aye, she assembled paper, a stylus, and a lap desk.

"Alas, I am no artist," he lamented, wanting to please her. Still, he began a fair etching of a handsome house and floor plan, her enthusiasm spurring him on. Half an hour later he had the details on paper, the walled garden with them.

"I'm enchanted," she said with a smile.

His hand stole across the table to hold hers, his signet ring glinting just as her posy ring caught the candlelight. "There's another matter not nearly as lighthearted."

"Such as?"

"If there's to be a war, the light will stay unlit. I want you to return to York. Better yet, Williamsburg, safe from enemy incursion and especially corsairs." He knew all too well the French and Spanish buccaneers, sea rogues who inspired fear and did far worse. "Take your maid with you."

"I shall. Lucy has left the almshouse for good. She wants to remain in our employ." Her face clouded. "So my time here as lightkeeper may be brief."

"Mayhap. For now there's enough crew remaining behind for a guard as well as an ample supply of powder and munitions. Your safety is essential and as assured as I can make it."

She squeezed his callused fingers. "If only I could ensure your own success, your well-being. If anything happens to you—"

"Nay, Esmée." He had hold of her hand more firmly now, and she seemed to lean into his strength. "God alone is our refuge. Our guide."

CHAPTER
forty-four

rost hardened the ground during the night, widening winter's icy grip. By the time Esmée ate her tea and toast, the sun had made a tentative appearance, a boon for the planned frolic at hand. Her heart gave an expectant leap only to fall like a stone at her next thought.

Henri's sailing was imminent.

Lucy began clearing the table, her usual query less cheery. "Did ye sleep well, mistress?"

Esmée set her cup down and stifled a yawn. "Excitement is a poor bedfellow, I'm afraid."

"I slept nary a wink myself, so I up and pressed yer gown and brushed yer cape, but unless it rains ye mayn't have need of it. Yer gown is too fetching to cover up."

"And your gown, Lucy?" In the rush, Esmée hadn't considered Lucy's attire. Did she even have a best dress?

The gentle query still left Lucy shamefaced. "I sold all I had to keep out of the almshouse but still ended up there."

"Well, we must send the *Intrepid* off royally, and I have just the gown for you." Esmée got up from the table and went to her bed-

242

chamber. "With your pale hair and skin, you'll look especially fetching in rose."

A trunk had her best gowns folded within. She'd not even thought to air them properly. The desired dress was at the bottom, lustrous and full, a gift from Eliza. Lucy was slender, and it likely needed alteration, something they could manage hurriedly with a few discreet pins. When she brought the garment to the kitchen, Lucy gasped.

"Fit for royalty, Miss Shaw, not for a girl from the almshouse!" Flushing, Lucy looked to her soiled apron. "Reminds me of the tale my mother told when I was small, complete with a fairy godmother, a pumpkin, and a glass slipper."

"Ah, the French fairy tale *Cendrillon*. In truth, you are the King's daughter, and 'tis all that matters." Smiling, Esmée smoothed a bold wrinkle that cried for ironing. "I want it to be yours."

Tears came to Lucy's eyes. For a girl so young, she'd endured much and hadn't yet lost the shadow of the almshouse.

"Best heat the iron to press it," Esmée encouraged. "I cannot wait to see you in it."

Lucy set the iron in the hearth near the flame. "Now, Miss Shaw, we must see to yer hair. No powder, to be sure. Spirals and a bit o' silk ribbon instead."

"Papillote curls?" They were Eliza's favorite. "I've some tissue paper and a pinching iron."

Lucy came alive in a way she never did when porridge making and pot scrubbing. "Captain Lennox will call ye his beautiful bride-to-be . . . *ma belle*."

So, she'd overheard the endearment.

Lord, let me hear it for always.

Henri had prayed for clement weather. Taken a frigid bath in a discreet cove. Donned his best suit of clothes. Forgotten breakfast. The empty jab to his ribs followed by a fierce rumbling reminded him of the celebratory feast to come.

"Have you any qualms, Captain, about your mission?" his new

sea chaplain asked him as they stood on the Flask and Sword's porch moments before the frolic was underway.

"Qualms?" Henri looked to the *Intrepid*, now at anchor offshore. "At five and twenty I would have been at sixes and sevens. At five and thirty I'm simply wanting it done."

"Splendid. Life's tragedy is that we get old too soon and wise too late, as Mr. Franklin said." Richard adjusted his cocked hat. "As for myself, I am in the prime of senility."

Henri smiled, appreciating his wit. It boded well for the coming voyage. His crew, old and new, was assembling. The festive air was undeniable. Cyprian had raided the slops chest again from all appearances, earning more than a few back slaps and guffaws. Henri and Richard entered the tavern and stood by the hearth, which glowed red-hot with burls of pine.

His sea chaplain removed his hat. "'Tis your lady, sir."

The hush that descended was akin to when a ship was sighted, that breathless, defining moment that determined friend or foe, all hands held captive. Henri stood taller, hands fisted behind his back as Esmée crossed the tavern's threshold with her father. He took her in, from her curled head to her buttery silk dress to her slippered feet. Her hair was woven with ribbon, curls cascading to the shoulders of her gown. A short, fur-lined cape covered her bodice. He spied pearls and shoes with gilt buckles.

When her gaze met his, he was overcome with love for her. And second chances. The emotion shining in her eyes raised such a knot in his throat, he wondered how he'd be able to voice the order to weigh anchor once it came.

The door shut on the wind and cry of gulls, and then the ensuing hours became a blur of delight. Punch. Sweet cake. Unending jigs and reels and country dances. Lucy in her gown had a ready supply of partners, Cyprian foremost.

When the first shades of evening began to gather, the merriment slowly faded. Though she'd danced with a great many men, Henri included, Esmée looked as lovely as when she'd first set foot in the Flask and Sword. Suddenly he wanted to be alone with her, if only to tell her what he couldn't withhold any longer. The governor's paperwork had been crystal clear.

He and Esmée exited the tavern, taking the path that would return them to the cottages. Tonight the heavens were spangled with stars, diamond bright, reminding him of their going up-scuttle atop the York townhouse long ago.

"Day after tomorrow we sail," he said.

Was she as loath to hear the words as he was to say them?

Without so much as a pause, she held up her hand and admired the posy ring. "When you are gone and all this seems like a dream, your gift shall remind me I am indeed to be married."

He came to a stop on the path. Moonlight cast her in silvery light. Tenderly he kissed her. "*Adieu, mon ciel étoilé.*"

Goodbye, my starry sky.

CHAPTER

forty-five

Early the next morn Esmée arose and did as she'd begun
to do every morning, crossing to the window to look out
at Henri's cottage and the lighthouse before dressing and
breakfasting. She'd just finished eating when Lucy answered the
knock at the cottage door. Henri stepped inside with a greeting, gaze
slanted toward the kitchen, where Esmée was rising from the table.

"Good morn to ye, Captain Lennox." Flushing furiously, Lucy
bobbed a quick curtsy before snatching up her cloak to fetch firewood
and hastening out the door.

"I do think she's afraid of me," Henri said with a slightly puzzled
look. "Or my exaggerated reputation."

"She's in awe of you, rather," Esmée told him with a smile, gesturing
to the refilled teapot. "Won't you join me?"

"How about a walk?"

In moments she was bundled up in her sturdiest shoes and cloak,
hood covering the remaining curls from the frolic. A walk would
do her good. She must do something to offset her moody thoughts.

A blast of wintry air buffeted them as they stepped outside, arm
in arm.

"A cold courtship," Henri said wryly, pulling his coat collar tighter.

She held on to her hood. "Good thing my heart is far warmer than the weather."

"We'll take the pine path instead of the beach."

There amid the evergreens they were somewhat sheltered from the wind.

"Feels like snow," he said, his breath a milky cloud.

"Am I wrong to wish we'd be snowbound?"

"Ships are rarely snowbound. But ice is another matter."

Would they have snow for Christmas? She wouldn't voice her melancholy that he'd be away for the holiday. Nor would she ask what they did to observe it aboard ship. Precious little, she wagered.

Now that they were away from the fire, the day felt bone-bitter. They walked on, the path winding in places and often picturesque, a cove here or there, the sky and ocean a shining pewter. Finally they came to a sandy rise where the trees gave way. She'd not been to the leeward side of the island. The view was breathtaking.

"'Tis the driest part of the island, protected from prevailing winds. A fine place for a foundation." Henri gestured to a rock border. "I had my midshipmen lay out stones to mark the boundaries."

"Our home," she breathed, a bit awed.

Arranged so plainly and paired with his sketches, the vision assumed a reality previously denied her. A blessed start.

"We'll bring over sheep and other livestock from Hog Island." He walked to what he called the garden spot, but she shook her head.

"*Two* gardens." The vision was clear as a painting in her head and heart. "A vegetable patch on one side and the formal walled garden on the other."

He smiled. "So be it, then. How do you want the dependencies?"

Smokehouse. Milk house. Laundry. A summer kitchen. They debated, rearranged, and amused themselves by laying out more stones. For a time they forgot the wind and weather and imminent departures. Paramount in Esmée's mind was making their last hours memorable. She'd not leave Henri with a sore memory like last time.

Ruddy-cheeked, eyes flashing, he was exhilarated in a way she'd seldom seen him. "We'll hire stonemasons rather than bricklayers. Put in gardens as soon as possible in spring. I'll leave it to you to order seed and plants from Bartram's in Philadelphia."

"I'll do all I can while you're away. Father has a great many connections and can arrange for shipping of building materials to the island."

Their shared excitement was palpable, adding an element of God-ordained joy to the winter's day. Pale sunlight broke through the clouds, brightening their vision. Their future.

"I've always wanted a stone house," she told him. "Brick is so common in Virginia. This island is better suited to stone."

"Potomac River stone and sand." He wrapped hard arms around her. "And we have the Norfolk house if you develop a taste for the city."

"I shan't." Standing on tiptoe, she kissed him. "Now that I'm here on the island, I never want to leave it."

"I once felt the same standing on the quarterdeck. But not any longer."

"If a ship has a name, then a house should." She thought of all the grand residences she knew across Virginia, including Mount Autrey. None held the slightest appeal.

"Ours will be a humble house. No enslaved, just indentures or those willing to work from the almshouse. Mayhap even a few of my crew." Henri stepped toward the pine path, holding her hand. "There's something else I need to show you not far from here."

He led her to a secluded grove, the pines so thick they nearly touched. Her attention shifted to the ground, where loose pine branches lay as if downed in a windstorm.

"Beneath those branches is a buried cache of prizes, including treasure from a sunken Spanish galleon." He looked over his shoulder toward the lighthouse. "And beneath a floorboard in my cottage there lies a map marking more."

His tone told her what his words did not. 'Twas vast. A king's ransom.

"Of which you gave the almshouse part," she said quietly, the pieces falling into place.

His eyes weren't on her but on their surroundings. Did he think someone might be watching? Listening? "If something should happen—if I don't return—"

Her fingers touched his lips in warning. "Say nothing of the sort."

"You'll have enough for two lifetimes." With a tug of her hand, he led her back toward their house's boundary stones and the open, windswept beach.

Upon hearing the *Intrepid* would sail with the tide, Lucy took the stockings and shirt she'd made for Cyprian and walked to the Flask and Sword to bid him goodbye. Esmée's father accompanied her, leaving Esmée and Henri alone. Likely this was his intent, as he knew how precious their remaining time together was. Supper awaited on the table in Esmée's cottage. A loaf of wheaten bread and Gloucester cheese. Potato soup as well as roast chicken and apple tansy.

"Lucy has outdone herself," Esmée exclaimed in gratitude as she and Henri sat down.

"It has the feel of the Last Supper," he replied, surveying the bounty. "A veritable farewell feast."

"I'd rather talk about our nuptials," she said, putting her serviette in her lap. "Shall we wed without ado upon your return?"

"Without ado, aye." Henri cut his meat as she sampled her soup. "Something small and private. Or do you wish otherwise?"

"I'm relieved, truly. Eliza's wedding was nothing short of a carnival."

Too many guests had crowded into their York parlor, and one man had suffered an apoplectic fit. The cake had collapsed in the heat, and a wharf rat had crossed the carpet, leading to a woman's fainting. Still, Eliza had shone, undaunted.

Henri winked before taking another bite. "You are as bold as your sister in your own right, rowing here and proclaiming your passion for me."

Amused, Esmée spooned her soup. "So you saw through my little ruse and appointed me lightkeeper anyway."

"I know an answered prayer when it comes, however cleverly disguised."

Their eyes met, the flickering candle between them.

"There's a saying you may well know," he said. "'Let those that would learn to pray go to sea.'"

Her throat tightened. "Perhaps we should pray now that we are not long parted. Or . . ." A new idea bloomed, however impossible. "You could take me with you."

"You would sail with me?"

"Rather that than be away from you, though I know women aboard are considered ill luck."

His face took on a studied solemnity. "I'd rather you mind the light. Guide me home. Your father wants you to spend Christmas with him in Williamsburg."

"Of course." Eliza wouldn't travel to York so near her confinement. Esmée and her father must go to her. The twelve days of Christmas leading to Epiphany in January were treasured by them all.

"There's an assistant keeper—a widower and former mariner from Norfolk—who'll stay in my cottage and spell you for your time on the mainland. George Haller."

"I'd rather think about next Christmas."

"Our first married Christmas, aye." His expression brightened. "In our new home right here, Lord willing. At least what's standing by then."

The tick of the clock chafed, tugging at Esmée's heart. She tried to grasp the present and savor its sweetness but already felt it slipping away like sand.

The only certainty about life was its uncertainty. Only God stayed steadfast. Only the Almighty could walk her through life's many changes. And when she felt overwhelmed, like now, she simply had to look back to see how faithful God had been, did she not? The heartaches and closed doors of the past had made the present more beloved.

She set down her fork. "Suddenly on the eve of your departure I want a great many answers."

"Such as?"

She pondered all she didn't know about him or had forgotten. "Your favorite color?"

His slow smile gave her butterflies. "The green of your eyes."

Was he ever at a loss for words? "Favorite place?"

"Other than right here, right now? Corfu off the coast of Greece."

Father had said the same. She could only imagine the beauty. "Best memory?"

"The spring we first met."

"Mine too." She looked to her posy ring, her fingers wrapped around the stem of her glass. "Best dish?"

"My mother's cassoulet."

"Best holiday?"

"Christmastide."

"Best book?"

"The Bible." He leaned back in his chair until it groaned. "Your turn, Esmée."

She smiled, trying not to dwell on the hands of the clock or the candles sinking lower in their holders.

"Best friend?" he asked, taking a drink.

"Kitty Hart. Other than you, that is."

"Foremost wish?"

"To marry you." Her voice held a touch of wistfulness. "To live here on the island with our children and savor every sunrise and sunset."

Their eyes locked.

We've not talked about children.

Heat filled her face as a smile came to his. Children. His thoughts ran ahead like hers, she knew it.

"A good half dozen of them is my hope," he said. "I've always wanted a son to call my own. And daughters."

He took the words right out of her mouth. 'Twas almost too much happiness to hold. Her soul overflowed with it. His gaze intensified. Was she making it harder, their parting? 'Twas not her intent.

His gaze canted toward a window. "'Tis time to mind the light."

One last time. Together.

forty-six

The cry of gulls woke her. For a moment Esmée drifted, eyes closed, before a heady reality rushed in. Today was the day of Henri's departure.

Snowflakes crystallized against the wind-beaten pane in icy elegance. All night the tower had illuminated a white world beyond the cottage, but she felt as unprepared for the cold as the events of the day. The next hour was spent in the usual routines of dressing and breakfasting that were now anything but normal. One look out the window at Henri's cottage, the chimney furiously puffing smoke, reminded her how cold he'd be aboard ship.

Lucy accompanied her to where the *Intrepid* lay at anchor. Men crawled over it like ants, readying for departure. Snow festooned the vessel like it was Christmas morn.

She would be strong. Brave. She would not let him see her sorrowful.

Snow turned the *Intrepid* into a ghost ship. Henri stood by the quarterdeck rail, turned away from Esmée rather than toward her.

No need to make their leave-taking more difficult than it already was. There was little time for it anyway, the holystoned decks a frenzy of activity. The crew was busy obeying Henri's order to put to sea, cutting the anchor and securing it to the side of the ship.

Goodbye, ma belle.

The sentiment was cut short by the exhilarating rush he always felt upon facing the open ocean, the wind a roar in his ears, snow-flakes stinging his skin. The cold drove all warm thoughts of Esmée away, at least temporarily. The *Intrepid* bore northeast in a squalling snowstorm, the waves hitting the ship's black sides and lifting the bowsprit skyward, sending a shudder through the vessel as it rolled then resettled into an even keel. His balance, finely honed over the years, took every pitch, roll, and heave in stride. Even the groans of the woodwork failed to unsettle him.

How many journeys had he made? He'd lost count of them all. He stood frozen in place by the capstan, a prayer for safety and wisdom on his lips, and looked up through white, stinging sleet, barely able to discern the lookout high above. A frostbitten business on such a day. Once upon a time he'd climbed the mizzen rigging and ratlines like Hermes, clutching his spyglass all the way. But now all he wanted was the leaping hearth's fire of the cottage and Esmée's company.

That night in his cold cabin, he sharpened a quill and opened his leather journal.

We got under sail with a snow. Heavy seas.

He would not pen his own feelings about the matter. *If I could have jumped overboard and swum back to the island, I would have.*

Their goodbyes had been whispered in the lighthouse shadows, a dozen lingering kisses in between. He'd pressed his lips to her hair. Her fragrant throat. The little hollow of her shoulder.

And then the next morn, once the *Intrepid* was far enough out that the island was reduced to a mere speck, he'd turned his back toward Esmée, not trusting his reaction. But her memory held, as real and intoxicating as if she'd been standing on the quarterdeck beside him.

All day Esmée had been restless. Had Henri really been away but a sennight? It seemed far longer. Sewing could not hold her. She had no taste for tea. A discarded novel lay at hand. By nightfall, a chill had trailed down her spine that had little to do with the change of weather. It sent her to her knees at sunset, a peculiarly scarlet sunset bright as holly berries. Or blood. Kneeling beside the trunk of letters Henri had left her, she bent her head, hardly knowing what needed praying for.

Lord, You are with him wherever he is. I know not. Please hedge him and his crew from harm and bring him back to me.

Henri missed the sound of birds singing. The drowsy warmth of a hearth's fire. The scent of baked bread. The sigh of the wind in the trees and firm ground beneath his feet. Not screeching gulls or the knifelike wind. Nor tasteless ship's biscuits and endless water—one moment blue and the next silver, always uncertain, at the whim of wind and weather.

But mostly he missed *her*.

Taking up his spyglass, he studied the handsome French frigate at a distance. Till now they'd not come to close quarters with the enemy. Just two false alarms from English merchantmen before this. But now . . .

His soul went still. "All hands clear the ship for action."

At his command, organized chaos ensued, everything scuttled on behalf of the guns. The galley's fire was put out. His own quarters became almost unrecognizable as furnishings were shoved aside and all munitions were prepared to the last detail.

Chasing the French had never been so straightforward. They'd been at sea only a sennight. Now with the enemy bearing toward them, he could nearly smell the powder and smoke. Already his body seemed to brace for the coming confrontation, the roar of cannon and oft fatal splintering of wood. His aim was not to sink the vessel but put the enemy cannons out of action and capture the crew and ship.

Before his steady eye, the frigate changed course. Seconds later the *Intrepid* gave chase. While they bounded after the *Sauvage* on a favorable wind, netting was fitted over the decks to shield the crew from debris, and numerous casks of water were prepared for fire. Cyprian and two other lads sprinted past, strewing sand everywhere. The lookout shouted what Henri had been prepared to hear. The enemy frigate was part of a fleet of five merchantmen, perhaps the very ones he'd been advised were carrying troops and provisions, important personages, and critical documents.

"Ship cleared for action, sir," came the call from the quarterdeck.

He steeled himself for what was to come. A battle fleet such as theirs might prevent an outright declaration of war and save the colonies the cost in untold lives and materials.

Still, despite the mounting melee, Esmée danced at the corners of his conscience, making what transpired more critical than it had ever been.

He swung his spyglass in another direction. More enemy ships amassed over the horizon now, the topsails in plain view. He trained his glass on them, his heart shifting from a dull thud to a roar between his temples. Five ships of war to dismantle. Could there be more? His crew worked feverishly as the *Intrepid* rolled, preparing to discharge shot fit to cut rope and tear sails in an instant.

In the chaos he'd forgotten the weather. The scent of rain filled his senses. The start of a squall? A rainstorm would shroud these ships and hinder the action. But better rain than snow. He shivered, more from foreboding than the cold.

Lord God Almighty, help.

Behind the *Intrepid* sailed a force of Royal Navy ships. Henri held the lead, gaining on his prey until the *Intrepid* was close enough to fire two shots across the French frigate's proud bow. The *Sauvage* heaved to with a great shudder and splintering of wood, its crew frantic and furious. His men gave a loud cheer, which was followed by a shuddering thud as one ball raced past him, making him reel. Another struck the *Intrepid*'s hull.

Through the smoke he could see the *Sauvage*'s main topmast

fall. In that moment, his own helmsman plummeted to the deck. Cyprian stumbled and stared down at the lifeless body, his own face masked in blood. At once Lucy's entreating face flashed to Henri's mind.

"Go below and tend to your wound," Henri yelled to Cyprian as shot poured forth all around them.

Nearly deafened, he barked orders as he sought to stay ahead of the storm and scatter the convoy, leaving the farthest-lying French ships to the Royal Navy. His prize was before him, the frigate that he sensed held the most important cargo, human and otherwise. His gaze swung to the frigate's deck, where a great many Frenchmen had fallen as the *Intrepid* ran alongside her, both pointed north.

"Lie down between the guns!" he shouted to his men on the main deck, mere seconds ahead of enemy shot ravaging them like a hailstorm.

He himself stayed standing while the *Sauvage* became incapable of the fight and its captain surrendered just as the sun sank lower on a now fiery horizon. With a few words, Henri sent an armed party aboard her. He stood by the taffrail, hands fisted behind his back, taking in every detail of the ship he'd just maimed. It was a masterpiece of French shipbuilding for the Marine Royale, launched from Brest most likely, a prize of extraordinary proportions for the British. Forty guns from the upper deck to the gaillards.

In minutes, the French captain faced him—grim, eyes flashing— and burst forth in a volley of fury that even Henri was hard-pressed to follow. Chest heaving, Henri continued to give orders as the British flag was hoisted and announced the frigate's capture. Rain began spattering, blessedly cool amid the heat of the fracas but making the decks a shocking stream of scarlet. Few of his men had been killed, but many were wounded, dulling the victory.

No more, Lord, no more.

A cluster of women appeared, huddled by the companionway. French officers' wives? They stared at him in mute misery, their stricken faces white as sailcloth. Choosing his words with care, he instructed them to board the *Intrepid*, but they hung back timorously as if going to the guillotine instead. Finally they made their way onto the deck, their rich silks and fur-lined capes held up above the mess as the captured officers and crew followed.

Even as the thunderous battle of other ships played out all around them.

CHAPTER

forty-seven

Shortly before Christmas, Esmée left the island in the company of her father and Lucy. They exchanged a cold, choppy journey in the wherry for a somewhat warmer ride in the coach, brass foot warmers filled with hot coals at their feet. For Williamsburg, the holiday season meant greenery adorning mantels and candles on windowsills. The snow that had sent the *Intrepid* sailing still lay upon the ground, half a foot deep now, freezing all but the holiday merriment.

Esmée hid her shock upon arriving at the townhouse and seeing Eliza again. Clad in a sultana, her hair undressed, feet swollen and face flushed, her sister lay upon a parlor sofa, her Angora cat, Dulcet, in her lap.

Truly, Eliza had lost her joie de vivre.

Taking Quinn aside, Esmée asked, "Have you consulted the physic of late?"

He nodded, then confessed as he readied to leave on business, "Dr. Anson is here nearly every day but says till the birth there's little to be done. By the ninth month, women tend to be overtaxed in every way."

In the days following, Eliza fussed continuously over a stray kitten.

Cried at underdone mutton. Rearranged the nursery thrice. Sent the servants to market for this or that at every whim. Pelted Esmée with fractious questions. Lambasted Quinn.

"A friend loveth at all times," Father muttered. "Rather, a husband and sister."

Then and there Esmée vowed to never try Henri so, not if she could help it.

"Did you read my advertisement in the *Gazette*?" Eliza asked her when they were alone. At Esmée's nay, her sister took up a paper. "'Wet nurse wanted immediately, a young healthful person of good character, with a plentiful show of wholesome milk, if from the country the more desirable. Good wages and advantageous terms.'"

"That would be Alice Reed from the almshouse," Esmée told her, taking out her embroidery. "She was brought to bed but two months ago with a son. She's fallen on hard times as her husband is away with Washington's army. Shall I seek her out on your behalf?"

"Is she gentle, quiet, and well-tempered?"

"She seems so."

"And her hair? Is it red? Redheads have a milk-curdling effect with their temper, according to Dr. Guillemeau of France."

Esmée hid her exasperation. "Dr. Guillemeau is dead, and his nonsense with him. Alice's hair is flaxen, anyway."

"What of her child-rearing principles? I cannot conscience the use of Godfrey's Cordial to quiet a baby."

"Rest your mind. Alice cannot afford such." Esmée worked a flower with silver thread. "Would you like me to send word to the almshouse and see if she's agreeable to your plan?"

Eliza affected her most pronounced pout. "I suppose so, though I do wonder what the wags will say when they learn an almshouse castoff is beneath my roof."

"They shall say 'tis your sister's doing."

"I suppose. But what else can I manage? I've had no success with a wet nurse as advertised."

"You'd do well to disregard the wags and dwell on Alice and how you both might benefit the other."

Eliza began a whipstitch on a handkerchief. "Sister, you seem to have an answer for everything and no trouble expressing it."

"Have you given serious thought to nursing your own child instead?"

"I have not." Eliza made a face and rang for tea. "Your bluestocking notions are most unwelcome. I shan't be tethered to an infant night and day."

"Then if you're sure, I'll seek out Alice on the morrow. She's friend to my maid, Lucy."

"Very well, then. I lack the time and temper to take care of it. My confinement is nearly at hand." She rang for the fire to be tended next, as she was cold, despite the shawl Esmée had settled round her shoulders. "Enough talk about mundane matters. I'd rather hear about Captain Lennox."

Esmée took her time answering. "Henri has been gone more than a fortnight in what is thought to be a two-month sailing." She bit back a sigh as she stitched. "Sealed orders."

"Sealed orders indeed. Quinn is quite tight-lipped about the matter. No doubt your stalwart captain is in pursuit of French ships, fooling them with false colors and all the rest."

"He's left me a sea chest of letters." Esmée felt aflutter even voicing it, the chest's tiny key on her chatelaine.

"Letters? From the past?"

"He began writing them years ago when we parted. I find it quite romantic. I've been saving them to read in his absence."

"And will you marry immediately upon his return?"

"'Tis the plan. On Indigo Island by his new sea chaplain."

"Speaking of sea chaplains, Nathaniel Autrey is coming to our holiday party."

"Oh? Is he well?"

"How blandly you ask about him. You'd rather marry a privateer and reside on an all but deserted island when you could live but a stone's throw from your sister at Mount Autrey."

"I would indeed."

Their conversation paused as a tea tray was brought. Esmée abandoned her embroidery, the room's drafts calling for a steaming cup. She poured and added sugar and cream to Eliza's, knowing just how she liked it.

"How goes it on the island?" Eliza took a sip. "You're the talk of the Tidewater, what with your sudden betrothal and being appointed lightkeeper."

"I can only imagine the tittle-tattle," Esmée said. "Keeping the light is all I'd hoped it would be, as is life on the island. Serene and simple and beautiful, even in winter."

"No sand fleas, at least, since 'tis cold." Dulcet jumped from Eliza's lap, jarring her cup. "Father said he can see the light from the town-house's rooftop in York."

"My hope is to help a great many at sea, to shed light—and hope—in a storm or some such calamity. And return Henri to me."

Lord, let it be.

CHAPTER
forty-eight

*L*ucy sat across from Esmée in the Cheverton coach, the liveried coachman and postilion as extravagant as the silver foot warmers at their feet.

"D'ye reckon Alice will take the work, Miss Shaw?" Lucy asked as the coach took a sharp corner. "'Twould be far better than the almshouse. Ever since I got shed of it I feel free as a lark."

"You're such a help to me, Lucy. I pray Alice can come to Williamsburg. 'Twould be a better arrangement for her and baby Alden, at least till her husband returns."

"I suppose a soldier in the backcountry is no better than a jack at sea."

Esmée raised a brow. "By jack, do you mean Cyprian?"

Lucy's chuckle was followed by a flush, her cheeks red as June's roses. "'Tis a terrible tussle to not think of him, Miss Shaw."

"A terribly delightful tussle." Esmée smiled as the coach lurched to a stop before the almshouse entrance. The buildings seemed less stark covered in snow, but the French encampment was widening, dense smoke hazing the air from countless fires.

They alighted and were promptly shown to the trustee's office.

Esmée sat down in an unfamiliar Windsor chair, eyes drawn to the new window curtains and other amenities. Henri's doing? Lucy remained standing by the door.

"What brings you out on such a frigid day, Miss Shaw?" The trustee's condescending manner toward almshouse residents turned to deference in her presence.

"I've come to speak with Alice Reed about a position in Williamsburg with my sister."

"Ah, Lady Drysdale? A timely arrangement." He looked to her purse. "'Tis unusual for you to visit empty-handed, Miss Shaw."

Did he expect a bribe? "Surely your recent windfall from an especially generous patron makes anything I might bring a mere pittance."

His eyes showed surprise, but he merely cleared his throat and called to an assistant in the corridor. "Summon Alice Reed."

Alice appeared in minutes, overjoyed to see Lucy. They embraced, and Esmée laid out Eliza's offer as best she could.

"A wet nurse, Miss Shaw? In Lord and Lady Drysdale's townhouse?" Wonderment softened her wan face. "How can I say nay?"

"You'll have bed and board, of course, generous wages, and company. A dozen servants are in Lord and Lady Drysdale's employ." Esmée paused. She mustn't paint too rosy a picture, given Eliza's moods and whims. "My sister can be temperamental at times, and you'd have the care and feeding of two babies night and day till weaning."

"I think my Johnny would be pleased with it, till he's done with his soldiering. And I get to see my dear friend besides." She looked to Lucy, who wore a wide smile. "Aye, then, and as soon as possible."

Relieved, Esmée gestured to the door. "'Tis snowing again. Best accompany us right away. Lucy can help collect your belongings and your sweet babe."

"Oh aye, Miss Grove is minding him till my meeting with ye is o'er."

"Please give her my regards." Esmée stood and glanced at the clock. "If we leave soon, we'll be in time for supper. You can settle in your dormer chamber across from Lucy's own."

Lucy was already unpinning the scarlet *P* on Alice's sleeve that marked her as a ward of the parish. Esmée felt a qualm for all who remained, but at least they were sheltered and fed, not freezing in some forgotten alley.

In a quarter of an hour they were underway, Lucy and Alice's excited chatter filling the coach to the brim. Esmée held Alden, now asleep and bundled in a woolen blanket smelling of lanolin. As was her habit upon leaving, Esmée looked back at the almshouse and said a prayer for those who stayed behind.

A lone figure in a worn matchcoat and hat stood by the woodpile, watching them. Jago Wherry. Was he remembering rowing her to the island?

He did not raise a hand in farewell.

CHAPTER

forty-nine

ather's earnest prayer echoed in the townhouse dining room on Christmas Day. Only the snap and pop of the fire and the press of wind against the windowpanes intruded on the stillness.

"God, which makest us glad with the yearly remembrance of the birth of Thy only Son Jesus Christ, grant that as we joyfully receive Him for our Redeemer, so we may with sure confidence behold Him, when He shall come to be our judge, who liveth and reigneth. Bless this food to our bodies, and be with those who are apart from this table and go down to the sea in ships, that do business in great waters. Bringeth them unto their desired haven, we pray. Amen."

Esmée's family echoed, "Amen."

Esmée felt a new tenderness toward her father for including the 107th Psalm. She'd read the Scripture over and over again, imprinting the holy words on her mind and heart. Doing so seemed to keep Henri close as she prayed those verses to the Almighty.

"A bountiful feast," Quinn was saying, presiding over the Christmas goose and roast beef with a look of satisfaction. "I've promised the kitchen servants a holiday after Epiphany, as they've worked so diligently of late."

The entire household had gone to bed and then awoken to the traditional "shooting in the Christmas" as boys about town fired their guns in celebration of the holiday. A few random pops could still be heard, reminding Esmée of the time she and Henri had begun to find their way back to each other the night of the illuminations on Palace Green.

"I'm hungry as a horse," Eliza said as dishes were passed. "This babe must be a boy, as he tumbles like an acrobat and swells my appetite."

"You'll be well fortified for our guests later today, then," Quinn replied, the dark half-moons beneath his eyes telling that he was getting as little sleep as his wife. "Not much company, just a few of our closest friends. I don't want to overtire you."

"Esmée is going to play the harpsichord on my behalf." Eliza seemed more her vibrant self. "I shall do my best lying on the sofa and conversing. But how I wish I were up for a little dancing!"

"Next season you will be." Father took both beef and goose, heavily layering them with gravy. "Think of what a year will bring. A wedding. A grandchild—perhaps two." He winked at Esmée. "I want this table bursting with them. Your mother would have been so delighted."

"Dear Mama. How she loved the Christmas season." Eliza raised her fork. "I take care to hang mistletoe in the hall for her every season. Did you notice, Father?"

"I did indeed. A thoughtful gesture. Perhaps your mother is even now looking down from heaven." His eyes misted in a rare display of emotion. "I miss her presence especially during the holidays. As I'm sure Esmée is missing Henri."

"God bless the *Intrepid*'s captain and crew," Quinn said between forkfuls. "How *does* one spend Christmas aboard ship?"

"With as much respect to the vessel as possible," Father replied. "An extra ration of rum, perhaps, for midshipmen, and the best Bordeaux claret for the officers."

Eliza eyed Esmée as she plied her fork with gusto. Was Eliza remembering the Christmases spent without Father?

"You were home for Mama's last Christmases, thankfully." Esmée smiled at him, wondering if Henri would miss the sea as Father did. "And you shall be present for those of your grandchildren."

"A toast to Christmases past and present." Quinn raised his glass, the crystal winking in the candlelight. "And our child, to be born in the new year."

They toasted, Eliza resting a hand on her waist and giving a slight wince. Was she still feeling early pangs?

"Tell me again the names you've chosen," Father said as a maid refilled his Madeira.

"In the unfortunate event it's a she," Eliza said, "we'll call her Ruenna after Quinn's mother, who is regrettably still in England on account of this fracas with the French."

Quinn nodded. "My parents are extremely pleased. As for a boy, 'twill be Philip after Grandfather Shaw."

"Not Barnabas?" Esmée teased. "After our very own papa?"

Eliza grimaced. "I care for that forename as little as I do Mama's."

"Well, my parents liked Barnabas, at least." Father studied his youngest daughter, merriment lightening his usually stern features. "So 'tis Ruenna and Philip. Splendid, both of them."

Eliza looked contrite. "I don't mean to offend you, Father."

He winked. "Is it too much to hope for twins?"

"Pish!" Eliza all but threw her napkin at him. "I'm thankful the Almighty gives most of us one infant at a time."

A wail erupted from the upper floors, drawing every eye to the high ceiling. "Good practice for what's to come," Esmée said of little Alden. "Though I must say he's a remarkably docile baby. And Alice can be a great help to you should you have questions."

"Any news of Alice's husband?" Father inquired.

"A letter of late has him at Fort Edward. But with the equipping of many frontier forts, that may soon change." Esmée didn't know if the missive brought more relief or concern. "He's been ill of late, as have many of the men, under winter camp conditions."

Quinn looked up from his plate. "I've heard there are to be no discharges and no more than two days' furlough granted them, which is of no use, given they are so far away on the frontier."

"Understandable since the frontier is beset with fighting," Father replied, taking another helping of beef. "There's a council of war occurring in New York with many colonial governors as we speak."

The men began debating Virginia's next move under the appointment of Colonel Washington as commander of the Virginia regiment. Good news, that. Washington was a very eligible bachelor, and rumors of his courting different belles abounded, but in truth, being a military man, he had little time for romance.

Esmée sipped her peach brandy and eyed the mincemeat tarts and plum pudding, trying to content herself in the moment, wondering what Henri was doing that very instant.

Thinking of her as she was him?

The holiday party commenced. Esmée nearly struck a wrong note at the harpsichord when Nathaniel Autrey entered the parlor. She was never sure of him, knowing him only slightly. Most men would have been offended by her refusal, but the sea chaplain seemed made of sterner stuff.

Esmée played on as a dozen guests chatted and toasted and laughed. Half an hour passed, and she cast Eliza a beseeching look. Her sister held court from the sofa she sat upon, finally giving a nod for the music to end. Eliza had confided that these select friends happened to be among Henri's foremost supporters. That alone cheered Esmée. A shame the captain couldn't be here among the very people who admired and espoused him.

When she arose from the bench to seek a quiet corner, Chaplain Autrey approached, bringing her a cup of punch. The thoughtful gesture touched her. Had he come alone? Or perhaps he'd needed a respite from the company of his doting aunts? Before she could cast about for an answer, he gave a small bow.

"Merry Christmas, Miss Shaw."

She thanked him and took a sip. "Merry Christmas to you. How goes it at Mount Autrey with your aunts?"

"A far cry from my seafaring days, but I've no complaint. How is it on Indigo Island without a chocolate shop to be had?"

"The lighthouse is an admirable trade. 'Twould seem we've exchanged places. You here and I there."

His gray eyes held hers for a decorous second. "And when is Captain Lennox due to return?"

"I cannot say." A chill settled round her heart. "His orders are secret."

"I wish him well. There's no worthier captain to be had on land or sea." His thoughtful reply bespoke many sailings and circumstances unknown to her. "I wish you both well."

"Your kindness is much appreciated."

"I've been meaning to return to the island. I've a debt to settle there with one of the crew. Soon the spring planting will be upon us and I'll not be able to get away."

"Perhaps Captain Lennox will be on hand to greet you then."

Quinn approached, flushed and garrulous. "My friend! How good of you to come on such a blustery day. I trust you and your kin at Mount Autrey are all well?"

As the men fell into easy conversation, Esmée finished her punch. Looking toward the door the servants used, she said, "If you gentlemen will excuse me, I have an errand elsewhere."

Belowstairs, the Chevertons' townhouse staff was making merry. Esmée could hear their hubbub before she'd made her way to a rabbit's warren of rooms. A butler, two footmen, and half a dozen maids, including all the kitchen staff save the French cook, were gathered around a large table where they took their meals. Piled high in the center were hot cross buns and a half-drunk bowl of punch.

Suspended from the ceiling was a string with a stick bearing an apple at one end and a candle at the other. Bold souls tried to bite into the fruit without being burned, much to the amusement of onlookers.

At Esmée's approach, the men stopped their game and the women fell silent. 'Twas rare for one of the family to make an appearance.

'Twas even unwanted ofttimes. But with spirits flowing freely and a mood of goodwill prevailing, the butler brought her a chair.

"I shan't keep you from your snap-apple long," she told them, setting a basket on the table. "In the spirit of Christmas, I've brought gifts. We are very thankful for the hospitality of this house."

"I daresay 'tis Shaw's chocolate," one of the maids called out, her words meeting with muted laughter.

Esmée began dispensing small tokens of appreciation that Eliza and Quinn had chosen with care and she and Father had added to. Small sacks of cocoa, clove-studded oranges, gloves, pockets, penknives, coins, pins, and lace.

Alice sat near the hearth, Alden asleep in her arms, Lucy beside her. They were smiling as the gifts went round. A sense of fullness stole over Esmée. Mama seemed especially near at such times. She sensed to her bones that Eleanor Shaw would have enjoyed this firelit moment. Had she not said, "At Christmas be merry, and thank God of all, and feast thy poor neighbors, the great with the small"?

Alice exclaimed over the wee bonnet and gown for Alden, while Lucy held up a length of lace for them both in the firelight's glow.

"Is it true, Miss Shaw?" one of the footmen said. "That yer to marry Captain Lennox and keep the light?"

"Ye prattling ingrate!" the housekeeper snapped, appearing in the doorway, her mobcap the largest thing about her. She wiped her hands on her soiled apron. "'Tis no more concern of yers than the garden snake."

With a smile, Esmée lifted the housekeeper's gift from the table and handed it to her, then made her way to the door. "A merry Christmastide to you all!"

CHAPTER

fifty

Their return to Indigo Island was delayed by rough weather. Finally, after two days waiting in York, a small sloop took them across the expanse of churlish water, leaving both Esmée and Lucy a bit green by the time they reached shore. Still, after all the feasting and fuss of town, Esmée felt a rush of elation upon returning.

Treading carefully on snow-slick rocks and steps, they reached the snow-covered cottage. Esmée threw open the door, wanting to shout, "Huzzah!" Cold as it was, it now felt like home, a place of happy memories. Lucy's cat, Tibby, greeted them with a yowl before curling up contentedly at their feet.

She and Lucy spent the rest of the day by the blazing hearth, drinking tea and planning their next tasks. The relief lightkeeper took leave by the vessel that had delivered them, promising to return again, weather permitting.

Esmée's work resumed at twilight. Head and heart full of what Henri had taught her, she climbed the steep tower steps alone. The relief keeper had cleaned the top thoroughly, even filled the compass lamps with oil, so she faced out to sea with a view unmarred by the smoke and fumes that quickly besmirched the glass. As far as she could see, silvery water flecked with foam rolled toward her in an incoming tide. She leaned forward, feeling like the figurehead on Henri's ship, penetrating the gathering shadows.

Oh, Henri, where are you in the deep?

A fragment of a Psalm quickly followed the lonesome question.

He maketh the storm a calm, so that the waves thereof are still.

Father had nearly lost his life in storms at sea. Henri had told her to expect shipwreck survivors—even lost souls—to wash up on shore during her tenure as lightkeeper.

Lord, prepare me for hard, heartbreaking things.

Since childhood she'd been haunted by the fate of the Boston lightkeeper. Upon returning to the island after church, he and his family had drowned when their boat capsized. Father had taken her to Boston's North Burying Ground, where the Worthylakes' triple headstone stood. Too much, perhaps, for a small girl to take in. She'd never forgotten.

"We'll build a chapel here," Henri had told her the day they'd looked at the boundary stones. "No crossing needlessly to Grace Church with all its risks and implications. Mayhap someday we'll even have an island parson."

Recalling it now, she began lighting the oil blazes, the fishy smell making her breath shallow. Each light flared, a small beacon of hope. Tallow candles, set on benches nearest the glass, remained unlit, saved for the stormiest weather when added illumination was needed. With the wicks trimmed, the oil would burn twelve hours and last through the night. All glowed gold, the windows agleam. By morn, all would beg for cleaning.

Though the wind that drove the waves beat upon the tower, nary a draft was felt. Below, the British flag was fully unfurled, its colors striking even in the twilight. She moved to a small desk where the logbook lay open, a quill and inkpot near at hand. The assistant keeper's script was small and tightly worded. She paged back to Henri's scrolling words, a beat of longing in her breast. He'd recorded the weather and wind direction, ships passing, and oil used.

Taking up the quill, she made her own entry.

8th January 1756. Northeast wind fresh.

She set down her quill and bent her head in prayer before the smoke and fumes hastened her down the steps. Taking a final look around the lit tower, she remembered Lucy had supper waiting.

Esmée smiled in anticipation as she approached the kitchen. "You spoil me." Bowls of thick barley stew with bread and butter graced the table, even a plate of molasses cookies. "I prefer molasses to the ever-popular jumbles."

"I'll make jumbles next, though they'll lack orange glaze." Lucy wrinkled her nose as she poured them both cider. "Nary an orange to be had."

"Perhaps the captain will return with citrus. He's partial to it."

Lucy sighed. "D'ye wonder night and day what they're about?"

"Captain and crew, you mean?" At Lucy's aye, Esmée nodded. "All the time. I pray continually for their safety and a speedy return to us."

"How many jacks are left on the island at Mistress Saltonstall's?"

"Half a dozen." Esmée buttered her bread. "Three injured and three able-bodied. The latter are to check on us daily, more so in foul weather."

"'Twill be good to have men about just in case." Lucy ate a few bites, her mind clearly on other matters. "Ye must think of yer dear sister too, soon to be in childbed."

"Any day now. Nor can I forget Alice and little Alden." Was Alice adjusting to town life? Rather, was Eliza patient and kind as her mistress? "Father promised to send word when the baby comes."

"I do hope 'tis a son." Lucy drew a spoon through her stew. "Lady Drysdale has her heart set on it."

Too much so. This was Esmée's worry. As for herself, she had no preference. She would be an aunt, at last. "Ruenna or Philip it shall be."

"Bonny names, both. Fit for a child with a silver rattle."

A silver rattle and an entire nursery overflowing with London-imported toys suited for a growing boy. Carved wooden soldiers and horses but no dolls. Balls and peg games but no miniature tea sets.

"I hope to have a babe o' my own someday." Lucy grew wistful.

"Now that I'm away from the almshouse I might stand a better chance. Is it wrong, d'ye think, to pray for a husband? Does the Almighty care about such?"

"Indeed He does." Esmée gave a reassuring smile. "Remember Adam and Eve? 'Twas not good for man to be alone, and so God made a help-meet."

"Glad I am of it, but I want to see ye wed first. Ye've waited so long and now have to wait longer still." A smile suffused Lucy's pock-marked features. "I suppose I'll soon be calling ye Mistress Lennox."

Yawning, Esmée stoked her bedchamber fire, then drew a chair nearer the heat and light of the hearth. A small leather sea chest, painted blue with flower medallions, was at her feet. She lifted the lid, releasing the scent of ambergris. Had Henri sealed his letters with perfumed sealing wax? The French were noted for such.

Her heart did a little dance as she bent nearer, breathing in the unique scent. Mounds of letters, stark white against the red seals made with Henri's signet ring, were a testament of his missing her. Each bore her name on the outside, penned in his unmistakable hand. She'd savored a dozen or so, each like the richest dessert.

She reached down and picked up an unopened one. Brought it close and breathed it in before breaking the brittle, fragrant seal.

19th April 1749

Dearest Esmée,

Four years. We have not spoken nor seen each other, yet you still seem nearer to me than the sea I sail upon. For all I know you have chosen another who, I am certain, is not a mariner. No matter our past, I choose to remember the good, for there was much of it in hindsight, if not the misspent words between us at the last . . .

CHAPTER

fifty-one

Esmée stood before the looking glass of her cottage bed-chamber, donning her cape before venturing out. Lucy was busy making bread in the kitchen, the earthy yeast scent promising a fresh loaf for supper.

"Yer going for a walk, mistress?" she called, waving a flour-covered hand.

"The sun calls for it after so much dreary weather. But our rain barrels are full at least," Esmée replied. "I shan't be long. I've letters to write and embroidery to finish."

Bidding her goodbye, Esmée stepped from the shuttered cottage into bright noon sunlight. The snow had melted as January pro-gressed, the wind banished with it. She sensed spring. Or was it only her woolgathering about her coming wedding?

With a last look at the lighthouse, she turned her back on it and began a slow walk to the beach. The tide was out, the water so flat it looked like a painted blue floor. She breathed in the salt air, thankful the time they'd been back on the island had seen no tempests nor foundering ships.

Her thoughts skipped forward, drawing her to the boundary stones. They were just as she and Henri had left them. She walked

275

the perimeter now, envisioning the parlor and hall, the staircase leading to bedchambers and the upper portico. They'd decided the most
basic details. Potomac River sandstone. Gambrel roof. Milk-paint
walls. Balustraded verandas like those Henri favored in the Caribbean
that tempered summer's heat.

She took in the view they'd have from the front of the finished
house. A lone sloop sailed into her line of sight, relying on the current
instead of the wind and heading toward York. She missed town not
a whit. Solitude suited her just as society suited Eliza.

She walked back onto the beach, eyes on the sand, the smallest
of breezes stirring her petticoats. Father always said the best shelling
happened at low tide after a storm. The tide was now turning, the sea
coming a little closer. Spying something purple, she bent and shook
the sand from a pansy shell, as Mama called them—or mermaid coins,
said Father. It was round and white with a petal design on top. Sadly,
Eliza had never shared her love of shelling.

Esmée walked in the direction of her cottage, wishing it were warm
enough to remove her shoes. For a time she forgot all about winter,
lost in the pleasure of the beach. A few shells later, she all but ran back
home, as carefree as a child. Into the parlor she went, the warmth of
the hearth nearly suffocating after her outing. Three loaves of bread
sat on the kitchen table. Had she been away so long?

Lucy's expectant face greeted her, a dab of flour on her chin. "What
have ye there, Miss Shaw?"

"Treasures of the deep." Esmée held out a conch shell, pink and
glossy. "If you place it to your ear you can hear the sea."

Lucy did so, eyes wide. "I do, aye!"

Esmée held up another shell. "Look at this scallop, orange as a
persimmon."

"The mantel looks magical with so many shells." Lucy set the
conch, the largest of them all, on one end. "Whilst ye were away,
two of Captain Lennox's crew rowed here from the tavern. The peg-
legged Tomkins and an African."

"I'm sorry I missed them," Esmée replied, removing her cape. "Is
all well on the island's opposite end?"

"Tomkins said his old bones foretell a tempest."

"A tempest?" Seasoned mariners were often able to predict the weather. Esmée was doubly glad for her beachcombing ahead of rough seas. "Two of the most able-bodied men will be quartering in the captain's cottage come any storms. Captain's orders."

"A tempest I can do without," Lucy exclaimed. "D'ye recall the last? 'Twas when I first came to the almshouse. Hail the size of turkey eggs!"

"I recall a massive sandbar lay in the Chesapeake when there'd been naught before. A great many ships ran aground. Did the crew say what needs to be done in preparation?"

"Batten down everything outside we can. Bring in more firewood to keep it dry. Secure the poultry and such." Lucy bent and added another log to the hearth's fire. "I do fret about our men at sea. What's to become o' them in a storm?"

"We shall keep praying for them." What more could they do? "One of my favorite biblical stories is Jesus calming the wind and the waves."

"Can ye read it to me tonight, Miss Shaw? After ye mind the light?"

"A lovely plan. Count on it."

CHAPTER

fifty-two

Esmée sat by the parlor window embroidering, carefully alternating between stem stitch and satin stitch, tiny leaves and vines unfolding before her unwavering eye in different hues of brown and green. Dear Mama had taught her well. Lucy's exclamation was proof.

"I've ne'er seen the like, Miss Shaw. And so fetching a fabric!"

"'Tis silk damask. I'm flowering a waistcoat for the wedding."

"The captain'll make a handsome groom, he will." Smiling, Lucy pulled up a chair and took out her own handwork. "I'm knitting more stockings. Seems like I'm ne'er warm enough even with the fire blazing night and day."

"There's a chill on the island with the wind coming from all directions."

A bob of her capped head led to a grimace. "I keep pondering what's been said about a tempest. Best prepare for such by dressing warmly, aye."

"Thankfully, all is well today. A mild south wind. Clear skies." Esmée looked up from her work to gaze through the glass. The lighthouse seemed to watch over them, casting a long shadow in the sun. "You should come up in the light on a starry night."

"Yer a brave soul climbing all those steps." Lucy busied herself with her needle. "A bit like a jack-tar climbing aloft to the lookout."

"Surely iron steps are better than a rope ladder."

Lucy chuckled. "Those jacks have a bit o' Hermes in them, they do, monkeying to the top."

"How *is* the mischievous creature, I wonder?"

"Livelier than a lamb in spring, no doubt." Lucy's thin frame shook with mirth. "He's missing Mistress Saltonstall by now. Or Cyprian, who had care of him till sailing."

Esmée plied a few more emerald-green stitches, finishing a leaf. She startled when Lucy rose abruptly from the table, jarring it and bringing their peaceful interlude to an end.

"By Jove . . . Is that yer father, Miss Shaw?"

Esmée looked again to the window as a small vessel drew up alongside the pier. Two jacks were tying up Father's Bermuda sloop, favored for its agility and speed. Had he news of Eliza?

Abandoning her embroidery, Esmée grabbed her cape hanging near the door. Lucy was on her heels, the cold air seeded with questions. By the time they reached the water, her father was helping a caped woman onto the main deck from the stern cabin below. Alice? An infant's cries shattered the stillness, startling a charm of finches in the near beach grass.

Esmée's insides turned to ice. With Father's help, Alice—her arms full of two bundles—stepped onto the pier. Her face was pale as frost, one arm jostling a crying babe. Father's strained face only added to Esmée's angst as he took one of the infants. She'd expected him at some point but not with babies. Nor Alice.

"Father, what has happened?" Esmée's voice sounded overloud. A bit breathless.

He simply stared back at her, unsmiling. When Lucy took one infant the blanket fell away, and they saw it was Alden. His fat fists punched the air and his round face was puckered, but he gave no cry.

While Alice and Lucy hastened to the cottage with the babies, Father came to a standstill on the dock. "Your sister, racked from a hard birth, lies gravely ill with the pox. One of the kitchen maids in their

279

employ has died of it. Now 'tis spreading through Williamsburg like fire and has reached York. Quinn is also ill, though not as ill as Eliza. He begged me to bring the babe to you straightaway for safekeeping. You know how hard the pox is on children."

Dismay nearly stole all speech. "Girl or boy?"

"A girl." His eyes glittered. "Your niece, Ruenna Cheverton."

Taking his arm, Esmée kissed his unshaven cheek as she fought back tears. "What a time you've had. Alice looks exhausted too, though I'm glad to see her standing. She survived the pox once upon a time, as her scarring shows."

"As have you and I, thanks be to God." His voice was rough with emotion. "You could have picked no better wet nurse, nor could the Almighty have provided one."

"Another praise, especially now."

He raised his eyes to the lighthouse. "If ever a structure seemed a beacon, a symbol of hope, 'tis Lennox's light on this day particularly."

"Come in by the fire and we'll get everything settled, the babies included. You must stay the night. Henri's cottage is readied for any visitors." Her words came in a rush as one thought tripped over another. "Are you hungry, Father? Lucy can serve tea and bread till supper . . ."

"Less than a sennight old and what a hard start you've had." Esmée leaned over the makeshift cradle, a dresser drawer layered with linens and blankets, and stared into the face of her newborn niece. "You are a beauty like your mama, though I do believe you have your father's mouth and brow."

Ruenna, quiet now after a feeding, blinked up at her as Esmée scoured her porcelain skin for any sign of the dread disease. The first flush of fever. An early rash. Father had said the babe was removed immediately from Eliza's arms at birth and placed in Alice's, a quick-witted act that might well have saved her.

But what of Eliza?

Taking Ruenna in her arms, Esmée marveled at how light she was, more like a doll. Were all newborns so tiny? Alden seemed like a giant at a few months older. Lord willing, he would be spared any illness, though time would tell. Thankfully, Alice had a healthy supply of milk for them both and seemed glad to be away from the townhouse and its shadows.

Esmée carried her niece into the parlor and sat down by her father near the hearth while Alice and Lucy visited in the kitchen, their low voices threaded with relief and joy at being together again.

Father took a sip of tea, finally settling down after his arrival an hour earlier. "I'd quite forgotten how taxing town is when a plague is set upon it. Since there is no pesthouse in all Virginia, the governor's council has decreed a fine of two pounds sterling to be paid for those housing any pox."

"How are your indentures?"

"Keeping to their quarters as best they can. I've closed Shaw's Chocolate and the coffeehouse till this passes by."

"You'll be returning to Williamsburg, I take it, till Eliza recovers?"

"As soon as possible. Heaven knows what awaits me when I do. Your sister is that ill."

She could only imagine the bustling capital now at a standstill. "Have you heard anything of the almshouse?"

"Supposedly the pox started amongst the French refugees, though it might be a malicious rumor."

Not all the specie in the captain's bequest could stave off smallpox. She bit her lip to stay a sigh and studied the baby in her arms. Reaching down, she released the chatelaine from her waist with her free hand and dangled the tiny silver lighthouse in the baby's line of vision. Though she was too young to grasp much of her surroundings, Ruenna's blue eyes fastened on it fleetingly.

"I know nothing about infants," Esmée lamented, returning the chatelaine to her waist. "All I can offer are my arms and a lullaby or two."

"That and feeding are about all a babe warrants aside from sleep." He leaned nearer, voice softening. "She's a beauty. Her father is quite smitten with her."

"Poor Quinn. Glad I am the physic and apothecary are near and his case is slight, if there is such a thing."

"He may well be on his feet by my return. He's always been hale and hearty." Father set his teacup aside. "I daren't say it, but if the babe sickens . . ."

Lord, nay. With no physic on the island . . .

"Oh, Father. Let's not think of such. We'll pray against it." She brought her niece nearer, marveling at her tiny lashes now closed in sleep, the peach hue of her skin. "She's safe as she can be right here. Please tell Quinn I shan't let her out of my sight except when I mind the light."

"How *is* the light?"

She smiled, wanting to reassure him. "I'm settling into a routine. At night when I do lie down to sleep, the light is so bright I wake up at once if it goes out, as it once did when the oil grew cold."

"Have you had to fire the fog cannon?"

"Twice. One of Henri's crew comes from the island's opposite end if warranted to perform that duty."

"Ah, Henri." He stared into the fire, seemingly far away, that wistful cast to his features telling.

Was he thinking of his own command? The days he spent far from hearth and home? His longing for the sea was palpable.

"If only we had the capability of knowing just where he was and when he'd return," Father confessed. "'Tis a risky mission. The future of the colonies might well depend on it."

"Perhaps he's spared the pox. I cannot recall if he's already had it." The possibility he had not sent a new terror through her. But surely all those ports, all those peoples, had made him immune already.

Lord, please, hedge him from harm, and all his crew.

Haunted, she kissed the baby's velvety brow as her initial shock faded over the unexpected arrival. There was little she could do about Henri. Or Eliza and Quinn. Providence had given Ruenna to her keeping, and she'd do her best to love and protect her in the meantime.

CHAPTER
fifty-three

ather left at dawn. He bid his first grandchild goodbye stoically, if reluctantly, before returning the sloop to York. Esmée wondered if he would ever see Ruenna again. If the babe sickened and died in her care, mightn't Quinn and Eliza blame her?

At least the wind and weather were favorable this morn, hastening his departure. Esmée stood on the pier and waved, a sinking feeling inside her. If ever she'd missed Father's strengthening presence, 'twas now.

She returned to a cottage lusty with the cries of both babies. Hurrying inside, she took Alden and amused him with her chatelaine while Alice fed Ruenna. As she listened to Alice recount Eliza's travail, the room grew still.

"'Twas dreadful, Miss Shaw." Alice's face was drawn with worry. "Lady Drysdale had such a time of it, laboring nigh on two days. The physic was called in at the first pains, then the midwife at the last, who said the babe had not yet fallen down . . ."

'Twas all Esmée could do to sit and listen to the details of her sister's travail. Eliza was not long-suffering in nature, yet she'd endured childbirth only to sicken with smallpox. Now, weakened from the birth as she was, would she even survive?

"Lady Drysdale's lying-in should have been far easier." Tears came to Alice's eyes as she finished feeding Ruenna. "It grieved me to see her babe whisked away into my keeping so soon."

"Merciful days," Lucy murmured in sympathy, poking at a gammon roasting on a spit. "How did her ladyship come by the pox?"

Alice's slim shoulders lifted. "Lord Drysdale suspected a kitchen maid brought it into the house. Every morn we were all summoned to Lady Drysdale's chamber to get our orders for the day, ye see. The poor maid was always there too, up till she sickened and died. But every house in Williamsburg seemed to have someone down with it, so who can say how it began?"

"We're thankful to have you on the island if not in the townhouse," Esmée reassured her. "And 'tis my job to make sure you're eating bountifully and resting."

Alice smiled a bit wearily. "My Alden doesn't seem to mind sharing, though it's a bit tricky minding two babes when both fuss to be fed."

They traded infants. Alden was awake and active, Ruenna asleep, her rosebud mouth white with dried milk.

"Have you enough clouts?" Lucy asked, moving from hearth to table.

"Admiral Shaw brought as many things as the coach and then the sloop could hold." Alice looked toward Esmée's bedchamber, where two trunks rested. "A shame we couldn't have carried away the babe's beautiful cradle with its silk hangings. A humble drawer seems sorely lacking."

"Thankfully, the babe doesn't mind a whit." Esmée settled back, wishing for a rocking chair. She was growing used to the feel of Ruenna in her arms, no longer on eggshells fearing she might drop her. That this was Eliza's child hadn't quite taken hold, not when she saw more of Quinn in her tiny features.

"She's a quiet little miss," Lucy remarked, reaching down to stroke Tibby's back.

"Glad I am of it when Alden is nothing of the sort," Alice mused, kissing him on the brow. "Right out of the womb he fussed. I do wonder though . . ."

Esmée looked up. Alice's hazel eyes held a timid question.

"D'ye think Miss Ruenna may have a touch of the pox? I fear for both babes. The pox steals away the young and old especially."

"I pray not." Feeling Ruenna's forehead, Esmée breathed another silent prayer. 'Twas trying enough worrying about Eliza and Quinn. And all of Virginia. What if one or both babies came down with the disease? She looked at Lucy quietly peeling potatoes. Had Lucy had the pox?

"I'm as like as the babies to come down with it." With a little moan, Lucy continued her simple task. "I've had other distempers but not the pox."

"You'll likely be well here on the island," Esmée sought to reassure her. "But if there's the first touch of fever . . ."

Lucy gave a bob of her fair head and set the potatoes to boiling. The aroma of roasting meat filled the kitchen, following Esmée out to the parlor as she moved to a window, Ruenna still in her arms. The gray landscape turned the lighthouse a starker white. Beyond it were two merchant vessels, a weighty presence in the water but toy-sized at such a distance.

Ruenna stirred and made a face. Despite feeling overwhelmed, Esmée chuckled then wrinkled her nose as an unmistakable odor overcame the more palatable aroma from the kitchen.

"I see you're going to cause me a great deal of fuss and bother during your stay," she said softly, moving toward the bedchamber. "Your grandfather was wise to bring a great many clouts."

Ruenna opened her eyes at the sound of Esmée's soft voice. She smiled. Or was it only indigestion? Despite the odor, Esmée's heart melted.

CHAPTER
fifty-four

29th January 1756. Cold day. Heavy NW gale toward night.

Esmée's light was snuffed thrice as she took a tin lantern up to the waiting lamps. Back to the cottage she went to kindle it again at the hearth's fire. Lucy and Alice, babies in arms, looked on, alarm in their eyes. The wind, steadily rising throughout the afternoon, had a particularly sharp, unfriendly feel. It moaned as it whipped round the cottage's corners and gabled ends, pressing against the windowpanes with such force Esmée feared they might shatter.

"First fog and now this," Lucy said before Esmée slipped back into the twilight.

Since early morn, passing ships had fired their cannons, and then the island's fog cannon answered with a sulfurous blast. The noise woke the babies and fretted Alice and Lucy. Even Esmée wanted to cover her ears. But at least she didn't have to man the cannon. Two of Henri's ablest crew, kept from sailing by a recurrent malarial fever, took on the chore without complaint.

Now at dusk, another boom sounded as the wind whipped Esmée's cape and petticoats, snatching off her hood as she made for the tower. With all her might, she slammed the door shut, preserving the lantern's light. Up the spiraling stairs she climbed, thankful for five-foot-thick stone walls, though she still heard the wind's wailing.

Was the wind worsening?

She hung the lantern from a hook and paused to look out on the surly Atlantic. A briny mist covered the glass, but it in no way dimmed her view of the blue-gray swells tipped a frothy white. The surf was encroaching where it had never been during her tenure as keeper, splashing over rocks and through sandy openings she'd thought impenetrable, closing in on the very foundation of the lighthouse.

Her stomach quavered as if pitched by the mounting waves. With a move so brisk it rattled her chatelaine, she began to light the lamps, praying they'd stay on, hoping they'd provide some sense of direction and bearing to any needy ship and keep them out of shoal waters. 'Twas her first storm as keeper. Would she weather it?

Where was Henri in this tempest?

She shut her eyes, caught between a prayer and a sigh. Oh, to have him by her side, capable and uncomplaining, not out on a vessel whose masts might be snapped by the wind's force and founder.

"Captain Lennox is the same in rough weather as if the seas were standing still," his quartermaster had once said in her hearing. "Dead calm."

She didn't doubt it. She wished for a mite of that composure. Her heart seemed to skip beats as she studied the waves, her breathing shallow. A motion below caught her eye, and she spied the two of Henri's crew who'd been manning the cannon. One made his way to the lighthouse while the other stood on the rocks and faced the surf. His bald head was covered with a brown Monmouth cap, a button on top. His hoary hand clutched it to his head lest the wind snatch it like her cape hood. He faced the sea as if to stand down the storm.

Chary, she returned her attention to the waves. As she hadn't heard any tread of steps on the stair, she started when Cosmos, one of Henri's ablest Scotsmen, appeared.

"Pardon, Miss Shaw." His gruff manner made his apology almost amusing. He came to stand beside her, his expression unreadable.

Reaching for the brass spyglass, he grunted his dismay. "A league or so distant is a Guineaman with her foremast cut away. Likely heavy laden with Africans."

"A slaver, then." The very word was bitter on her tongue even as compassion rent her heart. Who knew how many men, women, and children were aboard that vessel, taken by force. She'd once seen a child's shackles lying near the York wharves. Considered the most valuable cargo, children were stashed in a slaver's smallest spaces.

"The lot o' them are better off at the bottom o' the deep than in chains," he said. "The crew daren't launch their longboat even to save themselves. That she's lying bow to sea might keep 'er from breaking up."

Shaken, Esmée turned away from the struggle. Two of the lights had gone out. She rekindled them, fighting a swelling dismay as the wind lashed the tower with renewed force. It had been constructed with a bit of sway for hurricanes. Would it hold?

In a quarter of an hour the Guineaman was lost from view, the night thick and black as tar. Cosmos was still on watch, spyglass in hand.

Esmée nearly started again when he said, "Best return to the cottage and ready for worse."

"Worse?"

"The wind's mounting, the waves with it. There's nae telling what the storm's tide will do." His Scots burr was so thick she stumbled over his words. He raised the spyglass again. "At best, the Guineaman will run aground. At worst, she'll founder."

She looked out again as darkness pressed nearer. "God help them, then."

He looked straight at her. "If the hurricane doesna abate, the surf will be o'er this part of the island, washing into the cottage and even the bottom o' the lighthouse. Ye've got two bairns below, aye? Best bring them to the tower out o' the worst o' it."

She nodded, wasting no time in heading for the stair. But was it wise to bring the babies into the wintry blast? Had she no choice? The fumes from the pan lamps alone were an abomination.

She fought her way to the cottage, pushed and shoved all the way. Once inside, she found Lucy and Alice huddled by the hearth's fire, the babies swaddled and sleeping between them.

"Ye look tuckered out, Miss Shaw." Lucy stood as if wanting to help in some way. "I feared the wind would blow ye into the water."

"It nearly did." Gathering her wayward hair into a knot, Esmée secured it with the few remaining pins. "I come with hard news. Cosmos believes the water will soon rise and reach the cottage. 'Tis best if we all go to the tower."

Lucy shuddered. "Up those stairs to sit at the top with the light?"

"I'm afraid so. When the storm tide surges, we don't want to be here below."

"But, mistress, I'm nigh terrified o' heights. And what if the tower should fall into a heap o' rubble? Would we not be safer right here?"

Esmée's encouraging smile felt feeble. "Warmer but not safer, sadly." She began to move what she could atop tables and shelves. "Wrap yourselves in your warmest garments. I'll take Ruenna and lead you there."

She leaned over the baby's drawer bed, hating having to disturb her. Ruenna slept on peacefully, unaware of the danger. As Esmée picked her up, she marveled what a sennight's change could bring. Ruenna felt heavier, with no sign of the scourge that plagued her parents. Her prayers for both Quinn and Eliza seemed unending, her thankfulness that their daughter was out of harm's way ongoing, and now this . . .

She held Ruenna close against her bodice, her cape shielding them, head down in the wind and rain. Sand and shells stung her face and neck as she hastened to the lighthouse door, Alice and Lucy following with Alden. Cosmos was still in the light tower while the other crewman stayed on the ground, boarding up the cottage's windows and hammering with all his might.

Finally in the tower, Esmée tried to reassure Lucy, who stared at Cosmos and the lit pan lamps with trepidation. They'd begun to smoke badly, sending black tendrils into the air around them.

"You'll need these to cover your nose and mouth," Esmée told them, taking clean handkerchiefs from her pocket. She was glad for the benches where they could huddle together for warmth. Still holding Ruenna, she looked toward Cosmos, who was standing stalwart at the glass but likely couldn't see in the pitch blackness beyond.

"The Guineaman's closer," he said at a near shout above the wind's fury.

Ruenna began to stir, and Esmée took a seat, rocking her as best she could. In minutes Alden began to howl, the tense sound reverberating in the closed space and boxing their ears. No matter what Alice did, naught would quiet him. Soon Ruenna joined in, sending Cosmos down the stairs and out into the storm, whether from the noise or another matter Esmée knew not.

In the ghostly, flickering light, Lucy's face was drawn. Dear, steadfast Lucy who never complained but accepted her lot whatever befell her. Conversation was pointless with the din within and without. Another windy blast had Esmée trimming and relighting wicks, nearly overcome with smoke. Alice was crying quietly and trying to nurse Alden while Lucy soothed Ruenna as best she could.

Hands trembling, Esmée prayed, her words lost to the wind.

CHAPTER
fifty-five

s daybreak crept over the unsettled but vastly improved sea, Esmée felt alone in the tower. Alice and Lucy were half-asleep, huddled with the babies on benches. Cosmos and the other crewman were below. Just where, she didn't know. She stood at the glass and looked east, hoping for a flicker of sunrise, anything to temper the somber silver of water and sky. But she needed no sunrise to see the wreckage below.

Downed trees. Rocks and sand where there had been none before. The cottages stood stalwart though missing shingles. Her gaze trailed to the storm-scrubbed beach. Pressing her face nearer the glass till it fogged beneath her breath, she spied the two crewmen on the sand, paying attention to what seemed to be the hull of a ship, or what was left of it.

Nearly tiptoeing past the women and sleeping babies, Esmée descended the stairs, an eerie calm greeting her as she opened the door. Lungs and head clearing, she stepped outside. On the beach, shells and sea urchins amassed with tangles of seaweed. The air held a just-washed smell, briny and clean, but at her feet was wreckage. Soon she traversed shattered glass, trying to take in all she saw from the shipwreck.

Broken bottles. An intact green hourglass. A small chest. Rigging and wood. Coins. Even a tortoiseshell comb and buckled shoe. An apothecary's cup. She moved in the opposite direction of the men, along the south shore of the beach, her senses assaulted by the devastation. At least the wind and waves were spent, no longer a roar but a worn-out sigh.

"Miss Shaw." Cosmos stood behind her. "I urge ye to go inside. Captain Lennox would say the same."

She looked at him. He had been up all night like she, his bewhiskered face and bloodshot eyes holding a warning. True, Henri would not want her on the beach. She needed to return to the tower and tell the women to take the babies to the cottage.

"If ye've ne'er seen bodies wash ashore, I'd spare ye the horror."

She flinched. "From the Guineaman, I suppose."

"Aye. Expect it for days. Best keep to yer hearth's fire."

Nodding and heartsick, she turned back toward the cottage and lighthouse.

Though the cottage had been spared the storm tide, waves had licked the doorstep, leaving the wood frame wet. The brine seemed to penetrate the damp, cold interior but was quickly remedied by robust fires in the hearths. Lucy and Alice went about their tasks singing, the babies alert and content despite so long a night. Even Tibby seemed to have weathered the worst of it though was thoroughly soaked.

Changing into fresh garments, including a warm, quilted petticoat, Esmée looked at the bed longingly. For now, all she wanted was breakfast by the fire and a long cuddle with her niece.

Holding Alden on one hip, Alice stood by the kitchen window, shoulders bent, chewing on her lip as was her custom when worried. As Esmée entered, Lucy smiled wanly, taking the steaming teakettle to the table. Toast and quince preserves awaited.

"Come, the both of you, and breakfast with me," Esmée said.

They sat and Esmée said a prayer, her words laden with thankfulness and relief even as guilt rushed in that she had the luxury of breakfast with the wreck of the Guineaman beyond their door. But she didn't want to weight anyone else's spirits, so she struck a brighter tone.

A half-smile softened Alice's girlish features. "Yer a world apart from Lady Drysdale, Miss Shaw."

"Supping with the help, you mean?" Esmée looked at Ruenna, who flailed a wee hand, the dimples in her cheeks more apparent. "I daren't think what my dear sister would do if she found her firstborn in a dresser drawer."

They laughed, and Lucy said, "Is it true the ship's carpenter who stayed behind is making Miss Ruenna a proper cradle?"

"He said so, though I'm not sure how long she'll stay."

"We've a great many questions that beg answers," Alice said softly. "My mind is on the frontier and how my husband is faring fighting Indians and French."

Giving a rare sigh, Lucy poured the tea. "My thoughts are far out to sea."

"As are mine." Esmée spread her toast with the preserves before biting into the buttery goodness.

"'Tis the not knowing that nettles me. Forever wondering how they're faring out in the deep. And there's those in town with the pox besides—yer dear sister and husband. I wonder about the almshouse too." Lucy looked at Esmée entreatingly as Alice left the room at Alden's fussing. "I wish I could be more like ye, drawing comfort from Scripture, reading the holy words for myself."

Esmée set down her cup. The Bible lay open on the table, the twenty-third Psalm marked with a length of silk ribbon. Why had she not thought of it sooner? A bit shamefaced, she said, "I could teach you."

"I've tried to content myself with listening to ye read aloud." Dismay shadowed Lucy's features. "I'm too daft to learn, my pa always told me."

"Daft? Nay. If you want to learn, you will. We shall buy a Bible for both of you from the booksellers next time we're in York."

Lucy's shocked expression underscored the rarity of such a luxury.

"In the meantime, you can learn your letters. I've no slate, but we have paper. You can practice writing your name too."

"But what of my chores, Miss Shaw? And now with Alice and both babies . . ." Hope faded to confusion. "Is there time enough?"

"We'll make time. The three of us can manage better together. Alice can even join us if she'd like." Esmée looked toward Alice, who sat nursing Alden in the parlor. Her fair head was bent over her babe, eyes closed in weariness. "Though at present perhaps 'tis enough to be a mother."

"Alice can read but cannot write. She wants to answer her husband's letters in the worst way, but . . ."

"I can help her till she learns to pen her own letters." Finishing her tea, Esmée reached for Ruenna. She wore a soft linen gown embellished with ribbon and lace, the sewing exceptionally well-done.

"No sign of the pox, I pray." Lucy looked as distressed as Esmée had ever seen her. "It strikes fast, it does. Took my brother and mother straightaway." 'Twas the first time she'd ever spoken of it, tears close.

Esmée reached out and squeezed her hand. "Oh, Lucy. I cannot imagine. I'm more sorry than I can say."

Lucy blinked, digging in her pocket for a handkerchief. "I pray this wee one will thrive and reunite with her parents soon. 'Tis a grave task ye've been given."

Esmée felt that in spades. She kissed the bottom of Ruenna's tiny foot as she lay in her lap, then marveled as the baby grabbed hold of the finger where Henri's posy ring rested. Forgetting herself, Esmée made over her as if she were her own, singing an old French lullaby that was a favorite of her mother's.

"*Frère Jacques, Frère Jacques, Dormez-vous? Dormez-vous? Sonnez les matines. Sonnez les matines. Ding, ding, dong.*"

CHAPTER

fifty-six

The next sennight found Esmée standing by the graves of those who'd washed ashore after the storm. Six men, two women, and one child. Their final resting places were hastily dug, but the memory of the foundering Guineaman lingered long. Who knew what suffering had taken place that fatal night? The cries for mercy or attempts to be saved? Not even the lighthouse had aided them.

She bent and laid the silk flowers she'd made atop the sandy mounds. None other could be had in the barrenness of winter. Suddenly the island—home to her renewed courtship and future dreams—held a forlorn, wretched feel. Gray skies glowered, adding to her melancholy. That and no word of Eliza or anyone else left her at loose ends. Bending her head, she pondered the lost souls at her feet. And Henri, wherever he happened to be.

The graves were near the buried cache Henri had shown her. She looked toward the sheltering pines that marked it just a stone's throw away. Unseen treasure. But what did it matter if those who meant most were missing? Coin was cold comfort. True, it provided shelter and sustenance, but not family or fulfillment.

She turned away, the pleasant memory of shelling on the beach tattered beside the wreckage washing up. All she wanted at present was the hearth's fire and Ruenna in her arms. And her questions answered.

How was Eliza? Had Quinn recovered fully? She wondered about Father—how he was faring with Virginia all but shut down? Such outbreaks lasted for months and oft returned with a vengeance.

And Henri. Always Henri. Would this new voyage rekindle his love for the sea? Or was it as he said, that those days would soon be behind him?

She cut into the woods on the path that led to their future home. The ground was still soggy, and occasionally she veered round a fallen tree or branch. Before she reached the boundary stones she heard voices—the sound of labor and shouted directions. Coming into the clearing, she stopped beneath an oak, content to watch the work. One of Henri's crew waved at her.

She came closer, noting they'd built a partial wall. The kitchen garden enclosure? A little trill of delight lifted her melancholy.

Cosmos greeted her, wiping his hands on his leather apron. "We're at work with rock remaining from the lighthouse."

"'Tis a handsome wall that breaks the sea wind."

"We mean to finish that and a smokehouse and such before the captain's return, or toil till we've run out of stone."

"I long for spring and the first supply ship." She looked to the beach warily. She nearly couldn't broach the subject. "Have any more . . ."

He gave a yank to his Monmouth cap. "No more to bury, Miss Shaw. But that doesn't mean we're done. If another storm blows in . . ."

"I understand. You've all been such a mainstay. Captain Lennox will reward you handsomely for it."

"He's a generous man, the captain. If ye have need of anything, we're at your service."

She thanked him, and he returned to work whistling, further lightening her mood. She hastened back to the cottage, where she shuttered dark thoughts and spent an hour planning her garden and taking stock of the seed packets Kitty had given her, mostly flowers and herbs. 'Twas February and Candlemas, the month that required the attention of a gardener more than any other. What had Mama said? *If Candlemas day be fair and bright, winter will have another flight; but if it be dark with clouds and rain, winter is gone and will not come again.*

Weather permitting, she'd prepare her ground and sow salad herbs, mainly Silesia and imperial lettuces, by month's end. But the garden wall needed finishing before she set to work.

A cry arose from the drawer bed. Abandoning her seed, Esmée picked up Ruenna, who quieted at her touch. Recently fed, she couldn't possibly be hungry again. Finding the room cold, Esmée sought the warmth of the parlor and sat near the hearth, a sliver of trepidation accompanying what had become her usual routine. Gently she pulled back the baby's swaddling, searching for any worrisome sign.

Relieved, she placed Ruenna against her chest and shoulder, the warm bulk of her honey-sweet. All that Eliza was missing tugged at her. Each day brought telling changes to a child so young. Though the babe had been here but a fortnight, she was plumper and less wrinkled. Even her dark hair was curling at her crown.

Alice came into the parlor cradling Alden, smiling at them. "Ye've taken to Miss Ruenna like she's yer own."

"You set a worthy example," Esmée replied as Alice took a seat opposite, turning Alden around on her lap to face the fire. "His father would be proud."

"Aye, Johnny would be, as the imp looks just like him." Alice kissed the top of Alden's russet head. "I thank ye again for helping me pen a letter."

"Once Father returns we shall post it." Esmée took Ruenna's silver rattle from a basket and handed it to Alden. He shook it in his fat fist before bringing it to his mouth, the tiny bells tinkling.

"He's about to sprout a tooth. I can feel it on his gum." Alice settled back and looked to the kitchen, her thin frame less bony than before. "Lucy is determined to fatten me. She's baking ratafia cakes right now."

"I thought I smelled orange flower water." Esmée breathed in the delightful aroma coming from the bake oven. "We shall have a pleasant tea party, we three. Celebrate being here safe and sound together."

Alice nodded, gaze falling to her son. "If not for the island—and you and your father—where would we be? My own babe might have sickened and died. Here, away from the scourge, we're blessed indeed."

"D'ye think Alice will be here for a while yet, Miss Shaw?" Lucy called from the kitchen.

"At least till my sister has recovered and the smallpox fades." Esmée kissed Ruenna's soft brow. "My father should bring us news soon, I hope."

Alice looked toward a window. "The weather has settled, God be praised."

"We've much to be thankful for," Esmée replied. "Ratafia cakes. Healthy babes. Spring planting. The *Intrepid*'s return."

"I hope I'm here to see ye and the captain wed." Alice's smile broadened. "Lucy is sweet on one of the crew, aye? We might see two weddings come spring . . . and more babes the next."

Such happy talk pushed back every dark thought, at least for the present.

CHAPTER
fifty-seven

After Candlemas, the weather brightened. Nights were clear and cool, the stars so brilliant Esmée stayed longer in the lighthouse. By day, the sun beckoned her outdoors, though shelling had lost its allure, the memory of the wrecked Guineaman too fresh. But at least no wind frothed the water into a tempest. Some days the sea merely rippled and shone like blue silk.

The garden's stone fence was finished, so she trod the pine path to her future home, reveling in the enclosure warmed by winter's sun. Here she turned the sandy soil with spade and hoe, uprooting stubborn weeds in such a way Eliza would deem her a field hand. Her gloves protected her from the worst blisters, and soon she'd made a solid start. No seed planted yet, but still she rejoiced in what was to come as she returned to the cottage for tea.

Washing up, she sat down at the table, only to rise again as a knock sounded and Lucy went to answer. There on the threshold stood Henri's ancient ship's carpenter, toting a cradle mounted on rockers. He set it before the parlor fire, and Esmée brought linens, anxious to settle Ruenna in her new bed, as she would soon outgrow the dresser drawer.

"You've outdone yourself," Esmée told him, admiring the smooth pine and expertly carved crowns and anchors that embellished it, even the hood meant to keep away drafts. "'Tis a cradle fit for a nobleman's daughter."

"Not to mention the admiral's granddaughter." Hat in hand, he smiled, his grizzled face shining with pride in a job enjoyed.

"Father will be pleased. I expect him any day now."

"I'll start work on the second bed for Master Alden." He left, several tea cakes in hand.

The women returned to the hearth's warmth, Esmée enjoying her hyson while rocking the cradle with her foot. Soon Ruenna was fast asleep, snug as she could be within the bed's high, cushioned sides.

"A wee fairy she is." Lucy passed a plate of currant cakes before sitting down and pouring herself a cup of tea. "Almost a month old, aye?"

Esmée looked at the calendar pinned to the far wall, its numerals in boldface. "Three weeks as of yesterday."

Again her thoughts turned to Eliza and Quinn. Nary a word had come from Williamsburg. She'd expected Father before now. As for Henri, he'd been gone two months. Yet any day now she might see those linen sails she missed bearing down on the island. She turned toward the window in anticipation, expectation fragile as a spring flower inside her.

Sails were indeed in her line of sight. Two sails signifying a much smaller vessel than the *Intrepid*. Esmée set aside her tea, foot ceasing to rock Ruenna.

Father? At last. Did he bring good news?

She was out the door without her cape, so anxious was she to see him, only to turn around and ascertain Ruenna was still asleep and not too near the unattended hearth.

While Lucy and Alice hovered near the open door, Esmée hurried down the path to the pier. Paying scant attention to the deckhands aboard the sloop, she focused on her father. His back to her, he stood by the companionway, where a cloaked figure was emerging. Eliza?

In all black.

Eliza never wore black. She hated black. All the implications came crashing down as Father helped her onto shore. Eliza was in mourning.

Esmée's stomach flipped. By the time she reached them, another realization nearly had her casting up her accounts and left little time to hide her horror. Eliza had stepped onto the pier and looked straight at her, her face masked by a black veil. Just then the wind caught it and exposed once-smooth skin now horribly pitted, her very eyes inflamed. Some pox victims went blind . . .

Lord, I cannot bear it.

Eliza's veil settled back in place. Coming alongside her, Esmée took her arm while Father supported her on the other side. Questions Esmée couldn't ask sat like gravel in her mouth.

The cottage door stood open, but Lucy and Alice had vanished. Helping Eliza inside, Esmée and her father led her to a fireside chair, Ruenna near in her new cradle.

"I'll have Lucy bring you both tea." Hardly aware of what she said or did, Esmée removed her sister's wraps while a clatter went up in the kitchen.

Father kept on his greatcoat, his expression causing Esmée's heart to wrench harder. He looked down at Eliza, who stared vacantly into the fire. This was not her beloved, vibrant sister. This was a shell of Eliza, a fragile, miserable echo.

"Father . . ." Esmée looked at him imploringly, hands spread. Was Eliza listening? "What of Quinn?" Esmée whispered.

He swallowed with difficulty and hung his cape from a wall peg. "Though he seemed to rally, by the time I returned from bringing the baby to you, he was gone."

Gone. Such a small word for such enormous loss. It left her breathless. Quinn—an integral part of Williamsburg, from the House of Burgesses and governor's council to titled peer and attentive host, the pride of their very lives—now lay in the Bruton Parish graveyard. His absence tore a hole in everything they knew. Now Ruenna had no father, only a sickly, grieving mother. Death was never far, but never had it felt so personal since Mama's passing.

Numbly she watched as Lucy brought tea. Eliza said nary a word. Father took the chair beside her while Ruenna slept without stirring at one end of the hearth. Esmée felt hapless and uncertain, words of sympathy catching in her throat. Circling behind her father and Eliza, she took the empty chair by her sister, who was accepting a cup of tea from Lucy's hands.

"Despite everything, I'm glad you're here," Esmée began quietly once Lucy had retreated to the kitchen. She looked to the cradle. Ruenna wore the lace and linen gown she'd come to the island in, a matching cap on her head, the strings tied loosely beneath her chin. "Your daughter is well, thankfully. She has a felicitous disposition and cries little. She—"

"Looks just like her father." Eliza set down her cup with a clatter.

Esmée glanced at their father in a silent plea. He regarded his granddaughter with bloodshot eyes as if he'd not slept in a fortnight. What a time they'd had since they last parted. Esmée couldn't imagine the tears and the turmoil.

Drying her eyes, Eliza returned to her tea with a visibly set jaw, a handkerchief fisted in one hand. She did not raise her veil or look Ruenna's way again.

CHAPTER

fifty-eight

ather and Eliza took Henri's quarters with its two bed-chambers and larger parlor. Eliza made it quite clear Ruenna was to stay behind.

"I cannot have the care of an infant when my heart is broken. Not yet." She'd faced Esmée, the old fire in her eyes a mere flicker. "Perhaps not ever."

With that she'd hastened to Henri's cottage, Father in her wake. Esmée sensed Lucy's and Alice's unspoken relief when the decision was made.

In the ensuing days, Eliza was rarely seen, sleeping the hours away, trying to recover her health—or lose herself in slumber. Lucy would deliver their meals only to return posthaste. The easy amiability Esmée had once shared with her and Alice was now fraught with profound sadness. Even the weather grew stormy, washing more bodies from the Guineaman ashore.

Inking a quill, Esmée penned her uppermost hope during one of their lessons. "This too shall pass."

She wrote it in her light, scrolling hand, Lucy and Alice following with their own quills and paper. Esmée felt a glimmer of hope when

Alice suggested they write down what they were most thankful for, a challenging task amid their sadness. But quickly their gratitude was spelled out.

Birdsong. Cats. The Bible. Hyson tea. Warm bread. Jam. Companionship. Laughter. Firelight and starlight. The coming spring. Heaven.

That night, Esmée lingered in the tower, looking out on the vastness of the water and willing Henri back to her. Ensconced on high, she seemed to rise above the worries of the moment. She pulled another old letter she'd gotten from the sea chest out of her pocket.

7th June 1749

Dear Esmée,

Since we passed the island of Barbados we have had continuous contrary winds. We therefore mostly sailed with set sails and double-reefed topsails.

I have not written in some time. I have realized these letters, which you will likely never read, have instead become necessary to me. Somehow the simple stroke of writing your name brings you nearer despite the miles and circumstances that separate us. Though coastal Virginia fades in memory the longer I'm away, you remain steadfast. I see your eyes in the green of a Montserrat forest, your dark hair reflected in the black-sand beaches, your comely form in the wending hills and valleys of these lush islands. You once said I am all rigging and sails, not a whit romantic. Let this be proof I am not that which you claimed, not soulless but soulful, and still besotted.

She could almost hear him speaking, his penned words reflective of his voice. Longing swam through her in a giddy rush. All the years lost to them still stung like a sea urchin, but she sensed Henri was on his way back to her. Or so she hoped. Eliza had no such silver lining.

Setting aside his letter yellowed with age, she took out a blank sheet of new paper and inked her goose quill.

Dear Henri,

Words cannot express the depth of my missing you. Each day feels a year, each minute hours. Yet I am proud of your service to the colonies and am confident your mission will be a success.

All that has happened since you sailed breaks my heart. I cannot even commit my feelings to paper without spotting the page. Smallpox is making a misery of Virginia once again. Father and I are spared, as we have mild scars to show for it from years past. But dear Eliza has lost Quinn and is even now on the island with me, a scarred widow. Father is with us. I fear he is afraid to leave Eliza as if she might die of grief. I know not what to say nor how to comfort her. She has no interest in her newborn daughter. I pray to help her but cannot see my way clear.

Another heartache is that a ship foundered in a tempest a sennight or so ago . . .

The candle flickered, a glaze of gold before her tear-filled eyes. Her quill dropped and spattered ink. She laid her head against the table, another prayer rising in her heart.

Lord, help me help Eliza.

On the Sabbath, Esmée walked with her father on the beach. The tide was out, the sun making a blinding blue of the water. Signs of spring were taking hold, not only beach grass but a lone spot of color here and there poking out amid marshland and forest.

"I miss Grace Church," Esmée confessed, her arm tucked in his. "It seems strange on the Lord's Day to be absent."

"Sabbath services are suspended till the pox subsides." He bent to examine a piece of sea glass. "Henri told me he might build a chapel here, though he would be hard-pressed to find a clergyman to live on the island. 'Twould be an exceedingly small flock."

Esmée lifted her head to the sea breeze, trying to imagine it. She'd just shown Father the finished garden wall and boundaries of their future home. His approval meant the world to her. He'd also asked to see the graves. She bit her lip when tempted to tell him about the buried treasure.

"Has Mistress Saltonstall returned yet?" He was looking toward the Flask and Sword, whose twin chimneys could be seen puffing smoke.

"Not yet."

"Do you mind if your sister stays on with you for a time?"

Esmée hid her dismay. The sinking inside her turned to shame. She'd never been sure of Eliza even at her best, and now . . . "I thought perhaps she might want to return to the townhouse and the comforts of town."

"Your sister doesn't know if she's afoot or on horseback at present. In her grief she's incapable of any decision making, however small." His lined face seemed more so since Quinn's death, his periwig hiding the silver of his hair. "I was thinking your company might do her good. At the very least she needs to be near Ruenna."

The ache in Esmée's breast swelled. "But Eliza refuses to have anything to do with her."

"Give her time. Grief is a hard taskmaster." He pressed her gloved hand with his own. "Let us speak of more hopeful things. No doubt you are ever on the lookout for your captain. He's been cruising for some time now."

Her half-smile ended in a sigh. "Over two months, in fact."

"Which will soon have an end." His expression lightened. "I look forward to a wedding immensely."

"A wartime wedding, I fear."

"Aye. France is vying for empire not only in America but in Africa, India, and the Caribbean. 'Tis time to see it end. But it shan't end without another war."

"Which means Henri will be expected to sail again."

"Few are better qualified than he."

She digested this confirmation like a sour apple. Of course Henri would be expected at sea with war declared. As a captain's wife, she'd best get used to that. His talk of becoming a landsman was hopeful but unrealistic given colonial politics. Although Henri was no puppet, Dinwiddie was as intractable as a Scottish bulldog.

She finally said, "The governor and his family are well?"

"Dinwiddie's been ill for some time with something other than the pox. And as harried by contentions at the College of William and Mary and amongst the burgesses as by the French and their Indian allies."

"I feel for him."

Her father reached a hand into his weskit and consulted his timepiece. "Let us go have tea with Eliza—or attempt to, shall we?"

Tea no longer held the appeal it once did, but Esmée forged ahead. She must help rally her sister, and even their beleaguered father. "Of course. Lucy has made her favorite lemon cheese tarts. Hopefully that will help cheer her. And I'll open my best tea."

CHAPTER

fifty-nine

he lemon cheese tarts were brought alongside Esmée's tea chest, but would Eliza rouse herself and join them? Ensconced in Henri's parlor, Esmée promptly forgot the matter at hand. Wherever she looked seemed to whisper her beloved's name. There over the mantel was one of Henri's swords with its silken knot, beneath a map of the world. A handsome pipe and silver tobacco box rested on a near table. His upholstered chair, a rich blue brocade with a nautical theme, suited Father well. All carried Henri's distinctive style, his scent. She couldn't get enough of it.

In the other room Eliza could be heard readying herself. Without her maidservant it took considerable time. Father had said she had sickened as well and would hopefully recover. Till Eliza's return, the servants were being cared for by a physic and apothecary.

Esmée looked at the tea service that had been her mother's, artfully arranged on a silver tray. Lucy had brought it over before returning to their cottage, sending Esmée a sympathetic look. Alice carried Ruenna. Wide awake, she made cooing sounds from her basket and flailed her tiny limbs. Esmée couldn't resist leaning over and stroking her dimpled cheek, smiling down at her as she wished Eliza would do.

"I fear I have the look of an unmade bed." Eliza appeared, her unwashed hair in tangles and only half pinned up, sultana wrinkled, eyes red. "And I have no appetite."

"At least try a lemon cheese tart," Esmée coaxed. "Lucy made them with you in mind."

"I prefer a peck of toast." Eliza's gaze swept the tea table and landed on Ruenna. "Why is the child here? She should be by Alice's side."

Father patted the chair beside him. "We are family, Ruenna included."

Eliza sat with a frown. "She is so lively it tires me."

Grasping the handle of the teapot, Esmée bit back a hasty retort and poured her sister the first cup. "My chest of congou is nearly empty. Bohea it shall be for future teas."

"Such an infernal tax on tea, no wonder 'tis smuggled so," Father said, sipping from his saucer. "Lucy brews a perfect pot. She seems a hand at many tasks."

Esmée poured herself a cup. "I couldn't ask for better company—"

Eliza's unladylike snort clipped her words. "Really, Sister, to say a mere almshouse maid is good company borders on the ridiculous."

Father looked at his youngest daughter, his voice even. "Grief does not excuse insolence nor arrogance, Eliza. Not even Quinn would conscience that."

Her chin trembled. "And would you add to my grief with your untimely rebuke?"

"I am merely trying to return you to the world of the living." To his credit, he reined Eliza in as forthrightly as an admiral would a truant officer. "As your father, I would not see you inflict more suffering on yourself or others any longer. True, you are bereaved. Others are as well, myself included. True, you are scarred, but many are buried. As your mother oft said, the best of all healers is cheer."

Chastened, Eliza took a tart. At Ruenna's sudden cry, she started, a pained expression on her unveiled face.

Setting her cup down, Esmée reached for the baby, who smiled so wide her pink gums appeared. The tension in the room, which had been tempered by Father's wise words, ratcheted higher.

Ruenna was the image of Quinn. Dear Quinn. If not for him and his unwitting dinner invitation to Henri in the fall, Esmée might not be betrothed. How much she owed her brother-in-law. The latent realization left her wishing she'd thanked him before it was too late.

"She's a charming child, well content and getting plumper by the day," Father remarked. "Best enjoy her at every stage, as the first year flies away all too soon. Soon she'll be toddling about in a pudding cap."

Eliza jabbed her untouched tart with a finger. "I daren't think of the future. 'Tis too bleak."

"Bleak, my dear?"

"What have I?"

"Need I remind you that you are now one of the wealthiest widows in the colonies, not impoverished like so many?"

She brought her fist down on the table, rattling the china. "Would that I had Quinn and be destitute!"

A sullen silence fell. Esmée hardly tasted the delicious tart. Holding Ruenna in one arm, she resumed drinking her tea with her free hand, careful not to spill any.

Eliza continued undaunted. "I cannot imagine dancing or walking about or playing the harpsichord or anything I used to enjoy. Not without Quinn. He was so many things to me. Husband, confidant, advisor, a bulwark in every storm."

Father nodded gravely. "We will sorely miss him. Have you given any thought to returning to Williamsburg?"

"Nay." Eliza darted another look at Ruenna. "But this rusticated island is not the place for me either."

"You are always welcome to reside at our York residence. Your rooms are much as you left them."

Eliza added more sugar to her cup. "You are generous, Father, but I am foul company at present."

"You'll be in mourning, of course, wherever you go."

"A year at the outset." She shook her head in distaste. "I suppose this calls for a visit to the mantuamaker and milliner, as I'll be clad in black bombazine for an eternity. Not to mention we must blacken the townhouse. Coaches and chairs are to be covered in black cloth, and all the servants must wear shoulder knots of black silk ribbon. Even Ruenna shall be in all black."

At this Esmée nearly protested, but 'twas the custom, after all. Ruenna, thankfully, had not the slightest inkling what she wore. Esmée raised her eyes to Eliza, schooling the shock she always felt at her appearance.

"Being the bluestocking you are, I suppose you shan't postpone your wedding." Eliza's gaze held a challenge. "What say you, Sister?"

As Esmée finished swallowing a bite of tart, Father answered with vehemence, "Most certainly not. She and the captain have waited ten years and shan't delay a moment longer. I mean no disrespect to Quinn, but age and experience have taught me that some matters are best seized at once despite forms and customs."

"'Gather ye rosebuds while ye may, Old Time is still a-flying; and this same flower that smiles today tomorrow will be dying.'" Eliza quoted the old poem dry-eyed but with a bitter taint to her tone.

Ruenna gave another cry, and Esmée set down her cup and shifted the babe to her shoulder. "Shush, poppet."

"Does she need to nurse?" Eliza asked, eyes dark.

"'Tis not her hungry cry. She just had a feeding before Alice brought her over. Here, why don't you hold her?" Esmée made a motion to pass the baby to her, but Eliza held up her hands in protest.

"She would cry louder at my ravaged face." Chin trembling again, Eliza looked at her untouched tea. "Besides, you and Alice are the ones she needs. And once Alice weans her, she shall be in a nurse's care. 'Tis as it should be. Infants tire me so."

"Sister, please reconsider." Esmée returned Ruenna to her shoulder. "She needs her mother most of all, not a nurse."

Father tapped his fingers atop his chair arm, eyes on Eliza. "I must leave tomorrow. You'll have till then to decide whether you wish to remain here on the island or return to the mainland."

CHAPTER
sixty

*T*was a shimmering twilight when Esmée lit the pan lamps. She took up her quill and wrote in the logbook.

9th February 1756. Sea calm. Mild southwest wind. Lamp oil low.

Just that morn, two of Henri's crew who'd weathered pox in the past had returned with Father to York for supplies. She had enough oil for another sennight, or so she hoped. At least till their reappearance. She chided herself for letting supplies get so low.

Standing by the glass, Esmée looked down on Henri's cottage, where Eliza had chosen to stay on for an indefinite amount of time. Light rimmed the windows, making Esmée wonder what her sister did in Father's absence. His steadying presence was missed, especially where her sister was concerned.

Eliza's choice to stay surprised them all. She did not remain out of love for the island. A rustic outpost, she called it. She simply wanted to avoid the scrutiny of Williamsburg and York and so hid here, Esmée sensed, her grief over her pockmarked skin seemingly as great as her grief over Quinn. And there seemed no way to assuage it.

Lord, what would You have me do for my sister?

At a loss, she sat down and looked out the glass at a passing sloop. Lately her heart had ceased to catch over every ship, as if her hopes were fraying. Still, she stared at the handsome vessel till its lofty sails were swallowed up by darkness and seemed no more substantial than a moth's wings.

A half hour more and the tower shone bright as a lantern in the gathering darkness. Once the watery view was lost to her, she checked the lamps again, trimming wicks as needed.

"Miss Shaw."

The low voice nearly made her drop her candle. She spun, gaze fastening on a shadowed figure at the top of the stairs.

Jago Wherry?

He was heavily bewhiskered, his hat pulled low. His right hand clutched a pistol. A chill passed through her. She had no weapon here in the tower, only a flintlock pistol in the cottage.

"Why have you come?" she asked, her voice sounding stronger and more well-intentioned than she felt.

He took a step toward her, and she took a step back, bumping the desk behind her. "I've a need only ye can remedy."

"Speak plainly, sir." Her voice seemed to echo. "I must return to my cottage lest others come looking for me."

For the first time Esmée silently bemoaned Henri's crew at the island's opposite end.

"Not till ye hear what I'm after." Wherry stood betwixt her and the stairs. Caressing the weapon with his thumb, he smiled thinly. "I ken ye have knowledge of prizes secreted here on the island. And ye'll not be rid of me till ye show me just where."

How did he know? A sourness closed her throat. And what would he do if she didn't do as he bid? "Captain Lennox is due any day. If he finds you here wanting to steal from him, I shudder to think what your punishment will be."

Something inexplicable passed over his tight features. The reek of rum threaded the cold air. He'd been drinking, not enough to dull his wits or his limbs, but enough to make him dangerously reckless.

"Ye'll meet me at first light—alone—and take me to where the cache is buried."

She pondered this and her way out of it. Wherry was a canny man. She doubted he was alone in his nefarious dealings. "You're making a terrible mistake coming here and asking me such."

A low laugh. "I've half a dozen rogues and cutthroats in a near cove who consider it a handsome plan, not to mention some well-placed gents in Williamsburg. Beware my mates near at hand. When they're liquored they're prone to mischief. I'd hate to see them make sport with the other three women who keep ye company. Two babes wouldn't stand in the way."

"How dare you—"

"Oh, I dare, make no mistake. Weary o' the almshouse as I am, 'tis time to move on with coin in my pocket and that o' my companions."

Her stomach churned as her mind whirled. How to rid herself of him and his fellows was uppermost, but how to do it with so few of the crew near . . .

"I was leaving the French camp when I saw the captain leave the almshouse one night under cover o' darkness. No one said a word, but afterwards we were all the better for it." He spat a stream of tobacco on the pristine floor. "Everyone knows he's a prize master. Stands to reason he'd hardly miss what's cached right here. Word is he's after the French as we speak, taking more still. Needs be we poor folk have our day."

Esmée shook her head. "I cannot share what is not mine to give."

He all but lunged at her, grabbing her arm and pressing the pistol's cold steel against her temple. "Make no attempt to gain help at the Flask and Sword. We've timed our coming with care. Meet me at daybreak on the path that leads to the south beach. Come alone. If ye play me false ye'll not return to the light."

"Are ye all right, Miss Shaw?" Alice's voice penetrated Esmée's panic as she removed her cape at the door of the cottage.

A baby's cry spared her an answer. Alice moved toward Ruenna in her cradle near the hearth, giving Esmée a moment to gather her wits.

"All well here?" Esmée asked, crossing to the window to take another look at the light.

Jago Wherry had vanished as quickly as he'd come, making her wish their meeting was a bad dream. Her every nerve stretched taut, her stomach roiling. But for the moment Alice was holding Ruenna out to her with a slightly exasperated smile.

"The babe is fat as butter," she said as Esmée took Ruenna in her arms. "And she's been fed, so I don't know why she's cross."

Did the baby have a bit of Eliza's temper? Ruenna's blue eyes were awash with tears, her tiny fists bunched. She wailed as if she'd been pricked with a pin. Esmée made certain that wasn't the case, then cradled her closer, wanting to protect her at all costs.

Alice took Alden from his new cradle, his crying giving way to hiccups. "Just when we got the babes quieted for you, up they pop!"

Esmée took a steadying breath. "Have you seen my sister?"

Alice shook her head. "Lucy served her supper in the captain's cottage a half hour ago."

Taking a chair, Esmée studied the babe's delicate but flushed features, wishing Eliza would come in and console her. As it was, she was so distracted she could give little comfort.

"Would ye like a cup of chocolate, Miss Shaw?" Lucy came from the kitchen, all concern, as Alice excused herself to change Alden. "'Tis so chill in the lighthouse. Your cheeks are red as roses."

"Please," Esmée replied absently, though her supper sat uneasily, her head a-hammer. How would she manage the rich drink?

She studied Lucy's comely form as she went to the kitchen. Wherry had threatened harm to not only her but the women with her. How many of his fellows were with him? Were they even now watching the cottage?

Lucy returned, cocoa in hand. "Has any crew come from the Flask and Sword?"

"I haven't any idea." Esmée looked at her, startled. "Why do you ask?"

Lucy darted a look at the kitchen. "I spied a man coming out of the light. He had a familiar look about him."

An odd relief overrode Esmée's panic. "I'll not dissemble." She lowered her voice as Ruenna squirmed in her arms. "We are in a predicament. Jago Wherry has come seeking prizes."

"Wherry?" Lucy's alarmed words raised the gooseflesh on Esmée's arms. "Surely the old sot's bluffing?"

They stared at each other. Esmée couldn't risk their safety and oppose him. But neither could she betray Henri's trust and forgo the cache, though she was certain he would say it mattered little compared to their lives.

"I suppose Wherry's brought his cronies?" Lucy's eyes narrowed. "From the back alleys of York and the track, most likely. 'Tis spirits that embolden them to act so rashly and defy the captain, likely."

"Please, say nothing to Alice." Esmée heard her singing to Alden. "Pray for our protection and deliverance."

"God help us . . ." Lucy's usual paleness leached whiter. "There's the babes to think of—and her ladyship, who seems half-barmy, if ye pardon my saying so."

This was another of Esmée's fears, that her sister's disordered mind would refuse to right itself. No doubt the Eliza of old would rise to the challenge of outwitting Wherry if she got wind of his schemes. Or if she knew Henri's treasure was pinpointed on a map beneath the very floorboards of the cottage she now occupied.

Esmée's reply died in her throat when Alice reappeared with a smile, obviously none the wiser.

As cups were filled and the fire crackled and Ruenna finally began to settle, Esmée's mind spun. Might she lead Wherry to a false location and let him dig? Say the treasure had been taken when he turned up emptyhanded? But then what? If he became angry . . . if he knew she'd misled him . . .

Lord, a way of escape, please.

CHAPTER

sixty-one

The cold dawn added to Esmée's angst. Rain threatened, the
sea churlish. Sleepless and sharp-tempered, she walked the
path to Wherry's appointed meeting place with leaden feet.
Though she'd considered avoiding him, she sensed he would appear
at the cottage and thereby place the other women in more danger.
So she slipped out, telling Lucy to lock the door after her and not
unlock it till she returned.

Her silent prayers seemed to rise no farther than the clouds hanging above her head. When she spied Wherry waiting among the cover
of pines, her chest tightened till she couldn't breathe. Yet she held to
the Scripture that had come to her in the night, just as she clutched
the captain's pistol hidden in her pocket.

*The wicked plotteth against the just, and gnasheth upon him with his
teeth. The Lord shall laugh at him: for he seeth that his day is coming.*

She certainly felt gnashed upon. Then Wherry was at her back
with what she assumed was a primed, loaded weapon and a shovel.
He spoke little, his bloodshot gaze and shambling gait unnerving
her further. When they passed the copse of trees where Henri had
carefully stored his cache, she felt a momentary qualm. Should she

317

just give Wherry what he wanted? *Nay*, came a bone-deep conviction. She led him on down the path as far from the women and infants as possible.

"Hasten your steps, Miss Shaw." The gravelly voice was thick with drink. "I've no time to waste."

A sharp jab to the small of her back stole the last of her composure. She whirled on him, legs atremble beneath her quilted petticoats. His surprise flared as she thrust her own pistol in his leering face.

"Shall we have it out betwixt us first?" Her voice shook with heat. "I'm done with your threatening and demands."

"A foolish move." Their pistols were pointed at each other, only his hand was steadier. "My men are trailing us. If I say the word, ye'll have more than me to reckon with."

Could she believe him? She'd neither seen nor sensed anyone else. In the trice of her ruminating, he wrested the gun from her grasp, twisting her wrist and fueling her ire.

"Thou art unfit for any place but hell." She spat out the Shakespearean slur even as she prayed for deliverance.

On they went, two weapons now trained upon her. She stopped atop a dune. The storm surge had swept this side of the island, doing far more damage than to their own rocky point. When she gestured to a patch of sandy ground, he tossed aside the weapons and began digging, a mistrustful eye upon her.

Wrist aching, she watched him, standing well apart from his feverish work. At a gull's hollow cry, she scanned the surrounding brush and trees, searching, sifting. Wherry would soon tire of his fruitless search and turn on her.

Should she run?

Sleeplessness burned her eyes and left her cumbersome. A flicker of movement in the trees sent another tremor of alarm through her. His cronies? *Someone* was there, crouched just beyond a tangle of seagrass.

Wherry threw down his shovel in disgust, a great mound of sand the proof he'd been digging for naught. "Ye've fooled me, and there's but one fix for it." Taking up the pistols, he waved her on to walk in front of him again. "Mayhap yer of more value to me than buried treasure. What would yer admiral father give, I wonder, to see ye safely returned?"

In minutes they were alongshore in the island's smallest, most private cove, perfect for a hideout. Esmée stared at a sleek jolly manned by half a dozen crew. So Wherry hadn't lied to her. The men watched their approach, their wariness turning to outright disgust at seeing them emptyhanded. Had they truly expected chests of specie?

Esmée slowed her pace, only to be shoved from behind by Wherry, both pistols waving as he unleashed a string of epithets fit for the basest waterfront tavern. Another man grunted a few words to him from the jolly as they readied to push off.

With her aboard.

The realization ricocheted around her head but gave no motion to her leaden feet. She was shaking now, and another shove from Wherry left her stumbling in the sand. Rain began pelting down, a grumble of thunder overhead. Where would they take her? What demands would they make of her father?

Oh, heavenly Father, help me!

One buckled shoe came off in deep sand, and she bent to right it. At that moment, an ear-splitting crack sounded. Something whistled past her head, jarring her with its nearness. Wherry's pained howl stirred her to action. Grabbing up her skirts, she abandoned her shoe and started toward the nearest trees.

Another gunshot came, this one aimed at the shallop. A third shot sent a man overboard with a splash. Wherry's crew scrambled in all directions to take cover even as they put out to sea. Dangerously light-headed, Esmée looked on from where she crouched behind a thick pine. Wherry got to his feet, scarlet streaming in wide ribbons down his shirtfront. Another shot took off the club of his queued hair. He weaved atop the sand, taking a few staggering steps toward the jolly before collapsing on the beach.

Who had been the answer to her prayer?

Spent gunpowder burnt Esmée's nostrils as it carried on the damp air. An answering shot from the jolly hit a near tree, splintering the bark. The vessel withdrew into choppy water, minus two men.

"Miss Shaw!" A vaguely familiar voice bade her turn round even as the rustle of brush announced a man's approach.

Nathaniel Autrey? He stepped free of the beach grass, staring at her as if to ascertain she was unhurt.

She put a hand to her throat. "I've never been gladder to see someone!"

"Would you had said such upon my pursuit of you." His wry smile further reassured her as much as the smoking weapon in his right hand.

With a choked laugh, she stood on unsteady legs as he helped her to her feet. "You are unscathed, I hope, but understandably shaken." At her nod, his attention returned to the beach where Wherry lay. "God forgive me, but I could see no other way to aid you but take him down. Clearly his intent was to do you harm."

"He was bent on mischief. He threatened to harm the women and children." She leaned against the pine's trunk, winded. "However did you happen to be here at such a remarkable time?"

"Uncanny indeed. The Almighty gets all the credit. I was merely intent on paying a debt, the one I mentioned when I last saw you in the Drysdales' parlor over Christmas." He returned his gun to its holder beneath his frock coat. "I came over with the crew you sent to the mainland for lamp oil. And I bring good news from a trusted source. Captain Lennox's return is imminent, so I hoped to see him again as well."

Esmée's spirits took wing at the latter. *Henri home. Henri here.* 'Twas he who'm she'd be most glad to see when all was said and done.

Footsteps turned her on edge again till Cosmos and another crew member appeared.

"We heard the commotion from the tavern." Cosmos regarded them, alarm stitched into his bewhiskered face beneath his Monmouth cap. "We came as quick as we could."

"Which ain't quick enough given the state I'm in," the florid-faced master's mate muttered in apology as he rubbed his gout-stricken leg. "Needs be we see to burying the bilge-swilling blackguard. Or take 'im out in the captain's jolly at high tide."

All eyes turned to Wherry, who was clearly dead. Esmée's stomach twisted, and she swallowed hard even as Nathaniel took her elbow. "I'll return you to your end of the island," he said. "And I shall stay till the remaining crew at the Flask and Sword—or Captain Lennox—return."

CHAPTER
sixty-two

"You must stay on in the captain's cottage," Esmée told Nathaniel as they walked the path toward the lighthouse, far calmer than when he'd found her on the beach. "But first I must remove my dear sister."

"I suppose it can't be helped," he remarked, hat in hand. "I heard Lord Drysdale has been buried. A better man I've not found in all Virginia."

"Truly. We miss him sorely." Tears threatened at Quinn's mention, but she blinked them back. "Having you near will be a great relief to us all. But will it tax your aunts having you away? Mount Autrey needs you, surely."

"Mount Autrey and my aunts survived a great many years without me, including the pox. A few days or even a fortnight or longer won't change that." He looked toward the cottage in question. "Though I am loath to displace her ladyship."

"Think no more of it, please. We shall all be glad of your presence."

"I'll wait here by the pier then," he told her.

Esmée found Eliza sitting by the hearth's fire in her sultana, not abed as she so often was but still marked by the same forlorn expression. The remaining sores on her face were fading, but the scarring would remain. Near at hand was a Madeira bottle and cup. With a tick of alarm Esmée saw that it was half-empty.

"I'm happy to see you up." Esmée's voice sounded as washed-out as all the rest of her. "We've just come through a calamity, which I'll soon explain. For now, Chaplain Autrey is standing out in the cold and needs to lodge here in the captain's quarters while you return to us."

"Return? There's hardly room!"

"We've trundle beds in a pinch."

Eliza jumped to her feet. At once her hands flew to her face, revealing the gist of her thoughts. "But I cannot be seen. He will—I look a fright. I am not the woman he remembers."

"You are far more than your appearance, Sister." Esmée's words were soft. "He knows you're grieving and is thoughtfully waiting by the water till we move you."

Eliza hurried across the room and reached for her veiled bonnet and her cape. "I have no wish to exchange words with him so shall rush past straightaway."

"I'll have Lucy bring your belongings over then." Esmée took a poker, built up the fire, and added another log before following her.

In a quarter of an hour, the exchange was made, the former sea chaplain ensconced by his own fire with a book from the captain's library: *Travels into Several Remote Nations of the World.*

"Promise me you won't invite him to supper." Eliza was more animated than Esmée had recently seen her. "Though the chaplain was a friend to Quinn, I fear facing him would simply magnify my grief."

"You grieve more than a husband." Esmée saw past the ruse to the real heart of the matter. "You grieve your health." *And your beauty.*

Tears sprang to Eliza's eyes. They were alone in the parlor, Lucy and Alice in the kitchen with Alden amid a cacophony of crockery and cooing. Wherever Eliza was, they went elsewhere, not daring to trespass on her quicksilver moods. Ruenna slept in her cradle near the hearth, oblivious to her mother's angst.

"Tell me, Sister." Eliza's voice held a rare fragility. "Why is it the pox left you only lightly scarred but disfigured me completely? I feel naught but an abomination."

"The pox did not touch your soul," Esmée returned quietly. "Nor your spirit. Not unless you let it."

Eliza's chin firmed. "You evade the question."

"I was but a child when the pox struck—and lightly at that. I cannot say why it affected you differently as a woman."

"So you agree I am unsightly and unfit for company."

"I said nothing of the sort." Esmée gestured to a chair. Exhausted, she took the one opposite and said as much to herself as to Eliza, "Please sit and becalm yourself."

Eliza sat, shoulders hunched, her filmy veil hiding her features. "I recall a sermon Reverend Dawson gave before Quinn was taken from me, about prosperous worldlings being an affront to God. Do you think my pride—counting the world my darling—brought me low?"

"I have no cause to throw stones, Sister, not when my own ruinous vanity nearly cost me a future with Henri." This was said with such conviction Eliza fell silent. Esmée looked at her earnestly. "Please remove your bonnet so I can see your still-lovely face."

Though she could not see her sister's withering look, she felt it.

"One miracle at a time," Eliza retorted. "Is it not enough I am not abed but in a chair?"

"Would you care for tea?"

"Tea? Bah! Brandy is what I need."

"I have none," Esmée replied. She would not volunteer Henri's supply.

"Even arrack punch will do."

The smell of Madeira hung heavily about Eliza. "How will you explain to Captain Lennox your emptying his cellar?" Esmée asked.

This brought a momentary hush. "Spirits help temper my grief."

Esmée shook her head. "The Almighty is a far better tonic and leaves you with no headache after or any apologizing to do."

Eliza pulled off both bonnet and veil, revealing a tumbling mass of curls. "Is that Ruenna fussing?"

Esmée had hardly noticed, given their heated exchange. Stifling the urge to reach for Ruenna, she waited. Ruenna's cries grew more shrill. Alice appeared from the kitchen, but Esmée stilled her with a slight shake of her head. Casting Esmée a murderous look, Eliza got up and walked stiffly to the cradle.

Esmée held her breath. *Lord, be in this moment, please.*

"You mean to make a mother of me." Eliza picked Ruenna up and held her at arm's length. Alarmingly so.

Esmée had to lace her hands in her lap to keep from taking the babe. "Be at your ease. Ruenna loves to be held, talked to, and sung to."

Eliza cradled her awkwardly. "I am fresh out of lullabies."

"Remember the one Mama used to sing? 'Over the Hills and Far Away'?"

A softening touched Eliza's ravaged face. Esmée began to hum, focusing her gaze on the lighthouse beyond the window. In seconds Eliza began humming along with her, then gave way to song. Ruenna looked at her mother, quieting at the sound of her singing voice, which had always been lovely.

Spying a single tear coursing down Eliza's cheek, Esmée, worn to a thread by the morning's events, was nearly undone. The tear trailed to Eliza's chin, fell, and spotted the baby's linen gown.

They moved on to another lullaby, "Cradle Song," and for a few fleeting moments it seemed their beloved mother drew near.

And then, just as abruptly, Eliza swiped another tear away, the tender moment banished. "Why has Nathaniel Autrey come?"

Esmée took a breath, and the story poured forth.

Eliza, for a few rapt minutes, forgot her own misery. "That odious Wherry? From the almshouse? How fortuitous he was dispatched by the sea chaplain. I shudder to think what Captain Lennox would have done to him."

"Praise God we are safe." Esmée moistened dry lips and imagined Henri's reaction. "Now if the captain would return . . ."

Ruenna squirmed and gave a little cry, shattering Eliza's composure. She held the baby out to Esmée with a stony expression that signified she was done. Esmée took her niece, wanting nothing more than to retreat to her bedchamber and sleep till the lighthouse needed tending.

"I do wonder how Father is faring." Esmée placed Ruenna on her shoulder, patting the baby's back. In such times she missed Father fiercely.

"I suppose he'll soon return and want to take me back to the mainland. But I have no desire to return to Williamsburg. Not yet."

"You are always welcome here." Weary as Eliza made her, she was her beloved sister, after all. "I shouldn't want you to return to the townhouse till you and Ruenna are ready."

Eliza toyed with the bonnet in her lap. "Though I once called your island rustic, I rather like the seclusion. At least in my grief. And I must admit you are handling it quite well, despite having a nurse and two babies thrust upon you, not to mention an ill-tempered sister."

Well seemed an overstatement. Esmée withheld a sigh. *It is well with my soul, at least.*

A light footfall announced Lucy. "Are ye ready for dinner, milady? Miss Shaw?"

Eliza gave a curt nod, meeting Esmée's eyes with resignation, not refusal.

"Let's dine here by the fire, just the two of us." Esmée smiled at Eliza and then Lucy. "We'll invite Nathaniel Autrey to join us on the morrow."

"Very well, Miss Shaw. I'll take his victuals to him in the captain's quarters posthaste."

CHAPTER
sixty-three

*T*aking comfort from the light shining from Henri's cottage and the slim silhouette in a front window as Nathaniel smoked a pipe, Esmée returned to her lighthouse duties at twilight, the pistol Wherry had wrested from her in one hand, a lanthorn in the other. Though he was no longer a threat, his dark presence still seemed to linger. At the foot of the tower steps, she bent her head and thanked God again for His protection and blessing.

And Lord, lest I petition Thee to death, please hasten Henri's safe return and the healing of Eliza's torn heart.

Slowly she climbed the steps, glad to resume what she found to be a tranquil routine, and lit the lamps. She stayed on for a half hour to make sure they were burning properly, intending to return twice between eight o'clock and sunrise.

Taking up a quill, she wrote in the logbook.

10th February 1756. Cloudy, wind moderate, seas calm. Lamp oil abundant.

Would Henri return and find her on watch? Darkness was falling on the water, the inky night meeting the inky deep. How she missed the sunrises and sunsets on clear days. Not the bitterness of January and February. March held a whisper of warmth that heralded kinder weather.

A white sail caught her eye if not her heart. 'Twas a merchant vessel, gliding through the water like a swan, headed toward York or Norfolk or some other Virginia port. Something akin to a physical ache rent her heart. She'd gone through Henri's trunkful of letters twice, setting aside the most romantic. The scent of the French wax was fading. Other than his penned words, what did she have? Memories. Closing her eyes, she recalled a beloved one of years before from another lofty vantage point.

Henri had come to their townhouse to see her father, who wasn't yet home. With her mother and Mrs. Mabrey busy elsewhere, Esmée had shown him to her father's study, offering him refreshments and exchanging light banter, much to the amusement of the giggling housemaids behind the nearest door.

So heady was his company she felt flirtatious. Somewhat bold. Rather than leave him alone to wait for her father, she gestured to the ship's ladder at the middle of the west wall. "Would you enjoy a nighttime view of the harbor?"

His attention swiveled from her to the hatch in the ceiling. "Going up-scuttle?"

"'Tis the best observation point in all York," she replied as his eyes met hers again. "I much prefer it to dousing chimney fires."

Smiling, he looked to her petticoats, raising a silent question.

"Never mind my skirts. As Father says, labor like a captain, play like a pirate." At his chuckle she took a step toward the ladder. "You lead and I'll follow."

He did not hesitate. He climbed up the ladder, then pushed open the hatch as if he'd crafted it before reaching out a hand for her. She gathered up her petticoats in one fist while his firm hand pulled her upward.

Into the warm, velvety night they went, trading the study's leathery, smoky scent for the gambrel roof. In winter, the view was clouded by chimney smoke, but in summer, little marred the breathtaking seascape, countless stars bespangling the sky above and ship's lanthorns lighting the water below, softening countless hulls and spars.

Henri stood beside her, not letting go of her hand. Her heart beat like a drum at the pressure of his callused fingers. Moonlight silvered the rooftop, and the narrow walk between chimneys was enclosed with an ornate iron balustrade.

He pointed across the York River toward Gloucester Point. "Over there lies the *Relentless*."

She'd heard he was friends with Captain Perrin, who owned a plantation at the point, his private waterfront far less crowded than York's. "Are you a guest at Little England then?"

"Tonight, aye." He turned toward her with a slight smile, the night wind ruffling his dark hair and the tails of his frock coat. "The hospitality of the Perrins is only exceeded by that of the Shaws."

"High praise, given my father isn't at home." Her flirtatious banter seemed more invitation. Was he as delighted as she was that the admiral was away?

He reached for her other hand. Together they stood facing each other, fingers entwined. The still, starlit moment begged for intimacy. Her racing pulse was no match for the butterflies swarming her middle. Even in the dark she sensed his intent. She went willingly into his embrace as she would never have done by day in full view of all York.

The touch of his lips was surprisingly soft, given the strength of his arms. They enfolded her, drawing her against his chest. His mouth grazed her cheek . . . her hair . . . her lips. Then and there she lost her heart to him and felt a little thrill that no man had kissed her or held her till this. The moment had held a sweet purity she'd never forgotten.

She blinked and opened her eyes, the present darkness rushing in, the glass turning slightly smoky. But in her heart she was still up-scuttle with her handsome captain, the taste of his kisses all the sweeter in hindsight.

CHAPTER

sixty-four

You cannot possibly expect me to sit at table with Nathaniel Autrey and dine." Eliza's folded arms underscored her resistance. "Not even if he acts as our valiant protector for the time being."

"'Tis a courtesy we should extend," Esmée returned, setting a small vase of paper flowers on the table. "'Twill be good for us as well as him."

"*Good?* Rather, embarrassing. Mortifying." Eliza was near tears. "No doubt he will look upon me in revulsion."

"I am sure he will not. He's an experienced seaman and chaplain, remember, who is no stranger to suffering, having seen countless ports of call." Esmée spoke patiently but privately wearied of the ongoing battle with her sister. "You cannot spend the rest of your life shamed by your skin."

"How easy it is for you to say! The pox and my scars will always be an unwelcome reminder of the winter Quinn was taken from me. Of the beautiful life we lived before tragedy struck." Eliza raised her hands to her once smooth face. "Would that I could wear a veil from now till the day I die."

A knock spared them further conversation but led to the excruciating moment Eliza dreaded. Looking near bolting, she tensed as Esmée placed a reassuring hand on her shoulder. Esmée leaned down and kissed her sister's ravaged cheek as Lucy let the chaplain in.

To his credit, Nathaniel Autrey made a splendid supper companion, warming their ears with tales of his escapades sailing around the globe. Even Eliza seemed to forget herself for a time as she listened.

"How long will you stay on here?" Eliza asked as Lucy served apple tart for dessert.

"Till you've no more need of me," he said. "The captain's cottage is quite comfortable till I return to Mount Autrey."

"At least you are spared the mainland's plague," Eliza murmured, eyes downcast.

"I've already had the pox." His answer brought Eliza's head up. "But my scarring isn't as visible as it once was. The salt air and sun have been a blessed tonic."

Apparently forgetting herself, Eliza made a brazen study of his face. Esmée flushed at her sister's scrutiny. But Nathaniel simply enjoyed his dessert as if unaware of it, his easy manner a godsend.

Eliza's gaze returned to her. "I suppose Captain Lennox has weathered the pox too."

Esmée felt a renewed beat of alarm. Had he? Their ten-year separation yawned wide. She remembered no scars on his person. Esmée raised her shoulders, then looked to Nathaniel and saw uncertainty in his eyes.

"We shall pray to that end," he said quietly.

Excusing herself, Esmée went into her bedchamber, where a just-awakened Ruenna began to coo. Playing the doting aunt, Esmée brought her to the table. Tonight Ruenna was all smiles, looking about with lively blue eyes, rosebud mouth pursed.

"A veritable cherub," Nathaniel said with a chuckle.

"She is indeed." Esmée smiled, sitting the baby on her lap. "Soon she shall find her feet and run away from us."

They chatted a few minutes more till the conversation dwindled and Eliza stifled a yawn.

"I believe a turn on the beach will do me good after so fine a meal. If you ladies will excuse me . . ." Nathaniel gave a slight bow and bid them good night.

Esmée passed Ruenna to Eliza and retreated to the lighthouse. Looking down from her lofty perch, she observed the sea chaplain walking in the delicate twilight before returning to his lodgings, where he took up his usual pipe. He wasn't Henri, but his presence seemed to bring comfort, a sort of peace to their uncertainty and grief.

For now, 'twas enough.

CHAPTER

sixty-five

A fortnight passed. Esmée studied her calendar as signs of spring grew brighter and daylight stretched, enlivening all the nooks and crannies of the island as it slowly returned to life. Time's passage was made more memorable as Eliza began walking the beach with Nathaniel, her head covered in her usual veil and bonnet. In fair weather they could be seen deep in conversation as they walked back and forth, retracing their steps on the sand in full view of the cottages and lighthouse.

"What d'ye ken they're about?" Lucy asked one day, returning from outside with an apron full of eggs.

"Taking the air and grieving," Alice replied. "The chaplain with one of his ailing sheep."

From the bedchamber where she sat at her desk, Esmée listened, hope rising. Though she'd tried in vain to help her sister, comfort had finally come from someone else. A rush of thankfulness aided her writing an overdue letter.

Dear Father,

'Tis almost March and we are glad of the coming spring. Eliza shows some signs of improving, reckoning with her loss inwardly if

*not outwardly, though still making much of her scarring. Thank-
fully, God has sent us deliverance twice in the form of sea chaplain
Autrey. If not for him, I would be writing you an entirely different
letter. He will return to Mount Autrey once Henri arrives—any
day now—bringing you this letter when he does, as well as more
news that I shan't belabor here. I confess my impatience knows no
bounds where Henri is concerned, though I do find tending the
light satisfying if lonesome without him by my side.*

*I trust you are well. I pray for you and the indentures as well
as our friends in York, especially the almshouse. Lord willing, this
scourge will soon pass.*

The next day, Nathaniel went to the island's opposite end to visit
with former crew. Lucy and Alice busied themselves with their handwork in the sunlight beneath the cottage's eave, leaving Esmée alone
with Eliza and the sleeping babies inside.

Eliza sat staring into the fire while Esmée stitched clouts. Her
stomach rumbled in anticipation of supper, which promised game
pie if the kitchen smells were any indication. The ensuing silence was
tedious, and she almost wished the babies would awaken, the only
sound the loud ticking of the mantel clock.

Whereas once she and Eliza had shared nearly everything growing up as sisters, Esmée felt a widening chasm between them. Did
Eliza envy her future happiness? She daren't mention Henri and
his homecoming. Like salt in a wound it was, adding to her sister's
misery.

Eliza straightened her slumped shoulders, gaze never leaving the
fire. "Those for whom God has mercy in store He first brings into a
wilderness."

Esmée's needle stilled.

"Chaplain Autrey told me such." Eliza cleared her throat. "I pray
my wilderness is not too long nor too grievous. And that I learn my
lessons well lest I repeat them."

Another stitch and Esmée said, "God's mercy is great and comes to you, perhaps, in an island's refuge and a chaplain who's no stranger to the pox."

The fire snapped, sending a stray spark onto Eliza's skirt hem. She seemed to give no notice, though it left a small black spot. "Do you recall Mama's favorite verses?"

"Mama had many beloved verses. Which do you speak of?"

"'Favour is deceitful, and beauty is vain: but a woman that feareth the LORD, she shall be praised.' That is what comes to me at night when I cannot sleep, though I gave little thought to it before."

"Heaven itself is speaking to you then." Esmée rethreaded her needle. "'Strength and honour are her clothing; and she shall rejoice in time to come.' Notice it has nothing to do with how one looks."

"True, as does this—'the ornament of a meek and quiet spirit,' which is precious to God. Not outward adorning of hair and gold and dress." She sighed. "I am all about adornment."

"There is nothing wrong with being pretty. Being at your best." Esmée was moved by the distress in her sister's voice. "'Tis wrong to make a god of it. To usurp the place of the Almighty Himself with trifling matters."

"Which I have done. In spades."

"There are none of us righteous, not one."

"But there are some, like Quinn, who act righteously. Or attempt to live by what Scripture teaches." Eliza's voice shook. "Yet he was taken."

Quinn had been, in hindsight, having a soul awakening all his own. But before any of them realized what was happening, he was gone. Might his untimely death be of more consequence than his life?

Eliza took a handkerchief from her pocket, her husband's initials embroidered in blue thread. "Chaplain Autrey says there are those God loves so much He calls them home early."

Touched, Esmée paused. Had she not clung to one such Scripture in light of Mama's passing? "'Precious in the sight of the LORD is the death of His saints.'"

Eliza firmed her trembling chin. "Then I am glad Quinn was taken and not me. For I am no saint, nor am I at all sure of my standing with the Almighty. Perhaps that is His first severe mercy to me."

CHAPTER

sixty-six

The next day dawned uncommonly warm. Midmorning, Esmée left the cottage as the sun climbed in what Henri called a lapis lazuli sky. Eliza was walking the beach again, this time alone. Nathaniel sat beneath the eave of the captain's cottage, reading. Lucy was gathering wood for the cookfire, and Alice was inside the cottage, nursing the babies. 'Twas a fine time to slip away. The shadow she'd felt with Jago Wherry had finally passed.

The cove she sought was not far, sunlight shimmering on sand and sea with such blinding force Esmée narrowed her eyes beneath her straw hat. Henri had taken her here and told her it was the prettiest place on the island. She sat down on a piece of driftwood and removed her shoes and stockings.

Clenching her teeth, she waded into the cold water, foam rushing around her bare ankles. Once she and Eliza had chased the waves as children, running out onto the sand as far as they dared, then returning to shore before the water would break around them. Bunching up her skirts with her hands, she left sandy footprints as she followed the retreating sea, only to outrun it as it turned on a wave and rushed back to shore.

Next time I shall bring Eliza.

How carefree the sun made her. She felt like a girl again, enchanted with the water in all its sparkling liveliness. Again and again she raced the waves as the tide turned, casting off the lethargy of a long winter. Breathless and exhilarated and wet to the knees, she ventured forth again, only to stop completely and inexplicably. Transfixed, she turned toward the pines that clustered at her back.

Esmée.

Had she heard her name? The roar of the surf behind her snatched the word away, but as her gaze traveled up a sandy dune, her heart lurched. A man strode toward her, navigating the uneven ground with sure, swift steps.

Henri. Running. At long last.

All thought of the ocean left her head. A wave rushed her from behind, buckling her knees with its foamy force, knocking her down and taking her under. Choking on water, she felt her soaked petticoats pull at her even as her bare feet and fingers raked over sand and sharp shells and pebbles.

"Esmée!"

She stumbled, all the wind knocked out of her, and then hard hands encircled her waist, pulling her free of the surf. Henri lifted her and swiftly carried her to safety. He sat down hard on dry sand, sheltering her in his arms. She was a bedraggled mess, coughing up water, her heart leaping with joy.

He was smiling, his chest shaking with mirth as he smoothed back the tangled mass of her hair with one hand, his words warm on her cheek. "Comeliest mermaid I've ever seen, right here on my very own island."

She shut her eyes, swallowing down another sputter, and rested her head against his damp linen shirt. His heartbeat thumped as loud as her own. She felt she might burst with happiness.

"So much has happened." Her words came breathless, her nose stinging from salt water. "I hardly know where to begin. But all that matters now is that you're here, safe and sound."

"I wanted to surprise you." He held her closer, kissing her finger where the posy ring rested. His own signet ring caught the sun flashing in its fiery climb to noon. "The *Intrepid* is anchored off the south

337

side of the island. We docked at York briefly before coming here. Long enough to see your father and finish business with colonial authorities."

"Did you meet with success?" Her hopes hung on the word. Success and then retirement, at least from the naval world. 'Twas her highest hope.

"Aye, aside from half a dozen men lost."

"I'm so sorry."

"As am I." His voice dropped, then rebounded. "Our prizes include a French naval ship carrying war materials to Canadian militia, as well as a troop ship. Our greatest coup was capturing a French commander and his officers, including a copy of their war plans. These we delivered to Williamsburg to the governor's care."

Bold operations, all. She couldn't imagine the danger and complexities of overtaking war ships. "How is Father?"

"Glad to see us in port. Anxious about you and Eliza."

She nodded, her eyes on the roiling surf. "You heard about Quinn, then, and the baby and Eliza's being here."

"Your father told me. I cannot convey my shock and sorrow. But what most concerns me is you." His lips brushed her brow. "How you're faring with so much strife and then keeping the light too."

She raised a hand to his deeply tanned cheek, her own condition the least of her worries. The fatigue in his eyes . . . the loose folds of his shirt. His blue coat lay on the sand. He'd abandoned it coming after her. "You've lost a stone or so, to my eye. And you look exhausted."

"War wears one down." His smile was thin. "But with your company and care, I'll be in prime shape in no time."

She pushed herself to her feet, the sharp wind reminding her it was not yet spring. He stood too, retrieving her hat while she put on her stockings and shoes. Her skirts dragged on the sand as they left the beach hand in hand. Unable to contain herself, she turned to him, caught in a warm ray of sunlight, the fragrant pines ringing them.

"I cannot believe you've returned at last." Her hands were pressed to his chest. "I shan't believe it till you kiss me. Soundly."

He smiled as his arms went round her, undeterred by how damp she was. She shivered, more from pleasure than the chill. She leaned into him, seeking his beloved scent, his strength. His mouth was warm and insistent against her own, next trailing down her neck and the bare hollow of her shoulder till her very being stood on tiptoe.

"I've dreamed of this moment day and night away from you," Henri said. "It drove me half-mad."

"Kiss me again," she said, wanting to squeeze the last drop of joy from every hard-won moment.

"Have done with kissing. Marry me, Esmée." A flicker of uncertainty darkened his eyes. "If you're indeed sure of anchoring yourself to a man with salt water in his blood."

She threw her arms around his neck, determined to remove all doubt. "Let this be my answer." Pressing her lips to his, she kissed him with an abandon that brought them not simply body to body but soul to soul. The beach seemed to spin and fade, her awareness of him so complete it chased all else from consciousness. He kissed her back with equal fervor, and time came to a blessed standstill.

Breathless, he said, "Let us wed at once, then."

She smiled up at him, the sun in her eyes. "Nathaniel Autrey is on hand. He can have the honor."

"Ned?" Surprise enlivened his weary features. "Here?"

They began walking again, Esmée spilling out the whole story. "What's more, his coming seems to have helped revive Eliza."

"He understands loss. His own beloved died some time ago."

"The Almighty sent him as surely as you're standing here. I was at my wit's end about Wherry and then at my wit's end about Eliza. I still worry about her and Ruenna—"

"Ruenna?"

"Her wee daughter. She's the sweetest, prettiest babe."

The lighthouse was visible now, the sun striking the glass of the tower. He stopped for a moment, taking it in. She searched his face, seeking reassurance he was safe from the pox. Aside from faint, sun-weathered lines, his skin was smooth, no telltale marks of any scourge evident, past or present.

He brought her hand to his lips and kissed her fingers. "I've much to tell you, *ma belle*, but first a bath and a hot meal are in order."

CHAPTER

sixty-seven

Soon a bowl of hearty stew and crusty bread restored Henri. He and Ned had talked at length in his cottage while the women kept to theirs, preparing supper and minding the children. Lucy did slip out to reunite with Cyprian, who'd walked from the Flask and Sword, a gift of oranges and lemons in hand.

To Henri's surprise, a veiled Eliza had presented Ruenna to him with pride in her voice upon his return to the lightkeeper's cottage. Esmée wasn't far, arranging a table for four in advance of an early supper and minding the light. A linen cloth was laid, anchored by a pitcher of dried flowers, not the seaside goldenrod and sweet everlasting of summer.

Would Eliza join them?

He could sense Esmée's concern. Though he wished it could be just the two of them, he was grateful for Ned's engaging presence and Eliza's sincere if subdued welcome.

He stood by the hearth, adjusting to life outside wooden walls. After so many wintry weeks at sea, he couldn't seem to get warm.

Esmée lit the candles at table. She'd lost the look of a mermaid and drew his eye like solid ground for a drowning man, her figure in floral chintz a veritable garden, her curled hair beribboned.

She turned toward him with a smile. "Are you hungry, Captain Lennox?"

"Aye, for more than supper." He winked as Ned came into the cottage, accompanied by Eliza, her head down.

How proud she'd once been, the belle of any function, charming everyone near and far. Now he schooled his dismay to see her unveiled, her once flawless complexion a dim memory. Quinn's absence was especially felt, for he'd never been far from her side. It doubled Henri's intent to marry as soon as possible. Tomorrow was never promised. All they had was the enviable present.

"What news do you bring from the mainland?" Ned asked after saying grace.

"Very little." Henri took up a knife to carve the chicken and chose his words as carefully as he could before a newly bereaved widow. "April's legislative session has been postponed. Many shops remain closed in York and in Williamsburg as well."

Eliza raised her gaze. "Did Father say when he'd return to the island?"

Henri shook his head. "Till he does, he feels you and your daughter are safer right here."

"Wise of him." Esmée passed a basket of bread. "Eliza is welcome to stay as long as she likes. Besides, we'll have one less in our cottage soon."

"Which begs the question"—Ned smiled as he buttered his bread—"when will your nuptials be, and where?"

Esmée glanced at the window where clouds gathered, as if contemplating wedding on the beach. Next she looked to Henri as he finished with his carving.

"On the morrow." He didn't look back at Ned till she nodded in agreement. "The license to wed is in my pocket. We've only need of you to officiate before you return to Mount Autrey."

"My pleasure. I can think of no better sendoff," Ned told them.

"You've been good to stay on the last fortnight." Though Eliza's voice was calm, Henri detected a beat of dismay beneath. "I shall remember all your counsel."

"Keep close the Bible I gave you." Ned's features softened as he forked a first bite. "Within its pages you'll soon have need of little else."

Talk turned to the light, the last storm, and the moment the *Intrepid* overtook the French fleet. Esmée seemed on tenterhooks as Henri recounted the details.

"Your mission is finished then, at least for now," Ned said. "Virginia is never long satisfied."

"Our success has only intensified colonial officials' desire for further cruises, aye. Immediate ones." He could feel Esmée's eyes on him, the dismay his words wrought. "But we'll wed and have our honeymoon before any more pressures come to bear."

"A honeymoon at a pox-ridden time while tethered to a lighthouse is quite a feat." Eliza's voice held a touch of asperity. "I fear Virginia is still riven with the scourge."

Esmée reached for the saltcellar. "With things as they are, perhaps remaining here on the island seems best."

Warmth filled Henri's chest. "Given I've been away, the island is idyllic . . . and this meal likewise."

Smiling, Lucy murmured her thanks as she replenished their cups. The clink of utensils against pewter plates and the snap of the fire were the only sounds for several minutes. But it was a jubilant silence, lending to Henri's profound contentment to be home.

Ned eyed him with amusement. "Is it true Mistress Saltonstall is back on the island and has reopened the Flask and Sword?"

"She returned just yesterday, aye," Henri confirmed. "Hermes is beside himself."

"She's likely at her wit's end managing a full crew from the *Intrepid*, with no one wanting shore leave." Ned regarded him with a canny eye. "You look well, Captain. And what of your men? No maladies on board?"

Henri took another bite of chicken. "None, God be thanked. No scurvy either due to a short cruise."

"How long were you in port?" Ned persisted.

Long enough to catch the pox.

Was that what Esmée was thinking? He saw the joyous light in her eyes dim.

"Two days," he replied. "I suffered the pox soon after my impressment in the Royal Navy, if you're wondering. And it doesn't strike twice."

Esmée was regarding him over the rim of her glass with stark relief.

He smiled at her, knowing she'd be pleased at what had delayed him on the mainland. "I'm happy to say my time in York was more pleasure than politics. While there I spoke with stonemasons and ordered materials to begin building within a fortnight."

"Glad news indeed." Esmée's delight washed over him like a warm wave. "Your crew who remained behind have made a sturdy garden wall in your absence. I've even begun a small kitchen garden."

"How long will the house construction take?" Ned asked.

"Excavation of the cellar needs to happen first, then hauling the stone since it's not quarried here." Henri took a drink. "The double-pile plan and open staircase will take time, but I hope to see us at home there by winter."

As the men finished supper and moved nearer the hearth to continue their conversation, Esmée turned her attention to Eliza. The absence of a veil was no small matter. Though heavily powdered to cover the worst of the scarring and far quieter than before, Eliza seemed to have made a breakthrough of some sort.

"You seem better tonight, Sister." Esmée's voice was low, hardly heard over the men's robust conversation. She longed to draw Eliza out but always felt she walked a precarious line. "I'd like to see the Bible Nathaniel gave you. 'Tis kind of him."

"He said 'twas the least he could do, as Quinn and I were so hospitable to him upon his coming to Williamsburg and assuming his place at Mount Autrey. He's also indebted to us for introducing him to Quinn's cousin Elinor. They plan to wed next summer."

Elinor. Esmée had all but forgotten. The tears in Eliza's eyes spiked her alarm. Might she be too attached to the sea chaplain?

"I am happy for them." Eliza paused at the men's rumble of laughter over some matter. "I asked him what drew him to her as she is so plain. Of course, I did not say she was plain, though I've long thought it. And do you know what he told me?"

Held by her sister's shimmering eyes, Esmée waited.

"He said she has an inner beauty that can never be marred by age or disease, a gentle and quiet spirit of great price in God's sight. She is radiant to him, he told me. *Radiant.* And that, unquestionably, is far better than being beautiful."

"They are well suited, then. Both of them devout."

Eliza nodded and brought her serviette to her lips. "All this makes me wonder about my future." Her calm voice belied the emotion beneath. "My outward beauty is gone. I've done little to cultivate unfading beauty . . . or radiance."

"'Tis never too late. Spiritual beauty is something we should all aspire to." Esmée herself was convicted, her thoughts leaping ahead. "Perhaps 'twould be wise to cultivate Elinor's company once she becomes Mistress Autrey."

"Perhaps." Eliza looked at her hand, where the ruby ring Quinn had given her rested. "Given time, will any man want me?"

"The right man will." The words were out of Esmée's mouth before she'd given them thought, and they now became a silent prayer.

Eliza's eyes held doubt. "As for a second husband, the very thought sickens me. For now I need to consider returning to the townhouse and sorting through Quinn's belongings, his study, and his many papers. He was in some sort of a quandary before he fell ill. Some matter concerning the governor's council, other burgesses, and such . . ." Her voice trailed off, and she put a hand to her brow. "I feel a headache coming on."

Excusing herself, Eliza left the cottage. From where he stood by the hearth, Henri gave Esmée a concerned glance, but her smile offset it.

"So tomorrow is your wedding day." Nathaniel looked nonplussed

344

about Eliza's abrupt departure. "Are you going to observe custom and marry in the morn? Or do you need more time?"

"Time enough to give Mistress Saltonstall leave to concoct a bride's cake," Henri said. "I promised her."

Had he? Amused, Esmée discarded her notion of a small affair.

Nathaniel chuckled. "Your crew will want to be on hand, of course, for the frolic after. But what of the admiral?"

"Father knew he wouldn't be here, given the timing and circumstances," Esmée told him, regretful but resigned. "But he'll be happy to hear you married us."

With a knowing smile, Nathaniel reached for his wool coat hanging by the door. "If you'll excuse me, I'll hie to the Flask and Sword and alert Mistress Saltonstall that her services are needed. You won't mind being left alone, I daresay."

"Nay," Henri said emphatically, to Esmée's delight. Clearly, wedding cake was the last thing on his mind.

CHAPTER

sixty-eight

The bride's cake was hurriedly baked, a plump confection stuffed with dried fruit, spirits, and nutmeats. The punch was enlivened with citrus brought off the *Intrepid* and poured into an ornate silver bowl. Mistress Saltonstall was pleased to host the wedding reception at her ordinary and would try to keep Hermes calm amid all the fuss, Lucy told Esmée as she returned from helping at the tavern the next morn.

"Will the whole crew be at the nuptials, Miss Shaw?"

"Nay, only the festivities after."

"Glad I am to be part of it." Lucy's eyes misted. "Ye look like a bride. But more than that, ye look happy. Happier than I've ever seen ye."

"That I am," Esmée replied, embracing her.

Though the morning was one of fog and bluster, a gentle wind banished the clouds by midafternoon. Esmée left the cottage, followed by Eliza and Lucy. Alice remained inside by a window, minding the babies as the women walked down the beach to where Henri waited.

Esmée kept her eyes on Henri, struck by how commanding he was even away from the ship. The look that graced his face when he

346

saw her made her teary-eyed. He loved her. There could be no doubt. Why had she ever wondered?

Joining hands, Esmée and her groom stood on the stretch of sand before their house site, the sun fickle but warm upon their shoulders. Clad in her best lavender silk dress, lace cascading from her sleeves and pearls about her neck, she looked up at Henri, who was resplendent in black breeches and a fawn-colored coat. Freshly shaved, his hair trimmed and queued, and hinting of castile soap, he left her weak-kneed.

Eliza was somber in her black taffeta gown and hat, her veil swaying with the wind. She and Henri's sailing master, Tarbonde, stood as witnesses. The festive mood turned hallowed as Nathaniel read the age-old marriage rites, a Bible open in one hand. Though Esmée missed Father fiercely, not even his absence dimmed her happiness.

Henri looked down at her, his eyes conveying what he did not say. Did he sense her unspoken thoughts?

My love, you have my heart, my whole heart, from this day forward. There's been none but you, nor will there ever be, come what may. You are the Almighty's choice for me.

"You may kiss your bride, Captain Lennox," Nathaniel said at last.

Not one kiss but two sealed their vows, promising a night of bliss to come. The sun shone down as they began a walk to the Flask and Sword, determined to return by dusk to mind the light. Esmée looked forward to climbing the tower steps with Henri alongside. For now they led the small wedding party, though Eliza returned to the cottage to remain behind with Alice and the babies.

The fiddling could be heard from quite a distance. Esmée's anticipation quickened, though what she wanted was to be alone with her groom. But she wouldn't deny the crew their enjoyment of their captain in his newly married state. They went up the tavern's wooden steps into the taproom, where tables and chairs had been pushed back along the walls to allow for dancing. Huzzahs erupted at the sight of them. Hermes scampered hither and yon, not screeching but clearly excited by all the fuss.

Esmée's eyes went to the bride's cake and punch bowl, as she'd hardly eaten that morn. But such was forgotten as Henri led her out for the first dance. Lady Mary Menzies's Reel. There were no finely stepped minuets here. Just wild, happy romps where an abundance of men joined arms in a ring and cavorted around the two of them.

A sea breeze kept them cool, wafting in through wide-open windows. Cake was consumed and punch downed as the sun slipped west in a haze of pink and cream. With a look at the watch he kept in his pocket, Henri winked at her, signaling it was time to make their escape. And escape they did, just the two of them, while the merriment continued unabated.

"If only I could return you to our house and not our cottage," Henri said as they skirted the site.

She squeezed his hand. Lucy had helped her move all her belongings to Henri's that morning. "But your—*our*—cottage is quite cozy."

"Aye, that it is." His grin told her he minded not a whit. "The night is just beginning. Time enough to light the tower, then kindle our own fire."

She flushed, warmth drenching her. At the top of a sand dune they turned and took in the sunset, now little more than layered rose ribbons on the horizon.

He brought her hand to his lips. "Not long ago I was smelling black powder and dodging bullet lead. All this seems more mirage, Mistress Lennox."

"I pray the mirage never ends, Captain, and 'twill be smooth seas for us in the years to come."

He looked down at her, gathering her hands in his. "Now seems a good time to tell you I won't be returning to sea. I've told the governor the same. My maritime career is finished."

Finished. And said with such finality. "Are you . . . sure?"

"Without a doubt. My future is you. Our children. Indigo Island. And something tells me you'll not voice a single objection, *ma belle*."

Laughing, she snaked her arms around his neck as he swept her off her feet into his arms and walked toward the lighthouse standing stalwart in the distance.

CHAPTER

sixty-nine

Esmée opened her eyes to a rooster's crowing. Lying quietly, she pondered yesterday's events with a thankful heart, Henri's bulk warm and disheveled beside her. His boots stood near the bed along with his queue ribbon and her lavender gown. Raising a hand, she admired her posy ring, feeling every inch married. Would that they could stay abed all day. But life continued all around them, the sun streaming across the coverlet and rousing them to greet the day.

She must check in on the women and babies first thing. Eliza had mentioned leaving soon, perhaps with Nathaniel on the morrow. The jolly would return them to York. Would Alice and Ruenna leave too? If so, 'twould just be her and Henri here on their end of the island and Lucy in the adjoining cottage. Construction would soon begin. Esmée could plant the remainder of their garden and welcome summer when it came.

The rooster's renewed crowing brought Henri round. He blinked, eyes half-shuttered against the sun. And then he got his bearings, rolling toward her and tickling her without mercy.

She laughed till the tears came, her words breathless. "Stop, Husband, lest we bring all the islanders to our door!"

"Nay, *ma chérie*. We are honeymooning. They wouldn't dare."

To escape him, she rolled away and hung her feet over the side of the feather mattress. "I must see to your breakfast like I've dreamed of doing for years. Hot chocolate and toast for you to start."

He reached for her again, but she eluded him, dressing hastily in the silk gown she'd discarded. She wouldn't return to her workaday clothes just yet. Peering in his shaving mirror, she wound up her hair as best she could, secured it with pins, and topped it with a lace cap, aware he watched her every move.

He pushed himself up on one elbow. "You're blushing. It becomes you."

She blew him a kiss as she started for the kitchen, her stomach a-rumble. The cottage was chill. The hearth's fires had gone out in the night. She stirred the kitchen coals with a poker, then went in search of wood. And drew up short just past the threshold.

An unfamiliar boat, a sloop she did not recognize, was docking at the pier. Wariness needled her. One man in particular drew her notice. Was that the Williamsburg sheriff? His grim expression soured the high mood from their wedding day.

It was then she heard a feminine shout.

Eliza?

Her sister's voice crested before Eliza spun on her heel and returned to her cottage with an emphatic slamming of the door. Hard enough to make the dishes rattle, surely.

Esmée returned inside posthaste. "Henri," she called.

"I'm nearly dressed," he replied from the bedchamber.

"I fear we have company."

He entered the parlor but drew up short at the window. His face showed no surprise or alarm, though her own heart ticked like a wayward clock. When he stepped outside, she followed, standing with him to watch the men on board disembark.

"Go inside and I'll join you shortly." His low tone brooked no questions. No argument.

She pulled her attention from the sheriff to Henri's now guarded face. "All right."

Head down, she took the shell path to her former cottage. Eliza stood looking out the window. As soon as Esmée let herself in, Eliza whirled on her.

"Why is that blackguard Osborn here with his minion magistrates?" Eliza's eyes lit with cold fire. "They were skulking for half an hour before landing."

At her outburst, Alice and Lucy scurried to the kitchen, babes in arms.

Esmée joined Eliza at the window. "I sense their coming bodes ill."

"It can't be about Father or they'd have told me when I confronted them." Eliza crossed her arms. "I shouted at them in most unladylike fashion when they docked. Asked their intent. They said they came seeking the captain."

Esmée's stomach clenched. Had Henri hidden something from her?

Eliza remained at the window, her expression a picture of disgust. The sun climbed higher, calling out the tense expressions of the men deep in conversation. Lucy and Alice were speaking in low tones in the kitchen.

Esmée kept on her cloak and went to the fire, chilled by more than the cold morn.

"My, how stern the sheriff looks. I've rarely seen him sober." Eliza sniffed. "Well, the captain shall soon send them packing, I've no doubt."

But the men remained through toast and tea and the babies' next feeding. Eliza paced while Esmée dandled Ruenna in her lap, trying to pray her way through the untimely interruption.

"At last, they're leaving." Eliza released a pent-up breath and joined Esmée at the hearth.

In moments, a knock at the door signaled Henri. "No need to look *contrarie*," he said, eyes on Esmée. But she knew that look. He said no more, but she sensed he was withholding something so as not to alarm them. Or waiting to be alone with her before he enlightened her further. "The men are on their way back to the mainland."

To her amazement, Eliza did not question him further. If she had, he might not have heard her, for Ruenna began crying her loudest and Alice hurried in, intent on helping.

"You two are on your honeymoon," Eliza said, unsmiling. "No need to stay here a moment longer."

Esmée soon left the cottage with Henri, looking over her shoulder to see the unwelcome boat moving slowly west toward the mainland.

CHAPTER
seventy

This was not how she'd envisioned her honeymoon. The knot of disappointment inside Esmée widened to alarm as she stepped from the *Relentless*'s jolly onto the York dock with the help of Henri's firm hand. Eliza stepped out after them, her veiled hat aflutter. Lucy and Alice had remained behind on the island with the babies. They couldn't risk returning them to York with smallpox still a menace.

Esmée cast a look down Water Street to where the sign *Shaw's Chocolate* swung in the early March wind. The town seemed fractious today, the taint of tar and brine and fishmongers curling Esmée's nose under a leaden sky. The weather had kept them from returning yesterday, the wind contrary, the waves high.

A carriage took them up the hill to the Shaw townhouse. Patches of green burst through the gloom along with the first of spring's blooms, pear trees and daffodils foremost. So focused was Esmée on her inner turmoil that the colors seemed muted, a shadow of themselves. Few folks were about, lending to her worry the smallpox was far from over.

Esmée turned her postponed plans over in her mind as she would soil with a garden spade. She should be sowing sweet marjoram and hyssop and thyme in their kitchen garden and expecting the laborers to arrive with the building stones for their home. But instead they were headed to Williamsburg because her new husband had been accused of something nefarious.

Father was not at home, nor was he expecting them. Mrs. Mabrey greeted them and made them comfortable in the parlor. Henri wanted to wait and inform Father that they were en route to the capital.

Eliza seemed to turn inward, saying little, her expression a mystery beneath her veil. She wasn't wanting to return to the Williamsburg townhouse, to the place where she'd known such happiness with Quinn. She'd confided this when Henri had told them he must meet with authorities in Williamsburg. But at the last Eliza decided to accompany them. Perhaps putting off the inevitable somehow made it more painful as a widow.

Esmée, seated near the fire with Eliza, kept her eyes on Henri, who stood looking out a draped window. When the front door opened and shut with a familiar thud, she knew Father was finally home.

"Company—the very best kind." He came in, his pleasant expression somewhat guarded as he set aside his hat and walking stick.

They greeted him, and Henri spoke with a composed ease that made him all the more irresistible to Esmée. "First the good news. Your daughter and I are now wed as of day before yesterday, and your granddaughter is well and remains safely on the island with her nurse."

"My felicitations can wait. What, pray tell, is the bad news?" He looked in concern at his daughters. "My study might be best suited for such."

He and Henri passed through the adjoining door to the room in question, their voices a dull monotone once the door was closed.

"What mischief has led to this?" Eliza's sharp question unnerved Esmée further.

"I know little except that the sheriff and his men were sent by unnamed officials to summon Henri to the governor's chambers."

They fell silent as their father's voice grew more strident. Though she couldn't make out the words, she knew he was as confounded and disbelieving as she. Tea was served, and they made small talk with Mrs. Mabrey, who inquired about Ruenna.

The thoughtful question hung on the air. Eliza said nothing for several uncomfortable seconds, leaving Esmée to answer. "She's as bonny a babe as ever drew breath. Tiny but healthy and very fond of being held."

Did Eliza miss her? Esmée certainly did.

When Mrs. Mabrey excused herself, Eliza turned to Esmée in exasperation. "You think I'm a terrible mother, don't you?"

"Nay," Esmée replied calmly, countering her sister's sudden mood. "I think you're a grieving one."

Eliza set down her cup with a rattle. "The truth is I absolutely abhor returning to town. Even sitting here having tea and fielding questions, however well placed, is excruciating."

"Would you rather have remained on the island?"

"I have no choice but to return and try to get on with life as best I can. But I shan't resume any society, I assure you. Not looking like this." Her voice shook with emotion. "Thankfully, I am a woman of means and can shut the world out if I want to."

"I hope you do not, for your daughter's sake." Esmée would waste no words on behalf of Ruenna. "Quinn would have wanted you to live life to the fullest. 'Tis one of the reasons he married you. Your zest and—"

"All that has passed, along with my beauty. I am a shell of what I was, and you know it." She reached into her purse, withdrew a vial of hartshorn, and waved it beneath her veil, lapsing into sullen silence.

Soon Esmée and Henri were in Williamsburg, ensconced in Eliza's best guest bedchamber, and then Henri was on his way to the governor's palace. The townhouse had a forlorn feel. Quinn loomed large in memory, as he had in life. Reminders of him were everywhere. Most of the servants had been dismissed. Few remained to keep the elegant house, further adding to the echoing rooms.

True to her word, Eliza withdrew to her second-floor bedchamber. Esmée heard her door shut with vehemence from down the hall. The silence soon gave way to weeping. Should she go and offer comfort?

Uncertainty kept her from it. Eliza needed to grieve. Esmée sent another prayer heavenward, and the house quieted again.

Standing by a tall window, Esmée overlooked the townhouse garden with its lovely fountain and sundial and bricked paths. The paling fence kept out deer and other marauding creatures. One busy gardener remained to tend to spring's showiest flowers. All was as lovely as ever, yet everything had changed.

She sought a window seat and a book. But Eliza was not a reader, and Esmée daren't go downstairs to Quinn's study. Instead she began pacing back and forth upon the Turkish carpet, wishing it weren't a glaring red but a soothing blue. A low fire burned in the grate, but she longed to open a window. A clap of thunder scuttled her plan and sent her back to the hearth and a comfortable chair. Eliza's Angora cat sauntered in, leaping into Esmée's lap and purring fitfully.

Esmée missed the cottage's simplicity. The babies' noises. The teakettle's singing. Alice and Lucy's good-natured chatter. Henri's abode was richly masculine, and she missed that too. His sea chest rested near the door, and she fixed her eye on it, willing him back, craving the low timbre of his voice and his kiss.

Supper arrived on a tray. The French chef was still in the kitchen, thankfully. Loin of veal, salad, crusty bread, a dish of early strawberries and cream. She had little appetite but partook with a listening ear for Henri's return. Within minutes she was rewarded as the hall clock below chimed seven and the butler opened the front door.

Up the stairs her bridegroom came, slowly, without the usual spring in his step. She set down her fork and brought the serviette to her lips, ready to greet him when he came through the doorway.

Her smile slipped past her trepidation. "Welcome home, Husband."

Even if it was not their home. Nor their desire to be here.

A flicker of joy lightened his solemnity. "Home is wherever you are, aye." He shrugged off his greatcoat and laid it over the back of a chair. He was wearing his wedding suit, the finest clothes he had. As was his custom, he went to the washbasin.

"I'll have your supper sent up," she told him, pulling on a bell cord.

With a nod, he took the seat opposite her, but she sensed he was in no more of a mood to eat than she.

When she sat back down, he reached for her hand. "This isn't the sort of news I wanted to bring you, especially so soon after our wedding."

Their joyous joining on the beach seemed a lifetime ago. Had it only been two days?

She squeezed his hand. "I've sat here and wondered what would take you away from me for hours on end, and at last I shall have it."

"I met with Governor Dinwiddie first and then his council. It appears certain charges have been brought against me. One of them is spy—"

"*Spy?*" She spat the hated word out in disbelief.

"For the French. Also, it seems some planters—burgesses—have banded together with the intent of seeking revenge for my liberating the *Swallow* and its Africans all those years ago. They believe I remain a threat to plantation owners and Virginia's economy, not to mention other slaveholding colonies, with my crew of black jacks and my stance on slavery. They accuse me of enticing their Africans to run away and fomenting discontent for untold freedoms and that sort of nonsense."

She sat back, her stomach giving way. "Nonsense is the kindest word for it. 'Tis outrageous—laughable."

Henri cleared his throat and said evenly, "There are men powerfully placed who have aligned themselves against me."

"But there must be just as many honorable men for you who would call this matter mutinous and seek to end it."

"Perhaps." He released her hand and sat back, expression weary. "For now I am under house arrest here at Lord—*Lady* Drysdale's."

She felt she'd been struck in the face. House arrest? If only Quinn were here. Quinn would set matters aright. Quinn had been one of those men powerfully placed.

What other allies did Henri have?

CHAPTER

seventy-one

For the first time since leaving it, Esmée missed the chocolate shop. There was simply little to do at the townhouse besides a great deal of hand-wringing. She couldn't even fiddle with her chatelaine as she was wont to do, since she'd left it on the island. Most of Williamsburg remained shuttered, though the smallpox was said to be abating. Henri was in his third day of meetings at the palace, which left her on tenterhooks. With Eliza hiding in her bedchamber and sinking further into despondency, Esmée summoned a plan and knocked lightly on the bedchamber door. No answer. Gently she jiggled the doorknob. Locked.

Her voice was quiet but aggrieved. "Eliza, please let me in."

A groggy reply. Had Eliza been imbibing again? Or merely sleeping?

"Please open the door. I'm concerned about you and need to discuss what is happening with Henri."

Slow footsteps and then the door opened a crack. Eliza stared back at her, eyes swollen and bloodshot, hair in a frayed braid that dangled over one shoulder to her waist. Her sultana was stained. Wine, likely. Esmée spied an uncorked bottle near the bed.

Esmée pushed past her and threw open a window sash. The March wind roared in, stirring the drapes and cleansing the air. "I've sent for tea." She began arranging two chairs near the open window, then lifted the tea table and placed it there.

"My, Sister." Arms crossed, Eliza regarded her with grim amusement. "You're a veritable whirlwind when you want to be."

"Cook has been asking what you are hungry for."

"A pity, as I have no appetite."

"Would that you could say that about the wine instead." Lifting a dark green bottle, Esmée saw that it was French champagne. "Must I run your household for you and lock the wine cellar?"

With a derisive snort, Eliza collapsed into a chair. She toyed with the fringe of her sash, eyes down, as Esmée took a seat opposite her.

"You need to know what is happening all around you," Esmée began, needing an ally. "Henri has been placed under house arrest at your very residence." The ugly words even tasted bitter. "He's at the palace presently, enduring who knows what as we speak."

Eliza studied her through narrowed, incredulous eyes. "The same captain who only recently chased down an entire French fleet on behalf of Virginia's colonial government?" The cold irony in her tone fueled Esmée's ire. "And came away with countless sealed documents and high-placed prisoners of war, not to mention enemy ships?"

"At the moment all seem to have forgotten that. Henri says little to me about the proceedings. But I believe the word *spy* was mentioned."

"Spy? What blather!" Eliza sat up straight. "I recall hearing some hullabaloo about his championing of blacks when he returned to Virginia last fall. Several burgesses—most of them planters—were quibbling about his signing on black jacks as crew, thereby fomenting discontent among plantation slaves who wish to gain their freedom by sea."

"There are many black jacks, free and runaways, from all the colonies, even England."

"True, but England has no plantations or slave labor like America. And slave owners fear giving Africans *any* liberties lest it threaten

Virginia's very foundation . . ." Eliza's voice faded as tea was brought. "Close the door after you, Rose," she told the servant.

Esmée waited, hands folded in her lap, for her sister to serve. Eliza did so reluctantly. Taking up the silver teapot with an unsteady hand, she sloshed rather than poured tea into Esmée's cup.

"As we were saying," Esmée continued, wondering what else Eliza recalled, "matters have obviously come to a boil. But till now I knew nothing of it."

"Quinn certainly did—" At the mention of his name, Eliza broke off for an emotional moment before continuing. "He made mention to me of it when Henri left on his cruise. He said he was going to put down any trouble regarding it, and so I've thought little of it since."

Esmée stared at the plate of untouched pastries. She knew Henri had enemies, but as he'd been away for years till recently, she'd thought the animosity had died down. "Do you know who is involved? Did Quinn mention them by name?"

Eliza rattled off enough names to chill Esmée's blood. "The prosperous planters stand to lose the most if slavery is challenged. They have the governor's ear, of course. Two of the troublemakers are related to him by marriage." A shrewd glint shone in her eyes. "And I do wonder if a few of them weren't in cahoots with Jago Wherry. Two of Henri's opponents are in horrendous debt and could benefit from any and all prizes."

Stunned, Esmée sipped her tea without tasting it as her mind flooded with what she knew of maritime criminals and vice-admiralty courts. Though Eliza tried a pastry, she soon gave it up and left her tea unfinished, pleading a headache and saying she wanted to sleep.

Unable to stand the confines of the townhouse and wanting to be free of the house's black trappings that bespoke Quinn's passing at every turn, Esmée put on her cape and escaped into the windy spring afternoon. Sun broke through amassing clouds with a feeble light, illuminating gardens hemmed in by tidy fences and the few passersby traversing the cobblestone streets. She walked toward the governor's palace, her eyes roaming the building's brick face. Somewhere inside was Henri.

Eliza's confession threatened the small peace Esmée had held on to since they'd arrived in Williamsburg. Henri was careful with what he told her. She sensed his holding back, and it frightened her. She longed to ask him detailed questions but felt it only added to the trial before him. She'd not grill him as officials were doing behind closed doors. Her task was to stand by him. Love him. Pray for him.

Lord, please end this. Let truth prevail.

She bypassed the palace and turned right, continuing on in the windy afternoon. So sunk in her own private thoughts was she that she hardly heard a coach roll to a stop across the lonesome stretch of road.

"Daughter, what on earth are you doing on the outskirts of town?" Her father's concerned voice returned her to the present. "Join me in the coach. A storm is brewing."

Indeed, a storm within and without. Esmée looked at the sky, startled she'd walked so far so mindlessly. She'd passed the gaol with its forlorn sounds and smells, the courtyard overfull of the indigent and derelict. The usual pang of sympathy she always felt eluded her completely. She seemed as wooden as a ship's figurehead.

The postilion opened the door, and she settled opposite her father, escaping a lightning-lit landscape. "Why have you come?"

"I heard news—ill news—that the governor is being pressured by certain officials, mainly planters, who've invented charges against the captain. Henri may well be sent to Marshalsea in London for trial at the admiralty court there, thus relieving Virginia of responsibility—"

"*Marshalsea?*" The word was more epithet. Esmée stared at him, lips parted from the most grievous shock yet. "The place of pirates and rogues?"

"That or Newgate. But I'm hoping it's hearsay, and I've come to find out."

Her father never minced words, but for once she wished he would. She could only sit, stunned, as the coach picked up its pace and headed toward the heart of Williamsburg. Her heart seemed to keep time with the horse's hooves, her thoughts somersaulting over themselves in dismal abandon.

"How is your dear sister?" Father asked.

She barely heard his query. Her breath came short, her words scattered. "Eliza . . . she seems to have worsened back at the townhouse. She's begun to go through Quinn's belongings, his study and papers. I've offered to help, but . . . Eliza refused me outright. We visited his gravesite yesterday. Left flowers."

He nodded soberly as the coach turned down Nassau Street. Her gaze returned to the palace as she alighted from the coach. What if Henri wouldn't be coming back to the townhouse? What if he was immediately taken to a port and shipped to England? Hot tears blurred her vision. 'Twas all she could do not to go to pieces in front of her father.

"I'll see how Eliza is before I go to the palace and learn what's afoot," Father said.

They entered together, the butler taking their wraps. No supper smells. No other servants at hand.

"Lady Drysdale is upstairs in her rooms," the butler told them.

Father mounted the steps slowly as if pondering what to say to his youngest daughter once he knocked on the door. If ever Mama was needed, 'twas now.

Esmée passed into the guest chamber and shut the door. Her Bible lay open on the table, a silk ribbon marking the passage she'd been reading before her walk.

The scrap of Psalm was impressed on her heart, a promise to prevent her from falling apart.

In the day of my calamity, the Lord was my stay.

seventy-two

I've never seen Dinwiddie in such a quandary." Father returned from a private meeting with the governor and shook his graying head. "His own ill health is forcing a speedy end to the matter, either here or on English soil."

"Ill health be hanged!" Esmée exclaimed as he removed his hat. "Is there no one in all Virginia who supports my husband?" The exasperated words were tempered by grief. "Oh, that Quinn were here. Then all would be well."

She paced before the parlor hearth as the butler opened the front door to admit Henri himself. He joined them, his slight smile not at all reassuring, though his embrace was warm and heartfelt despite all that was against them.

He took a chair opposite Father by the hearth while Esmée settled on the stool beside him. A maid who had recovered from the pox brought steaming flip and announced supper would be served as soon as they wished. Eliza would not be joining them, pleading a headache. During the time they'd all been at the townhouse, she'd supped with them but once. Esmée had seen the light on in Quinn's study the last two nights. Was her sister unable to sleep and sorting through his things instead?

"How are you holding up under all the scrutiny?" Father asked Henri quietly.

"Well enough." Henri's weary eyes declared otherwise. "I'm most concerned about my crew—the Africans—who've been brought in for questioning. Though freemen, they risk being captured and sold into slavery the longer they're ashore. 'Tis a tenuous business."

"Indeed." Father heaved a sigh. "Dinwiddie and his council seem at sixes and sevens about the entire matter. I've yet to hear any formal charges against you. 'Tis a secretive business as well. The newspapers are printing all manner of false drivel, but most of it is in your favor."

"There are some who feel I'm more pirate than privateer, and no amount of argument or proof will convince them otherwise. And there are those who covet the prizes we've brought in."

"It all smacks of treachery and greed to me." Father stared into his steaming cup. "What of this about banning any outsiders—any spectators—from the proceedings on Friday?"

Henri lifted his shoulders in a shrug. "A precautionary measure, perhaps, as such matters always generate too much interest. But I'm going to request my crew be there. And you and Esmée, of course."

"If they deny you, 'twill be a means of furthering their dark deeds when exposing them to light could end the matter entirely." Esmée's heated remarks drew both men's attention. "I for one will be there. And on the very front row."

"I detect some of your sister's spirit in you," her father said, a beat of sadness in his tone. "Or what once was."

"She's no better?" Henri asked, holding Esmée's gaze.

She reached for his hand. How like him to deflect this serious business and ask about someone else. "She keeps to her rooms by day and Quinn's study by night. I've instructed the servants to serve her no more spirits other than medicinal tonics. She's as yet unable or unwilling to dine with us."

Sympathy shone in his eyes. Grief was a hard season, singular and unpredictable.

A slight commotion in the foyer drew Esmée's eye. When the butler announced Nathaniel Autrey, Henri got to his feet. The men embraced, emotion on both their weathered faces.

"Pardon the interruption, but I wanted to see the captain." Nathaniel took a near chair. "And inquire about Lady Drysdale."

Tears came to Esmée's eyes. Henri had few friends on land, away as he'd been. Quinn had been one of them, and now Nathaniel remained. Ned, Henri called him. His steadfast friend. "You're a most welcome interruption," she said.

"I second that." Henri leaned back in his chair, his reflective mood of moments before shifting. "Stay on for supper, at least."

The parlor air was laden with the smell of roast beef, and through the open door Esmée saw a maid setting the dining room table. Ned and Henri fell into conversation with her father while she excused herself and went upstairs to Eliza's bedchamber.

Not wanting to wake her sister, Esmée cracked open the door. Eliza sat before her dressing table, combing her waist-length hair. Freshly washed, it pillowed about her slim shoulders as it dried, the candlelight calling out every russet highlight.

Esmée entered, shutting the door behind her. "Nathaniel Autrey is here. I thought you might want to see him."

"Chaplain Autrey?"

"He's staying for supper. I hoped you would join us."

Setting her brush aside, Eliza leaned nearer the looking glass. Pots of powder and rouge lay open as if she'd been about to cover her scars. With a shudder, she turned away from her reflection and looked at Esmée seated next to her. "I have no heart for it."

"Please." Esmée was rarely so entreating where Eliza was concerned. "It might well be the last time we are all together."

Eliza's gaze sharpened. "Because Henri might be transported to England, you mean."

Esmée nodded, her whole world upside down. "There's Father besides. He's aged so much of late. Quinn's death has taught me we must never take each other for granted. Ever."

"A lesson I learned too late." Frowning, Eliza reached for some

Hungary water to rub on her temples. "Betimes I think these head-aches will crack my skull."

Esmée breathed in the rosemary-mint scent. "The physic will be here tomorrow."

"Why? No physic has the remedy for what ails me."

Esmée's gaze traveled from the rumpled bed to the bedside table, where a book lay open. A Bible. The one Ned had given her?

"I am missing my wee daughter."

Eliza's surprising admission returned Esmée's attention to her. How could she not miss her own flesh and blood? Yet not once had she mentioned Ruenna since they'd returned to Williamsburg.

"If I am seldom around her, she'll never think of me as her mother. I want Father to bring her to me as soon as it's safe to do so. Besides, I've been reading the papers." She gestured to the copies of the *Virginia Gazette* littering the plank floor. "The pox seems to be abating, according to the medical men. Alice must return too."

"Of course. Father and I would be overjoyed." A glimmer of light broke through the darkness. Esmée smiled, her first in days. "I'm sure Ruenna will be much changed even in the short time you've been apart."

"No doubt." Eliza picked at a stray thread on her sultana. "For now, I want you to give serious thought to living here with me if the worst happens."

The worst? Esmée's mind raced. Henri transported, hanged from the gallows, or perhaps drawn and quartered. A wave of nausea washed through her.

With a grimace, Eliza focused on a window that overlooked Palace Green. "I suppose the matter is to be decided day after to-morrow."

Esmée nodded. "Despite your gracious invitation, I cannot stay on here in Williamsburg. If Henri is to be transported, I will go with him to England."

Eliza turned back to her. Something rare passed over her sister's ravaged features. Fear. But instead of mounting a protest, Eliza seemed to withdraw once again, the pain in her head reflected in her glassy eyes. "Please give my regards to the company. I cannot possibly endure supper."

Heartsick, Esmée stood and leaned in, kissing her sister's once smooth cheek.

Lord, be my stay.

seventy-three

The governor's chambers were cold, the seats hard. Sunlight speared through the closed shutters, arrows of light across the polished floor. Nine o'clock. Esmée and her father were the first to arrive, Ned with them. As they sat near the front, Esmée saw the sea chaplain's lips moving as if in silent prayer.

Dinwiddie had yet to appear. One by one the governor's council members came in, all bewigged and powdered, some undeniably pompous, all eyes down. She knew of these men. Many of them were the most powerful in the colony, with wealth and connections that wove an impenetrable web, placing them above the law. Only two gentlemen were above reproach, men of integrity. Quinn's fellow barristers.

Lord Drysdale's usual place was left vacant. The heaviness in the chamber chilled Esmée to the marrow. Henri sat directly in front of them in a Windsor chair. His wide-set shoulders were unbowed, his manner untroubled. A murmur rippled through the room when his crew took seats in the gallery. Esmée was heartened by their presence. Not one of them seemed to be missing, though the black jacks were here at their own peril, their presence sure to infuriate the most prejudiced on the council.

Her father's shoulder pressed against hers, his low murmur reaching her ears. "I spy the printer for the *Virginia Gazette*."

Behind them, the squint-eyed owner had entered the chamber, a printer's devil with him. The word was that Dinwiddie and the council read and censored every word of each edition before circulation to the public. Would what was printed about these proceedings be fact or fancy?

The governor entered. Esmée felt a flicker of dismay. He looked old. Ill. However careworn and grim his countenance, she would not let it chip away at the promise stored in her heart. She laid hold of the memorized Psalm like a woman drowning.

He delivered me from my strong enemy, and from them that hated me: for they were too strong for me. They prevented me in the day of my calamity: but the Lord was my stay. He brought me forth also into a large place: he delivered me, because he delighted in me.

She fisted her hands in her lap. *Thank You, Lord.*

The chamber doors closed. An opening prayer was uttered. A mockery, Esmée thought. She looked at Henri's bowed head once the amen was said. What was rushing through her beloved's thoughts? Had he any inkling what might befall him here?

The governor addressed the chamber, his color high, his voice hoarse. "We are gathered here on this March day to decide the most suitable, expeditious course of action in the case of Captain Henri Lennox—"

A high voice erupted outside the sealed chamber. Some sort of commotion was brewing. A man's voice was cut short by a woman's strident tone. Then the gilded doors swung open, and every eye turned toward the back of the room. In walked Eliza, clad in all black, her step sure if hurried, a ream of papers clutched in both hands. The tap of her heels created a staccato echo in the large chamber. She looked neither to the right nor the left as she strode toward the front, past a great many astonished officials.

The governor stared at her as if trying to come to terms with her unexpected appearance. "Lady Drysdale . . ."

Eliza gave the most perfunctory of curtsies to Dinwiddie, the silk

369

of her sable skirts rustling, before facing the chamber with its now unsettled council members.

One bewigged gentleman shot to his feet, fury staining his features. "I beg of you, madam, to take leave of these proceedings at once. Sheriff! Bailiffs! Escort this—"

"I shan't be silenced," Eliza all but shouted, overriding him. The cold fire in her eyes mirrored the harsh mettle of her tone. "If you force me from these chambers, I shall bring all my powers and my late husband's powers to bear both here and in the halls of parliament, even before the king himself. Do not underestimate me. You shall hear me out."

She stepped onto the raised dais and took the podium. Lifting her chin, she scanned the chamber as if taking stock of each man present. Unveiled—without even a hint of powder—Eliza was a shocking sight.

"As widow to one of the foremost members of the governor's council, I now state my case. My husband's papers are before me. I have studied them at length since his passing. Before his death he compiled copious correspondence and documentation of matters essential to Williamsburg, as befitted his barrister standing." She looked down at the thick ream and took a deep breath. "If you think my husband's concerns and grievances died with him, you are sorely mistaken."

Eliza's gaze traveled to Henri. She gestured to him with a wave of her hand. "Here we have a man who has been named a French spy. A pirate. That he adamantly opposes slavery is crime enough, especially to you mammon-hungry Virginians with your presumptions of supremacy and inhumane trade of human beings. But I digress. My late husband held Captain Henri Lennox in the highest esteem. As a lawyer of prodigious skill, Lord Drysdale could find no taint associated with the captain's character or reputation. In fact, he was the first to recommend him to sail under a letter of marque and reprisal. He would have been appalled at the false accusations that now float about and besmirch this man's honorable name.

"Captain Lennox had no wish to become embroiled in what will undoubtedly become an international war. He was solicited to do so by the governor himself and council members here, who now prove themselves unworthy of the captain's trust." She spoke rapidly and flawlessly, though Esmée saw her hands tremble as she took hold of the podium's sides. "Having accepted so onerous a mission that could easily have led to his own demise, Captain Lennox instead chased down an entire French fleet on behalf of Virginia's colonial government and His Majesty the King and came away with countless sealed documents and high-placed prisoners of war, not to mention enemy ships." Her voice rose a notch. "The same captain who recently gave so many prizes to the parish almshouse that it has no need of funding for the next five years or better."

She held up an accounting book. Quinn had served as vestryman and overseen parish funds. When Eliza stated the bestowed sum, the stilted silence gave way to a shocked murmur.

"Who dares bring a charge against this man?" Again Eliza scanned the overflowing chamber. "I challenge the foremost accuser, Mr. Jeffries. With your fomenting violence and mayhem in your parish's last questionable election, will you cast the first stone?" Her gaze traveled to another man on the first row. "And Mr. Percy, owner of the largest number of slave ships in Virginia, who in the year 1753 killed two Africans in a drunken rage but was never brought to trial? And you, Mr. Taylor, who cries the loudest for liberty against taxes and tyranny yet has recently been discovered embezzling funds from various businesses in town—have you any inkling of true freedom, shackled as you are to enormous personal debt? Lord Drysdale has evidence— witnesses—that prove you were in league with Jago Wherry from the almshouse to further your avaricious purposes. Shall I enlighten the chamber as to how your actions threatened my dear sister and other vulnerable women and children on Indigo Island?" She stared at Taylor till he looked away. "Must I continue, councillors?"

Eliza set the book aside and looked to Quinn's papers. "I also have before me sound evidence regarding a conspiracy involving the murder of a customs inspector a twelvemonth ago that involves your illustrious family, Mr. Calvert. And then there is the matter of Mr. Byrd, who has incited rebellion in his very county with the intent to repeal a new tax. Not to mention Mr. Knox, who has attempted to bribe the Speaker of the House with ten thousand pounds tobacco. Then there is Mr. Burkhardt, who has taken a pen name to publish a scandalous libel on this government and the established church. Such smacks of treason, does it not?"

Esmée did not realize she had been holding her breath till her chest began to ache. Beside her, Father sat stunned. This was the Eliza of old, who seemed to gather momentum with each and every word, driven by a sort of holy zeal.

"Almighty God has a quarrel with you councillors. Has He not said, 'Woe unto you, hypocrites! for ye are like unto whited sepulchres, which indeed appear beautiful outward, but are within full of dead men's bones, and of all uncleanness'? Indeed, which of you will cast the first stone?" She gathered up Quinn's papers. "How dare you accuse Captain Henri Lennox of anything at all."

The entire chamber seemed to hold a collective breath as Eliza left the podium and strode down the aisle to exit through the door she had entered. It closed behind her with a resounding shudder, a proper exclamation point to her heated defense.

Tears gathered in Esmée's eyes, making Henri's back a blur of blue cloth. No one had yet said a word. The silence was ponderous and—could it be?—threaded with an undercurrent of shame, as if the entire assembly had taken a whipping.

Governor Dinwiddie finally stood, his face the scarlet of the red-coated soldiers at his command. He struggled to speak. Taking out a handkerchief, he dabbed at his brow, then looked to the council. "Gentlemen—though I use the term loosely—who among you will now cast the first stone, as Lady Drysdale so eloquently and truthfully put it? Join me in the antechamber at once."

An excruciating silence followed. Esmée fixed her eyes on the podium Eliza had vacated as council members slowly got to their feet and adjourned through a side door. Bending her head, Esmée shut her eyes.

Lord, You alone can deliver us. Not Dinwiddie. Not Eliza. Not even Quinn had he been here. God alone.

Molasses-slow minutes ticked by. Esmée raised her head, eyes on Henri's broad back. He sat stone still, gaze forward. She longed to go to him but daren't leave her seat and cause another commotion. Murmuring began in the chamber around her. What she would give to be a fly on the wall in the antechamber! Beside her, Father and Ned sat as stoically as Henri.

At the stroke of eleven, the governor reappeared. But not the council members.

Dinwiddie inclined his head to Henri. "Captain Lennox, you are hereby dismissed. The council shan't be taking any more of your time with its unwarranted charges and fomenting of libelous gossip. Your exemplary service to the colonies and crown cannot be understated."

Joy sang through Esmée. She shot to her feet with a rustle of her silk skirts, wanting to forsake this cold, accusatory chamber as fast as she could. But not without her beloved. Henri turned toward her, his eyes smiling though his face stayed stoic. Ned grabbed Henri's hand and shook it while Father let out a long, relieved breath.

"This calls for a celebration," Father said. "Let's hasten to the Edinburgh Castle tavern, which has just reopened. A celebratory beefsteak dinner seems in order. Shall we?"

Overcome, Esmée dried her eyes discreetly with a handkerchief. "A shame Eliza can't join us."

Her father nodded as they moved toward the door. "After a stellar performance of which Quinn would have been proud, your sister has earned her rest. But 'twill take me a sennight to recover myself."

Ned grinned and adjusted his cocked hat. "Lady Drysdale's delivery puts most pastors I know to shame. And a great many actors and actresses."

Father led their small procession. "Now seems the time to tell you I'm returning to sea." Catching Esmée's wide-eyed stare, he amended, "It seems the crown is in need of my services now that war with France is to be declared."

They exited the palace into a windy, sun-scented world. Henri picked a blossom from a flowering dogwood on Palace Green and passed it to her. Arm in arm they walked toward Duke of Gloucester

Street, elation in her step as she kept up with his long stride. Her father and Ned went ahead of them, deep in conversation.

"So, Mistress Lennox, what say you about our future?" Henri brought her gloved hand near and kissed it. "Shall we set sail tomorrow for our island? Resume our honeymoon?"

"Tomorrow?" She smiled. "I'm ready to return right now, though Father is intent on a little feasting and we must thank my sister."

"Thanks hardly seems enough," Henri said.

They walked on beneath flowering trees, still stunned by the turn of events. When they reached the tavern, fiddle music spilled from its open windows, joyous and lively, entirely fit for the occasion. While Father and Ned passed inside to seek a table, Henri removed his hat and stood alone with her in the tavern's entry.

"As I told you, I've retired as privateer and government agent." His sea-shaded eyes were as earnest as she'd ever seen them. "My future is yours. Ours. On the island, tending the light."

"God be thanked." She laid a hand on his smoothly shaven cheek, wanting to put distance between them and the mainland as soon as possible. "Let us be away to our island, then. Our future is bright."

Turn the Page for Chapter 1 of Another Captivating Story from Laura Frantz—
Available Now

On the eve of her wedding, Lady Elisabeth Lawson's world is shattered as surely as the fine glass windows of her colonial Williamsburg home. In a town seething with Patriots ready for rebellion, her protection comes from an unlikely source— if she could only protect her heart.

CHAPTER

one

MAY 1775

Elisabeth took a breath, breaking an intense hour of concentration. Mindful of the pinch of her stays, she straightened, the ache in her back and shoulders easing. In her apron-clad lap was the round pillow with the new lace she'd worked. Delicate as snowflakes, the intricate design was crafted of imported linen thread, now a good two yards of snowy white. She preferred white to black. All skilled lacemakers knew that working with white was kinder to the eye.

Raising her gaze, she looked out fine English glass onto a world of vivid greens broken by colorful splashes of blossoms. Elisabeth's favorites, butter-yellow roses and pale pink peonies, danced in the wind as it sighed around the townhouse's corners. Nearly summer at last. But not only almost June. 'Twas nearly her wedding day.

"*Oh là là!* What have we here?" Around the bedchamber's corner came a high, musical voice. "Surely a bride does not sew her own laces!"

"Nay, Isabeau. I've not patience enough for that."

"Not for an entire wedding gown, *merci.*" The maid rounded the four-poster bed as fast as her girth would allow, holding a pair of clocked stockings. "You have been busy all the forenoon and likely forgot 'tis nearly teatime with the countess. Lady Charlotte surely wants to discuss your betrothal ball. 'Tis rumored Lord and Lady Amberly will be there."

Elisabeth nearly smiled at her maid's flaunting of titles. A humble Huguenot, Isabeau was still as bedazzled by the gentry as the day she'd first landed on Virginia's shores. Elisabeth set aside her lace pillow and watched her maid pull two tea gowns from a large armoire.

"Are you in a blue mood or a yellow one?"

"Yellow," she said. Yellow was Lady Charlotte's favorite color, and Elisabeth sought to cheer her all she could. In turn, the governor's palace served up a lavish tea table that surely rivaled the British king's.

Glancing at the tiny watch pinned to her bodice, Elisabeth left her chair so that Isabeau could undress and redress her.

"'Tis such a lovely day, likely the countess wants a turn in the garden. Do you think her girls will be about?"

"I should hope so. Fresh air and exercise are good for them, though their father oft keeps them inside of late."

Isabeau darted her a fretful look. "On account of the trouble, you mean."

Elisabeth tried not to think of that. "The sun might spoil their complexion, Lady Charlotte says. And she's right, you know. Look at me!" Though faint, the freckles across the bridge of her nose and the top of her cheekbones gave her skin a slightly tarnished look that even ample powder couldn't cover. Her fault for slipping outside with her handwork in the private corner of the garden she was so fond of, forever hatless.

"You are *tres belle*, even speckled," Isabeau said, lacing her stays a bit tighter. "And you've won the most dashing suitor in all Virginia Colony, no?"

"One of them." Elisabeth swallowed hard to keep from saying more on that score too. Her fiancé, Miles Cullen Roth, was many things, but he was not cut of the same cloth as fellow Virginians William Drew and George Rogers Clark and Edmund Randolph.

Isabeau's voice dropped to a whisper. "Though I do wonder about love."

Elisabeth shot a glance at the cracked bedchamber door. Papa always said she gave the servants too much room to talk, but the truth was she preferred plain speaking to the prissy airs of the drawing room. "'Tis a business matter, marriage."

"So says your father." Isabeau frowned her displeasure. "I am a romantic. One must marry for love, no?"

"Is that the way of it in France?"

"*Oui, oui!*" her maid answered.

Though she was an indentured servant, Isabeau did not have a father who orchestrated her every move. Given that, Elisabeth could only guess the gist of Isabeau's thoughts. *I am free. Free to come and go outside of work. Free to marry whom I please.*

And she? Who was Elisabeth Anne Lawson? The reflection in the looking glass told her little. When the history books were printed and gathered dust, what would be said of her?

That she had the fortune—or misfortune—to be the only child of the governor of Virginia Colony, the earl of Stirling? Daughter of a firebrand mother who used ink and quill like a weapon? Possessor of a pedigree and dowry the envy of any colonial belle? Friend and confidante of Lady Dunmore? Wife of Miles Cullen Roth? Mistress of Roth Hall?

End of story.

The scarlet seal on the letter was as unmistakable as the writing hand. Noble Rynallt took it from his housekeeper and retreated to the quiet of Ty Mawr's paneled study. Sitting down in a leather chair, he propped his dusty boots up on the wide windowsill overlooking the James River before breaking the letter's seal.

> *Time is of the essence. We must take account of our true allies as well as our enemies. You must finagle a way to attend Lord Dunmore's ball 2 June, 1775, at the Palace. 'Tis on behalf of*

your cousin, after all. Gather any intelligence you can that will
aid our cause.

Patrick Henry

'Twas the last of May. Noble had little time to finagle. His cousin
was soon to wed Williamsburg's belle, Lady Elisabeth Lawson. He'd
given it little thought, had no desire to attend any function at the
Governor's Palace, especially one in honor of his nemesis's daughter.
Lord Stirling was onto him, onto all the Independence Men, and none
of them had received an invitation. But 'twas as Henry said, Noble's
cousin was the groom. Surely an invitation was forthcoming or had
been overlooked.

Noble frowned, thinking of the stir he'd raise appearing. Lord
Stirling was likely to have an apoplectic fit. But if that happened,
at least one of the major players barring Virginia Colony's fight for
independence would be removed. And his own attendance at the ball
would announce he'd finally come out of second mourning.

The unwrinkled copy of the *Virginia Gazette*, smelling of fresh
ink and Dutch bond paper, seemed to shout the matrimonial news.

Miles Cullen Roth's future bride, Lady Elisabeth Lawson, an
agreeable young Lady of Fortune, will preside at the Governor's
ball the 2nd of June, 1775 . . .

The flowery column included details of the much-anticipated event
right down to her dowry, naming minutiae even Elisabeth was unaware
of. As she turned the paper facedown atop the dressing table, her smile
faded. A ticklish business, indeed.

Isabeau, quick to catch her mistress's every mood, murmured, "The
beggars! I'd rather it be said you have a sunny disposition and Christian character. Or that you are a smidgen over five feet tall, flaxen

haired, and have all your teeth save one. And that one, *Dieu merci*, is a jaw tooth!"

"I *am* Williamsburg's bride," Elisabeth said as her maid pinned her gown together with practiced hands. "The locals feel they can print what they want about me. After all, I was born and bred in this very spot and have been catered to ever since."

"You don't begrudge them their bragging?" Isabeau studied her. "Having the particulars of one's dowry devoured by the masses seems shabby somehow."

"It does seem silly. Everyone knows what everyone else is worth in Williamsburg. There's no need to spell it out."

"Tell that to your dear papa," Isabeau answered with furrowed brow. "He had a footman pass out multiple copies of the *Gazette* this morning like bonbons on Market Square."

Unsurprised, Elisabeth fell silent. Turning, silk skirts swishing, she extended an arm for Isabeau to arrange the beribboned sleeve. Below came the muted sound of horse hooves atop cobblestones.

"Your intended? On time? And in such stormy weather?" Isabeau looked up at her mistress with surprised jade eyes.

Turning toward an open window, Elisabeth listened but now only heard the slur of rain. "Mister Roth promised he'd come. 'Tis all that matters. He didn't say when."

"How long has it been since you've seen him?"

"April," Elisabeth admitted reluctantly, wondering why Isabeau even asked. Her maid well knew, being by her side night and day. Isabeau's pinched expression was a reminder that Miles was not a favorite, no matter his standing in Williamsburg. Elisabeth dug for another excuse. "He's been busy getting Roth Hall ready for us, his letters said."

She felt a twinge at her own words, for his letters had been but two over six months. He sent unnecessary, extravagant gifts instead. Gold earrings in the shape of horseshoes. A bottle-green riding dress. Pineapples, lemons, and limes from his estate's orangery. A London-built carriage. So many presents she soon lost track of them. And not a one had swayed Isabeau's low opinion of him.

Despite his generosity, Elisabeth felt a sense of foreboding for the future. She did not want his gifts. She wanted his presence. If he was like her oft-absent father . . . 'Twas difficult to see clear to what she really hoped for. A happy home. A whole family.

"Your coiffure is *magnifique*, no?" The words were uttered with satisfaction as Isabeau produced a hand mirror for her to better see the lovely twisting of curls falling to her shoulders, the wig dusted a costly powdered pink. Twin ostrich feathers, dyed a deeper rose, plumed near her right ear.

"I don't know." Reaching up, Elisabeth slid free the pins holding the wig in place, displacing the artfully arranged feathers. "Powder is going out of fashion like patch boxes. Tonight I will move forward with fashion."

Her maid's brows arched, but she took the wig and put it on a near stand, where it looked forlorn and deflated. Catching a glimpse of herself in the mirror, Isabeau smoothed a silvered strand of her own charcoal hair into place beneath her cap. At middle age, she was still an attractive woman, as dark as Elisabeth was fair.

"We must make haste, no? But first . . ." Isabeau retrieved the ostrich feathers and refastened them in Elisabeth's hair while her mistress glanced again at the watch lying faceup on her dressing table.

Late.

Miles was nothing if not perpetually late, while she happened to be an on-time sort of person. Fighting frustration, she set down the hand mirror. "I wonder what Mama is doing tonight."

Isabeau looked up, a telling sympathy in her eyes. "Your *mère* will rejoin you when all this talk of tea and taxes blows over, no?"

Elisabeth had no answer. Mama had sailed to England—Bath—months ago. All this talk of tea and taxes had no end.

A soft knock sounded on the door, followed by another maid's muffled voice. "A gentleman to see you, m'lady, in the drawing room."

A gentleman? Not her intended? She smiled wryly. Likely the servants didn't remember Miles.

She went hot, then cold. Miles's visits were so few and far between, he seemed a stranger each time she saw him. Because of it they spent the better part of an hour becoming reacquainted at each meeting. Tonight would be no different. Perhaps they'd recover the time lost to them in the coach.

Isabeau steered her to the stool of her dressing table. With deft hands, she clasped a strand of pearls about Elisabeth's neck. The routine was reassuring. Familiar. Selecting a glass bottle, Elisabeth uncapped it, overwhelmed by the scent of the latest cologne from London. Rose geranium. Again Elisabeth peered at her reflection in the looking glass with a sense of growing unease.

Everything seemed new tonight. Her scent. Her shoes. Her stays. Her gown. She'd never worn such a gown, nor felt so exposed. Despite the creamy lace spilling in profusion about her bare shoulders, the décolletage was decidedly daring. Made of oyster-pink silk, the gown shimmered and called out her every curve. The mantua maker had outdone herself this time. Fit for Queen Charlotte, it was.

Moving to the door, she grasped about for a glimmer of anticipation. "I'd best not keep company waiting."

At this, Isabeau rolled her eyes. "I should like to hear Mister Roth say such!"

Isabeau followed her out, and they passed down a dimly lit hall to a landing graced with an oriole window and upholstered seat. The velvety blackness beyond the shining glass was splashed with rain, not pierced with stars, and the warm air was soaked. This was her prayer place. Isabeau paused for a moment as Elisabeth bent her head briefly before going further.

Then down, down, down the circular steps they went, Isabeau pulling at a stray thread or straightening a fold in the polonaise skirt before reaching the open door of the sitting room, its gaudy gold and scarlet overpowering and oppressive even by candlelight. The colors reminded Elisabeth of red-coated British soldiers. She stepped inside as Isabeau retreated. Her eyes shot to the marble hearth where she expected Miles Roth to be.

"Lady Elisabeth."

She swung round, her skirts sashaying, her head spinning as well. Mercy, her stays were tight. She'd eaten little at tea.

Behind her stood a man, the shadows hiding his features. She put out a hand to steady herself, missing the needed chair back by a good two inches and finding a coat sleeve instead. The gentleman looked down at her and she looked up, finding his dark head just shy of the wispy clouds skittering in blue oils across the ceiling. Whoever he was, he wasn't Miles. Miles was but two inches taller than she.

"Mister . . ."

"Rynallt. Noble Rynallt of Ty Mawr."

What? A recollection returned to her in a rush. Noble Rynallt was a distant cousin of Miles. So distant she had no further inkling of their tie. Quickly she calculated what little she knew of him. Welsh to the bone. Master of a large James River estate. Recently bereft of a sister. A lawyer turned burgess. The Rynallts were known for their horses, were they not? Horse racing? The finest horseflesh in Virginia, if not all the colonies.

She was certain of only one thing.

Noble Rynallt was here because Miles was not.

Surprise mellowed to resignation. She gave a small curtsy. "Mister Rynallt, what an unexpected pleasure."

"Mayhap more surprise."

She hesitated. He was honest, at least. "Is Mister Roth . . ."

"Delayed." He managed to look bemused. And apologetic.

She tried not to stare as rich impressions crowded her senses. A great deal of muscle and broadcloth and sandalwood. The cut of his suit was exceptionally fine, dark but for the deep blue waistcoat embroidered with the bare minimum of silver thread, a creamy stock about his neck. The color of his eyes eluded her, the remainder of his features failing to take root as she dwelt on the word *delayed*.

Dismayed, she anchored herself to the chair at last.

"He asked me to act as your escort till he arrives." He struck a conciliatory tone. "If you'll have me."

He had the grace to sound a bit embarrassed, as well he should. This was, after all, her betrothal ball given by Lord Dunmore at the Governor's Palace, with the cream of all Williamsburg in attendance. And she was coming not with her intended but with a . . . stranger.

Nay, worse. Far worse.

Yet good breeding wouldn't allow a breach of manners. She forced a small smile. "I thank you for the kindness. Will my intended's delay be long?"

"As brief as possible, I should hope," he replied, extending an arm.

No matter who Noble Rynallt was, his polite manner communicated that he had all in hand. Yet it failed to give her the slightest ease.

"As I rode in I noticed your coach waiting," he remarked as he led her down the front steps, past the butler to the mounting block. "I'll ride alongside on my horse."

Behind them the foyer's grandfather clock tolled one too many times. The ball had begun. Lord Dunmore hated latecomers.

They'd be fashionably tardy, at best.

ACKNOWLEDGMENTS

Where do I even begin?

People often ask me how to write a book, and I honestly tell them I don't know. It's a gift. What I do know is that my publisher, Baker Publishing Group, is extraordinary, from editorial to cover design to marketing and sales, and dedicated to bringing the most edifying fiction to readers. I'm always amazed to be part of that extraordinary process, and it's a pleasure to give a shout-out to the people who make my books better.

My agent, Janet Grant, a shining light in the industry. Andrea Doering, with her huge heart for readers. Jessica English, a wordsmith deserving of her name who, with an unswerving eye for detail, helps polish a book till print. The proofreaders, who catch every little error (or most). And my amazing marketing team, headed by Michele Misiak and publicist Karen Steele, to the sales reps and book retailers who give a book a place in a noisy world. And last but not least, Laura Klynstra, senior art director, who captured the mood and essence of *A Heart Adrift* with an exceptional cover.

A shout-out to my dear author friends, especially the irrepressible Pepper Basham, and fellow travelers who continually inspire me and make time spent on our Facebook group page "The Armchair Traveler" so much fun. Please join us!

Last but not least, a book would just sit on the shelf without readers and all those who share their love of reading through social media, reviews, gracious comments, etc. Beautiful bookstagrams especially make my world go round. Heartfelt thanks for your reading time and all else you do!

AUTHOR NOTE

Who would have thought a lifelong love of chocolate would lead to a novel about a chocolatier? But not chocolate as we know it. As has been said, "The past is a foreign country. They do things differently there." And that includes chocolate. Though I am not a chocolate historian, I quickly became intrigued by just how those American colonists developed a taste for cocoa. As so often happened, Benjamin Franklin was ahead of the trend, selling chocolate from his print shop as early as 1735. Even George and Martha Washington drank it as a favorite beverage. If you're wanting to learn more, Colonial Williamsburg is a wonderful resource both on-site and online for chocolate history, and if you crave a taste of historic chocolate, then American Heritage Chocolate might be a good start.

It's such a pleasure to set a novel in the richly historic area of Yorktown, which was once York, Virginia. Though it's hard to imagine what it must have been like in its heyday, one English traveler leaves us with a compelling impression from a letter published in the *London Magazine* in 1764: "Yorktown makes no inconsiderable figure. You perceive a great air of opulence amongst the inhabitants who have, some of them, built themselves houses equal in magnificence to many of our superb ones at St. James, as those of Mr. Lightfoot, Nelson, etc."

Today Yorktown is quieter but surely just as beautiful as it was then. The Hornsby House Inn's gracious hospitality and water views and York's wonderful museums make it come alive. Though Indigo Island is entirely fictitious, there are many islands that exist like it, including the historic Chincoteague with its wild ponies, which inspired me as I wrote this novel.

Ever since I was a child and watched *The Ghost and Mrs. Muir* (there's a novel too!), I've had a fondness for sea captains and an outright fascination for pirates. Of all my research materials, *Black Jacks: African American Seamen in the Age of Sail* by W. Jeffrey Bolster stands out as both compelling and educational, opening a door on a world unknown to many. Privateers such as Captain Henri Lennox played a critical part in the American colonies achieving independence and the formation of the United States Navy—no small feat.

Women lighthouse keepers became increasingly common from the colonial period onward, some serving astonishingly long periods of time and proving entirely capable. *Women Who Kept the Lights: An Illustrated History of Women Lighthouse Keepers* by Mary Louise Clifford was a favorite resource of mine, as was *The Lighthouse Keeper's Daughter* by Hazel Gaynor, a novel based on the life of England's legendary Grace Darling.

I never imagined writing a book about smallpox in the midst of a pandemic, but doing so gave me better insight into the history of disease and made me very thankful for modern medicine. My dear friend Ginger Graham, to whom this book is dedicated, lost her life to COVID-19 as this book neared print, giving me a very personal window on grief in a health crisis. I realized anew that life continues its usual pace even though the hole in your heart is huge. Eternal reunions must be magnificent. I'm so thankful for the hope we have in Christ.

If you've read my other novels, then you know how much I love to tuck children, especially babies, into books. It's fun to think of who or what Ruenna Cheverton might become when she grows up. Maybe she'll have a novel of her own someday. There's no doubt she'll have a fondness for a certain island and chocolate!

If you'd like to stay connected, please visit my website at www .laurafrantz.net, where you can sign up for my seasonal newsletter and find me via social media. And I'd love to have you join us at "The Armchair Traveler," a private Facebook page where we talk tea, travel, and books.

Till next time, happy reading!

Laura Frantz is a Christy Award and INSPY Award winner of thirteen novels, including *Tidewater Bride*, *The Lacemaker*, *The Frontiersman's Daughter*, *Courting Morrow Little*, *The Colonel's Lady*, and *A Bound Heart*. She loves to travel, garden, cook, and be in her office/library. When not at home in Kentucky, she and her husband live in Washington State. Learn more at www.laurafrantz.net.

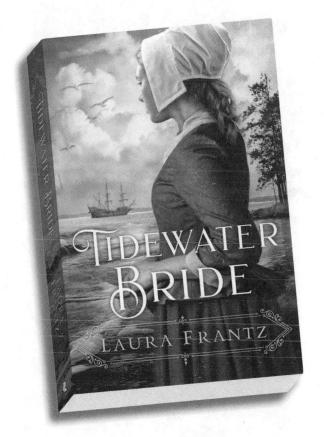

Their Stations Could Not Have Been More Different . . .

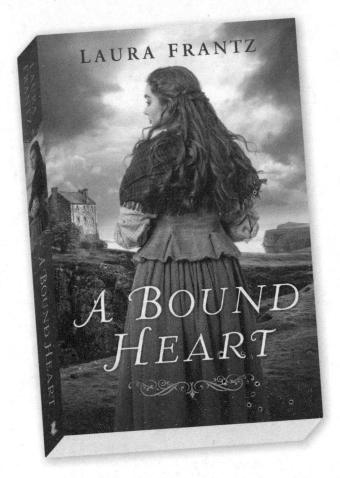

When a tragedy forces both a Scottish laird and a simple lass to colonial Virginia as indentured servants, can a love thwarted by tradition come to life in a new land?

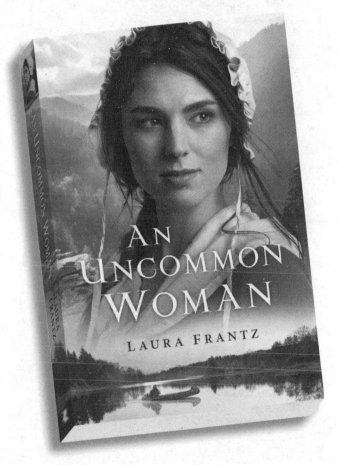

Can Love Survive the Secrets Kept Buried within a Tormented Heart?

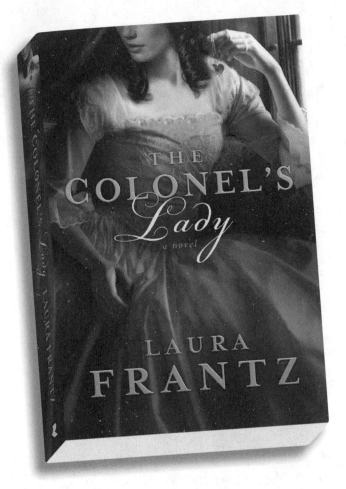

In 1779, a search for her father brings Roxanna to the Kentucky frontier—but she discovers instead a young colonel, a dark secret . . . and a compelling reason to stay. Laura Frantz delivers a powerful story of love, faith, and forgiveness in *The Colonel's Lady.*

MEET

LAURA FRANTZ

Visit LauraFrantz.net to read
Laura's blog and learn about her books!

f Enter to win contests and learn about what
Laura is working on now

y Tweet with Laura

P See what inspired the characters and stories

THE
SIXTIES
YEARS OF HOPE
DAYS OF RAGE

TODD GITLIN

BANTAM BOOKS · NEW YORK · TORONTO · LONDON · SYDNEY · AUCKLAND

THE SIXTIES
A Bantam Book
PUBLISHING HISTORY

Bantam hardcover edition / November 1987
Bantam trade edition / March 1989
Bantam revised trade edition / August 1993

Bantam Books are published by Bantam Books, a division of Random House, Inc. Its trademark, consisting of the words "Bantam Books" and the portrayal of a rooster, is Registered in U.S. Patent and Trademark Office and in other countries. Marca Registrada, Bantam Books, 1540 Broadway, New York, New York 10036.

PRINTED IN THE UNITED STATES OF AMERICA
BVG 20   19   18   17   16   15   14

FOR RUTH

CONTENTS

PART FOUR: **FORCING THE REVOLUTION**

Men fight and lose the battle, and the thing that they fought for comes about in spite of their defeat, and when it comes turns out not to be what they meant, and other men have to fight for what they meant under another name.

—William Morris

The age of lust is giving birth
Both the parents ask
The nurse to tell them fairy tales
On both sides of the glass
And now the infant with his cord
Is hauled in like a kite
One eye filled with blueprints
One eye filled with night

—Leonard Cohen

PREFACE TO THE NEW EDITION

All times of upheaval begin as surprises and end as clichés. Such is the fate of the great tidal swells of history—especially in a shorthand culture where insatiable media grind the flux of the world into the day's sound bites. Wondering where we stand in history, or even whether there exists a comprehensible history in which to stand, we grapple for ready-made coordinates. And so, as time passes, oversimplifications become steadily less resistible. All the big pictures tend to turn monochromatic.

The cultural reputations of whole decades are particularly crude. No sooner do we enter a year whose final digit is nine than the great machinery of the media is flooding us with phrases to sum up the previous ten years and characterize the next. The phrases are conveniences, of course, handles for unwieldy reality. They are also ideological code, a symbolic repertory for the perplexed. The prefabricated images are wheeled out to enshrine myths. And they accomplish this neatly when the catchphrases are simplistic—thus the Fifties are said to have been nothing but complacent, the Sixties nothing but glorious (or disastrous), the Eighties nothing but self-indulgent.

Perhaps no decade has suffered this absurd reduction more than "the Sixties," which in popular parlance has come to stand for a single seamless whole, an entity that presidential candidates and talk-show guests are pressed to take a position on. They must have been either wonderfully high times or else a catastrophe anyone was lucky to have survived. They were days of unbridled idealism or rampant destruction, youthful exuberance or degeneracy, moral intelligence or stupidity. They must have been an unsurpassed time of righteous revolt or an abyss from which only the triumph of Ronald Reagan rescued us. All the myths, left or right or neither of the above, today serve in part as alibis, rationales for the slogans of the present, relieving us of the need to understand the complex tendencies at work in the present and the obligation to do what can be done here and now.

There is a specific reason, of course, why "the Sixties" are still so heated a subject. To put it briefly, the genies that the Sixties loosed are still abroad in the land, inspiring and unsettling and offending, making trouble. For the civil rights and antiwar and countercultural and women's and the rest of that decade's movements forced upon us central issues for Western civilization—fundamental questions of value, fundamental divides of culture, fundamental debates about the nature of the good life. For better and worse, the ideas and impulses remain, transposed into other keys, threatening, agitating, destabilizing—and, in 1992, prevailing—as Bill Clinton brilliantly established that an antiwar activist with a feminist and a professional for a wife was, at the very least, not disqualified from the highest national leadership.

In this sense, the 1992 campaign was the latest in a generation-long sequence of contests over, among other things, the question of who won the Sixties. In fact, every national election since 1968 has been, at least on its symbolic plane, a cultural referendum. Thus, in 1992, a spokesman for President George Bush blamed Los Angeles's burning and looting (or, rather, "inner-city difficulties") on unspecified government programs of the Sixties, while Vice-President Dan Quayle singled out as the "unfortunate legacy of the baby-boomer generation" that it was at "war against traditional values." In the public limelight, George Will has made an expressive and self-validating career of deploring "the cult of self-validating expression" and declaring that "the central myth of the Sixties was that the wretched excess was really a serious quest for new values." The absorbing question in coming years is whether the Clinton administration—only the second *in sixty years* to be headed by a man who was never a commander or a soldier in World War II—can further both the libertarian and communitarian sides of the Sixties spirit without letting a bad economy and Republican nastiness drive wedges into their triumphant coalition.

In the interim, much of the talk about the Sixties has trivialized the stakes. Who isn't sick of hearing the songs and stories of Sixtiesiana, not to mention the rock 'n' rolling commercials? Young political activists who take inspiration from the civil rights and antiwar movements of the Sixties groan at the thought of one more Sixties song, one more anniversary news report about glory days gone by. The halo of "the Sixties" has weighed on them, as if nothing they might ever do in their own lives could match the deeds of the giants of yesteryear who stalked the earth leading casts of thousands. While the spirit of voluntary service (an underappreciated tradition in the Sixties) is reviving on campuses, many college students today, especially children of the New Left and the counterculture, regret having "missed the fun"; they are envious of AIDSless sex, communes, VW bugs, all that careless rapture—and who can blame them?

The unavoidable question, whether posed nostalgically or harshly, in disappointed or smug or prosecutorial tones, refuses to go away: What did "the Sixties"—the movements, the spirit—accomplish? I argue in the multiple endings of *The Sixties* that assessments of the meaning and impact of the past are always provisional, always colored by intervening history. Caught in the Ice Age, one's memories turn rosy—never more than when the recollected past is the moment of one's one and only youth as well as a searing and incandescent time. During the Reagan and Bush years, the prevailing answer was: *The Sixties were a bust.* Or the next worst thing: something to "put behind us," a fashion, "history" (to use the colloquial pejorative). Thus a savvy newsman on National Public Radio suggests disparagingly that the main thing that "the Sixties" changed is America's eating habits. A student on the Berkeley campus wonders bemusedly what to wear for the evening's "Sixties party" on Fraternity Row. Quaintness is the afterimage of bygone principles. It has been the right more than the left that has credited the Sixties movements with lasting accomplishments—a backhanded compliment indeed, to say that the movements trashed families, canons, standards, traditions, housewives, heterosexual dominion, and everything else holy.

The truth is that the movements were tremendously (at best, wondrously) complex and self-contradictory—no wonder they developed unevenly, no wonder it is difficult to pick out their consequences with any precision. At least equally important, they did not give birth to themselves, much as they sometimes fancied they had. The cultural, political, and economic currents that fed them also limited them. They had great successes and squandered great opportunities—unsatisfactory as this answer may ring to those who think, in Hollywood fashion, that history is either (choose one) a chorus of angels or a bummer.

So then, after all the qualifications, what *did* all the uprisings of the Sixties accomplish? A great deal for the good; and not nearly enough; and at a price. To reckon adequately with the successes, the limits, and the missed opportunities would require another book; here I wish only to offer a framework for thinking about the consequences and meanings of the Sixties insurgencies under four headings: social equality (race, gender, sexuality); wide-open "life-styles" (sex, drugs, rock 'n' roll); the limitation of national violence and the care of the earth; and the spread of democratic activity.

SOCIAL EQUALITY

• Whatever the subsequent disappointments and disillusionments, the civil rights movement relaunched the long, long trek toward racial equality. The movement's rise and fall, its transmutation from Southern nonviolence to black power, its insistence on the self-determination of the insulted and injured, was the template for every other movement of the decade. At stake was the rock-bottom principle of the Declaration of Independence, the rights of citizens not only to formal political participation (*e.g.,* the right to vote) but also to the dignity of social recognition (*e.g.*, the right to take a seat in the orchestra of a movie theater). White supremacy having been the original and besetting sin of the American nation, the struggle against it has been traumatic and unfinished and did not, could not, occur without a backlash.

For in mobilizing a mass opposition to race inequality, the movement for the rights of African (and other dark-skinned) Americans had to aggrieve many whites. It also intensified the counterresentments of the many white have-a-littles who felt hard-pressed by the dark-skinned have-nots—just at a time when the American economy was forfeiting its post–World War II dominance and starting downward. Instead of the class solidarity of a majority, there ensued racial panic, blockbusting, white flight, declining schools, resegregation, intractable ghettoes, and a shrinking tax base for the increasingly nonwhite cities. Once the lines of cleavage became economic, the fight for rising shares of a dwindling bounty made for lasting wedges.

Panic, rancor, recrimination: a situation tailor-made for the Republican politics of racial resentment. As long as race was a more salient fact than class in American lives, and the economy was in decline, the pursuit of racial justice for minorities had the partly unintended consequence of suppressing the deep but less acknowledged inequality of American life—the inequality of treatment by class—affecting life expectancy, health, education, and the many other goods of a modern society. Already back in the Sixties, even before busing and affirmative action polarized the population, Republican politicians had begun to make capital by splitting the white South off from the Democratic Party, undermining the liberal majority, composing a new alliance by convincing the white steelworker that he had more in common with the steel executive who moved the plant to Mexico than with the unemployed son of the black janitor. The partially integrated black middle classes abandoned the ghetto, leaving it more desperate. The result was to strangle the resources available for cities (meaning, increasingly, minorities) which in turn accelerated the rage and withdrawal of blacks, a rising rate of violent crime especially on the part of blacks (and the perception that it was rising even faster than it was), rampant fear, and a penchant for short-term "solutions" by force.

To abolish legal segregation, to bring African-Americans and their concerns into American politics and professional life, to enlarge the black middle-class—all this was long overdue, and crucial. But the aftermath of slavery remains grotesque and, since the Sixties, worsening. Now, men in Harlem live shorter lives than men in Bangladesh. Two-thirds of black households have zero or negative net financial assets, compared to thirty percent for whites. On top of the insults imposed by poverty and racial discrimination come the dangers imposed by criminals, disproportionately the hard-core, disproportionately black poor—who find in the drug trade the income and opportunity which they cannot find in the legitimate economy. Nihilism spirals. Punishment begets crime begets punishment.

"The problem of the twentieth century," wrote W. E. B. DuBois in

1903, understating the issue, "is the problem of the color line." The twenty-first century will begin on the same shaky footing.

• The women's movement broke down so many barriers as to have transformed American social relations (at least outside the U.S. Senate and its Judiciary Committee) beyond recognition. Careers opened up, laws were altered, assumptions about women's place were sent reeling. The movement for the civil rights of women succeeded brilliantly—so much so that many women under thirty take these conquests for granted and conclude that there remains no need for feminism. As a cultural force, likewise, if we compare the present with a generation ago, feminism has to be counted a tremendous success, whatever the rollbacks and the periodic declarations that, except for a few cranks, we're all "postfeminist" now. The women's movement, built on the irreversible entry of women into the work force, has remade much of daily life and language. The insistence on "chairperson" is easily mocked, but hardly cancels the moral advances in vocabulary marked by "sexism," "sexual harassment," "marital rape," "battered women," the public acknowledgment of incest—the very terms, and the activism attached to them, owe their currency to feminists. Whatever legal and judicial decisions are made on the right to abortion, the women's movement can take credit for having mobilized a vociferous pro-choice majority. The sex war is being fought on more equal terms—which doesn't keep it from being bloody.

Men, in general, have not been grateful for the chance to vary their styles of manliness and shed the skins of John Wayne, Superman, and that contemporary reincarnation of the Man of Steel and apostle of "family values," Arnold Schwarzenegger. How could there not have been backlash, in the face of a movement whose very object was to overturn the habits, laws, and power arrangements ingrained over centuries? Of course, as a cultural icon, the relatively prosperous dressed-for-success feminist has been far more visible than the nurse and the bus driver who have found advancement and dignity from the women's movement—but despite schisms of class and race, most women have benefited. Still, women's advances into the workplace have not been matched by men's advances into housework and child care.

Feminists now have to hold onto their, our, successes while opening up new territory. They cannot afford to cede "the family" to conservatives whose idea of helping children is to send them to orphanages while their mothers are forced off welfare; whose idea of helping young children is to veto public child care; who offer no remedy for the domestic violence of men but to throw more of them out of meaningful work. Happily, the era of Bill and Hillary Clinton stands to normalize feminism—not, God knows, to solve all the problems of women, but at last to take serious account of the troubles and conflicts that truly stifle their (and men's) lives.

• The right of men to love men and of women to love women is still embattled, but at least the fight is on.

Measured against the unapologetic oppression of prior decades, one must be impressed by the antidiscrimination victories of gay rights in employment and child custody, in general public standing. Of course, no one can say that gay men and lesbian women have become legitimate as long as they are the targets of violence for no other reason than that they claim the right to live differently. Police abuse and gay-bashing remain rife, for all that the press generally doesn't notice. Other forms of discrimination, both noisy and quiet, persist, although many ritual condemnations, as in the psychiatric profession, have been beaten back. Symbolically, same-sex lovers are still automatic outcasts in the eyes of Hollywood plotters looking for prefabricated plot devices. And AIDS, the epidemic whose name could barely be spoken by the Reagan White House until Rock Hudson died, has torn through the body of the gay world with a force that can scarcely be comprehended.

To much of America, as to most of the rest of the world, homosexual love is a disease, a sin, or a crime. Nonetheless, the question of what is normal sexual life has been thrown open among much of the population, never to be slammed shut. This longest of all transformations is well launched.

WIDE-OPEN "LIFE-STYLES"

• The counterculture of the young tried to combine two impulses at once —the libertarian and the spiritual. Over the past two decades, the two have split apart and the halves have hardened.

The libertarian side wanted to overturn repression in the name of id. Young bodies wanted release. The separation of sex from procreation was the prerequisite and the prod. Styles followed to suit—long hair, let-it-hang-out rock music, public cursing, gestures of wild affection and disaffection. All those currents continue. But desire unleashed is not necessarily desire fulfilled; it is more likely to be desire entertained. Anarchic anti-authoritarianism came to take the form of what Norman O. Brown called polymorphous perversity: teenage sex, sex released from procreation, oral and anal sex, aboveground pornography, profanity and obscenity in public discourse and media. But liberation also took forms cultivated by the consumer society. Marketers learned how to channel the demands of the senses. Much of the libertarian longing was processed into fashion by what might be called the rebellion industry. The commercialization of sex reached beyond prostitution to encompass sex shops, the X-rated movie and magazine industries, the sadomasochistic savagery of blockbuster movies, the sex-slave gimmickry of music television. As lids were thrown off, sexual tastes, like gourmet and musical tastes, proliferated. At the edge of popular culture, would-be musical and literary vanguards, from *Hustler* to rap, seemed driven by nothing more than the desire to transgress, to offend, to shock—the traditional trap of the avant-garde—while civil libertarians scrambled to protect the First Amendment but failed to offer the vision of a culture that would amount to more than cacophony.

Meanwhile, the transcendental promise of drugs was overwhelmed by their anesthetic use and the addiction that followed. The least discriminating "anything goes" attitude was assimilated into America's fun culture. As marijuana yielded to cocaine, drugs ceased to be peace-inducing and magic-making, became more dangerous and intoxicating. As the drugs became nastier, their sale became inextricable from organized violence. Devotional uses were supplanted by addiction, a fraudulent and momentary balm in a disorienting society that promises more fun, more goods, more deliverance than it can deliver.

The bitter truth, the irony of freedom, is that choice opens doors to anterooms—that is all. The good life always remains to be made. The freedom to divorce and to abort, normalized in recent decades, are inseparable from the main movement of modernity—toward "the pursuit of happiness"—but they cannot deliver happiness any more than emancipation could deliver slaves to the promised land. Every freedom comes wrapped in an anguish. But collectivist conservatives like George Will are wrong to declare that unbridled freedom was the sole principle of Sixties rebellion. For the other side of the counterculture was communitarian and—overused word—spiritual, a longing for group experience that would transcend the limits of the individual ego. Alongside the claims of the counterculture for instant ecstasy, there coexisted a craving for a sort of public love, a communal self-determination, access to one or another kind of God. Frightened by spiritual chaos, longing for community and links to past and future, many eventually found company among the varieties of institutional religion or religiosity—Christian, Jewish, "New Age." Here, widespread suspicion of central authority—of government as well as business, of orthodox medicine as well as the law—fuses with a suspicion of science and universal morality. The result is confusion: cultural multiplicity, authoritarian cults, nihilism. Strong cultural ferment goes accompanied by triviality and quackery. America's spongy culture of excess, cynicism, and sentimentality seems to absorb every tendency at once.

THE LIMITATION OF NATIONAL VIOLENCE AND THE CARE OF THE EARTH

• Until 1991, it could be said that the main legacy of the movement against the Vietnam war was America's reluctance to ship its troops abroad for long against left-wing revolutions. To serve as a veto force was no small achievement, though hardly the millennium. The empire fought back with surrogate strategies for securing Cold War victories. To avoid stirring up popular protest, the Pentagon supported clandestine proxy wars ("low-intensity conflict") in behalf of favored right-wing forces like those in El Salvador, Nicaragua, Guatemala, Indonesia, and the Philippines. Faced with legal obstacles in Nicaragua and Iraq, the Republican White House devised the Iran-Contra exercise and the pro–Saddam Hussein tilt to subvert the laws and the Constitution. Still, to the chagrin of the White House, full-blown war was staved off for more than fifteen years.

Eager to recover from the hamstringing of the executive branch, George Bush came to office committed to roust the hobgoblins of the "Vietnam syndrome." When his strategy of appeasing Iraq's Saddam Hussein broke down, he found the awaited opportunity to crank up America's military machine. With the Cold War melted down, he could use the tool of sanctions to mobilize the United Nations and to frame the Persian Gulf war in the language of collective security. Thus he overcame a significant split in public and Congressional sentiment and, locked in embrace with television, isolated a dwindling, deeply divided, and indeed largely self-isolating antiwar movement. In the end, he could crow that he had "kicked the Vietnam syndrome once and for all."

But perhaps his celebration was premature. Unlike Iraq—loathsome in the eyes of neighboring rulers, devoid of mountains and neighboring sanctuaries, and susceptible to air assault—most of the world's dictatorships and violent zones are not primed for quick American victories with minimal American casualties. The Vietnam syndrome may have been dented, but America is still reluctant to throw itself into long, murky wars. And, as I write, the debates over American intervention in Somalia and Yugoslavia signal the emergence of whole new questions about collective security and global obligations. Whatever the rights and wrongs, there is unlikely to be a replay of Vietnam.

• The tidal shift of opinion that began in the Sixties eased the way for an end to the Cold War. Indeed, had President John F. Kennedy seized available opportunities during his (and Nikita Khrushchev's) brief time in office, and not instead succumbed to the lure of adventure in the Indochinese jungle, the Cold War might even have ended several trillion fewer dollars sooner. Not until two more decades had been squandered did the unlikely convergence of Mikhail Gorbachev and Ronald Reagan turn the trick—principally because of Gorbachev's farsightedness. The peace movements of the Sixties and early Eighties deserve credit for helping create a climate in which it was politically advantageous for Ronald Reagan to step back from the doomsday talk of his earlier years—though not before he wrecked the American economy in a misguided quest for "military supremacy."

• Two decades after the unity of the earth was "discovered," there is general awareness that we live on a single, interlocked, fragile planet, and that the industrialized world bears the main responsibility for sustaining or destroying it. While clear-cutting corporations accuse chi-chi environmentalists of preferring spotted owls to people, local activists of every social class are at work to purge the earth of toxins. Environmentalist rhetoric has become central to political discussion, so much so that George Bush felt the need to present himself as an "environmental president," and Senator Al Gore announced to the 1992 Democratic Convention that "just as the false assumption that we are not connected to the Earth has led to the ecological crisis, so the equally false assumption that we are not connected to each other has led to our social crisis"—two points whose interconnection was first stated by the eco-anarchist movement philosopher Murray Bookchin in the early Seventies.

DEMOCRATIC ACTIVITY

• The principle of direct citizen action has become normal. No one is surprised or scandalized to see a demonstration anymore. Sit-ins and Washington rallies are everyday events, while direct mail and door-to-door solicitation suit the more bureaucratic needs of long-running lobbies and interest groups. Even the right mobilizes local movements—even to the point of civil disobedience, as with the militant wing of the anti-abortion movement. Still, unions are in precipitous decline, while single-issue groups are maligned as "special" when they represent millions of workers or women.

• Whatever the misleading cultural archetype of the Yippie-turned-Yuppie, as enshrined in *The Big Chill,* a significant proportion of Sixties activists pursue their original principles—usually by less photogenic, possibly more enduring, means. However, the sum is no more than the whole of the parts, and sometimes less. Too often, insurgent movements choose tactics for strictly theatrical purposes, as if for an unseen audience, and fail to devise forms of action that appeal outside the immediate circle. Aside from single-issue movements, the political outcomes are, so far, more apparent in state and local government than nationally—partly because of demographic shifts toward the suburbs, partly because New Leftists were hostile to the organization and hierarchy, the compromises and discipline of organized national politics.

• The troubling side of the movement's most countercultural, participatory spirit is a certain tendency toward know-nothing leveling. One hears the assumption that all knowledge is bankrupt, all claims to authority or objectivity fraudulent, all expertise a mask for raw power. There is a recklessness to this spirit which sometimes willingly risks the destruction of liberal institutions sooner than accept less than total victory. In education, alongside important achievements in opening up history, sociology, and literature to hitherto buried problems and vantage points, there are self-righteous new orthodoxies which, while hardly as widespread or uniform as the cultural Right maintains, do tend to stifle thought—as do right-wing orthodoxies in, say, economics.

• Movements that seek to represent underrepresented people too often harden into self-seeking. The result is balkanization fueled by a narcissism of small differences, each group claiming the high ground of principle, squandering moral energy in behalf of what has come to be called "identity politics"—in which the principal purpose of organizing is to express a distinct social identity rather than achieve the collective good. In this radical extension of the politics of the late Sixties, difference and victimization are prized, ranked against the victimization of other groups. We crown our good with victimhood. While conservatives claim to speak in the name of a majority, the standard-bearers of identity politics cultivate their own marginality, practicing a separatism that incapacitates them for alliances and collective improvements. When African-American nationalists single out Korean storekeepers or Jewish academics for their antagonism, racial purism veers toward fascism.

At their strongest, the movements of the Sixties amounted to an incomplete Reformation. As in sixteenth-century Germany, the urgent young, disgusted by the corruption of values, beat on the doors of established power in the name of reform. Rebuffed, they reconsidered not only their institutions but their identities, their nature, their mission. Their dissidence deepened. They developed rituals of self-transformation and unification. While diffuse and at times self-contradictory in their purposes, they were unified by a common enemy, and came to see themselves as a common onslaught on wrong-headed power—and alternatives to it.

In the Sixties, the power centers of American society lost connection with the depths of popular spirit and resisted the reform impulse. The movements coalesced into a heartfelt if frequently inchoate insurgency. Converging with the parallel uprisings of the young in many parts of the world—in Paris and Berlin, in Prague, in Mexico City—they challenged illegitimate authority of many stripes. They not only undermined illegitimate power, they honored the unity-in-diversity of the human project. Even when speaking the language of Marxism, they foreshadowed the collapse of Marxism as a globally unifying ideology of change. They groped toward new principles of revolt, new codes of authority. As in the case of the so-called Counterreformation, the power centers of society responded with fright—and calculation. They rebuffed the invaders but also, in some measure, reformed. In the course of this running battle, a new agenda of politics took shape.

So, too, in America. In the closing decades of the twentieth century, the centers of power likewise mix repression with reform. In the case of the Reformation and Counterreformation, a century and a half of confusion, travail, and bloodshed passed before the reformers worked out a form of coexistence with the established Church and the shape of the new world had become less unclear. We are thrashing around in that troubled aftermath, which is always, and perpetually, a beginning.

• • •

A final note on this edition: I have said too little in the pages to follow about the growth of the American right in the Sixties, about domestic policy initiatives and debates, about economic changes, about the impact of political assassinations, about international reverberations of America's student movements. But I have resisted the temptation to recast the book fundamentally, to interrupt the flow of the narrative for such major discussions, or to elaborate my subsequent views of many events and people I wrote about half a decade earlier. Instead, for this new edition, I have confined myself to making corrections, clarifications, updates and amplifications of fact, while respecting the book's essential unity.

T.G.
July–December 1992

THE SIXTIES

INTRODUCTION

On New Year's Eve, as 1958 slipped into 1959, I wasn't especially aware I was living in the dead, dreary Fifties. I was a high school senior about to turn sixteen. I had little sense of living in any kind of "Fifties" at all; I wasn't old enough to think in decades. I was simply living my life: striving for grades, wondering about sex, matching my exploits against those—real and imagined—of my rivals, watching the tides of adolescence rip through me. The only threshold I thought about was the one I would cross later that year, on the way to college. I was not living in history, but in biography.

Which is not to say I was devoid of political interests. I read *The New York Times* and my parents were liberal. I stayed up late on election nights and rooted for Democrats almost as passionately as I followed the New York Giants baseball team (until they broke my heart by running off to San Francisco in 1958). I thought President Dwight David Eisenhower was a genial deadhead, a semiliterate fuddy-duddy who deserved to be chastised almost as much for excessive golfing and tangled sentences as for embracing *Generalísimo* Franco. I thought Richard Nixon was sinister. I delighted in Jules Feiffer's worldly spoofs of Eisenhower's syntax, the phone company's arrogance, and the middle class's clichés. I liked Herblock's liberal cartoons, including one in which Bernard Baruch said that Eisenhower's stinginess with the military budget would make the United States "the richest man in the graveyard." A friend introduced me to H. L. Mencken's tilts at the philistine American "booboisie," and when I wrote the valedictory speech at the Bronx High School of Science later that year, the only quotation was from Mencken: "We live in a land of abounding quackeries."

My closest friends, the children of Jewish civil servants and skilled workers, held similar opinions. As we celebrated the coming of 1959, around midnight, in a fragment of news squeezed into Guy Lombardo's orchestral schmaltz, we saw the black-and-white footage of bearded Cubans wearing fatigues, smoking big cigars, grinning big grins to the cheers of throngs deliriously happy at the news that Batista had fled; and we cheered too. The overthrow of a brutal dictator, yes. But more, on the faces of the striding, strutting *barbudos* surrounded by adoring crowds we read redemption—a revolt of young people, underdogs, who might just cleanse one scrap of earth of the bloodletting and misery we had heard about all our lives. From a living room in the Bronx we saluted our unruly champions.

I was studious and clean-cut. I won scholarships and mathematics awards. In three years I cut one day of classes. At the Sputnik-era Bronx High School of Science, one of the alumni held up to us as a model was a physicist named Harold Brown, then a rising star among President Eisenhower's scientific advisers, later secretary of defense under President Jimmy Carter. I went off to Harvard that fall wearing a blue blazer. What was I doing cheering a bunch of bearded revolutionaries? What were ten thousand Americans doing in Harvard Stadium that April, chanting "Viva! Viva!" to the same Fidel Castro?

So much of America in the Fifties seemed content, so many of the old promises redeemed; why were middle-class children of the Fifties looking in such strange places for heroes? I was far from the only one, as it turned out, and my next ten years, if hardly typical of a whole generation's, belonged to a larger drama. In my sophomore year, 1960, I was swept up in a Harvard-Radcliffe peace group called Tocsin. I identified with a scatter of campus organizer-intellectuals who called themselves the New Left. In 1963, at twenty, I was elected president of their organizational center, Students for a Democratic Society, SDS, which numbered a grand total of six hundred paid members and harbored the modest ambition of shaking America to its roots. In the spring of 1965 I helped organize a Wall Street sit-in at the Chase Manhattan Bank against loans to South Africa, then the first sizable demonstration at the White House against the war in Vietnam—and soon thereafter smoked my first marijuana (which I had previously thought to be a demon "narcotic"). I was moved by the idea that "people should make the decisions that affect their lives," knocked on doors trying to organize Appalachian white migrants to Chicago into an "interracial movement of the poor," wrote for and sometimes edited "underground" newspapers, gave speeches against the war, went to interminable conferences, walked innumerable picket lines, visited Cuba and was stirred by it late in 1967, scampered through clouds of tear gas to get away from billy clubs and bayonets (and get near the action) at the Democratic Convention in 1968, then again at San Francisco State College and Berkeley's People's Park in 1968 and 1969. I started growing my first beard the day I came to California in the fall of

1967, then shaved it off aiming to ease my way past customs to and from Cuba. I saw a comrade gashed by a chunk of concrete as we integrated an amusement park in 1963, heard a racist mob scream itself shrill surrounding our nonviolent group, until we were rescued—and arrested—by the police. A few years later, I watched police destroy my camera after I snapped them illegally searching my car in Chicago; I saw our organizing office reduced to rubble when Chicago police turned it upside down in a raid for planted drugs. I sat through the conspiracy trials of my friends, watched others try to overturn a police van in the Chicago streets, knew still others were planting stink bombs in the Democratic delegates' hotel—and admired their courage. I dreaded guns, refused to smash windows—and at the same time learned to scorn nonviolence, which seemed helpless against the juggernaut of the war and the police. From mildly socialist I became "radical," "anti-imperialist," a partisan of "resistance," a half-serious advocate of "destroying America," and then, gingerly, ambivalently, found myself caught up in the collective hallucination (or was it?) of "the revolution."

And then the movement's—and my—forward motion was broken: In 1969, SDS, at the peak of its size and militancy, with some hundred thousand members, hundreds of chapters, millions of supporters, and under the intense scrutiny (to say the least) of the White House and the FBI, broke into screaming factions, one of which, the Weathermen, began to build bombs. One movement friend was assaulted (probably by a right-wing lunatic) and nearly killed; others were blown up, went underground, or died by their own hands. History, as Czeslaw Milosz has said in a different connection, came off its leash. The student movement, having spawned a women's movement which both denounced and continued it, marched into a cul-de-sac and disbanded. I was one of those old New Leftists, anathema to all factions, who was broken up by the movement's whirling destruction and self-destruction as much as I had been inspired—even formed—by its birth. Reproached for "revisionism" and dangerously "liberal" tendencies, I ended up identifying with something Martin Buber said about his friend the German socialist Gustav Landauer, murdered by soldiers in 1919: He "fought in the revolution against the revolution for the sake of the revolution."

By the early Seventies the upheaval was over—as mysteriously as it had appeared, and as worldwide. Neoconservatives wobbled between relief and vindication; old radicals felt mixtures of despair, regret, chagrin, pride, resolve, and got on with their lives. "The Sixties" receded into haze and myth: lingering images of nobility and violence, occasional news clips of Martin Luther King, Jr., and John F. Kennedy, Beatles and Bob Dylan retrospectives, the jumble of images this culture shares instead of a sense of continuous, lived history. "The Sixties": a collage of fragments scooped together as if a whole decade took place in an instant. It is to reclaim the actual Sixties from "the Sixties," from this big-bang theory of history, as well as to find out what I think, that I have written this book.

I have worked at the edge of history and autobiography, from inside and outside the Sixties, writing at different focal lengths, in first and third persons, hoping that by describing the texture of certain episodes I could gain in sharpness what I had to sacrifice in breadth, at other times backing off to expose a larger picture. So this is part historical reconstruction, part analysis, part memoir, part criticism, part celebration, part meditation. Pride, chagrin, embarrassment have their places, but beyond them, I hope to have evoked the spirit of the time from the interior, yet without succumbing to the hallucinatory giddiness of the late Sixties especially, whose sheer wildness, even now, seems the stuff of another century. At the hub is the youth movement, principally the white student part of it, and its self-conscious core, the New Left, which borrowed from the black movement the habit of calling itself "the movement." For along with the black movement (and under the mighty pressure of the Pentagon) the New Left became the dynamic center of the decade, pushing the young forward, declaring that change was here, forming the template for the revolts of hippies, women, and gays. I have stressed the strips of history I knew firsthand, taking my experience as primary evidence, material to be fathomed for the sake of a larger understanding. (In a few cases I lacked more than passing acquaintance but the segments were too important to pass over: the beats, the southern civil rights movement, the hippie scene.) The American youth upheaval was but part of a worldwide surge which cannot be explained simply by the baby boom, the economic boom, the growth and bureaucratization of universities, civil rights, the Vietnam war, Dr. Spock, the Democratic Party's defaults, the mass media, or any other single factor. It was partly a product of social structure—there had to be a critical mass of students, and enough economic fat to cushion them—but more, the upsurge was *made* from the living elements of a unique, unrepeatable history, under the spreading wings of the zeitgeist. A grander analysis would require painstaking international comparisons; I hope I have found at least a point of entry. The result is a kind of record of a conversation with myself, and with friends and comrades, teachers and students, colleagues and (sometimes) opponents, over the course of some twenty years of reflection about where the upheaval came from, how it developed, why it disbanded, what it did and did not accomplish, what was and was not possible, why apparently sensible people got swept into maelstroms, why solid landscapes dissolved into maelstroms, and what maelstroms are good and bad for.

Most of this book is organized around pivotal moments. Some were turning points in the life of the movement, episodes when the movement collided with surrounding forces, or when the movement's own tensions erupted: the SDS Port Huron convention of 1962, when the radical veteran Michael Harrington (age thirty-four) attacked the draft manifesto by Tom Hayden (age twenty-two), with fateful consequences; the clash between SNCC and Hubert H. Humphrey, Walter Reuther, and other liberals at the Atlantic City Democratic Convention of 1964; the confrontations of Stop the Draft Week in 1967, Chicago in 1968, People's Park in 1969; SDS's factional death in 1969; the Weatherman townhouse explosion and Kent State killings in 1970. Some were moments of truth when the movement's predicaments came clear, at least after the fact, though the incidents were not necessarily momentous in themselves: a 1958 debate between Jack Kerouac and the liberal editor James Wechsler; a speech by a radical professor during the Cuban missile crisis of 1962; a 1963 encounter between Tom Hayden and the editor of the social democratic journal *Dissent*, Irving Howe; Wechsler's attack on SDS on the eve of the first national antiwar demonstration in 1965; Ken Kesey's appearance at a Berkeley Vietnam protest in 1965; a 1967 New Left conference disrupted by countercultural toughs called the Diggers; the heckling of a representative of the women's movement on an antiwar platform in 1969. To establish the setting there are also prologues and entr'actes and side-stories: about the roots of the Sixties in the rock music, movies, spoofs, and folk culture of the Fifties, and in the suburbs and the H-bomb; about the freaks of the Haight-Ashbury and Lower East Side, about drugs and living together in unmatrimonial bliss, about Bob Dylan's odyssey and the San Francisco Sound and the Rolling Stones; about visits to Cuba and Vietnam; about the Black Panthers, government crackdowns, and the idea of The Revolution. And still I feel daunted by how many moments, collisions, social forces, movement predicaments I have had to bypass.

The course of the student movement was of course inseparable from its historical moment: affluence, civil rights, the Cold War, Vietnam; Kennedy, Johnson, Nixon; the assassinations of Kennedy, Malcolm X, King, and another Kennedy; worldwide upheavals seeming to promise the founding of a new age in the ashes of the old. From social tensions came a tumult of movements aiming to remake virtually every social arrangement America had settled into after World War II. Yet, from the beginning, the student movement also faced structural tensions, built-in dilemmas. From its attempts to resolve them came the movement's dynamics. Whatever answers the movement came up with, it was not free to choose the questions thrust upon it. One of my running meditations is precisely about how much freedom there was, under which circumstances, to make events come out differently than they did.

The unavoidable dilemmas are my leitmotifs. For example:

■ Because the Old Left had suffered political defeat and moral collapse in the Fifties, the New Left resolved to be a student movement and a left at the same time. Twenty-two-year-olds set out to change the world.

Starting from such ambition, the movement oscillated between narcissism (imagining itself to be the instrument of change) and self-disparagement (searching for the *real* instrument of change), eventually succumbing to the false solution of Leninism, which was the first in the guise of the second.

■ Because it rose from the ashes of the American left, the movement was inclined to feel that it had given birth to itself—and came to overvalue the power of sheer will, which had apparently created something from nothing.

■ The movement wanted to be both strategic and expressive, political and cultural: to change the world (end the war, win civil rights) while freeing life in the here and now. Sometimes these poles were compatible, sometimes not. The idea of the youth revolution was an exercise in finessing the difference.

■ The movement had to find the right relation to the American nation; having taken America's dream of itself seriously, it was quick to feel betrayed when the dream turned into nightmare, quick to relocate the promised land on some revolutionary soil elsewhere.

■ The rock 'n' roll generation, having grown up on popular culture, took images very seriously indeed; beholding itself magnified in the funhouse mirror, it grew addicted to media which had agendas of their own—celebrity-making, violence-mongering, sensationalism.

■ The movement took liberalism for granted, but at crucial junctures found itself obstructed by liberals. Once liberalism had sacrificed itself on the altar of the Vietnam war and race polarization, what were radicals to do?

■ Influenced by remnants of the Old Left, yet eager to make its own way, the New Left had to decide whether the holdovers were victims, instructors, exemplars, rivals, or opponents.

■ Nourished on cultural opposition, the New Left had to confront a counterculture that was in many ways more attractive than radical politics. Should it outflank? Accommodate? Especially in California, the hip-political synthesis—along with violence—was the siren song of the late Sixties.

I have tried to be guided by Alfred North Whitehead's injunction: "Seek simplicity and distrust it." The onetime mathematician in me yearns for crystalline conclusions, and at times this book records, and complicates, my best efforts at them. As I strain to comprehend—that is, to simplify—historical narrative is the form my distrust takes.

· · ·

Life is always lived in common, whatever rugged individualists may think, but in the Sixties it seemed especially true that History with a capital H had come down to earth, either interfering with life or making it possible; and that within History, or threaded through it, people were more than themselves, they were supercharged: lives were bound up with one another, making claims on one another, drawing one another into the common project. And so the boundary between memoir and history has to be blurred. I have tried to use my own recollections and records (I kept letters and journals) to bring some of the larger story alive. I have cross-checked and supplemented my memory, as much as possible, by interviewing several score of my contemporaries and consulting documents and published accounts. I have tried to convey the grain of other voices than my own, tried to be fair to those I have disagreed with (and to an earlier self, and those I agreed with but no longer do). Plunging into a tumult of memory, documents, interviews, I have tried to skirt the pitfalls of nostalgia and cheap second-guessing.

I have left traces of my debates with myself, for some of the outstanding questions of the Sixties do not settle themselves, if they can be settled at all, and I think there may be some value in the frictions I have felt, as actor, recorder, and analyst. The work of thinking out a position can be more valuable than the position itself—especially in a time when public matters are reduced to slogans, taken in capsules. It is a cliché that radical politics and culture suffer from excesses of certainty. (So, too, those of right and center.) True enough, polarization chews up doubt. But especially at the start, beneath the Sixties' dramatic displays of iron certainty, invisible from the outside, there were questions, endless questions, running debates that took their point from the divine premise that everything was possible and therefore it was important to think, because ideas have consequences. Unraveling, rethinking, refusing to take for granted, thinking without limits—that calling was some of what I loved most in the spirit of the Sixties.

ONE
AFFLUENCE AND UNDERTOW

The radical of the thirties came out of a system that had stopped and the important job was to organize new production relations which would start it up again. The sixties radical opened his eyes to a system pouring its junk over everybody, or nearly everybody, and the problem was to stop just that, to escape being over-whelmed by a mindless, goalless flood which marooned each individual on his little island of commodities.

—Arthur Miller

CORNUCOPIA AND ITS DISCONTENTS

THE WIDE OPEN SPACES OF AFFLUENCE

Groping for a sense of the zeitgeist has been an intellectual stock-in-trade since the ancient Greek thinkers, who discovered they were living in history. If they could name the immediate past, they could locate themselves in relation to it; they could perhaps comprehend and certainly criticize it. Kings, naturally, have always wanted to know where they stood in the winds of their time, and so, of course, have the opponents of kings, as well as those who simply wanted to make do in the crevices of power. Today, the habit of naming the zeitgeist has grown widespread, even frantic. As a convenience sport, it is most frequently practiced by journalists and publicists with deadlines to meet and headlines to write; there is profit in getting the right handle on the moment and making it marketable. Zeitgeist-mongering is the stuff of cocktail party chat for an age in which capsule stereotypes masquerading as ideas help us master the flood of incoming information. But the zeitgeist is an elusive wind, and the worst temptation is to oversimplify. There are many cross-breezes, eddies, local variations, rippling shifts of direction; even Sturm und Drang blows in fits and starts. The zeitgeist mutters, like the oracle of Delphi, and like the oracle it requires interpreters. What the zeitgeist mutters depends in good part on what questions it is asked.

"The Fifties" were multiple, of course, according to whether you lived on Manhattan Island or in Manhattan, Kansas, in Southern California or North Carolina; different too depending on whether you were eight or eighteen or fifty-eight, female or male, black or white, Irish Catholic or Protestant or Jewish, an electrical worker or a salesman of appliances or a housewife with an all-electric kitchen or the president of General Electric; and this is not yet to speak of differences in family style and personality. But one thing we know is that the presumably placid, complacent Fifties were succeeded by the unsettling Sixties. The Fifties were, in a sense, rewritten by the Sixties, as the Sixties have been rewritten by the Eighties.

I am going to look at the Fifties, then, as a seedbed as well as a cemetery. The surprises of the Sixties were planted there. I want to look closely at the culture and institutions of the Fifties, look at how the Fifties presented themselves to the young in general, and in particular to that minority who were about to claim the right, if not the capacity, to remake history: those of us who were born during or just after World War II; who were roughly eight to fourteen years old in 1956, when Dwight Eisenhower defeated Adlai Stevenson for the second time and "Heartbreak Hotel" was a smash hit; who were thus twelve to eighteen in 1960, when the sit-ins began and John Kennedy was elected President over Richard Nixon; who were then seventeen to twenty-three in 1965, when Lyndon Johnson began the systematic bombing of North Vietnam. I offer something of a composite of those who were middle- or upper-middle class in origin and poised to go to college in the late Fifties and early Sixties; and in particular those who spawned the civil rights and antiwar movements and the New Left within them, as well as the hippies and other cultural movers and shakers of the Sixties. How did we understand the world and ourselves in it? How did the spirit and structures of that decade shape our sensibilities? How, from closure, did openings come?

A first approximation: this generation was formed in the jaws of an extreme and wrenching tension between the assumption of affluence and its opposite, a terror of loss, destruction, and failure.

"Affluence": so much a word of the Fifties, with its cognate connotations of flow, flux, fullness. The word had already achieved currency by the time John Kenneth Galbraith published the bestselling *The Affluent Society* in 1958; it was far more American than "rich," harnessed as that brutal syllable is to its natural counterpart, "poor," thus bringing inequality to mind. "Affluence" sounds general, and in the Fifties it was assumed to be a national condition, not just a personal standing. Indeed, affluence was an irresistible economic and psychological fact in a society that had long since made material production and acquisition its central activities. The boom of 1945 to 1973, occasionally interrupted by recessions only to roll on seemingly undiminished, was the longest in American history. Starting late in war-blasted Western Europe and Japan, the boom rolled, however unevenly, through the rest of the industrialized world. But America was the richest, richer than any other country or bloc had ever been.

By 1945, the United States found itself an economic lord set far above the destroyed powers, its once and future competitors among both Allies and Axis powers. Inflation was negligible, so the increase in available dollars was actually buying more goods. Natural resources seemed plentiful, their supplies stable; only small think-tanks and obscure writers worried about whether they might ever prove exhaustible. And if, as some critics charged, the distribution of income had not materially changed since the Thirties, the fact remained that all segments of the population were improving their positions—not necessarily in relation to one another, but in relation to their pasts and those of their families. And it was the relation to the past that struck most people as the salient comparison. The Depression was over. And so were the deprivations of World War II, which also brought relative blessings: While European and Japanese factories were being pulverized, new American factories were being built and old ones were back at work, shrinking unemployment to relatively negligible proportions. Once the war was over, consumer demand was a dynamo. Science was mobilized by industry, and capital was channeled by government as never before. The boom was on, and the cornucopia seemed all the more impressive because the miseries of Depression and war were near enough to suffuse the present with a sense of relief.

The flush of prosperity and the thrill of victory also translated into a baby boom. The number of births jumped by 19 percent from 1945 to 1946, then another 12 percent the next year, and after settling down for three years boomed again and continued to boom into the early Sixties. More babies were born in 1948–53 than in the previous thirty years. The first boom could be understood as a makeup for wartime deprivations, but then why did it resume and, astonishingly, go on? As Landon Y. Jones has pointed out, the sustained boom took place only in the United States, Canada, Australia, and New Zealand, countries that were left unscathed by the war, blessed with land, robust with confidence, feverish with what Lord Keynes once called "relentless consumption." Couples were marrying earlier, starting their children earlier, and having more of them. The baby boom was widely touted as a tribute to the national glory. Whatever the exact explanation, babies were the measure and the extension of the economic boom; they were good for its markets; they were its pride; in some ways they were its point.

So affluence was not just an economic fact but a demographic one, and the demographic bulge matched the affluent state of mind. The idea of America had long been shaped by the promise of opportunity in a land of plenty, but at long last the dream seemed to be coming true. The world seemed newly spacious, full of possibilities. Americans were acquiring consumer goods at an unprecedented pace; indeed, with the housing boom, and the great treks from the country to the city, from the city to the suburbs, from the South to the North, millions of Americans were acquiring whole new spaces to live in. The cities were being "renewed," "redeveloped," their faces lifted, while the upbeat language of "renewal" concealed the injuries done to millions who were unwillingly shunted away from the valuable parcels of real estate they had called home; but there was presumably nothing to worry about, for wasn't progress (as General Electric advertised) our most important product, and didn't the language of affluence imply that there was room for all in the great gushing mainstream?

Most of the newly affluent were happy to forget, and the media had little interest in reminding them, that even with easy credit and higher incomes and the growing number of white-collar jobs, not everyone could afford a new house, a new car, TV set, high fidelity sound, or the rest of the appurtenances of the American good life. The evident fact remained: in the course of the Fifties, television, high fidelity, jet travel, and multiple cars became middle-class staples. Galbraith charged that private affluence was crowding out public goods, causing and obscuring the impoverishment of the public sector. If you looked at American schools, if you contrasted the condition of trains and subways with the condition of suburban houses and cars, you could see that public services were being starved, that public funds were going to fuel the boom in private spaces and private goods. For after 1945, the government had been enlisted in behalf of private comfort and convenience for the vast reaches of the middle classes. But who looked?

The Puritan utopia of a "city upon a hill" found its strange completion in the flatlands of the American suburb. For growing numbers, daily life was delivered from the cramp of the city, lifted out to the half-wide, half-open spaces, where the long-sought and long-feared American wilderness could be trimmed back and made habitable. The prairie became the lawn; the ranch, the ranch house; the saloon, the Formica bar. The postwar American families wanted space for stretching out, space for their children (and from them), space from their parents and in-laws; and they wanted their private domains loaded with the latest appliances: partly for the convenience, partly to confirm that they were making a fresh start, freed from Depression cramp. In 1945, a mere 19 percent of the people polled by *The Saturday Evening Post* said they were willing to live in an apartment or a "used house."

Fueled by federal financing, by low interest rates and mortgage guarantees for veterans, builders constructed vast suburban developments. Between 1946 and 1958, outside the farms, 85 percent of all new housing was built beyond the central cities. And when the vets and newlyweds beheld the grass and trees and the panoply of their private properties, they must have felt at least for a moment that the American dream had come true, that in America even the butchery of the war could have a happy ending. With the kitchen spilling directly into the dining room, the glass doors opening from the living room into the outdoor barbecue and play area, the picture window bringing the lawn right up to the wall-to-wall carpet, the ideal suburban home was an intertwining of nature and civilization; it was as if the suburban family had realized Karl Marx's vision of a blending of countryside and city. Magazines advertised these houses, television featured them, relatives admired and envied them, and the suburbanites reveled in the space—the "spaciousness"—of their new quarters, jumping at the chance to stuff them with washers and dryers, electric kitchens and garage openers and do-it-yourself workshops. Spread out laterally, like the lords of tiny manors, they enlarged their domains and cushioned their days with television, a kind of electronic upholstery. Apparently the whole world was at the fingertips of the American family.

And the family was the raison d'être of affluence, its point and its locale. The ostensible beneficiaries of all the plenitude were the most dependent members of the family unit: Mom, who would spend the bulk of her life supervising her conveniences, and the kids, who would grow up knowing how good the things of life could be. Dad's wage underwrote the whole family's division of labor and pleasures; after the jarring wartime years, when vast numbers of women were mobilized into jobs, women were now expected—and expected themselves—to secure the home front. This delicate bargain was secured by an unwritten contract, a division of labor, that was trumpeted through all the linkage networks of the modern mass media. Against the centrifugal pressures inherent in Mom and Dad's division of labor, the nuclear family was bound together through the cementing idea of "togetherness."

The suburb was of course inconceivable without quick, reliable transportation to work, and the instrument of choice, the incarnation of power, comfort, and freedom all at once, was the automobile. This was the time of the automatic transmission, of power steering, power brakes, and more powerful engines. The long stabbing fins, easily mocked, were only the extreme and outward signs that the car, like a yacht, was meant for cruising. The conspicuous adornment of chrome was a sign that America had metal to waste. And what could be more deluxe than to bring the car under one's own roof, in the two-car garage? Shopping and leisure were retailored for an age of easy access. The shopping center represented the possibility of consumption without limits, the logical extension of the department store. The drive-in theater, a bonus of auto-convenience, created a social space perfectly adapted for the newly mobile.

Improved roads also heightened the sense of freedom—even as the breadwinner followed the same route day after day. Even city dwellers could slip away to the countryside for weekends and summer vacations. The expressways were especially efficient conduits. And what the local expressway made possible every day, the interstate highway made possible on a national scale. The Federal-Aid Highway Act of 1956 authorized forty-one thousand miles of interstate roads, great sleek limited-access superhighways where nature was trimmed back for smooth passage, and Americans could begin to feel that the whole of their vast country was coming within reach. The open road had long been a symbol of American freedom from overcivilization; it meant adventure and sex and joyrides before it meant commuting. For now, few worried aloud about the congestion, the carnage and pollution which the private automobile brought with it, or about its consequences for the cities, or about the future of America's dependence on petroleum. The car was still the incarnation of personal power, freedom, leisure, sex, access, efficiency, ease, comfort, and convenience all wrapped in a single machine; both a symbol and a symptom of the American search for ways to liberate the self from social restraints. It was personal power in a private compartment tooling its way toward the horizon.

Middle-class Americans were becoming cultural omnivores, traveling abroad in growing numbers, visiting national parks and historical sites, going to theaters, museums, and concerts as never before. Cultural ambitions ratcheted upward; New York became the world center of the arts. Growing numbers of middle-class consumers felt it their responsibility to be au courant. They were accumulating coffee-table books, subscribing to *Saturday Review* and the Book-of-the-Month Club, buying records, briefing themselves about art. The wealthier were buying paintings, propelling Abstract Expressionists to stardom and unanticipated wealth; the less wealthy bought prints. Amateurs tried their hands at acting and choral singing, or tinkered with crafts at home. Painting by the numbers was one fad that all by itself contained the contradictory aspirations of the middle-class Fifties: creativity and security at the same time. Movie attendance shrank, largely because of competition from television, but campuses and museums spawned film (not just *movie*) societies, and by the late Fifties, amid the overall decline, Americans were for the first time getting to see a good number of foreign films: the British comedies starring Alec Guinness and Peter Sellers; Brigitte Bardot; then, in the cosmopolitan centers and university towns, Bergman, Fellini, the French New Wave, even the Russians.

For the multitudes who could afford the ticket, then, the payoff for hard work and a willingness to accept authority promised to be a generous share in the national plenitude. Even when the goods were not at hand, the ads cataloged a beckoning future. For decades, advertising had barraged Americans with images of a world without horizons, but now, in television, it had the most powerful and—in Madison Avenue's language—most "penetrating" conduit ever devised. In the early Fifties, when the tube was a new toy, people lined up in the streets to stare at the new models in store windows. Television rewarded, tantalized, cozened, flattered; it congratulated Americans for being so sensible or fortunate as to live in a land where television was available. For most viewers, television's world, however sanitized and upbeat, hovered close enough to the reality of their lives and their immediate aspirations to render the image of abundance plausible. No longer did you have to be a criminal poseur to believe, with Jay Gatsby, "in the green light, the orgiastic future that year by year recedes before us." Tomorrow we could *all* "run faster, stretch out our arms farther. . . ." And so, when the majority of Americans called themselves middle class, they meant at the least that they were on their way.

By way of a summary of the economic underpinnings, then: Where the parental generation was scourged by memories of the Depression, the children of this middle class in the late Forties and Fifties were raised to take affluence for granted. The breadwinners were acutely aware of how hard they had worked to afford the picture window, the lawn, the car, the Lionel trains; and since they could, most of them, remember a time when the sweat of their brow availed them little, they were flooded with relief and gratitude, and expected their children to feel the same. Many were the parents who policed their rambunctious children with when-I-was-your-age tales of the Depression. Here was generational cleavage in the making.

And yet children also live out potentials that lie dormant in their parents; the discontinuities can be overdrawn. For all their comforts, the middle-class parents were afflicted by "insecurity," to use another of the decade's code words. One was not supposed to feel "insecure." It was a mark of "maladjustment." Yet no matter how much consumer debt they piled up to feed their hunger for consumption, no matter how eagerly they accumulated space and goods to convince themselves that their self-sacrificial struggles had been worthwhile (and to placate the Puritan's nameless guilts), they were not always convinced that their well-upholstered consumer paradise was here to stay. Nor was it always self-evident that the price was worth paying. Many are the signs that Americans were ill at ease in Eden, and although they lay scattered throughout the culture, susceptible to rival interpretations, their cumulative weight is impressive. Strikingly, for example, Americans spent a growing portion of their incomes on life insurance. While disposable family income rose by a considerable 49 percent between 1950 and 1960, sales of individual life insurance policies rose by more than 200 percent in dollar value; and this did not even include the increase in employee-benefit plans. It is also worthy of note that the number of psychiatrists multiplied almost sixfold between 1940 and 1964; and presumably, although statistics are hard to come by, the number of patients who thought they needed their heads examined mushroomed accordingly. The temptation grew to define "maladjustment" as a medical problem susceptible to personal "cure."

The middle class's choice of everyday reading matter also tells us something of its preoccupations. Bestsellers, of course, do not directly transcribe popular moods, but their readers have to find the shifts palatable, recognize new styles of heroism as plausible. Between 1945 and the early 1950s, the typical bestseller hero was a go-getting individual who goes after what he wants, straightforwardly, and gets it. But starting with Sloan Wilson's *The Man in the Gray Flannel Suit* and Herman Wouk's *Marjorie Morningstar* (both 1955), among other bestsellers, success costs. A hard-driving man discovers conflicts between work and family commitments. Heroes no longer conquer, but try to adapt and balance. Success is no longer a good that justifies itself; now it has to be justified as an instrument of self-fulfillment.

Likewise, popular social criticism tells us a good deal about widespread middle-class apprehension. True, there was a curious rift dividing the writers of social analysis. Some prominent intellectuals, many of them ex-radicals, were busily settling their accounts with the postwar order. These celebrants of affluence, however uneasy, presumed that America was melting down to a single sea of national satisfaction. Their intellectual style was to celebrate American unity, "the American way of life"—singular, not plural. The dangers came from resentful arrivistes, authoritarian workers, brutish anti-intellectuals—ingrates, in short. The melting pot was invoked sentimentally, as an ideal, without irony: differences in America were meant to be melted down. America was "exceptional," exempt from European passions and dangers, as it had been spared not only fascism but the temptations of socialism and communism; there was only one "American way of life." Daniel Bell and Seymour Martin Lipset, socialists turned sociologists, wrote that we had attained that blessed state in which ideology was defunct, exhausted; social problems were now discrete, isolated, manageable by clear-headed professionals. And as important organs of intellectual opinion closed ranks, officialdom also closed doors. "Those who do not believe in the ideology of the United States," declared the attorney general of the United States, Tom Clark, in 1948, "shall not be allowed to stay in the United States." But when McCarthyism overreached, going after not just defenseless Communists and helpless innocents but the U.S. Army itself, it was beaten back, replaced by a more popular, plausible, and stable consensus that these intellectuals helped formulate: that America was the very model of the best possible society; that economic growth would make opportunity universal; that domestic differences could be bargained out; that Communism could be contained by a combination of military might and free enterprise.

The consensus intellectuals had their influence; they were much cited in popular journals, much honored in their professions. At least one of their journals was financed, as it turned out, by the Central Intelligence Agency. But later analysts, impressed by the chasm between the Fifties and the Sixties, may have set too high an estimate on their impact; they may have left more of a mark on their disciplines than on the public at large. At least they were not unopposed. In the early Sixties, the New Left also built up its oppositional identity, its hard-and-fast generational definition, by decrying this "dominant ideology." But in the process we overlooked our debts to the dissonant voices of the Fifties. What has to be remembered is that Bell and Lipset were not the authors of the *bestselling* Fifties polemics; and some of the popular social critics told a different tale indeed. For all their overemphasis on social equilibrium, the bestselling social critics agreed that the heroic individual was paying a steep price— in autonomy and meaning—for the security and comfort he was reaping from the managed, bureaucratically organized society. David Riesman's *The Lonely Crowd* (1950; paperback edition, 1953) delivered an elegy for the "inner-directed" Protestant soul and deplored the degradation of work, arguing that the new "outer-directed" America had forfeited the liberating potentials of leisure time for shallow conformity, and that even "peer groups," which buffered individuals against the citadels of power, could prove suffocating. C. Wright Mills's *White Collar* (1951) lamented the spread of the sales mentality and the ebbing of the independent middle class. William H. Whyte's *The Organization Man* (1956) deplored the displacement of the entrepreneurial ethos by smooth, manipulative adjustment. More radically, Mills's *The Power Elite* (1956) made the argument that history was in the hands of irresponsible corporate, political, and military circles. But even the less radical—usually ex-radical—critics agreed that authentic community and tradition were being flattened by a "mass society." Later in the Fifties, muckrakers scraped at the surface of the consumer society: Vance Packard in *The Hidden Persuaders* (1957), John Keats in *The Crack in the Picture Window* (1957) and *The Insolent Chariots* (1958), while John Kenneth Galbraith, of course, struck at the giddiness of *The Affluent Society*. "Conformity" became something else to feel anxious about, whether in books like Robert Lindner's *Must You Conform?* (1956) or *New Yorker* cartoons. The point is that some critical mass of readers wanted to be warned. And these books were lying on the coffee tables of many a curious adolescent.

In the years to come, many words would be spilled about the "generation gap," many of them in hysteria and bravado on each side. In retrospect, all the claims seem overblown—and yet, what about the fierce sense of difference? The young insisted that their life situation was unprecedented (and therefore they had no one to follow); the older, that they *did* understand, so well, and with so many years' advantage, that they knew better (and therefore should be followed). As many studies revealed, student radicals of the New Left shared many more sentiments and values with their parents than with the rest of American society. Children of the relatively democratic families of the educated middle class, they wanted to live out the commitments to justice, peace, equality, and personal freedom which their parents professed. But about the meaning of affluence there was a divide of experience which could never be erased. Parents could never quite convey how they were haunted by the

Depression and relieved by the arrival of affluence; the young could never quite convey how tired they were of being reminded how bad things had once been, and therefore how graced and grateful they should feel to live normally in a normal America.

The opportunities were real, however, and the revolts of the following decade would have been unimaginable without them. For the middle-class children who came of age in those years, there was an approved track for running faster and stretching farther: college and university training. Credentials were tickets—indeed, the only sure tickets—to the affluent society. The service sector of the economy was growing, the manufacturing sector shrinking. More employees than ever before were handling people and paper, not soil, ore, lumber, and steel. And if most of the white-collar workers—even most of the professionals—were performing repetitive labors in large organizations at less than spectacular wages, it still wasn't hard for them to feel, to know, that they were doing better than their parents did. They had reason to think that, with higher education, their children could move up higher still, perhaps to become secure, self-employed professionals like doctors and lawyers, even though the self-employed middle class was shrinking while the bureaucratized sector boomed. In this respect, the secretaries and clerks and low-level bureaucrats who made up the bulk of the white-collar sector shared the aspirations of the professionals and managers who made up the cream of it.

Even before the closing of the frontier, the American middle class had believed that education marked the route upward to membership in the republic of plenty. By the late Fifties, the demand from below for higher education was more than matched by a demand from above. The economic explosion detonated an educational one. During World War II, big science at the service of big government had begun to demonstrate what it could do for warfare: the Manhattan Project's atomic bomb was the supreme product of this partnership. And the Cold War extended the partnership into peacetime, in the form of what radicals called "the permanent war economy." Big industry systematically enlisted science both to organize itself and to develop and market the peacetime cornucopia of consumer goods. The centers of power wanted better-trained personnel and government-subsidized knowledge. To harness knowledge to power, no institution was more important than the university. In the permanent ideological as well as military mobilization which the Cold War and high-consumption economy promised, managerial styles would have to be taught; specific techniques for the manipulation of the physical world would have to be instilled; the American celebration would have to be refined and rendered plausible. But military arguments did the most to promote the cause of higher education. Especially after the Russians shattered American pride by getting into the heavens first with their Sputnik in 1957, public funds poured into the universities. "Intellect has . . . become an instrument of national purpose, a component part of the 'military-industrial complex,'" wrote Clark Kerr. Total spending on public institutions of higher education rose from $742.1 million in 1945 to $6.9 billion in 1965.

The universities boomed even faster than the college-age population. The result was that by 1960 the United States was the first society in the history of the world with more college students than farmers. (By 1969 the number of students had nearly doubled, to three times the number of farmers.) The number of degrees granted, undergraduate and graduate combined, doubled between 1956 and 1967. The proportion enrolled in public institutions rose especially fast. The elite universities still trained gentlemen, but increasingly the gentlemen were being trained as managers and professors, not bankers, diplomats, and coupon clippers with a taste for higher things. In the postwar meritocratic mood, there was more room—though still not as much as sheer academic merit would have commanded—for high school graduates like me whose background was not particularly gentlemanly. Science was our faith: Golly gee, Mr. Wizard. Knowledge solved problems; it *worked*. Even the pandemic fear of polio had a happy ending when Dr. Jonas Salk developed his vaccine in 1954; what miracles could not be wrought by scientific knowledge? (Nor was it lost on my family and friends that Dr. Salk, as well as Einstein and many atomic scientists, were Jews like us.)

So it was fully within the spirit of the moment when Alexander Taffel, the principal of the Bronx High School of Science, wrote in my class yearbook:

> About a century ago, the great editor, Horace Greeley, pointed the way of opportunity to the youth of his day in the words, "Go west, young man!" Today, there are no more undeveloped western territories but there is a new and limitless "west" of opportunity. Its trails lead through the schools, colleges and university to the peaks of higher learning. Never in history has there been so promising an opportunity for the young men and women who can make the ascent.
>
> As you of the class of 1959 go on to higher education, you are in full accord with the times. The road you are taking is not an easy one but you will find it interesting and rewarding. For those who pursue it with devotion and sincerity, the signposts everywhere read, "Opportunity Unlimited!"

TERRORS

Yet the affluent Fifties were, as I. F. Stone wrote, haunted. Conformity was supposed to buy contentment, cornucopia promised both private and public utopia, but satisfaction kept slipping out of reach. Opportunity meant competition; even the middle class had to wonder whether the great meritocratic race was really wide open. Plenitude beckoned, but there was no finish line, no place to rest and assure oneself, once and for all, "I've made it." And there were fears that could barely be kept at bay. The affluent society was awash with fear of the uncontrollable. The personal jitters matched the country's obsession with "national security." Republicans and Democrats disputed whether the primary agent of insecurity was internal or external Communism, but virtually the whole society agreed that the Soviet state posed a serious threat to peace and the American way of life. The daily newspaper, the TV news, *Time* and *Life* and *Reader's Digest,* and at school the *Weekly Reader,* were all full of thick red arrows and black tides swooping and oozing across the West. The Bomb, which felt like a shield in 1945, turned into a menace again in 1949, when the Russians exploded their own. The supporters of Senator Joseph McCarthy feared the Communist Party of the United States of America. Liberal and left-wing enclaves feared McCarthyism. Conservatives feared social dissolution, immorality, rock 'n' roll, even fluoridation. Intellectuals feared their own past, and the mass mind.

The middle class furnished its islands of affluence, but around it the waters kept rising. Popular culture and politics ran rife with foreboding. While the actual rate of juvenile delinquency probably declined in comparison with that of a half-century earlier, adults panicked. Juvenile delinquents haunted the imaginations if not the streets of the middle class; even if the barbarians could be kept away from the nation's gates, they might sneak into the house through the kids' bedrooms. Movies and comic books bent the prevailing insecurity into concrete fears of alien invaders who, descending from outer space or rising from the black lagoon, threatened the land, the lives, even the souls of harried America. Blobs, things, creatures, body-snatchers, and all manner of other monsters crept into the sacrosanct household, infiltrated the bodies and minds of loved ones, stole their personalities, left them as standardized, emotionless hulks who could be read as Communist or conformist or just plain alien, depending on the terms of one's ideological paranoia.

There may not have been a single master fear, but to many in my generation, especially the incipient New Left, the grimmest and least acknowledged underside of affluence was the Bomb. Everything might be possible? So might annihilation. Whatever the national pride in the blasts that pulverized Bikini and Eniwetok atolls, whatever the Atomic Energy Commission's bland assurances, the Bomb actually disrupted our daily lives. We grew up taking cover in school drills—the first American generation compelled from infancy to fear not only war but the end of days. Every so often, out of the blue, a teacher would pause in the middle of class and call out, "Take cover!" We knew, then, to scramble under our miniature desks and to stay there, cramped, heads folded under our arms, until the teacher called out, "All clear!" Sometimes the whole school was taken out into the halls, away from the windows, and instructed to crouch down, heads to the walls, our eyes scrunched closed, until further notice.

Sometimes air raid sirens went off out in the wider world, and whole cities were told to stay indoors. Who knew what to believe? Under the desks and crouched in the hallways, terrors were ignited, existentialists were made. Whether or not we believed that hiding under a school desk or in a hallway was really going to protect us from the furies of an atomic blast, we could never quite take for granted that the world we had been born into was destined to endure.

The Bomb also drew a knife-edge line between the generations. Our parents remembered World War II as The War, "The Good War," which, whatever its horrors, had drawn the country together and launched America upon its unprecedented prosperity. And if the memory of horrors lingered into peacetime, they associated the Bomb not so much with war as with the *end* of The War, deliverance for American boys spared the need to storm the beaches of Japan; and then, by the standard Cold War arguments, with the keeping of the postwar peace. The memory of Hiroshima and Nagasaki was either repressed or transfigured, forged into a shield against the hypothetically world-conquering Soviet aggressors. In government propaganda, the Bomb was either too terrible to be used or not so terrible that it couldn't be weathered. General-turned-President Eisenhower, the first professional military man to hold the office in three-quarters of a century, spoke soothingly of "Atoms for Peace," a slogan cheerfully used as an official postmark. If the Cold War was nerve-racking, the Bomb could tranquilize.

What was to become the New Left generation (at first only a small minority of the whole generation, of course) had a different angle of vision. For us, the future was necessarily more salient than the past. The Bomb threatened that future, and therefore undermined the ground on which affluence was built. Rather than feel grateful for the Bomb, we felt menaced. The Bomb was the shadow hanging over all human endeavor. It threatened all the prizes. It might, if one thought about it radically, undermine the rationale of the nation-state. It might also throw the traditional religious and ethical justifications of existence into disarray, if not disrepute. The Bomb that exploded in Hiroshima gave the lie to official proclamations that the ultimate weapon was too terrible to be used. It had been used. And worse was being prepared. We did not even know that genial Ike thought of the Bomb as a weapon like any other, one that might actually be used, one that, indeed, he threatened to drop in Korea and offered to the French in Indochina.

But this is one of those moments when I do not know exactly how many of "us" I am speaking about. There are no scientific-sounding numbers to wield. Much of the nuclear terror probably hovered just beneath the threshold of awareness. Several observers have reported what my own impressions and interviews confirm: children who grew up in the Fifties often dreamed, vividly, terrifyingly, about nuclear war. This cannot have been simply because of the presence of the Bomb: there were far more missiles in the Seventies, when college students were not dreaming the same dreams. To some extent it must have been the stress of amply reported East-West confrontations. As the air raid drills confirmed, the Bomb was not just a shadow falling on some distant horizon. Bombs were actually going off. H-bomb tests obliterated atolls in the South Pacific; A-bombs regularly scorched the Nevada desert. President Eisenhower was benignly reassuring, except that East-West relations failed to improve—culminating in the collapse of the summit conference of 1960, when the Russians brought down Francis Gary Powers's U-2 spy plane and Ike was caught in a lie. Such reassurances did not altogether reassure.

Popular culture, that ever-quivering barometer, also registered some of the anxieties that Washington sought to dissolve with official elixirs. In many science fiction films of the Fifties, the Bomb was conspicuously the offscreen nemesis. Aliens sometimes recognized the atomic peril before the stupid humans did; they came to help us, and if we didn't get the point (nations of the world, unite), so much the worse for us. *The Day the Earth Stood Still* (1951) portrayed an otherworldly agent sent to warn earthlings that they had better not loose their military destructiveness into the heavens; paranoid American soldiers panicked and shot him. In *Them!* (1954), as in low-budget Japanese releases, it was atomic testing that created the bug-eyed monsters in the first place. *On the Beach,* about the aftermath of thermonuclear war, was a bestseller in 1957; the star-studded movie of 1959, the first to show a bomb-blasted planet more or less "realistically," suggested (in a speech by Fred Astaire) that the prewar world had been to blame for not taking the danger seriously enough.

The same Bronx High School of Science yearbook which contained the principal's paean to opportunity included these words, not from ban-the-bomb activists (none of those were visible in the class of '59) but from the student editors:

> In today's atomic age . . . the flames of war would write *finis* not only to our civilization, but to our very existence. Mankind may find itself unable to rise again should it be consumed in a nuclear pyre of its own making. In years to come, members of this class will bear an ever-increasing responsibility for the preservation of the heritage given us. Those of us who will become scientists must make certain that the Vanguards and Sputniks of the future herald the coming of an era of light and not an epoch of never-ending darkness.

The Bomb was not the only offstage presence to shake what C. Wright Mills called the American Celebration. For Jewish adolescents in particular, the Nazis were not so long defeated, and Hitler was the most compelling of all bogeymen. "Camp" did not mean only a place to go for the summer. Protective parents were reluctant to remind us, but rumors and images and random facts did seep into our consciousness. Photos of camp survivors, not yet stereotyped, floated through popular culture like stray bones, and lodged, once in a while, in our collective throat. One of my grandmother's brothers had stayed behind in Lithuania when she, three sisters, and another brother came to America, for example, and I was vaguely aware that all but one member of his family had been murdered; I remember my excitement when we learned, in the early Fifties, that one of her nephews had turned up, having apparently run off to join the Red Army near Vilna as the Nazi troops approached. The Holocaust had not yet acquired that name, at least in my hearing; the catastrophe was simply a mangled piece of history, incomprehensibly real, unique to the twentieth century: our century. Meredith Tax, who grew up in the Milwaukee of the Fifties, has written: "Every night I looked under the bed for men from Mars, witches, and Nazis. My little brother slept with a German luger, war booty of my father's, unloaded but with magic potency." The heavily German-American Milwaukee had an active Nazi Bund during the war, as she points out, and so the main downtown street was full of "war memorabilia" stores displaying swastikas. But even in New York my father once or twice referred darkly to Yorkville, the German section of Manhattan, as if once, in prehistory, something terrible—I was not to know what—had happened there.

We were survivors, in short, or our friends were, without having suffered in the flesh, thanks to our (or our friends') grandparents for having journeyed halfway around the world to Ellis Island. But our luck was tainted, confused. For some parents, the relief they felt was another form and measure of America's bounty, the gift of affluence. But questions nagged: Why should we have been so lucky? How close was the close call? Again a spiritual gulf opened between the generations, a divide which led us in later years to our different ways of reliving World War II. Our parents had lived through these horrors. Later, childishly thinking them omnipotent, we wanted to know: How could they have let this happen? How could they not have known? Some felt tremors of guilt, perhaps just beneath the threshold, that they had let the slaughter take place without quite knowing, without making a point of knowing, without doing much, or anything, or in any case enough—but what would have been enough?—to help their European cousins, to press the sainted FDR to bomb the tracks to Auschwitz or open the immigration gates. One might even surmise that some of their guilt was later fought out over Vietnam, that the Jewish Cold Warriors of the Fifties and early Sixties were dead set on stopping Communism precisely because they had failed to stop the Nazis—whereas to me and people I knew, it was American bombs which were the closest thing to an immoral equivalent of Auschwitz in our lifetimes. When the time came, we jumped at the chance to purge ourselves of the nearest thing to the original trauma. And then atrocities committed by innocent America rang the old alarms—even if the parallels were drawn too easily, overdrawn, with crucial differences obscured.

(Killing peasants because they were supposed to be Vietcong, even destroying villages "in order to save them," as an American officer once famously said, was not the same as killing Jews systematically because they were Jews.) We were going to be active where our parents' generation had been passive, potent where (having once looked omnipotent) they had finally proved impotent. Then we could tell our parents: We learned when we were children that massacres really happen and the private life is not enough; and if not now, when?

So the generational divide was not just an economic but a spiritual fact. And if Jews were transfixed by their unforgettable knowledge, it was not only Jews who were haunted. Many gentiles (as well as Jews) converted the Holocaust into yet another reason to love America, but some brooded about what it implied for the human heart and the human project, even for redemptive dreams of affluence. The massacre of the Jews was a huge fact lying overturned, square in the middle of the through route to progress. There were some, or many, for whom the Holocaust meant that nothing—neither private satisfactions nor the nation's greater glory—could ever supplant the need for a public morality. There were Christians as well as Jews who concluded that they would never end up "good Germans" if they could help it.

INTIMATIONS

The fact of affluence and the terror of destruction: the tension was especially sharp among a minority: the largely urban and suburban, disproportionately Jewish children of the more-or-less affluent but discomfited middle class. And this minority was located within huge institutions, the elite but mass universities, which collected these forces, as a magnifying glass collects the rays of the sun, and brought them to a smolder. For neither economic tendencies nor even political issues by themselves could generate a student movement. First there had to be an igniting minority.

This early New Left of the early Sixties, which I will sometimes call the old New Left, the pre–Vietnam New Left, aspired to become the voice, conscience, and goad of its generation. It was never quite typical: it was morally more serious, intellectually and culturally more ambitious than the rest of its generation. It shared its generation's obsessions, and then some, but focused them in an original way. Itself ignited by the civil rights movement, it was the small motor that later turned the larger motor of the mass student movement of the late Sixties. Within a few years this minority created a tradition—a culture, a style, an approach to society, a set of tactics—that played itself out in the movement's subsequent history. It was on the achievements as well as the paradoxes and tensions of the old New Left that the later movement foundered.

The old New Left was acutely, even sentimentally, conscious that they were of a particular age. "We are people of this generation," the 1962 *Port Huron Statement* of Students for a Democratic Society opens, "bred in at least modest comfort, housed now in universities, looking uncomfortably to the world we inherit." But the authors of this document were aware that they were not altogether typical of their affluent peers. "Our work is guided by the sense that we may be the last generation in the experiment with living," they wrote. "But we are a minority—the vast majority of our people regard the temporary equilibriums of our society and world as eternally-functional parts."

This minority turned out to be, as Jack Newfield later wrote, "prophetic," but at the time they could not be sure. (Anyway, many people feel like prophets and turn out to be wrong.) They were not only willing to be marginal, they felt there was a kind of nobility in being devoted to the public good in an unconventional way. In a nation devoted to private pursuits, they believed in public action. In a culture devoted to the celebration of middle-class security, they labeled it smugness and expressed solidarity with people who were systematically excluded from a fair share in prosperity. The revelation that there were people blocked from affluence not only offended them, it discredited the dream—a dream they already felt ambivalent about, even estranged from. They felt cramped by the normal middle-class pursuits of career, family, and success, and they brandished their alienation as a badge. They were not satisfied to take up public participation as a sideline, whether in political parties, PTAs, or professional associations. Their peers wanted to make families; this tiny group wanted to make history.

The New Left, when it erupted, insisted that above all it was new, tailored to a new time, exempt from the vices that had afflicted the various factions of the Old Left. There was truth in the insistence. The Old Left had been shattered by McCarthyism, the Cold War, the postwar consensus, and its own moral obtuseness vis-à-vis the Soviet Union; partly for this reason, partly because of the prevailing fear of getting out of line, and partly because of the rewards of gray-flanneled conformity, there was (with few exceptions) a "missing generation" on the Left. Few were the radicals twenty to thirty years old in the Fifties who might have served as exemplars for the next generation, a link between experience and innocence. The self-flattering idea of a virgin birth enabled the early New Left to think its way past defeat, to break from both pro-Soviet and Cold War rigidities. From this reality came much of the famous New Left spunk, the impulse to go it alone. But the heady truth in this image of self-creation also concealed continuities. The movers and shakers of the Sixties did not invent a new political culture from scratch.

Even in the ranch-housed, well-laundered Fifties, while the bulk of the middle class busied itself with PTA meetings, piano lessons, and *The Saturday Evening Post,* there were, dotted around the country, enclaves where groups of adults carried on in opposition to prevailing values. Moreover, within the very mass youth culture which affluence made possible, the self-satisfied Fifties were crisscrossed by underground channels where the conventional wisdoms of the time were resisted, undermined, weakened. It was in these enclaves of elders and subterranean channels, rivulets, deep-running springs—or backwaters and swamps, depending on your point of view—that unconventional wisdoms, moods, and mystiques were nurtured.

With left-wing politics in a state of collapse, most of these oppositional spaces were cultural—ways of living, thinking, and fighting oneself free of the affluent consensus. Most were indifferent or hostile to politics, which they saw as yet another squandering of energy. But even the antipolitical enclaves opened a space for later and larger oppositions, both the New Left and the counterculture, oppositions compounded—however contradictorily—of politics and culture. The beats were the main channel; hostile to the postwar bargain of workaday routine in exchange for material acquisition, they devoted themselves to principled poverty, indulged their taste for sexual libertinism, and looked eastward for enlightenment. Overlapping, there were other tiny bohemias of avant-garde culture and political dissonance, notably the radical pacifists of *Liberation,* New York's Living Theatre, San Francisco's anarchist and East-minded poets, jazz connoisseurs, readers of *The Village Voice* and *Evergreen Review.* Battered remnants of the Old Left carried their torches for some kind of socialism, rejected the orthodoxies of the Cold War to one degree or another, and felt the national security state to be a menace rather than a guarantor of true-blue liberties; they maintained a "folk culture" in the absence of an actual folk. These were, to use the shorthand, subcultures where exotic practices attracted a hard core of rebels, a fringe of hangers-on, and a larger penumbra of the part-time, the tempted, and the vicarious participants. More narrowly political were the invisible communities clustered around the social-democratic *Dissent* and I. F. Stone's anti–Cold War *Weekly,* trying in different ways to think in the name of a Left that did not exist. In their studies, and among their students, obscure critical intellectuals like Paul Goodman, Herbert Marcuse, Norman O. Brown, William Appleman Williams, and Betty Friedan were writing the books, many of them not even published until well into the next decade, which set a tone for rebellion when rebels came up from the underground streams, looked around, and decided to make history. There was anger collecting in these nodes, but they also were governed by a happy sense of their distance from the normal. It was as if they were living in color while the rest of America was living in black and white. They radiated jarring signals to the next generation.

At the same time, usually less angry, certainly less focused, and far more extensive, popular music and the movies and other forms of mass-distributed culture began speaking in their own ways directly to the young, challenging the affluent society's claims that its social arrangements were sufficient nourishment for the human spirit. Some of the initiative came from the entrepreneurs of popular culture, who, to keep the mainstream entertained, scouted the margins, absorbing outsiders and outsideness, packaging them in marketable form, relaying the idea that authorities were questionable and that to be young was to be weird, angry, marginal, dispossessed. So hoods acquired a shadow life as folk heroes. But more important than the hoods themselves, their culture of delinquency turned out to be the outer edge of a more vast and amorphous teenage culture. To put it another way, what happened in the mid-Fifties is that the normal teenage culture borrowed the mystique of the subterraneans in order to express its own uneasy and ambivalent relation to the society of parents. The adolescent society depended on affluence—on time and money of its own to spend—but it also flirted with the harmless part of the culture of delinquency: the spirit of fun and adventure, the disdain for studies, the drinking, smoking, making out, swearing, staying out late. Never before had so many of the leisured young had a chance to spend so much so relentlessly to indulge their tastes. The marketplace sold adolescent society its banners. To call the resulting spectacle an "adversary culture" would be to lend it too much coherence and to miss its ambiguities. But this cultural display was certainly far from an uncritical embrace of the social order. Where the narrower enclaves and channels of the beats, the bohemians, and the remnant Left opened spaces for the New Left in the early Sixties, and for the pure counterculture later on, the shallower channels of the Fifties' teenage culture marked the territory for the far larger youth upheaval of the late Sixties.

Rock and roll and its dances were the opening wedge, hollowing out the cultural ground beneath the tranquilized center. Marlon Brando and James Dean embodied styles and gestures of disaffection. On the fringes, satirists of all kinds—*Mad,* Lenny Bruce, Tom Lehrer, Mort Sahl, Chicago's Compass and Second City cabarets—ridiculed a host of pieties. TV's Steve Allen and Sid Caesar and their offshoots and imitators carried some of the rambunctious spirit into the mainstream. Late in the decade, domestic avant-garde films as well as foreign dramas of dislocation helped a new college generation feel that angst was normal. As America exported Hollywood movies, it imported parables of estrangement.

Literary culture was also piled high with maps of a devastated social landscape; struggles with the absurd resounded in the heart of every half-alienated student. Lost souls and embattled antiheroes paraded their losses of meaning. J. D. Salinger's Holden Caulfield was revolted by "phoniness," and his other dislocated adolescents dabbled in Zen. In the legitimate theater, Arthur Miller's Willy Loman matched the spiritually uprooted souls of Riesman's and Mills's sociology. To Beckett's and Genet's and Ionesco's characters, the postwar cornucopia looked absolutely beside the point. Off Broadway, "communication" was problematic, "to-getherness" a bad joke, happy endings the real absurdity; and Grove Press's *Evergreen Review* carried the news outside New York. In *Lady Chatterley's Lover* and Henry Miller's *Tropic* novels, finally available over the counter, raw sex was posed as the oasis in an arid society. Existentialism started from the premise of meaninglessness, and then executed a brilliant judo move: it declared that *precisely because* humanity is deserted by God and values are not inscribed in the natural order of things, human beings are responsible for making their own meanings. (It followed, then, that authority would always have to prove itself, minute to minute. If Norman Mailer could bend existentialism to support John F. Kennedy in 1960, he could just as easily turn it against Kennedy's successor and the Vietnam war in 1965.) Book marketing itself pried open a new cultural space: Starting in 1952, first Doubleday and then other publishers began to publish serious nonfiction in paperback, so that avant-garde currents and European repertories—existentialism, the absurd, all manner of philoso-phy, history, and sociology—could circulate to the idea-hungry and college-bound.

UNDERGROUND CHANNELS

WILD ONES The future New Left read David Riesman and C. Wright Mills and Albert Camus, and found in them warrants for estrangement, but nothing influenced me, or the baby-boom generation as a whole, as much as movies, music, and comics did. On the big screen, on posters, and in popular magazines, America was mass-producing images of white youth on the move yet with nowhere to go. What moved the new sullen heroes was the famous rebellion without a cause, partly because McCarthyism and the Cold War had rendered cause anathema. But the very point of this particular rebellion was to claw one's way toward libertine self-definition. Disaffiliation came first. Alienated, made into aliens, the causeless rebels tried to revel in marginality. To them, the best the adult world had to offer was flimsy, phony, hypocritical. Figures of authority were *proprietors* without a cause. If it was necessary for young people to act unmanageable in order to sidestep the management, so be it; they were giving back to the society just what they got, but double. In return, the authorities looked askance. In the eyes of a managerial society and a therapeutic culture, the young and estranged were "juvenile" (i.e., not adult) and "delinquent" (i.e., deficient); they didn't deserve the dignity of real crooks.

The new specters on the movie screen were white-skinned, but they wore black motorcycle jackets and combed their hair with greasy kid stuff. They were private, hopeless, misunderstood—and heroic for all these reasons. First came Marlon Brando, cast as a motorcycle-riding gangster bent on disrupting a folksy American town in *The Wild One* (1953). To the ingenue's naïvely rational question, "What are you rebelling against?" Brando snarls his classic answer, "Whadda ya got?"—declaring that he is happy to be every bit as bad as his uncomprehending accusers (and victims) claim. To which the patronizing sheriff lamely answers back: "I don't think you know what you're trying to do, or how to go about it." Organized society expects a young man to have a purpose; pragmatism requires that he look to his methods. But rationalism to Brando—and to the film—is a collaboration between weaklings: a woman and a mild-mannered authority figure. To be without either purpose or technique is to be not only subversive but strong, autonomous. It is also, it turns out, romantic.

Perhaps because he was older (already twenty-nine when *The Wild One* was released), Brando never became the teen idol James Dean was. Dean's persona wasn't so angry; he was more the sensitive, brooding type. His masculine and feminine appeals were delicately balanced: to teenaged girls he was an awkward darling, to boys a lost companion of the soul. Dean's meteoric career, moreover, seemed the perfect embodiment of doomed, estranged youth. Considering his reputation, it is astonishing to realize that he lived only long enough to star in *three* movies before flaring out, with poetic justice, in an auto wreck at age twenty-four, in 1955. When he wrecked his custom racing car in a spurt of bravado on a California highway, only *East of Eden* had been released; *Rebel Without a Cause* opened three days later. But James Dean's importance as a loner *maudit,* an incarnation of lost hopes, soared at his death. His ghostly appearance in *Rebel Without a Cause* became a vivid symbol of how precarious was youth-who-had-everything. The road, promising everything, could take every-thing. Dean's martyrdom gave an aura both mysterious and grim to the famous scene in which he and his rival raced their cars to the edge of a cliff in a game of Chicken. A year after he died, as many as eight thousand fans a month were writing to the dead James Dean, more than were writing to any living star. In the Fifties, death on the road at high speed before one's time held the poignancy that had earlier been reserved for death in battle.

Rebel Without a Cause was therefore instant mythology, and it prefigures an astonishing amount of the oppositional mood of the Sixties, especially in what it displays of the dynamics of fathers and sons. The fathers' capacity to bring home the goods is not in question; everyone takes for granted that high school boys own cars. What is at issue is what fathers fail to provide: authority to boys, love to girls. Fathers without authority produce sons without purpose. When fathers are absent (Sal Mineo's Plato) or feminine (James Dean's Jim), the sons are thrown into aimless crime; a daughter (Natalie Wood's Judy) becomes a "bad girl" because *her* father, confronted with her tight-sweatered sexuality, pulls away. Dean's father, played by Jim Backus (best known as the voice of Mr. Magoo), wears a fur coat in one scene, an apron in another, and lets his loud-mouthed wife tell him what to do. "I don't ever want to be like him," says the disgusted Dean. Rather than give his son a model of manhood, the flabby Backus does nothing but provide ("Don't I buy you anything you want?") and permit ("Jim, did I ever stop you from anything?"). He doesn't understand that young Jim simply wants an old-fashioned father, strong enough to test himself against. When Jim goes so far as to engage Dad in hand-to-hand combat, he has to grab the pushover and force him to stand up—only to shove him down again and try to strangle him. Jim's mother wears the family pants, and her men resent her for it: trapped in her perfect house, stronger than Dad, but with nothing to do but carp, in a backhanded way she anticipates Betty Friedan's exposé of the suburban housewife's "disease with no name."

Against Dad's wishy-washy hypocrisy, Jim stands for directness. He is, as Plato says, "sincere," and he signals his sincerity by speaking in off-rhythm cadences, failing to finish sentences, erupting in anger. He grows up by becoming a good symbolic father himself—to the errant, eventually martyred Plato. His exercise of kindness and responsibility, however doomed, serves a purpose: it compels the fatuous Backus to reclaim his own rightful authority from his wife's usurpation. The possibility of benign authority is underscored by a good cop, who speaks a therapeutic language of sensitivity and human relations and does what he can to save the day. But this double redemption of authority comes too late for Plato, the rich and innocent waif who had been preoccupied with the end of the world. Despite the good cop's intervention, Plato is shot down by reckless police. The core of adult society remains unforgiving.

To the impassioned audiences of the time, not trained as film analysts, the intricacies of plot were probably less important than Dean's persona. Alongside the movies themselves, fan magazines kept his image in circulation. Between them, Dean and Brando gave the dislocated young a repertoire of stances and gestures. Unlike Clark Gable, Gary Cooper, or Humphrey Bogart, say, heroes who knew what they wanted and went after it, Brando and Dean went looking for trouble because they had nothing better to do. They were refusers, defined by what they weren't. Their halting speech was a sign of their essential confusion and passivity. Who needed to be articulate anyway? They said no, therefore they were.

As often happens in popular culture, Dean sharpened a vague mood, then amplified it with a precise sound and look. In Hibbing, Minnesota, for example, the young Robert Zimmerman devoured Dean's fan magazines. In working-class Detroit, David Wellman, later a New Left activist, remembers imitating Dean's haircut and his "sullen, sour, nasty, angry look"—one common interpretation, if not the only one possible. In the middle and late Fifties, Wellman wore motorcycle boots and a Sam Browne belt with sharpened buckle, aiming to look like a hood and freak out his father—a Communist, in this case. In Wellman's high school and college circles—he entered Wayne State University in 1958—Brando and especially Dean were romantic prototypes. In photos taken of Wellman in the late Fifties, he recalls, he was never smiling. "People said it was because of McCarthyism, because my father went to jail under the Smith Act. Hell no! It was James Dean. And his death was very heavy to me.

"He was Camus," Wellman adds, and the metaphor is worth pausing over for a moment. Needless to say, James Dean was no intellectual. His message was neither more nor less than his look and whatever his fans took it to mean. To many, that message meant: Live for the moment, without guarantees, in a world that doesn't deliver. Or more: Homelessness is the truth of the human condition when society, all organized, sanitized, and insured to provide security, denies the rock-bottom fact that life ends. So James Dean's reckless death put the seal on the myth of his life. Here was a mass-circulation version of the aura that in America later surrounded Camus, who was to die at forty-six *in an auto crash* (in the first week of 1960), thereby seeming to testify that rebellion is the essence of freedom because, after all, life is lived "for keeps." It was the looming fact of death, framing life, that made it possible—necessary—to mean something. Myself, I remember the M.I.T. freshman, a friend of my roommate, who when Camus died told me that *The Myth of Sisyphus* had saved him from suicide, and now he had to rethink his commitment to live.

This sense of a fatal connection to young martyrs, of death as the final refutation of plenitude, ran strong through all the phases of Sixties' culture. C. Wright Mills, for example, renewed the original impetus when he died in 1962, at age forty-five, of a heart attack—a natural cause, in a sense, but brought on prematurely when Mills burned himself out cramming for a national television debate over Kennedy's Cuba policy. Mills was a hero in student radical circles for his books, of course, but it was no small part of the persona for which he was cherished that he was a motorcycle-riding, cabin-building Texan, cultivating the image of a gunslinging homesteader of the old frontier who springs into virtuous action crying, "Don't tread on me!" The Christian passion of the wanderer who dies trying to help the uncomprehending was even affixed onto the assassinated John F. Kennedy, who succeeded, mythologically, in becoming both outsider and insider at once. The legend absorbed Malcolm X, Martin Luther King, and Bobby Kennedy in turn. Bob Dylan narrowly escaped his mythic fate when he succeeded in recovering from his 1966 motorcycle accident—but he was hurt badly enough to remind the counterculture that behind its charmed existence there were close calls. The myth of the doomed outsider surfaced again, in fictional form, with *Bonnie and Clyde* and *Easy Rider*. Finally, Jimi Hendrix, Jim Morrison, and Janis Joplin, by dying young, famous, and drugged, certified once and for all that ritual sacrifices were necessary to placate the battered gods of order.

James Dean's death inaugurated the idea that living fast is living right, and yet that there is something ineluctably poignant at stake when youth commits itself to go beyond limits. In the Sixties' own hand-made mythology, not just the media's canned summary of it, Dean's death was epochal. Dean, like Keats, was "half in love with easeful Death": that is what gave his death its sting. And James Dean's death erupted in the midst of an affluent society which was supposed to have had no more need of risk because it was organized to make happiness mandatory and adaptation the irresistible flagstone path of least resistance.

"WHAT, ME WORRY?"

In 1962, Paul Goodman remarked that a recent eastern high school poll had found *Mad* a close second to *Life* as the most widely read magazine. ("That is," he added deftly, "the picture magazine that publishes the slick ads, and the cartoon magazine that scoffs at them.") *Mad* appeared first in 1952 as the mock-grotesque *Mad* comics ("Tales Calculated to Drive You MAD: Humor in a Jugular Vein"), but in 1955, when comics came under fire for allegedly causing juvenile delinquency, was reincarnated in the tamer magazine form. *Mad*'s benign parodies started out mocking the formulas of popular comic strips, movies, ads, and the new living room fixture, television; eventually they turned their attention to suburbia, Eisenhower, the smugness of "the American way of life." If official America radiated health, *Mad* insisted on the importance of the "sick." (This was also the moment of "sick" jokes—"Mrs. Anderson, can Joey come out and play?" "But you know he has no arms and legs." "Yeah, but we need a second base.") If America was whiter-than-white clean, *Mad* played on the allure of the disgusting, pointing the finger at people picking their noses. If consumer culture achieved some of its power by taking itself hyperseriously, as the achievement of a high order of civilization, *Mad* pulled the plug and said, "Hey, the Lone Ranger, Wonder Bread, and TV commercials— even Marlon Brando—are *ridiculous*! Clark Kent is a creep! Superduperman can't get off the ground!"

No affirmations for *Mad:* it also scorned the possibility of any alternative to the scorned American way of life. It badgered nonconformists and high-cultured intellectuals along with Marlon Brando and "sick-making, soft-sell" advertisements. In "How to Be Smart," for example, *Mad* mock-recommended that pretentious types "cultivate a withering sneer." In "The Bulletin of Alfred E. Neuman University, 1958–59," it proclaimed "how ridiculous anthropology really is" for concerning itself with "nasty little people" with their "pygmy smell." In *Mad*'s world, the normal and the abnormal, the American and the un-American, were melted down in the universal solvent of silliness.

It was a popular attitude, this indiscriminate hilarity. On television, Sid Caesar, Steve Allen, and Ernie Kovacs played in the same key. They spoke through the boob tube about its own boobery. Not that their aesthetics were automatically left-of-center in a political sense. Kovacs's burlesque could even slide right over into racism, in a brilliant skit featuring three droll apes in a rock band called "The Nairobi Trio." At the same time, Stan Freberg was producing spoof records like "St. George and the Dragonet," ridiculing the hardened conventions of adult popular culture. In his "History of the United States," Freberg chided an "Un-British Activities Committee"; but he also mocked rock records like "Sh-Boom," "The Great Pretender," and "Heartbreak Hotel," echoing the conventional wisdom of adults that rock was simply incompetent. These amiable comics were teases, even of themselves, in sharp contrast to Lenny Bruce and the beats, scourges of bourgeois morality all. Endearingly, *Mad* even called *itself* trash: high-level trash, as if this were the appropriate level of comment in a trash culture. In junior high and high school, I devoured it.

Though *Mad* never sympathized with student radicalism, it playfully anticipated one of its curious features: it used the far-flung distribution systems of mass society to circulate a sense of self-disarming superiority. This was elitism with a bad conscience. *Mad* chided its mass of readers—each of them addressed as if more intelligent and discriminating than the average—for wasting time on the "idiotic garbage" produced by the "clods" at *Mad*. (It was hard to know exactly where the mockery meant to stop—which uncertainty helped to convey the absurdist effect.) With the help of *Mad* and its ilk, a subgeneration crystallized on the curious premise that, en masse, it was made up of singularly discerning, superior spirits—who were, at the same time, just plain knuckleheads. *Mad*'s club of nonconformists was committed to vulgar snobbery. And so *Mad*'s style was perfectly expressed in the slogan of its deliberately dopey-looking mascot, Alfred E. Neuman: "What, me worry?" In his grinning caricature of a cherub was the bubble-gum nihilism of the late Fifties—and its refutation.

It would be absurd to retrofit *Mad* and its electronic equivalents as subversive forces that by themselves, automatically, undermined middle-class values. Both radicals in search of a cultural pedigree and conservatives scouting for cultural subversion have given *Mad* too much credit. *Mad* was usually as sweet-tempered as it was sweeping, and it was no friend of political action; indeed, convinced that deviance and orthodoxy blurred together in a consumer culture, it giggled at all the plagued houses. But a more modest credit is due to all these instruments of hilarity. They pried open a cultural territory which became available for radical transmutation—as it was also available for a good-humored liberalism or an utterly apolitical cynicism. In a world that adult ideologies had defined as black and white—America versus totalitarianism, respectability versus crime, obedience versus delinquency, affluence versus barbarism, suburbia versus degradation and filth—they did help establish the possibility of gray.

"DELIVER ME FROM THE DAYS OF OLD"

The electric subcurrent of the Fifties was above all rock 'n' roll, the live wire that linked bedazzled teenagers around the nation—and quickly around the world—into the common enterprise of being young. Rock was rough, raw, insistent, especially by comparison with the music it replaced; it whooped and groaned, shook, rattled, and rolled. Rock was clamor, the noise of youth submerged by order and affluence, now frantically clawing their way out. The lyrics were usually about the anguish and sincerity of adolescent romance. But far more than any lyrics, it was the thump and throb and quaver of rock that electrified the young. Even the tamed stuff repackaged by clean-cut, crew-cut white bands went right into the body. Rock was itself a moment of abundance, energy in profusion. It was an invitation to dance, and at some fantasy level—just as the bluenoses protested—it was an invitation to make love. Even if the lyrics said so subliminally, the beat said it directly: *express* yourself, move yourself around, get going. Rock announced: Being young means being able to feel rock. Whatever it is you're in, kid, you're not in it alone; you and your crowd are where it's at, spirited or truculent or misunderstood, and anyone who doesn't get it is, well, square.

Rock's beginnings, of course, were black. Cultural segregation had the unintended effect of shoring up diversity by protecting the space in which a discordant subculture could thrive. Rock had its origins in blues and gospel, songs of travail and exultation written and performed by and for blacks, going back to the late nineteenth century. The blacks who migrated from the land to the cities in the Thirties and Forties brought with them their blues rituals of anguish and sex, search and release. Finding its way onto local record labels, sold in ghetto stores and played on black radio, this is what the record industry unsubtly called "race music" until the late Forties, when, embarrassed, it changed the label to "rhythm and blues," R & B. White radio considered R & B disreputable, and barred it. By now the music had changed, too: the accents were still southern, the voices raw and untrained, but the younger musicians, born or raised in the northern and western cities, played faster and more raucously. R & B was dance music, built on the singular style of the wailing or shouting or otherwise feelingful singer. Sometimes a lone saxophone was in effect a second voice, wailing, lamenting, rasping, mocking. Most of all, R & B was inescapably *rhythm,* built on a beat.

By the mid-Fifties, in spite of de facto segregation, small groups of white teenagers living in or near black neighborhoods in northern cities were buying these records that seemed sexy and made them want to dance. A Cleveland disk jockey named Alan Freed was the first to scout the new market. Told about these crossover sales by a store owner, he liked both the music and the commercial possibilities, and in June 1951, on his mostly white radio station, he started a rhythm and blues show for which he coined the euphemism "rock 'n' roll."

Rock 'n' roll was rhythm and blues whitened, in two senses. Rock brought the pulse of R & B to places where blacks themselves never dreamed of going; at the same time it blanched the music. The right technology was there at the right time to serve—and help form—the youth market. Even more than the saxophone or the electric guitar, the instrument that made rock culture possible was the radio, then a medium in search of a message. For in the early Fifties television was replacing radio as the ideal vehicle for advertising and mass entertainment. But if the family no longer huddled around the living-room radio console together, radios, plural, were now available for other purposes, especially as they became steadily cheaper and—with the advent of plastic cases and transistor models—more portable. Watching the handwriting on the screen, radio stations switched to low-cost, audience-segmented formats. Recorded music was ideal. Rock, augmented by jukeboxes, proved most ideal of all.

Rock lore justly repeats the tale about the white Mississippi boy, Elvis Presley, who learned rhythm and blues from blacks he heard on Memphis radio and in the clubs along Beale Street. As R & B took off, a white Memphis producer, Sam Phillips, had taken to saying, "If I could find a white man who had the Negro sound and the Negro feel, I could make a million dollars." Phillips coached Elvis in the vocal style of blues masters like Muddy Waters, B. B. King, and Howlin' Wolf. The black blues, with guitar throbs and drums, fused with the country-western hitches of Elvis's rangy, racy voice. Two styles of American restlessness smoldered together. Elvis's live shows—curling lips, rolling hips—ignited the screams of thousands of teenage girls across the South. Then a northern disk jockey was persuaded to try out Elvis's early records on the radio—in Cleveland, again—only to have his switchboard light up with an unprecedented frenzy of excited calls. These enthusiasts hadn't even seen Elvis sneer, shake, and swivel his famous pelvis. They were responding to a sound, an incandescence that seemed intimate, thanks to Sam Phillips's echo chamber recording technique, which made his voice sound as if it were ricocheting around inside the listener's skull. It was Elvis Presley, the white boy with the black beat and the hitch in his voice, who (to answer Barry Mann's question) put the bop in the bop-da-bop-da-bop. In two years, Elvis Presley, then on the RCA label, with national reach, sold more than 28 million records.

In the sphere of music as in the sphere of justice, white America was drawing its juice from blacks. To R & B purists, Elvis's rockabilly style was bleached blackness, vanilla-coated chocolate. As Greil Marcus reminds us, Elvis was imitating no one so much as himself, founding a sound more than inheriting one. Still, he skated close to many a cultural edge: class, sex, race. By the Tin Pan Alley standards of commercial pop music, Elvis and his promoters were committing cultural miscegenation. Now, thanks to the radio, Elvis, Carl Perkins, Jerry Lee Lewis, Buddy Holly, and other southern white boys coexisted with Chuck Berry, Little Richard, and Fats Domino, the wizards of R & B who would not have been permitted to break bread at the same lunch counter. The breakthrough year was 1955, when the airwaves rocked with Fats Domino's "Ain't That a Shame," Bill Haley and His Comets' "Rock Around the Clock," Chuck Berry's "Maybelline," and Little Richard's "Tutti Frutti." That same year, *The Blackboard Jungle* linked the boiled-down "Rock Around the Clock" with the dread juvenile delinquency. Joyriding, rampaging white youth made trouble for teachers and caused panic in the city while God-fearing crowds screamed back helplessly. That December 1, a seamstress and civil rights activist named Rosa Parks refused to give up her seat to a white man in a Montgomery, Alabama, bus and got arrested for refusing to "know her place," kicking off a bus boycott that established the power of nonviolence and catapulted Martin Luther King to national fame. The parallels between rock and civil rights were far from exact, but such imperfect coincidences are the updrafts on which the zeitgeist spreads its wings. What news photographers and television did for civil rights, breaking blacks out of their social ghetto, radio did in a different way for musical rights. And in both cases, black dependence on white goodwill carried the seeds of later resentments.

Black and white, the rockers also represented the South brought North. Music trailed demographics, and now, in a rush, caught up. Blacks and working-class whites had been fleeing the job-poor South for the industrial North for two decades, especially during World War II. Rock amounted to cultural carpetbagging in reverse, and it had important cultural and political counterparts in the mind of the white North. Since the Civil War, the South had played the part of the national feminine: sometimes genteel (*Gone with the Wind*), sometimes brooding, sexy, and violent (*Birth of a Nation, Tobacco Road*). In the midst of the rationalizing Fifties, the Montgomery bus boycott and the Little Rock school desegregation crisis disrupted the calm of national politics, and the North again saw the South as the incubator of the tempting and dangerous. The southern invasion started with the 1951 success of Elia Kazan's movie version of Tennessee Williams's *A Streetcar Named Desire;* Brando's uncouth Stanley Kowalski played out in a domestic setting the seething archetype which Elvis, the onetime truckdriver, would later take on the road for the kids. While northern middle-class parents were deploring the sexual innuendo of rock and loathing the racist white violence they saw on television, without any sense of irony they were trooping to the movies to see a succession of Tennessee Williams movies—five in five years starting in 1955—about sexual trauma, incest, and the barely suppressed passion and violence lurking in the family living room. Families fascinated by Williams's neurotic passions were the nests of rock and rockers. Youth, blackness, and southernness: three national symbols of the uncontrollable, unfathomed id-stuff surging beneath the suburban surface, fused into rock 'n' roll.

The rock market ballooned. The blues had been adult music, but now market-sensitive rock producers focused on teenage problems: desire, jealousy, loneliness, romantic mistreatment, misunderstanding by adults. To sing the market-tailored lyrics, the record companies hired whites to "cover" black songs, to sound (to young white ears) just black enough. They stripped down the beat, cleared up their enunciation, sanded off the grit of regional dialect and R & B realism. Bill Haley, for example, was a longtime country-western bandleader in search of a commercial style. Even the stylized spit curl hanging over his forehead marked him as a man whose wildness was deliberate and ornamental. He sounded cooked rather than raw. Yet his simplified beat was still emphatic enough—more than enough—to rouse dancers and irritate adults. Haley and other whites like him even desexed the lyrics. Joe Turner's 1954 R & B hit version of "Shake, Rattle and Roll," for example, said:

> Well you wear low dresses,
> The sun comes shinin' through.

The cover-version hit by Bill Haley and His Comets was sanitized:

> You wear those dresses,
> Your hair done up so nice.

White singers ran away with the mass market for years before blacks regeared to meet radio specifications and found their way into the white teenage heart.

Thus processed, rock quickly became the music of choice on records, on the radio, at afterschool and weekend dances. Concerts drew big teenage crowds, white and black, sometimes together. Rock movies harnessed the image of shakin', rattlin' and rollin' to teenagers' generational surge. The pulsating effect was the musical equivalent of petting. The lyrics were usually expressions of longing, even in the religious metier ("Crying in the Chapel," "Earth Angel," "Book of Love"), but language was only one channel through which the songs conveyed emotion. (That is why we shouldn't exaggerate the importance of expurgated lyrics, although the radio censors did so themselves. Most of the audience was probably less concerned with the nuances than were station managers.) White adults cringed at the strings of nonsense syllables which turned the voice into percussion and pure sound, a kind of sub- (or trans-) linguistic expression of the inexpressible, as in the memorable opening lines of the Silhouettes' 1957 "Get a Job":

Sha da da da
Sha da da da da
Ba do
Sha da da da
Sha da da da da
Ba do
Sha da da da
Sha da da da da
Ba do
Sha da da da
Sha da da da da
Bah do
Bah yip yip yip yip yip yip yip yip
Mum mum mum mum mum mum
Get a job.

In riffs like this, black or pseudoblack voices cut loose from the practical language of the wider world. They slurred their words, stylized their pronunciation ("*bay*-beh," "earth an-*gell*"). Choruses kept up the beat with nonsense ("*do*-wop, do-*wop*"). Singers grunted (Screamin' Jay Hawkins), shrieked (Little Richard), and whined (Shirley and Lee). What adult critics heard as incoherence, primitive regression, was indeed part of the music's appeal. But all these devices could be heard—*were* heard, by me entering into puberty, for one—another way: as distrust of language, distrust of the correct, distrust of practicality itself. Percussive language was a rush of sound so urgent it stuttered, as if to say: What we're feeling is so deep, so difficult, so amazing, it can only be expressed if we leave behind the middle-class manners, undo the lessons of school, stop *trying* to sound correct. With a catch in its collective throat, rock announced to unbelievers: Before your very ears we invent a new vocabulary, a generation's private language. Distrusting the currency, we coin our own.

To accomplish this, though, the music was not enough. The music had to be packaged—selected, produced, amplified, and channeled to the millions of teenagers looking for ways to declare who they were and were not. The packagers—producers, record company executives, disk jockeys, station owners, all in hot pursuit of market appeal—therefore had a great deal to do with defining what it meant to be a teenager in the Fifties. So did the naysayers, also adults: proprietors of the obsolete pop sounds, popular magazines who dismissed rock as regressive music, white southern churches who defined it as the devil's work, segregationists who boycotted what they thought was an NAACP plot. (In 1956, six men committed to keeping music segregated—one of them a director of the local White Citizens' Council—assaulted Nat King Cole in the middle of his concert at Birmingham, Alabama, thinking him a rock 'n' roller.) Parents who winced, like mine, "How can you stand that noise!" also helped define what it meant to like rock: If there had ever been any doubt, "that noise" now meant, "Something my parents can't stand." To the question, "How can you listen to that stuff?" the teenager answered, in effect: "I've got what it takes, and you, the old, the over-the-hill, don't."

In the late Sixties, it became fashionable for conservatives to blame the youth upsurge on Dr. Spock, whose bestselling manuals were supposed to have encouraged "permissive" parents to (in Spiro Agnew's words) "throw discipline out the window." Some liberals, more tolerant of the outcome, retained the explanation but changed blame to credit. As either charge or credit, however, the theory neglected three important facts. First, childrearing manuals had been telling parents to loosen restraints on their children as far back as the Twenties. Second, the mothers who bought millions of copies of successive editions of Spock's *Baby and Child Care* were receptive to his easygoing advice in the first place; their children were already at the center of household life. "Let's do it for the children" was the guiding spirit of the postwar period. Third, as the Seventies and Eighties made clear, it was entirely possible to raise children pliably without turning them into dissidents. But if there *was* a distinctly permissive parent who encouraged the young to "let it all hang out," it may have been less Mom and Dad than the disk jockey.

This presiding angel (or devil) of adolescence underwrote the sense of generational difference. He invaded the home, flattered the kids' taste (while helping mold it), lured them into an imaginary world in which they were free to take their pleasures. His stylized rapidfire language of melodramatic thrill and age-graded romance made them feel as much like insiders as their parents were outsiders. When his wild singsong voice excitedly announced that the next song was "going out for Joey and Janie, Barbara and Johnny and Karen and Beth and Mary Jo and all the seniors down at Seventy-seventh Street," Alan Freed or "Murray the K" Kaufman helped draw a charmed circle around youth and its obsessions. Even if—like me—you didn't date yet, and felt socially inept, you could consort with Joey and Janie, like what they liked, belong, by proxy, to their crowd. So the disk jockeys played an important part in extending the peer group, certifying rock lovers as members of a huge subsociety of the knowing. Even as I sat home doing my homework to the top forty countdown, I felt plugged in. For those of us who were ten or twelve when Elvis Presley came along, it was rock 'n' roll that named us a generation.

The shift was abrupt and amazing. One moment parents and children were listening together to the easygoing likes of Dean Martin's "Memories Are Made of This" or Rosemary Clooney's "Hey There" ("you with the stars in your eyes"), and gathering together on Saturday night to watch the regulars of *Your Hit Parade* cover the week's hits; the next, the spectacle of those crooners trying to simulate Elvis Presley and straddle the widening cultural chasm was too laughable to behold. True, earlier generations of parents had also been disturbed to see their children writhing with abandon, treating their bodies as erotic instruments, screaming at idols like Frank Sinatra. Popular music often serves to insulate young people against the authority of the previous generation, and the commercial search for The Latest makes generational tension over music virtually automatic. But in rock's heyday there was a special intensity on both sides. On one side, generational defiance: "Hail hail rock 'n' roll/Deliver me from the days of old" (Chuck Berry); "Rock and roll is here to stay" (Danny and the Juniors). On the other: Perry Como, Patti Page, Tony Bennett, adult fear and loathing. When teenagers screamed themselves hoarse at Frank Sinatra in the Forties, whatever quality it was that teens celebrated and editorialists deplored was the possession of a single skinny singer. Now both sides agreed that rock was all of a piece, love it or leave it.

The American mainstream greeted the challenge in its usual way: trying partly to expunge the menace, partly to domesticate it. And sometimes both at once: Ed Sullivan first insisted that Elvis Presley would never darken his Sunday night television variety door, then relented under commercial pressure and paid fifty thousand dollars for Elvis's three famous 1956 appearances. Contrary to youth culture myth, Elvis's famous pelvis was shown on the first two shows; it was only the third time that the censors refused to let the camera descend below his waist. No matter: with all the advance publicity, it wasn't hard for the viewers to imagine what all the fuss was about. In similar fashion, Dick Clark's *American Bandstand,* nationally telecast from Philadelphia beginning in 1957, when rock was already sinking into formula, went on distributing the music and flattening it at the same time. With his boyish, round-cheeked good looks, Clark was to Alan Freed as Pat Boone was to Fats Domino: a cover artist even a middle-class mother could love. After school every afternoon, *American Bandstand*'s smartly dressed and generally white teens rocked, snuggled, and showed off the latest steps and styles. Who cared if the only Negroes Clark showed on camera were bands lip-synching to the music? Even packaged for mass consumption, *American Bandstand* rolled over Beethoven and insisted rock and roll was here to stay, out in the suburbs and small towns where flesh-and-blood blacks did not tread.

With spread went normalization. By 1957, carefully overproduced teenage crooners like Frankie Avalon, Paul Anka, and Fabian were all the rage. How far was the mainstream from the margins? The critics' consensus is that when the likes of Bobby Vinton and Fabian rose to the top of the charts, the real music went into cryogenic death for several years until the Beatles kissed it back to life in 1963. But one can get excessively nostalgic for the Golden Age of Rock. The truth is that raw and cooked rock, the coarse and the refined, coexisted and interpenetrated from the beginning. Even Paul Anka was not a throwback to Perry Como. To this sixteen-year-old, Anka's wailing "Diana" of 1959—"I'm so young and you're so old/This my darling I've been told/I don't care just what they say/With you forever I will stay"—expressed as much rebellion as the Coasters' "Yakety Yak." Boy loves woman, boy talks back to father: two sides of the same Oedipal drama.

The initial outrage subsided. A wise cop in *The Blackboard Jungle* already knew that the rock-happy delinquents were like the rest of the world: mixed up and scared. But even sanded-down rock defined the new generation as sexy, noisy, uncouth—if not necessarily subversive. When Elvis Presley was inducted into the army in 1958, no questions asked, *Life* pictured him, newly crew-cut, happy in khaki, an icon of the rock and roller's ultimate normalcy. That sneering, vibrating kid denounced by teachers and preachers and politicians turned out to be a good American boy after all. Mainstream culture sighed in relief. Perhaps rock itself, like juvenile delinquency and awkward teenage self-consciousness, was nothing more than a "phase": "growing pains."

ENCLAVES OF ELDERS

"A CAMARADERIE OF LONELINESS"

In 1955, not long after Marlon Brando grunted "Whadda ya got," Allen Ginsberg read "Howl" to an enthralled audience in a San Francisco gallery (Jack Kerouac urging him on with shouts of "GO") and answered the well-meaning question "What are you rebelling against?" with a rumbling indictment:

> Moloch! Moloch! Nightmare of Moloch! Moloch the loveless! Mental
> Moloch! Moloch the heavy judger of men! . . .
> Moloch whose buildings are judgement! Moloch the vast stone of war!
> Moloch the stunned governments!
> Moloch whose mind is pure machinery! Moloch whose blood is running
> money! . . .
> Moloch whose eyes are a thousand blind windows! Moloch whose
> skyscrapers stand in the long streets like endless Jehovahs! . . .
> Moloch whose love is endless oil and stone! Moloch whose soul is
> electricity and banks! Moloch whose poverty is the specter of genius!
> Moloch whose fate is a cloud of sexless hydrogen! Moloch whose name
> is the Mind!

And for the first time in the American twentieth century, poetry read aloud became a public act that changed lives.

Despite the alarms sounded by the press and the intellectuals, there were never so many beats, perhaps a few thousand at the peak, not nearly so many as there were actual and aspiring rockers and, eventually, hippies. Most of the beats were inconspicuous; indeed, that was part of the point of being beat, whether that meant self-consciously beaten or beatified. Most of them dressed simply, as the sociologist Ned Polsky wrote, "in an ordinary working-class manner, distinctive only to middle-class eyes." Only a minority wore the notorious beards as badges of identity. Probably fewer than 10 percent, perhaps 150 in the entire country, published any writing at all.

But a handful of beat writers spread the news, retailing legends which both repelled and attracted the great washed. I will concentrate here on the famous among them, those who were ferociously articulate, wrote furiously, and—as virtually all the mass and not-so-mass media demonstrated in chorus—scraped an American nerve. America's crisis of spirit, they thought, required not just new thinking but right action. If the mind of Moloch, the false god, was "pure machinery," and its soul "electricity and banks," then the right action was to unplug. In the name of some larger Buddhist quest, they assailed the national obsession with family and property. They felt cramped by the postwar bargain of homes and mortgages, steady jobs, organized suffering; they wanted to run around, hang out, get away, find spiritual bedrock. If the true-blue Fifties was affluence, the beats' counter-Fifties was voluntary poverty. They aimed to refute the ranch house and the barbecue pit with plain apartments and strewn mattresses. They unplugged from the standard circuits of family, job, and good behavior in order to overthrow sexual taboos, to commit uncivil disobedience against a national dress code which required trimmed minds to match trimmed lawns. If Moloch was "the heavy judger of men," its towers a long line of "endless Jehovahs"—if Moloch was the harsh social superego making insupportable demands of the human spirit—then an intensely, polymorphously perverse life was the right rebuttal. With the help of the mainstream's moral panic, the beats' vivid, incessant writings carried word of their exploits and style everywhere. Astonishingly, these bad boys were anointed as shamans; through them, far greater numbers of the grumbling and disgruntled young learned to recognize one another. Myself, I was too young for the beats, too straight, too studious, and too timid, but I was impressed by high school classmates who spoke knowingly about going out on the road.

The road was their central symbol, Walt Whitman's open road that always led to the next horizon. Whenever the scene got dull or entangling, as sooner or later it always did, the beats took off from New York to Berkeley and San Francisco, Denver, Mexico City, or, on special occasions, Tangier. They were hitchhikers upon a landscape already occupied; they depended upon the automobile as much as did any garaged suburbanite, though Jack Kerouac, the poet laureate of the endless American highway, never learned to drive. Like many another American bad boy, he had to go to enormous lengths to deny his most profound and binding social attachment: his fierce dependence on the demanding mother to whom he always returned and with whom he spent his last, miserable, alcoholic days.

The beats were adept at turning established values against the society that enshrined them. Was this the era of worship, when families were supposed to "pray together" in order to "stay together"? The beats preached love, too, and spoke their own home-style Buddhist language of the spirit. Were the suburbs clannish about "togetherness"? The beats celebrated epiphanies of companionship in the form of their own selective and exclusive human buddyhood—a fragile community, for the buddies were always having lovers' quarrels. To Joyce Johnson, drawn to them while a student at Barnard College, the beat world stood for the chance "to be lonely within a camaraderie of loneliness." In their mythmaking imaginations, and in fugitive moments of reality, the beats were true brothers on the road together sharing wine, women, and mantras. Allen Ginsberg dreamed that the beat novelist John Clellon Holmes wrote him, "The social organization which is most true of itself to the artist is the boy gang." To which the waking Ginsberg added, "Not society's perfum'd marriage." Instead of martinis, they offered marijuana. Meditation and drugs were the vehicles of their spiritual experiments and ecstasies. Marijuana and wine by the jugful transformed the everyday into the extraordinary; for special occasions there were also peyote, mescaline, and barbiturates. According to Ned Polsky, about 10 percent tried heroin at one time or another.

To guard against what they saw as the deathly pallor of middle-class culture, the beats followed a traditional romantic and bohemian route: they sought out noble savages. Interracial sex was an affirmation of raw impulse against the overupholstered paleface mind. They grooved on white working-class men, familiar to Jack (né Jean) Kerouac from his French-Canadian upbringing; and on Mexicans and blacks, as in this incantation from *On the Road:*

> At lilac evening I walked with every muscle aching . . . in the Denver colored section, wishing I were a Negro, feeling that the best the white world had offered was not enough ecstasy for me, not enough life, joy, kicks, darkness, music, not enough night. . . . I was only myself, Sal Paradise, sad, strolling in this violet dark, this unbearably sweet night, wishing I could exchange worlds with the happy, true-hearted, ecstatic Negroes of America. . . .

Sex was the cusp in their manic-depressive adventures. The legends they wrote for themselves smashed through literary niceties and obscenity laws. They were blunt about sexual adventure: with women, with each other, with many partners, occasionally in groups—though if one is to judge from their writings, rarely more happily for long than the benighted suburbanites who gave them the creeps. Their prototype was the fast-talking "holy goof" and lumpenproletarian intellectual manqué Neal Cassady, who was Ginsberg's muse ("secret hero of these poems") and Kerouac's star (the model for Dean Moriarty in *On the Road* and the enlightened, angelic Cody in other books). Cassady's unrestrained talk was analogous to his prodigious sowing of seed, which qualified him for rhapsodies like Kerouac's: "'Oh, I love, love, love women! I think women are wonderful! I love women!' He spat out the window; he groaned; he clutched his head. Great beads of sweat fell from his forehead from pure excitement and exhaustion." Nor did it hurt Cassady's legend that he was sometimes married to more than one wife at a time. "Real life was sexual": this was the impression the beat world gave the young Joyce Johnson. "Or rather, it often seemed to take the form of sex. This was the area of ultimate adventure, where you would dare or not dare. It was much less a question of desire." Johnson, who had an affair with Kerouac, saw the beats bonded together in "some pursuit of the heightened moment, intensity for its own sake, something they apparently find only when they're with each other."

But Johnson, one of the women in the margins of the men's scene, is exaggerating to make a point—they also came to life in the act of writing. Their styles and ways of work were transcriptions of their ideals. In keeping with their refusal to separate art from life, they even devised appropriate technologies. Ginsberg resurrected Christopher Smart's long loping line; Kerouac typed his novel-length manuscripts on long, continuous rolls of paper feeding nonstop into his typewriter over strenuous days and weeks; William Burroughs scissored apart his manuscripts to slice up rational order. Their methods were extrapolated from the spontaneities of Rimbaud, the late Yeats, and the Surrealists, but the greatest influence was jazz, which sometimes accompanied the poetry readings. Kerouac insisted that language be "undisturbed flow from the mind of personal secret idea-words, *blowing* (as per jazz musician) on subject of image"; that there be "no periods separating sentence-structures already arbitrarily riddled by false colons and timid usually needless commas—but the vigorous space dash separating rhetorical breathing (as jazz musician drawing breath between outblown phrases)"; "not 'selectivity' of expression but following free deviation (association) of mind into limitless blow-on-subject seas of thought, swimming in sea of English with no discipline other than rhythms of rhetorical exhalation and expostulated statement, like a fist coming down on a table with each complete utterance, bang!"; that there be "no pause to think of proper word but the infantile pileup of scatological buildup words till satisfaction is gained. . . ."

The result, at its best, was a fierce kinetic prose, its leaps reproducing the discontinuity of the mind, its sheer onrushing velocity. Ginsberg's long poems—especially "Howl" and "Kaddish"—still crackle and inspire with their reclaimed emotion thirty years on. But a good deal of beat writing was flat, dry cataloguing. Even the best of the beat writers wrote interminable pages meant as tributes to the sacraments of experience, but reading (perhaps to unenlightened minds) like dull indiscriminate blurs, as if a burned-up world were showering them with a storm of sparks and ashes glimpsed through the windshield of a car hurtling down the road at high speed. They went to great lengths—literally!—refusing to observe hierarchies of value; life was a succession of stopping-off points, each just as sacred and (un)important as the others. All beginning and end was artifice, all life momentary—and exquisite. They were consistent, then, when, cultivating Rimbaud's "systematic derangement of the senses," they used *crazy* as an affirmation. Their exuberance knew despair. The trip, spree, rendezvous, binge landed in gloom. The fear of "schiz," of "flipping," was epidemic.

Necessarily they scorned conventional literary schooling, "colleges being nothing but grooming schools for the middle class non-identity," Kerouac wrote, ". . . rows of well-to-do houses with lawns and TV sets in each living room with everybody looking at the same thing." The "best minds" of Ginsberg's generation, "starving hysterical naked," "threw potato salad at CCNY lecturers on Dadaism." William Burroughs once told Kerouac, "I am shitting out my educated Middlewest background for once and for all." Especially at Columbia University, where Kerouac and Ginsberg met and where Lionel Trilling's gentility reigned supreme, literary studies emphasized cool distance, teeth-gritting irony, the decorous play of literary reference. Ex- and anti-Communism had widened into a general program of moderation. To even the erudite Ginsberg, who knew his literary sources, academia smelled of the fustiness of yellowing libraries and easy chairs. About academic critics Ginsberg wrote to his old college friend, the poet John Hollander: "The whole problem is these types want money & security and not ART."

So the beats should hardly have been surprised when academic and highbrow critics, who specialized in rational objection, rose to the bait. (The outsiders, blasting away at the dullards who commanded the culture's heights, still wanted the insiders to love them.) Although the poet Richard Eberhart generously greeted Ginsberg's work in *The New York Times Book Review,* and (through the fluke of a regular reviewer's vacation schedule) a *Times* pinch-hitter raved *On the Road* onto the bestseller list, the beat writers yelped when they were savaged from the heights of *Partisan Review.* Where the beats saw beatitude, Norman Podhoretz saw "a revolt of all the forces hostile to civilization itself," "a movement of brute stupidity and know-nothingism that is trying to take over the country from a middle class which is supposed to be the guardian of civilization but which has practically dislocated its shoulder in its eagerness to throw in the towel. . . . [W]hat juvenile delinquency is to life, the San Francisco writers are to literature."

The beats, of course, were no social theorists, but they were rooted in their moment, recoiling not only from squareness but from plenitude. The image of profusion recurs, most memorably in Ginsberg's "A Supermarket in California," which begins by invoking the master transcendentalist:

> What thoughts I have of you tonight, Walt Whitman, for I walked down the sidestreets under the trees with a headache self-conscious looking at the full moon.
>
> In my hungry fatigue, and shopping for images, I went into the neon fruit supermarket, dreaming of your enumerations!
>
> What peaches and what penumbras! Whole families shopping at night! Aisles full of husbands! Wives in the avocados, babies in the tomatoes! —and you, Garcia Lorca, what were you doing down by the watermelons?

Yet the pilgrimage to material plenitude only reminds Ginsberg of his loneliness. "When can I go into the supermarket and buy what I need with my good looks?" he asks in "America." Plenitude tantalizes, then thwarts. One thing Kerouac finds attractive in the poet Gary Snyder (who becomes the hero of *The Dharma Bums*) is that he "refuse[s] to subscribe to consumption." In a 1955 conversation Kerouac and Snyder even conjure up the hippie movement: "a 'rucksack revolution' with all over America 'millions of Dharma bums' going up to the hills to meditate and ignore society."

For real abundance was to be found in illumination; or in the flow of experience, culminating in illumination; in either case, in the act of transcribing the ripples of feeling into torrents of writing. In the act of writing, the god of prohibitions was dead and everything was permitted—and possible. What resulted, presumably, was an affluence of the soul: Cassady's "wild yea-saying overburst of American joy." And so Kerouac's notion of writing as "infantile pileup of scatological buildup" could be understood as a tactic for creating abundance from within. The unrevised associations of automatic prose would create an inexhaustible world. It was an old American story, from Walt Whitman's ecstatic catalogs to Henry Miller's gruff affirmations. Ginsberg concluded "Howl" with the bodily equivalent of the Emersonian idea that the self in its infinite variety is the source of all good:

> The world is holy! The soul is holy! The skin is holy! The nose is holy!
>   The tongue and cock and hand and asshole holy!
> Everything is holy! everybody's holy! everywhere is holy! everyday is in
>   eternity! Everyman's an angel!

But behind the celebration was a profound passivity in the face of experience, a passivity matched by the antipolitics of most beats. They knew they were "beaten," and wanted to make the most of defeat. Living in the rubble of a once-confident Old Left, they didn't want to change society so much as sidestep it. John Clellon Holmes made the point: "In the wildest hipster, making a mystique of bop, drugs, and the night life, there is no desire to shatter the 'square' society in which he lives, only to elude it. To get on a soapbox or write a manifesto would seem to him absurd." Politics, they declared, was yet another boring, pointless subassembly in the grotesque machinery of Moloch.* Their clubbiness echoed the general withdrawal from political activity; echoed the New Critics' strategy for extricating the literary text from historical context; echoed the do-it-yourself movement, which sent husbands into their basements to muster the small autarkies of leisure time; echoed, overall, the American infatuation with private stratagems for social troubles.

Among the well-known beats, Allen Ginsberg was exceptional in skating along the radical edge. When Ginsberg read the "Moloch" choruses of "Howl" to a Berkeley audience in 1956, there were boos and hisses each time he denounced the demonic superforce. In fact, much of beat quietism was savvy, only momentarily "beaten," unreconciled to Eisenhower and a permanent Cold War. What *was* to be done in the age of smiling Ike? The beat scenes in New York and San Francisco were interlaced with motley defeated ex-Communists and Trotskyists and anarchists, one eye cocked for changes in the political weather. Ginsberg's red-diaper vocabulary, even if wistful rather than militant about radical possibilities, was at least intelligible there. ("When will you be worthy of your million Trotskyites?/ . . . /America I feel sentimental about the Wobblies./America I used to be a communist when I was a kid I'm not sorry.") Thus, when the zeitgeist shifted direction, retreat passed out of style, and other beats grew steadily more forlorn, Ginsberg could make the transit into the political Sixties with grace, along with the onetime left-wing activist Gary Snyder and the poet-bookseller-publisher Lawrence Ferlinghetti (who in 1958 published *Tentative Description of a Dinner Given to Promote the Impeachment of President Eisenhower*). Still, differences should not be overestimated: the beats recognized one another as brothers, all taking cover in the crevices of a society they could not begin to imagine changing.

And then the brothers found themselves adopted by spiritual

---

*Kerouac in particular, though a kind of Franciscan pacifist, was no political radical. From his devout Catholic family he inherited a formidable anti-Communism. In 1956, on Desolation Mountain, longing for God, he read *The God That Failed* and vented his fear of "totalitarian beastliness," of "Russias and plots to assassinate whole people's souls." America, in contrast, with its football scores and its endless roads and endless promises of adventure, was "as free as that wild wind." Reading about the presidential campaign, he sneered at the liberals' darling, "Adlai Stevenson so elegant so snide so proud."

children—youth circles, especially high-school intellectuals who were far too estranged, even from their peers, to care about rock music. Some readers picked up Kerouac's Buddhism; probably many more took him as a guide to back-roads escape and backseat sex. The burgeoning commercial youth culture widened the beats' following, and they acknowledged their debt to it. Though partial to jazz, for example, Kerouac toyed with renaming *On the Road* "Rock and Roll Road," and dreamed of a movie version starring Marlon Brando as Dean Moriarty.

The beats, however, were at the mercy of the mass media, which, horrified and titillated, blew their lurid images far and wide. *Time* savaged Ginsberg. (No wonder Ginsberg, "obsessed by Time Magazine," asked in "America": "Are you going to let your emotional life be run by Time Magazine?") *Life* hatcheted "The Only Rebellion Around" (subtitle: "But the Shabby Beats Bungle the Job in Arguing, Sulking and Bad Poetry"), complete with a posed studio photo, spilling over more than a full page, of what the caption called "the well-equipped pad" featuring "beat chick dressed in black," "naked light bulb," "crates which serve as tables and closets," "Italian wine bottle," "beat baby, who has gone to sleep on floor after playing with beer cans," and "bearded beat wearing sandals, chinos and turtlenecked sweater and studying a record by the late saxophonist Charlie Parker." The police played their part, stirring up hysteria, most notoriously by arresting Lawrence Ferlinghetti in 1956 and charging him with selling obscene material including, among other items, "Howl." The results? Containment, yes. But what *Time* thought appalling about Allen Ginsberg made him sound appealing to the young Robert Zimmerman (soon to be Dylan) in Hibbing, Minnesota. The fourteen-year-old Jim Morrison copied passages from *On the Road* into his notebook and imitated Dean Moriarty's laugh.

The beats wrote on, energy undiminished. By 1960, Allen Ginsberg and Gary Snyder had left the country in serious pursuit of Buddhist enlightenment—returning later to bring ecological consciousness and engagé spirituality to the Sixties rebellion. But omnivorous mass media chewed the beats' reputations to pulp for popular horror and amusement. Trend-scouting gossip columnists like San Francisco's Herb Caen (who invented the patronizing label *beatnik*) converted the beats into comic relief. By the final days of 1959 a New York entrepreneur—himself a photographer in the beat scene—could make some money on the side by offering partygivers a "Rent-a-Beatnik" service. By that time, in college towns and big cities, even abroad, young folksingers, guitar pickers, and would-be expatriates—what David Matza has called "morose Bohemians"—were affecting black turtlenecks, tights, and jeans (black was the negation of affluence's false colors), going to poetry-with-jazz readings, sitting in cheap cafeterias drinking endless cups of strong coffee and talking about books and foreign films. Student intellectuals, trained in literary finesse, could disdain the beats' sloppier writing but still smoke their marijuana and absorb their reflected energy. By the early Sixties, for every full-time beat there must have been dozens of hangers-on, part-timers and weekenders—and high school straights like me—who dropped into the Village or North Beach or Venice, California, window-shopping for forbidden auras (as Jack Newfield wrote, "Bronx boys picking up Brooklyn girls on MacDougal Street in the Village"). Which meant that as a cultural insurgency the beat scene was finished. As the tourists arrived, the rents went up and the original beats moved on.

Sometimes subcultures like this soften into freakshows for the delectation of the cultural mainstream—bounded zones where more adventurous normals can indulge impulses usually kept in harness, and even the conventional can safely slum. The Fifties' subcultures might have hardened into self-enclosed spores. But other forces intersected: the dialectic of affluence and fear among the young; the growth of college campuses; the celebrity machinery of the media. Something was happening and Mr. Kerouac didn't know what it was. As the beats' energy rippled outward in the late Fifties, they left behind more than modish jadedness and touristic coffeehouses. *Evergreen Review* mixed the beats with European absurdists and other miscellaneous literati, and carried their word beyond their small circles. Some of the beat spoor rubbed off on other bohemians, even those like Paul Goodman who disdained the frantic and shapeless romanticism of the beats. Colonies of would-be artists hung out in the Village, listened to jazz, retreated to out-of-town enclaves like Woodstock and Sausalito. "Underground" films (like Kenneth Anger's homosexual-motorcycle pseudoepic, *Scorpio Rising*) drew long lines of students looking for images of exotic sex. Late-night free-form parties, spaghetti dinners and cheap Italian wine, talk of art and sex, the hovering possibility (and threat) of seduction . . . the whole scene lured teen-agers yearning to flee their middle-class parents—a Long Island high school girl named Barbara Jacobs, for example, wanting to be an artist, who spent the summer of her seventeenth year, 1955, in upstate Woodstock, and felt that *here,* at last, was the good life. Like many others, she was attracted to Brandeis University because, hospitable to the arts, it cultivated a bohemian atmosphere. Bohemianism overlapped with left-wing politics at Brandeis; students were divided into bohemian "Bos" and straight "Rahs." Jacobs, later a civil rights activist who attended the Port Huron convention of SDS, was "a semirespectable Bo"; another Brandeis contemporary who described himself as "semi-'bo'" was Abbie Hoffman, whose father later blamed Brandeis for his "corruption."

In 1958 and 1959, in coffeehouses and student unions scattered across the country, beat talk, pseudobeat talk, avant-garde talk, political talk, sex talk, and literature and art talk were buzzing and mingling, not always logically, at neighboring tables. The enclaves required low rents and high turnover, which meant that districts just off major campuses—

Columbia's Upper West Side, Berkeley's Telegraph Avenue—filled with hangouts. The circles of disengagement and reengagement overlapped; one might lead to another. Even beat antipolitics could be permuted into politics. One of the few to grasp this was David McReynolds, an activist of the avant-garde New York pacifist cluster called the War Resisters League. Listening with a third ear, McReynolds heard, beneath the beat disengagement, a desire to live a life in which personal action mattered:

> [The] beat generation by its very existence serves notice on all of us who are political that if we want to involve youth in politics we must develop a politics of action. The beat generation can understand Gandhi much better than they understand Roosevelt. They can understand Martin Luther King much better than they can understand Hubert Humphrey. They can understand the Hungarian workers much better than they can understand Mikoyan.

One of the legion of Jack Kerouac's readers was the editor of the University of Michigan student paper, a fervent existentialist named Tom Hayden, who said later he "was interested in the bohemians, the beatniks, the coffeehouse set, the interracial crowd, but I wasn't really part of them." Inspired by a reading of *On the Road,* Hayden set out in June 1960 to hitchhike around the country, "trying to mimic the life of James Dean," heading for San Francisco's North Beach and the Democratic Convention in Los Angeles. To get involved in politics at this point was "unimaginable" to him; he had never even seen a demonstration. In Berkeley, someone stuck a political leaflet into his hand and gave him a place to stay for a few weeks. He was told about farm workers, nuclear weapons research, and the House Un-American Activities Committee. Inducted into the ways of radical politics, he went to the Democratic Convention, marched in a picket line with Martin Luther King, stopped in Minneapolis to cover the National Student Association meeting, met southern sit-in leaders, and returned to Ann Arbor a political organizer. Kerouac's road, it turned out, might lead to some unexpected stopping-off points.

THE LIBERAL SUMMONS

There are moments when the zeitgeist struts on stage so theatrically it fairly screams. On November 6, 1958, in front of a boisterous, overflow, standing-room-only crowd at Hunter College, James A. Wechsler, the editor of the *New York Post,* the most reliably liberal big-city newspaper in the United

States, shared a platform with none other than Jack Kerouac.* Wechsler was a liberal with fire in his belly—"one of the few unreconstructed radicals of my generation," he called himself that night. Many left-wingers would have disputed Wechsler's claim to the embattled and noble label of "radical," but the point is that on this occasion, at least, Wechsler was proud to embrace it. At least it would distinguish him from the beats.

Radical or not, Wechsler was a perfect representative of the anti-Communist liberalism of his time. He had joined the Young Communist League in 1934, had been a leader of the Communist-controlled American Student Union, and had quit the YCL in 1937, when he was all of twenty-two. After World War II, he had plunged into the thick of the political wars then raging between pro-Soviet and anti-Communist liberals; he left the newspaper *PM* in 1946, charging it was run by Communists; he fought against Communists in the American Veterans Committee and the American Newspaper Guild; he was a founder of Americans for Democratic Action and an early member of the American Committee for Cultural Freedom (but left it in 1956, when he thought it was veering too far to the Right). In 1953, a series of anti-McCarthy articles in the *Post* earned him an appearance before McCarthy's Senate committee, where he was asked to name the names of other former or present Communists at the paper; and, reasoning that silence would work to McCarthy's benefit, he named names, to his later regret. He was fiercely committed to civil rights for Negroes; when the young Emmett Till was lynched in Mississippi, in 1955, he wrote a letter about the case strong enough to exasperate a cautious Adlai Stevenson. In 1958, by Wechsler's own account, he felt "out of touch" with the preoccupations of the young, including the beats, so tantalizing to his sixteen-year-old son and his son's friends.

That night at Hunter College, two worlds passed through each other like ghosts. By the time Wechsler arrived, a drunken Kerouac in checked lumberjack shirt and black jeans and boots was already reading his rambling, moving, anecdotal manifesto. "It is because I am beat, that is, I believe in beatitude," said Kerouac, swaying over the podium, "and that God so loved the world that he gave his only begotten son to it. . . . So you're all big smart know-it-all Marxists and Freudians, hey?" he jeered. "Why don't you come back in a million years and tell me all about it, angels? . . . Who knows, my God, but that the universe is not one vast sea of compassion actually, the veritable holy honey, beneath all this show of personality and cruelty." Kerouac talked Buddhism, nonviolence, and the love of all creatures, sliding saxophonically (sometimes subtly, sometimes obscurely) across the registers in a manner not calculated to

*The occasion was sponsored by Brandeis University. The other invited panelists, the British novelist Kingsley Amis and the anthropologist Ashley Montagu, were incidental to the main action.

make sense to the likes of James Wechsler. He swigged brandy. He celebrated "the glee of America, the honesty of America," its "wild selfbelieving individuality." He proclaimed that the beat generation was "a swinging group of new American men intent on joy," rooted in his father's wild parties and the exploits of his noble Breton ancestors, in Popeye and Laurel and Hardy. He deplored the blindness of media label mongers and those who concocted "beatnik routines on TV." He read a poem dedicated to Harpo Marx. He stomped offstage and dragged Allen Ginsberg out from the wings. Hearing Wechsler speak of "fighting for peace," Kerouac laughed, plucked up Wechsler's hat—"a Zen move," Ginsberg says—and circled the stage with it.

Wechsler did not begin to comprehend. To him Kerouac's performance was "a stream of semiconsciousness," "a union of madness and sadness." Kerouac sounded to him "like a jaded traveling salesman telling obscene bedtime stories to the young." Kerouac's writings were "raucous hedonism," "vulgar ramblings on a latrine wall." "I was grappling with a man from outer space," Wechsler wrote, "and it was only for the briefest of intervals that we even seemed to occupy the same mat." Wechsler was at times condescending, at times snide, dotting his comments with phrases like "I am obliged," "with due respect to Mr. Kerouac," "if I may say so." Kerouac, for his part, was belligerent: "Who's James Wechsler? Right over there. James Wechsler, you believe in the destruction of America, don't you? . . . I want to know what you do believe in. . . . I believe in love, I vote for love." The audience applauded. Kerouac had put Wechsler on the spot, and Wechsler's answering credo could hardly fail to be pompous: "I believe in the capacity of the human intelligence to create a world in which there is love, compassion, justice and freedom." Wechsler sputtered, "I think what you are doing is to try to destroy anybody's instinct to care about this world. . . . There is no valor in the beats' flight and irresponsibility." He disagreed with end-of-ideology theorists who claimed "that everything was settled by the New Deal and the Fair Deal, and that there really aren't any great differences in political life." For there were two outstanding issues that seemed to him "to be worthy of everything within us": the hydrogen bomb and the quest for human equality.

It would be an understatement to say that Wechsler was exasperated. "It is a sad thing about America now," he told the audience, "that what is regarded as the great revolt and the great representation of dissent and unorthodoxy is what is called the beat generation. . . . [A]fter listening to its spokesman tonight, I must say that I find myself groping in the darkest confusion as to what the hell this is about." From the hall came shouts of "Shame on you!"

The evening made a great impression on James Wechsler. He opened his next book with an account of it; indeed, he said it provoked him into writing the book in the first place. The book, *Reflections of an Angry*

Middle-Aged Editor, published in 1960, is a passionate liberal manifesto. It makes robust polemic against the Bomb, for racial integration and civil liberties, against the siren song of false affluence, against the trivialization of politics by television. It deplores a decline in public-mindedness, even in the trade union movement, whose revitalization Wechsler devoutly hopes for and does not expect. Although a Democratic president is about to be elected for the first time in eight years, Wechsler, like many liberal activists, expresses not even the most tentative jubilation about the credentials of John F. Kennedy.

His book is not forward-looking but haunted, and the specter that haunts it is none other than Jack Kerouac and his beat friends. Wechsler says at the outset that he wants to "explain what the rest of us look like to the beat and why it is they seem so self-righteously convinced that it is their elders who are the sad specimens." Again and again Wechsler bemoans the fact that the younger generation is not quickened by political combat. He knows which side the audience was on at Hunter College. The beats are more prominent than they deserve to be, he says, because they care, even if what they practice is "the cult of not caring." He is haunted by the fear that the young will desert the liberal cause and become "beatniks." He sees himself surrounded by "liberals suffering from tired blood, dismayed by their failure to communicate with the new generation, doubting their own strength, saddened by the seeming treacheries of men who win elections under their banner." He is tormented by the sense of being a failed political parent, wondering whether his cohort should bear the blame for the apathy of the young. He wonders "whether the confusions and disappointments of the last two decades have destroyed our will and desire to do anything, and whether we have communicated—however indistinctly and falteringly—to those younger than ourselves the sense that our failure justifies their apathy."

Wechsler's lament may seem overdrawn. One might think that in 1960 the precincts of liberalism should have been bursting with gusto. Was not the Eisenhower interregnum drawing to an end? Despite their suspicions of Kennedy money, Kennedy glamour, and Kennedy family connections to McCarthyism, despite long-standing attachments to Stevenson and Humphrey, many top liberals were anticipating a return to power with the Senator from Massachusetts. Liberalism should have been able to look forward to a robust future and a cheerful vindication. For over a quarter of a century, ever since Franklin Roosevelt came to power, American liberals had claimed title to the future. Their tones were optimistic, their rhetoric redolent of progress. It was this faith in unending progress that set them apart—or so they maintained—from conservatives. When Adlai Stevenson attempted to define liberalism, in a somewhat murky 1956 speech, he listed first the liberal's belief in the future: "He believes in the existence of the future as well as the past. . . . In answer to the conservative's classic question, 'Whither are we drifting?' the liberal says, 'We cannot drift, we must *go.*'"

Liberals did not altogether agree on philosophical underpinnings. Some thought society perfectible, although the influentials, chastened by Nazism, Stalinism, and the Bomb, and impressed by Reinhold Niebuhr's antiutopian theology, thought humanity fundamentally flawed and social action intrinsically subject to moral limitations. Both David Riesman and Paul Goodman deplored the dearth of utopian thinking now that liberals had grown fat from the postwar cornucopia. Innocent or chastened, however, liberals traced their common lineage to the Enlightenment. They believed that society could be understood and, once understood, rationally steered through responsible action. Reason was the name of their faith, and the government its instrument. Leaders were to embody reason by standing for moderation. But the brooding Wechsler caught a real deficiency in the liberal spirit, an undertow at work beneath the forward-looking rhetoric that cascaded through the speeches and articles of such liberal spokesmen as Arthur Schlesinger, Jr., Hubert Humphrey, and Adlai Stevenson. At just the moment when liberalism was apparently about to renew the mission it had inherited from Roosevelt and Truman, after eight long, demoralizing Eisenhower years and two humiliating defeats, why the tone of pathos, the sense of doubt, the "tired blood" which Wechsler observed in his generation?

Allow that Wechsler was exaggerating—for Kennedy's Camelot soon stirred much of the liberal blood. And yet Wechsler still deserves credit for suspecting, in his bones, that liberals could lose, were going to lose the young. (Not that Jack Kerouac was going to inherit them either; the beats' had their moment and were superseded.) As things turned out, Wechsler was absolutely right to be dismayed by his generation's "failure to communicate with the new generation," and to wonder about the fragility of what was being communicated. One key question about the Sixties is why it wasn't liberalism that reaped the harvest of the young's growing disgruntlement. Why a New *Left*? Why not a new liberalism? (Later we shall also ask, Why not a revival of the *Old* Left? And eventually, Why did the New Left refuse in the end to be New any longer?) Understanding requires a closer look at the experience of the liberal generation.

Most of the leading liberals of the Fifties were men (rarely women) who were born around World War I and came of political age during the Great Depression. They entered politics under the sign of the New Deal, which meant for them that the government was the natural ally of the common people at home and the natural enemy of totalitarianism abroad. Now middle-class themselves, though many came from working-class homes, they believed in government protection for trade unions, collective bargaining, works programs, Social Security—in short, a welfare state with a floor under it and some protection for the weak against the corporate rich whom Roosevelt called "economic royalists"; they wanted capitalism without its most brutal inequities and injustices. Some of them were onetime socialists or Communists, like Wechsler. Many were first-generation Americans; childhoods in poverty and parents' escapes from political oppression were fresh in their minds. Some were organizers, people of working-class origins who learned the political ropes in the parties of the Left and battled their way to positions of influence. A good many were professors or editors or writers or clergymen, college-educated men who were taught the power of human action by the government of Franklin Roosevelt.

In the Fifties, Adlai Stevenson, the veritable "egghead" and a reluctant politician, was their symbolic representative, but Franklin Delano Roosevelt was their permanent hero. For them the government was the prime instrument of collective will, the embodiment of political reason, the finest expression of public-spirited virtue—because the New Deal had established that kind of government. "Roosevelt taught us," one of them wrote a half-century later, "that in both spheres, domestic and foreign, 'government is the solution.'" Some were stirred by the suffering of the unemployed, some more offended by the irrationality of the market—committed, therefore, to create a government that would enforce a rational order. But whether motivated more by heart or by mind, they had a loyalty in common: the jaunty FDR delivered them from marginality, and they never forgot it. In the great ferment of New Deal legislation, some of them rolled up their sleeves and went to work drafting bills and writing speeches. These were heady times for idealists in their twenties, full of ideas and pragmatism, eager to apply themselves. Decades later they held reunions and celebrated their enlistment in the New Deal cause as among their finest hours.

One of this generation was Samuel Beer, briefly a speechwriter for FDR, later a professor of government at Harvard and simultaneously (in 1959–62) national chairman of Americans for Democratic Action. Beer turned twenty-one in 1932, just before Roosevelt's election. Reading his political memoir, I am struck by the same mood which carried me into the early New Left almost thirty years later:

> In 1932 I could have cast my vote for FDR. I did not. I did not vote at all. . . . I belonged to that huge pool of eligibles who were in the habit of not voting in those days, but who were later mobilized by Roosevelt. Insofar as these nonvoters were like me, they were smart-alecky college kids who felt themselves superior to the whole business of politics. We had been taught by Charles Beard that politics was simply business carried on by other means, and by Sinclair Lewis that businessmen were a bunch of Babbitts, and by H. L. Mencken that the American people as a whole were the "booboisie."
>
> Today [1984] we would be called alienated. Yet we became incorrigible followers of Roosevelt and the New Deal, and made the Democratic party the dominant majority party until well into the 1960s. We were a true political generation.

Theirs was the creed into which I and a majority of the early leaders of the New Left were raised. It was not terribly far removed from the creed that came to power in 1960 with John F. Kennedy, and "got the country moving again" after the political somnolence of the Fifties. By all evidence, it should have had a bright future, especially among the college-educated. It was, after all, well represented on campuses, where in 1956 60 percent of American college professors had supported Adlai Stevenson against President Eisenhower. But Sam Beer and the rest of his generation were fathers who lost their political children. (The social democrats who had still grander hopes—who hoped that the unions would stir up a European-style social-democratic movement that would push beyond welfare-state liberalism—also ended up bereft of political progeny.) Their students and sometimes their biological children were among the founding generation of the New Left. The son of an economist who helped write the Social Security Act founded Students for a Democratic Society. The son of another liberal economist, a member of Harry S. Truman's Council of Economic Advisers, coordinated SDS's community-organizing projects, then helped organize the demonstrations that disrupted the 1968 Democratic Convention in Chicago. My own parents, high school teachers and not activists, were committed New Dealers of the Roosevelt-Truman-Stevenson stripe; my father hung pictures of Lincoln and FDR on his office wall. How could the liberal generation, so well situated, apparently so clear in its purposes, fail to pass on its mission to its young?

Part of the answer is that the liberal generation half-succeeded. In politics, nothing is so unsettling as half a success. After a catastrophe, the next generation rebuilds from scratch. After a heroic victory, they inherit the triumph. But half a success tantalizes and confuses: it dangles before the eyes a glaring discrepancy between promise and performance. The liberal generation stood for opening access to the regime of affluence, which sent their children to college, where they learned to find names and remedies for the spiritual poverty they attached to that selfsame affluence. Liberalism stood for equality, but lacked the means, or the will, or the blood-and-guts desire, to bring it about. The leadership, if not all of the base, also stood for permanent Cold War mobilization, which to many in the next generation seemed much too dangerous. So liberalism accomplished enough to launch the next generation—not enough to keep them.

The leading liberals after World War II thought they knew the way to social justice. They wanted to extend the New Deal, to buffer the majority of people against the abuse of power in a capitalist economy. They detested monopoly and liked public services. Capitalism itself, the private control (though with public regulation) of the economy, they endorsed with greater or lesser enthusiasm. For some it was a matter of first principles—Hubert Humphrey, for example, the son of a druggist, always took it as an article of faith that private property was the cornerstone of liberty. Others, more reluctant, concluded from the history of the Soviet Union that socialism meant authoritarianism, or totalitarianism; in any event, it was unnecessarily disruptive medicine in an America that didn't need socialism to head toward equality or deliver the goods. In the crucial campaign year of 1948, the compendium of their economic wisdom was entitled *Saving American Capitalism;* its editor, the prominent liberal economist Seymour E. Harris, introduced the book—intended to serve as a bible for the Truman administration—by saying, "Like the National Association of Manufacturers and the United States Chamber of Commerce, we too are anxious to save capitalism." In the Thirties, socialism had appealed to many of them not so much on ethical or philosophical grounds but pragmatically and by default—because in the Depression, capitalism had thrown millions out of work and reduced them to penury. Capitalism didn't *work*.

But the economic boom of World War II and its aftermath convinced the leading liberals that they didn't need to go out on a political limb for socialism. Capitalism could be saved through an extension of New Deal principles, could promote prosperity and political democracy at the same time through an adroit use of Keynesian economics, a limited welfare state, and collective bargaining. As long as investment and productivity were increasing, increased business profits would finance increased wages; workers would buy more goods and keep the boom fueled. With class conflict institutionalized in the form of collective bargaining, the unions would be integrated into this state-supervised capitalist economy. By hitching liberalism to growth, liberals would keep the allegiance of a hardheaded public accustomed to bread-and-butter results. If the government could manage the economy with fiscal and monetary policies, minimize unemployment and control inflation, and satisfy the working class by giving it a share in material progress, who needed socialism?

Surveying the postwar boom, most prominent liberals were convinced not only that America was prosperous—who could doubt it?—but that it was becoming steadily more equal. Economic growth was apparently the solvent for social problems, which would be addressed by skilled managers. Class conflict would not need to get out of hand. If some people were left out of the mainstream, if there were still (in a common phrase) "pockets of poverty," these were exceptional; they could soon and easily be taken care of. Social problems were, in another well-worn phrase, "unfinished business." The American model of well-managed capitalism was a model for the rest of the world; it would bring middle-class democracy in its wake; in any event, it was still preferable to the depredations of Stalinism.

This last point was the key to the mood of postwar liberalism: increasingly, before all else, at least in leading pronouncements, it was anti-Communist. All its other passions were nestled in this obligatory one. It outlasted McCarthyism by agreeing that America was besieged; the difference was that liberalism thought the principal menace lurked *outside.* "It is still up to us," Seymour Harris wrote, "to prove that capitalism is not but a passing phase in the historical process from feudalism to socialism." In the public arena, the same note was mandatory. To take one of a myriad examples: Hubert Humphrey's famous debut in national politics—his passionate speech on behalf of a strong civil rights plank at the 1948 Democratic Convention—began with a reference to the American airlift against the Soviet blockade of Berlin. "Our demands for democratic practice in other lands will be no more effective than the guarantee of those practices in our own country," Humphrey said, adding: "Our land is now, more than ever before, the last best hope on earth." To put this rhetoric down to simple opportunism would, I think, be playing false with the liberals' passion. They were not hypocrites. They were not violating principle. For the most part they had been anti-Communist for years, although during the war years they had submerged the impulse in the interest of the U.S.-Soviet alliance—they, the White House, and many others in the upper reaches of American power, including *Life* magazine and Hollywood's Jack Warner.

The liberal leadership's anti-Communist fervor was not reserved for resounding phrases on ceremonial occasions. Anti-Communism was the very crucible of their political identity. They were activists, not political philosophers, these pragmatists-on-principle, and it was in the postwar battles that they defined themselves. They collaborated with their opposite numbers in the fellow traveling Left to draw a line in the dirt: Either one was anti-Communist (in which case one supported the main lines of American foreign policy) or one subscribed to the Popular Front (in which case one either wholeheartedly subscribed to Soviet foreign policy or, in the name of unity on the Left, refused to say that one did not).

This is not the place to assess the moves and countermoves by which the Cold War hardened in the immediate postwar years. Suffice to say that the Cold War, like a powerful electromagnetic field, induced its domestic counterpart. The Roosevelt heritage divided along sharp lines. The "progressives"—among them the war-swelled numbers of the American Communist Party—blamed a rightward-veering American foreign policy. In their view, the Truman administration was violating wartime Roosevelt-Stalin accords, the West was acting aggressively, and the tightening Soviet grip on Eastern Europe—insofar as they acknowledged it at all— was a legitimate effort to protect Soviet security. The anti-Communist "liberals" supported Truman's containment policies, and more: They became convinced, with good reason, that wherever the two camps coexisted within the same organizations, the disciplined, single-minded Communist-liners and their apologists would be able to dominate debate, smuggle in their hidden agendas, and stifle the more easygoing liberals. Even rank-and-file liberals whose priorities were domestic had grown weary of factional wars against Stalinists—and Trotskyists—who were boring (in both senses) from within group after group. Standing up against Communism became organized liberalism's driving purpose. The camps dug in.

The Cold War came home. Move spiraled into countermove. In May 1946, the prominent liberal activist James Loeb threw down the gauntlet in a much-noticed letter to *The New Republic*. Liberals, said Loeb, would have to decide whether East-West tensions were solely the West's fault, whether economic security should be pursued to the exclusion of intellectual freedom, and whether those who answered no could work with Communists who thought yes. Late in December, Popular Front advocates founded a new national organization, Progressive Citizens of America. A few days later, the anti-Communists founded *their* new organization, Americans for Democratic Action, ADA. ADA's founding statement supported "the general framework of present American foreign policy" more vehemently than it supported anything else, and closed by "reject[ing] any association with Communists or sympathizers with communism in the United States as completely as we reject any association with Fascists or their sympathizers." As the whole political center of gravity slid to the Right (the 1947 Taft-Hartley Act required that union leaders swear they were not Communists, for example), most liberal leaders slid with it. Under pressure from the Catholic Church, the CIO unions were ripped apart, the Communists defeated or expelled. The American Veterans Committee and many other political groups were riven. Local Democratic parties were split by threat and counterthreat. Caucuses were organized; politicians maneuvered and countermaneuvered. Mailing lists were stolen, partisans hooted down. In battle after battle, the postwar liberals crushed the progressives. Within the ADA, the aggressive Cold Warriors triumphed over the activists who, while anti-Communist, preferred to take their stand for domestic reforms. Positions polarized. As in the larger Cold War, each side mirrored and caricatured the other. The liberals denied that American policy bore any substantial responsibility for worsening East-West relations. The progressives refused to blame the Russians for anything: At the founding convention of the Progressive Party in 1948, for example, a mildly worded proposal stating that no nation's foreign policy should be beyond criticism was roundly defeated by Communist-liners.

The Cold War in American liberalism replayed the breakdown of the wartime alliance, and in retrospect it is hard to see how the progressives could ever have competed successfully, if for no other reason than that Stalin was the pro-Communist Left's worst enemy. In Central Europe, Truman and Stalin traded hostile moves. But the American moves took place behind closed doors, and were easily forgotten by liberal observers. They included, for example, what Stalin could legitimately regard as American reneging on Lend-Lease, on credits, and on the promise of billions of dollars in German reparations. By contrast, the Russian seizures of power in Poland, Hungary, and Czechoslovakia were transparently, horribly repressive. In 1948, the Berlin blockade and the Communist coup d'etat in Czechoslovakia undermined whatever auld lang syne credit the progressives still retained.

Henry Wallace's 1948 Progressive campaign for the presidency was the progressives' last hurrah. When Wallace went down to humiliating defeat, with a mere 2.4 percent of the popular vote, the Popular Front alternative shriveled to a shadow of its wartime self. Liberal housecleaning routed what McCarthyism and self-doubt did not; the ranks of Soviet sympathizers dwindled, and among visible writers only a few social democrats and hardy independents, like I. F. Stone and C. Wright Mills, refused to let the combination stampede them into Cold War orthodoxy. Liberals like Arthur Schlesinger, Jr., who had been warning against Soviet-lining Communists for years, felt vindicated. A good many liberals were troubled by Senator Joe McCarthy and his fellow inquisitors, by House Un-American Activities Committee hearings and their local equivalents, by the questionable trials of Alger Hiss and Julius and Ethel Rosenberg, by the spectacle of Communists and fellow travelers and principled leftists and liberals hounded out of universities, out of teaching and other jobs. But others seized the hour and joined the punitive edge of the anti-Communist crusade: In 1954, for example, Senator Hubert Humphrey, vice chairman of ADA, liberal's liberal, candidate for reelection, in a move that was part tactical ploy and part ideological metooism, devised and sponsored the Communist Control Act, which would have made membership in the Communist Party a criminal act. (According to his biographer, Humphrey's measure "infuriated his ADA friends, but mostly they looked upon it as a momentary aberration and forgave him.")

Whatever their reactions to American society's great purge—and they ranged from the horrified to the apologetic—when the dust cleared, the liberals had essentially cornered the left-of-center world of American politics. Yet the Eisenhower years were still hard for them. Adlai Stevenson, their standard-bearer, was clobbered in two successive elections. Even worse, their spirit was stalled. They were, Bert Cochran wrote, "demoralized and in retreat." They had fought for material security, and now the American economy had rewarded their crusade with suburbanized affluence, which was not precisely what they had had in mind. They went on talking the old New Deal language of equality and justice, but the old slogans seemed stale. And where they were passionate, about the evils of Communism, they were trapped in a terrible bind. They were committed to the Cold War, but victimized by the passions the Cold War ignited. As Cochran put it, the liberals "had grown conservative but were frightened by the furies of McCarthyism, and they were choking in the thickening know-nothing atmosphere." Rank-and-file liberals with impeccably anti-Communist credentials were smeared by gossips, harassed by threatening phone calls, or found the *Daily Worker* left on their doormats by local vigilantes—all for daring to organize in the Parent-Teachers Association and like groups. Even the ADA, which excluded Communists, was controversial.

In the Thirties, liberals had rested their hopes on the unions and the state. But in the Eisenhower years, the state was no longer theirs, and the gloss had worn off the unions, whose "countervailing power," as John Kenneth Galbraith termed it, had been set back by Taft-Hartley, by the purge of the Communists, by the shrinkage of the blue-collar work force, and by Eisenhower's antagonism. The unions had grown bureaucratized, committed more to bread-and-butter gains than crusades for justice. The merger of the AFL and CIO in 1955 betokened the normalization of the latter, not the radicalization of the former. Now, cleansed of the Communist taint, liberals beheld a society afflicted by a malaise they could not grasp. They too had been reading *The Lonely Crowd* and *The Organization Man* and wondering whether the well-upholstered world of "other-directed" man, the world that liberal capitalism had made, was the world their hearts had once beat for. Wistful for new crusades, liberals spoke of "the quality of life."

This was a middle-class mood and they were unabashedly middle-class people. A good number of them were established, or about to be. They held respected positions in journalism, the academy, and liberal organizations. If the unions no longer made their blood race, if sweeping utopian visions now had to be ruled out as illusions or, worse, invitations to Stalinism, the liberals could fall back on themselves. Perhaps their own success represented the good society, or progressively unfolding reason, at work. Many of them lived lives which depended on language and knowledge, after all. Many of them were Jews, the children of impoverished immigrants, and they had made a place for themselves in America, it seemed to them, against long odds, by turning to good use their intelligence, their command of acquired knowledge. There was good reason why they were thrilled by Adlai Stevenson, whose elegant phrases made them feel that a materialistic America deserved a well-schooled tongue—the source of their own status. Although Stevenson was twice beaten by Eisenhower, he swept a new generation of liberals into politics—the California Democratic Council, a revived Independent Voters of Illinois, reform Democratic clubs in machine-dominated New York City, groups that kept liberal politics alive and also became proving grounds and sometimes allies for parts of the New Left.

Many of the liberals were content to surrender their old values like outworn suits. Cheerfully disillusioned with socialist and Stalinist dreams, they signed up for the American Celebration by concluding, with the ex-socialist Seymour Martin Lipset, that America was a country in which "leftist values" already prevailed. They could dream trimmer dreams. Having carved out personal niches, they now had something to lose. And here was another source of the generational chasm. Some of their children, feeling disaffiliated, identified with the dispossessed. Organized liberalism, by contrast, had made its bargain with affluence; it passed on its ideals to its children, but spoke in the voice of the proprietor, or his expert-priest. The liberals were not guilty of that famous Sixties cliché, a "failure to communicate"; in the unspoken language of property and complacency, they "communicated" all too well.

Whatever James Wechsler's forebodings, most of the liberals went over to John F. Kennedy's side when he won the 1960 nomination. They came to power with him, and he spoke for them in his inaugural address, in the self-conscious accents of a generation: "Let the word go forth . . . that the torch has been passed to a new generation of Americans—born in this century, tempered by war, disciplined by a hard and bitter peace, proud of our ancient heritage." How strikingly different is this tone from the keynote of the tiny New Left's manifesto eighteen months later: "We are people of this generation, bred in at least modest comfort, housed now in universities, looking uncomfortably to the world we inherit." But notice: both are speaking the language of generations. In John F. Kennedy's manifesto the strenuous life is rearing up—and riding for a fall; in the obscure *Port Huron Statement* there is a brooding. The proud have come to power, but the uncomfortable are beginning to gather.

LEFT REMNANTS, RED DIAPERS

I, for one, was a liberal youth, raised by liberal parents, dreaming liberal dreams, moved by liberal heroes, who threw himself into political activity and moved leftward in the early Sixties. If the New Deal generation was going to hold the loyalty of its successors, it should have been able to hold people like me—teenagers who sat before the TV set on election nights cheering the Democrats (all but the southerners) and thronged into the Bronx's Grand Concourse to hear Adlai Stevenson orate in 1956. One reason the New Dealers failed to hold their own was that the liberal summons had some political competition.

I arrived at Harvard in the fall of 1959. My freshman year, I schooled myself in the pursuit and perfection of first-year-away-from-home alienation. I read *The Catcher in the Rye* and *Lady Chatterley's Lover,* saw Bergman's *The Magician* twice, signed a telegram opposing the execution of Caryl Chessman at San Quentin, shot pool (not very well) after dinner, and played poker (better) almost every night. Ostensibly I was studying mathematics, which came easily and lacked soul. Actually I was excited by philosophy and moved by Dostoyevsky, Nietzsche, Kafka, and most of all Camus's *The Myth of Sisyphus*. During the summer of 1960, I continued reading in this vein—principally Camus's *The Rebel* and Kafka's diaries—on the long commute to my job, programming one of the early desk-size computers for the Monroe Calculating Machine Company in suburban New Jersey. My free-floating alienation here discovered alienated labor: the machine I was programming was stupid, the work uninspiring, my co-workers affable but narrow. Conveniently, I fell in love.

The object of my affections, whom I shall call Madeleine, was a red-diaper baby: the daughter of onetime Communists. This may sound like falling-into-the-clutches, but it did happen this way. I was seventeen and in every sense ready for clutches of this sort. My political attitudes were muddled. Earlier that summer, I'd been wearing a Stevenson button, and when I saw Kennedy trounce my hero for the Democratic nomination, on television, I cried. I had heard on the radio that real liberals like Eleanor Roosevelt were leery about Kennedy—thought he was too confirmed a Cold Warrior, for one thing—and so I was ready to listen to lefter voices. Now, as Madeleine and I dawdled around on long summer weekend afternoons, next door to my parents' place in upstate New York, I got into the habit of picking up the left-wing weekly newspaper her parents subscribed to, the "progressive" *National Guardian*. I don't remember any enthusiasm for the *Guardian*'s rather apologetically pro-Soviet slant; *The Nation* or *The New Republic* might have served my purposes, and indeed did so in liberal families. I liked the fact that the *Guardian* was undisguisedly dissident.

To the more or less liberal youth of my generation, with no family tradition of activism to draw on, red-diaper babies were frequently our first contacts with the forbidden world of wholesale political criticism. They had grown up breathing a left-wing air; their sense of being different, touched by nobility and consecrated by persecution, was magnetic; they had a perch from which to criticize. I had no inkling of this at the time, but I have subsequently learned from interviews that, romance aside, mine was a common experience: The majority of the original New Leftists were not the children of Communist or socialist parents, but sometime in adolescence were touched, influenced, fascinated, by children who were. From them the rest of us absorbed, by osmosis, the idea and precedent and romance of a Left.

In fact, as far back as junior high school, I was tantalized, intrigued, by the idea of a Left. Then too, my corruptor was the child of a onetime left-winger. In 1955 or 1956, one of my best friends, whom I shall call David, played for me a record that came in a jacket unlike anything I'd seen before—black and white, no names, no credits, the only words a headline: THE INVESTIGATOR. The reverse side was a blank white. Like a magazine wrapped in the proverbial plain brown wrapper, *The Investigator* exuded an aura of irresistible taboo. The author, I learned years later, was Reuben Shipp, a Canadian who had worked in American radio until blacklisted, then deported. First broadcast in Canada, then smuggled onto a disk, *The Investigator* came as a "ray of hope" into the households of the American Left—so remembers Jessica Mitford.

The unnamed Investigator did a splendid rendition of Senator Joseph McCarthy's giggle and his blustering, wheedling tone. After perishing in a plane crash, the Investigator finds himself in Heaven, which, appallingly, is running wild with subversive elements like Socrates, Thomas Jefferson, and John Milton. He takes charge of ideological purification, subpoenas these worthies, and, unimpressed by their ringing self-defenses, deports them "from Up Here to [significant pause] Down There." ("Naturally they say the same thing," he explains. "They're part of the same conspiracy.") He also subpoenas a succession of Karl Marxes, who on interrogation turn out to be Karl Marx the watchmaker, Karl Marx the piano tuner, and Karl Marx the pastry chef, whereupon *all* persons named Karl Marx are deported. The political atmosphere, needless to say, is chilled. But the Investigator runs out of important witnesses and ends up subpoenaing the Chief, intoning that "there is no one so high as to be immune from investigation." His voice cracking, he takes to ranting, "I am the Chief!" which hubris sends him pell-mell down to The Other Place, shrieking, "I'm the Chiefffff!"—only to be refused entry by the Devil himself.

Although I did not understand this at the time, *The Investigator* was typical of Popular Front anti-McCarthy culture, which presented McCarthyism as an assault on all free thought—which it was, though of course McCarthyism gnashed its teeth over certain lines of thought in particular. But the thinness of the American radical tradition, the residues of Earl Browder's Stalin-era line ("Communism is twentieth-century Americanism"), and the habits of Stalinist duplicity, along with the terrors of McCarthyite inquisitions, led Popular Front culture to defend Thought in general, not socialism in particular. *The Investigator* placed Karl Marx, whoever he was, on the side of the diffuse heresies with which, time after time, humanity had battered (with eventual success) against the princes of narrow-mindedness.

It was taken for granted around my house that McCarthy was a force of evil, though not much was said about him (or any other politician, for that matter). I watched pieces of the 1954 all-day live broadcasts of the army-McCarthy hearings on our new television set, enthralled as McCarthy tried to dig himself out of a hole by impugning the record of one of the army's attorneys until the impeccably patrician Joseph Welch, the army's chief attorney, got the better of the bully by asking the famous question, "Have you no sense of decency?" It was a showdown even better than *High Noon,* itself an ex-Communist's parable about McCarthyism. McCarthy's comeuppance is the most-remembered televised event among the early New Left generation; it meant there were limits to bullying, that the bad guys, once exposed, could be stopped because, like the Investigator, they didn't know where to stop. But what made the saga of Joseph McCarthy all the more real to me was my friend David's father. David confided that in the Thirties, a long-gone time whose heroism was poignant because ancient, his father had joined a Communist group at City College—or so his employer had come to believe. Twenty years later, his employer had gotten wind of this sin; he had been forced to change not only jobs but careers. The details were vague. Like many red-diaper babies, David knew little about his father's political past. In the haunted Fifties, parents did not speak of these things, and children—and children's friends—did not ask. But the fact that David's father had to shift to a second-best career jarred me.

In the fall of 1956 David and I made the move to the Bronx High School of Science, and he introduced me to my second political artifact. The big political event that fall was Adlai Stevenson's speech on the Grand Concourse; I was madly for Adlai. In the spring, the big event on the Concourse was something different: David and I went to see a double bill of Brigitte Bardot movies, all the rage. That day, or another like it, we stopped to rummage in a bookstore, and David pointed out to me a paperback called *Heavenly Discourse,* by one Colonel Charles Erskine Scott Wood. Not that David was full of politics; he, like me, was far more interested in the empyrean realm of differential calculus, and the enjoyment of all sorts of curves. We talked about logarithms much more than we ever talked about the logic of history. I bought the book, the first in my life I can remember spending scarce cash for. The very act of buying a book was as risqué, as much a *rite de passage,* as seeing a Bardot movie.

Heavenly Discourse consisted of dialogues originally written for the pre–World War I *Masses;* most of them were published only in 1927, though, in book form, because Woodrow Wilson's wartime government withdrew the magazine's mailing permit and forced it to fold. In Colonel Wood's heaven, the likes of Tom Paine, Mark Twain, Mary Wollstonecraft, Voltaire, Rabelais, Socrates, Confucius, and other paragons of freethinking, free love, bohemianism, pacifism, socialism, and all-around wisdom disported themselves with God and Jesus in the realm of eternal ideas, aiming their wit at thickheaded goons the likes of the warmongering President Wilson, the fundamentalist William Jennings Bryan, and the censorious Carrie Nation and Anthony Comstock. *Heavenly Discourse,* like *The Investigator,* represented one big ecumenical radicalism against one big enemy. I suddenly understood that McCarthyism had a history.

Like Wood's purehearted heroes, I was devoted to freethinking dilettantism; like most callow academic achievers, I cared more about the existence of ideas than about their consistency. But there were patterns. While my main preoccupation was going to the top of my class, I sympathized with underdogs and suspected the masses. During the tenth grade, a dissenting English teacher, a substitute, blessedly excused us from the *Silas Marner* imposed upon every other tenth grader, and had us read instead *A Tale of Two Cities* and *Les Misérables.* I was enthralled by embattled heroes, whether aristocratic or impoverished. When we read American poets, I loved most of all Walt Whitman and Carl Sandburg;

Whitman's omnivore ego, sounding its barbaric yawp, appealed to both my solitude and my desire to feel at home among Americans, and I liked the idea of Sandburg's folksy if abstract "the people, yes," who would eventually triumph over all the philistines and merchandisers. I read through Tom Paine's collected works, which my father had bought in the Thirties, and Howard Fast's Popular Front novel, *Citizen Tom Paine,* a library find; I was moved to tears by the fate of the great pamphleteer eventually spurned by the Americans for whom he had harbored such hopes, and whose ashes were scattered, "for the world was his village."

Colonel Wood's version of heavenly thinkers striving to redeem humanity for the good carried me to George Bernard Shaw, another white-bearded demigod on whom I wrote a paper in a creative-writing class my junior year. Shaw convinced me that socialism, the common ownership and planning of socially produced property, was simply the twentieth-century version of common sense. But there was a paradox. Apparently socialism was an ideology for discriminating people: the thinking man's ideology, to paraphrase a commercial slogan of the time. Through no fault of socialists themselves, then, socialism was opposed to the society of ordinary people. Wood's and Shaw's heroes—like Tom Paine and the glorious dead of *The Investigator*—were apostles of popular salvation martyred by the populace. The people as ingrates, the elite as spurned prophets: I was bothered, moved, and probably more than a bit attracted by the contradiction; indeed, the whole New Left can be seen as an extended attempt to find a solution to it. In a more severe spirit, I devoured H. L. Mencken, whose glorious broadsides against American philistinism were perfectly suited to upward-bound Jewish boys and girls, for we were fearful of the anti-intellectual, goyish, McCarthyite mass of Americans and at the same time eager to get in on elite culture.

Communists and ex-Communists were the largest blocs of the Left holding on to their niches by their fingernails in the Fifties, but there were other radical holdovers, and one of them affected me in a curious way. One sweltering spring day in 1958, the word went around my school that a socialist rally was going to take place outside, that afternoon. I knew instantly I wanted to be there. An actual socialist here and now, in the Bronx! I would have to cut class during the last period, something I, as a well-behaved boy, had never done, but it turned out that many of my friends were planning to go.

When the hour arrived, the street, astonishingly, was filled with students. Across the street, standing on an honest-to-God soapbox, a young man in a dark suit and tie was giving a rational, step-by-step exposition of what, years later, I could recognize as the theory of surplus value—that all value derives from labor, not bosses. I hadn't been standing there long, taking in this oversimple elegance of Marxism 1A, when from behind me eggs began to fly. Unbelievable! I wheeled around. The eggs were being flung by one of the more disagreeable Science boys I knew: a rah-rah booster type, active in student government, notable for wearing loud madras sport jackets to school. One egg flew by the speaker and splattered against a brick wall; he ducked; the other one hit him on the back and proceeded to drip, slowly, down his suit.

The socialist went on unfazed. "Charlie Wilson," he said, referring to the General Motors president turned secretary of defense, renowned for his statement that "What's good for General Motors is good for the country"—"Charlie Wilson put nothin' into that car." It seemed eminently reasonable. The speaker went on to say some kind words in favor of Swedish social democracy. A young child pushed toward him screaming: "Dirty Communist, go back to Russia!" One of my classmates shouted out, "We don't wanna have open minds!" I had thought what was bad about *Russia* was that it was harsh on free thought.

On my way home on the bus, shaken, I scribbled the somber, pretentious phrases of what I think was my first poem, called "Egg-Stain," soaked in sarcasm toward "The American Way." I'd learned in a small way something red-diaper babies had already learned, something I hadn't picked up from George Bernard Shaw's otherwise persuasive drawing-room Fabianism—that ideas have consequences; that people who make a point of flouting popular prejudices shouldn't necessarily expect public acclaim for their trouble.

Years later, I found out that the rally at Bronx Science had been organized by a small Marxist group called the Young Socialist Alliance, then a stopping-off point for red-diaper babies on their way out of the Communist Party with their parents. (Later it became explicitly Trotskyist.) With Khrushchev's speech denouncing Stalin's crimes at the Soviet Party Congress of 1956, whatever McCarthyism and affluence had left unspared in the Church of World Revolution was defunct, leaving a melange of sects scrambling for the mantle. Not all the enclaves of the Old Left derived from the Communist Party and its front groups; various Trotskyist remnants were vigorously if complexly anti-Soviet, which did not, however, protect them from the harassment of the FBI and the campus cold-shoulder. Trotskyist and social-democratic splinter groups spoke of socialism, and often argued for a labor party along Western European lines; Communist and ex-Communist groups spoke of the "progressive" cause, and usually tried to work through the Democratic Party. But regardless of political position, most of America's puny Marxist sects spoke self-enclosed languages. They had lost virtually all their base in the labor movement. And yet they insisted that organization—*their* organization—was all-important. Steve Max, briefly part of the Young Socialist Alliance, later entertained his comrades in early SDS with a story about walking across Washington Square Park with another YSAer who, seeing a DO NOT WALK ON GRASS sign, dutifully kept to the side-walk. "Why pay attention?" Max asked. "That's a *capitalist* DO NOT WALK

ON GRASS sign." The reply: "We don't believe in individual acts of heroism."

Within a year after Khrushchev's tirade against Stalin in 1956, followed by his brutal suppression of the Hungarian uprising, the American Communist Party numbered a mere 5,000 or 6,000 members—down from its peak of 60,000–80,000 during and after World War II, and 43,000 as late as 1950. In 1951, top Party leaders were convicted of "teaching and advocating the overthrow of the United States government by force and violence" under the Smith Act; the Party, fearing the worst, sent many other leaders into hiding, isolating them from one another. The Party line twisted toward revolutionary delusions at a time when members were suffering from the McCarthyite purge; thousands dropped out in disgust. Finally, with Khrushchev's speech, most of the cadres who had resisted knowing about Stalin's crimes heard enough to persuade them to exit en masse. The remaining Party faithful turned further and further inward, preoccupied with internal purity, living in what one former Party official has called "a mental Comintern," with what another former member has called a "fortress mentality."

As a political force, the Communist Party and its satellites were spent, but what survived through the Fifties was a social world and a cultural enclave. Persecuted, devoid of a live social movement, the Communists drew their world more snugly about them. They had long since composed a world unto themselves; now it tightened. Partly for financial reasons, their doctors and dentists and lawyers were Communists or sympathizers. The friends with whom they spent social weekends were other Communists. Their babysitters were Communists. They sent their children to Jewish shuls, where they were taught Yiddish, Yiddish culture, and politics, and to special summer camps (like Kinderland and Wo-Chi-Ca, which stood for "Workers' Children's Camp," not a Seneca chief) where they learned union and folk songs and were graced by visits from cultural heroes like Paul Robeson and Pete Seeger. They took their children to picket lines (one red-diaper child I interviewed thought they were barbecues). Some even lived in neighborhoods where, in the Old Left's heyday, virtually everyone turned out for the May Day parade. Most former members, the peripheral and the sympathizers, turned their backs on the internecine strife, which enabled them to sustain a rosy memory of the Party, the Popular Front, and "progressive" politics in general. Those in middle-class professions, for whom Party membership no longer squared with the rest of their lives, remained members in their hearts, and kept up their old subcultural bonds. Many, perhaps the majority, never thought through what had gone so catastrophically wrong in the Soviet Union, or in their own subservient Party. They were no longer Communists, but they were not exactly anti-Communist. As the McCarthyite storm passed, many kept up their old contacts, rolled up their sleeves, and enlisted in civil rights and other single-issue causes.

The life of the Old Left was self-enclosed, but the other side of self-enclosure is firmness—even rigidity—of identity. One of the Old Left's major legacies was the sense of a world divided between us and them. *We* were different, special. *We,* however isolated in the United States, were part of "a worldwide community"—led, of course, by "the socialist countries," the Soviet Union usually ranked foremost (despite what were euphemistically called "mistakes"). *We* lived by distinct values: justice, equality, peace. *They,* the rest of America, were persecutors, or pawns in the hands of neocolonialists, or (the few "advanced" ones) more or less "developed." *They* were reaping the harvest of affluence, but right here in America *we* were victims of war—or, the children of the Party core were told, conquerors on the side of the future. In 1949, one boy told his parents he had heard in school that "our side lost in China." "No," said his father, "our side won." Children absorbed all of this and made sense of it in various ways, but my sense is that what they absorbed most—less from ideology than from the home experience—was the sense of a we/they world. In one survey of fifty-six red-diaper babies in the early Eighties, the sense of "difference" was ranked most significant, the sense of the "worldwide community" was ranked third, the sense of values fourth. Many took in a powerful moralism: there are rights and wrongs, and it is important to live by the rights. This sense affected even the children of parents who had long since dropped out of left-wing politics, who discovered the truth about their parents only later, when they were activists themselves.

According to the survey, the second most salient aspect of the red-diaper identity was fear; and in my own interviews with red-diaper babies, fear is what they recall more vividly than anything else. D., whose father went underground, was taught never to open the door without asking who was there, and never to use names on the phone. V. knew FBI men were waiting outside her door, waiting to serve her mother with a subpoena to testify before the House Un-American Activities Committee; her father was driven out of his career as an actor and had to take up selling bathroom equipment. R., whose father went underground, remembers his mother telling him that his father was away "helping people," from which he concluded that his father was a fireman. R. remembers coming home from school to find his mother sprawled across her bed, weeping— Julius and Ethel Rosenberg had just been executed. Red-diaper children were often kept in the dark for years about just what their parents were doing, or had done—all the more so when their parents were mysteriously away from home for months on end, except for fugitive visits. But they all heard a great deal over the dinner table about the "ruling class" that rode roughshod over American workers, about the "class struggle," the Cold War, McCarthyism, civil rights. They knew there were books and magazines that had to be hidden from outsiders. Many of those who were Jewish absorbed a sense of trauma added to the echoes of the Holocaust;

there were things in the world too painful to think about. Some of them grew up in working-class, integrated communities, fusing their sense of otherness with that of black friends. Many came to cherish their protected social zone, the summer camps above all. They might be isolated during the year, ostracized by schoolmates, even beaten up, but at camp they were among friends, safe, normal.

Some of the children felt both terrified and neglected, and turned against politics as they matured. But a large number gravitated easily into the New Left. Many brought Old Left styles with them—hostility toward Western imperialism and a sardonic attitude toward America's democratic and pacific pretensions, coupled with a lingering nostalgia for the Soviet Union as a fallen but still noble ideological homeland—and many also rebelled against the hand-me-down pieties. Some were so traumatized by their childhood experience that, when they later moved into the New Left, they held back from leadership, cautious lest by becoming visible they might endanger their own careers. Some were cautioned by their parents not to get arrested, for that might draw attention to the family name. Some later decided that the Communist Party had failed because it had played the tail to the New Deal's dog; or that the subpoenaed Communists should have declared that yes, they were Communists and proud of it; or that their parents, taking up careers and moving to the suburbs, had "sold out"—and they rebelled by becoming *more* revolutionary when the New Left afforded them the opportunity. Others concluded that they had to become more coalition-minded, more anti-Soviet, less dogmatic, or more spiritualist. Burdened with secrets to keep, some grew up resentful, some excited, but all knew they belonged to a virtual secret society of the elect.

The larger world was prattling on about affluence, but here were people cut out of the celebration. They were internal exiles, an outlaw culture and proud of it. To people like me, alternately offended and unimpressed by Communism but in search of a mooring for my own sense of difference, that was appealing. One thing I liked about my feisty girlfriend Madeleine was her feisty, intellectual parents. They read, they talked about the world. (Once I showed up at her house carrying the ex- and anti-Communist Arthur Koestler's autobiography, and her father twitted me; but that was also a way of taking me seriously.) They were cultural émigrés, but safely middle-class—not nearly as threatening as the beats.

Most of all, their subworld had cultural appeal. Madeleine brought me the gift of folk music. This was the main bridge between red-diaper babydom as a whole and the rest of their generation. From the Forties through the early Sixties, the music of the Weavers, Woody Guthrie, and others was an embattled minority's way of conjuring an ideal folk. The Old Left was confined to its enclaves, but it could invent an artificial "people" to sing about; folk music was "for the masses" the way the

Communist Party had stood for "the people," whether the actual people embraced it or not. The folk taste could also be a way of expressing distance from and disdain for mainstream popular culture, yet without the avant-garde aura of jazz; thus the continuing Swarthmore College folk festivals of the Fifties. In 1960, folk was coming out of its hermitage; Harry Belafonte had Americanized Caribbean songs; the Kingston Trio was in vogue, with its slick, upbeat, pop version of folk ballads; around Harvard Square, Joan Baez began reviving the Elizabethan folk tradition. But Madeleine's Forest Hills, Queens, version of folk was rooted in the cultural soil of the Communist Party, whose postwar "cultural workers" carried on the tradition of audience participation "hootenannies." Banished from the mass media, Pete Seeger, the rest of the Weavers, and a few lesser lights warmed the hearts of the faithful at left-wing summer camps, sympathetic campuses, civil rights rallies and small meetings. Among Madeleine's circle of friends, there were songs of rough-and-tumble proletarians, like "Sloop John B." ("I want to go home/Please let me go home/I feel so break-up/I want to go home.") There were political song-parables like "If I Had a Hammer," "This Land Is Your Land," and "The Banks Are Made of Marble." The Popular Front was dead, but the idea of it could be sung. The sentimentality of folk music was a measure of the Old Left's distance from the actual working class. The political generation of the Fifties was missing, but folk was the living prayer of a defunct movement, the consolation and penumbra of its children, gingerly holding the place of a Left in American culture.

Aside from the songs, the greatest achievement of the scattered Old Left of the Fifties was to keep up what Irving Howe called "steady work," and to wait. There were non-Communists who worked in the Henry Wallace campaign, opposed blacklists and deportations and lynchings, supported racial integration. Their roots were in the wartime resistance against fascism; they were not given to doctrine. They did not necessarily like the CP but they did not want to crusade against it. The smallest actions required courage: The early Fifties were a time when a Queens woman, a refugee from the Nazis, could be hounded out of her PTA for urging the group to take up a collection for UNICEF at Halloween. In the hills of Tennessee, a former Socialist Party organizer named Myles Horton ran the Highlander Folk School, with workshops for southern civil rights workers (one of whom was Rosa Parks) under the nose of the Ku Klux Klan, providing a safe haven for civil rights visionaries from a variety of Old Left backgrounds, including Ella Baker, later the presiding spiritual and political mother of SNCC, and Anne and Carl Braden, indefatigable Louisville organizers. (Carl Braden spent a year in jail for refusing to testify before HUAC.) Ripples crossed: In 1947 Horton's wife Zilphia learned an old gospel song called "I'll Overcome" from striking North Carolina tobacco workers, turned it into "I Will Overcome," and taught it to Pete Seeger, who converted the title to "We Shall Overcome," added lines like "We'll walk hand in hand," and spread it around. A couple of teachings later, in 1959, "We Shall Overcome" landed back at Highlander with a singer-organizer named Guy Carawan, who taught it to civil rights workers—all without benefit of records or radio.

In New York, outside the old CP circles, the minuscule Old Left remnants debated more than they sang. In the late Fifties, all the activists could easily have fit into a single musty walkup loft near Union Square, and often did. Their political culture was one of Talmudic disputation; they argued out correct lines with the ferocious energy of itinerant rabbis hoping to scrape up a congregation. What they had instead of living movements were symbolic confrontations. Each had a lineage which had harbored heroic hopes for the Left, whether in the Soviet Union or in the American Thirties; each was prone to blame the others for the ensuing debacle. There was an alphabet soup of tiny self-fissuring socialist and Trotskyist sects, of whom the most talented exceptions to the missing generation gravitated to and through Max Shachtman's orbit, in flight from both Stalinism and the American capitalist celebration. Shachtman, once one of Trotsky's secretaries, was by all accounts a riveting orator, impressing radicals from Irving Howe to Bayard Rustin. To the Right, the moribund social democrats of the League for Industrial Democracy sent organizers (including James Farmer, Gabriel Kolko, Aryeh Neier, and André Schiffrin) to the unfavorable student hinterlands, where some of the main events of the Fifties were debates—for example, at Brandeis University, between Irving Howe and the then-Communist Howard Fast in the winter of 1955–56, and between Howe (pro) and Herbert Marcuse (equivocal) on the Hungarian revolution in the fall of 1956. (Brandeis was one of perhaps only three campuses which experienced much political continuity from the Fifties into the Sixties—the others were Madison and Berkeley.) All the way into the early Sixties, the buzz of sectarian remnants stayed most alive in New York City's political-cultural pressure cooker (which is why SDS, started by midwesterners and aspiring to be homegrown but saddled with a New York national office because that was where its parent group was, eventually had to move its offices to Ann Arbor and Chicago). In the conservative mood, all these groups adapted to their ecological niches in the wilderness—each isolated in its purity, insisting on its difference from the others. And some took on protective coloration—the Student League for Industrial Democracy abandoned the word *socialist* for *liberal*. Whatever the politics, all agreed that the pivotal events were taking place overseas, whether in Hungary or, later, Cuba.

Not least, there were the placemarkers, the grouplets who tried in competing ways to find a voice for becalmed socialism, to wind their way beyond both Stalinism and liberalism. "When intellectuals can do nothing else they start a magazine"—thus Irving Howe on the founding of the anti-Communist, anti-McCarthyite, democratic socialist quarterly *Dissent* in 1954. With a circulation of a bare few thousand, *Dissent* quickly became a polemical center for radical outriders of American intellectual life, railing against Popular Front evasions, yet still a place where Howe and A. J. Muste, say, could debate C. Wright Mills's critique of the Cold War, where Norman Mailer could trumpet "The White Negro," where Herbert Marcuse and Erich Fromm could debate Marcuse's *Eros and Civilization*, where Paul Goodman could make his anarchist raids on contemporary centralization and where, in 1960, Michael Walzer could celebrate the North Carolina sit-ins. Harsh-toned, proud to display its twentieth-century scars, much of it written in a somber tone of aftermath, *Dissent* prided itself on its freedom from illusion, its ability to face what Howe later called "the sheer terribleness of our time." Writing about Albert Camus in 1961, Howe noted that Camus, like the rest of the Democratic Left, had failed "to move from abstract position to a concrete program and then from a concrete program to an active politics. . . . This was *our* dilemma: the one we felt to be an essential part of our experience." *Dissent*'s pathos was to represent a dangling ethics, another form of culture, really, but not—not yet?—a movement.

The most buoyant of the holdouts, and probably the most influential do-it-yourselfer of the Fifties, was the one-man grouplet I. F. Stone, who started his four-page *Weekly* newsletter in 1953 with 5,300 subscribers and his wife as circulation manager. "Izzy" specialized in ferreting out neglected facts in government hearings and wire-service reports, making sense of the news, showing week to week how the government fudged and obfuscated. Gradually he built up his mailing list with reports on the McCarthyite persecutions and a running critique of the Eisenhower-Dulles foreign policy; he survived some four hundred cancellations in 1956 when he went to Moscow for the Party Congress and painted an unpretty picture of the Soviet Union. Willfully uninterested in the Left's internal polemics, Jeffersonian about civil liberties, Marxist (but not Leninist) in his hopes for a socialist working class, a romantic of the heart and an Enlightenment skeptic of the head, Izzy had formed his political views as a partisan of the Popular Front against fascism; he saw no reason to change now. Unlike the socialist intellectuals of New York, he had grown up in a small town and he was used to living in the wilderness. In an America of giant news corporations, he was an authentic loner, something of a holdover from the America of Charles Erskine Scott Wood. The *Weekly* was appealing partly because Stone's colorful, literate prose style didn't sound like a corporate product; it read like something edited at home, which it was.

TWO
THE
MOVEMENT

Why not simply the *current* left? What makes it new?
—Carl Oglesby

LEFTWARD KICKING AND SCREAMING

1960   History rarely follows the decimal system as neatly as it did in
1960. Suddenly the campus mood seemed to shift. Without
question a major reason was that the end of the Eisenhower era
was looming; whatever doubts attached to John F. Kennedy, one could
anticipate a thaw, a sense of the possible. What had been underground
flowed to the surface. After all the prologues and precursors, an
insurgency materialized, and the climate of opinion began to shift, the
way spring announces itself with scents and a scatter of birdsong before
the temperature climbs to stay. And then it was as if, all over the country,
young people had been waiting for just these signals.

In Greensboro, North Carolina, on February 1, four black (then
known as Negro) students from North Carolina Agricultural and
Technical College, wearing jackets and ties, sat down at a Woolworth's
whites-only lunch counter, claimed their right to be served, and refused to
leave. Contrary to movement legend, these four—Ezell Blair, Jr.,
Franklin McCain, Joseph McNeil, and David Richmond—did not spring
full-blown from the abstract idea of resistance to segregation. They had
belonged to the Youth Council of the National Association for the
Advancement of Colored People (NAACP), and knew of earlier sit-ins in
Durham, North Carolina, and elsewhere. (Indeed, without benefit of mass
publicity or a mass base, but with the help of black churches, the
NAACP, and the Congress of Racial Equality, there had been sit-ins in at
least sixteen cities since 1957.) They had been nourished in a tradition of

liberation passed on to them by parents, ministers, and teachers; by an active NAACP; by the Montgomery bus boycott, the Southern Christian Leadership Conference (SCLC) and its leader Martin Luther King; by participants in earlier Freedom Rides; by the writings of black heroes; by a television documentary about Gandhi. The four returned on February 2 with twenty-five other young people, some wearing ROTC uniforms. Twice as many went back to Woolworth's the day after that; by the fifth day, there were more than three hundred. Their audacious refusal to "know their place" touched off a wave of sit-ins at lunch counters across the urban South. The word spread through church networks and civil rights movement clusters, and within days sit-ins were organized in other cities in North Carolina; within two weeks, the same impulse brought sit-ins to other southern states. A generation had been reared to expect that the 1954 *Brown* v. *Board of Education* decision truly spelled the end of segregation; by 1960, it was clear that popular action was necessary. Meanwhile, in northern cities, blacks and whites organized picket lines at local Woolworth's outlets. Within two months, sit-ins had been organized in fifty-four cities in nine states. The civil rights stalwart Ella Baker called a conference of sit-in activists; in April that conference organized the Student Nonviolent Coordinating Committee (SNCC) to fight segregation through direct action.

And under the rotunda of San Francisco's City Hall, on May 13, another body of upstarts insisted on their right to attend hearings of the House Un-American Activities Committee. Kept outside the hearing room, the demonstrators, most of them students, sat down in the rotunda and started to sing "We Shall Not Be Moved," a song of the Thirties. The police attacked them with high-pressure fire hoses, clubbed them, and hurled them down the marble steps, charging one demonstrator with a felony charge they could not, in the end, make stick. The anti-HUAC demonstrations also brought to the surface a tradition that had been in the making for several years: an underground stream combining Berkeley campus politics, local anti-HUAC sentiment, and the relatively strong local Communist Party and its fellow travelers.

Thinking to capitalize on the disruption, HUAC produced *Operation Abolition,* a film which scrambled footage and invented facts to present the Committee as the victim of a Communist-run campaign. Its soundtrack and pictures met at odd angles. Posing in front of a faked backdrop of the Capitol dome, Committee members with small-town demeanors spoke clumsily of "well-trained Communist agents" mobilizing their "dupes" to discredit the Committee, while their footage showed no such thing. Kept out of the hearing room, demonstrators chanted, "What are you afraid of?" and, "Open the doors!"—hardly signs of conspiracy or insurrection. The police, called "especially trained" (twice for good measure), looked brutal. The demonstrators, called "unruly," sang "The Star-Spangled Banner" and were shown being washed down the steps. To anyone not convinced that HUAC had the corner on truth, the unfriendly witnesses sounded heroic. And so *Operation Abolition* proved a camp favorite and an inspiration to campus activists more than a cautionary tale. Civil liberties activists accompanied it to campuses, even refuted it with their own film, *Operation Correction*—pointing out along the way that one reason "identified Communists" had been present was that the Committee had subpoenaed them. But the refutation was scarcely necessary. The Committee radiated thickheadedness and ineffectuality; the anti-Committee Left stood for eloquence and humor. When liberal audiences heard the congressmen's grade-B gangster movie lines and *Dragnet*-style melodramatic music, they laughed. The mere appearance of a Communist on the screen no longer provoked universal horror. The Committee could still punish—merely being served with HUAC subpoenas cost several San Francisco teachers their jobs—but it was losing its power to intimidate. The lumbering Committee had made a recruiting film for a New Left that barely existed.

Between the sit-ins and the anti-HUAC demonstration, the Fifties expired. The sit-ins were the main dynamo that powered the white movement, galvanizing the little nodes of opposition that had been forming in New York City, in the Boston and San Francisco Bay areas, in Chicago's Hyde Park, in Ann Arbor and Madison—wherever the booming universities, thick with students, were promoting the value of reflection, cultivating intellectual alienation, and providing sites for both. The sit-ins could only have reverberated across the country (as did the news of San Francisco three months later, though less so) because there were already cultural and political enclaves, zones of negativity, which had withstood the leveling pressures of affluence and, now that McCarthyism was no longer in the saddle, were ready to move. But without the civil rights movement, the beat and Old Left and bohemian enclaves would not have opened into a revived politics. Youth culture might have remained just that—the transitional subculture of the young, a rite of passage on the route to normal adulthood—had it not been for the revolt of black youth, disrupting the American celebration in ways no one had imagined possible. From expressing youthful *difference,* many of the alienated, though hardly all, leaped into a self-conscious sense of *opposition.*

McCarthyism and the Old Left together had discredited the idea of a general multi-issue Left. The result was that the New Left made its appearance in the guise of single-issue movements: civil rights, civil liberties, campus reform, peace. But beneath was a common élan, a tangle of common principles, eventually a generational identity: New Left, meaning neither Old Left nor liberal. Over the next years, this opposition groped for a language and a way of understanding itself. Aiming to become a political force, it had to work out its relations to other forces— entrenched enemies, possible allies, and political parents. The black student movement had to come to terms with the bastions of the civil rights movement—the long-lived NAACP and the clergymen of Martin Luther King's Southern Christian Leadership Conference. The budding white student movement had to feel out its relations to the Communist and social-democratic sectors of the Old Left, and to organized liberals. Both, crucially, had to figure out where they stood in relation to the Kennedy and then Johnson administrations. The history of what became the New Left in the early Sixties is in large part the history of these struggles for self-definition.

But first there had to be a *movement:* that which moves. The common chord in Greensboro and San Francisco was direct action. Following these precedents, what came to call itself "the movement" was a fusion of collective will and moral style. The movement didn't simply demand, it *did*. By taking action, not just a position, it affirmed the right to do so; by refusing to defer, it deprived the authorities of authority itself. How did you "join" the movement? An old-fashioned question from unhip reporters and congressmen, to which the answer was: You put your body on the line. Actions were believed to be the guarantees and preconditions of ideas. The New Left's first raison d'être was to take actions which testified not only to the existence of injustice but to the imperative—and possibility—of fighting it. The second was to take action in common, and to constitute, in here-and-now community, the future commonweal itself. First, though, came the decision. The movement was not going to take evil lying down—this practical moralism was a good part of the movement's appeal. As many studies have shown, most of the movement's young people, black or white, took their parents' liberal or radical values seriously. They tended to think that, in succeeding, their parents had failed—some by giving up, some by settling for material rewards, some by beating their heads against stone walls. Now they wanted to live out what their parents had repressed or abandoned.

This generation was haunted by history. They had been taught that political failure or apathy can have the direst consequences; they had extracted the lesson that the fate of the world is not something automatically to be entrusted to authorities. The red-diaper babies among them were often especially eager not to be cowed; their own passivity might confirm their parents' defeats. The black students, whose parents and teachers had stood up firmly and quietly against the humiliations and terrors of white supremacy, had felt strong enough to stop putting up with the Jim Crow their parents had been forced to eat. The Jews—but not the Jews alone—were not going to walk into any more gas chambers, or see any other good Germans go on about their business. All wanted to redeem their parents' ideals in the face of their parents' failures. All breathed the intellectual air of existentialism: action might not avail, but one is responsible for choosing. And so, from under the dead hand of history, they leaped to a paradoxical conclusion: that history was alive and open. Once touched by the example of others taking history into their own hands—there, Cubans, and here, in the American South, blacks—they took the leap of faith expressed in the words of one civil rights song:

One man's hands can't tear a prison down
Two men's hands can't tear a prison down
But if two plus two plus fifty make a million
We'll see that day come round
We'll see that day come round.

Action in common was not just a means, it was the core of the movement's identity. An astonishing break with the mood of the Fifties, which
counseled adjustment, acceptance, and moderation at every turn. In this
sense, the New Left had a practice and a spirit before—or more than—it
ever had an ideology. At its luminous best, what the movement did was
stamped with imagination. The sit-in, for example, was a powerful tactic
partly because the act itself was unexceptionable. What were the
Greensboro students doing, after all, but sitting at a lunch counter, trying
to order a hamburger or a cup of coffee? They did not petition the
authorities, who, in any case, would have paid no heed; in strict Gandhian
fashion, they asserted that they had a right to sit at the counter by sitting
at it, and threw the burden of disruption onto the upholders of white
supremacy. Instead of saying that segregation ought to stop, they acted as
if segregation no longer existed. That was the definitive movement style,
squarely in the American grain, harking back to Thoreau's idea of civil
disobedience, to the utopian communards' idea of establishing the good
society right here and now—but also to the pragmatists' insistence that
experience is the measure of knowledge, and the do-it-yourselfers' (and
entrepreneurs'!) belief in getting down to business.

UNEASY IN AN ANTEROOM IN CAMELOT

Small groups of scouts cracked the self-satisfaction of the affluent society and
declared that history-making was their business. Now this spirit moved
on to the issue to end all issues: the Bomb hovering just over the horizon.
If it was possible to act on behalf of racial equality and civil liberties,
wasn't there a chance that collective action could prevent the ultimate
catastrophe?

Mickey Flacks, then a student at the City College of New York and
later one of the early SDS cadre, recalls that in May 1960 someone—not
the old-line left-wing student groups she knew—called a campus
demonstration against a civil defense take-cover drill. She expected that
"the usual suspects" would show up to be counted. To her amazement,
hundreds stayed aboveground to demonstrate. When a dean appeared to
collect the offenders' registration cards, the demonstrators, instead of
running away, crowded around him to make sure *their* cards were
included. The Old Left remnants on campus had been fighting to keep

their membership lists secret from the administration; here were students insisting on giving out their names!

More underground streams were surfacing. For years the Bomb had been invulnerable to normal politics. Some liberals had poked away at the usual clogged channels. During the 1956 presidential campaign, Senator Hubert Humphrey held hearings on disarmament; a few weeks later, candidate Adlai Stevenson proposed a moratorium on bomb tests, only to be savaged by President Eisenhower and the nation's editorial writers. When the Russians launched the first intercontinental ballistic missile and Sputnik, in 1957, they blasted the national pride and stoked a national panic. Liberals flailed away, helpless to arrest the momentum of the arms race.

Enter the spirit of direct action. Small knots of New York pacifists, intermixed with avant-garde artists and intellectuals, demonstrated against civil defense drills and bomb tests as far back as 1955, sometimes getting arrested in the course of their moral witness. In 1956, the onetime Trotskyist turned pacifist A. J. Muste pulled together a group to publish the monthly *Liberation,* which pieced together a synthesis of Gandhian nonviolence and "Third Camp" plague-on-both-their-houses socialism. The editorial board, which included Dave Dellinger and Bayard Rustin, worked out editorial positions and action plans at the same meetings. In 1958, Muste also founded the Committee for Nonviolent Action (CNVA), a network of pacifists who in 1958 and 1959 tried to sail small boats into Pacific bomb-test zones and ritualistically climbed over the fences of missile bases. A more respectable opposition formed among liberal celebrities and intellectuals: A newspaper ad against bomb tests late in 1957 led to a blue-ribbon National Committee for a SANE Nuclear Policy, which spawned some active local chapters.

A variety of well-known writers also took cognizance of the Bomb. John Kenneth Galbraith expressed a larger intellectual gloom when he wrote, early in *The Affluent Society:* "No student of social matters in these days can escape feeling how precarious is the existence of that with which he deals. . . . The unearthly light of a handful of nuclear explosions would signal [Western man's] return to utter deprivation if, indeed, he survived at all." Galbraith's Bomb was the threat to the affluent society, while Allen Ginsberg's was its extension, Moloch's phallic instrument: "America when will we end the human war?/Go fuck yourself with your atomic bomb." Was the problem of nuclear weapons rooted in bad political-military strategy or a fundamentally wrong-thinking civilization? Galbraith's Bomb and Ginsberg's, the reformist and the radical challenge, later quarreled for imaginative possession of the ban-the-bomb movement.

Student sentiment quickened. In 1958, as thousands in Great Britain marched on the nuclear base at Aldermaston, a Student SANE formed in the United States. In the spring of 1959, the American Friends Service

Committee spun off a midwestern Student Peace Union, which the next year went national with a grand total of 150 members scattered among fifty campuses. By 1962 the SPU numbered 2,000, by 1963, 4,000. Even aloof Harvard had a Student SANE chapter in 1959–60, my freshman year, albeit one so quiet I never heard of it at the time. Still, Student SANE and the SPU mobilized only a small fraction of the subsurface anxiety. Even where the student groups failed to reach, there were new tremors. I was one who felt them.

Back in Cambridge for the 1960–61 school year after my summer with Monroe Calculating Machines and Madeleine, I discovered I was breathing different air, and not for private reasons alone. Although John F. Kennedy was outdoing Richard Nixon in sounding alarms about a purported "missile gap," dissidents were taking heart from the impending change of administration. Walking through Harvard Square, I saw a poster tacked on a telephone pole. The Committee for a SANE Nuclear Policy was sponsoring a rally October 1 at the Boston Arena starring Erich Fromm, the liberal Governor G. Mennen ("Soapy") Williams of Michigan, and Steve Allen, with music by Pete Seeger and Joan Baez. The previous year, I might have passed such a notice with barely a glance, but this one was irresistible. Several of my friends, who had also gotten through freshman year without strong political feelings (even about the southern sit-ins), were independently planning to go. Boston SANE was reviving too. Many of the new leaders, graduates of Brandeis now studying at Harvard, had been inspired by the recent Woolworth's pickets in support of the southern sit-ins. "After all," one later wrote, "if one could march for Negro rights, why not for disarmament as well?" That August, SANE began sending soapbox speakers to the Boston Common during rush hour. (Passersby yelled "Where's Castro?"; "Go back to Russia"; "You aren't real Americans"; "Draft dodgers"—and occasionally "That takes guts" and "Keep it up—I'm with you.")

The night of October 1, the arena was jammed with six thousand people. Somebody threw an egg at Steve Allen. Soapy Williams said that John F. Kennedy was on the side of peace—which, from talks with Madeleine and another red-diaper friend, and from reading the *Guardian,* I doubted. SANE gave everyone a packet of readings (including an excerpt from C. Wright Mills's *The Causes of World War III*) and a button: a black X over a mushroom cloud.

The next day, on the serving line at Quincy House, I was wearing the button, and a stranger with an unplaceable accent (southern Indiana, as it turned out) suggested I join him for lunch. Thus was I organized, imposingly enough by a senior. His name was Robert Weil and he was the chairman of Tocsin, a new Harvard-Radcliffe peace group whose idea, as best I could make out, was not to take positions but to expedite whatever projects its members wanted to undertake. Weil himself was a pacifist who had taken part in a CNVA protest, but Tocsin itself was not pacifist.

The name notwithstanding (an alarm bell of the French Revolution), it was not in any sense radical either. Indeed, the group had no particular position on the rights and wrongs of Cold War and military issues. I found the group's agnosticism strangely appealing; it was an ingenious way of catering to the prevailing style of tough-minded Harvard individualism. Weil told me Tocsin was sending carloads of students to Vermont to work for the incumbent congressman, William Meyer, a forester and, of all things, a pacifist who had been elected with a handful of other peaceniks in the Democratic wave of 1958. The next thing I knew, I was on my way to Brattleboro (in a station wagon belonging to David Riesman, one of Tocsin's faculty advisers) for a weekend of knocking on doors.

The contact with actual citizens was bracing, and I agreed to organize subsequent expeditions to Vermont. Came November, Meyer lost badly, but who thought we were going to turn the arms race around overnight? Tocsin made me feel useful, gave me good company, books to read, intellectual energy. I was boosted onto the executive committee, dazzled to find myself among articulate juniors and seniors. An endearing crowd they were, quintessentially Harvard, several of them preppy, prematurely serious and whimsical at the same time, like Fitzgerald characters mysteriously outfitted with a social conscience. It was as if they had been born, raised, and schooled to talk sense into the thick heads of power, if not themselves to rule. During summers, while I was practicing mathematics for large corporations, they were off to Africa to teach refugees or practice journalism, contracting malaria and coming under gunfire, all in good causes. What we had in common, this seventeen-year-old son of Bronx high school teachers and the children of corporate executives and newspaper editors, was that we felt not only endangered but insulted when power behaved stupidly.

After all, Harvard in 1960 was fully—and smugly—aware of its proximity to power. During the era of (as *The Harvard Crimson* always called him) John F. Kennedy '40, Tocsin thought we had a right too to expect that now, at last, intelligence was going to reign. More than a few of the faculty were shuttling to Washington; Henry Kissinger, professor of government, taught seminars on defense policy and was in the habit of pronouncing, "Everything is more complex than it seems," which some of us liked to render, "Everything is more complex than it *is*." The Tocsin leadership set out to master the technical arguments well enough to play in the big leagues. When we decided to hold an all-day "walk" to express "concern" about bomb tests and the arms race in general ("walk" sounded more genteel than "march"), only forty Tocsin members, in eight groups of five, were permitted to be official "walkers." To prepare, we spent weeks in study groups poring through learned arguments about inspectable test bans, minimum deterrents, first- and second-strike capabilities. Our meticulously argued leaflet got some unofficial help from the incoming president's science-adviser-to-be, Jerome Wiesner, a family friend of our vice chairman, Peter Goldmark. Good Harvard-Radcliffe boys and girls, we behaved as if we lived in a community of reason.

The walk, on December 6, was a huge success. A thousand students and a few faculty wore blue armbands to signal their sympathy. At lunch tables all over Harvard, students debated the issues we'd posed; a demonstration was a novelty, like a tornado in Massachusetts. Three of our leaders flew off to Washington to visit with friendly congressmen and deliver our proposals for a test ban to State Department officials. Samuel Beer, professor of government and ADA chairman, addressed our rally and anointed us. Outside our rally, a group of right-wingers hung a long banner quoting Bertrand Russell: "I'D RATHER CRAWL TO MOSCOW ON MY KNEES THAN DIE IN A NUCLEAR WAR." (They were members of Young Americans for Freedom, organized that September at William F. Buckley's family manor in Connecticut.) We felt the double thrill of having enemies along with friends. And I crossed a personal divide. My parents found out what I was doing with my Harvard education and were not pleased. I spent hours disputing with my father. Eventually he said my arguments mostly made sense, but I shouldn't be the one to be acting on them. I felt vindicated.

Tocsin's inner circle, like a cabinet in exile, was saturated with politics. We devoured books and articles both polemical and technical. Teetering between the two, I was swept up by C. Wright Mills's radical critique of the Cold War—his argument that "the balance of blame" was shifting from East to West, in *The Causes of World War III*. Still an aspiring mathematician, if only by default, I was stirred by Robert Jungk's cautionary tale about the Manhattan Project, *Brighter Than a Thousand Suns,* with its implicit call for the social responsibility of science. I grew partial to Gandhi. Yet moralism pure and simple felt lame, so I threw myself into practical Tocsin. I spent days compiling notes on treatises by Herman Kahn and other heavy thinkers of arms race theology. Tocsin deferred to professors who were lobbying for sweet reason. We did the leg work to solicit signatures for faculty ads against civil defense and the arms race. (There was one chastening and memorable moment. The famously iconoclastic literary historian Perry Miller refused to sign one mild ad, grumbling that things had gone too far, we wouldn't do any good. I was shocked—both that the great man thought things had gone so far, and that he would weasel out of signing.) At lunch tables, over many cups of coffee, we debated "the balance of blame" and the intricacies of nuclear strategy. And then Washington jolted us out of balance at the Bay of Pigs.

In our circle there were varying degrees of sympathy for Fidel Castro. C. Wright Mills's cri de coeur, *Listen, Yankee!*, made an impact, but the view that impressed me most was that of Robert Paul Wolff, a young philosophy instructor and the only faculty member at Harvard in 1961 who taught the work of Marx in a rigorous way. Wolff, something of an anarchist, visited Cuba and reported that the revolution had accomplished great good for the majority—even though it was not a society that intellectuals would want to live in. We were, like Wolff, sympathetic to revolutionary change but disabused of illusions about paradise abroad. We applauded I. F. Stone when he came to Cambridge to speak with unillusioned sympathy about Castro's Cuba, and I subscribed to his beacon *Weekly,* which taught me, as it taught many of my contemporaries, that the government lied.* I liked the fact that Stone was alert to Fidel's authoritarian tendencies; he had an eye for the tragic as the United States mobilized against what President Kennedy called a "dagger" ninety miles off Florida.

Even Harvard's dissidents took the Kennedy administration personally. To the social-democratic and left-liberal instructors, the Bay of Pigs was not just a crime, it was a violation of the implied contract binding John F. Kennedy '40 to Harvard. A group of young instructors and graduate students (among them Wolff, Martin Peretz, and *Dissent* affiliate Michael Walzer, all teachers of mine) organized a rally against the invasion. Three hundred students heard history professor H. Stuart Hughes call upon his former colleague Arthur Schlesinger, Jr., to resign from the administration. The spectacle of Adlai Stevenson lying at the United Nations and Schlesinger serving as a figurehead liberal was sickening. To make things worse, we worried (as did Norman Mailer in an influential piece in *The Village Voice*) that Kennedy's truculence was forcing the daring Castro to subordinate himself to the Soviet Union.

So my friends and I grew steadily more estranged from Kennedy liberalism, and yet without sidling up to the Soviet Union.** Reading with horror about Lenin and Leninism, I was coming to think that the rebel's task was necessarily quixotic, bittersweet: to work against the old regime, and then, after a brief celebration, to go into opposition against the new. Permanent opposition was the rebel's way to avoid the corruptions of power, remain an underdog. Both principle and practicality demanded that we keep a distance from the peace propaganda of the USSR. In April 1961, Tocsin decided on an act of indisputable evenhandedness: We organized a caravan to New York City and picketed the Soviet Mission to the United Nations, urging them to act constructively at the Geneva test-ban talks and specifically to accept the principle of inspection. There were people in the Tocsin ranks, mostly red-diaper babies, who were offended; one friend screamed at me the night before,

---

*Stone says that when he gave speeches at Harvard in the Fifties, his audiences were older townspeople, veteran leftists—and barely a student. But students were very much in evidence in 1961.

**And when *Dissent* published a pamphlet by Michael Walzer attacking the CIA but supporting a democratic radical alternative to Castro, I shared their apprehensions about Castro but thought it naïve in the extreme to expect the United States, with its imperial history in the Caribbean, to install a radical democrat in Havana. And what gave the United States—"we" in Walzer's language—the right to try?

like a sloganeer in a bad Cold War melodrama, "The Soviet Union is the greatest hope for peace in the world!" Twenty-five of us picketed the Russians, to no apparent effect. At least we could say that we'd "told it to the Russians."

Some of the Tocsin leadership, unabashed reformers, felt like the Cambridge outpost of enlightened Washington; others, reformers by default, myself among them, thought ourselves their left flank. At times we were seduced by the prospect of influence, at times we simply played our strongest hand. But in either case, although we did not think of it this way, we were playing our part in that postwar rapprochement of government and higher education which Kennedy had refined to a mystique. At the highest levels of Camelot, the idea was that will and intelligence would be united and placed at the service of a reinvigorated superpower. The arms race would be made more efficient, counterinsurgency leaner and tougher: reason would be more muscular, more manly, while manliness would become wittier, more elegant. Robert S. McNamara, the former Harvard Business School professor with the steel-rimmed glasses, was technocratic reason and cynical vigor (to use one of Kennedy's favorite words) in person; we saw ourselves as counterwill and counterintelligence. Harvard professors—not least the liberals and arms controllers we were close to—were commuting to Washington so frequently to consult for the administration that they might as well have organized a private air shuttle service; the Tocsin high command constituted itself the student counterpart. More than once we made expeditions to Washington to meet with young low-level officials and friendly congressional assistants who formed an informal left-liberal caucus in Washington. We wanted to know what we could do to make a difference, and these might be the people to tell us. It was heady stuff for world-savers still in their teens, getting taken seriously in middling-high places.

Heady too for a generation of liberals then in their mid-twenties, spotted throughout the Kennedy bureaucracies, quickly outgrowing their own early hopes, isolated in the middle levels of power, alarmed about the drift of American policy. Garry Wills has argued that Kennedy and his immediate circle operated as "guerrillas," trying to outmaneuver their own bureaucracy; the young liberals were an outmanned version of the same, jockeying around the margins of Camelot, testing the limits of rationality and conscience. We were their naïve but promising younger political brothers. One of these bright and disaffected young men was Marcus Raskin, an assistant to McGeorge Bundy on the staff of the National Security Council, maneuvering to stop Kennedy's civil defense program; we needed to run a gauntlet of phone clearances to get to see him in the Executive Office Building, next to the White House. Another was the legislative assistant to the liberal Representative Robert Kastenmeier of Wisconsin, Gar Alperovitz, who urged us to try to mobilize the sleeping American public to pressure the administration to move toward disarmament initiatives. That Raskin, Alperovitz, and others in their circle took us seriously swelled our heads, of course; it also encouraged us to think strategically about just what we might accomplish. No pure and simple moralists were we; the very chance of having an effect was already a transport to the realm of real politics.

From many discussions in Cambridge and Washington we distilled a rudimentary political analysis; having a political analysis certified us as serious. (All the way through the Sixties, an "analysis" was a ticket to the elite world of movement cadres. It was a sign that one was not beholden to authorities, that one was potentially an authority oneself. To be without an "analysis" was to be dependent on those who "had" one.) Our analysis was this: The American and Soviet elites were divided between pacific and belligerent sectors. The two great powers were wired together: a rise in the fortunes of one side's belligerents would boost the influence of the belligerents on the other side, and vice versa. Kennedy was a political animal; without pressure from his Left, he would remain the prisoner of the military, the Dixiecrats, and what David Riesman called the "bomber liberals," of whom Senator Henry Jackson of Washington State and Boeing was the archetype. From this analysis, a strategy followed. If mainstream Americans—in churches, unions, business and civic groups, high schools—could be mobilized, liberal members of Congress would no longer feel constrained by their retrograde constituents, and Kennedy would have "permission" to end the arms race. We were educators, "disseminating 'downward' and suggesting (and prodding) 'upward.'" Alperovitz impressed this strategy upon us so forcefully, we dubbed it "alperovitzing." It harnessed our energy and desire to be useful to our sense of indispensability.

Back in Cambridge in the fall of 1961, we set up a speaker's bureau and did a bit of alperovitzing, but the world was getting too dangerous too fast, and we felt impatient. At their Vienna summit in June, Kennedy and Khrushchev had come to loggerheads. Tension mounted over divided Berlin. Aggressive moves on one side generated aggressive countermoves on the other. In July, Kennedy called for a crash fallout-shelter program, boosted the military budget, doubled draft calls, and called up the army reserves. In August, the Berlin Wall went up and the Russians announced they would resume nuclear tests in the atmosphere. Kennedy gave his imprimatur to a *Life* magazine feature on civil defense, and the United States started testing. Some of us started fidgeting for direct action.

We weren't the only ones to feel the pull. It was widely reported that the fallout from bomb tests was poisoning grasslands, lacing cow's milk with strontium 90 and other radioactive isotopes. A group of professional women in Washington, D.C., circulated a statement against bomb tests and for disarmament. Galvanized, some fifty thousand women demonstrated around the country against the resumption of tests on November 1, 1961. (Many Tocsin people and our Brandeis Student SANE counterparts joined the Boston-area march.) This was the beginning of the

Women Strike for Peace movement, and a harbinger of a still more profound women's movement to come.

Now it felt less like giving Kennedy "permission" to push past the Cold War impasse, more like letting him know he was going to have to reckon with a political force to his left. Angry and more than a little desperate, Peter Goldmark and I decided to organize a march on Washington as soon as possible: February 16–17, 1962. Tocsin set out to improvise a political alliance.

First we knit together a Boston Area Coordinating Committee in which we shared leadership with the Brandeis Student SANE people. The two political cultures could not have been more different. The Brandeis leaders were red-diaper babies; they counterbalanced the Harvard politics of pragmatic maneuver. Brandeis was ensconced in radical history. Radical émigré professors of various stripes were conspicuous. By 1961, Brandeis already had seen a half-decade of left-wing politics, much of it organized around the followings of rival professors, especially the social democrat Irving Howe and the revolutionary Marxist Herbert Marcuse. While the Tocsin elite was discussing the intricacies of inspection systems for a test ban, Brandeis SANE was passionately debating responsibility for the Cold War. The red-diaper babies at Brandeis lived—as one of them put it years later—"in a we/they world of political paranoia"; in their eyes, the "high-powered" Tocsin group "moved around as if knighted."

Next, needing a national base, we talked the national Student Peace Union into cosponsorship, along with Student SANE and a minute group called Students for a Democratic Society. At planning meetings in New York, the War Resisters League's staff diplomat, David McReynolds, successfully brokered our differences in style—we respectable, though more ambivalent about Kennedy's power than showed from outside; SPU, with its roots in the "Third Camp" wing of the Old Left, forthrightly moralistic and wholeheartedly estranged from Kennedy liberalism. We insisted from the start on not just picketing the White House but lobbying officials—to "prove our credibility," as a later lingo put it. A skeptical SPU, properly suspicious of our accommodating politics, went along. Respectful of selected elders, we accumulated an ecumenical list of notable sponsors (many of them literary lights, such was our bent) and printed it on our stationery: the likes of Hannah Arendt, W. H. Auden (who handwrote me that he supported unilateral disarmament), Van Wyck Brooks, Henry Steele Commager, Norman Cousins, Jules Feiffer, Robert Hutchins, Alfred Kazin, Robert Lowell, A. J. Muste, Eleanor Roosevelt, Bayard Rustin, Ben Shahn, Norman Thomas, Mark Van Doren, Richard Wilbur, and Edmund Wilson.

Passionate as was the impetus, the tone of the enterprise remained moderate. I straddled a political divide. Interminable Harvard-Brandeis meetings, and the influential counsel of Michael Walzer (my "section man" in a social science course), produced the official "call": opposition to the resumption of nuclear tests and to the civil defense program; an appeal for "unilateral initiatives," tension-reducing moves, like the removal of

American missile bases in Turkey, which the United States could make in hopes that the Russians would reciprocate; support for economic aid to the Third World, the better to bolster alternatives to Soviet-style Communism. The statement (neither widely read nor cited in the press) ended up reading as if it had been stitched together—which it had.

The two-day demonstration drew—by various accounts—between four thousand and eight thousand students to Washington in a snowstorm; we had hoped for a thousand or two. It was the largest White House demonstration since the effort to stop the execution of the Rosenbergs in 1953. Photos reveal earnest short-haired young men wearing jackets and ties, even while picketing the White House, marching to Arlington National Cemetery to lay a wreath on the Tomb of the Unknown Soldier, and rallying at the Washington Monument to hear Norman Thomas, nuclear physicist William Higinbotham, and United Auto Workers official Emil Mazey. A reporter from *The Harvard Crimson* drew a contrast to the "traditional 'peace' activity," presumably in the style of Student SANE, with its "old images—beards, guitars, a political philosophy tinged with the rosy hue of the nondemocratic left." The approved picket signs threw some of Kennedy's slogans back at him: "Let us call a truce to terror"; "Neither Red nor Dead but alive and free." Another said: "Mr. Kennedy: We Support Your Words, Now Give Us a Chance to Support Your Actions." One hundred fifty Young Americans for Freedom counterpicketed with "Better Brave than Slave" and "A Test a Day Keeps the Commies Away."

By prearrangement, delegations lobbied most of the members of Congress and a considerable number of administration officials. A few dozen of us were suffering through the pomposities and irrelevancies of middle-level bureaucrats in the State Department auditorium at the moment when President Kennedy, with his fine eye for public relations, dispatched a liveried White House butler with a huge urn of hot coffee to the demonstrators picketing in the snow—who proceeded to debate whether drinking the President's coffee amounted to selling out. (The pragmatists won the debate, drank the coffee, and felt heartened by Kennedy's gesture. Over at the State Department, I felt chagrined. We didn't want to be patronized; we wanted Kennedy to meet with us, not keep us warm. But of course I was already warm.)* Later, a group of us met in the White House basement with national security adviser McGeorge Bundy, Kennedy speechwriter Ted Sorensen, and science adviser Jerome Wiesner, in what felt to me at the time like a dialogue of the moral with the deaf. Bundy, trying to sway us toward the strategy of creating "permission," said he appreciated the counterweight we had thrown against "the Cold Warriors," but defended the White House's fallout-shelter program and invoked the hoary realist's maxim, "Politics is the art of the possible."

*Jules Feiffer appreciated the ironical position Kennedy's gesture put us in. He later sent me an unpublished cartoon in which a picket carries a picket sign that reads "COFFEE."

Demonstrators who remembered the benighted Fifties were delighted with the turnout, encouraged by the access to government offices and the occasional ripple of agreement. But some of us felt the official reactions had ranged from "barely concealed condescension to political dismissal." Peter Goldmark grumbled aloud that the officials "had not even bothered to read our policy statement." Now what? In stray late-night moments during months of day-in, day-out work, we had fretted about what we called "the February 18th problem"—what to do next. For a chosen few, semi-influence still beckoned: In March, after Kennedy decided to resume nuclear testing, Jerome Wiesner, the key test-ban campaigner in the White House, asked for our help, whereupon Peter Goldmark and I wrote a crisp, mild memo (try harder in the negotiations, and stop waving the big stick); Wiesner said he took it to a meeting of the National Security Council. More heady stuff, yet nothing seemed to follow. We had apprenticed to insiders, fine-tuned our expertise, made the right friends, tried to influence the right people, spoken their language—now where were the signs that knowledge meant power? I read avidly, even wrote for, the erudite *Newsletter* of the Council for Correspondence, published under David Riesman's aegis, but the academics who wrote there were also displaying various shades of bleakness.

I was finding it harder to keep my personal truce between two warring sensibilities. More and more I acted reformist but felt radical. Even as a part-time insider, peering inside the world of power, I was flooded with existential alienation. I read technical treatises about nuclear strategies; at the same time I read some Marx and was impressed. I read romantic novels about wartime resistance movements in Europe, and wrote a long paper attacking the idea that there could be such a thing as "the national interest." I thought—and argued in print—that the entire structure of deterrence was "bound to fail," and that it "must be condemned not merely because some upper-story bricks are loose, but because the foundation is rotten." At the very same time, I thought—and also argued in print—that a minimum nuclear deterrent would be less dangerous than the so-called counterforce strategy for building up the American missile force, aiming at Russian bases, and preparing to fight an "acceptable" nuclear war. In a paper I wrote that summer for the Liberal Study Group cosponsored by SDS and Campus Americans for Democratic Action at the National Student Association (sign of the times, the name of this lobby and the nature of this coalition), I repeated the argument for a minimum deterrent, and tried to persuade activists to prime themselves to win arguments about nuclear strategy.

I ask myself now, how could I think both these ways at once? I still saw hope in a strategy of reforms, and none in any alternative. To set out to remake America root and branch seemed a sure path to irrelevance. There were radical graduate students at Berkeley (Robert Scheer, Maurice Zeitlin, and David Horowitz among them) beginning to publish a journal called, indeed, *Root and Branch*, but in Cambridge's reformist air that seemed romantic and imprecise. If radical transformation was no more than a pious wish, the only choice was to attach my romantic feelings about resistance and fundamental change to the tiny dramas of reformism, push them to their limit, and be glad for the chance. Perhaps a more *methodical* approach to reform would work. . . . At the beginning of the summer of 1962, for example, Marcus Raskin told me that a demonstration against civil defense in front of the White House in the first few months after May 1961 (when Kennedy first broached the subject) might have succeeded in scotching the program. I thought this important enough to detail in my journal, adding: "Best to come in at *start* of (long-running) decision like . . . [civil defense]—then your attitude is 'part of the calculus.'" Then came Raskin's larger conclusion: "You can't meddle with what JFK considers 'national interest.'" Then my disgusted conclusion: "But—eating away at the edges won't give you anything but a stomach ache." I argued with myself: Wasn't it best to walk the last mile for practical reforms? Raskin thought so, but that year, blasted for dangerous liberalism by congressional Republicans, he was forced out of his job. How did you know when you had reached the last mile?

For me, two milestones, one private, one excruciatingly public, made radical politics appear necessary, even possible. In 1962, one of our young insider Washington friends—Arthur Waskow, another former assistant to Representative Kastenmeier—invited me to be a summer research fellow at a modest Washington think-tank called the Peace Research Institute. Waskow was writing a book (eventually published as *The Worried Man's Guide to World Peace*) about how the peace movement could change government policies; my job was to interview officials, congresspeople, journalists, and lobbyists, and gather their wisdom. One day Waskow and I went to the Pentagon and made our way through the tangle of corridors to interview Adam Yarmolinsky, McNamara's special assistant for civil defense. To my horror, there was a child's drawing of a battleship taped to the glass in Yarmolinsky's bookcase. A small thing, no doubt normal in a capital obsessed by the mystique of PT-109, yet it meant to me, somehow, that clever arguments were beside the point, that the people in power really took their games for granted. No matter if they spoke with rigor and erudition. No matter if they were blessed—like Adam Yarmolinsky, the son of two eminent writers—with impeccable liberal credentials.* As the diminutive Yarmolinsky stood behind his desk and defended the administration's civil defense program, the world went obvious on me. *Men such as this were not going to be persuaded to be sensible.* They were grotesque, these clever and confident men, they were unbudgeable, their language was evasion, their rationality unreasonable, and therefore they were going to have to be dislodged.

If ever I might have wanted to fashion myself into a hipster playing it cool through long rounds of office politics to boost my chances of influence, someday, in the corridors of Camelot—if ever I had felt twinges

*Yarmolinsky had also organized the anti-Communist caucus of the American Veterans Committee after World War II.

of that impulse, I abandoned them that day. I left the Pentagon a convinced outsider.

In the short run, what could this mean if not electoral politics? At the end of the summer, I spent a day working for Village Independent Democrats in Greenwich Village (their antimachine ticket was headed by a liberal named Ed Koch). I rang doorbells for the peace-minded Congressman William Fitts Ryan in upper Manhattan. Back at Harvard for the fall, and now elected chairman of Tocsin, I was thrilled that we could fill an auditorium for an introductory meeting and pull in 130 members. Many of the Tocsin faithful turned out to campaign for Stuart Hughes, who had decided to run for the Senate against the family scions Ted Kennedy and George Cabot Lodge—the standard-bearer of *our* Harvard against *theirs* of the upper-crust management styles and Green Berets. But although I liked Hughes himself and his unilateralist politics, I couldn't get excited about his prospects. Hughes's political base was flimsy. It was heartening that delegates to the state AFL-CIO convention gave our debonair candidate a warm reception; I heard black voters sound sympathetic during one canvass in Boston; but whites in a different district said they'd never heard of *any* of the candidates, even Kennedy.

A more patient soul might have thought that peace campaigning needed time. But the movement had already acquired a history, and with it a loathing of repetition. Meetings were dull, and knocking on doors, after the initial frisson of an encounter with "ordinary people," unrewarding. Moreover, my friends and I were imprisoned by our own recruiting strategy. The louder we sounded the alarm—the veritable tocsin—the more frightening seemed the apocalypse we were warning against, to us if no one else. For two solid years now, we had been living with the sense that apocalypse was hanging just over the horizon. We had immersed ourselves in the official speeches and congressional transcripts and technical papers in which the experts routinely, banally, rehearsed the world's catastrophe. Kennedy's and Khrushchev's bellicose maneuvers were the drumbeat of our one and only youth. The sense of crisis seemed interminable. A movement is a passion: it has to keep moving or it withers. We may have been on the move, but it felt to me like impasse.

My political equilibrium was ready to tip: ready for the Cuban missile crisis, my second radical milestone.

"DESTRUCTIVE CRITICISM OF A DESTRUCTIVE SYSTEM"

In the official mythic version, the missile crisis was at once the world's climactic moment and the supreme test for the Kennedy high command: serious men in shirtsleeves debating through all-night meetings, cultivating the right toughness and the right moderation, proving themselves strenuous enough for the nuclear age and ourselves lucky enough to have deserved, for "one brief shining moment," such steady hands. This is supposed to have been the moment when the nuclear age proved viable. Apocalypse was, after all, averted. Kennedy resisted the counsel that would have bombed the missile sites or invaded Cuba; his precision was vindicated by Khrushchev's decision to withdraw his missiles. When the chips were down, the superpowers wised up. But the hindsight is pat, a luxury. Another ending was possible, the ending of all endings, and then we would not be alive, most likely, to challenge the official myth.

Kennedy gave his "quarantine" (better called by a less medicinal term, blockade) speech on Monday night, October 22, 1962. For six days, time was deformed, everyday life suddenly dwarfed and illuminated, as if by the glare of an explosion that had not yet taken place. Until the news was broadcast that Khrushchev was backing down, the country lived out the awe and truculence and simmering near-panic always implicit in the thermonuclear age. At colleges in New England, some students piled into their cars and took off for Canada until further notice.

In the basement of Quincy House, the Tocsin core watched Kennedy's speech on television, then launched into—what else?—a meeting. For the first time, we were seriously divided. According to the dominant Tocsin outlook, which I shared, this was just the sort of emergency the arms race was bound to produce. Khrushchev's missiles were analogous to the American missiles in Turkey; they were a shortcut to catch up with the Americans. Since the missiles represented no clear danger to American life and limb (the Russians already had ICBMs, after all), the blockade was indefensible. The Marxists, principally red-diaper babies, who had not spoken up as a bloc before, said the heart of the matter was that Khrushchev was trying to protect *Cuba*. How could we oppose Kennedy's blockade, they wanted to know, without at the same time rising to the defense of the Cuban revolution, which was his true target?

I think I opposed the Marxists that night—by temperament and politics, I wanted to find the narrowest possible grounds (and therefore largest possible political base) for opposing Kennedy. But the argument from the Left gnawed at me. Kennedy's move *was* out of all proportion to any reasonable fears of Khrushchev's missiles. Kennedy was furious *at Cuba* for defying him. I had my critical sympathy with Castro's Cuba, but until that night I had succeeded in keeping it sealed away from Tocsin. Revolutionary Cuba touched my heart; Tocsin was about mind and effectiveness.

The phone brought the news: the national hysteria made protest both necessary and dangerous. Gar Alperovitz called from Washington to say we had to demonstrate if civil liberties were going to be preserved. At Indiana University, a handful of antiadministration picketers were heckled, chased by a mob of two thousand students, finally forced to take refuge in a library. At Cornell, two professors were forced off the platform by stones and clumps of dirt. At the University of Minnesota, professors were splattered by eggs and oranges. In Ann Arbor, Michigan, four hundred demonstrators organized by SDS and Women for Peace passed out a leaflet urging an end to the "game of Chicken, with mankind on the bumpers." Condemning the Russians for their provocative move, and urging that the missiles be withdrawn, they also demanded that the United States guarantee Cuba's safety and accept the "inevitable revolutions coming throughout Latin America in the Sixties." Six hundred students jeered at them, hurled eggs and stones (at Tom Hayden among other speakers), and blockaded their line of march. (A few of the attackers were so revolted by the attack, they joined the protesters.) In major cities there was virtually no dissent. In Atlanta, for example, the grand total of demonstrators, mostly civil rights activists, was thirty; one of them, Alice Lynd, was fired from her child-care job as a result.

What was Tocsin to do? We debated whether to cosponsor a Boston-wide open-air rally on Saturday—assuming we should live till Saturday—and a Tocsin member passed me a note headlined: "DEMONSTRATION IS WRONG!" (History mocks our innocence: two years later this conservative became assistant national secretary of SDS.) Our main response, though, was a Wednesday-night rally. Stuart Hughes was one obvious choice of speaker. A friend brought up the name of Barrington Moore, Jr., who held a research appointment, taught only seminars, and was reputed to be something of a Marxist éminence grise. Moore sent back word that he would be happy to speak and, moreover, wished to have forty-five minutes.

Across the street from our rally, Martin Luther King was speaking that night in a larger hall. (We sent an emissary to him, asking him to combine the two rallies and address them jointly, but he declined.) Each rally drew a capacity crowd of a thousand or more and a larger overflow. Outside our hall, several dozen anti-Castro émigrés who had showed up late banged on the doors and windows. In one corner, right-wingers from Young Americans for Freedom hoisted black umbrellas, intimating that we were Munich-minded equivalents of Neville Chamberlain, and hissed sporadically throughout the evening.

The mysterious Barrington Moore, Jr., dressed in a three-piece suit, gold watch-chain dangling across his lean frame, looked for all the world like the Boston banker his father had been. Calmly he stood at the podium and in plain sentences dismantled my politics. Trying to take existential heart, I had stood there a few minutes earlier and rattled off the news of demonstrations around the country. Now Moore was saying, in the most reasonable of tones, that the only sensible protest was "critical exposure." "The standard pacifist reaction," he said, "stressing the horrors of war, with an appeal to the United Nations . . . is utterly inadequate. . . . It doesn't expose the roots of the situation. It merely contributes to the general mystification."

I was aghast. We had spent two nights trying to work out precise proposals to distribute on the Boston Common, as if they mattered, and here was Moore telling us that

> the attempt to make practical proposals, constructive proposals, moderate and realistic proposals, is the most unrealistic thing you can do at this point. . . . It just looks silly. In the government, they know a great many more of the facts than you do. . . . Leave the constructive alternatives to Bundy. . . . He has an interest in surviving that is probably at least as strong as ours.

We had to understand, Moore said, that the Cuban revolution was the latest in a line that began with the French revolution and continued through the Russian and the Chinese. A few years later, such grand tours of History were commonplace, but that electric night, with humanity hanging in the balance, Moore seemed to be bringing us fresh Old Testament truth. People did not say these things! We were wasting our time and dodging the truth, Moore said, unless we "face the fact that at least in regard to the backward nations, the United States is a bastion of reaction. . . . In other words, if there is a protest, to make sense, it has to take the form of destructive criticism of a destructive system." What was required to save the world, finally, were "simultaneous revolutions in the United States and the Soviet Union."

Moore was in the midst of his homily when Stuart Hughes, fresh from another speech, strode onto the stage—and inspired a standing ovation. Moore broke off his critique of pathetic, ineffectual protest, walked over to Hughes, and shook his hand warmly. No matter that Hughes, in his own talk, issued his own "concrete proposals" and called upon us to be "the loyal opposition." I was moved by the handshake; in person if not in logic, a rapprochement of critical analysis and practical politics might be possible.

Moore's ideological bomb went on exploding for days. When the rally ended, my friends and I went back to my room and stayed up for hours debating the implications of his speech. If Moore was right, what did Tocsin and its politics matter? We had put aside our romantic attachments to socialism, anarchism, resistance, and staked everything on the chimera of practicality. Now, when push came to shove, the powers in Washington—and Moscow—couldn't care less what a darling bunch of articulate college students thought. The great powers could drag the world to the brink of annihilation whenever they damned well pleased. That night, for me, Tocsin went up in smoke.

On Friday, I drove off to a Washington demonstration with Robb Burlage, a graduate student in economics full of hilarity and Texas sass, along with an SDS buddy of his and another Tocsinite, all of us ready to die a happy if premature death. (Just as we piled into Robb's '55 Chevy, a friend came up and asked if we'd heard the latest news on the radio:

Kennedy was said to have called Congress into special session. We bought a bottle of wine and spent hours telling one another the self-dramatizing stories of our lives, until, distracted, we ran out of gas just south of Baltimore.) Robb, formerly the editor of the University of Texas newspaper, was the one-man New England outpost of Students for a Democratic Society. He scouted out local talent, and dazzled us with his omnivorous intelligence, his rapidfire punning, and his knack for seeing how every wisp of political work was part of a hypothetical whole.

In Washington, we hooked up with some of the SDS inner circle from Ann Arbor: Tom and Casey Hayden, Dick and Mickey Flacks. We heard I. F. Stone tell a meeting that an invasion of Cuba was imminent and that thousands of years of civilization were hanging by a thread; we sent Fidel Castro a telegram urging him to dismantle the missiles. I felt my center of gravity shift toward SDS. There was a warmth these people exuded—a moral warmth, if that makes any sense—and I loved the clean passion in their prose. The previous spring, I had read the draft of what became their *Port Huron Statement,* had felt that their statement of values and attack on the American bleakness spoke for me (though the programmatic particulars got tedious, and I didn't read to the end); only timidity and my commitment to take up my job in Washington kept me from flying off to their convention in Michigan. In the flesh, they personified intelligence at the service of moral clarity. I wanted to be like them, with them. These exalted, clear, somehow devout souls so loved the world. . . . My most vivid memory: When we heard the joyous Saturday night radio news that Khrushchev was withdrawing the missiles and the crisis was subsiding, Mary Varela, a Catholic student activist from Boston, ran into a cathedral to give thanks. I felt as though I'd come home.

Over the next weeks, I went through the motions as chairman of Tocsin, but against the feeling that the organization's purpose was played out. My closest friends in the group were, like me, painfully aware of our nearly complete isolation from the rest of the country and our lack of power to influence the course of events. Stuart Hughes drew all of 1½ percent of the Massachusetts senatorial vote. At best, we were irrelevant; in some quarters, people like us had been assaulted as traitors. The consensus we had basted together for the February 1962 demonstration had come apart. If we were to forego the slim hope of influence on a rational Establishment, now that the apparently practical was revealed to be impractical, then what? Committed to "destructive criticism," we were also without moorings—

Except in the living idea of a student movement. The student movement itself, by default, would have to become the base of whatever potential power could be organized against the drift toward war. A month after the missile crisis, SDS held a regional conference at Harvard Divinity School: "The Role of the Student in Social Change" it was called, the quotation marks included on the indifferently mimeographed agenda, as if the writer were self-conscious about this daring and still tentative idea. A caravan of heavyweights—Al Haber, Tom Hayden, and Paul Potter—drove in from Ann Arbor, and again I was more than impressed by the caliber of these individuals: I felt graced to be in their company.

I was particularly taken by Potter, a sinew-lean midwesterner with burning globes for eyes, past vice president of the National Student Association, impeccably middle-American. Potter exuded a sense of having earned the right to every eloquent syllable he spoke with his own hard-won thoughtfulness. Looking for a safe harbor on the radical side of the political watershed, I thought these new politics must be right if someone as dignified as Paul Potter, his manner deliberate but never academic, had found fresh language to say that we and the Cuban revolutionaries were somehow fighting the same battle.* Hayden was coiled, relentless, an intellectual boxer coming out of the crouch. His acne-pitted face and quick eyes made less of an impression than the fluidity of his speech. He seemed to have read everything. Hayden's every word seemed chosen; he never hesitated, never stumbled, as he crisply assaulted the social science establishment, especially the idea of "the end of ideology" then in circulation from the influential sociologists Daniel Bell and Seymour Martin Lipset. Haber, mild and slow-spoken in a way that suggested infinite care, spoke on "American Imperialism and the Emerging Nations." (How astonishing to see these words in 1962!)

I have kept the notes I made for my own little talk on "Peace." The Barrington Moore mood is evident. We have to face up to the fact that "peace has no social base"—no social institution wants it enough. Peace requires "changing the international system, but that is, it seems, out of our hands." We would have to make ourselves "relevant" to "labor, Negroes, intellectuals"; we would have to "link issues." We would have to fight "the alienation of men from the decision-making process"; without any illusions about our strength, we would have to "struggle for the means of struggle."

It is the tone of these notes that interests me: full of yearning for a movement that could comprehend, in both senses, all the American nightmares and injustices. I had already been influenced by the idea of participatory democracy, in which, as *The Port Huron Statement* says, "the individual [should] share in those social decisions determining the quality and direction of his life," and "society [should] be organized to encourage independence in men and provide the media for their common participation." This metaphysics of participation could only have made sense if there was already an arena in which to participate—the movement itself. The idea of participatory democracy made it possible to leapfrog over the

---

*In a letter around that time, Potter wrote about the missile crisis in terms similar to mine: "What the crisis did was make clear the fact that American power had reached the point of *menace*. America had to be curbed. . . . My feelings after were that you sensed yourself as part of a tiny, but very just minority. Enormous frustration at our inability to convince people."

futility of Tocsin-style reform. If reform was blocked, the movement itself could be the point of the movement. One of SDS's slogans was, "The issues are interrelated," and I was also reflecting that. "The issues arise together and need to be addressed together": this was how Hayden put it. In Robb Burlage's weekly SDS study group, which met in the back room of a local bar, I read Paul Goodman's just-published *Growing Up Absurd* and liked its way of groping for a total analysis. There and in *The Port Huron Statement* I liked both the longing for a total explanation and the uncertainty as to what it might be.

One thing was clear: Tocsin was too confining a vessel. In February, I resigned as chairman. In my last semester before the abyss of commencement, unencumbered by the responsibility for the next demonstration and the next after that, I could finally try to think straight! In a seminar with Stuart Hughes, I was riveted by European ideological novels—among them Malraux's *Man's Hope,* de Beauvoir's *The Mandarins,* and Hermann Hesse's *Steppenwolf,* so far from being a cult book it was not yet available in paperback. I took a course on modern China, thought romantic thoughts about Mao and Chou En-lai, and especially about the 1919 student movement in which the Chinese Communist Party had originated, and also about the briefly flourishing intellectuals of the "hundred flowers" period, brutally uprooted for flowering too vigorously. I also read about the Hungarian rebels of 1956, on whom my roommate Chris Hobson was writing an undergraduate thesis; we were disgusted when over the lunch table one of the red-diaper Marxists of Quincy House tried to convince us these revolutionaries were "fascists."

I wrote earnest poems about the need to break through to some more authentic reality. I met unimaginably brave civil rights workers from SNCC and set up a rally for them at Harvard. I worked on a big Boston march in support of the southern movement. I watched police with cattle prods and dogs attack Birmingham demonstrators on television, and felt guilty about not doing enough. I went to Bogart movies (the two-week Bogart festival had become an exam-time institution at the Brattle Theatre): I was overpowered by *Casablanca,* of course, but also by *To Have and Have Not* and even the hypersentimental *Key Largo* and *Passage to Marseilles,* all allegories about the passage from cynicism to political commitment. I also loved Truffaut's *Shoot the Piano Player,* I think because it illustrated so brilliantly how things don't work out as you plan; I needed the irony to hedge my passionate bets. At Tom Hayden's urging, I visited Ann Arbor for two days, met more of the SDS group, and felt the holy communion again listening to Pete Seeger's "We Shall Overcome" in the Flacks living room. The trip cinched my decision to go to graduate school at the University of Michigan—not so much to study political science (my ostensible purpose) as to breathe the air of the SDS circle. In a last-ditch effort to yoke my expertise to my passions, I wrote a mathematics thesis called "Archetypical Mathematical Models in International Relations."

My last week in Cambridge, I wrote a paper for Stuart Hughes in the form of a playlet called "Six Characters in Search of Commitment." Figures from *Man's Hope, The Mandarins, Steppenwolf,* and *All Quiet on the Western Front* debated the urgencies of politics. My heart was with the hesitant heroes who, without illusions, even against their better judgment, chose to plunge themselves into the miserable and necessary life of society; but I also understood Harry Haller, Hesse's Steppenwolf, once an organizer against World War I, now an outsider content to live furtively in the social margins, alert to magic. I drew my epigraph from the most powerful allegory I knew: "It's still the same old story/A fight for love and glory/A case of do or die/The fundamental things apply/As time goes by."

I had come to my restlessness by my own route, but my quirk was not mine alone. All over America, little knots of students were looking for ways to forsake the predictable paths of career, propriety, family. Some were going south to work with SNCC; some into northern ghettoes, to run tutorial projects or start free schools with the Northern Student Movement; some, suspected by the "serious" movement people, into the Peace Corps; some simply *out,* to live by themselves, think, write. Without thinking about it, we all took the fat of the land for granted.

Sometime that spring, Leo Szilard, the atomic physicist who in 1939 convinced Albert Einstein to write to President Roosevelt urging a crash program to develop the atomic bomb, asked me avuncularly what I was going to do when I graduated. Appalled by Hiroshima and the arms race, Szilard had organized a fund-raising group to finance peace candidates in senatorial elections (one of his first beneficiaries was George McGovern of South Dakota). I had gotten to know Szilard when he gave a speech in Cambridge and kept in touch with him on visits to Washington. I gave him a pompous schoolboy answer about studying political science in order to understand society, blah blah blah. . . . "Don't study society," Szilard proclaimed, echoing Marx. "Change it!"

Then, in June, just after commencement, I went to the SDS convention in a camp near the Hudson River at Pine Hill, New York, and for reasons I didn't quite understand, among people I scarcely knew, but loved, in an organization with which I had identified my hopes but had never worked in, at age twenty I found myself—let myself be—elected president.

5

THE FUSED GROUP

"A BAND OF BROTHERS STANDING IN A CIRCLE OF LOVE"

The curious thing is that I went to the Pine Hill convention without the slightest intention of getting involved in SDS. I went to see people I cared about.

On the last day, Tom Hayden declined to run for a second term as president, and Robb Burlage also declined the nomination, claiming personal obligations, leaving Rennie Davis and Paul Potter and me, also desirous of living our private lives, to drop out too. While the delegates squirmed, Rennie, Paul, and I walked around on the lawn, discovered we all craved a certain distance from politics, and tried to figure out whose life would be disrupted least. I had barely met Paul, had never met Rennie at all before the convention. I thought of my "Six Characters in Search of Commitment," and felt an obligation to these strangers. The bond made my decision for me.

I had been to only one previous national SDS gathering: a meeting of the National Executive Committee that spring of 1963. The official talk had been all business, nothing momentous. The main thing that struck me then was that at the party afterward one of the original Ann Arbor people was crying her eyes out because she and her boyfriend were breaking up.

A strange thing to remember, and yet this is what moved me most about the SDS circle: everything these people did was charged with intensity. They moved and attracted me as people in the same spirit that *The Port Huron Statement* first moved and attracted me as a manifesto. It wasn't just that they were bright, though bright they were, and mostly without the polish and snobbery and arrogance that often went with brightness at Harvard. They were at once analytically keen and politically committed, but also, with a thousand gestures of affection, these unabashed moralists cared about one another. They lived as if life mattered profoundly, as if—this is hard to say without sounding mawkish, yet it seemed this way at the time—as if you could actually take life in your hands and live it deliberately, as if it were an artwork. They seemed to live as if life were all of a piece, love and commitment indivisible.

Rather a rhapsodic project for a national organization with all of eleven hundred members and a dozen chapters if that! The few dozen of the elite spoke of making SDS an "ideological home" for activists from civil rights and peace and university reform movements. To my eyes, they personified those movements and that home. Inducted into the inner circle, I was clued into the news of who was breaking up and taking up with whom in the extended family. In a way, it was by being made privy to the mesh of personal relations that I *was* inducted. Even in private life, there was a collective passion to find the right thing to do—a kind of erotics of morality. Most of them were a few years older than I; they seemed adult about romance and suffering where I was unlucky and inept and mostly inexperienced. I did have a chaste penchant for one lovely woman in particular, the girlfriend of one of the leaders, but, absurd as it sounds from this distance, I was really falling in love with a cadre—though this is too harsh and purposive a word; the SDS elite was more like what Kurt Vonnegut, Jr., called a "karass," a far-flung network joined in a common destiny. Organized one by one, face to face, most of the early SDS people were drawn into the circle and kept there by powerful personal bonds—bonds which were more important than political analyses or positions. "Brute love," the newcomer Carl Oglesby said he felt upon being elected president of SDS in 1965. People who didn't feel the same charge found it hard to break into the inner circle of power.

So there was substance, real life, behind the language of love, which the movement spoke without embarrassment. "Love is the central motif of nonviolence," said SNCC's founding statement at its outset. *The Port Huron Statement* discussed "human relationships" before it got to the *political* principle of participatory democracy:

> *Human relationships* should involve fraternity and honesty. . . . [H]uman brotherhood must be willed . . . as the most appropriate form of social relations. Personal links between man and man [sic] are needed, especially to go beyond the partial and fragmentary bonds of function that bind men only as worker to worker, employer to employee, teacher to student, American to Russian. . . .
>
> Loneliness, estrangement, isolation describe the vast distance between man and man today. These dominant tendencies cannot be overcome by better personnel management, nor by improved gadgets, but only when a love of man overcomes the idolotrous worship of things by man.

Notice that "human brotherhood must be *willed*": it does not come naturally. Over the next few years the principle came to be honored in the breach, and eventually a good deal of the community of the SDS elite unraveled in disputes of ideology and personality. What is interesting is that the passion was so strong in the first place.

The SDS circle had founded a surrogate family, where for long stretches of time horizontal relations of trust replaced vertical relations of authority. Letters, still the premium linkage, were round-robin affairs, passed on among brothers and sisters, full of well-wishing. "A band of brothers standing in a circle of love"—this was James Forman's phrase for SNCC, popularized by Staughton Lynd, its sexual exclusivity not yet apparent. True, the circle faced outward, to a world that had to be remade. But the movement constantly tended to become its own end, its own "program"; more energy flowed into maintaining the collective bond than into making clear where it wanted to take the world, and how. The movement was in this way a living protest against both isolation and fragmentation. There was a longing to "unite the fragmented parts of personal history," as *The Port Huron Statement* put it—to transcend the multiplicity and confusion of roles that become normal in a rationalized society: the rifts between work and family, between public and private, between strategic, calculating reason and spontaneous, expressive emotion. At the same time, at least for some of us, the circle evoked a more primitive fantasy of fusion with a symbolic, all-enfolding mother: the movement, the beloved community itself, where we might be able to find, in Kenneth Keniston's words, "the qualities of warmth, communion, acceptedness, dependence and intimacy which existed in childhood. . . ."

Which is to say that in some measure some of us were bent on overcoming the traumas of our own troubled families. By rough count, as many as one-third or one-half of the early SDS elite came from visibly broken or unstable families: a disproportionately large number for that generation. But even those who grew up in more stable families shared the fervent desire to find a community of peers to take seriously and be taken seriously by. In no strict sense was the movement simply a surrogate for amniotic bliss. If vulgar psychoanalytic interpretations were sufficient, the early SDS circle might have been a religious cult or a utopian commune, not the complicated and paradoxical, inward- and outward-facing community it was.

Moreover, the movement's élan and language were utterly American. It did not speak in Marxese dialects. If anything—mixed blessing!—the SDS Old Guard were steeped in a most traditional American individualism, especially the utopian edge of it expressed in the mid-nineteenth century middle-class transcendentalism of Emerson and Whitman. They were striking and distinct figures, the ethereal Potter with his androgynous style, the uproarious Burlage, the burning Hayden never at a loss for cogency—far from the faceless herd viewed with such alarm (and so predictably!) by the Fifties' "mature" critics of social movements. Who were Emerson's "representative men" if not these intensely rugged individualists? When Hayden wrote his master's thesis on C. Wright Mills, another lone radical from the American heartland, he gave it a subtitle that expressed his own utter Americanism: "Radical Nomad." The movement family was irresistible to me precisely because its members, one by one, were extraordinary.

Thus one of the lasting movement paradoxes: longing for fusion, we were equally fearful of it. I, among others, lived out this ambivalence in a decade-long dialectic between total immersion and skittish withdrawal. The internal drama also entered into SDS ideology, for *The Port Huron Statement* ingeniously sketched a vision of human nature which made it possible to straddle. Even before the singing its psalm to "human relationships," SDS affirmed (with the automatic sexist language of 1962) this lyrical idea of human nature:

> We regard *men* as infinitely precious and possessed of unfulfilled capacities for reason, freedom, and love. . . . Men have unrealized potential for self-cultivation, self-direction, self-understanding, and creativity. It is this potential that we regard as crucial and to which we appeal, not to the human potentiality for violence, unreason, and submission to authority. *The goal of man and society should be human independence: a concern not with image {or} popularity but with finding a meaning in life that is personally authentic.* . . .

Only in America could an organization of the Left have sounded such ringing praise of "human independence." Emerson, the prophet of self-reliance, could have trumpeted the selfsame notes.

And so SDS's allure was condensed, for me, into the symbolic sight of a woman crying at a party. I was beginning to sense, dimly, that the SDS circle was not just any family: it was an incestuous clan. My first year in Ann Arbor, a member of the Old Guard, fresh from one of the quickie entanglements that "campus traveling" made possible, said to me half-ironically: "The movement hangs together on the head of a penis."* The circle was made of triangles, consummated and not, constantly forming, collapsing, reforming, overlapping. The sexual intensity matched the political and intellectual; or was it the other way round? Each national meeting was not only a reconnection among people who, after all, lived scattered across the country; it was also an enclave in time where the normal social rules were suspended. No national meeting took place

---

*The same woman whose tears made such an impression on me—she was one of the few women in the early SDS circle—was regaled with the same motto by another Old Guardsman at Port Huron. Lacking a language for her complaint in 1962, she still felt annoyed by this sexist way of describing a sexy reality in which she, after all, shared happily. But who would have dreamed, then, of saying, "The movement hangs together in the depths of a vagina"? Not only were women outnumbered, but such language might have made the homoerotic implication of male bonding too uncomfortably stark.

without its sexual liaisons—and integral to them, the protracted, anguished, frequently all-night discussions about where the new and old relationships should go from there. Some of these dramas bumped on, semipublicly, for years. Many a time, the big reason why so-and-so of the Old Guard didn't play much part in a particular meeting was that, alongside the workshops and plenary sessions, he (or less frequently, she, there being fewer women in the inner circle from the start) was back in the bunk, tending to personal affairs.

This was the decade of the Pill, after all; we were young; the so-called sexual revolution was not simply media hype. But the extraordinary thing was that *The Port Huron Statement*'s appeal for "honesty" was not empty. Lovers almost always forged and disbanded their romances out in the open, and tried to be kind. Such was the norm, at least, and it was remarkably honored. The exceptions—as when a married SDS leader fell into extramarital love and abandoned his wife—shocked the community precisely because they were violations of the prevailing decency.

I was drawn into a circle of energy, then, whose bonds were intellectual and moral, political and sexual at once. I must have half-imagined the chance I might be admitted—not so much to sex as such, I think, but to the mutual love and reliance and the sense of possibility which sex can stand for. Even to be in the presence of all this transpersonal libido awed me. That it should accompany intelligence and political passion seemed to prove that thought, morality, and feeling could form a whole way of life.

Robb Burlage used to say SDS ought to change its name to Students for a Small Society. Sex was less a motive than a cement. The movement's coherence required a circle of triangles. The vulgar way to say it was that the clan was consolidated through the exchange of women—yet one should not cheapen or oversimplify. These were accomplished people, "junior achiever" types—newspaper editors, student government leaders, academic stars, big men (and women) on campus—trained in the ways of competition. Only the strongest personal bonds could have held the Small Society together. The sexual criss-cross meant generational force, meant innocence, meant starting fresh—and meant the grand illusion that we, the *New* Left, could solve the problems of the Left by being young.

THE IMPORTANCE OF BEING ANTI-ANTI-COMMUNIST

Port Huron was the first time our politics surfaced. [The League for Industrial Democracy] could tolerate searching young minds but not a group of people who were four-square against anti-Communism, eight-square against American culture, twelve-square against sell-out unions, one-hundred-twenty-square against an interpretation of the Cold War that saw it as a Soviet plot and identified American policy fondly.

—Al Haber

But SDS did not forge its identity in love and trust alone. It was hurt into independence. As this "band of brothers and sisters" struggled for a language and vision adequate to its historical moment, the parent organization, the League for Industrial Democracy (LID), tried to impose its own. What resulted was a collision, inevitable and fateful, between a would-be New Left, bound for glory, and a leftover segment of the moribund social-democratic segment of the Old Left, huddling around its embers. From the "child's" point of view, nothing was more important than its claim to be taken seriously; from the "parent's" point of view, nothing was more important than the question of what to say and do about Communism and Communists. Precisely because anti-Communism was the core of the LID's faith, it became the fulcrum of SDS's heresy. The "child" flexed its muscles; the "parent" clamped down, losing its chance of control. The New Left declared independence and won it, but not without a price. It turned out to be more difficult to start afresh than the upstarts had imagined.

That SDS began as the student department of the League for Industrial Democracy was in one way a fluke, in another the most melodramatically apt of circumstances. For the LID—the *lid,* as SDS came to call it—was the musty relic of a bygone past. One of a galaxy of New York–based offices rotating around the shell of the Socialist Party, the LID could trace its lineage to the Intercollegiate Socialist Society of 1905, whose first president was Jack London and which numbered Upton Sinclair, John Reed, and Walter Lippmann among its adherents. But many years and sectarian battles later, its abiding passions were a vigorous anti-Communism and a celebration of trade unions. In the early Sixties, the LID was not much more than a letterhead and a budget, an executive committee in search of a membership—but it did have one entry into the future, a student affiliate which the assiduous Al Haber, virtually single-handedly, had stirred into existence, renaming it Students for a Democratic Society. In September 1960, one board member wrote to the head of the LID Executive Committee: "Since last May, the LID has not even made a pretense of activity. . . . I do not think we can afford to prolong the current inactivity unless we resign ourselves to the LID as a functionless sponsor for SDS activities"—this at a time when SDS had barely begun. He proposed, "in all seriousness," a conference starting with the topic, "HAS THE OLDER GENERATION ANYTHING LEFT TO SAY?"

Like the liberals of James Wechsler's ADA, the social democrats of the LID needed a youth organization to establish a toehold in the future—and to impress the unions, chiefly the International Ladies Garment Workers, from which they raised funds. The LID preferred a youth affiliate that was a paper replica of itself. As Al Haber said, they wanted neat meetings, coherent chapters, the orderly collection of dues. What they got was Haber, a stolid-seeming visionary who spoke of the campuses as the base for a "radical liberal" force and who dropped out of the University of Michigan to create a hypothetical SDS. The slow-spoken and studious Haber had gravitated to jazz and folk music at the University of Michigan; he approved of the beats, read *Evergreen Review* and *I. F. Stone's Weekly*. His memoranda were extensive and amazingly methodical, orderly little encyclopedias of political points and tasks. Balding, round-faced, brooding, he had something of the sweet and retiring look of a wise man; he spoke slowly, as if making room for his listeners in the spaces between his words. But the LID didn't like the fact that in 1961, for example, Haber planned to send a civil rights newsletter to a mailing list ten thousand strong, which he had compiled from campus petitions and such. Faced with the possibility that their student department would be flooded with potentially mindless activists (with potential risk to their tax exemption as an educational organization), they fired him. When they relented and took him back (partly because Haber's father, an economist with impeccable credentials, intervened to vouch for him), they forbade SDS to hold a convention in 1961. But Haber persisted. Starting with his small circle of friends at Michigan—Sharon Jeffrey, Bob Ross, Dickie Magidoff, and the student newspaper editor Tom Hayden—he drew in Dorothy Dawson and Robb Burlage from Texas, Paul Potter and Rennie Davis from Oberlin, and other campus live wires. The circle widened. In December 1961 Tom Hayden was appointed to draft a manifesto for a June convention at the Michigan AFL-CIO camp in Port Huron, north of Detroit. It was time for SDS to declare what it was about.

In later years, the founders of SDS basked in the glow of solidarity they felt at Port Huron, the exhilarating sense that in reworking Hayden's draft and producing their *Port Huron Statement* they had collectively found the language for a fresh political start. Most of the Old Guard remembered above all the glow of solidarity: the sense that they had "found home," had "signed up to a good world." Some remember singing civil rights songs and "feeling high the whole time" even if they felt overwhelmed by the collective intellect and incompetent to enter into the inner circle. Some remember nights too intense for sleep, workshops followed by drafting sessions, and finally the twenty-four-hour-long plenary when they finished revising their declaration—all fifty pages of it, about one page per delegate—and went outside to watch the sun come up over Lake Huron, and felt pure exaltation. At the end of five days, says Rebecca (Becky) Adams, "I think we knew we'd done something big." Fighting for language, they were founding their intellectual and political home.

It was not a moment for modesty. But amid this shimmering feeling that the New Left had succeeded in giving birth to itself, two major conflicts erupted at Port Huron: what to do about a Communist and what to say about Communism. The gnarled politics of the Fifties were not going to wither away on their own.

First, a seventeen-year-old named Jim Hawley showed up, uninvited, representing the Progressive Youth Organizing Committee (PYOC), a group set up by the Communist Party, and asked to be seated as a nonvoting observer. Delegates Richard Roman and Rachelle Horowitz were incensed at the thought that SDS would tolerate such a presence; they were officers of the Young People's Socialist League (YPSL), the "Third Camp" Socialist Party group, and their wing of the YPSL saw SDS (and the LID's budget) as a worthy arena for maneuver. To most other delegates, the debate over something so innocuous as the official "seating" of observers was "silly," a "relic" of obsolete bureaucratic rules. To Roman and Horowitz, says Steve Max, seating Hawley was "like recognizing Cuba. . . . For the rest of us, it wasn't anything." To Max, the argument was simply the product of a culture clash. To Sharon Jeffrey, such issues were scarcely "paramount," but although she had grown up in a militant trade-unionist family that steadfastly took the anti-Communist side in the United Automobile Workers' factional wars, she wasn't afraid that factional history would repeat itself; she wanted Hawley seated. "It gave people a new way of seeing things to have a Communist in the room," she said years later. "It was raising consciousness. My position was, if we're going to get along in the world, we have to be able to talk to anyone." To the Texan Robb Burlage, not cued in to the Left's internecine history, the issue was simply "baffling." Hawley didn't speak on his own behalf, didn't talk politics; what was really going on?

What was going on was that SDS didn't want to be told whom it could and couldn't let observe. By a lopsided vote, Hawley was permitted to observe, with the stipulation—so the SDS leadership wrote later—"that this indicated neither approval nor fraternal relations with him." In fact, the convention proved way over Hawley's head; he felt "like a kid." Indeed, this walking symbol of Popular Front politics was just out of suburban high school, where he had been a civil rights and peace activist in the Communist Party orbit (though not a member himself). By his own testimony, years later, he knew "zilch about SDS." Cowed, traumatized by having been thrust to the center of attention, he spoke not a word in public and left Port Huron before the convention ended. His silence only illustrated the Old Left tendency to look like victims rather than conveyors of a politics to be debated—a self-protective Popular Front tendency that did nothing to clarify political issues.

The Hawley issue was pure symbolism, but in politics symbols *are* substance whenever groups take them seriously—especially when they collide. The other symbols at issue were Tom Hayden's words. Port Huron was the scene of a late-night brouhaha over the draft manifesto. Michael

Harrington—the thirty-four-year-old veteran of socialist and sectarian wars of the Fifties, and a leading member of the LID's Student Activities Committee—saw red. A fluid orator, Harrington argued strenuously that Tom Hayden's draft wasn't critical enough of the Soviet Union—that it "seemed to imply the United States was the prime source of evil in the Cold War."

How did the document read? Hayden had indeed decried the way Americans "have abstracted Russians to demonic proportions, projecting upon them all blame for the Cold War," choking off "rational and full debate." Russia, he wrote, was "a conservative status quo nation state. . . . The forceful take-over of East Europe signalled not the first stage of European conquest but a clumsy and brutal establishment of a security zone by a harassed and weakened nation." Radical and liberal elders were using their obsession with Communists to "mask . . . their own timidity," "trying to 'get by' in a society that would be hostile in the extreme were they to ever let down their anti-communist shield." Their "paranoid quest for decontamination" and "replays of the old fights" contributed "to the mood of public hysteria," and were thus more dangerous than "the small cluster of people who, tired of Official America, project their wishful humanism onto the Soviet Union." Hayden might have been anticipating Harrington's response. But there was real bait for Harrington to rise to. He must have been horrified that Hayden would refer to trials, executions, and invasions in Eastern Europe as "irresponsibility" and "small and large denials of human dignity." With Hungary still burning in his heart, Harrington could not have warmed to Hayden's statement that "the savage repression of the Hungarian Revolution was a defensive action rooted in Soviet fear that its empire would collapse."

If SDS didn't take a harder line against the Russians, Harrington said, the LID was going to "go through the roof." He also thought the draft far too harsh toward liberals and, in particular, labor unions, which in his eyes were the only conceivable center of a united left-liberal coalition. You didn't wash labor's dirty laundry in public if you expected to work with them—not to mention taking the LID's money. As he put it later, "if one dismissed the entire American labor movement and the liberal middle class, what hope was there of ever building a majority coalition that could transform the most powerful and imperial capitalist power in human history?" SDS *said* it wanted to "realign" the Democrats into a liberal party, forcing the southern "Dixiecrats" to merge with the Republican Right; but who was going to do the realigning?

As the beer flowed, Harrington took on all comers. To some SDSers, he was patronizing, unimaginative, long-winded. Robb Burlage, predisposed to admire this elder-brother figure, found him guilty of "some special pleading which I didn't exactly understand." Becky Adams found him impressively stylish but domineering. Sharon Jeffrey thought he "fueled the flames." But for all the qualms, Harrington proved more persuasive than he knew. When the convention broke into workshops to revise the document, his criticisms lingered.

But Harrington left Port Huron before the workshops got to work. The discussions he missed felt sublime to the SDS core. The workshop on values decided that the document ought to state its principles—by far its most memorable and influential section—at the outset, before proceeding to policies. The values were all-American in their attempt to fuse individualism with participatory democracy; but whatever the instability of the mixture, there was no way it could be confused with sympathy for Communism. The one serious argument that broke out there was about whether humankind was really infinitely perfectible. In the economics group and the final plenary, though, Robb Burlage was disappointed: he thought it high time to get more specific about positive programs.

The final document did display a seam—joining utopian values to reform proposals at the leftmost reaches of liberalism and social democracy. Was it seam, though, or rupture? *The Port Huron Statement* exhibited the same divide that ran through every political declaration, from the League for Industrial Democracy to the political parties—the distance between ends and means, between the rhetoric of the desirable and the agenda of the attainable. Later on, it was charged against the student movement that it lacked a positive program—as if any political force in American life had more of one. But no one truly expected the Democratic or the Republican Party to live out its Fourth of July rhetoric. Radicals, aiming higher, are judged by higher standards—by protectors of the status quo, and by themselves. The movement bristled at the accusation, and suffered from the split, because the values it proclaimed were so luminous, so ambitious; because it insisted that means were ends.

. Port Huron's big controversy burst out at the workshop on anti-anti-Communism, chaired by Becky Adams, the earnest former student body president at Swarthmore College. The daughter of a civil libertarian Republican corporate lawyer in Marin County, California, Adams herself not long before had trembled at being asked to sign a petition against the McCarran Act: a single false move, after all, might jeopardize a career. No generational rebel, she was, like most SDSers, living out her parents' latent values—her father's civil libertarianism, her mother's democratic-mindedness. "I wanted very badly to have a meeting of the minds," she recalls, but the minds in her workshop ranged from the crusading anti-Communist YPSL chairman Richard Roman to the red-diaper baby and former Old Left activist Dick Flacks. Adams didn't know much about Soviet crimes; she pooh-poohed Roman's litany. Above all she wanted the New Left to say what it was *for.* Even though she had been bothered by some of the draft's blithe dismissals of anti-Communism—she wanted to make it clear that SDS was civil libertarian and not pro-Communist—she was put off by Roman's style. "This was the first time I was exposed to

Socialist Party provocations," Adams recalls. "It seemed to me that Roman's only interest was in getting his language into the statement. It was obvious he was on a mission for his Party. He was insensitive and stubborn. He repeated himself again and again. You couldn't get through the workshop in that style."

Dick Flacks, for his part, was ecumenical too. The LID's concerns, he thought, should be part of the New Left grand synthesis. Revising Hayden's language, he says, "I tried to figure out the minimum Dick Roman would accept."

Port Huron was Flacks's epiphany. Characteristic of his Old Left generation (he was born in 1938), he had started out in student politics by submerging his own radicalism. His Popular Front approach had been to nudge liberals toward a more committed liberalism: In 1955, while active in the Communist Party's youth organization, the Labor Youth League (LYL), he had been elected president of the Brooklyn College Young Democratic Club.* Disquieted by Hungary, antagonistic to Stalin, Flacks had been "thrilled" by Khrushchev's 1956 speech denouncing Stalin's crimes; finally he could say out loud what he already thought, that Stalin was atrocious and the entire Soviet system "questionable." He concluded that the LYL should break with the Communist Party. But the Party moved first, and disbanded the LYL; most of his peers never went back to active politics.

While in graduate school at Michigan, Flacks got involved in civil rights and peace work; the larger non-Communist Left was his lifeblood. But he held back from leadership for fear that his past would prove "discrediting." Then Flacks encountered the Ann Arbor SDS circle. Clearly not Communists, "these people were from America." At first Flacks trod lightly, defensively, in SDS too, but he—and his wife, Mickey, also a red-diaper activist—were relieved to discover that these straight-arrow Americans welcomed them precisely *as* red-diaper babies, to be "supported and brought into the synthesis," as he put it later. When the Port Huron convention voted to seat Jim Hawley, Flacks says, "I knew we were home."

At home, Flacks thought, no voice on the Left should be excluded. Resolute anti-Communism should be given its due—alongside Hayden's critique of hysterical anti-Communism. He asked Roman, in so many words, what the statement should say against Communism, and incorporated many of his points, resulting in a passage that pulled no punches:

> As democrats we are in basic opposition to the communist system. The
> Soviet Union, as a system, rests on the total suppression of organized

---

*Note to supporters of loyalty oaths: A friend of his, also a member of the Labor Youth League, simultaneously became president of Students for Democratic Action, which, like its parent organization, the ADA, had an exclusion clause.

opposition, as well as a vision of the future in the name of which much human life has been sacrificed, and numerous small and large denials of human dignity rationalized. . . . The Soviet state lacks independent labor organizations and other liberties we consider basic. . . . Communist parties throughout the rest of the world are generally undemocratic in internal structure and mode of action. Moreover, in most cases they subordinate radical programs to requirements of Soviet foreign policy. The communist movement has failed, in every sense, to achieve its stated intentions of leading a worldwide movement for human emancipation.

But Flacks retained Hayden's point that Soviet "tyrannies" and "oppressive institutions" did not mean that the Soviet Union was inherently expansionist. Russia was "becoming a conservative status quo nation state," not the aggressive monster beloved of Cold War orthodoxy. He kept Hayden's critique of "unreasoning anti-communism" which obstructed "tentative, inquiring discussion about 'the Russian question.'"

Surely, Flacks thought, the LID would be satisfied now! Both the draft and the final document were studded with slams at the Soviet bloc. (For example: "The conventional moral terms of the age, the politician moralities—'free world,' 'people's democracies'—reflect realities poorly, if at all, and seem to function more as ruling myths than as descriptive principles"; ". . . the dreams of the older left were perverted by Stalinism and never recreated.") When the convention approved the essence of his revision (leaving the final wording up to a "styles committee"), Flacks felt for one long exhilarating moment that SDS had averted a collision with the LID, had left the Fifties (and Forties and Thirties) behind, had found a fresh language—beyond both pro-Communism and anti-Communism—adequate to the moment.

Most of the sleepless brothers and sisters exulted too. "We were very aware we were taking a position different from the LID's," Sharon Jeffrey recalls with a laugh, "and we were very willing to do it." But Robb Burlage, the Texan half-outsider, remembers feeling "the beginnings of an anxiety" as the sun came up over the shores of the Port Huron consensus, for Roman and Horowitz, whom he liked, "weren't sharing in the sense of sunrise. It was very sunset to them."

The sense of triumph was short-lived. Michael Harrington went back to New York—along with another ex-Shachtmanite, Donald Slaiman of the AFL-CIO—and sounded the alarm to the LID staff. Rachelle Horowitz, of the YPSL faction in SDS, told him the convention had ratified the draft manifesto without making any changes. In fact, Harrington realized later, "SDS had responded quite generously to my criticisms. But before I found that out, I committed myself, emotionally and politically, to attacking the SDS leaders—my friends and comrades." As Shakespeare knew, accident slides into tragedy. Why was Harrington quick to assume the worst?

Harrington was pivotal, for he was the one person who might have mediated across the generational divide. Among the older, largely Jewish trade unionists, he was the LID's one younger hope ("the 'oldest young socialist' alive," he joshingly called himself); he was as much a man of the Fifties as they were of the Thirties—a one-man stand-in for the "missing generation." At the same time, he was excited about the impending New Left. He was close to Hayden, had drunk and traveled with him, had gone to his wedding—they were both fluent-tongued, fervent, middle-class Irish Catholic boys from the Midwest. Harrington had just published an article in *Dissent,* in fact, cautioning democratic socialists not to come crashing down on the just-radicalized New Left—to remember that their romanticism toward Fidel, however "fuzzy," was not "a finished ideology" but a "complex feeling" that had to be "faced and changed" but could not be done so "from a lecture platform," "through a recital of the old categories or by a magisterial act." "The persuasion must come," he wrote, "from someone who is actually involved in changing the status quo here, and from someone who has a sympathy for the genuine and good emotions which are just behind the bad theories." But anti-Communism was Harrington's emotional touchstone. He had formed his politics with the brilliant and bitter Max Shachtman, who had suffered the anguish of seeing his revolution—forever, by rights, *his* revolution—perverted. And there was the irrevocable fact of generation. Harrington was a mature twenty-eight when the Hungarian revolution—the living, burning epitome of his politics—was crucified by the Red Army. To the radicals of SDS, on the contrary, "Hungary" was ancient history, something out of their early teens; it signified not so much a crushed revolution as a tattered banner in the Cold War, and roused their hearts far less than Fidel Castro and the Bay of Pigs. Moreover, Harrington had come into radical politics at a time when the Left was minuscule, self-enclosed, doctrinal. Those who learn to make their homes in the wilderness can bristle when the next generation has the audacity to dash toward the promised land. It was hard for Harrington to admit that he was "no longer the youthful maverick of the 1950s." The title had passed to the brash New Left, and he felt—he *was*—threatened.

Whereupon the LID rushed to judgment. Whatever one wants to say about the "balance of blame" for the Cold War, the LID resorted—in SDS's words—to "a morally dubious intrusion by a paternal hand." Their tone was legalistic and hysterical at once, their maneuvers the blind and rageful blunders of petty proprietors fearful of losing their franchise to the new boys and girls on the block—which guaranteed exactly that outcome. The LID Executive Committee met (without notice to Haber, an ex-officio member) and decided that the convention had not only been unrepresentative (too many delegates from Ann Arbor) but had "disagreed with us on basic principles and adopted a popular front position." Without having seen the final document, LID executive director Vera Rony told her board that the SDS convention had "adopted a policy statement which placed the blame for the cold war largely upon the U.S. and affirmed that the Soviet Union was not an expansionist power and was more disposed to disarmament. . . . In addition, Communist youth observers were seated at the convention and given speaking rights."

Whereupon the LID leaders summoned SDS defendants to a "hearing" in New York. Harrington played the role, Haber said years later, of the Grand Inquisitor. Much was made of the excessive voting power of the Michigan delegation at Port Huron, when in fact they had only one-fifth of the convention votes. Harrington, speaking for an organization that was nothing but an executive committee and a letterhead, hammered away on the theme that the convention was illegitimate: "There is no SDS as a functioning organization with a political life. It does not exist. How can you get a representative convention from a non-organization? On only ten days' or two weeks' notice, a document of cosmic scope was given to delegates. It requires a year's discussion." Hayden bounced back that SDS needed a political position before it could grow.

So it went. Harrington said that the seating of Jim Hawley amounted to "United Frontism," long discredited. Another LIDer, Harry Fleischman, wanted to know, "Would you give seats to Nazis too?" Rony focused on the document: "There's no mention of the Russians breaking the test ban; *no reference*. . . . Hungary is dismissed, the Berlin wall, nuclear testing. It's here, we can read it: the bias against criticizing the Soviet Union. You don't mention their faults." Fleischman added that the document lacked a "single standard. It lambastes the U.S. and taps the Soviets on the wrist." Hayden denied the charge, insisting the document's "Values" section imposed a single standard. Haber reminded the prosecutors that the final document had not yet been edited (it would be ready within a week) and that Harrington's and Slaiman's objections had been "taken to heart."

The LID tribunal was not impressed. An hour passed, and Rony called Haber with the verdict. The LID was throwing SDS staffers Haber, Hayden, and the newly hired Steve Max (the son of a Communist, after all, and once a teenage member of the Communist-sponsored Labor Youth League) off salary. From now on the parent organization would have to approve all SDS documents; Dick Roman was to be SDS's interim secretary, replacing Haber. At the same time, without breathing a word to Haber, the LID cut off all SDS funds and took direct action to keep exclusive access to that most crucial of all organizational resources, the mailing list: they changed the lock on the SDS office door.

Flabbergasted and furious, most of the SDS National Executive Committee gathered from near and far in Steve Max's Riverside Drive apartment. Nothing could have done more to fuse this group, already bonded at Port Huron. They listened to a tape of the hearing, then met around the clock for two days and nights, camping out on the floor, living on pizza. Outlanders like Burlage and Potter had to be briefed on the ins and outs (mostly outs) of left-wing history. There was talk about sneaking the SDS mailing list out of the office before the LID could lock it up. Memories fade and clash about whether the deed was actually done. Flacks thinks someone was dispatched to get the list; Haber, for one, thinks no one got it but somebody should have.

The moment of truth came in a confrontation between the Shacht-manite Tom Kahn and the SDS regulars. Kahn had been elected to the NEC as a sop to his YPSL faction, but his sympathies were plainly with the LID. The LID had a perfect right to the SDS files, said Kahn. More-over, people were going to call SDS "Communist"; wasn't SDS in touch with known pro-Castroites? "People are going to attack us," said Kahn. Hayden turned to Kahn and said, disgustedly, "Yeah, and you're going to be one of them." There was a collective gasp. "Treacherous," Hayden called Kahn, and threw a pencil at him. "Our greatest enemy is not HUAC or the Right, it's you. You will try to destroy us." Paul Potter concluded on the spot that Kahn and Dick Roman were "the enemy," the LID "paranoid."* So much for the hope that SDS was going to be the Grand Synthesis on the Left.

After two days in Max's apartment, the SDS phalanx, welded into a unit (less Roman and Kahn, one of whom voted against and the other abstained), resolved to stand their ground and appeal their way back into the LID. If they could weather the immediate crisis, they could still use the LID affiliation and spare themselves the agony of a wholehearted, career-damaging public attack. Whereupon they spent three more twenty-four-hour days drafting a twenty-seven-page single-spaced appeal to the full LID Board. The fury of its composition is forever inscribed in the appeal's improvised look: The writing and typing were parceled out, so that the mimeographed brief came out in a patchwork of styles and typefaces, mixing a due-process technical defense with substantive political argument. The basic problem, it concluded, was that the LID was unwilling to accept SDS as the voice of "a different generation."

The appeal succeeded in cooling the larger LID Board into compro-

---

*For his part, Kahn, the son of a manual laborer from Brooklyn, was full of class resentment of an SDS elite which he remembered, years later, as coming from "Ivy League–type" schools, although only two of them were graced, or tarnished, with that affiliation. "I thought they were sort of playing a lot of intellectual games," he says. "I thought they were elitist, their attitude towards the labor movement, the liberal establishment. They were very wrapped up in their own political and intellectual creativity. They really believed that they were defining the goals of the generation, setting forth the new political doctrine. And to a large extent they succeeded. I, in that sense, probably underestimated them." Kahn went on to become executive secretary of the LID, a speechwriter for Hubert Humphrey in 1968 and Senator Henry Jackson in 1972, and a top aide to presidents George Meany and Lane Kirkland of the AFL-CIO.

mise. Former Sarah Lawrence College president Harold Taylor, who had been at Port Huron, led the forces of moderation; Norman Thomas, among others, also sympathized. Although the LID still insisted Haber play the sacrificial lamb, the office was returned to SDS and *The Port Huron Statement* was permitted to stand. But the clash was burned into the organization's primal memory. The tale of the magnificent manifesto written around the clock by a convention that stayed up to watch the sun rising over Lake Huron, followed in short order by the saga of the brilliant brief worked up by sleepless cadres fighting off a sneak attack by paranoid elders—this was the stuff of SDS's founding legend. Although I wasn't yet involved in the organization, I have my own myth-sized memory: I was having dinner with Haber and Hayden in my Washington apartment, early in July, when they got the call from New York alerting them that the LID had summoned them to the emergency hearing. They left for New York, as I recall, without finishing dinner. Summary hearings, legalistic diatribes, locking a staff out of its office: This sounded to me like an Alice in Wonderland version of what I had read about the long-gone internecine left-wing strife of the Thirties. It was not the sort of thing to make my heart beat fast for the "democratic Left."

The patchwork could not last. Errors and accidents aside, two generations glowered at each other across a deep historical divide of experience as well as belief.

To the LID: Anti-Communism was at the core of political identity. Bitter battles with Communists had been their proving grounds. There was an LID board member who at one meeting tore at his shirt to show Al Haber the scars Communists had inflicted on him at a Madison Square Garden rally more than a quarter of a century before. In the League for Industrial Democracy, the danger of cooperating with Communists had long since been settled: In 1935, their student department had deserted the parent organization, helped form the Communist Party–lining American Student Union, and been submerged. Almost three decades later, the experience still quivered in the LID's institutional memory. And that history served their present interest. The unions which supported the LID—especially the International Ladies Garment Workers and Walter Reuther's United Automobile Workers—had signed up for the duration with American prosperity, demanding only a fairer share. Anti-Communism, alongside its intrinsic merits, was more than a matter of principle: it underwrote the postwar social contract. Curiously, too, the specter of Stalinism safeguarded the LID's standing as proprietor of a democratic Left. Stalinism was a spent force in American life, but its lingering aura enabled the feeble LID to feel important. Soviet aggression in Hungary was alive to them not simply because the Hungarian revolutionaries deserved all the solidarity in the world—a good enough reason in itself—but also because there was no longer a real American movement to stir the blood. It was absolutely central to these anti-Communists that their student group play what Harrington later called "a pro-American, Cold War, State Department kind of role."

Meanwhile, *to SDS:* The formative fact was the domestic void. Despite ritualistic incantations to "the trade union movement," the Old Left—Marxists and social democrats alike—had lost their popular base. Why take anti-Communist moralism seriously when the old moralists had so little to show for it? Anyway, the old pro-Communist Left was more a ghostly remnant than a live rival. Outside the lurid imagination of the House Un-American Activities Committee, who could fear such a shriveled ghost? At the same time, there were huge new facts. Stalin, after all, was dead, and Khrushchev had brought a thaw if not full spring. If the Russians were such a military threat, the Soviet bloc so monolithic, how account for Tito's successful break in 1948 and the growing rift between Russia and China? The Soviet system had so little hold on the SDS founders, they couldn't take it seriously, even as an enemy; it was an aged and obsolete "dinosaur," not a monster in its prime.

What haunted this generation was not the specter of Communism but the force and mood of McCarthyism. When Becky Adams was growing up civil-libertarian in Marin County, California, for example, suspect books were being publicly burned, and she was revolted; if this was anti-Communism, she thought, then anti-anti-Communism became a moral necessity. Communism was a remote abstraction, anti-Communism a clear and present rampage against *any* American Left. Intellectuals were cowed, radicals purged, students largely submissive. All radical and utopian thought was suspect: didn't respected intellectuals warn that it was utopian passion as such, the very will to believe, that had blinded them to Soviet crimes? SDS reversed this logic. If the prevailing view was that all utopias were mortally wounded by the horrendous example of Soviet Communism, the early New Left theory was that any resurrection of utopia was going to require a dampening of anti-Soviet passion.

So anti-Communism, the LID's automatic reflex, became SDS's dirty word. But why didn't SDS settle for a more careful anti-Communism? Why not what Harrington later called "a progressive, Leftist anti-Communis[m]"?

There was much more of a discriminating opposition to Soviet-style Communism in *The Port Huron Statement* than Harrington could acknowledge then. In standing up for détente and recognizing that both sides were complicit in the Cold War, SDS was only a year ahead of President John F. Kennedy. But SDS's view of revolutions was indeed more muddled. Unlike Harrington's Trotskyists, who had watched the socialist dream devour its dreamers in the Soviet Union, SDSers weren't old enough to have had their primal hopes dashed. Children of the open spaces of the Fifties, their sense of plenitude craved a reason to believe that the world was not finished, that the history of socialism, so savagely sidetracked after 1917, could start again freshly. However hostile to the USSR, SDS devoutly wanted Third World revolutions to overturn the Soviet model, whose crimes were taken to be the results of overcentralization and encrusted bureaucracy, even gerontocracy.

Thus the particular importance of Castro's Cuba for the New Left. Cuba was the revolutionary frontier, the not-yet-known. Here, apparently, was the model of a revolution led by students, not by a Communist Party—indeed, in many ways against it. The triumph over a brutal American-sponsored dictatorship had been improbable, dramatic, hard to categorize. In its early years, moreover, Castro's Cuba with its several newspapers and freewheeling style seemed far from both Stalinism and stolidity. On trips to Cuba in 1959, 1960, and 1961, before U.S. government restrictions made travel harder, Americans like Paul Potter mixed with Cuban students, identified with their esprit and their defiance of the Colossus of the North. Even the National Student Association expedited these trips; so, on a smaller scale, did the budding Students for a Democratic Society, which provided a desk in its office for a group arranging travel to Cuba. Fidel Castro might turn out to be a dictator, but in *The Port Huron Statement*'s words, anticolonial revolutions embodied "individual initiative and aspiration" along with a "social sense of organicism"—precisely the image New Left activists had of themselves as they took history in their own hands. Widely circulating tracts by Jean-Paul Sartre and C. Wright Mills made the same hopeful case.

The proper attitude toward Third World revolutions, then, was what SDS called "critical support." *The Port Huron Statement* anticipated "more or less authoritarian variants of socialism and collectivism" in the Third World, but said Americans could help the cause of democracy "not by moralizing" but by identifying with them critically and working to keep them independent. (What radicals should say about revolutionary regimes which *didn't* protect dissent was left dangling.)

At the same time, SDS didn't want to bog down in passing resolutions for or against anyone's pet regimes. The way to break with the Cold War was not to leap from one side to the other. Even to dwell on politics abroad was the politics of the armchair, a surrogate for activity, and for it SDS reserved the ironic term *statementism*. An American radical's first and overwhelming priority was radical change in America.*

So this ungainly double negative, anti-anti-Communism, was for the New Left what anti-Communism was for postwar liberals and social

---

*A younger Michael Harrington had once argued this way himself, for example against an American Committee for Cultural Freedom which was obsessed with "absolute freedom in Russia (where the ACCF does not yet have any influence)" and yet ambiguous "with regard to freedom in the U.S. (where it does have influence)." No one saw the snag in this argument: The movement wanted to be a voice of universal morality, beyond all boundaries, yet when it refused to be anti-Communist on purely pragmatic grounds ("our job is in the U.S."), it forfeited its claim to universality. The turn to international revolution in the late Sixties—including revolution in the U.S.—was an abstract and futile way to regain the moral mantle.

democrats: the crucible of a political identity. Obviously there was more at work than a strictly rational dispute (although it was that too); the SDS/LID imbroglio also amounted to a family fight. *One* of the dynamics of transgression was Oedipal, as the partisans of patriarchal order declare triumphantly, but their crude version of this notorious parricide is nothing more than a simplistic way of discounting the revolt of the sons (not to mention daughters, who get short shrift from the oversimplifiers).* Generational politics takes two generations to play; each was spoiling for a fight on precisely the ground closest to the other's heart. So part of the answer to Harrington's question, why not a leftist anti-Communism, is that too many fine distinctions between different varieties of anti-Communism would have dampened SDS's abiding passion: to start afresh. In this sense the appeal brief was disingenuous, a legalistic response to a quasi-judicial kangaroo court. But if SDS was in some ways naïve (especially in failing to anticipate the parental onslaught), the LID was vindictive. The vigorous children had to fight back the possessive fathers to go out into the world on their own.

Thus the vertical dimension of SDS's revolt. There was also a horizontal dimension: what to do about old Communists and their children, as actual persons. To the LID, respect or affection for Communists or fellow travelers was simply beside the point; what counted was political principles, period. You could like a Communist-liner as a drinking buddy but you were still bound to exclude him and his positions from your organization, even your convention. But for SDS the question was not so much what to think as how to change life. This was the legacy of bohemia, deepened in the exalting experience of the fused group, solidified by the belief that the old answers led into the political desert—thus it would take transgression to break new ground. The pro-Communist Old Left was moribund *as a Left;* it therefore looked like a series of individuals, to be taken (or left) one at a time. There were individuals of Old Left vintage who had earned the respect of SDS leaders. They were courageous civil rights activists in the South, peace activists in the North. They might or might not be members of the CP, but who cared? They were to be judged by their actions, not their memberships. SDS also rebelled against an impersonal society by refusing to respect the normal boundary between private feeling and public position. At the very least you didn't want to purge miscreants, especially if you weren't sure

---

*Even Sophocles's story is far more complicated than is dreamt of in neoconservative philosophy. The original "back story" begins, let us recall, with Laius receiving news from an oracle that a son of his, not yet born, is going to grow up to kill him. When Oedipus is three days old, Laius therefore pierces his ankles, pins them together, and casts him into the wilderness to die. The son survives, but, years later, an oracle tells him he is fated to sleep with his mother and murder his father. Horrified, Oedipus flees. One day he happens upon a carriage-drawn old man who tries to force him out of the road. The coachman pushes Oedipus, who strikes back; the old man attacks Oedipus, who batters back and kills this man who, of course, turns out to have been Laius. Father and son, each desperate to escape from a dire fate, end up fulfilling it. The moral difference is that Laius fulfills the first prophecy by leaving his son to die, while Oedipus fulfills the second in the course of trying to avoid doing wrong to his father.

where the truth lay in the first place. Social democrats were right to abhor totalitarianism, but their tempers were distorted, as Barbara Haber put it, by the "rabid anti-Communism at the center of their lives." Communists, in contrast, could be "nice." The self-righteousness of the right-minded was offputting in a way the wrong doctrine was not. This sort of calculus was not something the veterans of the ideological wars of the Thirties and Forties could view with equanimity—nor, since they lacked standing as a living Left, could they easily sway the New Left by pontificating at them.

And then, crucially, SDS had an active respect for some particular children of the Old Left, above all the red-diaper babies of the Old Guard itself: principally Dick and Mickey Flacks and Steve Max, bright, knowledgeable, dedicated, full of lore about the multiple absurdities as well as decencies of the Communist side of the Old Left, yet living links to a radical past that, however "perverted by Stalinism," as *The Port Huron Statement* put it, was at least devoted to radical change. The majority of SDSers, from liberal or social-democratic backgrounds, had been drawn (like me) to red-diaper babies as living, breathing carriers of the radical tradition, conscientious objectors to the American Celebration. Then again, what was to fear? In the heady days of the dawning Sixties, who cared whether stodgy, obvious *Communists* came around? Communists and fellow travelers were heavy-handed, thick-headed, laughably attached to their cautious formulas—some of these, in fact, not so different from the LID's ("liberal-labor coalition," "support the party of the workers"). They were glued to electoral politics, glued to the Democratic Party; they didn't hear the music of direct action. Anyway, there were few live Communists in sight,* no sign of any antidemocratic influx into SDS, no apparent danger that Old Left authoritarians could ever count for anything in an organization so resolutely anti-Soviet. In this mood, to exclude observers, even members, seemed absurdly fearful. And as Sharon Jeffrey typically, gleefully, puts it, "I didn't have fear in me!"

New Left pluck was built on a supreme faith in the power of face-to-face persuasion—the pure liberal nineteenth-century rationalism of John Stuart Mill, unscarred by factional wars. For two years, Al Haber had sparred with the LID over the proper way to deal with "Stalinoids"; he respected their energy and commitment, wanted to keep channels open, thought it possible to win them over one at a time. In the good society which SDS hoped not only to bring about but to *be,* good arguments would surely defeat bad. From conversation would come conversion. In any event, the overriding need was to leave the Thirties and Forties in their grave, to start again. By calling itself a New Left, SDS could automatically solve, transcend, the problems of the Old.

Could the post–Port Huron collision have been avoided? Probably not for long. With good-faith diplomacy, and under calmer political

---

*At Port Huron, during the debate on seating Jim Hawley, one observer said to Mickey Flacks, "You mean to say there's a Communist in this room? I want to see this guy. I've never seen a Communist."

circumstances, tempers might have been soothed for a time; the two sides might have negotiated a truce, a modus vivendi. But with so much at stake, on both sides, there wasn't much interest in finesse, let alone experience at it. SDS, with far less experience, bent more; the LID, with far more experience, panicked more—in this sense the LID was more deeply at fault. But given the two camps' fundamentally different political histories, and the aggravating pressure of events over the next few years, the odds were that sooner or later any truce would have collapsed. The tensions were too severe.

For SDS, barely founded, the crisis was formative—a rite of passage. The fused group was welded together in that heat. The LID's "inquisition made the SDS paper Executive Committee into a group committed to an organization," said Al Haber years later. "That attack is what made our community real." "It taught me that Social Democrats aren't radicals and can't be trusted in a radical movement," Tom Hayden told Jack Newfield. "It taught me what Social Democrats really think about civil liberties and organizational integrity." SDS won, more or less. Victory left them cocky, and scarred in ways they didn't understand. For anti-anti-Communism, the fulcrum of independence, could become an imprisonment. The LID, by reacting hysterically, had made it vastly more difficult for SDS to establish itself in the clear light of affirmation.

The New Left habit of negation was learned all too well from the social democrats themselves, who proved more anti-Communist than democratic and excluded themselves from the movement. Most of the LID, in the meantime, learned its own tribal lesson: This was the moment when the bad children showed their true colors. For Tom Kahn, soon to become executive director of the LID, it spurred the conviction "that to the extent the student left separated itself from the traditional liberal coalition, it would go off the deep end in every possible respect." All parties felt they had passed a point of no return.

One final irony. The LID thought SDS was being sucked into the vortex of the Communist-bound Old Left, but the Old Left, trapped in its own dogmas, refused to be impressed. The two most widely circulated organs of the independent Old Left were *Monthly Review* and the *National Guardian*. Just after Port Huron, Dick and Mickey Flacks happened to run into *Monthly Review* co-editor Leo Huberman at his fellow editor Paul Sweezy's vacation house on Martha's Vineyard. Still glowing from SDS's convention, they regaled Huberman with the news. "Are they socialists?" Huberman wanted to know. "I don't know," Dick Flacks said. "Some are, some aren't." "If they *are* socialists," Huberman said, "what are they doing about it?" Flacks bridled: what, after all, was socialism exactly? Huberman said it was a planned economy under government control. "You expect Americans to get excited about a planned economy?" Flacks asked. What really counted, in Huberman's eyes, were the Cuban revolution and Cheddi Jagan's socialist government in Guyana. "Anyway,"

Huberman said, "this is all academic because ten years from now we'll have a nuclear war." Flacks threw up his hands—all Huberman was offering the young was a vision of closed America surrounded by the revolutionary wonders of the Third World.

Flacks, meanwhile, had covered Port Huron for the *National Guardian* (and had been pleased when Haber and Hayden told him that was acceptable). He sent in a long report on the proceedings, but all that appeared was a three-line item: SDS had held a founding convention. He wrote a long letter of protest. A *Guardian* editor wrote back that they hadn't had the space, and moreover that SDS should have understood that the *Guardian* still suffered from the wounds of exclusion; why hadn't they been put on the Port Huron program? They had passed their own bill of attainder: to them, the youth group of the profoundly anti-Communist LID could not have been up to any good. Flacks, disgusted, concluded that the *Guardian* was living in the past; the New Left was going to have to make its own way.

AIN'T GONNA LET NOBODY TURN ME 'ROUND

RADICALS AND THE LIBERAL GLOW

One of the core narratives of the Sixties is the story of the love-hate relations of radicals and liberals. To oversimplify: Radicals needed liberals, presupposed them, borrowed rising expectations from them, were disappointed by them—*radically* disappointed—infuriated by them, made trouble for them, then concluded that liberals—suspicious, possessive, and quellers of trouble—were "the enemy." Liberals were the most receptive, sometimes admiring enemies; they might argue, or scheme, but they wouldn't shoot. Competing for the same constituency, liberals in turn could capitalize on radicals' political energy, but they grew just as disappointed, just as angry, when radicals wouldn't see reason their way. On two main testing grounds the New Left worked out its uneasy attitude toward liberals (and vice versa). One was the East-West confrontation and the problem of Communism—which in 1964–65 became compressed into the problem of Vietnam. The other was the question of liberals' attachment to the civil rights movement—in particular to SNCC, the movement's radical edge.

If Port Huron was skeptical about the future of organized liberalism, SDS's Pine Hill convention of June 1963 was even more so. The brotherly and sisterly love I went there to revel in was a love that felt its strength in opposition to established liberals; and no inspiration was more important than the civil rights surge. For northern supporters were swept into

SNCC's force field. SNCC moved us, seized our imaginations. From 1960 on, SDS felt wired to these staggeringly brave, overalled, work-shirted college students and the local people who were their inspirations, recruits, allies, raisons d'être. SNCC had suffered, SNCC was *there,* bodies on the line, moral authority incarnate. "[T]hose Negroes are down there," Tom Hayden wrote of McComb, Mississippi, in the fall of 1961, "digging in, and in more danger than nearly any student in this American generation has faced. . . . When do we begin to see it all not as remote but as breathing urgency into our beings and meaning into our ideals?" SNCC-SDS connections were thick.* Hayden spent months traveling around SNCC projects that fall, firing off vivid descriptions to the SDS mailing list (later gathered into a pamphlet, *Revolution in Mississippi*). Writing to Al Haber after attending a SNCC meeting in Mississippi, Hayden welcomed the new, more militant SNCC that had carried direct action into the terrorized hinterland: "In our future dealings we should be aware that they have changed down there, and we should speak their revolutionary language without mocking it, for it is not lip service, nor is it the ego fulfillment of a rising Negro class." The southern movement, he said, had "turned itself into the revolution we hoped for, and we didn't have much to do with its turning at all." SNCC was "miles ahead of us, looking back, chuckling knowingly about the sterility of liberals. . . ." A few weeks later, in McComb, Mississippi, Hayden and Paul Potter, equipped with stringers' credentials from James Wechsler's *New York Post,* got punched around by a local ultra while trying to help SNCC workers.**

And the SNCC-SDS alliance was strategic, not just moral. In the Port Huron analysis, and subsequent speeches and articles by Hayden, the South's reactionary politics held the rest of the nation in thrall because the Dixiecrats faced no serious political opposition in the one-party South. Therefore they accumulated seniority; therefore they dominated the key committees of Congress. To identify with SNCC was not only an act of solidarity, it was an alliance with brothers and sisters against the old white men who deadlocked the Democratic Party and fueled future wars.

Through SNCC, the South came North. Whenever civil rights

---

*North–South connections were thick in general. Among Al Haber's first SDS recruits outside Ann Arbor were the white Texans Dorothy Dawson (later Burlage), Sandra (Casey) Cason (later Hayden), and Robb Burlage. Chuck McDew, SNCC's second chairman, attended Port Huron; SNCC workers Casey Hayden, Jim Monsonis, and Bob Zellner, along with SNCC cofounder Tim Jenkins (later NSA national affairs vice president) were SDS officers up through 1963; other SDSers (including Betty Garman, Mary Varela, and Casey Hayden again after 1963) went south to work in SNCC, and stayed there for years—several up through the bitter days when whites were expelled. And of course many non-SDS northerners also went South.

**Because a photographer was on the scene, the beating drew national publicity and a Washington press conference. Afterward, Potter, then national affairs vice president of the National Student Association, was privately furious. With a blow across the kidneys, a cut lip, and a bloody nose—so Potter wrote to his brother—two white boys had become a cause célèbre. Just a few weeks before, in a neighboring county, the Negro farmer Herbert Lee had been shot dead by a Mississippi State representative—without any national notice whatsoever. (See p. 141 below.)

workers were shot at, assaulted, and indicted, SNCC relayed the word to Friends of SNCC groups, SDS chapters, and other sympathizers. We invited southern heroes to speak on our campuses. In northern movement circles, the names of SNCC leaders became legendary, along with the sites of SNCC's passion, the Delta, Parchman Penitentiary, and the rest. The southern martyrs became our saints; cherishing them, we crossed the Mason-Dixon line of imagination, transubstantiated. In emergencies, we mobilized our slender networks, activated our phone trees, called the Justice Department, implored friendly members of Congress to intervene, sent telegrams of protest.

And so, in the year between 1962's Port Huron and 1963's Pine Hill conventions, as SNCC's staff grew to 200 organizers and the Birmingham demonstration electrified a national television audience, SDS was swept with excitement about the movement's prospects. During 1963, according to one estimate, 930 civil rights demonstrations took place in at least 115 cities in 11 southern states; over 20,000 people were arrested. The country was bubbling with what the 1963 SDS convention document, *America and the New Era,* called "local insurgency." In the North, CORE, the Congress of Racial Equality, and NSM, the Northern Student Movement, were organizing in the ghettoes. Belatedly, President Kennedy was paying attention; liberals were forced to address the movement's agenda. The 1963 SDS convention's first day of speeches by older-than-student luminaries could be called, without too much self-consciousness, "New Left Day."

America and the New Era lacked the lilt and drive of *The Port Huron Statement,* partly because the Port Huron values and rhetoric were already in place. But it did show how SDS was symbiotically connected with the very Kennedy liberalism it aimed to transcend. Drafted by Dick Flacks, the document half-recognized that the new insurgency presupposed the New Frontier. "The new era" (a lame Old Leftish atavism) referred to Kennedy's promising, vigorous attempt to manage a world whose old stabilities had broken down. Kennedy got credit for recognizing that international and domestic crises required an active response, even if that response was "mediating, rationalizing, and managerial," a policy of "aggressive tokenism." Abroad, the New Frontier had the virtue of working toward "political stabilization" with the Russians; it was deeply committed to avoiding nuclear war—although it showed no interest in general disarmament. Just a few days before the convention, in fact, Kennedy gave his most pacific speech, at American University. "Let us re-examine our attitude toward the Cold War," Kennedy said, eight months after the Cuban missile crisis, "remembering that we are not engaged in a debate, seeking to pile up debating points. We are not here distributing blame or pointing the finger. We must deal with the world as it is. . . ." He called for East-West accommodation, announced that test-ban negotiations would begin soon, and proclaimed that the United States would cease nuclear testing in the atmosphere as long as other nations did likewise. Yet SDS smelled trouble in Kennedy's commitment to military counterinsurgency in the Third World—although Kennedy said he accepted anticolonial revolutions and nonalignment policies as legitimate, "the Administration has not yet abandoned its resolve to meet revolution with force if necessary, and this means the sure devastation of country after country in the Third World, as Vietnam, for instance, is now being destroyed."

At home, said *America and the New Era,* the Kennedy administration was mired in what—following the Wisconsin Marxists of *Studies on the Left*—SDS called "corporate liberalism," meaning that Kennedy was tinkering with the corporate economy in order to maintain it. His Keynesian economics was mixed with "faith in the essential genius of the American corporate system." Kennedy was skimpy with jobs, health, and antipoverty action. Central economic planning was necessary, but the New Frontier was inching, if anything, toward an "elitist" brand of national planning under corporate aegis. Kennedy had supported Negro voter registration in the South; indeed, the day after his American University speech, he had finally, ringingly, spoken out for civil rights as "a moral issue . . . as old as the scriptures and . . . as clear as the American Constitution." But his programs could not begin to touch the Negroes' need for jobs and job equality, housing, school integration, and the right to vote.

And the traditional liberal-labor forces? Faced with the civil rights upsurge, they were weak, overly polite, and defensive. Automation—the economic bugaboo of many manifestos in the early Sixties—was rapidly eroding the traditional industrial sources of union strength, while reformers were trapped within "the limitations of the Democratic Party." Liberals had let their militance decay. They had to take some of the blame for the political stalemate, for a "style of politics which emphasizes cocktail parties and seminars rather than protest marches, local reform movements, and independent bases of power" was doomed to political weakness. The "hope for real reform" lay with "the re-creation of a popular left opposition—an opposition that expresses anger when it is called for, not mild disagreement."

On that note, SDS ended its last consensual manifesto.

Even in 1963, *America and the New Era* was striking for what it omitted as well as what it said. Much more than *The Port Huron Statement,* it stood silent about the world outside American borders. The explanation for this silence points to later troubles. There was a workshop on foreign policy; fresh from Tocsin, with a reputation for expertise, I was appointed its chairman. There we debated the degree to which "American imperialism" could be held responsible for tyranny and poverty in the Third World. American imperialism was *the* issue, some argued in Old Left tones; I, as best I recall, took the position that it was *an* issue, albeit an important one. In the end, with no consensus in sight, we decided not to write a report at all. Better agnosticism—or ambivalence—than division.

Afterward, no one noticed that anything important was missing. A manifesto was now only a puff of smoky words. After 1963, in fact, SDS conventions stopped trying to produce sweeping analyses. One reason was that in subsequent years the organization came to focus on action programs. But successive leadership circles also intuited that if SDS strained too hard to describe the world it wanted, rifts might emerge. The fused group made its claims; consensus was best preserved by smothering conflict. "In a world where countless forces work to create feelings of powerlessness in ordinary men," said *America and the New Era,* "an attempt by political leaders to manipulate and control conflict destroys the conditions of a democratic policy and robs men of their initiative and autonomy. . . . In the long run, the encroachment of the engineered consensus will permanently frustrate the long human struggle to establish a genuinely democratic community." Wise words. In a small but significant way, SDS proceeded to muffle itself, to slip toward precisely what it criticized in smooth, orthodox America.

Pine Hill was happy, though, about the promise of "the new insurgency." There was an exuberant sense of a political space opening up, movements converging, community expanding. If "the issues were inter-related," as SDS liked to proclaim, it was partly because the people were. Even my own election as president was considered a sign that yet another constituency was coming around to the grand synthesis: Just after the convention, Paul Potter wrote that in my person SDS was reaching outside the Ann Arbor group, to "eastern intellectuals"; I was the first top officer whose main work had been for peace, not civil rights.

We were warmed by the dawn of what Marcus Raskin has called "the We Shall Overcome period of American life"—the fourteen months from American University to the Gulf of Tonkin, a moment when the democratic promise came alive, the arms race, racism, and poverty seemed solvable problems, and the New Left looked as though it might push liberalism beyond its old limits. Kennedy's American University speech convinced us that the old Cold War was thawing. The axis of international confrontation was now rotating from East–West to North–South; the dangers of counterinsurgency were real, but at least thermonuclear war seemed to have been staved off. So we left Pine Hill exhilarated. Not only was the society moving in the right direction, but we had a privileged understanding of it. I remember the thrill and vindication a number of us felt when we got our first look at a *New York Times* after several days in the woods without one. The front page was full of news about Kennedy's détente with the Russians, about civil rights demonstrations, about the middle-class discovery of poverty (for which Michael Harrington's book, *The Other America,* was heavily responsible). *The New York Times* might as well have been printed on tea leaves, so avidly did we inspect it for clues not only to what the Establishment was thinking, but to the nature of reality itself, not to mention our own fates.

That whole year was full of signs of opening. The movement against the Bomb subsided with détente and the test ban, but the civil rights movement continued unrelenting. And the movement moved North. A few weeks after the convention, I was one of the SDSers who got swept into a July Fourth demonstration to integrate a whites-only amusement park in the suburbs of Baltimore, Maryland, the northernmost state of the South. It was my first taste of the spirit of the southern movement. We launched ourselves with freedom songs from a Negro church, where the good citizens in their Sunday finest smiled upon us as if we were visiting diplomats, and I could begin to feel an approximation of what Martin Luther King had called "the beloved community." Prominent white church leaders were in the front lines. After decorously stepping across a line the police had drawn on the sidewalk, we were carted away. In the democracy of the local jail I was moved to meet a real prisoner, a soft-spoken Negro man up on larceny charges. He maintained that a racist witness had falsely identified him, and I believed him. His modesty and dignity struck me as preferable to the egocentric clamor of my fellow demonstrators, some of whom had made private arrangements to get themselves bailed out early while the rest of us huddled up head to foot for a night on the cold concrete floor. I wondered what had become of the beloved community.

Three days later, I went back to Baltimore County for more. This time, while the main arrests were going on in an orderly fashion at the police line in front, twenty of us forded a stream at the rear and sneaked in. A white teenager spotted us and hurled a chunk of concrete which hit one of our group—an organizer for the Northern Student Movement—just above the eye. Blood streaming down from what, for all anyone knew, was the eye itself, she turned to the rest of us and yelled, "Let's get into the goddamned park!" Now there were only seven of us—two Negro, five white—the others having been left behind in the fracas. We plunged in. Turning a corner, we ran up against a white mob. Before we could make a move, another mob pushed up behind us. To our left was a wall, to our right a high fence. The taunts started: "Nigger lovers!" Uncountable time elapsed. The mob started shoving from behind. Our line stumbled, held. We said nothing. I thought of singing, then thought better of it. After who knows how long, the cops arrived and led us away. Then and only then did we sing "We Shall Overcome." It was official: I was in *the movement*.*

Gwynn Oak was, of course, a weak echo of the bloody movement

---

*The next day the Baltimore County executive called the second demonstration "hasty and immature" (orderly steps were being taken to desegregate the park in due time, after all) and said we were victims of "emotional self-hypnosis." His name: Spiro T. Agnew.

down South. Northern activists were excruciatingly aware of the terror being inflicted by the white South wherever civil rights workers penetrated. It would take an entire book to describe the bombings, beatings, and tortures, the assassinations well known and obscure, of the early Sixties. This extraordinary terrorism extended the ordinary terror with which white power had held down the Negro population for a century after emancipation. Shaken by sit-ins and Freedom Rides and voter registration, an entire social system, fighting for its violent life, went into convulsion. Negroes of the Deep South stepped out of the shadows to shake the pillars, even as they shook with their own fear. In churches, on marches, in prison, through all the spasms of liberation, they sang *"We will never turn back," "Ain't gonna let nobody turn me 'round," "Keep your eyes on the prize, hold on," "We shall overcome."*

And the Kennedy administration, that incarnation of normal politics and the liberal promise, moved crabwise. In the years to come, blacks in sharecropper shacks and tenement apartments throughout America would adorn their walls with portraits of the martyred John F. Kennedy. But in the crucial years 1961–64, when the civil rights movement was searching for strategies and working out its political identity, the federal government at key junctures proved a halfhearted ally. Tantalizing with the promise of change, timid in performance—a volatile mixture indeed.

A COLLISION OF POLITICAL CULTURES

The promise and the timidity were two facets of a larger political culture, what might be called custodial or managerial liberalism. Beneath the language of justice, in SDS's eyes, the liberal manager is a custodian of order. Whenever movements rock the boat, his imperative is to hoist it back on an even keel. Where the movement takes sharp action, he fears above all a sharp right-wing *reaction*. To neutralize the danger, he prefers to proceed with caution, gradually—"with all deliberate speed," in the language of the Supreme Court's 1954 school desegregation decision. Social issues are fine for idealists to crusade about, but politics is the art of the possible. He faces "real world" problems: how to get what he can while he maintains, consolidates, expands his political base. So the managerial imperative is a matter of principle, but it is also the custom of his tribe. In a complex world of conflicting interests, what choice is there but to balance the many competing claims of their representatives? The militancy of masses may have its time and place—to muscle an issue onto the political agenda—but then it gets out of hand, loses sight of its goal. So the manager believes the place to settle political problems is in the back room. For many reasons he feels uncomfortable on the streets, comfortable where arms can be twisted and squeezed, backs scratched, palms greased, dissonant voices coaxed and orchestrated, deals made. How else are limits to be respected in a democracy?

The New Left's political culture reared up opposed. It presupposed the liberal promises—wielded them, in fact, as bludgeons against the failings of liberal performance. What liberal managers called seeing reason, the New Left called rationalizations for unjust power. The method of politics was at least as important as extrinsic results. The New Left style was an extension of a much older small-d democratic tradition. It wanted decisions made *by* publics, *in* public, not just announced there. It valued informality, tolerated chaos, scorned order. Clamor was the necessary overture to a genuine harmony. The motto might have been Frederick Douglass's 1857 cry: "Those who profess to favor freedom and yet deprecate agitation are men who want crops without plowing. . . . Power concedes nothing without a demand; it never did and it never will." Clamor was the weapon of the weak, the voice of the voiceless. What passed for neutral order actually secured the privileges of the few. "Normal" channels were clogged, civility therefore expendable. If nonviolent direct action resulted in violence, even against the demonstrators themselves, so be it; the issue had to be forced, the price had to be paid, to crack through the fraudulent facade. Speaking of the white supremacists who met civil rights demonstrations with savagery, SCLC's James Bevel put it this way: "Maybe the Devil has got to come out of these people before we will have peace. . . ."

Alongside political strategy, there was an expressive side to the movement culture, rooted in the subterranean ethos of the Fifties, and in a longer-run revolt against the containment of feeling and initiative in a society growing steadily more rationalized. Participatory democracy entailed the right of universal assertion. It meant inserting yourself where the social rules said you didn't belong—in fancy meeting halls if you were a sharecropper, off limits and off campus if you were a student. The expressive tendency was in revolt against all formal boundaries and qualifications, which it saw as rationalizations for illegitimate or tedious power. It couldn't abide the life of waiting in line—or even the bureaucracy of its own organizations. One small example: After Pine Hill, Lee Webb was elected SDS's national secretary—its chief bureaucrat— despite his declaration of "moral dislike for [the] administrative process"; he proceeded to leave the national office as often as possible to throw himself into civil rights demonstrations with the Swarthmore chapter in Chester, Pennsylvania.

Expressive politics wanted the pain to stop, now. In the Gandhian form of expression, you wagered your body as the sign of your witness. In the later Sixties, a less restrained expressive dramaturgy emerged. Demonstrators should refuse to sit still; politics should shake, rattle, and roll, move body and soul. Gandhian or raucous, expressive politics wanted you to "put your body on the line"—not only to win demands, but *to feel good*. It wanted to "do what the spirit say do," as a SNCC song put it. It trusted feeling and wanted to "let it all hang out." The implicit theory of expressive politics was that the structures of private feeling begin before the individual, in capitalist acquisition and the patriarchal family; public in its origins, private feeling should therefore be expressed where it belongs, in public. Its faith was that a politics of universal expression would make the right things happen—*and* be its own reward.

A caution: Strategy and expression, far from being pure alternatives, are coordinates like latitude and longitude; any action partakes of both, in degrees hard to measure. *All* politics, oppositional or establishmentarian, proceeds from a mélange of motives. So it was not always crystal-clear just when the movement was acting strategically, when expressively. One person's demonstration of feeling was another's stratagem. When the movement couldn't tell what it was accomplishing (which was the case much of the time), its strategic and expressive motives grew especially tangled.

But note: The belief that political style is central to political substance—a fetishism of style, to those dismayed by the idea—was not something plucked by the New Left out of thin air. We shared it, in fact, with Kennedy's managerial liberalism. Managers claim reason and sneer at the opposition's "irrational" tactics, but obscure their own prideful attachments to the symbols of power. They have their own quite emotional needs to hold on to the social territories where their writs run. The New Left's disruption of established procedure was a counterpolitics to the managed world of institutions—a system which professes the glory of democracy while its bureaucratic rules mask the ways in which correct procedure has taken on a weight of its own. The New Left thought America was a society whose cost-benefit analyses and body-counts mask systematic violence. People who are offered channels that don't lead where they are supposed to lead usually feel fatalistic at first. Then, if they come to think they have a right and a need and a chance to go where the channels are supposed to go, they may end up not only dredging their own channels, but declaring them to be precious and fundamental— precisely because they are the only channels where the movement flows freely. On both sides, channels become identity.

So two political styles faced off in the early Sixties: one managerial and liberal, the other participatory and radical. I have exaggerated the differences between them, perhaps—in the manner each came to see the other. But division is not necessarily the stuff of social explosions. Managerial liberalism might have kept the upper hand and dampened the insurgent political culture *if it had delivered on its promises*. But it defaulted. And therefore two political cultures, each claiming the same political ground, were on a collision course.

JUSTICE AND THE DEPARTMENT

THERE'S A TOWN IN MISSISSIPPI CALLED LIBERTY.
THERE'S A DEPARTMENT IN WASHINGTON CALLED JUSTICE.
   —Sign in Jackson civil rights headquarters, summer 1964

Even two historians sympathetic to President Kennedy can say nothing kinder for his race policy than to refer to its "peculiar pace . . . : conciliatory, slow, incremental reform punctuated in the end by dramatic televised responses to the great civil rights events of the day." What is striking is how little this assessment differs from Victor Navasky's critical summary of the administration's first two-and-a-half years in office:

> From 1961 to 1963 Robert Kennedy had no civil rights program in the sense that he had an organized-crime program. Civil rights was in the rear ranks of the Kennedy Administration's early priorities. "I did not lie awake worrying about the problems of Negroes," Robert Kennedy freely conceded in later reminiscing. And as each crisis surfaced, the [Attorney] General confidently approached it on the assumption that it was a temporary eruption which he and his remarkable team could cool. . . . His most visible and most significant civil rights activities were responsive, reactive, crisis-managing, violence-avoiding. He and his people were cool, creative, imaginative, effective and risk-taking reactors, and they should be credited with converting the freedom rides into an ICC order desegregating interstate bus travel; with calling out the troops to back up court orders integrating Ole Miss (in response to James Meredith's initiative) and the University of Alabama (Governor Wallace in the doorway notwithstanding); with not calling out the troops and nevertheless preventing a racially explosive Birmingham from exploding into a bloody race war. But the civil rights program of the new Administration was more limited than John Kennedy's campaign rhetoric would have suggested or than civil rights activists hoped.

Activists in the Deep South, daring to take the Bill of Rights at face value, kept banging up against the Kennedy brothers' caution. At the time of the 1961 Freedom Rides, for example, when civil rights crusaders were having their skulls cracked, their clothes set afire, their teeth kicked in, their bus blown up, all for daring to take seriously a Supreme Court decision banning segregation in bus terminals, the administration's response was late and ambivalent. A year after the 1960 Greensboro sit-in, CORE, the Congress of Racial Equality, had a new national director, James Farmer, and an idea for forcing federal action. No less an authority than the Supreme Court had just ruled that segregated interstate terminals were unconstitutional, just as it had ruled fifteen years earlier that interstate buses had to be integrated. "Our intention," Farmer said, "was to provoke the southern authorities into arresting us and thereby prod the Justice Department into enforcing the law of the land."

In good Gandhian fashion, Farmer gave advance information of CORE's plans to the President, the attorney general, and FBI director J. Edgar Hoover. Robert Kennedy said later that the information never got to his desk; the first he knew of the Freedom Ride was when a mob turned over the integrated bus and burned it outside Anniston, Alabama, on May 14, 1961. When a second bus reached Birmingham later that day, it was met by a mob led by Ku Klux Klansmen carrying pipes, chains, and baseball bats. Not a single policeman appeared. One of the Klansmen was a paid FBI informant who had briefed his "handler" about the Klan's plans, whereupon the Birmingham FBI office had sent a teletype to J. Edgar Hoover about the impending ambush. Hoover therefore knew that police chief Bull Connor had promised the Klan enough time to attack the Freedom Riders, whom Connor wanted beaten until "it looked like a bulldog got a hold of them." Hoover notified no one and did nothing. A sixty-one-year-old Freedom Rider was left permanently brain-damaged by the beating he suffered.

To President Kennedy, busy preparing for his Vienna summit with Nikita Khrushchev, civil rights was worse than distracting, it was divisive. The Berlin crisis was brewing. Front-page photos of mayhem in Alabama were giving American racial policy a bad press the world over. The President's first reaction to the news of the Freedom Ride was therefore to growl at his civil rights adviser: "Tell them to call it off. Stop them!" The Cold War was top priority; what business did these agitators have kicking up a fuss about bus stations? Still, the crisis had to be managed. To his credit, the President sent a representative, John Seigenthaler, to Alabama. For days the governor, a Kennedy supporter, refused to return phone calls from either the attorney general or the President; finally he promised to protect the Freedom Riders on the next leg of their journey. Armed state troopers did accompany their next bus to Montgomery—only to melt away as soon as the bus arrived. With no local police in sight, the waiting mob ran amok, bashing Freedom Riders and reporters with fists, sticks, metal pipes, and baseball bats, setting one person afire. Seigenthaler, on the scene, saw two women slapped around and tried to help them into his car. He was jumped, beaten unconscious, and left lying on the ground by the police for twenty-five minutes before they drove him to a hospital. FBI agents stood around taking notes.

Rioters took turns smashing one Freedom Rider in the head while others chanted, "Kill the nigger-loving son of a bitch"; he lay bleeding, in shock, with a damaged spinal cord, for more than two hours before he was taken to the hospital. The police commissioner of Montgomery declared: "We have no intention of standing guard for a bunch of troublemakers coming into our city."

John F. Kennedy was painfully aware that he had won election by a mere 119,000 votes—by the grace of Chicago mayor Richard J. Daley and his Illinois machine, many believed. The white South had deserted the Democratic Party and had to be wooed back. Once in office, Kennedy kept his distance from congressional liberals. He appointed southern segregationists to the federal bench, and for almost two years delayed signing a promised executive order to ban racial discrimination in federally assisted housing. But now the state of Alabama was openly and brutally defying federal authority, and the managerial imperative had to be asserted. However eager Kennedy was to cover his political flank in the white South, he finally felt compelled to send federal marshals to protect the battered Freedom Riders.

In Montgomery, the day after the bus station riot, Martin Luther King and James Farmer were addressing a huge church rally. Again a white mob gathered. Again Negroes were beaten. Whites threw stones, bottles, stench bombs, and firebombs through the church windows. Inside, the congregation tried to barricade the doors, but the mob kicked them open. Just then the marshals materialized, like movie cavalry—this time called out to protect the Indians. Even then, in the midst of the siege, the attorney general asked the Freedom Riders to observe a "cooling-off period." Happy to have provoked Washington into acting at last, Farmer sounded off to King: "We have been cooling off for three hundred fifty years. If we cool off any more, we will be in a deep freeze. The Freedom Ride will go on." Eventually, the governor sent the Alabama National Guard to rescue the congregation and the outnumbered marshals. Robert Kennedy petitioned the Interstate Commerce Commission to ban discrimination in interstate bus stations; four months later, the ICC complied.

But the Freedom Rides left the Kennedy administration fearful that civil rights hotheads would set the South to boiling again. More confrontation would mean more bloodshed, more racial polarization, further jeopardizing Kennedy's standing in the South. As soon as the Freedom Ride crisis was quelled, therefore, Robert Kennedy went to work persuading the major civil rights groups to shift from direct action to voter registration. It was a tempting proposition, this alliance of convenience—the Kennedy Democrats stood to gain, but so did civil rights; on his own, Martin Luther King had already been thinking along the same lines. Administration officials proceeded to line up funds from their friends in the liberal foundations.

That June, Robert Kennedy met with representatives of CORE,

SCLC, SNCC, and the National Student Association, and unveiled his master plan. "If you'll cut out this Freedom Riding and sitting-in stuff," the attorney general said, "and concentrate on voter registration, I'll get you a tax exemption"—provoking a shouting match with one of the SNCC people. The core issue concerned protection for would-be voters and civil rights organizers. Only protection against reprisals could make the bargain tenable to the movement. Individuals close to the administration later denied that any promise had been made in so many words. From an insider point of view, to expect any such promise was naïve; the organizers must have succumbed to wishful thinking. But Martin Luther King left the meeting convinced that SCLC, CORE, and SNCC had been guaranteed "all steps necessary to protect those rights in danger." Timothy Jenkins, then vice president of the National Student Association (and later, at Port Huron, elected for a year to SDS's National Executive Committee), recalled "very vividly" that one administration official—he thinks it was Harris Wofford—said "that if necessary in the course of protecting people's rights to vote, that the Kennedy Administration would fill every jail in the South." Lonnie King, a SNCC organizer, remembered that "Bobby pledged marshals and what have you to help us out."

SNCC was split. A direct-action faction wanted to keep up mass demonstrations, fearing that the quieter work of voter registration would stall their momentum, while any practical results would serve mainly to gild Kennedy's image. Others in SNCC thought that, Justice Department or no, voter registration was the logical next step toward changing the balance of political power in the South. If the foundations would fund it and the Justice Department would protect it, all the better; Jenkins argued that this was the only way to get the Justice Department to go to court against repressive state and local governments. After a summer of wrangling, with Lonnie King and some other direct actionists resigning in protest, SNCC finessed the conflict. The incoming executive director, James Forman, convinced doubters that voter registration in the Black Belt would meet with such hard-core resistance, would so disrupt the old patterns, it would amount to direct action in itself. Ella Baker, the longtime southern activist who had midwifed SNCC into existence, convinced both sides they could coexist in the same organization.

In the fall of 1961, the bargain was struck. A Voter Education Project was established, funded by the foundations; Attorney General Kennedy intervened with the Internal Revenue Service to procure a rapid tax exemption. SNCC was skeptical, but it would act *as if* the federal government could be taken at its word, would see how far official power and liberal money would go.

The civil rights groups divided up the front lines of the South; SNCC took hardcore Alabama and Mississippi. SNCC's Robert Moses had already arrived in McComb, in embattled southwest Mississippi, to set up a voter-registration school. While the Kennedys were tacking and veering, Moses and other SNCC organizers lived with daily terror. In dusty towns and on back-country highways they were running the gauntlet of sheriffs and night riders, facing arson, bombings, beatings, brutal jail conditions, assassinations, and an avalanche of threats— knowing that the terror was at least tolerated, often instigated, even inflicted directly with fists and bullets and electric prods, by the local representatives of the law. The writ of the First Amendment, with its freedoms of speech and assembly, did not run through the Deep South, no matter that the Fourteenth Amendment forbade any state to "abridge the privileges and immunities of citizens of the United States." In Amite County, near McComb, for example, Negroes were the majority, 3,560 of them of voting age, but only one had succeeded in registering, and he had never voted.

What was the law worth? Even apart from the bargain they thought they had struck with the Justice Department, SNCC workers were primed about their rights. Looking for legal protections, SNCC lawyers dis- covered Reconstruction-era federal laws on the books since 1870 prohibiting any attempt to impede citizens in their exercise of rights guaranteed under the Constitution or U.S. law. SNCC supporters, confronting doubters, could rattle off section and title numbers to clinch the case. And it was encouraging that sympathetic subalterns at the Justice Department would take calls from menaced SNCC workers filing complaints. SNCC organizer Charles Sherrod could assure a group of southwest Georgia Negroes that the federal government was "as close as the telephone." A civil rights worker could tell a frightened congregation in Greenwood, Mississippi: "The government is with us. The Department of Justice is with us." Knowing that Washington sometimes kept an eye on things, local officials did relent at times.* Under the glare of publicity, federal power was sometimes deployed against particularly egregious officials; for example, when Robert F. Kennedy called for a "cooling-off period" during the heat of the Freedom Rides, he simultaneously went to federal court seeking to enjoin Birmingham chief Bull Connor and other police from interfering with interstate travel.

But in the face of everyday terror, spotty federal intervention seemed less than sufficient. The normal sight was of local FBI agents standing by, taking notes, while SNCC workers were being bashed bloody. The FBI was in the habit of working with local officials; personal attitudes aside— many were southern whites—they weren't about to antagonize their partners in law enforcement. Hoover, like a feudal chief, even refused to attend Robert Kennedy's staff luncheons. According to one civil rights lawyer, the FBI "would interrogate a black and scare him out of his pants. They'd interrogate a white sheriff and then report his version straightfaced without 'evaluating' it."

---

*On one occasion, for example, in August 1961, Bob Moses drew a reduced sentence (on a fraudulent charge) when a McComb jailer heard him phone a complaint, collect, to the Justice Department.

Or worse. In August and September 1961, Bob Moses and two other SNCC field secretaries working to register voters in and around McComb were brutally beaten. Then a Negro farmer named Herbert Lee, the father of nine, an NAACP member who braved the terror to attend voter meetings and drive Moses around the county, was shot dead, in broad daylight, by a state legislator named E. H. Hurst. There were several Negro eyewitnesses, one of whom, Louis Allen, told a coroner's jury, in a courtroom full of white farmers carrying guns, that Lee was wielding a tire iron and that Hurst had shot him in self-defense. Soon thereafter, Allen told Bob Moses that he had been instructed to lie, that he had now told the FBI the truth, and that he would repeat it to the grand jury if he could get protection. The Justice Department—which protects witnesses who agree to testify against organized crime—told Moses they could offer no protection to Louis Allen. Nine months later, the deputy sheriff broke Allen's jaw while he was in custody. A year and a half after that, Allen was ambushed, shot in the face by two loads of buckshot, and killed. No one was ever charged.

Instead of taking on the FBI, Attorney General Kennedy prodded, coaxed, and outflanked it, congratulating himself on small victories like a middle manager outfoxing his clumsy superior, not a cabinet member (and the President's brother!) dealing with a staff subordinate. Above all else, he aimed to avoid a showdown with J. Edgar Hoover. Thus the FBI, when it did yield, was able to exact a *quid* for its *quo*—including the wiretapping of Martin Luther King. The Kennedys, guerrillas of government, were usually not so retiring in the face of recalcitrant bureaucrats; why such uncharacteristic deference? Garry Wills's hypothesis is that the Kennedys knew that Hoover was in possession of tape recordings from 1941 in which John F. Kennedy chatted about his naval intelligence work with a Danish lover suspected of Nazi connections—an affair that cost the young Kennedy his position in naval intelligence. Or perhaps the Kennedys thought the top national cop politically untouchable. In any event, the Kennedys' servility toward Hoover seemed the perfect expression of the futility, or helplessness, or hypocrisy, of managerial liberalism.

Under movement pressure, gradually and gingerly, Robert Kennedy did nudge the FBI into a more aggressive posture. During his years at the Justice Department, the number of FBI agents in Mississippi soared from three to more than one hundred fifty. The Bureau did infiltrate the Ku Klux Klan. To bitter-end whites, the FBI became the "Federal Bureau of Integration." In July 1964, after the murders of civil rights workers Michael Schwerner, Andrew Goodman, and James Chaney (the first two northern whites) near Philadelphia, Mississippi, it even opened a field office in the state capital. But even then, J. Edgar Hoover was not going to let *his* Bureau get pushed around by uppity blacks demanding that the authorities deliver on their rights. When Hoover opened his Mississippi office, he conferred with the governor, the mayor, the head of the state highway patrol, the local police chief—the entire local white-supremacist political establishment, in short—and then told a press conference that the protection of civil rights workers was strictly a local matter. Civil rights workers were not reassured.

SNCC organizers were scouring the back country of the Mississippi Delta and southwest Georgia, trying to coax sharecroppers to dare register to vote knowing that all of them might be ambushed and shot to death for their pains. The niceties of the Kennedys' restraint, their federalist scruples about challenging the southern states' rights, their refusal to alienate the Dixiecrat South, all seemed beside the point. Any positive gestures from Washington the movement understood as halfhearted responses to its own militancy; at worst, Kennedy stood convicted of exploiting the movement for dubious political ends. Between 1961 and 1964, SNCC repeatedly, doggedly, sometimes desperately appealed for federal help. Their appeals were usually unavailing. Until the Voting Rights Act of 1965, the Justice Department only twice took legal action on behalf of assaulted civil rights workers.

Organizers who had staked their strategy on promises of protection felt betrayed. They weren't privy to, or interested in, Robert Kennedy's management problems, or the in-house politics of the Justice Department and the FBI. They had either taken Kennedy at his word or had felt it necessary to act as if they did, to stand a chance of breaking the cycle of fear in the rural South. Harold Fleming, one of the foundation executives behind the Voter Education Project, said later that "not protecting the kids was a moral shock, more than a cold-blooded, calculated reckoning. It was bruising and deeply emotional. To have the FBI looking out of the courthouse windows while you were being chased down the street by brick throwers deeply offends the sensibilities. So people wept and cursed Robert Kennedy and [Assistant Attorney General] Burke Marshall more than the FBI, whom they never had any confidence in to begin with.

"Project yourself back to '61 or '62," Fleming added. "There was a totally unjustified euphoria. The climate of expectation was created not by the Kennedys with an intention to deceive, but by the ethos of the moment. The feeling was: After Ike, at least we'll have an activist Administration. We were all unsophisticated about power. We thought it was there to be used. This was exciting. We didn't know about the inhibitions of power. . . . [E]verybody overestimated the capacity of the Administration to intervene in an unlimited way. And everybody underestimated the prospective need for intervention. The sense of betrayal which came later, was the inevitable hangover from the binge. . . ."

Fleming's "we," the liberal elite of foundation executives, labor and church leaders, and legislators, made the mistake of thinking they were "*part* of the Administration"—an illusion that SNCC organizers could not begin to harbor. The youth of SNCC were on fire; they were not in a mood to hear about the fire department's difficulties arranging the transport of water. In the meantime, Robert Kennedy's staff—as Victor Navasky has written—"brought with them the code of the Ivy League Gentleman, which involved, among other things, the assumption that negotiation and settlement are preferable to litigation; the idea that winning in a higher court is preferable—for precedential purposes—to winning in a lower court; the notion that reasonable men can always work things out; patience at the prospect of endlessly protracted litigation; the preference for defined structures, for order. . . . Without disputing the dynamism, good will, ingenuity or capacity of these men, without underestimating the unique benefits of an Ivy League education, without suggesting that they were genteel assembly-line products who thought and felt alike, one can still argue that the system by which they defined themselves predisposed them to peaceful coexistence with present injustice—especially where they could see light at the end of the appellate tunnel."

Then, in the midst of a long series of disappointments, the Justice Department committed one absolute betrayal. In August 1963, a federal grand jury indicted nine civil rights activists in Albany, Georgia, charging them with obstructing justice and perjury for picketing a supermarket owned by a white man who had recently served on a federal jury. That jury, all white, had acquitted a rural sheriff who had been charged with shooting a handcuffed Negro prisoner four times. Albany supermarkets had been picketed for more than a year, as part of a general boycott, and the picket signs around this particular store said nothing about the sheriff's trial; they simply demanded that Negroes be hired. It was not Attorney General Kennedy who had brought these charges, but he had refused to exercise his authority to quash them. Moreover, the same Federal Bureau of Investigation which had proved royally disdainful of Albany's Negroes when they were brutalized by local officials had supplied at least thirty-eight agents to help prosecute the civil rights workers. In the presence of a Justice Department representative from Washington, the U.S. attorney argued that the civil rights workers would get a fair verdict from an all-white jury, and proceeded to drive all Negroes off the jury by peremptory challenge. Slater King, president of the Albany Movement, and one of those indicted, wrote: "It seems to be a great disparity when my pregnant wife is kicked to the ground and beaten by a police in Camilla, Georgia. She later loses the baby and yet the Federal Government says that there is nothing that they can do." All but one of the nine were convicted; some were sentenced to up to one year in jail, although eventually the convictions were reversed on appeal. The same month, in nearby Americus, three SNCC field secretaries and a CORE worker were charged with inciting insurrection, which in Georgia was a capital crime.

The national media spotlight was not drawn there, but the movement's own channels made these cases notorious.

What commandeered the TV cameras that spring were the thousands of Negro demonstrators in Birmingham, and Bull Connor's cattle prods, fire hoses, and police dogs that greeted them. The national liberal conscience was galvanized; civil rights groups now found themselves the cutting edge of a coalition of unions, churches, and students. White police and racist mobs were now the conspicuous disorder that Kennedy had to manage. When Governor George Wallace grandstanded against Negro admissions at the University of Alabama, Kennedy federalized the Alabama National Guard and faced him down.

A. Philip Randolph, the Negro trade unionist who had founded the Brotherhood of Sleeping Car Porters, and Bayard Rustin, the Negro pacifist and adviser to Martin Luther King, seized the opportunity to propose a March on Washington for Jobs and Freedom. Aided by the League for Industrial Democracy's Tom Kahn, Rustin mobilized King, James Farmer, and SNCC's John Lewis, along with the NAACP's Roy Wilkins, church leaders, and the UAW's Walter Reuther, among others, into the perfect model of the liberal-labor coalition. Fearful as always of losing control, worried lest an unruly demonstration could "give some members of Congress an out," President Kennedy tried to talk the organizers out of marching, but Randolph, King, and Farmer convinced Kennedy that they could control the crowds. SNCC, with some support from CORE, proposed civil disobedience, including sitting down in the streets, sit-ins in the offices of southern members of Congress, mass arrests; but any thought of civil disobedience was discarded at Wilkins's and Reuther's insistence. SNCC proposed demonstrations at the Justice Department; the other groups vetoed the idea. Kennedy, placated, pledged to introduce sweeping new civil rights legislation, including provisions for desegregating public facilities and for withholding federal funds from discriminatory programs.

Faced with a polarized public, Kennedy at last seemed to be delivering on the civil rights rhetoric of his 1960 campaign. SNCC, however, was underwhelmed, for the Justice Department wasn't enforcing laws that were already on the books. Although the attorney general had consistently argued that he didn't have the authority to protect civil rights workers, the new bill failed to contain any new authority along these lines; indeed, when a House subcommittee later tried to amend the bill to give it to him, he testified against the amendment, and the new language was removed.

Some SNCC organizers accompanied local people to Washington; others derided the March, just as they had long derided Martin Luther King as "De Lawd." On August 28, the nearly quarter of a million people who came to the Lincoln Memorial, one-third of them white, were a walking advertisement for racial integration. Negroes from the Deep South, brought to Washington by SNCC and CORE organizers, took heart: perhaps there *was* a national conscience after all. They were on the national stage, and there was apparently a national audience.

To the media, indeed to the bulk of the participants at the time, the memorable speech that day was Martin Luther King's unsurpassable vision:

> I have a dream that one day on the red hills of Georgia the sons of former slaves and the sons of former slaveowners will be able to sit down together at the table of brotherhood. . . .

What brought tears to their eyes, and has brought tears to millions of eyes since, was his glorious peroration:

> When we let freedom ring, when we let it ring from every village and every hamlet, from every state and every city, we will be able to speed up that day when all God's children, black men and white men, Jews and Gentiles, Protestants and Catholics, will be able to join hands and sing in the words of that old Negro spiritual, "Free at last! Free at last! Thank God almighty, we are free at last!

The cadences rolled out over this utopian camp-meeting of "all God's children," of sharecroppers and students, trade unionists and professionals, and, via the television cameras, over a nation converted for one brief moment into a national revival, aching to be redeemed from the legacy of enslavement.

But for SNCC's trajectory (and by reflection SDS's) the most important speech that day was the one that wasn't delivered in its entirety. Chairman John Lewis of SNCC softened his words after the Catholic archbishop of Washington let it be known that he would otherwise withdraw his support. At the last minute, inside the Lincoln Memorial, a committee rewrote Lewis's speech. The prepared text, already distributed to the press, had him saying: "In good conscience, we cannot support the Administration's civil rights bill, for it is too little, and too late. There's not one thing in the bill that will protect our people from police brutality." Even as delivered there was strong criticism: "True, we support the Administration's civil rights bill, but this bill will not protect young children and old women from police dogs and fire hoses. . . ." Lewis told of the government's inaction when police assaulted Slater King's pregnant wife, and wrote but didn't deliver the statement that "the Albany indictment is part of a conspiracy on the part of the Federal Government and local politicians in the interest of expediency." He called the movement "a serious revolution," albeit a "nonviolent" one. He wrote but didn't say: "The next time we march, we won't march on Washington, but we will march through the South, through the Heart of Dixie, the way Sherman did. And we will make the action of the past few months look petty."

He wrote but didn't say: "I want to know—which side is the federal government on?"

John Lewis had been a seminary student. He had preached in the churches of rural Alabama since high school. Many times beaten and arrested, he was the nonviolent gospel incarnate. If John Lewis was speaking this language, it should have been clear that the moment of SNCC's ambivalence toward federal power was passing. Battered SNCC field secretaries were already asking why, if they were going to be battered, it should be in the name of integration and nonviolence. As the liberal-labor-Kennedy coalition reached high tide, it was difficult to imagine a plausible alternative. But a growing number of militants were starting to pay close attention to an avenging angel named Malcolm X, a Black Muslim who spoke of armed self-defense, dismissed the "Farce on Washington," and asked: "Who ever heard of angry revolutionists swinging their bare feet together with their oppressor in lily-pad park pools, with gospels and guitars and 'I Have a Dream' speeches?" Within two years, few of the SNCC stalwarts bothered asking, even rhetorically, which side the federal government was on.

WHITE SHIELD, WHITE HEAT

Only when metal has been brought to white heat can it be shaped and molded. This is what we intend to do to the South and the country, bring them to white heat and then remold them.

—Bob Moses, November 1963

Vivid days like August 28, 1963, become watersheds. The next day, everyone agrees that time has parted into time before and time after. The conflicts come in the interpretation. What has become possible and impossible now? What else is to be done?

Many of the SNCC workers returned from Washington convinced that the age of Jim Crow was fading. Little doubt remained that Kennedy's civil rights bill, inadequate and even retrograde as it was, was going to pass. (It passed, in fact, after a filibuster, the following summer, when Kennedy himself was dead.) But most of SNCC now thought desegregation a bourgeois business at best; symbolically, what good was the right to eat a hamburger when the Negro couldn't afford one in the first place?* If liberal-labor allies were problematic, perhaps others could be found: That month Stokely Carmichael of SNCC met with Tom Hayden and proposed that SDS organize poor whites to ally with SNCC's poor blacks in a class-based alliance—and SDS agreed to try. But the interracial movement of the poor was a long shot. SNCC's main idea was to build local power bases for the mass of Negroes, the impoverished ones. For that, it was necessary to get the vote. Again, Mississippi was the key. Negroes constituted a majority in more than one-third of Mississippi's counties; overall, they were over 40 percent of the state population. Bob Moses had dug in and recruited a cadre of talented, energetic young Mississippi Negroes. Shortly after the March on Washington, SNCC agreed to pursue a "one man, one vote" campaign in Mississippi, and to pour all necessary resources into it.

Moses's cadre possessed courage beyond measure, but to this point, after two years of voter registration, they had few voters to show for their labors. Between 1961 and 1963, 70,000 Mississippi Negroes tried to register; only 4,700, a mere 5 percent of Mississippi's voting-age Negroes, succeeded. In November, the Voter Education Project cut off almost all the funds it had been sending into Mississippi, arguing that the money would be better spent in less hard-bitten states, and criticizing the Justice Department for failing to back the drive with lawsuits and protection. To crack Mississippi would require new tactics. To accomplish the Kennedys' own strategy—voter registration—in the face of the administration's failure to provide protection, the movement would have to force the very confrontation that the Kennedys' strategy had been intended to avoid. Timid liberalism had outfitted the commandos who were wearying of liberal promises.

SNCC teetered on a knife-edge paradox of its own. To register voters, it would have to force precisely that federal intervention which increasingly it doubted possible. It would have to act against its doubt, as if the Justice Department's hesitant liberals might be compelled to be *real* liberals. That was its radical wager, the rock-bottom "as if" which defines the dilemma of a radical movement acting in a liberal political culture.

As a student of Camus, Bob Moses must have appreciated that this exercise in the absurd was Sisyphean—as Sisyphean as it was necessary. The movement's agonies and cross-currents took up residence in this Harlem-born Harvard philosophy M.A. who had quit his job teaching math in a

---

*It wasn't only SNCC militants who raised such questions. The LID's Tom Kahn wrote a pamphlet, "The Economics of Equality," which asked: "Did the *right* to use public accommodation amount to much without the *means* to exercise that right? What difference did the integration of hotels and restaurants make to the unemployed black workers?" Once economic reform became the goal, though, the routes diverged. One pointed toward the solidarity of the excluded (thus Tom Hayden and Carl Wittman's 1964 SDS paper, "An Interracial Movement of the Poor?"), the other toward a liberal-labor-civil rights coalition (whose most influential and controversial formulation was Bayard Rustin's "From Protest to Politics," published in *Commentary* in February 1965).

prep school to work for SNCC at bare subsistence. Moses was the quintes-
sence of SNCC and its foremost saint, trusted by northern supporters as by
Mississippi organizers and sharecroppers for courage, clarity, and selfless
incorruptible grace. His move into Mississippi, his steadiness, and his
defiance of murderous deputies were the stuff of movement legend.
Stokely Carmichael told Robert Penn Warren about a time in Mississippi
when he and Moses and a third SNCC organizer were followed by three
cars: "The men in the cars had guns hanging out of the windows. George
started off driving. Bob asked why he was driving so fast. George said:
'God dammit, Moses, we're being chased.' Bob looked back and could see
the headlights. He said: 'Well, they won't bother us.' And Bob turned
over and went to sleep." "I thought Bob Moses . . . was Jesus Christ in
the flesh," wrote Anne Moody, a young Mississippi CORE organizer. "A
lot of other people thought of him as Jesus Christ, too."

Born in 1935, Moses was several years older than the students, at an
age when a few years' difference amount to a generation. He was
something of an older brother to a movement suspicious of fathers. He
read Camus in college, reread *The Rebel* and *The Plague* in jail, and cited
them in public. He absorbed from Camus the idea that the Negro should
be "neither victim nor executioner," and that race hatred was a universal
plague to be found and fought in every human heart.

The light-skinned Moses's slight frame and large, somber eyes gave
him an ascetic look. His voice was mild, even-toned. He spoke slowly,
plainly, pausing frequently to gather his thoughts, or to think things
through one more time, giving the impression that every occasion was
unique and required something unique of him. He lacked high-flown
rhetoric, or adornment, or what is conventionally called charisma—but
charisma is the property of a specific culture, and what passes for charisma
in one setting goes over poorly in a culture that honors something
different. The reporter Nicholas von Hoffman called Moses "an outstandingly poor speaker" whose "cadences are monotonous" and "words . . .
unimaginative" compared with the "huge-voiced men who thrill people
with the King James Bible English they learned in a thousand Baptist
churches." Von Hoffman was accurate, but he missed the point. Moses
was "perhaps the most trusted, the most loved, the most gifted
organizationally of any southern Negro leader" *precisely because* he seemed
humble, ordinary, accessible. The early New Left distrusted flourishes. It
wanted elemental talk, not grand rhetoric.

In voice and gesture, Moses did more than anyone else to create the
premium movement style: diffidence over bravado; quiet assertion rather
than driving crescendos; plain, halting speech rather than rolling phrases.
He liked to make his points with his hand, starting with palm down-
turned, then opening his hand outward toward his audience, as if
delivering the point for inspection, nothing up his sleeve. The words

seemed to be extruded, with difficulty, out of his depths. What he said seemed *earned*. "He's like someone you only read about in novels," a Freedom Summer volunteer said. "He has great currents of moral perplexity running through him." Unintimidated, so was he curiously unintimidating. He believed in leading by example; he seemed to sacrifice himself on behalf of the universality of the democratic impulse. To teach his unimportance, he was wont to crouch in the corner or speak from the back of the room, hoping to hear the popular voice reveal itself. If persuaded to the platform, he was in the habit of asking questions. To preach from the rostrum he deemed manipulative, especially when the folks in the audience were uneducated. His leadership style spread throughout the movement, including SDS in the North, and as Moses's mannerisms separated themselves from the flesh-and-blood Moses they sometimes lent themselves to a cultivation of the inarticulate. When imitators stumbled on, vaguely and interminably, the plainspoken stop-and-start style became a caricature of itself. Worse, in the hands of leaders less scrupulous than Moses, the self-abnegating style of participatory democracy didn't eliminate leadership, only disguised it. The de facto leaders were still influential; followers were swayed willy-nilly. Diffident leaders in disguise couldn't be held accountable, and ended up more manipulative than when they stood up tall, made their authority explicit, presented solid targets.*

It is a semantic curiosity, if not the zeitgeist's trick, that the movement's chief exponent of this tender and ambivalent style of leadership should have carried the name of the primal liberating patriarch in Western history. His namesake, of course, wasn't permitted to enter the Promised Land; he didn't survive the wilderness.

The March on Washington seemed to have infused local activists with new élan, but SNCC workers were exhausted. The March on Washington also provoked a renewal of Mississippi terror: a new Society for the Preservation of the White Race had been stitched together statewide, able to organize as many as eighty cross burnings in a single night. The perennial problem returned: how to crack the Mississippi terror? Moses and others devised a twofold strategy. To take a step toward political power, the Council of Federated Organizations, or COFO (with SNCC the pivotal component, CORE strong in one congressional district, and SCLC and the NAACP nominal partners), founded the Mississippi Freedom Democratic Party, mostly Negro but open to people of all races. The MFDP tried to attend official Democratic Party meetings, and when repelled, pro-

---

*The LID's Tom Kahn tried to convince me of this in 1965 or 1966; as a loyalist of participatory democracy, I argued back. Events of the late Sixties convinced me that, up to a point, Kahn was right: accountability matters more than the leaderless style. But there are no formulaic solutions to the conundrums of authority.

ceeded (with SNCC's leadership) to hold its own precinct and county gatherings.

Influenced by the peripatetic freelance organizer Allard Lowenstein, who brought news of South African tactics, Moses also decided to import white students from the North. At the beginning of November, COFO staged a Freedom Ballot. Disenfranchised Negroes cast unofficial votes in a symbolic election, demonstrating for all the world to see that it wasn't for lack of desire that they failed to cast their duly sanctioned ballots. Lowenstein organized a hundred students from Stanford and Yale to swoop into Mississippi to help. Over eighty thousand Negroes cast their Freedom Ballots for Aaron Henry, the Negro head of the Mississippi NAACP, and Edwin King, the white chaplain of Tougaloo College, for governor and lieutenant governor, respectively. By Mississippi standards, relatively little violence resulted. The reason, SNCC concluded, was that the white students had attracted northern reporters in their wake. The white shield had also been deployed successfully when white and Negro ministers had demonstrated in Greenwood the previous spring without violence. Moses was heartened. Shortly after the Freedom Vote, he and Lowenstein began to discuss bringing a larger wave of white students to Mississippi for the summer—as hostages, in effect, for the national conscience and triggers for federal intervention.

The assassination of President Kennedy on November 22, 1963, did nothing to diminish Moses's resolve or his sense of what was necessary. If anything, Lyndon Johnson would need to be pushed even more than Kennedy; whoever sat in the White House, local power would have to be created. Still, the assassination made politics more volatile, the liberal-radical tension more severe. Kennedy, for all his hesitations, was at least a known and malleable quantity. When the assassin's bullet struck its target, some civil rights activists, especially those from the Deep South, were distraught; others, disoriented, dazed, blank. Many New Leftists speculated about right-wing and CIA conspiracies; on the cui bono principle, some wondered, in late-night broodings, at Lyndon Johnson's role as inheritor. A SNCC staff member coauthored one of the first speculations about discrepancies in the official story about Lee Harvey Oswald. Kennedy could be appreciated better in his absence; hadn't the strongest attacks on him before his death come from his Right? Within a few weeks it became apparent that Johnson was committed to Kennedy's domestic policies, if anything with greater vigor and a more sweeping popular mandate. But the tension between radicalism and managerial liberalism was fundamental and outlived the martyred Kennedy.

It was one week after Kennedy was killed that Moses spoke of the "annealing process," bringing Mississippi to a "white heat." Already the strategy was ambiguous. Were the white students to function as a white shield or the conduits of white heat?

The Mississippi Summer Project never resolved this tension. Nor did

it ever assuage the suspicion of some Negro organizers that the white
students would swamp the local Negro leadership, overwhelm them with
skills and arrogance, then leave the movement disrupted when the
autumn came and college called. It took a personal appeal from Moses to
talk SNCC staff out of their initial opposition. But the three hundred
volunteers, five-sixths of them white, did draw the media spotlight—and
white heat as well. While SNCC organizers at the training session in
Oxford, Ohio, were still warning the volunteers of the dangers of back-
road Mississippi, CORE organizers Mickey Schwerner and James Chaney,
and volunteer Andrew Goodman, were reported missing, presumed dead,
near the town of Philadelphia. Even before the three bodies were
unearthed from a dam on August 4, the summer project was shadowed by
violence. By one tally, there were three other civil rights murders in
Mississippi that summer, as well as eighty people beaten, thirty-five shot
at (with three injured), thirty-five churches burned down, thirty homes
and other buildings bombed (seventeen in McComb alone), and a
thousand arrests.

Despite white violence, the white shield was a partial success. The
missing Schwerner, Chaney, and Goodman brought Mississippi terror into
screaming headlines for the first time. By the end of the summer, Moses
reported that harassment had subsided in most of Mississippi, although
many SNCC people thought that the guns many Negroes were quietly
carrying (legal in Mississippi) were a more powerful deterrent than the
presence of FBI men. Yet the shield rubbed at an old movement wound.
While many Negroes were grateful for the help of whites—in voter
registration, freedom schools, and many another summer project—many
others were enraged that killings, beatings, and jailings were worthy of
the ministrations of the media, the FBI, and the Justice Department only
when whites were in jeopardy. Herbert Lee was memorialized in a civil
rights song and in Bob Moses's talks on the campuses of the North, not on
the front page of *The New York Times*. Who could believe that the Negro
James Chaney of Meridian, Mississippi, would have become a national
martyr on his own?

ATLANTIC CITY

More than eighty thousand Mississippi Negroes joined the Freedom Democratic Party
(MFDP) that summer.* Not only did the
counterparty have right on its side, but there seemed a fighting chance it
could displace the lily-white official party, many of whose delegates were
pledged to Barry Goldwater, and whose leader, Governor Paul Johnson,
had been in the habit of proclaiming from the stump that NAACP stood

*Of the seventeen thousand who filled out registration forms, only about sixteen hundred were
permitted onto the official voting rolls.

for "Niggers, Alligators, Apes, Coons, and Possums." In early August more than eight hundred MFDP members held a statewide convention, nominated sixty-eight delegates (including four whites) to the Democratic Party Convention in Atlantic City, and pledged allegiance to the national party and its platform.

"'Optimism' among Mississippi veterans," wrote the volunteer Sally Belfrage, "is a quality so muted as to be barely discernible." But who knew what might prove possible on the boardwalk of Atlantic City? Some in SNCC, including Bob Moses, had big strategic hopes. Like SDS (and Michael Harrington, Tom Kahn, Bayard Rustin, and other social democrats), they could imagine "realigning" the Democratic Party, establishing a new left-of-center majority. SNCC field secretary Cleveland Sellers wrote about the strategic sense he and Bob Moses shared: "We were thinking far beyond Atlantic City. If our venture there was successful, we intended to utilize similar tactics in other Southern states, particularly Georgia and South Carolina. Our ultimate goal was the destruction of the awesome power of the Dixiecrats, who controlled over 75 percent of the most important committees in Congress. With the Dixiecrats deposed, the way would have been clear for a wide-ranging redistribution of wealth, power and priorities throughout the nation."

Even those who doubted the official Mississippi Democrats could be unseated, like SNCC's adviser Ella Baker, thought the attempt worth making, "an alerting process." SNCC's pessimists, sending their caravan of buses and battered cars northward, thought of Atlantic City as one more necessary exercise in dramaturgy. MFDP delegates, many of whom had never been out of Mississippi, were more innocent. Fannie Lou Hamer, vice chairman of the delegation and a sharecropper's wife who had been thrown off the plantation and beaten for leading a vote drive, took the bus north "with all of this hope." Some three-quarters of the delegates were small farmers. They came a long way with their depositions on voter discrimination, their pictures of Negro living conditions, their lists of churches burned and bombed. They took with them the car in which Chaney, Goodman, and Schwerner had been riding when they were ambushed and killed. "When we went to Atlantic City," Mrs. Hamer said later, "we didn't go there for publicity, we went there because we believed that America was what it said it was, 'the land of the free.' And I thought with all of my heart that the [official delegation] would be unseated in Atlantic City. . . ."

At first, a conscientious America seemed to be paying them heed, and even longtime SNCC staff members found themselves hoping against hope. On top of the publicity, a summer of lobbying seemed to be paying off. The MFDP had become the sentimental favorite of the liberals in several northern and western delegations. Ten percent of the Credentials Committee could force a minority report, carrying the issue to the convention floor; eight delegation chairmen on the floor could then force a roll-call ballot, shaming many delegates into voting for the MFDP.

And thanks to live television, previously voiceless people were able to speak to America over the heads of the usual managers. The afternoon of August 22, the Credentials Committee heard the passionate testimony of Fannie Lou Hamer, who told what had happened when she led a group of Negroes to register in Senator James O. Eastland's hometown:

> I was carried to the county jail. . . . And it wasn't too long before three white men came to my cell. . . . I was carried out of the cell into another cell where they had two Negro prisoners. The state highway patrolman ordered the first Negro to take the blackjack. The first Negro prisoner ordered me, by orders from the state highway patrolman, for me to lay down on the bunk bed on my face, and I laid on my face. The first Negro began to beat, and I was beat until he was exhausted. . . . After the first Negro . . . was exhausted, the state highway patrolman ordered the second Negro to take the blackjack. The second Negro began to beat and I began to work my feet, and the state highway patrolman ordered the first Negro who had beat to set on my feet and keep me from working my feet. I began to scream, and one white man got up and began to beat me on my head and tell me to "hush." One white man—my dress had worked up high—he walked over and pulled my dress down and he pulled my dress back, back up. I was in jail when Medgar Evers was murdered. All of this is on account we want to register, to become first-class citizens, and if the Freedom Democratic Party is not seated now, I question America. . . .

Fannie Lou Hamer's testimony was TV's close-up equivalent of its devastating 1963 footage of Birmingham's cattle prods, water hoses, and police dogs. This was probably the first time the networks had transmitted a Mississippi Negro's story at length. It was irresistible, uncensored television, and one of the people who thought so was Lyndon B. Johnson. In the middle of Mrs. Hamer's testimony, on the spur of the moment, Johnson called a press conference. Dutifully, the cameras cut away from Mrs. Hamer to the President of the United States. But the tactic backfired: that night, in prime time, the networks broadcast Mrs. Hamer's whole testimony. Delegates were flooded with telegrams. The next day, Johnson made an offer. The MFDP delegates could be "honored guests" on the convention floor—without votes. "A zero," thought Joseph L. Rauh, Jr.

Joe Rauh, longtime ADA and Democratic Party stalwart, adviser to Hubert Humphrey, general counsel of Walter Reuther's United Automobile Workers (UAW), was the MFDP's counsel. He asked the Credentials Committee, "Are you going to throw out of here the people who want to work for Lyndon Johnson, who are willing to be beaten and shot and thrown in jail to work for Lyndon Johnson?" But sooner than chase after Negro voters, Johnson hastened after southern whites. Five of the regular southern delegations had proclaimed they would walk off the floor if the MFDP was seated. There were few enough Negro voters; where else could they go? Johnson was more worried about his right flank. Steeped in decades of realpolitik, he was acutely aware that George Wallace had picked up 30 percent or more of the Democratic primary votes in Wisconsin, Indiana, and Maryland. He needed the loyalty of Dixiecrat committee chairmen to push through his Great Society program. He could clinch liberal and labor support by dangling the vice-presidential nomination before their darling, Hubert Humphrey. Johnson was busily staking out his personal claim to the postassassination Democratic Party; he needed the liberals, but he was not a man to brook defiance from upstarts, whether Ho Chi Minh, Bobby Kennedy, or Fannie Lou Hamer.

Whether or not Johnson made Humphrey's support of his position on the MFDP an explicit condition for his nomination, Humphrey got the message and set out to round up the liberals.* Some of them did not need their arms twisted. Walter Reuther, for one, had been unsympathetic to the MFDP from the beginning. For months Reuther had tried to talk Rauh—who was, after all, the UAW's principal lawyer—out of representing the Freedom Democrats. At one point, in July, Rauh had given a speech to the MFDP, detailing the numbers of delegates they needed to win their challenge. Reuther had phoned Rauh to say, "The President called. He was very upset with you. Lyndon thinks if we seat those people, Goldwater will win." "Oh come on, cut out this shit," Rauh said. "Goldwater isn't going to beat Johnson and you know it." "What'll I tell Johnson?" Reuther asked. "Tell him that I'm an incorrigible son of a bitch that you can't control," Rauh said. "I should tell Johnson that I don't control my own general counsel?" "Look, Walter," said Rauh, "I am acting not as your general counsel, but as a citizen. I've got a private law practice. If you want to fire me, for Christ's sake, be my guest." Reuther was "so fucking mad," Rauh recalls, "you could fry an egg on his heart."

In Atlantic City, the MFDP promptly rejected Johnson's offer to make them guests without votes. Johnson, impressed by the breadth of the MFDP's support and eager to avoid a public fuss on his televised convention floor, began to float a new idea: two MFDP delegates would be seated alongside the regulars. While a special subcommittee headed by Minnesota Attorney General Walter Mondale went off to deliberate, Johnson's operatives set about twisting arms in the Credentials Committee. According to Rauh, one Negro California delegate was told "that her husband wouldn't get a judgeship if she didn't leave us, and the Secretary

---

*Humphrey, however, had no good reason to fret about the right. In May, Humphrey wrote to a friend, "President Johnson right now has universal acceptance—he occupies the center." Early in the summer a Humphrey poll showed a Johnson-Humphrey ticket drubbing a hypothetical Goldwater-William Scranton ticket with more than 70 percent of the national vote.

of the Army told the guy from the Canal Zone that he would lose his job if he didn't leave us." A New York delegate had her job threatened. The MFDP's support began draining away. Johnson knew that. He also knew that the national civil rights leadership was weakening. For the FBI had bugged Martin Luther King's and Bayard Rustin's rooms as well as MFDP, SNCC, and CORE headquarters. Fifty FBI men were deployed in Atlantic City, some posing as reporters, with NBC credentials, to ferret information from activists "on background." Every hour the FBI was delivering up-to-date information to Johnson aides Walter Jenkins and Bill Moyers.

The liberal-labor establishment pulled out the stops to talk the MFDP into accepting Johnson's two-delegate plan. At Johnson's behest, Walter Reuther slipped away from talks aimed at settling an impending strike in Detroit, and flew to Atlantic City to join Humphrey in Johnson's persuasion squad. Bayard Rustin persuaded Martin Luther King that the Johnson compromise amounted to a major victory, that to spurn it would amount to a "no-win policy." Rustin took at face value Johnson's campaign slogan, "We seek no wider war," arguing "that the peace of the world is more important than race at this moment, and the Negroes had to realize that Lyndon Johnson was the great candidate for peace, and if we wanted peace in the world, we had to support him and not upset the convention"—although Johnson, in the wake of a half-provoked, half-fabricated shooting incident in the Gulf of Tonkin, had just two weeks earlier procured a blank check for the Vietnam war from an acquiescent Congress. Roy Wilkins told Fannie Lou Hamer: "You're ignorant, you don't know anything about politics. I been in the business over twenty years. You people have put your point across. Now why don't you pack up and go home?" Mrs. Hamer also recalled this encounter with Hubert Humphrey:

> All that we had been hearing about . . . Hubert Humphrey and his stand for civil rights, I was delighted to even have a chance to talk with this man. But here sat a little round-eyed man with his eyes full of tears, when our attorney at the time, Rauh, said if we didn't stop pushing like we was pushing them and trying to get the . . . fight to come to the floor, that Mr. Humphrey wouldn't be nominated that night for Vice President of the United States. I was amazed, and I said, "Well, Mr. Humphrey, do you mean to tell me that your position is more important to you than four hundred thousand black people's lives [the Negro population of Mississippi]?" You see, this was blows to me, really blows, and I left out of there full of tears. . . . He didn't give too much of an answer.

The morning before the Credentials Committee was due to vote on Johnson's proposal, Bob Moses asked the MFDP delegation whether they would accept the seating of just two of their delegates. Rauh urged staying open to the impending compromise. Aaron Henry, the delegation's official head, supported it. But many of the delegates, and the SNCC organizers who influenced them, viewed Henry as their titular head only; as statewide leader of the NAACP he brought them some of the old-line Negro middle-class cachet, but the NAACP as a whole was not central to the MFDP. Ella Baker argued against a "sellout" designed to save Hubert Humphrey's career. Fannie Lou Hamer asked "what kind of moral victory" it would be to be seen on television when the delegates were "subject to being killed on our way back" and "the masses of folk are taking the same hell." Listening to Rauh and Henry, she felt sick: "We didn't come all this way for no two seats!"

So the MFDP told Johnson no. But watching the tide turn against them, they declared that they would accept a compromise that had been floated by Congresswoman Edith Green of Oregon: any Mississippi delegate who affirmed loyalty to the national ticket would be seated.* But Green's plan was a dead letter. Johnson wouldn't relent. Thanks to the FBI, he had the informational edge. He had victory in hand; therefore he had the liberal-labor coalition in hand. Ever since the New Deal, the standing of the unions and the liberals had rested on their capacity to deliver the goods to their constituencies; they, and the social bargain they stood for, were lost without access to presidential power.

Rauh was the man in the shrinking middle. A Washington labor lawyer since the New Deal, Rauh was—in the words of his old friend James A. Wechsler—"what Heywood Broun must have had in mind when he referred to the species 'congenital liberal': a large, warm, forceful and resourceful man who was probably more responsible than any other individual for the sustained existence of those formidable initials ADA. . . ." The consummate liberal activist, Rauh was vehemently anti-Communist in the name of liberal ideals—ever since 1939, when he had watched line-changing Communists try to obstruct American aid to Great Britain after the Hitler-Stalin pact. Yet he was also steadfastly opposed to anti-Communist inquisitions, and had defended Wechsler, Lillian Hellman, and Arthur Miller, among others, when they were dragged before McCarthy and HUAC.

Rauh was also Humphrey's left-hand man. As Democratic Party leader from the District of Columbia, he had shared Humphrey's fight for

---

*This was a variant of a hint Joe Rauh had dropped in his brief for the MFDP. "If you look at my brief," Rauh says, "which was approved by Moses and everybody else before it was filed, it's perfectly clear that it's heading for the seating of both, because the appendices are just reeking with the examples of seating both." One of those examples was the seating of two Texas delegations in 1944, one of them including Congressman Lyndon B. Johnson. "I wanted Johnson to see what the right compromise was," he says. "So I hinted at the compromise as early as the brief we prepared, long before the convention," and repeated the hint again and again. It would have been a good deal, Rauh thought, because "if they'd offered it to both of us, we'd take it and the other side wouldn't." But for exactly that reason, when Johnson sounded out his southern governor friends John Connally of Texas and Carl Sanders of Georgia on the idea of a two-delegation compromise, Connally said, "If you seat those black buggers [in another version, "baboons"], the whole South will walk off." "In other words," as Rauh put it later, "the real resentment is not against the exclusion of Paul Johnson's crowd. The real resentment is against the inclusion of our crowd."

a civil rights plank at the Democratic Convention of 1948. Now Humphrey, on the verge of the vice presidency, was fearful that troublemakers on the Left would cost him his chance. In Atlantic City, the two men met every night. With the two-delegate proposal in the air, Rauh insists that he kept driving a hard bargain on behalf of the MFDP: "I said, 'You've got to get more, we haven't got enough yet.' And he would say, 'I can't get you any more, but I'll try.'"

In private, Rauh had advised the MFDP to accept the compromise. But he went to the decisive Credentials Committee meeting committed to represent their uncompromising position. No sooner had the meeting started than Detroit's Negro congressman Charles Diggs alerted him that Detroit's political heavyweight, Walter Reuther, wanted Rauh to call him, right that minute. Such was Reuther's clout that he could arrange to have the meeting recessed while Rauh went out to a phone booth. Reuther told Rauh that Johnson, through Mondale's subcommittee, was going to put forward a new compromise: Aaron Henry and Ed King, the Negro chairman and white vice-chairman of the MFDP delegation, would be seated as delegates at large, away from the Mississippi section of the floor. The regular Mississippi delegation would be seated *if* they pledged to support the Democratic ticket in November. Starting in 1968, no delegation could be seated unless Negro voters were enfranchised. Then and there Reuther ordered Rauh to support the compromise. Rauh was impressed with the second and third points, which he assumed Reuther had bargained for. He was sure the lily-white delegation would refuse to endorse Johnson; they had already said they would. Still, Rauh told Reuther he had promised Aaron Henry that he wouldn't abandon the MFDP position without Henry's approval.

When Rauh got back to the committee room, he discovered he was not only outnumbered but outmaneuvered. He asked Mondale to postpone the vote so he could find Aaron Henry. Mondale was amenable, but Johnson's people insisted on going ahead without delay. They bulldozed the Johnson plan through by voice vote. Rauh tried and failed to get a postponement, then a roll-call vote. With the stalwarts down to a handful, Rauh shouted his no.

Outside, Mondale had first claim on the TV cameras. A frustrated Rauh waited his turn, then told reporters he had voted against the compromise and would now see what could be done to force a fight on the convention floor.

Radical and liberal political cultures were colliding again. At the instant Rauh was telling Reuther that he needed to find Aaron Henry, Henry was sitting a few feet away from Reuther, and Reuther wasn't letting on. While the Credentials Committee was in progress, Humphrey, Reuther, Bayard Rustin, and Martin Luther King were closeted in a hotel room with Henry, Ed King, and Bob Moses. Ed King thought it inherently paternalistic of Johnson to name the at-large delegates over the heads of the delegation itself. In his comparatively mild manner, he pushed for a modification in the compromise: Break the two at-large votes in half, then apportion the four half-votes to Henry, King, Fannie Lou Hamer, and another Negro woman, Victoria Gray. Then, according to Ed King, "Humphrey said, 'The President has said that he will not let that illiterate woman speak on the floor of the Democratic convention.' Bob Moses exploded. . . . He told Humphrey that he was a racist." Ed King thought "the real issue was that she was too emotional a speaker, and they were just afraid to have her as a delegate." Reuther reminded Martin Luther King how much money the UAW had given him over the years. About Rauh, this most fiery of the nation's labor leaders said, "That man worked for us, and we'll break him if we have to, destroy him. We'll fire him if he goes and keeps working for you people." A furious Humphrey told Moses, "Now look, Moses, anything you tell those people they're bound to do. . . . I know you're the boss of that delegation," to which Moses said the delegation would have to talk about it. The liberal managers weren't willing to let the MFDP speak in its own accent at the price of their control. They assumed that Moses's power over his constituents was like Lyndon Johnson's power over his.

At this point, the television report on the Credentials Committee meeting came on. Mondale gave his account. Humphrey, Reuther, and the others listened as the reporter went on to declare that the vote for the Johnson plan had been unanimous.

Bob Moses, furious, stood up. "You cheated," he said to Humphrey, and stormed out of the room, slamming the door. He didn't stay to hear Rauh say he had, in fact, voted no.

By the time Aaron Henry and Ed King got back to the MFDP delegation—said King later—"the SNCC people had gone mad. They were convinced that Ed King and Aaron Henry and Bob Moses had made a deal—because there it was on television." Rauh said later, "If the television account had been accurate, [Moses] had every right to be violent. I would have broken my word to him." The last threads of the radical-liberal bond were frayed; it took only bad reporting and bad timing to break them. Paradoxically, as they had gathered momentum in Atlantic City's early days, SNCC and the MFDP for all their radicalism and cynicism had let themselves hope—and therefore they felt betrayed, and went looking for traitors. By now the SNCC people were inclined to distrust Rauh anyway. Hadn't he tried to talk the MFDP into accepting a compromise? Although it isn't clear how much SNCC knew at that moment, Rauh's own position was indeed compromised. He may have voted against the Johnson proposal, but he had also exulted in another TV interview that "to call [the Johnson proposal] a loss is a mistake. . . . I think we've made a terrific gain. At a convention you always say there'll be no compromise. You get the best you can and you quit." Normal politics, in Rauh's eyes. Typical liberal sell-out, in SNCC's. For their taste Rauh was altogether too close to Humphrey and the rest of the liberal-labor establishment in the first place; some of them thought Rauh had cut a deal with the future vice president during their late-night tête-à-têtes. Nor did SNCC trust Rauh's middle-class allies Aaron Henry or Ed King. King himself was convinced "Rauh would not have made any move without our permission"; but why should Rauh have needed to consult with Henry, SNCC organizers asked, when the MFDP as a whole had already gone on record against what they considered a "back-of-the-bus" compromise? Some of the details of the Johnson-Reuther compromise were new, but the principle had already been settled.

Rauh had waited since 1948 to see the color line broken in the Democratic Party; he could wait till 1968. The MFDP's fight, in his eyes, was simply "a continuation" of the old struggle. To Bob Moses and Fannie Lou Hamer, however, 1964 was something quite different: the principle was that *these delegates* should not be turned back. What entitled the sharecroppers to seats was not their claim to justice alone but the quality of their suffering, the intensity of their bond, the witness that their entire lives bore forth. From SNCC's point of view—and most of the delegation's—waiting until 1968 was out of the question. It would represent a retreat to the NAACP's long-suffering wait-till-the-more-propitious-moment philosophy. The appetite for justice had been whetted, and the small farmers who were the majority of the MFDP delegation didn't see why they should sacrifice for the future one moment longer. At such moments, the symbols of privilege loom large. While Martin Luther King and other notables were ensconced in fancy hotels—why should they have anything less than the delegates?—MFDP representatives were staying at the shabby Gem Motel. Several SNCC staff workers were sleeping in the same Union Baptist church where the MFDP delegates took their meals and held their meetings.

Rauh told the press he was "disappointed," but said "we shouldn't forget that we made great progress." "This proves that the liberal Democrats are just as racist as Goldwater," proclaimed SNCC's Stokely Carmichael. In SNCC's eyes, Johnson, Humphrey, Reuther & Co. were not only pushing the MFDP onto the back of the symbolic bus, but, to add insult to insult, were taking it upon themselves to name the second-class passengers.* That night, the MFDP delegates, using borrowed credentials, smuggled themselves onto the convention floor, seized Mississippi's vacant seats, locked arms, and sat-in. Security police mobilized to evict them; Johnson, fearing a televised brawl, let them stay.

The credentials decision was a fait accompli, but the liberal and civil

---

*Many years later, when Rauh finally sat down with Moses to hash over Atlantic City, he expressed his belief that the MFDP might have reacted differently if the seats had gone to Henry and Fannie Lou Hamer. Moses thought it possible. But Rauh cautions: "I don't say it would have been [different] and [Moses] didn't say it would have been." Earlier, during the credentials fight, liberals had floated another possible compromise, giving the MFDP delegation two votes to share as a whole. Moses had not rejected the idea out of hand, but his interest was moot—the offer was never forthcoming from Johnson.

rights notables still weren't satisfied. Humphrey persuaded Aaron Henry to let Martin Luther King and Bayard Rustin address the delegates once more. They wanted the MFDP not only to acknowledge the inevitable but to endorse it. Liberal paternalism sought the willing acquiescence—even better, the enthusiastic embrace—of the weak. There was a short-term tactical side: proving reliability to the White House by guaranteeing decorum on the convention floor. There was strategy: trying to cement the MFDP into the liberal–labor–rights coalition of the future. There were personal motives as well: eminences like Humphrey and Walter Reuther wanted to be appreciated, even loved, for their devotions to the cause of civil rights. They *meant* their stated or unstated preface, "After all we've done for you . . ." Getting bills passed wasn't sufficient reward; neither were the pure pleasures of maneuver in the corridors of power. Gratitude was the coin in which insiders had to be paid. Gratitude from below certified that through all their backstage dealing, their consciences remained intact.

The next morning, at the notables' behest, the MFDP delegation, seething with feelings of betrayal, met to reconsider Johnson's offer. One after another, the leaders of the liberal-labor-civil-rights coalition trooped to the rostrum of the church to plead with the MFDP delegation. Joe Rauh said it "wasn't a bad deal." Martin Luther King rose to the heights of his eloquence—so testified no less a witness than the unreconstructed Stokely Carmichael. As a Negro leader, King said, he wanted the MFDP to accept the compromise: it would help the prospects for Negro voter registration throughout the South. If he were a Mississippi Negro, though, he would vote against it. King relayed a message from Humphrey: If they accepted, then the Civil Rights Commission would at long last hold hearings in Mississippi, unofficial seats on the floor would be found for the entire delegation, Johnson would meet with them, and the Democratic Party would leave segregation behind. Bayard Rustin's argument was that it was time for the movement to move "from protest to politics." People in politics had to give up the luxury of the pure moral act; politics always entailed compromise. The civil rights movement had to move toward economic reforms, for which it was going to need an alliance with people like Reuther and Humphrey—presumably on their terms. "You're a traitor, Bayard, a traitor! Sit down!" SNCC organizer Mendy Samstein yelled from the audience, while a Negro organizer tried to hush him. CORE's James Farmer equivocated, calling rejection of the compromise "morally right but politically wrong," reminding the MFDP delegates that turning it down would mean going it alone as a third party in hostile Mississippi. Michael Schwerner's widow, Rita, said the movement should scrap its hopes of getting anywhere in the Democratic Party.

Bob Moses's soft voice was the one that rang loudest in that old church, speaking to delegates whom he had done more than anyone else to bring to this crossroads—and he opposed the deal. So did SNCC's director, James Forman. At one point Moses met with Bayard Rustin and other high-level people in a corner of the church, but when the discussion turned to another possible compromise Moses walked out—high-level dealing would violate the principle that the people should decide. Then, in a meeting closed to SNCC organizers and all other outsiders, the MFDP delegates voted 64–4 against, once and for all.

Still, the Johnson plan proved too much for the official Mississippi delegation; they walked off the floor in protest. Some MFDP delegates, using borrowed credentials, smuggled themselves again into the convention hall, but this time the shrewd guards had removed the vacated Mississippi seats, leaving the Freedom Democrats standing awkwardly on the floor. When Johnson and Humphrey were nominated by acclamation, the cluster of Negro farmers in a corner was barely noticeable amid the flag-waving and the cheers.

The MFDP delegates went home to Mississippi terror and limited choices. In the short run, where else could they go but to the national Democrats? The Johnson-Humphrey ticket swamped Goldwater, who despite the liberal panic won only his native Arizona and five states in the Deep South—including Mississippi with 87 percent of the vote, although the MFDP remained loyal. Many of the MFDP delegates stayed with the party long enough to reap the proceeds of Johnson's Atlantic City concession. At the embattled Democratic Convention of 1968, they were official. "When we had an integrated delegation from Mississippi walk on the floor in 1968," Joe Rauh said years later, "that was one of the high points of my lifetime."

But the world they were integrated into was a different world, in good measure because of the rupture at Atlantic City. The party was integrated, the movement no longer. The SNCC-CORE polite boardwalk vigil of 1964 was the overture to the Chicago street riots of 1968. By 1968, virtually none of the veterans of Mississippi Summer and Atlantic City remained to welcome Fannie Lou Hamer's triumphal march onto the convention floor.

For SNCC and its supporters, including SDS, Atlantic City flashed the testament: Moment of Truth. The very name became synonymous with liberal betrayal. To the New Left, Atlantic City discredited the politics of coalition—between militants and the liberal-labor establishment, between whites and blacks, between youth and elders. (The Berkeley slogan, "Don't trust anybody over thirty," more dearly beloved by reporters than by eighteen-year-olds themselves, was coined by a CORE organizer, Jack Weinberg, just back on campus from Mississippi Freedom Summer. At that, reporters mistook Weinberg's point. Enamored of the phrase, they omitted the context. Weinberg was insisting that the Free Speech Movement, far from following a Communist line, was suspicious of older *Communists*.) Apparently the right response to being consigned to the back of the bus was to arrange for a bus of one's own. To Stokely Carmichael, "the major moral . . . was not merely that the national conscience was generally unreliable but that, very specifically, black people in Mississippi and throughout this country could not rely on their so-called allies. . . . Black people would have to organize and obtain their own power base before they could begin to think of coalition with others." Cleveland Sellers: "The national Democratic party's rejection of the MFDP at the 1964 convention was to the civil rights movement what the Civil War was to American history: afterward, things could never be the same. Never again were we lulled into believing that our task was exposing injustices so that the 'good' people of America could eliminate them. We left Atlantic City with the knowledge that the movement had turned into something else. After Atlantic City, our struggle was not for civil rights, but for liberation."

Both liberals and radicals fused means to ends, and so Atlantic City was a watershed on both sides. In an influential broadside against his old *Liberation* comrade Bayard Rustin, Staughton Lynd relayed the SNCC view that Atlantic City represented the betrayal of direct democracy, the rights of ordinary people. "The meaning of Atlantic City," Lynd wrote, was that "coalitionism" was "elitism," built on the assumption that "major political decisions are made by deals between the representatives of the interests included in the coalition," with men like Bayard Rustin "the national spokesmen who sell the line agreed-on behind doors to the faithful followers waiting in the street. . . . What was at stake," Lynd added, "as it seemed to the SNCC people there, was not so much the question, Should the compromise be accepted? as the question, Are plain people from Mississippi competent to decide? Rustin, Martin Luther King and Roy Wilkins answered the latter question: No. . . . But what [the MFDP and SNCC] learned at Atlantic City was simply no longer to trust these 'national civil-rights leaders.' . . . They learned, so . . . [Bob Moses said] in November, that the destiny of America was *not* in their hands, that they should seek their own objectives, 'let the chips fall where they may.'" Moses spoke of setting up a shadow government in Mississippi which Mississippi Negroes would honor instead of white rule. The SNCC rhetoric slid into the apocalyptic registers. The movement felt free—obliged, even—to skid off on its own.

The liberal-radical rift widened from there too fast for anyone to straddle. A case in point: Joe Rauh. For six months, throughout an entire General Motors contract negotiation, Walter Reuther didn't talk to Rauh, still his chief counsel. Bob Moses didn't speak to Rauh either, or answer his letter, for fifteen years.

THE REVOLUTIONARY PASTORALE

Atlantic City and the Gulf of Tonkin together, in the fateful month of August 1964, drew a sharp line through the New Left's Sixties. Before, liberalism posed a dilemma. After, it was an obstacle. Now that the movement had resolved to shake loose of the liberal managers, what followed?

The movement's expressive side, for one thing. A politics, too—eventually, the politics of going it alone, or looking for allies in revolution. But also the perfecting and proliferating of identities: culture as politics: the idea of "liberation"; the movement as a culture, a way of life apart. Cultural transformations already at work in the Fifties picked up speed. Subsurface tendencies showed themselves, shaping the rest of the decade: campus reform; black power; seeds of counterculture; the women's movement; the withering away of nonviolence. The North continued to follow the South.

SNCC had been a culture as well as a politics from the time Bob Moses settled into Mississippi. The urban sitters-in of 1960 wore uniforms of respectability: jackets and ties, white blouses and skirts. It was their part to look civilized, after all, as unreconstructed racists poured bottles of ketchup down their backs. Then, in 1961 and 1962, the SNCC organizers who fanned out into the Black Belt were powerfully affected by the most impoverished and disenfranchised Negroes: what began as strategy became identity. SNCC organizers, mostly city-bred, picked up the back-country look of Georgia and Mississippi: denim jackets, blue work shirts, bib overalls. One SNCC poster showed a sharecropper sitting in front of his shack, a torn hat shading his face: "One Man, One Vote." SNCC's clothes were physical markers of solidarity. The standard SNCC wage was ten dollars a week, a practical and ideological fact—it insulated SNCC from the pressures of big-money donors—as well as a spiritual one.

"What happens with students in our movement," Bob Moses told Robert Penn Warren, "is that they are identifying with these people . . . who come off the land—they're unsophisticated, and they simply voice, time and time again, the simple truths you can't ignore because they speak from their own lives." Other Negro leaders, Moses said, were "for the kind of meeting where you get well-dressed, cleaned-up Negroes. They don't want the other people. They're embarrassed. Those people don't speak English well. They grope for words." These ill-educated back-country men and women were the first in their counties in generations to dare register. To make the attempt, they had to brave the beatings and bombings of nightriders. To qualify for the state's deliberately tortuous version of literacy, under a Jim Crow law of 1890, they had to interpret whichever of the Mississippi Constitution's 285 sections the registrar chose. The souls who dared try register to vote under these conditions could not pronounce the word *register*. They said "reddish."

Years later, Mario Savio, who worked in Mississippi during the glorious and terrifying Freedom Summer of 1964, said that the simple word *reddish* summed up the moral force of SNCC. The boldness of unlettered heroes was part of the spirit that summer volunteers like Savio and Jack Weinberg brought back to the Berkeley campus that fall—along with a respect for the power of civil disobedience, a fierce moralism, a lived love for racial equality, a distaste for bureaucratic highhandedness and euphemism, a taste for relentless talk at intense mass meetings on the way toward consensus. There were already five years of student protest to build on at Berkeley, but the usual organizers did not expect much to flare up that fall. A demographer might have noticed that 1964 was the year the first cohort of the baby boom was reaching college in force (freshman enrollments were up 37 percent that fall), but still, no one expected students to rise up en masse. Mississippi was the ignition. When University of California administrators knuckled under to local right-wing politicians and refused to permit the recruitment of civil rights demonstrators or the raising of movement money on campus, Savio, Weinberg, and others recognized a paternalism familiar from Mississippi and Atlantic City. On October 1, 1964, Jack Weinberg sat down at his "unauthorized" recruitment table in Sproul Plaza, violating campus rules, and was arrested; the police put him in the back of their car; other students sat down and blocked it for thirty-two hours; Savio among others spoke from its roof; and the Free Speech Movement—a movement of students claiming for themselves something of the innocence that went with the word *reddish*—was born.

The romance of intellectuals for the poor and uneducated is not new, of course. Consider the various ways of anthropology, Gauguin, Cubism, anticolonialism, and Malraux (and Jack Kerouac, as we saw). The whole of modernity is streaked with a passion for the premodern. The political form is especially potent: Ever since Rousseau and the Enlightenment, from the French Revolution through the Russian Narodniks who tried to organize peasants in the 1870s, from Tolstoy to James Agee, from Thoreau to Gandhi, a strain of radical intellectuals has insisted not only that simple people, especially peasants, are entitled to justice but that they are unspoiled repositories of wisdom, insulated from the corruptions of modern urban commercial life; that despite the injuries meted out to them, or perhaps because of those injuries, they remember something about living which the prosperous have forgotten. The ideals of equality and fraternity meet in the presence of the noble savage. A pastorale becomes the folk belief of populist revolutionaries; Marx's scorn for "the idiocy of rural life" is alien to them. Displaced, ill-at-ease, they seek precedents for their own fused group. Inspired by the solidarity of the resisting oppressed, they convince themselves that simplicity is the cultural soil from which a new society, purged of marketeering impersonality and trivial excess, grows. In the extreme form of the revolutionary romance, this simplicity fuses with what looks like absolute commitment: the peasants, pushed to the wall, have nothing to lose; not only their revolt but their ordinary lives become exemplary.

What existentialist radicals of the New Left cherished was variously what they saw as the stoicism, wholeness, community, and expressiveness of the poor farmer, which stood as alternatives to suburban blandness, middle-class impersonality, and folding-spindling-and-mutilating universities. Jane Stembridge, a onetime theology student from Virginia, one of the early SNCC staff members, a poet, and a consistent opponent of strategic thinking and tight organization in SNCC, knew that "poverty negates the strength/of being poor." But in 1965, in an internal SNCC memo, she wrote that in contrast to revolutionaries, who in their adherence to the "party line" are "afraid to be free," rural Negroes had "a closeness with the earth . . . a closeness with each other in the sense of community developed out of dependence . . . the strength of being poor." Howard Zinn's influential book on SNCC made much of the group's "renunciation, without the pretense of martyrdom, of the fraud and glitter of a distorted prosperity. It is also a recapturing from some time and place long forgotten of an emotional approach to life, aiming, beyond politics and economics, simply to remove the barriers that prevent human beings from making contact with one another." In a sympathetic review of Zinn, Tom Hayden wrote from SDS's Newark Community Union Project that SNCC's "strength comes from the humanism of rural people who are immune to the ravages of competitive society." Hayden added: "The honesty, insight and leadership of rural Negroes demonstrate to the students that their upbringing has been based on a framework of lies." The alternative to the false promises of coalition was "the construction of alternative institutions—freedom schools, cooperatives, the FDP—which carry at least the seeds of a new consciousness." The movement's hope was to preserve its worthy alienation while deploying it against the pyramids of power, not squandering it in withdrawal as the beats did.

So it was that the community organizers of SDS's Economic Research and Action Project (ERAP), inspired by SNCC (via the Carmichael–Hayden conversation of August 1963), transposed the pastorale into an urban key by digging in among black and white ghetto-dwellers of the North in the summer of 1964. At the same time three hundred northern students were flocking to Mississippi, SDS recruited a hundred more to move into the slums of Newark, Chicago, Cleveland, Philadelphia, and half a dozen other cities, looking to stir up an interracial movement of the poor. Most went back to school at the end of the summer, but others came and stayed a year or two, which passes for permanency at age twenty-two. There were strategic notions: We believed automation was about to send the economy into crisis, dumping millions out of jobs, stoking up poor white backlash against blacks unless we created a class-based alternative on the Left. Some of the ERAP strategists, unlike Hayden, thought the poor could build a fire under the liberal-labor establishment, keeping it honest. But the expressive motives were at least equally strong: middle-class guilt, and the search for a congenial Other.

And so most of SDS's practiced cadres vacated the campuses in 1964 and 1965. ("Ghetto-jumping," ERAP's antagonists in SDS called it, preferring electoral politics and campus work.) In a world where gouging landlords and local tycoons were tied to Democratic machines professing liberal values, the organizers diverged even further from the tainted liberal-labor establishment. Not for the first time, the tendency was led by Tom Hayden. Paul Potter wrote privately, early in 1965: "Tom seems to be moving closer and closer to a position that the liberal establishment (if not all liberals) constitutes the most dangerous enemy we confront. Without debating that point of view, it should simply be pointed out that it stands in direct and polar opposition to the public attitude of SDS in the past. We have tried to be fraternal critics of liberal institutions and organizations. . . . We have avoided direct and personal confrontations in favor of arguments over issues, and we have searched for common ground and not the numerous bases of division." No longer.

In the ERAP projects, expenses were kept down and the organizing groups fused by installing the organizers in staff apartments, proto-communes inspired by SNCC's "freedom houses." Spending money was scarce, but the projects were devoted to peanut-butter-and-jelly lunches and macaroni dinners by mystique as well as necessity. In a few cases, the obligatory giant-size peanut butter jar was supplemented with a steak or two swiped from the local supermarket. Some organizers wanted to go further, forcing themselves to eat on the welfare budget—twenty-five cents per person per meal, or less. I felt the force of the spirit of pastorale myself, or its literary equivalent. Having learned in the SDS summer project in Chicago during the summer of 1964 that I hated knocking on doors, trying to entice people into an organization difficult to explain, I came back in 1965 with my then-wife to work on a book about the Appalachian migrants whom our ERAP friends were trying to organize. In the spirit of James Agee's *Let Us Now Praise Famous Men* and Oscar Lewis's *The Children of Sanchez,* the idea was to become instruments of the voiceless voices, those who if not exalted by suffering, exactly, still spoke with dignity. Their stories would show, at least, that poverty was not the fault of the poor.

FLOATERS AND HARDLINERS

As SNCC and SDS loosed the restraints of respectability, new dilemmas surfaced. The habit of participatory democracy was hard to stop. If all authority was suspect, why not the authority of the organizers themselves? The revolutionary pastorale easily slipped into an anguish. By what right did outsiders, these self-appointed partisans of the future, disturb the fragile equilibrium of the oppressed, exposing them to the reprisals of landlords, welfare bureaus, and police? When outsiders knocked on doors and tried to mobilize people around immediate issues, keeping their radical agendas in abeyance, was this not manipulation? When the outsiders had degrees from fancy colleges, and knew how to talk a good show, were they another breed of colonizers not so different, perhaps, from the highfalutin liberals, the social workers, the war-on-poverty operatives from Washington?

A tormented few quit organizing altogether. But a larger number of SNCC and ERAP organizers (and some who migrated from one organization to the other) stayed, and became a loosely knit anarchist caucus, a counterculture in the making. In the post–Atlantic City mood, they resonated to Jane Stembridge's poems, one of which denounced "all executive committees," and to Bob Dylan's line, "Don't follow leaders, watch the parking meters," from "Subterranean Homesick Blues." SNCC began to divide into self-proclaimed "hardliners," mostly black, and the group, half-black, half-white, they derided as "floaters," "philosophers," "existentialists," "anarchists," and "freedom-high niggers." As early as 1965, the floaters were describing their mission in the prophetic words, "Do your thing." They sang, "Do what the spirit say do," an early SNCC motto, with particular relish. Against them, James Forman, for one, complained about "an ailment known as local-people-itis—the romanticization of poor Mississippians. This carried with it the idea that local people could do no wrong; that no one, especially somebody from outside the community, should initiate any kind of action or assume any form of leadership." In the only somewhat jaundiced eyes of hardliner Cleveland Sellers, who wanted a more disciplined and centralized organization, "They were 'high' on Freedom, against all forms of organization and regimentation. . . . No one ever knew for certain what they were going to do or where they might turn up next. They were great talkers, who generally ended up dominating those meetings and conferences they saw fit to attend. . . . They loved to bring meetings to a screeching halt with open-ended, theoretical questions. In the midst of a crucial strategy session on the problems of community leaders in rural areas, one of them might get the floor and begin to hold forth on the true meaning of the word *leader*. . . . I considered them impractical. SNCC was not a debating society. It was an action organization." You did not decide on a demonstration simply because of the "freedom-high argument" that it made you feel good.

Sellers has described one confrontation, in October 1964, when battle fatigue from Freedom Summer and disillusionment from Atlantic City brought simmering factionalism to a boil. Sellers and two other hardliners got wind of a floater caucus meeting one night. They rushed over. A hush fell when the three of them walked in. Casey Hayden was saying: "Do you remember when you were a child? Do you remember how people oppressed you, not with chains or anything, but because they were always trying to get you to do things you didn't really want to do?"

"What has that got to do with SNCC and the work before us?" Sellers yelled at her. "We are trying to move people from one place to another.

Sometimes we have to coerce them. Sometimes we have to shame them. They're frequently afraid and reluctant to do the things we want, but that's the way it is. We are not oppressors. We aren't doing anything we should be ashamed of. We *have* to establish priorities. Getting people to deal with their fears and insecurities is a SNCC priority. There's nothing wrong with that! We don't need to get hung up on a lot of philosophy. What we ought to be discussing is strategy and programs. Where are your programs?"

SNCC's floaters and their SDS equivalents weren't politicians in any conventional sense—all the less so after Atlantic City discredited the big-league politics of coalition. They only felt comfortable working on a scale they could control: among themselves. It wasn't in their characters to relish the movement's own back-room decisions and power plays, the compromises and deferred dreams of practical politics. Few such characters were active in the New Left in the first place; as the baby-boom generation reached the campuses, antiauthority flourished all the more, and the movement attracted people who liked to float.

At the same time, SNCC was tilting toward an angry nationalism. The Selma-to-Montgomery March led by Martin Luther King in March 1965 was the high-water mark of integrationism. Its televised dignity, juxtaposed to racist violence, spurred Johnson to declare "We Shall Overcome," and push through an overdue Voting Rights Act. But SNCC militants felt betrayed by King's decision to draw back from confrontation. Moreover, the reforms once and for all deprived SNCC of its old strategic rationales. After public accommodations came voter registration; after voter registration came—what? Blacks had rioted in Harlem in the summer of 1964; in August 1965 came an enormous and bloody uprising in Watts; perhaps the anger released in such "rebellions"—as SNCC called them—pointed the way to SNCC's future in the cities. Racial antagonism, stoked by Freedom Summer and Atlantic City, burst through to the surface.

Late in the fall of 1965, a newly elected hardliner SNCC Executive Committee told the floaters on the staff that they had to start complying with rules (specifically, to report on their activities) or be thrown off the payroll forthwith. Arriving at a staff meeting, the floaters burned their meal tickets and refused to register, provoking a near-brawl. But they were outnumbered and outorganized. SNCC's center of gravity was tilting toward black nationalism. In 1965 and 1966, SNCC's white staff—almost all of them floaters—were forced out. Expelled from their political home, burned out, most left the South. Doubly uprooted, they looked up from the pits of their pain for transcendence, and turned to marijuana—already widespread in Mississippi in 1964—and to LSD, the just-spreading drug that promised to unleash the spirit even more than a mass meeting in the Delta swelling with "We Shall Overcome."

As the old SNCC exploded, it threw off centrifugal energies like a dying star. Some of the ex-SNCC outcasts turned to antiwar work. (One of them, a Stanford student named Dennis Sweeney, in 1967 was one of the founders of The Resistance, the major national network of draft resisters.) Some, like Casey Hayden, tried to organize poor whites. Some migrated to low-rent districts which were on their way to becoming the hippie enclaves of New York City, Vermont, and San Francisco. (One floater extraordinaire, Abbie Hoffman, opened a store on Manhattan's Lower East Side to sell Mississippi co-op-made goods.) Veterans of freedom houses, these pioneers of the counterculture were partial to the collective life. Some devoted themselves to cultivating the authentic. At an SDS meeting in 1965, just after the first big march against the Vietnam war, an ex-SNCC floater, a black man, tried to talk us student radicals into the virtues of "soul sessions," something akin to what would later be called encounter groups. Organizing be damned; how dare we presume to organize anyone else before we got straight about who we were and how we felt? In their revolt against hierarchies, the floaters also floated something extraordinary: a women's movement. Late in 1964, Mary King and Casey Hayden of SNCC wrote an anonymous memo protesting the fact that women were automatically consigned to menial office tasks, were not heeded at meetings, were undervalued, and undervalued themselves, like blacks up against whites. Stokely Carmichael's famous response line, "The position of women in SNCC is prone," was actually spoken in jest, but although Carmichael himself sympathized with the protest, plenty of SNCC men did not. A year later, Hayden and King extended their argument into a modest manifesto they mailed around the movement, where it was greeted by tremors of recognition. From the beginning, hadn't SNCC's idea, and SDS's, been that a subject people had the right, the duty, to master their own fate?

Black nationalism, hippiness, feminism: the old movement unities were certainly breaking down.

"THE MAN WITHOUT THE UNIFORM"

With Freedom Summer and Atlantic City, the burdens of SNCC leadership staggered Bob Moses. He had worked in Mississippi— and Mississippi had worked in him—for more than three years. At a time when battle fatigue was normal for organizers who had been there three *months,* his nerves and spirit were worn ragged. "The man without the uniform," Jane Stembridge wrote, "is wearing only scars." In 1961, Moses had cast his lot with voter registration against direct action, as if protection would be forthcoming from Kennedy's Washington. The wager was one thing but the murder of Herbert Lee was another, bitter and irreversible. He felt responsible. Three years later, he threw his whole weight and prestige behind the white heat/shield strategy. During the Freedom Summer training session in Oxford, Ohio, when Chaney, Schwerner, and Goodman were discovered missing, he spoke of J. R. R. Tolkien's Frodo, corrupted by the Ring of Power he carried. Now Moses felt frayed by what felt to him like liberal-labor betrayal. What more illusions could he imagine or endure?

From the beginning, Moses had wanted to be a catalyst, not a formal leader. Even under the best of circumstances, the dilemmas of leadership were severe. Now, with no route visible out of the strategic wilderness, he retreated. Late in 1964, he resigned as head of the unified Mississippi movement and moved to Alabama, telling a reporter he had become "too strong, too central, so that people who did not need to, began to lean on me, to use me as a crutch." Early in 1965, Moses stood up at a SNCC staff retreat to announce that he would no longer be known as Robert Moses. He would be Robert Parris, after his middle name, which was his mother's maiden name. He spoke of his mother, who had once broken down under family strain and the strain of being poor. He passed around a hunk of cheese and an empty bottle of wine, as if to say that in this ceremony of his abdication, no one should expect miracles.

The tenuous ground he tried to occupy had turned to quicksand. Soon this exemplar of integration resigned from SNCC altogether. Robert Parris's last political acts in the United States were speeches and marches against the war boiling up in Vietnam. His self-abasing style, tailored to dusty Delta towns, was already beginning to be drowned out by apostles more in tune with the stridencies of ghetto streets: a line of succession that proceeded from Malcolm X to Stokely Carmichael and Rap Brown and eventually to Huey Newton and Eldridge Cleaver. Under pressure from the draft, Robert Parris Moses banished himself to Tanzania, to teach, and stayed away from America for more than a decade.

"NAME THE SYSTEM"

OLD STYLES IN ACRIMONY

Despite the post–Port Huron imbroglio of 1962, it was only reluctantly, fitfully, that SDS dissolved the bands that bound it to the social-democratic Left and the liberal-labor coalition. In 1963, we weren't so cocky or desperate, yet, as to think we could go it alone. There were well-disposed social democrats who also hoped, as Irving Howe later put it, "there might be a joining of two generations of the Left." So it was that in October 1963 a group from SDS met with a group of *Dissent* editors, Irving Howe and my old teacher Michael Walzer (Howe's former student) among them. We would talk to anyone who would talk to us about the modest undertaking of changing the world.

Perhaps this stab at amity was ill-starred by its setting: the elegant Upper East Side Manhattan home of Joseph Buttinger, an editor and patron of *Dissent* who had been one of the leaders of the Austrian Socialist Party and its underground resistance against Hitler. Later he became one of the first American scholars of Vietnam. Although I wasn't aware of it at the time, Buttinger was married to the psychoanalyst Muriel Gardiner, the courageous heiress who had rescued many Jews in prewar Vienna, and whom many now regard as the model for Lillian Hellman's famous "Julia." Most of the first floor of their house was taken up by a library; there was a private elevator. I was dazzled.

The gemütlich Buttinger and the taut, indignant Howe played grandfather and father, the elders scouting the upstarts; Tom Hayden, Lee

Webb, Paul Potter, Steve Max, and I played the rambunctious youth. I have carried for years a memory of this occasion's sting. Howe has written about it himself, twice in fact: in a *New Republic* article and again in his memoir. We have both felt the pain of what failed that day. More than twenty years after the fact, we talked over that afternoon, and I have also discussed it with Hayden. Generations crystallize around their memories. So do political rifts.

Howe has set the scene nicely: "At this meeting two generations sat facing each other, fumbling to reach across the spaces of time. We were scarred, they untouched. We bore marks of 'corrosion and distrust,' they looked forward to clusterings of fraternity. We had grown skeptical of Marxism, they were still unchained to system. We had pulled ourselves out of an immigrant working class, an experience not likely to induce romantic views about the poor; they, children of warm liberals and cooled radicals, were hoping to find a way into the lives and wisdom of the oppressed." Is it the fate of the middle-aged to read the present in the flickering half-light of their youth? When Howe's group heard SDS contrast participatory democracy to representative democracy, it was "as if somehow the two were contraries." The *Dissent*ers winced: "It sounded a little too much like the fecklessness of our youth, when Stalinists and even a few Socialists used to put down 'mere' bourgeois democracy." Even worse, Howe thought, "was the readiness of SDS people to excuse the lack of freedom in Cuba, a country that seemed to them the home of a better or more glamorous kind of communism. They, in turn, made quite clear their distaste for our 'rigid anticommunism' and our lack of responsiveness to the new moods of the young."

Confrontations tear deepest when they are one-to-one. Hayden made the biggest impression on Howe, and their collision made the lasting impression on them, and on me. Of the SDS group, Howe wrote, Hayden was "the most rigid, perhaps even fanatical." Fanatical? Does this signify anything aside from passion you disagree with? In truth Hayden was a dynamo. The two of us shared a house that year; I was awed by his nonstop schedule, and asked him once how he kept it up; he replied, apparently without irony, "I have an ideology." But Howe was reacting to more than Tom's intense commitment: "Hayden did not suffer from illusions about the democratic character of North Vietnam or Cuba; he spoke with the clenched authority of a party leader. . . ." In Howe's recollection, Cuba was the flash point. As he saw it, Hayden defended Castro's Cuba, whereupon *Dissent* editor Emanuel Geltman lost his temper—"rose to Tom's bait, in a way," as Howe put it—and launched into his own diatribe. All these years later, Howe could admit that he and Geltman, while correct about Cuba, were "heavyhanded and didactic and no doubt patronizing, or at least so it must have seemed to you people. . . . We came on as know-it-alls." Hayden's "hard" quality, his "tremendous self-assurance," his casting himself as "a hero of history," "unnerved us a little bit."

In the memory I have carried with me for years—equally selective, no doubt—the "clenched authority" was shared but the edge went to Howe. The debate about Cuba left no imprint on me. What has stuck in my mind is another moment: Hayden expounding the pure Gandhian theory of nonviolence—the idea that loving your enemy while suffering his violence not only changes society but redeems the enemy himself. You had to love everyone, Hayden insisted, in the voice of his southern experience. To me, this was Hayden at his most eloquent, the New Left at its most stirring. The question wasn't academic; Hayden was wrestling with this question because around that time his draft board was interrogating him about the absoluteness of his nonviolence. What I remember most vividly is Howe, the hard-nailed disbeliever, sneering: "Could you love a fascist, Tom?" Backed into a corner, Tom insisted he could indeed. Howe, aghast, declared that he couldn't love Hitler.

Two decades after the fact, I ask Hayden about this as he takes a break from a state assembly committee hearing in the Capitol building in Sacramento. "I don't know if I could then love a fascist or now love a fascist," he says, "but if Irving Howe insisted that I couldn't then, I would probably say I could. It's that kind of unhealthy dynamic that I remember the most."

When I exchange fragments of memory with Irving Howe, we are two grizzled veterans. I am the same age, forty-two, that Howe was in 1963. We agree about more today than we did when I was twenty. I know what it is like, now, to be attacked from my left—how galling when the attacker is twenty years younger, how hard to forge the link between innocence and experience. Howe says he was exasperated by Hayden's illogic: "How can you be in favor of Castro, who speaks of exporting revolution to South America, and then also be in favor of nonviolence?" To be attacked by the same person from both right and left at the same time got on Howe's nerves. In fact, there is a way to make sense of the contradiction: Above all, Hayden was inspired by, and loyal to, the handfuls of students who had succeeded in making history, whether through sitting-in at southern lunch counters or storming the Moncada barracks in Cuba.

To the SDS contingent, Howe and his colleagues stood, precisely, for *dissent:* naysaying from the side of the parade. However noble, they were reconciled to their failure to change the course of history; they were indeed, as Howe said, "antiheroes of history," while we yearned to see history go our way for once in the twentieth century.* Moreover, by dint of being intellectuals, they were, in our eyes, inactivists. They *had*

*In 1967, with just this distinction in mind, the Berkeley activist Steve Weissman set out to edit a volume of original New Left essays to be entitled, self-consciously, *Beyond Dissent.* Typically, half the authors never wrote their essays, and the book never saw print. Touché Department: Howe edited a 1970 collection called *Beyond the New Left.*

politics; we *were* politics. We wanted to know what people were prepared to do; what they thought was secondary. Like it or not, these vigorous anti-Communists were cousins of the state socialist *Monthly Review* editor Leo Huberman, who had offended Dick Flacks on Martha's Vineyard after Port Huron. They shared a position: in the armchair. All of them were waiting until that ever-receding moment when pure politics would shimmer into existence. They were the utopians, we the realists. *We* were out organizing the masses, or at least we aspired to be. It didn't matter to us that Howe went to some of our meetings, spoke at some rallies, or (least of all, perhaps) published a journal which had embraced the early student movement.

About to flee the university in search of a revolutionary populace, we scorned "mere" intellectuals unless—like C. Wright Mills and Paul Goodman—they broke unequivocally with the tone and texture of established America. Mills with his outlaw Texan-in-New-York persona— his motorcycle, his handwrought house in the country, his bad odor in the academy, not to mention his assault on "the power elite"—possessed the unreconciled allure that Hayden, in the master's thesis on Mills he was writing at that moment, referred to in his title: "Radical Nomad." Goodman was the insider's outsider, the peripatetic freelance philosopher, enormously learned yet economically and socially (and sexually, though we didn't know it yet) a man of the margins. We loved them for their bad manners.* Compared to them, or their reputations, men like Irving Howe and Joseph Buttinger, for all their talk of socialism, seemed to us altogether *settled*.

For which the lovely Buttinger house, of course, fairly screamed as symbol. As we left, Buttinger took Tom and me aside and gave us copies of a thick book he had written about the collapse of the underground socialist opposition to Hitler's *Anschluss*. The title was *In the Twilight of Socialism*. I was touched by his grandfatherly gesture, and both moved and uneasy about the title. Tom and I exchanged knowing glances. We sensed Buttinger's kindness and tolerance, respected his heroism. But through no fault of his own, history had condemned him to be a loser. Not for us elegies to the twilight; for us the celebration of sunrises! (Which didn't stop us from going to Buttinger's family foundation, the next spring, for a few thousand dollars to help us set up an ERAP training institute—a request he graciously granted.) By the time I learned that Buttinger had been one of the earliest American supporters of Ngo Dinh Diem (although he had turned actively against him in 1962), I was ready to say, Aha, that's where social democracy can take you.

For years I have thought that the *Dissent* people forfeited an

---

*Actually, I was considerably more enamored of Goodman, and his bad-boy reputation, before meeting the man. He came to Ann Arbor in the winter of 1965, fresh from Berkeley, and gave a speech heralding the Free Speech Movement as the vanguard proletariat-in-training of the knowledge industry. He was blunt about knocking SDS as old-fashioned left-wing dreamers, hung up on the poor. A version of his speech ended up in—where else?—*Dissent*.

opportunity that day. Howe too concludes that they were guilty of a "tactical incapacity," that they "should have played it more calmly, more quietly. . . . We should have expressed the difference with Tom, but we shouldn't have made it into an immediate ideological confrontation." Hayden thinks the dynamic was "profoundly generational" and that "a little love and respect would have gone a long way"; Howe doubts that much collaboration was in the cards anyway. But I am struck most by how much they agree about the importance of style. Howe could be "a very brutal debater," says his onetime student Martin Peretz; "nastier than the others," says Hayden. But the harsh, moralistic style was characteristic of Howe's entire political crowd. Hayden attributes it to "the New York intellectual culture, and a style of debate that I still don't think is helpful in arriving at the truth or arriving at consensus." "People like Harrington and myself," Howe says, by the early Sixties "really had a social democratic politics, but we didn't yet have a social democratic style." These seasoned scrappers, trained in the Talmudic disputation characteristic of Trotskyism, could not sit there sagely while we, young and inexperienced *pishers,* apparently ducked the lessons of Stalinism.

Howe says today that another reason for the head-on collision, "paradoxically—and that we couldn't have understood at that time—was that we were so eager to make a connection. The thing was so important to us that we overloaded, so to say." They had high hopes for us because we might—who knows?—embody the possibility of the mass movement they believed in. We represented their tendrils into the future. At the same time, I would add, all but Buttinger were young enough to feel that we might be a threat. Their democratic Left was small and weak, but for ten years it had been theirs. They wanted us to need them, and resented the fact that, as the student movement grew, we didn't. For the New Left, there was no worse limbo to which an enemy could be consigned than the outer reaches of "irrelevance." What could be more unkind, to a onetime Trotskyist, than to threaten to sweep him into—Trotsky's malevolent phrase—"the dustbin of history"?

After the meeting, both sides tried to put on diplomatic faces. Paul Potter and I wrote a report on SDS which *Dissent* published. Later I submitted to Howe an exchange Arthur Waskow and I had written about American expansionism. Howe rejected it, I believe for its epistolary style, but he seemed genuinely interested in getting me to write about the Vietnam war. Either because *Dissent* was plunged into the outer darkness of "irrelevance," or because I was daunted at the prospect of spelling out precisely what I thought—or because the first reason enabled me to mask the second—I passed up the invitation. Hayden and Howe tangled on other occasions, each rising to the other's poisoned bait. At a New York debate, Hayden said that you couldn't call the countries of Eastern Europe totalitarian. "What would *you* call them, Tom?" asked Howe with great scorn and to great effect, filling Hayden with rage and contempt.

In the summer 1965 issue of *Dissent* came Howe's blast against what he called "New Styles in 'Leftism,'" an essay that was crucial in drawing the social democrats' line against the New Left. "New Styles" spotted an "extreme, sometimes unwarranted, hostility toward liberalism"; an impatience with the old debates about Stalinism; "a vicarious indulgence in violence"; unconsidered enmity toward a vaguely defined "Establishment"; "an unreflective belief in 'the decline of the West'"; "a crude, unqualified anti-Americanism"; and "an increasing identification with that sector of the 'third world' in which 'radical' nationalism and Communist authoritarianism merge."

"New Styles" had the keen and partial truth of caricature. It pointed to the importance of style, posture, gesture, dress, in defining the New Left revolt, although underplaying the importance of style in defining all manner of modern attitudes—even, holy of holies, those of intellectual life. As sociology it gave possibly the first notice in print that the "inordinate difficulty in communication" between the two generations was a consequence of the missing radical generation, "the generation that would now be in its late thirties, the generation that did not show up." I ask myself, therefore, why I was so annoyed by Howe's piece at the time. Partly, I think, because it was smug, dismissive, and badgering. ("You cannot stand the deceits of official anti-Communism? Then respond with a rejection equally blatant. . . . You are weary of Sidney Hook's messages in *The New York Times Magazine*? Then respond as if talk about Communist totalitarianism were simply irrelevant or a bogey to frighten infants.") Today, Howe recognizes that there were *two* quite different political styles at work against social democracy—one of individual moral rectitude along the lines of Thoreau, the other "Leninist-Maoist." "One of the reasons that we had difficulty coding the whole phenomenon of the Sixties," he says, "is that at first we couldn't see the interweaving of these two . . . and secondly, even if we could see it, we didn't know how to cope with this." At the time, though, Howe couldn't say anything generous about the New Left without quickly canceling it, even in the same sentence. Another part of the trouble was that, up through the end of 1966, Howe held on to the idea that the U.S. had legitimate purposes in Vietnam; even as he grew disabused of the war, he was still, as Jeremy Larner points out, reluctant to offend his old Shachtmanite comrades Bayard Rustin and Tom Kahn, *Dissent*'s right wing, who were holding on to a hard-line position. (Michael Walzer and David McReynolds, meanwhile, argued straightforwardly for immediate withdrawal in *Dissent*'s pages.) But partly, I think, I recoiled from "New Styles" because I feared that too much of Howe's description was accurate, or might turn out to be, something I couldn't bear to recognize, let alone act on. For if Howe were right, what followed, so it seemed to me then, was high-level politicking for a few and the armchair for the many. After Atlantic City and the Gulf of Tonkin, the liberal-labor coalition, that presumed alternative to the "revolutionary" style, seemed no alternative at all.

Hindsight tantalizes. Might it have been useful to keep up relations with *Dissent*? Might a continuing tie have encouraged those of us in the New Left who tried to keep the movement from running off its rails? Pleasant it would have been to try, instructive to have the benefit of their thinking, but such a tie would probably not have altered the movement's larger direction. As the Vietnam war spilled its venom into American life, whatever bridge might have been built between *Dissent* and the New Left would probably have collapsed. It would have taken a surplus of wisdom all around to keep the two sides from ending up tilting against each other, like jilted lovers huddled in bitterness, launching curses into the void.

"A FRENZIED ONE-SIDED ANTI-AMERICAN SHOW"

. . . we must tread delicately on the Vietnam question because lots of SDS people are far from being for withdrawal. . . .
—Paul Booth to Paul Potter, July 1, 1964

The demand [of the March on Washington to End the War in Vietnam] will be non-specific since there is dispute within SDS as to whether we should be for withdrawal, negotiation, U.N. presence or whatever; but the important thing is to state the overriding demand: end the war.
—Todd Gitlin to Martin Peretz, January 19, 1965

On the eve of this weekend's peace march on Washington, several leaders of the peace movement have taken clear note of attempts to convert the event into a pro-Communist production. . . . Americans may reasonably differ with some aspects of the President's course. But, especially in the aftermath of Mr. Johnson's call for "unconditional" negotiations, there is no justification for transforming the march into a frenzied one-sided anti-American show.
—Editorial, *New York Post*, April 17, 1965

. . . those people who insist now that Vietnam can be neutralized are for the most part looking for a sugar coating to cover the bitter pill. We must accept the consequences that calling for an end of the war in Vietnam is in fact allowing for the likelihood that a Vietnam without war will be a self-styled Communist Vietnam. . . . I must say to you that I would rather see Vietnam Communist than see it under continuous subjugation of the ruin that American domination has brought. . . . [I]n a strange way the people of Vietnam and the

people on this demonstration are united in much more than a common concern that the war be ended. In both countries there are people struggling to build a movement that has the power to change their condition. The system that frustrates these movements is the same. All our lives, our destinies, our very hopes to live, depend on our ability to overcome that system.
—Paul Potter to the March on Washington to End the War in Vietnam,
April 17, 1965

[The *Post* editorial was] a very clever smear. . . . It makes me sick to read it. . . . The article portends much of what is to come. Some people are clearly going to link us to the far left sectarian groups and rub our faces in the same mud that is slung at them. . . .

I guess I like being on that fence that makes SDS both risky and relevant. . . .
—Paul Potter to his mother and brother, May 3, 1965

SDS compressed a lifetime of politics into a handful of years—or rather, it was compressed into us. We were force-fed with history. The pace of change was dizzying—still feels that way, even at two decades' remove. Some of the vertigo can be traced in these five quotations. Ten months separate the last from the first. But they belong to two different political universes.

The short explanation is: Lyndon Johnson's Vietnam policy, which ratcheted decisively upward during those months. First came the Gulf of Tonkin incidents of August 2–3, 1964. Johnson had long since readied a congressional resolution authorizing him to "take all necessary measures" to protect American forces and "prevent further aggression." After he assumed office, American ships helped the South Vietnamese mount clandestine raids against North Vietnam in the waters just off their coast. As an American destroyer nosed offshore, probing Hanoi's defenses, North Vietnamese gunboats opened fire. The Americans destroyed them. Then a nervous commander imagined a second attack. Johnson, guarding his right flank against Goldwater, found the moment auspicious for reprisals; he launched sixty-four sorties against North Vietnamese bases and an oil depot, and brought his resolution before Congress. Liberal doubters were assured that the President had no intention of getting drawn into a land war; the Tonkin Gulf resolution passed the Senate with two dissenting votes (Wayne Morse of Oregon and Ernest Gruening of Alaska), the House of Representatives unanimously.

The Gulf of Tonkin and Atlantic City in the same month: the combination fatefully turned the movement. Johnson's twin triumphs crushed whatever possibility remained of a radical-liberal-labor coalition. Committed to the welfare-warfare beneficence of his hero FDR, Johnson hadn't the faintest idea that his war also passed a death sentence on his Great Society and killed his chance for a second full term. Cold War liberalism was forced to choose between the two terms of its definition, and chose war. The puny radicals Johnson thought he was sweeping aside came back to devastate him. The movement's whole constellation of attitudes for the rest of the decade was shaped by its experience of liberal default.

With the Tonkin Gulf resolution in hand, Johnson was ready for Step 2: the steady bombing of the North beginning on February 7, 1965, on the heels of a Vietcong attack on the American barracks at Pleiku. Years later, national security adviser McGeorge Bundy said that Pleikus were "like streetcars," they came along every so often; the administration had been waiting for the right moment to expand the war. U.S. Marine units in full combat regalia, no longer isolated "advisers," started to pour into South Vietnam, followed by tens of thousands of other combat troops. Again, there was barely a squeak of liberal dissent.

A brief version of SDS's antiwar trajectory from then on would read: We were outraged; isolated; suspicious of those who damned us or counseled caution. The defaults and assaults of liberals and social democrats blew us leftward; so did SDS's increasingly plausible commitment to go it alone; so did the growing social base for alienation on the American campus. Were the results inevitable? That is a question for metaphysics, not this more modest inquiry. But many forces certainly lined up in the same direction.

In late December 1964, when SDS decided to organize a national demonstration against the war, I didn't think of it as our major foreign policy project for the spring. My pet project, actually, was a sit-in at the Chase Manhattan Bank, protesting its loans to South Africa, which helped shore up the regime. The issue was both morally compelling and intellectually interesting, raising the question of American business's role in foreign policy. CHASE MANHATTAN, PARTNER IN APARTHEID, read our buttons, which the bank went to court to enjoin us from wearing. But Vietnam also made its moral claims. And so Paul Booth and I, the coordinators of SDS's Peace Research and Education Project, invited I. F. Stone to give a speech about Vietnam at the December National Council meeting. We talked about circulating a declaration that would say: "I will not be drafted until the U.S. gets out of Vietnam."

Revulsion against the growing war was our main motive, but we were also looking over our left shoulders. As the campus mood tilted leftward, competition was setting in. First came the W. E. B. DuBois Clubs, dominated by the children of Communist and fellow traveler activists, especially strong on the West Coast. We mocked them as Da Boys, called them "doctrinaire," and suspected their tricky tactics, including hiding their sponsorship of meetings to which SDS was invited. At one point national secretary C. Clark Kissinger, a veteran of ideological wars at the University of Wisconsin (and no relation to the future secretary of state), lamented that "the Worker keeps running stories on demonstrations cosponsored by DuBois and SDS. Some of them we never even heard of until we read about it in the Worker. Unfortunately, the LID also read about it in the Worker." Kissinger also sagely wrote that "Da Boys . . . only exists where there is a concentration of kids from old left homes (e.g. Wisconsin, Minnesota, Antioch, NYC, etc.). In contrast to this SDS is able to crop up most anywheres (e.g. North Texas State, Western Kentucky State, Tufts, etc.) . . . [But] second generation radicals . . . are able to organize circles about our bushy tailed kids brought in by reading the PHS [*Port Huron Statement*]."

If DuBois wasn't enough, there also materialized in the spring of 1964 the May 2nd Movement (M2M), named after a New York City antiwar demonstration. It wasn't entirely clear yet, except to the cognoscenti, that a majority of M2M's leadership came from the Progressive Labor Movement (PLM, or PL for short), a 1962 Maoist breakaway from the Communist Party. In the fall of 1964, M2M circulated a "We Won't Go" petition.* Many in SDS agreed with it. If SDS hoped to be the campuses' main act on the Left, plainly we would have to confront the war head-on. Clark Kissinger, the first SDS bureaucrat to bring a relish for order and infighting to the job, thought SDS could get a jump on the competition by being the first to call for a national rally in Washington. If we could attract two or three thousand students, we could not only send Johnson a message, we could "build SDS."

After much debate, SDS shelved the "We Won't Go" statement, along with a proposal to send medical supplies to the National Liberation Front (NLF). SDS's electoral-politics faction, which had successfully pushed for a "Part of the Way with LBJ" slogan the previous September, worried that SDS would be tarred with a pro-Communist brush. Many thought a march too tame; to the ERAP contingent, it was too national; still, the idea of a demonstration in Washington on April 17, during spring vacation, passed.

What, then, would we demonstrate for? Booth and I submitted a resolution. We finessed our doubts about Communist-led movements by saying that the war was a "civil war," the NLF "an indigenous rebel movement." As in *The Port Huron Statement,* we rooted for "neutralist forces" and "democratic revolutionaries," worried that "the American military presence and the continuing backing for right-wing regimes" had under-

*An earlier version, calling upon students not to fight in Vietnam, had been published in the *National Guardian* and the *New York Herald Tribune* by an ad hoc committee headed by PLer Philip Abbott Luce. Perhaps its greatest effect was on the Federal Bureau of Investigation, which set out to interrogate the signatories. In one case the FBI called the parents of a Haverford student—how they got the parents' number remains a mystery—and terrified them, which was no doubt one of their purposes. The student agreed to meet the FBI men on a street corner, wearing a yellow carnation—he too had read spy novels. They interrogated him for an hour or more about his motives and those of other signers, scaring him so badly he never signed another petition or joined an organization despite his radical sympathies. Luce soon changed sides and blasted the New Left before the House Un-American Activities Committee.

cut them, and thought the NLF, "despite its Communist leadership, may still be the major vehicle of these [democratic] revolutionaries." Then we tried to force together the different positions about what to do, in a kind of arithmetic sum of two incompatible positions:

> We believe there is only one alternative to escalation—American withdrawal from South Vietnam. We believe there is only one chance for democracy and development in South Vietnam—a negotiated settlement of the war. Accordingly, we call on President Johnson to withdraw American troops from their undeclared war, and to use American influence to expedite a negotiated neutralist settlement in that beleaguered country.

The discussion bobbed and weaved. Finally somebody moved to maximize turnout while minimizing division with a baby-simple statement, which passed overwhelmingly: "SDS advocates that the U.S. get out of Vietnam for the following reasons: (a) the war hurts the Vietnamese people; (b) the war hurts the American people; (c) SDS is concerned about the Vietnamese and American people." Anyone who endorsed the three-point position was welcome to march.

In keeping with our eclectic strategy, we chose an official list of slogans, a hodgepodge including "War on Poverty—Not on People," "Ballots Not Bombs in Vietnam," "Self-Determination for Vietnam," "Freedom Now in Vietnam," and *both* "Withdraw Now" and "Negotiate." Marchers would be permitted to bring signs identifying their cities or campuses, but not their organizations. Peace groups like the Student Peace Union and Women Strike for Peace were permitted to "co-sponsor," the DuBois Club and M2M only to "endorse." I. F. Stone and Senator Ernest Gruening quickly agreed to speak at the rally. The official call, hoping to appeal to a broad opposition, maintained that the war was "fundamentally a civil war," as well as "losing," "self-defeating," "dangerous," "never declared by Congress," and "hideously immoral." Campus interest ballooned after Johnson began the regular bombing of the North in February. SDS drew (for the first and last time) a long, respectful piece in *The New York Times,* headlined: "The New Student Left: Movement Represents Serious Activists in Drive for Changes."

Then once again the gooseflesh rose in the LID. The specter of "United Frontism," laid to troubled rest after the post–Port Huron inquisition, again rustled its robes. In the eyes of the LID's Tom Kahn, for example, SDS, having slipped away from the liberal-labor alliance, was sliding irrevocably into the gravitational pull of the hereditary Marxist-Leninist Left. To Kahn the situation presented a precise analogue to the orthodox Cold War view of an either/or world. A student movement could never really go it alone; it was bound to become the satellite of one side or the other. SDS, having escaped the correct orbit, was on the verge of choosing the wrong, Communist, side. Could the Left ever establish itself in American life unless it appealed to the majority *on its Right*? Did not the principal danger lie on the Right, as Johnson in his own way believed, always conceiving that his war moves were ways of deflecting pressure for still more destructive moves?

Port Huron hadn't been terribly public, and the LID's parental inquisition had been kept in the family. This time SDS was out in the world; so was the response. On Friday, April 16, the day before the march, a group of peace movement notables released to the press a statement affirming "interest and sympathy" toward the march, hoping for self-determination and free dissent in Vietnam, lauding Lyndon Johnson for presumed moves in this direction—and then the kicker: "In the effort to register such concerns with our government and people, we welcome the cooperation of all those groups and individuals who, like ourselves, believe in the need for an independent peace movement, not committed to any form of totalitarianism nor drawing inspiration or direction from the foreign policy of any government." Among the signatories were not only leaders of the Student Peace Union (an endorser of the March) and the pacifist Fellowship of Reconciliation, but, surprisingly, SDS friends A. J. Muste and H. Stuart Hughes, along with Bayard Rustin and SDS's erstwhile defenders in the LID, Norman Thomas and Harold Taylor.*

The best to be said for this eleventh-hour warning was that the elders were desperate to build a maximum bloc against the war. But it could not have been simple prudence which led the statement's galvanizer, Turn Toward Peace leader Robert Gilmore, to tell I. F. Stone the outlandish tale that the students intended to urinate on the White House. The open letter mixed political platform-building with pure panic, and once again sorely damaged the standing of SDS's critics. As Martin Peretz, the heiress Anne Farnsworth (from whom Peretz had raised twenty-five thousand dollars to help finance the March), and another donor, Mrs. Gardner Cox, wrote in an open letter:

> It is of interest . . . that the very men who are so concerned with totalitarian influences are themselves prepared to censure any activity which falls within what they consider their purview and with which they might disagree. Will not the libertarians allow a plurality of opinion in the peace ranks, and even a plurality of style? Particularly as the commitment of SDS to liberty and democracy is above reproach. Or will any independence on the part of the young be used as an excuse to shower opprobrium on what they do?

---

*Thomas and Hughes subsequently apologized to SDS, and when pressure was put on Senator Gruening to withdraw from the Washington Monument rally, Taylor persuaded him to stay.

To make matters worse, on the very day of the March the liberal *New York Post* ran a hysterical editorial quoting the open letter and referring to "attempts to convert the event into a pro-Communist production" and "a frenzied one-sided anti-American show." To continue the saga of liberal anti-Communism, the *Post's* editorial page was edited by the "angry middle-aged editor" James A. Wechsler.

Wechsler's frenzied exercise may not have kept a soul away from Washington. Twenty or twenty-five thousand people, mostly students, streamed around the White House on April 17. It was the largest peace march in American history. But if the statement and the editorial failed to dampen what we celebrated as a glorious day of public opposition, many of us were sickened by what Paul Potter called liberal anti-Communism's "very clever smear." When the celebration had faded, and SDS found itself flooded with recruits and uncertain what to do next, Potter wrote with foreboding that the *Post* editorial "portends much of what is to come."

"IF THEY WERE SERIOUS"

The radical-liberal rift also burst into the open at the Washington Monument. "Love Me, I'm a Liberal," sang Phil Ochs, the folksinger, with a sneer.* I. F. Stone didn't like it. He'd been a liberal himself all these years, he told the crowd. Senator Gruening, who had voted against the Tonkin Gulf resolution, was a liberal. "I've seen snot-nosed Marxist-Leninists come and go," said Stone.

Bob Moses, now Parris, also spoke, saying that the prosecutors of the war were the same people who refused to protect civil rights in the South. But the New Left position emerged most sharply in the closing speech by SDS president Paul Potter. Potter insisted with characteristic honesty that "we must accept the consequences that calling for an end of the war in Vietnam is in fact allowing for the likelihood that a Vietnam without war will be a self-styled Communist Vietnam. . . . I must say to you that I would rather see Vietnam Communist than see it under continuous subjugation or the ruin that American domination has brought." Potter's reason was fundamentally different from Old Left pro-Communism.

---

*Typical verse:

I vote for the Democratic Party
They want the U.N. to be strong.
I attend all the Pete Seeger concerts,
He sure gets me singing those songs.
And I'll send all the money you ask for
But don't ask me to come on along.

So love me, love me, love me—
I'm a liberal.

Potter caught the spirit of New Left thinking, as the picket-sign slogans did not. For one thing, he was not allergic to a tragic vision; unlike Old Left purists and liberal sugar-coaters, Potter acknowledged that the choice in Vietnam was agonizing, that the result was not likely to be the best of all possible worlds, and that moral choices had consequences which were not necessarily intended. What was striking was the manner in which he identified with the Vietnamese revolutionaries nevertheless.

Potter's speech was pure New Left, at once electrifying and vague in its invocation of "the system" of which the war was but a symptom, a system of generalized brutality and domination that had not yet been given its proper name. In a soaring, impassioned summation of what SDS stood for, he declared:

> We must name that system. We must name it, describe it, analyze it, understand it and change it. For it is only when that system is changed and brought under control that there can be any hope for stopping the forces that create a war in Vietnam today or a murder in the South tomorrow or all the incalculable, innumerable more subtle atrocities that are worked on people all over—all the time.

"If the war has its roots deep in the institutions of American society," Potter asked, "how do you stop it? . . ." His answer was SDS's all-purpose answer to many vexing questions (including the classic "What do you people want?"): change your life, "build a movement." In theory, the movement itself was going to be that means in which the luminous end was inherent. It would be the solvent of all its internal contradictions. The collective will would be self-fulfilling. "Twenty thousand people," Potter said, "the people here, if they were serious, if they were willing to break out of their isolation and to accept the consequences of a decision to end the war and commit themselves to building a movement wherever they are and in whatever way they effectively can, would be, I'm convinced, enough." In the presence of Potter's spectral eloquence, several thousand people, for that moment if none other, probably believed it. The sheer fact of being there, in that hushed communion, seemed so remarkable to begin with; who knew what else might turn out to be possible?

Potter's peroration provided the key to the New Left's evolving identification with Vietnamese guerrillas halfway around the world:

> . . . in a strange way the people of Vietnam and the people on this demonstration are united in much more than a common concern that the war be ended. In both countries there are people struggling to build a movement that has the power to change their condition. The system that frustrates these movements is the same. All our lives, our destinies, our very hopes to live, depend on our ability to overcome that system.

The crowd was stunned; then stood and applauded long and hard. Many of us felt that we ourselves—searchers and strugglers—had truly been named.

Over the subsequent years, SDS did variously "name the system." "Corporate liberalism," Potter's successor Carl Oglesby called it in another memorable (and even more influential) speech that fall, distinguishing bad, "corporate" liberals from good, "humanist" liberals. Soon "imperialism" and "capitalism" became the terms of choice, stressing the war's linkage to America's wealth and global reach. Years later, Potter recounted that a friend of his had remarked

> how far we had come from the name-the-system speech in 1965, since we were now unembarrassed to say what we all knew then—that the system is capitalism. . . . I didn't feel free to say that capitalism was not the name I was looking for in 1965. . . . I did not fail to call the system capitalism because I was a coward or an opportunist. I refused to call it capitalism because capitalism was for me and my generation an inadequate description of the evils of America—a hollow, dead word tied to the thirties. . . . I talked about the system not because I was afraid of the term capitalism but because I wanted ambiguity, because I sensed there was something new afoot in the world that we were part of that made the rejection of the old terminology part of the new hope for radical change in America.

What Potter thought "afoot in the world," the "name for ourselves" he was groping for, was self-definition and self-determination against all forces of management from on high.* Vietnam was a screen onto which he projected the American New Left's political culture, its struggle for self-definition against managerial power. "The people of Vietnam" slid imperceptibly into "people struggling to build a movement," which in turn, over the next few years, could blur into the North Vietnamese and National Liberation Front apparatus. Without knowing much about the particulars of Vietnam, Potter assumed—as many of us did—that the Vietnamese revolutionaries were a more victimized and better organized version of ourselves. If, like myself, we knew that Ho Chi Minh had massacred the Vietnamese Trotskyists, we buried the information in parentheses. If there was a single system of domination in the world—management—then it neatened the world to assume that the forms of resistance were equivalent. Then the opposition in America was that much less alone in the world. One oppression, one revolution: unthought

---

*Potter was typically Old Guard SDS in his insistence that the movement be collective and individualized at once. In a May 3 letter, he recommended a *Life* magazine picture of the March because "people don't seem to be reacting as a mass, . . . expressions and reactions are individuated."

through, in the heat of the war, this oversimplified logic swept through the New Left.

The pressure toward this sort of identification was fierce. Much of it came from the new generation that swooped into SDS in the wake of the March on Washington. (*Generation* is an extreme term, but from close up, campus populations undergo major shifts every two or three years.) Several years younger than the Old Guard, they tended to come from the Midwest and Southwest, they were not Jewish, they were more likely to come from working-class families, and they were less intellectual, less articulate (Carl Oglesby being a crucial exception on this score). They kidded about standing for "prairie power." Many hailed from frontier country, had long, shaggy, swooping mustaches, wore blue work shirts and cowboy boots, and smoked marijuana at a time when the Old Guard was either faintly curious or frightened of it. Children of Goldwater voters, students at schools that hadn't progressed to paternalism, sometimes veterans of the armed forces, they were instinctive anarchists, principled and practiced antiauthoritarians. Many had broken with their parents—had been driven to, once they got labeled "nigger-lovers" or "liberals" or "Communists" simply for supporting civil rights. Once outlawed from family and town for what northerners would have considered mild positions, they encountered no obstacles to moving further leftward. They didn't have to be talked out of relying on the liberal-labor coalition; they distrusted its eastern-style moderation from the start. If the U.S. government told them it was good to fight Communism in Southeast Asia, that seemed a good prima facie reason to sympathize with the Vietcong, for didn't the authorities call *them* Communists too?

Moreover, the hinterland generation was not—in Carl Oglesby's words—"intellectually forewarned" of an American propensity toward empire-building. They were brought up to believe in American institutions; unlike the grandchildren of immigrants, they had not started out disposed to be alienated. When they discovered alienation, they looked to Thomas Pynchon more than Karl Marx, John Lennon more than V. I. Lenin. They had inherited neither Stalinism *nor a bitter anti-Stalinism* as what Oglesby years later called "a personal burden." They had started out innocent, credulous about America: and thus the news of American violence in Vietnam came as an utter shock, a radical challenge to their fundamental morality. Therefore, the newer SDSers later would prove quicker than the founders to gravitate toward violence of their own— "their trauma had no prelude," as Oglesby says.

The Old Guard, preoccupied with ERAP and the we-happy-few mystique of the early years of face-to-face organizing, failed to take these "prairie people" into our old-boy networks—and perhaps could not have succeeded, given the cultural differences. Whereupon a generational chasm opened up within the student movement, reproducing the one that was opening up in the wider society.

But the prairie people were by no means wholly responsible for the identification Potter evoked at the Washington Monument. In some measure we were all feeling it. For me the turning point came not because of Vietnam but because of Santo Domingo—or rather, the televised version of it. A week after the March on Washington, generals allied with the previously elected and ousted social-democratic president of the Dominican Republic, Juan Bosch, launched an assault on the incumbent regime. President Johnson claimed first that American lives were in danger, then that Communists were going to turn the country into "another Cuba." Within days, twenty-two thousand American Marines and airborne troops were occupying the capital city of Santo Domingo. I remember turning on NBC News, watching young Dominicans riding a ramshackle tank scrawled PUEBLO as it wheeled around the city, making a last stand against junta troops protected by the Americans. Choked by fellow-feeling I wrote a clumsy poem, which ended: "O Santo Domingo! I would gladly walk your streets/with your young lovers, bearing only a rifle and a sad song." The U.S. was throwing its armed might against *us*. I felt for the first time that I belonged to a "we" that had no choice but to fight against America's armed power. Four months earlier, I had signed my name to an SDS resolution that referred to the United States government as "we." From now on, whenever I spoke of my country and its government, the pronoun stuck in my throat.

Another bellwether: For two years, since I had graduated from college and moved Left with SDS, my old friend Chris Hobson, much more knowledgeable about the Third World than I, had been tending my anti-Communist conscience. "Vietnam worries me," he wrote, for example, in February 1965. "I can't really get enthused about the Viet Cong—maybe I am too influenced by our propaganda. But even if we won I don't see much ahead for South Vietnam—no more than if they won, which is little enough." Right after April 17, he thought that our bad press (from Max Lerner in the *New York Post* and James Reston in *The Times*) was "partly our own fault for obscuring the real issues with a lot of liberal gobbledegook (Stone-Grueningite Sub-tendency) and having slogans like 'Freedom Now in Vietnam.'" But when I sent him my Santo Domingo poem, he wrote back that "somehow the simple fact, that they are us, never had occurred to me, though I was for them all the time. . . ." Juan Bosch and his supporters were not, in fact, Marxist-Leninists like the Communists of Vietnam. But the more important thing was that the United States was acting like an empire, and that fraternity with revolutionaries abroad had become compelling.

And therefore a curious nonevent at the National Teach-In on May 15 also struck me hard. A month before the March on Washington, a group of young University of Michigan instructors thought the time had come for radical antiwar action, and proposed a campus strike, to be coupled with off-campus classes about the war. Hearing of this, Republican state legislators screamed, the university administration fretted, and the faculty antiwar group swelled with more cautious souls, whereupon the radicals were talked into an apparently more moderate tactic, a free-for-all colloquium at night (thus not interfering with classes) in which local experts would teach about Vietnam: a "teach-in," the political philosopher Arnold Kaufman called it. Some three thousand students attended Ann Arbor's all-night teach-in; the atmosphere was electric, and copies sprang up on campuses everywhere—even in Europe and Japan. The State Department even agreed to send out speakers, most of whom got trounced. With its emphasis on educational process, its overcoming of barriers between faculty and students, the teach-in was characteristically New Left.

Whereupon an all-day National Teach-In, in Washington, was organized two months later, to be piped by radio and television around the country, with Johnson defenders up against the cream of antiwar expertise. National security adviser McGeorge Bundy was to represent the administration. We looked forward to the comeuppance of the nation's leading official intellectual. But at the last minute Bundy absented himself. Johnson had sent him on an errand—to Santo Domingo. To me, the most significant thing about the National Teach-In was the man who wasn't there. While we were arguing rights and wrongs, the men in power, heedless, were off settling the affairs of small, weak nations. Now I could close a letter to Hobson, only half in jest, "Crush i*********m, with love."

ENTER PROGRESSIVE LABOR, LAUGHING

Two months after the March on Washington, Paul Potter was already uneasy with the position he had taken there. In a paper for the June SDS convention, Potter evoked the shade of George Washington. SDS up to this point had avoided "foreign entanglements." It had wanted to organize people inductively, step by step, according to "immediate grievances." But in four months, all seemed to have changed. New members were streaming into SDS on the premise that it was an antiwar organization, or ought to be. As a result, Potter wrote,

> the pressure has increased for us to begin to take positions on foreign policy questions that are much more detailed and specific than we have ever wanted to undertake before. Increasingly, people who I speak to not only oppose the American intervention in Vietnam, but actively identify with the National Liberation Front and the Viet Cong . . . although the complexities of making judgments about those forces on the basis of confused, incomplete and almost universally ideologically distorted

information remains as difficult as ever. We tend to be suspicious of sources that depict the Viet Cong as depraved or some such and accepting of sources that support our growing inclination that they are popular, humane and even democratic. Perhaps, although I am not certain, we will come soon to a juncture where we have to decide whether we support the Viet Cong or some other revolutionary group politically.

Potter, a radical pragmatist in the grain of William James and John Dewey, wanted SDS to return to its original epistemological spirit—its insistence on working from the world at hand, refusing to accept second-hand versions:

I am worried about the situation in which we begin to make critical and difficult judgments about groups that are thousands of miles away operating in environments and under conditions that we have never perceived or witnessed. I am also worried about a situation in which the involvement of people in SDS depends on their identification with movements outside of the country which they cannot participate in or develop through.

SDS's business was domestic change, Potter concluded, and so we should leave foreign revolutions to foreign revolutionaries (and their American supporters like M2M), and stay out of Cold War disputes.

The convention did default on Vietnam, though not principally for Potter's reasons. Held at a camp near the northern Michigan town of Kewadin, it was flooded by recruits who had joined SDS only weeks or months before. Prairie anticentralism ran high. Plenary sessions were chaired by people who had never chaired meetings before; votes went uncounted, credentials unchecked. The pressure against *any* national program was considerable; having just organized the largest antiwar demonstration in American history, SDS seriously contemplated abolishing its offices of president and vice president. Many of the Old Guard were preoccupied with ERAP and unable or unwilling to think seriously about campus activities; some, as in earlier days, were obsessed with personal dramas of separation and recoupling. Moreover, not even those who thought the war was SDS's key issue knew what to do about it. With liberals impotent or coopted, and the country enthusiastic about Johnson's martial moves, we brooded. Perhaps all that could be done was to "build a movement" that would be able to stop "the seventh war from now." Staughton Lynd proposed "nonviolent revolution" as the alternative to the Bayard Rustin position, which he called "coalition with the Marines," but that felt to me a romantic gesture: leaping into the grave.

Kewadin was most noteworthy for two benchmarks on SDS's long march away from its origins. It was the first convention at which the cadres of a Marxist-Leninist party showed up to participate and inspect. There may not have been more than a dozen members of Progressive Labor on the lawns and beaches of Camp Maplehurst, but to the Old Guard they were conspicuous—sometimes by the lameness of their anti-imperialist rhetoric, sometimes by the lameness of their efforts to tiptoe around it. Now that SDS was going places and moving leftward, PL sniffed out a recruiting ground.

Kewadin's other achievement was to strike the "exclusion clauses" from the SDS constitution (and thus the membership card). Two amendments were circulated by Clark Kissinger. Since Port Huron, the preamble had said that SDS "put forth a radical, democratic program counterposed to authoritarian movements both of Communism and the domestic Right"; Kissinger proposed a change to ". . . a radical, democratic program whose methods embody the democratic vision." Another clause had read:

> SDS is an organization of democrats. It is civil libertarian in its treatment of those with whom it disagrees, but clear in its opposition to any totalitarian principle as a basis for government or social organization. Advocates or apologists for such a principle are not eligible for membership.

Kissinger moved that "totalitarian" be changed to "anti-democratic" and that the last sentence be struck altogether. The exclusions were relics of a bygone era, he argued, and good riddance to them. In Washington, while accepting cosponsorship from other groups, SDS had reserved the right to dictate the March's policy and slogans. But by changing the membership clauses, SDS was going considerably further: it was welcoming one and all, including the members of a disciplined cadre organization, into the deliberations that would produce the policy in the first place. No caution would be allowed to keep the organization beholden to its anti-Communist elders.

Faint opposition there was. When Kissinger first proposed the changes, a Princeton member named David Garson wrote a cogent argument against it:

> I think that this is very wrong in principle and in tactics. In principle because we do believe in democracy and moreover *have some standards,* however minimal, to judge whether a system is democratic. We do not share basic values with those who see democracy in Russia, China, or Cuba, all of which are clearly lacking in civil liberties for *organized* political opposition, which is essential for any standard of democracy. (This is not to say that we cannot critically defend countries like Cuba. I personally would rather live in Cuba than anywhere else in Latin America.) . . . Tactically, however, the strategy is far worse. I think it will force not only a break with LID but with most of the left liberals

with whom I at least want to work. The fact of the matter is that if we are to grow into a large movement we have to appeal to, recruit, and radicalize liberals. These liberals will be concerned with the issue of Communism. . . . I'm not against working with Communists if they want to support any of *our* programs, like the March, but I insist that we as an organization be critical of them.

Only a few, if anyone, paid attention. Atlantic City, and the peace leaders' attack on the April 17 March, had fatally undermined what would have been a tenuous position in the best of circumstances. With prairie power on the march, who cared what a lone Princetonian thought? The LID's Tom Kahn, a futile emissary, argued that the constitutional changes, on top of SDS's general drift to the Left, would fatally rupture the bond between the youth and the parent organization. If any clincher was needed, Kahn's point was it. The capacity of a disciplined cadre to take over or paralyze a mass organization had been amply demonstrated in the Left of the Thirties and Forties, but that thread of history was either lost—like most other knowledge of what had happened in ancient times, i.e., before 1960—or glibly discounted as a useless relic, or worse, a recrudescence of bankrupt "anti-Communism" (the very term now becoming a curse word). The amendments passed overwhelmingly.

It would have been in bad taste to note the irony: SDS stripped itself of its strongest line of defense at just the moment PL was moving in. But who could believe there was anything to fear? SDS now had several thousand members on paper and many more in spirit; PL numbered a few hundred, if that. Anyway, we were the *New* Left, vigorously antiauthoritarian, purely American, no suckers for a bunch of tightassed Stalinists. Prairie power innocence merged with post–Port Huron cockiness to double our faith that rambunctious small-d democracy was bound to prevail; the Nietzschean mood was that, as incoming president Carl Oglesby later put it, "democracy is nothing if it is not dangerous." Meanwhile, a year earlier, PL had declared itself no longer a mere Movement but a Party. The Progressive Labor *Movement* had had a bohemian flair, but the *Party,* to "organize the working class," set about to get disciplined. "Bourgeois tendencies"—long hair, beards, marijuana, cohabitation without benefit of matrimony—had to be dispensed with. Eight months after Kewadin, PL dissolved the relatively unruly M2M, and its cadres promptly flocked into the happy hunting ground of SDS. "In principle," Steve Max wrote to me, "an agent for the FBI and an agent for PL are the same thing. Both have our welfare at heart and both are dispatched by the same manipulative mentality."

It was the symbolism of antiexclusion that mattered, of course; no one in SDS would ever have scrutinized anyone's wallet to see which cards he or she was carrying. But why should SDS have chosen this moment to throw open its doors? On top of all the motives and conditions operating since 1960—the breakdown of the Stalinist monolith, the enthusiasm for Cuba, the disgust with McCarthyism and its replicas, the desire to start afresh, the absence of a buffer generation between ourselves and the generation of the Thirties, the generational bravado—there was now the promise of something new in the world: a genuine rollicking free-form movement of American youth.

From the start, SDS had known in its bones that it was a tiny minority among students who were themselves a minority. It followed that the student movement had to go in search of longer levers of change. Thus the successive strategic notions: Port Huron's idea of realigning the Democratic Party into a vehicle of the liberal-labor alliance; the short-lived vision of the university as a repository of socially responsible reason in an unreasoning land; ERAP and its hopes for an "interracial movement of the poor"; even PL's idea of a "worker-student alliance" that would send students to organize the industrial working class. For all the differences, such lines of thought were attempts to solve the same rock-bottom problem: the country was vast, the New Left small.

The largely unconscious intuition of 1965 was this: Suppose the New Left were only *apparently* small. Suppose it were actually the thoughtful, active "vanguard" of a swelling social force, one that embodied the future forming in the cocoon of the present the way Marx's proletariat was supposed to do. Suppose that SDS stood for students-as-a-whole, and students-as-a-whole stood for *the young*. The first major cohort of the baby boom, the postwar babies of 1946, turned eighteen in 1964; between 1964 and 1970, 20 million more turned that magical corner. America's young were not only multiplying, not only relatively rich, not only concentrated on campuses and—thanks to the mass media—visible as never before. Suppose they were, en masse, in motion, breaking out of the postwar consensus, out of complacency, out of good behavior and middle-class mores, out of the bureaucratic order and the Cold War mood. Then the unthinkable might be actual, the unprecedented possible. You could safely kick out the jams, dissolve the old hesitations, break with adults, be done with compromises, *get on with it*. Not only did the imagery of popular culture belong to the young, but political upheaval, even—dare one think it?—"revolution." With a bit of subconscious imagination, the longhaired, dope-smoking Texans who showed up at Kewadin could be seen as the advance guard of the new generational armies.

If you were disabused of the liberal-labor coalition, you were already disposed to search out a self-sufficient movement of the young. But you didn't have to strain your eyes to see signs of youth upheaval everywhere. The Free Speech Movement . . . the March on Washington . . . the prairie-fueled SDS boom . . . and here and there, the low-rent districts on the coasts where dropouts were beginning to congregate. John F. Kennedy, with his call to ideals, was already the fading memory of their childhoods; Vietnam was getting tattooed into their adolescence. The subterranean youth culture of the Fifties was coming of age.

THREE
THE SURGE

"Everybody Get Together"

ALL-PURPOSE APOCALYPSE

Nothing put the category *youth* on my own political map more resoundingly than a song called "Eve of Destruction."

In August 1965, within five weeks after its release, "Eve of Destruction" surged to the top of the sales charts. It was, disk jockeys said, the fastest-rising song in rock history. Even in an age when commercial fads materialize overnight, a success like this was amazing. For "Eve of Destruction" took off while a good many stations were banning it—including all of the ABC network's—and a good many others were playing it only infrequently. This was a song which a vociferous group of campus barnstormers called the Christian Anti-Communist Crusade said was "obviously aimed at instilling fear in our teenagers as well as a sense of hopelessness," helping "induce the American public to surrender to atheistic international Communism."

Written "as a prayer, for my own pleasure" by a nineteen-year-old named P. F. Sloan, "Eve of Destruction" began with two funereal thumps of the kettledrum, leading into a pounding drumbeat. Then the surly voice of Barry McGuire ground out a thunder-and-brimstone sermon:

> The Eastern world, it is explodin'
> Violence flarin', bullets loadin'
> You're old enough to kill but not for votin'
> You don't believe in war but what's that gun you're totin'
> And even the Jordan River has bodies floatin'

Then the refrain:

> And you tell me over and over and over again, my friend,
> You don't believe we're on the eve of destruction.

There had been no song remotely like this one in the decade-long history of rock music, although the objections of the Christian Anti-Communist Crusade suggest that here, at long last, was the song fundamentalists had been anticipating through all their years of panic, the one that would confirm their dire prophecies about the dark, inexorable logic of "nigger music." Nothing could have been in starker contrast to the previous year, 1964, when the Number 1 hits had included the Shangri Las' "Leader of the Pack," the Beach Boys' "Deuce Coupe" and "California Girls," the Supremes' "Baby Love," and the Beatles' "A Hard Day's Night"—all bouncy. "Eve" was strident and bitter, its references bluntly topical—no precedent for that, not even in Bob Dylan's allegorical "Blowin' in the Wind." Its structure came from folk: simple guitar strum, repeated refrain, forced rhymes. With an off-balance rhythm, it wasn't much to dance to; it brooded. McGuire's voice started with a whimper but got surlier as it went along, punctuated by the occasional ripping whine of a Dylanesque harmonica. The all-purpose apocalypse took in the Bomb— "When the button is pushed there's no runnin' away/There'll be no one to save with the world in a grave"—and even civil rights, which by now, with the passage of the Voting Rights Act that spring, had become an apple-pie issue:

> . . . Handful of Senators don't pass legislation
> And marches alone can't bring integration
> When human respect is disintegratin'
> This whole crazy world is just too frustratin'. . . .
> Look at all the hate there is in Red China
> Then take a look around to Selma, Alabama. . . .

Protest even engendered protest. An ad hoc group called the Spokesmen recorded an answer song, "Dawn of Correction"—which flopped.

The Christian Anti-Communist Crusade was on the right track about what the song implied, though wrong that its *aim* was to demoralize. Growing numbers of the young had to have been demoralized in the first place or they couldn't have relished McGuire's growls. Students of popular culture later tried to downplay the significance of the lyrics,* but the

---

*A study of a sample of undergraduates at the time showed that only 14 percent understood the song's "total" theme; 44 percent understood it "partially." A junior college survey showed 36 percent interpreting the song correctly.

lyrics conveyed only part of the song's meaning. Pop music devotees react to the mood of a song whether or not they grasp the lyrics. The sound carried the point: "Eve of Destruction" didn't well up with all-American high spirits; its drumbeat wasn't martial but ominous.

If any doubt was left about what the song meant, the superintendents and interpreters of popular culture (including right-wing alarmists) went to work to clear things up. Shortly after "Eve of Destruction," a hearty ditty called "Ballad of the Green Berets," sung by Staff Sergeant Barry Sadler, rose to the top of the charts in march tempo with a display of rat-a-tat-tat. That fall of 1965, Chicago's leading rock station sponsored a "battle of the Barrys," McGuire versus Sadler. On the decisive day, listeners were invited to call in and cast a ballot for their favorite: "Eve of Destruction" or "Green Berets." "Berets" won—by a single vote out of thousands cast. For promotion's sake, at least, the programmers of WCFL knew there was circulation to be gained by hyping their contest as if an entire culture were at stake. Plainly a new constellation of moods was in the air. "Eve of Destruction" seemed to certify that a mass movement of the American young was upon us.

"I CAN'T GET NO"

Not out of the blue, of course. Bob Dylan had groaned out his triptych of wasteland passions and rebellions for two years now, in the albums *The Freewheelin' Bob Dylan* and *The Times They Are A-Changin'*. The Zimmerman boy from up-country Minnesota had adopted a name that was both literary (the besotted and lyrical Dylan Thomas) and true-gritty American (*Gunsmoke*'s Marshal Matt Dillon), had gone to Greenwich Village and picked up a following with his folk anthems and antiestablishment gags. The tiny New Left delighted in one of our own generation and mind singing earnest ballads about racist murderers ("The Lonesome Death of Hattie Carroll"), the compensatory racism of poor whites ("Only a Pawn in Their Game"), Cold War ideology ("Masters of War" and "With God on Our Side"). Insiders knew Dylan had written the chilling "A Hard Rain's Gonna Fall" during the Cuban missile crisis, evoking the end of the world; the anthem "The Times They Are A-Changin'" sounded like a musical version of the "new insurgency" rhetoric of *America and the New Era*. To make it all more marvelous, Dylan did all this not on the marginal, faintly do-it-yourself Vanguard or Folkways label, redolent of Pete Seeger and the fight against the blacklist, but on big-league commercial Columbia Records. Teased by the idea of a popular movement, we admired Dylan's ability to smuggle the subversive into mass-circulated trappings. Whether he liked it or not, Dylan *sang for us:* we didn't have to know he had hung out in Minneapolis's dropout-nonstudent radical scene in order to intuit that he had been doing some hard traveling through a familiar landscape. We followed his career as if he were singing our song; we got in the habit of asking where he was taking us next.

It was a delight but not altogether a surprise, then, when Dylan dropped in on SDS's December 1963 National Council meeting. We were beginning to feel that we—all fifty of us in the room—were the vibrating center of the new cyclonic Left. Alger Hiss came to visit the same meeting, and drew an ovation; Allard Lowenstein also dropped in, and sat in the corner, anonymous. Dylan arrived unceremoniously with a Mississippi civil rights lawyer, sat shyly in the back, listened to a discussion about our plans for community organizing, and said nothing. (We'd been alerted he was coming, and decided not to put him on the spot with a public introduction.) A recess came, and Dylan told a group of us he'd be interested in working in one of our incipient ERAP projects. (Too exciting to believe! This proved we were the center!) But Dylan warned us to be careful—of him. A few weeks earlier, just days after the Kennedy assassination, he told us, he had appeared at the banquet of the Old Leftish Emergency Civil Liberties Committee. He thought he'd been invited to sing; he didn't know he was about to be given their Tom Paine Award. "Then I see these bald-headed, pot-bellied people sitting out there in suits," he told us. He tanked up at the backstage bar, contemplated the assemblage, then "went crazy," ranted that old people in furs and jewels should retire, announced that he could see some of himself in Lee Harvey Oswald, and stalked off the platform. He was half warning us, half apologizing for his bad-boy behavior.* In the meantime, Dylan said he would sing some benefit concerts for SDS. (But afterward he didn't answer our letters or phone calls.)

Dylan wasn't just putting on; or if his political commitment was a put-on phase designed to catapult him to stardom, as he said in a later and cynical incarnation, he was probably putting himself on as well. The woman he lived with on and off for years worked for CORE. He sang to Negroes in the Mississippi cotton fields (there is a touching sequence from this trip in the Pennebaker-Leacock documentary *Don't Look Back*). He visited movement organizers in the mining country of eastern Kentucky, where he wrote "The Chimes of Freedom Flashing." And so his next album, *Another Side of Bob Dylan*, struck the politicos as something of a personal betrayal, especially the line directed at the onetime lover: "I've heard you say many a time that you're better than no one and no one is better than you/If you really believe that, you know you have nothing to win and nothing to lose."

---

*In another version of the Tom Paine Award episode, Dylan reworked the experience to sound purely and simply dismissive of the spectacle of ridiculous old-fart left-wingers: "All they can see is a cause, and using people for their cause."

Through all this, Dylan's albums were never big successes by American pop standards (they sold better in England). When two of his songs made the top ten—"Blowin' in the Wind" and "Don't Think Twice, It's All Right"—it was in sweetened versions by Peter, Paul and Mary. By contrast, the astonishing trajectory of "Eve of Destruction" signaled a new mentality on a grand scale, stretching far beyond Berkeley and Ann Arbor and Swarthmore and other havens of the educated. For popular music was suddenly brooding and snarling all over the place. That same month, folk's princess, Joan Baez, broke into the hit parade for the first time in five years of recording, with an elegiacal Phil Ochs ballad called "There But for Fortune," which oozed universal compassion, included sympathy for winos, and referred to "the city where the bombs had to fall," which I took to mean Hiroshima. Dylan had just converted to electrified folk-rock—a few hundred purists (out of twenty thousand fans) had booed him when he unveiled the new style at the Newport Folk Festival in July— and his commercial instinct was rewarded: the folksinger who wanted to be a rock 'n' roll star finally burst through to Number 1 with the private, electric, rocked-up hostilities of "Like a Rolling Stone." His stylistic breakthrough made "Eve of Destruction" and all its folk-rock successors possible, in fact, by "dragging [folk] screaming," as Charlie Gillett writes, into the pop world, breaking the back of orthodox folk music in the process.

And if these sullen bursts weren't enough, what they followed to the Number 1 spot were the grinding riffs of the Rolling Stones' "Satisfaction," which announced its intent with a guitar lick that sounded like a sour buzz saw, and never stopped snarling. The verses were hard to understand—in fact they were digs at the banality of radio, TV, and advertising, if you could decipher them—but it was hard to miss the sexual insinuation of the repeated "I can't get no satisfaction"; the *interruptus* of "And I try, and I try, and I try"; the dare and taunt in the stop-starting "I can't get no—"; the strut of all kinds of pleasure-hungry, thwarted, ravaged and—what the hell—ravaging selves proclaiming once and for all that no one was going to stop them when they cruised into the world to get whatever it was they hadn't gotten. Angrier than the Stones' earlier blues, and far more popular in the States, "Satisfaction" was a cross-class yelp of resentment that could appeal to waitresses and mechanics and students, all stomping in unison. The Stones' rough-tough bad-boy personae were as much a contrivance as the Beatles' famous sweetness; with the help of clever counselors, the Stones discovered to their own satisfaction just how vast was the market for *badness*.

"FAR FROM THE TWISTED REACH OF CRAZY SORROW"

Eve of destruction; no satisfaction . . . and a third motif went rippling through the baby-boom culture: adhesive love, that luminous remedy without which the popular imagination of the young would have dissolved into nothing more than paranoia and rampant aggression. If the apocalypse was impending, your every hope for pleasure thwarted; if you found yourself "on your own, no direction home, like a complete unknown" (Bob Dylan's version of alienation in "Like a Rolling Stone"); if this was a dog-eat-dog world, as Dylan seemed to be sneering, it was still possible to imagine transcendence.

Popular culture conjured up both private and public compensations, actually. One theme was implicit in the double entendre of Dylan's next hit single, "Rainy Day Women #12 and 35": "Everybody must get stoned," meaning both that the great man incurs the wrath of the uncomprehending mob (as at Newport), and that the way out is through the magic of wonder drugs, especially marijuana, just then seeping out of its black and Hispanic, jazz-minded enclaves to the outlying zones of the white middle-class young. Dylan's taunt had its hard edge; there was a more persuasive, utopian version in his dreamy spring 1965 "Mr. Tambourine Man," a myth of pure sensuality which was also widely and laughingly interpreted, at least in Ann Arbor's hermeneutic circles, as an ode to a dope dealer, but was really a traditional Romantic vision:

> Yes to dance beneath the diamond sky with one hand waving free
> Silhouetted by the sea
> Circled by the circus sands
> With all memory and fate
> Driven deep beneath the waves
> Let me forget about today until tomorrow
>
> Hey, Mr. Tambourine Man, play a song for me
> I'm not sleepy and there is no place I'm going to
> Hey, Mr. Tambourine Man, play a song for me
> In the jingle-jangle morning I'll come following you.

Thus did Dylan lilt of absolute liberty in an infinite present time severed from the past: this was the transcendentalist fantasy of the wholly, abstractly free individual, finally released from the pains and distortions of society's traps, liberated to the embrace of nature and the wonder of essential things, in an America capable of starting the world again.

Although Dylan sang "Mr. Tambourine Man" as sweetly as he was able, the lyric was still scarred by the rough edges of his voice; as with "primitive" painting and sculpture, the roughness, coupled with innocence, was part of the attraction: Dylan had earned his fantasy. For side 1 of his last pre-electric album, *Bringing It All Back Home,* was full of nightmare visions, not least the sadistic torments of "Maggie's Farm." Once you had paid your dues—Dylan seemed to be saying—and made your escape from Maggie's Farm, then you could cavort down to the beach with Mr. Tambourine Man. "Mr. Tambourine Man" was all the more luminous and poignant because on the Hieronymous Boschian side 2 of *Bringing It All Back Home* it led directly to "Gates of Eden," "It's Alright Ma (I'm Only Bleeding)," and "It's All Over Now, Baby Blue."

Stoned, my friends and I and many another movement circle would fish Dylan's torrent of images, confirming our own revolts and hungers. As Dylan lurched through the doggerel stations of his personal cross, his bêtes noires were a gallery of our own grotesques. Even his irony about his own failed flight from the straight world spoke for an anguish we shared about the ambiguities of privilege: "Disillusioned words like bullets bark/As human gods aim for their mark/Make everything from toy guns that spark/To flesh-colored Christs that glow in the dark/It's easy to see without looking too far/That not much is really sacred. . . . But though the masters make the rules/For the wise men and the fools/I've got nothing, Ma, to live up to. . . . For them that must obey authority/That they do not respect in any degree/Who despite their jobs, their destinies/Speak jealously of them who are free/Do what they do just to be/Nothing more than something they invest in. . . . Money doesn't talk, it swears/Obscenity, who really cares/ Propaganda, all is phony." ("It's Alright Ma [I'm Only Bleeding]" alone donated dozens of headlines to the just-invented underground press.) And this "Baby Blue" with whom it was "all over," was it possibly America itself? Dylan's celebration of the solitary singer burst upon educated circles like ours in Ann Arbor just as high school seeker-intellectuals were discovering Hermann Hesse's *Steppenwolf,* equally a celebration of magic among the illuminati for the benefit of the lone wolf (once himself, like Dylan, an antiwar partisan).

"Mr. Tambourine Man" went down especially well with marijuana, just then making its way into dissident campus circles. The word got around that in order to "get" the song, and others like it, you had to smoke this apparently angelic drug. It wasn't just peer pressure; more and more, to get access to youth culture, you had to get high. Lyrics became more elaborate, compressed, and obscure, images more gnarled, the total effect nonlinear, translinear. Without grass, you were an outsider looking in.

"Circles" was the right word for the developing counterculture, in fact, because marijuana and music made up a collective ritual. It didn't matter that Dylan's lyrics, for example, were celebrations of strictly private experience; by playing the music together we transformed it into a celebration of our own collective intimacy, love, hilarity. In groups— rarely anything so formal as a preannounced "party"—we would sit around, listening, awed, all sensation, to Dylan's or somebody else's images bursting one out of the other like Roman candles, while we jabbered and giggled at anything at all ("Can you dig it?"), the afternoons and evenings seeming to stretch, the present liquidly filling all time past and time future, not just the words but the spaces between notes saturated by significance, the instruments sounding in the ear more distinctly than could have been imagined before. The songs drifted on, and on, leisurely, taking their sweet time; no longer were they being written for efficient two-minute jabs on AM radio.

The point was to open up a new space, an *inner* space, so that we could *space out,* live for the sheer exultant point of living. Go to class stoned; shop for food stoned; go to the movies stoned—see, all is transformed, the world just started again! On these luminous occasions, the tension of a political life dissolved; you could take refuge from the Vietnam war, from your own hope, terror, anguish. Even if you weren't "political," you had something in common with those who were: the ideal of an aesthetic existence, existence for its own sake, seemed within reach. Drugs planted utopia in your own mind. Call it a spiritual search? Fine, if you please. Or the ultimate giggle. Or both. In any event, grass seemed to have outfitted us with a more acute set of senses. Taste buds multiplied a thousandfold: pass the peanut butter, M & Ms, whipped cream, pepperoni. Light took on properties of its own: take a look through this prism, this kaleidoscope, check out the color TV. And sex . . . sex was ethereal. Did anybody ever do this before? The straights talk about martinis, but they're so uptight, they don't know how to wonder, they don't know what they're missing. *They don't get the joke.* Love is already here. "I'd love to turn you on. . . ."

New popular experience breeds new clichés. "Oh wow," "out of sight," "far out," or the more intense "far fucking out" (or "far fucking Rockaway," in the cynical-affectionate words of a journalist friend rejuvenated by grass)—these were easily parodied attempts to express the fact that delight was possible, the world was not entirely signed, sealed, and delivered over to the powers of instrumental reason. "Weird" was an easy label for the mysteries that opened up while you were stoned; then, banal and overused, it enshrined the strangeness of real unfolded- unspindled-unmutilated life, the sort of strangeness you could domesti- cate, like a house pet. Domesticated strangeness also showed up in "flashes" of free association. Stoned consciousness darted, flowed, went where it wanted to go, freed of rectilinear purpose and instruction. Routine talk seemed laughable; weird juxtapositions made perfect sense;

sense made no sense at all. Rarely did dope flashes look as good the morning after, but who cared? Meanwhile, virtually nothing was *really* weird, because anything might prove significant, or hilarious, or both— "Do . . . you . . . believe . . . this?"—just as anything you looked at, *really* looked at, might be transfigured in the seeing. The universe was drenched by meaning. Stoned people called up WBAI in New York to argue earnestly about what Dylan meant by "The pump don't work 'cause the vandals took the handles," or some other line. "He's rewriting the Bible," a Berkeleyite told me once in all seriousness. So Dylan's cascading lyrics matched the marijuana experience of snapping the normal links, breaking the usual associations, quilting together patterns from rags. The combination of a joint, the right company, and the right long-playing record seemed to have redeemed the traditional Romantic promise, Blake's "eternity in an hour": to see and feel truly the grain of the world, the steady miracle ordinarily muffled by busyness but still lurking in the interstices, a revelation of your astonishing existence in an electric universe. The everyday had been converted into the extraordinary.

As one cut on a less-than-best-selling album, Dylan's 1965 fantasy remained the property of small circles of the disaffected *initiati*. But "Mr. Tambourine Man" soon achieved a national audience in the crisper, smoothed-down, mechanical L.A. single version recorded by the Byrds. This was folk-rock's first commercial hit, danceable with or without a diamond sky or indeed any deep comprehension of Dylan's words at all. Plainly there was a national teen market for the spacy lyric, the invitation to drop out into a kingdom of druggy satisfaction—even the Byrds' metronomic version (created by professional backup sessionmen brought in by the producer to give the Byrds a steadiness they ordinarily lacked!) retained some of Dylan's original meaning. "Take me on a trip/Upon your magic swirling ship"; "Take me disappearing/Through the smoke rings of my mind"—the message, however imperfectly translated, got across.

"SMILE ON YOUR BROTHER"

"Mr. Tambourine Man" was the individualist's fantasy writ large: the hippie as lone ranger. The other utopia that swooped into popular music at the same time was that of the hippie as communard: the ideal of a social bond that could bring all hurt, yearning souls into sweet collectivity, beyond the realm of scarcity and the resulting pettiness and aggression. With the benefit of hind-hearing one can even hear the tribal love-sound foreshadowed in the exuberant innocence and joie de vivre of the Beatles' early harmonies: "Love Me Do," "From Me to You," "She Loves You," "I Want to Hold Your Hand," "All My Loving." Like the Stones, the Beatles had discarded their earlier, raunchier, black-based blues in order to rise as stars for the teenage audience. But as they brought new jubilation to the traditional "I'll-do-anything-for-you" puppy-love theme, they also succeeded in tapping a deeper sensibility. Their own love-quartet—at least the version retailed to the adoring hordes live and in Richard Lester's mock documentary *A Hard Day's Night*—could be taken to embody the ethic of brotherly love: harmony through diversity.

But the idea of a loving society only took full shape with what publicists called the San Francisco Sound, especially the Jefferson Airplane's languid invocation: "Hey people now/Smile on your brother/ Let me see you get together/Love one another right now." Already a staple at Bay Area concerts in 1965, released nationally on their first album in August 1966, and eventually popularized in a version by the Young-bloods, "Let's Get Together" brought religious yearning into Sixties pop. Unlike religiosities such as 1953's smash "I Believe" and the 1958 gospel hit "He's Got the Whole World in His Hands," the Airplane's sermon implored the beloved community to take the whole world in *their own* hands and remake it under the sign of love: "You can make the mountains ring/Hear the angels cry. . . . You hold the key to love and fear/All in your trembling hand/One key unlocks them both/It's at your command."

Yet there was something curious here. One second the Airplane told their audience that everything was up to them; the next, they veered toward a kind of Taoist fatalism: "Some will come and some will go/We shall surely pass/When the wind that left us here/Returns for us at last/We are but a moment's sunlight/Fading on the grass." Their wistfulness fought against the frantic all-for-the-future self-sacrifice of the Protestant ethic, but equally against the profound existentialist will which the counterculture itself tried to coax forth. The counterculture made immense demands on young multitudes unplugging from the normal social circuits—and hedged its bets with mysticism. If "logic and proportion have fallen soggy dead," as the Airplane sang later, there was still a transcendent logic to fall back on.

Thus the looming popularity of astrology, the I Ching, and other founts of mystical wisdom and explanation. The stars (or the Book of Changes, or the chakras, or the more esoteric systems of yoga, Sufism, etc. to which the real cognoscenti graduated) were all at once a relief, a link to a mysterious past, a connection to the ultimate, a guarantee of personal meaning, a grid of "rationality," and an alibi. The burden of existential-ism could be backbreaking; no wonder the Airplane's hand was "trembling." Who, on the other hand, could get all worked up trying to push the stars around? They simply *were*. If you believed, you gained access to ancient stockpiles of lore, once left pulverized and scattered by the bulldozer age of science and industrialism, the shards miraculously preserved to provide proof of the continuing life of the spirit. Moreover, the fact that the constellations sent forth their cosmic emanations to shape your life was the very proof—otherwise lacking—of your significance down here in San Francisco on Planet Earth.

Normally, schools, corporations, armies, and other institutions provide people with enough everyday rationality to get by. If the question arises, "Why do things this way?" the workaday answer springs up: "Those are the rules. That's the way we do things around here." Or, "That's the way we've always done it." Or, "It makes sense because the authorities say so." The multitudes of young dropouts lost the cushion of those rules, even if it was a cushion they were happy to have chucked. Their new cushions, embroidered with hip lingo, were at once ancient and avant-garde; the personally tailored star-charts were distinguished from the banalities of the supermarket checkout stand and the syndicated newspaper columns with which the hoi polloi had to content themselves. The question of the hour was, "What's your sign?" ("Flashing yellow," I used to like to answer.) Astrology, the I Ching, etc., were perfectly suited for transcendental alibis because their instructions were so vague. If you didn't like what was written in your heavens, the skilled chart-maker could always remind you that "the stars impel, they don't compel," and get off the hook. If the I Ching coins turned up an abstract lesson you couldn't grasp or didn't like, you could stretch for another interpretation, or toss the coins again. These were systems you could relax into.

Coupled-up love had long been a staple of pop music. Now, for the first time, the normal culture of teenagers was becoming infiltrated by grander ideals: freedom, license, religiosity, loving community. Blurry as the pop images were, they added up to intimations of a different way of life. Thanks to modern mass media, and to drugs—perhaps *the* most potent form of mass communication—notions which had been the currency of tiny groups were percolating through the vast demographics of the baby boom. *Life, Time,* and the trendspotters of the evening news outdid themselves trumpeting the new youth culture. As with the beats, the cultural panic spread the news and image of hippiehood. Alarmists and proselytizers alike collaborated in the belief that American youth en masse were abandoning the stable routes of American society and striking out onto unprecedented trails (or into unprecedented thickets). Even as the editors deplored the current excesses (although the Luces themselves had taken LSD, and it was a *Life* article that stimulated a psychologist named Timothy Leary to try his first psychedelic mushrooms), they were usually less than scrupulous in reminding their audience that most of the young were not, after all, dropping acid and fleeing to the Haight-Ashbury. There was enormous anxiety about whether the prevailing culture could hold the young; and on the liberal side, anxiety about whether it deserved to. It became easy to imagine that the whole of youth was regressing, or evolving, into—what? Barbarism? A new society unto itself, a Woodstock Nation? A children's crusade? A subversive army? A revolutionary class?

Astonishingly soon, Governor George Wallace and Dr. Timothy Leary agreed that what was at stake was nothing less than Western Civilization, the only question being whether its demise was auspicious.

BEING-IN

The tension between the individualist ethos of "Mr. Tambourine Man" and the communality of "Let's Get Together" was, for the time being, submerged in a great surge of animal joy. The emerging counterculture longed for both, for the fusion of the two. Why not have it all? Contradictions were a drag. The old world was coming to an end, and square logic with it. So let the good times roll! It was time for Better Living through Chemistry.

Human culture is ingenious. When people believe incompatible things at the same time, the contradictions become lived out, institutionalized, in rituals and habits. The counterculture thus devised institutions in which hip collectivity and the cultivation of individual experience could cohabit. Among them:

■ The Acid Tests. What could be more private than a drug trip? But both the defrocked Harvard professor Timothy Leary in the East and the let-it-all-hang-out novelist Ken Kesey in the West agreed that the miracle drugs should be ingested in company; moreover, that they were truth serums, agents of change that would tear apart the flimsy stupidities of life and get down to universals. Thrown out of Harvard in 1963 for tampering with unwary undergraduates, Leary and his colleague Richard Alpert took their drug experiments to a millionaire heir's mansion in upstate New York, a quasi-religious ashram for what Leary called the International Federation for Internal Freedom, where psilocybin was superseded by the even more mind-blowing chemical LSD. At first Leary and Alpert specialized in ancient wisdoms, cosmic imagery, Eastern meditations, and *The Tibetan Book of the Dead,* but Leary, eager to save the world in a flash, was also adept at arousing the media with slogans like "Tune in, turn on, drop out" and "Get out of your mind and into your senses." In the San Francisco Bay Area, Kesey, who had been turned on to LSD by a Veterans Administration hospital experiment in 1960, wrote *One Flew Over the Cuckoo's Nest,* with its romance of crazy-like-a-fox heroes up against the Combine (a.k.a. System), and founded a countercombine of Merry Pranksters.

How to summon up the enormous innocence, not to say heedlessness, of the Pranksters? In their reckless abandon, their sheer ingenuity and bravado, they were strangely of a piece with the nodules of the civil rights movement and the New Left—not in ideology, obviously, but in the absolute audacity it took for a small squad to seize the moment and believe they could actually change the world with exemplary acts. (The real achievement of Tom Wolfe's prose in *The Electric Kool-Aid Acid Test*, still unsurpassed as a chronicle of the counterculture, is not simply its breathless sense of fun but its capacity to evoke the animal magnitude, and nuttiness, of what the Pranksters were about.) In the summer of 1964 a dozen Pranksters careened around the country in a beat-up Day-Glo–painted super-stereo'd bus named FURTHER, gobbling and smoking vast quantities of drugs, freaking out local citizens (thus carrying the good tidings to the democratic multitude), having a high old time punctuated with bursts of stark raving madness. With mythic appropriateness, FURTHER's cannonball driver was none other than the beat hero, pill-popping, nonstop talker and wild man Neal Cassady. The Pranksters were indeed a wilder, western, electronic, vastly more raucous version of the beats—in large part because LSD, destroyer of tidy psychic worlds, was their thing. "Freak freely" was the idea: drop acid, smoke grass, eat speed, whatever drug was around, paint your faces, paint your scene, change everything, go after cosmic unity, "tool up for some incredible break-through," as Tom Wolfe summed it up, but whatever happened, *go with it* in hot pursuit of the old bohemian vision, enlightenment by any means necessary. "Either you're on the bus or off the bus."

By the fall of 1965, Kesey and friends, back in the Bay Area, were passing the word and the acid, come one, come all, first to friends, then to all comers, in public happenings they called Acid Tests. The dozens, then hundreds who caught wind of these occasions were given the purest LSD (still legal in California), treated to costumes, paint, pulsating colored lights, Prankster movies, barrages of sound and music, weirdly looped tape-recorders, assorted instruments, a flood of amplified talk. For Kesey, like Leary, was a proselytizer at a moment when millions were seeking a way to live beyond limits; he had a "vision of turning on the world," electrifying it courtesy of the most advanced products of American technology. The Pranksters had fantasies of slipping LSD into the public skin with solvents; and eventually, in Watts, while Kesey himself was on the lam in Mexico from marijuana charges, other Pranksters dispensed Kool-Aid spiked with LSD, didn't notify the novices, and treated one woman's bad trip by having her rant over the PA system to the dazzled, dazed assemblage. But the Watts test made *Life* magazine. Maybe there were no limits to the numbers of people who could be turned on; then all the inmates could take over the asylum.

■ The Pranksters were irregulars, with irregular schedules; they organized events as they pleased, on a moment's notice. In the hands of a hip household quaintly called the Family Dog, and the entrepreneur Bill Graham, who got the idea while he was business manager of the New Leftish San Francisco Mime Troupe, the Acid Tests evolved into Trips Festivals and scheduled concerts, with a new sound—spacy, unbounded whorls, not discrete songs: acid rock. By the fall of 1965, young people were flocking to San Francisco ballrooms every weekend to dance, to listen, just to be there, usually stoned, in the all-over sensual massage. By projecting light through glass slides smeared with swirling paints, artists created light shows—an evolution from the Pranksters' colored lights. Strobe lights turned the dancers into unearthly mobiles themselves. Just so, the acid-inspired swirls of the new-style psychedelic posters were barely comprehensible, but that was precisely their point: they turned letters into art-objects themselves, liberated them from the burden of literal signification. In the new dances, individuals didn't touch; they communed, dug each other by occupying the same space. The bands got their names from the sort of inspired and often inexplicable juxtapositions that came in dope flashes: Iron Butterfly, Quicksilver Messenger Service, Jefferson Airplane (a major theme: transport and flight), Big Brother and the Holding Company, the Grateful Dead, Electric Flag. Or they shined up the banalities of everyday life by stuffing them with double entendres: Loading Zone, Cleveland Wrecking Company. For special occasions (and word traveled fast), the concerts moved outdoors, and what could be more appropriate, for wasn't music part of nature, and was there any purpose higher than the celebration of being young in the fullness of time, with no reason to be anywhere else in the world?

■   In January 1967, the San Francisco Bay Area effusion was summoned to a "Human Be-In," also known as "A Gathering of the Tribes." The attempt was to bring together political radicals and acid devotees, in Golden Gate Park, to celebrate what the editor of a new freak paper, the San Francisco *Oracle,* called "a union of love and activism previously separated by categorical dogma and label mongering."

Not a union too easily consummated. All such collaborations were suspect from the start, for beneath the giddy New Age rhetoric a fierce competition was shaping up between the radicals and the hippie-gurus, jealous-eyed world-savers, each eyeing the young unplugging from school and job and flag, jamming into the Haight-Ashbury, up for grabs. The *Oracle* itself normally leaned away from politics and toward psychedelic-looking headlines, Eastern arcana, dope news, and personal testimonials to New Age drugs; it was designed, its editor said, "to aid people on their trips." It didn't look like the staid, linear Left: it was printed in many colors, with some pieces set in pictorial shapes, as if to say that words had to take second place to images. A few old beat-turned-countercultural hands, especially Allen Ginsberg and Gary Snyder, believed devoutly in a confluence of politics (on behalf of the outside and the future) and psychedelia (on behalf of the inside and the present), but the Haight-Ashbury merchants, rock impresarios, and dope dealers who financed the *Oracle,* and the hip influentials who starred in the media, were antipolitical purists. For Leary and Alpert, all political systems were equal oppressors and power-trippers. Political news was game-playing, a bad trip, a bringdown, a *bummer.* Indeed, all social institutions were games;

the LSD game was simply the best game in town. The antidote to destructive games was—more playful games. Hadn't Bob Dylan sung, "It's only people's games that you've got to dodge"?

For their part, hearing the siren songs of the counterculture, political radicals polarized. Some, mostly PL types, lashed themselves to the mast of Puritanism. Drugs, they thought, were bourgeois self-indulgences, distractions from discipline. But many more radicals—especially in Berkeley—were stunned by the wonders of marijuana and LSD. Even if they feared that the Haight-Ashbury stood for an unsupportable "flower-child innocence," that drugs "divorced the will from political action," the force of acid itself could not be denied, or forgotten, or assimilated. It hung there, apart from the rest of experience, *terra incognita,* a gaping hole in their mental maps. Just as graduate students had dipped into North Beach coffeehouses ten years earlier, so now did Berkeley antiwar activists join the crowds grooving over to the concerts at the Fillmore and Avalon ballrooms on the other side of the Bay, and screw colored bulbs into their lamps for hometown dance parties. Perhaps it was no longer necessary for politicos to defend themselves against the media charge of being beatniks; perhaps looking shaggy and sandaled was something to be proud of. And as with everything that had happened in Berkeley since the Free Speech Movement, the instigators (like the reporters) quivered to the feeling that as Berkeley went today, so would the rest of America go tomorrow.

If you watched with an optimistic eye—was not All One?—perhaps all revolutions would converge. There were sporadic experiments in synthesis, and some grand failures. In October 1965, the organizers of Vietnam Day, the round-the-clock antiwar teach-in on the Berkeley campus, invited no less a guru than Ken Kesey, who showed up in Day-Glo regalia, sized up the crowd and the bombastic speakers as some kind of ego-clamoring fascist rally, and announced that "you're not gonna stop this war with this rally, by marching. . . . That's what *they* do," marching was *their* game, whereupon he honked a chorus of "Home on the Range" with his harmonica, a back-woods American boy to the end, and told the fifteen thousand antiwarriors the only thing that would do any good was to "look at the war, and turn your backs and say . . . Fuck it." This was not what the organizers wanted to hear on the verge of a march into fearsome Oakland to confront the army base.

But a year later, quicksilver Berkeley seemed to be building sturdier bridges between freaks and politicos. In December 1966, Berkeley antiwar protestors tried to evict a Navy recruiting table from the student union. The police intervened. Afterward, at a mass meeting to discuss a campus strike, someone started singing the old union standby, "Solidarity Forever." Voices stumbled, few knew the words. Then someone started "Yellow Submarine," and the entire roomful rollicked into it, chorus after chorus. With a bit of effort, the Beatles' song could be taken as the communion of hippies and activists, students and nonstudents, all who at long last felt they could express their beloved single-hearted community. (It did not cross the collective mind that "Yellow Submarine" might also be taken as a smug anthem of the happy few snug in their little utopia.) One who felt vindicated in that musical moment was the Free Speech Movement veteran, ex-mathematician, poet, leafleteer and romantic, Michael Rossman. Rossman, though a red-diaper baby, was the most original and least formulaic spokesman for the movement's transcendent side—a man who respected the God-force of acid too much to issue programmatic statements about it. Rossman promptly ran off a leaflet which showed a little submarine adorned by the semi-psychedelic words "NO CONFIDENCE" (in the university administration, that is) with this explanation:

> The Yellow Submarine was first proposed by the Beatles, who taught us a new style of song. It was launched by hip pacifists in a New York harbor, and then led a peace parade of 10,000 down a New York street. Last night we celebrated the growing fusion of head, heart and hands; of hippies and activists; and our joy and confidence in our ability to care for and take care of ourselves and what is ours. And so we made a resolution which broke into song; and we adopt for today this unexpected symbol of our trust in our future, and of our longing for a place fit for us all to live in. Please post, especially where prohibited. We love you.

So it seemed no mean symbolic rapprochement when on January 14, 1967, there gathered on the same platform in Golden Gate Park Allen Ginsberg chanting Hindu phrases to the young hordes; Gary Snyder, converted to Buddhism, blowing on a conch shell; Timothy Leary chanting, "Turn on, tune in, drop out"; Jerry Rubin, who had risen to celebrity as leader of the militant Vietnam Day Committee in Berkeley, appealing for bail money, to no apparent effect; and the usual bands playing. Off the platform, where most of the action characteristically was, twenty thousand young people, more or less, reveled, dropped acid, burned incense, tootled flutes, jingled tambourines, passed out flowers, admired on another, felt the immensity of their collective spectacle. Berkeleyites and Haight-Ashbury weirdos gawked at one another. A group of anarchists called the Diggers, of whom more later, passed out thousands of tablets of highest-quality (and now-illegal) LSD, manufactured for the occasion by the renowned acid chemist Augustus Owsley Stanley III, known universally as Owsley; and handed out thousands of free sandwiches made from turkeys that Owsley donated too. The police treated the spectacle with benign neglect.

While the micrograms flowed freely, the Hell's Angels guarded the microphone. The Angels, malevolent shaggy toughs, were the counterculture's resident bad guys, stark embodiments of California's stark media-pumped nightmare, striking fear into even the hippest middle-class heart, making Marlon Brando's wild ones look like Mickey Mouse.

And therefore to make peace with the undisputed barbarians was a challenge no countercultural vanguard could refuse, for to succeed would mean making peace with the bogeymen of the freaks' collective psyche, proving that they had snipped the last umbilical cord binding them to the suburbs. To federate with the Angels, even better, would be to prove that lambs and lions could make a home together on the outskirts of town (while reminding the worried mother in yourselves that you weren't the *real* barbarians). The Angels, for their part, garnered LSD from the Pranksters and respect from Haight Street hipsters. They were not easily tamed, of course. The bad boys wanted to be ultragood patriots. When the Vietnam Day peace march from Berkeley was stopped at the Oakland line on the way to the army terminal, the day after Kesey's performance, the Angels roared in to bash the marchers, apparently with the collusion of Oakland police. By the time of the Human Be-In, though, they had become fixtures of the Haight-Ashbury, celebrated by Allen Ginsberg as the current version of the "saintly motorcyclists" of whom, a decade before, he had howled.

The media delighted in the infinitely photogenic Be-In; whatever this strangeness was, it was certainly A Story. "Hippie," the beats' once-derogatory term for the half-hip, caught on, circulated by the mass media, which alternated scare stories with travelogues of local color. Using affordable offset presses, the counterculture conjured its own channels, weekly or occasional papers sold on the street by the reserve armies of the runaway young: the *Oracle* for the hippies; Berkeley's ejaculatory left-wing *Barb* for the politicos. A failing San Francisco FM station, KMPX, began to play lengthy album cuts for the growing hip population, all night long, and found its listenership turning up (and, probably, on). The be-in was apparently becoming a way of life.

Hard-core counterculturalists were not persuaded to abandon the ways of the spirit for the ways of power. The guru Alan Watts told the *Oracle:* "whenever the insights one derives from mystical vision become politically active, they always create their own opposite . . . a parody." But politicos did not abandon their efforts to fuse the technologies of personal transcendence with the passions of politics. That spring, Jerry Rubin ran for mayor of Berkeley, calling for an end to the war, support of Black Power—and the legalization of marijuana—all with psychedelic posters. His campaign manager was Stew Albert, a bohemian ex-PLer with curly blond locks and a guileless manner who had turned Rubin on to marijuana and for years enjoyed flirting with the idea of a hip-radical fusion. Even in PL's palmy days, Albert hadn't seen much contradiction between bohemianism and radical politics: his attitude was, "After the revolution, we'll be beats again." As the campaign wound on, Rubin wanted to play less and win more; he put on a jacket and tie and started to talk straighter, though not straight enough to win more than 22 percent of the vote.

Rituals on the be-in model even started filtering into the American interior. Prairie-power SDSers were among the carriers. In the fall of 1965 SDSers at the University of Oklahoma were smoking marijuana, and in 1966 a few of them were arrested for it. (When the arrest drew comment in the press, the national organization debated whether to defend them or, rather, proclaim that their personal habits were their own business and leave them to their own devices. No position could be agreed upon.) At the University of Texas, SDS and a new underground paper called the *Rag* organized "Gentle Thursday," a day for smiling on your brother and festooning the old jet parked in front of the ROTC building with signs saying "MAKE LOVE, NOT WAR" (a favorite slogan that year, this clever attempt to deploy pleasure for political purposes) and "FLY GENTLY, SWEET PLANE." On Mother's Day, the be-in even arrived on the shores of Lake Michigan, in benighted Chicago, courtesy of a newly organized underground paper called the *Seed*. One young woman who painted her legs in great psychedelic swirls for the occasion was a University of Chicago law student, civil rights activist, and acid-lover named Bernardine Dohrn.

Other politicos, including myself, were edgy. We'd been smoking grass regularly since an organizer brought the habit from Berkeley at Christmas of 1965; but we feared that utter frivolity would short-circuit American youth's still tenuous sense of moral obligation to the world's oppressed. Love should feel ashamed, I thought, when it was founded on privilege. The hip-youth-drug thing, whatever it was, was beyond our control, and we must have sensed that the disciplines of politics (including our own) were in danger of being overwhelmed. Paradigm case: There was talk in those days that the scraped interiors of banana skins, dried and smoked, would get you high: "Mellow Yellow," in the vernacular and the Donovan song immortalizing it. Just before the Chicago Be-In, I joked about organizing a group to pass out leaflets saying that "The Bananas You Smoke Were Picked by Men Earning So-Many Cents a Day and Whose Land Was Taken Away by United Fruit." I wasn't quite grouchy enough to write the leaflet, but I did spot a young woman wearing a Chiquita sticker on her forehead, and sourly raised the issue of United Fruit's exploitation of Central American labor. "Oh, don't be so hung up on United Fruit," she said. (Soon thereafter I wrote an "Open Letter to the Hippies" making my case, circulated that fall to underground papers via the new Liberation News Service.) Political forebodings notwithstanding, the *Seed* trumpeted afterward that this modest event was "the Midwest's confirmation that She, too, belonged within the folds of Love that have gathered the tribes together everywhere across the continent. . . . The crowds relaxed, forgot the cold, the police, the hate, war, and all the petty flaws that keep men's scattered souls from uniting in love."

The utopian meanings might be disputed, but it was hard to miss the fact that the young everywhere seemed to be deserting their scripts. Even in the Midwest, for example, casual hitchhiking became a premium mode of transport for the young; people flashed the antiwar V-for-victory sign at strangers. Friends of mine driving through Michigan in a car with California plates were honked at by the car in the next lane; barreling down the expressway, the driver rolled down his window, grinned, and passed the strangers a joint. Robb Burlage wrote me from Washington with a new lyric, "Which Drug Are You On, Boys?" to the tune of the classic Thirties class-struggle song, "Which Side Are You On?" ("My father owns a drugstore/He's in the bourgeoisie/And when he comes home at night/He brings a drug to me/Which drug are you on, boys?/Which drug are you on?") What did it all mean?

Interpreters and organizers went to work interpreting and organizing. At the risk of oversimplifying the currents of 1967: There were tensions galore between the radical idea of political strategy—with discipline, organization, commitment to results *out there* at a distance—and the countercultural idea of living life to the fullest, *right here,* for oneself, or for the part of the universe embodied in oneself, or for the community of the enlightened who were capable of loving one another—and the rest of the world be damned (which it was already). Radicalism's tradition had one of its greatest voices in Marx, whose oeuvre is a series of glosses on the theme: change the world! The main battalions of the counterculture—Leary, the Pranksters, the *Oracle*—were descended from Emerson, Thoreau, Rimbaud: change consciousness, change life! (In a 1966 speech at a Boston church, for example, Allen Ginsberg claimed the mantle of Thoreau, Emerson, and Whitman for his own millennial yawp: that every American over age fourteen and in good health should take LSD at least once. "If there be necessary revolution in America," he said, "it will come that way.") There were hybrids: change the world *by* changing your life! Perhaps each style of revolt would soften the edges of the other. Perhaps logical knots were only illusions of the overly rational mind.

Despite these tensions, there was a direct line from the expressive politics of the New Left to the counterculture's let-it-all-hang-out way of life. Some of the SNCC "floaters" followed it, in fact, when they shifted to LSD; SDS's prairie-power generation of 1965 saw no barrier between radical politics and drug culture. The New Left's founding impulse said from the start: Create the future in the present; sit in right now at the lunch counter, as if race didn't count. Historically the traditions were tangled, intertwined. The synthesizers took up a grand American tradition of trying to fuse public service and private joy: *The Masses,* for example, the pre–World War I magazine that brought the cultivation of self and youth cheek to jowl with socialism, feminism, and the antiwar crusade (and published my old inspiration Charles Erskine Scott Wood). Now there was a populace on which to dream: the unleashed young. On the verge of the 1967 "Summer of Love," many were the radicals and cultural revolutionaries in search of convergence, trying to nudge the New Left and the counterculture together, to imagine them as yin and yang of the same epochal transformation.

"WHAT IT IS AIN'T EXACTLY CLEAR"

Youth culture seemed a counterculture. There were many more weekend dope-smokers than hard-core "heads"; many more readers of the *Oracle* than writers for it; many more cohabitors than orgiasts; many more turners-on than droppers-out. Thanks to the sheer numbers and concentration of youth, the torrent of drugs, the sexual revolution, the traumatic war, the general stampede away from authority, and the trend-spotting media, it was easy to assume that all the styles of revolt and disaffection were spilling together, tributaries into a common torrent of youth and euphoria, life against death, joy over sacrifice, now over later, remaking the whole bleeding world.

Of preconditions in society there were many, but the core of what came to be called the counterculture was *organized*—by intellectual entrepreneurs, streetcorner theorists of postscarcity, campus dropouts with advanced degrees, visionary seekers quickened by drugs. For every Timothy Leary, Richard Alpert, or Ken Kesey there were a dozen of the unfamous. Cloistered at first like monks preserving ancient rites in the midst of the Dark Ages, they later took their shows on the road to bring enlightenment to the young: today the Haight-Ashbury, tomorrow the world. Expert chemists like the Bay Area's Owsley, who set up underground laboratories and fabricated potent and pure LSD tablets in the hundreds of thousands, were not in it just for the money; they kept their prices down, gave out plenty of free samples, and fancied themselves dispensers of miracles at the service of a new age—"architects of social change" with a "mission . . . to change the world," in the words of one of Owsley's apprentices, toward which end Owsley helped, for example, to finance the Grateful Dead. A goodly number of small-scale entrepreneurs first dipped into the marijuana or acid trade as true believers helping their friends; only later did some of their businesses grow into the impersonal operations of big-time dealership. "Counterinstitutions" mushroomed, offering excitement, collectivity, and employment: underground newspapers; pamphleteering publishers; rock bands and promoters; hip FM radio; all manner of cooperatives; drug distribution networks; crash pads for runaways; free medical clinics; antiauthoritarian free schools.

The ideologues of the counterculture found ready listeners, of course. Above all means of communication were the electric ones: drugs, rock, mass media, pumping the cultural entrepreneurs' news into a receptive baby-boom generation, captivated audiences gathered in colleges and high schools—even in the armed services. (In 1967, more American troops in Vietnam were arrested for smoking marijuana than for any other major crime.) Millions, cushioned by affluence, desirous of fun or relief, out of joint, were in an experimental mood. In the Thirties, Woody Guthrie had sung of "pastures of plenty"; in 1967 his son Arlo sang, "You can get anything you want in Alice's Restaurant." (In thirty years the image of plenitude had shifted from agriculture to consumption.) Only fifty or seventy-five thousand young pilgrims poured into the Haight-Ashbury for the Summer of Love, but they were at the center of the nation's fantasy life. Music, dress, language, sex, and intoxicant habits changed with breathtaking speed. Countercultural entrepreneurs couldn't help thinking that enlightened youth were going to bring down Pharaoh and found the New Jerusalem.

In fact, they had gotten hold of some sociological truth. Dope, hair, beads, easy sex, all that might have started as symbols of teenage *difference* or *deviance,* were fast transformed into signs of cultural *dissidence* (or what both protagonists and critics considered dissidence, which amounted to the same thing). As the styles spread, their secondhand versions seemed to swell into a whole cultural climate. Consider the outward looks, the wild and various antiuniforms that took on especial meaning as the nation sent its armed forces off to war. Boys with long and unkempt hair, pony tails, beards, old-timey mustaches and sideburns; girls unpermed, without rollers, without curlers, stringy-haired, underarms and legs unshaven, free of makeup and bras. To orthodox eyes, this meant slovenliness and sexual ambiguity (like many of the androgynous-sounding rock voices); to the freaks themselves, a turn from straight to curved, from uptight to loose, from cramped to free—above all, from contrived to natural. A beard could be understood as an attempt to leap into manhood, even to age into one's own grandfather—thus to become spiritual father to one's own failed, draggy Dad. Clothes were a riot of costumes, with preferences for the old and marginal, which meant the unspoiled: India's beads, Indians' headbands, cowboy-style boots and hides, granny glasses, long dresses, working-class jeans and flannels; most tantalizingly, army jackets. Colors were pulled toward both plain and fancy—toward psychedelic disorder, homemade to suit via tie-dying, and toward the unadorned, basic, earthy: blues, grays, greens, browns. Food tended toward the "organic," simple ingredients, unrefined. Beads and amulets, for both sexes, represented the primitive. The antiuniforms became uniform.

Feeling "out there," giddily launched into uncharted territory, abandoned in history ("lost in a Roman wilderness of pain/all the children are insane," as the Doors put it), disordered by a fragmented culture, trying to invent roots, the freak entrepreneurs turned to bypassed worlds. Freak culture was a pastiche, stirring together intoxicating brews from extracts of bygone tradition. Thus the fascination with Eastern religions, especially in the Westernized versions of Hermann Hesse. Thus identification with the American Indians, who were, as Bennett Berger has pointed out, triply attractive: oppressed, "nobly savage" (wise enough to regard drugs as sacraments, too), and more deeply American than anyone else. What were the natural, the primitive, the unrefined, the holy unspoiled child, the pagan body, if not *the repressed,* the culture from the black lagoon, the animal spirit now reviving from beneath the fraudulent surface of American life, for which the most damning word possible was *plastic*? Get back, as the Beatles would sing, to where you once belonged.

Even more than in the Fifties, mass-circulation youth music seemed impenetrably, exclusively coded now. Self-respecting hits now had to be written by the singers themselves; what self-respecting shaman would hire a ghostwriter? Concerts ran from the Grateful Dead's acid-spacy interminables to the raunchy chants ("Gimme an F . . . U . . . C . . . K") and antiwar bluntness ("One, two, three, what are we fighting for?") of Country Joe and the Fish. Even the Beach Boys surged into the top forty of the annus mirabilis 1967 with the druggy "Good Vibrations," along with the Doors' Dionysian "Light My Fire" (their name was inspired by a line of William Blake's borrowed by Aldous Huxley for his prose poem to mescaline, *The Doors of Perception*); the Jefferson Airplane's "White Rabbit" ("one pill makes you taller/and one pill makes you small/ and the ones that mother gives you/don't do anything at all"); Scott McKenzie's plastic-hippie "San Francisco" ("if you're going to San Francisco/be sure to wear a flower in your hair"); Procol Harum's spooky, arcane "A Whiter Shade of Pale," which seemed to require either a Ph.D., or drugs, or both, for clarification; the Beatles' "Strawberry Fields." . . . And then, stunningly, came their brilliant, intricate *Sgt. Pepper's Lonely Hearts Club Band,* with its touching, backhanded tribute to the English music-hall tradition. If *the Beatles* were getting high with a little help from their friends, loving to turn you on, flying with Lucy in the sky with diamonds, then just what was marginal anymore, where was the mainstream anyway?

Yet authorities proceeded to define these ways of youth as illicit, immoral, dangerous. The Fifties panic over juvenile delinquency, having slid into a horror at "beatnik" demonstrators, now took the form of a drug-crazed–hippie scare. As in the Fifties, the labels stuck and the victims converted them into badges of identity. If you were bashed over the head and labeled a freak, well then, you were reminded why you had felt like a freak and gravitated toward drugs and weirdness in the first place. If you had started out smoking dope, growing your hair, discarding your bra partly to join the crowd and partly to shock adults, if you had gone along for the ride because it seemed the most interesting ride in town, only to end up getting harassed and busted, it was natural to ask questions about the society that was treating you like a freak. Police busted dope-smokers, dealers, the keepers and occupants of crash pads, troublemakers and innocents at rock concerts, and a lot of other young people whose looks they didn't like. Restaurateurs threw young longhairs off their premises. City officials deployed housing-code violations, zoning and vagrancy laws, and all manner of obscure regulations against them. With some justification, headlines screamed against what *Life* called "LSD: The Exploding Threat of the Mind Drug That Got Out of Control"; they also sensationalized scientific claims that acid destroyed chromosomes. The Senate Subcommittee on Juvenile Delinquency held hearings on the dangers of LSD; liberals denounced Timothy Leary for urging everyone to turn on and then washing his hands of all the bad trips. As old authorities lost their hold, politicians got mileage out of denouncing student radicals and hippies and black militants, all clumped together as battalions undermining the rule of the father-state and the family's own father. The personable Ronald Reagan, singled out as a plausible California gubernatorial candidate by a group of right-wing businessmen, won the 1966 Republican nomination and then parlayed antiblack, antiobscenity, and antistudent backlash, along with time-for-a-change sentiment, into a million-vote victory against the two-time incumbent, Pat Brown. (The freak population, meanwhile, affected indifference. From the spring of 1966 through the November election, the *Berkeley Barb* mentioned Reagan exactly once, and then only in passing.) Newly elected, the governor said a hippie was someone who "dresses like Tarzan, has hair like Jane, and smells like Cheetah." Parents complained about their children's looks, threatened to cut their hair, worried they would run away, placed ads in the underground papers to find them. Newspapers and television vacillated between shrieking about the hairy menace and cooing over how cute the kids were; proclaiming that hordes of fledgling hippies were about to wander to the Haight-Ashbury for the Summer of Love, they guaranteed it would happen.

Drugs, rock 'n' roll . . . sex: they were amalgamated, whether as liberation or scandal. There probably was more youthful sex, although reliable information is hard to pinpoint; what is certain is that the sense of a sexual revolution was fueled by vastly more public *talk* about sex, accelerating with *Playboy* and the end of the Hollywood Production Code in the Fifties, the overthrow of book censorship in the early Sixties. The birth control pill, spreading year by year from 1960 on, made sex virtually procreation-free, helped undermine parental (and in loco parentis) control over teenage sexual bodies. Starting then, and accelerating through the mid-Sixties, thousands of students moved off campus, popularizing that old bohemian custom of housekeeping without matrimony—and most assuredly without parental approval. Parents were shocked, and so were other parental authorities: the conspicuous cohabitation of a Barnard student and her boyfriend, and the university's crackdown, was a newsworthy item as late as 1968. (But within a few years, according to a study at the decidedly middle-American Penn State, about half of the seniors reported they had "lived with" someone of the opposite sex.) Meanwhile, interracial couples, rarities not so long before, became common sights around northern campuses and hippie ghettos. Sex was not simply a pleasure but a statement.

But freer pleasures brought more retribution and more fear: of the knock at the door, the "narc" at the party, the sweep down Haight Street, the summons to the dean—not to mention Mom and Dad, who might find your pills or diaphragm, smell your grass, find the wrong undergarments in the hamper. If you were politically active, there was yet more reason to worry—about being watched, bugged, tapped. The sheer knowledge that smoking pot was illegal, and that the police were on the lookout for it, injected routine apprehension into the marrow of everyday life. Teenagers who casually indulged these tastes, even as hedonists and crowd-followers, found themselves labeled outsiders, even criminals. Why were the authorities cracking down on harmless indulgences, they wanted to know? What was it about *these* authorities that marijuana—an acceptable sacrament in Morocco and India and elsewhere—should so disturb them? The crackdown may have contained the counterculture, but it also weakened the *authority* of authorities.

As drug trips became commonplace, less care was taken with their settings. Especially given a bad mind-set and an uncongenial setting, drugs were capable of driving anxiety to a high pitch. Drug tourism (and perhaps expectations of trouble) led to bad trips—very rare with marijuana, more common with hashish, most common of all with LSD, especially the amphetamine-laced or otherwise polluted stuff increasingly sold on the street in the later Sixties. A sizable number of the experimenters lived through episodes of acute terror, the memory of which could be hard to shake. Newspapers played up the catastrophe stories, of course, but people under the influence *did* jump out windows under the misapprehension that they could fly—even Richard Alpert did it once— and many young people, their egos fragile from the start, could not assimilate the ego loss that the gurus touted. Groups of "chemical freaks" formed, with indiscriminate tastes for barbiturates and amphetamines— speed—as well as LSD, mescaline, and whatever else was around. "Speed Kills," said street graffiti, but amphetamines spread. In the presence of bad trips and overarching fear, the youth culture had need of a term to describe the vague sensation of surrounding menace: "paranoia." The feeling became so commonplace, it worked its way into one of the key lyrics of 1967, the Buffalo Springfield's edgy, ambiguous, portentous "For What It's Worth": "Paranoia strikes deep/Into your life it will creep/It starts when you're always afraid/Step out of line and the man will come and take you away"—written by Stephen Stills after he watched a TV news piece about police smashing longhairs who were demonstrating against storekeepers who refused to serve them on Sunset Strip.

As sex lost the sheen of taboo, it was violence that took on the frisson. The sepulchral voice of the Doors' Jim Morrison, like an echo in a marble mausoleum, fused the two in his eleven-minute "The End." ("Father, I'm going to kill you/Mother I'm going to . . ." he screamed on the record; ". . . fuck you," it came out the first time he performed it live, smashed on a huge dose of LSD.) Hip ideologues might pin all the violence on the cops, but most of the young on the streets knew better. With the demographic youth bulge came more young criminals, and crimes; with illegal drugs came "burns," gang muscle, street wars. For the children of the suburbs, this was an unexpected shock. Drug-crazed murderers and LSD-inspired suicides did sell papers, but that didn't mean they weren't happening. Three months after the Haight-Ashbury Be-In, a group of savvy leafleteers who called themselves the Communication Company wrote about "Uncle Tim's Children":

> Pretty little sixteen-year-old middle-class chick comes to the Haight to see what it's all about & gets picked up by a seventeen-year-old street dealer who spends all day shooting her full of speed again & again, then feeds her 3000 mikes [micrograms of LSD, twelve times the standard dose] & raffles off her temporarily unemployed body for the biggest Haight Street gang bang since the night before last. . . .
>
> Rape is as common as bullshit on Haight Street. Kids are starving on The Street. Minds & bodies are being maimed as we watch, a scale model of Vietnam. . . .
>
> Are you aware that Haight Street is as bad as the squares say it is?

The white kids' less-than-delighted neighbors in the low-rent youth enclaves, moreover, were usually blacks (as in the Haight-Ashbury) and Hispanics (as on the Lower East Side). To them, the freaks were the invaders. The hippies proclaimed their culture was universal; they didn't see why they should concede much to people who had other ideas. Maybe straight society was right, the blacks were getting too pushy and riotous. . . . Inevitably there were turf fights, culture wars, and neither protagonists nor police were always subtle in handling them. Parks and festivals, scarce resources, were especially contested areas. Typically, on Memorial Day 1967 in Tompkins Square Park on the Lower East Side, Puerto Ricans were fuming because, as Don McNeill wrote in *The Village Voice*, "they had heard the 'LSD music' and they thought that the hippies were taking over the park. . . . [A] group of Puerto Ricans came to the bandshell and demanded Latin music. Some words were exchanged, and a scuffle started. . . . The kids then . . . knocked over a couple of sanitation barrels, and began to work on a Latin beat. A tall blonde, Wendy Allen, went up to protest. The kids attacked her and tore her clothes. A mob formed around her and hurtled toward the park entrance at East 7th Street and Avenue B. There, a police sergeant rescued her and summoned reinforcements." The crowds confronted each other until heavily armored police arrived to disperse them, sealing off the park for the night. There were summit meetings to cool out these frictions. Savvy organizers and underground papers—many of whose writers came from the New Left—tried to analyze the situation into peace and placate all sides, with some success. But the points of division remained: scarce goods; hippie racism; the resentment of white slummers by people of color.

And to nudge the sense of paranoia and apocalypse onward there was also, not least, the Vietnam war. Youth culture stared and trembled at the enormity of what was happening on the other side of the world. By June 30, 1967, there were 448,800 American troops stationed on Vietnamese soil. With draft calls up, and student deferments pared down in 1966, the war moved a lot closer to the hitherto exempt, and the student antiwar movement boomed as a direct result. But even beyond the students and the militantly opposed, the war was a steady, hovering curse. Many of the freaks knew soldiers, had been soldiers themselves, or feared becoming soldiers. With the test ban, the Bomb had receded to the status of an abstract threat, but the Vietnam war was actual, nothing potential or abstract about it; napalm was scorching actual flesh, bombs were tearing apart actual bodies, and there, right there, were the traces, smeared across the tube and the daily paper—every day you had to go out of your way to duck them. The New Age was streaked with nightmares.

Thus the bewilderment about where the world was tending. "There's something happening here/What it is ain't exactly clear": so began the Buffalo Springfield's "For What It's Worth," relaying youth culture's confusion. Developments broke so fast, who could absorb them, let alone insert them into the mind's polarities of left/right, politics/culture, rational/irrational (or, for that matter, strategic/expressive)? Extravagance was common currency. Whatever was happening, it was far out, too much, out of sight.

So youth culture became the hope, and therefore the target, of countercultural entrepreneurs and New Left organizers alike. But major differences were masked.

According to youth culture proper, the enemy was adults, their institutions and culture.

According to countercultural entrepreneurs, the enemy was the established culture, or civilization itself, neither of which was necessarily organized by age.

According to the New Left, the enemy was the political and social system, and/or the dominant institutions, and/or the inhabitants of the commanding heights.

According to liberal reformers, the enemy was particular policies.

In all the excitement, the rush of events, the multiple paranoia and hysteria, the mad overlap of millennarian hopes, profound tensions were obscured. But the stakes were high, and therefore so was the pressure to imagine the situation starkly. There are moments in history when the sense of extremity takes on a life of its own. The media said the stakes were high, the police said so (and the FBI, in terms the New Left barely began to grasp), politicians said so, Vietnamese and Cuban revolutionaries said so, black rioters laying waste to Watts and then the Newark and Detroit ghettos seemed to say so, SNCC chairman Stokely Carmichael and then the Black Panthers said so. Was not the old order, however one understood it, passing? That all these uprisings should have materialized in the first place from anesthetized America was altogether astounding. From various angles, insurgents mused: What if, whether they knew it or not, young whites smoking grass and students burning draft cards and blacks burning storefronts were detachments in common battle against a single occupying army?

The moment carried many names, aliases: "the new age," "the age of Aquarius," according to hip gurus; "from protest to resistance," according to the war-attuned politicos of SDS. If necessary, said Allen Ginsberg, there should be "a mass emotional nervous breakdown in these states once and for all." But all these voices of, or for, the young agreed we were on a knife edge in national if not global (or cosmic) consciousness. It was not a moment for thinking small.

9

PUBLIC NUISANCES

[After the triumph of Soviet Russia and bureaucratic American trade unions] power itself was now the spook, and the only alternative, if humankind was to show a human face again, was to break the engagement with the future and, above all, the psychic power upon people which the future held—and that was sublimation itself. You lived now, lied now, loved now, died now. And the thirties people, whether radicals or bourgeois, were equally horrified and threatened by this reversal because they shared the same inner relation to the future, the same self-abnegating masochism which living for any future entails. . . .

—Arthur Miller

THE THEATER OF OUTLAWS

The Haight-Ashbury drew all manner of avant-gardes in search of constituencies who might be ready to think big. The organizers with the greatest flair called themselves Diggers.

They practiced street theater, with performances and leaflets as their two forms. They declared "The Death of Money and the Birth of Free," trudged down Haight Street as pallbearers wearing five-foot animal masks and carrying a coffin, giving away flutes and flowers, mocking the law banning "public nuisance," which they said was only "new sense." They raised money from Owsley, and stole sides of beef which ended up in the stew they ladled out every afternoon for a year at 4 P.M. in the Panhandle of Golden Gate Park. They broke a donated brick of marijuana into baggies, went into Haight-Ashbury stores, and yelled, "Free marijuana. Does anybody want this?" They ran a Free Store with "liberated goods," and gave out "free money." They burned dollar bills. They erected a twelve-foot-square "Free Frame of Reference"—walk through it and remind yourself how constructed consciousness is. They put on the media by exchanging names, claiming credit for some demonstrations, disowning others. One of them, Peter Berg, once convinced each of two reporters, one from *The Saturday Evening Post,* the other from *Time,* each having dressed down for his foray into the wild and mysterious Haight, that the other was the manager of the Digger Free Store. (The two interviewed each other for some time before they caught on.) They shanghaied the Grateful Dead into giving a free concert in Golden Gate Park. To protest an execution at San Quentin, they butchered a horse.

"We were doing a piece of theater called the Diggers," Peter Berg said years later, "and it involved the audience." There was theater, indeed, in their background. Berg, the most book-learned of the bunch, had roots as a beat poet, then wrote plays and acted in the San Francisco Mime Troupe. (In the first "guerrilla theater" piece he wrote, American MPs simulated beating German POWs to death in the middle of Berkeley's Sproul Plaza, with no announcement that this was Theater; in the second, *Search and Seizure,* an acidhead subverted the police by being so stoned he simply didn't know he was being interrogated.) Emmett Grogan, an ex-junkie, had also acted with the Mime Troupe; he and Billy Murcutt were working-class Irish boys from Brooklyn. Billy Fritsch was a longshoreman married to the beat poet Lenore Kandel. Others came and went.

There was considerable theory to the Diggers' practice. Though they became famous for giveaway services and acquired a reputation as Robin Hoods, they were not social workers any more than SNCC or ERAP organizers were. They were anarchists of the deed, and their flair, in the full spirit of the time, was to carry a romantic idea to its logical endpoint. Not that they were romantic about the dropouts flooding into the Haight-Ashbury; they thought that "hippies" were cute, unserious, and innocent, "white kids who weren't that hip." A decade older than most hippies, the Diggers moved into the Haight deliberately to infuse the new culture with their ethos. It was time to live in a world beyond scarcity, they thought, and they wanted to bring the news: live off the abundant fat of the land. Or, in the words of a leaflet, "SEW THE RAGS OF SURPLUS INTO TEPEES."

"The executive branch of the hippie movement," a sympathetic minister called them, wishfully. The Diggers were a cadre organization, actually—radical existentialists, artists of the will. They didn't *demand* because, as they saw it, demanding was dependency, it taught that authorities are legitimate enough to be targets of demands. Don't demand food, they said; get the food and give it away. They had no illusions about loving the world into a new shape with a smile, a two-finger V, a chestful of buttons, and a psychedelic shop. "When Love does its thing," they proclaimed in an early broadside, "it does it for itself, not for profit. . . . To Show Love is to fail." They had a theory of society in which theatrical disruptions and recreations were central. Social institutions, left to themselves, calcified into "horizontal and vertical pyramid hierarchies boxed and frozen for coordinating programmed corpses." Life took place in breaking through the "games," making life happen—why not now?—by force of sheer audacity. As the young journalist Don McNeill wrote, "The Diggers declared war on conditioned responses. They blew minds by breaking subtle mores. They practiced public nuisance." LSD was useful because it might remind you of childhood's lost "tense of presence," but drugs by themselves wouldn't change the world. For that there would have to be action that would—in a phrase Berg pulled out of a theater history book—"create the condition it describes." History was theater if you "assumed freedom"; the protagonists who made things happen were "life-actors"—life was their act—who "amped" their theater by pumping it into the right audience in the right place at the right time.

Since history could be picked up by the scruff of the neck and made to dance, the Diggers dredged up precedent wherever they could. They took their name from the seventeenth-century English revolutionaries who declared their faith in Love and "endeavour[ed] to shut out of the Creation, the cursed thing, called *Particular Propriety,* which is the cause of all war, blood-shed, theft, and enslaving Laws, that hold the people under miserie." Those righteous small-c communists thought the way to celebrate universal divinity was to unearth glory here and now by treating all the earth as a "Common Treasury," and they proceeded, without asking permission, to treat it that way; at a time of great privation they took over common land and, by God, started to dig it. Beyond protests and demands—although eventually, after being run off the common lands, they humbly addressed their utopian proposals to Oliver Cromwell—the original Diggers weren't satisfied to disobey authority civilly; they utterly ignored it. From the Futurists and Dadaists of the early twentieth century, the twentieth-century Diggers derived the precedent of artists injecting art like some wild drug into the veins of society; from the civil rights movement came the as-if, the idea of forcing the future by living in it, as if the obstacles, brought to a white heat, could be made to melt.

The Diggers were prone to compression: compressed language (Ezra Pound: "DICHTEN = CONDENSARE"), compressed history, compressed events. Their prose style, descending from Pound via Allen Ginsberg and Gary Snyder, was breathless, extravagant, desperate, as if they had only an instant to pass on the latest bulletin before moving on to the next emergency. Like hip admen they floated pithy slogans like "Today is the first day of the rest of your life" (originally a line from the beat poet Gregory Corso, actually) which as a caption to a poster showing a little girl marveling at the ocean found its way onto many a hip wall. They were either/or and they liked hard-and-fast formulations: "if you're not a digger/you're property"; "if you Really believe it/do it." And although the Diggers loathed the media for faking experience, they were willing to use them as public address systems. When they were trying to scare up resources to take care of the anticipated Summer of Love influx, for example, they happily participated in a community press conference. ("Huge Invasion" was the *San Francisco Chronicle*'s tag, over "HIPPIES WARN S. F." in gigantic black letters at the top of the front page. Whereupon the Diggers passed out photocopies of the article with an addendum that read: "Two predictions absolutely free: I. They won't believe it till it happens. II. When it does, they'll try to bust it.")

In June 1967, Paul Krassner, editor of *The Realist* and a countercultural impresario with a raunchy sense of humor, mentioned to the Diggers that he was going to an SDS conference in Michigan. What an opportunity to take the Digger show on the road! Visions of freaking out the stodgy New Left! Emmett Grogan liked the idea of disrupting, "calling the white radicals' bluff." Peter Berg, who had read *The Port Huron Statement* (he thought it "pallid" and "elusive"), was mildly less antagonistic; he thought the Diggers might make some converts, but he agreed that the New Left was square and hypocritical—middle-class kids comforting themselves with plans for the future while supporting themselves with checks from Mommy in their dull-eyed present. An SDS conference might be interesting enough to warrant blowing its collective mind.

There was no time like the present. They got in a car with plenty of whiskey and wine and speed pills, and drove at breakneck speed from San Francisco to the middle of Michigan.

A COMIC COLLISION

What the Diggers drove cross-country toward was not, in fact, an SDS conference, though the distinction was lost on them. It was the SDS Old Guard's attempt to regather an extended version of the original fused group.

The Old Guard was trying to think big in its own way. We were not giddy about the youth surge; but we too had been infected by the sense that something unprecedented was upon us.

We were rather sobersided easterners and midwesterners, nothing hippie-dippie about us. In 1967, I doubt whether a single one of the Old Guard had sampled the mystery drug LSD. Most were leery even of marijuana. (When Tom Hayden saw me weaving under the influence of grass at a party during the 1967 SDS convention, he gave me a suspicious look, as if to say that no serious radical should be messing around with this stuff.) We had streamed off the campuses, many of us into ERAP projects, a few into professional careers. In various ways we had tried to dig in, on a small scale, "for the duration." But that spring we were more than usually restive. Plunging off campus to find a constituency large and committed enough for radical change, we had kicked away our onetime base. In our middle and late twenties, we felt too old for *Students* for a Democratic Society. With the benefit of a bit of experience in the larger world, we knew that students, no matter how many and how estranged and militant, hadn't the leverage, by themselves, for enormous social change. It was, moreover, dawning upon the community organizing wing, at least subliminally, that ERAP's much-touted "interracial movement of the poor" was not materializing, at least not fast enough to outrun nationalism among blacks and George Wallace's popularity among whites. To win the simplest reforms—housing repairs, a traffic light at a dangerous intersection, more money for welfare recipients and their children than 22 cents per meal (the Chicago rate)—proved herculean. It was a moment when many on the Left wanted to push outward. Some organized Vietnam Summer, a canvassing program to channel antiwar activists into the untouched heart of middle-class America. An older cadre including Marcus Raskin and Arthur Waskow put together a National Conference for New Politics (NCNP), which aimed to be a new coalition in the making; some anticipated a national effort to form an electoral campaign against Johnson, with hopes that Martin Luther King and Dr. Benjamin Spock would be the candidates.

What some of the Old Guard wanted was a post-SDS, some sort of organization to fuse political passions and professional commitments for onetime student activists. The movement's heart was still ecumenical: come one, come all. Whatever your skill and calling, there was a place for you. For poets and fiction writers, SDS had spun off a literary magazine called *Caw!* (after Whitman). For architects, computer specialists, artists, you name it, there was New York City's loose-knit federation, Movement for a Democratic Society. For journalists, including myself, there were meetings to organize a radical newsweekly. Playwrights, take your work out on the road to SDS projects! (This was the scheme that had first drawn an Ann Arbor dramatist named Carl Oglesby to SDS.) City planners, draw up plans that community groups can embrace! For every hundred schemes, a handful materialized—but never mind, the spirit of One Big Movement was alive. In June there was a conference to coordinate "Radicals in the Professions": incipient doctors, lawyers, teachers, planners. But old SDSers felt that something more sweeping, something national, was needed. As early as 1964 Dick Flacks had proposed that SDS expedite an organization of alumni; the SDS National Council had sagely nodded approval, and nothing had happened, graduate students, young professors, and community organizers all having other priorities. But an Old Guard kernel in Chicago had been searching, in fits and starts, for a way to act collectively as political intellectuals. We put together a conference we called, mock-grandly, "Back to the Drawing Boards."

We didn't quite agree on what we wanted: electoral politics, post-student organization, a canvass of the state of local activity and movement ideology. The incumbent SDS officers, of the prairie-power persuasion, suspected the Old Guard of social-democratic heresies; I tried to convince them that the conference wasn't "a plot of aging, jealous sell-outs to deliver the movement into NCNP." At bottom, the "Drawing Boards" group wanted to rally old faces and see what they had to say to one another. We put out the word, however vague, to old SDSers, young radical professionals and intellectuals, antiwar activists, and lo and behold, a couple of hundred agreed to spend a June weekend at a camp in the woods between Kalamazoo and Grand Rapids, Michigan, to discuss next steps. It was exactly five years since Port Huron.

What everyone remembers from Drawing Boards is the melodrama, or farce. Tom Hayden was giving the keynote speech in the wood-beamed camp dining hall. The context was emergency: the war was burning, the ghettos were burning. Hayden was mixing militant rhetoric and reform goals. On the one hand, with the radical upsurge, rifle practice was the next step; we might need to know how to break off friendships and become urban guerrillas. On the other, radical organizers had to consider joining Johnson's war on poverty, boring from within, for was not the Economic Opportunity Act making a pass at participatory democracy with its commitment to "maximum feasible participation of the poor"?

As in the opening scene of a horror movie, rain was pouring down. The door burst open and three men barged in. "Is there a fuckin' lawyer here? We need a lawyer."

Confusion and astonishment in the hall. Hayden ground to a halt.

One of the invaders wore a leather vest, another a fur hat. The one in the vest, long-legged and long-jawed, called himself Emmett Grogan. They were the Diggers, they said. They represented all the kids fleeing to the Haight-Ashbury to act out their vision. They had just driven all the way from San Francisco, stopping exclusively at Phillips 66 gas stations because that was the credit card they had hustled; they had been nabbed by the highway patrol for swimming naked in the Platte River, then nabbed for speeding, then narrowly squeaked out of a shoplifting episode and a barroom brawl . . . and then, just down the road, their car had skidded into a canal, and now one of their comrades was in jail.

A lawyer in the audience volunteered to go off with Grogan to do his lawyerly thing.

By now enough of the assembled had recovered from their shock to demand, Who are you guys? The one in the fur hat, Billy Fritsch, started banging his tambourine in time. Questions came from the dumbfounded audience, quivers of interest and fear. What are you doing here? What are you about? Are you provocateurs? More than one person in the audience thought of *The Wild One*.

Peter Berg, short and coiled, calling himself Emmett Grogan, started to talk, prowling across the room as if it were a stage. Someone came up front to turn on a tape-recorder. Berg grimaced with his actorly face. This is not going to be tape-recorded, he roared, because if you tape-record it, you're not going to listen. This isn't for posterity, it isn't literature! The New Left didn't know what was happening, Berg laid out in jumbled illumination; it was abstract, ineffectual, hopelessly middle-class, irrelevant, derivative—without Vietnam, without Cuba, there wouldn't be any New Left at all. What were your politics anyway? You could be a rich dentist and protest against American intervention. The only thing worth doing was to make up your own civilization! "Property is the enemy— burn it, destroy it, give it away. Don't let them make a machine out of you, get out of the system, do your thing. Don't organize students, teachers, Negroes, organize your head. Find out where you are, what you want to do and go out and do it. The Kremlin is more fucked up than Alabama. Don't organize the schools, burn them. Leave them, they will rot." Look at the Diggers, taking direct action. They had a community of people who needed help in San Francisco, and they were helping with free food, free crash-pad housing, free clothes, a free information switchboard, free medicine, free tie-dying. *That* was politics.

Yells from the audience: That's not much! What gives you the right to come in here and criticize us?

His legal mission successfully accomplished, Grogan returned, jumped up on a table. "We're trying to understand you," one woman said. "Are you a mother?" Grogan asked. "Yes." Grogan: "You'll never understand us. Your children will understand us. We're going to take your children." He leaped down, kicked over the table, smashed down a chair. He knocked down one woman and slapped around some others, or went through the stage motions—accounts disagree. "Faggots! Fags! Take off your ties, they are chains around your necks. You haven't got the balls to go mad. You're gonna make a revolution?—you'll piss in your pants when the violence erupts. You, spade—you're a nigger, what are you doing here? Your people need you. There's a war on. They got fuckin' concentration camps ready, the world's going to end any day." Grogan unrolled a scroll of wrapping paper, declaimed a poem by Gary Snyder called "A Curse on the Men in the Pentagon, Washington, D.C.," including the line, "I hunt the white man down/in my heart." Periodically the Diggers turned off the lights, and Grogan held a flashlight under his face for horror-movie effect.

"If the CIA wanted to disrupt this meeting," yelled straight ex-SDSer Bob Ross, sitting in front, "they couldn't have done it any better than by sending you." Grogan, grimacing, leaped over to Ross, shook his finger at Ross's nose, and barked out, "What an ugly face!" Ross assumed that Grogan was anti-Semitically singling out what Ross called his "misshapen Jewish nose."

One of the Diggers announced that he was going to chase women. He was going to spread love. He wanted to get laid by one of the SDS ladies, he said. At one point he crawled around the floor and moaned, "Nobody wants me. Nobody wants to go to bed with me. I'm a poor dog that nobody wants."

"Please give us back our meeting," somebody said.

Eventually one of the Grogans announced that they had fuckin' guns and fuckin' bows-and-arrows in their fuckin' car, and that the next morning they'd be leading fuckin' target practice.

Whereupon Mickey Flacks said, "There isn't going to be any fucking if you people don't register." This brought the house down, and the opening plenary session of Back to the Drawing Boards came to an end.

A quirk, in a way, this farcical showdown. But quirks also explode into moments of truth. For the interesting thing about Drawing Boards is what didn't happen there. What has to be understood—what tells us a truth about where the New Left was tending in 1967—is why dozens of experienced organizers, who had set up the conference with a sense of high if vague purpose, permitted three Diggers to derail it. Even after the Diggers left the next morning, the conference never gathered momentum, never broke out of the Diggers' gravitational field. No organization was founded, no further plans sketched. That failure prefigured a larger chasm between political and cultural radicals—and also indicates why the New Left's attempt to outgrow the student movement never got off the ground.

The Diggers, for their part, full of stagecraft and menace, fueled by class resentments as well as politics, knew how to take over a crowd. "We were a pretty swaggering bunch in those days . . . cocky and outrageous, and sometimes rude, disrespectful," as Peter Berg says. ("Insufferably self-confident" is how the journalist Nicholas von Hoffman puts it.) The New Left was not into street theater, let alone streetfighting. The Diggers had the advantage of planning and surprise; they had spent days on the road putting together their performance (although not the accident that gave them their dramatic entrée). A few of the Old Guard, myself included, were distracted by marital crises. But earlier conferences had weathered worse.

No, the Old New Left didn't quite accept the fact, but its moment had passed. SDS, under prairie-power leadership, was moving "from protest to resistance," the premise being the idea long in the making that radicalized youth culture presaged a movement that could go it alone, building to the young and left, with limited reliance on coalitions to the elder and right. The swelling war seemed to discredit anything less than "resistance"; and there was now a mass youth base for upping the ante of militancy, which might even impress the middle class. Thus there were both strategic and expressive motives for leaving the Old Guard behind. Of all the New Left, we at Drawing Boards were the most hostile to Marxism-Leninism *and* the most skeptical of the political significance of new cultural styles. Yet even we were cowed by anyone who said he was a revolutionary. The Diggers, who liked to talk about freeing "the Digger in yourself," were our anarchist bad conscience, and so they paralyzed us.

We shared in the antileadership mood—our own countercultural roots again. We had built a politics on the accusation that liberals were hypocritical: thus we made ourselves vulnerable to the charge that we were hypocritical ourselves. We had cast ourselves adrift from conventional ideas of legitimate authority, but we possessed no clear authority principle to mobilize against the Diggers' takeover style. Most of the Old New Leftists who believed in formal leadership had long since been discredited by their belief in boring from within the Democratic Party. If the conference organizers had linked arms, say, and rallied the audience to throw the Diggers out, they might indeed have been thrown out. But the idea never dawned. The fact that the Diggers were left free to do their particular thing was both cause and effect of Drawing Boards' fragility. It was the SDS alumni crowd who were shaken, intrigued, and tempted by the Diggers, not the other way around.

The Diggers got exactly the effect they had angled for. Some of the SDS alumni were turned on by their theater of cruelty, some were transfixed, some repelled. The Old New Left not only was incapable of pulling anything together, its seams were showing. Bob Ross, for example, came away absolutely convinced that the Diggers represented antipolitics, "frenetic madness," "disaster" pure and simple. Some said the hippies would be "co-opted" by a business culture: wasn't there already a hot-dog stand in the Haight-Ashbury selling "love burgers," a Bay Area radio station advertising its "flower power"? Others were fascinated by the Diggers' flair and force. Many saw portents of trouble in a New Left out of control.

THE THEORY AND PRACTICE OF YIPPIE

If the Digger diatribes sound a bit familiar, it is probably because a version of their rap became household lore—a television version.

One of those agog about the Diggers at Drawing Boards was a former civil rights organizer with a clown face who had moved to the Lower East Side to open a store selling the products of Mississippi cooperatives, until he was eased out when SNCC went for Black Power, and Stokely Carmichael advised him to hurl his formidable energies into the antiwar movement. Abbie Hoffman did that. He grew his brown curly hair long, discovered LSD, and rollicked through the swelling Lower East Side hip scene, an East Coast sort of street Digger (complete with Broadway-Catskill shtick and a Massachusetts accent), organizing against police brutality, picketing here and there, social-working on behalf of the dropouts, trying to cool out violent scenes, joining community goodwill committees, then trying to disband them. ("Think of it," he said once. "A committee disbanding after two days. It'd be a whole turn in American political life.") Digger emissaries from the Haight had started showing up in Manhattan in the spring of 1967, "received in the hippie community like visiting royalty," as the astute Don McNeill wrote in *The Village Voice*. "They rapped to a series of meetings about free stores and fucking the leaders and turning-on Puerto Ricans, but between their visits the momentum would die and the torch would be snuffed." Abbie was one of the turned-on, although by Haight-Ashbury standards the Lower East Side imitation-Digger scene was uninspired. In beads, boots, bellbottoms, and Mexican cowboy hat, Abbie Hoffman flew to Kalamazoo with Central Park Be-In organizer Jim Fouratt (in purple pants) and Paul Krassner, to make the scene at Drawing Boards.

"A monumental meeting, probably never to be repeated," Abbie called the Diggers' freak-out performance. In *Revolution for the Hell of It*, published under the name "Free," he rhapsodized about the Diggers (exaggerating their violence as he went), and about staying up talking all night with them, getting stoned, while the Old New Leftists, "shitting, really scared of acid . . . losing control, Marx with flowers in his hair, can't deal with contradictory stimuli, simultaneous bombardment . . . slept all night very soundly. . . ." "Abbie was starry-eyed," Peter Berg recalls. "It was like a revelation had been committed to him." When the Diggers took off, Abbie and his fellow travelers stayed on. "The seminars drag on . . . a total bore . . ." Abbie recorded. "Jim and I are avoided, except by a small group. They do socialism, we blow pot in the grass, they do imperialism, we go swimming, they do racism, we do flowers for everybody and clean up the rooms." Bob Ross has another memory: the gay Jim Fouratt coming up to him the next day, trying to argue him into the politics of Love, and to prove the point kissing him full on the lips, making Ross feel he was "the first New Left victim of sexual harassment."

From Drawing Boards, the Diggers pushed on to New York City. A TV talk show host named Alan Burke had invited Peter Berg to be his guest. Berg, who had read his Marshall McLuhan, went on the air with hijacking in his heart. He launched into a lecture on the unreality of media portrayals. Watching people on the box, he said, you put yourself in a box. Did Berg know someone named Emmett Grogan? Burke asked. "No," said Berg, "there is no one named Emmett Grogan. There is, however, an *Emma Goldman* in the audience." At this point an older woman in the audience got up, perplexed, and asked what young people stood for these days. "Emma can handle your question," Berg said, and told the cameramen to focus on "Emma," a Digger plant who approached the microphone carrying a box, opened it, took out a pie, and shoved it right in the straight woman's face. Burke turned white. Berg addressed the audience and the camera: "This is how you get out of the box. You stand up, and you at home can join me in this. Stand up, and start walking to get out of the box. Now, here I go, now, just keep the camera on me, and I'll keep walking." He walked to the exit door, opened it, looked right into the camera, said, "Now turn off your television sets and go to bed," and walked out.

Berg later maintained that his stunt was what started Abbie Hoffman thinking about the curious notion of organizing through . . . television. But the priority matters less than the confluence. For the movement as a whole, countercultural and political alike, this was just the moment when the media were becoming problematic. To become a political force was to become media fodder: a fact at once inescapable, important, and confusing. Plainly the media helped define the collective sense of reality which underlay politics. The nightly news was bringing images of bloody war into the living room—was that the revelation of an awful reality, a trivializing of that reality, an obscuring of the war's imperial core, or all three? Administration spokesmen periodically blamed the press for insufficient patriotism, but the worst of the news of the Vietnam war, reported in *Liberation* and other movement journals, generally wasn't deemed fit to print in *The New York Times*. As black ghetto riots polarized race feeling, the white movement got its share of flamboyant coverage. The media had discovered youthful protest, and in the process bent the images toward the sensational. The problem arose: what should one do with inquiring reporters? Credentials were scrutinized with increasingly narrowing eyes. Just a month before Drawing Boards, a *New York Times* reporter had converted an extravagant metaphor into this front-page lead: " 'We are working to build a guerrilla force in an urban environment,' said the national secretary of the left-wing Students for a Democratic Society, Gregory Calvert, one day recently. 'We are actively organizing sedition,' he said." Distortions were being committed by professionals: what should we make of that?

Even Drawing Boards had brought some of these cross-currents to the surface. After the Diggers left, Nicholas von Hoffman, covering the event for *The Washington Post,* got up to say his notebook had been stolen. Word got around that the spunky Carol McEldowney, veteran of early SDS and now ERAP cadre, had (with accomplices) "liberated" this instrument of establishment scrutiny. For hours the meeting buzzed over whether the offending notebook should be returned. Was von Hoffman, a sympathizer and a former community organizer himself, an ally (in fact, he had had to convince skeptical editors that the meeting was worth covering at all)—or an unwitting tool of the Establishment? Protracted and earnest discussions ensued, in public, until the perpetrators were persuaded to return the notebook. Here was 1967 New Left ambivalence in perfect microcosm: even the more rambunctious among us could be persuaded, after hours of participatory democracy, to be nice to liberals. Pulled between the Diggers and a *Washington Post* reporter, the Old New Left lost ground to the countercultural side. The express train of antiauthority was hard to brake.

. . .

Therefore the antics of Abbie Hoffman were hard to stop or outdo. If the New Left didn't believe in its own leadership—if leaders denied they were leaders and the rank-and-file thought leadership illegitimate—then the movement, in effect, turned over to the media the capacity to anoint leaders in its name. Abbie's story is that he stumbled into the spotlight. In August, two months after Drawing Boards, he led a group to drop dollar bills on the floor of the New York Stock Exchange, watching the brokers scramble for them and the ticker tape stop dead, then burning bills for the hordes of reporters as they asked their uncomprehending questions. It wasn't original: the Diggers burned money first, at a demonstration outside the druggy-spiritualist paper *East Village Other*. This time, although no one called the reporters beforehand, the word got around in a flash anyway. Thus did Abbie Hoffman the dramatist grasp that The Hippies were one of the Hottest Stories in town. Next time, and the time after that, he could lure them with a phone call or a flashy press release.

One stunt led to another. Soot bombs going off at Con Edison headquarters . . . The army recruiting booth in Times Square plastered with "SEE CANADA NOW" . . . A tree planted in the middle of a Lower East Side street (the second tree Abbie uprooted, that is; the first one died during the transplant) . . . Joints of marijuana mailed to three thousand people selected "at random" from the phone book, one of whom happened to be a TV newsman . . . Reporters loved Abbie Hoffman; he was quotable, colorful, guaranteed good copy. "Recognizing the limited time span of someone staring at a lighted square in their living room," he wrote later, "I trained for the one-liner, the retort jab, or sudden knockout put-ons." Abbie (né Abbott) and Jerry Rubin, like Abbott and Costello, might as well have been sent over from Central Casting.

With the counsel of Ronnie Davis, the founder of the San Francisco Mime Troupe, Jerry Rubin had already discovered the theatrical virtues of costuming. Subpoenaed by HUAC, he had appeared in an American Revolutionary War uniform, stoned, blowing bubbles, making headlines, and (with the help of his fellow subpoenaees, the Nazi-saluting, finger-giving, put-on artists of PL, still in its bohemian phase) puncturing the bubble of the feared Committee's fearsomeness. He arrived in the East to coordinate the October 1967 antiwar demonstration in Washington, just in time to join Abbie's desecration of the Stock Exchange temple. Abbie's theatrics—he was wearing flowers in his hair when they met for the first time—gravitated toward Jerry's politics. But it would be mistaken to make too much of their differences. "Personally," Abbie wrote later, "I always held my flower in a clenched fist. A semi-structure freak among the love children, I was determined to bring the hippie movement into a broader protest."

The Hoffman-Rubin offspring was a politics of dis*play*. Jerry, weary of orderly demonstrations, wanted to confront the Pentagon. Why stop, he asked, at what had become the predictable semiannual antiwar show of strength? Weren't these mobilizations like working for a living, just another case of sacrificing the vivid, vibrating present on the altar of some hypothetical future? The movement's twice-yearly body count, for the sake of impressing a dubious "public opinion," had the worst possible attribute in the eyes of a subculture devoted to killing conventional time: it was boring. New tactics were called upon to infuse the movement with countercultural spunk. Since five-sided shapes were evil, why not apply for a permit to levitate the Pentagon, then invite witches and incantations to do the deed?

Abbie and Jerry proceeded to discover that the authorities could be trusted, in their own self-protective hysteria, to raise the stakes. Like skilled judo wrestlers, they could flip huge and clumsy opponents by using their own weight and ineptitude against them. When the Washington police announced they were ready to use a new stinging, temporarily blinding spray called Mace, Abbie sprang into symbolic counteraction, announcing a new drug, "Lace," ostensibly "LSD combined with DMSO, a skin-penetrating agent. When squirted on the skin or clothes, it penetrates quickly to the bloodstream, causing the subject to disrobe and get sexually aroused." Before bemused reporters, two couples sprayed each other with water pistols full of a fluid actually called "Schwartz Disappear-O!" imported from Taiwan, which was as good as its name: it made purple stains, then disappeared. The couples proceeded to tear off their clothes and make love, not war.

The point was to get reported, it didn't matter in what spirit, through what frame. In fact, if the point was to force the authorities to rise to the bait, to commit their cumbersome bulk and lose their balance, then the more offensive the image, the better. If someone was attracted by watching the story, great. If someone was alarmed, also great. Jerry's contributions tended to evolve in this direction: "to grab the imagination of the world and play on appropriate paranoias," in announcing the Pentagon demonstration, for example, "we needed the help of Amerika's baddest, meanest, most violent nigger—then [SNCC's] H. Rap Brown. . . . We began the press conference by identifying the Peace Movement with the Detroit and Newark riots. The newsmen quickly asked Rap if he would bring a gun to the Pentagon. He answered: 'I'd be unwise to say I'm going with a gun because you all took my gun last time. *I may bring a bomb, sucker.*'" No one brought a bomb, of course, and the only people who brought guns to the Pentagon that October were the federal marshals who occasionally poked their bayonets and bashed their rifle barrels into the symbolic siege.

It remained only to turn up the spotlight, broadcast the image far and wide. To Rubin, "A new man was born smoking pot while besieging the Pentagon, but there was no myth to describe him. There were no images to describe all the 14-year-old freaks in Kansas, dropping acid, growing their hair long and deserting their homes and their schools. . . . The Marxist acidhead, the psychedelic Bolshevik. He didn't feel at home in

SDS, and he wasn't a flower-power hippie or a campus intellectual. A stoned politico . . . A streetfighting freek [sic], a dropout, who carries a gun at his hip. So ugly that middle-class society is frightened by how he looks. A longhaired, bearded, hairy, crazy motherfucker whose life is theater, every moment creating the new society as he destroys the old." A mélange of Digger, prairie power, heaven's demon, in short: Rubin's ideal of himself.

Like all purist pioneers, the Diggers thought the popularizers violated the spirit and missed the point. The Diggers were virtually anonymous, came and went; Abbie and Jerry collaborated with the media, became celebrities. The Diggers wanted to expose the media as fraudulent; Abbie and Jerry wanted to go through the channels, use them for good ends, take the theater to the enemy camp. Abbie did collect food, clothing, and blankets on the Lower East Side, then trucked them through police lines to Newark blacks when the ghetto was cut off during the ferocious riots of August 1967. But that was his last performance from the old Digger repertory. Within a few months, a decade in drug-hyped wind-tunnel time, the Digger idea of direct service toward a new society in the making was submerged by the Prankster idea of organizing a youth revolution electronically. Why think small and slow? On December 31, 1967, Abbie, Jerry, Paul Krassner, Dick Gregory, and friends decided to pronounce themselves the Yippies. (The name came first, then the acronym that would satisfy literal-minded reporters: Youth International Party.) They would coax, goose, entice, and dazzle thousands of freaks to Chicago for the August Democratic Convention, create there a "Festival of Life" against the "Convention of Death," a "blending of pot and politics . . . a cross-fertilization of the hippie and New Left philosophies." In an age of instant panaceas, commercial promises of instant gratification, this was the first instant organization, if in fact it was an organization at all. The underground press as well as the Establishment media, relaying the prophecy, would fulfill it. The myth would "inspire potential yippies in every small town and city throughout the country to throw down their textbooks and be free." Slogans: "We will burn Chicago to the ground!" "We will fuck on the beaches!" "We demand the Politics of Ecstasy!" "Acid for all!" "Abandon the Creeping Meatball!" Yell Yippie! at the moment of orgasm.

Rubin and Hoffman went to great lengths to commandeer the media, which had their own reasons for playing along. But chutzpah aside, their siren song of hip-Left harmony was a consummation with a logic. Since revolutionaries couldn't count enough real allies for a revolution, they conjured images—images that permitted them to elude, for a while, the difficulties of practical politics. Yippie followed directly from the belief that the turned-on baby-boom generation was already "the revolution" in embryo; that what the media were calling its "lifestyle" prefigured a kind of small-c communism remaining only to be taken up by the rest of sluggish America. With the pleasure principle as their guide, Rubin and

Hoffman committed themselves to two *as if* propositions. First, act as if the young everywhere were dropping out and slouching toward Chicago to be born, and they would, in fact, appear in Chicago on cue. "The myth is real," Rubin wrote, "if it builds a stage for people to play out their own dreams and fantasies." The Diggers' "create the situation you describe" had been transformed into the huckster's "People all over America are switching to . . ." The myth, properly amplified, would engineer the impression that the State was losing its capacity to govern. Thus the second proposition: act as if the State were falling apart, and it would fall apart. In Chicago, "we'd steal the media away from the Democrats and create the specter of 'yippies' overthrowing Amerika." As if specters overthrow nations once the latter have been renamed to make them sound Germanic.

Sometimes the Yippies seemed to think that the media were transparent channels. Abbie: "The media in a real sense never lie when you relate to them in a non-linear mythical manner." The young, after all, were the first generation who could not remember a time before television. "Runaways are the backbone of the youth revolution," Abbie decided. "A fifteen-year-old kid who takes off from middle-class American life is an escaped slave crossing the Mason-Dixie line. . . . **It seems America has lost her children.**" The young were so primed to escape middle-class banality, like runaway slaves, that with just a flash of the new Yippie image they could be enticed, presto, to join up. "We tear through the streets. Kids love it. They understand it on an internal level. We are living TV ads, movies. Yippie!" It followed that "once you get the right image the details aren't that important. Over-analyzing reduced the myth. A big insight we learned during this period was that you didn't have to explain why. That's what advertising was all about.* 'Why' was for the critics." Drugs were the guiding metaphor, the pole of experience around which all their other images orbited. Everything Abbie and Jerry said about television, they might have said about drugs. If drugs were usually used to keep people tranquilized, the right drugs, rightly used, would flood you with ecstasy and the giggles, open your eyes to the true nature of things.

At other moments, Abbie recognized that the media didn't simply reproduce reality, they distorted and muffled it. Far from transparent, they were smoked glasses, funhouse mirrors. Justifying his Yippie stunts on talk shows, he wrote: "The goal of this nameless art form—part vaudeville, part insurrection, part communal recreation—was to shatter *the pretense of objectivity* . . . rouse viewers from the video stupor." There was no such thing as bad publicity. But whether wearing a flag-shirt, uttering dirty words, or violating the aplomb of the master of equanimities, Abbie and Jerry had to perform according to the media's standards for newsworthy stunts: flamboyant, outrageous, mock violent,

*Indeed, after Chicago, Abbie and Jerry received job offers from three advertising agencies.

"anti-American." They had to outrage according to the censors' definition of outrage. They were trapped in a media loop, dependent on media standards, media sufferance, and goodwill. These apostles of freedom couldn't grasp that they were destined to become clichés.

In the process, they also contributed to the very polarization of counterculture and radical politics which they claimed to overcome. "Ideology is a brain disease," Jerry wrote of the left-wing sects, Progressive Labor above all, who doubted the gospel of the youth revolution and preferred their own versions of working-class romance. "The left turns Communism into a church with priests defining 'the line.'" These dogmatic Puritans stood for sacrifice, not fun. They turned people off—they were also, Puritans might have said, competition for the holy grail of revolution. Their meetings were deadly boring. Not only that, the "ideological left" was "made up of part-time people whose life-style mocks their rhetoric. . . . How can you be a revolutionary going to school during the day and attending meetings at night?" The ideal Yippie, by contrast, would live a seamless life, totally committed. "Act first. Analyze later. Impulse—not theory—makes the great leaps forward." Freaks of the world unite; you have nothing to lose but your brains. Jerry was right about the tedium of Old Left true-believing politics, of course, right to recognize that the New Left in 1967 was already careening in that direction. But his own impulses were hardly free of ideology—flaunting the NLF flag, embracing "white middle-class youth as a revolutionary class," etc. Meanwhile, not a few partisans of the counterculture saw that the jester had aspirations toward priesthood himself. Envy, unacknowledged, churned through the movement's ultrademocracy.

But even many who sniped at Rubin and Hoffman, like the original Diggers, shared their fundamental premises. For the Yippie affirmation of impulse was squarely in the American vein—back to Walt Whitman's barbaric yawp from the rooftops. The new wrinkle was to assert that the very act of engorging the self, unplugging from all the sacrificial social networks, would transform society. An audacious notion, that id could be made to do the work of superego! Yippie electronics wanted to short-circuit the obstacles, "break on through to the other side," bring to completion the gambit of the Pranksters and Diggers. Arthur Miller caught the innocent spirit of the counterculture's extraordinary gambol: "If responsibility can be reached through pleasure, then something new is on the earth."

And yet there was a less innocent side to the Yippie sublime. When the freaked-out children insisted on frolicking in their parents' world, the freaked-out parental bullies were bound to rise to the bait.

The collision came at Grand Central Station, midnight, March 22, 1968. What better place to stage a grand symbolic confrontation over the possession of time and space? From the Yippie point of view this was the frantic hub of the straight world's working life. Abbie's Yippies called for a celebration of the spring equinox, the media amplified the word, and that night six thousand people streamed into the great vaulted cavern to celebrate the natural cycle of seasons. But if a great number of the celebrants were there to whoop "Yippie!" and play with balloons, not everyone felt benign. A few kids climbed onto the roof of the information booth to lead incendiary chants: "Long Hot Summer!" "Burn, Baby, Burn!" Someone unfurled a banner: "UP AGAINST THE WALL, MOTHER-FUCKER!" Two cherry bombs went off. Someone tore off the hands from one of the clocks on top of the information booth. Having seized the straight world's space, like NLF guerrillas roving at night through rice paddies which Saigon patrolled during the day, some of the hips were now commandeering its time. It was an evocative image; during the Paris Commune, workers shot up the clocks.

The trouble was, fifty cops were waiting outside—"quivering in formation," as *The Village Voice*'s appalled Don McNeill put it. Without warning or order to disperse, they charged into the crowd, smashing people with nightsticks. People fell trying to run the gauntlets; cops kicked them where they lay sprawled. A soda bottle flew out of the crowd; five cops grabbed one seventeen-year-old—the wrong one, according to a reporter eyewitness—and started beating him with their sticks; the crowd chanted, *"Sieg Heil!"* Two cops looked at Don McNeill's press credentials and then "cursed *The Voice*, grabbed my arms behind my back, and, joined by two others, rushed me back toward the street, deliberately ramming my head into the closed glass doors, which cracked with the impact." A squad went for Abbie Hoffman; trying to protect him, a twenty-two-year-old Yippie was thrown through a plate-glass door; the broken glass severed the tendons and nerves of his left hand. Abbie himself was clubbed on the back until he was unconscious. "It was the most extraordinary display of unprovoked police brutality I've seen outside of Mississippi," said a lawyer from the New York Civil Liberties Union. Some called it a "police riot." McNeill was mainly horrified by the police, but he also blamed the Yippies for dodging the obligations of leadership—they failed to anticipate, lacked megaphones, and led their masses into a trap. "It was a pointless confrontation in a box canyon," concluded McNeill, innocence lost, "and somehow it seemed to be a prophecy of Chicago."

ARMED LOVE IN FAT CITY

Alongside the Diggers, there emerged a profusion of named and unnamed clusters of smart rough cultural revolutionaries, aiming to carry the avant-garde spirit of the arts—Surrealism, Dada, Artaud—into the streets. Their common thrust was to overcome the distances between art and everyday life, artists and audience. The Lower East Side, overstuffed with young uprooteds trying to root, was hospitable to guerrilla theater and similar interruptions. So was the historical moment: Vietnam and riots smashing up America's innocent image of itself; drugs smashing up the quotidian; prosperity taken for granted; social connections coming unstuck. Even the larger New York art scene was filling up with happenings, Performance Art, Conceptual Art: the idea made act.

One Lower East Side cluster, formed in the fall of 1967, became movement legend. Their name alone guaranteed it: Up Against the Wall, Motherfucker, taken from a line in a poem by beat-turned-black-nationalist LeRoi Jones. (The next line was: "This is a stick-up.") Cultural revolutionaries weren't content to name themselves as a Committee "for" This or That—"for" something out there, separate from themselves; they wanted to embody direct statement. Their theoretical inspiration was a hybrid of European anarchism (especially the idea that there is no higher principle of organization than free association) and the Marxism of the Frankfurt School, whose best known exponent was Herbert Marcuse, according to whom mass entertainment distracted attention from the "one-dimensional" closure of society, while high art had sunk into an affirmation of the status quo. The Motherfuckers' core idea was organizational: the "affinity group," "a street gang with an analysis." In theory, affinity groups were all-purpose: fighting units in the midst of riots, "armed cadres at the centers of conflict" during "the revolutionary period itself," intimations of the new society after the revolution.

The affinity group suited free-floating radicals who were childless, jobless, out of school, freebootingly male, and given to high-powered theoretical debates. The Motherfuckers included the anarchist publisher of a magazine called *Black Mask;* a Dutchman from the brilliant, difficult, sectarian group of Europeans called Situationists, who liked to theorize about "the society of the spectacle"; an actor-artist who was the stepson of Herbert Marcuse himself; another actor from a Lower East Side theater troupe; an organizer from Movement for a Democratic Society, an attempt to form a poststudent radical enterprise in New York (he thought straitlaced SDSish politics needed a strong dose of cultural radicalism); and a dropout filmmaker from the U.S. Information Agency. Their actions were less survivalist than the Diggers', more aggressive, more hostile to high art and intellect. When garbagemen went on strike and the stench of garbage overflowed the Lower East Side, the Motherfuckers carried a load of garbage on the subway to the just-inaugurated Lincoln Center. (They talked macho, but at this stage only one rambunctious fellow had the nerve to dump the garbage in the fountain.) In the style of Dada, the spirit was: bring the garbage to the real temple of garbage, an upper-class mausoleum that uprooted the inconveniently located poor and kept art sealed away from "the people." At another point, they performed a street-theater piece to defend Valerie Solanis, an underling in Andy Warhol's arts factory who had shot Warhol in the name of her one-woman Society for

Cutting Up Men, S. C. U. M. Over time they talked themselves into toughness, practiced the martial arts, urged hippies to interfere with police (already "pigs") trying to make busts, barged into the office of underground papers, threw their weight around. Their slogan was "Armed Love"; they used for a logo the exotic (Moroccan?) smoker who appeared on packets of Zig-Zag cigarette papers.

In New York's whirl of avant-garde molecules, the Motherfuckers mixed with other ginger groups—what were later called "collectives"—of artists-manqué-turned-revolutionaries. There was Liberation News Service, shipping parcels of syndicated articles to the burgeoning underground press. There was the underground *Rat,* which let the Motherfuckers lay out their own full-page spreads: one, for example, included a picture of the rifle-toting Geronimo and another of a revolver juxtaposed to the old art-school slogan, "We're looking for people who like to draw." There was Newsreel, a collective of filmmakers rolling out quick films about exemplary movement actions. (An early one was *Garbage,* about the Lincoln Center "action.") Newsreel's idea was that there was no time for art films aiming to please armchair-sitting cineastes, no point in argumentative exposés aiming to win over naïfs. With experience and contacts in New York's film world, they could beg and borrow film stock, make films that were grainy and looked improvised (modeled on National Liberation Front films edited under fire), distribute on their own. At the beginning of every Newsreel, their logo stuttered to the sound of a machine gun: film was a weapon.

The Motherfuckers, like the Diggers, held milky student politics in contempt, but went even further in taking their show to the straight Left. They constituted themselves the Lower East Side chapter of SDS, which in true ecumenical spirit (no applicants for an SDS charter were ever refused) welcomed them. They journeyed to the SDS National Council meeting in Lexington, Kentucky, at the end of March 1968, where at a plenary session the Motherfuckers took the stage, and while two of them held up a brick wrapped in gold foil, the third smashed it in half with a karate chop, explaining passionately: we are going to smash capitalism, smash the state, *just like that.* They wowed a gaggle of gullible midwesterners by telling them they had organized the patients in the terminal ward of a New York hospital to become the cutting edge of The Revolution—nothing to lose, right? At the June SDS convention, they seemed to be having the best time: dressing in black, giving outlandish anti-PL speeches, waving the black flag of anarchism while straight SDSers waved the red, and passing out a leaflet pushing affinity groups, illustrated with a drawing of men and women joined in a circle of oral sex.

Many were the new SDSers thrilled that tough hippies were taking the time to bother with stodgy SDS. Progressive Labor and its principal opponents in the SDS leadership were building up their titles to the revolutionary future, lining up on behalf of their various Marxism-

Leninisms. What an Old Left drag! Enter the Motherfuckers, postbeat, postbiker, would-be Hell's Angels with manifestos, like the Diggers deploying direct action against strategy, extravagance against tedium. "Cultural revolution" looked like a plausible alternative to the thick-headed mumbo-jumbo artists, top-heavy with jargon and Old Left ideas of organization. *Direct action,* that was the New Left idea at its best! Wasn't it growing obvious that a revolution by and for youth was ricocheting around the world? In Amsterdam, the Provos (for Provocateurs) were publicly smoking grass, taunting police, smokebombing Princess Beatrix's wedding procession, leaving white bicycles all over town for anyone to ride, even winning elections. In China, Red Guards were beating up bureaucrats, making professors wear dunce caps. By the spring of 1968, Columbia had ignited. Most stunning of all, behold the first post–industrial revolution to celebrate "ALL POWER TO THE IMAGINATION"— Paris's May, destined (were it not for the treasonous Communist Party) to seize the imagination of the twenty-first century as the 1789 version had the nineteenth.

10

FIGHTING BACK

A PROLOGUE TO THE LATE SIXTIES

On April 17, 1965, when 25,000 students marched in Washington against the Vietnam war, there were about 25,000 American troops in Vietnam. At the end of 1965 there were 184,000 troops; at the end of 1966, 385,000. By the end of 1967, the number was 486,000, and 15,000 had been killed, 60 percent of them in the single year 1967. Those were the prominent figures, numbers of Americans. Figures about the air war and the Vietnamese casualties were, and remain, far harder to come by. In 1967 the air force was flying two thousand sorties per week. That year alone, the U.S. defoliated 1.7 million acres in South Vietnam. By the end of the year more than a million and a half tons of bombs had been dropped on the North and the South together. That year the San Francisco *Oracle* claimed a national circulation of one hundred thousand. On April 15, a New York crowd variously assessed at anywhere from 125,000 to 400,000 heard Martin Luther King denounce the war, but not a single congressman or senator would sponsor or speak. Congress passed war appropriations by huge majorities. George Wallace laid plans to run for the Democratic nomination for President.

How can I convey the texture of this gone time so that you and I, reader, will be able to grasp, remember, believe that astonishing things actually happened, and made sense to the many who made them happen and were overtaken by them? Statistics are "background," we do not feel them tearing into our flesh. The years 1967, 1968, 1969, and 1970 were a cyclone in a wind tunnel. Little justice has been done to them in realistic fiction; perhaps one reason is that fiction requires, as Norman Mailer once said, a sense of the real. When history comes off the leash, when reality appears illusory and illusions take on lives of their own, the novelist loses the platform on which imagination builds its plausible appearances. Readers caught in a maelstrom want to recover distance. No wonder the fiction that young freaks and radicals read in those years tended toward postmodern weirdness, the false calm of allegory, or the eerie simplicities of the saucer's-eye abstraction: Thomas Pynchon, Kurt Vonnegut, Jr., Hermann Hesse.

Years later, I still struggle to recollect in tranquillity. But it is no easy thing to reconstruct the hallucinatory state in which the space between illusion and plausibility has shrunk to the vanishing point. Reality was reckless, and so there is the temptation to dismiss it—say with the cliché of compilation, snippets of pure spectacle, in the style of a ticker tape or a clunky documentary: draft card burnings . . . the Pentagon . . . Stop the Draft Week . . . the Tet offensive . . . the McCarthy campaign . . . Johnson decides not to run for another term . . . Martin Luther King killed . . . Columbia buildings occupied . . . Paris . . . Prague . . . trips to Hanoi . . . Robert Kennedy killed . . . Democratic Convention riots . . . hundreds of students massacred in Mexico City . . . Miss America protest . . . Nixon elected . . . deserters, flights to Canada and Sweden, mutinies, "fragging" in Vietnam . . . Eldridge Cleaver underground . . . San Francisco State, Berkeley, Harvard, Stanford, etc., etc. besieged . . . People's Park . . . police shootouts with Black Panthers . . . student, freak, black, homosexual riots . . . SDS splits . . . Woodstock . . . women's consciousness-raising . . . the Chicago Conspiracy trial . . . Charles Manson . . . Altamont . . . My Lai . . . Weatherman bombs . . . Cambodia . . . Kent State . . . Jackson State . . . a fatal bombing in Madison . . . trials, bombings, fires, agents provocateurs, and the grand abstractions, "resistance," "liberation," "revolution," "repression"—to name only some of what was swirling. Images spewed forth from television every night, hyping excitement and dread and overload and the sense of America at war with itself. The matter-of-factness of a list does not diminish the knowledge that "reality," an exercise in surreal theater, had to be slipped into quotation marks.

The liberal-labor coalition fragmented past the point of recognition. Urban blacks rioted. The backlashing Right gathered momentum. Students moved to the Left, and as the youth movement grew, so did the idea of fighting back against the State. So did the idea of a single world revolution. Of forcing a confrontation between the forces of light and the forces of darkness. Of cultural secession: carving out zones where the new culture could feel and test its strength—Black Power, women's power, gay power . . . while State power gathered for its own showdowns.

"WHAT DOES WHITEY DO?"

For the New Left, the summer of love was the summer of desperation. By the end of July 1967, eighty-three people were dead (twenty-six in Newark, forty-three in Detroit) and thousands wounded in scores of black riots (or "rebellions," as we insisted they be called). Detroit was in flames, snipers were shooting, forty-seven hundred U.S. Army paratroopers occupied the flaming ghetto along with eight thousand National Guardsmen, and it was reported that some poor whites, Appalachians like the ones the SDS projects were still trying gamely to organize in Chicago and Cleveland, had joined the assault. During the Detroit showdown I wrote from Chicago to Carol McEldowney in Cleveland:

> All of us are on the brink of madness, and so much the worse that we are all marginal to what is going on. Andy [Kopkind] called last night, checking in, reporting that Washington was about to blow, the mood crackling up and down the length of 18th St., and we talked about the end of the movement as we've known it; so we live in the space between the end of the movement and the beginning of revolution. Of course ("of course") the insurrections are not revolution, but they sound like it and the fires burn close to revolution, as close as we have seen. "Oh Mama, can this really be the end?/To be stuck down here in Uptown while the blacks go wild again."

Relatively sober soul that I was, haunted and horrified by violence, I mentioned having gotten together with a few others to "make crazy plans" to distract the Chicago police in case the black ghetto erupted. (Bluster more than plans, actually. But it is interesting that the freelance organizer most enthusiastic about diversionary actions later surfaced as an FBI informant.) I closed: ". . . and wear a flower in your gunbelt."

This sort of desperation and bravado (with boosts from various police agents) rippled through radical circles across the country. Carol McEldowney wrote me back from Cleveland, for example:

> I talked last night with a local black guy—a real man of the streets—about the riots. Trouble, by the way, is rumored for tonight. This guy plans to firebomb a rotten tenement building. His chief complaint was that things aren't organized—anyplace. He thought the riots should start systematically in the suburbs, should utilize tactics like cutting power lines, and strongly felt there should be efforts to get all the black

boys in Vietnam to drop their guns and come on home. Probably not a typical guy—but the question remains, what does whitey do? He was really turned on by the integrated aspect of Detroit. I've been wondering what I'd do if and when a riot broke in [the Cleveland ghetto of] Glenville.

The Vietnam war seemed to be coming home.

The war itself went on, swollen and unrelenting, like an irreversible plague. By the spring of 1967, Johnson had been boosting both air strikes and ground combat for two years. Some more coalition-minded people in and around the New Left, including early SDSers like Lee Webb and Washington hands like Gar Alperovitz, had organized Vietnam Summer, with the idea of putting students, mostly, to work mobilizing new, largely middle-class forces against the war and in favor of a larger radical program. Perhaps seven hundred people had worked more or less full-time in Vietnam Summer, and up to twenty thousand part-time. To what effect? Not much was visible—not as visible as televised carnage, at any rate. But radicals had doubted all along whether a summer project could accomplish much when most of the cadres would go back to school in the fall. It was like Mississippi Summer without the SNCC and CORE cadres who would keep up the arduous work. No one had anticipated that this sort of slow nibbling would actually end the war, but by September the radicals tended to conclude that few Americans cared enough about the war to do what was necessary—whatever that was—to end it.

Most of the New Left pulled inward, toward self-rectification. The politics of identity swept across the movement. Black nationalists argued that blacks, oppressed as a caste, deserved representation as a caste. Attempts to create political alliances therefore fell afoul of bombast and purification rituals. At the chaotic National Conference for New Politics convention in a Chicago hotel over Labor Day weekend, some three hundred blacks in a conference of two or three thousand demanded—and in an orgy of white guilt were granted—half the votes on all resolutions, including a condemnation of Israel for the Six Day "imperialist Zionist war." Jews with attachments to Israel, even ambivalent ones, saw kneejerk anti-Semitism. There were radicals with anti-imperialist credentials fully in order who had felt called upon to fight for Israel in what seemed to them a war of national self-preservation; and did not even Fidel Castro say that to speak of driving a whole nation into the sea was unconscionable? Martin Luther King, Andrew Young, and Julian Bond made appearances at the New Politics convention and quickly absented themselves. Meanwhile, representatives of a radical women's caucus were hooted down.

There were police agents at work in the black caucus—possibly a good many, for the major organization behind the conference was the Communist Party, surely the most heavily infiltrated organization in the United States. But provocateurs could not have fanned the flames of reckless nationalism had not those flames already been burning. The season of rage had arrived; in the aftermath of Newark and Detroit, there was no real chance for a genuine alliance of equals. And black militancy held the New Left in thrall. In September, the authorities were called "pigs" in SDS's *New Left Notes* for the first time. We were preoccupied with the hardening of official power and the question of our courage to meet it; across the country, in hundreds of late-night conversations, in small boasts and self-interrogations, we asked ourselves whether "when the time comes," which might be tomorrow, we were ready to do "whatever it takes." Andrew Kopkind, the clearest journalistic chronicler of movement moods, began an article in *The New York Review of Books* with the thumpingly accurate sentence: "To be white and a radical in America this summer is to see horror and feel impotence." ("Together," he added, "the active, organizing, risk-taking white radicals would fill a quarter of a big football stadium.") In Berkeley, the radical organizer Frank Bardacke wrote, "despair became a cliché among young white radicals. Many of us in Berkeley talked incessantly about political impotence. We were enthralled by apocalyptic novels like *The Crying of Lot 49* and *Cat's Cradle.* The New Left looked sick . . . near death."

We were drawn to books that seemed to reveal the magnitude of what we were up against, to explain our helplessness. Probably the most compelling was Herbert Marcuse's *One-Dimensional Man,* with its stark Hegelian dirge for the Marxist dream of an insurgent proletariat: a book of the Fifties, really, though not published until 1964 (paperback 1966). Gradually its reputation swelled among the New Left for its magisterial account of a society that, Marcuse argued, had lost the very ability to think or speak opposition, and whose working class was neutered by material goods and technology. Some unimaginable radical break, some "Great Refusal," was apparently impossible but deeply necessary. Impossible and necessary: that is how we felt about our task.

It was in that spirit that many also pored over Régis Debray's *Revolution in the Revolution?,* first published as the summer 1967 issue of *Monthly Review,* which sold out its printing. Debray, a well-born French *gauchiste* jailed in Bolivia, had written the theory to accompany Che Guevara's (and Fidel Castro's) practice. The idea was that political and military leadership should fuse to form a *foco,* a rural guerrilla unit, freed of the caution and urban bias of traditional Latin American Communist parties. Debray was not talking about the flatlands of Berkeley but about the high plateau of Bolivia (not that his confident advice proved so apt there either). But during this overheated summer a critical mass of American New Leftists toyed with his detailed prescriptions as if they were metaphors for their own future: small bands of revolutionaries should not be tied to larger parties or fronts, which cannot understand their practical problems; the *foco,* winning victories, is "the 'small motor' that sets the 'big motor' of the masses in motion." The idea spread that at least symbolically, it was more important for intellectuals to acquire the right guerrilla boots than to debate the right books. At a moment when conventional channels seemed blocked, there was intense concentration on the powers of the will. The New Left had always valued the power of the deed to blowtorch through an apparently frozen situation; now a desperate intensity heightened the feeling that with sheer audacity we must—and therefore could—bull our way past the apparent obstacles. Debray popularized a Fidel Castro slogan: "The duty of the revolutionary is to make the revolution." Debray's *focos* seemed to lead the way out of Marcuse's labyrinth.

The unstated background murmur: Liberals had defaulted, even the good ones were helpless, they made lousy allies. Liberals! The very word had become the New Left's curse. The litany crystallized: Atlantic City— LID—*New York Post.* Then, in the spring, *Ramparts* had spilled the lurid details about liberals in the National Student Association who for years had taken money from the CIA and run a secret recruitment program. Liberal foundations were found to have served as conduits as well. Carl Oglesby's 1965 distinction between "corporate" and "humanist" liberals was getting murkier.

Frank Bardacke described the movement's sea change. The antiwar movement had successfully "dramatize[d] the existence of a sizable minority who opposed the war, thereby stimulating a debate about it," he wrote, but even the respectable opposition seemed ineffectual. Martin Luther King thundered against the war, but Johnson seemed unrestrained. Robert Scheer pulled 45 percent of the Democratic primary vote on an antiwar platform in Berkeley and Oakland in 1966, running against a pro-Johnson liberal—which might have been encouraging, for a first outing, but this was one of the most antiwar districts in the country; could Vietnam wait for piecemeal change at this rate? If you monitored elections, the more conspicuous fact was that Ronald Reagan had swept with ease into the governor's mansion in Sacramento. Anyway, as Bardacke said, radicals believed in a political community "for whom voting is only one of many public acts." Hippies, who might once have looked like an alternative to normal politics, looked "scared, lonely, and frantic. . . . Some of my friends," Bardacke wrote, "started playing with guns as a way to forget their own hopelessness. . . . But the guns just depressed me." Whatever the revolutionary fantasies of whites watching Detroit in flames on television, "the talk of running guns to the ghetto was the hopeful nonsense of young white men who could not admit that we actually had nothing to offer the people in Detroit." And the constant chatter about sabotage, de rigueur at radical parties, was nothing more than "complete fantasy." Meanwhile, SDS-style community organizing was at a dead end.

The only radical work with life in it, Bardacke wrote, was active opposition to the draft. There was The Resistance, founded at Berkeley and Stanford, burning or turning in draft cards, promising to fill the jails with civil disobeyers who insisted on "putting their bodies on the line."

The Resistance was gathering momentum, chapters spreading across the country, organizing toward a mass turn-in of draft cards for October 16, the now-traditional date for coordinated antiwar actions. Closer to the New Left spirit of trying to cross the class boundary, there were sporadic attempts to help working-class opponents of the war. But the class barriers were real. Like it or not, most students were still shielded from induction. Most of the young men reached by draft counseling were middle class.

In keeping with what one Resistance organizer called "vicarious intoxication by the summer riots," a group of Bay Area radicals decided that the only way to break out of the charmed middle-class circle and attract working-class kids to the antiwar movement was to show muscle. The working class, after all, supplied most of the cannon fodder. The developing New Left theory was that even the working-class kids who weren't victims of war propaganda stayed away from the Left because they saw radicals as pushovers. Suppose they *were* ready to resist; what was the Left going to do for them? High school graduates and dropouts didn't have student deferments, after all. Some radicals, like Berkeley's Mike Smith, wanted to inspire a GI movement against the war: "It was every revolutionary's dream: to get the soldiers to lay down their guns." Moreover, wasn't the Black Panther Party for Self-Defense growing in Northern California by carrying guns, following the police, refusing to be scared, thereby impressing young ghetto toughs? Hadn't SNCC organizers and Mississippi, Alabama, and Louisiana blacks long since carried guns for self-defense, abandoning nonviolence on anything but tactical occasions, though without advertising the fact? The movement's antiwar tone was shifting from sympathy for slaughtered Vietnamese to identification with powerful Vietnamese whose victory would surely come. To get serious, it seemed, whites had at least to declare their *right* to defend themselves. Anyway, peaceable antiwar protesters had been bashed by police while picketing Lyndon Johnson in Los Angeles's Century City just that June, so of what avail was mannerliness? Those who took this tack said they had spotted inductees raising clenched fists of solidarity as they were being bused through induction center picket lines. Fearful of isolation, Bay Area militants convinced themselves they could break through their self-enclosure by raising the stakes.

Whence the week of October 16 was declared Stop the Draft Week, to block off and shut down the downtown Oakland building to which potential inductees were bused from all of Northern California. At last protest would go beyond the merely symbolic; at the very least, an obstructive demonstration could "gum up the works for quite a while." "By our decree there will be a draft holiday," one poster modestly announced. David Harris, the charismatic former Stanford student body president who was one of the quadrumvirate who had started The Resistance, argued vehemently for keeping up the movement's high moral tone, and against anything that might smack of fighting the police. The streetfighting tendency thought The Resistance gutsy and inspiring but mired in moral witness; why risk five years in jail for burning your draft card, to no apparent political end? The factions parceled out the week. The pacifists would have Monday for a conventional sit-in; they would keep the police apprised of their plans, they would sit down, go limp, get carried away. After that, the militants were on their own.

FROM PROTEST TO RESISTANCE

I moved to California at the beginning of October 1967. I came to lick my wounds, to recover from the breakup of my marriage and two bruising years in the white slums, to start a book about the Appalachian exiles, to retreat from the consequences of a bleak political diagnosis, to plot next moves, and not least to see if I was in love. I was. And like many another migrant in those years, I came to shed restraints. California felt like deliverance in every way. "The West is the best," Jim Morrison sang (ironically?), and so it seemed to this eastern boy suddenly lifted from brutal Chicago to perch on the cliffs of the Carmel Highlands and look out to sea contemplating Asia in flames. At the edge of the continent, I was overwhelmed by disbelief at the luminosity of the light, which seemed to radiate from within every tree and stone in the late afternoons; I was delirious at the monarch butterflies of October. The day I arrived, I started growing a beard and—unaware that I was anticipating *Easy Rider*—threw my watch in a drawer. I was flooded with relief to discover that imperial America did not stretch out forever.

In those years I used to keep over my desk a quotation from Thoreau: "The memory of my country spoils my walk." I had filed for draft exemption as a conscientious objector two years before, had been turned down, knew that my appeals were going to come to naught, and then what? I knew the Pentagon demonstration was coming up, and wondered which of my friends were going and who was going to get hurt. I was shaken by the news, first reported October 10, then apparently corroborated with a photograph of the corpse the next day, that Che Guevara had been captured and killed. Che the irreconcilable, restless moralist, embodiment of permanent revolution, the eternal international-ist (or exile, for he was Argentine by birth), matching my own sense of estrangement. . . . If Che could be killed, then "the revolution" was more vulnerable than the Left wanted to think.

On October 16 the ritual sit-in took place on schedule in downtown Oakland, with 124 arrested, including Joan Baez, all walking sedately into the paddy wagons in what one newspaper called a "charade." The Alameda County Board of Supervisors obtained an injunction against a campus rally to launch the Tuesday action, and six thousand students defied it. I read about the sit-in, and The Resistance's turn-in of some four hundred draft cards at the San Francisco Federal Building, and felt moved, even guilty for not being there (Thoreau to Emerson: "What are you doing *out* there?"), but not quite galvanized. But the Tuesday event was the confrontation I had known, in my bones, was coming. The next day I picked up the *San Francisco Chronicle* to behold a banner headline—"Cops Beat Pickets. THE BIG DRAFT BATTLE. Oakland Draft Protest. A Bloody Attack by Police—Clubs, Tear Gas, Boots. Many Are Injured—20 Arrested." And this lead: "Police swinging clubs like scythes cut a bloody path through 2500 antiwar demonstrators who had closed down the Oakland Armed Forces Examining Station yesterday for three hours." A big front-page picture showed two Oakland cops, each with a club in one hand, spraying the incapacitating chemical Mace with the other. The article was replete with accounts of laughing cops, "their hard wooden sticks mechanically flailing up and down, like peasants mowing down wheat"; cops beating doctors and priests, and students trying to protect other students; cops singling out reporters and photographers for clubbings and Macings. Some demonstrators had responded by throwing cans, bottles, and smoke bombs.

Che's death was one more reason why I couldn't stay away. There was going to be a follow-up action that Friday; my lover and I drove up to the Bay Area for it. Long before dawn, the day felt supercharged; simply to be awake in the gray dark, on the way into mysterious Oakland to "stop the draft," meant that the sense of rendezvous was irreversible. We grinned and flashed Vs at all the longhairs astonishingly streaming down across the Berkeley–Oakland line in their Volkswagen bugs and late-Fifties Chevies, and crawled with care past Oakland police cars, and tried to pretend we weren't afraid.

On what was now enshrined as "Bloody Tuesday," the organizers had expected the cops simply to seal off the downtown area around the induction center. Two police spies had attended planning meetings, and knew the organizers had a sitdown in mind.* It was hard to resist the conclusion that the cops had deliberately suckered them. On Friday many came ready for "mobile tactics," modeled partly on French student actions, partly on ghetto riots. At a launch-point park, instructions circulated: stay in the streets and keep moving. There were motorcycle helmets, construction hardhats, shields. A Berkeley sporting-goods store was said to have sold out of protective cups. Many people smeared their faces with Vaseline, reputed to protect against Mace. One SDS organizer passed out ball bearings to scatter on the street, the better to deter police

---

*It gradually dawned on the organizers that these two short-haired gentlemen didn't fit, but they were reluctant to point the finger—after all, weren't they trying to organize working-class toughs? Eventually, suspicion peaked. Early Tuesday morning, one of the organizers drove the two deviants to a remote section of the Oakland hills, gave them a pair of binoculars, and told them to keep lookout. They materialized next as witnesses for the prosecution at the conspiracy trial of the organizers, known as the Oakland 7.

on horseback. In the predawn chill, a playful and resolute crowd estimated variously at between four and ten thousand, probably twice as many as on Tuesday, proceeded to choke off at least ten square blocks around the induction center.

We deployed for hours against more than two thousand cops, in a kind of scrimmage, or was it warfare? "An amalgam of riot and high school high jinks," a reporter called it. The cops charged. Some got surrounded, some broke ranks to bash or Mace. The crowd retreated to seize more intersections. When the cops pulled back to redeploy, the crowd took back the block, sealed it off from traffic, spray-painted the pavement and sidewalks. People hauled parked cars into the streets (the U.S. attorney's, for one), disconnected their distributors, let the air out of their tires, punctured them; and hauled anything else that could be moved: benches, newspaper racks, parking meters, garbage cans, trees in concrete pots. ("Careful with the trees!" onlookers cried out.) Crowds pulled the wires out of a public bus here, a Coca-Cola truck there. One bus was commandeered, emptied, and pushed into a line of cops. I saw a group mount a truck, stand one foot away from a line of Oakland cops, clubs at the ready, and burn draft cards in their faces. (After their bad press Tuesday, the cops were on a tight leash.) I watched a crowd block off a white truck in mid-intersection, saw the driver shrug good-naturedly— what did he care about a delay in his daily rounds when he was forced to punch a time clock for The Man? Some demonstrators were put off, even near tears by the casual assault on property, at least according to the *Chronicle:* "'For God's sake, stop it,' a bearded youth shouted to his contemporaries as they dragged and pushed a car out into an intersection at Clay and 13th streets. 'Don't you understand you're defeating the whole movement. You're going to kill us with the public!' They paid no attention to him." From time to time, a metallic blare came from a police bullhorn: "In the name of the people of the state of California . . ." "WE ARE THE PEOPLE!" came the immediate roar. We looked for signs of popular approval, and noted that black onlookers seemed friendly.

Demonstrators were festive, exultant—precisely what had been reported about black riots and deplored by white politicians. The streets and sidewalks were coated with slogans, of which the most popular were variations on CHE IS ALIVE AND WELL IN OAKLAND. The windows of parking meters ("don't follow leaders . . .") were painted opaque, some green lights sprayed red. Late in the morning, word went around that the National Guard was about to be called, and the organizers, not wanting to take a chance on getting a lot of people hurt, decided to leave. The crowd disbanded. A column marched back to Berkeley, singing antiwar songs, whistling "When Johnny Comes Marching Home Again." In Oakland, the induction buses finally went through, a few hours delayed.

The organizers were elated. On Bloody Tuesday, only a few people had fought back. One organizer, for example, had wrested a billy club from a charging cop, hit him in the face with it, then scampered away. The wife of another had succeeded in leading a group to free her husband—not once but three times—from the grip of the cops. Other demonstrators, meanwhile, had contented themselves with restatements of Christian nonviolence. A monitor, "his lip torn by a riot stick," had told a reporter, "We will be back on Wednesday. We can bleed just as long as the cops can swing." But by Friday a watershed had been crossed. The point now was to conduct yourself in a disorderly way, close off the streets, retreat when attacked, make interesting trouble, and protect yourself. Exhilaration became a mystique of The Street: The street belongs to *us*, the insurgents, not to *them*, the custodians of power and the tenders of commerce. As Frank Bardacke put it, "We blocked traffic and changed the streets from thoroughfares of business into a place for people to walk, talk, argue, and even dance. We felt liberated and we called our barricaded streets liberated territory." If we half-remembered that we were not quite all of "the people," at least we had not been cowed by the authorities' claim to speak in the name of *their* official "people." For those who had grown up fearing what "the people" can accomplish when they run amok, "WE ARE THE PEOPLE!" amounted to self-protective wishfulness. The mirage was vivid enough to overcome the question George Wallace and Richard Nixon and Spiro Agnew shortly set out to answer: Who are all those *other* people?

What should we name this thing that had happened? "Militant self-defense," said the organizers. "We consider ourselves political outlaws," Bardacke wrote. "Insurrection," I gushed in letters to friends: "It was not revolution, but it *was* insurrection in the legal sense and in the spirit. . . . Anarcho-syndicalism in vivo, vindicated. . . . Leaders were everywhere. Ordinary students became something else . . . barricading the intersections on their own, without a signal from leaders. . . . If balls are not equivalent to revolution—they are not—they are prerequisite to an honorable resistance. . . . The old movement symbol was the overhauls; now it's the hard-hat. It comes in handy, or heady, in this resistance. Now I take the idea of resistance damned seriously. . . ."

And more of my expressive politics with a vengeance: ". . . the white movement came into its own last week. I hear that some SNCC guys were saying, after Washington [the Pentagon demonstration], OK boys, you've become men now, we're ready to talk. They're right. . . . So into the grave we leap together, or into something. . . . Of course the politics of the Oakland insurrection like those of the Mobilization are hazy. The point is that people have demonstrated their seriousness. . . . No one has yet really decided to put the induction center out of commission, but I think the time is not far off. Should blacks in Oakland move, . . . whites can throw the cops into all sorts of disarray, even knock radio stations, telephone stations, etc. out of action . . . as if to say, we take a lot of shit and we know this is not revolution but for Christ's sake there are some things that are ours—these color TVs, or these intersections—and we will take them if only for a while; we will give them back (under threat of the Guard) but we will not give ourselves back to authority, because we have changed ourselves—the verysame picnic atmosphere that Gov. Hughes found so reprehensible in Newark. Of course I romanticize. . . . [T]he motion from 'protest to resistance' is halting and reversible; yet still I think something has changed."

Blocking the intersections to stop the buses declared, in effect, "this is the sort of power we have, it may be hollow but we intend to use it. . . . On the streets, [the cops] were often outmaneuvered by one *foco* or another (and the Berkeley mystique is no bullshit: the best political minds are also the military directorate . . .)." Hollowness as power, indeed! The person who wrote these words, myself, was half-aware of the contradiction, just as he knew that Régis Debray's *focos* had nothing to do with Berkeley. Delaying the buses was symbolic; the draft machinery simply worked a few hours overtime. But when in doubt, why be patient? Better to suspend disbelief. If we had already accomplished one astonishing thing, stopping business-as-usual, then why not two? If we had no good evidence that raising the ante had an effect, there was no evidence that milder tactics worked either.

This as-if mood was all-surrounding. Which raises the question of the part played by drugs, especially LSD, whose glory and terror is precisely to suspend the sense of the real. If trippers thought they were meeting God or dissolving their egos, experiencing cosmic love or watching the boundaries between things shimmer, did drugs dispose them to think that the world and their place in it was more fluid, less predictable, than they would otherwise have imagined? A question as tantalizing as it is impossible, alas, to answer. True, LSD percolated through the New Left, especially its inventive California wing, at just the same time as the surge in militancy. It is also one of the truisms of drug research that the impact of psychedelics, even of marijuana, depends heavily on one's mind-set and the social setting. But drugs or no drugs, young radicals in 1967 were feeling acute pressures to raise the stakes—from the war, from blacks, from an identity in flux. We had started the decade with grand if not grandiose hopes, with no help from drugs; now drugs certainly did nothing to diminish the feeling of political possibility—or impending apocalypse. The need to make a difference felt extreme, and so did the cost of failing, at least failing to try to one's utmost. That is why the sense of unreality was intoxicating, not paralyzing.

The willful suspension of disbelief was the spiritual heart of the new militancy. It had many uses. It warded off fear. Most of the organizers of Stop the Draft Week were surprised at how brutal the cops turned out to be on Bloody Tuesday; to the last minute, these notorious radicals had remained innocent about what the authorities would do about a threat to the smooth running of the draft machine. Suspending disbelief was also a way to suspend what otherwise might have been an imprisoning sense of our isolation in America: the nagging apprehension that as we toughened up, fought back, and mobilized more of the young, we were at the same time stretching to the outer rim of what our generation, by itself, could accomplish. The perception was roughly: We are so many, yet, since the war rages, so helpless. To keep from being paralyzed by fear, we had to believe that what we were leaping into was the unknown; that we had outdistanced known reality, therefore also the judgment of elders and cool heads and internal restraints.

The total political amalgam—the war, the alienated youth boom, the overextension and collapse of liberalism—defined a new terrain, as surreal as it was unprecedented. Reality shimmered. Extremities of hope led to extremities of despair, and this cycle fogged our vision. That is why perceptions could shift so radically from one moment to the next. The honest Frank Bardacke, for example, gave vent to the prevailing mood when he acknowledged that "Americans did not understand our message. They called us vandals and said the demonstration was chaos"; then immediately shifted to the language of strategy: "And if we can actually convince them that we can cause chaos in this country as long as the war continues, so much the better. We may have even stumbled on a strategy that could end the war"; then, in the next breath, worried: "But maybe we have only moved one step closer to the concentration camps. If we succeed in organizing something like Stop the Draft Week again, the Government will begin to consider organizing a Stop the Left Week"; and in the next breath, determined: "But that is a risk we have to take."

The surge "from protest to resistance," as that fall's slogan had it, swept across the country, concentrated on the two coasts but not limited to them, provoked by a common mood, at times amplified by mechanical imitation. Indeed, on the day after Oakland's Bloody Tuesday, after a day of unobstructive picketing, SDS and other activists at the University of Wisconsin blocked a recruiter from the Dow Chemical Company, manufacturer of napalm. When they got bashed by club-swinging riot police, thousands of students rallied, surrounded the police, freed demonstrators from their grip, let the air out of paddy-wagon tires, got tear-gassed and Maced, and fought back with rocks and bricks, sending seven policemen to the hospital along with sixty-five students. That fall, there were forty large campus demonstrations against military and Dow recruiters, at least half of them attempting active interference with the recruiters, followed by police intervention. On November 14, as limousines brought the foreign policy elite to hear Secretary of State Dean Rusk at a New York banquet, more than five thousand people gathered for a peaceful protest, while SDS cadres—recruited by a leaflet saying, "The Revolution Begins at 5:30"—hooted, threw bottles, bags of paint and cow's blood, then dumped trash baskets, dented fancy cars, and swarmed through intersections in an Oakland-style effort to disrupt. A December New York City action, designed to seal off the induction center, drew on both Pentagon and Oakland models. The lesson of the Pentagon, said a leaflet, was that soldiers could be won over to our side. Oakland's lesson was to stay loose in the streets.

But as Michael Ferber and Staughton Lynd later pointed out, the lessons clashed. At the Pentagon, after the initial confrontation, demonstrators sat nonviolently, tried to convert the soldiers, chanting "Cross the lines and join us!" and "We love you!" They sang "Yellow Submarine" and stuck flowers in the barrels of rifles that carried fixed bayonets. For the most part, even when MPs and federal marshals attacked brutally, with rifle butts and bayonets, the civilly disobedient didn't fight back. A former Green Beret turned resister spoke to the troops about the history of Vietnam. Two soldiers broke ranks; one passed out cigarettes to demonstrators; of these events was legend spun. Movement people were beginning to see that soldiers were potential allies, or at least not hard-bitten enemies. "Certainly we were unruly; that is, we were determined to cross the line drawn by illegitimate authority," wrote a scrupulous observer, the writer George Dennison. "That done, the protest was almost classically nonviolent." In Oakland, by contrast, despite a few attempts at proselytizing cops, the prevailing style was to taunt or elude the armed antagonists, not to try to convince them of anything but the demonstrators' ferocious resolve. In subsequent movement discourse, however, the two models tended to blur into one grand idea: push hard, turn up the heat, confront, fight back.

The government fought back too. In January 1968 the district attorney of Alameda County, California, indicted seven of the Oakland organizers (Frank Bardacke, Terry Cannon, Reese Ehrlich, Steve Hamilton, Bob Mandel, Jeff Segal, and Mike Smith) for conspiracy to trespass, to commit a public nuisance, and to resist, delay, and obstruct police officers. (But he refrained from indicting two key females, evidently deeming them less capable of mayhem, or fearing juries would be less likely to convict.) The Oakland 7, as they were instantly dubbed, were the first in a long line of New Left organizers who became known by their number and the place of their transgression. (As in most of these cases, the lawyers eventually made mincemeat of the charges, after months of expense and effort, and won acquittals.) During the Oakland 7 trial, in the winter of 1968–69, the visiting SDS officer (and self-proclaimed "revolutionary communist") Bernardine Dohrn told Steve Hamilton that Stop the Draft Week was one of the events that had convinced her that it was time for the antiwar movement to do battle in the streets. Hamilton remembers thinking there was a danger in her romance of the working-class young. Militant actions, he thought, couldn't take the place of grass-roots organizing. But who could wait?

A year or two was a vast time in the lives of twenty-one-year-olds. Besides, what was at stake now wasn't an abstract future, participatory democracy versus managerial liberalism, a good society versus a bad or an ambiguous one. Look at TV, *Newsweek* or *Time:* Interspersed between the ads for the American way of life, here was *this* child seared by napalm, *this* suspect tortured by our freedom-loving allies, *this* village torched by Marines with cigarette lighters, *this* forest burned to the ground . . . a seemingly endless procession of pain and destruction. So much punishment inflicted by one nation against another: the sheer volume of it seemed out of line with any official, self-contradictory, incomprehensible reasons of state. There had to be something radically, unredeemably wrong at the dark heart of America. By the late Sixties many of us had concluded the problem wasn't simply bad policy but a wrongheaded social system, even a civilization. The weight of decades, or centuries, even millennia had to be thrown off overnight—because it was necessary.

WHAT DO THESE PEOPLE WANT?

Fighting back could be defended, arguably, as part of a strategy for ending the war, since neither civil disobedience nor Establishment grumbling seemed sufficient by itself. But the militant surge was more than strategic: it was at least as much the expression of an identity, a romance, an existential raison d'être. The mood of embattled defiance responded to the war and the suppression of ghetto riots; it also carried a life and a logic of its own. This political generation's decade had started with a rising hope—and its undertow, fury at the denial of hope and terror at the prospect of annihilation. Then came seven years of disillusion with liberalism, a disillusion that was neither preordained by our primal feelings nor simply a shadow of them: disillusion with real Kennedys, real civil rights defaults, and most of all a real war fought in the name of the rock-bottom principles of Cold War liberalism. The vision of participatory democracy was utopian, literally nowhere, ungrounded in actual prospects. The New Left's affirmative commitments were murky, then, but one thing was not: the passion to end the war. Little to build, much to stop: the sum was an impulse to smash up the machine, to jam the wheels of the juggernaut, and damn the consequences. "My fear of America's stability is bleeding away," I wrote a friend just after Stop the Draft Week, "in the combination of white militance and cop stupidity. This has no 'political' meaning in the old sense. It has plenty of meaning if we want to stop America—if we submerge or even abandon intentions of changing the country purposively, and switch instead to modes of activity which shatter ordinary patterns of expectation. Mass violence of the Oakland sort is then entirely relevant. (And of course costly; somebody is going to get killed one of these days.)"

The red thread winding through my recollections and letters of that summer and fall is the idea of stopping the war by stopping America in its tracks. There were other moods at work in the New Left of the late

Sixties, but this was a strong one. Strategy flirted with nihilism. To a friend who effused about the radical potential of American working-class culture, I came back with my own Diggerlike motif: "Don't dig America, dig it up." My teasing defense of patience was "Rome wasn't destroyed in a day." On Bloody Tuesday, before I'd even heard the news from Oakland, I wrote to an old SDSer: "The politics that makes sense to me now aims to stop this country, not change it; to help revolutionaries, not pretend to be them."

My friends and I found it hard to imagine that America was susceptible to radical change. The majority seemed entrenched, devoted to conserving what property they had accumulated or looked forward to accumulating. I noted with an Aha! something Lyndon Johnson said on a 1966 swing through Asia: "There are 3 billion people in the world and we only have 200 million of them. We are outnumbered 15 to 1. If might did make right they would sweep over the United States and take what we have. We have what they want." After two years in a poor white community, while trying to convince myself of the prospects for "an interracial movement of the poor," I had few illusions about the ability of class consciousness to override either white racism or patriotic gore. I avidly followed New Left historians' efforts to root us in an American past, with American heroes—the Revolutionary War seamen celebrated by Jesse Lemisch; the radical artisans celebrated by Staughton Lynd; the Populists; Debs's Socialists. But in the end, while these excavations moved me, I found myself thinking the quest for American roots forced and sentimental.* Hadn't the United States been founded in slavery and a quite literal genocide against the Indians? It seemed that the decent traditions were as good as dead in the American breast. America stood damned by original sins, compounded by an impressive history of imperial expeditions. Manifest Destiny and the forging of national identity seemed far more salient than class consciousness. "America is a crime," I concluded with no apparent irony. Against the weight of this history, if we thought we could stand for a positive ideal, we were kidding ourselves. The only affirmative position was negation. To put it mildly, this was not the mood to generate ideas about a reconstruction of politics. The best that could be claimed for it was the purity of a scourging—the aesthetic of the apocalypse, not a political vision.

In the middle and late Sixties, you could get a sure laugh in New Left circles by intoning a mock version of the reporter's earnest (or liberal's exasperated) inquiry, "But what do these people want?" The question was utterly reasonable but seemed to us absurdly naïve—or worse, intended to

---

*In fact, early in 1969, I set out to write a children's book (later abandoned) celebrating the Sons of Liberty. The biographical subject I was drawn to—whom I took to be representative of the sad fate of the American promise—was one Isaac Sears, a formidable anti-British rabble-rouser who prospered during the Revolution and then became a pillar of the new Establishment, dying, in fact, on the first U.S. trade mission to China.

discredit. From our hermetic point of view, it was sufficient to be on the side of the angels, certified by Vietnam and race and poverty and our own sense of mission. In fact, there was a dilemma in our objectives that was hard to face. The early New Left program mixed liberal reforms with visionary ideals of participatory democracy. The reforms were substantive, participatory democracy was procedural, and there was always a tension between them. As civil rights and antipoverty reforms became national policy, the idea of participatory democracy grew both more prominent and hazier. It had the virtue of distinguishing us from managerial liberals; it gave voice to a widespread suspicion of bureaucratic organization and central authority. But it disguised our own real power relations and posed profound conundrums. Disbelieving in any principle of authority, including that of its own leaders, SNCC and SDS rested their case on slogans like "Let the people decide," which begged the questions of how leaders could be held accountable, of whether anything "the people" wanted was right, and of which people ought to be deciding which particular issues. SDS's last serious effort to clarify what it stood for, in December 1965, failed badly. Asked to write a statement of purpose for a *New Republic* series called "Thoughts of the Young Radicals," I agonized for weeks about what it was, in fact, I *wanted*. The movement's all-purpose answer to "What do you want?" and "How do you intend to get it?" was: "Build the movement." By contrast, much of the counterculture's appeal was its earthy answer: "We want to live life like this, voilà!"

Participatory democracy was the ideology of a middling social group caught between power and powerlessness, and soaked in ambivalence toward both. The principal property of educated radicals was its knowledge credentials. We were angry at managers whose power outran the knowledge that would entitle them to legitimate authority. We were queasy about dominating the voiceless, yet we knew that education had equipped us to fuse knowledge and power as professionals. We believed in equality but experienced superiority. Fearful of giving up the de facto authority we possessed by virtue of education and articulateness, we were unwilling to pin ourselves down to policies and formal authority. Still, left to these pressures alone, the New Left would have been strained, but might have evolved toward a reformist social democracy mixed with direct action. As it was, the war made its demands on us, and stripped our politics bare.

I puzzled endlessly about *who we were*. It was my passion to think out loud with people of a similar bent; personally, I preferred running off at the mouth (or typewriter) late into the night to running in the streets. An intellectual preoccupation with the nature of our maelstrom was also a way of trying to cope with velocity and runaway emotions; this was how I scrambled to assimilate the enormity of what was happening in the world. Throughout the late Sixties I looked forward most to long conversations with Carl Oglesby, conversations which felt like fragments of one long conversation starting when we spent the overnight bus ride from Ann Arbor to Washington for the April 1965 March on Washington telling each other the stories of our lives. The lean, taut, Ohio-born Oglesby, with his trimly bearded Lincolnesque profile, was eight years my elder. A produced playwright with roots in a working-class childhood and a bit of a beat past, he first gravitated to the SDS crowd, in fact, to talk about putting together a radical theater troupe. The fact that he wrote plays and acted was by no means incidental to Oglesby's style; the man was a dazzling talker and stunning writer of Faulknerian cadences, adept at turning anecdote into high drama. Never having been trimmed back by graduate school, he was universally curious and intellectually independent in the high style of the autodidact. Working as a writer for a Pentagon-funded think-tank, supporting a wife and three small children, he took the time to master the history of the Cold War. His flair with words— along with his respectable age (thirty), his family normality, his willing-ness to drop out of the military industry, and his midwestern proto-prairie origins—catapulted him to the presidency of SDS in 1965; his momen-tous November 1965 Washington speech on Vietnam as a liberals' war brilliantly stated the New Left's leftward turn. In the spring and summer of 1967, in Chicago and Ann Arbor and Yellow Springs (it was part of the drama of these conversations that they would start in one place and con-tinue in another, a movable bull session), Oglesby and I had some long talks which convinced me that the New Left had to be seen as a part of a history of movements against progress. The Communist-centered Old Left, starry-eyed about industrialization, had delivered itself over to dreadful illusions about Stalin. Liberals and social democrats, for their part, had let their own belief in Western-style progress blind them to the dark side of the American dream. We were going to be wiser than all the glib, myopic optimists we despised.

Meanwhile, our skepticism about power would shield us from pure nihilism. That fall, from Carmel, I wrote one letter after another about the need to "stop America," adding that we had to be "alert, exquisitely alert, to the dangers inherent": "There are risks as yet unexplored: the CP [Communist Party] trap of becoming tail on the foreign dog; discourag-ing people who still want to organize Americans." As this mood grew, the main danger would be "fixing our work too rigidly to one star or another (China, the North [Vietnam], NLF, OLAS [the Cuban-sponsored Organi-zation of Latin American Solidarity]), and running into changes of line, etc. We are better protected than movements of the 20s and 30s in two ways: we're not centralist (quite the opposite, congenitally), and we're more interested in small countries and small movements than in great powers. Still, the danger is there."

Sensing the danger was one thing, averting it was another. If the goal was "stopping America," after all, then the risk of isolating yourself from potential allies by aligning with "small countries and small movements" could easily be overlooked. Anyway, those potential liberal-labor allies of whom social democrats spoke were altogether too potential, not very actual. Compared to hypothetical allies, the "small countries and small movements" had two supreme virtues: they found themselves at the wrong end of American guns, and they actually existed.

Earlier that fall, I had talked with Tom Hayden about the coming disruptions. It was our style then to speak in ironies, as we watched ourselves slide into an all-or-nothing politics we both longed for and dreaded. I said jokingly, "Remember when we used to talk about values?" Hayden grinned and replied, "Remember when we used to talk about organizing people?" It was one of those not infrequent moments when Hayden stated something many of us felt and stretched it one important inch. In the backs of our heads, we had given up on the America that existed. But still I wrote, "we have to force ourselves, carefully, compulsively, rigidly, not to give up on the possibility of *intentional* change, i.e. reconstruction." Not a very attractive project. We had to believe because it was absurd.

"How to pursue it practically?" that letter ended. "I don't know. Temperamentally I am more interested in stopping Leviathan. . . ." That was the tone that ascended. Temperament took charge. "Year of the Heroic Guerrilla," the Fidelistas called 1968. I got into the habit of writing it beneath the date of my letters, sometimes whimsically—"Year of the Up-Tight Intellectual" was one variant. At the turn of 1969, I was writing the dateline "Year of the Heroic Convict."

THE OTHER SIDE

"ALL FOR VIETNAM"

As the war became more militant, so did the antiwar movement—in demands, in spirit, in tactics. Between 1965 and 1967, as American troops in Vietnam doubled and redoubled and redoubled twice more, most antiwar movers and shakers shook off their leftover faith in negotiations and endorsed immediate withdrawal. When doubters asked, "How can we get out of Vietnam?" the quick answer was: on boats. But the New Left wing, young and sick at heart at what it reasonably took to be empire flexing its muscles, moved beyond rebellion against American foreign policy. Much of the leadership, and some of the rank and file—it is hard to say exactly how many—slid into romance with the other side. To wear a button calling for "Victory to the National Liberation Front," to wave an NLF flag or shout, "Ho, Ho, Ho Chi Minh/The NLF is gonna win," meant more than believing that the NLF was the most popular force in South Vietnam, or that Vietnamese had flocked to it for compelling reasons, or that it represented the least bad practical alternative for Vietnam—all defensible propositions. It meant feeling the passion of the alignment and placing it at the heart of one's political identity. It meant finding heroes where the American superstate found villains and pointed its guns. It meant imagining comrades riding to *our* rescue.

This was *a* tendency, not the only one, not final or unopposed even in SDS. Its significance was certainly inflated by the prowar Right and by the attentions of a demagogic press. Although almost always greatly outnumbered by American flags turned to patriotic antiwar use, NLF flags seized a disproportionate share of the media spotlight at the giant antiwar marches. And so a too-uncomplicated endorsement of Third World revolutions—and revolutionary organizations—built a firebreak around the New Left part of the antiwar movement, sealing it off from the underbrush sympathy of the unconvinced. Surely those NLF flags were part of the explanation for one of the stunning political facts of the decade: that as the war steadily lost popularity in the late Sixties, *so did the antiwar movement.* At the growing edge of the New Left, it was as if there had to be a loyalty oath for working against the war, or American dominion in general. The napalm had to be stopped for the correct reasons. Strategy-minded antiwar liberals rudely reminded us that we were forfeiting the respect of Americans who were turning against the war but were unwilling to do so at the price of their own sense of patriotism. But the hell with them! Which side were they on, anyway?

The consequence of the New Left's Third World turn—both product and impetus of our isolation—was yet more isolation. But the reporters had not invented those NLF flags out of proverbial whole cloth. Desperate for moral companionship—America having forfeited our love—a part of ourselves looked with respect, even awe, even love, on an ideal version of ourselves who we thought existed—*had* to exist—out there in the hot climates. We needed to feel that someone, somewhere in the world, was fighting the good fight and winning. Better: that the world's good guys formed a solid front. Even better: that out of the rubble, someone, somewhere, might be constructing a good society, at least one that was decent to the impoverished and colonized. If the United States was no longer humanity's beacon—and if the movement was not building a new society itself—the light had to be found outside. The melodrama of American innocence was alive and well in the anti-American left. Henry Luce had been deluded when he anticipated "the American Century"; we thought this was going to be the *anti*-American Century, just as pure, just as irresistible, with a different although equivalently happy ending.

And always there was the war, which we took to be the definitive moral test of America's intentions toward the vast poor and dark-skinned world. The Third Worldist movement route began in McComb, Mississippi, and led to the Mekong Delta. With the United States pulverizing and bullying small countries, it seemed the most natural thing in the world to go prospecting among them for heroes. Their resistance was so brave, their enemies so implacable, their nationalism so noble, we could take their passions, even their slogans and styles of speech, even—in fantasy—their forms of organization for our own. And so we identified with victims who were in the process of repossessing their homelands, as we were straining to overcome our own sense of homelessness. We loved them for what we took to be their struggle for independence, as we were struggling—no mere hackneyed word—for our own. We started out feeling the suffering of peasants, defending their right to rebel, and ended up taking sides with the organizations and leaders who commanded the rebellion—all the while knowing, in anguish, that guerrilla organizations usurp the freedom which rebels are willing to die for, yet also knowing, also in anguish, that without organization (even, often, the wrong organization: dictatorship in embryo) all the bravery in the world is squandered. Some of us took seriously the dreadful histories that Communist groups had imposed, and some didn't, but the New Left tendency was to agree that American occupation was so clear and present an evil—a *homegrown* evil—that the other side would have to be forgiven its crimes. Even the movement's antiutopians thought the future of "the other side," and the morality of guerrilla war, were questions to be left until later, luxuries, or, worst of all, potential weapons in the hands of the napalmers, the question for the present being simply whether the guerrillas, or the enemy nation (the two were often confused), were entitled to have any future of their own. The issue became *how we felt* more than *what would end the war.* We would settle for nothing less than a cleaning of the historical slate.

And so, increasingly, we found our exemplars and heroes in Cuba, in China, in the Third World guerrilla movements, in Mao and Frantz Fanon and Che and Debray, most of all—decisively—in Vietnam. It no longer felt sufficient—sufficiently estranged, sufficiently furious—to say no to aggressive war; we felt driven to say yes to revolt, and unless we were careful, that yes could easily be transferred onto the Marxism-Leninism which had commandeered the revolt in the interest of practicality. Apocalypse was outfitted with a bright side. If the American flag was dripping napalm, the NLF flag was clean. If the deluded make-Vietnam-safe-for-democracy barbarism of the war could be glibly equated with the deliberate slaughter of millions in Nazi gas chambers—if the American Christ turned out to look like the Antichrist—then by this cramped either-or logic the Communist Antichrist must really have been Christ. America had betrayed us; the war, Carl Oglesby movingly said in 1965, "broke my American heart." Only true-blue believers in the promise of America could have felt so anti-American. Ours was the fury of a lover spurned. But a fury so intense, left to itself, would have consumed us. "Don't you want somebody to love?" as the Jefferson Airplane sang. So we turned where romantics have traditionally turned: to the hot-blooded peoples of the subtropics and the mysterious East. The Manichaean all-or-nothing logic of the Cold War was conserved, though inverted, as if costumes from Central Wardrobe had been rotated.

No formal links were forged, of course. What I am about to describe about the New Left's relations with revolutionary movements abroad has nothing in common with the notion that the antiwar movement "stabbed America in the back," obstructed an otherwise splendid and attainable victory on behalf of freedom and democracy in Vietnam; nor with the claim that the many and grave crimes of the victorious revolutionaries retroactively justify the crimes of the expeditionary forces, or the specious logic that sent them to Vietnam (it is far more likely that the longer the war went on, the crueler the victors became). Nor, finally, is there a shred of truth in the paranoid view that the movement was controlled or financed by The Enemy (leave aside that no war was declared), whether Hanoi, Moscow, or as Secretary of State Dean Rusk used to say, "Peiping." That shallow premise was the inversion of quite a different fact: it was the *Saigon* government that depended on funds from abroad. No less a personage than Lyndon Johnson was obsessed by the theory of foreign direction; what else could explain these unruly young? Pressed by Johnson on the eve of the Pentagon siege to investigate the peace movement's international connections, the CIA reported back that "many [leaders] have close Communist associations but they do not appear to be under Communist direction," and that "connections between . . . US activists and foreign governments are limited"—whereupon Rusk said the CIA simply hadn't searched well enough, and Johnson was reportedly so unhappy he shook his finger in the face of CIA director Richard Helms and said, "I simply don't understand why it is that you can't find out about that foreign money." Members of Congress more than once proclaimed that "superior forces," "manipulators," "architects behind closed doors" were responsible for antiwar protests; that they had been "cranked up" in Hanoi. What the officials could not grasp was the convoluted linkage of spirit—or the depth of our revulsion, or the lengths to which unbridled revulsion could run.

Visits to "the other side" started as explorations and diplomatic missions and became pilgrimages. If bumper stickers said "America, Love It or Leave It," we eventually accepted the dare: spiritually, we left. We had started the decade "spiritually unemployed," in a phrase Robb Burlage had reinvented from Van Wyck Brooks; toward the end, it seemed that the best way to feel useful was to settle into a sort of alliance with the real revolutionaries. I remember a conversation circa 1966, in which my anti-Stalinist movement friend Chris Hobson and I felt moved by the Cultural Revolution in China, which we saw as old Mao's last-ditch effort to crush state bureaucracy, to shake off the heavy hand of Stalinism. (We didn't know, or chose to overlook, the fact that Stalin remained prominent in Maoism's pantheon.) In 1967, Paul Potter gave a speech supporting the Cultural Revolutionaries on the grounds that the Chinese purgers of corruption, like us, were bands of brothers and sisters seeking meaningful work.

But the supreme repositories of New Left trust were the Vietnamese revolutionaries, especially the National Liberation Front cadres of the South. The whole movement felt the pull of these devoted, long-suffering people. Those lucky enough to meet them came away with an "NLF high." Not everyone yielded to it in the same way, not every report was equally glowing, not every private attitude as uncritically positive as the speeches. Essentially, though, the New Left agreed that the North Vietnamese, however authoritarian, were the legitimate heirs of a fundamentally just anticolonial war against France; and even if "Uncle

Ho" had at times resorted to ugly methods, there was still the NLF, with its aura of autonomy. However dominated by the Communist Party, the NLF was still a *front*, a coalition, fundamentally independent of Hanoi, which we believed (with good reason) had even discouraged its formation in 1960. There were doubts, but it was suspicious indeed that most of the nasty charges came from the State Department and its academic supporters. The war had narrowed discussion to either-or, and the naysayers had discredited themselves by placing their anti-Communism at the service of napalm.

Anyway, attitudes were cheap; what counted was *stopping the war*. Information was ammunition. News about life and death in Vietnam was hard to come by. In the prevailing discourse, the war was fought against voiceless abstractions: Communism, Hanoi, infiltration, Ho. The American media either repeated U.S. government claims or, when they were skeptical, failed to convey how the world looked to "the other side." Given the demonology that prevailed on both sides, Communist sources were unavailable to the American public; travel to Hanoi was forbidden by both U.S. and North Vietnamese governments. One reason to build bridges was practical: information pure and simple. But of course information is never pure and simple. Hanoi and the NLF passed out the information that served them, and true, we were innocents abroad—yet about the war itself, their scourge and ours, they brought mostly plausible testimony. There was no testimony like their territories themselves.

Major contacts began in July 1965. A delegation of ten American women, organized by Women Strike for Peace, met in Indonesia with six high-ranking North Vietnamese and three NLF women, including the impressive Mme. Nguyen Thi Binh, later the NLF's foreign minister and chief negotiator. The NLF delegates said they had had to walk for two weeks just to get out of South Vietnam, and their undeniable suffering lent force to the rosy picture they painted of the Front. The Northerners spoke convincingly, in frightening detail, of the repeated bombing of hospitals, schools, churches, and villages. They described fragmentation bombs that peppered the body with tiny pellets which scattered under the skin of the victims and which surgery could not remove. Back in the States, such stories were blithely dismissed by American reporters. I was married at the time to one of the American delegates, Nanci Hollander; I was moved to tears by NLF accounts of the bombardment raining down on them in their countryside tunnels. If half of what they said was true, even a quarter of it, then even if their picture of Front politics was disingenuous, the war went real now. There were witnesses, individuals with names and faces at stake, asking for help.

At Christmas 1965, during a bombing "pause" declared by President Johnson, Tom Hayden and Staughton Lynd accompanied the American Communist historian Herbert Aptheker on the first wartime American trip to Hanoi.* From then on, many of the movement's missions to "the other side" had a second purpose: informal diplomacy. "Fact-finding about 'the other side's' negotiating positions for ending the war was our principal purpose," Lynd and Hayden wrote, for at the time the Johnson administration was systematically undermining North Vietnamese moves toward peace talks. Lynd, a Quaker whose sweet-tempered generosity was the stuff of movement legend, was inspired by the example of Dr. George Logan, the American Quaker physician who traveled to revolutionary France in 1798, brought its views back to President John Adams, won the release of imprisoned American seamen, and helped avert war with the United States. Lynd and Hayden stayed in Hanoi for two weeks, met with North Vietnamese officials, witnessed some bomb damage, and wrote a short book called *The Other Side*. Lynd was thirty-six, Hayden twenty-six, and this was Hayden's first trip outside North America.

Most of *The Other Side* recounted the world views of their North Vietnamese hosts; the authors remained politely in the background, like masters of ceremonies. At some points the authors wrestled self-consciously with the Left's grim lineage of self-deception: "We are conscious of the ways in which some intellectuals during the nineteen-thirties sought to excuse the evil side of Soviet communism, and we have made every effort to avoid those habits of thought. . . . We are not arguing that First Amendment liberties thrive in North Vietnam, and we do not believe we are Sartres who require a Camus to remind us of the existence of slave labor camps. . . . On the whole we think the information given us was accurate," they wrote, "although our hosts were superficial in describing certain of the grimmer aspects of their revolution's history. . . ." They tried to honor the distinction between *explaining* something and explaining it *away*. And yet they frequently took at face value their hosts' claims about North Vietnam's achievements. At certain moments, searching for points of resemblance between Vietnamese Communism and the American New Left, they bent over backward to give their hosts the benefit of the doubt. For example: "We suspect that colonial American town meetings and current Vietnamese village meetings, Asian peasants leagues and Black Belt sharecroppers' unions have much in common, especially the concept of a 'grass-roots' or 'rice-roots' democracy." They strained to render the strangeness of Communist Vietnam familiar, to force it into the terms of their own experience. Impressed by the character of some of their hosts, they were moved by "the possibilities for a socialism of the heart." They were disarmed by assurances that a postwar Vietnam would be democratic in a Western sense.

---

*Aptheker had been approached by the North Vietnamese (it was probably the last time the American Old Left was Hanoi's main link to the United States); he in turn approached Lynd, then teaching at Yale, who in turn recruited Hayden. SDS, initially approached by Aptheker, didn't want to be associated with him.

Today, rereading Lynd's and Hayden's book for the first time in almost twenty years, I find its refusal to honor the standard Cold War demonology touching, naïve, and saddening all at once. Lynd himself calls it "a poor book." He already had reasons to suspect the North Vietnamese, in fact, but muted his doubts in the writing. While in Hanoi, he had been asked to address a cultural congress; he reluctantly complied, feeling it would be awkward to refuse. (The dean of Yale Law School had cautioned Lynd, then an assistant professor of history at Yale, not to do anything to "embarrass" the university—though how he knew about Lynd's impending trip was not exactly clear, since Lynd had not made it public.) After Lynd left North Vietnam, Hanoi released the text of his remarks to the world press, and a few sentences ended up in *The New York Times*—stripped of Lynd's light voice and tone of Quaker modesty. It "left a bad taste in my mouth," Lynd says, that Hanoi had left him exposed. For another thing, Lynd recalls, "I went out of my way to ask them whether North Vietnamese troops were fighting in the South. I subsequently became absolutely convinced that there were North Vietnamese troops fighting in the South in large numbers at the time that we were there. They may very well have been persons who originally came from South Vietnam and had volunteered to return and so forth and so on, but the long and the short of it is that there were armed troops going from the North to the South and it was a question that I had asked in writing, in as blunt a way as I could, and the answer was no, and I felt that I had been lied to. I think I had this sense of uneasiness from the outset, and that it was perhaps a year or two later that I concluded that I had been snookered."

But even errands on behalf of peace have their own momentum. Diplomacy is a game in which all appearances can be reduced to ulterior motives, and only ulterior motives count. Nothing is quite what meets the eye; all' statements and omissions are coded for effect. Aside from wanting to ferret out information, Hayden and Lynd—and all other travelers to the Eastern bloc from this moment on—were committed to keeping lines of communication open. Paul Potter was in touch with Hayden after his return, and among Potter's letters I find this note: "Staughton and Tom are trying to write a book on their trip to North Vietnam . . . and are at the moment tied in knots over the question of how critical they can be of the North Vietnamese. On the one hand they do not want to appear as the apologists for anybody and on the other they fear that the North Vietnamese given their total engagement in the war will misinterpret any criticism that they may choose to make—seriously undercutting the possibility of similar future contacts."

Lynd took little pleasure in the diplomatic role. One of the movement's few elder statesmen—he came of political age in the early Fifties, a member of the otherwise "missing generation"—he had lived in voluntary communities and was comfortable with right living, "speaking

truth to power," as the Quakers say, whether on a picket line in Atlanta
during the Cuban missile crisis or as director of the Freedom Schools
during Mississippi Freedom Summer. His private, traumatic moment of
truth came a few months after returning from Hanoi, in the spring of
1966. Bertrand Russell had decided to organize an international tribunal
to gather and publicize evidence about American war crimes in Vietnam,
and Russell's American representative, Russell Stetler, formerly of the
May 2nd Movement, came to New Haven to feel out Lynd as a prospective
member. "A crime is a crime," Lynd remembers telling Stetler, "no matter
who commits it, and it would be my judgment that the Tribunal would
be more credible if it would permit witnesses to appear before it, alleging
crimes by any side." When the sums were added up, Lynd argued, "the
crimes of the United States and the government of South Vietnam would
be seen to be overwhelmingly greater than those of the National Liberation Front or the government of North Vietnam, but more credibly so."
"If anyone were to torture prisoners, that would be a crime, right?" Lynd
asked Stetler. "Anything is justified that would force the American
invaders into the sea," Stetler replied. It was at that moment, Lynd
recalls, "that I realized that this beautiful movement, that I thought I
was part of, was going someplace where I didn't want to go." It was, for
him, "the beginning of the long loneliness of the late Sixties and early
Seventies."

That summer, Lynd traveled to Geneva for an international meeting,
but the ambience was all too disturbingly familiar. "This is the
international Communist banquet circuit," he thought, "and I have seen
this before. I felt if there's one place that we've all been, it's what
happened in the 1930s and thereafter vis-à-vis the Soviet Union. My first
political experiences had to do with . . . defining how I felt toward the
American Communist Party and various front groups of the American
Communist Party." Thus fortified, Lynd found himself moving in a
direction opposite to the younger, blither, angrier, more wishful New
Left. The movement was coming to a boil. The avant-garde of the antiwar
movement, growing impatient with scruples, raged against America like
a drunkard against his bottle. We inverted the traditional American
innocence, and located the "city upon a hill" in the jungles of the Third
World. Rage against the war required a counterbalance: as not only
America but the movement itself became less lovable, we looked for
populations (and movements) that were more so—the more remote
culturally, the better, since less could be understood about them. Uneasy
with this turn, with media-bestowed celebrity, and with diplomacy in
general, Lynd eased himself out of the spotlight and turned to local
organizing.

Why should it be easy to reckon with the movement's troubled, troubling, wrong moves? But caution: Hindsight can have it too easy. Every
simple categorical statement is also a form of forgetting. Lynd, today a labor

lawyer, rightly says: "There's a Scylla for every Charybdis. One doesn't exactly want to derogate the impulse for solidarity; one doesn't want to stand in the way of whatever would help Americans to get beyond the parochialism and cultural-bound point of view that all of us, the left included, have." The danger was that decent impulses grew tunnel-narrow in the course of defensiveness and infatuation. And even if, miraculously, we could have thought our way through the entire cycle of action and reaction which was the Cold War, the dominating script of that time, still, how would we ever have gotten beyond the respective alibis to the main point, which was to stop violence? Hayden and Lynd were Americans awed, cowed, obliged by their visit to a country under brutal American bombardment. Of course, romance was not the only response to revulsion; it should have been possible (*was* possible: some antiwarriors did it) to face the grim truth of what the West had wrought in Indochina without glorifying the victim-resisters or overlooking the tragedies that the victors furthered. Still, the past is not the present read backward; the Vietnamese reign of terror in "re-education camps" and against boat people after America was expelled in 1975 is not necessarily what would have taken place if the war had ended with a decade's less destruction and bitterness. Then I remind myself—as Lynd and Hayden did—of the killing of thousands of peasants, kulak-style, in North Vietnam, and the imprisonment of thousands of others in forced labor camps, in 1955–56 (a "mistake" Hanoi had owned up to, after the fact). As the Right indeed said, Hanoi had a history of brutality—although as the Right never asked, why should antipersonnel bombs have been the proper response to a vicious land policy? Were the instruments of terror supposed to persuade Hanoi to act more kindly? Let us remind ourselves too that the regime of Ngo Dinh Diem in the South was no slouch at torture, at the forced evictions of multitudes to "strategic hamlets," at the repression of former Vietminh cadres waiting for the reunification elections promised by the Geneva accords for 1956 (none of which Saigon had owned up to). . . .

So does the spiral snake around. Those who want simple conclusions should forget politics and stick to arithmetic. Of only one thing have I no doubt: that the war poisoned Vietnam, poisoned its politics and its culture as well as its crops and its soil. Lynd and Hayden were absolutely right to say that "if the United States is genuinely concerned to promote freedom for the North Vietnamese, it should stop bombing them."

The State Department revoked Lynd's passport. (Eventually the Court of Appeals for the District of Columbia restored it.) Lynd went back to teaching at Yale; in 1967, having been denied tenure, he was persuaded by Rennie Davis to join a new organizers' training school in Chicago. In his passage to local activism, he ended up crossing paths with Hayden, who had returned to the SDS-founded community organization in Newark but was dogged by the need to do something about the war. Hayden's dilemma was typical of what afflicted SDS-style radicals in those years—one felt bound to work on a manageable scale *here,* albeit lacking a plausible vision of a new society, all the while feeling obligated to revolutionaries *there,* on the other side of the world, but without a clear way to make that obligation practical. And then, with the rise of race consciousness in the ghettos—including all kinds of black nationalisms, from dashikis and Afros and "black is beautiful" to militant politics—what were whites working in black ghettos to do? Although Hayden and other Newark organizers were able to function there during the July 1967 riots, plainly the time of white organizers in black ghettos had expired. For a whole generation of New Left organizers, the antiwar movement—and Third World revolutions—were becoming more alluring partly because the war was metastasizing and partly because they were losing their base.

Whether sensitive to the limits of brief excursions or not, Americans who met with revolutionaries abroad came back surrounded by a singular aura. They were in demand at rallies. Their passion had an apparently firm ground. Their mission was to widen their circle, organize other trips. Accordingly, in September 1967, Hayden and Dave Dellinger put together a kind of movement-to-movement summit conference, a grand encounter with high-level North Vietnamese and National Liberation Front delegations in Bratislava, Czechoslovakia. The Americans, forty of them, included experienced antiwar organizers like Dellinger, early SDSers (most of them now community and antidraft organizers) like Rennie Davis, Carol McEldowney, Dick Flacks, and Nick Egleson, and radical journalists like Andrew Kopkind and Sol Stern. Many had not been abroad before; at the age when many of their peers routinely took passage to Europe, they had been organizing the poor.

The Vietnamese made an extraordinary impression. They were warm, charming, calm, and well organized to a fault: they toasted and lectured in a formal style—Communist? experienced revolutionary? culturally Vietnamese? diplomatic?—that sometimes bothered casual Americans. They were effusive in their gratitude to the antiwar movement and their faith in "the American people," at the same time they insisted that their struggle was their own and that history was on their side. Whatever their suffering—one Vietnamese woman was carrying two hundred pieces of American shrapnel in her body—they seemed free of bitterness; they told their heart-rending stories in moderate tones. An American friend wrote me this paraphrase: "Each family digs bunkers for each member of the family; but, when an air raid comes, then 3 of your children go to other families, and vice versa—so that, if there is a direct hit, then if you had 5 children, then at least you'll have 2 left. 'You see,' the man says smiling, 'we must find ways to divide the suffering among the nation.'" "Their most extreme form of expression," my friend went on, was "the cold, didactic, slightly harsh and disciplined speech of long-time party members (Mme. Binh)."

The Americans were moved—so much so, some felt called upon to declare their ringing solidarity on the spot. One proclaimed that the antiwar movement was "the National Liberation Front behind LBJ's lines," and that like the slaves in Stanley Kubrick's movie who refused to give Spartacus away, each one of them would tell the interrogators, "I'm Spartacus!" (More than one American complained afterward that the rousing rhetoric was out of place when the Vietnamese themselves were so modest.) Dave Dellinger told the Vietnamese at one point, "You are Vietnamese and you love Vietnam. You must remember that we are Americans and we love America too, even though we oppose our government's politics with all our strength." At which one American groaned and others looked embarrassed. Little by little, alienation from American life—contempt, even, for the conventions of flag, home, religion, suburbs, shopping, plain homely Norman Rockwell order—had become a rock-bottom prerequisite for membership in the movement core. The New Left felt its homelessness as a badge of identity by now; damned if it was going to love what it had spiritually left.

Strange partners indeed, these marijuana-smoking Americans and ascetic Asian revolutionaries, united by B-52s! (Some Americans tried to finesse the difference by bruiting it about that the Northerners' "Dien Bien Phu"–brand cigarettes contained small amounts of marijuana. This news was not supposed to be spread, however, for it would discredit the ascetic Vietnamese.) The then-journalist Christopher Jencks, covering the meeting for *The New Republic,* was struck by "the extent to which [the young radicals] identified with the Viet Cong," and astutely observed:

> This New Left sympathy for the NLF is not based on any similarity of style or of temperament. The Vietnamese revolutionaries we met were not the joyless communist *apparatchiks* whom the Soviet Union would send to such a meeting, but they were dignified, restrained, disciplined and apparently selfless—about as unlike the loose-tongued, anarchistic, spontaneous Americans as any group could conceivably be. It was easy to respect their courage and patience under incredibly difficult conditions, and to find them personally charming, but it would not be very easy for a young American to establish an intimate personal friendship with or psychological understanding of such strangers. Nor do I think most of the Americans at Bratislava would find life in post-revolutionary Vietnam congenial; on the contrary, I suspect most would find themselves in opposition fairly soon. *The common bond between the New Left and the NLF is not, then, a common dream or a common experience but a common enemy: the US government, the system, the Establishment. The young radicals' admiration for the NLF stems from the feeling that the NLF is resisting The Enemy successfully, whereas they are not.*

From Bratislava, seven of the Americans—including Hayden, Rennie Davis, and Carol McEldowney—went on to Hanoi, where they were thunderstruck as Hayden and Lynd had been, and by many of the same things. Rennie Davis was hit hard by "the magnitude of the war and the incredible human struggle and the widespread Vietnamese attitude toward the American people. In a crowd I'd be announced as an American. Immediately there was spontaneous applause. It could *not* have been programed." He was astonished to discover that Norman Morrison, the American Quaker who had burned himself to death on the steps of the Pentagon to protest the war in 1965, was a national hero. Several Americans came back from Bratislava and Hanoi wearing aluminum rings—cast, they were told, from the scrap of an American bomber shot down during a raid. A few had bomb casings and antipersonnel pellets, material souvenirs of the damage. Davis came back to the States transfigured, his old commitment to slow, steady local organizing shattered; he resolved, like Hayden before him, to hurl himself into anti-war work. Over the next few years, several dozen antiwar Americans— young New Leftists, black militants, professors and writers, filmmakers and folksingers and actors—undertook the circuitous trip to Hanoi.* By the end of the war, several score other Americans met with North Vietnamese and NLF delegations in Montreal, Havana, Budapest, and Paris. Many came back wearing the mysterious aluminum rings—signs that the American techno-juggernaut was not, after all, invincible; signs of engagement if not marriage.

The travelers became familiar figures in the movement's little world. Their stories of damage and courage were as compelling as they were predictable. Many had to take shelter from air raids—an unaccustomed thing for any American, all the more so when the bombs were American. They were dazzled and inspired. Those granted an audience with prominent leaders felt graced; it was like being given the Keys to the Revolution. "It was like being caught up in some splendid fairy tale of revolution peopled with live heroes and heroines," wrote Elinor Langer, who went to an East-meets-West meeting in Budapest in the fall of 1968. "Each of them was wonderful: physically beautiful, warm, sensitive, smart." There were revolutionary fantasies, as Andrew Kopkind wrote of having been ushered into a private meeting with Mme. Binh at Bratislava: "I was to be appointed a master spy, I was to visit the Liberated Zones, I was to receive the Revolutionary Word." Often they came away convinced that the officials and semiofficials they met—universally referred to as "the Vietnamese"—were a species apart, a virtual new breed of human, not

---

*Several escorted captive bombardiers back to the United States. Neither North Vietnam nor the antiwar movement benefited much from the prisoner releases, partly because few of the POWs were persuaded of Hanoi's case and partly because the Pentagon took the freed POWs off the hands of the antiwar people as soon as possible. On one occasion, in early 1968, Daniel Berrigan and Howard Zinn accompanied three released flyers on a plane that stopped in Laos on its way out of Hanoi. The American ambassador in Laos came on board the plane, delayed it, and left no doubt in the flyers' minds that their government expected them to leave the company of Berrigan and Zinn and fly back to the States with the air force. They did.

only representative of the will of their populations (something only the American government, bombing to break that will, doubted) but a model for the world's revolutionary future: even our own.

Most of all, the travelers came back resolute: *something,* something *else,* something *more* had to be done to stop the war. For many reasons—I shall come back to this—it always took a complex argument to think that the movement was getting anywhere against the war; and complex arguments are not easy to feel. But the returned travelers had an acute problem of their own. The stakes of the war had become vastly more vivid. They had set foot on its ground, felt the force of real combatants who were exemplars as well as victims. After Bratislava, as Andrew Kopkind put it, "I was no longer merely 'against the war,' but struggling in solidarity with Vietnamese revolutionaries." On American soil, the antiwar movement was embattled, liberals and the apathetic roused themselves only slowly, and otherwise business went on as usual. In November 1967, for example, only 10 percent of Americans polled favored withdrawal from Vietnam—and this after two and a half years of demonstrations, teach-ins, petitions, sit-ins, electoral campaigns, you name it. The discrepancy between America and enemy Vietnam was unbearable; many of the returning travelers went into shock. How could these two worlds exist on the same planet? The nation which trumpeted the worth of the individual was bombing the nation which not only stood for community and equality but—partly thanks to the bombing— apparently practiced it. Responsibility seemed clear: to overcome the almost unimaginable distance between the bombers and bombed. The route of honor led into the caldron. Feelings pared themselves down to slogans. Tom Hayden expressed the far limits of a larger mood when he wrote: *"Our task: an all-out siege against the war machine. Our watchword: All for Vietnam."*

Questions that might have emerged in calmer times about the political nature of "the other side" felt like distractions and were swept into the shadows. If you thought too hard about what your allies stood for, you would be playing Washington's game. About revolutionary coercion you didn't want to know; the bad news would only complicate what had to remain child-simple to justify one's departures from normal life. The only serious question was, How could you possibly do enough? "My god," said one of the Americans in Budapest, "I'll eat peanut butter the rest of my life if that's what it'll take to help these people be free." "The one problem, of course," Andrew Kopkind wrote, "was what I, or anyone, was supposed to do with this new sense of revolutionary solidarity. Nothing that young Americans were doing (that is, nothing that seemed possible for me) seemed appropriate to the comradeship entrusted to us. And simply feeling guilty was, as people used to say, a stone drag." Guilt simmered, and projects came to a boil, and most of all, young influentials of the New Left, enraged by the casual crimes of their own country, lacking a good society of their own making, could not shake off the pull of that odd identity: a metaphorical "National Liberation Front behind Lyndon Johnson's lines."

"NO PARADISE"

Many were the New Left travelers who came back from Cuba burdened by inspiration, too. I was one. My experience was not typical in every respect, but it testifies to the power of the journey to the East.

Just before moving to California, and just after my friends came back from Bratislava, in September 1967, I traveled to Expo in Montreal. It was my first trip outside the United States (except for a few hours driving across part of Canada in college); to breathe un-American air for three days felt to me like liberation. (The company of a certain young woman, and the hope of persuading her to fall in love with me, helped too.) I was dazzled by the multimedia Canadian and Czech pavilions, which were influenced by Marshall McLuhan and other avant-garde wizards, but what moved me most was the modest Cuban exhibit, showing no industrial goods or technological wonders, only a modernist photo-essay juxtaposing photographic blow-ups to fragments of poetry exalting the continuity of the fight against Batista with the revolutionary present. After a short conversation with the Cuban guide I swapped a JOBS OR INCOME NOW button for her Cuban pin. On the plane coming home, my companion translated for me K. S. Karol's interview with Fidel Castro in *Le Nouvel Observateur,* in which Fidel anticipated abolishing money and spoke of the superiority of moral over material incentives. A man after my own heart! I raved about the pavilion and the interview for weeks, and wrote a poem pitying Americans who couldn't understand how glorious it would be to abolish money ("the pilot pities the eagle for having no parachute").

A couple of months later, now settled in California and fortified by Stop the Draft Week, I was accepted onto an SDS delegation to Cuba. Knowing I was inclined toward infatuation and therefore unwilling to let myself off lightly, I tried self-inoculation. I brushed up my high school Spanish, read critical as well as adoring books, and made a list of questions: What did intellectuals think of restrictions on civil liberties? What kind of democracy prevailed in the Party and in unions? Was there any workers' control? Would there ever be institutionalized factions (with mass bases) in the Party? I knew all about the terrible and laughable history of Westerners (Lincoln Steffens, George Bernard Shaw, H. G. Wells, Sidney and Beatrice Webb) making their pilgrimages to the East and trapping themselves in apologies; it wasn't going to happen to me.

I traveled with Carl Davidson, then one of the leaders of SDS. In Mexico City, we were accosted several times near the Cuban embassy—

where we were getting our visas—by a mysterious thirtyish American who said he'd come back from Vietnam, didn't like what America was doing there, didn't like what America was doing in Cuba either, knew how to run bulldozers and other heavy equipment, and wanted to place his knowledge at the service of brave little Cuba. Couldn't we put in a good word for him, get him a visa? Likely story! We were amused at the skulduggery, surprised at its crudeness, flattered and apprehensive to be the targets. Then there were the routine pictures snapped by a photographer with an ostentatious Graflex at the Mexico City airport as we waited to take off on Cubana de Aviación.

We arrived in Cuba just after Christmas, in time for the Cultural Congress of Havana, an international bash bringing together luminaries from First, Second, and Third Worlds. It was heady stuff for a first overseas visit. There were intelligent papers mimeographed on cheap paper in Spanish, French, and English, about cultural imperialism, the formation of a new man under socialism, even (mirabile dictu!) the importance of literary freedoms. The left-wing intelligentsia of Europe and Latin America turned out in force. Sartre canceled at the last minute because of illness, but Julio Cortazar and David Siqueiros attended; it was said that someone had accosted Siqueiros in an elevator, accused him (accurately) of involvement in the assassination of Trotsky, and kicked him in the shins. Russians, Bulgarians, and East Germans wrote deadening propaganda pamphlets and hulked about in double-breasted suits, looking inaccessible. Our Cuban hosts did not skimp. Delegates hob-nobbed, ate and drank spectacularly well. The visitors slept high above the waterfront at the Habana Libre (formerly Hilton). The Trinidad-born writer C. L. R. James, a noble independent radical, was said to have protested the splendor of the Congress when so many Cubans were poor; I sympathized, though I would have hated to give up the Cuba Libres and crab and shrimp cocktails that started every meal.

I got away from the hotel as much as possible, and wandered through Havana, sometimes without my guide, improvising ramshackle conversations in my so-so Spanish. I even escaped Havana for several days, and toured more factories than I'd ever seen in the United States. I went to an exemplary farm where workers honest-to-God sang as they marched off into the fields. I visited a training school for teachers in the Sierra Maestra (I got a kick out of posing for a picture wearing my U.S. Army fatigue jacket outside the cave where Che Guevara was supposed to have directed guerrilla actions against Batista). I worried about whether these sites were typical, then decided not to worry; when in doubt, I usually shone the best possible light on what I saw. Mostly I saw energy, amazing commitment. Ordinary people seemed both mobilized and relaxed; it was that famous Latin revolution-with-a-beat. A cane cutter in Oriente Province told me straight-faced, "Anyone who fights imperialism is our brother," but cheerfully acknowledged that the work was backbreaking and he'd happily do something else for the revolution. A tractor driver told me, matter-of-factly, that he had been working for twenty-four hours straight: "The people in Vietnam don't sleep, why should we? We're doing the same work." (Tom Hayden, also along for the Cultural Congress, said wryly he had heard the same thing in North Vietnam— from a cadre so exhausted he could hardly keep his eyes open.) The Party-line press was awful, but I was still impressed with how carefully people read it. An airplane mechanic said he would give me his copy of the paper as soon as he finished his painstaking reading of Régis Debray's speech of self-defense: "It's important." I was moved to read on a billboard, "REVOLUCIÓN ES CONSTRUIR"—especially moved since I thought our own task in America was to destroy the destroyers. Intimations of workers' control of production in the future impressed me more than the Communist Party's (Fidel's?) monopoly of political power. The most disturbing thing I saw was at the one school I saw in session, near the Sierra Maestra (most schools were out, for the Christmas holidays). As soon as our touring group walked into the classroom, the students rose and chanted in unison: "The slogan for today is: We will fulfill production for Company Number One!" One of the major slogans in Cuba that winter was, "We will make men like Che." "This is not," I wrote in my journal, "the way to make men like Che."

Trying to keep honest, I searched high and low for an authentic counterrevolutionary. I found an older man who didn't like the Leninist catechism being impressed upon his children, but convinced myself he was an authentic socialist who would be pleased by Fidel's latest reforms. In a working-class section of Havana I got into a conversation with a street sweeper who had earned a prettier penny in the days of the American casinos. Introducing myself as a *norteamericano* journalist, not a *ruso*, I asked him how he felt about the Revolution. "I can't say anything against the Revolution," was his answer. Aha! I thought; I'd finally found one. Did he mean he was afraid? No, not at all, he begged to clarify. There was *nothing to say* against the Revolution.

My guide, a medical student named Marilú who had been found too rambunctious for the Party, was still a Party-liner; she thought there were no reasons why workers would ever strike against a workers' state, and was appalled to hear that SDS chapters were free to act on their own. When I asked why so many of the Che Guevara posters plastered around Havana had been ripped, Marilú blamed the wind, which I doubted blew so selectively. Yet for all her impressive resolve to defend the island revolution, Marilú told more or less counterrevolutionary jokes. (For example: In the year 2000, a little boy is going through an old photo album. He sees a photo of a line waiting in the street. "Grandpa," he says, "what's that?" "Well, in the early years of the Revolution, there wasn't enough to go around, so people lined up for goods." "What are they waiting for here, Grandpa?" "Well, the sign says they're waiting for meat." "Grandpa, what's 'meat'?") Stalinist bogeymen seemed conspicuous by their absence. Like any good *norteamericano* liberal, or Communist, Marilú tried to counsel us toward political patience. At one point she tried to convince Carl Davidson and me that we should love our working class, while we tried to convince her of the half-truth that much of the American working class had benefited from slavery and the slaughter of the Indians. Likewise, the North Vienamese delegates we met with one day told the Americans, "We have faith in the conscience of the American people." "Sometimes I wish we had as much faith," Davidson told them. The Vietnamese laughed: "We have faith that you can *awake* the conscience of the American people." Cubans were horrified to learn that Americans were reading Régis Debray as a guide for the United States.

The upbeat mood was infectious, and it didn't hurt that there were long black Cadillacs to whisk us around. We were told about moral incentives for work and the campaign against bureaucracy; no one said it, but my willful imagination champed at the bit, wondering if a threshold *had* been crossed on the way to a higher civilization. (After one Cultural Congress session I sat down on a bus next to the British historian Eric Hobsbawm, who argued knowingly that the Cuban dependency on sugar production was leading them to disaster; I dismissed this as old-fashioned conservative Marxist grumpiness.) I was taken with the modernist posters and documentary films, the billboards invoking Che and proclaiming "VIETNAM, WE ARE WITH YOU." My favorite, standing behind Fidel as he dedicated a new town outside Havana, read: "CUANDO LO EXTRAOR-DINARIO SE CONVIERTE EN COTIDIANO, ES QUE EXISTE UNA REVOLUCIÓN." ("WHEN THE EXTRAORDINARY BECOMES EVERYDAY, THAT'S A REVOLUTION.") It was as if the surrealist (and countercultural) dream of the interpenetration of art and life had come to power.

The Cubans were the most heterogeneous of delegations to the Cultural Congress. There were cultural power brokers who spoke in too-familiar euphemisms; there was Carlos Franqui, onetime director of the rebel radio and editor of a postrevolutionary newspaper, who won my heart when he said during a workshop that there were times in the Sierra Maestra when the insurgents would have given up rifles for books of poetry. (He went into exile not long afterward, and years later published a scathing book about Fidel as tyrant.) I spent long evenings with a group of Cuban writers and filmmakers who were my age (I turned twenty-five the night of Fidel's new town speech). We gobbled ice cream at the glorious Coppelia emporium and gabbed about movies and cultural theory, the dangers of socialist realism, the nature of democracy, the ins and outs of the revolution's treatment of intellectuals, homosexuals (there had been labor camps in the early Sixties but Fidel had disbanded them, I was told) and other deviants. I was delighted to hear that Isaac Deutscher's three-volume biography of Trotsky was due for a Cuban edition, although publication had been delayed in "temporary" deference to the Russians, who had just celebrated the fiftieth anniversary of the October Revolution. The Russians had just started shipping oil, and my friends seemed well aware of the dreadful Marxist-Leninist history it was their task to avoid. For a time these free spirits had edited *El Caimán Barbudo* ("The Bearded Alligator"), the literary supplement to the daily Young Communist paper (where they had published Rosa Luxemburg as well as other heretical Marxists); *El Caimán* had just been snatched away from them by orthodox types who called them "elitists" and preferred to publish doctrinaire (and unthreatening) writings from the Cuban hinterlands. I had no trouble deciding which side I was on. But I was impressed that these young intellectuals weren't bitter; they had lost one battle, they thought they would win others. (I went to interview the winning faction too. They were dull hacks, but it was still impressive that they could insist that the free spirits were *not* counterrevolutionary.) Unlike the culturally alien Vietnamese whom the New Left met at Bratislava, the young Cubans demonstrated that it was possible to be committed and questioning at the same time. Even our poetic styles—loose-jointed rhythms, Brecht's bluntness, Borges's beat-skipping—seemed similar. "There is a worldwide shared sensibility among the young," I wrote in my journal, "taking its force from pain and rejoicing and its variance from circumstances." If I were Cuban, I thought, I would be like them. By accident of birth, I was destined to destroy, they to construct.

One day Tom Hayden, Carl Davidson, Dave Dellinger, and I brainstormed about demonstrations at the Democratic Convention in August, and joked about how delighted HUAC would be to know our little cabal was having this conversation in *Havana*. Movement tensions also came with us. Ralph Featherstone, Willie Ricks, and Bob Fletcher were there from SNCC; Ricks, who had promoted the "Black Power" slogan in Mississippi the year before, was bristling with hostility toward whites, and Featherstone, an old comrade, intervened at one point when Ricks got nasty. Cuban officials, who had given Stokely Carmichael the royal treatment when he had stood up in Havana and called for revolution in the United States at an international conference six months earlier, wondered why Carmichael now proclaimed that socialism was irrelevant to blacks. Everywhere we went, the news that we were "*revolucionarios norteamericanos*" brought revolutionary *abrazos*.

We were, in short, both flattered and dazzled. I questioned much of what met my eye, but the Cubans I met were so compelling, and the relief from the burdens of opposition so great, I usually overrode my skepticism. Perhaps the neighborhood Committees for the Defense of the Revolution, for example, were benign block clubs to gather complaints, administer inoculations, and such; then again, perhaps they were control outposts for the state security apparatus. When in doubt, I shrugged, hoped for the best, and submerged the problem. Like any revolutionary tourist, I thought little about what I didn't get to see; I walked on the bright side, sampling some combination of reality and wishful thinking—to this day I do not know exactly in which proportions. From what I can gather, the turn of 1967–68 was a relatively benign moment in Cuba. Fidel Castro, far from pandering to the Soviet Union, was denouncing it for insufficient revolutionary zeal in the Third World. My Coppelia friends acknowledged that several years earlier, homosexuals had been rounded up and sent into forced labor, but said that Fidel had put a stop to this barbarism. The poet Heberto Padilla had not yet been jailed, beaten, and forced to confess to having fed information to two independent left-wing French writers (whom Castro slandered as CIA agents). About police bullying and the torture of political prisoners I had not yet any idea. What was palpable was the pain of reentry to my homeland, whose trade embargo and violence (not to mention dozens of assassination attempts, not yet publicly known) were certainly not helping Cuba's chances for independence. At the Mexico City airport, having a drink with Dave Dellinger and Robert Scheer, I looked out the window and saw a billboard advertising Cutty Sark. I had to change seats: after twenty-three days where public space was turned to revolutionary use, capitalist propaganda disgusted me. Briefly in Chicago on my way back to California, I started to babble about Cuba to Greg Calvert, then national secretary of SDS; Greg said he'd never seen me so free of cynicism.

I helped set up other trips to Cuba, gave enthusiastic talks and wrote enthusiastic articles which I dotted with maybes. (The best began on a reflective note: "We look to Cuba not only because of what we sense Cuba to be but because of what the United States is not. For generations, the American Left has externalized good: we needed to tie our fates to someone, somewhere in the world, who was seizing the chances for a humane society. Perhaps we need an easy diversion from the hard business of cracking America. Now we dig Cuba. . . . We preserve our quick optimisms with fantasies of an assault on *our* barracks, a landing in *our* yacht, a fight in *our* mountains.") I wrote one white-heat paean for SDS's *New Left Notes,* explaining to Carl Davidson that it was the first of a hypothetical two-parter, the second of which would treat, among other topics, "the vitality of critical consciousness" and "excesses of discipline and their future." Although I wrote to Davidson twice urging him to print a blurb about the coming attractions—"it wouldn't be hard for somebody to get very wrong ideas by assuming the article was complete as printed"—he ran the piece without the blurb, for whatever reason. I never got around to writing my follow-up (about the controlled press and mind-numbing pedagogy, among other troubling things)—doubts were low priority.

I tried to keep up correspondence with my newfound Cuban friends. Upsetting things happened. On January 18, before leaving Havana, I had mailed a letter to a man I had met at the Cultural Congress, a professor from Santiago de Cuba. He wrote back to me in California: my letter had arrived on April 10. I wrote to the Cubans via a friend in Canada, but even so my letters seemed inordinately delayed. Then came confusing news. Just after I left Cuba, the regime threw into jail the members of a so-called "microfaction" of old-time Communists charged, of all things, with spying for the Soviet Union. This seemed not necessarily a bad sign—but still a bit puzzling. Then Castro announced a "revolutionary offensive" against bars, nightclubs, small businesses, and miniskirts. In the spring, I asked my Coppelia friends what they thought of the efflorescence of freedom going on in Dubcek's Czechoslovakia. To my delight, one of them, whom I shall call Pedro, wrote back that he liked it: ". . . in the same way there is no possible coexistence with aggression (e.g. Viet Nam war, Bay of Pigs, etc.), there is no possible coexistence [with] countries that won't change their thinking patterns inherited from the Comintern times and that will take rapid action against heresy (as they have done with us—the Soviets, the Chinese, etc.). . . ." There was also a sour note: I had sent Pedro a poem I had written on the occasion of reading Trotsky's *History of the Russian Revolution;* he liked it, but added: "—silly thing—L. D. Bronstein's [Trotsky's original] name is still tabu here." What did that make of the claim that Deutscher's biography was about to see print in Havana?

Sometime that year, for reasons never disclosed, Fidel Castro cut short his movement away from the USSR. Soviet troops marched into Czechoslovakia on August 20. I was just about to fly to Chicago for the Democratic Convention protests. I was disturbed to hear that Fidel had given a bloated, tortured speech acknowledging that "not the slightest trace of legality exists" for the invasion, yet refusing to condemn it—for "the Czechoslovak regime was heading toward capitalism and was inexorably heading toward imperialism." (Amazingly, he had criticized the Russians for setting out the wrong arguments—failing to make "any direct accusation against Yankee imperialism for its responsibility in the events in Czechoslovakia.") In Chicago during the horrendous convention week I was one of those who thought the Hog Butcher of the World had been transformed into "Czechago"; I identified wholeheartedly with the Czech students who refused to cooperate with the Russian invaders. In June Pedro had written me: "These are really hard years and everyone should see them like they are. No paradise, no all-is-well, no smile-with-strong-arm-and-broad-neck. We make history and also suffer it. . . ." What exactly had he been trying to tell me?

Within a year, influentials in SDS were saying I was "unreliable"—too unreliable to be included in planning for the Venceremos Brigade, which American radicals sent to Cuba to cut sugarcane starting in late 1969. (The same commissars were forcing Carl Oglesby—who had thought up the idea of the Brigade in the first place—out of the Brigade and SDS leadership altogether, for being "insufficiently revolutionary.") The "proof" of my counterrevolutionary tendencies was the fact that I had spent too much time with Pedro, who had acquired a bad reputation for hanging out with Americans. At first I was flabbergasted, then stung, indignant, and disgusted—but by that time also resigned: there was no way to stop the movement's own loyalty oaths. I lost touch with the Coppelia writers. I have often wondered what became of them.

"Leave this Europe where they are never done talking about Man," wrote Frantz Fanon, "yet murder men everywhere they find them, at the corner of every one of their own streets, in all the corners of the globe." That is how we felt, touring the revolutions. America, onetime precedent and promiser of liberation, was taking up the white man's burden, with anti-Communism as its *mission civilisatrice*. The official United States of America projected its demons onto foreign shores; anti-Americans did the same with our angels.

Which is probably why the May 1968 incandescence in Paris and Prague Spring, each electrifying in its own way, didn't rank as high as Third World revolutions for the late New Left: although Paris in particular filled the air with the ozone of impending revolution, it was neither sufficiently exotic nor charged with white-skin advanced-nation guilt, albeit more relevant to our actual circumstances. Periodically travelers came back from Europe with news that the New Left was international—was informally, in fact, a New International—and that Americans, released from obligations to Old Left parties, were at the center of it. My aforementioned friend at Bratislava wrote me from Rome in November 1967 that "the new generations (plus the particular alliances they make in their particular countries) are the (we hope) 'revolutionary class.' This is a class that *dramatically* cuts across national lines, we have more in common with the young Italians (etc.) than with say anybody except the young in America. . . ." French and West German radicals began to visit more often. News trickled in of Dutch Provos, of antiwar protests in Britain (where they were sometimes led by Americans) and Australia. Perhaps, if the French *gauchistes* had been able to unite with the workers to bring down de Gaulle in the glorious spring of 1968, we might in the end have rotated our axis of fascination from North-South to East-West.

But the war, if nothing else, took the focus away from the First World. Our passionate alliance with the profoundly other side was psychological balm; Vietnam and Cuba confirmed that we had been right all along to feel displaced at home. And not only because the Third World revolutionaries seemed (thanks to some reality, some arranged hospitality, and some suspension of disbelief) more civilized than the napalming would-be civilizers. They proved there were models of revolution other than the Soviet kind. And most of all they demonstrated that victims could be transfigured into victors; their success might rub off on First

World novices. They taught that small revolutionary bands could apparently—this is Tom Hayden's word—"paralyze" powers grown fat and lazy and uncomprehending. Just after returning to California, I read Che's *Memoirs of the Revolutionary War.* I was charmed and tickled by the revolutionaries' luck at the time of their landing in 1956. (They misread constellations, miscalculated their position, and could have been wiped out with a couple of helicopters. Seventy of the eighty-two who landed were quickly killed, wounded, or taken prisoner.) Their incompetence planted questions in my mind about what was to be learned from such a chancy victory . . . but such questions were quickly suspended. We had been trying to be tough-minded existentialists, committed to the movement more for the good fight than the triumph; I wore existentialist purity like a scarf of thorns. On the other hand, it was nice to know somebody, somewhere, could win.

And so "the Vietnamese" (as if there were no other Vietnamese but the NLF and Hanoi cadres), "the Cubans," Mozambicans, Angolans, Maoists, and the courageous, noble, quixotic ghost of Che were looking over our shoulders in the dramas of the late Sixties, as language shifted from "protest" to "resistance" and then to "revolution." To think we were "the NLF behind LBJ's lines" was, of course, the voice of pure fantasy, or pure wish: as if, once we practiced the patience (*not* the tactics) of guerrilla armies—once we created their kind of party or organized their kind of front—we might ourselves, one day, overcome. For now, that borrowed identity seemed to shine a pure light on us, our love and our hate. It preserved the drama of black hats and white hats by reversing them. It confirmed that we were worthy of being the enemies of the American state. To be at the wrong end of the big guns—it was how we had always known things were going to turn out.

FOUR
FORCING THE REVOLUTION

The New Left was a series of epiphanies.
> —Michael Rogin

We've got something going here and now we've just got to find out what it is.
> —A member of Columbia SDS, just after the seizure of a building and a dean, April 23, 1968

1968

THE POLITICS OF EXTREMITY

How to stop the war, or (as a growing segment of the New Left was putting it) make the revolution? If it wasn't clear what would work, it seemed clear to the New Left what wouldn't. "Having tried available channels and discovered them meaningless," Tom Hayden told the National Commission on the Causes and Prevention of Violence in October 1968, "having recognized that the establishment does not listen to public opinion—it does not care to listen to the New Left—the New Left was moving toward confrontation. The turning point, in my opinion, was October, 1967, when resistance became the official watchword of the antiwar movement."

"Available channels" having apparently failed, much of the New Left set out to dig its own trenches, or grave. Within antiwar circles, exponents of moderation pointed to growing numbers at mass rallies and argued that popular opinion was shifting: In November 1967, for example, 36 percent of the voters supported withdrawal from Vietnam on the San Francisco ballot, and 39 percent in Cambridge, Massachusetts. Always the militants felt the force of the rhetorical question: Is this the absolute best we can do for the Vietnamese? Superimposed on strategic hunches were tropisms. One impulse for confrontation came from the desperate feeling of having exhausted the procedures of conventional politics. A second line of radical thinking was that militancy could coax moderates along, and actually widen the antiwar coalition. A third was that the war was soon to be settled by the rational wing of the Establishment; radicals should therefore return to the issue that most requires radicals, the issue of race. The conclusions were the same: turn up the militancy. Beneath the blur of strategic intuitions, something else was stirring. In the spreading cross-hatch where the student movement and the counterculture intersected, a *youth* identity said, in effect: To be young and American is to have been betrayed; to be alive is to be enraged. The same demonstrations which were driven by strategic purpose were also insurgent youth culture's way of strutting its stuff, or, as it might have preferred to say, staking out room to breathe in an alien land. What resulted was an *unavailable* channel—the mirage of "the revolution."

What evolved from the blur of strategy and identity was a movement that was, in a sense, its own program. It did not merely want you to support a position; it wanted you to dive in, and the more total the immersion, the better. The link between feeling and action was a short fuse. Actions were undertaken—so it was commonly said—to "dramatize" convictions, and judged according to how they made the participants feel. There were actions which made you feel good ("highs") and actions which made you feel not so good ("bummers")—both terms borrowed from drug jargon. It was the immediate experience that counted most. To squeeze meaning out of (at best) ambiguous results was a large part of what a movement leader did. Even actions which made you feel not so good could be reinterpreted as momentary conquests of liberated space, exercises in "training" and "survival." Even a trial forced upon its unwilling defendants could be converted—if you were willing to hold the biased norms of the courtroom in contempt—to an exhibition of the youth movement's identity. These actions were the New Left's rituals, mirrors, festivals of self-recognition.

The "resistance" that first declared itself in Oakland and the Pentagon, expressing at one and the same time a fury against the war and a frantic joy at being itself, involved only a minority of the antiwar movement. Meanwhile, mass marches, student strikes, pickets, petitions, orderly sit-ins, and civil disobediences continued apace, and grew. But the militant sector grew steadily more prominent, partly because the turn to confrontation produced headlines. There unfolded a long-running action theater: theater of the whole. Its incandescent high points ran from Oakland and the Pentagon through Columbia University, the Chicago convention, San Francisco State, People's Park, Kent State, plus hundreds of local student strikes, sit-ins, confrontations, melees—clashes whose images still loom large in the collective memory of what "The Sixties" looked and sounded like. The landscape was cluttered with landmarks and watersheds. How many memories begin: "After Chicago . . ."; "After People's Park . . ." How many others are punctuated: "After Johnson took himself out of the race . . ."; "After the King assassination . . ."; "After Bobby Kennedy was killed . . ." It is scarcely movement people alone who remember the politics of the late Sixties as a succession of exclamation points.

One can see the late Sixties as a long unraveling, a fresh start, a tragicomic *Kulturkampf*, the overdue demolition of a fraudulent consensus, a failed upheaval, an unkept promise, a valiant effort at reforms camouflaged as revolution—and it was all of those. Whatever the image, the contending forces labored under a cloud of impending doom, or salvation, or both. Everything could be lost, everything could be gained. How is it possible to hazard a strictly political account of even the single apocalyptic year 1968 without casting at least a sidelong look at the surrounding culture of politics? On every side, extremity was the commonplace style. To Lyndon Johnson, who longed to establish himself as the deserving heir of Franklin Roosevelt, the war in Vietnam was nothing less than a crusade for freedom. His programs amounted to nothing less than a *war* on poverty, a *Great* Society. From Barry Goldwater's "Extremism in the pursuit of liberty is no vice" (the Republican Convention of 1964) to "Burn, baby, burn" (Watts, 1965), from "Eve of Destruction" (1965) to the Doors' "The End" (1967), from *Bonnie and Clyde* (1967) to "Today's Pig Is Tomorrow's Bacon" (the spring 1968 headline of a radical newspaper in Richmond, California), the rhetoric of showdown and recklessness prevailed. The end always lay near. The zeitgeist screamed until it was hoarse.

In that setting, the movement's rites became epiphanies. Confrontations were moments of truth, branded into memory, bisecting life into Time Before and Time After. We collected these ritual punctuations as moments when the shroud that normally covers everyday life was torn away and we stood face to face with the true significance of things. Each round was an approximation of apocalypse, in the original meaning: a revelation of the way things actually stand. The language of showdown, shootout, and faceoff tripped easily to movement lips, that of heroism, tragedy, cataclysm to pundits' typewriters and politicians' press conferences—on every side everything was written in portentous headlines. We dramatized ourselves while the whole of American political culture did the same: Richard Nixon trundled out "the new Nixon," and Hubert Humphrey, announcing his presidential candidacy three weeks after the assassination of Martin Luther King, burbled: "Here we are, in a spirit of dedication, happiness, the politics of purpose, and the politics of joy." Washington spoke of bringing Hanoi to its knees; we spoke of smashing the State, the State of smashing us.

To work out the meanings of the movement's rites was the calling that kept you busy during the boring meetings and factional disputes that hung heavy between phases of Armageddon. The sense of an identity bubbled up, an ideal of grand fusion between radical politics and counterculture—drugs, sex, rock 'n' roll, smash the State. The confrontation at the Democratic Convention in Chicago was the grand climax of this state of mind. Music drove it home. Martha and the Vandellas' exuberant 1964 "Dancing in the Street" was a piece of early Motown which white radicals found congenial, but by the summer of 1968 the more common anthem was the Rolling Stones' snarling "Street Fighting Man," without which no dance party was complete. Everyone missed the irony of Mick Jagger's lament that "in sleepy London town there's just no place for street fighting man"; during the Democratic Convention, Chicago's leading rock station, loyally counterinsurgent, refused to play the Stones' song, preferring the Beatles' newly released put-down, "Revolution," which cautioned: "If you go carrying pictures of Chairman Mao/You're not gonna make it with anyone anyhow."

The hip-radical identity coalesced in the underground newspapers, over a hundred of them in 1968, which hundreds of thousands, then millions, read. "THE YEAR OF THE COP" headlined the *San Francisco Express Times* on February 22, 1968; "THE YEAR OF THE BARRICADE," proclaimed the May 30 cover, trumpeting Paris and San Francisco State as "INSURRECTIONS OF THE WEEK." In 1968 came underground "comix," above all R. Crumb's "Mr. Natural" and Gilbert Shelton's "Fabulous Furry Freak Brothers," celebrating hip radicalism, popular culture, paranoia, and fantasy, and mocking them by turns. In the iconography of the underground press, *they* were uptight, uniformed, helmeted goons; *we* were loose, free, loving freaks. *They* harrumphed about law and order; *we* desecrated their temples. *They* threw tear gas canisters; *we* threw them back. *They* swung their clubs; *we* threw rocks and trashed windows. *They* brought up their battalions of National Guardsmen; *we* sang, "We Shall Not Be Moved." *They* put us on trial; *we* denounced "Amerika," with its Teutonic look, or "Amerikkka." Eventually, *they* fired, and *we* were wounded, killed. *We,* being young, were going to beat, or at least outlive, *them.*

SLEEPING DOGS

At the risk of belaboring the obvious: while the slogans and justifications were deceptively simple, the movement's motives were intricate. Even years after the fact, motives were tangled, perhaps impenetrably. The political and cultural situation of the late Sixties was so volatile that the results of actions were particularly hard to compute. Mild actions might permit mass slaughter on the other side of the world; violence on the streets might spark the McCarthy and Kennedy reform campaigns; an election campaign might lead to assassination. The road to the right result was paved with unintended consequences. History was beside itself with perverse turns. Still, there developed styles of thinking—or prayer—which might serve to guide, or rationalize, action. It was as if the Buddhist idea of "right action" had been imported from the mysterious East along with the incense and Nepalese hashish—that one should take action in the right spirit, without regard to consequence, and let the chips fall where they may.

In this murk, one theme resounded: the virtue of polarization. There was satisfaction in making the enemy reveal his true nature. This motif had been strong in the southern civil rights movement, even in the extravagant form of James Bevel's religious notion (above, p. 134) that you had to make the Devil show himself, had to bring out the Klan sheets hidden beneath the business suits, before the beloved community could take shape. Jerry Rubin set out another version of what became a New Left folk belief: "A movement cannot grow without repression. The Left needs an attack from the Right and the Center. Life is theater, and we are the guerrillas attacking the shrines of authority, from the priests and the holy dollar to the two-party system."

The particular version that haunted me, though, was Tom Hayden's. In June 1967, just before Drawing Boards, Hayden and I attended a *Liberation*-sponsored conference on antiwar strategy at the University of Chicago, with Dave Dellinger, Staughton Lynd, and Philip Berrigan among others. Even the militants had lacked for a strategy. Hayden and I left together. As we drove up the Outer Drive, Tom said our project now was to "arouse the sleeping dogs on the Right."

It would take confrontation, disruption, Tom went on. If and only if the country polarized sharply enough, the war would have to end. The elites would insist. The forces of rationality, weak and sleepy though they were, would attend to the barks, wake up, wise up. As Hayden recreates his 1968 thinking, years later: "Since the country, provably, has no soul that is operational, no conscience that works, only a kind of tattered remnant of a democratic tradition that doesn't prevail when the chips are down—given that, then you have to make a cold calculation . . . to raise the internal cost to such a high level that those decision-makers who only deal in cost-effectiveness terms will have to get out of Vietnam. . . . The cost in terms of internal disruption, generational conflict, choking off the number of reliable soldiers, the number of willing taxpayers—just make a list of everything they need to fight the war, and calculate what you can take away from them." The movement was "no longer the beloved community," as Hayden put it. The idea was now to "figure out what cost we can impose" upon the "heartless, cost-calculating decision-makers." It was most certainly not—in his tendentious description of the alternative—to become "obsessed with finding ways to make the antiwar cause respectable to the editors of *The New York Times*."

Hayden was not alone in thinking like a high commander; this was close to the strategic idea of "causing chaos" that Frank Bardacke was to articulate after Stop the Draft Week (above, p. 254). If "revolutionary" activities were necessary to bring about a "reformist" goal, so be it. Hadn't polarization in the South led, in the end, to civil rights laws? In movement rhetoric, the Mason-Dixon Line had become the Canadian border; the Pentagon was the Ku Klux Klan with napalm. Radicals who felt this way didn't appreciate the difference: the civil rights laws had presupposed a national moral consensus, but there was no such agreement on the wrongs of the Vietnam war. Movements like generals mislearn lessons and refight old battles; if Dean Rusk thought Vietnam was Munich, much of the movement thought Chicago was Mississippi—or the early days of Nazi Germany. Hayden was strategic, but at least equally moralistic: like others in the movement, he was obsessed by a passion not to be like "the good Germans." "I guess I thought the best of the good Germans were probably people who in their time were working on parliamentary reform, trying to keep their jobs, trying to keep their family and not make too many waves . . . but didn't see the big picture, that there was no possibility of peaceful reform." Left to itself, the war, he thought, would evolve toward genocide, and the government would have to crush the Left.

There was a link missing in the logic—for if social democrats and Communists had cooperated before 1933, they might have kept Hitler from coming to power. In fact, the German Communists had said *"nach Hitler uns"*—"after Hitler, ourselves"—thereby guaranteeing their destruction. But in 1968, desperation spoke louder than logic. If repression was coming anyway, then the risks of confrontation seemed beside the point. In the combat mood that came to dominate the movement, to talk about risks was to capitulate, period. As soon as the choice was framed as a choice between giving in to fear and defying it, then each ritual event was framed as a test of personal commitment. The outcome was foreordained: Most activists discovered a point beyond which they would not go, while at each stage a critical mass swallowed its fear and declared full speed ahead. The reform-through-polarization motif had another unintended consequence: it drew a sharp line between planners and troops. Planners were more apt to have a strategic reason for sacrifice, while the rank and file, who had to do most of the sacrificing, were correspondingly less devoted to it.

Whole movements have their demons. First in the South, then in the Newark ERAP project, Hayden, for one, had learned the lesson that the empowerment of the weak required a confrontation with enemies— sitting-in at the courthouse, picketing the landlord. Now, in effect, he was extrapolating to the antiwar movement. But at a perhaps deeper level, his sleeping dog notion was at the service of a motive he called "existential." Years later he put it to me this way: "Not being able to be Vietnamese—those people were taking the brunt of the punishment—the least one could do would be to stand in front of the war machine . . . to the extent possible. I guess not going as far as suicide, but trying to find some way to confront it where you would definitely pay a price, but the larger result would be that the system would pay a price for inflicting that punishment on you.*

"I would not have done something simply on existential grounds," Hayden insists. "That would have been total romanticism." He draws a distinction between his 1968 stance and a different idea that was also in the air in the late Sixties: the wealthy man's son's idea that social rebirth and the shedding of class privilege came through rebellion. (One fellow traveler of the Motherfuckers put it this way: "You don't begin to be free until your own blood is being shed at the end of a baton.") "I was drawn to do things that were romantic but could also have a rationale to them," Hayden says. "Romantic in the sense that I think it is noble to stand up against an evil, and that we don't get many opportunities in the normal course of life to do anything that's noble at all. But without a purpose or plan or strategy, it would be self-serving or foolish." He pauses, reflects. "To what extent it was a rationalization as opposed to rational is another question. It was probably sometimes a rationalization." Hayden was trying to merge "soul" with "strategy"—a typical movement stretch.

VARIETIES OF ANTIWAR EXPERIENCE

Strategies always exist in relation to other strategies. Confrontation, then, in relation to what?

Flowing from the pacifist tradition were various forms of civil disobedience. Draft resistance, which started in earnest in 1967, continued until President Nixon phased out the draft in 1972–73. Draft card burnings and turn-ins were regular events, enraging the flag-wavers and inspiring even those in the movement who were doubtful about the utility of the tactic. Some 5,000 men turned in their cards in public, and many more did so without fanfare. Over 200,000 were accused of draft offenses, more than 25,000 were indicted, of whom 8,750 were convicted and 4,000 were sentenced to prison. (Most won parole after six to twelve months behind bars; some served four or five years.) More than 10,000 went underground; many fled via underground railroads to Canada and elsewhere. Semiorganized networks passed the resisters, and armed-forces deserters, from one safe place to another. A quarter of a million never registered in the first place. One hundred seventy-two thousand successfully ran the gauntlet of investigation to become conscientious objectors.

*There is an echo here of Mario Savio's famous words: "There is a time when the operation of the machine becomes so odious, makes you so sick at heart, that you can't take part; you can't even passively take part, and you've got to put your bodies upon the gears and upon the wheels, upon the levers, upon all the apparatus and you've got to make it stop. And you've got to indicate to the people who run it, to the people who own it, that unless you're free, the machine will be prevented from working at all." Note that both these rationales for quasi-crucifixion were uttered by young men raised in Catholic homes.

Draft resistance was also the hub for support activities from those ineligible for the draft. In December 1967, Dr. Benjamin Spock, the Reverend William Sloane Coffin, Marcus Raskin, Mitchell Goodman, and Michael Ferber were indicted for "counselling, aiding and abetting" draft resistance; many supporters over draft age followed in their wake. "Girls Say Yes to Men Who Say No" was a movement slogan that later embarrassed and angered the proto-feminists of the New Left, but in 1968, when the women's movement was just aborning, it accurately registered the difficulties women faced when they insisted on participating. There was also what Francine du Plessix Gray called "the ultra-resistance," a wave of more aggressive and clandestine actions against property: the pouring of blood and paint onto draft records; burning them with homemade napalm; destroying files of Dow Chemical and General Electric, companies actively engaged in the war effort. Most of these incidents were organized by radical priests and nuns, starting with Father Philip Berrigan and three colleagues a few days after Stop the Draft Week and the Pentagon. Some submitted to trial and imprisonment; some went underground. Thousands of young men owed their de facto draft exemptions to sorties that destroyed their files. The larger antiwar movement greatly admired this direct-action derring-do, but mostly from outside.

The Christian-inspired witness of the late Sixties was crisscrossed by regular episodes of antiwar normality: peaceable assemblies, striving for the utmost legality, accepting of the rules laid down by authorities, trying to cement maximum coalitions. The organizers of these events dutifully applied for parade permits, worked out routes in negotiations with the police, encouraged American and discouraged Vietcong flags. They went out of their way to keep from alienating unionists or frightening away the mothers who brought their tots in strollers. The events borrowed from established dramaturgy: they began with parades, a patriotic tradition, and ended with platform speakers. The point was obvious: to swell the ranks, to impress upon public officials and the media the fact that the movement was growing larger and broader. It was no mean feat to patch together the coalitions of pacifists, Trotskyists, Communists, and freelance radicals who created the occasions for standing up to be counted.

These events were, in effect, lobbies in the streets. Much of the organizers' energy, accordingly, went to assembling the proper cast of speakers to represent actual and hypothetical constituent groups. Dr. Spock, for example, could speak to suburban parents; Martin Luther King could hope to reactivate the moral coalition of the civil rights movement. Much energy, too, went to thrashing out the precise demands which the demonstration would stand for. Would it be "unconditional negotiations," a slogan popular in 1965 and 1966, whatever it meant, exactly—except, perhaps, a signal to Lyndon Johnson that he should not dismiss the peace movement's "nervous nellies" quite so cavalierly? A halt to the bombing of North Vietnam—a demand adopted by Johnson at certain pivotal moments, but leaving unopposed the furious bombardment of the South Vietnamese countryside, not to mention the expeditionary force of a half-million American troops? Increasingly the demand for unconditional withdrawal came from more than the New Left. For example, three to five thousand largely middle-class women marched in Washington on January 15, 1968, calling for immediate withdrawal, cosponsored by such mainstream groups as the YWCA and the National Council of Jewish Women along with Women Strike for Peace. The movement's center moved leftward.

The grand total of protesters grew steadily from 1965 into the early Seventies. Even the October 1967 siege of the Pentagon by a thousand or so militants was, numerically speaking, a sideshow to the tranquil assembly of fifty or a hundred thousand at the Lincoln Memorial the same day. Huge, orderly antiwar mobilizations took place twice a year, usually in New York and San Francisco, supplemented by local versions; there were antiwar candidates to support, newspaper ads to sign, lobbying expeditions, antiwar propositions to put on local ballots. On April 26, 1968, up to a million college and high school students took part in a national student strike. Profuse and varied were the efforts to give the antiwar movement a presence in common American life, from the tough-talking militance of draft-resistance organizers in working-class communities to the plainspoken work of antiwar workers in unions, town meetings, local party caucuses, and in the heart of the military itself. Truly the movement against the Vietnam war was a broad-based antiwar mobilization of a sort rarely if ever before seen in the blood-soaked history of the world.*

In the eyes of the militants, the millions who poured into the parades hoping to see their bodies count against the bloodshed mattered less than the body count in Vietnam piling up even faster. The peaceful demonstrations *had been done;* they were losing wagers on the lingering possibility that normal politics might still matter. Around SDS, it became chic to call the plodding marchers "peace creeps," turning around a taunt that American Nazis had thrown at SDS. Early on, even Carl Oglesby, no fan of the barricades, sneered at the "wilderness of warmed-over speeches and increasingly irrelevant demonstrations." Public opinion, as registered in polls, turned steadily against Johnson, although measuring it was a tricky business, it depended on exactly what question was asked. The percentages who thought getting into the war had been a "mistake" leaped from 32 percent in February 1967 to 46 percent in October, then

---

*At a conference on Vietnam in 1983 I went out on a limb and called the movement against the Vietnam war the most successful antiwar movement in the history of the world, whereupon Roger Hilsman, formerly President Kennedy's assistant secretary of state for Far Eastern affairs, remarked to me that there had been, in fact, one still more successful: the Bolshevik Revolution. Not strictly speaking an antiwar movement, of course, but he had a point.

inched up to 49 percent in April 1968, and kept rising from there. But huge majorities were still against withdrawal, and sentiment also grew for *harsher* measures. Congress kept passing war appropriations, the troop count passed a half-million, the bombs streamed down, and Lyndon Johnson gave no sign of reconsidering his commitment to the killing. Vice President Hubert H. Humphrey, the fallen angel of Cold War liberalism, told an audience of military suppliers that the Pentagon marchers were "incredibly ridiculous," that they gave aid and comfort to the enemy; and told the American embassy staff in Saigon that the Vietnam war stood in the line of Valley Forge and Yorktown and Dunkirk, that Vietnam would be "marked as the place where the family of man has gained the time it needed to finally break through to a new era of hope and human development and justice. . . . This is our great adventure—and a wonderful one it is!"

THE LOYAL OPPOSITION

Gadfly liberals thought ahead. In the fall of 1967, Allard Lowenstein tried to recruit an antiwar standard-bearer for a Dump Johnson movement. But even liberal senators who deplored escalation—Frank Church of Idaho, George McGovern of South Dakota, Robert Kennedy of New York—were lukewarm, at best, about challenging the incumbent President in the upcoming primaries. There was no precedent for a successful run of that sort. No less a liberal eminence than the ADA's Joseph Rauh preferred a campaign for a peace plank in the 1968 Democratic platform. In the person of its reluctant leaders, liberalism was imprisoned: by appreciation for Johnson's Great Society; by timidity and decorum; by fear of failure. They preferred the problems of insiders to the problems of outsiders; during the Eisenhower years they had felt like exiles, and now that they had come in from the cold, they didn't want to go back there again.

And then suddenly it seemed that liberalism might be coming back for its seventh or eighth life. The collapse of the national third-party option at the National Conference for New Politics left a clear field for liberals who wanted to work against the war where they were comfortable, within the Democratic Party. Lowenstein and like-minded liberals worked feverishly to stir up the juices of antiwar Democrats, building on the party's old Stevenson base—ADA, the California Democratic Council, New York Reform Democrats. On November 30, 1967, Senator Eugene McCarthy of Minnesota, impressed by the widening base of respectable activists, announced he was running for President against Johnson and against the war. Lowenstein's vision of disinterested citizens pushing American politics to its limit corresponded to McCarthy's ideal of a high-minded polis, the small-r republican village which had been undermined by corporate, presidential, Pentagoned America.

The hard-driving Lowenstein had a knack for galvanizing bright, competent, earnest, well-placed, go-getting young men and women—student government presidents, college newspaper editors, seminarians, Peace Corps returnees. By upbringing, training, and ambition, these children of affluence were *winners*. They had been raised and schooled to believe in the promise of America and they hated the war partly because it meant that the object of their affections, the system that rewarded their proficiency, was damaged goods. They were the inheritors of the vision of a moral America, and they did not want their moral capital squandered. Jeremy Larner, a McCarthy speechwriter, described them as "American optimists at heart: . . . the 'A' students in their high schools and colleges. Politically they were inclined to some romanticization of the NLF, Ché Guevara, and Malcolm X. But whether they came with beards to shave or not, these were kids who reacted against the violent anti-Americanism of the New Left, whom they far outnumbered. Though they hated the war and the draft, they still believed that America could be beautiful—if it would live up to its own principles." They were the children the liberal generation had always wanted, the heirs James Wechsler (face to face with Jack Kerouac in 1958) had despaired of: a "government in exile," McCarthy called them. They included the children of influentials, even high administration officials: included, in fact, McCarthy's own children, especially his daughter Mary, who was active in the antiwar movement at Radcliffe and pressured him for months, in the words of journalists, "not to go down in history as one of those who had supported Lyndon Johnson and the war." Unswayed by the siren song of LSD, disaffected by cultural revolution, these straight insurgents wanted to rescue their country from its emergency. In style and method they resembled activists of the nascent SDS and groups like Tocsin in the early Sixties—one of Lowenstein's key allies, Curtis Gans, was an early SDSer-turned-ADAer, in fact. They flashed the antiwar V long past the time, in 1968 and 1969, when their New Left counterparts had switched to the clenched fist.

The war crashed down upon these Competent Young Adults as it did upon the New Left. Self-interest wasn't the point, at least in any pure sense: as good students they were deferred from the draft. With Jack Kennedy murdered, they had no hero to bind them; yet in memories of an idealized Camelot they had an image of a recent Golden Age to vivify the promise of liberalism. In the vulgarities and bellicosity of Lyndon Johnson they beheld the upstart, the usurping betrayer of their dead hero's grace and style. (Their mood thus fueled the 1966 popularity of Barbara Garson's play *Macbird,* in which Johnson played murderous Macbeth to Kennedy's martyred Duncan.) For the New Left leadership, swooping rapidly leftward from 1965 on, had left a yawning vacuum to its immediate right. As Dylan and the Rolling Stones and the Doors roared toward an apparent counterculture-radical crossroads, there remained the thoughtful and perturbed students inspired by the Beatles and Beach Boys and Simon and Garfunkel. These wistful pragmatists were, in Larner's words, "terribly grateful to have a chance to do something real"—so grateful they were willing to shave and dress up: "Clean for Gene."

No one roused the liberal will more than Allard Lowenstein. Lowenstein was the quintessential Cold War liberal activist.* Elected president of the National Student Association in 1950 with a rousing speech supporting the American intervention in Korea, he was anti-Franco, antiapartheid, a mover and shaker on many fronts. In 1963–64 he had thought up the Mississippi Freedom Ballot and (with Bob Moses) Freedom Summer, only to watch the movement drift off to his Left; he campaigned against SNCC's decision to take help from the National Lawyers Guild (which refused to exclude supporters of the Communist Party), only to be rebuffed. Now he was on the move making the war issue safe for liberalism, crisscrossing the country in search of support, drafting a critical letter to Johnson from a hundred student-body presidents here, prodding divinity students to demand changes in the draft law there. Like McCarthy and Robert Kennedy he thought the war mistaken and unwinnable but opposed complete withdrawal and favored "de-escalation," negotiations, and some sort of power-sharing arrangement. He worried about what he called the New Left's "new politics of alienation," about its misapplication of southern-style direct action to the infinitely more difficult task of creating a winning national reform program. He feared that without a compelling channel into the political system, a whole generation would end up having to choose—in the words of Harvard's Greg Craig, a Lowenstein ally—"between Staughton Lynd and Lyndon Johnson." "There's a lot of room for innovation within the democratic system," Lowenstein told *The Wall Street Journal* in the fall of 1967, "but the general strain of liberalism in this country is passive. . . . This is dangerous because it leaves it up to the radicals to act."

But if Senator Eugene McCarthy was the white knight of the loyal opposition, it was a strange life indeed liberalism was coming back to. Part of what made the senator attractive to the Concerned Young Adults was that he was a *reluctant* crusader. Very much the intellectual ironist, antibombastic to the core, the only published poet in the U.S. Senate,

---

*Contrary to insinuations, there is no good evidence Lowenstein was on the Central Intelligence Agency's voluminous payroll. True, over the years he kept the loyalty of top NSA alumni and their liberal activist ilk, including those who were "witting" to the CIA's longtime subsidy of the NSA's international division, as revealed by *Ramparts* magazine in 1967. The conspiracy-mongers who twist facts as they prowl for evidence of subsidy are asking the wrong question, assuming as they do that anti-Communism has to be bought, that it is not a passion. What is important is that Lowenstein fervently believed in the resilience of the American political system, and with equal fervor feared that those more radical than he would prevail.

McCarthy was given to astringency, as in this line from his 1967 "Lament of an Aging Politician": "Stubbornness and penicillin hold/the aged above me." His bons mots ran in the same key; asked to comment on Michigan governor George Romney's remark that the army had "brainwashed" him in Vietnam—a remark which knocked Romney out of the running for the Republican nomination—McCarthy quipped, "I think in that case a light rinse would have been sufficient." (McCarthy's press aides prevailed upon reporters not to quote him.) In the eyes of the thousands of young activists who flooded into New Hampshire and Wisconsin, McCarthy resembled some ideally elegant version of themselves, the witty outsider ill-at-ease in politics. Some had fond memories of his stirring nominating speech for Adlai Stevenson at the 1960 Democratic Convention—"Do not turn your back upon this man!"—not knowing what Kennedy supporters could never forget: that he had ended up supporting Lyndon Johnson against Jack Kennedy, and stayed close enough to Johnson to be a frontrunner for vice presidential running-mate in 1964 up to the last minute, when Johnson rewarded Humphrey for his service in the Atlantic City–Mississippi credentials fight.

To career liberals like Lowenstein, McCarthy's was a most diffident crusade. The candidate damned the war but hung back. He was noble about the problem of race but squeamish about campaigning in the ghettos and vague about what could be done to redress inequality; in fact, he had voted only unevenly liberal in the Senate, had made few waves there. He showed no enthusiasm for the sweaty stuff of campaigning; he thought gladhanding smacked of demagoguery. When Martin Luther King was assassinated he did not speak out in grief and anguish; he did not speak out at all. He mused about the curses and ironies of power more than he hungered for it. He did not cultivate the press. He did not cultivate even his own campaign workers. Johnson supporters said McCarthy was still nursing resentment at the way Johnson had humiliated him by dangling the vice presidency before him at Atlantic City; and perhaps there was something to the suspicion that McCarthy's motives for running were more complicated than unvarnished idealism.

And yet for all his wryness and distance, McCarthy's unorthodox campaigners remained devoted. The newsworthy "Clean for Gene" commandos who caravanned into the early state primaries from a hundred campuses (not least the Ivy League) smelled victory. They were willing to be polite and patient. In New Hampshire, the shaved and spiffed-up ones went door to door (three visits to each house, plus two phone calls), while the hairier ones stayed back at headquarters stuffing envelopes. They noted the excitement McCarthy kindled among suburban reformers, and were not noticeably bothered by the lack of response their candidate stimulated among the working class. In hawkish New Hampshire there wasn't much of a working class anyway.

TET   At the start of the Vietnamese New Year, Tet, on the last day of
———   January 1968, the Tet offensive erupted, and overnight the
imagery of the war had to be radically redrawn.

For years the Johnson administration had been reassuring the public
that there was light at the end of the proverbial tunnel. Meanwhile, night
after night for hundreds of nights, the newspapers had described and the
television cameras had shown American troops slogging through treacherous countryside, shooting, shot at, searching and destroying, "pacifying."
It proved disconcerting to people schooled in the World War II style of
warfare that American advances into the countryside could not be neatly
marked off on the map, that territory secured during the day reverted to
the NLF at night; but at least the Americans and their Saigon allies held
the cities, and Pentagon spokesmen could point to the mounting body
counts of enemy dead, which the media dutifully relayed as signs of
progress. Surely the Vietcong were withering away.

Suddenly, the Tet cease-fire was shattered, and for days which
stretched into weeks images without precedent seized the small screen:
gunfire and rockets bursting in Saigon and all other major cities and
provincial capitals; NLF commandos invading the U.S. embassy grounds,
killing GI guards, seizing Saigon's major radio station, assaulting the
presidential palace, attacking major American bases, highways, police
stations, prisons. Communist forces took the old capital of Hué and
then—prolonging the shock—held it for twenty-five days; U.S. Marines
and Saigon troops recaptured the city only at the cost of an air and artillery
bombardment that killed 5,000 Communist troops as well as an untold
number of civilians, while 150 Marines and 400 Saigon troops died as
well. (Then the Americans unearthed mass graves: 3,000 people had been
killed by the NLF as Saigon collaborators. Then the Saigon forces who
retook the city reciprocated by assassinating suspected *Communist* allies.)
Battlefield death was concentrated as never before: 2,000 American
fatalities, 4,000 Saigon Vietnamese, in a single month. Therefore
Communist atrocities made less of an impression than the fact that the
Communists had the capacity to inflict them.

To the NLF leadership, as it turned out, the Tet offensive was far from
a glorious military success. Their losses in both regular troops and
political cadres were immense: so much so, in fact, that the Southern-
based NLF never recovered its strength. (Then the survivors were
decimated by the CIA's "Operation Phoenix" program for assassinating
cadres. Tet and Phoenix together meant that the NLF command was outnumbered by Northerners for the duration of the war, whence whatever

chance they had of retaining Southern autonomy in a reunified Vietnam was crushed.) After the war, a top North Vietnamese general told the reporter Stanley Karnow: "In all honesty, we didn't achieve our main objective [in the Tet offensive], which was to spur uprisings throughout the south. Still, we inflicted heavy casualties on the Americans and their puppets, and that was a big gain for us. As for making an impact in the United States, it had not been our intention—but it turned out to be a fortunate result." The NLF and North Vietnamese seemed to be every-where they weren't supposed to be, all at once. General William West-moreland stood square-jawed before the television cameras to assure the public that the Communists' "well-laid plans went afoul," but American politics was not impressed.

Instead, the country went into shock. Tremors jolted the pragmatic case for the war, for in American politics there is no more drastic criticism to be made of a policy, whatever its moral dubiousness, than that it proves conspicuously ineffective. Tremors jolted the moral side too, for no more devastating criticism can be made of a president, whatever his policies, than that he lies. The war had been marketed at home, after all, as a victory waiting to happen. National leaders had declared that the national fate was tied to Vietnam, little calculating that the blood tie went both ways. A nation that commits itself to myth is traumatized when reality bursts through—in living color. American politics was now hostage to events on the other side of the world. Where the movement's armies of the night had failed to turn American policy, now the black-pajama'd armies had shunted the political initiative to the doubters. Newscasters were visibly shaken. "What the hell is going on?" asked Walter Cronkite when he heard about the offensive. "I thought we were winning this war." In a New Hampshire campaign speech, Senator Eugene McCarthy acidly summarized the prevailing liberal reaction to Tet:

> In 1963, we were told that we were winning the war. In 1964, we were told we were winning the war. In 1964, we were told the corner was being turned. In 1965, we were told the enemy was being brought to its knees. In 1966, in 1967, and now again in 1968, we hear the same hollow claims of programs and victory. For the fact is that the enemy is bolder than ever, while we must steadily enlarge our own commitment. The Democratic Party in 1964 promised "no wider war." Yet the war is getting wider every month. Only a few months ago we were told that 65 per cent of the population was secure. Now we know that even the American Embassy is not secure.

For months Robert Kennedy had been agonizing whether to jump into the race against Johnson. In the best of all possible timetables, 1972 looked like his year. This time around, he and the older family advisers were afraid he would be dismissed for fighting a grudge match against the usurper of the family throne. They doubted he could garner the support of mainstream politicians. Nor were they impressed by the electoral value of volunteers, however clean-cut. Kennedy's more rambunctious friends and staff members urged him to get out ahead of the country's antiwar upsurge, yet Kennedy himself seemed bent on personifying liberalism's crisis of hesitation. He was disinclined to take the chance. But Tet provoked him into giving his strongest speech yet against the war. "Our enemy," he said, "savagely striking at will across all of South Vietnam, has finally shattered the mask of official illusion with which we have concealed our true circumstances, even from ourselves."

Tet, in short, breathed life into languishing American liberalism— just as it deflated Lyndon Johnson. In the six weeks following the first Tet attacks, Johnson's overall approval ratings plunged from 48 percent to 36 percent, and approval of his handling of the war from 40 percent to 26 percent. The bloodiness of the war sank in as never before: Network footage of civilian casualties and urban destruction jumped almost fivefold during the two months of Tet fighting, footage of military casualties almost threefold. The chief of South Vietnam's national police held his gun to a prisoner's head and shot him to death—in front of an Associated Press photographer and an NBC cameraman; the picture landed on many an American front page. Journalists hitherto reluctant to depart from Washington's conventional wisdom suddenly viewed the war with alarm. "What is the end that justifies this slaughter?" cried James Reston of *The New York Times* on February 7. "How will we save Vietnam if we destroy it in the battle?" No less a personage than Walter Cronkite got up from behind his desk, flew an inspection tour to Vietnam, and then, in a half-hour CBS special report that aired on February 27, declared that the only "realistic, if unsatisfactory" conclusion was that "we are mired in stalemate" and that "the only rational way out" was "to negotiate not as victors, but as an honorable people who lived up to their pledge to defend democracy and did the best they could." *Time, Newsweek,* the *New York Post,* the *St. Louis Post-Dispatch,* and no less a beacon of respectable opinion than *The Wall Street Journal* chimed in to like effect, but no one resonated like Cronkite, who even now stoutly maintained that the war was about "defending democracy." Presidential press secretary George Christian said later that when Cronkite spoke, "the shock waves rolled through government."

Tet reverberated through the rest of the country too, and the dominoes fell on Washington. On March 10, *The New York Times* reported that the military was asking for 206,000 more troops to supplement the 510,000 already in Vietnam—and that the administration was divided about whether to supply them. On March 12, the New Hampshire returns, counting Republican crossovers, gave McCarthy 28,791 votes to Johnson's 29,021—a margin of 230 votes for a sitting president seeking his party's renomination. Reporters and McCarthy campaigners alike failed to make much of a poll showing that 60 percent of these McCarthy voters wanted *more* military action in Vietnam, not less. Indeed, just after the first Tet attack, the national percentage of self-described hawks *rose* from 56 percent to 60 percent against a mere 24 percent who called themselves doves. Still, once the citizenry had rallied round the flag, Johnson had no easy move to keep them rallied. Escalation would cost more, run the risk of war with China, and fuel the right's appetite for victory. With the administration racked by debate, Johnson hunkered down and said little. In March, the percentage of hawks plummeted to 41 percent, doves soared to 42 percent. American opinion was volatile, to put it mildly. What was clearly discredited was Johnson's attempt to manage the war without calling up the reserves, declaring war, or pulling out one or another military stop. If there was to be war, Americans wanted to win it.

Four days later, having decided the Democrats were already so deeply split he couldn't be blamed for splitting them, Robert Kennedy declared his own candidacy for the presidential nomination. If the timing of his announcement troubled some of his supporters and enraged McCarthy's, well, politics was a cruel game, and let the memoirists take the hindmost.

"A GIANT STAMPEDE"

In the view from the top, the crisis was military and political and economic all at once. Lyndon Johnson, riding the crest of the boom, had gambled that he could war in Vietnam and on poverty at the same time. To win the glory of completing the New Deal, he refused to trim back his Great Society to pay for a war he imagined to be an extension of the New Deal abroad. (When, in 1965, Johnson tried to quiet Ho Chi Minh by offering him a billion-dollar Mekong Delta development program patterned after the Tennessee Valley Authority, he couldn't for the life of him fathom why this tinhorn dictator was denying him the chance to show himself even more benign than FDR. After all, *Johnson* had once parlayed a Texas dam into supreme power in the U.S. Senate. Why couldn't Ho take the hint?) Floating on cornucopian currents, Johnson had taken the easy way out in 1966, claimed the Vietnam war would cost $10 billion in fiscal year 1967 (on the assumption the war would end by June 30, 1967!), and gone into deficit financing—for that year, in fact, the war cost *$20* billion. In 1967 Johnson had to add on a 10 percent tax surcharge. How often could he resort to that sort of squeeze?

The premise of plenitude was just as naïve for Lyndon Johnson as for Arlo Guthrie's Alice's Restaurant. The concealed bill for the war began to come due in the form of inflation. The balance of payments deficit swelled. Periodic reports of peace feelers sent the stock market *up*. With news of impending increases in the military budget, the dollar started to quiver in the international market. Speculators flocked to gold. Rumors flew that the United States would be forced to devalue the dollar. The day Robert Kennedy announced his candidacy, the London gold market had to close in order to stanch the drain on American reserves.

Lyndon Johnson, who lived for gratitude, beheld his world crumbling. If Vietnam were not bad enough, North Korea had captured an American intelligence ship, the *Pueblo*. He was widely seen as a liar and, just as bad, a failure. He had given his all for paternalistic liberalism—his strategy for winning the gratitude of the masses since the Thirties—but no one appreciated the largesse. He had delivered the Civil Rights Acts of 1964 and 1965, intoning "We Shall Overcome," but the blacks, ingrates all, had turned to riot. His dream of presiding over an international Great Society was shattered. He had fought for aid to education, only to have students everywhere chant what he called "that horrible song": "Hey, hey, LBJ, how many kids did you kill today?" His family and aides were distressed by the pickets. He had to alter his travel plans at the last minute, even cancel speeches. He could avoid demonstrations only by speaking on military bases. "I was being forced over the edge by rioting blacks, demonstrating students, marching welfare mothers, squawking professors, and hysterical reporters," he told Doris Kearns. "And then the final straw. The thing I feared from the first day of my Presidency was actually coming true. Robert Kennedy had openly announced his intention to reclaim the throne in the memory of his brother. And the American people, swayed by the magic of the name, were dancing in the streets. The whole situation was unbearable for me. . . . I felt that I was being chased on all sides by a giant stampede coming at me from all directions."

Johnson's private demons demanded a high order of devotion; when his acts of beneficence were not rewarded by obedience, he resorted to punishment. The infinite love he needed was precisely what he could not compel: from neither blacks nor students nor intellectuals nor Ho Chi Minh. He thought, with some reason, that the media and the snotty Ivy League kids sneered at him because he sounded like a hick, not a Kennedy. But quirks of personal history aside, there was an ideological meaning to Johnson's crisis. He had catered to the Right, in Vietnam, while his popularity eroded to his Left; and in the end he could not give the Right the victory he had promised them. It was left to Lyndon Johnson to play out the impossible legacy of Cold War liberalism, to stretch its self-contradictory formulas to the breaking point.

In times of national crisis, the pragmatism of America's managers is formidable. The technocrat Robert McNamara had lost heart for the war. On March 1, 1968, Johnson replaced him with Clark Clifford, a canny high-priced Washington lawyer and an insider's insider since the Truman years. As Johnson sank into self-pity and paranoia about reporters and students and blacks, Clifford, hitherto no dove, brought bad news. The war of attrition was "hopeless." Instead of signing on to Johnson's war scenario, Clifford told him in late March that among his "friends in business and the law across the land," men who had supported the war until a few months ago, "there has been a tremendous erosion of support [for the war]. . . . [T]hese men now feel that we are in a hopeless bog. The idea of going deeper into the bog strikes them as mad. They want to see us get out of it. These are leaders of opinion in their communities. What they believe is sooner or later believed by many other people. It would be very difficult—I believe it would be impossible—for the President to maintain public support for the war without the support of these men." Johnson's most trusted counselors were telling him he had to do something dramatic to capture the "Peace with Honor" vote or he would be clobbered in the primaries.

Clifford thought Johnson "needed some stiff medicine," which could only be delivered by the bluest of blue-ribbon experts, men whose credentials established them as virtual proprietors of American foreign policy. And so he persuaded the President to sit down with the informal advisory group known as the Wise Men, a Who's Who of the elite of the Truman, Eisenhower, Kennedy, and Johnson administrations, who had been meeting periodically since July 1965 and blessing Johnson's war strategy: Dean Acheson, George Ball, McGeorge Bundy, C. Douglas Dillon, Cyrus Vance, Arthur Dean, John McCloy, General Omar Bradley, General Matthew Ridgeway, General Maxwell Taylor, Robert Murphy, Henry Cabot Lodge, Abe Fortas, and Arthur Goldberg. These impeccably trustworthy gentlemen, not a scruffy student or black radical or even a Robert Kennedy or Gene McCarthy devotee in the crowd, were troubled by America's economic decline. They hated to see the country jeopardize its Atlantic alliance in pursuit of an apparently hallucinatory victory across the Pacific. They met in the White House and heard bad news from middle-level government officials, and they believed it: Saigon was corrupt and overwhelmed, the war was going badly, there were many more Vietcong than they had been led to believe. Cyrus Vance, Johnson's deputy secretary of defense, later described the Wise Men's wisdom: "We were weighing not only what was happening in Vietnam, but the social and political effects in the United States, the impact on the U.S. economy, the attitude of other nations. The divisiveness in the country was growing with such acuteness that it was threatening to tear the United States apart." They knew a bad investment when they saw one, and they hated throwing good money after bad.

The Wise Men read Johnson the riot act. It wasn't unanimous, George Ball said later, but the "general sentiment" was, "Look, this thing is hopeless, you'd better begin to de-escalate and get out." Johnson looked "shocked." "The meeting with the Wise Men served the purpose that I hoped it would," Clifford said later. "It really shook the president."

The antiwar movement, had it known, might have felt mightily vindicated. Just a few months earlier, Frank Bardacke had written that "if we can actually convince them that we can cause chaos in this country as long as the war continues, . . . [w]e may have even stumbled on a strategy that could end the war." Tom Hayden's sleeping dogs had awakened, all right. Thanks to the backlash against blacks at least as much as to the antiwar upsurge, the loudest of the dogs was named George C. Wallace. Wallace was in the habit of saying things like, "If any demonstrator lies down in front of my car when I'm President, that'll be the last car he lays down in front of." Demonstrators and hippies, he said, should be "drug before the courts by the hair of their heads and thrown under a good strong jail." On the ballot as a third-party candidate, Wallace was drawing 15 percent in the polls, and rising.

Johnson later maintained he had toyed for months with backing out of the race. On March 28, the Wise Men confirmed his worst fears. Johnson's speech three nights later, March 31, was pure electricity. He dampened the war, as the Wise Men had urged. He declared a halt to the bombing above the 20th parallel, and turned down the request for 206,000 new American troops. He spoke of beefing up the South Vietnamese army—what the next President would call "Vietnamization," and the antiwar movement would call "changing the color of the bodies." And then, declaring that "this country's ultimate strength lies in the unity of our people," that "there is division in the American house now," that nothing, not even "personal partisan causes," should distract him now from the search for peace, he announced: "I shall not seek, and will not accept, the nomination of my party for another term as your President." Nothing became his presidency like the leaving of it.

At the grass roots, there was jubilation. Activists let themselves hope against hope that light was streaming from the end of a seemingly endless tunnel. Horns were honked and parties spilled into the streets in Berkeley, Madison, wherever students congregated—although some Lefter-than-thou movement organs and underground papers found Johnson's announcement beneath notice. McCarthy workers, gearing up for another showdown in Wisconsin, were ecstatic. ("I don't think they could stand up against five million college kids just shouting for peace," the candidate said. "There was too much will-power there.") Two days later, McCarthy drew 412,000 votes in Wisconsin to Johnson's 253,000, and if anything, the polls suggested, Johnson's withdrawal had averted still worse defeat. The stock market soared; Washington, like the antiwar campuses, turned euphoric. McCarthy and Kennedy forces immediately began to worry whether the king's abdication had damaged the prospects of the insurgent princes. Antiwar leaders worried how the news would affect the prospects for future demonstrations. Was the bombing pause the beginning of the end of the war, or a trick to build the case for a subsequent escalation?

THE DECAPITATION OF THE HEROES

THE LAST BLACK HOPE

Nineteen sixty-eight was no year for a catching of the breath. No sooner had the euphoria settled than the political fever soared again. In two strokes, liberalism, as Tom Hayden put it years later, was "decapitated."

On April 4, Martin Luther King was assassinated in Memphis. That night, eighty riots broke out. Federal troops were dispatched into Baltimore, Chicago, Washington, and Wilmington. Chicago's mayor Richard J. Daley—the same who growled openly when King came to Chicago in 1966 to organize for open housing—ordered the police to shoot to kill arsonists and to maim looters.

King's following had fallen off in the years leading up to his death. His moment had passed. Since the triumph of his Selma campaign, which culminated in the 1965 Voting Rights Act, he had turned to the urban poor, but his strategy of nonviolence, national publicity, and coalition-building seemed unavailing. Just a week before his death, his hopes for a nonviolent march in Memphis, in support of striking garbage workers, had been dashed by the window-smashing of a few dozen black teenagers. King had become a hero without a strategy—but a hero he undeniably was at a moment when the larger movement craved heroes and disowned them with equal passion. For liberals, even for many black militants and radicals, he was the last black hope. When he was murdered, it seemed that nonviolence went to the grave with him, and the movement was "free at last" from restraint.

Most of the New Left had long since given up its commitment to nonviolence. But it was one thing to think of Martin Luther King as passé, another to think of him as murdered. I think that for the white New Left as for the ghettos, at some level we knew he stood for our better selves, and the rage and grief we felt when he died was the same sour rage blacks felt when they torched their neighborhoods the night of April 4. Bernardine Dohrn, for example, who had done legal work with King's open housing campaign in Chicago, was—according to a friend—

> really stunned. I must admit that I was fairly jaded by then, and I remember saying that with King dead, the Panthers and the other militants would have a clear field to lead the revolution. But Bernardine was sincerely moved, and she began to cry. She cried for a while and she talked about Chicago, when she had worked with King. She said she hadn't always agreed with him, but she responded to him as a human being. Then she went home and changed her clothes. I'll never forget that—she said she was changing into her riot clothes: pants. We went up to Times Square, and there was a demonstration going on of pissed-off black kids and white radicals. We started ripping signs and getting really out of hand and then some kids trashed a jewelry store. Bernardine really dug it. She was still crying, but afterward we had a long talk about urban guerrilla warfare and what had to be done now—by any means necessary.

THE ACTION FACTION

The movement, reeling, found fresh inspiration. Nineteen days after King's assassination came the student occupation of buildings at Columbia University, in protest over two specific issues: the university's sponsorship of war-related research, and its quasi-colonial disdain for the black community with the building of a gymnasium (with a separate entrance for the ghetto) in a public park. For years the haughty, old-school President Grayson Kirk had stonewalled the upstart radicals. As a campus reporter put it, "In the midst of prosecuting 26 nonviolent demonstrators who had protested construction of the Morningside Park gym, Columbia held a memorial for Martin Luther King. The memorable scene: Grayson Kirk standing silent as everyone else joined hands and sang 'We Shall Overcome.' Two days later President Kirk made his first statement on the Vietnam War and urged that the country 'extricate' itself from the conflict. His main objection: the war was elevating civil disobedience into a virtue." Early in 1968, the intellectually sophisticated "praxis axis" that had dominated the SDS chapter, arguing for educational "base-building" on campus, was supplanted by an "action faction" led by a tough-talking junior named Mark Rudd. Long-standing movement tensions now crackled with a new fury. For Rudd, it was disruptive action that changed students' heads—"raised consciousness," in a phrase becoming popular. To the "praxis axis," Rudd and his comrades were foolhardy "action freaks." Rudd could argue that the "praxis axis" had little to show for its patience.

The confrontation at Columbia signaled four important transformations in the student movement. First, deference and civility were resoundingly dumped. The day before the occupation, Mark Rudd wrote an open letter to President Kirk which closed with a line of LeRoi Jones, "whom I'm sure you don't like a whole lot": "Up against the wall, motherfucker, this is a stick-up." (It is interesting to note the civility preserved in Rudd's polemic, however: the grammatically correct "whom.") Weary of rebuffs, SDS and the black students simply took matters—and university buildings, and even (as an afterthought) a dean—into their own hands. The dynamic of events swept power into the hands of the less compromising; the black students' more militant style carried the white radicals along. (Even after the first building was taken, Rudd at first opposed barricading it.) Some of the occupation forces specialized in desecrating symbols; they smoked Grayson Kirk's cigars, drank his sherry, leafed through his books (discovering many uncut pages), and after five days of occupation left a mess. They pirated, or "liberated," documents, promptly smuggled to the underground *Rat,* which showed that the university administration was secretly maneuvering on behalf of classified war research and against community groups. Still, the movement committed no violence against persons, press accounts of vandalism were wildly exaggerated, and most of the physical damage was probably done by police.

Second, the festival moved onto the authorities' home grounds. Counterculture and New Left met, however uneasily, in the corridors of the occupied buildings. Women stayed overnight. The movement was still aspiring to "the beloved community"; students surfeited with campus individualism were still breathing the spirit of SNCC's old slogan, "Freedom is an endless meeting"; the occupiers felt the onrushing euphoria of a "freedom high" in their own improvised space. In the course of that week occupied Columbia saw romances, ideological and tactical debates, and a wedding. Freelance organizers like Tom Hayden and the Motherfuckers came by to breathe the tonic air and preach. Hayden was crucial in holding together Mathematics, the most militant of the improvised communes; the freewheeling Motherfuckers dazzled Rudd.

Third, the powers did not cede graciously. After eight days of oscillation and failed negotiations, Kirk called in the police. In the middle of the night, more than a thousand conquered the buildings, arresting 692, three-quarters of them students. As at the Grand Central Station Yip-In a month earlier, their brutality was unrestrained; before the eyes of horrified bystanders, more than a hundred students and others—including faculty trying to buffer—were injured, along with fourteen policemen. True enough, the barricaded occupiers were a force difficult to dislodge, although the clubs and brass knuckles that the police employed were scarcely necessary. (Mayor John V. Lindsay criticized "excessive force" by some police.) Part of the brutality, moreover, reflected a kind of class war SDS had not reckoned with: working-class cops' resentment of the children of privilege. Student opinion at large, already sympathetic to the student demands, turned decisively against the hardened university administration. Seeking to draw a line against what Kirk even before the occupation had called "turbulent and inchoate nihilism," the administration lent authority to SDS's hunch that repression nudged "the revolution" along.

Finally, as even uninvolved students could not help but note, the press built a containing wall against the radical tide. A. M. Rosenthal, assistant managing editor of *The New York Times,* broke with the tradition that insulates editing from reporting and produced a front-page by-lined story condemning the students' loutish behavior, quoting Kirk: "My God, how could human beings do such a thing?" (It did not pass unnoticed that the *Times*'s publisher was a member of the Columbia Board of Trustees.) *Newsweek* editors axed their own reporter's story, although he was an eyewitness, in favor of the *Times*'s version. The press cast a blind eye at Columbia's owning slums, cooperating with the military, disdaining students; apparently it agreed with the radicals that "the issue is not the issue."

For the moment, Columbia's liberators were heady with success. In their self-accelerating euphoria, there was no such thing as bad publicity. The police bust led to a student strike; campus support mushroomed. The bust and the *Times*'s distortions, in tandem, seemed to confirm SDS's notions that the university was a bastion of reaction and that students were "radicalized" at the point of a billy club—a prevalent misjudgment that confused (in Carl Oglesby's words) "radical insight, radical commitment of the whole person, and on the other hand, amazing spikes of rage and terror." Underground papers ran a picture of a sweet-faced and slightly dazed-looking college boy, blood streaming down over his forehead, displaying his shaky but triumphant two-fingered *V.* The *Rat*'s cover said "HEIL COLUMBIA" and showed a swastika'd helmet resting on a colonnaded building marked "TPF [for the elite bone-crushing Tactical Patrol Force] Library." In *Ramparts,* Tom Hayden called for "two, three, many Columbias."

From the mainstream point of view, SDS was irresponsible to blame the nearest authorities for the sins of the larger society; Kirk was to be faulted for poor management, but SDS was guilty of manipulating issues and trampling civility underfoot. There was truth to the charge, though SDS could respond that a university involved in war research had done its own trampling. Among themselves, radical leaders at Columbia and other embattled universities were quite prepared to admit that "the issue is not the issue." They knew that in order to mobilize a mass of students, they had to point their fingers at the hinge where the university intersected some large evil; they had to cast university authorities (often eager to oblige) in the villain role, and to that end, nothing was more compelling than to dare them to call the police. Reform-minded protesters set out to reconstruct Columbia, but for SDS changing the university was now beside the point. The occupation was a ritual of unmasking. *Of course* Columbia had its seats in the boardrooms of power; *of course,* push comes to shove, they would mow down whoever stood in their way, from ghetto blacks to antiwar students. Meanwhile, weren't Stokely Carmichael and Rap Brown and the Black Panthers and anonymous blacks waving guns? Weren't students and workers building barricades in Paris? Liberal values evaporated in the scales. All that mattered was to build a base for the glimmering revolution.

Taped to an administrator's wall during the occupation was the hand-lettered sign: "WE WANT THE WORLD AND WE WANT IT NOW!" It was a paraphrase of a line from Peter Weiss's brilliant, popular *Marat/Sade,* in which the inmates rehearse taking over the asylum.

DEAD CENTER

The week of the Columbia uprising, Hubert Humphrey entered the race for the presidential nomination, proclaiming "the politics of joy" against those Irish bearers of bad tidings, Kennedy and McCarthy.

It was a mark of New Left pride to sneer at arrivistes seeking deliverance within the two-party system. At the end of March, Marvin Garson, who had started the weekly *San Francisco Express Times* with money from his wife's *Macbird,* heard a Robert Kennedy speech opposing withdrawal and urging Saigon to boost its draft calls, and called this "the vaguest, emptiest speech I have ever heard, and I have heard Lyndon Johnson speak on numerous occasions." From Berkeley, which probably had more leftists per capita who opposed working in the Democratic Party than any other city in the country, came the initiative for a Peace and Freedom Party, in loose coalition with the Black Panthers, gathering seventy-one thousand signatures to get on the fall California ballot.

California radicals watched the Kennedy-McCarthy debate on May 31 with scorn and groans. Kennedy was plainly pandering for votes to his Right. McCarthy called for a coalition government in South Vietnam, including the National Liberation Front; Kennedy implied that McCarthy wanted to impose "coalition with the Communists" on Saigon. McCarthy said he wanted to build public housing in the suburbs, and Kennedy came back on the low road: "You say you are going to take ten thousand black people and move them into Orange County." It was not an impressive spectacle.

Kennedy won the California primary, and that night was murdered. The Kennedys aroused feelings about destiny; I was far from the only person to hear the news with some sick sense that Bobby's murder had been fated. I oscillated between *Oh no* and *Of course;* an early radio report said that the assassin was dark-skinned, and I remember hoping the bastard wasn't going to turn out to be black—that was all we needed. In the following days, some movement people didn't know whether the assassination was surrealism or tragedy. "Don't waste your vote for Kennedy," Marvin Garson had written before the shooting; "KENNEDY SHOT AGAIN," was the postassassination headline at the *Express Times,* where surrealism was always sliding over the edge into bad taste. Some on the New Left wanted to brazen it out: thus Sandy Archer of the San Francisco Mime Troupe was quoted in Garson's article with the reaction, "It's a very interesting event. Get out of Vietnam." Who, the Left, mourn a liberal? We could not see a thread of hope or a spark of consolation in any politician or celebrity. In my own article for the *Express Times* the next week, sorrow was the tone—I called for a voter write-in of the Kennedy and King names in November.

And then, at Kennedy's casket in Saint Patrick's Cathedral, Tom Hayden held his Cuban fatigue cap in his hand and wept. It became a famous tableau. Knowing Hayden's scorn for the electoral process—"Why are you a whore for McCarthy?" was his greeting to Jeremy Larner during the California primary campaign—a good many movement people thought Hayden had, thereby, betrayed the movement's radicalism. For my part, I was a bit baffled. I remembered the contempt with which Hayden had told me of a meeting he and Staughton Lynd had with Bobby Kennedy, early in 1967; Kennedy, he said then, had been fixated on the dangers of a "bloodbath" in South Vietnam if the Communists succeeded in taking over. A few days before Bobby Kennedy was killed, Hayden had called him "a little fascist" to my face. It was easy for movement people, including myself, to charge Tom with hypocrisy, but the kneejerk reaction, justified or not, missed something important. I think many of us were divided like Hayden, but in a way we refused to acknowledge. We still wanted the system to work, and hated it for failing us.

Today, Hayden acknowledges that he "liked and was drawn to Robert Kennedy"—liked his ability to scrap, to transform himself; was drawn to "that part of him that was also"—like Hayden himself—"fundamentally disenchanted and troubled, because he had been through violence." "A voice in me," Hayden says, "tells me that somehow, some way, Kennedy would have wrested that nomination; that he was a man of destiny, and that he would have been elected president, even though the odds were incredibly long at the time, I'm sure." (Not pure wishfulness: there are sober analysts who think that at the last minute Kennedy might have pulled together a majority of the delegates in Chicago.) But Hayden the connoisseur of driving will was at odds with Hayden the theorist of American society's gridlock: Kennedy's "ability to persevere and win did not fit in with my analysis of our society." The assassin dissolved the contradiction. Kennedy's assassination proved to Hayden that his "analysis of society did not go far enough and that our society was even worse in terms of the opportunities for peaceful change than I had thought." Things were worse than that. With Kennedy dead, the life went out of McCarthy. During the following weeks, McCarthy's antiwar staffers looked on disgusted as their hero proceeded to take leave of his own campaign. What McCarthy's devotees didn't know was that, three days after the assassination, McCarthy had gone to Humphrey and met with him secretly for an hour, fishing for a policy change that would justify his dropping out. Humphrey didn't satisfy him, but McCarthy all but dropped out anyway. With his chance gone of squeaking through by breaking a Kennedy-Humphrey stalemate, the giant-killer had lost heart for the fight. Once more, a liberal hero had found reasons to buckle under.

Still, it was not with unmixed joy that we cast aside the last shriveled hopes for peaceable reform. Most New Left radicals were, in the end, reluctant revolutionaries. Hayden's reaction to Kennedy's assassination was comparable to Bernardine Dohrn's to the murder of Martin Luther King six weeks earlier; he redoubled his energy toward the impending showdown in Chicago. With King and Kennedy dead, a promise of redemption not only passed out of American politics, it passed out of ourselves. The rage released in us was partly a rage at the burden we were left with. Hayden felt it this way: "So now it was time to take your turn in the line of people who would probably be repressed, brutalized or killed." Oglesby says: "When these two heroes were killed, the movement was silenced. The whole procedural foundation of our politics was shattered." What was the point of "speaking truth to power" now? We were on our own, and what we half-felt along with the stark aloneness was not simply excitement, it was terror.

To think about the enormous repercussions of the assassinations of 1968, we need to backtrack to the imagery and mood of a more general Armageddon, for which the triggering moment is the assassination of 1963. Kennedy, King, Kennedy: they sometimes felt like stations in one protracted murder of hope.

There are times when an entire culture takes the shape of a single event, like rows of iron filings lined up by the force of a magnet. What is assassination, after all, if not the ultimate reminder of the citizen's helplessness—or even repressed murderousness? Instantly the killing creates an abrupt contest between Good and Evil, albeit with the wrong ending. The country had weathered the assassination of a president three times before, but every assassination is special in its own way; it must be for good and profound reason that virtually every aware person can remember exactly where and when he or she heard the dread news of November 22, 1963. John F. Kennedy had been relatively young, his death untimely in the extreme. The educated young felt his call, projected their ideals onto him. His murder was felt as the implosion of plenitude, the tragedy of innocence. From the zeitgeist fantasy that everything was possible, it wasn't hard to flip over and conclude that nothing was.

This was, after all, the first assassination in the age of television, even the first to be captured on film—the home movie of an instantly famous furrier named Abraham Zapruder, some frames destined to appear in *Life,* others to be brandished by assassination researchers. Thanks to the wonders of instant replay, television drove the event, and its grotesque sequel—Jack Ruby's live on-camera assassination of Lee Harvey Oswald— like a nail into the collective brain. Mysteries multiplied. John F. Kennedy's murder was untimely and shocking, yes, but also peculiarly hard to comprehend (who *was* Oswald? what did he want? who, if anyone, did he work for?); hence it begged for symbolic deciphering. American culture struggled to make sense of the apparently senseless. Fatalism flourished; the power of the will to prod history in the right direction was blunted. One common conclusion was that even the steadiest of institutions, the august presidency, was fragile indeed. The Camelot legend was recycled: moments of grace and glory don't last. Some would-be rationalists resolved to cling to President Johnson in the storm, to find a compensatory good in the horror; others cringed from the graceless successor, who could never measure up to the dead Kennedy.

From the national mélange of rational optimism and free-floating paranoia, and in the face of widely cited mysteries drifting foglike from cracks in the official accounts of the assassination, there emerged conspiracy theories galore. The Warren Commission Report, released on September 27, 1964, was shoddy enough, but something else was operating to discredit it: a huge cultural disbelief that an event so traumatic and vast in its consequence could be accounted for by a petty assassin. Popular books, starting with Mark Lane's 1966 bestselling *Rush to Judgment,* punched holes in the Warren Commission's finding that Oswald was the lone assassin. Serious journals like *The New Republic, The New York Review of Books,* and *Ramparts,* not to mention the more sensationalist underground papers, regaled their readers with tale after tale about exit wounds, gunshots from the grassy knoll, missing frames of the Zapruder film, the accuracy of Mannlicher-Carcano rifles, exotic Cuban émigrés, mysteriously murdered witnesses, double agents, double Oswalds. Many objections to the official line were convincing, but one had to become a full-time assassination obsessive to keep up with the intricacies. Not to be outdone, the far Right looked to Oswald's Russian period and his ostentatious Fair Play for Cuba connections, covering up its hatred of the living Kennedy by clambering onto the side of the dead one.

There was trauma for young radicals too. In the months and years after November 22, 1963, Tom Hayden, Dick Flacks, and I were given to playing with the concept of Oswald as "lurker." History, which *we* aspired to make, was now being made behind our (and virtually everyone else's) backs; we were fascinated by the conspiracy theories, impressed by their critiques of the Warren Commission, doubtful of the single-assassin idea though unconvinced of any specific conspiracy. For years thereafter, late at night, amid our sage analyses of political forces, the thoughts of lurkers would leap up, and we would muse about the havoc these apparently marginal men had wrought. We who were proud of having shed every last illusion about John F. Kennedy shared in the national trauma; up to the last possible moment we held on, white-knuckled, to the scraps of hope for legitimate heroes. Our intuition knew better than our passions that radicalism and liberalism were joined in a symbiosis.

Then the Kennedy trauma was compounded by the assassination of Malcolm X in February 1965. In the official version, it was a simple case of loyal Black Muslims shooting down the apostate; but movement people duly noted that Malcolm on his recent trip to Africa and the Middle East was departing from his racial purism and pulling closer to the white Left. A number of white New Leftists who had met Malcolm had been impressed with his thoughtfulness, his apparent freedom from personal prejudice. Although there had been rumblings of danger, Malcolm had been left unprotected by the police; how could we fail to wonder whether there was a government claw in his death?

Some black activists adopted Malcolm as a martyr to black separatism, others to world revolution. His death fueled both. By the time Martin Luther King was shot down, there was no way to resurrect the nonviolence he had stood and died for.

VIOLENCE SHOCK

The enlightened Establishment's great men gunned down, a self-proclaimed black revolutionary gunned down, common people gunned down: there was an eerie democracy of sudden death. The southern civil rights movement had been deeply bloodied, of course. Dozens of blacks were killed in the urban riots of the North from 1964 on, and, as we have already seen, the riots of the summer of 1967 magnetized the imagination of white radicals. Then, early in February 1968, black students in Orangeburg, South Carolina, demonstrating outside a bowling alley that wouldn't permit them inside, were fired upon by police. Thirty-three were wounded; three died.

Meanwhile, it was widely—and, as it turns out, accurately—surmised that the FBI, military intelligence, and police Red Squads in cities like New York and Chicago, were busily tapping phones, recruiting informers, and occasionally planting dope on activists. Rumors began to fly that the government was going to prepare—had prepared?—concentration camps for use in a hypothetical national emergency. Drugs inflated the spirit of Armageddon, but with conspiracy trials in progress from Boston to Oakland, who could really be certain the pipe nightmares were only that? Under the headline "LOTS OF COINCIDENCES," Bob Novick noted in the *Express Times* that in the previous week "the S. F. P. D. broke up an anti-war picket line at the Fairmont after tolerating such lines for many years"; cops were routinely Macing and clubbing on Haight Street; and four warrantless cops had burst in on Eldridge Cleaver and questioned him at gunpoint. Then he felt called upon to caution against conspiracy tales, "atrocity stories and paranoia-producing articles about police brutality and concentration camps." Not all the rumors were wrong by any means. The CIA *had* joined the surveillance operation. I didn't know—until I sent for my FBI records years later—that there really was a Security Index to expedite roundups, and I had been honored with a place in it.

A whole movement culture looked over its shoulder. At the *Express Times,* to take one example, there worked an early draft card burner and Resistance founder, Lenny Heller, an intense and darting talker (in the style of the man he took his name from, Lenny Bruce) with a knack for rapping out the larger mood, viz.:

> If you want to be a revolutionary you have to be awake, you can't have one minute's peace, you're alive every single moment. . . . When you hear a sound, the sound of the wind, the footsteps right at the door—not a wasted motion. It is intense, and there are distortions that take place under that intensity. When you see a cop you have to size him up. I mean he's the enemy, and every time the Gestapo walks in, you go through changes. It's a very scary feeling to think that every phone is tapped, so it's not tapped, it's just the idea that you have to be conscious of that, you have to be conscious of that, you feel that there's a microphone, you know there's been too many investigations. Every place I go someone has talked to the FBI.

Rank-and-file devotees to nonviolence were defecting in droves. Lenny worried about prison. What was the point of brazening it out for martyrdom? When I met him early that summer, amid the marijuana fumes that filled the warehouse from which the *Express Times* emanated, he was specializing in reports on the street battles that were becoming de rigueur in Berkeley and environs. In the paper's lower-case anti-ego style, his by-lines were "lenny the red-and-black," "lenny the head," "lenny the black-and-blue."

The first of those streetfights, at the end of June, was Berkeley's introduction to barricades and my introduction to the Berkeley style. In a year proceeding under the sign of "two, three, many Vietnams" and "two, three, many Columbias," it was, appropriately enough, an echo of the Paris insurrection; imitation was the better part of valor. (At Columbia, in fact, a second student insurrection in May borrowed tactics directly from the French New Left.) To support the French insurrection that seemed, miraculously, to have united revolutionary students and workers, the decidedly uninsurrectionary Trotskyist Young Socialist Alliance held a rally on a Telegraph Avenue streetcorner. The police lined up; after a long face-off, a few demonstrators threw a few rocks; the police barraged them with tear gas, and beat whomever they caught. Bottles, rocks, and bricks came back at them; a few demonstrators heaped up barricades, lit bonfires; the police charged; the barricade-tenders retreated.

The next night, a crowd gathered for more of the same. This time the speechmakers said that the issue was not just freedom of assembly but the right to liberate Telegraph Avenue for "the people," and the barricades went up early. "People were saying 'riot' like they really liked the word," wrote "lenny the red-and-black." "They were caressing it like 'rebel.'" Hundreds of police charged, and the air was choked with the acrid fumes of tear gas. Rioters hurled rocks and bottles and smashed bank windows. Political discrimination among commercial establishments did not altogether prevail: the window of Cody's Books, whose proprietor was a friend of the movement, was shattered as well. For hours the crowd played cat-and-mouse with the cops. Someone threw a Molotov cocktail and, in Lenny's words, "a highway patrolman went up like a scarecrow." The cops, enraged, beat heads; thirty-one demonstrators were hospitalized (along with a dozen police, including the burned highway patrolman) and many more of the injured didn't go to the hospital.

A friend and I drove over from San Francisco to scout out the scene, and scurried around in the fumes, taking refuge in friendly apartment buildings, feeling exhilarated, awkward, stagy all at once. It was easy to fancy that the Telegraph Avenue street people were "white niggers," a quasi-ghettoful of the hip in search of their liberated space. At the same time, I knew it was absurd to claim, as the chants did, "We are the people." Lenny wrote scornfully that while ambivalent rioters chanted "Walk. Walk. Walk," edging away from the worst concentrations of tear gas, the "bourgeois press" misreported that what they were saying was "War." Scornful of the Trotskyists, who worried about antagonizing people, his long exuberant report also touched on a central political problem for the new insurgency: "The barricades were democracies, given that you wanted to build one." In passing, too, he grasped the pathos of this festival of outlaw identity: "It was an exceptional feeling to dance in the crosswalk of a revolutionary street, but torture to know it's a tease": once again, politics *as if*. But the *Express Times* headlined "WAR DECLARED/ Foe Strikes Berkeley, Boston," with a red-tinged photo of lurid gas clouds and the caption: "Enemy Troops Deploying on Telegraph Avenue. Allies Put Up Fierce Resistance, Then Fell Back." A month later, Lenny was celebrating a riot of dope-smoking suburban high school kids, provoked when the owners of the shopping center where they hung out called the cops: "Young Pacifica—Revolutionary Surprise!"

The dread of confrontation was curling over, yin to yang, into anticipation. In November, the month Richard Nixon was elected President of the United States, Lenny Heller, draft resister, began publishing a staccato fantasy novel, serial style, in the *Express Times*. "The day the White Revolutionaries took their guns onto Telegraph Avenue, Friday July 4th, 1969": so it began. Half in bravado and half in apprehension, Lenny called his tale *Berkeley Guns*. There is a point at which imagination threatens to slide over into self-fulfilling prophecy. When two sides collaborate at the same prophecy, the odds of self-fulfillment go up geometrically. More than one side was preparing to play at Armageddon, not least the side with the guns.

Violence was endlessly talked about, feared, skirted, flirted with. The social psychologist Kenneth Keniston astutely wrote around this time that *"the issue of violence is to this generation what the issue of sex was to the Victorian world."* It remained true, to the decade's bitter end, that most of the New Left thought of violence as the harsh currency of the twentieth century, not the means of liberation. But violence also became the threat and the temptation around which the whole movement, whatever its actual disinclination to pick up stones or guns, revolved. Violence organized the movement's fantasy life—and, through the mass media, the whole society's. It was as if the assassinations, the riots, and the war distilled all the barely suppressed violence seething through American life. Palpably, just as Rap Brown said, violence *was* "as American as apple pie." The eruptions of public violence fused murder with madness, tore the heart out of rational faith, felt like some kind of historical repressed returning with a vengeance. A drifter named Richard Speck killed eight Chicago student nurses on July 14, 1966; the ex-Marine Charles Whitman shot twelve people dead from the top of the University of Texas tower on August 1, 1966—apparently unmotivated crime stirred up a sense of the precariousness of life. Cultural energy clustered around the terror (and the allure) of sudden death—most poignantly, and stylishly, in 1967's *Bonnie and Clyde,* with its romance of doomed killers and choreographed slaughter, displaying assaults on the body as stark facts far more vivid and incomprehensible than any possible causes. America's iconography had come a long way from the innocence of *On the Road* and *The Wild One*—and not just because of technological advances in the representation of gore.

For the rest of the decade there was a lingering sense of playing in overtime, wondering when the game was going to end in sudden death. First in the somber progression, we—and I mean not every individual in the New Left, but a critical mass that included parts of people like me who still cherished nonviolence and felt a terror of real bloodshed—we felt the violence in the world like a sharp instrument on our psychic skins. The enormity of what was happening in the world, even packaged in media images, swept us into a kind of voyeuristic complicity. Traces of Auschwitz and Hiroshima were still detonating like slow-motion time bombs. The fear of ultimate planet-death, to which Vietnam often seemed an extended prologue, produced psychic defenses: an inner bravado, a fascination with precisely what was feared, eventually a powerful identification with people who seemed to be fighting back and winning. Only then did protected youth strip off their protection and expose themselves to the billy clubs: Vietnamization. And then a daring possibility opened up: Why not seize upon violence, why not will what had first been experienced as a terrible destiny?

As much as anyone, Tom Hayden embodied these moods and advanced them. By the middle of 1968 he—like many others in the movement—was suffering from a state that could be called violence shock. Looking back from the calm of the mid-Eighties, he reconstructs this terrible sequence: First, violence in the South, which touched him directly enough to be unforgettable. Then everyday violence in the Newark ghetto, especially the violence meted out by the police. (In March 1965, after only nine months in Newark, Hayden already had inflamed reactions to the police. Protesting loans to South Africa, forty-one SDSers sat on the sidewalk in front of the Chase Manhattan Bank headquarters near Wall Street, mannerly, well dressed, and with arms linked, until, one by one, we were lifted not ungently into the paddy wagons. As I sat awaiting my turn, I heard Hayden yelling, from the plaza above: "Fascist cops!") Then his trips to North Vietnam, where he saw the antipersonnel bombs, the napalm and white phosphorus, and came under bombardment himself. Then the Newark riots, where twenty-six blacks were killed, two of them before his eyes. Then police clubs against antiwarriors. Then the assassinations. Overall, "it just had to have been a terrible stripping away of my feelings down to the rawest possible point," Hayden says.

Rage was becoming the common coin of American culture. There are cultures in which people are not seared by acquaintance with bloodshed; their martial traditions steel them. But despite Rap Brown's rhetoric, violence was scarcely "as American as apple pie" for middle-class American youth. This was a generation not only impatient, not only primed for plenitude and instant gratification, but protected. We were unacquainted even with street crime in a way that today defies belief. (In the private housing development where I grew up in the Bronx, the police were elderly men who strolled about without so much as a nightstick. Our standard joke was: "What does your father do for a living?" "Nothing, he's a Parkchester cop.") The Bomb was a menace but a dangling one, not only abstract but oddly impersonal. Vietnam, whose flattened TV images were the culture's cliché, was at once remote and queerly, heartbreakingly present. So were the ghetto firestorms. So violence and the threat of violence became stark and factual to us in an eerie way—as abstractions. Having stepped into the aura of violence, many of the middle-class young were stunned into a tolerance, a fascination, even a taste for it. I doubt that movement cadres grew up any more—or less—rageful than an equivalent population of law school students, more "violence-prone" than ROTC cadets or bomber pilots. Perhaps less so—whence the shock of Vietnam. Our emotions were flooded. Along with Lyndon Johnson and Richard J. Daley and James Earl Ray, Ronald Reagan and J. Edgar Hoover and Sirhan Sirhan, "Eve of Destruction" and *Bonnie and Clyde,* Green Berets and Black Panthers and the N.Y.P.D., we were churning in a sea of rage.

And rage sometimes dovetailed with strategy. When in doubt about the rational course of action, people choose the strategy that "feels right." Tom Hayden had, as we have seen, a strategic rationale for a confrontation in Chicago. It was probably on his mind, and some other planners', more than the rank and file's. But my guess is that most of the demonstrators who went to Chicago were driven, like Hayden, to test themselves. It was a matter, he says, of "finding out how far you were willing to go for your beliefs, and finding out how far the American government was willing to go in suspending the better part of its tradition to stop you. You wouldn't know without entering the amphitheatre." You would go because *not* going would tell the powers that be that you had broken your head against the Vietnam wall; you would go as if your going would teach them a lesson. Hayden was "expecting death, expecting the worst." I told friends I was going to Chicago with the instinct of the moth for the flame.

THE CRUNCH

Chicago became Götterdämmerung because all the protagonists thought polarization served their larger purposes. Everyone hardened—the phallic imagery is deliberate. The movement's irresistible force collided with Mayor Daley's immovable object, while the television cameras floodlit the clash into national theater. Self-fulfilling prophecies coiled around each other like vines. It was as if everyone were playing out a fantasy version of Vietnam: act tough, try to intimidate, win over the center with a show of force, draw the other side into acting every bit as monstrous as you said it was.

Given the movement decision to go to Chicago, Daley had by far the greater latitude to keep the peace, and infinitely the greater armament: the purported demonstrators' weapons he displayed afterward were largely improvised (the pièce de résistance was a black widow spider in a jar) or decidedly nonlethal—not a single gun. Therefore by far the greater responsibility for the spilling of blood was the mayor's. Daley hewed to the hard line from the start. Hoping to keep demonstrators out of Chicago in the first place, he talked tough, refused to grant permits, and called up his troops. Afterward, as his warrant, the mayor brandished death threats against the major candidates and himself. Even had there been such threats—and no evidence was ever produced—what was the danger of all-night sleepers miles from the convention site, or demonstrators across the street from the delegates' hotel? What were squads of police charging into a crowd going to do about hypothetical gunmen? No, the assassination card was the last refuge of a man with power but not arguments. Judging from their conduct, Mayor Richard J. Daley and the Chicago police headed full tilt toward a riot. It is impossible to know how many movement people surged into the Chicago streets eager to fight; probably a few hundred at most. More were willing to fight back under attack. The great majority of the demonstrators simply wanted to march and chant, to stand up and proverbially be counted; when the cops charged, gassed, smashed, they ran.

Part of the New Left wanted a riot, then, but the streetfighters could not by themselves have brought it about. For that they needed the police. The sleeping dogs sat bolt upright, howled, bared their teeth, bit.

LURCHING TOWARD CHICAGO

Marching across the Potomac River en route to the Pentagon in October 1967, Rennie Davis and Dave Dellinger had started talking about some sort of militant nonviolence at the upcoming Democratic Convention. The movement could continue its turn "from protest to resistance," and present a sort of alternative convention to the eyes of a watching world. As far as Dellinger was concerned, the Pentagon confrontation confirmed the power of nonviolence; the radiant image of the young antiwarrior sticking his flower into a soldier's gun barrel confirmed his hopes. Soon Tom Hayden joined the planning for Chicago. But the rest of the movement held back, fearful of being drawn into a trap. No one had illusions about the Chicago police or federal authorities—less and less as bloody 1968 wore on—and it was common knowledge that organizers had talked loosely about disrupting the Democratic Convention, forcing it to a halt unless it voted to stop the war. Leaders of the National Mobilization Committee to End the War in Vietnam (familiarly known as "the Mobe") were adamant about proceeding nonviolently—on the record they were unanimous—but some worried that disruptions by marginal affinity groups could "open the door for provocateurs." Meanwhile, the SDS leadership, though not in principle averse to confrontations, was deeply suspicious of Hayden and Davis, thought they might be stalking horses for the hated liberals in the Democratic Party; along with many local Chicago organizers (including my old comrades from JOIN, the ERAP project in Uptown), the SDS officers were also afraid that the police, once stirred up during convention week, would come after *them* once the outside agitators had slipped out of town.

Yet since Johnson was sure to run for a second term, and the Vietnam issue was likely to be smothered in Democratic Party unity, movement eyes turned toward Chicago as the irresistible arena for—something. Hayden and Davis opened a Chicago office for the Mobe in February, and wrote a proposal for "nonviolent and legal" demonstrations; they were speaking the Mobe's language, but there were disturbing overtones. In the last week of March, just as the Wise Men were meeting in the White House, a movement conference at a YMCA camp near Chicago heard

Hayden and Davis present their idea of an "Election Year Offensive," but couldn't agree what to do about it. At one point Staughton Lynd argued against a national spectacle in favor of a strategy of digging in and creating local groups, and won a vote to that effect; Hayden kept the meeting going for another two hours, waited for attendance to thin out, and got the original vote rescinded. Fresh from the Yip-In at Grand Central Station, Abbie Hoffman, Jerry Rubin, and friends arrived to trumpet the Yippie platform—including the abolition of pay toilets, to the consternation of the straight Left—then declared themselves bored with the meeting, announced that their "Festival of Life" would go on, and scampered out. In the end, the conference failed to formulate a goal which might be worth the possible massacre, and broke down in confusion.

When Johnson plucked himself out of the race, confusion mounted further. "When Johnson dropped out," Rennie Davis told Marvin Garson, "that nearly killed it. It was mid-May before you could even get the thing discussed." One reason was that life was flooding back into the Democratic Party like blood to a sleeping limb. Another was that Mayor Daley was devoted to making the city look forbidding. Daley's "shoot to kill" order during the riots after King's assassination was one thunderous statement to potential demonstrators. A few days later, sympathetic whites marched in protest against the police attacks in the ghetto, and the cops battered and tear-gassed them, too. Then, on April 27, while a hundred thousand marched placidly and predictably against the war to New York City's Central Park, Daley's police waded, clubbing and Macing, into a crowd of several thousand equally placid in downtown Chicago.* Daley denounced "hoodlums and Communists." In this supercharged atmosphere, rock stars and counterculture heroes were not flocking to the Yippies' hypothetical "Festival of Life"; even Jerry Rubin was thinking of calling off his show.

Then Robert F. Kennedy was killed, and the idea of massive protest in Chicago regained its rationale and momentum.** Hayden and Davis tried to reassure the media that they wouldn't try to stop the convention from taking place, but the police and federal agents who were monitoring their moves inflated their ambiguous hints of violent confrontation into an unambiguous threat to the convention. The more staid middle-class troops of the antiwar movement were not wholly reassured any more than the authorities; Dellinger argued repeatedly in Mobe councils that Hayden's and Davis's ambivalent statements about "self-defense" were

---

*Years later, a former Chicago cop told Abe Peck, "Each one of us was told that we had to make an arrest. I couldn't believe it. There was nobody bad there."

**The SDS office remained suspicious that the Left was being set up as the liberal Democrats' stalking horse, even though there was no candidate left to stalk for. In the end, though, SDS couldn't afford to lose the chance to recruit, and urged its cadres to come to Chicago to organize "McCarthy kids."

dangerous, and took the position that demonstrators would not be welcome unless they were willing to be nonviolent.

The Yippies, meanwhile, were drumming up their own put-ons, to the displeasure of Hayden and Davis and the alarmed delectation of the media. If humorless editors and city officials were tempted to take Rubin and Hoffman at their word, all the better. What they issued blithely as fantasies, claims, and predictions became "plans" in the media and "threats" to the managerial mind. (But what other kind of mind could be expected to be running Chicago?) When they announced they were going to slip LSD into the water supply, presto: banner headlines. (Mayor Daley rose to the bait and sent a twenty-four-hour-a-day guard to patrol the reservoirs.) When Hoffman twitted city negotiators that he'd call the whole thing off and leave town for $100,000, the *Chicago Tribune* screamed: "Yippies Demand Cash From City."

The rest of the Yippies' dummy agenda reads like a pastiche of John Birch and Marx Brothers fantasies of the anarchist left: faking delegates' cards; setting off smoke bombs in the convention hall; fucking in the parks and on the beaches; floating nude, a mass of flesh, in Lake Michigan; releasing greased pigs; planting Yippie agents in hotel and restaurant kitchens, and drugging the delegates' food; painting cars to look like taxis and kidnaping delegates to Wisconsin; getting female Yippies to pose as prostitutes and dose the delegates' drinks with LSD; getting "hyper-potent" male Yippies to seduce the delegates' wives, daughters, and girlfriends (the great majority of delegates being male); walking the streets dressed as Vietcong; burning draft cards en masse with the flames spelling out "BEAT ARMY." Outrageous talk was cheap. What better way to inspire young longhairs to smash up everything holy? Best of all, from the Yippie point of view, the mayor might be provoked into acting like a caricature of lummox authority run amok.

Hayden and Davis, meanwhile, were playing out a complicated strategy of their own. Among militants, Hayden and Davis talked tough. Face to face with the city administration, they requested permits—the Mobe for parades and rallies, both the Mobe and the Yippies for sleeping in the parks. There was a practical reason: In the face of mounting publicity about Chicago's military preparations, they knew their only chance of coaxing tens of thousands to Chicago was to persuade the city to grant permits. But there was also an apple-pie innocence these reluctant revolutionaries couldn't shed. It was their doubleness that led Staughton Lynd, for one, to tell Hayden that "on Monday, Wednesday, and Friday [Hayden] was a National Liberation Front guerrilla, and on Tuesday, Thursday, and Saturday, he was talking to Robert Kennedy and Galbraith and was on the left wing of the Democratic Party, and it just wasn't together."

Through May, June, July, and August, the organizers negotiated in good faith with city officials. A high Park District official had said in the spring that facilities would not be made available to "unpatriotic" groups, but the organizers still expected that if the First Amendment did not suffice, at least the city's desire to prevent a riot would prevail at the last minute. The city, however, was unyielding. (Liberals fared no better than radicals: Allard Lowenstein's Coalition for an Open Convention tried to reserve Soldier Field, the city stadium, only to be informed that the official Democrats had reserved it for the entire convention period—for President Johnson's birthday.) As city officials stalled, Rennie Davis enlisted the aid of the Justice Department's top mediator, Roger Wilkins, convincing him that permits would keep violence down; Wilkins believed him but got nowhere with Mayor Daley, who had been advised by the Secret Service to keep demonstrations away from the convention site. The staff of the underground paper *Seed,* the New York–based Yippies' designated proxies in Chicago, carried on their own fruitless negotiations; the high police command said the 11:00 P.M. curfew was absolute, although in fact it was normally not enforced. A week before the convention was to open, the Mobe filed suit in federal court for parade and park permits; the complaint was assigned to District Judge William J. Lynch, Mayor Daley's former law partner, who dismissed it. Yet the organizers still thought the city would have the wisdom to make informal concessions once the longhaired thousands began to slouch into the parks.

Stalling on permits, Daley proceeded with fortifications. The convention site itself, the Amphitheatre, was sealed off with barbed wire. All twelve thousand Chicago police were placed on twelve-hour shifts. Five to six thousand National Guardsmen were mobilized and put through special training with simulated longhair rioters. A thousand FBI agents were said to be deployed within the city limits, along with innumerable employees of military intelligence and who knew which other local and federal agencies.* Six thousand U.S. Army troops, including units of the crack 101st Airborne, equipped with flamethrowers, bazookas, and bayonets, were stationed in the suburbs.

All this well-publicized armament, along with the movement's own provocative talk, intimidated the antiwar multitudes around the country. In the absence of a crystal-clear and universal commitment to nonviolence, the early enthusiasm melted away. "In my recruiting trips around the country," Dave Dellinger wrote later, "the two questions I was always asked were: (1) Is there any chance that the police won't create a bloodbath? (2) Are you sure that Tom and Rennie don't want one?" From Hayden and Davis, Dellinger extracted promises that they wouldn't

---

*In 1978, CBS News attributed to army sources the claim that "about one demonstrator in six was an undercover agent" during convention week in Chicago. Common sense, for what it is worth, says this sounds excessive, like the typical braggadocio of military intelligence in the Vietnam years. But suppose it exaggerates by a factor of five or ten. The number would still be extraordinary and its possible implications sizable, given how few provocateurs it takes to provoke a riot in a delicate situation.

advocate violence. He hoped solidarity would prevail: "We thought that if we could hold the Mobe together," he says years later, "we could minimize the damage." But riddled by dissension, the Mobe made little effort to bring thousands to Chicago until a month beforehand, and by then it was too late. The Yippies lost ground, too. By the beginning of August, Chicago's underground *Seed* resigned as the Yippies' outpost and warned: "Many people are into confrontation. The Man is into confrontation. . . . Chicago may host a Festival of Blood. . . . Don't come to Chicago if you expect a five-day Festival of Life, music and love." Tom Hayden was fraying: he and Rennie Davis were being tailed, around the clock, by plainclothesmen conspicuously displaying their guns and growling threats. Paranoia and aggression were two sides of the common coin: Hayden went so far as to denounce *Seed* editor Abe Peck as a CIA agent. Gene McCarthy, having lost the nerve to fight his Minnesota-mate Humphrey now that Johnson had taken himself out of the running, urged his supporters to stay away from Chicago; a warning from Daley that McCarthy might end up the target of an assassination attempt—a warning that may have originated with the FBI—may have added to his squeamishness. Blocked from access to Soldier Field, Lowenstein dropped his idea of a rally, saying the city seemed "determined to have a confrontation that can only produce violence and bloodshed." The week before the convention, signs sprang up around Lincoln Park, the major Yippie hangout: PARK CLOSES AT 11 P.M. The Mobe was conducting Japanese snake-dancing lessons, very photogenic if decidedly sloppy, for the benefit of excited cameramen in the park.

Convention week had felt like trouble from the beginning. (In those days we were training ourselves to feel hardboiled, to face an apocalyptic future with sangfroid, so even my sentences were becoming clipped, Raymond Chandleresque.) I knew Chicago cops: knew they had planted dope on JOIN's premises—SDS's Chicago community organizing project—to set up a bust and give them an excuse to wreck the office in 1966; remembered how they had broken a camera of mine when I snapped a picture of them illegally searching my car one time. From San Francisco I had long talks with Hayden and Davis on the phone; I knew their thinking too, and sensed the vibes. Just before the convention opened, I wrote a front-page headline for an eleventh-hour *Express Times* advance piece on Chicago: "If you're going to Chicago, be sure to wear some armor in your hair." (We ran it with a photo of a longhair, saluting, wearing a hardhat.) Hayden was unhappy about public forebodings, mine among them, but the warnings piled up. You stayed away if you wanted to avoid trouble and you went if you couldn't stay away. Most of the movement stayed away. The fear, the squabbling, maybe above all the lack of permits, took their toll. The tens of thousands of demonstrators once trumpeted did not materialize. A few thousand did, three or four thousand on most days, up to perhaps eight or ten thousand at the peak on Wednesday, August 28. By educated guess, at least half came from

Chicago and environs. Law enforcers outnumbered demonstrators three or four to one.

Necessity therefore forced Hayden and Davis and other strategists to improvise a new scenario. Small threats would trigger Daley's paranoia, and the clumsy forces of order would disrupt *themselves*. As convention week began, Hayden spelled it out: The befuddled forces of repression were unable to "distinguish 'straight' radicals from newspapermen . . . [or] rumors about demonstrations from the real thing." Therefore "the threat of disorder, like all fantasies in the establishment mind, can create total paranoia . . . at a minimum, this process will further erode the surface image of pseudo-democratic politics; at a maximum, it can lead to a closing of the convention—or a shortening of its agenda—for security reasons." Like a lighter, quicker judo opponent, unruly street activists could use the peabrain hulk's size against him. It was at least an idea.

It wasn't especially mine, but by then I really didn't have one. Like many old hands, I shared a sense of fate and complicity, not a strategy. For me Chicago was the unavoidable rendezvous. I knew the city, and I would see friends. There was loyalty to the SDS Old Guard, but more: the old incestuous love. It was still possible—barely—to think of the Old Guard as "the movement," and "the movement" as the circle to which I belonged and, at its moment of truth, had to return. That movement's fate felt like my own. I think it was feelings like this that drew a good many early SDSers to Chicago, whatever their qualms about Hayden's and Davis's thinking. Convention week was the culmination of their summer's political work in community-based draft resistance, GI organizing, and other such projects, but it was also their showdown. To attract a range of demonstrators, the Chicago organizers set up "movement centers" (often in churches) free to plan their own actions; the decentralism was appealing to New Left veterans. I was too skittish to go to Chicago as a wholehearted organizer, though; I needed my own place to stand. I wanted to be an honest witness to the breakthrough, or catastrophe, or whatever it was going to be—to take it seriously, let it seep into my bones without getting them cracked in the process. I had no illusions about being a streetfighter—I was somewhere between not believing in it and not feeling tough enough—so I arranged to give myself a semilegitimate niche: I would hang out with my radical journalist friends and write for the daily *Wall Poster* which *Ramparts* had decided to publish as a service to the demonstrators and a general guide to the logistical and ideological lay of the land.

Chicago sweltered, the Russian tanks clanking through Czecho-slovakia clanked through our heat too, and I felt as though the whole world was on a knife-edge. The first news I heard at the *Wall Poster* office was that a Sioux teenager named Dean Johnson had been killed by police in Old Town, the hip neighborhood near Lincoln Park; it was reported that, accosted by the police, he had reached into his pack and pulled out a pistol. The second was that forty-three black GIs at Fort Hood, Texas, fearing assignment to ghetto duty, had refused to accompany their units to Chicago, and were being held in the pen. WELCOME TO CZECHAGO. RICHARD J. DALEY, MAYOR.

THE CALDRON

What exploded in Chicago that week was the product of pressures that had been building up for almost a decade: the exhaustion of liberalism, the marauding vengefulness of the authorities, the resolve and recklessness of the movement, the disintegration of the Democratic Party. But Chicago threw all the elements into chemical reaction, and redoubled the pressures; from that week on, potentialities became actual. The movement emerged committed to an impossible revolution; the Right emerged armed for power and a more possible counter-revolution; liberals barely emerged at all. Chicago confirmed that no centers were going to hold, no wisdom was going to prevail. It wiped out any lingering doubt that the logic of the Sixties—of both the movement and the mainstream—was going to play itself out to a bitter end. Two decades later, the polarizations etched into the common consciousness that week are still working their way through American politics.

A thorough chronicle of August 25–30, 1968, clash by clash, would sit heavily upon an already long book, for unlike the movement's previous epiphanies these events went on for a full week, and there were no fewer than three major battlegrounds.* The important thing, anyway, is not the whole wild sum of events but the main thrust, and what it meant for the movement and American life at large. The bare facts are these: (1) In Lincoln Park, on the North Side, adjoining Chicago's hip neighborhood,

---

*All these years afterward there seems little point to marshaling a vast string of facts once again. We have as one point of reference the blue-ribbon blow-by-blow Walker Report (to the National Commission on the Causes and Prevention of Violence), which amassed heaps of information from thousands of eyewitnesses in the course of coming to its famous conclusion that what happened in Chicago was a "police riot." For its sheer volume of testimony to the brutality of the police, the Walker Report remains valuable. Yet it was not the mission of Daniel Walker, an enlightened corporate lawyer, to penetrate to the movement's dynamics or the meaning of events. Moreover, walking a political tightrope, bending this way and that to achieve "balance," as if the truth were the sum of everyone's testimony, Walker took at face value many uncorroborated police accounts, and suggested at times that the chanting of "Kill the pigs" and "Your wife sucks cock" and other such phrases was enough to account for indiscriminate carnage. Walker tended to blame the mayhem on the excesses of individual cops getting out of line. The folklore lives on in the precincts of the Right: that the cops, besieged by bags of urine and excrement, and by vile language they had presumably never heard in the locker room, acted with justification. A better grounded and more significant judgment has been rendered by the Chicago novelist John Schultz, whose splendid and undeservedly neglected *No One Was Killed,* closer to the streets, changes the frame: In a number of crucial instances it wasn't a matter of individual police running amok; with officers present and discipline apparently holding, there is good reason to believe that they were ordered to assault the crowds.

the cops, as promised, cleared out the park with tear gas and clubs, leading to street warfare on Sunday, Monday, and Tuesday nights. (2) In Grant Park, across the street from the downtown Conrad Hilton Hotel, where the delegates stayed, the movement faithful gathered every night, and occasional violent clashes took place until on Wednesday a great deal of blood flowed for the networks' conveniently positioned cameras, and "the whole world" (America, anyway) proverbially watched. (3) Miles away, in the Amphitheatre—the major field of action for the Democrats and the TV cameras, and therefore for the rest of the country—a peace plank was defeated, liberals proclaimed their disgust, and Hubert H. Humphrey was nominated to lead a broken party.

Some essentials, then. Who beat whom? In brief, again and again, the police came down like avenging thugs. They charged, clubbed, gassed, and mauled—demonstrators, bystanders, and reporters. They did it when there were minor violations of the law, like the curfew; they did it when there were symbolic provocations, like the lowering of an American flag; they did it when provoked (with taunts, with rocks, and, at times, they claimed, with bags of shit); in crucial instances, like the assault outside the Hilton Hotel Wednesday evening, they did it when unprovoked. Sometimes, in the heat of their fury, the police took little or no trouble to distinguish between provocateurs and bystanders. Sometimes they singled out longhairs. Monday night in Lincoln Park, they slashed the tires of some thirty cars bearing McCarthy stickers. They bashed reporters so devotedly that they guaranteed themselves a bad press. More than five demonstrators were injured for every policeman, and a large proportion of the police injuries were to hands—suggesting that they were hurt while colliding with the flesh and bone of demonstrators.

Those who braved Chicago were determined, at the least, not to be intimidated. Among them were some two or three hundred—many more than the nonviolent stalwarts like Dave Dellinger anticipated—who welcomed the fights on the street, and a few who came intending to damage some strategic piece of property. At the beginning of the week, for example, Dellinger went to an SDS movement center where he heard an organizer giving a pep talk about streetfighting; addressed as "Mr. Dellinger"—the kiss of death—he tried to talk the *enragés* out of violence. But even then the benign-minded Dellinger didn't realize how extensive the violence would turn out; the term *trashing* had not yet entered the movement vocabulary. The fighters were a small minority of the demonstrators, of course. Given the small total of demonstrators in the city, though, the proportion bent on fighting and fighting back was high—high enough to provoke the easily provoked police; especially high because, as opposed to the usual fifty-fifty male-female balance in demonstration ranks, men outnumbered women in the Chicago street actions by eight or ten to one. Some arrived in affinity groups, ready to test themselves in turf fights. Others beheld the police charging and for the first times in their lives picked up stones and wheeled into the streets for mobile tactics. In the churning chaos, it was impossible to seal off and control the fighters. For days, in the heat of the park confrontations, Mobe and Yippie cadres repeatedly tried to cool out the *enragés*—only to be greeted by taunts of "Fuck the marshals!" and "Marshals are pigs!" or clubbed out of action by the cops for their pains. All in all, they were about as effectual as Allen Ginsberg chanting Om in Lincoln Park to soothe the cosmically troubled vibrations. The stage had been set by some leaders and the city officials together, but now the household names— Hayden, Davis, Rubin, Hoffman—were no longer writing the script.

At the movement centers, there was a continuous blur of meetings, but most of these were exercises in an obsolescent movement form, and had little or nothing to do with what actually happened on the streets. Who had the initiative, then? "Yippies," said the press, but precious few of the longhairs assumed that label. "Park People," we dubbed them. Some were movement toughs in affinity groups, but most were new to the movement. Theirs was the politics of turf; anyone who wanted to take their turf away was a pig. They were proud to be freaks, playing out the logic of juvenile delinquency, the beats, James Dean, Hell's Angels; the very idea of "the movement" or "political authority" was laughable to them. John Schultz talked to two agitators, both native Chicagoans, who were as responsible as anyone for the first confrontation with the cops, Sunday night in Lincoln Park. One was an actor who taunted the Yippies as cowards; the other a fourteen-year-old NFL–flag-waving boy from an Italian "greaser" neighborhood, whose political career consisted of *one* previous demonstration. This same boy was active in the crowd that climbed onto the statue of a Civil War general in Grant Park the next day and precipitated another clash. Some of the official leaders, having advised against violence, scampered about in the riotous streets chortling "Beautiful, beautiful"—"as if watching an electrical storm," in Schultz's words—while they tried to make out what was happening. After all, especially when the streets fill with tear gas, the fog of streetfighting is as thick as the famous fog of war. The "leaders" were leading no one.

Old-timers tingled to see the movement open up. In their rush toward militancy what they had feared, more than anything else, was isolation. Now they beheld allies and wanted to swing with them. "Youth Will Make the Revolution," gushed one improvised poster that went up in the SDS movement center near Lincoln Park. Those of us who felt oppressed more than impressed by the way things were sliding out of control bit our tongues. A mystique was born. The Park People went as far beyond SDS's Prairie People as the Prairie People had gone beyond the Old Guard. In the stale iconography that swirled like tear gas through Chicago, the Park People were the symbolic proletariat. When the cops attacked, they led the action into the streets of Old Town; threw gas canisters back at the cops (a few brought oven mitts for this purpose);

darted through the traffic, blocked the streets with trash baskets, trashed police-car windows with bricks and rocks, rocked police cars and paddy wagons and tried to overturn them, got their licks in at isolated cops when they could. Heavy among the Park People were "greasers," motorcycle toughs, no-nonsense Chicago working-class teenagers, along with a handful of Chicago organizers simulating them. Even more than the runaway slave-surrogates of Abbie Hoffman's revolutionary dream, the greasers were as far as you could get from middle-class values and still be white; hence they were romantic heroes, the Pretty Boy Floyds and Tom Joads of this hour, and their presence was taken to be a sign that the white movement was getting "serious," serious enough to break out of its class-bound bubble, serious enough to be taken seriously by the Panthers and other black heroes. Jerry Rubin, for one, took on as bodyguard a freshly bearded, leather-vested biker who later turned up to testify against him during the conspiracy trial—and there is no reason to assume he was a singleton, for undercover cops could play greasers better than they could play movement intellectuals.

The greasers in Lincoln Park were joined by hard-core hippies and freelance militants drawn by the chance to transgress by raising the enemy banner. They had their own version of movement mythology: a woman in army fatigues, for example, arguing that nonviolence hadn't worked in the civil rights movement "and it isn't going to work now." There were also a few streetfighter cadres, the Motherfuckers from New York and others who came to disrupt Chicago's business as usual, although they didn't have the capacity to do much of that. I knew two people who brought little steel spikeballs which looked like sharpened versions of jacks, and scattered a few of the nasty things in Loop traffic now and then, hoping to puncture tires and tie up traffic. Three old movement hands released stink bombs in the Hilton, leaving an aroma that mixed with the vomit later brought up by tear gas; the lobby stank for days. Another painted slogans on the door of the CIA office in the Federal Building. At the SDS movement center, one chapter leader urged small groups to drift down to the Loop with Molotov cocktails and rocks. A few freelance detachments deployed themselves around the city; one affinity group went to suburban Evanston to firebomb a draft board, only to watch its Molotov cocktail (perhaps the only one actually thrown all week) shatter uselessly against a wall. Viewed on a revolutionary scale, of course, this was penny-ante stuff. In the parks, at least, the heavy fighters were outnumbered by the kids with the McCarthy buttons, the rank and file of disillusioned liberalism, no longer quite so clean for Gene now that their candidate seemed sunk.

Was it streetfighting or revolution? Was the feeling desperation or exultation? The barricades in Lincoln Park Monday night were part Eisenstein, part Paris—so what was real? Nightsticks, gas, and defiance, bravery and bravado. And what was good? Caught in conflicts of loyalty, those of us who felt qualms about particular tactics muffled our voices for fear of derailing the onrushing movement. Paul Cowan, who covered the action for *The Village Voice,* has written: "I remember watching, amazed, as kids a year or two younger than me threw rocks and slabs of sidewalks at the police, hoping to provoke reprisals. I filed a story about that—and then asked [editor] Dan Wolf to kill it when the police fought back against anyone who happened to be on the streets. In other words, the police riot seemed to me a far greater evil than the fact that some kids had wanted to provoke it. I didn't want my story to dilute that impression." One day the *Wall Poster* sent me to cover a Mobe meeting, where I heard Tom Hayden speak, in chillingly cavalier tones, about street actions which would run the risk of getting people killed. Others in the Mobe thought the risks were too great and the ethics wrong, and spoke up for nonviolent witness. Still, the words had been spoken. I had to choose my own words. The *Wall Poster* was the main conduit to the thousands who slept and gathered at the movement centers and in the streets. I felt obliged to warn them to proceed with caution ("don't follow leaders"), but with indictments certain to come, and old loyalties still alive, I didn't want to name names. I stared at a typewriter in the *Wall Poster* office for hours before deciding to use the quotes. Then, a day or two later, I was buying a disguise for Hayden to help him stay "underground" while the cops were looking for him, and setting up his network TV interview, false beard and all. Those were days in which Hayden appeared, *moraliste extraordinaire,* in the dreams of more than one Old New Leftist; chanting "Free Hayden" at a demonstration outside Chicago police headquarters one afternoon (Hayden had been arrested for letting the air out of a police tire), Bob Ross and I grinned at each other and agreed we had always known it would come to this.

The astounding fact is that as we returned again and again, with barely any sleep, in clothes caked with sweat, to streets saturated with tear gas, playing dangerous cat-and-mouse games with shotgun-toting cops (who were, by Monday night, shooting into the air)—through all the terror and doubt the uncanny sense spread that we were *winning.* Weren't the cops beating the reporters onto our side? Weren't residents of the neighborhood around Lincoln Park sheltering the wounded? One morning I was walking near the *Wall Poster* office in the West Side ghetto when a black kid, no older than twelve, cheerfully yelled: "You gonna kill a cop?" Monday night I flagged down a car to get the victim of a police beating to a movement infirmary. (It was best to avoid hospitals, where the cops might be waiting.) A couple drove us, all concern and efficiency, no explanations needed. They were shorthaired, well dressed, they sported a McCarthy flower emblem on their VW bug. Had we stumbled into a people's war against the cops, in which every repressive move by the authorities would ricochet back at them?

I spent long evenings from Tuesday on at the nonstop rally—without permit—in Grant Park, across Michigan Avenue from the Hilton, where the Park People were outnumbered by McCarthy kids and movement cadres. Peter, Paul and Mary sang "This Land Is Your Land," and for a moment you could almost believe it. When Georgia state senator (and ex-SNCC) Julian Bond, speaking in Grant Park, asked supporters in the huge bleak hotel to flash their lights in sympathy, many did—didn't that prove we weren't isolated? Speeches appealed to the McCarthy kids: learn from this debacle that the established reform channels are dried up, that the police are only the shield for the whole system; join us. The TV cameras whirred from their platforms over the street, the powerful lights catching us in their beams from time to time, chants cranking up— "Dump the Hump!"—and subsiding, the police on their twelve-hour shifts glaring, everyone waiting.

And suddenly, Tuesday night, six hundred National Guardsmen materialized, in full battle dress, rolling down the faded elegance of Michigan Avenue in jeeps outfitted with barbed-wire cages, stopping between us and the Hilton to relieve the police. My feelings cascaded: astonishment (on a couple of hours' sleep a night, I hadn't reckoned on the exhaustion of the cops), then fright, then euphoria—the late Sixties' definitive sequence of feelings. We had outlasted the cops; the Guard was full of middle-class draft evaders; we would be safer now. And another image: we were like the Czechs, at that moment confronting Soviet tanks. (Whatever the "soft on the Russians" charge, our loyalties were clear; a Mobe group had gone to picket the Polish consulate.) We were comparably noble up against a machine that was comparably bankrupt. The lines were drawn, the storybook confrontation pure, although whether it pointed toward revolution or counterrevolution wasn't at all clear and didn't seem to matter. I remember an eerie satisfaction: *At last. We've shown they can only rule at gunpoint. The world is going to see.*

The Guardsmen deployed at the edge of the park, facing us, with their young faces and their bayonets fixed, and they stood there for the rest of the night, trying to avoid eye contact, while demonstrators, mostly women, walked along their line, looking for the more receptive ones, lecturing them about the war, hoping to convince them they were on the wrong side.

On Wednesday the delegates, unimpressed by the fact that 80 percent of the primary voters had voted for antiwar candidates, defeated the peace plank by a vote of 1,567¾ to 1,041¼. With Johnson and Daley pulling strings behind the scenes, and party hacks overrepresented, it was a foregone conclusion that Hubert Humphrey would be nominated that night. Ten thousand people gathered for the legal rally at the Grant Park bandshell. A hundred cops marched up in formation. A youngster lowered the American flag; the police swooped in, clubbing; a group of men stepped out of the crowd, finished taking down the flag, and raised some kind of red cloth in its place. Most of the crowd felt "shame and anger," John Schultz writes. Dave Dellinger has said he found out that the first flag-lowerer was a small-town Wisconsin kid carried away by "innocent enthusiasm," but Schultz describes the follow-up group as strangely "huskier than most Yippies or students," and adds sagely that "the Yippies, who were daring enough to do the work of provocation themselves, did not need any police-assigned provocateurs or CIA assignees or what have you: nevertheless, throughout Convention Week the feeling was never stronger that the weird color guard was composed of plainclothesmen." The cops formed a wedge and charged; Rennie Davis, trying to cool things down, was clubbed senseless; Park People fought back, a few having pulled up the slats of park benches and hammered nails into their ends. The chants shifted from "Hell no, we won't go" and "Peace now" to "Pigs are whores" and "Pigs eat shit." Dellinger tried to organize the bulk of the people into a nonviolent march toward the Amphitheatre, for which no permit had been granted, and which the police and the Guard promptly blocked. As the crowd scurried around looking for a safe way out, a distraught Tom Hayden, fresh from the sight of his dearest comrade Rennie stretched on the ground unconscious with blood all over his face, took the microphone and shouted: "The city and the military machinery it has aimed at us won't permit us to protest in an organized fashion. Therefore, we must move out of this park in groups throughout the city, and turn this overheated military machine against itself. Let us make sure that if blood flows, it flows all over the city. If they use gas against us, let us make sure they use gas against their own citizens."

The crowd, sealed off on three sides, surged blindly north, trying to find a way out of the cul-de-sac, but the National Guard was posted on the bridges connecting this part of Grant Park with Michigan Avenue, and they blocked the way with machine guns, they rammed panic-stricken demonstrators with rifle butts, they blockaded cars that had nothing to do with the demonstration but were simply trying to get across the park. A network television camera recorded a Guardsman in extraterrestrial-looking gas mask halting one driver (no demonstrator), telling her to turn around, getting enraged by her hesitation, then poking a grenade launcher into her child's face. And the Guard in their masks sprayed vast clouds of tear gas from converted flamethrowers slung on their backs, the gas filling the park in every direction and wafting across Michigan Avenue to the Hilton, where eventually it disturbed Hubert Humphrey in his shower.

Eyes burning, lungs filling with this corrosive stuff, throats feeling as though we had swallowed steel filings, hundreds of demonstrators streamed north until we found a blessedly unguarded bridge and crossed over onto Michigan Avenue, where the gas was still thick but at least it was possible to run, who knew where, run as fast as you could, hoping to reach some hypothetical safety. I stopped at a water fountain to dab at my eyes, soaked my handkerchief, wrapped it around my nose, looked up and recognized—Jules Feiffer. A circle closed for me: In high school, I devoured books of Feiffer's cartoon strips, a bible of alienation. My dearest possession was a cartoon he had sent me at the time of the 1962 Washington march, in which a demonstrator pickets the White House with a sign reading "COFFEE." Now Jules Feiffer was a McCarthy delegate from New York, we were breathing the same gas, I introduced myself, we decided to run together. As we dashed past the Hilton, Feiffer suggested we duck through a revolving door into the cocktail lounge, to get away from the gas, and we did.

Inside, conversation was buzzing and waitresses hovering, the street noise and gas screened away behind plate glass. Feiffer was hailed by Studs Terkel, Chicago's energetic leprechaun, and the bleak-looking William Styron, in town for *Esquire*. Feiffer asked me what I wanted to drink; I ordered a Bloody Mary. The waitresses wore tiny Gay Nineties dresses with miniskirts and deep décolletages; this was the Haymarket Lounge, "a place," said its advertising, "where good guys take good girls to dine in the lusty, rollicking atmosphere of fabulous Old Chicago." On a TV screen in the corner of the Haymarket Lounge, Paul Newman, a McCarthy delegate from Connecticut, was blasting the Vietnam war. The delegates had to *do something,* I jabbered to Feiffer. And Jules Feiffer, my hero, said he was scared. *Jules Feiffer* was scared. He sounded scared. The cocktail waitress arrived with her automatic smile, her vivid cleavage, and my second Bloody Mary. Styron was talking about how awful everything was. I guzzled my drink and stared outside. The gas was billowing thicker than before and people were streaming past, in and out of sight, as if they were behind the glass in an aquarium. I excused myself, stumbled through the Haymarket Lounge and the stench-filled lobby, and ran back out onto Michigan Avenue.

At the corner of the Hilton, a little later, two phalanxes of cops blocked what was left of Dave Dellinger's would-be march, and after a series of scuffles they scythed into the crowd in apparent unison, smashing heads and limbs and crotches, yelling "Kill, kill, kill," spraying bystanders and demonstrators with Mace, squeezing the trapped, terrified crowd until one demonstrator wearing boots had the presence of mind to kick through the window of the Haymarket Lounge, shattering it, and some people scampered and others were shoved through, many slashed by glass, only to be pursued inside and then clubbed and knocked around again by police screaming "Get out of here, you cocksuckers." One Mobe organizer who tried to restore order was battered between his legs and on his head (twenty-two stitches) as he tried to negotiate a truce with the deputy superintendent of police. The melee spilled into the surrounding streets for hours, but it was the assault in front of the Hilton that became famous, it was concentrated and it took place directly under the TV lights, seventeen straight minutes with the crowd chanting "The whole world is watching," the pictures seeping into the convention hall itself, where Senator Abraham Ribicoff of Connecticut denounced the police's "Gestapo tactics" and Mayor Daley yelled something which the TV sound couldn't pick up but lip-readers later decoded as "Fuck you you Jew son of a bitch you lousy mother-fucker go home."

A while later, I ran into some journalist friends who were walking around Grant Park with Fred Dutton, formerly one of Robert Kennedy's close advisers, now a Democrat insider without portfolio, who invited us up to his room in the Hilton to watch the roll-call vote on the presidential nomination. At the hotel door, my friends, in jackets and ties or reasonable facsimiles thereof, passed through the checkpoint easily enough, but I was wearing a sweaty white shirt and smelled of the afterodor of tear gas, so a cop grabbed my shoulder. "Get your hands off him!" Dutton roared from behind me. "He has more right to be here than you do!" The startled cop unhanded me, and I followed the others through the revolving door and upstairs to watch the bad news.

Everything about Chicago sprouted symbolic meanings. Dutton's gesture spoke to me of the decency of liberalism, however disenfranchised. A candlelight parade of three hundred antiwar delegates later that night also displayed the side of liberalism which was repelled by the victorious Humphrey, whose HHH insignia had come to resemble barbed wire. If I had stopped to think about it, my little incident at the door of the Hilton might also have suggested how dependent we still were on the liberals we had by this time grown adept at whipping. New Left radicalism was a vine that had grown up around liberalism, they had sprung from the same energy and soil of possibility, and although by now the two represented different cultures, different styles, different ideologies, like it or not they were going to stand or fall together.

At the end of the week, many a demonstrator assumed that battered liberals had no choice but to shift Left and join us. The McCarthy people had spilled out into the streets—not because anyone had persuaded them to be anti-imperialist but because the Democrats' doors had been slammed in their faces. After he went down to defeat, Senator McCarthy himself made a pilgrimage across the street to Grant Park, and greeted the "government in exile"—having abandoned them months earlier. In the dawn hours Friday, the cops honored the McCarthy staff on the fifteenth floor of the Hilton by raiding their headquarters, tossing several staffers out of bed, breaking a club over one's head. It was said that members of the loyal opposition in a fit of disgust had thrown heavy objects out their window—even a typewriter, by one reliable account. Clean for Gene did not impress the police; McCarthyists and Maoists were interchangeable in the eyes of the law. Humphrey and Daley between them had apparently cemented the alliance between loyal and disloyal oppositions.

There was another reason why the people I knew came out of convention week feeling triumphant: the sheer thrill and relief of having survived. Before Chicago, even the wildest street actions were no more than interruptions in everyday life, brief suspensions of the rules. Now the week stretched into eternity and the cinematic sequence of gas, clubs, TV cameras, meetings, street moves felt like normality. Chicago was the movement's sealed-off world pushed to some nth degree of emergency, so that people going to work seemed the freaks. We were awash in the purity of the we-versus-them feeling on the streets, the crazy battlefield sense that all of life was concentrated *right here,* forever. And there was also the thrill of knowing that the cameras had picked up the action, not only on the streets but in the convention hall, where Daley's goons manhandled Dan Rather and Mike Wallace, and an uncharacteristically ruffled Walter Cronkite lashed out at the security "thugs." Wasn't it obvious that the viewers were going to see matters the way we did, from the wrong end of a billy club, and that they would conclude that these rampaging police, defending a corrupt political system, discredited it? Maybe Jerry Rubin was half-right when he talked about the suburban kids who would watch the Yippie theater mesmerized and rush off to sign up on our side. . . .

To our innocent eyes, it defied common sense that people could watch even the sliver of the onslaught that got onto television and side with the cops—which in fact was precisely what polls showed. As unpopular as the war had become, the antiwar movement was detested still more—the most hated political group in America, disliked even by most of the people who supported immediate withdrawal from Vietnam. McGeorge Bundy had been right to tell Lyndon Johnson, in November, just after the Pentagon and Stop the Draft Week: "One of the few things that helps us right now is public distaste for the violent doves. . . ." Apparently the majority agreed with Bundy that whoever swung the clubs, we were to blame.

But our giddiness kept us from reckoning with the majority of the "whole world" that, watching, loathed us. The collective euphoria about Chicago masked a tremendous confusion about the nature of the American reality and our own impact on it. Were we on our way to The Revolution or to concentration camps? Was it Revolutionary Year Zero or fascism's Last Days? The movement's metaphors were pulling in contrary directions. "We were all going direct to Heaven, we were all going direct the other way. . . .": Dickens's phrases, transcending their decline into cliché, capture the garish mood that sweeps down when great and terrible things seem equally and inseparably real. Elinor Langer has recalled that as the police were bludgeoning the crowd up against the window of the Haymarket Lounge that Wednesday: "Running and stumbling to get away, maybe to regroup, half the crowd looked up at the police and soldiers, shot out their arms, and shouted 'Heil Hitler.' The other half of us waved our arms to the soldiers and shouted 'Join us.' In the middle of Chicago, at the nominating convention of one of America's two major parties, half of us thought we were in Germany and half of us thought we were in Russia." Or was it Czechoslovakia?

THE AFTERTASTE OF TEAR GAS

Meanwhile, back in the United States, if the two-party system was frozen against reform, the most tempting metaphor, by default, was revolution. We had to be in the early stage—1905, I called it. Many were the liberals who, as John Schultz put it, "under the club, acted as revolutionaries in Chicago without ever becoming radicals"—ready to hate the cops and to fight, in other words, if hazy about the balance of forces and vague about what to build. "Radicalized," we called them, and that is what they called themselves and felt they were—at Columbia, Chicago, and dozens of smaller and less luminous confrontations. SDS boomed; that fall, at least 100 of its 350 to 400 chapters were new. Scandalized journalists in Chicago, spurred by editorial blue-pencils as well as police billy clubs, started a *Chicago Journalism Review* to criticize their papers, and similar efforts sprouted in New York and elsewhere. Television news, having brought the majority more bad news than it wanted to see, rapidly backpedaled from its criticism of Daley and the Democrats—which only went to prove that the Establishment media were, well, part of the Establishment. In recoil from their overwhelming defeat, the liberal pros in the Democratic Party rolled up their sleeves and set out to take advantage of rule changes to bring blacks and women into the party, to pry nominations away from the urban machines, to give greater weight to primary votes. Even in Chicago, Mayor Daley's televised spectacle of savagery was the prologue to his last hurrah; enough white liberals were sufficiently incensed to join the legions of unrepresented blacks in a reform effort that, a decade later, overturned the Chicago machine.

Having unmasked the Democrats as Democrats, the late New Left convinced itself that the movement's unpopularity was either skin-deep or a proof of our revolutionary mettle, or both. The discourse in SDS was warped into simplistic formulas and the tones were abrasive; people who worried about the new turn couldn't see how to get a word in edgewise. At an SDS gathering right after convention week, outside Chicago, the lines were clearly drawn. The Progressive Labor bloc thought Chicago had alienated the working class, on which they relied to "make the revolution"; they continued to push their "base-building" line, arguing for "worker-student alliances." The anti-PL National Office group felt that the strategy of "resistance" was vindicated and the mysterious Park People were the vanguard of the developing revolutionary forces. There were a few of us old New Leftists, without much organizational base, who abhorred the streetfighting turn while also thinking PL's fetishism of the working class romantic nonsense; I for one argued vaguely against "mobilizing" and in favor of something called "organizing," though in full knowledge that ERAP had trickled to an end and that the only organizing work with momentum was directly targeted against the war, notably in the GI coffeehouses dotted around army bases. "Organizing," sneered Mark Rudd in return, "is just another word for going slow." He was right; and at the edge of Armageddon nothing more damning could have been said. Sublime indifference to any evidence that a tactic was adventurist (to use the Old Left term for *risky*) was now the hallmark of revolutionary seriousness. Chaos in the streets was an arguable strategy for the not-so-modest purpose of ending the war; now it was being touted as more: a prologue to revolution.

A couple of weeks after Chicago, I was worried enough about the penchant for wildness to write a piece for the *Express Times* called "Casting the First Stone," beginning: "Watch the man who casts the first stone. He may be a cop." I ticked off facts, rumors, and questions about agents provocateurs, and worried that "delicate judgments in these raging days are falling afoul of a fetishism of the streets: that is why we have a hard time telling the cops from the desperados. We are living through some profound crisis of masculinity, explained but not wholly justified by the struggle to shake off middle-class burdens of bland civility. The guy who hits hardest and moves fastest begins to look like the biggest revolutionary cock; it doesn't seem to matter whom he hits, where he runs." The piece was widely reprinted in the underground papers, the *Rat* among them; I happened to be in New York, at its ratty Lower East Side headquarters, when a group of Motherfuckers roared in and growled at me for discrediting the righteous tactics of righteous brothers. Never mind that I had taken pains to caution that "the police would like nothing better than to have all militancy discredited under suspicion of provocative trickery, all trust shattered by curse and countercurse." To the streetfighting men, I was a watery holdover from the discredited old New Left, dangerously soft on liberals, undermining the toughness that we had to develop now to prime ourselves for the coming struggle.

I ended my piece saying that it didn't matter much whether a dangerous character was on the police payroll; what mattered was clarity and "political discipline. Know what you want to do, and then you have solid ground to refuse to follow people who take you where you don't want to go. Use strategy as a code to define provocateurs." A too delicate hint that it was time to think about what this movement *wanted;* but the truth was that I lacked a strategy as much as anyone. The movement's survival was hardly a political program for Americans. The fact was that we were living in a bubble, talking to ourselves, reading texts drawn from nineteenth-century Germany or turn-of-the-century Russia or twentieth-century Cuba or some other twilight zone—Narcissus admiring himself in a TV screen. The America that worked for a living and had something to protect—something "law and order" might protect—was abstract, offscreen. The New Left had taught the liberals something about the ruthlessness of official power, but now had little to offer but more proofs of the obvious. Chicago's presumed success trapped the believers in a self-fulfilling spiral: If one Chicago was a splendid victory, then two, three, many would be more splendid still. We had committed ourselves to "demystifying" institutions, but once the mask of legitimacy was stripped away to reveal brute force—at Columbia, in Chicago—then what? If present power was the servant of elites, how to accumulate future power to displace it and rule more justly? Clarity might have answered: The movement, whatever it says, has no serious intention of ruling; we are once and for all a *youth* movement, aiming to reform our elders, and if they will not reform, there is no alternative but to throw ourselves down on the floor and scream—to act, in fact, "like children." That, at least, would have been honest. But the late New Left thought of itself more grandly. Increasingly the movement's answer to all questions was: abandon the institutions; "*decide* to possess power"; make "the revolution."

From the beginning, the movement's commitment to action had been almost deliberately naïve: change would come quickly because it was necessary and because it was right. In naïveté lay strength; the movement cracked the pall of the Fifties, after all, by underestimating obstacles. Now, the movement's will and moral seriousness, unhinged from real possibilities, hardened into our own cage.

All fall, student groups heckled the candidates, principally the hapless Humphrey. SDS blustered about a student strike on election day; in some states, movement people campaigned for Eldridge Cleaver and Jerry Rubin on a Peace and Freedom ticket. While the movement clamored "We told you so," mainstream politics was making a presidential campaign. Humphrey, far behind Nixon in the polls and worried about losing the working class to George Wallace, took the Left for granted—Johnson's 1964 argument: where else could they go?—and cultivated the party's right wing. Just after the convention he told CBS's Roger Mudd: "I think the blame [for blood in the streets] ought to be put where it belongs. I think we ought to quit pretending that Mayor Daley did anything wrong. He didn't. . . . The obscenity, the profanity, the filth that was uttered night after night in front of the hotels was an insult to every woman, every mother, every daughter, indeed, every human being, the kind of language that no one would tolerate at all. You'd put anybody in jail for that kind of talk. And yet it went on for day after day. Is it any wonder that the police had to take action?" Twenty-four hours later, in another TV interview, Humphrey proclaimed no fewer than four times that Daley's police had "overreacted"—the season's shibboleth for criticizing police technique without appearing to go over to the cause of the demonstrators.

Waffling did not improve Humphrey's reputation. Neither did his refusal to peel himself away from Johnson on the war. To the campaign's end the vice president was imprisoned by a Cold War Manichaeism that viewed every contraction of the American sphere of influence as a triumph of evil, every extension of American power, at whatever cost, as an unadulterated good. What Humphrey failed to appreciate is that he forfeited precisely the middle-class liberals whose electoral labors were the necessary wherewithal of Democratic Party campaigns. He had won a pathetic 3 percent of the New York primary vote, for example, but it took him far too long to realize that he needed the liberal warhorses, and even then his position softened only microscopically. Nixon polls just before the election showed that only four in ten of McCarthy's erstwhile supporters, and only half of Robert Kennedy's, were ready to vote for Humphrey. Not until the last days of the campaign did Johnson, still Humphrey's master, go through the motions of appealing to the Democratic Left. He announced a total halt to the bombing of North Vietnam and the beginning of peace talks. Humphrey proceeded to gain in the polls day after day, but ran out of days.

Most likely many of the antiwar liberals voted with their feet and stayed home on election day, helping keep turnout comparatively low. Some habitual Democratic voters may have returned to the fold at the last minute, especially after Nixon's speech of October 24 decrying "a gravely serious security gap," a purported Soviet lead over American weapons. But even the old Nixon-hating passion could not outweigh the doubts whether Humphrey's policies in Vietnam would turn out any different from Nixon's; little was said during the campaign to distinguish the two. And Humphrey's default was matched by McCarthy's. In the later words of McCarthy's frustrated campaign manager, Blair Clark, the peace Democrats' reluctant standard-bearer "put minimum pressure on Humphrey to break with LBJ on the war and when he finally endorsed him, it was so late and so weak that it failed to win Humphrey the votes that would have elected him." In the end, Humphrey lost by a mere 510,000 votes, two-thirds of 1 percent of the popular vote, although the electoral college margin was much greater; still, had Humphrey picked up 55 more electoral votes (say, Wisconsin, Oregon, and California, lost to Nixon by a total of 334,000 votes), the decision would have been thrown into the House of Representatives, where he probably would have won. The antiwar Democrats might have made the difference.

Yet in the emotional hangover of Chicago, not to mention the war, it would have felt like the height of masochism for anyone central to the movement to vote for Hubert Humphrey. Barely thinkable even to suggest such a thing! To contemplate shoring up the Democratic Party at this juncture would have required a degree of political calculation foreign to the movement's dominant state of mind. If once we had needed the space of liberalism in which to flourish, well then, we thought we could dispense with it now—we had better be able to, because it was giving way. Three weeks before the election, typically, I gave a speech to a big teach-in at the University of Washington in Seattle. The Cold War temperament had created an unwinnable war and an unquenchable thirst for anti-Communism; the welfare state had failed to satisfy the poor while inciting the Right; liberalism had thus slit its own throat. "We are moving toward the generational strike," I proclaimed. "We face in our lifetimes the cold and hard choice between two . . . alternatives: fascism or an American revolution." In the shadow of Humphrey's default, with the war burning on, I wasn't the only radical who felt more comfortable in the clarity of an all-or-nothing scenario than sloshing around trying to keep in power a morally squalid liberalism against which to fight. A fierce moralism had brought us into opposition in the first place, and the same moralism didn't brook the politics of lesser evils; even the promise of Great Society benefits to the poor wouldn't persuade us to enter into what Staughton Lynd had called "coalition with the Marines." I hadn't voted for president in 1964 and I didn't vote in 1968.

The day after election day, I found myself at a rally on the campus of San Francisco State College, where a student strike had just started. Gauntlets were thrown, demands were made: for autonomous ethnic studies programs, for open admissions for students of color, for the retention of a Black Panther official as an instructor. Humphrey-hater as I was, I was struck by the fact that not one speaker found the election of Richard Nixon worthy of mention.

Viewed from the San Francisco Bay Area, Washington politics is always a continent removed. But the silence about Nixon reflected more than the normal geographical-cum-cultural distance: it displayed the distance between the movement's sideshows and the place where power was actually deployed. It was also a shrug of despair and fatalism, as if to say: *Of course* Richard Nixon has just been elected President of the United States; we always knew it would come to this. Anyone who came of political age in the Fifties should have known that the election of *Richard Nixon* was worthy of note; but the pall of that decade was now either forgotten (what did twenty-year-olds remember of Hiss and Checkers?) or assumed to be the essential nature of the unmasked American capitalist order. And so the Great Society expired without a tear from the New Left. If the center couldn't hold, that was its own fault and its own problem. We were hell-bent for the promised, not the compromised, land.

THE SPRING OF HOPE, THE WINTER OF DESPAIR

Everything was at stake, anything seemed possible, there was the promise of universal liberation, there was the profaning of everything holy, the end of time was approaching, nothing was changing, there was a leap toward equality, there was a degradation of standards, there was disgust with the Pentagon's perversion of reason, there was a flight from the rigors of intellect, there was the revelation that America benefited from the misery of the poor countries, there was the glorification of Third World tyrannies, there was the unmasking of capitalism, there was the reflex that capitalism was the root of all evil, there was a revulsion against vast and impersonal violence, there was violence that was going to end all violence, there was an opening of doors, there was a closing of minds, there was psychedelic rapture, there was the scrambling of brains by bad drugs and too many drugs and the siren song of madness, there was a search for fresh language, there was an epidemic of cant, there was universal love, there was the right to say "fuck" on the movie screen. For every face of authority, there was someone to slap it.

Dickens is irresistible, for in 1968, 1969, 1970, polarizations were the common syntax, extremities were ordinary, reality was a blur, contradiction was commonplace. More than one war, indeed, came home.

I was hardly alone in taking Chicago as a revelation that there was "no turning back." Much of the movement felt that way. So did local and federal authorities, all the more so once Richard Nixon took over the

White House. The Chicago melodrama was a dry run for the longer-running collision between the movement and official power. In the year after August 1968, it was as if both official power and movement counterpower, equally and passionately, were committed to stoking up "two, three, many Chicagos," each believing that the final showdown of good and evil, order and chaos, was looming. During that year and the next, the political edge of the opposition proceeded in two keys at once. There were confrontations with power, aiming to unmask illegitimate authority, to give aid and comfort to its victims, and to "build the movement." Alongside, in communes and collectives, there were the exuberant, fitful, and flawed attempts to live a new way of life.

The battles raged, known by their sites like scenes from a war or Stations of the Cross. Campus confrontations tore up San Francisco State, Berkeley, Harvard, and Stanford, to name only some of the better-known and most bitter cases. . . . At Cornell, black students threatened by racist cross-burnings took over a building and later walked out clenching their rifles in front of the cameras. . . . All across the country Black Panthers shot it out with police, with more police dying than Panthers, but the list of martyrs piled higher. . . . The Black Panther and bestselling author Eldridge Cleaver, facing felony charges from a shootout with Oakland police in which another Panther, "Little Bobby" Hutton, had been killed, went underground, surfacing first in Cuba, then in Algeria. Communist leaders had gone underground in the Fifties, but outside their immediate circle they were pariahs. Cleaver was a folk hero. . . . Just after Chicago, an early phalanx of the women's liberation movement picketed the Miss America pageant, dumped some of the more confining pieces of underwear in a trash barrel, and became known forevermore as "bra-burners." . . . The Justice Department wheeled out conspiracy charges and created the Chicago 8: Rennie Davis, Dave Dellinger, Tom Hayden, Abbie Hoffman, Jerry Rubin, the lesser-known activists John Froines and Lee Weiner, and—surprise guest!—the Black Panthers' Bobby Seale, whose contribution to the Chicago events had been two uneventful speeches during a stay lasting less than twenty-four hours; and there came, in many other cities, many miscellaneous busts and lesser indictments of many a smaller "conspiracy," which as movement etymologists liked to point out meant "breathing together." . . . In May, Berkeley's People's Park brought police shotguns into action, for the first time a white was shot and killed on the scene of a confrontation, and a largely white city was occupied by the National Guard. . . . In July, homosexuals responded to the bust of a gay bar in Greenwich Village by fighting back against the police.

In the course of 1968–69, there were well over a hundred politically inspired campus bombings, attempted bombings, and incidents of arson nationwide, aimed at ROTC buildings, other campus and government buildings, high schools, even electrical towers. In the spring of 1969 alone, three hundred colleges and universities, holding a third of

American students, saw sizable demonstrations, a quarter of them marked by strikes or building takeovers, a quarter more by disruption of classes and administration, a fifth accompanied by bombs, arson, or the trashing of property. Journalists recognized the movement as a running story, like Vietnam. Rare was the day when the major newspapers failed to devote at least an entire page to tracking its fever chart. Every week the underground press recorded arrests, trials, police hassles and brutalities, demonstrations against the war, demonstrations of blacks and then Hispanics and other people of color and their white allies, demonstrations by GIs against the war, crackdowns by the military . . . and there were more of these underground papers, and their radio equivalents, all the time. By July 1969 the Los Angeles *Free Press* sold 95,000 copies a week, the *Berkeley Barb* 85,000, *The East Village Other* 65,000—all up from 5,000 or fewer in 1965.

But none of this was more than the newsworthy surface of a social upheaval. The once-solid core of American life—the cement of loyalty that people tender to institutions, certifying that the current order is going to last and deserves to—this loyalty, in select sectors, was decomposing. Not even the extravagance, the confusion and sometimes moral dubiousness of the opposition could keep the schools and the army and the family from losing their grip on the young. The liberal-conservative consensus that had shored up national satisfaction since 1945—the interwoven belief in economic growth, equality of opportunity, and the Cold War—had fallen afoul of black revolt and Vietnam, and it was as if once the keystone of the arch was loosened, the rest of the structure teetered. As fast as you could say "legitimacy crisis," people lacking the slightest affiliation with the organized Left were saying to hell with the rules, redefining (as C. Wright Mills had once hoped) private troubles as public issues, viewing old bonds as bondage and snapping them, going public with their varieties of suffering. During the school year 1968–69, according to the principal of the Bronx High School of Science, as many as fifty seniors dropped out—to do politics, to live in communes . . . or for no discoverable purpose. (Most never went back to school and proved hard to track.) Harvard in 1968 found it advisable to repeal its rule on the wearing of jackets and ties in the dining halls. In Vietnam, while some troops followed orders to the point of massacring civilians, others "fragged" particularly tough officers. Anthropologists declared their independence of the CIA, city planners consulted for community organizations; physicists tried to find work outside the military; graduate students protested requirements. High school students wore forbidden buttons, seminary students joined the Ultra Resistance, wives left husbands, husbands left wives, teenagers ran away from parents, priests and nuns married (sometimes each other), and people who didn't do these things talked with, and about, people who did. As soldiers confronted officers, so did reporters confront editors; doctors, hospitals; patients, doctors; prisoners, guards; artists, curators. From subversive questions welled up picket lines, sit-ins, a vast entangled web of organizations, collectives, publications, conferences, a great storm of nonnegotiable demands and radical caucuses and participatory democracy and "getting my head together."

The black and student revolt was general now, and part of the reason was that the first cohorts of student rebels were now carrying their defiance into jobs and professional schools. But revolt was also generalizing because authority had been knit together—because, in other words, the bureaucrats and generals and fathers had rested their legitimacy on a single "American way," so that when the rationales of the Pentagon and the University of California could no longer be taken for granted, the habit of doubt and defiance threatened to unravel the whole fabric. Authorities looked vulnerable when they gave in and arbitrary when they didn't, and in either case seemed arbitrary and incompetent and even immoral. The same corrosive questions came up over and over again, what SNCC people had once called "the movement questions": Who decides? Who is qualified?

Of course the prevailing litany of holy subversion was not as new as it imagined. It resumed American traditions. It was one more sweeping wave in the extension of the great democratic and republican ideas (lowercase both times): that maximum participation in the shaping of the public weal was desirable, and that any voice was as valuable as any other in the absence of any commanding reason to the contrary. The centrality of the *res publica,* the public thing, took the form of insisting that the personal was political—that power was present in every aspect of everyday life, from housework to homework, from final examination to medical examination. All assaults on authority could count on the presumption of innocence; all authority started out with the presumption of guilt.

And surely the time of rectification was at hand! Look at the signs: Because of Vietnam and the radical crisis, the intellectuals were defecting to the Left, as *The New York Review of Books* made plain, bashing the draft and Grayson Kirk and of course Nixon, regularly publishing Noam Chomsky on the war and Andrew Kopkind on the movement and even Tom Hayden on the Newark riots, going so far as to run a drawing of a Molotov cocktail (complete with proportions of the ingredients) on its cover. Political elites were deeply divided, and the Democrats, the party of stability through reform, had apparently lost both their Left and their Right. The media, ever alert to extremity, were deepening the sense of crisis. *Fortune* devoted a special issue to "American Youth: Its Outlook Is Changing the World," and worried over a Daniel Yankelovich poll in October finding that 42 percent of college students said they were unconcerned with college's practical benefits; that of them, more (20 percent) identified with Che Guevara than with presidential candidates Nixon (19), Humphrey (16), or Wallace (7); and that, in all, some 750,000 students identified with the New Left, "suggest[ing] a potential for disorder in our society that has barely been tapped." In Paris, the *gauchistes* had been subdued by the grotesque combination of the Communist Party and the Gaullist Right, but black-pajama'd Vietnamese guerrillas were still on the move and the young Red Guards were still sweeping across China. In the radical imagination, the university, easily shaken by relatively small numbers, became a prototype for society as a whole—or at least raised the question: What if students and their allies threw themselves into all the gears? Couldn't they bring the entire works to a crashing halt? Hadn't they come close enough in France, one of those First World countries where the very possibility of revolution was supposed to have been a dead letter? True enough, students were young people with energy to burn and relatively little to lose; true, the army was troubled but soldiers were not deserting en masse; but still, five years ago no one would have thought things would come *this* far, and five years hence . . . who knew? From experienced quarters there came tough-minded soliloquies about hidden strengths in the ancien régime, but underneath grew a sublime faith that the old sturdy-seeming walls might just be papier-mâché and that the right trumpet blast—*the* correct analysis, *the* correct line, *the* correct tactics—might bring them crashing down.

THE LANGUAGE OF THE MILLENNIUM

Accordingly, the movement's language hardened into blunt instruments. From the Black Panthers, white leftists borrowed the slogan "Power to the people," generously stretched by the Panthers to "Power to the people! Black power to black people!" This was reassuring to whites, although it did leave open the question of what happens when racist whites fight for the power to keep blacks out—an issue that later became a live one in school busing fights. Then came "people's war," borrowed from Vietnam, although even revolutionists found it hard to fit to the United States with a straight face. (When a 1969 Progressive Labor headline said "People's War Is Invincible," for example, the joke went around Harvard SDS that PL had misspelled "Invisible.")

But above all figures of speech loomed one supreme talisman: The Revolution. In the summer of 1969, for example, the embattled Black Panthers urgently called for a "United Front Against Fascism," but kept up their faith with the notion that 1970 would be "The Year of the Revolution." To invoke The Revolution was to claim title to the future; to see beyond raids and trials and wiretaps and empire and war and guilt; to justify the tedium of mimeographing one more leaflet, working out one more position, suffering through one more insufferable meeting. *The* Revolution: The name of our desire became firm and precise—never mind the absence of a vision of reconstruction—by dint of the definite article. Through the magic of a phrase, the students and lumpen-proletarians of this unprecedented "post-scarcity" society were joined to Parisian communards of 1871 and Muscovite workers of 1917 and Vietnamese peasants (and Parisian students) of 1968. To speak of The Revolution was automatically to acquire a pedigree, heroes, martyrs, allies, texts, and therefore anchorage—no mean achievement for this unmoored movement floundering around in an unfathomably rich and violent America. It was to take heart, and mind, from Marx, Bakunin, Lenin, Sacco and Vanzetti, Wilhelm Reich, Che, Mao, Fidel, Ho, from Brazil's urban underground or Guatemala's guerrillas slipping into villages to show the Indians that the military regime was not omnipotent—take your pick, they were all professionals who had fought against the odds and hadn't quit. (If you hated Stalinism, you could work up your own genealogy—Rosa Luxemburg, Emma Goldman, Trotsky, assorted other combinations—and *they* could qualify, arguably, as The Revolution's authentic lineage.) It was to overlook distinctions between Vietnam (where Ho had led a nationalist movement against no fewer than three invading armies since 1930) and Bolivia, say, where Che was not able even to speak the language of the impoverished Indians—let alone distinctions between the Third World and the First. To speak of The Revolution was to postpone vexing questions about socialism, anarchism, democracy. The Revolution was a solvent for strategic doubts, moral qualms, and internecine skirmishes. When disputes erupted, "Comes the revolution!" could mean "Later for that—much later."

What made the revolutionary mood possible was more than apocalyptic events: it was the collective willingness to suspend one's better judgment. We had been to college, after all, had studied sociology and read history, knew that in the classical revolutions three things happened: there was a revolutionary class or coalition, the establishment was not only deeply divided but incapable of keeping order and delivering the goods, and the police and army crumbled. No less an authority than Barrington Moore, Jr., took to the pages of *The New York Review of Books* to remind us of these home truths. But if you were suitably inflamed to begin with, Moore's very title, "Revolution in America?" confirmed that the feasibility of revolution was the right question. Anyway, hadn't every revolution— every successive phase in The Revolution—been unprecedented in its time and its own way? Hadn't the odds always been long? All that remained was to identify the protagonists—the Third World? blacks? industrial workers? working-class toughs? salaried professionals? the young as a whole? In any event, wasn't it clear by now that revolution, even if not imminent, was indispensable? Even the "reformist" goal of ending the war seemed impervious to "reformist" tactics. "A revolution is probably necessary if rationality is to be restored to a society that thinks it has been operating rationally," wrote Richard Poirier in *The Atlantic,* speaking of youth as "a cultural force that signals . . . the probable beginnings of a new millennium."

To invoke The Revolution was, in short, to acquire prepackaged identity, international sweep, and historical precedent for a breathtaking exercise of will. Black, white, male, female, democrats, antidemocrats, children of suburbs and ghettos—if in all our diversity, all our conflicts of style and objective, we were destined in world-historical Hegelian fashion to live out fragments of the true and single Revolution, then obstacles and even disasters could be seen as transitional, the errors and sins just friction in the machinery. The Revolution was an eschatological certainty, a given, a future already unfolding—History cresting the flotsam and jetsam of mere history. If we failed to see it, it was only because our experience and interests and therefore our visions were partial. Thus the importance of ceremonial moments when the benign (if at times brutal) necessity of History made itself manifest—the epiphany of *The Battle of Algiers,* for example, when the Left, black and white unusually together, would crowd into art-film houses to behold the counterinsurgent French sounding like Americans with their rhetoric of pacification and the damned of the earth overcoming scruples and setting off bombs in the cafés. It was a time suited to the poem found over many a movement desk in which Bertolt Brecht told posterity, "Alas, we/Who wished to lay the foundations of kindness/Could not ourselves be kind./But you, when at last it comes to pass/That man can help his fellow man/Do not judge us/Too harshly." The present was a "transitional period" on the Midnight Special to a better place. Later, as sectarian wars boiled up from the collective unconscious of The Revolution, revolutionaries could flatter themselves that if they themselves failed to be kind, it was a great pity—but not a disqualification from the throne of History. The Revolution was the ultimate alibi.

What followed from the revolutionary metaphor, and the utopianism flaming within it, was a corollary usage: the Marxist-Maoist language of "contradiction." Built into the term was the premise that the world is, at least potentially, a coherent logical system in which conflicts are kinks destined to be straightened out. "Contradictions" existed between "forces," between gigantic abstractions like classes, and there was something reassuring about that too, for it meant that individuals who took the "incorrect" position now and then were simply miseducated and could be brought around; the flood tide of reason was *ultimately* (one of Marx's and Engels's favorite weasel-words when they wrote in their prophetic mode) not to be denied. The word *contradiction* confirmed one's knowingness; whence its spread, even among novices who wondered, in private, what they were really talking about. In public, late SDS and Black Panther leaders brandished the word with a smile and an air of condescension, hinting that *they* were in possession of the philosopher's stone.

The Left was crisscrossed, however, by chasms of experience and ideology not so easily wished away.

THE BOGEY OF RACE

Nothing made the idea of revolution more vivid to the white Left than the Black Panther Party. *Image:* Eldridge Cleaver writing in *Ramparts* how he fell for the Panthers when he saw Huey P. Newton hold a shotgun on a San Francisco cop in front of the *Ramparts* office, and face him down. *Image:* Rally after rally, on the steps of the Oakland courthouse where Newton was held without bond on the charge of killing an Oakland policeman, the paramilitary teenagers in black berets and leather jackets chanting "The Revolution has co-ome, it's time to pick up the gu-un," with "Off the pig!" tossed in on the back-beat. *Image:* The emblem of the stalking Panther, drawn to make it look curiously pussycatlike. *Image:* Police bulletholes in the window of the Panther office, the photos circulating widely. The Panthers had more than a swagger, they had organization, presence, martyrs.

Huey Newton and Bobby Seale founded the Black Panther Party for Self-Defense in 1966. Arguing that white police forces amounted to occupying armies in the ghetto, they patrolled Oakland ghetto streets carrying the California Penal Code and unconcealed guns, then legal, at the ready. When thirty Panthers carried rifles into the state capitol in Sacramento on May 2, 1967, to protest a bill that would make it illegal to carry unconcealed weapons, they were automatically big news. Their eagerness to face off against the police gave them high visibility and ghetto youth appeal, but precisely that visibility generated gunplay. In October 1967, just after Stop the Draft Week, Newton was arrested and charged with murder. (Eventually he was convicted of voluntary manslaughter, but his conviction was reversed because of a judge's error, and after two more inconclusive trials he was freed—after three years in jail.) In April 1968, the Panthers' seventeen-year-old treasurer, Bobby Hutton, was killed in a shootout with Oakland police, and Eldridge Cleaver, their most eloquent recruit, and other top Panthers were arrested. The Panthers were at risk by dint of their organizing strategy, but at least they could claim a base in the otherwise unreachable black lumpen-proletariat, and wear the mantle of Malcolm X.

From the white Left side, the Panthers were a godsend. Most of the New Left, having been galvanized by the civil rights movement, still extended moral title to black leadership. But when SNCC proclaimed

Black Power in 1966, though the white Left took their side,* it was difficult to stay enthusiastic—for while Stokely Carmichael and Rap Brown were becoming national celebrities and bogeymen, SNCC organizers were abandoning the grass roots and the organization was decomposing, a process only accelerated by a short-lived SNCC-Panther "merger" or "alliance" in 1968.** Moreover, Carmichael, feted in Cuba and North Vietnam in 1967, was disillusioned by Castro's and Ho's hostility toward black separatism, and in February 1968 scandalized the white Left and the Panthers by proclaiming to a Free Huey Newton rally in Oakland that "Communism is not an ideology suited for black people, period, period. Socialism is not an ideology fitted for black people, period, period."

Black separatism was on the upswing; black radical candidates for cross-race alliance were scanty. Yet, if revolution was imminent, the black underclass, rioting in the streets, were the plausible cadres. Who seemed to represent those specters better than Huey Newton, Bobby Seale, and Eldridge Cleaver, these intelligent brothers in black leather jackets, James Dean and Frantz Fanon rolled into one, the very image of indigenous revolutionary leadership risen from the underclass and certified in prison? In a series of prison interviews widely circulated in the movement press, Huey Newton—primed with reading matter by white leftists—discoursed fluidly about socialism, anticolonialism, anti-imperialism, and world revolution. Cleaver could write—a bestseller, no less. The Panthers were streetwise, disciplined, fearless, Marxist-Leninist, revolutionary, and, most miraculously of all, at a time when most other black militants donned dashikis and glowered at whites, they welcomed white allies. (Even in the early days Newton and Seale had raised funds hawking copies of Mao's Little Red Book on the Berkeley campus.) There was no rival black leadership on the national horizon. So by 1968 the main white movement "heavies" chose the Black Panther Party as their leading black heroes and allies. Alongside the posters of Che Guevara ("At the risk of seeming ridiculous, let me say that a true revolutionary is guided by feelings of love") and Malcolm X (pointed arm outstretched, Old Testament fire in his eyes—and the hint of a twinkle), there appeared on movement walls the poster of Huey Newton in a black beret, seated in a fan-shaped wicker throne, spear upright in his left hand, rifle in his right.

It was also exciting to deal with leaders who could deliver a whole organization overnight. They called themselves a party, but the Panthers were closer to an outlaw political gang—precisely the unit which had

---

*In June 1966, only days after Stokely Carmichael's proclamation of Black Power, I myself drafted SDS's ringing declaration of support, which made two main points: (1) integration presupposed "the integrity of the dominant (white) culture," although the latter was "essentially racist"; (2) whites were obligated to build white movements which could "at some point ally with the black movement for common goals."

**The Panthers called it a "merger," SNCC an "alliance." Whatever it was, it dissolved rapidly amid mutual recriminations and, according to some reports, brandishing of weapons and threats of gunplay.

exercised such a powerful hold on the dissident imagination since the beats and Brando and the Cuban *barbudos*. The Panthers walked in the footsteps of Hell's Angels and Diggers and Motherfuckers and Parisian "groupuscules"; they were the incarnation of what Marvin Garson called the "revolutionary gang." In the person of the Panthers, then, the anarchist impulse could be fused with the Third World mystique, the aura of violence, and the thrust for revolutionary efficiency. The Panthers were tailor-made for the romance; the young, tough, crime-seared "brothers on the block" replaced the "band of brothers in a circle of love," even though their militaristic drills could look a bit chilling to the less-than-wholly convinced. Apologies were made: If they were menacing ("Free Huey or the sky's the limit!"), well, that was the style of the street, and anyway, how else could the oppressed get justice? If they were authoritarian, didn't a movement of street brothers reared in hellish circumstances require an iron discipline? If their cartoonist, Emory Douglas, was free with Jewish stars on his "Zionist pigs" (a.k.a. "kosher nationalists") in the Panther paper, one would be willing to look the other way—as I was—after Communications Secretary Kathleen Cleaver smiled and acknowledged that "Emory's not too swift about politics." If their base in the ghettos was possibly tenuous, wasn't every other group's too? Weren't the Panthers at least *on the move*? But mostly the Panthers' claims weren't challenged at all.

The Panthers' "nitty-gritty" audacity, matched against the patent brutality of the police, could make their gun-toting "self-defense" look excusable, even alluring. By late 1968 they were going national, recruiting talented and energetic ghetto youth across the East and Midwest, obviously exploiting a real ghetto mood. Among whites it was the mixture of prowess and martyrdom that served them most compellingly, though. The press, under- and aboveground, was full of reports of Panthers shot down in gun battles with police or with rival groups of a black nationalist persuasion (like US in Los Angeles) later shown to have ties with local police and the FBI.* During 1968 and 1969 there were thirty-one raids on Panther offices in eleven states. The provocative Panthers often played innocent,** but no fair-minded observer could deny that they were being shot down. Panther leaders sometimes knew that

---

*Edward Jay Epstein, writing in *The New Yorker*, later cast considerable doubt on widely circulating Panther and press claims that twenty-eight Panthers were killed by the police in 1968–69. But while succeeding in discrediting most of the inflated Panther claims, Epstein tended to take Panther accounts at their worst while taking self-serving police accounts at face value. Documents subsequently unearthed by the post–Watergate Church Committee, by Frank Donner, and others establish the part played by the FBI and local police forces in exacerbating the Panthers' internal and external tensions, heightening paranoia, procuring arms and explosives, instigating violence, and helping set up the Panthers as police targets—with plenty of help from the tough-talking gun-waving Panthers themselves, of course.

**In 1980, Eldridge Cleaver, now reincarnated as a born-again Christian and a follower of the Reverend Sun Myung Moon, told a reporter that the April 1968 shootout which killed Bobby Hutton and sent Cleaver to jail (and eventually underground and into exile) began with a Panther ambush of the police.

their cadres were responsible for a good deal of mayhem, but under siege—in a ghetto under siege as a whole—they covered up for their own. Nerves frayed; by the summer of 1969 the Berkeley headquarters staff were getting three hours sleep a night, which was not conducive to clearing their minds.

At a time when the hierarchy of sacrifice certified revolutionary virtue, the Panthers were irresistible allies, and knew it. In that supercharged atmosphere, there was a law of the Transferability of Revolutionary Credentials. Late New Left factions played the Panther card to certify themselves as righteous revolutionaries. (The same law cemented alliances between SDS cadres and the Young Lords Organization in Chicago and New York, the Brown Berets in California, and other Hispanic grouplets.) In March 1969, SDS declared the Panthers "the vanguard of the black liberation struggle," leading the independent black radical Julius Lester to denounce SDS for its "presumption." So the white-Panther alliances amounted to shadow plays, backroom liaisons between leadership cadres more concerned with revolutionary stances than political bases. I played a minor part, for example, in a short-lived 1969 alliance between a handful of Bay Area white radicals (organized by Tom Hayden) and the Panther leadership. Originally Eldridge Cleaver's idea, the modestly named International Liberation School included medical training (sorely needed by the Panthers), martial arts, and "political education," or "PE," for which Hayden invited me in. "PE" as I understood it was to have included American politics, power structure analysis, a history of the Cold War, etc., but after a couple of sessions in this vein, interest slackened and my class dissolved. "PE" as the Panthers understood it was a close reading of Mao's *On Liberalism* and other such samples of philosophical baby talk. One session, at the Panthers' Berkeley headquarters, featured a catechism in the scripture of Mao's vinyl-covered Little Red Book, and my vivid memory is of Chairman Bobby Seale's voice hardening as he browbeat a Panther woman into confessing her insubordinate "liberalism." I had admired and liked Seale, sided with him, defended him; my feelings sank. Driving home, the woman I lived with said that the exercise had convinced her that she herself, sigh, was that dangerously individualist brand of sinner, a liberal. She was braver than I, or less conflicted. But I was queasy too; I wasn't prepared to admit that part of me had never left the liberal camp; and yet dropping out of the pro-Panther orthodoxy would have felt like betrayal. I wrote to a friend: "Everyone was too quick to say, 'Oh, yeah, sure, ah, I am and always have been a Marxist-Leninist.' " Ghettoites and Ph.D.'s in Leninist study groups and "free universities" were huddling under two wings of the same zeitgeist. Fortunately, the International Liberation School withered away without demanding any more contortions.

For all that the Panthers were folk heroes, the rhetoric of revolution could not begin to bridge the real chasm between white middle-class radicals and the black poor. The depth of that chasm revealed itself in the disastrous New York City school fight of the fall of 1968. In the eyes of black parents and their Establishment supporters, the teachers were conservators of their own privilege, miserably failing to teach impoverished black children. In the eyes of many of the largely Jewish teachers, blacks were bad students, period; moreover, the black parents were barging in and infringing on their prerogatives just at the moment when the union had established itself, improved teachers' salaries and working conditions, and wrested some control from the WASP Establishment. Statesmanship was not in evidence on either side; the collision was virtually inevitable. The local governing board in the Brooklyn district of Ocean Hill/Brownsville moved to transfer some white Jewish teachers; the teachers' union retaliated by striking the entire city for most of the fall semester. Most New Leftists automatically supported the parents, though a few raised eyebrows at the sight of the Ford Foundation under McGeorge Bundy backing school decentralization.

This fight I would rather have ducked, but I happened to visit New York that fall. My parents and sister, never militant before about politics of any kind, were members of the teachers' union—all picketing their schools, in fact. A radical student at the Bronx High School of Science invited me to look in on "liberation classes" going on at my alma mater in support of the Ocean Hill parents. Without telling my family where I was going, I crossed the teachers' picket lines at Science with a gulp and spent a pleasant day with the three hundred students and twenty teachers (about one-tenth normal attendance) who were conducting what looked like serious classes (without tests), keeping up decorum (though Aretha Franklin records were playing for the blacks in study hall), frowning on smoking, and cleaning up in the absence of the striking janitors. (At a nearby community center, the striking teachers were holding what they called "freedom schools"—*with* tests.)

The visit moved me—it felt like a kind of liberation from the pettier aspects of high school—but it was another "movement high": dramatic as personal experience, of limited use for politics. Delighted by my day with the liberators, I minimized the acrimony crackling on both sides. The strike dragged to an end, but bitter feelings rumbled on for years. White teachers who supported the Ocean Hill board stewed as they remembered the way some of their colleagues race-baited them; strikers gnashed their teeth over the black teacher who read (on Julius Lester's radio show) an anti-Semitic poem dedicated to union president Albert Shanker. The radical vision of a participatory democracy with small-scale units and client-centered services presupposed a society, a community of values, that simply did not exist. Who could believe without a herculean stretch of the will that if radicals magically came to power they could harmonize the righteous demands of black parents and white teachers all at once? "Freedom Now" settled no conflicts of interest. Black Skin Good, White Skin Bad settled the question for some SDSers, but the movement was riddled with doubters who wondered just which power rightly belonged to just which people.

THE FRAGILE PARADISE OF PEOPLE'S PARK

From its beginnings, the student movement had oscillated between two principles. It had started as a movement *for others*—a support for blacks, Cubans, and Vietnamese who were victims of privation and violence and whose revolt seemed elemental. An impulse that began as altruism then spawned a movement *for itself,* a revolt of the white young who wanted to overcome their own alienation and shape their own lives—as in the Free Speech Movement and the counterculture. If the New Left proved unable to straddle the chasm of race or to propose new policies for work or education or welfare in the larger society, its hip wing was at least able to set out models for its own kind: two, three, many Berkeleys.

The fusion of movement and counterculture flourished best in Berkeley, a café-cluttered college town of a hundred thousand people, big enough for urban ailments, small enough to imagine transformed. The Berkeley campus of the University of California attracted a critical mass of young seekers, and the culture was tolerant enough, the climate benign enough, the interstices ample enough to sustain the freak colonies while drawing in fresh pilgrims with every season. Dropouts and visionaries and hustlers—sometimes all three in a single skin—found a place to drop into. More came from the East Coast now—"New York types," the police called them. The Left could be comfortable there, with its own tradition. (After the Chicago confrontation, Tom Hayden, for example, moved to Berkeley and soon became nonleader of a succession of communes culminating, in 1970, in one called the Red Family, which in turn spawned a child-care operation called Blue Fairyland.) In 1969 Berkeley already had a full decade (vast time by movement calendars) of protest and cultural ferment to take credit for—the student political party SLATE, the anti-HUAC demonstrations and civil rights sit-ins, the Free Speech Movement, the Vietnam Day Committee, the Scheer campaign, hippies, barricades, trashings, a long and violent Third World strike, the *Barb,* nonprofit left-wing radio station KPFA, a Free Clinic (staffed partly by Vietnam medics), a Free Church, free schools, study groups, collectives of doctors, lawyers, therapists, auto mechanics, filmmakers, gardeners, architects, a panoply of political groups. The tradition had become a way of life. The student body had shifted toward the hip and radical, with fraternities and sororities losing half their population between 1964 and 1972. (Market demand was so slack, one off-campus commune called COPS—Committee on Public Safety—could afford the rent on a vacated fraternity house.) The radicals were hipper in Berkeley, the hippies more combative, and there were enough of each, and all the possible hybrids, to feed any utopian vision imaginable.

The search for a confluence was like the search for a Holy Grail. For all the political ferocity of the time, the movement wanted to go beyond disruption just as the hippies wanted to go beyond private trips. The movement's countercultural side, like the anarchist Wobblies, longed to create the new society in the womb (or ashes) of the old. A superficially plausible (though wrong) sociological argument emerged to bolster that hope. A critical mass of the disaffected young were becoming expert at living off the fat of the economy. There were more of them than ever before. Through drugs, rock music, and sexual freedom, the dropouts were attracting straighter students. Against the corporate-military-professional future for which the university was training ground, perhaps what was developing was the embryo of a postindustrial, postscarcity society, in which work would be undertaken not for the extrinsic reward of the paycheck but for its social good and intrinsic satisfactions. To the hip radicals and the radically hip, dropouts and runaways were the vanguard of the leisure class, and the South Campus area along Telegraph Avenue—with its cafés, repertory cinema, funky shops, dope dealers, wide side-walks, leaflet-plastered telephone poles, sojourning blacks and bikers, and some of the best bookstores in America—seemed to prefigure a society in which the arts and crafts would flourish, and people would sip cappuccino in the morning, criticize in the afternoon, smoke dope and make love at night.

It takes two to make a turf fight, and the university and the police were eager to play. To the university administration, hungering for expansion room, the South Campus area looked like crime, blight, and "hippie concentration." Here was the ideal site for new dormitories. When it became apparent that state money was not forthcoming for that purpose, the university discovered a "desperate need" for an intramural soccer field, whereupon, in 1967, it rushed the regents into a decision and promptly exercised the authority of eminent domain to buy for $1.3 million three acres of old brown-shingled frame houses just off Telegraph Avenue, four blocks south of the campus. In June 1968, it condemned the houses and demolished them, leaving a muddy trash-strewn parking lot. This oblong block of blight remained that way, undeveloped and with neither money nor plan for early development, for ten months.

The following April, a prominent local mover and shaker named Mike Delacour conceived the idea of converting the grim space into a park, for in his view the street community needed a turf of its own, a public place for rock concerts and general rendezvous. The tall and lanky Delacour, with shoulder-length hair, had made his way from General Dynamics missile work to Berkeley, where he rolled up his sleeves and went to work for the Vietnam Day Committee and the Peace and Freedom Party. A practical, hands-on sort, weary of organizational infighting, he crossed over to the hip side of the street and opened the Red Square dress shop, a few steps from what was now the wasteland of the parking lot. There he convened some hip freelance radicals to talk about the idea of a park, and they proved as enthusiastic as he. In a few days' time, with a few hundred dollars raised from Telegraph Avenue merchants, they carted in a truckload of sod and plants, and this small group—a "revolutionary gang" indeed—proceeded to start digging People's Park in a corner of the vacant lot.

The felt need for a commons, a communal space, outran the organizers' dizziest expectations. Within days hundreds of people were working in this improvised utopia. Work was joy, not a job. Local longhairs tamped down the sod next to students, housewives, neighbors, parents. Fraternity boys mixed with freaks; professors shopped for shrubs; graduate students in landscape architecture came by to propose designs. On weekends up to three thousand people a day came to carry sod, to plant, to install swings, slides, a wading pool and a sandbox, to cook and eat huge vats of stew and soup, to drink and to smoke marijuana, to play; someone made seven-foot-high letters spelling K N O W, straight out of *Yellow Submarine.* Decisions were improvised and casual, sometimes lengthy, but conflicts got resolved, work got done; the proverbial hundred flowers bloomed, yet within an overall design. People's Park amounted to the spirits of the New Left and the counterculture in harmonious combination; it was a trace of anarchist heaven on earth. It redeemed visions of the cooperative commonwealth—Indians tilling the common lands, seventeenth-century Diggers—from time immemorial. Beneath all the divisions of straight versus hip and student versus nonstudent, People's Park in the Northern California spring touched some deep hunger for a common life. It consolidated the community, made it palpable. It was an answer (however fugitive) to the question, "What do you people want?" I wrote, in the rhetorical tone of the moment: "As substance and sign of a possible participatory order, as the living and hand-made proof that necessary institutions need not be overplanned, absentee-owned, hierarchical—as such the Park came to stand in many minds as one tantalizing trace of a good society, as the practical negation of American death, as a redemption worth fighting for."

The freelance Yippie Stew Albert, who attended Mike Delacour's original meeting, expected at first that the university would let the park be—it was "such a gentle thing," a community project readymade, in his terms, for "cooptation." Even when a reporter put it to him that the university would not stand idly by while squatters infringed upon its property, he thought the worst that might happen was a mass arrest. Like many of the rake-and-file, Ruth Rosen, a graduate student in history and editor of a campus newspaper supplement, saw People's Park as a constructive alternative to futile antiwar streetfighting. The park was no assault on academic activities; as long as it was not menacing, not too flamboyantly druggy, surely the university would look kindly on these constructive labors—after all, they improved the property. Surely the university, still living down the Free Speech Movement and later skirmishes, had no desire to tarnish its name again. Most of the organized Left, the "politicos," avoided the park altogether: it sounded unserious, hippy-dippy; it wasn't the right issue; what did planting tomatoes have to do with the working class or the Vietnam war?

Others, however, expected trouble from the beginning—and savored the possibility of a head-on collision with the university. The provocation was the park itself. At least two people who attended the initial meeting recall that their initial motive was to give the anticipated summer riot a clear focus and a political enemy. No sooner had the park decision been made than Frank Bardacke (just acquitted of conspiracy charges stemming from Stop the Draft Week) wrote one of the classic leaflets of the Sixties, "WHO OWNS THE PARK?" It was printed over the daguerrotype image of Geronimo holding his rifle across his chest, and it eloquently tracked the history of the land from the Costanoan Indians to the Catholic missionaries who "ripped it off in the name of God" to the Mexican government "who had guns and an army" to the American government who "had a stronger army" and who sold it to white settlers, and so down to the "rich men who run the University of California." It ended: "We are building a park on the land. We will take care of it and guard it, in the spirit of the Costanoan Indians. When the University comes with its land title we will tell them: 'Your land title is covered with blood. We won't touch it. Your people ripped off the land from the Indians a long time ago. If you want it back now, you will have to fight for it again.' " "If they leave us alone, we have a park," one park activist told me at the time. "If they try to take it back" (he said with a grin), "we have a riot!" There were a few acid-saturated Telegraph Avenue habitués ready and eager to fight. But the park people in general were far from pugnacious. They wanted *the actual park,* and the university's property rights be damned; even people who at first grumbled that the park was a gimmick (including Marxists who complained that "workers can't relate to a park") and others who initially had thought of the park only as the pretext for a riot, soon fell in love with the palpable green ground. "I planted this land with love / and confrontation in my heart, also a bit / of romantic self-consciousness," wrote Michael Rossman, always the Berkeley movement's most honest voice.

To the university administration, People's Park was nothing more or less than a dare. Neighbors complained about late-night bongo drumming, public sex, and drugs. Four weeks went by. Governor (and ex-officio Regent) Ronald Reagan thought the way to deal with revolutionaries—and please Southern California crowds—was to crack down; he had been trying to centralize the regents' (and his own) power over the nine-campus university system. Pressure was mounting on Berkeley chancellor Roger Heyns to assert property rights and *do something.* The regents were to meet next on May 16.

Heyns gave the order. Before the sun came up on May 15, the police sealed off eight square blocks while a crew bulldozed the gardens and threw an eight-foot fence around People's Park. At a noon rally of several thousand on campus, student body president-elect Dan Siegel said, "Let's go down there and take the park," and the crowd, as if poised for the cue, poured down Telegraph Avenue toward the fence. Some trashed the Bank of America window, street people opened a fire hydrant, the police threw tear gas, rocks were thrown in return (causing no serious injuries)— apparently another round of the long-running fight for control of the streets. Then a squad of Alameda County sheriff's deputies in blue jump-suits appeared, the special units who had been dubbed "Blue Meanies" after the pleasure-hating villains of *Yellow Submarine*—such whimsy during those bitter days says something about the spirit of the moment—and amid rampant disbelief the deputies lifted shotguns to their shoulders and opened fire. (Alameda County sheriff Frank Madigan said later that "the radicals had developed an antidote for tear gas." Governor Reagan's version was that the shotguns were issued after a policeman was stabbed—not seriously— near the fence.) For several hours they emptied their loads of birdshot and buckshot into crowds, they shot people running away from crowds, they shot passersby and reporters, they fired at students simply walking around on the campus. After two rocks were thrown from a rooftop—neither coming close to any deputies, according to eyewitnesses—they shot into a group standing on the adjacent roof of the Telegraph Repertory Cinema, cutting down two men: an artist named Alan Blanchard, who was permanently blinded by birdshot, and a visitor from San Jose named James Rector, whose belly was torn apart by a load of buckshot. In all, at least fifty (by some accounts, at least a hundred) demonstrators were shot. Four days later, Rector died.

It was one thing to theorize about the university's commitment to its property, but no one had anticipated shotguns. The community went into shock, terror, fury. That night, Governor Ronald Reagan sent three thousand rifle-bearing National Guardsmen into Berkeley. From a "liberated zone" Berkeley was converted into an occupied territory under martial law: streets blocked off to all but proven residents; bayonets fixed; public gatherings of more than three people prohibited; a nightly curfew. Partisans of the park started a "People's Park Annex" on public land on the other side of town, only to see it torn up by rampaging police. Other tiny instant parks flourished briefly, then were uprooted too. In the course of the next week, a thousand people were arrested (two hundred on felony charges) while demonstrating or leafleting, or simply rounded up on the street and in stores. At one point a Berkeley cop shoved Frank Bardacke, hands cuffed behind his back, down on the street, held his gun against Bardacke's head, cocked it, held the gun there—then threw him into the police car, punched him in the ribs, and forced him to sing "The Star-Spangled Banner." One day a National Guard helicopter flew low over a huge but peaceful campus rally and after a perfunctory warning blanketed the entire campus, all square mile of it (including the campus hospital and nearby schools), with tear gas. Activists bought gas masks and helmets. Some women walked up to the Guard bayonets and stuck flowers in the barrels of their rifles; people collected stories of Guardsmen flashing the V, and at least one such photo made the rounds. (But one prominent activist walked down a Guard line at the end of a day of demonstrations trying to demoralize them—on the model of Vietnam—with the mantra, "See you again tomorrow, see you again tomorrow. . . .") On May 30, upwards of twenty-five thousand marched peacefully through Berkeley to the park, while the bayoneted Guardsmen lined the fence and police sharpshooters manned the rooftops. A small minority of radicals wanted to tear down the fence with their bare hands; the Guard wouldn't shoot—or would they? The balloons, the nervous festivity, reminded the militants of a funeral procession. They saw May 30 as the day they lost control to liberals and pacifists, as they had in the antiwar movement. The Guard left after seventeen days, but the fence stayed.

No one could resist analogies to Vietnam, for the authorities played the parts they would have been allotted in a New Left scenario of imperial occupation. Photos of a grinning cop lounging on a slide brought up images of Ugly Americans in their expeditionary uniforms. Guardsmen posted a sign saying FORT DEFIANCE, bringing Bardacke's leaflet to life. Then helicopters, indiscriminate bombing, the campus as free fire zone! Robert Scheer wrote in *Ramparts* that the intramural playing field had amounted to a " 'strategic hamlet' of clean-cut soccer players—a positive deterrent to subversion—in the very heart of the enemy camp." Chancellor Heyns, who ordered the fence installed and then flew off to a conference, leaving events in the hands of the police, called the original land seizure "unjustified aggression," and more than once sounded (as Scheer said) "like a Secretary of State . . . apologizing for possible excesses of the troops." A grim-faced Governor Reagan, for his part, maintained that the revolutionaries had left bamboo spikes in the park, and told the regents there were two alternatives only: crush the insurrection or surrender. Heyns maintained he was in the position of a business manager working for "a conservative landlord . . . confronted with an unauthorized tenant." The radical view was that university officials, however dismayed by the shootings, had fronted for escalation. Scheer made the point that the majority of the regents who had bought the land were appointees of the Democratic governor Pat Brown. Just as liberal presidents had fancied that their "limited" war in Vietnam was a way of placating the Right, so had the benign administrators hoped to satisfy Reagan with some ill-considered counterinsurgency. "The policy begins with 'reasonable' men," Scheer wrote, "as it did in Viet-Nam and in Berkeley, but it must always end with the hawks. . . . However much they demur later on, the Heynses unleash the Reagans." No one felt the polarization more keenly than one of the Brown-appointed regents, who said: "The Board offered repression and no solutions. The center keeps shrinking, and we are the provocateurs." This was Fred Dutton, formerly of the Robert Kennedy campaign, the same who had saved my neck in Chicago.

On the street side, the Vietnam analogy was susceptible to different colorations. Talk of self-defense escalated. After the helicopter raid, a few activists approached local Vietnam veterans to find out what kind of gun it would take to shoot down a helicopter, although no one went so far as to procure one, and the Guard helicopters, heavily criticized by other police agencies, didn't return. Some activists procured handguns to keep at home. Usually, though, the rhetoric of self-defense took milder forms. To refute Marxists who sniffed at the park because Berkeley wasn't an oppressed colony, I wrote an editorial for an emergency wallposter likening the park people to heroic Vietnamese, and relaying the rumor that the way to keep helicopters away was to fly kites. (What merited attention, though, was the other side of the wallposter: movement artist Frank Cieciorka's full-page drawing of a red rose in the form of a fist smashing through the pavement, which ended up posted in many a Berkeley window.) Others in the movement cautioned against overworking the analogy and forgetting the actual Vietnamese: Bernardine Dohrn flew in to deliver that message at a rally. Even cooler antiwar heads felt the same way: Professor Franz Schurmann returned from a meeting with NLF and North Vietnamese delegates to caution the movement against ceding the antiwar issue to liberals and neglecting the terrible air war being escalated by Nixon under cover of Vietnamization.

What did the park mean? Movement heavies claimed moral and even political victory. "We won the war for the children of California," Frank Bardacke exulted, at a time when Governor Reagan's popularity in the state was undiminished. In one common revolutionary scenario, repression showed how oppression had worn thin; next would come the preliminary stages of guerrilla war. To Stew Albert, his wife Judy Clavir, Tom Hayden, and other revolutionaries, this was an auspicious moment to release a "Berkeley Liberation Program" (it was published in the *Barb* the day of the May 30 march), a call for affinity groups to "make Telegraph Avenue and the South Campus a strategic free territory for revolution"; "turn the schools into training grounds for liberation" ("students must destroy the senile dictatorship of adult teachers and bureaucrats"); "destroy the University unless it serves the people"; "protect and expand our drug culture" ("establish a drug distribution center and a marijuana cooperative"); "break the power of the landlords"; "tax the corporations not the working people"; "defend ourselves against law and order" ("abolish the tyrannical police forces not chosen by the people. . . . The people of Berkeley must arm themselves and learn the basic skills and tactics of self-defense and street fighting. All oppressed people in jail are political prisoners and must be set free"); "create a soulful socialism" (communes, shared housekeeping, and vanguards "who lead by virtue of their moral and political example" rather than by manipulation); and "unite with other movements throughout the world to destroy this motherfucking racistcapitalistimperialist system"—a hodgepodge of revolutionary bravado, radical reform, and the mirror image of the Reaganite nightmare. The Liberation Program unwittingly displayed the decline of the movement's vision since Port Huron; although fragments eventually spun off to become part of the program of Berkeley's electoral Left, its shrill and hackneyed phrases failed to speak to, or for, a shell-shocked community.

What got the most publicity, of course, was the call to paramilitary training. The *Berkeley Tribe,* newly split off from the *Barb,* ran a cover photo of a hip young couple in the woods, she carrying a baby and a gun, he pointing a rifle. (The headline: "JOIN THE NEW ACTION ARMY!") Gun graphics poured through the underground press. But target practice, however defensively intended, was not an alluring political plank even in Berkeley, where the question of whether to learn to shoot split movement groups during the months after the National Guard left. Doublethink spread: act as if this was a revolutionary situation and it would become one. The armed State would see to that; nevertheless, the State was a paper tiger. The State had the guns; the State would wither away. One sign of the phantasmagorical mood was *Ice,* a full-length fiction film written and directed by Robert Kramer, one of the founders of Newsreel and one of its more accomplished and articulate practitioners. Set in an indefinite future (the U.S. is a police state, the U.S. Army is at war against a Mexican revolution) but shot naturalistically in Newsreel's no-frills style, *Ice* depicted a national network of armed collectives laying paramilitary plans under cover of movement filmmaking. In one scene, the revolutionaries rounded up residents of Washington Square Village in lower Manhattan, as if they were Guatemalan peasants, and lectured them about the impending revolution. Newsreel, alarmed by *Ice's* "adventurism," refused to release the film under its name. Nonetheless, at living room screenings, *Ice* had its influence; Stew Albert was one inspired by the fantasy. In the *Tribe* that summer, only half in jest, he recommended Sam Peckinpah's brutal *The Wild Bunch* as "a revolutionary film" because it showed you had to "pick up the gun."

People's Park also left quite different legacies. It pushed forward what was coming to be known as the ecological spirit. At a campus teach-in during the National Guard occupation, Gary Snyder first read his "Smokey the Bear Sutra" (". . . And he will protect those who love woods and rivers,/Gods and animals, hobos and madmen. . . . /Will help save the planet Earth from total oil slick. . . .") The defense of the park linked old-style upper-crust "nature-lovers" with Sierra Club mountaineers and political insurgents. But most of the park-lovers were mild souls depressed and horrified by the bloodshed. The last thing they wanted was to "pick up the gun," and if that was what politics was going to require of them now, many preferred to flee politics altogether. (Myself, I went off for my first visit to Yosemite National Park, to get a sense of what was at stake, what had to be preserved.) The park that was supposed to fuse movement and counterculture ended up driving a wedge between them.

What Berkeley parochialism concealed from the movement notables was that People's Park was the last glimmering hope for a glad-eyed movement, one that would be ecumenical, constructive, and combative all at once. Some terrible line had been crossed. "People's Park ended the movement, really," Stew Albert acknowledges. "The repression was so brutal." For those who paid attention to Berkeley, the sense of white exemption died there, a full year before Kent State. And one small incident suggested to me how fatally insular was Berkeley's uprising. Soon after the National Guard went home, some activists, anticipating that hordes of young freaks were going to flood into town for the summer, persuaded the city to lease them (for one dollar) a cluster of abandoned buildings to use as crash pads. The faithful marched there one day to take proud possession of what was now to be known as People's Pad. But why were these buildings abandoned? It turned out that their former tenants had been evicted—to make way for redevelopment. Those former tenants were impoverished blacks, supposedly the other half of a revolution in the making.

Hip self-help was one thing, but a community organized across class and race lines was another. Between a murderous State and an indifferent or vindictive majority, the counterculture had bumped up against its limits; as the Marxist jokesters said, you could not build socialism in one park. The youth subculture, including its radical segment, was a *sub*culture, an enclave trying to live out "post-scarcity consciousness" in a society still obsessed with scarcity. Liberated territory was a fantasy, but to face that fact head-on would have meant owning up to real limits and vast confusion about the movement's whole trajectory. The movement-for-itself had come far enough to recognize that it was scarcely capable of maintaining itself, let alone making a revolution. The movement-for-others embraced the rhetoric of world revolution, but was at a loss for actual allies. There was more repression than revolution, more fear than ebullience. To acknowledge these truths was to feel paralyzed. Denying them made it possible to keep the revolutionary mirage alive. There was much despair, much talk about impending fascism, much fidgety waiting. For what rough beast?

16

WOMEN: REVOLUTION IN THE REVOLUTION

Objectively, the chances seem nil that we could start a movement based on anything as distant to general American thought as a sex-caste system. Therefore, most of us will probably want to work full time on problems such as war, poverty, race. The very fact that the country can't face, much less deal with, the questions we're raising means that the movement is one place to look for some relief. . . .
—Casey Hayden and Mary King, November 18, 1965

Goodbye, goodbye forever, counterfeit Left, counter-left, male-dominated cracked-glass-mirror reflection of the Amerikan nightmare. Women are the real Left.
　　　　　　　—Robin Morgan, February 9, 1970

On January 19, 1969, the antiwar National Mobilization Committee marked the inauguration of Richard Nixon—or "inhoguration," as it was called—with a march and rally in Washington. In the chaos that followed Chicago, only a few thousand demonstrators turned out; a scatter of objects was hurled helplessly at Nixon's official caravan. That night, under the Mobe's circus tent, two speakers from the growing women's movement were on the platform: SDS veteran Marilyn Salzman Webb and New York radical feminist theoretician Shulamith Firestone. It was the usual movement practice to incorporate constituencies by giving them slots on the program—a pluralist move that made for long rallies. There were two women (along with others bearing mock voter registration cards) because there were already two women's positions bitterly antagonistic to each other. The radical feminists had wanted to skip the occasion, having concluded that all men kept all women down; Webb, an organizer of one of Washington's first women's consciousness-raising groups, had insisted that women keep taking their case to the larger movement. The radical feminists wanted to tear up voter registration cards on the platform, symbolizing that suffrage had failed women; Webb and her comrades decided to destroy theirs as well—to repudiate electoral politics across the board.

Marilyn Webb was twenty-six, slender, attractive. Although she had years of movement experience—she had organized a Head Start project in Chicago while a graduate student in psychology, and had spoken before black congregations—this was the first time she had addressed a multitude on a ceremonial occasion. "We as women are oppressed," she said. "We, as supposedly the most privileged in this society, are mutilated as human beings so that we will learn to function within a capitalist system." As she warmed to the subject, pandemonium broke out in the crowd below her. She plunged on, denouncing a system that views people as "objects and property"—and a cheer went up. She heard shouts: "Take her off the stage and fuck her!" "Take her down a dark alley!" "Take it off!" This was not a burlesque joint, this was the movement she knew and loved. She finished, shaken, and Shulamith Firestone went to the microphone and attacked—not just capitalism, but men, and not just capitalist men, but the men in front of her, "revolutionary" men. "Let's start talking about where you *live,* baby," she roared, to boos, "and wonder whether . . . capitalism and all those other isms don't just begin at home. . . . Because we women often have to wonder if you mean what you say about revolution or whether you just want more power for yourselves."

It was not clear, exactly, which men were yelling and shoving down there. But it was clear to Marilyn Webb who was interrupting, telling her to get the women to stop, they were going on too long, they were going to start a riot. It was Dave Dellinger, presiding. Dellinger was as respected as anyone in the antiwar movement. Happy survivor of pacifism's dog days, editor of *Liberation,* he was a sturdy, smooth-shaven, indefatigably even-tempered man in his mid-fifties with a wide-open smile and an even New England twang. Veteran of a hundred sectarian battles, this coalition-builder's coalition-builder looked unscarred, benignly solid and out of place among angry young longhairs. At stormy demonstrations he was normally an eye of grown-up calm. He had been willing to give the women their chance, but the result, as he had feared, was divisiveness. Ellen Willis, one of the New York feminists on the stage, was outraged: "Why isn't he telling *them* to shut up?"

"I realized," says Marilyn Webb, "that if there was a riot about to start, something very important was happening here." Ellen Willis was shaking: "If radical men can be so easily provoked into acting like rednecks," she wrote soon thereafter, "what can we expect from others? What have we gotten ourselves into?" Later, Webb, Firestone, and the other women repaired to Webb's apartment for a postmortem. The radical feminists told Webb: See, we went along with you, we told you this would happen, now you're going to have to separate from the men's movement. Such arguments had been raging throughout the New Left for months. Webb had resisted the separatist arguments. She had been active in SDS since 1965. She was married to Lee Webb, one of the SDS Old Guard, now on the staff of the Institute for Policy Studies. She was a reporter for the *Guardian*. She hadn't wanted to embarrass the movement men in public. "These were my brothers," she thought. It was no fault of men that, like women, they had been trained for their parts in the system of male supremacy. Even if men treated women's activities as if they were PTA auxiliaries, off to the side of serious political work; even if men were not holding up their end of housework and child care; even if women were blocked in their careers—men and women were still brothers and sisters in One Big Movement.

The argument raged. Then Marilyn Webb's phone rang. She heard giggling in the background, and an obviously disguised woman's voice said: "We're calling from Lanier Place [the SDS staff apartment]. If you or anybody else like you ever gives a speech like that again, we're going to beat the shit out of you. SDS has a line on women's liberation, and that is *the line.*" It sounded to Webb like one of the Washington SDS people with whom she had been tangling for months—probably, she thought, Cathy Wilkerson, formerly of Swarthmore SDS and the SDS national office, who had been arguing in their women's group against independent women's action like the Miss America protest, on the grounds that the concerns of women were petty compared to the imperative of the Revolution. Wilkerson and some of her friends were on their way into the gathering cyclone called Weathermen.

"Just fuck off," Marilyn Webb yelled into the phone. "Don't set foot in here again. I'm going to beat the shit out of you if you do. Don't call me anymore." She hung up, went back to her meeting, and declared that her ambivalence was resolved and that she was now convinced that there had to be a separate women's movement. Webb's group, sans Wilkerson, went on to set up an abortion counseling center, and in February 1970 a feminist newspaper called *off our backs.*

Many years later, Marilyn Webb and I concluded that she had been the victim of a government impersonation. Government agents had known just which button to push.*

---

*In August 1988, at an SDS reunion in upstate New York, Marilyn Webb and I were startled to be told by Cathy Wilkerson that she had not made any such phone call. I discussed the story at length in detail with Webb, Wilkerson, and Mike Spiegel, Wilkerson's former colleague in the SDS Washington office, and found (as did Webb) the following considerations decisive: For one thing, Wilkerson stoutly maintained that she did not make such a call and would never have identified herself as "Lanier Place"—she would have used her name. For a second, she was sure that, at the time of the phone call, she had been out on the street, harassing limousine-driving inauguration guests. For a

By this time, even without government dirty tricks, other New Left women were well on their way to the same separatist conclusion.

No "contradiction" in the late New Left was as charged with implications for the future as that between women and men. As always there was a history of prefigurations—only recognized as such after the fact. Mickey Flacks, for example, could think back to New Year's Eve, the turn of the year from 1962 to 1963, when the tiny SDS National Council in Ann Arbor was rushing through its agenda and got knotted up because one monomaniac insisted on debating SDS's position on, of all things, China, while the women groused in the kitchen about when the year-end party was going to start, for it was *New Year's Eve.* In silence Casey Hayden pointedly wandered in and out of the meeting, but the men ignored her attempt at a discreet signal. Midnight approached. Finally Casey marched out of the kitchen and ostentatiously stood in the midst of the men, facing the wall. The meeting finally got her point, and ended.

That year the SDS heavies were in the habit of taking *Friday nights* for a study group in the Hayden basement, and Casey Hayden and Mickey Flacks would sometimes repair upstairs and gripe about the disappearance of their private lives inside the insatiable maw of the movement. Such flares of annoyance were a long way from women's liberation, but it was striking that they were talking at all. New Left women felt the pinch of a discrepancy between their potential and their position in the movement. To start with, many of the northerners had grown up in relatively egalitarian families—most from the Old Left, influenced by the Communist Party's opposition to what it called "male chauvinism." Their mothers usually worked outside the home, many in jobs as good as their fathers'. Their parents took girls' intellects as seriously as boys', and assumed that the girls would go to college. In the South, most white civil rights activists found a surrogate family in campus church groupings where the idea of the oneness of humanity found a refuge. Like the rest of their generation, the New Left women went to college and graduated in unprecedented numbers; although men still continued to outnumber women in the student population as a whole, the difference was shrinking. Women were the rising gender.*

third, as evidence of government attention, she and Spiegel recall that during these months, the Lanier Place phone was frequently, mysteriously, out of order before and during Washington demonstrations. For a fourth, we now have documented proof that at least from 1968 on, police provocateurs were frequently using forged and anonymous written and phoned threats to inflame political antagonisms in the New Left, the Black Panther Party, and elsewhere. An FBI memo of July 5, 1968, entitled "Counterintelligence Program, Internal Security, Disruption of the New Left (Cointelpro-New Left)," included among "suggestions for counterintelligence action . . . . 2. The instigating of or the taking advantage of personal conflicts or animosities existing between New Left leaders." The government agent who impersonated Wilkerson would have to have been extremely skilled, for she had a distinctive, low-register voice. Government documents give ample evidence of agents' skills in such matters.

*For example, the number of women eighteen to twenty-four enrolled in college increased by 47 percent between 1950 and 1960, then by another 168 percent from 1960 to 1970, while the number

Moreover, the ideology of the New Left was a permanent incitement to internal revolt. The manifestos harped on universal equality and participation, the inseparability of ends and means, goals and process. From C. Wright Mills came the notion that personal troubles are connected with social issues. And the movement had not only a public rhetoric of egalitarianism, but a public rhetoric of honoring its rhetoric—in public and behind closed doors. The attack on hypocrisy was its raison d'être. At its core the movement disputed the premise that politics was to be entrusted to professionals except on election day. Both SNCC (especially its "floater" side) and SDS had a passion to make life whole: to bring political commitment into private life, to make private values count in public, thus to avoid what they saw as the treacherous liberal schism between public postures and private evasions and hierarchies. They refused to reserve politics for cocktail parties and hundred-dollar-a-plate occasions. They did not want to be white liberals with black maids. The movement, in short, encouraged revolts against its own authority in the name of its own values; it had a built-in bad conscience. If the brothers, like the fathers before them, turned out to be frauds, there was no stopping the fury of revelation.

Finally, the early women in SDS had taken initiative, taken risks, exercised some leadership in the movement. They knew how it felt to be taken seriously in a civil rights group or an SDS chapter—wherever face-to-face organizing counted. Sharon Jeffrey, for example, was one of the first Ann Arborites recruited by Al Haber into the tiny SDS circle. As the daughter of Democratic Party stalwarts (her mother was a top United Automobile Workers organizer and the Democratic Party committee-woman for Michigan), organizing came easily to her. She was central to the Michigan SDS chapter, recruited activists (like Rennie Davis) on other campuses, and went on to become a key organizer of tutorial projects in the Northern Student Movement. Barbara Jacobs (later Haber) organized Woolworth's picket lines at Brandeis and was active in the Baltimore chapter of CORE. Dorothy Dawson (later Burlage), an early SDS recruit at the University of Texas, was a leading civil rights activist; she and Sandra Cason (later Casey Hayden) organized voter registration projects through the YWCA and the National Student Association. As students in Chicago Marilyn Salzman (later Webb) and Heather Tobis (later Booth) had been active in a study group that became an SDS chapter. Many of these women felt that movement men took them seriously in ways the world of school and work did not.

Moreover, when most key SDS people gravitated to the ERAP projects in northern ghettos, from 1964 to 1967, many of the women proved to be more

---

of men enrolled at the same age rose by only 21 percent from 1950 to 1960 and another 145 percent by 1970. And these figures understate the difference, for the number of women *staying* in school to earn a bachelor's degree rose by 35 percent between 1950 and 1960, while the number of men graduating *fell* by 24 percent (in part a function of the phasing-out of the G.I. Bill of Rights); from 1960 to 1970 the number of women graduating rose by another 146 percent while the number of men rose by 96 percent.

effective organizers than many of the more celebrated men. The demoralized and skeptical poor were not eager to march; people had to be organized one at a time. Speechmaking, manifesto-writing, analyzing the economy or the history of liberalism—the premium talents of the university and the café; the *men's* talents—were not much use over coffee at some welfare mother's kitchen table. It was the female organizers who were best at hanging out with the local women, listening, commiserating about problems with men and welfare, drawing out stored-up resentments. The women of the community, in turn, became the pillars of the local groups.

By contrast, the poor white men most attracted to radical politics were mostly angry young toughs and older alcoholics. They came and went. Among the hillbillies of Uptown in Chicago, for example, much of the male organizers' energy went into work with "young guys" who hung out on streetcorners, liked cars, sex, and fighting, got fired up against the police in spurts, and were not reliable cadres. Some were the "greasers" and "Park People" who loomed large during the 1968 Democratic Convention demonstrations. The more stable men were also more vulnerable: one local leader led a 1966 march against police brutality (alienating local householders in the process), only to run into flak from his wife, get fired from his job, and drop out. Some had too much trouble with the law: one renowned gang leader was coaxed into the movement against police brutality, but forced to flee the state when the cops turned up the heat. No one organized easily in the poor white sections of Chicago and Cleveland, or the Newark ghetto, but the women, one step at a time, got further than the men.

Thus background, education, ideology, and experience all primed the New Left women for equality. Yet their experience in the national movement was confusing, grating. It wasn't so much that they were underrepresented among national SDS officers—which they were, although no one counted, and women were also underrepresented in other political organizations. (*But SDS wasn't supposed to be just another political organization,* women would say later.) There was a disgruntlement that ran deeper than statistics. SDS women felt obscurely uneasy. Men sought them out, recruited them, took them seriously, honored their intelligence—then subtly demoted them to girlfriends, wives, note-takers, coffeemakers. Although Casey Hayden, Becky Mills, Mickey Flacks, Sharon Jeffrey, and Mary Varela played significant parts at Port Huron, and Carol McEldowney was central in Ann Arbor thereafter, the SDS Old Guard was essentially a young boys' network. One to one, true, the women felt respected. Man-woman friendships were common, intense platonic connections. But in public, at the big national meetings, women had trouble making themselves heard. Many times they didn't want to bother. Most were more timid than the men, less commanding, less adept at parliamentary procedure. To speak up at large gatherings they would have needed encouragement, but encouragement was not the premium SDS style. There were psychic penalties for women who transgressed. A man interrupting a woman sounded normal, a woman interrupting a man violated caste. Ambition, expected in a man, looked suspiciously like ballbusting to the male eye. An aggressive style, which might pass as acceptably virile in a man, sounded "bitchy" in a woman—especially since the SDS men affected a gentle manner and didn't have to strain to get attention.

Early SDS was, as Paul Potter put it, "both fraternal and competitive"—a mixture both effervescent and bewildering, especially in a movement that espoused equal standing and had to cope with the obdurate fact of unequal talents. As Potter added, the fraternity was acknowledged, the competition was not. Neither was the unequal distribution of gifts—for the most part the women were not the writers or speakers the men were. The original circle of SDS male heavies were well read, well spoken, adept at circulating in a man's world. Trained to excel, the Old Guard were hardly averse to shining: indeed, to succeed in the movement required a show of personal prowess, for it was the stirring speech that might move multitudes, the stellar pamphlet that might widen the movement circle, the comprehensive prospectus that might raise the needed money, the show of articulateness that might attract the prestigious outsiders. If women were less competitive, they experienced the deficiency as a personal problem. If (like less aggressive or less talented men) they couldn't speak or write well enough, they blamed themselves, or confined themselves to private resentments about nasty individual X or Y. If they weren't sure how competent they were, the burden was on them to prove themselves. When men withdrew, they were seen as having personal problems; when women withdrew, or showed a sullen resentment, they *became* less competent, and seemed subtly to confirm that women in general were the weaker sex. In 1964, for example, Carol McEldowney wrote me of having "endured many feelings of insecurity and inferiority, largely in the intellectual realm." At one meeting she "felt ignorant, incapable of making intelligent contributions, tongue-tied, and just generally pissed at myself"—and resentful of the elite who could discourse with apparent ease about "American foreign policy, imperialism, SDS's theoretical position, Brazil, ad nauseam. . . . I have trouble saying this to people because the standard response is, 'oh, stop being silly,' which does nothing, absolutely nothing, to reassure me. . . . The damn thing of it is that I'm sure many other people in SDS feel as I do. . . ." In 1965, several of her old friends, myself included, tried to persuade her to become national secretary of SDS, and failed—this experienced and highly competent woman was overwhelmed at being considered in the first place.

At the heart of the matter were the befuddlements of sex. To be at once the comrades and bedmates of power, in an egalitarian climate, was unsettling. What was a woman supposed to make of her lover's remark, "The movement hangs together on the head of a penis"? Were women simply the conduits of men's bonds? The unacknowledged truth stung, even if one was too much the "good girl" to say so out loud. Discomfort had to be submerged. Men were also puzzled: were they interested in women as lovers or as political co-workers? Men in stable couples liked feeling proud of their women—all the better if their women were renowned for political talents—but also craved their femininity, their cooking and typing. Women cherished affiliations with the heavies, which gained them entry to the informal high-level meetings; quietly they also resented being there on male sufferance. They had arrived, but not quite; just what *was* expected of them?

They imagined themselves in a "beloved community" but lived in couples. There was sometimes a sense that couples were only small-scale stand-ins for some unlivable omnisexuality; movement weddings were celebrations of the whole community. But day to day somebody wrote leaflets and somebody else mineographed them, washed the dishes, took out the garbage. Within couples, the commitment to honesty was a matter of generational pride: we were going to surpass our hypocritical parents. But men still held power—including the ultimate power to dissolve the couple, for men left women more often than women left men. In the background, silent, lurked the fact that women were responsible for birth control and suffered through the abortions—not only the terrible procedures themselves, but the fright of having them done illegally, secretly, at risk. There were the apartments in New York from which the woman would be escorted by an unknown person to an unknown address in New Jersey. There were the special flights to Puerto Rico and Mexico. There was, at best, the dedicated doctor in a Pennsylvania mining town, the typed unsigned letter: CHECK INTO THIS MOTEL, BE AT THIS ADDRESS AT THIS HOUR OF THIS DAY, BRING SO MANY HUNDREDS OF DOLLARS.

The SDS women were disconcerted, then, but their discomfort had no name, was not yet a grievance. It became an *issue* at a moment when the Old Guard was particularly vulnerable and the desire for face-to-face politics particularly strong. In 1965, with the success of the Washington antiwar march, SDS was flooded with new members who thought of it as an antiwar organization pure and simple. The Old Guard had lost coherence and traction: we were no longer students, we were unaccustomed to a mass movement, our intellectuality was devalued, and many of us had moved on to ERAP projects. Wanting SDS to rethink its essentials—and revert to a style we could feel halfway at home in—several of us organized a December conference, at the University of Illinois in Champaign-Urbana, to enfold the recruits and renew the SDS point of view on everything.

Into this moment of transition there poured fifteen hundred mimeographed words called "Sex and Caste: A kind of memo from Casey Hayden and Mary King to a number of other women in the peace and freedom movements"—a characteristically modest title for a slow-acting time bomb, arguing that women, like blacks, were an oppressed caste in society *and in the movement.* The authors were formidable figures: Casey Hayden a revered founding mother of SDS, she and Mary King both SNCC stalwarts. Their "freedom high" faction having lost the power struggle in SNCC, their proto-feminist appeals having been ridiculed there, they were carrying the discussion to the wider movement. Their paper arrived a month before the December conference. Several of the SDS women—and some men—read it with a shock of recognition. "Sex and Caste" was included among the conference papers.

The Illinois conference floundered. The intellectual plane was both high and muddled; in the thick of the speechmaking, no one seemed to be paying attention to anyone else. There were, for the first time, race tensions—a Texas delegate punched out for a racist remark; an interloping Chicago black gang member menacing white women. A workshop was announced to discuss the problems of women in the movement, and it drew most of the women veterans (*these are our lives we need to talk about*) and many of the Old Guard men as well (*these are the women we love, what are they talking about?*). The initial discussion was delicate—*were* women a subordinated caste in SDS? Few women doubted it. Most men denied it; some, guilty and confused, said it wasn't their fault. After a while, some of the women said they couldn't talk about these difficult matters in the presence of men, and there were enough of them and the force of the mood was strong enough that they picked up and moved to another room, where, feeling the frisson of having crossed some invisible line, they stayed for hours, reading the Hayden-King memo out loud, talked in personal terms about their humiliations in SDS, about child-rearing, sexual exploitation, the roots of their subjection in marriages and movement offices. They were dazzled to discover they held grievances in common.*

For a moment the women had reconstituted the old face-to-face SDS, that sacred circle of trust. But face-to-face organizing was a waning style in a movement of mass marches, press conferences, hundreds of chapters, giant and anonymous conventions. For a year and a half after Illinois, the women deferred to more urgent issues, Vietnam and black power.** They were reluctant to press their disgruntlement, to ignite the men's rancor. But their issues, submerged, had a subterranean life amid the greater cultural upheaval. SDS grew perhaps tenfold between 1965 and 1967. As the movement swelled, everyone embraced the tribal principle that the oppressed should group together and fight on their own behalf. In 1966 and 1967, separatism was in the air. Blacks, students, Vietnamese, hippies, it was said, should stand apart. Even the image of the revolutionary gang expressed the desire to "make

---

*Meanwhile, the men, chagrined, puzzled, and fascinated, along with women who agreed that separatism was incomprehensible, went on talking by themselves. Barbara and Al Haber were among them, sitting on the veranda of the student union. The evening deepened as the argument proceeded about whether women were essentially passive. It grew chilly. Barbara proposed that the group continue the discussion around the corner, away from the wind. No one noticed. She raised the point two or three times; talk ambled on. Her husband nudged her and said, "Watch this." He repeated the same proposal in the same tone of voice. Everyone moved.

**There were exceptions, although the targets were not movement men. In 1966, for example, a friend of SDS's Heather Tobis at the University of Chicago was raped at knifepoint in her room, and when she went to the student health service for a gynecological exam, she was told such exams were not covered in her plan, and given a lecture on her promiscuity. Tobis and other women sat in at the health service to change the policy.

the revolution" for one's own kind on one's own scale. Yet as the movement galloped headlong, the space left for personal feelings was shrinking.

The sense of grievance simmered. The antidraft movement aggravated sexual difference, echoing the draft itself. "Girls say yes to boys who say no" was a cute slogan, but many women felt humiliated by the pressure to make themselves over into a women's auxiliary. Women new to the movement weren't bound by old loyalties to their men, and even old loyalties were wearing thin. When women brought a resolution for what was now called "the liberation of women" to the floor of SDS's 1967 convention, parliamentary manuevering chewed it up. (In the spirit of the time, women could argue for being taken seriously only by declaring that they had a "colonial relationship to men.") After a debate punctuated by hoots and catcalls, the convention passed a watered-down resolution, which was published in SDS's *New Left Notes,* as Sara Evans points out, "alongside a cartoon of a girl—with earrings, polkadot minidress, and matching visible panties—holding a sign: 'We Want Our Rights and We Want Them Now.' SDS had blown its last chance."

That year, in Chicago and in New York, small groups of women—sparked by SDS and SNCC veterans—started meeting in what became known as consciousness-raising groups. They took inspiration from the peasants' "speak bitterness" groups of the Chinese revolution, publicized in William Hinton's just-published chronicle *Fanshen;* but without quite realizing it, they had another reason to reconstitute the face-to-face group—they were trying to wriggle out from under the movement's vast scale and its abstractions. Soon, women in New York and then Boston and San Francisco, keeping to small groups, were theorizing. In bursts of energy and exhilaration they circulated papers whose titles became famous: "The Myth of the Vaginal Orgasm," "The Politics of Housework," "The Personal Is Political," collected under the ringing titles *Notes from the First Year* (1968) and *Notes from the Second Year* (1970). Men denied the charges, grew defensive, felt remorseful, tried encouragement. Many worried out loud: Was not all this talk about bedroom and dishwashing a great distraction from the war, the working class, the politics of The Revolution? There were attempts at cooptation (women are, after all, one revolutionary battalion among others); from the utterly unreconstructed came ridicule. Women ridiculed back: One cartoon showed a woman holding a screaming infant, washing a sinkful of dishes, saying into a telephone, "He's not here, he's out helping the struggle of oppressed people."

Men were caught up short by the eruption of women's rage. In fact, during the years of New Left acceleration, a critical mass of women felt their situation worsening. In the mid-Sixties, the sexual revolution surged through the New Left as everywhere else. The Pill became routine; men and women took to bed with alacrity. At first, to women as to men, easy sex felt like freedom, and experienced men felt like teachers. "What got me involved," one Free Speech Movement woman has said to embarrassed and approving giggles, "was these exciting older men." The movement, along with the rampant counterculture, was a sexy place to mix. Common bonds could be presupposed; strangers were automatically brothers and sisters. Meetings were sites for eyeplay and byplay and bedplay. Some leaders in effect recruited women in bed—what Marge Piercy in a classic polemic called "fucking a staff into existence." Women might be attracted by a show of sensitivity or an aura of bravery, but in any case there were staffs that were, in effect, serial harems. Packing more clout as the heavies' consorts than on their own, women were willing to play along—hoarding their resentment.

As the movement heated up, its celebrities notched more conquests. The smoldering mixture of danger and notoriety seemed to make men more predatory. The style of long-drawn-out heartfelt triangles yielded to furtive hit-and-run. One married heavy kept a notebook rating his many encounters. While I was traveling in Cuba, a movement buddy tried to seduce the woman I lived with. No real surprise; he was renowned as a miniskirt-chaser. I, in turn, was a basically monogamous sort, and yet, in the tomorrow-we-may-die summer of '68, I indulged in a series of clandestine one-night stands of my own, two of them (one potentially serious, one strictly a lark) with women who were in the process of leaving comrades of mine. The atmosphere was reeking of barricades, the burning possibility (and temptation) of death, the desperate passion to "break on through to the other side"; was not one of Paris's slogans, "The more I make revolution, the more I make love"? Street-fighting man outnumbered streetfighting woman, but in the dark he could impress any number of her more retiring sisters. If the earth was going to glorious hell, sexual conquest was the garden (or last ditch?) of earthly delights. Orgasm was the permanent revolution, the grand finale that led to the next grand finale; or was it that The Revolution was orgasm writ large? With their knack for riding the zeitgeist, the Rolling Stones seized the transition—from 1966's "Let's spend the night together" to 1969's "War and tears, it's just a shot away. . . . Love, sisters, it's just a kiss away. . . ."

And the libertine counterculture, elevating liberty over equality, lacked even the New Left's bad conscience. From the beat boys' gang to Kesey's bus and Leary-Alpert's mansion, men's ideal was the guru, women's the Earth Mother. Women were expected (and expected themselves: no conspiracies here) to step off their pedestals, take off their bras, put on long dresses, and bake bread. In 1968, the druggy White Panther Party manifesto declared: "Fuck your woman so hard till she can't stand up." Liberation News Service excised the offending line, but the word and the text got around. Women were revolted, along with most movement men; five years earlier, the violence of the fantasy would have been unthinkable anywhere in the movement's orbit.

It was now, indeed, that the movement's male stars became known as heavies, with the double connotation of big shots and bad guys. They were minor-league celebrities with a shot at the big leagues. Many of their egos, as Barbara Haber has put it, "metastasized." By the late Sixties there were a few dozen men who stood out as incarnations of The Revolution, so that to sleep with them was the equivalent of taking political communion; and they cut a considerable swath. These "engorged egos" had fewer scruples about making promises, turning women against one another, dividing and ruling. In the rush toward the phantasmagorical revolution, women became not simply a medium of exchange, consolidating the male bond, but rewards for male prowess and balm for male insecurity. The fantasy of equality on the barricades shattered against the reality of the coffeepot and the mimeograph machine. As Marge Piercy put it in her searing diatribe, "The Grand Coolie Damn," the old movement style of intensely caring relations was probably doomed anyway, on the ground of political efficiency: "But there is also a point beyond which cutting off sensitivity to others and honesty to what one is doing does not produce a more efficient revolutionary, but only a more efficient son of a bitch. We are growing some dandy men of steel nowadays."

The other side of the truth was that the tough-talking men of steel, committed to their revolutionary mirage, were losing their grip on reality. Which is one explanation for why the independent women's movement spread as fast and as furiously as it did. Sisterhood was powerful partly because movement brotherhood was not. The women's groups reacted against movement machismo—*and also copied it* with their own version of revolutionary apocalypse—but either way, feminist rage thrived on the sense that the men ostensibly running the show (giving the speeches, calling the demonstrations, editing the papers) were vulnerable. The heavies, beneath the prevailing bluster, were losing their troops; the State had them on the defensive. Most were guilt-ridden sexists anyway, and realistic enough to know that The Revolution wasn't close enough to wash away their sins.

Reality, in short, began to crash through. The Alameda County deputy sheriffs could kill at People's Park, and for all the movement's rhetoric there was nothing that could be done about it. It was the movement, not imperialism or the State, that was apparently a paper tiger. The movement was banging up against its limits, although the cadres of the various factions kept on making wishful music about people's war, worker-student alliances, global revolution, armed struggle, Woodstock Nation—whistling hymns in the dark. As the rhetoric became more flagrantly and insupportably revolutionary, women, I think, were the first to grasp, subliminally, that the male-run movement was moving nothing but itself. Even the macho, besieged Black Panthers encountered a women's revolt in 1969–70, although these rebels stayed within their organization.

And yet women's liberation took over some of the mood, the hope, the fury and extravagance of the male-run movement from which it was breaking, and nowhere more than in Robin Morgan's diatribe, "Goodbye to All That," printed in an all-women's issue (February 9, 1970) of New York's underground *Rat.* Movement women in New York had been offended by a long series of *Rat* articles about "pussy power," headlines like "Clit Flit Big Hit" (for a story on clitoral orgasm), and classified ads for female flesh, whereupon a coalition of women (radical feminists, Weatherwomen, and the self-proclaimed WITCHes of a guerrilla theater squad calling itself Women's International Terrorist Conspiracy from Hell) took over the paper for a special issue. That issue included a defense of guerrilla warfare in terms now familiar, but the talk of the movement was Robin Morgan's ad hominem diatribe.

"White men are most responsible for the destruction of human life and environment on the planet today," wrote Morgan, a poet who had been active in the antiwar movement. "Yet who is controlling the supposed revolution to change all, that?" Against the tyranny of the tribe of white males, Morgan offered a recycled version of the Left's hierarchy of suffering: "It seems obvious that a legitimate revolution must be led by, *made* by those who have been most oppressed: black, brown, and white *women*—with men relating to that the best they can." And then the political became personal. The rest of her piece was an inspired list of male sins and crimes, including the "WeatherVain" with its "Stanley Kowalski image"; the Chicago Conspiracy defendants (spotted "lunching with fellow sexist bastards Norman Mailer and Terry Southern in a bunny-type club in Chicago" with "Judge Hoffman at the neighboring table—no surprise: *in the light they are all the same*"); Abbie Hoffman and Jerry Rubin and Paul Krassner and a gaggle of other luminaries by name and in lurid (and sometimes distorted) detail. She savaged hippies and sexual revolutionaries, declared that men were *"fucked up"* but not *"oppressed,"* and trashed "the simplistic notion that automatic freedom for women —or non-white people—will come about ZAP! with the advent of a socialist revolution." The point was that women were sick of waiting until "after the revolution." "It is the job of revolutionary feminists to build an ever stronger independent Women's Liberation Movement, so that sisters in counterleft captivity will have somewhere to turn, to use their power and rage and beauty and coolness in their own behalf for once, on their own terms, on their own issues, in their own style—whatever that may be." Movement rage mixed with movement present-mindedness ("change *each day of your life right now*") and was leavened by movement solidarity ("Sisterhood Is Powerful"). "Goodbye to All That" went with the male-run movement's melody, but with a different lyric: "Women are the real Left."

One of the bizarre features of 1969, 1970, and 1971 was this deep divide in experience: the time was agonizing for movement men, exhilarating for tens of thousands of women. There were not just separate movements but separate calendars. Women had been the cement of the male-run movement; their "desertion" into their own circles completed the dissolution of the old boys' clan. While men outside the hard-line factions were miserable with the crumbling of their onetime movement, women were riding high. With amazing speed they spawned not only theory but practice—a web of women's health collectives, clinics, legal centers, newspapers, therapeutic groups, communes, publishing houses, bands, abortion counseling services, battered women's shelters, rape counseling centers, legislative campaigns, professional caucuses. There were a myriad of ways to be "in the movement," from sexual experimentation as "political lesbians" (to avoid collaborating with the enemy) to journal-keeping à la Anais Nin, yet all vying for the mantle of correctness. There were also a myriad of uncertainties, carried over from the old movement: Was it sisterly to sleep with the husband of someone in your women's group? Was it "correct" to stay in graduate school? But faith remained that history was beginning afresh, that The Revolution (now in its feminist incarnation) would work out the "correct" answers and resolve all "contradictions." One didn't have to agree that all women constituted a "Fourth World," as some maintained, to feel that sisterhood was, indeed, powerful, that this commune or collective or "relationship" or theory was hastening the Last Days of Patriarchy.

It was the season of the "rectification of names," when a vast profusion of customs hitherto thought "natural" were redefined as "sexist." Male heavies were heckled in public by women they had worked with, or over, for years. The bitter idea floated that a delegation of women should stand up in the courtroom where the Chicago 8 were on trial and shout, "These men are being tried for the wrong reasons!" But even more extensive and explosive were the reverberations in living room, kitchen, and bedroom. The movement household had never been a terribly private space, but now it was officially "an arena of struggle." The war came home. Clumsily, men set out to cook, sweep, and make sure their lovers had orgasms. "Chicks" were upgraded to women; traditionalists who insisted on the generic "man" for the human race had to apologize. Wolf-whistles and dirty jokes were suppressed. In 1971, Tom Hayden, trashed by his Berkeley lover and fellow Red Family communards for self-aggrandizing activities and "male chauvinism," left Berkeley altogether.

The rectifications did not prevent an extraordinary number of movement couples from coming uncoupled, though. For years men, if pressed, had claimed that jealousy was a female hangup. Now women returned the disfavor, refusing to be "possessed." Jealousy was a male hangup. Women's liberation echoed the countercultural cry, "Smash monogamy." Only when women freed themselves from male proprietors, it was argued, could they come into their own. Romantic love was "bourgeois." Love might be possible some bright day in the future, but first came revenge. At times the smashing of couples left individuals happier and women more powerful; often what got smashed were psyches. But the revolution was not for people with failed nerves. It was "too late to turn back."

By 1969, the male-run movement was in convulsions, of which the women's movement was as much a product as a cause. Might women have salvaged the self-destroying Left had they stayed inside it, not organized autonomously? Would they have injected sanity and clarity into a movement by this time sorely lacking in a sense of the real? Possibly in the short run, probably not for long. The centrifugal forces were too fierce. The old movement was coming apart because of its commitment to an impossible revolution, and everything that followed—passionate hairsplitting, irresponsible leaders, desperado strategy, insupportable tactics. Indeed, women of the Left gloried in that all-or-nothing spirit, and suffered from it as well. From the embers of the old movement, a new one rose scorching—sisterly, factional, wild, egomaniacal, furious with insight and excess, the voice of millions of women, living survivors of the death and transfiguration of the New Left.

THE IMPLOSION

As one young SDS activist put it recently, after a certain
amount of frustration you decide that at least you can
make yourself into a brick and hurl yourself.
                              —Staughton Lynd, Summer 1969

THE ANTIWAR STALEMATE

Strategy for The Revolution was difficult to work up but easy to talk about, for The Revolution was as abstract as it was nebulous. You could cite authorities (Lenin said X), brandish shreds of personal testimony (I heard a black say Y, a worker say Z), lead cheers for the latest action (numbers are growing, struggle is sharpening). But questions of practical strategy—in particular, how to end the war—required a firmer grounding in reality. Before the perpetual question "What is to be done?" comes "How are we doing?" And on this score, in the summer and fall of 1969, the antiwar movement was in the dark.

Richard Nixon, master strategist, had fastened on a three-pronged project of which the antiwar movement was only dimly aware. First, he had resolved to extricate the war—political dynamite, as Lyndon Johnson had discovered—from American politics. In May 1969, Nixon announced the withdrawal of 25,000 troops, and by the end of the year he had brought home a total of 65,000. On November 3, he gave a name to his policy: "Vietnamization," turning the burden of ground combat over to the Saigon army. In 1970 another 140,000 Americans came home. With draft calls peaking, and the number of eligible males swelling, Nixon moved toward a draft lottery and indicated that he was going to phase out the draft altogether. In fits and starts, he talked peace with Hanoi and the NLF in Paris. He convinced TV network news that "the story" was "We Are On Our Way Out of Vietnam"—fully four years before the last American combat troops left Vietnam.

Meanwhile, Nixon accelerated the concealed war, the one that pulverized Indochina but cost few American casualties. In March 1969, aiming to impress Hanoi with the possibility that he would stop at nothing, he began bombing Cambodia—in secret. Over the next fourteen months, he authorized 3,600 flights which dropped 110,000 tons of bombs on neutral Cambodia. He bombarded North Vietnam, and threatened still more furious attacks upon Hanoi and its infiltration routes south. His goal, like his predecessors', was at the least to keep from losing the war while he was in office; or at most, as Seymour Hersh has argued, to bomb his way to victory. Nearly 10,000 Americans died in Vietnam during 1969. More than 20,000 Americans, and several hundred thousand Vietnamese, died while the war was "winding down." All told, between 1965 and 1973, Nixon and Johnson dropped more than eight million tons of bombs on Indochina—more than four times what the U.S. dropped during all of World War II.

Third, to keep his hands free, Nixon tried to crush as much as possible of the antiwar movement, along with black militants. The FBI had finally come to the conclusion that the New Left was a force to be reckoned with, not just an infiltration zone for the Communist Party. New Leftists were gradually added to J. Edgar Hoover's Security Index, a master file of candidates for roundup "during a national emergency." (Our whereabouts therefore had to be updated every few months. We were often tracked down through "pretext calls" by FBI agents. "Because of GITLIN's background as a writer," my favorite memo reads, "it is not believed to be in the Bureau's best interest to interview him at this time.") The CIA's Operation Chaos (formerly the Special Operations Group), for movement surveillance, grew. The Nixon administration used militants (including agents provocateurs) to taint moderates, on the principle that the more destructive the protest, the easier it was to discredit. It authorized wiretaps, grand jury investigations, felony prosecutions. It contrived to plant nasty stories and otherwise worsen the already bad press which the New Left was receiving. It tried to intimidate news media deemed too sympathetic to the protests, and harassed the underground press. The FBI and other agencies opened mail, pressured employers, landlords, and printers, forged letters to provoke or deepen intramovement quarrels, and schemed to spread suspicion that some leaders were government informers—a practice apparently so common there was a special term for it, "bad jackets." State and local police contributed their own burglaries, stole mailing lists, instigated harassment by landlords and disconnection by phone companies. Eventually, even mild liberals were placed on a White House "enemies list." With Nixon trying to spin an aura of statesmanship, the "bad cop" rhetoric was assigned to Vice President Spiro T. Agnew, who contributed blasts against "small cadres of professional protesters," "nattering nabobs of negativism," and the "effete corps of impudent snobs who characterize themselves as intellectuals." Indeed, Agnew proclaimed his own version of the "sleeping dogs" strategy: "If, in challenging, we polarize the American people," he said on October 30, 1969, "I say it is time for a positive polarization . . . a constructive realignment. . . . It is time to rip away the rhetoric and to divide on authentic lines. It is time to discard the fiction that in a country of 200 million people, everyone is qualified to quarterback the government."

The antiwar movement was like an audience gathered for a performance taking place behind drawn curtains. There were offstage screams. Once in a while, a functionary would appear in front of the curtain and announce that difficulties were being tended to. It was obvious that, since Tet, the war had divided the political, economic, media, and even military elites—and equally obvious that these divisions were not forcing the U.S. out of Vietnam. The question was whether to widen or intensify the protest. Moderates wanted to augment the numbers and galvanize supporters in Congress and the media. They marched, lobbied, wrote letters, campaigned for immediate withdrawal —what had been the "radical" position in the mid-Sixties. On October 15, 1969, came their supreme moment, the Moratorium, a day on which millions decided not to do business-as-usual, but took part in a cascade of local demonstrations, vigils, church services, petition drives, replete with respectable speechmakers and sympathetic media fanfare. On November 15 came a huge Mobilization in Washington, up to three-quarters of a million demonstrators, coinciding with a second national Moratorium. Then—hiatus. The moderates stalled, the leadership didn't know what to do for an encore.

The antiwarriors had become accustomed to defeat. That the worst escalations might be averted or postponed was abstract surmise; the solid fact was that bombs were falling. No one outside the White House suspected that the October 15 Moratorium, and the promise of more of the same on November 15, helped abort Nixon's secret summer ultimatum to Hanoi: either accommodate to his bargaining terms by November 1 or he would launch an unprecedented new assault, including, as Seymour Hersh has written, "the massive bombing of Hanoi, Haiphong and other key areas in North Vietnam; the mining of harbors and rivers; the bombing of the dike system; a ground invasion of North Vietnam; the destruction—possibly with nuclear devices— of the main north–south passes along the Ho Chi Minh Trail; and the bombing of North Vietnam's main railroad links with China." There were military arguments against the feasibility of this barrage, but Nixon was also deterred by the protest. While letting it be known that he would spend November 15 in front of the White House TV watching the Washington Redskins' game, the President was convinced that—as he later put it—"after all the protests and the Moratorium, American public opinion would be seriously divided by any military escalation of the war." But more and more of the movement was succumbing to bitter-end rage. By 1970 even the antiwar movement's longtime campaigners—adult, relatively patient, immune to America's cornucopian promises—felt burned out by frustration and factionalism.

The younger, more radical activists were more utopian and apocalyptic to start with, and experience seemed not to reward their small supplies of patience. All the more reason for them to "intensify the struggle," as Eldridge Cleaver put it—and not just in the name of ending the war, but increasingly for "Victory to the NLF" and against a system of which the Vietnam war came to seem a necessary consequence. Every day the blood spilled, the radical anaylsis gained credibility. For if the war went on despite massive and widening protest, despite economic drain and political unpopularity, if liberals and "rational imperialists" like Johnson's Wise Men could not liquidate it as a bad investment, it had to be more than a "mistake"—had to be not only a crime but a symptom. From the principle that effects are commensurate with causes, it seemed to follow that some enormous machinery was at work, call it imperialism. Once resistance sprang up, imperialism led to mass slaughter, for if the guerrillas swam among the people like fish in water, as Mao said, the imperialists would try to win by drying up the lake. Perhaps, then, the Vietnam war was the linchpin of the entire imperial order. Perhaps the "domino theory" was valid after all, although not as the policymakers meant it: if they lost in Vietnam, they *would* inspire revolutionary movements throughout the Third World. If the White House thought Vietnam was the sine qua non of American power, it was.

If everything was at stake in Vietnam, it was easy to conclude that whoever opposed imperialism was on the side of the angels, and that the angels, arrayed in a single choir, were about to usher in the millennium. Emotion scoured the mind to black and white. The logic came down to this: The world was neatly divided into revolutionaries and counterrevolutionaries; the task was no longer ending the war but "winning" it, which, thanks to the North Vietnamese and the NLF, was within reach. From early SDS on, hadn't the New Left point been victory, not moral witness? Counselors of patience and coalition, those who doubted that a revolution was on the American agenda, were accused of having made their peace with a savage society. The militants, whether from early or late SDS, thought they were pragmatists, learning from experience that when you beat your head against a wall often enough there is something to be said for turning to dynamite. This late New Left no longer called itself a New Left—it even spat at such sentimental mush. As early as the summer of 1968, SDS national secretary Mike Klonsky was using "New Left" as a pejorative. "When I got involved in SDS," Klonsky said years later, "I haven't read the Port Huron Statement. . . . I got involved because Calvert and Davidson came out to L.A. and they said, 'Put your body on the line,' and 'From protest to resistance,' and so on, and the next thing I knew, I was the field secretary."

What had been the movement was increasingly the Left, period—the current incarnation of a historical perennial; or a prologue to that apocalypse to end all apocalypses, The Revolution.

THE REVOLUTIONARY LOOP

So the no-longer-new Left trapped itself in a seamless loop: growing militancy, growing isolation, growing commitment to The Revolution, sloppier and more frantic attempts to imagine a revolutionary class, growing hatred among the competing factions with their competing imaginations, growing vulnerability to repression. Students for a Democratic Society, the movement's main organizational web, became its final battlefield. As the organization was pulled apart by cannibal factions, most of the remnants of the old New Left stood aside, demoralized, gazing in fascinated horror as sideshow theatrics became the movement's main act. How could the organization that began by echoing Albert Camus and C. Wright Mills end with one faction chanting, "Ho, Ho, Ho Chi Minh, Dare to Struggle, Dare to Win," while members of the other waved their Little Red Books in the air and chanted "Mao, Mao, Mao Tse-tung"? The comic-book crudeness of the sloganeering at this point was self-evident to anyone with a residual hold on reality—anyone who appreciated how many enemies the movement strategy of "fighting back" was arousing, how many "sleeping dogs" were barking precisely because the movement had aroused them.

The Old Guard stood dumbstruck, as if at the scene of a bloody accident. The perpetrators were not aliens. They were familiar—indeed, horrifying and enthralling, precisely because they were familiar. Several of the leading Weathermen had been visible in and around SDS for a number of years. The Weathermen were the New Left's "id," said Tom Hayden. They were "my children," said Carl Oglesby: he had taught them, inspired them, loved them. And what they caricatured was equally familiar—the politics of the late New Left.

All the versions of that politics attempted to force a revolutionary solution to a fundamental problem. If morality and eschatology agreed that there had to be a revolution, there had to be someone to make it. The New Left's torment—the torment of all radical student movements—was that relatively privileged people were fighting on behalf of the oppressed: blacks, Vietnamese, the working class. Committed to a revolution it did not have the power to bring about, the movement cast about for a link with forces that might have the power. But none did. For all the slackening in the loyalties which bound people to the social order, for all the demonstrations and dropping out and divisions among the governing forces, there was no revolutionary crisis. Yet to give up the revolutionary dream would have been to confront a situation without precedent in the history of the modern Left. The working class was conservative, more or less, the privileged were radical. What could be made of *that*?* Unwilling to give up the revolutionary dream, the New Left factions convinced themselves that The Revolution had already begun, and proceeded to conjure up abstract and imaginary allies: allies either nonexistent (revolutionary white youth, industrial workers) or unreliable (Black Panthers) or remote (Vietnamese, Chinese). The more abstract these hypothetical allies, the more serviceable for the revolutionary myth.

The Weathermen, in other words, were an extension—not the only imaginable one, but the most rageful—of bad, abstract politics by other means. They were the purest consequence of a syllogism: The Revolution had to be; there was no one to make it; therefore it had to be forced. They finessed the flaws in their vision and resolved to bull past obstacles with sheer nerve. They were the pure New Left in a way—self-enclosed, contemptuous of liberalism, romantic about Third World revolutions, organized in small squads, exuberant with will, courageous, reckless, arrogant, burning to act *as if* anything might be possible. And ideologically, they shared the growing movement notion that the bulk of Americans were bribed by affluence into supporting the system. Three SDS theorists wrote an influential pamphlet in 1968 arguing that consumption amounted to wasteful "domestic imperialism"—still, only one of the three, David Gilbert, came to conclude that the American working class was hopelessly integrated into capitalism's strategy for stabilization and that terror was therefore legitimate. Most of the movement still observed limits, moralities, barriers between politics and violence. To convert weak ideas into desperado politics, it was necessary to let rage off the leash.

The details of SDS's late days matter less than the logic, but traces of the history—the "begats" of successive factions—display the logic unfolding.

The Weatherman faction coalesced as SDS girded for its June 1969 convention. The faction organized by Progressive Labor was growing—less a consequence of its "Maoism," whatever exactly that was (it was certainly different from the barricade romanticism of the French "Maoists"), than of its availability as a counterforce to the "resistance" mood of 1967–69. With its talk of "base-building" and "worker-student alliance," its short hair and suspicion of rock 'n' roll (to avoid offending "the workers"), PL positioned itself as a straitlaced alternative to the raucous go-it-alone sentiment surging

---

*I put it this way in the summer of 1969: ". . . an inescapable choice presented itself: Either the post-scarcity left would comprehend its own unprecedented identity as a social force, elaborate that identity into a vision and program for the campus and the youth ghettos, and use its reality as a strength from which to encounter anti-colonial and working-class energy and to devise common approaches—or it would turn from its identity, throw the vision out with the narrowness of the class base, and seek an historically pre-packaged version of revolution in which students and *déclassés* intellectuals are strictly appendages or tutors to the 'real' social forces. Either it would take itself seriously as a visionary force, conscious of post-scarcity potentials with revolutionary and democratic goals, or it would buy clarity on-the-cheap, taking refuge in mirror-models of the underdeveloped socialisms of Russia and the Third World. Either it would accept the awesome risk of finding new paths—or it would walk the beaten trails, pugnacious and sad. A grave choice, where the stakes are immense; but the pounding pressure of the State leaves no time for placid reflection." To get a hearing in the movement I had to speak—indeed, to think—the apocalyptic language of "post-scarcity" and "revolution."

through the rest of SDS. Few of the delegates to PL's founding convention came from the industrial working class, but inexperience boosted the fantasy: it equipped PL's sympathizers to think that by taking a summer job in a factory (a "work-in") they could bring correct politics to the historically predestined agency of change. Not surprisingly, PL's major strength within national SDS came from that citadel of privileged guilt, Harvard. If you intuited that insurgent students—even numbering in the millions and even featured on the nightly news—were no substitute for a wider political base, PL looked plausible. With its disciplined cadres and prepackaged quotations from Mao, PL was at least a way of making a pass at clarity.

PL helped Marxize SDS, and PL fattened, parasitically, as Marxism and then Marxism-Leninism became SDS's unofficial language. "In about a six months period," as Greg Calvert later put it, "suddenly everybody in SDS said, 'I am a Marxist,' or 'I am a Marxist-Leninist.' . . . People you never would have suspected of having read Marx at all suddenly became 'Marxists.' Overnight." Behind that mass conversion was a hunger. Marxism as a practice, traditionally, was among other things the historically certified attempt to solve a perennial problem: to reconcile the privilege of socialist intellectuals with their commitment to take the side of the oppressed. If Marxism had no good solution—if, indeed, the failure of the pre–World War I social-democratic parties is what brought Lenin to the fore and made the rest of the history of socialism revolve around the baleful precedent of his success—at least Marxism acknowledged the problem. Lenin went further and made the bearers of theory indispensable. And so in the late Sixties the student movement cast about for a usable Marxism.

One possible option was to declare the movement itself the crucible of a revolutionary class. After PL, Marxism entered SDS as a way to make respectable the idea of the movement for itself. This was the tack of a 1966 pamphlet by the prairie-power leader Carl Davidson, "A Student Syndicalist Movement," arguing that students were being trained as future managers, technocrats, and technicians, that the universities were factories whose product was knowledgeable labor, and that when students tried to take power in those factories they were igniting a sort of anticipatory strike in the core of society.* Then came what was jocularly known as the "Port Authority Statement": Early in 1967, a small New York faction imported French Marxism and argued in a long polemic that professionals and technical workers were themselves a "new working class," the cutting edge of this stage of capitalist development, the true creators of wealth who, with help, would come to see that to be free and happy they needed to overthrow superfluous capital. Students were labor in embryo. The important thing was to sustain the principle

---

*Davidson's hope became capitalism's fear. The editors of *Fortune*'s special issue on youth (January 1969) warned business to work harder to accomodate themselves to students' reform passions. Max Palevsky, president of Scientific Data Systems, told *Business Week* that the student movement "certainly bodes ill for industrial discipline. If this kind of irrationality spreads to industry, the results will be disastrous."

put forward in February 1967 by SDS national secretary—and Davidson's ally —Greg Calvert. "The liberal reformist is always engaged in 'fighting someone else's battles.' " Calvert said. "Liberal consciousness is conscience translated into action for others." On the contrary, "radical or revolutionary consciousness . . . is the perception of *oneself* as unfree, as oppressed—and . . . leads to *the struggle for one's own freedom in unity with others who share the burden of oppression. . . .*"

But none of these attempts to place students at the storm center of radical social change proved persuasive. For one thing, if the "new working class" was the core of the production system of the future, why were student radicals coming from the ranks of sociologists and English majors, not engineers? And if students were training to be managers or well-paid professionals, in what sense were they suffering? Were boredom and powerlessness comparable to the wounds of the Vietnamese or the starvation of Guatemalan peasants? What if the logic of their individualist revolt led no further than sex, drugs, rock 'n' roll, and dodging the draft? *Precisely because there were so many students in motion it was self-evident that students did not suffice,* that other forces were needed to make The Revolution. The problem remained not just what was to be done, but who was to do it.

By 1969, then, all the factions of SDS strutted about as self-appointed vanguards in search of battalions: PL's working class, the Weathermen's Third World, the Revolutionary Youth Movement's working-class youth. They spoke in Marxist-Leninist tongues because there was, as Carl Oglesby wrote, *"no other coherent, integrative, and explicit philosophy of revolution."* But more: Leninism was a kind of solution—as spurious as it was ingenious—to the core problem: so big, the student movement was too small to remake America root and branch. It had to cast about for a group big and strategically placed enough to do that. Which raised another problem: the revolutionaries had to remain indispensable. After all, they were either born into privilege or schooled to believe they were entitled to it. Knowledge was their key to mastery. Eureka, Leninism!—the classic way to enable would-be vanguards to finesse the contradiction between their aspirations and their capacities. Titleholders of irreplaceable theory, keepers of perpetual flames at the tombs of revolutionary ancestors, the Leninist groupings could fancy themselves the vanguard of a revolutionary class, could justify holding power in the course of The Revolution—and why stop there? So Leninism gave would-be theorists the most honored of places. With perverse brilliance it preserved the anarchist taste for the small group and welded it to a time-honored strategy for successful revolution. The vanguard was the gang transmuted into the Party.

THE LOGIC OF SECTARIANISM

Enter the Weathermen. The sixteen-thousand-word position paper from which they took their name, called "You Don't Need a Weatherman to Know Which Way the Wind Blows" after a little-known Bob Dylan line, argued that you *did* need one after all, and they were it. It swooped from giddy Third Worldism to a call for "antipig self-defense" movements and "cadre organization" on the way to a "Marxist-Leninist party" and "armed struggle." From Chinese defense minister Lin Piao's famous 1965 polemic came the notion that just as the Chinese revolutionaries had first mobilized the peasantry and surrounded the cities, now the Third World revolution was going to surround the imperialist metropolis; it was just a matter of time before the United States—the imperialist mother country itself—was engulfed in revolution. The Weathermen closed with Lin Piao's title, "Long Live the Victory of People's War."

Who knows how many of SDS's hundred thousand or more members actually read this clotted and interminable manifesto, which raised obscurity and thickheadedness to new heights? But the Weathermen didn't recruit through force of argument so much as through style. Their esprit was undeniable. They were good-looking. They had panache. They radiated confidence as if to the manner born. Nor did it spoil their mystique that, like some of the PL leaders, several of the Weathermen came from wealth: Bill Ayers, the son of the chairman of the board of the Commonwealth Illinois electrical combine; David Gilbert, the son of a toy manufacturer; Diana Oughton, the daughter of a small-town Illinois banker and Republican state legislator, and great-granddaughter of the founder of the Boy Scouts of America. Most of the Old Guard, by contrast, were children of public-school teachers, professors, accountants, and the like; a higher proportion of the prairie-power group came from working-class families. But contrary to popular impression, most of the Weathermen were not the spoiled children of the rich. What drove them was not so much class origins but magical fury. Theory permitted them to abase themselves before a sterotyped Third World, and yet hold on to their special mission. They presented themselves as the refutation of PL, which was tactically stolid, morally stodgy (no drugs, no living in sin), and shockingly unenamored of the Black Panthers and Ho Chi Minh. In accord with the prevailing sociology of the Fifties and Sixties, they thought the bulk of the American working class—all but the young angries—had been bought off. They scorned the notion "that there is a magic moment after we reach a certain percentage of the working class, when all of a sudden, we become a working-class movement. We are already that if we put forward internationalist proletarian politics." Presto! Who needed the working class?

At the core of the Weathermen mystique stood SDS's interorganizational secretary, Bernardine Dohrn, who combined lawyerly articulateness with a

sexual charisma—even more than her chorus line looks—that left men dazzled. At SDS's 1968 convention Dohrn picked up a national following when
she declared she was a "revolutionary communist" with a small c. She fused
the two premium female images of the moment: sex queen and streetfighter.
(Indeed, of all the factions, the Weathermen were the most alluring to
women, who could prove themselves now by slinging revolutionary jargon
and kicking ass with the best of the men.) Once installed in the SDS office,
she agreed to put aside feminism for The Revolution. Compared to Bernardine Dohrn, the famous Mark Rudd was a minor Weathermen adornment, if a
major one by media lights.

These hip outlaws made revolution look like *fun*. One of the signers of
their manifesto, Gerald Long, had raved about *Bonnie and Clyde* for the *Guardian*, likening the "consciousness-expanding" outlaws to Frantz Fanon and the
NLF hero Nguyen Van Troi. The Weathermen relished LSD. They liked
orgies. Although their formal position papers were as leaden as all the other
factions', they were not allergic to wit, on which they placed heavy hands.
They were given to headlines like "Hot Town: Summer in the City, or I Ain't
Gonna Work on Maggie's Farm No More." In *New Left Notes* (soon renamed
Fire) they ran pictures and articles celebrating the presumed guerrilla exploits
of a five-year-old child named Marion Delgado, who had once derailed a train.
Their top command was—what else?—the "Weatherbureau." Proud of their
roots in youthful innocence, they sang songs like "I'm dreaming of a white
riot" (to the tune of "White Christmas"), and from *West Side Story*, "When
you're a red you're a red all the way/From your first party cell till your class
takes the state," and to the tune of "Maria": "The most beautiful sound I ever
heard/Kim Il Sung . . . /I've just met a Marxist-Leninist named Kim Il
Sung/And suddenly his line/Seems so correct and fine/To me/Kim Il Sung/Say
it soft and there's rice fields flowing/Say it loud and there's people's war
growing/Kim Il Sung/I'll never stop saying Kim Il Sung." Giggling at their
own fanaticism, they also affected themselves superior to it. During the People's Park battle, for example, a visiting Weathermen delegation criticized the
Berkeley wallposter group I belonged to because we had failed to conclude
our editorial with a resounding "Power to the People!" A few days later, I
heard two of them at a party, stoned, going on about Chairman Mao having
said this, Chairman Mao having said that. "Where did the Red Book come
from?" I finally exploded. "Heaven?" They exchanged a look of stoned knowingness, and rolled their eyes. The blond Jeff Jones, formerly of Antioch
College, cherubic as the Southern California surfer he had once been, smiled
at me and hissed, "Yesssss!" Then the two of them cracked up at the straight-
man rube.

"They knew they were crazy," said Carl Oglesby (who knew them better
than anyone else of the old SDS) years later. "Terry [Robbins] and Billy
[Ayers] had this Butch Cassidy and Sundance attitude—they were blessed,
they were hexed, they would die young, they would live forever, and at their
most triumphant moment they would look over their shoulders, as Butch and

Sundance looked back at their implacable pursuers, and say more in admiration than in dread, 'Who *are* those guys?' I believe they thought they looked cute, and that everybody would know it was basically a joke. The next minute, they were lost in it and couldn't get out."

Althought the Weathermen loathed the old New Left—they lashed out at "so-called 'Movement People'" as "this kind of right-wing force, this weirdness that's moving around," infected by pacifism and morality—they still cried out to be taken as sole heirs of the original SDS. They had credentials, mostly from the SDS of 1966 and after—SDS campus travelers like Washington's Cathy Wilkerson (ex-Swarthmore) and the Midwest's Terry Robbins (ex-ERAP); the onetime Columbia chapter influentials John Jacobs, Ted Gold, and Dave Gilbert, as well as the media shooting star Mark Rudd; the longtime civil rights and ERAP organizer (turned August 1968 Chicago Hilton stink-bomber) Kathy Boudin; the Ann Arbor Children's Community School organizer Bill Ayers ("CHILDREN ARE ONLY NEWER PEOPLE," read their happy-face button). Many of them had been swept away at staggering speed: A mere two years earlier, Gilbert had been one of the authors of the "Port Authority Statement," Boudin an organizer of welfare mothers in Cleveland, Ayers a campaigner for an antiwar resolution in the American Federation of Teachers. . . . On the movement's breakneck timetable, they could claim to have tried everything short of revolutionary violence.

SDS's 1969 convention, its last, met in the cavernous Chicago Coliseum, amid a veritable counterconvention of reporters (excluded), FBI agents (equipped with long lenses on the third floor of a vacant building across the street), and hundreds of police milling around, in and out of uniform, snapping pictures. Of the fifteen hundred delegates, perhaps a third were controlled by PL. Perhaps another third were divided between the Weathermen and their short-term allies, the upholders of a rival version of a Revolutionary Youth Movement—RYM II for short, in the arcane jargon of the time. (Among the RYM II supporters was a Bay Area faction passing out a pamphlet called *The Red Papers* adorned with portraits of Marx, Engels, Lenin, and Stalin.) The remaining third were baffled newcomers, dazed rank-and-filers, and other tendencies casting anathema on all the leading factions—most inventively a grouplet of anarchists passing out Murray Bookchin's corrosive pamphlet *Listen, Marxist!* with its cover pictures of Marx, Engels, Lenin, and Bugs Bunny.* The rest of the organization—tens of thousands of national members, and who knew how many members of individual chapters—voted with their feet and stayed away. So did almost all the old and middle-period hands of SDS. Reports filtered back from Chicago as if from another planet— or rather, from a moon in orbit around one's own, for that bone-white light, that silver deathliness, had the familiar look of reflected light.

---

*There was already a tradition for the expression of rank-and-file disgruntlement through stunts. At the 1968 convention, a Motherfucker nominated a garbage can to run against one of the national office's slate of ponderous leftists. The garbage can narrowly lost.

The funeral had its farcical aspects. To score points against PL, the Weathermen-RYM II coalition trundled out Third World allies; representatives of the Young Lords, Brown Berets, and finally, of course, the Black Panthers, whose Illinois minister of information in the course of a diatribe against the "armchair Marxists" of PL suddenly launched into a celebration of "pussy power," proclaiming that "Superman was a punk because he never even tried to fuck Lois Lane." (The anarchists' Bugs Bunny cartoon turned out more realistic than they could have imagined.) Another Panther took the stage to endorse "pussy power" and to add, à la Stokely Carmichael, that the correct position for women in the movement was "prone." The crowd, aghast, hooted. The next day, the Panthers returned and read an ultimatum: PL had to change its line or "they will be considered as counter-revolutionary traitors and will be dealt with as such." It sounded like a burlesque of the left-wing mumbo jumbo of earlier decades, but no one laughed. PL chanted "Smash redbaiting, *smash redbaiting,*" "Read Mao, *Read Mao.*" But these were only curtain-raising preliminaries to the grand climax: the Weathermen and RYM II caucused, then decided to expel PL and its allies for being "objectively anticommunist" and "counterrevolutionary." "Long live the victory of people's war!" were Bernardine Dohrn's parting words before leading seven hundred fist-waving delegates out of the convention hall, chanting, "Ho, Ho, Ho Chi Minh," into their own rump SDS. The Weathermen had no qualms about dismantling the largest organization of the New Left, indeed, the largest American organization anywhere on the Left in fifty years. The rest of an agonized, bewildered movement could be sloughed off like old skin. They reveled in the thrill of cutting loose—true outlaws at last.

Hilarious, this debacle, but no one could laugh it off. There was too much at stake, and tragedy that repeats itself too often becomes numbingly banal. In the course of the previous year, name-calling had become SDS's premium style. Whole issues of *New Left Notes* were filled with columns of factional denunciation, written in clumsy Marxoid code. "Brotherfucking," I called it, and wrote to a Cuban friend that "these fights among brothers depress me enormously. The Left is its own worst enemy here . . . and often I'm glad we're in no position to take power: if we did, the only honorable sequel would be abdication." One small but exemplary moment: the arraignment of almost five hundred demonstrators, including my civil-libertarian self, who had gone to a January 1969 rally banned by fiat at San Francisco State College. I had been skittering around the edges of the campus strike for months, writing articles, working on a campus wallposter, comforting the wounded, outside-agitating in an effort to organize an alternative to the PL caucus in the SDS chapter, and then, during the bust, watching a cop blithely steal my address book for my pains. Now, in court, I heard the clerk call my name. As I walked to the front of the courtroom one of the PL people hissed, "Revisionist!" A small thing, but demoralizing. All the veterans had stories like that.

"On every quarter of the white Left, high and low," as Carl Oglesby wrote, "the attempt to reduce the New Left's inchoate vision to the Old Left's perfected remembrance has produced a layer of bewilderment and demoralization which no cop with his club or senator with his committee could ever have induced."

Still more demoralizing, it dawned upon Oglesby and me and others of our ilk that the sectarian furies were more than an epidemic of nasty manners. The intellectual squalor and moral collapse of the SDS leadership followed, in fact, from their common and long-growing commitment to revolution from on high—which was the only place it could have come from in this decidedly unrevolutionary circumstance.

True sectarians are in the habit of disputing one another's positions in earnest, endlessly, humorlessly, as if the concepts deserve to be taken at face value; too little attention has been paid to sectarianism as a phenomenon in its own right, a force capable of fueling wild energies on behalf of positions that seem, to all but partisans, incomprehensible. Political sectarianism is the fight for possession of a sacred thing, i.e., The Revolution. The more appealing the fantasy, the more vicious the sectarian ravages. For the force of sectarianism is one result of an inflated belief in the power of revolutionaries. The silent reasoning goes like this: (1) The need or the situation is revolutionary. But (2) behold! The Revolution is not upon us. Therefore (3) it follows that the masses (workers, students) are being misled by bad revolutionaries—who must be as powerful as we would like to be, as we *would* be if not for *them*. In 1969 the revolutionaries' only property was the idea of The Revolution embodied in The Organization. Thus the overriding importance of taking over SDS. Thus the ferocity of the factional struggle.

Tom Nairn put it well in an analysis of the May '68 movement in France:

> Where ideas are all, the upholder of a contrary thesis becomes automatically an enemy—indeed, the most vicious of enemies, since his 'position' is the most direct contestation of the vital truths. Where the revolution is reduced to this poverty, every scrap matters: every opinion, every attitude, every individual adhesion to this or that idea must be fought over like a bone. Antagonism becomes hatred, and polemic is turned into degenerate abuse.

When history is not performing the way the script decrees, then the sectarian conceives

> a bottomless faith in organization, in the ability of the group to accomplish by sheer drive and hard energy all that 'history' is failing to do. The fierce, arid tension of this subjectivity is then interpreted as the revolutionary spirit, the right fighting atmosphere. . . . This and all the other traits of sectarian Marxism indicated—its arrogance, its violent élitism, its instant and cutting condemnation of all deviations from

the 'line,' its chronic substitution of insult for argument, its mystique of exclusive worker militancy, the cult of organization—reflect the basic, previous defensiveness of such movements. That is, its underlying historical task of . . . keeping alive the consciousness of revolution across the 'Hell-black night' of the last decades.

Language became a cudgel in this shadow play—which is why PL's and the Weathermen's pronouncements, mind-numbingly derivative and frequently self-contradictory, far from damaging their claims to revolutionary virtue actually certified them. Each side agreed there was a "primary contradiction" in the world; they disagreed only about what it was. Simpleminded on the surface, obscurantist on further inspection, these pronunciamentos read like encrusted imitations of Stalinist polemics from bygone decades, or bad translations from the Chinese. *That they were bad writing was essential to their purpose.* Their leaden abstraction served to distract from intractable realities— above all, the widespread public distaste for revolutionary violence. Murk enabled the sectarians to mask (even from themselves) what they intended to do. As George Orwell noted, it is easier to speak of killing someone if you muffle the intention in a batting of polysyllabic abstractions. The clumsily translated quality of Weatherprose also certified that the writers belonged to the club of successful revolutionaries. I open the "Weatherman" document at random and find this sentence: "As a whole, the long-range interests of the noncolonial sections of the working class lie with overthrowing imperialism, with supporting self-determination for the oppressed nations (including the black colony), with supporting and fighting for international socialism." The prefabricated phrases spare the trouble of genuine thought, but more: they are easily parroted by those who want to feel privy to Important Questions. They are like a tourist's handbook phrases, instantly conveying a false sense of membership in an alien culture—in this case, the culture of World Revolution. (Thus too, the Weathermen's postschism document embraced the People's Republics of North Korea and Albania. Ignorance wasn't an excuse—it was a requirement.) Impenetrable outside the charmed circle of believers, the phrases amount to ritual incantation for the cadres. They ratify the division between vanguard and ignorant mass—the vanguard, by definition, are the people who can read, or abide, the priestly phrases. The Weathermen quickly learned to spice their proclamations with snappier exhortations to "kick ass" and "kill the pig," but they never shed the belief that political power in The Revolution grows out of a barrel of grandiose slogans.

KICKING ASS

The Weathermen proceeded to launch theory into practice. Their first project was to inspire white working-class youths to join The Revolution. They organized squads to barge into blue-collar high schools in Pittsburgh, Milwaukee, Boston, and other cities, pushing teachers around, binding and gagging them, delivering revolutionary homilies, yelling "Jailbreak!" The kids were bewildered; in Boston, five hundred high school students countermarched on Northeastern University to fight *against* the revolutionaries. Some two hundred Weatherman organizers spent the summer trying to convince tough white teenagers in Detroit, Columbus, Pittsburgh, Boston, and elsewhere that they were tougher, hence deserved to be followed into battle against "the pigs"—as if all that was holding the young multitudes back from an uprising was the fear of losing. They carried National Liberation Front flags through July Fourth celebrations, planted them in the sand at lakeside beaches, barged into hamburger joints and schoolyards, talked about "kicking ass" and "getting us a few pigs," and dared the local kids to fight. In the fall, ostensibly to impress Harvard-hating high schoolers, twenty Weathermen marched on Harvard's Center for International Affairs—known for counterinsurgency research—and smashed windows, yanked out phones, shoved secretaries, and beat three professors, for which the ringleader was subsequently sentenced to two years in prison. If the Weathermen stuck it out —as one of them, Shin'ya Ono, a former Columbia graduate student in political science, wrote—the kids would learn that "their only choice is either joining the world revolution led by the blacks, the yellows, and the browns, or being put down as US imperialist pigs by the people of the Third World, as has already happened to three hundred thousand working-class Amerikans in Vietnam."

Not being Vietnamese peasants, working-class kids did not think they had to choose. A handful joined up for the chance to vent some class spleen, but the rest thought the Weathermen were maniacs. They threw punches at them, even drove them out of their neighborhoods—and still the Weathermen claimed victory. The children of the upper classes were gleeful about the taste of blood, even if it was their own. To be outnumbered and martyred testified to their vanguard status. Their RYM II allies soon abandoned the alliance and went off to find their own working-class base—the first of a series of factional splinterings that culminated, years later, in the founding of a minuscule Revolutionary Communist Party.

Unfazed, the Weathermen plunged on toward a grand October assault in Chicago under the slogan, "Bring the war home!" The Pentagon and Chicago August '68, they said, marked "the conception and birth of a white mother country anti-imperialist movement. A movement conceived in battle and willing to die in battle." Now it was time to act "not only against a single war . . . but against the whole imperialist system that made that war a necessity," to plunge into a new style of "anti-imperialist action in which a mass of white youths would tear up and smash wide-ranging imperialist targets such as the Conspiracy Trial, high schools, draft boards and induction centers, banks, pig institutes, and pigs themselves." The point was "not primarily to make specific demands, but to totally destroy this imperialist and racist society." Fighting in the streets would train the fighters, would take "the first step toward building a new Communist Party and a Red Army," would "do material damage so as to help the Viet Cong." It would even reinforce the mass antiwar movement: "The ruling class would have to consider the probability that the longer they drag their feet in admitting defeat and getting out of Vietnam, the more the candle-holding type [of peace marcher] will join the ranks of the crazies on the streets." After several such actions, they thought they could "build a core of ten to twenty thousand anti-imperialist fighters" who would stir up still more "local and national mass kick-ass anti-imperialist street fights" and "give the ruling class a tremendous kick"—so tremendous that, in combination with the Vietcong's victories, the U.S. would be forced to pull out of Vietnam within six months. In July, a Weatherman group met with North Vietnamese and NLF delegations in Cuba and came away convinced that the Vietnamese had thrown away their customary caution* and endorsed the streetfighting tack.

Each Weatheraction could be interpreted, bent, in such a way as to redouble the Weathermen's giddiness. There were no limits. "If it is a world-wide struggle," the cocky twenty-four-year-old Bill Ayers told a Weatherman gathering in late August, "if Weatherman is correct in that basic thing, that the basic struggle in the world today is the struggle of the oppressed people against U.S. imperialism, then it is the case that nothing we could do in the mother country could be adventurist, nothing we could do, because there is a war going on already, and the terms of that war are set." The snag was that they were too tiny, and the United States too vast and recalcitrant, for the American phase of the seamless world revolution to offer much "material aid" to the people's armies of the Third World. If working-class youth weren't hip enough to recognize the Weathermen as their vanguard, so much the worse for them. "The more I thought about that thing 'fight the people,' " said Ayers, "it's not that it's a great mass slogan or anything, but there's something to it." You could win over the toughs by being tougher—beating white privilege and male supremacy out of them and "out of ourselves" in the process. Polarization was good. Those who doubted were "movement creeps," "right-wingers," "these old 'Movement people.' " Students were "wimpy," said a boot-stomping Mark Rudd to an unimpressed audience at Columbia. "I

---

*The usual conclusion from meetings with the Vietnamese was that the movement ought to be more ecumenical. For example, Terry Cannon of the Oakland 7, in January 1969: "Last fall I met with our comrades in the NLF in Budapest, and I learned one thing clear and hard as a stone: there is no such thing as a revolutionary tactic."

hate SDS," said Rudd that fall, "I hate this weird liberal mass of nothing-ness."

Children of privilege were rediscovering the virtues of command. They relished the "ass-kicking" their childhoods had denied them. "We began to feel the Vietnamese in ourselves," wrote Shin'ya Ono. "We're bullets in the guns of the Third World," another Weatherman bragged. But the way they toughened themselves was more like a Fifties horror story of juvenile delin-quency: one collective, sealed off behind chicken wire, proved itself by smash-ing tombstones in a cemetery, and killing and eating a cat. On one occasion, Illinois Black Panther chairman Fred Hampton called the Chicago action "Custeristic," worried that it would bring the wrath of the police down on the ghetto, called Mark Rudd "a motherfucking masochist," and knocked him to the ground. For years the movement had been cultivating a hierarchy based on sacrifice. It suffered from what Jerry Rubin called "subpoena envy." Wounds were credentials. The Weathermen pushed this middle-class notion one step further, concluding that the old "parlor game" movement had been "defeatist" because it feared that winning a battle would bring down the heavy hand of repression. "It was as if the movement made a secret, unspoken agreement with the ruling class not to struggle beyond certain limits," Ono wrote. The Weathermen thought they had freed their minds for "a life-or-death revolutionary struggle for power."

The "mass of white youths" failed to materialize in Chicago on October 8 for what was now known as "Four Days of Rage." The two or three hundred people who showed up in Lincoln Park to "bring the war home" were almost all students and ex-students, equipped with helmets, goggles, cushioned jack-ets, and medical kits, armed with chains, pipes, and clubs, the men outfitted with jockstraps and cups. They had convinced themselves, and aimed to convince everyone else, that the movement was precisely the nightmare which the police had fabricated a year before. ("They looked exactly like the people we [the Conspiracy defendants] were accused of being," thought Tom Hay-den.) They psyched themselves up with *Battle of Algiers* war whoops and chants of "Ho Chi Minh," and to the astonishment of more than two thou-sand police—who must have known that the vast majority of the demonstra-tors of August 1968 had been peaceful until roused—they charged onto the upper crust Gold Coast, trashing cars and windows, smashing into police lines. "Within a minute or two," Shin'ya Ono wrote, "right in front of my eyes, I saw and felt the transformation of the mob into a battalion of three hundred revolutionary fighters." The police fought back in kind, shooting six of the Weather soldiers, arresting two hundred fifty (including forty on felony charges), beating most of them, sticking them with $2.3 million worth of bail bonds requiring $234,000 in cash bail. The fighters injured enough cops (seventy-five), damaged enough property, precipitated enough arrests and headlines ("SDS WOMEN FIGHT COPS," "RADICALS GO ON RAMPAGE"), and out-lasted enough fear to talk themselves into a fevered sense of victory.

In the aftermath, they were shaken by casualties and defections—and revved themselves up yet again. Their most thorough published account, by Shin'ya Ono, blithely contradicted itself: "Militarily and tactically, it was a victory"; then, in the same paragraph, "mass street action is a necessary, but a losing, tactic." But again the Weathermen found a way to finesse their confusion: the sharpness of the clash confirmed that the apocalypse was impending. They were awed by their own audacity and by the thrill of having lived out their fantasy, having "done it in the road." To be against the war was too easy, too namby-pamby, they argued: "THE VIETNAM WAR ISN'T THE ISSUE ANY MORE. Mainly because the war is over. . . . What we say when we demonstrate about the war isn't that the U.S. should end the suffering or brutality. We tell people about how the VC have won. It's not so much that we're against the war; we're for the Vietnamese people and their victory."

Meanwhile, the mass antiwar movement was showing its strength, commanding the spotlight. A week after the Days of Rage came the immense October 15 Moratorium. A November 15 Moratorium was in the works, coupled with a mass demonstration in Washington. Bill Ayers and three other Weathermen—"flat and grim in their shades and work clothes and heavy boots," as Jeremy Larner, an eyewitness, described them—told Moratorium leaders that a $20,000 payment toward their Days of Rage legal expenses might avert violence in the Washington streets. The Moratorium organizers, who had the impression they were being blackmailed, said no. On November 13, the Weathermen went into the streets, led a splinter march on the South Vietnamese embassy, fought with the police, trashed store windows, garnered headlines. On November 15, 1969, perhaps three-quarters of a million people, the largest single protest in American history, a veritable mainstream, flowed through the streets to the Washington Monument. Senators George McGovern and Charles Goodell gave speeches; John Denver, Mitch Miller, Arlo Guthrie, and the touring casts of *Hair* sang; Pete Seeger led the throng in choruses of "Give Peace a Chance." But the breakaways wanted more. Led by Jerry Rubin and Abbie Hoffman—then on trial as part of the Chicago 8— several thousand militants marched on the Justice Department, complete with NLF flags. Smoke bombs, rocks, and bottles brought forth the obligatory tear gas. The "Amerikan" flag came down, the NLF flag went up. The militants dispersed through a gassed city, building barricades and setting fires. Attorney General John Mitchell, gazing out upon the spectacle, said it "looked like the Russian Revolution." (Movement militants like to cite that quote to certify their path—as if the attorney general was an expert on revolutions.) The Nixon White House, which had tried for weeks to tar the entire antiwar movement with the brush of violence, was delighted. Over the protest of the news staff, the Justice Department sideshow took the lead over the mass march on the *CBS Evening News*.

But unlike the other sects, forever selling their newspapers on the fringes of the crowd, the Weathermen were not willing to settle for parasitical influence. Martyrdom could not satisfy them forever. They were impressed by the Tupamaros, the Uruguayan urban guerrillas who robbed banks and kidnapped the rich to finance their movement; they reveled in the terror tactics displayed in *The Battle of Algiers.* To push on to the next phase, and abort doubt, they had to forge, at white heat, a world apart. So they withdrew from friends and former comrades, and sealed themselves off airtight. The world having failed their analysis, they rejected it. The whole movement had been self-enclosed for a long time, progressively more so into the late Sixties, for turning toward revolution usually meant turning away from family and the wrong friends, dropping contact with disquieting ideas, confounding books, critical magazines. Of course, the more insulated we were from counterarguments and complicated reality, the easier it was to hold on to abstract revolutionary schemes. The Weathermen developed this hermetic tendency to a coarse art. The revolutionary loop closed.

In the furious Weathergroups, inconvenient individualism got reduced to pulp; battered egos were welded into the Weathermachine. Couples were disbanded by fiat; everyone was to sleep with everyone else, women with men, women with women, men with men. Weatherwomen wrote articles celebrating their victories over monogamy. The point was to crash through the barriers to revolution by creating a single fused life: "People who live together and fight together fuck together." Collective drug sessions, and protracted rounds of "criticism-self-criticism," adapted from Maoism, broke down "bourgeois" inhibitions. (The LSD ritual was also intended to flush out police infiltrators, but at least one FBI informer succeeded in passing the "acid test.") And then, having "smashed monogamy," the Weathermen turned around and experimented with celibacy, as if to prove they were will incarnate, more powerful even than sex.

WHEN PROPHECY FAILS

All summer and fall of 1969, what remained of the New Left buzzed with rumors and dismay and horror about the Weathermen; and while most of the movement was appalled ("You don't need a rectal thermometer to know who the assholes are," was a Wisconsin SDS slogan), and the Weather ranks never grew beyond a few hundred, they held the rest of the Left enthralled. Freelance collectives split over whether to join or imitate them. At just the moment when antiwar action was peaking, most SDS chapters broke apart, floundered, or collapsed. Imitators formed their own collectives: "Mad Dogs" in New York, "Juche" (the North Korean slogan for self-reliance) in Cambridge, Massachusetts. Sympathizers in Washington and New York met to figure out what beliefs they shared with the Weathermen and to wonder aloud if they had the guts to run with them. (Some humor surfaced in Berkeley, though: Frank Bardacke, Sol Stern, and friends formed a commune called "Fisherman." Their slogan: "You don't need a fisherman to know something's fishy." Their T-shirt showed a hand gripping a fish—a "clenched fish.") Those who disappeared into the Weathermachine spoke bitterness to recalcitrants who wouldn't fol-low. "If you don't do it our way, you're up against the wall"—that was how Kathy Boudin told off one of her old comrades, himself a self-described "militant internationalist." ("You're so hostile and fucked-up," he yelled back. Those were the last words they exchanged.) They convinced themselves that other activists would be inspired "to re-examine the nature of their revolutionary commitment . . . and to struggle harder," but most of the "struggling" took place between, and within, the movement's battered psyches.

To go with the Weathermen was to take flight from political reality. To go against them was to go—where? Women could take refuge, find commu-nity and political purpose in the women's movement. But most of the old New Left men—those who weren't on trial or immersed in defense commit-tees—felt paralyzed. In the name of what compelling strategy for ending the war could we oppose the Weatherpeople? The weather felt as though it had become the climate. We could not imagine any life without the movement, but the movement no longer held any life for us. The demonstration rituals felt stale and—for militants—increasingly dangerous. Anyway, the occasional demonstration, whether nonviolent or not, could not satisfy our need for an insurgent life all of a piece. What we wanted—what we had lived for the better part of a decade now—was a movement which was both a whole way of life and the cutting edge of change. Now the sects, the Weathermen most of all, had run off with the cutting edge. Some veterans, burned out by the infighting, brooding with visions of impending apocalypse (concentration-camp roundups, urban riots), found this a propitious moment to slip off into communes in Vermont, Mendocino, and their equivalents. They talked about offing the pig and joked about "liberated bases"; what they did was feed their livestock. Beneath the rhetoric, they kept up their whole way of life by relinquishing any illusion that they could shape history.

On the intellectual's premise that to comprehend was to feel liberated—or was comprehension only the next best thing?—I worked on and off for months on a long essay about the movement's crisis. But the harder I looked at the movement's history, the less I saw simple error, the more I saw the Weathermen embodying the worst of both poles of the movement's long-standing built-in dilemma. Their guilty Third Worldism was a caricature of the "politics-for-others" stance, their arrogance an extension of "politics-for-selves." The white movement had been guilty of a "failure of nerve"; now it should take its "postscarcity" identity seriously while recognizing its limits, all the while disowning the false solution of Leninism. In the meantime, I criticized "assuming you are the revolution if you say so; getting to like the taste of the word 'dictatorship' (of the proletariat, over the proletariat, over anyone); getting so pleased with being correct that you don't like being corrected; substituting rhetoric and slogans for analysis and appeals; kicking your friends as practice for your enemies." In columns for the *Guardian* and articles for the underground papers, I railed against sectarianism in the name of a cooler anti-imperialism. *If only* the movement would wise up! All well and good, but appeals to movement will amounted to ineffectual moralism, and I half-knew it.

All my thinking had been predicated on the intelligence of the movement itself as the embryo—like the classical Marxian proletariat—of a new society taking shape in the shell of the old. Now the premise decomposed. Therefore, the more predestined the Weathermen and the SDS crackup seemed, the more depressed I felt. "Can't separate things," I wrote Chris Hobson: "grief over SDS & all that; sense of displacement from 'the movement'—which seems to require quotation marks now; . . . discovering that I had believed in the movement *itself* (you're right: an elitist belief) as embodiment as well as instrument of dreams; having lost faith, I don't know just what I believe in now." Around the country, my comrades were making their own agonizing reappraisals. One spent days building wooden model airplanes. Whenever I brought up the subject of SDS's collapse, to see whether anything could be resurrected by old-timers, he threw up his hands. I couldn't blame him. But we were not much good for each other. Our exhaustion and impotence congealed into yet another political fact. The sects had triumphed by default—and our defeat became one more bludgeon with which to beat ourselves.

Some argued rationally against particulars in the Weatherman manifesto —who exactly *was* the hypothetical vanguard, for example? Carl Oglesby pointed out the Weathermen's incoherence: "Sometimes the vanguard is the black ghetto community, sometimes only the Panthers, sometimes the Third World as a whole, sometimes only the Vietnamese, and sometimes apparently only the Lao Dong [North Vietnamese Communists] Party. Sometimes it is a curiously Hegelian concept, referring vaguely to all earthly manifestations of the spirit of revolution." Some endorsed the Weatherman notion that imperialism was a system from which all white (and why only white?) Americans benefited, and picked away at the Weathermen's backfiring tactics, their romance with the Third World, their male chauvinism. But the counterarguments, deep or shallow, were beside the point. The Weathermen were a scourge, not an argument. They were the foam on a sea of rage. The same rage disarmed their opponents. Worst of all, in the revolutionary mood, no one could imagine how to translate compelling refutations into a compelling political practice.

No alternative theory or action crystallized from the murk of the collective despair. Too much of the criticism came in the name of some less melodramatic but still abstract vision of The Revolution. *They're crazy,* one heard, *but you have to admit they've got guts. Anyway, are you quite so sure they're wrong? And what is going to bring down American imperialism? And what are you, we, going to do about it?* It was hard to summon up the standing to criticize. Were not critics tainted by their love of private life? Did not many white New Leftists feel, in the ferocity of their political frustration, that private life was a niche protecting what Tom Hayden too called "the pseudo-radicalism of the white left"? Hayden, for one, concluded that "the New Left was rapidly becoming the old left, a comfortable left, with too many radicals falling into the ruts of teaching and monogamy, leaving Che and Malcolm and Huey only as posters on their walls." With Malcolm and various Cuban posters on my wall, I took it personally.

Thousands in the movement's most experienced networks bled from the bludgeons of Weatherguilt. "Gut-checking"—scrutinizing one another for leftover "bourgeois attitudes"—became the movement's favorite parlor game. And what one didn't do to one's comrades, one could do to oneself. There was a tale about an activist in Santa Barbara who wondered aloud whether it was counterrevolutionary to watch the sunset. I remember telling a friend that even if American prosperity did rest on the exploitation of the Third World— a cardinal movement premise in 1969—a politics built on guilt was not to be trusted. "Where would we be without guilt?" was his retort, and that stopped me. We, the collectively privileged—he himself was the son of a wealthy doctor—could not be trusted. Touché, I thought, though my own parents were high school teachers. A modest tuna sandwich had the power to remind me that I'd read somewhere that the tuna catch came from the waters of countries like Peru whose people didn't have enough protein to eat. I dreamed about the Weathermen and the Conspiracy defendants. In dreams, they weren't berating me; old comrades were partners again. They were *doing something.* What was I doing?

"Do you find the word incredible is no longer useful?" I wrote Chris Hobson after the Days of Rage. The sheer facts were stupefying. Kathy Boudin and I had been good friends in the mid-Sixties, when she was neither stupid nor foolhardy. I knew many of the other Weathermen. They were not geniuses but not dopes either—at least not any dopier than any of the other sectarians. Big consequences surely required big causes, but my common sense failed to comprehend their wildness. Casting about, I turned to *When Prophecy Fails,* the classic of social psychology published in 1956. Leon Festinger, Henry W. Riecken, and Stanley Schachter investigated a millenarian cult which believed that on a certain date a great flood would engulf the land, but they would be carried off in time by flying saucers. When the great day came and neither flood nor saucers materialized, many believers fell away, but some devotees found a way to make sense of the "cognitive dissonance." The absence of saucers became a signal that they were coming later—and so the believers redoubled their commitment. Around this time, I ran into a friend who had also been a friend of Bernardine Dohrn. She told me she had found a book that made the Weathermen comprehensible: *When Prophecy Fails.*

"WE HAVE TO CREATE CHAOS"

The Weatherlogic ground on, relentless. In blind faith and paranoia, the barbarians made ready to go underground. "We have to create chaos and bring about the disintegration of pig order," proclaimed their invitation to a Christmas 1969 "National War Council" in Flint, Michigan. America was Rome and they talked of changing their name to the Vandals, again taking inspiration from Dylan: "the pump won't work 'cause the vandals took the handles."

Inside Flint's ghetto ballroom, a huge cardboard machine gun hung from the ceiling. A twenty-foot poster depicted bullets attached ecumenically to the Weathermen's enemies' list: Mayor Daley, Humphrey, Johnson, Nixon, Ronald Reagan, the *Guardian*—and Sharon Tate, recently murdered by Charles Manson's gang while eight months pregnant. The slogans were "Piece Now," "Sirhan Sirhan Power," "Red Army Power." The sessions, amid whoops and karate displays, were dubbed "wargasms." Bernardine Dohrn apologized for the Weathermen's having gone "wimpy" after the Days of Rage. Three weeks before, the Illinois Black Panther leader Fred Hampton had been murdered in his sleep during an armed assault on the Panther apartment by Chicago police; the Weathermen should have burned Chicago down, said Bernardine. She recommended a new attitude: "We were in an airplane and we went up and down the aisle 'borrowing' food from people's plates. They didn't know we were Weathermen; they just knew we were *crazy.* That's what we're about, being crazy motherfuckers and scaring the shit out of honky America." Mark Rudd contributed this pensée: "It's a wonderful feeling to hit a pig. It must be a really wonderful feeling to kill a pig or blow up a building." "JJ," a onetime Columbia strategist, said: "We're against everything that's 'good and decent' in honky America. We will burn and loot and destroy. We are the incubation of your mother's nightmare." The more theoretically inclined Ted Gold said that "an agency of the people of the world" should be set up to run the United States once imperialism went down to defeat; when a critic objected that this sounded "like a John Bircher's worst dream," Gold replied: "Well, if it will take fascism, we'll have to have fascism." Charles Manson, exulted Bernardine Dohrn, truly understood the iniquity of white-skinned America: "Dig it! First they killed those pigs, then they ate dinner in the same room with them, then they even shoved a fork into the victim's stomach. Wild!" Flint's favored greeting was four slightly spread fingers—to symbolize the fork.

Flint's "group psychosis"—so one participant later called it—was a public rite to exorcise the Weathermen's last doubts. Their experiments in ego-smashing had succeeded. Having unmade and remade themselves, they had resolved to disband what was left of SDS and go it alone. After Flint, their collectives broke into smaller groups, Debrayist "focos," the better to weed out infiltrators and faint-hearts. They dropped from sight, about a hundred people in all. Only loosely connected, the affinity groups made their plans.

Over the next few months, Weatherpeople rarely surfaced among unbelievers. When they did, one of their themes was that all white babies were tainted with the original sin of "skin privilege." "All white babies are pigs," one Weatherman had insisted in Flint. Robin Morgan recounts that one day a Weatherwoman saw her breastfeeding her baby son in the *Rat* office. "You have no right to have that pig male baby," said the Weatherwoman. "How can you say that?" said Morgan. "What should I do?" "Put it in the garbage," was the answer.

On March 6, 1970, Cathy Wilkerson's father, a radio-station owner, was vacationing in the Caribbean. Cathy had grown up without her father, grown up without much money, in fact, a bit of a juvenile delinquent. Then her father had paid her way to Swarthmore College, where she'd joined SDS. Now, in what she later called "a sort of guerrilla action," she had made off with the key to his West Eleventh Street townhouse, just off Fifth Avenue. There, a group of Weathermen were manufacturing pipe bombs and bombs studded with roofing nails—makeshift copies of antipersonnel bombs like those the United States was dropping in Vietnam. Someone connected the wrong wire. The house blew up, igniting the gas mains. Cathy Wilkerson, Kathy Boudin, and several other Weathermen staggered out of the rubble and disappeared. That night, Ted Gold's crushed body was identified. Diana Oughton's had to be identified from the print on a severed fingertip. There wasn't enough of Terry Robbins's body left to identify; only a subsequent Weatherman communiqué established that he was the third who died. Enough dynamite was recovered, undetonated, to blow up a city block. By some reports, including the police's, the roofing-nail bombs were intended for use at Columbia University; the Weathermen deny it. There is another claim that they were planning to bomb an army noncommissioned officers' dance at Fort Dix, New Jersey. The Weathermen have never said—they insist they will never say—what the target was going to be.

"WE'VE GOT TO TURN NEW YORK INTO SAIGON"

It was, and is, too pat: "the Sixties blew up." If the townhouse had blown up on February 1, it could have rounded out an exact decade since the Greensboro sit-ins. Indeed, the quest for precise symbolism might back up to the wee hours of New

Year's Day, 1970, when three Wisconsin activists stole an ROTC plane and dropped three bombs—which failed to explode—on an army ammunition plant outside Madison. ("The Vanguard of the Revolution," they called themselves.) The habit of thinking in decades is hard to break. So is the sense of inevitability, and the search for a neat lesson. What conclusion would be commensurate with this disaster? That what goes up must come down? What begins in ideals ends in destruction? If nonviolence is dead, anything is permitted?

The turn toward deliberate violence against property was already well along, the explosions amplified, as usual, by the mass media. By conservative estimate, between September 1969 and May 1970 there were some two hundred fifty major bombings and attempts linkable with the white left—about one a day. (By government figures, the actual number may have been as many as six times as great.) The prize targets were ROTC buildings, draft boards, induction centers, and other federal offices. As far as is known, almost all these acts were committed by freelance bombers and burners, though the Weathermen, the most organized phalanx, were probably some inspiration to greener terrorists. For every bomber and arsonist there were several who mulled over the idea. The members of one Berkeley commune liked to go out at night, for example, randomly trashing Safeways (in support of striking farm workers) or banks (against imperialism); massive retaliation might be imminent, they thought, and for that contingency they kept a Molotov cocktail in the basement, designed to the specifications of the *New York Review of Books* cover of 1967. A San Francisco grouplet, impressed by the attention the media paid to political explosions, hoarded dynamite and talked seriously about blowing up Grace Cathedral (which had been a refuge for antiwar meetings) as an act of protest.

As antiwar militants turned against imperialism, attacks turned to the headquarters of multinational corporations. On February 4, a riot in Isla Vista, outside Santa Barbara, in protest against the guilty verdicts in the Chicago Conspiracy trial, culuminated in the burning of the local branch of the Bank of America. (A student explained, "It was the biggest capitalist thing around.") Five nights after the townhouse explosion, bombs went off in the Manhattan headquarters of Socony Mobil, IBM, and General Telephone and Electronics; a note to the press denounced "death-directed Amerika." No one knows how many people committed all these acts; probably only a hundred or two, including police agents. (The most famous was Thomas Tongyai, "Tommy the Traveler," who expertly posed as an SDS organizer in upstate New York and taught militants how to make Molotov cocktails to burn down a campus ROTC building.) Many antiwar militants were reduced to cheerleading. "The real division is not between people who support bombings and people who don't," wrote Jane Alpert, herself a secret member of a freelance bombing collective, "but between people who will *do* them and people who are too hung up on their own privileges and security to take those risks."

The West Eleventh Street disaster sobered the surviving Weathermen and probably saved more lives than it cost. Just afterward, the network of Weatherman groups convened for an emergency summit meeting. In a supercharged atmosphere, they rejected any further antipersonnel tactics and decided to centralize. They tried appointing themselves the vanguard of the freak culture; in September they tried to secure that reputation by helping Timothy Leary escape from the California federal prison where he was serving a drug sentence. The twenty or so bombs they set off subsequently (including one that blew up New York police headquarters and another a U.S. Capitol bathroom) killed no one; the Weathermen (now feminized as the Weather Underground) phoned warnings. Dwindling numbers of cheerleaders went on rejoicing. But the townhouse shook the ground under the whole movement. The freelance bombings up to that point had killed no one. The Weathermen, like it or not, were national figures; three people were dead; and New York was the world's media hub. As word spread about what was being manufactured in the townhouse, there was the toll of an ending, the subliminal sense that what blew up was not just three people but the movement's innocence and its larger logic.

But still there is a missing link. How exactly does one get from murky theory about the world revolution to blasting caps and roofing nails? Not just through a wrongheaded political analysis. Not just by mistake, or the malignant habit of abstraction, or hermetic self-enclosure. It asks too much of any strictly political logic, either the Pentagon's or the Weathermen's, that it should explain the building of bombs whose use is to kill civilians at random. Nor can individual biographies account for the way revolutionaries can shade into nihilism. There is something not quite explained by the notion of forcing an impossible revolution. For even if one is willing to sever means from ends, it is not easy to forget the practical fact that the State possesses the vast majority of the guns. The war had kindled a loathing for "Amerikkka," but the Weathermen were traveling to the far reaches of loathing. Their immensely bad ideas and dreadful tactics must have had a root in some larger upheaval of the movement's collective psyche. Charles Manson, the fork, the Weathermen as vandals and scourges—we have stumbled into the realm of the demonic.

A curious slogan, "Bring the war home." Curious too, the particular slant Ted Gold gave it in a talk with an old Columbia comrade he met in the West End Bar on Broadway not long before he died. As things stood, Ted Gold said, the Vietnam war was an abstraction; liberals could afford to sit back and let it happen on the other side of the world. "We've got to turn New York into Saigon," he said.

"Smashing the pig means smashing the pig inside ourselves, destroying our own honkiness": so went their last aboveground communiqué. They wanted to be "bad"—"We are the incubation of your mother's nightmare"—the way the Vietcong and the Panthers were "bad." As the movement had felt from the start that it had to give birth to itself, so had the revolutionary child metamorphosed into its own harsh parent, out to "smash" the retrograde, hesitant self. Revolutionary logic, tied in knots, led to a bad imitation of Pentagon logic. They could not see that the dread "pig inside ourselves" that had to be "smashed" was not just "male chauvinism, individualism, competition," but the imperial attitude which insisted that villages had to be destroyed in order to save them. The best to be said for the Weathermen is that for all their rant and bombs, in eleven years underground they killed nobody but themselves.*

DEATH CULTURE

The townhouse was the flash point for an implosion still greater and more horrendous. The Weathermen heightened the general self-hatred, darkened the darkness that already spilled over the Left. No end to the war, no end to the trials, no end to being white or American; no end to guilt for not being on trial, or dead, or for not being a Weatherman, or for not having stopped them. . . . It was as if the whole of the Left, and the counterculture as well, discovered bottomless guilt and death around them and inside them, not always able to tell which was outside and which inside. In the poisoned, sectarian atmosphere, even political trials—those time-honored occasions for solidarity—ceased to unify. With so much harshness and suspicion and death in the air, it was not easy to find a life-principle. Beneath the billowing clouds of rhetoric, the Left's real-life problem was simplifying down to a single earthy one: how to keep the terror at bay.

Everyone had a casualty roll call in 1969–70. Here is mine:

■ Early in May 1969, a man who called himself a reporter telephoned my old SDS friend Dick Flacks, then an assistant professor of sociology at the University of Chicago, and asked for an interview. Flacks, who had been visibly active against the war, agreed to meet the man in his office. He had never seen him before. After a few moments of conversation, the man took a crowbar and smashed Flacks's skull and his right wrist. A student found him by chance, lying in a puddle of blood, his hand almost severed. Newspaper

---

*In the late Seventies, several schisms later, most of the Weather Underground—including Dohrn, Ayers, Wilkerson, and Jones—surfaced and turned themselves in. But on October 20, 1981, a remnant underground group including David Gilbert, Judith Clark, and Kathy Boudin robbed a Brink's truck in Rockland County, north of New York City, killing a guard and two police officers (including the county's first black policeman) in the process. Gilbert and Clark were found guilty of murder and sentenced to seventy-five years in prison; Boudin, pleading guilty of robbery and murder, was sentenced to twenty years to life.

editorials had been fulminating that radical professors were responsible for student rebellion.*

■ The day after the Weathermen's Days of Rage, the police arrested Charles Manson outside Los Angeles and charged him and his harem-commune with the grisly Tate-LaBianca murders. Monstrous, but what did it mean? In those plummeting days, every stark fact was pressed into world-historical significance: teenage vandalism became "Blows Against the Empire," guerrilla attacks permuted into fronts of the single world revolution. For the mass media, the acidhead Charles Manson was readymade as the monster lurking in the heart of every longhair, the rough beast slouching to Beverly Hills to be born for the next millennium. At year's end the Weathermen too boasted a family resemblance, never mind that Manson's gang tried to pin the murders on blacks, hoping to foment race war. Jerry Rubin caricatured the caricature, paid Manson a visit in prison, and wrote: "I fell in love with Charlie Manson the first time I saw his cherub face and sparkling eyes on national TV. . . . His words and courage inspired [me] . . . and I felt great the rest of the day, overwhelmed by the depth of the experience of touching Manson's soul. . . ." The Los Angeles *Free Press* let Manson write a column, and ran free ads for a recording he made; another underground paper, *Tuesday's Child*, depicted him as a hippie on the cross.

Marvin Garson looked at the hypnotic-eyed photo of Manson on the cover of *Life* magazine and proclaimed the portent: "Charles Manson, *son of man.*" I argued with him, but the media image was not altogether dismissable. Not so long before, long hair had portended good. Even politicos like me, who pooh-poohed the hippies' pretensions, were glad they were there, pleasant and peaceable if not smashers of the State. Manson was a unique monster. But around that time, visiting a friend in Mendocino, I heard a couple of cowboy-booted longhairs whoop it up about going into town to find whores, and suddenly realized that the yahoo streak in the counterculture was the resumption of one of the less salutary of American traditions.

■ Meanwhile, on Halloween night, 1969, my bony Jewish-Afro'd freak friend Marshall Bloom, the cofounder of Liberation News Service, sat in his beat-up Triumph Spitfire in western Massachusetts, reading the paper, running exhaust through a hose, and died. Marshall Bloom, twenty-five years old, former editor of the Amherst student paper, leader of student revolt at the London School of Economics, was the incarnation of counterculture whimsy. Ripoffs were his art form. Once he drove across the country in his Sgt. Pepper–style frock coat staying at motels, saying that he was the advance man

---

*Flacks recovered, went on to become a professor at the University of California, Santa Barbara, and to write extensively on the student movement, but never regained full use of his hand. The attacker was never found.

for a rock band which would arrive the next day, and they would settle the bill together; then waking up at four in the morning and driving off. Ripoffs became habit: In the summer of 1968 he and cofounder Raymond Mungo and their hang-loose hippie faction of LNS wearied of the Marxist half of their collective, made a down payment on a farm, and absconded with money, printing press, and mailing list from bad-vibes New York. ("The movement had become my enemy," Mungo wrote later, "the movement was not flowers and doves and spontaneity, but another vicious system, the seed of a heartless bureaucracy, a minority Party vying for power rather than peace.") The New York faction raided the farm, terrorizing and beating Marshall, but after the dust settled, LNS/N.Y. and LNS/Mass. started publishing their separate weekly mailings, Mass.'s polyform, less gray, hippier than New York's. In his droll way Marshall told me that the proper strategy for revolution in America, since America lacked a peasantry, was to populate the countryside with an artificial peasantry—ourselves. Over the next year, the farm and the neighboring farmers became the main preoccupation of LNS/Mass.

I visited Marshall in the rolling hills near Amherst in September 1969. We picked cucumbers, fried slices of eggplant, drove to nearby Amherst College, his alma mater, to inspect a piece of equipment for his possible acquisition, and talked about the movement turning ugly. Marshall said it was important to distinguish between "opinions," which were cheap, and a "point of view," which came with accretion, preferably in the country. Even if the bucolic image was overripe, I was willing to find peace and wisdom in unlikely places. I was more of a rationalist and a politico than Marshall, less of a hippie, but we appreciated each other.

So on my return to California I started fiddling with a poem for him, rhapsodizing about the cucumber harvest by folks "who a year ago didn't know a furrow/From a hole in the ground." Late in October I mailed the poem. A few days afterward, a friend called to say that Marshall was dead. The communards found nude-boy magazines in his room; people said he was a closeted and shamefaced "gay celibate," and speculated that the implications of the Stonewall gay riot, the new message of gay pride, hadn't sunk in. Some said he had never recovered from the violent LNS schism. For me, Marshall Bloom died of the movement's sins.

■ Early on the morning of December 4, on the West Side of Chicago, the police shot down Fred Hampton and Mark Clark of the Illinois Black Panthers. Hampton, the state chairman, was killed in his bed. Although the police claimed the Panthers had instigated the shootout, it quickly became clear that the Panthers had fired at most a shot or two while the police riddled the walls with a hundred bullets.

■ Woodstock, in August, had been the long-deferred Festival of Life. So said not only *Time* and *Newsweek* but world-weary friends who had navigated the traffic-blocked thruway and felt the new society aborning, half a million strong, stoned and happy on that muddy farm north of New York City. If the youth culture was too squishy to become a people's army, surely it was at least a luminous prefiguration of the cooperative commonwealth, Abbie Hoffman's "Woodstock Nation," People's Park writ large, that possible and impending good society the vision of which would keep politicos honest. And so when the Rolling Stones announced their own West Coast free concert, at Altamont, near San Francisco, I had to go.

The tale has been told many times of how, at Altamont, among three hundred thousand fans, the Hell's Angels, serving as semiofficial guards, killed a young fan, black, who had a white date and the temerity to offend the Angels (by getting too close to them, or their motorcycles, or the stage), and then, at some point, pulled a gun—all the while Mick Jagger was singing "Under My Thumb." I heard about the killing that night, on the radio, having left before the Stones took the stage. But by the time I left, in the late afternoon, Altamont already felt like death. Let it sound mystical, I wasn't the only one who felt oppressed by the general ambience; a leading Berkeley activist told me he had dropped acid at Altamont and had received the insight that "everyone was dead." It wasn't just the Angels, shoving people around on and near the stage, who were angels of death. Behind the stage, hordes of Aquarians were interfering with doctors trying to help people climb down from bad acid trips. On the remote hillside where I sat, stoned fans were crawling over one another to get a bit closer to the groovy music.

Afterward everyone was appalled and filled with righteous indignation. But exactly who or what was at fault? On a practical plane, there were movie-rights squabbles; greed had played its part in preventing adequate preparations. But the effect was to burst the bubble of youth culture's illusions about itself. The Rolling Stones were scarcely the first countercultural heroes to grant cachet to the Hell's Angels. We had witnessed the famous collectivity of a generation cracking into thousands of shards. Center stage turned out to be another drug. The suburban fans who blithely blocked one another's views and turned their backs on the bad-trippers were no cultural revolutionaries. Who could any longer harbor the illusion that these hundreds of thousands of spoiled star-hungry children of the Lonely Crowd were the harbingers of a good society?

That night, lying in bed, I was struck by a bolt of panic so strong, it felt as if my mind were trying to blast away from my body. Too much Altamont, too much bad politics, too much grass added up to a bad "set" and a worse "setting." A few days later, in fear and trembling, I wrote a piece for Liberation News Service called "The End of the Age of Aquarius." "If there is so much bad acid around," I asked, "why doesn't this contaminated culture, many of whose claims are based on the virtues of drugs, help its own brothers and sisters? Why do the underground papers leave it to the media narcotizers to deplore the damaging possibilities of bad drugs? . . . Freedom, in the aggregate, turned out to be a spectator sport. . . ." The star-struck crowd was "turned on, not to each other, not to the communal possibilities, but to the big prize, the easy-ticket—the 'good trip.' The age of Aquarius was invented by the same hypesters who believe that television invented the 'global village.' Maybe it did, but then it was the same mean village which Sinclair Lewis wrote to death, a town of petty gossip and quiet desperation." I wondered "whether the youth culture will leave anything behind but a market."

People's Park, even if not the outskirts of Eden, had been an attempt to create; Altamont—even Woodstock—was a ritual consecrated to consumption.

■ In March 1970, three days after the townhouse explosion, in the small Maryland town of Bel Air, a bomb blew up the car carrying Ralph Featherstone and "Che" Payne of SNCC, and killed them. According to their comrades, Featherstone and Payne had gone to Bel Air to set up security for Rap Brown, about to go on trial for inciting to arson; the bomb had probably been intended for Brown, who promptly went underground. The FBI and Maryland state police claimed that Featherstone and Payne had intended to plant the bomb in the courthouse. I hadn't seen Featherstone since Cuba, and I knew people changed, but I couldn't imagine him anything other than sweet-tempered, a cooling influence. It was reasonable to surmise that SNCC was heavily infiltrated by informers, perhaps by agents provocateurs.* At the time, at least it was reasonable to think Featherstone had been murdered. In any case, to mourn.

■ On August 24, 1970, a bomb planted by the Madison, Wisconsin, New Year's Gang blew up the army's mathematics research building, killing a graduate student who was working late: the white student movement's first innocent casualty. This headquarters of war research had been a focus of Madison's nonviolent protest for years. The bombers were veteran activists—a tiny minority, true, but they played out a logic. In the illumination of that bomb the movement knew sin.

Anxiety and despair were most of what I knew. My world had exploded, ten years of the movement; I had lost the ground I walked on. Two nights after the townhouse explosion, I dreamed I was with the Conspiracy defendants, arguing against bombs, while blacks threw boomerangs at our rally; and I was not the only one to keep dream-appointments with the disaster. In the movement rhetoric of that hour, *we* were life and *they* were "the death culture," "Amerika," the Combine out of control, its death lust having surged beyond any rational political motives. The movement core were Manichaeans as well

* One small example: FBI documents, subsequently released, establish that SNCC's staff meeting of December 1968 was attended by *two* FBI informers.

as utopians; our sense of innocence required all-or-nothing thinking, and innocence was the motor of our collective passion. What Altamont was for the counterculture, the townhouse was for the student movement: the splattering rage of the "death culture" lodged in the very heart of the "life force." Whence the shock when it proved impossible to draw a hard and fast line between the two. The revolutionary mood had been fueled by the blindingly bright illusion that human history was beginning afresh because a graced generation had willed it so. Now there wasn't enough life left to mobilize against all the death raining down.

FADEOUT

On the surface, the student movement went on unabated. Campus attitudes tilted more strongly, indeed more radically, against the war. In the fall of 1969, 69 percent of a Gallup Poll of students called themselves "doves"—twice as many as in the spring of 1967. More and more students seemed to realize that "Vietnamization" was not tantamount to ending the war, and concluded—a few years behind SDS—that the war was not merely an isolated "mistake." According to one survey, the percentage of students who agreed with the statement, "The war in Vietnam is pure imperialism," jumped from 16 percent in the spring of 1969 to 41 percent in April 1970—*before* the invasion of Cambodia— while the number strongly disagreeing fell from 44 to 21 percent. The percentage of students calling themselves "radical or far Left," 4 percent in the spring of 1968, rose to 8 percent in the spring of 1969 and 11 percent in the spring of 1970. Without any central coordination, protests nonviolent and violent accelerated throughout the year, chiefly against the war—fully 9,408 incidents of protest, according to the American Council on Education, 731 of them involving the police and arrests, 410 involving damage to property (ROTC buildings and the like), 230 involving violence to persons.

When Richard Nixon, having shored up his nerve with several viewings of the film *Patton,* announced the American "incursion" into Cambodia on April 30, 1970, students went into action. By May 4, a hundred student strikes were in progress across the country. At Kent State University in Ohio, students burned down the ROTC building. Nixon denounced "these bums, you know, blowin' up the campuses." On May 2, a mass meeting at Yale called for a national student strike; the next day, editors of eleven student newspapers, and the National Student Association, joined them. Students at Brandeis University set up a National

Strike Information Center. Then, on May 4, National Guardsmen at Kent State responded to taunts and a few rocks by firing their M-1 rifles into a crowd of students, killing four, wounding nine others. Kent State was a heartland school, far from elite, the very type of campus where Richard Nixon's "silent majority" was supposed to be training. Carl Oglesby had gone to school at Kent State; Terry Robbins had organized there for SDS.

The dam broke. Strikes broke out at about 30 percent of the nation's twenty-five hundred campuses, demonstrations at more than half. There were demonstrations at schools large and small, public and private, secular and religious, four-year and two-year, although disproportionately at the larger and more elite universities. Probably between 50 and 60 percent of the students in the United States took part; at least a million students probably demonstrated for the first times in their lives during that month of May. Even more than a third of all students who called themselves "middle-of-the-road" demonstrated against the invasion of Cambodia. On May 9, the Mobilization brought over one hundred thousand people to rally in Washington on only ten days' notice, although plans for civil disobedience—around a White House shielded by sixty buses—dissolved in confusion; the Mobe steering committee feared that a sit-down by thousands would get some people killed, and they were not willing to bear that burden. The more militant and violent protests spread too. Thirty ROTC buildings were burned or bombed during the first week in May. National Guard units were mobilized on twenty-one campuses in sixteen states. Police were evidently overheated. On May 14, at Jackson State College in Mississippi, amid tensions apparently unrelated to the war, the police let loose a shotgun fusillade into a women's dormitory, killing two students and wounding nine—who, being black, inspired far fewer headlines, or demonstrations, than the killings at Kent State.

All in all, it was by far the largest number of students ever to demonstrate in a single spasm. Aftershocks went on rumbling. At least seventy-five campuses stayed closed for the rest of the school year, with hundreds of thousands of students leafleting in the surrounding communities, working for peace candidates, and—with interest in "student power" running strong—"reconstituting" their courses to address the international crisis. Lobbying in Washington for an immediate end to the war, students were joined by respectables: a thousand lawyers, thirty-three university heads, architects, doctors, nurses, a hundred corporate executives. Two hundred fifty State Department employees, including fifty Foreign Service officers, signed a statement against administration policy. The enormity of the uprising broke Nixon's will. As Henry Kissinger put it later, "The very fabric of government was falling apart. The Executive Branch was shell-shocked. After all, their children and their friends' children took part in the demonstrations." Nixon felt compelled to announce that the Americans would go no further than twenty-one miles into Cambodia, and that most of them would leave Cambodia by mid-June, the rest by July 1. Kissinger thought Nixon had yielded to "public pressures."

The antiwar movement had come back to life as a veto force. Militants ignited moderates. With social order at stake, Congress moved with alacrity to grant eighteen-year-olds the right to vote. Senators Frank Church and John Sherman Cooper introduced a measure cutting off funds for American forces in Cambodia after June 30, and on June 30 the Senate passed it. But to many who had been working against the war for five years, this was puny consolation. The wheels of Congress cranked slowly, producing too little, too late. Even after the post-Cambodia explosion, the Cooper-Church amendment died in House-Senate conference. The McGovern-Hatfield amendment, which would have cut off funds for American troops in Southeast Asia, was defeated 55–39 in the Senate on September 1. Public opinion, measured in polls, sided with Nixon's strategy of Vietnamization, periodic escalation, quiet bombardment, and Paris talks. Of what avail were moderate strategies? The dynamic sweeping antiwar students toward more radical measures was still in force—except that more radical measures seemed futile as well.

In fact, the post-Cambodia uprising was the student movement's last hurrah. Activism never recovered from the summer vacation of 1970. During the academic year 1970–71 there were fewer demonstrations than the year before; in 1971–72, fewer still. True, there was more antiwar protest than met the television-watching eye. During 1970–71 there were still almost as many student demonstrations as during 1968–69. A Washington rally in April 1971 drew half a million people. But in the eyes of mass media that measured each rally by the size and militancy of the last, and in the movement's own eyes, the threshold of awareness was stratospherically high now. Demonstrations declined at the old centers of protest, and press coverage declined precipitously. One study concluded that only 10 percent of all "severe protests" received national press coverage in 1970–71, compared with 40 percent in 1968–69. Antiwar demonstrations were "old news" now. The media helped restore order by blacking out demonstrations and playing up moderate tactics like the "Princeton Plan," in which universities gave students a two-week fall furlough to work in the 1970 congressional campaigns. The general impression was that the campuses were "quieting down."

Jaded and craven media aside, however, antiwar activity did slacken. Yet the paradox was formidable: The center of opposition moved to Congress, and the base of antiwar *opinion* continued to widen. In surveys, more and more students opposed the war, a growing percentage of them from less privileged backgrounds and less elite campuses. Why didn't their sentiment flare into action?

One often hears that the decisive move was Nixon's decision to end the draft and begin withdrawing troops. By 1970, male students were being assigned lottery numbers; at any given moment, almost half could feel safe. Draft calls proceeded to dwindle. The premise is that students had gone into action against the war to save their skins. But pure self-interest is not always the supreme human motivation, and the waning of the draft only partly explains the waning of antiwar activity. The draft in its heyday triggered more legalized dodging—more stopgap schoolteaching careers, more early childbearing—than demonstrations. The campus antiwar movement was never a simple function of students' fear of the draft. Recall first that the student movement sprang up at a time when student deferments were safe. SDS attacked the 1966 exam by which the Selective Service System sought to draft student underachievers. (Mike Locker and I wrote a counterexam on Vietnam which SDS chapters distributed outside the building where the official exam was being administered.) The next year, SDS exposed a Selective Service memo showing that the government was deliberately using the draft as an instrument of class privilege—to keep students busy acquiring approved skills. Recall too that thousands of students were willing to close down their own escape hatches in revulsion against the war. Typically, in the post-Cambodia spring of 1970 alone, twenty-five hundred Berkeley students turned in their draft cards—and so on around the country. Moreover, it is not even clear whether the draft-prone were more protest-prone. Studies at Columbia University and the University of California, Santa Barbara, show that vulnerability to the draft was not statistically related to opposing the war, although other studies show the opposite. Conceivably, opposition to the war fueled opposition to the draft more than the other way round. Finally, if the war was of concern to students only insofar as they were draftable, why were women as opposed to the war as men? Why did draft-exempt women risk so much?

For men in college, private exits were fairly easy to find—deferments in protected jobs, exemptions for actual or feigned homosexuality, actual or feigned medical conditions, actual or feigned nuttiness. Only 12 percent of male college graduates saw service in Vietnam, compared to 21 percent of high school graduates; only 9 percent of the college graduates saw combat, half the percentage of the high school graduates. And if that were not enough, college men might have been reassured by the low conviction rate for draft resisters ("only" 8,750 out of 570,000 "draft offenders," about 1.5 percent, were ever convicted). The most that can be said is that the slackening of the draft weakened the less committed's incentive for opposing the war. The students who made up the fringes of the crowd may have decided to stay home—no help to the organizers' morale. The same is true for Nixon's Vietnamization strategy as a whole—after all, *American* combat deaths did plunge from two hundred per week in May 1970 to thirty-five in May 1971. Except for fitful moments of escalation, like 1972's April mining of Haiphong and Christmas bombing of Hanoi, Nixon learned how to keep the level of urgency muted. But the more committed activists were not so impressed by the changing of the color of the corpses; it took more to knock them out of action.

Perhaps, then, the political power of the Nixon administration—its power to compel acquiescence if not campus enthusiasm—ultimately grew out of the barrels of its guns? Techniques of repression and intimidation were by now profuse. The first official comment on Kent State (a command performance, Henry Kissinger tells us) was White House press secretary Ron Ziegler's remark that the killings "should remind us all once again that when dissent turns to violence it invites tragedy." John Mitchell's Justice Department, with eager local assistance, pumped out special antiradical grand juries, subpoenas, surveillances, wiretaps, campus spies, riot training, high-tech weapons. The army ran its own parallel operations, infiltrating a vast range of meetings and demonstrations, setting up dummy journalist teams, cooperating with right-wing vigilantes.

The FBI had been slow to take the New Left seriously in its own right. Before the spring of 1968, J. Edgar Hoover seems to have cared about the New Left mostly as an undefined something that the American Communist Party might be infiltrating; only with the Columbia rebellion did Hoover target the New Left for an FBI "COINTELPRO"—counter-intelligence program—of its own. (Taking no chances, army intelligence had already launched its own far-reaching surveillance and infiltration programs.) Hoover scrambled to make up for lost time. In 1969 and 1970, the FBI accelerated its dirty tricks: newspaper leaks of manufactured "disinformation,"* the harassment of contributors and celebrity allies, faked letters sowing discord between blacks and whites, even between husband and wife. A month after the shootings at Kent State, Nixon moved to centralize domestic intelligence and counterinsurgency programs in his own hands. At Nixon's behest, White House assistant Tom Charles Huston, former chairman of Young Americans for Freedom and a veteran of military intelligence, proposed a new White House unit to authorize telephone taps without warrants, break-ins, mail-openings, and informers (a good many of which, please note, were already in effect without "authorization"). Only bureaucratic jealousy aborted the Huston Plan: the crusty J. Edgar Hoover was fearful of losing his special access to

---

*A trivial but suggestive example from my FBI files: Early in 1970, I was invited to be a "radical scholar in residence" at Vanderbilt University in Nashville, Tennessee. When this was reported in the campus paper, the Chicago FBI office told the San Francisco FBI office—in amazing syntax—to "furnish Memphis with recent background information, physical description, photograph of subject, as well as any public source type information which would tend to characterize the subject for any derogatory information in this regard." As it turned out, I didn't go to Nashville, and nothing derogatory—to my knowledge— materialized. An example with dire consequences: The Los Angeles FBI office planted in a gossip column the smear that the actress Jean Seberg was pregnant by a Black Panther leader. Her husband, the writer Romain Gary, successfully sued Newsweek for libel, but Seberg's baby was stillborn, Seberg cracked up, and after a series of suicide attempts on the anniversary of the stillbirth, she killed herself in 1979.

the White House, and annoyed at the implication that the FBI hadn't put its police powers to good use. With Hoover looking over his shoulder, Nixon also knew that if he ordered the Huston Plan into effect he would be giving Hoover leverage that he, Nixon, might regret; it was shrewder to continue the counterinsurgency with less fanfare. But no bureaucratic quarrels kept local police forces from feeding movement paranoia and demoralization. Agents of local Red Squads, knowing that movement organizers A and B were at odds, for example, built up tensions by denouncing B to A's allies, and vice versa. The movement didn't know the details of these behind-the-scenes maneuvers, but some of its direst intuitions proved to be sound.

Surveillance and crackdowns were bad enough, but the FBI was often amateurish, its technology clumsier than the paranoid movement came to think. In the end, nothing intimidated like official violence. Once the initial shock and rage wore off, Kent State proclaimed to white activists nationwide what People's Park had said to Berkeley a year before: The government is willing to shoot you. Since demonstrations were likely to turn to trashings, and trashings could create the pretext for shootings, were demonstrators supposed to buy guns in turn? At this point, logic dead-ended. To the vast majority of movement people, resorting to guns was both unconscionable and tactically stupid. So, helpless fury turned to spleen or withdrawal—and ultimately spleen was only the prologue to withdrawal. It was double or nothing, and to many old movement hands the answer was nothing.

Nor did it hearten antiwarriors that the sleeping dogs of the Right, having awoken, were baring their teeth. On May 8, 1970, two hundred hardhatted construction workers chanting "Kill the Commie bastards" descended upon an antiwar rally near Wall Street and beat up seventy students. Aroused by the patriotic scent of blood, prowar hardhats turned out in the thousands over the following weeks, earning their leader the post of secretary of labor in Nixon's cabinet. Other unions were defecting from Cold War orthodoxy, but none could command the hardhats' media razzle-dazzle. Polls showed that the nation thought "campus unrest" a more important problem than the war. The dovishness that showed up in surveys coexisted with a moral panic against antiwar activists; the national pragmatism which thought the war ought to be liquidated as a bad investment, a "mistake," a "mess," was incensed at students who insisted it was a crime.

And therefore Nixon's guns and the no-longer-silent majority's panic felt like harbingers of a far worse repression. The atmosphere filled with diatribes. Vice President Agnew called for "separating [the 'impudent snobs'] from our society—with no more regret than we should feel over discarding rotten apples from a barrel." Agnew's "positive polarization" was the prevailing official mood. On April 7, 1970, Governor Ronald Reagan of California, asked about campus militants, said: "If it takes a bloodbath, let's get it over with. No more appeasement." (Later that day, his press secretary said this was merely a "figure of speech.") Exactly what did Attorney General Mitchell mean when he said, "This country is going so far right you are not even going to recognize it"?

Sometime in the mid-Seventies I heard Herbert Marcuse tell an approving Berkeley crowd: "The movement did not die, it was murdered!" That was too simple, I think. The repression was vivid, ugly, demoralizing, but the movement collaborated in its own demise. At People's Park and Kent State, the authorities acted just the way radicals had predicted in our worst moods. Could the imperial State be expected to lie down and let a popular movement trim back its foreign policy? But an exhausted movement had lost its moral edge, and with it the capacity to console and rally its afflicted.

No one should belittle the emotionally and financially draining trials (and fear of trials),* the millions of dollars drained into bail bonds, the wiretaps (and fear of wiretaps), the infiltrators (and fear of infiltrators), the bullets, the fear of bullets. But let us be reminded how much more intimidating the U.S. government can be—has been—in wartime. During World War I, for example, President Woodrow Wilson banned antiwar and socialist publications from the mails, prosecuted most radical leaders under the Espionage Act, deported many others, raided scores of organization offices and meetings, and broke strikes with the U.S. Army. Mobs tarred and feathered IWW organizers, and dumped others in the desert without food or water. Draft "shirkers" were trapped by soldiers who sealed off whole downtown areas in major cities and arrested all draft-age men who were out of uniform unless they gave good reasons then and there. In January 1920, the Palmer Raids rounded up some ten thousand radicals (and bystanders) *in two days*. In those years, moreover, juries were usually quick to side with the prosecutors. Or consider the bombings, lynchings, arson attacks, and shootings unleashed upon black organizers in the South. The first repression was successful, the second ultimately not. In comparison to both, the repression of the late Sixties and early Seventies was mild—though fierce enough to demoralize a movement that had lost its faith and clarity and resilience.

There were also counterforces that helped, and might have helped more. During the Nixon years, juries remained relatively unimpressed with the government's cases against radicals. Many convictions—including the Chicago Conspirators'—were eventually overturned by higher courts. An excess of paranoia blinded the movement to that even more fierce paranoia, Nixon's, which drove him to violate liberal democracy's own rules, and ruptured his ties to much of the Establish-

*In February 1970, for example, the Chicago Conspiracy defendants were convicted on various charges and sentenced for contempt by the contemptuous judge Julius Hoffman. The convictions were eventually reversed on appeal.

ment. Desperately insecure in his White House bunker, Nixon eventually brought himself down with one too many break-ins, one too many wiretaps; had he confined himself to harassing and prosecuting radicals, he might have sidestepped his appointment with Watergate. Nixon had to hold back just as Johnson did—not out of goodwill, but for lack of a political consensus to enable him to declare war, override the separation of powers, and crush the opposition all at once. In the end, Nixon's counter-revolution was as airy, as impossible, as the movement's revolution.

Movements that are serious about radical change expect reaction from powerful interests. They do not necessarily cave in when power refuses to yield graciously. What is curious—curiously American, curiously middle-class—is the *innocence* of the New Left. When the movement was in good humor, it knew how to joke some of its fear into the ground. (Even in the Harvard Tocsin days, my friends and I used to twit the hypothetical FBI men on the other end of the phone. For years the phone in the SDS national office had a message taped onto the receiver: "THIS PHONE IS TAPPED." Documents later pried out of the FBI show this wasn't sheer self-importance.) Into the late Sixties it was possible to joke about government agents. (At its 1968 convention SDS announced a fraudulent workshop on sabotage, to divert police spies—with apparent success.) Then much of the banter wore away, and so did the movement's tensile strength. An elusive thing, the spirit of a movement. Southern sheriffs had battered civil rights workers, vigilantes had swarmed the countryside, and yet the civil rights movement had kept up morale with freedom songs, religious ritual, personal bonds that gave body to transcendent purpose. The late New Left was stripped of the integuments of solidarity, while there was just enough liberal democracy in America to preserve the innocent liberalism in the would-be revolutionary heart. Innocence is the tribute which American radicals pay to their deepest American faith in the happy ending.

Repression was damaging, painful, limiting, but not decisive—at least not according to the hard information available. What shriveled the late movement, and repelled antiwar students, was not so much repression as the movement itself—the hubris of a youth movement furious at its limits, desperate at being let down by the authorities, thus flinging itself into the revolutionary maelstrom. The sense of desperation was nothing new. For years the antiwar movement had talked itself out of desperation with one plan after another; the movement had bathed doubts in balms of solidarity. Now the beloved community had degenerated into a caricature of everything idealists find alienating about politics-as-usual: cynicism, sloganeering, manipulation. The leadership groupings were giddy with their various styles of hopelessness. Far from being an inducement to political action, a consolation and reward for a thousand sacrifices, the organized movement, such as it was, had deliquesced into a swamp that only the most dedicated—or masochistic—would bother to try slogging through. Jerome Karabel has put it well: In 1970 the fratricidal remnants of SDS were "the only New Left that students born around 1952 had ever known."

The crucial fact is that, once SDS imploded, there was no national organization to keep the student movement boiling, to channel antiwar energy into common action, to keep local organizers in touch with one another, to provide continuity from semester to semester. The women's movement was alive, but there was no intellectual center for a more general politics which was at once radical and practical. (Thus Earth Day of April 22, 1970, brought environmental concerns into the political mainstream but passed without any coherent radical criticism.) Student movements are chronically unstable: part of their membership rotates out every year; freshmen always have to be recruited afresh. But in the sectarian fratricide and the rush to revolution, no one was recruiting. The spectacle of the post-SDS factions hurling incomprehensible curses at one another was not inviting to newcomers. Neither was the turn to violence and mindless disruption. The media, drawn to the most violent antiwar actions, helped taint even more moderate actions; why should newcomers to antiwar politics want to associate themselves with "turning New York into Saigon"? Or with the Yippiesque slapstick of the three hundred longhairs who invaded Disneyland on August 6, 1970, stormed Tom Sawyer's Island, raised the NLF flag over its fort, and chanted "Ho, Ho, Ho Chi Minh"?

A movement less attractive, an administration at once more cooptive and more repressive, a war apparently impervious to protest—all these factors took their toll on the student mood. A Harris poll reported the first drop since 1965 in the percentage of students calling themselves "radical or far Left"—from 11 percent in the spring of 1970 to 7 percent in the fall. From spring to fall, the middle-of-the-road category leaped from 26 to 34 percent, and the "conservative" and "far Right" groups, which had been sliding steadily since 1968, from 15 to 19 percent. Students were stampeding away from the New Left. The grand antiwar mobilizations went on—gathering up to half a million people for a Washington march in April 1971, for example—but the interim marches subsided. On the campus, the movement ceased to be *the* place where the brightest and spunkiest congregated. There was a long sputtering.

The Catholic "Ultra Resistance" went on destroying draft records, and movement veterans like Dave Dellinger and Rennie Davis went on civilly disobeying. Others burned out, having worked too long too hard for too little satisfaction. But in large measure, from 1971 on, the antiwar initiative passed into new hands.

There were the active-duty soldiers (and to a lesser extent sailors and airmen) who deserted, went AWOL, filed as conscientious objectors, published newspapers, agitated, drugged themselves out, demonstrated (sometimes in uniform), rioted, sought sanctuary, were insubordinate in large and small ways, committed sabotage, even "fragged" their officers and mutinied in or on the way to Vietnam. The various styles of home-front disaffection—the counterculture, black nationalism, New Left radicalism, and general (not necessarily coherent, not necessarily polite) up-yours antiauthoritarianism—swept into the largely working-class armed forces. The people's army of the American democratic republic (albeit a people's army lacking the college-educated, no mean exception) went into spasm. "The Collapse of the Armed Forces" was the title of an article not in the *Guardian* or the *Berkeley Barb* but the *Armed Forces Journal,* where a former Marine colonel wrote in June 1971 that "the morale, discipline and battle-worthiness of the U.S. armed forces are, with a few salient exceptions, lower and worse than at any time in this century and possibly in the history of the United States." During fiscal year 1971, for every hundred soldiers, there were seven desertions and seventeen AWOL incidents; twenty smoked marijuana *frequently,* ten used opium or heroin *regularly*. The breakdown was grave enough to impress upon Defense Secretary Melvin Laird the need to speed up the withdrawal of ground troops. Over and above the military breakdown was direct political organizing in the armed forces, risky, evanescent, but extensive enough to generate over 250 antiwar newspapers and scads of organizations and on one occasion—"Armed Farces Day," May 15, 1971—simultaneous demonstrations at nineteen bases. Hundreds of movement veterans worked with the GI movement, setting up coffeehouses for support, raising funds, publicizing cases, staffing the elaborate desertion and exile networks—although there too sectarianism and official repression imposed limits.

There were antiwar Vietnam veterans whose moral standing for opposing the war was unlike any other. Early in 1971, in Detroit, over a hundred Vietnam Veterans against the War testified publicly about the war crimes they had seen, though the news media paid little attention. In April, a thousand of them lobbied, camped out on Washington's Mall in defiance of a Justice Department injunction, and then, calling the names of their dead buddies, hurled their medals onto the Capitol steps, electrifying the jaded media.

Then Daniel Ellsberg became the first war planner to change sides, releasing the Pentagon Papers to the press, producing ample evidence, for those who had failed or declined to see, that the antiwar movement had been right all along about government deceptions—wedging the press into a legal confrontation with Nixon, and drawing Nixon into a fateful burglary (of Ellsberg's psychiatrist's office) to discredit Ellsberg and, through him, as the White House's Charles Colson put it, "discredit the peace movement."

And at long last, Congress took up the slack. Liberal antiwar activists—Moratorium organizers, clergy, the no-longer-CIA-subsidized National Student Association—kept up the pressure; some burned out or turned local, like their radical counterparts. With antiwar sentiment (though not demonstrations) surging from the maelstrom into the mainstream, a network of old New Leftists led by Tom Hayden (with the considerable support of Jane Fonda and lesser celebrities) found it an auspicious time to lobby in Washington; in 1972 and 1973 their Indochina Peace Campaign helped the liberal pressure groups prevail upon Congress, at long last, to cut government financing for the war.

Then, in 1972, a coalition of antiwar reformers and Democratic insiders succeeded in nominating Senator George McGovern as sacrificial Democratic lamb—aided, without their knowledge, by Nixon's dirty tricksters, who helped to bring down the frontrunning Senator Edmund Muskie's campaign in New Hampshire. The candle-carrying vigilers of 1968 had carved out a place, however tenuous, "inside the system"—in the halls of a party that could not do without them any more than it quite knew what to do with them. The Party had waited so long to listen to its dissidents, its mainstream had been discredited, while the amateurs, having turned rowdy, could be dismissed as uncompromising purists. The McGovern campaign, deserted by the Johnson-Humphrey wing of the Party—by backlashing white ethnics and Cold War unions—proved a catastrophe. If the alternative to forcing an impossible revolution was a reform campaign buried beneath the Nixon landslide, what was the moral?

Nixon's victory proved pyrrhic too, of course. A man of notorious clumsiness, Nixon tripped himself up with his high-tech paranoia. Thanks to the White House tapes, and who knows what other help, the system—the combination of the courts, the Congress, and the press— "worked." The war fizzled to its uninspiring end. At the last, there was no Nixon and no national will to intervene again and keep Vietnam divided. The movement could claim its victories—but there was not much movement to do the claiming, only a few small rallies, a collective sigh of relief, and Chinese boxes full of endings.

19

CARRYING ON

Everything changed; the world turned holy;
  and nothing changed:
There being nothing to change or needing
  change; and everything
Still to change and be changed . . .
  —Thomas McGrath

The riptide of The Revolution went out with the same force it had surged in with, the ferocious undertow proportionate to the onetime hopes.

Forces of New Left magnitude culminate in counterforces. No iron law of history, that would be too pat, but there is no denying the cyclical tendency. After 1789 and 1848 in Europe, and 1968 around the world, activists cooled, beaten and disappointed *in the measure they were once hopeful and desperate*. The Right counterorganized. Not in the United States alone: the French May *événements* receded; the West German New Left fizzled out into Baader-Meinhof terrorism, and the Right mandated the *Berufsverbot*, the purge of leftists from the professions; guerrillas in Bolivia, Guatemala, Brazil, Uruguay, and Argentina came to naught, or worse, aroused support for military putsches. The world did not change utterly. Meanwhile, in the United States and elsewhere, the movement, that surrogate world of electricity and solace, had become a source of anguish itself. It failed, or half-succeeded, but in the process squandered its own values. People were pushed away: repelled by the infighting, the power moves, the harshness, the sense of futility. And they were pulled away: attracted to the once forfeited, now alluring satisfactions of private life. Many carried on with politics or cultural pioneering, looking to other movements and institutions that stood a chance to remedy the old errors. Those whose political work was episodic in the first place were most likely to retreat to private life—all the more so as they ascended toward what the Hindus call the householding stage of life.

The recessional worked its way throughout the culture. It *became* the culture; the surge of disappointment didn't have to be felt firsthand to be felt. In the minds of the next generations, the movement in the broad sense got saddled, deservedly and not, with forbidding reputations of various and not necessarily consistent kinds: (1) it flopped; (2) it was excessive; (3) it was so huge and thrilling, mere mortals of latter days felt dwarfed in comparison. So in an antipolitical culture did the New Left—fused in later imagery with the demographic bulge of "baby boomers," all drugs and rock and sex and riotous high jinks—get dismissed as the bygone "lifestyle" of a generation, like a set of discarded clothes or a groovy nostalgia trip, a theme for collegiate parties: in either case a fashion, not an at least partly sensible way of life.

Fantasy revolutions, withdrawals, media-driven dismissals . . . all the easy reactions obscured the more elusive and ambiguous results, the triumphs and precedents that the New Left left behind as it broke up. From furious hopes came political reforms and cultural shifts—along with backlashes and perplexities equally real. For in the Seventies and Eighties the dogs of privilege and panic were no longer asleep. As the political center continued to hollow out, the Right mobilized to exploit the failings of that liberalism which had both made possible and incensed the New Left. At least in the short run, the Right had stronger American traditions to draw on: symbols of righteous and wounded national might, the mystique of the marketplace, and ironically, the appeal of family decorum as an island in that very marketplace. The Right, in other words, made sense to the very forces that were threatened and stranded by the movements of the Sixties. Now that the postwar boom had unraveled in economic crisis, the Right also stood ready with a program of good-for-business economic growth arrayed against discredited welfare-state liberalism—to which the Left, by now a grab bag of movements for social and cultural change, had no coherent alternative. Make no mistake: the various clumps of the Left were still a force, especially in the cities, especially with respect to the rights of individuals. Protection of the biosphere and of reproductive rights became majority positions, though they were submerged by probusiness economics. But as a whole the Left was outorganized. Genuflections toward History and Revolution could not make its social programs popular, its economics palatable, its mystique potent.

SETTLING IN

The war subsided, and so, for students and no-longer-students, did the urgency of politics. Not that the students of the early Seventies and the veterans of the late movement were reillusioned with the powers that be. They distrusted the corporations and the national government. They flocked to the Sierra Club and Ralph Nader. They gloated over the 1974 Watergate hearings and Nixon's resignation. Absent any coherent radical critique, many of the casual demonstrators and weekend hippies were convinced that the system worked well enough, although the more radical movement veterans noted with I-told-you-so bitterness that Nixon's bombing of Indochina was not considered an indictable cause for impeachment.

The idea of The Revolution languished, to be supplanted by the practical pursuit of reforms, what the West German radical Rudi Dutschke called "the long march through the institutions"—a romantic phrase for grounding radical change in work that is of this world. A substantial number of movement veterans went on organizing full-time in factories and fields, in trade unions, in local politics—a number impossible to calculate, but probably comparable, by rough guess, to the numbers working full-time in radical politics during all but the peak New Left years. (Since they were outside the media spotlight, the whole looked like less than the sum of the parts.) Most of the organizers were convinced that the New Left's fatal mistake had been to burn its bridges to the multitudes whose lives were dominated by scarcity. Some harbored classical Old Left ideals of working-class revolution, but most were willing to think of themselves as unabashed reformers, availing them- selves of whatever room they found for lobbying, running for office, creating local, statewide, and regional organizations. As revolutionary visions subsided, many became crisp professional lobbyists: environmen- talist, feminist, antiwar. A good number succeeded in winning local office, most of them in the Democratic Party. All were compelled to play by the political rules in an unfavorable political climate: to formulate programs, at last, and push them across in a time of tax revolt and shrinking revenues. Radical rhetoric had to strain ("new populism," "economic democracy," "free spaces," and later, "rainbow coalition") for coherence. The vision of One Big Movement dissolved into—or, optimists would say, became realized in—distinct interest groups.

Activists both hard-core and peripheral flocked to ecology-minded groups, especially those fighting nuclear power. Only a small fraction of longtime activists stayed with the Marxist-Leninist sects. Purified of counterculture and expressive politics, some of these hoarders of the Correct Idea calcified into out-and-out cultists; some, more solid, on the Trotskyist side, worked to bring actual workers into radical union caucuses, cavalierly indifferent to the pathos that befalls Marxism when it lacks an insurgent working class and thus comes to resemble religion without God. A few devoted themselves to the cause of prison reform: some hardheadedly in pursuit of justice, especially in the wake of the Attica massacre of 1971, but others with a romantic attachment to pris- oners as the *real* lumpenproletariat for The Revolution—this side reaching farcical and finally disastrous collapse with the ragtag Symbionese Liberation Army that kidnapped Patricia Hearst, most of whom died in televised flames in 1974.

No one can know quite how unsettling the movement's and counterculture's internal strains would have proved all by themselves, for they became urgent at just the time when the fat of the land was drying up. The political and spiritual contraction was matched—partly caused, partly reinforced—by the end of the great economic boom of 1945–73. Economists still debate whether the OPEC price hike and the oil crisis of 1973 triggered or simply furthered the inflationary spiral. In any event, "stagflation"—the unanticipated combination of low growth, low productivity, and rising prices—rapidly closed out the era when affluence could be taken for granted. Inflation frightened not only the fixed-income middle class but their children, who had postponed, for who knew how long, their entrance into the economic mainstream. Economic distress fueled the meritocratic scramble for scarce positions in medical and law school, or in the professoriat—precisely the scramble which the baby-boom radicals and hippies had fled years before. With the cost of housing booming, the young could no longer assume that in the natural course of things they were going to live more grandly than their parents. As economic surplus dried up, the general sense of spaciousness withered. Japan's rise and America's sliding trade position brought out chauvinistic and social Darwinist impulses throughout the culture. Competition fueled caution. Out of school, the erstwhile demonstrator lost family subsidy. When postgraduate employment could no longer be taken for granted, life in the margins lost much of its glamour. Family life, devalued for years, looked more attractive; one could conduct politics by sending checks to the good causes that flooded one's mailbox weekly. The life cycle as well as the slump said: Lower expectations, dress up, get down to business. The long march through the institutions, as Russell Jacoby said, might turn out to look more like the protracted search for a job. It was time to go straight, from marijuana to white wine, from hip communes to summers on Cape Cod. And if the return of scarcity chastened the Sixties veterans, its impact was all the stronger on the generation of students arriving in college after 1973. There was no war to galvanize opposition, no compelling black movement to inspire white conscience. Imperceptibly, the Sixties slid into the Seventies, and the zeitgeist settled down.

ENCOUNTER CULTURE

Out of radical disillusion with America's plenitude and promises and imperial drive, there had evolved a movement to force a total change, a movement with its own plenitude and promises, fueled by a rage born of its own innocence and disillusion. In the eyes of the students of the Seventies, along with movement veterans of the Sixties, that movement had turned into something else to be disillusioned with. As the movement imploded, a good many New Left veterans, especially stranded men, went into retreat. We *were* overcome. Even early in the Sixties, civil rights workers, bone-weary as Sisyphus, burned out regularly. There was the humor of the trenches: who didn't sometimes need what the army called "rest and recreation"? It was assumed that a healthy movement was going to be there to return to: a whole way of life, a church. When that assumption went up in smoke, political projects remained, reform institutions dug in, but not the movement itself as a living, portable destination. If the movement no longer satisfied, if it made too many demands of a depleted self, what arrived was a full-blown crisis of faith. It was both stunning and baffling simply to discover oneself alive, the world spinning on, changed but unchanged.

And so the youth movement's collapse left not only political wreckage but a spiritual and psychological crisis—and not only for the onetime hard core, but for the larger penumbra of part-time activists and the less-committed young middle class as well. Many verities had collapsed fast in the Sixties, and no vigorous way of life had grown up in their place. Confusion abounded. Traditional authority had lost its hold, but what alternative principles should replace it? Affinity groups and consensus decision-making could replace top-down command relations and "ego-tripping" celebrities, as in the women's and antinuclear movements, but what were movements to do when the demand for round-the-clock commitment led to domination by reckless elites, or when national issues demanded large-scale coordination, or when the leaders who did emerge were savaged for abusing their fame? Feminism did not prove immune from revolutionism, or the sectarianism that followed, or plain overwork, and so some of the beleaguered pioneers of the women's movement burned out in turn. Those who had banked on a political revolution that turned out not to be imminent wanted relief from the imperious superego that beat at them saying, It is you yourselves—your will, your commitment, your politics—who failed. They were primed to side with the Marquis de Sade in Peter Weiss's brilliant dramatization of these debates, *Marat/Sade:* "Marat/these cells of the inner self/are worse than the deepest stone dungeon/and as long as they are locked/all your Revolution remains/only a prison remains/only a prison mutiny/to be put down/by corrupted fellow-prisoners."

In short, as the movement link between past and future snapped, the present had to be filled with meaning by other means. Whereupon a good many movement veterans gravitated toward the milieu which in the late Sixties had begun to call itself "the human potential movement." This melange of encounter groups, therapies, and mystical disciplines promised to uncover authentic selves, to help people "live in the present," "go with the flow," "give themselves permission," "free themselves of shoulds," "get in touch with their feelings," "get in touch with their bodies"—promises of relief for besieged individuals burdened by obligations; promises of intimate personal relations for those who had lost the hope of God or full community; promises of self-expression for the inhibited and cramped, the bored and spoiled. Professionalized counterculture, transcendentalism for an organizational age, this tangle of therapies, spiritual and physical practices by the early Seventies had spun outward from its hub at the Esalen Institute on the Big Sur coast of California and spawned a virtual transcendence industry whose crucibles were "workshops" in therapeutic and spiritual technique: confrontational "encounter," gestalt therapy, bioenergetics, meditation, massage, breathing—and, not least, easy recreational sex. Those who had converted their psyches into experimental stations for drugs, whether pharmacological or ideological, hoped to find equanimity—or ecstasy—by more natural means. The fault, they felt, must not be in ourselves but in our musculature (thus "Rolfing" to realign the body); bad diet (thus vitamins and organic food); bad breathing from early psychic trauma (thus bioenergetics); bad breathing and bad orgasm from a bad society which caused the original psychic trauma (thus Wilhelm Reich's original version of bioenergetics); bad karma from previous lifetimes (thus various forms of meditation). However you defined the problem, your task was to "work on yourself." If there was going to be a New Age at all, it was going to come—going to have to come—from the purification of the self.

It was easy for the prudent, puritanical, and Marxist, especially on the East Coast, to dismiss the "California touchie-feelie" style as bourgeois self-indulgence, but harder to quarantine the human potential spirit. Techniques that flourished in California soon cropped up on New York's Upper West Side and in Harvard Square, and not just on the coasts: To take just one example, at Hobart College in upstate rural New York, not known as a center of cultural innovation, in early 1970 the campus was swept by seventy-two-hour weekend "sensitivity training" marathons; erstwhile politicos suddenly swung over to "the internal trip." In the early Seventies it seemed that no ex-movement household was complete without meditations, tarot cards, group therapies, the *Tao Te Ching,* and the writings of Alan Watts on Zen, Fritz Perls on gestalt therapy, Wilhelm Reich on the recovery of the body, Idries Shah on Sufism, R. D. Laing on the truths of madness, Baba Ram Dass's invocation to *Be Here Now*—and most of all, Carlos Castaneda's parables of an intellectual's skeptical yieldings to the Yaqui shaman Don Juan. Gurus made their pilgrimages. Public appearances by Baba Ram Dass (the former Richard Alpert), Fritz Perls, Chögyam Trungpa, Werner Erhart, Arthur Janov, John Lilly, Swamis Satchidananda and Muktananda, and a host of lesser-known demigods became events of the season, where jubilant insiders seemed possessed of secrets of living denied lesser mortals.

In 1890, the defeated Sioux became convinced that if they practiced a certain circle dance, with rituals of purification, the ghosts would intervene to protect them from the white man's bullets and drive away the conquerors. A so-called Ghost Dance movement swept across the Great Plains, as in other desperate times and places indigenous people defeated in war have been drawn to the supernatural. The impulse to collective expression, blocked on the plane of human action, gets diverted toward the spiritual. The human potential movement sprang from countercultural visions; it was also the continuation of expressive politics by other means. With secular revolution discredited as an escape from the "iron cage" of narrow rationality, individual subjectivity promised to reinvent a shattered world: Act *as if* the world were not a prison, and your life will be made whole. If society was impenetrable and politics a simple reshuffling of elite credentials, the self could still be transformed at will—even if, in Zen-like fashion, what was required was the will to wrestle out of the grip of the demon will itself. The ingratiating paradox of some of the new practices was that they outfitted mysteries with a scientific halo while preserving their magical (even Third World) allure of otherness. Thus the fascination with past lives, spiritual "auras," extrasensory perception, suppressed goddesses, "women's knowledge" (believed to have been the true basis of "witchcraft" in the Middle Ages), and the like. Scorned by military-industrial czars and political would-be vanguards alike, the wizards of subjectivity retained their oppositional glow.

In the early Seventies, the journey to the interior preoccupied a good half of my old movement friends—not just in California. Some shopped, some flirted, some fell head over heels in love. It was our Ghost Dance. Systems that some took up for the temporary licking of wounds, or anesthesia, for others became substitute faiths, self-enclosures extending the movement's now obsolete self-enclosure. (No one who hadn't participated was entitled to criticize. This traditional defense of closed systems was shared by Freudian psychoanalysis, Reichian therapy, and Maoism—"If you want to know the taste of a pear, you must change the pear by eating it yourself.") These sects not only stabilized shaky selves, they had the side value of channeling devotees back to conventional middle-class existence, giving them rationales for putting aside the travails of politics. For the less rigid, the Americanized present-mindedness of Baba Ram Dass and the ontological skepticism of R. D. Laing were way stations for "working on themselves." But for others, meditation succeeded meditation, guru succeeded guru in a futile lurch toward ever-receding enlightenment. Devotees of Ho Chi Minh continued their journeys to the East with irreproachable masters like the guru Maharaj Ji—or, more modestly, with D. T. Suzuki and Zen. One old movement friend, living in a yoga ashram surrounded by beatific pictures of her guru, cheerfully granted the resemblance to the days when her walls were adorned with images of Malcolm X and Che. An early SNCC staffer joined Nichiren Shoshu, a Japanese cult that endlessly intoned a single meditation mantra. In a country retreat, ex-SDSers devoted themselves to confrontational group therapy sessions. Bruce Davis, a Hobart College SDS leader who spent two years in trials and factional squabbling—he had been indicted for campus ROTC firebombings for which training and materials had been supplied by the police provocateur called "Tommy the Traveler"—concluded "we were as crazy as anything we were trying to change," and passed from jail to community organizing to primal therapy to spiritual healing. For my part, I was curious about the books, comforted by some of the practices, skeptical about the claims, appalled by the dogmas. I studied T. S. Eliot's *Four Quartets* and tried to imitate it in a book-length poem about the demise of the movement. I took down my own Malcolm X and Cuban posters, replaced them with Van Gogh, Degas, and Renoir.

The sea change from politics to personal salvation and the cultivation of personal relations also gave movement men, at the turn of the decade, a way to cope with women's liberation. Sulking, they organized "men's groups." Political subjects came up, but it was the therapeutic spirit that rode highest. Men's groups tried consciousness-raising, asking what we had lost in a lifetime confined to stereotyped male roles. The group I belonged to was pulled in two directions at once: coping with our various sexual imbroglios, and speaking our own bitterness against women who done us wrong. Over time, the group degenerated into gripe sessions. (Around 1972, we used to joke about installing a blinking neon beer sign in the window on meeting nights.) It was a holding action, a way of soothing wounds and greasing our withdrawal from politics. In truth our political will was sapped.

KICKING BACK

The turn from radical politics reverberated on campuses and throughout the counterculture as well. As the antiwar movement subsided, many students found it an opportune moment to trade in their activism for a ticket to the less risky, more pleasurable counterculture. It would not be altogether untrue to say that the teenage side of the counterculture—the drugs, sex, rock 'n' roll, "personal liberation" side— was the Sixties' version of the fraternity-sorority culture of the Fifties. The youth culture which had swooped into antiwar action in 1965 found more placid and private ways to strut its generational stuff. Altamont spelled the end of utopian illusions, but marijuana remained a diversionary staple. Drugs became more self-consciously "recreational"—used for fun rather than transcendence. In California, students who might have been tempted to "kick ass" in 1969 started speaking of "kicking back" in the sun with a can of beer.

As usual, popular music tracked the shifting youth mood. The new message was: Turn on, tune in, give peace a chance—or, in a related key, cool out. The Rolling Stones' rage, the Jefferson Airplane's shrillness, the Doors' sepulchral edge dwindled; music couldn't stay at millennial pitch any more than politics. What developed was a music to coax the breakneck imagination down to earth—even if that meant inventing an America in which one could sink roots, and a self capable of sinking them there. Sometimes the new message was blunt: During the antiwar Mobilization of November 15, 1969, as hundreds of thousands sang John Lennon's "Give Peace a Chance" lullaby at the Washington Monument, no less a figure than David Crosby (of Crosby, Stills, and Nash, formerly of the Byrds), announced to a rally in San Francisco's Golden Gate Park, "Politics is bullshit!"

The search for musical soil ran parallel to the revolutionaries' search for a stable constituency in which the dangling self could plant itself. You could hear the prefigurations, as so often, in Bob Dylan. As early as 1967, *John Wesley Harding* sounded an uncustomarily smooth note: modest celebrations, calm questions, tentative answers. The rasp was gone from Dylan's voice, the creeps and geeks banished from his tales. Some credited Dylan's shift to his recovery from a near-fatal motorcycle accident, but his well-tuned antennae were also at work, anticipating. After a brief return to urgency in the bootlegged "Basement Tapes" circulating in 1969, he slid over to Tin Pan Alley pieties ("Love is all you need/It makes the world go round") in the 1969 *Nashville Skyline*, including a duo with no less a mainstream idol than Johnny Cash. To partisans who remembered his acoustic heartfelt period, Dylan's calm sounded smug, tranquilized. To settle his quarrel with the world, he had filed away his passions. Joan Baez also borrowed the sweet twang of country-western guitars; so did Arlo Guthrie, who by 1972 had removed himself from the no-man's-land of Alice's Restaurant to the heartland "City of New Orleans."

Musical imagination, in short, was trying to conjure a separate peace. The personal and rooted was more appealing than the political and outré. No more floating free in far-out space. The Band emerged, consummate and muted rock-and-rollers (with cachet as Dylan's onetime backups) who overlaid a southern gospel sound with an apropos weariness and an agonized nostalgia for sometime, someplace, obscure. (Who better to fabricate roots in America than four Canadians and a boy from Arkansas?) The jacket of their first album, *Music from Big Pink*, showed these down-home boys mixing with just plain friends and neighbors in the heart of small-town America, as if to say, Nothing to be scared of here, Mom. Creedence Clearwater Revival produced a rougher version of the same sound. For balladeers, the post-'70 generation turned to musicians like Carole King, Carly Simon, Neil Young, Elton John, James Taylor, Cat Stevens, and the Moody Blues, melodious in their various up- and downbeat ways, committed in common to "mellowing." Hard rock and soft ballads went their separate ways, as in the late New Left; with "feminine" styles on the rise, white women soloists played a larger part in the popular music of the early Seventies than they had in the Sixties. Private consolation was the thing: In 1970 and 1971, Simon and Garfunkel had a hit with "Bridge Over Troubled Water," Carole King with "You've Got a Friend," Kris Kristofferson with "Help Me Make It Through the Night."

The zeitgeist was consistent. Rock culture convulsed with the rest of the youth movement. Early in 1970 the Beatles released "Let It Be," which in the season of the townhouse explosion seemed a plausible alternative to the Rolling Stones' "Let It Bleed." Before 1970, no serious rock musicians could have sung straight-faced about "whisper[ing] words of wisdom." For comfort, the Beatles had moved from the Maharishi to Mother Mary, and she was only a last stopping-off point. To the youth culture's passionate spectators, the Beatles' breakup was traumatic in the way the breakup of SDS had been for the student movement. Then, in 1971, John Lennon racked the Sixties' heart with the stunning "I-don't-believe" chants of "God," renouncing everyone and everything from "Kennedy" to "I Ching" and "Beatles" in one dying fall after another, ending with the therapeutic afterthought, "I just believe in me," and the privatized "Yoko and me, that's reality." In the fall of 1970 Jimi Hendrix and Janis Joplin dropped dead of drug overdoses, and a few months later Jim Morrison collapsed and died, perhaps of drink, perhaps of drugs—all at age twenty-seven. Celebrity, one of the Sixties' headiest drugs, was evidently not so tonic. For eighteen- or twenty-year-olds seeking signs of grace in popular culture, the promises of deliverance had worn to a shine. Woodstock Nation's symbols peeled away from their Aquarian meanings and became banal with popularity. Joints of marijuana were served at dinner parties. Drugs and long hair fanned out from the middle class into the working classes; southwestern truckdrivers who sang along with Merle Haggard's "We don't smoke marijuana in Muskogee" began wearing ponytails.

The counterculture was not simply a trendy substitute for fraternity partying, of course. The thousands of communes, underground papers, free schools, food "conspiracies," auto repair and carpentry collectives, women's centers and health groups and alternative publishers, required commitment. Where there were thirty free schools in 1967, there were as many as eight hundred in 1973, not counting the versions implanted within official school systems. The legions who dropped out of college to work in the margins, whether in the post office or a rock band, were not just larking around. Counterinstitutions were ways of settling down for the long haul. The collective equivalent of "just Yoko and me" was the self-consciously modest project: socialism in one free school. If all else failed, there was pleasure in "survival" in one country house. Macramé, weaving with string, was the summary symbol of the new spirit: make the most of the materials at hand. "Small is beautiful" was the slogan of the mid-Seventies. Dozens of my Harvard classmates wrote for our tenth anniversary class report, in 1973, about "cultivating our garden," the traditional middle-class way of renouncing the world. Was the hip farm, with its freer-form style of family and conventional male-female division of labor, really so different?

Then were the stereo-laden hippies of Vermont and western Massachusetts, of Sonoma and Mendocino and Santa Cruz counties in California, yet one more generation of rural refugees fleeing (and thereby extending) the metropolis in search of grass and trees and clean air for their kids? Not quite so simply. Their exodus bore traces of the communal ethos. Ecological politics continued, with its practical side, organic farming. Here and there, the all-or-nothing fervor persisted; one former Motherfucker bought some land and, having concluded from a study of the history of agriculture that the root of all hierarchy was the plow, tilled his soil with a stick. Hip agribusiness developed, fueled by a market for health foods and drugs: by the Eighties, marijuana in Northern California was said to be the state's largest cash crop. New generations of freaks made lives for themselves in the countryside, selling crafts, growing pot, living in the margins. Every July Fourth since 1972, thousands of them—twenty-eight thousand in 1984, in Northern California's Modoc County—gathered at a different country site for the Rainbow Family Peace Gathering, some berobed, some nude, smoking grass and chanting Om and celebrating their strangeness. Year after year the "Deadheads" among them showed up for Grateful Dead concerts, mixing with suburbanites in their professionally tie-dyed shirts. Group marriages, cooperating couples, gay and lesbian communes, and collective farms led by gurus lived out their economic and sexual alternatives to the nuclear family. Still, even the more communal white projects bumped up against limits of race, class, sexual politics, and sheer practicality. Black and Hispanic parents preferred traditional 3-R schooling to the slack laissez-faire of free schools or the middle-class initiative of the home-schooling movement. Hip whites who bought land in northern New Mexico were met with enmity, even violence, by Hispanics. Hip women who had disdained the women's movement were revolted by male supremacy in the commune. Children had to be raised, crops planted, jealousies coped with. Breaking down lines of property and hierarchy, establishing order—that irresistible bogey—while avoiding lines of traditional authority, was a perpetual battle. Communes came and went. The ones with religious commitments survived longest.

On the surface, the counterculture had valued being over doing, expressing over accomplishing. But it never lost its practical edge—in the Diggers' "serve-the-people" spirit, for example, even in much-scorned "hip capitalism." When millenarian hopes were dashed, the old instinct for workmanship resurfaced. Those who had dropped out of professional careers found that they still cared about excellence along with freedom. The fugitives from meritocracy rediscovered merit. Middle-class dropouts looked for ways to drop partway back in. Recognizing that right action is not accomplished by hostility to authority alone, the counterculture discovered the importance of "skills." All the "correct lines" in the world couldn't make the engine cylinders run on time. It was one thing to dislike medical exams that kept you in the dark, but whoever taught gynecological self-examinations had to know what she was doing. Woodstock Nation fused with entrepreneurship, eco-consciousness with high-tech, the ideal of self-reliance with country hip to produce *The Whole Earth Catalog*, the Sears catalog for the New Age, with its array of "tools for living" from wood stoves to computers, all recommended with the motto, "We *are* as gods, and might as well get good at it." (While much of the New Left had scorned the 1969 moon landing as a techno-irrelevancy if not an exercise in imperial distraction and space colonialism, the *Catalog* ingeniously displayed an extraterrestrial photo of Planet Earth to conjure up splendid finitude.) Gradually, as the market became more affluent, the scale and splendor of hip capitalism ratcheted up. Hip and radical electronics whizzes founded Silicon Valley computer firms. A rugged Berkeley emporium called Whole Earth Access became the city's leading all-purpose department store. Celestial Seasonings Teas were bought out by the Dart & Kraft food conglomerate. By the Eighties, the B.A.'d, professional, high-earning yuppie as a social type was numerous enough—though far less prevalent than the media made out (there were probably no more than four million in the mid-Eighties)—to sustain thousands of chic restaurants and shops, aerobics clubs, organic products lines, therapy centers, clinics, boutiques, and alternative weeklies wobbling uneasily between investigative reporting and shopping tips.

High-markup health food combines and free schools that teach reading only when children "want" to learn are easily mocked, but the impact of countercultural values was both more sweeping and more elusive than the jokes could register. The revaluation of values rippled outward, in two directions. The chaos of American culture—and the counterculture in particular—sent some people fleeing toward absolute authority, gurus with systems of total discipline of whom the Reverend Jim Jones and his Jonestown inferno stand as a paranoid end point. On a larger scale, the ideals of cultural plurality and participatory democracy remained alive, cultural standards against which to criticize the workplace, the polity, and the household. Homosexuals, still embattled, could begin to claim self-respect and civil rights long denied them. Gay pride was no empty phrase when it took the form of mass marches, political blocs, and visible turf in San Francisco, Greenwich Village, West Hollywood, et al. A loose antiauthoritarianism was normalized—in the knowing, scattershot form of *Saturday Night Live*, in the ease of unpunished cohabitation, as well as in the corrupt and sloppy grade inflation that became a regular feature of school and university life. Yet only the most sentimental ex-hippie could fail to recognize the prices paid on the road to the new freedoms: the booming teenage pregnancy rate; the dread diseases, particularly AIDS, that accompanied the surge in promiscuity; the damage done by drugs; the undermining of family commitment, which, although it could hardly be blamed on human-potential do-your-thingism altogether, could not be said to have been resisted by it either. As early as 1972, feminists warned that women were not safe walking through People's Park. There were rapes.

Of all the countercultural and New Left values, the ones that radiated farthest were the mores affecting women. The women's movement extended far beyond the original feminist and New Left circles; the explosions of utopian and revolutionary sentiment, once channeled, drove the engines of reform. With the help of affirmative action, women broke into politics, law, pulpits, occupations, sports; to varying extents they changed the habits of speech, of the household and the bedroom. They won their greatest victories on the American path of least resistance: individual rights. Because men and institutions resisted radical challenges, they accomplished far less in the realm of economic equality. They failed, for example, to win public responsibility for child care (which would free women from the burden of presiding over domestic duties even when they work); they failed to compel higher-earning men to share their earnings with ex-spouses and children after divorce. Some women broke job barriers, others broke into poverty. Meanwhile, the New Left side of feminism, with its radical critiques of the isolated family, plunged into ideological free fall. In a way, like the New Left, the women's movement also underestimated the white-knuckled intensity with which men and women alike would hold onto old institutions—the nuclear family above all—when the rest of society offered so little anchorage.

For many—who knows, perhaps most—of the movement veterans, some version of New Left politics continued, but in a chastened, confused, and antiapocalyptic key. As the economy foundered in the Seventies, and the movement's moral imperatives grew more burdensome, many wearied of the life of the professional radical; we scooped together our bona fides (I enrolled in Berkeley's Ph.D. program in sociology in 1974, for example, after nine years out of school), or resumed half-completed dissertations, or otherwise set out on the track that middle-class upbringing and education had prepared us for before Sixties politics had intervened. We became professionals and managers, and made the acquaintance of credit cards and small domestic pleasures. (Hunter S. Thompson: "When the going gets tough, the weird turn pro.") From the next generation of lawyers, professors, journalists, teachers, clergy, planners, doctors, and nurses came invigorated professions—public interest law, legal help and initiative for the poor and powerless; radicalized, feminized religion in the mainstream denominations; in medicine, family practice, self-help, patients' rights; in journalism, a small boom in investigation; in the universities, ferment in the social sciences and humanities (along with cant and intellectual masturbation, the academic equivalent of vanguard revolutionism). Sometimes the participatory spirit was combined with an ethic of service and knowledge—as in legal aid and medical clinics for workers, midwife collectives, solar energy, marketing cooperatives for small farmers, socially responsible investment. As we acquired a modicum of authority, antiauthoritarian politics, needless to say, became more complicated. The long march through the institutions meandered through labyrinths: Which authority is just, which policies are right? What happens when liberty collides with community, equality with democracy? Which compromises are justified toward which ends? The long march grew longer. Still, although professionalized reform was a far cry from all-absorbing activism, it was decidedly more stable and in some ways, within limits, more effective. What was far more visible, of course, was the money-grubbing and chic self-absorption so much beloved by I-told-you-so journalists, as if a whole generation had moved en masse from *"J'accuse"* to Jacuzzi; Jerry Rubin's move to Wall Street in the early Eighties garnered more publicity than all the union organizers and antinuclear campaigners among New Left graduates put together.

IN SEARCH OF AN ENDING

A biography ends with a death; the history of a war with an armistice; a scientific article with a call for more research; a balance sheet with a bottom line; a cautionary tale with a moral. Any finality I can imagine for this book seems false, for I write not just about history but imprisoned within it, enclosed within the aftermaths of the Sixties, trying to peer over the walls. The outcome and meaning of the movements of the Sixties are not treasures to be unearthed with an exultant Aha!, but sand paintings, something provisional, both created and revised in historical time. Why assume history has a single direction, posing clear answers to the question of where it is tending? History seems to me less cunning than clumsy, a tangle of unintended consequences, and so it would be absurd to claim that subsequent developments were "caused" purely by the New Left, as if the movement were a solitary unmoved mover charging across an open field.

If I had been coming to conclusions in the early Seventies, my foreground would have been at odds with itself: part taken up with grief and the Ghost Dance, part with relief that the war was finally coming to an end, part with the ambiguous triumph of Watergate, and part with regret that the New Left remnant had succumbed to what some Marxists would call a "false consciousness" about itself. As an impossible revolution it had failed—how could it have succeeded?—but as an amalgam of reform efforts, especially for civil rights (ultimately for Hispanics, Native Americans, and other minorities as well as blacks) and women's rights and the environment and against the war, it had been a formidable success.

During the Jimmy Carter years I would have been struck by the persistence of those successes *and* the intensity of the rollback. The antiwar movement's veto power had become symbolized, even institutionalized, as a sort of disease labeled the "Vietnam syndrome," and as a result Washington was leery of military intervention. Congress had set some limits on the imperial presidency. But the Right was lashing back, and groups like the Committee on the Present Danger were seizing upon the frustration of America's defeat in Vietnam and winning support for an armament surge. Orthodox authorities, hard-pressed, were giving way to unorthodox authorities, like theocratic fundamentalists. Still, the movement's antiauthoritarianism was abroad in ways that were not frivolous—in the currency of ideas about workers' control, in the contest against sexism in the domestic division of labor, in congressional investigations of the CIA, in investigative journalism and the wholesale use of the Freedom of Information Act. If black, student, and women's activism had subsided, at least some of their demands had been institutionalized. A reformer's heart could take satisfaction from Jimmy Carter's concern for human rights, from his unpanicked response to a revolution in Nicaragua, from the growing clout of consumer activists and environmentalists, from the beginnings of steady-state energy in the wake of the oil crisis, from the obstruction of nuclear power in the wake of the Three Mile Island accident.

From the mid- to late Eighties, the sweet and wild dreams of the Sixties seem as remote as the nightmares. The counterrevolution seems to have outorganized the revolution. While middle-class whites protected themselves with private schools and suburban boundaries, backlash against the black movement (tactically inspired by it, curiously) rallied the hearts of squeezed working-class whites who were fighting to protect what they had, and acquire more, in the teeth of competition and crime and sheer resentment from below. The fraternities and sororities filled again, the most accomplished undergraduates swept into business and law, the law students into corporate firms. (So much for the theory that permissive childrearing, or huge impersonal campuses, automatically radicalized students.) Real estate speculation triumphed over political speculation. In ghettos and steel towns as well as college towns, collective action was eclipsed—though not universally—by private pursuits, retreats, anxieties, greeds. Ronald Reagan swept to the White House as the defender of verities against upstarts, as he had swept to the governor's mansion in Sacramento in 1966 bearing that same torch, taking advantage of the blunders of a tired liberal governor, astonishing not only radicals but many liberals, all of them drastically underestimating the force of conservative impulses.* Twice running, the nation's shrinking

---

*In 1966, the two-term Democratic governor Edmund G. (Pat) Brown so underestimated candidate Reagan, he leaked to the press information detrimental to Reagan's competitor during the Republican primary.

electorate willed itself to believe in a mellifluous teller of fairy tales about a restored America whose Marines would always slog ashore to plant the red-white-and-blue on the beach. The Right, awash in money, unencumbered by antiauthoritarianism, proved—for a time, at least—more successful at coalition-making than the Left, which was not only undisciplined but seemed committed to staying that way. Robust, coherent liberalism—the liberalism of the helping-hand state—was in rubble.

Who could have expected a reformation without a counterreformation? Only naïfs who thought history moved onward and upward in a straight line. Still, the force of the recoil was extraordinary. Anyone who went to sleep in 1968, with Eldridge Cleaver's *Soul on Ice* leading the bestseller list and *The Graduate* first at the box office, and woke up in 1985 to behold *Iacocca* and *Rambo,* and Cleaver as an apostle of the fire-breathing anti-Communist Unification Church, would be entitled to some astonishment. The movement's victories, real as they were, seemed to dwindle with time—both because they were partial and because they came to be taken for granted. Blacks became police chiefs and bankers, and could drive across Mississippi in the same cars as whites without risking death; but proportionately at least twice as many blacks were out of work as whites, and the ghettos were training grounds in desperation. College students went on interracial dates with seeming nonchalance, yet there were campus cross-burnings. Thirty-two years after the Supreme Court declared that racially separate schools were intrinsically unequal, Linda Brown Smith, the girl in that case, now forty-three and a grandmother, was back in court to argue that the schools of Topeka, Kansas, were still segregated. Women were no longer bound to kitchen and playpen, but as some dressed for success, millions had no choice but to raise their children alone. In Vietnam, the toll had been stopped at more than 850,000 "enemy" and 400,000 civilians dead (by *conservative* estimate), 1 million wounded, millions of refugees; but while napalm was no longer searing children, the aftertaste of peace was bitter, for in short order the NLF (decimated by Tet and the CIA's systematic assassinations) was submerged by Hanoi's cadres, thousands of Vietnamese were in concentration camps for political crimes, and hundreds of thousands had taken to the high seas for life in exile. And which was the more imposing fact—that America organized, armed, and trained the counterrevolution in Nicaragua, or that President Ronald Reagan, at the height of his popularity, still had so much trouble overriding the "Vietnam syndrome"?

Disappointment too eagerly embraced becomes habit, becomes doom. Say what we will about the Sixties' failures, limits, disasters, America's political and cultural space would probably not have opened up as much as it did without the movement's divine delirium. (Better, to be sure, if we could have had the delirium without its demonic side—if history would have permitted pure goodness, which is doubtful.) This side of an ever-receding millennium, the changes wrought by the Sixties, however belea-guered, averted some of the worst abuses of power, and made life more decent for millions. The movement in its best moments and broadest definition made philosophical breakthroughs which are still working themselves out: the idea of a politics in which difference (race, gender, nation, sexuality) does not imply deference; the idea of a single globe and the limits that have to be set on human power. However embattled, however in need of practical policy, these ideas sketch out a living political vision. A sort of shadow movement remains alive. . . . To which another voice says: *not nearly enough.* The ideas of the Sixties remain murky, full of conundrums. A generation giddy about easy victories was too easily crushed by defeats, too handily placated—but uneasily, and for how long?—by private satisfactions.

The movement was played out, but at the same time America's sense of divine exemption from Old World fates wore thin. The consensus that led to Vietnam was cracked, never to be restored, whatever the longings. And who can deny that the old political vocabularies are impoverished? Most self-proclaimed "conservatives" are Manichaeans waving one flag or another on behalf of their belligerent innocence. Liberals, facing taxpayer revolt against their fifty-year-long affiliation with kindly government, are reluctant to call themselves by a discredited name, while their trade-union base—some one-eighth of the work force—has eroded below its 1920 level. Multibillion-dollar corporations lay claim to free speech; some feminists (antipornography) and black activists (anti-*Huckleberry Finn*) oppose it. Students who think about their careers first and call themselves "conservative" endorse "liberal" social values. Mainstream churches committed civil disobedience by organiz-ing sanctuaries for Central American refugees; Sixties veterans created a counterworld within Judaism; the Catholic Church, bastion of the Vietnam war, became the most sizable organized opposition to the nuclear arms race. Most American political attitudes are not neatly laid out on a simple left-right continuum; they are hybrid varieties, self-contradictory at their core. They have not yet found their language. The most prevalent use of "radical," meanwhile, is as a Southern California surfer's term for a particularly good wave.

The odds have been against the Left in laissez-faire-loving, race-divided, history-burying America from the start. The two-party system, so-lidified by law, militates against the ideological margins—even as the parties lose their hold on the voters. The New Left, like its predecessors, failed to create lasting political forms; when SDS was torn apart, so was the chance for continuity. In the Seventies, affinity group models of par-ticipatory democracy helped discredit Leninist politics, but often at the price of discrediting leadership and lucid debate altogether. Whipsawed between anarchism and Leninism, the New Left failed to produce the political leaders one might have expected of a movement so vast: it de-valued too much intelligence, was too ambivalent about personal prowess. The millennial, all-or-nothing moods of the Sixties proved to be poor training for practical politics. The premium the movement placed on the glories and agonies of the pure existential will ill equipped many of us to slog away in coalitions in a society crisscrossed by divisions, a society not cleanly polarized along a single moral axis, a society not poised on the edge of radical change. Therefore, for both long-standing and recent reasons, a substantial Left has been conspicuous by its absence since the McGovern debacle. When Nixon and then Reagan went too far in their efforts to damage or circumvent legitimate opposition, and suffered the crippling of their war-making powers, there was no Left to say: These are the consequences of imperial passion run amok. With its moderating genius, the political system worked to contain the scandals as matters of lawbreaking, bad judgment, bad character, shoddy administration.

Power and greed need to be leashed, democracy given a chance; but why should Americans want a total Left? What used to call itself socialism in power chilled the heart. Anti-interventionism can no longer be innocent, it must be an anti-interventionism without illusions, for what excuse can there be, in the closing years of the twentieth century, for overlooking the injuries done to human freedom and dignity not only by the Soviet Union but by Castro's Cuba and the Chinese Cultural Revolution? An honorable Left which wants to give credit to revolutions where credit is due cannot blithely pass the blame for revolutionary crimes to their enemies; the staggering carnage left by the Khmer Rouge—ideologues par excellence, not just murder machines started up by the West—should have sunk any lingering idea of a single, indissoluble, automatically noble Revolution. (But neither should revulsion toward the Khmer Rouge expunge the fact that their victory was expedited by America's anti-Sihanouk moves and its terror bombing in the countryside. American planes dropped over 250,000 tons of bombs on Cambodia during the seven months beginning in February 1973—50 percent more than the tonnage dropped on Japan in all of World War II.) There are no clean hands. The idea of a unitary Left destined to save the world because it was born on the side of the angels is grotesque blindness. Even benign social democracy, when it comes to power in Western Europe, loses much of its allure if for no other reason than that capital goes on strike and a weak economy cannot satisfy the demands an aroused democracy makes.

Globally, after the great popular upheavals against communism in 1989–90, the open eye sees the vast anticlimax of utopian capitalism, fundamentalism, nationalism. If the glimmering idea of the Left has failed to finesse all the terrible quandries of an honorable politics, then, what can be said of the counterculture? I take a train north from New York City. One young man reads a pamphlet called "How to Meditate." Another, in a red T-shirt, bears around his neck a medallion with a picture of the guru Bhagwan Rajneesh. A forty-five-ish woman proclaims drunkenly: "I don't care about money, I care about self-realization." The New Age has been, to say the least, neutralized—

the form of absorption that pleases pluralists as much as it infuriates the apostles of a humanity reborn.

• • •

And now? My generation numbers teachers more activist (for the moment) than their students, rock stars more antiestablishment than their audiences: this is mind-boggling for a generation who believed that youth had the privilege of vision. But the Sixties' returns are not in, the activists now in their thirties and forties and early fifties by no means finished. At this writing, one-time antiwar demonstrators live in the White House; others are dotted through all levels of government, education, nonprofit organizations, and professions. There are Greens, and Greenpeace, and campaigns for political prisoners, and thousands—not enough—of little, local movements full of intelligent democratic boisterousness. There are movements waiting to happen, movements that will imitate, and transcend, and sometimes caricature those of the past (it will be hard at times to tell which), movements that do not necessarily spring from the old social categories or speak the old languages—at least not if they are alive to their moment. And still there are no guarantees that noble purposes will produce the best of all possible results. We strain to foresee, but history refuses to purify the results of our efforts in advance. It is not a promissory note: Pay to the bearer, on demand, after years of good works, the best of all possible worlds.

Still, those who deplore the mess and wildness of social movements should ask themselves whether the world's managers, left to their own devices, can be trusted to cease torturing and invading peoples who are inconvenient to them; to cease driving peasants off their lands and into starvation; to keep the rain forests and battered species alive; to sustain the planet Earth and preserve us from industrial poisoning. And even after the Cold War, states can scarcely be trusted to brandish the Bomb forever, comforted by the fantasy of perpetual safety through perpetual threat to destroy whole populations. On one side, there remains the perennial trap of thinking the old dilemmas can be outmuscled by the good luck of youth; on the other, the trap of thinking the future is doomed to be nothing more than the past; between them, possibly, the space to invent.

"It was not granted you to complete the task," said Rabbi Tarfon nineteen hundred years ago, "and yet you may not give it up."

ACKNOWLEDGMENTS

I am grateful to the following, whom I interviewed and/or who speculated out loud with me about what happened, why it happened, and what it meant: Stew Albert, Gar Alperovitz, Danny Beagle, Robert N. Bellah, Larry Bensky, Peter Berg, Marshall Berman, Victoria Bonnell, Robb Burlage, Richard Busacca, Blair Clark, Judith Coburn, Bruce Davis, Dave Dellinger, Claudia Dreifus, Mickey Flacks, Richard Flacks, Hardy Frye, Allen Ginsberg, Bob Gottlieb, Alan Haber, Barbara Haber, Steve Hamilton, Michael Harrington, Hyman Hartman, Jim Hawley, Tom Hayden, Christopher Z. Hobson, Irving Howe, Sharon Jeffrey, Jeff Jones, Tom Kahn, Michael Kazin, Paul Krassner, Elinor Langer, Jeremy Larner, Gerda Lerner, Al Levitt, Straughton Lynd, Robert Machover, Dickie Magidoff, Steve Max, Rebecca Adams Mills, Jessica Mitford, Carolyn Nichols, Martin Peretz, Marcus Raskin, Joseph L. Rauh, Jr., Ruth Rosen, Robert Ross, Kirkpatrick Sale, Franz Schurmann, Mike Smith, I. F. Stone, Meredith Tax, Don Villarejo, Myrna Villarejo, Nicholas von Hoffman, Arthur Waskow, Steve Wasserman, Marilyn Webb, David Wellman, Peter Wily, and Ellen Willis, Leni Wildflower made Paul Potter's papers available to me, and Richard Flacks lent me his own. Clayborne Carson, Irving Howe, Dickie Magidoff, and David Wellman gave or lent me various obscure and valuable materials. Paul Lichterman and Tom Wells were my research assistants. Tom Wells compiled the index.

The friends and colleagues whom I most wanted to read at least parts of the manuscript and argue with me were usually the people who had the least time to do so. For both the encouragement and the criticism my gratitude is therefore double: Peter Davis, W. Russell Ellis, Hardy Frye, Herbert J. Gans, Allen Ginsberg, Jeremy Larner, Joan Levinson, Robert Machover, David Plotke, Joseph L. Rauh, Jr., Franz Schurmann, Steve Wasserman, Tom Wells, and especially Carl Oglesby. Most of all, time and again I was encouraged and challenged in matters of form, argument, and fact by two wise and exacting readers: Elinor Langer and Staughton Lynd.

Like anyone who plows these fields, I owe a debt to writers who have worked some of them before in their own ways, especially Clayborne Carson: Lewis Chester, Godfrey Hodgson, and Bruce Page; Sara Evans; Charlie Gillett; Abbie Hoffman; Martin Lee and Bruce Shlain; Don McNeill; Greil Marcus; Abe Peck; Charles Perry; John Schultz; Tom Wolfe; Nancy Zaroulis and Gerald Sullivan; and above all, Kirkpatrick Sale.

At Bantam, Carolyn Nichols put me in touch with Tobi Sanders, my editor, who was unfailing with support, criticism, and tolerance. As the book was going to press, Tobi died in an auto accident. She was a friend as well as an editor with guts; I shall miss her.

The staff at Bantam—especially Barb Burg, Elizabeth Chapman, Fran Fisher, Francie Nuelle, Donna Ruvituso, Richard Sandomir, Susie West, Jaye Zimet, and again Carolyn Nichols—were helpful in myriad ways, as was my agent, Roberta Pryor.

From start to finish, the burden of all my obsessions, doubts, relivings, and fanatical work fell on Ruth Rosen. Only the one who lives with the author knows how pale a word is "encouragement" for the compound of listening, criticism, forebearance, close reading, steadiness, and faith—and again forebearance—that she delivered. Tough mind, tender heart: I and this book have been graced by her.

NOTES

EPIGRAPH

PAGE

xi   **William Morris:** *A Dream of John Ball and A King's Lesson* (London: Longmans, Green, 1886), p. 31.

xi   **Leonard Cohen:** "Stories of the Street."

PREFACE

xiv   **George Will:** "Slamming The Doors," *Newsweek,* March 25, 1991, pp. 85–86. In a subsequent column (*Los Angeles Times,* July 15, 1992, p. B7), Will, stalwart defender of the right of corporate executives to move their factories anywhere in the world they please, blames the post-1960 left for advocating "more 'rights' for Americans to throw sharp elbows against one another, and less deference to social norms."

INTRODUCTION

2   **Harvard Stadium:** *New York Times,* April 26, 1959, p. 3.

2   **paid members:** Kirkpatrick Sale, *SDS* (New York: Random House, 1973), p. 663.

3   **"fought in the revolution":** Martin Buber, *Pointing the Way,* trans. Maurice Friedman (London: Routledge and Kegan Paul, 1957), p. 120.

1. CORNUCOPIA AND ITS DISCONTENTS

9   **Arthur Miller:** Introduction to Ken Kesey, *Kesey's Garage Sale* (New York: Viking, 1973), p. xv.

12   **assumption of affluence:** Edward Shils ("Dreams of Plenitude, Nightmares of Scarcity," in Seymour M. Lipset and Philip G. Altbach, eds., *Students in Revolt* [Boston: Houghton Mifflin, 1969]) has pointed to the role of affluence in forming the consciousness of the student movement, stressing the relation between affluence and authority.

13   **baby boom:** Landon Y. Jones, *Great Expectations: America and the Baby Boom Generation* (New York: Ballantine, 1981), pp. 20–23, 26–27, 396.

13   **land of plenty:** David Potter, *People of Plenty* (Chicago: University of Chicago Press, 1954).

14   **American suburb:** My discussion is indebted to Gwendolyn Wright, *Building the*

PAGE

16   **interstate roads:** Godfrey Hodgson, *America in Our Time* (Garden City, N.Y.: Doubleday, 1976), p. 51.

17   **life insurance:** U.S. Bureau of the Census, *Statistical Abstract of the United States: 1976* (Washington, D.C.: U.S. Government Printing Office, 1976), p. 499, tables 811–12.

17   **number of psychiatrists:** Robert Castel, Francoise Castel, and Anna Lowell, *The Psychiatric Society* (New York: Columbia University Press, 1982), p. 60.

18   **typical bestseller hero:** Elizabeth Long, *The American Dream and the Popular Novel* (London: Routledge and Kegan Paul, 1985), pp. 63, 82, 91.

18   **Daniel Bell:** *The End of Ideology: On the Exhaustion of Political Ideas in the Fifties* (Glencoe, Ill.: Free Press, 1960).

18   **Seymour Martin Lipset:** *Political Man* (Garden City, N.Y.: Anchor, 1963). See also Pells, *Liberal Mind*, pp. 131–33, 138.

18   **"Those who do not believe":** In David Caute, *The Great Fear* (New York: Simon and Schuster, 1978), p. 15.

18   **Central Intelligence Agency:** The journal financed by the CIA was *Encounter. New York Times*, April 27, 1966; Christopher Lasch, "The Cultural Cold War," in *The Agony of the American Left* (New York: Vintage, 1969), pp. 98–110.

19   **popular social critics:** Long, *American Dream*, pp. 150–64.

20   **"permanent war economy":** Walter J. Oakes, "Toward a Permanent War Economy?" *Politics* 1 (February 1944), pp. 11–17.

21   **"Intellect":** Clark Kerr, *The Uses of the University* (New York: Harper and Row, 1963), p. 124.

21   **Total spending:** Cyril Levitt, *Children of Privilege: Student Revolt in the Sixties* (Toronto: University of Toronto Press, 1984), p. 31.

21   **number of students:** U.S. Bureau of the Census, *Statistical Abstract of the United States: 1976*, pp. 115, 375; Milton Viorst, *Fire in the Streets: America in the 1960s* (New York: Simon and Schuster, 1979), p. 164.

21   **number of degrees:** Levitt, *Children of Privilege*, p. 31.

22   **rate of juvenile delinquency:** David Matza, "Subterranean Traditions of Youth," *The Annals of the American Academy of Political and Social Science* 338 (November 1961), p. 104.

23   **genial Ike:** On his attitudes toward the atomic bomb in general, and its possible use in Korea: John Colville, *The Fringes of Power* (London: Hodder and Stoughton, 1985), p. 685. On Indochina: Georges Bidault, in Peter Davis's film *Hearts and Minds*.

23   **children who grew up:** Personal communication, David Riesman, 1975.

24   **science fiction films:** Susan Sontag, "The Imagination of Disaster," in *Against Interpretation* (New York: Dell, 1969), pp. 220–22.

24   **"In today's atomic age":** Gil Einstein and Elaine Digrande, "From the Editors," *Observatory*, Bronx High School of Science (New York, 1959), p. 6.

25   **"Every night":** Meredith Tax, "Speak, Memory: Primo Levi's Living History," *Voice Literary Supplement*, March 1986, p. 12.

25   **Jewish Cold Warriors:** This suggestion comes from Michael Rogin.

27   **Their peers:** The terms of this sentence are adapted from Richard Flacks, "Making History vs. Making Life," *Sociological Inquiry* 46 (1976).

27   **"missing generation":** Irving Howe, "New Styles in 'Leftism,'" reprinted in Howe, *Beyond the New Left* (New York: McCall, 1970), p. 23.

29   **harmless part:** Matza, "Subterranean Traditions," p. 116.

29   **"adversary culture":** Lionel Trilling, *Beyond Culture* (New York: Viking, 1965), pp. xii–xiii; Daniel Bell, *The Cultural Contradictions of Capitalism* (New York: Basic, 1976), pp. 40–41.

2. UNDERGROUND CHANNELS

32 eight thousand fans: Ezra Goodman, "Delirium Over Dead Star," *Life*, September 24, 1956, p. 75.

33 Zimmerman: Anthony Scaduto, *Bob Dylan* (New York: Grosset and Dunlap, 1971), p. 9.

35 Paul Goodman: *Utopian Essays and Practical Proposals* (New York: Vintage, 1964), p. 278.

35 "withering sneer": Reprinted in *Son of Mad* (New York: Warner 1973), n.p.

35 "nasty little people": In Albert B. Feldstein, ed., *William M. Gaines' The Mad Frontier* (New York: Signet, 1962), p. 35.

36 Freberg: Charlie Gillett, *The Sound of the City*, rev. and expanded ed. (New York: Pantheon, 1983), p. 60.

36 *Mad* too much credit: Tony Hiss and Jeff Lewis, "The 'Mad' Generation," *New York Times Magazine*, July 31, 1977, pp. 14ff.; Stanley Rothman and S. Robert Lichter, *Roots of Radicalism* (New York: Oxford University Press, 1982), p. 108.

38 Alan Freed: Gillett, *Sound*, p. 13.

38 Memphis radio: Albert Goldman, *Elvis* (New York: McGraw-Hill, 1981), pp. 101–5.

38 In the clubs: Greil Marcus, "Lies About Elvis, Lies About Us," *Voice Literary Supplement*, November 18–24, 1981, citing Margaret McKee and Fred Chisenall, *Beale Black and Blue* (Baton Rouge: Louisiana State University Press, 1981).

38 "If I could find": Marcus, ibid., p. 16, citing Jerry Hopkins, *Elvis* (New York: Simon & Schuster, 1971) and his own telephone interview with Marion Keisker, Phillips's co-manager at Sun. I thank Marcus for setting me straight that the widely quoted version of this remark on p. 110 of Goldman's *Elvis* (with "nigger" for "Negro" and "boy" for "man") distorts Phillips's commitment to racial equality.

38 Phillips coached: Arnold Shaw, *The Rock Revolution* (New York: Crowell-Collier, 1969), p. 15.

38 echo chamber: Gillett, *Sound*, p. 27.

38 RCA label: Shaw, *Rock Revolution*, p. 16.

38 Greil Marcus: *Mystery Train: Images of America in Rock 'n' Roll Music* (New York: Dutton, 1976), pp. 179–82.

39 national feminine: In French writing of the nineteenth century, the European "South"—Spain, Italy, Egypt, North Africa—played a similar part in national iconography. See César Graña, *Bohemian versus Bourgeois: French Society and the French Man of Letters in the Nineteenth Century* (New York: Basic, 1964), pp. 131–34.

40 "Well you wear": Quoted in Gillett, *Sound*, pp. 20–21.

41 "Sha da da da": Adapted from Richard Goldstein, *The Poetry of Rock* (New York: Bantam, 1969), p. 29.

42 Nat King Cole: Gillett, *Sound*, pp. 17–18.

42 "throw discipline": Spiro T. Agnew, address of April 28, 1970, Fort Lauderdale, Florida, reprinted in John R. Coyne, Jr., *The Impudent Snobs: Agnew vs. the Intellectual Establishment* (New Rochelle, N.Y.: Arlington House, 1972), p. 319.

42 Some liberals: Christopher Jencks, "Is It All Dr. Spock's Fault?" *New York Times Magazine*, March 3, 1968, pp. 27ff.

42 the Twenties: Paula S. Fass, *The Damned and the Beautiful: American Youth in the 1920's* (New York: Oxford University Press, 1977), pp. 102, 106–7.

43 Ed Sullivan: Douglas T. Miller and Marion Nowak, *The Fifties: The Way We Really Were* (Garden City, N.Y.: Doubleday, 1977), p. 410; Goldman, *Elvis*, p. 203.

43 pelvis: Goldman, *Elvis*, p. 203; Robert Palmer, "Elvis Presley: Homage to a Rock King," *New York Times*, November 18, 1984, pp. 21, 23.

44 newly crew-cut: Goldman, *Elvis*, p. 270.

3. ENCLAVES OF ELDERS

45 In 1955: My discussion of the beats benefits from the enlightening criticism of Allen Ginsberg in telephone conversations of May 20 and 29, 1987.

45 Jack Kerouac urging: Michael McClure, *Scratching the Beat Surface* (San Francisco: North Point, 1982), p. 13.

45 a few thousand: Ned Polsky, "The Village Beat Scene: Summer 1960," in *Hustlers, Beats, and Others* (Chicago: University of Chicago Press, 1985), p. 174.

46 "in an ordinary working-class manner": Polsky, *Hustlers*, p. 147.

46 fewer than 10 percent: Ibid., p. 174.

46 They felt cramped: Dennis McNally, *Desolate Angel: Jack Kerouac, the Beat Generation, and America* (New York: McGraw-Hill, 1979), p. 136; Barbara Ehrenreich, *The Hearts of Men* (Garden City, N.Y.: Anchor/Doubleday, 1983), pp. 52–67.

46 never learned to drive: Joyce Johnson, *Minor Characters* (Boston: Houghton Mifflin, 1983), pp. 195–96.

47 demanding mother: McNally, *Desolate Angel*, passim.

47 "camaraderie of loneliness": Johnson, *Minor Characters*, p. 27. See also Thomas Parkinson, "Phenomenon or Generation," in Parkinson, ed., *A Casebook on the Beat* (New York: Crowell, 1961), p. 278. Compare Norman Podhoretz's half-perceptive, half-lurid remark in the December 1958 *Esquire* (p. 150): the beats were a "conspiracy" to replace civilization with "the world of the adolescent street gang."

47 "boy gang": Allen Ginsberg, in Johnson, *Minor Characters*, p. 79.

47 heroin: Polsky, *Hustlers*, pp. 161–62.

47 "At lilac evening": Jack Kerouac, *On the Road* (New York: Signet, 1957), pp. 148–49.

48 "holy goof": Ibid., p. 160.

48 "secret hero": Allen Ginsberg, "Howl," in *Howl and Other Poems* (San Francisco: City Lights, 1956), p. 12.

48 "Oh, I love": Kerouac, *On the Road*, p. 117.

48 "Real life was sexual": Johnson, *Minor Characters*, p. 30.

48 "some pursuit": Ibid., p. 171.

48 "undisturbed flow": Jack Kerouac, "Essentials of Spontaneous Prose," *Evergreen Review*, Summer 1958, pp. 72–73, reprinted in Parkinson, ed., *A Casebook on the Beat*, pp. 65–66.

49 "schiz": Johnson, *Minor Characters*, p. 83.

49 "colleges being nothing": Jack Kerouac, *The Dharma Bums* (New York: Signet, 1958), p. 39.

49 "best minds": Ginsberg, "Howl," p. 15.

49 "I am shitting": William Burroughs, in Jack Kerouac, *Desolation Angels* (New York: Coward-McCann, 1965), p. 311.

49 "The whole problem": In Jane Kramer, *Allen Ginsberg in America* (New York: Random House, 1969), p. 177.

49 Eberhart: Richard Eberhart, "West Coast Rhythms," *New York Times Book Review*, September 2, 1956, p. 7.

49 *Times* pinch-hitter: McNally, *Desolate Angel*, p. 240.

49 "a revolt of all": Norman Podhoretz, "Where Is the Beat Generation Going?" *Esquire*, December 1958, pp. 148–50.

50 "subscribe to consumption": Kerouac, *Dharma Bums*, p. 97.

50 "rucksack revolution": Kerouac, *Desolation Angels*, p. 62.

50 "wild yea-saying": Kerouac, *On the Road*, p. 11.

50 "The world is holy!": Ginsberg, "Footnote to Howl," *Howl*, p. 21.

51 "In the wildest hipster": John Clellon Holmes, "'This Is the Beat Generation,'" *New York Times Magazine*, November 16, 1952, p. 22.

PAGE
51 "totalitarian beastliness": Kerouac, *Desolation Angels*, pp. 18–19.
51 "Adlai Stevenson": Ibid., p. 113.
51 When Ginsberg read: Johnson, *Minor Characters*, p. 116.
51 "When will you": Ginsberg, "America," in *Howl*, p. 31.
52 Kerouac toyed: McNally, *Desolate Angel*, p. 235.
52 movie version: Ibid., p. 212. Kerouac thought the beats' hijacking of literature from the academy was comparable to the way rock 'n' roll lifted music "from Tin Pan Alley to the folk." McNally, *Desolate Angel*, p. 298.
52 *Life*: Paul O'Neil, "The Only Rebellion Around," *Life*, November 30, 1959, pp. 114–30.
52 Zimmerman: Anthony Scaduto, *Bob Dylan* (New York: Grosset and Dunlap, 1971), p. 13.
52 Morrison: Jerry Hopkins and Danny Sugerman, *No One Here Gets Out Alive* (New York: Warner, 1981), pp. 11–12.
52 Rent-a-Beatnik: Joseph Morgenstern, "Beatniks for Rent," *New York Herald Tribune*, May 1, 1960, reprinted in Fred W. MacDarrah, ed., *Kerouac and Friends* (New York: Morrow, 1985), pp. 243ff.
52 "morose Bohemians": David Matza, "Subterranean Traditions of Youth," *The Annals of the American Academy of Political and Social Science* 338 (November 1961), p. 117.
53 "Bronx boys": Jack Newfield, *A Prophetic Minority* (New York: New American Library, 1966), p. 45.
53 Paul Goodman: *Growing Up Absurd* (New York: Vintage, 1960), chap. 9.
53 Barbara Jacobs: Interview, Barbara Haber, November 17, 1984.
53 "semi-'bo'": Abbie Hoffman, *Soon To Be a Major Motion Picture* (New York: Perigee, 1980), pp. 23, 27.
54 "[The] beat generation": David McReynolds, "Youth 'Disaffiliated' from a Phony World," *Village Voice*, March 11, 1959, in MacDarrah, ed., *Kerouac and Friends*, p. 215.
54 "interested in the bohemians": In Milton Viorst, *Fire in the Streets* (New York: Simon and Schuster, 1979), p. 166.
54 "trying to mimic": "Tom Hayden: Rolling Stone Interview," by Tim Findlay, *Rolling Stone*, October 26, 1972, p. 38.
55 "unreconstructed radicals": James A. Wechsler, *Reflections of an Angry Middle-Aged Editor* (New York: Random House, 1960), p. 9.
55 McCarthy's Senate committee: Wechsler, *Reflections*, p. 168; Victor S. Navasky, *Naming Names* (New York: Viking, 1980), pp. 58ff.
55 Adlai Stevenson: Walter Johnson, ed., *The Papers of Adlai E. Stevenson* (Boston: Little, Brown, 1972), p. 22.
55 "out of touch": Wechsler, *Reflections*, p. 4.
55 That night at Hunter College: Marc D. Schleifer, "The Beat Debated—Is It Or Is It Not?" *Village Voice*, November 19, 1958, reprinted in MacDarrah, ed., *Kerouac*, pp. 79–80; Kerouac, "The Origins of the Beat Generation" (based on his Hunter College speech), originally published in *Playboy*, June 1959, pp. 31–32, 42, 79, reprinted in Parkinson, ed., *Casebook on the Beat*; McNally, *Desolate Angel*, pp. 258–59; Newfield, *Prophetic Minority*, p. 44; telephone conversations, Allen Ginsberg, May 20 and 29, 1987.
56 "a Zen move": Telephone conversation, Allen Ginsberg, May 20, 1987.
56 Wechsler did not begin: Wechsler, *Reflections*, pp. 5, 6, 7, 11, 13; Schleifer, "The Beat Debated," pp. 79–80; Newfield, *Prophetic Minority*, p. 44.
56 "Shame on you!": Wechsler, *Reflections*, pp. 10–11.
57 robust polemic: Ibid., pp. 38–39.
57 "explain what the rest": Ibid., pp. 18, 16–17, 221, 223, 234.

PAGE
57 "He believes": Adlai E. Stevenson, *The New America*, eds. Seymour E. Harris, John Bartlow Martin, Arthur Schlesinger, Jr. (New York: Harper and Bros., 1957), p. 256.

58 humanity fundamentally flawed: Richard H. Pells, *The Liberal Mind in a Conservative Age* (New York: Harper and Row, 1985), pp. 136–38; Richard Fox, *Reinhold Niebuhr* (New York: Pantheon, 1985).

58 David Riesman: "Some Observations on Community Plans and Utopia," in *Individualism Reconsidered* (Glencoe: Free Press, 1954), pp. 70–75 (written in 1946–47).

58 Paul Goodman: "Utopian Thinking," *Commentary*, July 1961, reprinted in *Utopian Essays and Practical Proposals* (New York: Vintage, 1964), pp. 3–21.

58 Leaders were to embody reason: Pells, *Liberal Mind*, p. 146.

59 learned the political ropes: Richard Flacks, *Making History vs. Making Life* (New York: Columbia University Press, forthcoming).

59 "Roosevelt taught us": Samuel Beer, "Memoirs of a Political Junkie," *Harvard Magazine*, September–October 1984, pp. 165–70.

59 "In 1932": Ibid., p. 165.

60 American college professors: Lawrence Howard, "The Academic and the Ballot," *School and Society*, vol. 86, no. 2141 (November 22, 1958), p. 416.

60 The leading liberals after World War II: This discussion is indebted to Godfrey Hodgson, *America in Our Time* (Garden City, N.Y.: Doubleday, 1977), pp. 78–83.

60 Hubert Humphrey: Carl Solberg, *Hubert Humphrey* (New York: Norton, 1984), pp. 75–76; John Earl Haynes, *Dubious Alliance: The Making of Minnesota's DFL Party* (Minneapolis: University of Minnesota Press, 1984), pp. 123–24, 204.

61 "anxious to save capitalism": Seymour E. Harris, ed., *Saving American Capitalism* (New York: Knopf, 1948), p. 4.

62 "It is still up to us": Ibid., p. 4.

62 "last best hope": Solberg, *Hubert Humphrey*, p. 18.

62 *Life:* The issue of March 29, 1943, was devoted to apologias for the Soviet Union.

62 Jack Warner: Warner's production of *Mission to Moscow* (1942), like the memoir by Ambassador Joseph P. Davies from which it derived, apologized for Stalin's Moscow trials. See William L. O'Neill, *A Better World* (New York: Simon and Schuster, 1982), pp. 59–60, 75–78.

62 the very crucible: Haynes, *Dubious Alliance*, and Mary Sperling McAuliffe, *Crisis on the Left: Cold War Politics and American Liberals, 1947–1954* (Amherst: University of Massachusetts Press, 1978).

62 moves and countermoves: The literature is, of course, voluminous. The strengths of both orthodox and revisionist views emerge in Daniel Yergin, *Shattered Peace* (Boston: Houghton Mifflin, 1977).

62 rank-and-file liberals: Personal communication, Herbert J. Gans, December 3, 1986.

63 In May 1946: James Loeb, letter to the editor, *The New Republic*, May 13, 1946, p. 699.

63 "the general framework": Curtis D. MacDougall, *Gideon's Army* (New York: Marzani and Munsell, 1965), vol. 1, pp. 121–22.

63 American Veterans Committee: Michael Straight, *After Long Silence* (New York: Norton, 1983), pp. 234–39.

63 Local Democratic parties: For a case of intimidation by the pro-Communist Left, see Solberg, *Hubert Humphrey*, p. 113. On the general atmosphere, a good case study is Haynes, *Dubious Alliance*.

63 a mildly worded proposal: MacDougall, *Gideon's Army*, vol. 2, p. 571.

63 American reneging: Yergin, *Shattered Peace*, pp. 64–65, 94, 95–97, 227–29, 297–300, 330–32.

64 "infuriated his ADA friends": Solberg, *Hubert Humphrey*, pp. 158–59.

PAGE

64 "demoralized": Bert Cochran, *Adlai Stevenson: Patrician among the Politicians* (New York: Funk and Wagnalls, 1969), p. 9.

64 "had grown conservative": Ibid., pp. 242–43.

64 *Daily Worker*: Interview, Barbara Haber, November 17, 1984.

65 "quality of life": Pells, *Liberal Mind*, pp. 130ff.

65 new generation of liberals: Cochran, *Adlai Stevenson*, p. 161.

65 Seymour Martin Lipset: *Political Man* (Garden City, N.Y.: Anchor, 1963), p. xxi.

67 Reuben Shipp: Interview, Al Levitt, April 5, 1986.

67 "ray of hope": Interview, Jessica Mitford, March 27, 1986.

69 *Heavenly Discourse:* Charles E. S. Wood, *Heavenly Discourse* (New York: Vanguard, 1927). Years later I learned that the young Wood had been an Indian fighter, the jailer—and then friend—of Chief Joseph of the Nez Percé, before leaving the army and acquiring renown as a civil libertarian lawyer.

71 Trotskyist remnants: Frank J. Donner, *The Age of Surveillance* (New York: Vintage, 1981), pp. 195ff.

72 Communist Party numbered: Irving Howe and Lewis Coser, *The American Communist Party: A Critical History* (New York: Praeger, 1962), p. 497; David Caute, *The Great Fear* (New York: Simon and Schuster, 1979), p. 185.

72 Party line twisted: Howe and Coser, *American Communist Party*, p. 488.

72 "mental Comintern": Joseph Starobin, *American Communism in Crisis, 1943–1957* (Cambridge: Harvard University Press, 1972), pp. 103, 224, 232.

72 "fortress mentality": Jessica Mitford, *A Fine Old Conflict* (New York: Knopf, 1977), p. 116.

72 what survived: The following discussion is based on my interviews where not otherwise attributed.

72 drew their world: Mitford, *Fine Old Conflict*, p. 117.

72 doctors and dentists: Navasky, *Naming Names*, passim.

72 social weekends: Linn Shapiro, "Beginning the Exploration: Taking Over the Family Business," in Judy Kaplan and Linn Shapiro, eds., *Red Diaper Babies: Children of the Left*, privately printed, 1985, p. 2.

72 They sent their children: Kaplan and Shapiro, *Red Diaper*, p. 54.

72 turned their backs: Starobin, *American Communism*, pp. 224ff.

72 members in their hearts: Kaplan and Shapiro, *Red Diaper*, p. 36.

73 "developed": Ibid., p. 49.

73 one survey: Ibid., p. 120.

73 the survey: Ibid.

74 ostracized: Kim Chernin, *In My Mother's House* (New York: Ticknor and Fields, 1983), pp. 225ff., 255ff.; Kaplan and Shapiro, *Red Diaper*, p. 10.

74 at camp: Kaplan and Shapiro, *Red Diaper*, pp. 14, 15, 20, 21, 25, 28.

74 turned against politics: Chernin, *Mother's House*, pp. 291–92; Kaplan and Shapiro, *Red Diaper*, p. 35.

74 subpoenaed Communists: Kaplan and Shapiro, *Red Diaper*, p. 19.

75 warmed the hearts: R. Serge Denisoff, *Great Day Coming: Folk Music and the American Left* (Urbana: University of Illinois Press, 1971), p. 166.

75 a Queens woman: Interview, Gerda Lerner, March 21, 1988.

75 "We Shall Overcome": David King Dunaway, *How Can I Keep from Singing: Pete Seeger* (New York: McGraw-Hill, 1981), p. 222.

76 At Brandeis University: Interview, Jeremy Larner, May 5, 1987.

76 Student League for Industrial Democracy: Kirkpatrick Sale, *SDS* (New York: Random House, 1973), p. 689.

76 "When intellectuals": Irving Howe, *A Margin of Hope* (New York: Harcourt Brace Jovanovich, 1982), p. 234.

77 Howe noted: Irving Howe, review of Camus, *Resistance, Rebellion and Death, Dissent*, vol. 8, no. 2 (Spring 1961), p. 211. On *Dissent* I am also indebted to David

PAGE

Plotke's unpublished paper, "Marxism in the United States, 1960–1980: Culture and the Problem of Politics."

77   **"the sheer terribleness":** Ibid., p. 244.

77   **I. F. Stone:** Interview, I. F. Stone, March 2, 1985.

4. LEFTWARD KICKING AND SCREAMING

79   **"Why not":** Carl Oglesby, ed., "The Idea of the New Left," in *The New Left Reader* (New York: Grove, 1969), p. 1.

82   **Within two months:** William H. Chafe, *Civilities and Civil Rights: Greensboro, North Carolina, and the Black Struggle for Freedom* (New York: Oxford University Press, 1980), pp. 99–120; Aldon D. Morris, *The Origins of the Civil Rights Movement* (New York: Free Press, 1984), pp. 188–201.

82   **Ella Baker:** Clayborne Carson, *In Struggle: SNCC and the Black Awakening of the 1960s* (Cambridge: Harvard University Press, 1981), pp. 19–20.

82   **"We Shall Not Be Moved":** R. Serge Denisoff, *Great Day Coming: Folk Music and the American Left* (Urbana: University of Illinois Press, 1971), p. 168.

82   **underground stream:** David Horowitz, *Student* (New York: Ballantine, 1962).

84   **many studies:** The first of these was Richard Flacks, "The Liberated Generation: An Exploration of the Roots of Student Protest," *Journal of Social Issues* 23 (1967), pp. 52–75.

86   **Hubert Humphrey:** Carl Solberg, *Hubert Humphrey* (New York: Norton, 1984), pp. 185–86.

86   **Small knots:** Judith Malina, *The Diaries of Judith Malina, 1947–1957* (New York: Grove, 1984), pp. 377, 442ff.; Nat Hentoff, *Peace Agitator: The Story of A. J. Muste* (New York: Macmillan, 1963), p. 157.

86   **In 1958:** Hentoff, *Peace Agitator*, pp. 150–57.

86   **"No student":** John Kenneth Galbraith, *The Affluent Society* (Boston: Houghton Mifflin, 1958), p. 5.

86   **"America when":** Allen Ginsberg, "America," *Howl and Other Poems* (San Francisco: City Lights, 1956), p. 31.

87   **the SPU:** George R. Vickers, *The Formation of the New Left* (Lexington, Mass.: D. C. Heath, 1975), pp. 28, 51.

87   **Passersby yelled:** N. Gordon Levin, "Boston SANE," *New University Thought*, Spring 1962, p. 123.

90   **Stone was alert:** For example, "Two Months Before the Bay of Pigs," in I. F. Stone, *The Haunted Fifties* (New York: Random House, 1963), pp. 339–47 (first published February 27, 1961).

90   *Dissent* **published:** Michael Walzer, "Cuba: The Invasion and the Consequences" (New York: Dissent Publishing, June 1961).

91   **Garry Wills:** *The Kennedy Imprisonment* (Boston: Little, Brown, 1982), part 5.

92   **"disseminating 'downward'":** Todd Gitlin to Roger Fisher, August 25, 1961 (author's file).

92   **Kennedy called:** David Burner and Thomas R. West, *The Torch Is Passed* (New York: Atheneum, 1984), pp. 120–21.

93   **"in a we/they world":** Interview, Victoria Bonnell, October 12, 1984.

94   **"traditional 'peace' activity":** Steven V. Roberts, "Project Washington," *Crimson Review*, March 2, 1962, p. 8.

94   **approved picket signs:** Ibid., p. 9.

94   **Another said:** "Nuclear Testing: Youth For and Against," *New York Herald Tribune*, February 18, 1962.

94   **Young Americans for Freedom:** George Thayer, *The Farther Shores of Politics* (New York: Simon and Schuster, 1967), p. 171.

95   "barely concealed condescension": Christopher Z. Hobson, in Amy Perry, "Harvard/Radcliffe Students for a Democratic Society, 1960–1972," unpublished undergraduate thesis, Department of History, Harvard University, 1986, p. 14.

95   "had not even bothered": In Joseph Russin, "Peace Marchers Coolly Received in Washington," *The Harvard Crimson*, February 16, 1962, p. 1.

95   "bound to fail": Todd Gitlin, essay-review of Arthur I. Waskow, *The Limits of Defense*, in *Council for Correspondence Newsletter*, May 1962, p. 11.

96   Yarmolinsky had also organized: Harris Wofford, *Of Kennedys and Kings* (New York: Farrar, Straus and Giroux, 1980), p. 297.

97   A movement is a passion: Paraphrased from the film *Le Milieu du Monde*, written by Alain Tanner and John Berger.

98   protest both necessary and dangerous: The following facts about protest during the missile crisis, and quotations, are from my unpublished 1963 article, "Dissent During the Crisis," and from my interviews with Dickie Magidoff, February 9, 1985, and Staughton Lynd, October 5, 1985.

102   "What the crisis did": Paul Potter, undated letter (late 1962) (Potter papers).

5. THE FUSED GROUP

105   The Fused Group: This is Sartre's term (*Critique of Dialectical Reason* [London: NLB, 1976], pp. 345–404), but I am taking the liberty of appropriating it while leaving Sartre's precise meaning (and baggage) behind. Sartre refers to an action-group that forms in the midst of upheaval in the streets; I mean the movement elite with its powerful sense of unity and mission.

106   eleven hundred members: Kirkpatrick Sale, *SDS* (New York: Random House, 1973), p. 663.

106   "Love is the central": In Clayborne Carson, *In Struggle: SNCC and the Black Awakening of the 1960s* (Cambridge: Harvard University Press, 1981), p. 24.

106   *"Human relationships"*: Students for a Democratic Society, *The Port Huron Statement*, mimeographed ed., 1962, pp. 3–4 (author's file).

107   "unite the fragmented": Ibid., p. 4.

107   rifts between: Kenneth Keniston, *The Uncommitted* (New York: Dell, 1965), pp. 241–72.

107   "the qualities of warmth": Ibid., p. 191.

107   vulgar psychoanalytic interpretations: Lewis Feuer, *The Conflict of Generations* (New York: Basic, 1969); Stanley Rothman and S. Robert Lichter, *Roots of Rebellion* (New York: Oxford University Press, 1982).

108   "We regard *men*": *Port Huron Statement*, p. 4 (emphasis added).

109   "Port Huron was": Al Haber, December 31, 1969, interview with George Abbott White (Potter papers).

110   Intercollegiate Socialist Society: Sale, *SDS*, pp. 674, 676.

110   "Since last May": Memo from André Schiffrin to Frank Trager, September 28, 1960 (SDS papers, Series 1, no. 7). Spelling corrected.

111   As Al Haber said: Material on Haber is from my interviews of March 27–28, 1985, unless otherwise attributed.

111   "radical liberal": Al Haber to Frank Trager, March 11, 1961, in Sale, *SDS*, p. 24.

111   "signed up to a good world": Interview, Barbara Haber, November 17, 1984.

111   "I think we knew": Interview, Rebecca Adams Mills, March 17, 1985.

112   two major conflicts: This account draws from Sale, *SDS*, pp. 47–59; Jack Newfield, *A Prophetic Minority* (New York: New American Library, 1966), pp. 131–36; Michael Harrington, *Fragments of the Century* (New York: Saturday Review, 1973), pp. 143–50; and interviews with Alan Haber, Barbara Haber, Sharon Jeffrey, Richard Flacks, Mickey Flacks, Robb Burlage, Steve Max, Michael Harrington, Rebecca Adams Mills, and Tom Kahn. Unless otherwise attributed, all quotes are from my interviews.

PAGE

112 "silly": Interview, Steve Max, April 14, 1985.

112 "relic": Interview, Robb Burlage, April 14, 1985.

112 "It gave people": Interview, Sharon Jeffrey, February 13, 1985.

112 "baffling": Interview, Robb Burlage, April 14, 1985.

112 stipulation: Memo from SDS National Executive Committee to LID Executive Committee, July 12, 1962, p. 5 (author's file). The convention also voted to grant observer status to the representatives of two student Christian groups, and seated representatives of the Young Democrats and SNCC as voting delegates.

112 "like a kid": Interview, James Hawley, April 20, 1985.

113 "seemed to imply": Harrington, *Fragments*, p. 145.

113 "have abstracted Russians": [Tom Hayden], "Draft Paper for S. D. S. Manifesto," 1962, pp. 22–23 (author's file).

113 "mask . . . their own": Hayden, "Draft," pp. 20–21.

113 "paranoid quest": Ibid., p. 21.

113 "irresponsibility": Ibid., pp. 22–23.

113 "go through the roof": In Sale, *SDS*, p. 60; interview, Richard Flacks, December 24, 1984.

113 "if one dismissed": Harrington, *Fragments*, pp. 146, 147.

115 "As democrats": *Port Huron Statement*, pp. 25–26.

116 Russia was: Hayden, "Draft," pp. 22–23.

116 "unreasoning anti-communism": *Port Huron Statement*, p. 25.

116 "The conventional moral terms": Ibid., p. 3; Hayden, "Draft," p. 28. This sentence and the next loom larger in the final version because the convention voted to move the draft's "Values" section up to the front.

116 "dreams of the older left": *Port Huron Statement*, p. 3; a minor modification of Hayden, "Draft," p. 29. For other examples, see *Port Huron Statement*, p. 20 (Hayden, "Draft," p. 15); p. 30 ("Draft," p. 32); p. 36 ("Draft," p. 37); pp. 22, 33 (referring to "the totalitarian regime of East Germany").

116 "and we were very aware": Interview, Sharon Jeffrey, February 13, 1985.

116 "beginnings of an anxiety": Interview, Robb Burlage, April 14, 1985.

116 Michael Harrington went: Interview, Michael Harrington, April 13, 1985.

116 "SDS had responded": Harrington, *Fragments*, p. 147.

117 "oldest young socialist": Harrington, "The American Campus: 1962," *Dissent*, vol. 9, no. 2 (Spring 1962), p. 164.

117 close to Hayden: Sale, *SDS*, p. 65.

117 "a finished ideology": Harrington, "The American Campus," pp. 165–66.

117 Max Shachtman: Harrington, *Fragments*, pp. 60–77.

117 "a morally dubious intrusion": Memo from SDS National Executive Committee, p. 22.

118 "adopted a policy statement": Memo, Vera Rony to LID Executive Board, n.d. (between July 6 and July 12, 1962) (SDS papers, Series 1, no. 9).

118 Whereupon the LID leaders: Notes taken at SDS/LID hearing by Robb Burlage, July 6, 1962 (SDS papers, Series 1, no. 9).

118 Flabbergasted and furious: This discussion is based on interviews with Robb Burlage, Richard Flacks, Al Haber, Tom Hayden, Tom Kahn, and Steve Max.

119 Potter concluded: Interview with George Abbott White, January 3, 1970 (Potter papers).

119 single-spaced appeal: Memo from SDS National Executive Committee, pp. 14, 16, 21, 22.

119 The appeal succeeded: Sale, *SDS*, pp. 60–68.

120 In 1935: Ibid., pp. 682–84.

121 "a pro-American": In Sale, *SDS*, p. 691.

121 All radical and utopian: Richard H. Pells, *The Liberal Mind in a Conservative Age* (New York: Harper and Row, 1985), pp. 76ff.

121 "a progressive, Leftist": Harrington, *Fragments*, p. 145.

PAGE

122 "individual initiative": *Port Huron Statement*, pp. 37–38.

122 Jean-Paul Sartre and C. Wright Mills: *Sartre on Cuba* and Mills's *Listen, Yankee!* were published as inexpensive paperbacks in 1961.

122 "more or less authoritarian": *Port Huron Statement*, p. 22.

122 A younger Michael Harrington: Michael Harrington, "Liberalism—A Moral Crisis: The American Committee for Cultural Freedom," *Dissent*, vol. 2, no. 2 (Spring 1955), p. 122.

123 discounting the revolt: Lewis Feuer, *The Conflict of Generations* (New York: Basic: 1969); Stanley Rothman and S. Robert Lichter, *Roots of Rebellion* (New York: Oxford University Press, 1982).

124 "rabid anti-Communism": Interview, Barbara Haber, November 17, 1984, referring to her professor Irving Howe at Brandeis.

124 Haber had sparred: Al Haber, "Memorandum on the Students for a Democratic Society," May 20, 1961 (SDS papers, Series 1, no. 10); Memo from SDS National Executive Committee, p. 5.

125 LID's "inquisition": Interview, Alan Haber, March 27, 1985.

125 "It taught me": In Newfield, *Prophetic Minority*, p. 134.

125 Tom Kahn: Interview, Tom Kahn, March 5, 1985.

125 Just after Port Huron: Interview, Richard Flacks, December 24, 1984.

6. AIN'T GONNA LET NOBODY TURN ME 'ROUND

128 "Those Negroes": Tom Hayden, *Revolution in Mississippi* (New York: Students for a Democratic Society, 1962), p. 21.

128 "In our future dealings": In Clayborne Carson, *In Struggle: SNCC and the Black Awakening of the 1960s* (Cambridge: Harvard University Press, 1981), p. 176.

128 Potter wrote to his brother: Paul Potter to Norm Potter, n.d. (1961) (Potter papers).

128 Herbert Lee: Howard Zinn, *SNCC: The New Abolitionists* (Boston: Beacon Press, 1964), pp. 73–74.

129 930 civil rights: Southern Regional Council figures cited in Carson, *In Struggle*, p. 90.

129 "mediating, rationalizing": Students for a Democratic Society, *America in the New Era* (1963), excerpted in Massimo Teodori, ed., *The New Left: A Documentary History* (Indianapolis: Bobbs-Merrill, 1969), pp. 175–76, 177–78.

129 "political stabilization": *New Era*, in Teodori, p. 176.

130 SDS smelled trouble: Ibid., p. 178.

130 "corporate liberalism": Ibid., p. 177.

130 "elitist": Ibid., p. 178.

130 "a moral issue": In William H. Chafe, *The Unfinished Journey* (New York: Oxford University Press, 1986), p. 213.

130 "the limitations": *New Era*, in Teodori, p. 179.

130 "style of politics": Ibid., p. 181.

131 "In a world": Ibid., p. 177.

131 "We Shall Overcome period": Interview, Marcus Raskin, March 3, 1985.

132 "the beloved community": In Cleveland Sellers, with Robert Terrell, *The River of No Return: The Autobiography of a Black Militant and the Life and Death of SNCC* (New York: Morrow, 1973), p. 35.

132 Spiro T. Agnew: *Baltimore News-Post*, July 8, 1963, p. 1.

133 managerial imperative: The phrase comes from a work in progress by W. Russell Ellis.

134 "Those who profess": Frederick Douglass, August 4, 1857, in Philip S. Foner, ed., *The Life and Writings of Frederick Douglass*, vol. 2 (New York: International, 1950), p. 437.

PAGE

134 voice of the voiceless: "We are the voiceless voice" was a motto of the Japanese Zengakuren student movement in the early Sixties. David Riesman, personal communication, 1962.

134 "Maybe the Devil": In Zinn, *SNCC*, p. 14.

134 "moral dislike": Minutes of SDS National Executive Committee meeting, June 1963, Nyack, N.Y. (SDS papers).

135 theory of expressive politics: One history-minded locus of this idea was Norman O. Brown's *Life Against Death* (Middletown, Conn.: Wesleyan University Press, 1959); a therapeutic version was Abraham Maslow's *Toward a Psychology of Being* (Princeton: Van Nostrand, 1962).

136 THERE'S A TOWN IN MISSISSIPPI: Nicholas von Hoffman, *Mississippi Notebook* (New York: David White, 1965), p. 28.

136 peculiar pace: David Burner and Thomas R. West, *The Torch Is Passed* (New York: Atheneum, 1984), p. 177.

136 "From 1961 to 1963": Victor S. Navasky, *Kennedy Justice* (New York: Atheneum, 1971), p. 97.

136 Freedom Rides: Harvard Sitkoff, *The Struggle for Black Equality, 1954–1980* (New York: Hill and Wang, 1981), pp. 97–113.

137 "Our intention": In Sitkoff, *Struggle*, p. 98.

137 Farmer gave advance information: James Farmer, *Lay Bare the Heart: An Autobiography of the Civil Rights Movement* (New York: Arbor House, 1985), p. 197.

137 Robert Kennedy said: Harris Wofford, *Of Kennedys and Kings: Making Sense of the Sixties* (New York: Farrar, Straus and Giroux, 1980), p. 151.

137 Hoover therefore knew: Ibid., p. 152.

137 permanently brain-damaged: Sitkoff, *Struggle*, p. 102.

137 Vienna summit: Ibid., p. 107.

137 "Tell them to call": In Wofford, *Of Kennedys and Kings*, p. 153.

137 John Seigenthaler: Navasky, *Kennedy Justice*, p. 20; Wofford, *Of Kennedys and Kings*, p. 152; Sitkoff, *Struggle*, p. 104.

137 FBI agents: Wofford, *Of Kennedys and Kings*, p. 154.

138 "We have no intention": In Sitkoff, *Struggle*, pp. 103–5.

138 huge church rally: Sitkoff, *Struggle*, p. 107; Farmer, *Lay Bare*, p. 206.

138 "We have been cooling": In Farmer, *Lay Bare*, pp. 205–6.

138 Robert Kennedy went to work: Wofford, *Of Kennedys and Kings*, p. 159.

138 liberal foundations: Ibid.; Carl M. Brauer, *John F. Kennedy and the Second Reconstruction* (New York: Columbia University Press, 1977), p. 14.

139 "If you'll cut out": Farmer, *Lay Bare*, p. 219.

139 insider point of view: Harold Fleming, in Navasky, *Kennedy Justice*, pp. 117–18.

139 "all steps necessary": Sitkoff, *Struggle*, p. 114.

139 "very vividly": Timothy Jenkins, in Howell Raines, ed., *My Soul Is Rested* (New York: Bantam, 1978), p. 245.

139 "Bobby pledged": Lonnie King, in Raines, *My Soul*, p. 246.

139 If the foundations: Carson, *In Struggle*, pp. 39–42; Sitkoff, *Struggle*, pp. 114–16; Lonnie King, in Raines, *My Soul*, p. 246.

139 Jenkins argued: Zinn, *SNCC*, p. 59.

139 SNCC finessed the conflict: CORE had a similar debate and resolved it the same way. August Meier and Elliott Rudwick, *CORE: A Study in the Civil Rights Movement, 1942–1968* (New York: Oxford University Press, 1973), pp. 174–75.

139 In the fall of 1961: Wofford, *Of Kennedys and Kings*, p. 159.

140 Amite County: Jack Mendelsohn, *The Martyrs* (New York: Harper and Row, 1966), p. 24.

140 federal laws: Zinn, *SNCC*, pp. 194, 195.

140 "as close as the telephone": In Carson, *In Struggle*, p. 85.

140 "The government is with us": In Anne Moody, *Coming of Age in Mississippi* (New York: Dell, 1968), p. 92.

PAGE
140 "cooling-off period": Zinn, *SNCC*, p. 52.
140 Moses drew a reduced sentence: Ibid., pp. 67–68.
140 FBI agents: For an example, see Moody, *Coming of Age*, p. 374.
140 Kennedy's staff luncheons: Navasky, *Justice*, p. 100.
140 "interrogate a black": In Navasky, *Kennedy Justice*, p. 103.
141 E. H. Hurst: Mendelsohn, *The Martyrs*, pp. 21–37; Robert Penn Warren, *Who Speaks for the Negro?* (New York: Random House, 1965), pp. 93–94.
141 *quid* for its *quo*: Navasky, *Kennedy Justice*, pp. 107, 155.
141 guerrillas of government: Garry Wills, *The Kennedy Imprisonment* (Boston: Little, Brown, 1982), pp. 35–36.
141 tape recordings from 1941: Ibid., pp. 20–21; Peter Collier and David Horowitz, *The Kennedys* (New York: Summit, 1984), pp. 122–24; Richard Sid Powers, *Secrecy and Power: The Life of J. Edgar Hoover* (New York: Free Press, 1987), p. 359.
141 "Federal Bureau of Integration": von Hoffman, *Mississippi Notebook*, p. 28.
141 opened a field office: Navasky, *Kennedy Justice*, p. 101.
142 When Hoover opened: Ibid., pp. 106–7.
142 Justice Department only twice: Pat Watters and Reese Cleghorn, *Climbing Jacob's Ladder: The Arrival of Negroes in Southern Politics* (New York: Harcourt, Brace and World, 1967), pp. 61–62.
142 "Project yourself back": Harold Fleming, in Navasky, *Kennedy Justice*, pp. 117–18.
143 "brought with them the code": Navasky, *Kennedy Justice*, p. 163.
143 In August 1963: Howard Zinn, *The Politics of History* (Boston: Beacon, 1970), p. 192.
143 refused to exercise his authority: Brauer, *John F. Kennedy*, p. 289.
143 thirty-eight agents: Zinn, *Politics of History*, p. 193.
143 "It seems to be": Letter from Slater King to Constance Baker Motley, in Brauer, *John F. Kennedy*, p. 289.
144 Randolph, King, and Farmer: Sitkoff, *Struggle*, p. 160.
144 civil disobedience: Farmer, *Lay Bare*, p. 243.
144 SNCC proposed: Carson, *In Struggle*, p. 92.
144 new civil rights legislation: Farmer, *Lay Bare*, p. 243.
144 Although the attorney general: Zinn, *SNCC*, pp. 207–8.
144 Some SNCC organizers: Interview, Mickey Flacks, December 24, 1984.
145 "I have a dream": In Sitkoff, *Struggle*, pp. 163–64.
146 "I want to know": John Lewis, in Joanne Grant, ed., *Black Protest: History, Documents, and Analyses, 1619 to the Present* (Greenwich, Conn.: Fawcett Premier, 1968), p. 375.
146 John Lewis: Carson, *In Struggle*, pp. 21–22.
146 Battered SNCC: Ibid., p. 83.
146 "Who ever heard": Malcolm X, in Sitkoff, *Struggle*, p. 165.
146 "Only when metal": Bob Moses, in *I. F. Stone's Weekly*, December 9, 1963.
147 Stokely Carmichael: Kirkpatrick Sale, *SDS* (New York: Random House, 1973), p. 102.
147 Negroes constituted: Sitkoff, *Struggle*, p. 169.
147 SNCC agreed to pursue: Carson, *In Struggle*, p. 97.
147 Tom Kahn: In Tom Brooks, *Walls Come Tumbling Down: A History of the Civil Rights Movement, 1940–1970* (Englewood Cliffs, N.J.: Prentice-Hall, 1974), p. 219.
147 "An Interracial Movement of the Poor?" Reprinted in Mitchell Cohen and Dennis Hale, eds., *The New Student Left* (Boston: Beacon, 1966), pp. 180–219.
147 Rustin's: *Commentary*, February 1965, reprinted in Bayard Rustin, *Down the Line* (Chicago: Quadrangle, 1971), pp. 111–22.
147 Between 1961 and 1963: U.S. Commission on Civil Rights, Hearings on Voting (Washington: Government Printing Office, 1965), p. 10.

PAGE

147 Voter Education Project: Watters and Cleghorn, *Climbing Jacob's Ladder,* pp. 213–14.

148 "The men in the cars": Stokely Carmichael, quoted in Warren, *Who Speaks,* p. 403.

148 "I thought Bob Moses": Moody, *Coming of Age,* p. 252.

148 "an outstandingly poor": von Hoffman, *Mississippi Notebook,* p. 34.

149 "He's like someone": Sally Belfrage, *Freedom Summer* (New York: Fawcett Crest, 1966), p. 32.

149 eighty cross burnings: Anne Romaine, "'We Come From a Distance' (The Story of the Mississippi Freedom Democratic Party Through the Convention of 1965), An Oral History," Charlottesville, Virginia, 1969, p. 83.

149 Freedom Democratic Party: Carson, *In Struggle,* pp. 108–9.

150 Freedom Ballots: Ibid., pp. 97–98.

150 Greenwood: Ibid., p. 97.

150 assassin's bullet: Moody, *Coming of Age,* pp. 352–55.

150 SNCC staff member: Jack Minnis and Staughton Lynd, "Seeds of Doubt," *The New Republic,* December 21, 1963, pp. 14–20.

151 personal appeal from Moses: Staughton Lynd, personal communication, 1985, citing what he was told in 1967 by CORE's Dave Dennis.

151 By one tally: Pat Watters of the Southern Regional Council, cited in Carson, *In Struggle,* pp. 122, 322.

151 many SNCC people thought: Carson, *In Struggle,* p. 123.

152 "Niggers, Alligators": Paul Johnson, in Merle Miller, *Lyndon: An Oral Biography* (New York: Ballantine, 1981), p. 478.

152 Of the seventeen thousand: Carson, *In Struggle,* p. 117.

152 "'Optimism'": Belfrage, *Freedom Summer,* p. 251.

152 "We were thinking": Sellers, *River of No Return,* pp. 208–9.

152 "an alerting process": Ella Baker, in Romaine, "'We Come,'" p. 419.

152 "with all of this hope": Fannie Lou Hamer, in Romaine, "'We Come,'" p. 252.

152 small farmers: Ed King, in Romaine, "'We Come,'" pp. 200–201.

152 They took with them: Sellers, *River of No Return,* p. 108.

152 "When we went": Fannie Lou Hamer, in Romaine, "'We Come,'" p. 253.

153 "I was carried": Fannie Lou Hamer, in Brooks, *Walls Come Tumbling Down,* p. 248; Sitkoff, *Struggle,* p. 181.

153 "Are you going to throw": Joseph L. Rauh, Jr., in Sitkoff, *Struggle,* p. 180.

154 Johnson was more worried: Sitkoff, *Struggle,* p. 182.

154 Reuther had phoned Rauh: Interview, Joseph L. Rauh, Jr., March 6, 1985.

154 Humphrey wrote: In Carl Solberg, *Hubert Humphrey* (New York: Norton, 1984), p. 244.

155 According to Rauh: Joseph L. Rauh, Jr., in Romaine, "'We Come,'" pp. 335–36.

155 A New York delegate: Interview, Joseph L. Rauh, Jr., March 6, 1985.

155 the FBI had bugged: Testimony of Cartha DeLoach in "Intelligence Activities," vol. 6, Hearings before the Select Committee to Study Governmental Operations with Respect to Intelligence Activities, U.S. Senate (1975), pp. 174–80, 495–510; Allen J. Matusow, *The Unraveling of America: A History of Liberalism in the 1960s* (New York: Harper and Row, 1984), p. 141; David J. Garrow, *Bearing the Cross: Martin Luther King, Jr., and the Southern Christian Leadership Conference* (New York: Morrow, 1986), pp. 347–48.

155 At Johnson's behest: Rowland Evans and Robert Novak, *Lyndon B. Johnson: The Exercise of Power* (New York: New American Library, 1966), pp. 476–78.

155 Bayard Rustin: David L. Lewis, *King: A Biography,* 2nd ed. (Urbana: University of Illinois Press, 1978), p. 253.

155 "no-win policy": Rustin, "From Protest to Politics," in *Down the Line,* p. 117.

155 "that the peace of the world": Ed King, in Romaine, "'We Come,'" p. 304.

PAGE

155   Roy Wilkins: Fannie Lou Hamer, in Romaine, "'We Come,'" p. 253.

156   "All that we had been hearing": Ibid., pp. 253–54.

156   "what kind of moral victory": Fannie Lou Hamer, in Romaine, "'We Come,'" pp. 270–71.

156   Ella Baker argued: Telephone interview, Joseph L. Rauh, Jr., March 24, 1987.

156   "If you look at my brief": Interview, Joseph L. Rauh, Jr., March 6, 1985; Rauh, in Romaine, "'We Come,'" pp. 335, 340; Sitkoff, *Struggle*, p. 182.

156   "what Heywood Broun": James A. Wechsler, *Reflections of an Angry Middle-Aged Editor* (New York: Random House, 1960), p. 14.

157   Rauh insists: Interview, Joseph L. Rauh, Jr., March 6, 1985.

158   according to Ed King: Romaine, "'We Come,'" pp. 307–9, 311.

158   Bob Moses, furious: Ed King, in Romaine, "'We Come,'" p. 309.

158   "the SNCC people had gone mad": Ibid., p. 311.

158   "If the television account": Interview, Joseph L. Rauh, Jr., March 6, 1985.

158   had let themselves hope: Arthur I. Waskow, "Notes on the Democratic National Convention, Atlantic City, August 1964," mimeographed paper, pp. 25–26 (Waskow collection, State Historical Society of Wisconsin).

158   another TV interview: Shown in Part 5 of Henry Hampton's documentary *Eyes on the Prize.*

159   King himself was convinced: Ed King, in Romaine, "'We Come,'" p. 311.

159   why should Rauh: Mendy Samstein, in Romaine, "'We Come,'" p. 298.

159   Several SNCC staff: James Forman, *The Making of Black Revolutionaries* (New York: Macmillan, 1972), pp. 390–91.

159   "disappointed": Interview, Joseph L. Rauh, Jr., March 6, 1985.

159   "This proves that": Stokely Carmichael, in Brooks, *Walls Come Tumbling Down*, p. 249.

159   seized Mississippi's vacant seats: Milton Viorst, *Fire in the Streets* (New York: Simon and Schuster, 1979), p. 265.

159   "I don't say": Interview, Joseph L. Rauh, Jr., March 6, 1985.

159   liberals had floated: Waskow, "Notes," pp. 14–15.

160   "wasn't a bad deal": Interview, Joseph L. Rauh, Jr., March 6, 1985.

160   Martin Luther King rose: Lewis, *King*, p. 253.

160   As a Negro leader: Ed King, in Romaine, "'We Come,'" p. 317; Garrow, *Bearing the Cross*, pp. 349–50.

160   Speeches: Meier and Rudwick, *CORE*, p. 281; Sitkoff, *Struggle*, p. 184; Waskow, "Notes," pp. 29–32. Curiously, Farmer fails even to mention Atlantic City or the MFDP in his otherwise forthcoming autobiography, *Lay Bare the Heart*.

160   James Forman: Forman, *Making*, p. 393.

160   At one point: Interview, Gar Alperovitz, March 2, 1985.

161   meeting closed to SNCC: Forman, *Making*, p. 395.

161   standing awkwardly: Viorst, *Fire in the Street*, pp. 266–67.

161   Mississippi terror: Lawrence Guyot, in Romaine, "'We Come,'" p. 96.

161   "When we had": Interview, Joseph L. Rauh, Jr., March 6, 1985.

161   reporters mistook: Interview, Jack Weinberg, by Mark Kitchell (1985), for the film *Berkeley in the Sixties*.

161   "the major moral": Stokely Carmichael and Charles V. Hamilton, *Black Power* (New York: Vintage, 1967), p. 96.

162   "The national Democratic party's: Sellers, *River of No Return*, p. 111.

162   "The meaning of Atlantic City": Staughton Lynd, "Coalition Politics or Nonviolent Revolution?" *Liberation*, June–July 1965, p. 19.

162   shadow government: "Moses of Mississippi Raises Some Universal Questions," *Pacific Scene* 5 (February 1965), p. 4, in Carson, *In Struggle*, p. 126; Lynd, "Coalition Politics," p. 19.

162   Walter Reuther didn't talk: Interview, Joseph L. Rauh, Jr., March 6, 1985.

PAGE
163   back-country look: Sellers, *River of No Return*, pp. 53–54.
163   One SNCC poster: This poster (photo by Danny Lyon) was singled out for comment by Tom Hayden, "SNCC: The Qualities of Protest," *Studies on the Left* 5 (Winter 1965), p. 118.
163   SNCC wage: Carson, *In Struggle*, p. 71.
163   Jim Crow law of 1890: Romaine, "'We Come,'" p. 28.
163   "reddish": Warren, *Who Speaks*, p. 98.
164   Free Speech Movement: Max Heirich, *The Beginning: Berkeley 1964* (New York: Columbia University Press, 1970).
164   "idiocy of rural life": Karl Marx and Friedrich Engels, *Manifesto of the Communist Party* (New York: International, 1948), p. 13.
165   "poverty negates": Jane Stembridge, "The Dark," in Todd Gitlin, ed., *Campfires of the Resistance: Poetry from the Movement* (Indianapolis: Bobbs-Merrill, 1971), p. 27.
165   "closeness with the earth": Jane Stembridge, "Some Notes on Education," in Carson, *In Struggle*, p. 155.
165   "renunciation, without the pretense": Zinn, *SNCC*, p. 237.
165   Hayden wrote: Tom Hayden, "SNCC: The Qualities of Protest," pp. 123, 119, 120.
166   "Tom seems to be": Paul Potter to Clark Kissinger, Tom Hayden, Carl Wittman, Rennie Davis, Dick Flacks, Todd Gitlin, Paul Booth, January 22, 1965 (Flacks file).
166   instruments of the voiceless voices: The outcome was Todd Gitlin and Nanci Hollander, *Uptown: Poor Whites in Chicago* (New York: Harper and Row, 1970).
167   "hardliners": Sellers, *River of No Return*, p. 131.
167   "local-people-itis": Forman, *Making*, p. 422.
167   "They were 'high'": Sellers, *River of No Return*, pp. 131–32.
167   Sellers has described: Ibid., pp. 134–35.
168   burned their meal tickets: Ibid., pp. 142–46.
168   marijuana: David Harris, *Dreams Die Hard* (New York: St. Martin's/Marek, 1982), p. 67; Carson, *In Struggle*, p. 149.
169   Abbie Hoffman: Abbie Hoffman, *Soon to Be a Major Motion Picture* (New York: Perigee, 1980), pp. 79, 81–82.
169   King and Hayden: Mary King, *Freedom Song* (New York: Morrow, 1987), pp. 443–55, 456–68, 567–74.
169   Stokely Carmichael's: Ibid., pp. 451–52.
169   battle fatigue was normal: Belfrage, *Freedom Summer*, pp. 203–5.
169   "The man without the uniform": Jane Stembridge, "The Man without the Uniform," in Gitlin, ed., *Campfires of the Resistance*, p. 26.
169   He felt responsible: Jack Newfield, *A Prophetic Minority* (New York: New American Library, 1966), p. 81.
170   Tolkien's Frodo: Staughton Lynd, personal communication, 1985.
170   "too strong, too central": Bob Moses, in Lerone Bennett, Jr., "SNCC: Rebels with a Cause," *Ebony*, July 1965, p. 148, as quoted in Carson, p. 156.
170   his mother: Sellers, *River of No Return*, pp. 138–39; Nancy Stoller, "The Ins and Outs of SNCC," *Studies in Brandeis Sociology*, Brandeis University, n.d., p. 18, quoting her own 1965 letter.

7. "NAME THE SYSTEM"

171   "there might be a joining": Irving Howe, *A Margin of Hope* (New York: Harcourt Brace Jovanovich, 1983), p. 292.
172   "At this meeting": Ibid., pp. 291–92.
172   "as if somehow": Ibid., p. 293.
172   "the most rigid": Ibid., pp. 292–93.
172   "Hayden did not suffer": Irving Howe, "The Fleeting New Left: Historical Memory, Political Vision," *The New Republic*, November 9, 1974, p. 26.
172   "heavyhanded and didactic": Interview, Irving Howe, April 15, 1985.
173   Hayden was wrestling: Interview, Tom Hayden, August 20, 1985.
173   Howe, aghast: Interview, Irving Howe, April 15, 1985.

PAGE
173   "I don't know": Interview, Tom Hayden, August 20, 1985.
173   "How can you be": Interview, Irving Howe, April 15, 1985.
173   "antiheroes of history": Ibid.
174   Ngo Dinh Diem: Robert Scheer, *How the United States Got Involved in Vietnam* (Santa Barbara: Center for the Study of Democratic Institutions, 1965), pp. 23–25; Joseph Buttinger, *Vietnam: The Unforgettable Tragedy* (New York: Horizon, 1977), pp. 35, 39–52.
175   "tactical incapacity": Interview, Irving Howe, April 15, 1985.
175   "profoundly generational": Interview, Tom Hayden, August 20, 1985.
175   Howe doubts: Interview, Irving Howe, April 15, 1985.
175   "a very brutal debater": Interview, Martin Peretz, March 5, 1985.
175   "the New York intellectual": Interview, Tom Hayden, August 20, 1985.
175   "People like Harrington": Interview, Irving Howe, April 15, 1985.
175   "paradoxically": Ibid.
175   Hayden walked out: Interview, Jeremy Larner, March 12, 1987.
176   "New Styles": Irving Howe, "New Styles in 'Leftism,'" reprinted in Howe, ed., *Beyond the New Left* (New York: McCall, 1970), pp. 19–32.
176   "inordinate difficulty": Howe, "New Styles," p. 23.
176   "You cannot stand": Ibid., p. 22.
176   "One of the reasons": Interview, Irving Howe, April 15, 1985.
176   Howe held onto: Irving Howe, "Vietnam: The Fruits of Blindness," *Dissent,* Fall 1963, p. 314; "Vietnam: The Costs and Lessons of Defeat," *Dissent,* Spring 1965, pp. 151–55; "Vietnam: The Politics of Disaster," *Dissent,* November–December 1966, pp. 660–75.
176   Jeremy Larner: Interview, Jeremy Larner, March 12, 1987.
176   Michael Walzer: Michael Walzer, "Comment," *Dissent,* Spring 1965, pp. 155–56.
176   David McReynolds: David McReynolds, contribution to Vietnam symposium, *Dissent,* Autumn 1965, pp. 401–3.
177   "we must tread": Paul Booth to Paul Potter, July 1, 1964 (SDS papers, Series 2A, no. 30).
177   "The demand will be": Todd Gitlin to Martin Peretz, January 19, 1965 (SDS papers, Series 2A, no. 59).
177   "those people who insist": Paul Potter speech, April 17, 1965 (SDS papers, Series 2A, no. 60).
178   "a very clever smear": Paul Potter to Eve and Norm Potter, May 3, 1965 (Potter papers).
178   Tonkin Gulf: Stanley Karnow, *Vietnam: A History* (Harmondsworth, England: Penguin, 1984), pp. 360–76.
179   "like streetcars": McGeorge Bundy, in Karnow, *Vietnam,* p. 411.
179   W. E. B. DuBois Clubs: C. Clark Kissinger to Todd Gitlin, July 23, 1964 (author's files); Kissinger to Paul Booth, October 23, 1964; Kissinger to Bob Ross, November 20, 1964 (SDS papers, Series 2A, nos. 23, 29).
180   a Haverford student: Interview with a signer who wishes to remain anonymous.
180   SDS shelved: Kirkpatrick Sale, *SDS* (New York: Random House, 1973), pp. 170–72.
180   Booth and I submitted . . . "SDS advocates": SDS papers, Series 12A, no. 12.
181   "The New Student Left": For a discussion of this piece, see Todd Gitlin, *The Whole World Is Watching: Mass Media in the Making and Unmaking of the New Left* (Berkeley: University of California Press, 1980), pp. 35–39.
181   Tom Kahn: Interview, Tom Kahn, March 5, 1985.
182   peace movement notables: SDS papers, Series 2A, no. 48.
182   Among the signatories: Sale, *SDS,* p. 178; SDS Work List mailing, May 27, 1965 (author's file).
182   outlandish tale: Open letter from Martin Peretz, Anne Farnsworth, Mrs. Gardner Cox, SDS Work List Mailing, May 1, 1965 (SDS papers, Series 2A, no. 48).

PAGE

182 "It is of interest": Peretz, Farnsworth, Cox letter, May 1, 1965.

183 "portends much": Paul Potter letter, May 3, 1965 (Potter papers).

183 "I've seen": Interview, C. Z. Hobson, April 27, 1986.

185 "how far we had come": Paul Potter, *A Name for Ourselves* (Boston: Little, Brown, 1971), p. 101.

185 "people don't seem": Paul Potter to Eve and Norm Potter, May 3, 1965 (Potter papers).

186 "prairie power": Sale, *SDS*, pp. 204–8; Gitlin, *Whole World*, pp. 130–31.

186 "their trauma": Carl Oglesby, personal communication, October 30, 1986.

186 old-boy networks: Robert J. Ross, "Primary Groups in Social Movements: A Memoir and Interpretation," *Journal of Voluntary Action Research* 6 (July–October 1977), pp. 139–52; Gitlin, *Whole World*, pp. 131–33.

187 "O Santo Domingo!": Todd Gitlin, "Watching NBC News," *Liberation*, June–July 1965, p. 28.

187 "Vietnam worries me": C. Z. Hobson letters to Todd Gitlin, February 20, April 27, and n.d., 1965 (author's file).

188 "Crush i*********m": Todd Gitlin to C. Z. Hobson, May 17, 1965 (author's file).

188 "the pressure has increased": Paul Potter, "SDS and Foreign Policy," SDS convention working paper, June 1965 (SDS papers, Series 2A, no. 16).

189 abolishing its offices: Sale, *SDS*, pp. 206–8; SDS papers, Series 2A, no. 35.

189 "nonviolent revolution": Staughton Lynd, "Coalition Politics or Nonviolent Revolution?" *Liberation*, June–July 1965, pp. 19–20.

190 Kissinger moved: Sale, *SDS*, p. 665.

190 "I think that this": David Garson memo, SDS convention papers, June 1965 (SDS papers).

191 The amendments passed: Sale, *SDS*, pp. 210–12.

191 "democracy is nothing": Carl Oglesby, speech to *National Guardian* dinner, in *National Guardian*, November 20, 1965, p. 6.

191 "an agent for the FBI": Steve Max to Todd Gitlin (n.d., 1965) (author's file).

8. EVERYBODY GET TOGETHER

195 within five weeks: R. Serge Denisoff and Mark H. Levine, "The Popular Protest Song: The Case of 'Eve of Destruction,'" *Public Opinion Quarterly* 35 (Spring 1971), p. 119.

195 many stations were banning: R. Serge Denisoff, *Sing a Song of Social Significance*, 2nd ed. (Bowling Green, Ohio: Bowling Green University Popular Press, 1983), p. 162.

195 "obviously aimed at instilling fear": In Denisoff, *Sing a Song*, pp. 155–56.

195 "as a prayer": Telephone interview, P. F. Sloan, January 27, 1990.

197 sample of undergraduates: Denisoff and Levine, "Popular Protest Song," pp. 117–22.

197 junior college survey: Denisoff, *Sing a Song*, p. 162.

197 adopted a name: Robert Shelton, *No Direction Home: The Life and Music of Bob Dylan* (New York: Morrow, 1986), pp. 49–50.

198 radical scene: Anthony Scaduto, *Bob Dylan* (New York: Grosset and Dunlap, 1971), p. 36.

198 Dylan told a group of us: Interview, Richard Flacks, February 8, 1985. See the transcript of Dylan's Tom Paine Award remarks in Shelton, *No Direction Home*, pp. 200–201.

198 "All they can see": Bob Dylan, in Scaduto, *Bob Dylan*, p. 163.

198 mining country: Shelton, *No Direction Home*, p. 241.

199 "dragging [folk] screaming": Charlie Gillett, *The Sound of the City*, rev. and expanded ed. (New York: Pantheon, 1983), p. 287.

PAGE

199   market for *badness*: Philip Norman, *Symphony for the Devil* (New York: Linden/ Simon and Schuster, 1984), p. 112.

203   Byrds' metronomic version: Gillett, *Sound*, p. 338.

205   the Luces: Martin A. Lee and Bruce Shlain, *Acid Dreams: The CIA, LSD, and the Sixties Rebellion* (New York: Grove, 1986), pp. 71–73.

206   Thrown out of Harvard: Ibid., pp. 96–102.

206   Kesey: Ibid., pp. 119–20.

207   "Freak freely": Charles Perry, *The Haight-Ashbury: A History* (New York: Random House, 1984), p. 13.

207   "tool up": Tom Wolfe, *The Electric Kool-Aid Acid Test* (New York: Bantam, 1968), p. 147.

207   "Either you're on": Ibid., p. 74.

207   Acid Tests: Perry, *Haight-Ashbury*, pp. 34–35.

207   "vision of turning on": Wolfe, *Kool-Aid*, p. 203.

207   Watts test: Ibid., pp. 253–54.

208   "a union of love": In Perry, *Haight-Ashbury*, p. 122.

208   "to aid people": Allen Cohen, in Abe Peck, *Uncovering the Sixties: The Life and Times of the Underground Press* (New York: Pantheon, 1985), p. 37.

208   financed the *Oracle*: Peck, *Uncovering*, p. 37.

208   Political news: Perry, *Haight-Ashbury*, p. 124.

209   "flower-child innocence": Michael Rossman, *The Wedding Within the War* (Garden City: Anchor, 1971), p. 161.

209   Vietnam Day: Wolfe, *Kool-Aid*, pp. 195–200.

210   "The Yellow Submarine": Rossman, *Wedding*, p. 164.

210   Hell's Angels: Perry, *Haight-Ashbury*, p. 125.

211   "whenever the insights": Alan Watts, in Peck, *Uncovering*, p. 38.

211   Jerry Rubin: Milton Viorst, *Fire in the Streets: America in the 1960's* (New York: Simon and Schuster, 1979), p. 428.

211   Stew Albert: Interview, Stew Albert, July 18, 1985.

212   "Gentle Thursday": Peck, *Uncovering*, p. 59.

212   "The Bananas You Smoke": Todd Gitlin to Staughton Lynd, May 3, 1967 (author's file).

212   "the Midwest's confirmation": Peck, *Uncovering*, p. 50.

213   "Which Drug": Robb Burlage to Todd Gitlin, April 4, 1967 (author's file).

213   every American over age fourteen: David Zane Mairowitz, *The Radical Soap Opera: Roots of Failure in the American Left* (New York: Avon, 1976), pp. 181–82.

214   weekend dope-smokers: Kenneth Keniston, *Youth and Dissent* (New York: Harcourt Brace Jovanovich, 1971), pp. 230ff.

214   "architects of social change": Tim Scully, in Lee and Shlain, *Acid Dreams*, p. 147.

214   Grateful Dead: Lee and Shlain, *Acid Dreams*, p. 146.

215   more American troops: John Steinbeck IV, in Lester Grinspoon, *Marihuana Reconsidered* (Cambridge: Harvard University Press, 1971), p. 97.

215   Summer of Love: Don McNeill, *Moving Through Here* (New York: Knopf, 1970), p. 137; Perry, *Haight-Ashbury*, p. 293.

215   androgynous-sounding: Bennett Berger, *Looking for America* (Englewood Cliffs, N.J.: Prentice-Hall, 1971), pp. 128–29.

216   Bennett Berger: *Looking for America*, p. 123.

216   *Doors of Perception*: Jerry Hopkins and Danny Sugerman, *No One Here Gets Out Alive* (New York: Warner, 1980), p. 45.

216   Fifties panic: James Gilbert, *A Cycle of Outrage: America's Reaction to the Juvenile Delinquent in the 1950s* (New York: Oxford University Press, 1986), p. 142.

217   *Life*: In Lee and Shlain, *Acid Dreams*, p. 150.

217   scientific claims: Maimon M. Cohen, Michelle J. Marinello, and Nathan Back, "Chromosomal Damage in Human Leukocytes Inducted by Lysergic Acid Diethylamide," *Science* 155 (1967), pp. 1417–19; S. Irwin and J. Egozcue, "Chromosomal

Abnormalities in Leukocytes from LSD-25 Users," *Science* 157 (1967), p. 313; Lee and Shlain, *Acid Dreams*, pp. 154–55.

217   **politicians got mileage:** Richard Bunce, "Social and Political Sources of Drug Effects: The Case of Bad Trips on Psychedelics," *Journal of Drug Issues*, Spring 1979, p. 227.

217   **Ronald Reagan:** Lou Cannon, *Reagan* (New York: Perigee, 1982), pp. 103–17.

217   **"dresses like Tarzan":** Ronald Reagan, in McNeill, *Moving*, p. 154.

217   **Barnard student:** Deirdre Carmody, "Co-ed Disciplined by College Becomes a Dropout at Barnard," *New York Times*, September 4, 1968.

217   **Penn State:** Dan J. Peterman, Carl A. Ridley, and Scott M. Anderson, "A Comparison of Cohabiting and Noncohabiting College Students," *Journal of Marriage and the Family*, May 1974, p. 347.

218   **India:** Grinspoon, *Marihuana*, pp. 331–33.

218   **acute terror:** Bunce ("Social and Political Sources," p. 218) cites a national survey of young men: Of those who ever used psychedelics, 50 percent of those who started between 1961 and 1967 said they had ever had a bad trip. The rate tends to decline with later starting dates (to 32 percent of those who started in 1973–75), from which Bunce concludes that bad trips were in part a function of the supercharged political atmosphere and resulting "paranoia." But 32 percent is still a considerable proportion.

218   **Richard Alpert:** Lee and Shlain, *Acid Dreams*, pp. 101–2.

218   **"chemical freaks":** Manuel R. Ramos, "The Hippies: Where Are They Now?" in Frank R. Scarpitti and Susan K. Datesman, eds., *Drugs and the Youth Culture* (Beverly Hills: Sage, 1980), pp. 237–38.

218   **written by Steven Stills:** Gillett, *Sound*, p. 344.

219   **". . . fuck you":** Hopkins and Sugerman, *No One Here*, p. 96.

219   **"Pretty little sixteen-year-old":** In Peck, *Uncovering*, p. 47.

219   **Tompkins Square Park:** McNeill, *Moving*, pp. 100–101.

220   **hippie racism:** David T. Wellman, *Portraits of White Racism* (Cambridge, England: Cambridge University Press, 1977), pp. 194–215.

220   **448,800 American troops:** Melvin Small, "The Impact of the Antiwar Movement on Lyndon Johnson, 1965–1968: A Preliminary Report," *Peace and Change*, vol. 10, no. 1 (Spring 1984), p. 7.

221   **"a mass emotional nervous":** Allen Ginsberg, in Perry, *Haight-Ashbury*, p. 123.

9. PUBLIC NUISANCES

222   **"power itself was now":** Arthur Miller, introduction to Ken Kesey, *Kesey's Garage Sale* (New York: Viking, 1973), p. xv.

222   **They practiced:** All information about the Diggers not otherwise attributed comes from my interview with Peter Berg, July 19, 1985.

222   **They declared:** Martin A. Lee and Bruce Shlain, *Acid Dreams* (New York: Grove, 1985), p. 170.

223   **Grateful Dead . . . horse:** Lee and Shlain, *Acid Dreams*, p. 173: Don McNeill, *Moving Through Here* (New York: Knopf, 1970), pp. 125–30.

223   **"SEW THE RAGS":** Communications Company leaflet, n.d. (Spring 1967): Bancroft Library, University of California, Berkeley, Social Action Collection, Communications Company file.

223   **"The executive branch":** Rev. Leon Harris, in "'Huge Invasion': HIPPIES WARN S. F.," *San Francisco Chronicle*, March 22, 1967, p. 1.

223   **"When Love does its thing":** Digger leaflet, in Charles Perry, *The Haight-Ashbury: A History* (New York: Random House, 1984), p. 260.

224   **"horizontal and vertical":** Ibid., p. 261.

224   **"The Diggers declared":** McNeill, *Moving*, p. 125.

PAGE

224 "tense of presence": Digger leaflet, in Lee and Shlain, *Acid Dreams*, p. 183.

224 "endeavour[ed] to shut out": Gerrard Winstanley, et al., June 1, 1649, in Digger leaflet, n.d. (1967): Bancroft Library, Social Action Collection, Communications Company file.

224 righteous small-c communists: Christopher Hill, *The World Turned Upside Down* (Harmondsworth, England: Penguin, 1972), chap. 7.

225 "Two predictions": Digger leaflet, March 22, 1967: Bancroft Library, Social Action Collection, Communications Company file.

225 "calling the white radicals'": Emmett Grogan, *Ringolevio: A Life Played for Keeps* (Boston: Little, Brown, 1972), p. 385.

227 "a plot of aging": Todd Gitlin to Carol McEldowney, n.d. (probably May or June 1967) (author's file).

227 As in the opening: Parts of this account are drawn from "Free" (Abbie Hoffman), *Revolution for the Hell of It* (New York: Dial, 1968), pp. 33–36; Grogan, *Ringolevio*, pp. 385–402; Nicholas von Hoffman, "Hippiedom Meets the New Left: A Study in Language Barriers," *Washington Post*, June 19, 1967, p. A3; and from my interviews with Peter Berg, Dick Flacks, Mickey Flacks, Paul Krassner, Elinor Langer, Dickie Magidoff, Bob Ross, Steve Max, Don Villarejo, Myrna Villarejo, and Nicholas von Hoffman.

228 "Property is the enemy": Peter Berg, in Hoffman, *Revolution*, p. 35.

228 "Faggots!": Emmett Grogan, in Hoffman, *Revolution*, p. 35.

230 clown face: Fred Halstead, *Out Now!* (New York: Monad Press, 1978), p. 314.

230 "Think of it": Abbie Hoffman, in McNeill, *Moving*, p. 99.

230 "received in the hippie": McNeill, *Moving*, pp. 125–26.

231 beads, boots: Hoffman, *Revolution*, p. 34.

231 "A monumental meeting": Ibid., pp. 34–36.

231 "The seminars drag": Ibid., p. 36.

231 "the first New Left": Telephone interview, Bob Ross, June 12, 1985.

231 Alan Burke: Interview, Peter Berg, July 19, 1985.

232 "'We are working'": Paul Hofmann, "The New Left Turns to Mood of Violence in Place of Protest," *New York Times*, May 7, 1967, p. 1.

233 If the New Left: Todd Gitlin, *The Whole World Is Watching: Mass Media in the Making and Unmaking of the New Left* (Berkeley: University of California Press, 1980), chap. 5.

233 Diggers burned money: Interview, Peter Berg, July 19, 1985.

233 no one called: Abbie Hoffman, *Soon To Be a Major Motion Picture* (New York: Perigee, 1980), p. 101.

233 A tree planted: McNeill, *Moving*, p. 120.

233 Soot bombs . . . Joints of marijuana: Hoffman, *Motion Picture*, pp. 108–9, 111–12.

233 "Recognizing the limited": Ibid., p. 116.

233 Subpoenaed by HUAC: Jerry Rubin, *Do It! Scenarios of the Revolution* (New York: Simon and Schuster, 1970), pp. 64–65.

233 flowers in his hair: Milton Viorst, *Fire in the Streets: America in the 1960's* (New York: Simon and Schuster, 1979), p. 430.

233 "Personally, I always": Hoffman, *Motion Picture*, p. 99.

234 "Lace": Ibid., p. 132.

234 "to grab the imagination": Rubin, *Do It*, p. 69.

234 "A new man was born": Ibid., p. 82.

235 the Diggers thought: Interview, Peter Berg, July 19, 1985.

235 Abbie did collect: Hoffman, *Motion Picture*, p. 98.

235 The name came first: Interview, Paul Krassner, April 7, 1986.

235 "blending of pot": Hoffman, *Revolution*, p. 102.

235 "inspire potential yippies": Rubin, *Do It*, p. 83.

235 "We will burn Chicago": Hoffman, *Revolution*, p. 102.

PAGE
236 "The myth is real": Rubin, *Do It*, p. 83.
236 "The media in a real sense": Hoffman, *Revolution*, p. 92.
236 "Runaways are the backbone": Ibid., p. 74. Boldface in original.
236 "We tear": Ibid., p. 80.
236 "once you get": Hoffman, *Motion Picture*, p. 108.
236 Indeed, after Chicago: Ibid., p. 146.
236 "The goal of this nameless": Ibid., p. 114. Emphasis added.
237 "Ideology is a brain disease": Rubin, *Do It*, p. 113.
237 "ideological left": Ibid., p. 114.
237 "Act first": Ibid., p. 116. Boldface in original.
237 "white middle-class youth": Ibid., p. 114.
237 "If responsibility": Arthur Miller, introduction to *Kesey's Garage Sale*, p. xvi.
237 Grand Central Station: McNeill, *Moving*, pp. 225–26.
238 Abbie Hoffman himself: Hoffman, *Motion Picture*, pp. 142–43.
238 "It was a pointless": McNeill, *Moving*, pp. 224–30.
239 "a street gang": "Affinity Group: A Street Gang with an Analysis," Motherfucker leaflet (1968?), reprinted in Peter Stansill and David Zane Mairowitz, eds., *BAMN (By Any Means Necessary): Outlaw Manifestos and Ephemera 1965–70* (Harmondsworth, England: Penguin, 1971), p. 156.
239 "armed cadres at the centers": Stansill and Mairowitz, *BAMN*, p. 156.
239 high-powered theoretical: Interview, Bob Gottlieb, November 1, 1985.
240 Liberation News Service: Raymond Mungo, *Famous Long Ago: My Life and Hard Times with Liberation News Service* (Boston: Beacon, 1970); Abe Peck, *Uncovering the Sixties: The Life and Times of the Underground Press* (New York: Pantheon, 1985).
240 "We're looking for people": Motherfucker leaflet (1968?), in Stansill and Mairowitz, *BAMN*, p. 160.
240 They wowed a gaggle: Interview with a midwestern participant who wishes to remain anonymous.

10. FIGHTING BACK

242 Troop figures: Loren Baritz, *Backfire* (New York: Morrow, 1985), pp. 145, 176; Stanley Karnow, *Vietnam: A History* (New York: Penguin, 1984), p. 512.
242 air force: William H. Chafe, *The Unfinished Journey* (New York: Oxford University Press, 1986), p. 290.
242 the U.S. defoliated: Gabriel Kolko, *Anatomy of a War: Vietnam, the United States, and the Modern Historical Experience* (New York: Pantheon, 1985), p. 145.
242 million and a half tons: Karnow, *Vietnam*, p. 512.
242 San Francisco *Oracle*: Martin A. Lee and Bruce Shlain, *Acid Dreams* (New York: Grove, 1985), p. 185.
242 On April 15: Nancy Zaroulis and Gerald Sullivan, *Who Spoke Up? American Protest against the War in Vietnam* (Garden City, N.Y.: Doubleday, 1984), p. 110.
244 U.S. Army paratroopers: Abe Peck, *Uncovering the Sixties: The Life and Times of the Underground Press* (New York: Pantheon, 1985), p. 64.
244 FBI informant: Testimony of Thomas Edward Mosher, Hearings before the Subcommittee to Investigate the Administration of the Internal Security Act and Other Internal Security Laws, of the Committee on the Judiciary, U.S. Senate, 92nd Congress, 1st Session, Part 1, February 11, 1971, p. 6; T. Edward Mosher, "Inside the Revolutionary Left," *Reader's Digest*, September 1971, p. 53.
244 "All of us . . . gunbelt": Todd Gitlin to Carol McEldowney, July 25, 1967 (author's file).
244 "I talked last night": Carol McEldowney to Todd Gitlin, July 29, 1967 (author's file).

PAGE

245 Vietnam Summer: Kenneth Keniston, *Young Radicals* (New York: Harcourt, Brace and World, 1968), pp. 4–8.

245 Fidel Castro: "True revolutionaries never threaten a whole country with extermination. We have spoken out clearly against Israel's policy, but we don't deny her right to exist." Fidel Castro in an interview with K. S. Karol, September 1967, in Robert Scheer, "A Nasser Thesis," *Ramparts*, November 1967, p. 85.

245 New Politics convention: Zaroulis and Sullivan, *Who Spoke Up?*, pp. 128–29.

245 women's caucus: Sara Evans, *Personal Politics* (New York: Vintage, 1980), pp. 198–99.

245 police agents: Two Chicago police infiltrators supporting the black caucus demands were identified by the longtime Chicago activist Sidney Lens. Zaroulis and Sullivan, *Who Spoke Up?*, p. 129.

246 Andrew Kopkind: "They'd Rather Be Left," *New York Review of Books*, September 28, 1967, p. 3.

246 Frank Bardacke: "Stop-the-Draft Week," *Steps*, December 1967, reprinted in Mitchell Goodman, ed., *The Movement Toward a New America* (Philadelphia: Pilgrim Press, and New York: Knopf, 1970), p. 476.

246 Régis Debray: *Revolution in the Revolution?* (New York: Monthly Review Press, 1967), pp. 70, 84.

247 "dramatize[d] the existence": Bardacke, "Stop-the-Draft Week," p. 476.

248 "vicarious intoxication": Stuart McRae, "Oakland Week," *Resist*, December 1967, in Michael Ferber and Staughton Lynd, *The Resistance* (Boston: Beacon, 1971), p. 142.

248 "It was every revolutionary's": Interview, Mike Smith, July 6, 1985.

248 "gum up the works": Steve Hamilton, in Ferber and Lynd, *Resistance*, p. 140.

249 "charade": *San Francisco Examiner*, October 16, 1967.

250 "Bloody Tuesday": My discussion of Stop the Draft Week is based on interviews with Steve Hamilton and Mike Smith; the *San Francisco Chronicle, San Francisco Examiner,* and *Daily Californian* for October 16–23, 1967; Bardacke, "Stop-the-Draft Week," p. 477; and my recollections and correspondence.

252 "his lip torn": *San Francisco Chronicle*, October 18, 1967.

252 "We blocked traffic": Bardacke, "Stop-the-Draft Week," p. 478.

252 "Militant self-defense": Oakland 7 defense leaflet, n.d. (1969?): Bancroft Library, University of California, Berkeley, Social Action Collection, Oakland 7 file.

253 mind-set and the social setting: Norman E. Zinberg, *Drug, Set, and Setting: The Basis for Controlled Intoxicant Use* (New Haven: Yale University Press, 1984), pp. 1–18, 135–71.

254 Frank Bardacke: "Stop-the-Draft Week," pp. 478–79.

254 University of Wisconsin: Kirkpatrick Sale, *SDS* (New York: Random House, 1973), pp. 369–73.

254 large campus demonstrations: Ibid., pp. 380–81.

254 Dean Rusk: Ibid., p. 378.

255 a leaflet: Ferber and Lynd, *Resistance*, p. 145.

255 "Certainly we were unruly": George Dennison, "Talking with the Troops," *Liberation*, November 1967, reprinted in Goodman, *Movement*, pp. 473–74.

255 proselytizing cops: Bardacke, "Stop-the-Draft Week," p. 478.

255 prevailing style: Ferber and Lynd, *The Resistance*, p. 146.

257 "There are 3 billion": "The President's Remarks to Troops and Speech to Korean National Assembly," *New York Times*, November 2, 1966, p. 16.

257 Revolutionary War seamen: Jesse Lemisch, "The American Revolution Seen from the Bottom Up," in Barton J. Bernstein, ed., *Towards a New Past: Dissenting Essays in American History* (New York: Pantheon, 1968), pp. 3–45.

257 radical artisans: Staughton L. Lynd, "The Mechanics in New York Politics, 1774–1785," in *Class Conflict, Slavery, and the United States Constitution* (Indianapolis: Bobbs-Merrill, 1967), pp. 79–108.

PAGE
258 profound conundrums: Robert Dahl, *After the Revolution? Authority in a Good Society* (New Haven: Yale University Press, 1971).

259 one letter after another: Todd Gitlin to Don McKelvey, October 16, 1967; Todd Gitlin to Carl Davidson, October 24, 1967; Todd Gitlin to Robert Kramer, October 23, 1967, and November 21, 1967 (author's file).

260 "we have to force": Todd Gitlin to Carol McEldowney, November 28, 1967 (author's file).

11. THE OTHER SIDE

261 demagogic press: Todd Gitlin, *The Whole World Is Watching: Mass Media in the Making and Unmaking of the New Left* (Berkeley: University of California Press, 1980), pp. 118, 182, 229.

262 struggle for independence: The best statement of this position is Carl Oglesby, "The Revolted," chap. 6 of his "Vietnamese Crucible: An Essay on the Meanings of the Cold War," in Oglesby and Richard Shaull, *Containment and Change* (New York: Macmillan, 1967), pp. 140–56.

263 exemplars and heroes: Some of this discussion derives from Todd Gitlin, "Seizing History," *Mother Jones*, November 1983, p. 38.

263 where romantics: César Graña, *Bohemian versus Bourgeois: French Society and the French Man of Letters in the Nineteenth Century* (New York: Basic, 1964), pp. 131–34.

264 CIA reported back: Charles DeBenedetti, "A CIA Analysis of the Anti-Vietnam-War Movement: October 1967," *Peace and Change* 9, 1 (Spring 1983), p. 35.

264 Rusk said the CIA: Thomas Powers, *The Man Who Kept the Secrets: Richard Helms and the CIA* (New York: Pocket Books, 1969), p. 315. Johnson was reportedly: Hugh Sidey in Merle Miller, *Lyndon: An Oral Biography* (New York: Ballantine, 1980), p. 594.

264 Members of Congress: Nancy Zaroulis and Gerald Sullivan, *Who Spoke Up? American Protest Against the War in Vietnam, 1963–1975* (Garden City, N.Y.: Doubleday, 1984), p. 142, quoting Sen. Frank Lausche (D-Ohio), Rep. Gerald Ford (R-Michigan), and others. See also Tom Hayden, *Rebellion and Repression* (New York: Meridian, 1969), pp. 121ff.

264 "NFL high": Elinor Langer, "Notes for Next Time," *Working Papers*, Fall 1973, p. 65.

265 American media: Daniel C. Hallin, *The "Uncensored War": The Media and Vietnam* (New York: Oxford University Press, 1986).

265 travel to Hanoi: Zaroulis and Sullivan, *Who Spoke Up?*, p. 66.

266 "Fact-finding": Staughton Lynd and Tom Hayden, *The Other Side* (New York: New American Library, 1966), p. 7.

266 undermining North Vietnamese moves: Franz Schurmann, Peter Dale Scott, and Reginald Zelnik, *The Politics of Escalation in Vietnam* (Greenwich, Conn.: Fawcett, 1966).

266 "We are conscious": Lynd and Hayden, *Other Side*, pp. 13, 212.

266 "On the whole": Ibid., p. 11.

266 "We suspect that colonial": Ibid., p. 200.

266 "socialism of the heart": Ibid., p. 63.

267 Lynd himself calls it . . . "snookered": Telephone interview, Staughton Lynd, October 5, 1985.

267 "Staughton and Tom": Paul Potter to Eve Potter and Norm Potter, May 27, 1966 (Potter papers).

267 Lynd took little . . .: Telephone interview, Staughton Lynd, October 5, 1985.

268 drunkard against his bottle: Paraphrasing Todd Gitlin, "Watching NBC News," *Liberation*, June–July 1965, p. 28.

PAGE

268 Every simple categorical: Paraphrasing T. W. Adorno's "All reification is a forgetting," from Max Horkheimer and T. W. Adorno, *Dialectic of Enlightenment* (New York: Herder and Herder, 1972), p. 230, translation amended by Martin Jay in *The Dialectical Imagination* (Boston: Little, Brown, 1973), p. 267.

269 killing of thousands: Lynd and Hayden, *Other Side*, pp. 202–12; Stanley Karnow, *Vietnam: A History* (New York: Penguin, 1984), pp. 225–26.

269 former Vietminh cadres: Karnow, *Vietnam*, pp. 227–30.

269 "if the United States": Lynd and Hayden, *Other Side*, p. 213.

270 one Vietnamese woman: Raymond Mungo, *Famous Long Ago: My Life and Hard Times with Liberation News Service* (Boston: Beacon, 1970), p. 10.

271 "You are Vietnamese": Dave Dellinger, in Christopher Jencks, "Limits of the New Left," *The New Republic*, October 21, 1967, pp. 19–20.

271 "identified with the Viet Cong": Jencks, "Limits of the New Left," p. 19. Emphasis added.

272 Rennie Davis was hit: Zaroulis and Sullivan, *Who Spoke Up?*, pp. 131–32.

272 Daniel Berrigan and Howard Zinn: Daniel Berrigan, "Journal to Hanoi," *Liberation*, March 1968, pp. 33–34.

272 "It was like being caught": Langer, "Notes," p. 65.

272 "I was to be appointed": Andrew Kopkind, "The Sixties and the Movement," *Ramparts*, February 1973, p. 32.

273 "I was no longer merely": Ibid.

273 In November 1967: Melvin Small, "The Impact of the Antiwar Movement on Lyndon Johnson, 1965–1968: A Preliminary Report," *Peace and Change*, vol. 10, no.1 (Spring 1984), p. 7.

273 *"Our task":* Tom Hayden, "All for Vietnam," *Ramparts*, September 1970, p. 48. Emphasis in original.

273 "My god": Langer, "Notes," p. 65.

273 "The one problem": Kopkind, "The Sixties," p. 32.

275 I got away from the hotel: This discussion draws on Todd Gitlin, "Cuba and the American Movement," *Liberation*, March 1968, pp. 13–18.

277 scathing book: Carlos Franqui, *Family Portrait with Fidel* (New York: Random House, 1984).

278 Carmichael now proclaimed: Stokely Carmichael, "A Declaration of War," *San Francisco Express Times*, February 22, 1968, pp. 6–7.

278 revolutionary tourist: The phrase derives from Hans Magnus Enzensberger, "Tourists of the Revolution," in *The Consciousness Industry*, trans. Michael Roloff (New York: Seabury, 1974), pp. 129–57.

279 far from pandering: Tad Szulc, *Fidel: A Critical Portrait* (New York: Morrow, 1986), pp. 604–6.

279 Heberto Padilla: Personal communication, Heberto Padilla, July 1981; K. S. Karol, "Convertible Castro," *The New Republic*, January 19, 1987, p. 29.

279 "We look to Cuba": Todd Gitlin, "Cuba and the American Movement," *Liberation*, March 1968, p. 13.

279 "it wouldn't be hard": Todd Gitlin to Carl Davidson, February 16, 1968 (author's file).

280 Sometime that year: Karol, "Convertible Castro," pp. 28–29.

280 "any direct accusation": Fidel Castro, in *Granma*, English language ed., August 25, 1968, pp. 1–4.

281 "Leave this Europe": Frantz Fanon, *The Wretched of the Earth*, trans. Constance Farrington (New York: Grove paperback, 1968), p. 311.

282 "paralyze" powers: Interview, Tom Hayden, August 20, 1985.

12. 1968

283 "The New Left": Michael Rogin, personal communication, c. 1972.

283 "We've got something going": Stu Gedal, in Jerry Avorn et al., *Up Against the Ivy Wall* (New York: Atheneum, 1968), p. 52.

285 "Having tried available": Tom Hayden, *Rebellion and Repression* (New York: Meridian, 1969), p. 30.

285 In November 1967: Fred Halstead, *Out Now! A Participant's Account of the American Movement Against the Vietnam War* (New York: Monad Press, 1978), pp. 348–49.

285 the issue of race: Carl Oglesby, in Kirkpatrick Sale, *SDS* (New York: Random House, 1973), pp. 418–19.

287 "Here we are": Hubert Humphrey, in Lewis Chester, Godfrey Hodgson, and Bruce Page, *An American Melodrama: The Presidential Campaign of 1968* (New York: Viking, 1969), p. 146.

288 underground newspapers: Abe Peck, *Uncovering the Sixties: The Life and Times of the Underground Press* (New York: Pantheon, 1985), p. 86.

288 motives are tangled: To make judgment still more difficult, Hannah Arendt has argued that human action intrinsically entails unpredictable and irreversible consequences. *The Human Condition* (Chicago: University of Chicago Press, 1958), pp. 42–43, 144, 188–89, 220.

289 "A movement cannot grow": Jerry Rubin, in *Militant*, January 8, 1968, cited in Halstead, *Out Now!*, pp. 406–7.

289 "Since the country . . . a rationalization": Interview, Tom Hayden, August 20, 1985.

291 "There is a time": Mario Savio, in Max Heirich, *The Beginning: Berkeley 1964* (New York: Columbia University Press, 1970), pp. 199–200.

291 Draft resistance: Michael Ferber and Staughton Lynd, *The Resistance* (Boston: Beacon, 1970), chap. 9; Nancy Zaroulis and Gerald Sullivan, *Who Spoke Up? American Protest Against the War in Vietnam 1963–1975* (Garden City, N.Y.: Doubleday, 1984), p. 414; Lawrence M. Baskir and William A. Strauss, *Chance and Circumstance: The Draft, the War and the Vietnam Generation* (New York: Vintage, 1978), pp. 69, 5, 30, 104–5.

292 "the ultra-resistance": Francine du Plessix Gray, "The Ultra-Resistance," *New York Review of Books*, September 25, 1969.

292 Father Philip Berrigan: Ferber and Lynd, *Resistance*, chap. 14.

292 constituent groups: Halstead, *Out Now!*, passim.

293 On April 26, 1968: Ibid., pp. 386–87.

293 "wilderness of warmed-over": Carl Oglesby, "Peace Activism in Vietnam," *Studies on the Left*, January–February 1966, p. 54.

293 percentages who thought: Melvin Small, "The Impact of the Antiwar Movement on Lyndon Johnson, 1965–1968: A Preliminary Report," *Peace and Change*, vol. 10, no. 1 (Spring 1984), p. 7.

294 "incredibly ridiculous": Hubert Humphrey, in Carl Solberg, *Hubert Humphrey* (New York: Norton, 1984), pp. 311–12.

295 "American optimists at heart": Jeremy Larner, *Nobody Knows: Reflections on the McCarthy Campaign of 1968* (New York: Macmillan, 1970), p. 37.

295 "government in exile": Eugene McCarthy, in ibid., p. 52.

295 "not to go down": Chester et al., *American Melodrama*, p. 76.

296 "terribly grateful": Larner, *Nobody Knows*, p. 37.

296 crisscrossing the country: Richard Cummings, *The Pied Piper: Allard K. Lowenstein and the Liberal Dream* (New York: Grove, 1985), pp. 327, 337.

296 "new politics of alienation": Allard Lowenstein, in ibid., pp. 312–13.

PAGE

296 "between Staughton Lynd": Greg Craig, in ibid., p. 341.

296 "There's a lot of room": Allard Lowenstein, in ibid., p. 354.

296 insinuations: Most recently Cummings, *The Pied Piper*. See the refutation by Hendrik Hertzberg, "The Second Assassination of Al Lowenstein," *New York Review of Books*, October 10, 1985, pp. 34–41.

297 "Lament of an Aging": Eugene McCarthy, in Chester et al., *American Melodrama*, p. 71.

297 "I think in that case": Eugene McCarthy, in ibid., p. 101.

297 supporting Lyndon Johnson: Albert Eisele, *Almost to the Presidency: A Biography of Two American Politicians* (Blue Earth, Minn.: Piper, 1972), pp. 201–4, 206–12, 216–17.

297 Martin Luther King: Larner, *Nobody Knows*, p. 66.

297 "Clean for Gene": Chester et al., *American Melodrama*, p. 97.

298 Tet cease-fire: My account of Tet is based principally on Karnow, *Vietnam: A History* (New York: Penguin, 1984), pp. 523 ff.

299 "In all honesty": Ibid., p. 545.

299 "What the hell": Walter Cronkite, in Don Oberdorfer, *Tet!* (Garden City, N.Y.: Doubleday, 1971), p. 158.

299 "In 1963, we were told": Eugene McCarthy, in Chester et al., *American Melodrama*, p. 93.

300 "Our enemy, savagely": Robert F. Kennedy, in ibid., p. 117.

300 In the six weeks: Karnow, *Vietnam*, p. 546.

300 Network footage: Daniel C. Hallin, *The "Uncensored War": The Media and Vietnam* (New York: Oxford University Press, 1986), p. 171.

300 *Time, Newsweek*: Doris Kearns, *Lyndon Johnson and the American Dream* (New York: Harper and Row, 1976), p. 336.

300 "the shock waves rolled": George Christian, quoted by William Small, *To Kill a Messenger: Television News and the Real World* (New York: Hastings House, 1974), p. 123.

301 Reporters and McCarthy campaigners: Chester et al., *American Melodrama*, p. 145.

301 self-described hawks: Hallin, *"Uncensored War,"* p. 168; Allen J. Matusow, *The Unraveling of America: A History of Liberalism in the 1960s* (New York: Harper and Row, 1984), p. 391.

301 Johnson had no easy move: Hallin, *"Uncensored War,"* p. 169.

301 percentage of hawks: Matusow, *Unraveling*, p. 391.

301 parlayed a Texas dam: Robert A. Caro, *The Years of Lyndon Johnson: The Path to Power* (New York: Vintage, 1983), pp. 458–68, 577–78, 627–28.

301 deficit financing: Matusow, *Unraveling*, p. 160.

302 peace feelers: Chester et al., *American Melodrama*, p. 39.

302 winning the gratitude: Caro, *Lyndon Johnson*, p. 273.

302 "that horrible song": Kearns, *Lyndon Johnson*, p. 340.

302 distressed by the pickets: Melvin Small, "Impact of the Antiwar Movement," pp. 8–9.

302 alter his travel plans: Ibid. See, for example, *New York Times*, November 14, 1967, as cited in ibid., p. 18, n. 20.

302 "And then the final straw": Kearns, *Lyndon Johnson*, pp. 343, 340.

302 technocrat Robert McNamara: Loren Baritz, *Backfire: A History of How American Culture Led Us into Vietnam and Made Us Fight the Way We Did* (New York: Morrow, 1985), p. 182.

303 "hopeless": Clark M. Clifford, "A Viet Nam Reappraisal," *Foreign Affairs*, July 1969, p. 613.

303 "friends in business": Harry McPherson, *A Political Education* (Boston: Little, Brown, 1972), pp. 433–35.

PAGE

303   Johnson's most trusted: Theodore H. White, *The Making of the President, 1968* (New York: Atheneum, 1969), pp. 110–11.

303   "needed some stiff medicine": Clark Clifford, in Herbert Schandler, *The Unmaking of a President: Lyndon Johnson and Vietnam* (Princeton: Princeton University Press, 1977), pp. 254–55.

303   They met in the White House: Ibid., pp. 259–65; Chester et al., *American Melodrama*, pp. 419–20.

303   "We were weighing": Cyrus Vance, in Townsend Hoopes, *The Limits to Intervention* (New York: David McKay, 1969), pp. 215–16.

303   "general sentiment": George Ball, in Merle Miller, *Lyndon: An Oral History* (New York: Ballantine, 1980), p. 613.

304   "The meeting with the Wise Men": Clark Clifford, in Schandler, *Unmaking*, p. 264.

304   "if we can actually": Frank Bardacke, "Stop-the-Draft Week," *Steps*, December 1967, reprinted in Mitchell Goodman, ed., *The Movement Toward a New America* (Philadelphia: Pilgrim Press, and New York: Knopf, 1970), p. 478.

304   "If any demonstrator": George Wallace, in Chester et al., *American Melodrama*, p. 283.

304   Wallace was drawing: Ibid., p. 293.

304   "this country's ultimate": Lyndon Johnson, in Kearns, *Lyndon Johnson*, pp. 348–49.

304   "I don't think": Eugene McCarthy, in White, *Making*, pp. 124–25.

304   McCarthy drew: Chester et al., *American Melodrama*, p. 137.

304   The stock market: White, *Making*, pp. 93–94; Kearns, *Lyndon Johnson*, p. 349.

13. THE DECAPITATION OF THE HEROES

305   his hopes for a nonviolent: David L. Lewis, *King: A Biography*, 2nd ed. (Urbana: University of Illinois Press, 1978), pp. 380–83.

306   "really stunned": In Lindsy Van Gelder, "Bernardine Dohrn Is Weighed in the Balance and Found Heavy," *Esquire*, April 1971, p. 168.

306   "In the midst of prosecuting": Paul Starr, "The Explosion Had a Long Fuse," *Columbia Daily Spectator, Connection* supplement, May 10, 1968, p. C3.

307   Mark Rudd: Jerry Avorn et al., *Up Against the Ivy Wall* (New York: Atheneum, 1968), p. 27.

307   as an afterthought: After the first edition of this book was published, Michael Engber, now a dean at the City University of New York and in 1968 a graduate student in mathematics at Columbia and no activist, wrote me as follows: "I was in Hamilton Hall when Dean [Henry] Coleman was 'taken hostage' . . . the truth is that Coleman took himself hostage. No one had given any thought to keeping him there until he came out of his office and asked Mark Rudd, 'Am I to understand that I am not to be permitted to leave?' Mark said 'no' but repeated the question to the assemblage with surprise in his voice. The same Mark who got the 'whom' right in the letter to Grayson Kirk also clearly got Coleman's peculiarly inverted syntax right too. We shouted out a mixture of yeses and nos that, to my ears at least, leaned a little to the nos. When Mark hesitated to announce the will of the majority, Coleman jumped right in with, 'In that case, all of those who don't wish to keep me prisoner had better leave.' And so we did. And so he was." Michael Engber to Todd Gitlin, May 3, 1988. Coleman's own account of the incident appears in Avorn et al., *Up Against*, pp. 49–51.

307   Even after the first building: Ibid., pp. 61–63.

307   desecrating symbols: Michael Stern, "Twisting the News: Perspective or Prejudice?" *Columbia Daily Spectator, Connection* supplement, May 10, 1968, pp. C6–7.

PAGE

307   left a mess: Robert S. Stulberg, "Report Buildings Vandalized After Students Leave," *Columbia Daily Spectator*, May 2, 1968, p. 7; Stern, "Twisting," pp. C6–7.

308   Lindsay criticized: "Lindsay Criticizes Brutality By Police Tuesday Morning," *Columbia Daily Spectator*, May 3, 1968, p. 3.

308   "turbulent and inchoate": In Avorn et al., *Up Against*, p. 25.

308   the press built: Stern, "Twisting," pp. C6–7; Todd Gitlin, *The Whole World Is Watching: Mass Media in the Making and Unmaking of the New Left* (Berkeley: University of California Press, 1980), pp. 274–75.

308   *Newsweek* editors: Herbert J. Gans, *Deciding What's News* (New York: Pantheon, 1979), p. 347, n. 32.

308   "radical insight": Personal communication, Carl Oglesby, October 30, 1986.

309   "WE WANT THE WORLD": Jerry Avorn, "If Grayson Kirk Were Alive. . . ," *Columbia Daily Spectator, Connection* supplement, May 10, 1968, p. C3.

309   "the vaguest, emptiest speech": Marvin Garson, "Vietnam: Bobby Does It Better," *San Francisco Express Times*, March 28, 1968, p. 1.

309   Kennedy-McCarthy debate: Lewis Chester, Godfrey Hodgson, and Bruce Page, *An American Melodrama: The Presidential Campaign of 1968* (New York: Viking, 1969), pp. 339–49.

310   I called: Todd Gitlin, "Mourning Becomes Electronic," *San Francisco Express Times*, June 12, 1968, p. 8.

310   "It's a very interesting": Sandy Archer, in Marvin Garson, "Kennedy Shot Again," *San Francisco Express Times*, June 6, 1968, p. 1.

310   at Kennedy's casket: Tom Hayden, "Rolling Stone Interview, Part 1," *Rolling Stone*, October 26, 1972, p. 50.

310   "Why are you a whore": Tom Hayden, in Jeremy Larner, *Nobody Knows: Reflections on the McCarthy Campaign of 1968* (New York: Macmillan, 1970), p. 118.

311   McCarthy had gone to Humphrey: Albert Eisele, *Almost to the Presidency* (Blue Earth, Minn.: Piper, 1972), pp. 338–39; Blair Clark, "The Politics of Futility," *Washington Post*, Outlook Section, July 17, 1988.

311   "When these two heroes": Personal communication, Carl Oglesby, October 30, 1986.

313   a government claw: A recent circumstantial hint in this direction is contained in James Farmer, *Lay Bare the Heart: An Autobiography of the Civil Rights Movement* (New York: Arbor House, 1985), pp. 230–38. On Malcolm X's trip, see Alex Haley, *The Autobiography of Malcolm X* (New York: Ballantine, 1973), pp. 340–41.

313   black students in Orangeburg: Clayborne Carson, *In Struggle: SNCC and the Black Awakening of the 1960s* (Cambridge: Harvard University Press, 1981), pp. 249–50.

314   FBI, military intelligence: Frank J. Donner, *The Age of Surveillance* (New York: Vintage, 1981); Paul Cowan, Nick Egleson, and Nat Hentoff, *State Secrets: Police Surveillance in America* (New York: Holt, Rinehart and Winston, 1974).

314   planting dope: For an example of a setup marijuana raid as early as 1966, in the Uptown neighborhood of Chicago, see Todd Gitlin and Nanci Hollander, *Uptown: Poor Whites in Chicago* (New York: Harper and Row, 1970), pp. 392–94.

314   Under the headline: Bob Novick, "Lots of Coincidences," *San Francisco Express Times*, January 24, 1968, p. 2.

314   The CIA: Thomas Powers, *The Man Who Kept the Secrets: Richard Helms and the CIA* (New York: Pocket Books, 1979), pp. 315, 468.

314   "If you want to be": Lenny Heller, in Tom Farber, *Tales for the Son of My Unborn Child: Berkeley, 1966–1969* (New York: Pocket Books, 1973), p. 79.

315   At Columbia: Gitlin, *Whole World*, pp. 194–95.

315   To support the French: Steve Chain, "Telegraph Avenue in Berkeley: After the Barricades, Let the People Decide," *Ramparts*, August 24, 1968, pp. 22–27; Lenny

PAGE

the Red-and-Black [Lenny Heller], "War Zone Report," *San Francisco Express Times*, July 3, 1968, pp. 9–11; Lenny the Head [Lenny Heller], "Young Pacifica—Revolutionary Surprise!" *San Francisco Express Times*, July 30, 1968.

316 *"the issue of violence"*: Kenneth Keniston, *Young Radicals* (New York: Harcourt, Brace and World, 1969), p. 248. Emphasis in original.

317 movement cadres: Stanley Rothman and S. Robert Lichter (*Roots of Rebellion: Jews, Christians, and the New Left* [New York: Oxford University Press, 1982]) have argued that New Left activists were distinctly rage-prone from an early age, but the evidence is far from convincing (see Richard Flacks's review in *Society*, January/February 1984, pp. 89–92); and even if the predisposition could somehow be established, the political focus of this predetermined rage would remain to be explained. Why New Left politics? Why not, say, frantic music, nihilist violence, or sheer militarism?

318 When in doubt: Stan Kaplowitz, "An Experimental Test of a Rationalistic Theory of Deterrence," *Journal of Conflict Resolution* 17 (September 1973), pp. 535–72.

318 "expecting death": Interview, Tom Hayden, August 20, 1985.

14. THE CRUNCH

320 As far as Dellinger: Telephone interview, Dave Dellinger, November 3, 1986.

320 "open the door for provocateurs": Sidney Peck, in Nancy Zaroulis and Gerald Sullivan, *Who Spoke Up? American Protest Against the War in Vietnam, 1963–1975* (Garden City, N.Y.: Doubleday, 1984), p. 175.

321 Staughton Lynd argued: Telephone interview, Staughton Lynd, October 5, 1985.

321 Fresh from the Yip-In: Todd Gitlin, "Chicago Showdown: Hog Butcher Is the Pig," *San Francisco Express Times*, July 31, 1968, p. 15.

321 "When Johnson dropped out": Rennie Davis in Anonymous [Marvin Garson], "If you're going to Chicago, be sure to wear some armor in your hair," *San Francisco Express Times*, August 21, 1968, p. 1.

321 A few days later: John Schultz, *No One Was Killed: Documentation and Meditation: Convention Week, Chicago—August 1968* (Chicago: Big Table, 1969), p. 194.

321 even Jerry Rubin: Milton Viorst, *Fire in the Streets: America in the 1960's* (New York: Simon and Schuster, 1979), p. 447.

321 a former Chicago cop: In Abe Peck, *Uncovering the Sixties: The Life and Times of the Underground Press* (New York: Pantheon, 1985), p. 106.

321 Hayden and Davis: Gitlin, "Chicago Showdown," p. 15.

321 Dellinger argued: Dave Dellinger, *More Power Than We Know* (Garden City, N.Y.: Doubleday 1975), p. 121.

321 SDS office: Kirkpatrick Sale, *SDS* (New York: Random House, 1973), p. 473.

322 When they announced: Abbie Hoffman, *Soon To Be a Major Motion Picture* (New York: Perigee, 1980), p. 154.

322 When Hoffman twitted: Hoffman, *Motion Picture*, p. 152. The Walker Report (Daniel Walker, *Rights in Conflict: The Violent Confrontation of Demonstrators and Police in the Parks and Streets of Chicago During the Week of the Democratic National Convention of 1968* [Washington: National Commission on the Causes and Prevention of Violence, 1968]), says the sum was $200,000 (p. 40).

322 Yippies' dummy agenda: Walker, *Rights*, pp. 49–50.

322 "on Monday, Wednesday": Telephone interview, Staughton Lynd, October 5, 1985.

323 Roger Wilkins: Lewis Chester, Godfrey Hodgson, and Bruce Page, *An American Melodrama: The Presidential Campaign of 1968* (New York: Viking, 1969), p. 519.

323 normally not enforced: Ibid., p. 520; Schultz, *No One*, p. 76.

323 Mobe filed suit: Walker, *Rights*, pp. 31–40.

PAGE
323 Stalling on permits: Gitlin, "Chicago Showdown," p. 15; Zaroulis and Sullivan, *Who Spoke Up?*, pp. 182–83.

323 CBS News: CBS News Special, *1968*, broadcast August 25, 1978; transcript, p. 28. Copyright 1978 CBS Inc. All rights reserved.

323 "In my recruiting trips": Dellinger, *More Power*, p. 122.

324 "We thought that if": Telephone interview, Dave Dellinger, November 3, 1986; Walker, *Rights*, p. 17.

324 "Many people are into": In Peck, *Uncovering*, pp. 109–10.

324 Gene McCarthy: Walker, *Rights*, p. 28. On FBI involvement with assassination rumors, see Judith Clavir Albert and Stewart Albert, *The Sixties Papers* (New York: Praeger, 1985), p. 32 and p. 60, n. 55.

324 Lowenstein dropped: Chester et al., *American Melodrama*, p. 519.

324 The week before: Schultz, *No One*, p. 49.

324 By educated guess: Walker, *Rights*, p. 53; Schultz, *No One*, p. 70.

325 Hayden spelled it out: Tom Hayden, in *Ramparts Wall Poster*, August 25, 1968, quoted in Walker, *Rights*, p. 17.

326 "police riot": Walker, *Rights* passim.

326 ordered to assault: Schultz, *No One*, pp. 193ff.

327 slashed the tires: Ibid., p. 116.

327 More than five: Chester et al., *American Melodrama*, pp. 601, 602.

327 Dellinger went to: Telephone interview, Dave Dellinger, November 3, 1986; Walker, *Rights*, p. 4.

327 men outnumbered: Schultz, *No One*, p. 204n.

328 "Fuck the marshals!": Ibid., p. 95.

328 John Schultz talked: Ibid., pp. 83–91. Quotations from pp. 90–91.

329 a woman in army fatigues: Ibid., p. 150.

329 heavy fighters were outnumbered: Ibid., p. 71.

330 "I remember watching": Paul Cowan, "Subterranean News," *Columbia Journalism Review*, September/October 1985, p. 58.

330 I heard Tom Hayden: Todd Gitlin, "MOB Debates Street Plans," *Ramparts Wall Poster*, August 26, 1968.

331 defeated the peace plank: Chester et al., *American Melodrama*, pp. 580, 584.

332 "innocent enthusiasm": Dellinger, *More Power*, pp. 70–71.

332 "huskier than most": Schultz, *No One*, p. 171.

332 The cops formed: Ibid., pp. 169–77.

332 "The city and the military": Tom Hayden, *Rebellion and Repression* (New York: Meridian, 1969), p. 163.

332 The crowd, sealed off: Schultz, *No One*, p. 184.

333 "a place," said its advertising: In Walker, *Rights*, p. 173.

333 At the corner of the Hilton: Walker, *Rights*, pp. 158–86, esp. p. 169; Chester et al., *American Melodrama*, p. 583; Schultz, *No One*, pp. 190–211; Zaroulis and Sullivan, *Who Spoke Up?*, pp. 193–96; interview, Jeff Shero, August 26, 1988.

333 One Mobe organizer: Sidney Peck, in Zaroulis and Sullivan, *Who Spoke Up?*, pp. 194–95.

335 what polls showed: In the first week of September, the Gallup Poll showed 56 percent approving of the police, 31 percent disapproving. (*The Gallup Poll*, vol. 3 [New York: Random House, 1972], p. 2160.) A University of Michigan Survey Research Center poll in November (John P. Robinson, "Public Reaction to Political Protest: Chicago 1968," *Public Opinion Quarterly*, vol. 34, no. 2 [Spring 1970], p. 2) showed that only one-quarter of people with opinions thought the police used too much force, while one-third thought they didn't use enough.

335 antiwar movement was detested: Howard Schuman, "Two Sources of Antiwar Sentiment," *American Journal of Sociology*, vol. 78, no. 3 (November 1972), pp. 513–36.

335 "One of the few things": McGeorge Bundy memorandum for the President,

PAGE

November 10, 1967, in President's Appointment File/November 2, 1967/Lyndon B. Johnson Library; cited in Charles DeBenedetti, "Lyndon Johnson and the Antiwar Opposition," unpublished ms., p. 27, from his forthcoming study of the antiwar movement in America, 1955–1975.

335   "Running and stumbling": Elinor Langer, "Notes for Next Time," *Working Papers*, Fall 1973, p. 68. The first chant was actually "Sieg Heil!"

336   "under the club": Schultz, *No One*, p. 217.

336   at least 100: Sale, *SDS*, pp. 478–79.

336   rapidly backpedaled: Godfrey Hodgson, *America in Our Time* (Garden City, N.Y.: Doubleday, 1976), pp. 370–76; Todd Gitlin, *The Whole World Is Watching: Mass Media in the Making and Unmaking of the New Left* (Berkeley: University of California Press, 1980), pp. 213–16.

337   "Watch the man": Todd Gitlin, "Casting the First Stone," *San Francisco Express Times*, September 25, 1968, p. 2.

338   "*decide* to possess": From an SDS leaflet to McCarthy supporters in Chicago, in Sale, *SDS*, p. 474n. Emphasis in original.

338   "I think the blame": Hubert Humphrey, in Carl Solberg, *Hubert Humphrey* (New York: Norton, 1984), p. 370.

339   He had won: Solberg, *Hubert Humphrey*, p. 342.

339   Nixon polls: Chester et al., *American Melodrama*, p. 737.

339   Nixon's speech: Ibid., p. 722.

339   Blair Clark: "The Politics of Futility, 1968: How Gene McCarthy Sank the Peace Movement—and Himself," *Washington Post*, Outlook Section, July 17, 1988.

339   Humphrey lost: U.S. Bureau of the Census, *Statistical Abstract of the United States: 1976* (Washington: Government Printing Office, 1976), pp. 452–55.

340   "We are moving toward": Todd Gitlin, notes for Seattle speech, October 1968 (author's file).

15. THE SPRING OF HOPE, THE WINTER OF DESPAIR

341   "no turning back": Todd Gitlin to "Rafael Otero," December 20, 1968 (author's file).

342   In the spring of 1969: Kirkpatrick Sale, *SDS* (New York: Random House, 1973), pp. 503–4, 512–13.

343   By July 1969: Abe Peck, *Uncovering the Sixties: The Life and Times of the Underground Press* (New York: Pantheon, 1985), p. 183.

344   *Fortune* devoted: *Fortune*, January 1969, pp. 70–71, 175.

345   1969 Progressive labor headline: Interview, Michael Kazin, June 6, 1985.

346   "post-scarcity": Todd Gitlin, "The Dynamics of the New Left," part 1, *Motive*, October 1970, p. 49; Murray Bookchin, *Post-Scarcity Anarchism* (Berkeley: Ramparts Press, 1971).

346   Barrington Moore, Jr.: "Revolution in America?" *New York Review of Books*, January 30, 1969, pp. 6–12.

346   "A revolution is": Richard Poirier, "The War Against the Young: Its Beginnings," in *The Performing Self* (New York: Oxford University Press, 1971), pp. 148, 152; first published in *The Atlantic*, October 1968.

347   "Alas, we": Bertolt Brecht, "An Die Nachgeborenen," trans. H. R. Hays, in Brecht, *Selected Poems* (New York: Grove, 1959), p. 177.

348   Cleaver writing in *Ramparts*: Eldridge Cleaver, "A Letter from Jail," *Ramparts*, May 1968, pp. 20–21.

349   "Communism is not": Stokely Carmichael, "A Declaration of War," *San Francisco Express Times*, February 22, 1968, pp. 6–7, reprinted in Mitchell Goodman, ed., *The Movement Toward a New America* (Philadelphia: Pilgrim and New York: Knopf, 1970), p. 182.

PAGE

349 I myself drafted: "Resolution on SNCC, passed by National Council of Students for a Democratic Society," June 18, 1966 (author's file).

349 threats of gunplay: Clayborne Carson, *In Struggle: SNCC and the Black Awakening of the 1960s* (Cambridge: Harvard University Press, 1981), pp. 278–86.

350 "revolutionary gang": Marvin Garson, "Revolutionary Gangs," *San Francisco Express Times*, June 26, 1968, p. 2; "Going Beyond Democracy," *San Francisco Express Times*, July 3, 1968, p. 2; "Free Street Movement," *San Francisco Express Times*, July 10, 1968, p. 2.

350 ties with local police: Frank Donner, *The Age of Surveillance* (New York: Vintage, 1981), pp. 222–24.

350 thirty-one raids: Kate Coleman, "Souled Out," *New West*, May 19, 1980, p. 20.

350 Edward Jay Epstein: "The Panthers and the Police: A Pattern of Genocide?" *The New Yorker*, February 13, 1971, pp. 44ff., reprinted in *Between Fact and Fiction: The Problem of Journalism* (New York: Vintage, 1975), pp. 33–77.

350 Church Committee: U.S. Senate, Select Committee to Study Governmental Operations with Respect to Intelligence Activities. Hearings, 94th Congress, 1st Session, 1975, vol. 6, Book III, "The FBI's Covert Action Program to Destroy the Black Panther Party," pp. 185–224.

350 Frank Donner: *Age of Surveillance*, pp. 221–32.

350 began with a Panther ambush: Coleman, "Souled Out," p. 20.

351 "the vanguard of the black": Sale, *SDS*, p. 546.

351 "presumption": Julius Lester, "From the Other Side of the Tracks," *Guardian*, April 19, 1969, p. 22.

351 "Everyone was too quick": Todd Gitlin to Norm Fruchter, April 22, 1969 (author's file).

352 New York City school fight: Maurice R. Berube and Marilyn Gittell, eds., *Confrontation at Ocean Hill-Brownsville* (New York: Praeger, 1969); William L. O'Neill, *Coming Apart: An Informal History of America in the 1960's* (New York: Quadrangle, 1971), pp. 183–87; Robert Rossner, *The Year Without an Autumn: Portrait of a School in Crisis* (New York: Richard W. Baron, 1969).

352 "freedom schools": Todd Gitlin, "The Liberation of Bronx H. S. of Science," *San Francisco Express Times*, November 13, 1968, reprinted in Goodman, ed., *The Movement*, p. 289.

353 "New York types": Interview, former Berkeley police chief William Beall, by Mark Kitchell, 1986.

353 fraternities and sororities: Max Heirich, *The Spiral of Conflict: Berkeley 1964* (New York: Columbia University Press, 1969), p. 63.

354 It takes two: My account of People's Park draws on my interviews with Stew Albert, July 18, 1985, and Ruth Rosen, January 4, 1986, along with other participants who prefer to remain anonymous; my conversations, observations, interviews in May–June 1969, including one with Regent Fred Dutton; Mark Kitchell interviews with Frank Bardacke, William Beall, and Joel Tornabene; Robert Scheer, "The Battle of Berkeley: The Dialectics of Confrontation," *Ramparts*, August 1969, pp. 42–49, 52–53; editors of *Ramparts*, "Rampage: A Detailed Investigation into Shotgun Tactics," *Ramparts*, August 1969, pp. 54–59; Roger W. Heyns, address to Berkeley Division Academic Senate, May 23, 1969 (Academic Senate, University of California, Berkeley); Todd Gitlin, "White Watts," *Hard Times*, no. 33, May 26–June 2, 1969, pp. 1–3; Todd Gitlin, "The Meaning of People's Park," I, *Liberation*, July 1969; John Simon, "The Meaning of People's Park," II, *Liberation*, July 1969 (the latter two reprinted in Goodman, ed., *The Movement*, pp. 506–7, 509–10); William J. McGill, *The Year of the Monkey: Revolt on Campus, 1968–69* (New York: McGraw-Hill, 1982), pp. 154–94. Partly because of Berkeley's distance from the national media centers, People's Park gets short shrift in most

PAGE

histories of the Sixties, including Sale, *SDS*, O'Neill, *Coming Apart*, and Godfrey Hodgson, *America in Our Time* (Garden City, N.Y.: Doubleday, 1976).

355 "As substance and sign": Todd Gitlin, "The Meaning of People's Park," I, in Goodman, ed., *The Movement*, p. 506.

356 history of the land: Frank Bardacke, "WHO OWNS THE PARK?" reprinted in Goodman, ed., *The Movement*, p. 505.

356 "I planted": Michael Rossman, "Poem for a Victory Rally in a Berkeley Park," in Todd Gitlin, ed., *Campfires of the Resistance: Poetry from the Movement* (Indianapolis: Bobbs-Merrill, 1971), p. 252.

357 a Berkeley cop shoved: Interview, Frank Bardacke, by Mark Kitchell, 1985.

358 "'strategic hamlet'": Scheer, "The Battle of Berkeley," p. 46.

358 "like a Secretary of State": Ibid., p. 53.

358 bamboo spikes: McGill, *Year of the Monkey*, p. 166.

358 "a conservative landlord": Heyns, address to Academic Senate.

358 "The policy begins": Scheer, "The Battle of Berkeley," p. 53. On Vietnam strategy, see Daniel Ellsberg, *Papers on the War* (New York: Simon and Schuster, 1972), pp. 42ff.

359 Franz Schurmann: "The NLF Asks the American Left: 'Where Are You Now That We *Really* Need You?'" *Ramparts*, August 1969, pp. 14–22.

359 "We won the war": Frank Bardacke in *San Francisco Good Times*, a film by Allan Francovich.

359 repression showed how oppression: Paraphrased from a talk by Terry Cannon before the Commission of Inquiry in behalf of the Oakland 7, University of California, Berkeley, January 1969; published as "Brothers and Sisters . . . ," *San Francisco Express Times*, January 18, 1969, reprinted in Goodman, ed., *The Movement*, p. 229.

359 Berkeley Liberation Program: *Berkeley Barb*, May 30, 1969, and *Leviathan*, Summer 1969; reprinted in Goodman, ed., *The Movement*, pp. 512–13.

360 Stew Albert was one: Interview, Stew Albert, July 18, 1985.

360 "And he will protect": Anonymous [Gary Snyder], "Smokey the Bear Sutra," in Gitlin, ed., *Campfires of the Resistance*, p. 79.

361 "People's Park ended": Interview, Stew Albert, July 18, 1985.

16. WOMEN: REVOLUTION IN THE REVOLUTION

362 "Objectively, the chances": Casey Hayden and Mary King, "Sex and Caste," in Sara Evans, *Personal Politics* (New York: Vintage, 1980), p. 237.

362 "Goodbye, goodbye forever": Robin Morgan, "Goodbye to All That," *Rat*, February 9–23, 1970, pp. 6–7, reprinted in Judith Clavir Albert and Stew Albert, eds., *The Sixties Papers* (New York: Praeger, 1985), pp. 515–16.

362 On January 19, 1969: My description of this event draws on interviews with Marilyn Webb, Cathy Wilkerson, Mike Spiegel, Judith Coburn, Dave Dellinger, and Ellen Willis, as well as the texts of the Webb and Firestone speeches, and Jane Adams, "Factionalism Lives," in *Voice of the Women's Liberation Movement*, no. 6 (February 1969), kindly made available to me by Jo Freeman; and on Ellen Willis, "Up from Radicalism: A Feminist Journal," *US*, no. 2 (New York: Bantam, 1969), p. 114.

362 a scatter of objects: Nancy Zaroulis and Gerald Sullivan, *Who Spoke Up? American Protest Against the War in Vietnam* (Garden City, N.Y.: Doubleday, 1984), pp. 209–10.

365 Mickey Flacks: Interview, Mickey Flacks, April 6, 1986.

PAGE

365 New Left women felt: Ibid.; Evans, *Personal Politics*, chap. 5.

365 In the South: Evans, *Personal Politics*, chap. 2.

365 documented proof: See, for example, Frank J. Donner, *The Age of Surveillance* (New York: Vintage, 1981), pp. 220–26, 232–33, 236–37; and Ward Churchill and Jim Vander Wall, *The COINTELPRO Papers* (Boston: South End, 1990), chaps. 5–6, passim. In the case of the Black Panther Party, the FBI efforts probably had lethal consequences.

365 FBI memo of July 5, 1968: Reproduced in Brian Glick, *War at Home* (Boston: South End, 1989), p. 80.

365 number of women: Computed from Tables 3/13, "Undergraduate Enrollment, 18-to-24-Year Olds: 1940–1972, By Sex and Race," and 3/17, "Bachelor's, Master's, and Doctor's Degrees Earned: 1940–1972, By Sex," in Executive Office of the President, Office of Management and Budget, *Social Indicators* (Washington: U.S. Government Printing Office,), pp. 105, 107.

366 the early women: Interviews with Sharon Jeffrey, Barbara Haber, Marilyn Webb; Evans, *Personal Politics*, chap. 5.

367 work with "young guys": Todd Gitlin and Nanci Hollander, *Uptown: Poor Whites in Chicago* (New York: Harper and Row, 1970), pp. 375–97; Evans, *Personal Politics*, chap. 6.

367 underrepresented: Evans, *Personal Politics*, p. 112.

368 "both fraternal and competitive": Paul Potter, in ibid., p. 110.

368 "endured many feelings": Carol McEldowney to Todd Gitlin, November 18, 1964 (author's file).

369 discomfort had no name: The reference is to Betty Friedan's concept of "the problem that has no name," in *The Feminine Mystique* (New York: Norton, 1963), chap. 1.

369 SDS was flooded: Todd Gitlin, *The Whole World Is Watching: Mass Media in the Making and Unmaking of the New Left* (Berkeley: University of California Press, 1980), p. 25.

370 Illinois conference: Evans, *Personal Politics*, pp. 161–69; interview, Marilyn Webb, October 25, 1985.

370 SDS grew: Kirkpatrick Sale, *SDS* (New York: Random House, 1973), p. 341.

370 Barbara and Al Haber: Interviews, Barbara Haber, November 17, 1984, and Alan Haber, March 28, 1985.

370 Heather Tobis: Heather Tobis Booth at a conference on student movements, Columbia University, November 8, 1986.

371 When women brought: Sale, *SDS*, pp. 362n.–363n.; Evans, *Personal Politics*, pp. 190–92; *New Left Notes*, July 10, 1967.

371 critical mass of women: I am indebted to Ruth Rosen for insights on the changing sensibility of women in the Sixties.

371 "What got me involved": Kate Coleman at panel discussion on Sixties movements, University of California, Berkeley, October 12, 1984.

372 "fucking a staff": Marge Piercy, "The Grand Coolie Damn," *Leviathan*, Summer 1969, reprinted in Mitchell Goodman, ed., *The Movement Toward a New America* (Philadelphia: Pilgrim, and New York: Knopf, 1970), p. 59.

372 "Fuck your woman": Chicago *Seed*, vol. 3, no. 3, cited in Abe Peck, *Uncovering the Sixties: The Life and Times of the Underground Press* (New York: Pantheon, 1985), p. 208.

372 Liberation News Service excised: Peck, *Uncovering*, p. 339.

372 "metastasized": Barbara Haber at panel discussion on Sixties movements, University of California, Berkeley, October 12, 1984.

372 "engorged egos": Ibid.; also see Piercy, "Grand Coolie," p. 59.

373 "But there is also": Piercy, "Grand Coolie," p. 57.

374 long series of *Rat* articles: Peck, *Uncovering*, p. 212; Morgan, "Goodbye," in Albert and Albert, eds., *Sixties Papers*, p. 510.

374 "White men are most": Morgan, "Goodbye," in Albert and Albert, *Sixties Papers*, pp. 509–16. Morgan made a historical error when she wrote that "the so-called Sexual Revolution . . . has functioned toward women's freedom as did the Reconstruction toward former slaves—reinstituted oppression by another name." In fact, Reconstruction was a boon to the freed slaves, which was why the southern whites worked so hard to dismantle it.

375 Only when women freed: See Milton Viorst, *Fire in the Streets: America in the 1960's* (New York: Simon and Schuster, 1979), pp. 492–93.

376 injected sanity and clarity: The affirmative was asserted by Barbara Haber during a panel discussion on the Sixties, University of California, Berkeley, October 12, 1984.

17. THE IMPLOSION

377 "As one young SDS activist": Staughton Lynd, "A Program for Post-Campus Radicals," *Liberation*, August–September 1969, p. 44.

377 Strategy for The Revolution: This chapter draws extensively from Todd Gitlin, "New Left: Old Traps," *Ramparts*, September 1969, reprinted in Harold Jacobs, ed., *Weatherman* (Berkeley: Ramparts Press, 1970), pp. 105–9, and Todd Gitlin, "White Heat Underground: Weathermania," *The Nation*, December 19, 1981, pp. 657, 669–74.

377 he had resolved: Loren Baritz, *Backfire: A History of How American Culture Led Us into Vietnam and Made Us Fight the Way We Did* (New York: Morrow, 1985), pp. 203–4.

377 In 1970: Ibid., p. 204.

377 "We Are On Our Way": Edward Jay Epstein, *News from Nowhere: Television and the News* (New York: Random House, 1973), pp. 17–18.

378 In March 1969: This was what Nixon told H. R. Haldeman he called "the Madman Theory. . . . I want the North Vietnamese to believe I've reached the point where I might do *anything* to stop the war. We'll just slip the word to them that, 'for God's sake, you know Nixon is obsessed about communism. We can't restrain him when he's angry—and he has his hand on the nuclear button'—and Ho Chi Minh himself will be in Paris in two days begging for peace." H. R. Haldeman with Joseph DiMona, *The Ends of Power* (New York: Times Books, 1978), p. 83.

378 Over the next fourteen: Baritz, *Backfire*, p. 203.

378 His goal: Daniel Ellsberg, *Papers on the War* (New York: Simon and Schuster, 1972), pp. 42ff.

378 bomb his way to victory: Seymour M. Hersh, *The Price of Power: Kissinger in the Nixon White House* (New York: Summit, 1983), p. 51.

378 Nearly 10,000: Stanley Karnow, *Vietnam: A History* (New York: Penguin, 1984), p. 601.

378 More than 20,000: Baritz, *Backfire*, p. 200. On the difficulty of computing Vietnamese deaths, see Guenter Lewy, *America in Vietnam* (New York: Oxford University Press, 1978), appendix A. I have used a conservative estimate taken from Lewy, p. 453.

378 between 1965 and 1973: James William Gibson, *The Perfect War: Technowar in Vietnam* (Boston: Atlantic Monthly Press, 1986), p. 319.

378 The FBI had finally: Frank J. Donner, *The Age of Surveillance* (New York: 1981), pp. 178–79, 232ff. Until the spring of 1968, the FBI's program for SDS was called

PAGE

"COMINFIL, STUDENTS FOR A DEMOCRATIC SOCIETY." (Chicago FBI file 100–42064, airtel of August 23, 1966, obtained by the Alliance to End Repression and the American Civil Liberties Union; author's file.)

378 New Leftists were gradually added: FBI document in Chicago FBI file 100–42064, n.d.; Donner, *Age of Surveillance*, pp. 162–67.

378 CIA's Operation Chaos: Thomas Powers, *The Man Who Kept the Secrets: Richard Helms and the CIA* (New York: Pocket Books, 1979), pp. 315–20, 468.

378 agents provocateurs: Gary T. Marx, "Thoughts on a Neglected Category of Social Movement Participant," *American Journal of Sociology* 80 (1974), pp. 402–42.

378 It tried to intimidate: Todd Gitlin, *The Whole World Is Watching: Mass Media in the Making and Unmaking of the New Left* (Berkeley: University of California Press, 1980), pp. 269–79.

378 The FBI and other agencies: Geoffrey Rips, *The Campaign Against the Underground Press* (San Francisco: City Lights, 1981), pp. 55–135; Ward Churchill and Jim Vander Wall, *The COINTELPRO Papers* (Boston: South End, 1990), chap. 6.

378 State and local police: See Thomas Powers, *Diana: The Making of a Terrorist* (Boston: Houghton Mifflin, 1971), p. 107; Robert Wall, "Five Years As a Special Agent," in Paul Cowan, Nick Egleson, and Nat Hentoff, with Barbara Herbert and Robert Wall, *State Secrets: Police Surveillance in America* (New York: Holt, Rinehart and Winston, 1974), pp. 247–57; Donner, *Age of Surveillance*, p. 28; Rips, *Campaign*, pp. 51ff.

378 "small cadres of professional protesters": Spiro T. Agnew, in John R. Coyne, Jr., *The Impudent Snobs: Agnew vs. the Intellectual Establishment* (New Rochelle, N.Y.: Arlington House, 1972), p. 248.

378 "If, in challenging": Spiro T. Agnew, in ibid., pp. 258–59.

379 The antiwar movement: Some passages of this discussion are drawn from Todd Gitlin, "Seizing History," *Mother Jones*, November 1983, pp. 32ff.

379 Moratorium: Nancy Zaroulis and Gerald Sullivan, *Who Spoke Up? American Protest Against the War in Vietnam* (Garden City, N.Y.: Doubleday, 1984), pp. 269–73.

379 Nixon's secret summer: Hersh, *Price of Power*, p. 120.

379 "after all the protests": Richard M. Nixon, *RN: The Memoirs of Richard Nixon* (New York: Grosset and Dunlap, 1978), p. 402.

380 "New Left" as a pejorative: Kirkpatrick Sale, *SDS* (New York: Random House, 1973), p. 473.

380 "When I got involved": Mike Klonsky, SDS reunion, August 1988.

381 New Left's "id": Tom Hayden, *Trial* (New York: Holt, Rinehart and Winston, 1970), p. 94.

382 "domestic imperialism": Dave Gilbert, Bob Gottlieb, and Susan Sutheim, "Consumption: Domestic Capitalism" (New York: Movement for a Democratic Society, 1968), in Massimo Teodori, ed., *The New Left: A Documentary History* (Indianapolis: Bobbs-Merrill, 1969), pp. 425–37. SDS published a later version by Gilbert as a pamphlet entitled "Consumption: Domestic Imperialism."

382 availability as a counterforce: Sale, *SDS*, pp. 397–99.

382 "an inescapable choice": Todd Gitlin, "New Left: Old Traps," *Ramparts*, September 1969, reprinted in Jacobs, ed., *Weatherman*, p. 107.

383 "In about a six": Greg Calvert, speech to SDS reunion, Hell, Michigan, August 1977.

383 *Fortune*'s special issue: Daniel Seligman, "The Freedom to Be Idealistic" and "A Special Kind of Revolution," *Fortune*, January 1969, pp. 60, 175.

383 Max Palevsky: In *Business Week*, May 3, 1969.

384 "The liberal reformist": Greg Calvert, *Guardian*, March 25, 1967, in Sale, *SDS*, p. 318. Emphasis in the original.

PAGE

384 *"no other coherent"*: Carl Oglesby, "Notes on a Decade Ready for the Dustbin," *Liberation*, August–September 1969, p. 6, still the most perceptive and scintillating analysis of the movement's demise. Emphasis in the original.

385 "You Don't Need": Karen Ashley et al., "You Don't Need a Weatherman to Know Which Way the Wind Blows," *New Left Notes*, June 18, 1969; reprinted in Jacobs, ed., *Weatherman*, pp. 51–96.

385 Diana Oughton: Powers, *Diana*, p. 11.

385 "that there is a magic": Ashley et al., "You Don't Need," in Jacobs, ed., *Weatherman*, p. 73.

386 Dohrn picked up: Sale, *SDS*, p. 451.

386 *Bonnie and Clyde*: Gerald Long, "A Revolutionary Hollywood Film," *Guardian*, September 9, 1967.

386 "Hot Town": Bill Ayers and Jim Mellen, "Hot Town: Summer in the City, Or I Ain't Gonna Work on Maggie's Farm No More," *New Left Notes*, April 4, 1969, reprinted in Jacobs, ed., *Weatherman*, pp. 29–38.

386 Marion Delgado: Sale, *SDS*, p. 605n.

386 they sang songs: Anonymous [Ted Gold?], "Weatherman Songbook," in Jacobs, ed., *Weatherman*, pp. 351–58.

386 "They knew they were crazy": Personal communication, Carl Oglesby, October 30, 1986.

387 "so-called 'Movement people'": Bill Ayers, "A Strategy to Win," *New Left Notes*, September 12, 1969, reprinted in Jacobs, ed., *Weatherman*, p. 188.

387 sole heirs: Andrew Kopkind, "The Real SDS Stands Up," *Hard Times*, June 30, 1969, reprinted in Jacobs, ed., *Weatherman*, pp. 19, 26.

387 SDS's 1969 convention: Sale, *SDS*, pp. 557–58.

387 Of the fifteen hundred: Ibid., p. 564.

388 To score points against PL: Ibid., pp. 563–74.

388 "these fights among brothers": Todd Gitlin to "Rafael Otero," December 20, 1968 (author's file).

389 "On every quarter": Oglesby, "Notes," p. 15.

389 "Where ideas are all": Tom Nairn, "Why It Happened," in Angelo Quattrocchi and Tom Nairn, *The Beginning of the End* (London: Panther Books, 1968), pp. 131–33, quoting from Antonio Gramsci.

390 As George Orwell: George Orwell, "Politics and the English Language," *Horizon*, April 1946, reprinted in Sonia Orwell and Ian Angus, eds., *In Front of Your Nose, 1945–1950: The Collected Essays, Journalism and Letters of George Orwell*, vol. 4 (New York: Harcourt Brace Jovanovich, 1968), pp. 136–37.

390 "As a whole": Ashley et al., "You Don't Need," in Jacobs, ed., *Weatherman*, p. 65.

391 "Jailbreak!": Some Chicago teenagers recruited into a "jailbreak" action in Milwaukee were arrested there and then abandoned by the Weathermen. Interview, Marilyn Katz, August 29, 1988.

391 in Boston: Roy Bongartz, "Three Meanies," *Esquire*, August 1970, pp. 112ff.

391 twenty Weathermen marched: Ibid.; Sale, *SDS*, p. 602.

391 "their only choice": Shin'ya Ono, "You Do Need a Weatherman to Know Which Way the Wind Blows," *Leviathan*, December 1969, reprinted in Jacobs, ed., *Weatherman*, p. 236.

391 children of the upper classes: Milton Viorst, *Fire in the Streets: America in the 1960's* (New York: Simon and Schuster, 1979), p. 481.

391 RYM II allies: Ibid., pp. 492–94; Sale, *SDS*, pp. 580–88.

391 "Bring the war home!": Anonymous [Weatherman], "Look At It: America 1969," *New Left Notes*, August 1969, reprinted in Jacobs, ed., *Weatherman*, pp. 167, 168, 172.

PAGE
392 "give the ruling class": Ono, "You Do Need," in Jacobs, ed., *Weatherman*, pp. 237–40.
392 In July: Powers, *Diana*, p. 131.
392 "The more I thought": Ayers, "Strategy to Win," pp. 184, 191–92, 193.
392 Students were "wimpy": Mark Rudd, in Sale, *SDS*, p. 601.
392 "Last fall I met": Terry Cannon, "Brothers and Sisters . . . ," *San Francisco Express Times*, January 18, 1969, reprinted in Mitchell Goodman, ed., *The Movement toward a New America* (Philadelphia: Pilgrim, and New York: Knopf, 1970), p. 229.
393 "I hate SDS": Mark Rudd, in Bongartz, "Three Meanies," p. 114.
393 "We began to feel": Ono, "You Do Need," in Jacobs, ed., *Weatherman*, p. 241.
393 "We're bullets: Telephone interview, Michael Kazin, May 17, 1992.
393 one collective: Powers, *Diana*, p. 144.
393 Fred Hampton: Sale, *SDS*, p. 602, citing *People's Tribune* (Los Angeles), March 1970.
393 "It was as if": Ono, "You Do Need," in Jacobs, ed., *Weatherman*, p. 254.
393 "They looked exactly like": Hayden, *Trial*, p. 92.
393 "Within a minute or two": Ono, "You Do Need," in Jacobs, ed., *Weatherman*, p. 256.
393 police fought back: Ibid., pp. 255–74; Sale, *SDS*, pp. 603–12.
394 "Militarily and tactically": Ono, "You Do Need," in Jacobs, ed., *Weatherman*, p. 271.
394 "THE VIETNAM WAR ISN'T": Anonymous [Weatherman], "Washington, November 15, 1969," *Fire*, November 21, 1969, reprinted in Jacobs, ed., *Weatherman*, p. 276.
394 Bill Ayers: Jeremy Larner, "The Moratorium—A View from the Inside," *Life*, November 28, 1969, p. 57; Jack Rosenthal, "Violence Threat Laid to Radicals," *New York Times*, November 18, 1969, p. 21; interview, Jeremy Larner, July 19, 1986.
394 On November 13: Zaroulis and Sullivan, *Who Spoke Up?*, p. 284.
394 On November 15: Ibid., pp. 286–92; Anonymous, "Washington, November 15, 1969," in Jacobs, ed., *Weatherman*, p. 282.
394 John Mitchell: Paul Delaney, "Mitchell's Wife Says He Likened Protest to 'Russian Revolution,'" *New York Times*, November 22, 1969.
394 Over the protest: Gitlin, *Whole World*, p. 227.
395 they rejected it: Powers, *Diana*, p. 124.
395 turning away: Ibid., pp. 99–100.
395 "People who live together": A Weatherwoman, "Inside the Weather Machine," *Rat*, February 9–23, 1970, reprinted in Jacobs, ed., *Weatherman*, p. 325.
395 one FBI informer: Sale, *SDS*, p. 625n.
395 "You don't need": Ibid., p. 615.
395 At just the moment: Ibid., pp. 615–17.
396 "to re-examine": Ono, "You Do Need," in Jacobs, ed., *Weatherman*, p. 273.
396 long essay: Todd Gitlin, "The Dynamics of the New Left," *Motive*, October 1970, pp. 48–60, and November 1970, pp. 43–67; excerpted in "New Left: Old Traps," reprinted in Jacobs, ed., *Weatherman*, pp. 105–10.
396 "assuming you are": Gitlin, "New Left: Old Traps," p. 107.
397 "Can't separate things": Todd Gitlin to Chris Hobson, October 22, 1969 (author's file).
397 "Sometimes the vanguard": Oglesby, "Notes," pp. 16–17.
397 Some endorsed: For example, Bread and Roses (Boston), "Weatherman Politics and the Women's Movement," reprinted in Jacobs, ed., *Weatherman*, pp. 327–36.

PAGE

397   "the pseudo-radicalism": Hayden, *Trial*, p. 93.

398   "Do you find the word": Todd Gitlin to Chris Hobson, October 22, 1969 (author's file).

399   "group psychosis": Interview, Jeff Jones, April 5, 1986.

400   Only loosely connected: Ibid.

400   "All white babies": In Sale, *SDS*, p. 628.

400   "You have no right": Robin Morgan, in Abe Peck, *Uncovering the Sixties: The Life and Times of the Underground Press* (New York: Pantheon, 1985), p. 217.

400   On March 6, 1970: Liberation News Service, "Stormy Weather," *San Francisco Good Times*, January 8, 1970, reprinted in Jacobs, ed., *Weatherman*, pp. 341–50; Powers, *Diana*, pp. 1–5; Sale, *SDS*, pp. 3–5, 626–30; Kirkpatrick Sale, "Ted Gold: Education for Violence," *The Nation*, April 13, 1970, reprinted in Jacobs, ed., *Weatherman*, pp. 470–83; Zaroulis and Sullivan, *Who Spoke Up?*, p. 313. Interview, Cathy Wilkerson, Aug. 19, 1988.

400   Fort Dix: Peter Collier and David Horowitz, *Destructive Generation* (New York: Summit, 1989), p. 100.

400   insist they will never: Interview, Jeff Jones, April 5, 1986.

401   New Year's Day, 1970: Zaroulis and Sullivan, *Who Spoke Up?*, p. 301.

401   By government figures: Sale, *SDS*, p. 632.

401   A student explained: Richard Flacks and Milton Mankoff, "Why They Burned the Bank," *The Nation*, March 23, 1970, p. 340.

401   Five nights after: Homer Bigart, "Many Buildings Evacuated Here in Bomb Scares," *New York Times*, March 13, 1970; Andrew Kopkind, "The Radical Bombers," *Hard Times*, March 23, 1970, reprinted in Jacobs, ed., *Weatherman*, p. 500.

401   Thomas Tongyai: Ron Rosenbaum, "Run, Tommy, Run!", *Esquire*, July 1971, pp. 51–58.

401   "The real division": Jane Alpert in *Rat*, March 20, 1970, quoted in Jane Alpert, *Growing Up Underground* (New York: Morrow, 1981), p. 246.

402   they rejected: Interview, Jeff Jones, April 5, 1986.

402   "Smashing the pig": [Weatherman], "Revolution in the 70s," *Fire*, January 30, 1970, reprinted in Jacobs, ed., *Weatherman*, p. 451.

404   arrested Charles Manson: Ed Sanders, *The Family* (New York: Avon, 1972), p. 388.

404   "I fell in love": Jerry Rubin, *We Are Everywhere* (New York: Harper and Row, 1971), pp. 238–40.

404   Los Angeles *Free Press*: Peck, *Uncovering*, p. 227.

405   "gay celibate": Interview, Judith Coburn, October 16, 1984.

405   never recovered: Harvey Wasserman, in Peck, *Uncovering*, pp. 201–2.

405   Fred Hampton: Ibid., pp. 223–24; Frank J. Donner, *The Age of Surveillance* (New York: Vintage, 1981), pp. 226–30.

405   "The movement had become": Raymond Mungo, *Total Loss Farm* (New York: Bantam, 1971), p. 11. For a fine, unromantic appreciation of Marshall Bloom, see Stephen Diamond, *What the Trees Said* (New York: Delacorte, 1971).

405   raided the farm: On the split and the raid, see Raymond Mungo, *Famous Long Ago: My Life and Hard Times with Liberation News Service* (Boston: Beacon Press, 1970), pp. 163–82.

406   Hell's Angels: Greil Marcus, "History Outside of History," *Harper's*, December 1988, p. 23; Stanley Booth, "Arguing Over Altamont," *Harper's*, March 1989, p. 7; Booth, "Still Arguing," *Harper's*, June 1989, p. 9.

406   "The End of the Age of Aquarius": Todd Gitlin, "The End of the Age of Aquarius," *Liberation*, December 1969, reprinted in Thomas King Forcade, ed., *Underground Press Anthology* (New York: Ace Books, 1972), pp. 100–11.

407   Ralph Featherstone: Kopkind, "Radical Bombers," in Jacobs, ed., *Weatherman*,

PAGE

p. 498; Clayborne Carson, *In Struggle: SNCC and the Black Awakening of the 1960s* (Cambridge: Harvard University Press, 1981), p. 297.

407   **FBI informers:** Carson, *In Struggle*, pp. 293, 344.

18. FADEOUT

409   **Gallup Poll:** Cited in Seymour Martin Lipset, *Rebellion in the University* (Boston: Little, Brown, 1972), p. 43.

409   **According to one survey:** Yankelovich survey findings, cited in ibid.

409   **percentage of students:** Harris survey findings, cited in ibid., p. 49.

409   **protests nonviolent and violent:** Kirkpatrick Sale, *SDS* (New York: Random House, 1973), pp. 632–33.

409   **Nixon denounced:** *New York Times*, May 2, 1970.

410   **dam broke:** Information about actions after Kent State, unless otherwise attributed, comes from Rob Wrenn, "May 1970 and the Decline of the Student Movement," unpublished paper, University of California, Berkeley, pp. 14–15, citing Urban Research Corporation, *On Strike . . . Shut It Down!: A Report on the First National Student Strike in U.S. History* (Chicago, 1970), and Richard E. Peterson and John A. Bilorusky, *May 1970: The Campus Aftermath of Cambodia and Kent State* (New York: Carnegie Commission on Higher Education, 1971); Lipset, *Rebellion*, pp. 45, 90; Jerome Karabel, "An Empirical Analysis of Differential University Response to the Invasion of Cambodia," unpublished paper, Harvard University, 1971; and Sale, *SDS*, pp. 636–38.

410   **more than a third:** Harris survey findings, cited in Lipset, *Rebellion*, p. 47.

410   **Mobilization brought:** Nancy Zaroulis and Gerald Sullivan, *Who Spoke Up? American Protest Against the War in Vietnam, 1963–1975* (Garden City, N.Y.: Doubleday, 1984), pp. 322–28.

410   **Lobbying in Washington:** Henry Kissinger, *White House Years* (Boston: Little, Brown, 1979), pp. 512–13.

410   **"The very fabric":** Ibid., p. 513.

411   **Kissinger thought:** Seymour M. Hersh, *The Price of Power: Kissinger in the Nixon White House* (New York: Summit, 1983), pp. 194–95.

411   **Activism never recovered:** Wrenn, "May 1970," p. 31; Alan E. Bayer and Alexander W. Astin, "Campus Unrest, 1970–71: Was It Really All That Quiet?" *Educational Record*, Fall 1971, pp. 301–13; Jerome Karabel, "The Decline of the American Student Movement," unpublished paper, Harvard University, 1974, pp. 60ff.

411   **less privileged backgrounds:** Richard Flacks and Milton Mankoff, "The Changing Social Base of the American Student Movement," *Annals of the American Society for Political and Social Science* 395, May 1971, pp. 54–67.

412   **to save their skins:** James Fallows, "What Did You Do in the Class War, Daddy?" *Washington Monthly*, October 1975, pp. 5–19.

412   **Columbia University:** Allen H. Barton, "The Columbia Crisis: Campus, Vietnam and the Ghetto," *Public Opinion Quarterly* 32 (Fall 1968), pp. 333–52.

412   **Santa Barbara:** Robert B. Smith, "The Vietnam War and Student Militancy," *Social Science Quarterly* 52 (June 1971), pp. 133–56.

412   **other studies:** Charles F. Longino, "Draft Lottery Numbers and Student Opposition to the War," *Sociology of Education* (Fall 1973); Mark Levine and Serge Denisoff, "Draft Susceptibility and Vietnam War Attitudes," *Youth and Society* (December 1972).

412   **private exits:** Lawrence M. Baskir and William A. Strauss, *Chance and Circumstance: The Draft, the War, and the Vietnam Generation* (New York: Vintage, 1978), pp. 5, 9; Wrenn, "1970," pp. 40–41; Karabel, "Decline," p. 3, n. 13.

412   *American* combat deaths: Zaroulis and Sullivan, *Who Spoke Up?*, p. 372.

PAGE

413 **Ron Ziegler's remark:** In Kissinger, *White House*, p. 511.

413 **John Mitchell's:** Sale, *SDS*, pp. 642–46.

413 **The army ran:** Frank J. Donner, *The Age of Surveillance* (New York: Vintage, 1981), pp. 295–300, 306–14; Nick Egleson, "The Surveillance Apparatus," in Paul Cowan, Nick Egleson, and Nat Hentoff, with Barbara Herbert and Robert Wall, *State Secrets* (New York: Holt, Rinehart and Winston, 1974), pp. 7–16; Ron Rosenbaum, "Run, Tommy, Run!", *Esquire*, July 1971, p. 53.

413 **Hoover target the New Left:** Donner, *Surveillance*, pp. 232–36. Army Intelligence surveillance of SDS activists is mentioned in FBI files at least as early as 1966.

413 **In 1969 and 1970:** Ibid., pp. 232–40.

413 **A trivial but suggestive:** FBI airtel from SAC, Chicago, to SAC, Memphis, February 9, 1970, obtained from Chicago FBI by the Alliance to End Repression and the American Civil Liberties Union; author's file.

413 **An example with dire consequences:** Donner, *Surveillance*, p. 237.

413 **Tom Charles Huston:** Ibid., pp 262–68; Thomas Powers, *The Man Who Kept the Secrets: Richard Helms and the CIA* (New York: Pocket Books, 1981), pp. 317–19.

414 **Nixon also knew:** William R. Corson, *The Armies of Ignorance: The Rise of the American Intelligence Empire* (New York: Dial/James Wade, 1977), p. 417.

414 **FBI was often amateurish:** Egleson, "Surveillance Apparatus," *State Secrets*, p. 77. My own FBI files—at least the ones I was able to procure under the Freedom of Information Act—are riddled with irrelevancies and errors.

414 **May 8, 1970:** Zaroulis and Sullivan, *Who Spoke Up?*, pp. 333–35.

414 **Vice President Agnew:** Spiro T. Agnew, in John R. Coyne, Jr., *The Impudent Snobs: Agnew vs. the Intellectual Establishment* (New Rochelle, N.Y.: Arlington House, 1972), p. 259.

414 **April 7, 1970:** Ronald Reagan, in "'Bloodbath' Remark by Gov. Reagan," *San Francisco Chronicle*, April 8, 1970, p. 1. The *Los Angeles Times*'s version of the quote was: "If it's to be a bloodbath, let it be now. Appeasement is not the answer." (Ed Meagher, "Reagan Assails Militants, Then Tempers Words," *Los Angeles Times*, April 8, 1970, p. 3.).

415 **Attorney General Mitchell:** John Mitchell, in Jonathan Schell, *The Time of Illusion* (New York: Knopf, 1975), p. 124.

415 **During World War I:** William Preston, *Aliens and Dissenters* (Cambridge: Harvard University Press, 1963), pp. 75–180; Irving Howe, *Socialism in America* (New York: Harcourt Brace Jovanovich, 1985), pp. 42–43.

415 **Draft "shirkers":** Nicholas von Hoffman, "Watergate Under the Bridge," *The New Republic*, July 16–23, 1984, p. 30.

415 **Palmer Raids:** Preston, *Aliens*, pp. 220–21.

416 **1968 convention:** Sale, *SDS*, p. 456n.

417 **"the only New Left":** Karabel, "Decline," p. 61.

417 **no national organization:** Sale, *SDS*, pp. 616–19. Years after the fact, Jeff Jones, formerly one of the Weathermen, acknowledges that the destruction of SDS was an "error." Interview, Jeff Jones, April 5, 1986.

417 **The media, drawn:** Todd Gitlin, *The Whole World Is Watching: Mass Media in the Making and Unmaking of the New Left* (Berkeley: University of California Press, 1980), chap. 6.

417 **Yippiesque slapstick:** Charles T. Powers and Bill Hazlett, "Yippies' Outburst Shuts Disneyland; Riot Police Called In for First Time," *Los Angeles Times*, August 7, 1970, p. 1.

417 **Harris poll:** Lipset, *Rebellion*, p. 49.

417 **active-duty soldiers:** David Cortright, *Soldiers in Revolt* (Garden City, N.Y.: Anchor/Doubleday, 1975).

PAGE

418   "the morale, discipline": Col. Robert D. Heinl, "The Collapse of the Armed Forces," *Armed Forces Journal*, June 7, 1971, p. 30.

418   for every hundred: Cortright, *Soldiers*, p. 24.

418   Melvin Laird: *San Francisco Examiner*, January 17, 1971.

418   "Armed Farces Day": Cortright, *Soldiers*, pp. 55, 83.

418   Early in 1971: Zaroulis and Sullivan, *Who Spoke Up?*, pp. 354–58; Fred Halstead, *Out Now! A Participant's Account of the American Movement Against the Vietnam War* (New York: Monad Press, 1978), pp. 605–7.

418   "discredit the peace": Charles Colson, memo to Nixon, in H. R. Haldeman with Joseph DiMona, *The Ends of Power* (New York: Times Books, 1978), p. 116.

419   Indochina Peace Campaign: Zaroulis and Sullivan, *Who Spoke Up?*, pp. 410, 412; Halstead, *Out Now!*, pp. 689, 704.

419   waited so long: Thanks to David Plotke for this point.

19. CARRYING ON

420   "Everything changed": Thomas McGrath, *Letter to an Imaginary Friend* (Chicago: Swallow, 1970), p. 95.

420   cyclical tendency: The most sophisticated version of a cyclical argument—arguing that private dissatisfactions lead to public action, and public dissatisfactions back to private life—is Albert O. Hirschman, *Shifting Involvements: Private Interest and Public Action* (Princeton: Princeton University Press, 1982).

423   Russell Jacoby: Lecture to Institute for Socio-Cultural Studies, Berkeley, California, c. 1976.

424   burned out: Robert Coles, *Farewell to the South* (Boston: Little, Brown, 1972), p. 273.

424   "Marat/these cells": Peter Weiss, *The Persecution and Assassination of Jean-Paul Marat As Performed by the Inmates of the Asylum of Charenton Under the Direction of the Marquis de Sade* (New York: Pocket Books, 1966), p. 131.

425   intimate personal relations: Christopher Lasch, *The New Radicalism in America* (New York: Knopf, 1965), pp. 101–2, 108; Richard Sennett, *The Fall of Public Man* (New York: Vintage, 1978), pp. 337–40.

425   Esalen Institute: Stuart Miller, *Hot Springs* (New York: Viking, 1971).

425   Hobart College: Ron Rosenbaum, "Run, Tommy, Run!", *Esquire*, July 1971, p. 58.

425   the defeated Sioux: Weston La Barre, *The Ghost Dance: Origins of Religion* (New York: Delta, 1972), pp. 227–48.

426   "If you want to know": Mao Tse-tung, "On Practice" (July 1937), *Selected Works*, vol. I, pp. 299–300, in *Quotations from Chairman Mao Tse-tung* (Peking: Foreign Languages Publishing House, 1966), p. 209.

427   "we were as crazy": Telephone interview, Bruce Davis, September 19, 1985.

428   white women soloists: Charlie Gillett, *The Sound of the City*, rev. and expanded ed. (New York: Pantheon, 1983), p. 410.

429   free schools: Allen Graubard, *Free the Children* (New York: Pantheon, 1972), pp. 40–41; Joyce Rothschild-Whitt, "Alternative Institutions as Collectively Controlled Workplaces: Some Dilemmas," paper presented at the annual meeting of the American Sociological Association, Chicago, 1976.

430   "cultivating our garden": Todd Gitlin, "The Children of John F. Kennedy," *Village Voice*, July 12, 1973.

430   Rainbow Family: Phil Garlington, "The Return of the Flower Children," *California*, October 1984, pp. 81–83, 137–38.

430   Children had to be raised: Bennett Berger, *The Survival of a Counterculture*

PAGE

(Berkeley: University of California Press, 1981); Graubard, *Free the Children*; Ann Swidler, *Organizations Without Authority* (Cambridge: Harvard University Press, 1979).

431   **no more than four million:** Computed by the author and Jerome Karabel on the basis of income statistics, defining a yuppie as college-educated, in a professional or managerial occupation, and with family income of at least $40,000 a year—a low cut-off yielding a high outer limit.

432   **they failed to compel:** On the dramatic decline of women's incomes after divorce, see Lenore Weitzman, *The Divorce Revolution* (New York: Free Press, 1985).

432   **men and women alike would hold:** Kristin Luker, *Abortion and the Politics of Motherhood* (Berkeley: University of California Press, 1984), chap. 7.

432   **"When the going gets":** Hunter S. Thompson, quoted by Stuart Ewen, lecture at West Coast Critical Communications Conference, Stanford University, c. 1976.

433   **legal aid:** Jerold S. Auerbach, *Unequal Justice: Lawyers and Social Change in Modern America* (New York: Oxford University Press, 1976).

433   **I-told-you-so journalists:** For example, Charles Krauthammer, "The Revolution Surrenders: From Freedom Train to Gravy Train," *Washington Post*, April 12, 1985, p. A25.

434   **Committee on the Present Danger:** Jerry W. Sanders, *Peddlers of Crisis* (Boston: South End, 1983).

434   **Edmund G. (Pat) Brown:** Lou Cannon, *Reagan* (New York: Perigee, 1984), pp. 109–10.

435   **Thirty-two years:** Bill Shaw, "Brown vs. Board of Education: 35 Years Later, It's Still Not Settled," *San Francisco Sunday Examiner and Chronicle*, December 21, 1986, p. A-6.

435   **the toll:** Guenter Lewy, *America in Vietnam* (New York: Oxford University Press, 1978), pp. 107–8, 445, 453; Gabriel Kolko, *Anatomy of a War: Vietnam, the United States, and the Modern Historical Experience* (New York: Pantheon, 1985), p. 200.

436   **below its 1920 level:** Irving Bernstein, *The Lean Years: A History of the American Workers 1920–1933* (Baltimore: Penguin, 1966), p. 84.

436   **American political attitudes:** Craig Reinarman, *American States of Mind: Visions of Capitalism and Democracy among Private and Public Workers* (New Haven: Yale University Press, 1987), chap. 9.

437   **Cuba:** Aryeh Neier, "Castro's Victims," *New York Review of Books*, July 17, 1986, pp. 28–31; Armando Valladares, *Against All Hope* (New York: Knopf, 1986); Jorge Valls, *Twenty Years and Forty Days: Life in a Cuban Prison* (New York: Americas Watch, 1986).

437   **Chinese Cultural Revolution:** See, for example, Liang Heng and Judith Shapiro, *Son of the Revolution* (New York: Knopf, 1983).

437   **their victory was expedited:** William Shawcross, *Sideshow: Kissinger, Nixon, and the Destruction of Cambodia* (New York: Simon and Schuster, 1979); Michael Vickery, *Cambodia: 1975–1982* (Boston: South End, 1984), pp. 288, 325–26.

437   **American planes dropped:** Nayan Chanda, *Brother Enemy: The War after the War* (San Diego: Harcourt Brace Jovanovich, 1986), p. 68.

INDEX

About the Author

TODD GITLIN is professor of sociology at the University of California, Berkeley. He is author of *The Whole World Is Watching* and *Inside Prime Time*, and a novel, *The Murder of Albert Einstein*, as well as editor of *Watching Television*. His articles on politics and culture have appeared in *The New York Times*, *Harper's*, *The Nation*, *Mother Jones*, *The New Republic*, *Dissent*, *Tikkun*, and many other periodicals and newspapers.